*Less managing. More teaching. Greater learning.*

## INSTRUCTORS...

Would you like your **students** to show up for class more **prepared**? *(Let's face it, class is much more fun if everyone is engaged and prepared...)*

Want ready-made application-level **interactive assignments,** student progress reporting, and auto-assignment grading? *(Less time grading means more time teaching...)*

Want an **instant view of student or class performance** relative to learning objectives? *(No more wondering if students understand...)*

Need to **collect data and generate reports** required for administration or accreditation? *(Say goodbye to manually tracking student learning outcomes...)*

Want to **record and post your lectures** for students to view online?

## With McGraw-Hill's *Connect*™ *Marketing*,

### INSTRUCTORS GET:

- Interactive Applications – **book-specific interactive assignments** that require students to APPLY what they've learned.
- Simple **assignment management**, allowing you to spend more time teaching.
- **Auto-graded** assignments, quizzes, and tests.
- **Detailed Visual Reporting** where student and section results can be viewed and analyzed.
- Sophisticated **online testing** capability.
- A **filtering and reporting** function that allows you to easily assign and report on materials that are correlated to accreditation standards, learning outcomes, and Bloom's taxonomy.
- An easy-to-use **lecture capture** tool.

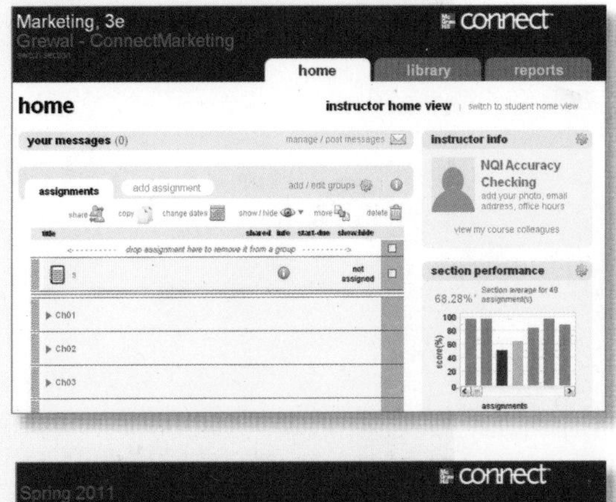


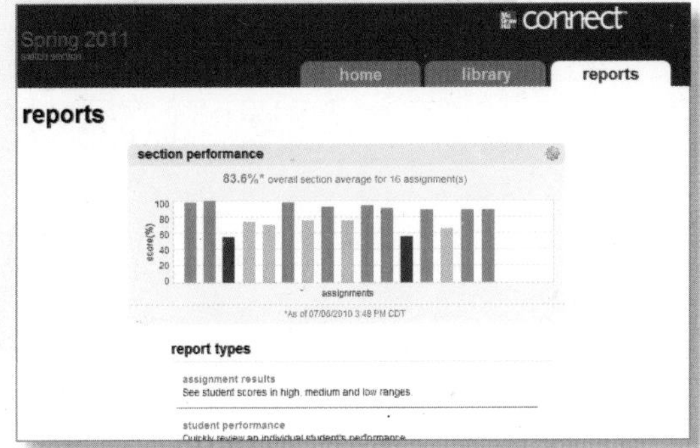

## STUDENTS...

Want an online, **searchable version** of your textbook?

Wish your textbook could be **available online** while you're doing your assignments?

### *Connect™ Plus Marketing* eBook

If you choose to use *Connect™ Plus Marketing*, you have an affordable and searchable online version of your book integrated with your other online tools.

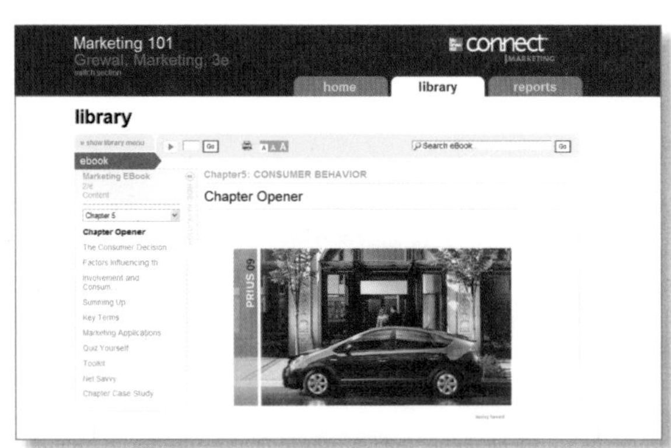


### *Connect™ Plus Marketing* eBook offers features like:

- Topic search
- Direct links from assignments
- Adjustable text size
- Jump to page number
- Print by section

## STUDENTS...

Want to get more **value** from your textbook purchase?

Think learning advertising should be a bit more **interesting**?

### Check out the STUDENT RESOURCES section under the *Connect™* Library tab.

Here you'll find a wealth of resources designed to help you achieve your goals in the course. You'll find things like **quizzes, PowerPoints, and Internet activities** to help you study. Every student has different needs, so explore the STUDENT RESOURCES to find the materials best suited to you.

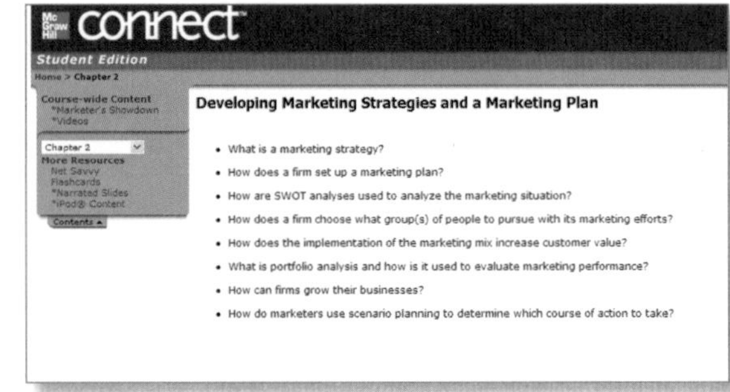

# ADVERTISING AND PROMOTION

## AN INTEGRATED MARKETING COMMUNICATIONS PERSPECTIVE

9e

George E. Belch & Michael A. Belch

*Both of San Diego State University*

# McGraw-Hill Irwin

ADVERTISING AND PROMOTION: AN INTEGRATED MARKETING COMMUNICATIONS PERSPECTIVE

Published by McGraw-Hill/Irwin, a business unit of The McGraw-Hill Companies, Inc., 1221 Avenue of the Americas, New York, NY, 10020. Copyright © 2012, 2009, 2007, 2004, 2001, 1998, 1995, 1993, 1990 by The McGraw-Hill Companies, Inc. All rights reserved. No part of this publication may be reproduced or distributed in any form or by any means, or stored in a database or retrieval system, without the prior written consent of The McGraw-Hill Companies, Inc., including, but not limited to, in any network or other electronic storage or transmission, or broadcast for distance learning.

Some ancillaries, including electronic and print components, may not be available to customers outside the United States.

This book is printed on acid-free paper.

1 2 3 4 5 6 7 8 9 0 WVR/WVR 1 0 9 8 7 6 5 4 3 2

ISBN 978-0-07-340486-8
MHID 0-07-340486-1

Vice president and editor-in-chief: *Brent Gordon*
Editorial director: *Paul Ducham*
Publisher: *Doug Hughes*
Executive editor: *Michael Ablassmeir*
Executive editor: *Sankha Basu*
Executive director of development: *Ann Torbert*
Development editor: *Kelly I. Pekelder*
Editorial assistant: *Andrea Heirendt*
Vice president and director of marketing: *Robin J. Zwettler*
Marketing director: *Amee Mosley*
Marketing manager: *Katie Mergen*
Vice president of editing, design, and production: *Sesha Bolisetty*
Project manager: *Dana M. Pauley*
Senior buyer: *Carol A. Bielski*
Interior designer: *Cara Hawthorne, cara david DESIGN*
Senior photo research coordinator: *Jeremy Cheshareck*
Photo researcher: *Jennifer Blankenship*
Senior media project manager: *Susan Lombardi*
Media project manager: *Suresh Babu, Hurix Systems Pvt. Ltd.*
Cover design: *Cara Hawthorne, cara david DESIGN*
Interior design: *Cara Hawthorne, cara david DESIGN*
Typeface: *10.5/12 Times Roman*
Compositor: *Lachina Publishing Services*
Printer: *Worldcolor*

**Library of Congress Cataloging-in-Publication Data**

Belch, George E. (George Edward), 1951-
Advertising and promotion: an integrated marketing communications perspective / George E. Belch & Michael A. Belch.—9th ed.
p. cm.
Includes index.
ISBN-13: 978-0-07-340486-8 (alk. paper)
ISBN-10: 0-07-340486-1 (alk. paper)
1. Advertising. 2. Sales promotion. 3. Communication in marketing. I. Belch, Michael A. II. Title.
HF5823.B387 2012
659.1—dc22

2010040703

www.mhhe.com

*To Our Families*

*and*

*To the memory of*
*Dr. Ken Canard Marino*
*Rico Di Toro*
*Buckeye Murray (and his dog)*

# ABOUT THE AUTHORS

## Dr. George E. Belch

George E. Belch is professor of marketing and chair of the marketing department at San Diego State University, where he teaches integrated marketing communications, strategic marketing planning, and consumer/customer behavior. Prior to joining San Diego State, he was a member of the faculty in the Graduate School of Management, University of California, Irvine. He received his PhD in marketing from the University of California, Los Angeles. Before entering academia, Dr. Belch was a marketing representative for the DuPont Company. He also worked as a research analyst for the DDB Worldwide advertising agency.

Dr. Belch's research interests are in the area of consumer processing of advertising information as well as managerial aspects of integrated marketing communications. He has authored or coauthored more than 30 articles in leading academic journals including: *Journal of Marketing Research, Journal of Consumer Research, Journal of Advertising,* and *Journal of Business Research.* In 2000, he was selected as *Marketing Educator of the Year* by the Marketing Educators' Association for his career achievements in teaching and research. He also received the Distinguished Faculty Member Award for the College of Business Administration at San Diego State University in 2003.

Dr. Belch has taught in executive education and development programs for various universities around the world. He has also conducted seminars on integrated marketing communications as well as marketing planning and strategy for a number of multinational companies including Sprint, Microsoft, Qualcomm, MP3.com, Fluor Daniel, Square D Corporation, Armstrong World Industries, Sterling Software, Siliconix, and Texas Industries.

## Dr. Michael A. Belch

Michael (Mickey) A. Belch is a professor of marketing at San Diego State University and is also co-director of the Centre for Integrated Marketing Communications at San Diego State. He received his undergraduate degree from Penn State University, his MBA from Drexel University, and his PhD from the University of Pittsburgh.

Before entering academia he was employed by the General Foods Corporation as a marketing representative, and has served as a consultant to numerous companies, including McDonald's, Whirlpool Corporation, Senco Products, GTI Corporation, IVAC, May Companies, Phillips-Ramsey Advertising and Public Relations, and Daily & Associates Advertising. He has conducted seminars on integrated marketing and marketing management for a number of multinational companies and has also taught in executive education programs in France, Amsterdam, Spain, Chile, Argentina, Colombia, China, Solvenia, and Greece. He is the author or coauthor of more than 40 articles in academic journals in the areas of advertising, consumer behavior, and international marketing including: *Journal of Advertising, Journal of Advertising Research,* and *Journal of Business Research.* Dr. Belch is also a member of the editorial review board of the *Journal of Advertising* and the *Journal of International Advertising.* He received outstanding teaching awards from undergraduate and graduate students numerous times. He also received the Distinguished Faculty Member Award for the College of Business Administration at San Diego State University in 2007.

# PREFACE

## THE CHANGING WORLD OF ADVERTISING AND PROMOTION

Nearly everyone in the modern world is influenced to some degree by advertising and other forms of promotion. Organizations in both the private and public sectors have learned that the ability to communicate effectively and efficiently with their target audiences is critical to their success. Advertising and other types of promotional messages are used to sell products and services as well as to promote causes, market political candidates, and deal with societal problems such as alcohol and drug abuse. Consumers are finding it increasingly difficult to avoid the efforts of marketers, who are constantly searching for new ways to communicate with them.

Most of the people involved in advertising and promotion will tell you that there is no more dynamic and fascinating field to either practice or study. However, they will also tell you that the field is undergoing dramatic transformations that are changing the ways marketers communicate with consumers forever. The changes are coming from all sides—clients demanding better results from their advertising and promotional dollars; lean but highly creative smaller ad agencies; sales promotion and direct-marketing firms, as well as interactive agencies, which want a larger share of the billions of dollars companies spend each year promoting their products and services; consumers who no longer respond to traditional forms of advertising; and new technologies that may reinvent the very process of advertising. We are experiencing perhaps the most dynamic and revolutionary changes of any era in the history of marketing, as well as advertising and promotion. These changes are being driven by advances in technology and developments that have led to the rapid growth of communications through interactive media, particularly the Internet and mobile phones.

Companies from outside the traditional advertising industry are rapidly changing the process of making and delivering advertising messages to consumers. Marketers are looking beyond traditional mass-media advertising to find new and more effective ways to communicate with their target audiences. They recognize there are numerous ways to reach their current and prospective customers and bring them into contact with their products and services. Many marketers view the Internet ads as a more cost-effective way to reach specific target markets and measure the results of their marketing efforts. Major changes are taking place in the way marketers are using the Internet for marketing communications including new applications that facilitate interactive information sharing and collaboration and bilateral, as opposed to unilateral, communication. Web 2.0 developments mean that Internet users are no longer limited to the passive viewing of information and can interact with one another as well as change website content. These applications have been given to social networking sites, video sharing sites, wikis, blogs, and online communities which have all experienced explosive growth. Five years ago Facebook, Twitter, YouTube, and LinkedIn did not even exist and MySpace was only a year old. However, Facebook now has more than 500 million members, Twitter boasts over 40 million, and more than 100 million videos are viewed each day on YouTube, including many of the TV commercials and other promotional videos created by marketers. Nearly every company or organization has a Facebook and Twitter page that they use to keep in constant contact with their customers and these tools, along with other types of social media, have become an integral part of most marketers' marketing communications programs. However, the increased use of the Internet and social media is only the latest in a number of fundamental changes that have been occurring in the way companies plan, develop, and execute their marketing communications programs.

For decades the advertising business was dominated by large, full-service Madison Avenue–type agencies. The advertising strategy for a national brand involved creating one or two commercials that could be run on network television, a few print ads that would run in general-interest magazines, and some sales promotion support such as coupons or premium offers. However, in today's world there are a myriad of media outlets—print, radio, cable and satellite TV, and the Internet—competing for consumers' attention. Marketers are looking beyond the traditional media to find new and better ways to communicate with their customers because they will no longer accept on faith the value of conventional advertising placed in traditional media. Major marketers are moving away from a reliance on mass-media advertising and are spending more of their marketing communication budgets in specialized media that target specific markets. Companies are also spending more of their monies in other ways such as event marketing, sponsorships, cause-related promotions, and viral marketing. Advertising agencies are recognizing that they must change the way they do business.

In addition to redefining the role and nature of their advertising agencies, marketers are changing the way they communicate with consumers. They know they are operating in an environment where advertising messages are everywhere, consumers channel-surf past most commercials, and brands promoted in traditional ways often fail. New-age advertisers are redefining the notion of what an ad is and where it runs. Stealth messages are being woven into the culture and embedded into movies and TV shows or made into their own form of entertainment. Many experts argue that "branded content" is the wave of the future, and there is a growing movement to reinvent advertising and other forms of marketing communication to be more akin to entertainment. Companies are using branded entertainment as a way of reaching consumers by creating short films that can be viewed on their websites, arranging product placements, and integrating their brands into movies and television shows to promote their products and services.

A number of factors are impacting the way marketers communicate with consumers. The audiences that marketers seek, along with the media and methods for reaching them, have become increasingly fragmented. Advertising and promotional efforts have become more regionalized and targeted to specific audiences. Retailers have become larger and more powerful, forcing marketers to shift money from advertising budgets to sales promotion. Marketers expect their promotional dollars to generate immediate sales and are demanding more accountability from their agencies. The Internet revolution is in full force and new ways to communicate with consumers are constantly being developed. Many companies are coordinating all their communications efforts so that they can send cohesive messages to their customers. Some companies are building brands with little or no use of traditional media advertising. Many advertising agencies have acquired, started, or become affiliated with sales promotion, direct-marketing, interactive agencies, and public relations companies to better serve their clients' marketing communications needs. Their clients have become "media-neutral" and are asking that they consider whatever form of marketing communication works best to target market segments and build long-term reputations and short-term sales.

This text will introduce students to this fast-changing field of advertising and promotion. While advertising is its primary focus, it is more than just an introductory advertising text because there is more to most organizations' promotional programs than just advertising. The changes discussed above are leading marketers and their agencies to approach advertising and promotion from an integrated marketing communications (IMC) perspective, which calls for a "big picture" approach to planning marketing and promotion programs and coordinating the various communication functions. To understand the role of advertising and promotion in today's business world, one must recognize how a firm can use all the promotional tools to communicate with its customers.

## TO THE STUDENT: PREPARING YOU FOR THE NEW WORLD OF ADVERTISING AND PROMOTION

Some of you are taking this course to learn more about this fascinating field; many of you hope to work in advertising or some other promotional area. The changes in the industry have profound implications for the way today's student is trained and educated. You will not be working for the same kind of communication agencies that existed a few years ago. If you work on the client side of the business, you will find that the way they approach advertising and promotion is changing dramatically.

Today's student is expected to understand all the major marketing communication tools: advertising, direct marketing, the Internet, interactive media, sales promotion, public relations, personal selling, as well as social and consumer-driven media. You will also be expected to know how to research and evaluate a company's marketing and promotional situation and how to use these various functions in developing effective communication strategies and programs. Marketers are also increasing their attention on the determination of return on investment (ROI) of various IMC tools as well as the problems companies face in attempting to make this evaluation. This book will help prepare you for these challenges.

As professors we were, of course, once students ourselves. In many ways we are perpetual students in that we are constantly striving to learn about and explain how advertising and promotion work. We share many of your interests and concerns and are often excited (and bored) by the same things. Having taught in the advertising and promotion area for a combined 50-plus years, we have developed an understanding of what makes a book in this field interesting to students. In writing this book, we have tried to remember how we felt about the various texts we used throughout the years and to incorporate the good things and minimize those we felt were of little use. We have tried not to overburden you with definitions, although we do call out those that are especially important to your understanding of the material.

We also remember that as students we were not really excited about theory. But to fully understand how integrated marketing communications works, it is necessary to establish some theoretical basis. The more you understand about how things are supposed to work, the easier it will be for you to understand why they do or do not turn out as planned.

Perhaps the question students ask most often is, How do I use this in the real world? In response we provide numerous examples of how the various theories and concepts in the text can be used in practice. A particular strength of this text is the integration of theory with practical application. Nearly every day an example of advertising and promotion in practice is reported in the media. We have used many sources, such as *Advertising Age, Adweek, Brandweek, The Wall Street Journal, BusinessWeek, The Economist, Fortune, Forbes, Sales & Marketing Management, Mediaweek, Promo,* and numerous online sites such as eMarketer, Mashable, MediaPost.com, and ClickZ News to find practical examples that are discussed throughout the text. We have spoken with marketing and agency personnel about the strategies and rationale behind the ads and other types of promotions we use as examples. Each chapter begins with a vignette that presents an example of an advertising or promotional campaign or other interesting insights. Every chapter also contains several **IMC Perspectives** that present in-depth discussions of particular issues related to the chapter material and show how companies are using integrated marketing communications. **Global Perspectives** are presented throughout the text in recognition of the increasing importance of international marketing and the challenges of advertising and promotion and the role they play in the marketing programs of multinational marketers. **Ethical Perspectives** focus attention on important social issues and show how advertisers must take ethical considerations into account when planning and implementing advertising and promotional programs. **IMC Technology Perspectives** focus on how changes and/or advances in various areas are impacting the field of integrated marketing communications.

Each chapter features beautiful four-color illustrations showing examples from many of the most current and best-integrated marketing communication campaigns being used around the world. We have included more than 350 advertisements and examples of numerous other types of promotion, all of which were carefully chosen to illustrate a particular idea, theory, or practical application. Please take time to read the opening vignettes to each chapter, the IMC, Global, Ethical, and IMC Technology Perspectives, and study the diverse ads and illustrations. We think they will stimulate your interest and relate to your daily life as a consumer and a target of advertising and promotion.

## TO THE INSTRUCTOR: A TEXT THAT REFLECTS THE CHANGES IN THE WORLD OF ADVERTISING AND PROMOTION

Our major goal in writing the ninth edition of *Advertising and Promotion* was to continue to provide you with the most comprehensive and current text on the market for teaching advertising and promotion from an IMC perspective. This new edition focuses on the many changes that are occurring in areas of marketing communications and how they influence advertising and promotional strategies and tactics. We have done this by continuing with the *integrated marketing communications perspective.* More and more companies are approaching advertising and promotion from an IMC perspective, coordinating the various promotional mix elements with other marketing activities that communicate with a firm's customers. Many advertising agencies are also developing expertise in direct marketing, sales promotion, event sponsorship, the Internet, social media, and other areas so that they can meet all their clients' integrated marketing communication needs—and, of course, survive.

The text is built around an integrated marketing communications planning model and recognizes the importance of coordinating all of the promotional mix elements to develop an effective communications program. Although media advertising is often the most visible part of a firm's promotional program, attention must also be given to direct marketing, sales promotion, public relations, interactive media, and personal selling.

This text integrates theory with planning, management, and strategy. To effectively plan, implement, and evaluate IMC programs, one must understand the overall marketing process, consumer behavior, and communications theory. We draw from the extensive research in advertising, consumer behavior, communications, marketing, sales promotion, and other fields to give students a basis for understanding the marketing communications process, how it influences consumer decision making, and how to develop promotional strategies.

While this is an introductory text, we do treat each topic in some depth. We believe the marketing and advertising student of today needs a text that provides more than just an introduction to terms and topics. The book is positioned primarily for the introductory advertising, marketing communications, or promotions course as taught in the business/marketing curriculum. It can also be used in journalism/communications courses that take an integrated marketing communications perspective. Many schools also use the text at the graduate level. In addition to its thorough coverage of advertising, this text has chapters on sales promotion, direct marketing and marketing on the Internet, smart media, and publicity/public relations. These chapters stress the integration of advertising with other promotional mix elements and the need to understand their role in the overall marketing program.

## ORGANIZATION OF THIS TEXT

This book is divided into seven major parts. In Part One we examine the role of advertising and promotion in marketing and introduce the concept of integrated marketing communications. Chapter 1 provides an overview of advertising and promotion and its role in modern marketing. The concept of IMC and the factors that have led to its growth are discussed. Each of the promotional mix elements is defined, and an IMC planning model shows the various steps in the promotional planning process. This model provides a framework for developing the integrated marketing communications program and is followed throughout the text. Chapter 2 examines the role of advertising and promotion in the overall marketing program, with attention to the various elements of the marketing mix and how they interact with advertising and promotional strategy. We have also included coverage of market segmentation and positioning in this chapter so that students can understand how these concepts fit into the overall marketing programs as well as their role in the development of an advertising and promotional program.

In Part Two we cover the promotional program situation analysis. Chapter 3 describes how firms organize for advertising and promotion and examines the role of ad agencies and other firms that provide marketing and promotional services. We discuss how ad agencies are selected, evaluated, and compensated as well as the changes occurring in the agency business. Attention is also given to other types of marketing communication organizations such as direct marketing, sales promotion, and interactive agencies as well as public relations firms. We also consider whether responsibility for integrating the various communication functions lies with the client or the agency. Chapter 4 covers the stages of the consumer decision-making process and both the internal psychological factors and the external factors that influence consumer behavior. The focus of this chapter is on how advertisers can use an understanding of buyer behavior to develop effective advertising and other forms of promotion.

Part Three analyzes the communication process. Chapter 5 examines various communication theories and models of how consumers respond to advertising messages and other forms of marketing communications. Chapter 6 provides a detailed discussion of source, message, and channel factors.

In Part Four we consider how firms develop goals and objectives for their integrated marketing communications programs and determine how much money to spend trying to achieve them. Chapter 7 stresses the importance of knowing what to expect from advertising and promotion, the differences between advertising and communication objectives, characteristics of good objectives, and problems in setting objectives. We have also integrated the discussion of various methods for determining and allocating the promotional budget into this chapter. These first four sections of the text provide students with a solid background in the areas of marketing, consumer behavior, communications, planning, objective setting, and budgeting. This background lays the foundation for the next section, where we discuss the development of the integrated marketing communications program.

Part Five examines the various promotional mix elements that form the basis of the integrated marketing communications program. Chapter 8 discusses the planning and development of the creative strategy and advertising campaign and examines the creative process. In Chapter 9 we turn our attention to ways to execute the creative strategy and some criteria for evaluating creative work. Chapters 10 through 13 cover media strategy and planning and the various advertising media. Chapter 10 introduces the key principles of media planning and strategy and examines how a media plan is developed. Chapter 11 discusses the advantages and disadvantages of the broadcast media (TV and radio) as well as issues regarding the purchase of radio and TV time and audience measurement. Chapter 12 considers the same issues for the print media (magazines and newspapers). Chapter 13 examines the role of traditional support media such as outdoor and transit advertising, the Yellow Pages, and promotional products, as well as the tremendous increase in the use of nontraditional branded entertainment strategies such as product placements and product integration.

In Chapters 14 through 17 we continue the IMC emphasis by examining other promotional tools that are used in the integrated marketing communications process. Chapter 14 looks at direct marketing. This chapter examines database marketing and the ways companies communicate directly with target customers through various media including direct mail, infomercials, and direct-response TV commercials. Chapter 15 provides a detailed discussion of marketers' increasing use of interactive media, including the Internet and wireless technologies to market their products and services. We examine the increasing use of blogs, mobile, paid search, and other digital media strategies. We also give attention to how the Internet is used to implement various IMC activities including advertising, sales promotion, and even the selling of products and services. Chapter 16 examines the area of sales promotion including both consumer-oriented promotions and programs targeted to the trade (retailers, wholesalers, and other intermediaries). Chapter 17 covers the role of publicity and public relations in IMC as well as corporate advertising. Basic issues regarding personal selling and its role in promotion strategy are presented in Chapter 22, which is available online in this edition.

Part Six of the text consists of Chapter 18, where we discuss ways to measure the effectiveness of various elements of the integrated marketing communications program, including methods for pretesting and posttesting advertising messages and campaigns. In Part Seven we turn our attention to special markets, topics, and perspectives that are becoming increasingly important in contemporary marketing. In Chapter 19 we examine the global marketplace and the role of advertising and other promotional mix variables such as sales promotion, public relations, and the Internet in international marketing.

The text concludes with a discussion of the regulatory, social, and economic environments in which advertising and promotion operate. Chapter 20 examines industry self-regulation and regulation of advertising by governmental agencies such as the Federal Trade Commission, as well as rules and regulations governing sales promotion, direct marketing, and marketing on the Internet. Because advertising's role in society is constantly changing, our discussion would not be complete without a look at the criticisms frequently levied, so in Chapter 21 we consider the social, ethical, and economic aspects of advertising and promotion.

## CHAPTER FEATURES

The following features in each chapter enhance students' understanding of the material as well as their reading enjoyment.

### Learning Objectives

Learning objectives are provided at the beginning of each chapter to identify the major areas and points covered in the chapter and guide the learning effort. We also indicate where specific learning objectives are covered within the chapter and how the discussion questions are keyed to the objectives.

### Chapter Opening Vignettes

Each chapter begins with a vignette that shows the effective use of integrated marketing communications by a company or ad agency or discusses an interesting issue that is relevant to the chapter. These opening vignettes are designed to draw the students into the chapter by presenting an interesting example, development, or issue that relates to the material covered in the chapter. Companies, brands, and/or campaigns featured in the opening vignettes include Volkswagen's PunchDub campaign; social media campaigns used to introduce the Ford Fiesta automobile to the U.S. market and the addition of a new flavor to the Mountain Dew soft drink product line; "The Man Your Man Could Smell Like" campaign for Old Spice body wash, Subway's "Five Dollar Footlong" promotion, as well as IMC campaigns used by Under Armour, the New York Jets, and Lady Gaga. Some of the chapter openers discuss current topics and issues impacting integrated marketing communications such as the rapid growth and popularity of social media; changes occurring in traditional media including television, magazines, and newspapers and how they are impacting their use by advertisers; public relations problems faced by companies such as Toyota and BP, the world's most popular global and regional brands; proposals to regulate product placement in television shows; and the veracity of claims made for athletic toning shoes.

### IMC Perspectives

These boxed items feature in-depth discussions of interesting issues related to the chapter material and the practical application of integrated marketing communications. Each chapter contains several of these insights into the world of integrated marketing communications. Some of the companies/brands whose IMC programs are discussed in the IMC Perspectives include Hyundai, Domino's Pizza, Dos Equis, GEICO, Google, Sun Microsystems, ESPN, and Macy's. Issues discussed in the IMC Perspectives include the challenges of building brands in a recession, the changing role of account executives in advertising agencies; the role of neuroscience in studying the processing of advertising messages; changes in the measurement of viewing audiences for television commercials; how companies use the purchase funnel to manage and guide their IMC programs; the use of music to enhance the effectiveness of TV commercials; theories on why infomercials are effective; efforts of consumer groups to prevent marketers from sending them unsolicited direct mail; and the debate over the advertising practices of the food and beverage industries including proposals to impose a tax on soft drinks.

### Global Perspectives

These boxed sidebars provide information similar to that in the IMC Perspectives, with a focus on international aspects of advertising and promotion. Some of the companies/brands whose international advertising programs are covered in the Global Perspectives include Asics, Samsung, Procter & Gamble, and PepsiCo. The Global Perspectives also discuss topics such as the challenges of developing marketing communication programs in China, the Cannes International Advertising Awards, celebrities who appear in commercials in Japan while protecting their image in the United States, communication problems in international advertising, the issue of whether the country of origin for products is important to college students, and developing IMC programs to reach consumers in third-world countries.

### Ethical Perspectives

These boxed items discuss the moral and/or ethical issues regarding practices engaged in by marketers and are also tied to the material presented in the particular chapter. Issues covered in the Ethical Perspectives include subliminal advertising, the battle between television networks and advertisers over tasteful advertising, whether advertisements should appear on the covers of magazines, unethical practices by Internet marketers, problems regarding marketers' use of rebates, and controversies arising from the increase in advertising of hard liquor on television, as well as the growth in direct-to-consumer advertising of prescription drugs.

### Technology Perspectives

These boxed items provide detailed discussions of how changes and advances in technology are impacting the practice of integrated marketing communications. Some of the issues covered in the IMC Technology Perspectives include the various ways developments related to Web 2.0 are impacting IMC; how technology is changing the role of brand managers; the targeting of early digital adopters by marketers of high tech products and services; how many creative campaigns are now moving to the Internet through the use of online videos and webisodes; the need for a creative revolution in online marketing and advertising; how social media are being used in various areas of IMC such as sales promotion and for user-generated content advertising and promotions; and how marketers are using various tools provided by Google such as the AdWords online search advertising and AdSense contextual advertising programs.

### Access to AdForum and Relevant Exercises—New to This Edition

A valuable feature new to the ninth edition is our partnership with AdForum which makes available a database of tens of thousands of advertisements from around the world including television commercials, print ads from magazines and newspapers, and various types of digital ads. Instructors who choose to incorporate AdForum into their classes will gain access to these ads for themselves and their students. *AdForum Exercises* are provided at the end of each chapter which direct students to a playlist of ads that are relevant to the material covered and asks them specific questions about them. Incorporating AdForum into the new edition allows students to gain valuable insight into how the material covered in each chapter can be applied to the development of various types of advertisements and other forms of IMC. Students gain access to the AdForum database through Connect.

### Key Terms

Important terms are highlighted in boldface throughout the text and listed at the end of each chapter with a page reference. These terms help call students' attention to important ideas, concepts, and definitions and help them review their learning progress.

### Chapter Summaries

These synopses serve as a quick review of important topics covered and a very helpful study guide.

### Discussion Questions

Questions at the end of each chapter give students an opportunity to test their understanding of the material and to apply it. These questions can also serve as a basis for class discussion or assignments. The discussion questions are also keyed to the learning objectives for the chapter.

### Four-Color Visuals

Print ads, photoboards, and other examples appear throughout the book. More than 400 ads, charts, graphs, and other types of illustrations are included in the text.

## CHANGES IN THE NINTH EDITION

We have made a number of changes in the ninth edition to make it as relevant and current as possible, as well as more interesting to students:

- **Updated Coverage of the Emerging Field of Integrated Marketing Communications** The ninth edition continues to place a strong emphasis on studying advertising and promotion from an integrated marketing communications perspective. We examine contemporary perspectives of integrated marketing communications that have been developed by those doing research and theory development in the area. We also consider developments that are impacting the way marketers communicate with consumers, particularly through the use of social media and viral techniques. Innovative social media-based campaigns for Mountain Dew and the Ford Fiesta, which rely heavily on user-generated content, are featured, and attention is given throughout this edition to ways marketers are utilizing Facebook, Twitter, and other tools. New technologies such as digital video recorders and the convergence of television, computers, mobile devices, and the Internet are changing the way companies are using advertising along with other marketing tools to communicate with their customers. In this new edition we examine how these cutting-edge developments are impacting the IMC program of marketers.
- **Updated Chapter on the Internet and Interactive Media** The ninth edition includes up-to-date information on the Internet and other forms of interactive media and how they are being used by marketers. The Internet chapter has been revised to reflect the impact of developments related to Web 2.0 while updating information regarding Web 1.0 from the last edition. We discuss the use of various Web 2.0 tools that facilitate interactive information sharing and collaboration including social media (Twitter, Facebook, and LinkedIn) and user generated content including videos (YouTube), blogs, and podcasts. Specific examples of how companies are using these tools in their IMC programs are provided. We discuss a number of new Internet-based tools and strategies used by marketers, including paid search, behavioral targeting, RSS, and the use of social and consumer-driven

media. This chapter discusses the latest developments in areas such as audience measurement and methods for determining the effectiveness of Internet advertising. Discussion of the emerging role of the Internet as an important integrated marketing communications tool and of the ways it is being used by marketers is integrated throughout the ninth edition.

- **Technology Perspectives—New to This Edition** In this edition we are introducing a new feature called *IMC Technology Perspectives.* These boxed items are designed to focus attention on how changes and advances in technology are impacting the practice of integrated marketing communications. When the new millennium began, technology was just beginning to impact the practice of integrated marketing communications. The Internet was still constrained by technological limitations such as bandwidth problems, and most consumers were accessing the Web via dial-up telephone services such as AOL, NetZero, and EarthLink. Search engines such as Google, Yahoo, and MSN were in their infancy; products such as the Blackberry and the iPod were just being launched; and YouTube, Facebook, and Twitter did not even exist. However, technology has advanced tremendously in the past five years as there has been rapid penetration in devices such as digital video recorders, smartphones, and high definition TV sets. Most consumers now have a third screen in their lives in the form of some type of mobile device such as a smartphone. As we enter the second decade of the new millennium, electronic readers are becoming part of the lives of many consumers and traditional media such as magazines and newspapers are developing digital versions of their publications which will include full-screen and full-color interactive advertising messages. For most marketers social media tools such as Facebook and Twitter have become a basic part of their IMC programs. The purpose of the new technology perspectives is to provide students with insight into how advances in technology are impacting the strategy and implementation of IMC programs.
- **New Chapter Opening Vignettes** *All* of the chapter opening vignettes in the ninth edition are new and were chosen for their currency and relevance to students. They demonstrate how various companies and advertising agencies use advertising and other IMC tools. They also provide interesting insights into some of the current trends and developments that are taking place in the advertising world.
- **New and Updated IMC Perspectives** All of the boxed items focusing on specific examples of how companies and their communications agencies are using integrated marketing communications are new or updated, and they provide insight into many of the most current and popular advertising and promotional campaigns being used by marketers. The IMC Perspectives also address interesting issues related to advertising, sales promotion, direct marketing, marketing on the Internet, and personal selling.
- **New and Updated Global and Ethical Perspectives** Nearly all of the boxed items focusing on global and ethical issues of advertising and promotion are new; those retained from the eighth edition have been updated. The Global Perspectives examine the role of advertising and other promotional areas in international markets. The Ethical Perspectives discuss specific issues, developments, and problems that call into question the ethics of marketers and their decisions as they develop and implement their advertising and promotional programs.
- **Contemporary Examples** The field of advertising and promotion changes very rapidly, and we continue to keep pace with it. Wherever possible we updated the statistical information presented in tables, charts, and figures throughout the text. We reviewed the most current academic and trade literature to ensure that this text reflects the most current perspectives and theories on advertising, promotion, and the rapidly evolving area of integrated marketing communications. We also updated most of the examples and ads throughout the book. *Advertising and Promotion* continues to be the most contemporary text on the market, offering students as timely a perspective as possible.

## SUPPORT MATERIAL

A high-quality package of instructional supplements supports the ninth edition. Nearly all of the supplements have been developed by the authors to ensure their coordination with the text. We offer instructors a support package that facilitates the use of our text and enhances the learning experience of the student.

### Instructor's Manual

The instructor's manual is a valuable teaching resource that includes learning objectives, chapter and lecture outlines, answers to all end-of-chapter discussion questions, and further insights and teaching suggestions. Additional discussion questions are also presented for each chapter. These questions can be used for class discussion or as short-answer essay questions for exams.

### Manual of Tests

A test bank of more than 1,500 multiple-choice questions has been developed to accompany the text. The questions provide thorough coverage of the chapter material, including opening vignettes and IMC, Global, Technology, and Ethical Perspectives.

### Computerized Test Bank

A computerized version of the test bank is available to adopters of the text.

### Instructor CD-ROM

This exciting presentation CD-ROM allows the professor to customize a multimedia lecture with original material from the supplements package. It includes the Instructor's Manual, PowerPoint presentations, test bank, and computerized test bank.

### Home Page

A home page on the Internet can be found at www.mhhe.com/belch9e

It contains downloadable supplements for instructors and a wealth of study tools for students. Adopters will be able to communicate directly with the authors through the site (contact your McGraw-Hill/Irwin representative for your password).

### Video Supplements

A video supplement package has been developed specifically for classroom use with this text. The first set of videos includes two DVDs with more than 300 television and radio commercials that are examples of creative advertising. It can be used to help the instructor explain a particular concept or principle or give more insight into how a company executes its advertising strategy. Most of the commercials are tied to the chapter openings, IMC and Global Perspectives, or specific examples cited in the text. Insights and/or background information about each commercial are provided in the instructor's manual written specifically for the videos. The second set of videos contains longer segments on the IMC strategies of various companies. Three new video cases have been produced for the ninth edition. The first video focuses on the PunchDub campaign created by the Deutsch LA advertising agency for Volkswagen of America. This integrated marketing campaign was created to increase awareness of Volkswagen's product line in the U.S. market and discusses how Volkswagen uses traditional media advertising as well as the Internet and other digital media tools. The second new video focuses on the innovative social media campaign called "The Fiesta Movement" which was used by the Ford Motor Co. to introduce the new Fiesta subcompact automobile to the United States market. The third new video is for PepsiCo's Mountain Dew brand and examines the "Dewmocracy" campaign which is another social media–driven initiative that the company used to add a new flavor to the product line for the popular soft drink. The video focuses on how the collective intelligence and user-generated content from loyal Mountain Dew drinkers were used to develop the flavor, packaging, and name as well as the advertising to launch the latest addition to the brand franchise. The video supplement package also includes two videos produced for the eighth edition. These include a video focusing on the integrated marketing communications for Under Armour, one of the most successful new companies in the athletic shoe and performance apparel industries. The final video case features Google and examines how this dynamic company has changed the use of the Internet as an advertising and marketing tool with programs such as its AdWords online search advertising, AdSense contextual ads, and YouTube, the video-sharing website that it now owns.

## MCGRAW-HILL *CONNECT™ MARKETING*

### Less Managing. More Teaching. Greater Learning.

McGraw-Hill *Connect™ Marketing* is an online assignment and assessment solution that connects students with the tools and resources they'll need to achieve success. *Connect™ Marketing* helps prepare students for their future by enabling faster learning, more efficient studying, and higher retention of knowledge.

### McGraw-Hill *Connect™ Marketing* Features

*Connect™ Marketing* offers a number of powerful tools and features to make managing assignments easier, so faculty can spend more time teaching. With *Connect™ Marketing* students can engage with their coursework anytime and anywhere, making the learning process more accessible and efficient. *Connect™ Marketing* offers you the features described below.

#### Online Interactives

Online Interactives are engaging tools that teach students to apply key concepts in practice. These Interactives provide students with immersive, experiential learning opportunities. Students will engage in a variety of interactive scenarios to deepen critical knowledge on key course topics. They receive immediate feedback at intermediate steps throughout each exercise, as well as comprehensive feedback at the end of the assignment. All Interactives are automatically scored and entered into the instructor's gradebook.

### Student Progress Tracking

*Connect*™ *Marketing* keeps instructors informed about how each student, section, and class is performing, allowing for more productive use of lecture and office hours. The progress-tracking function enables you to:

- View scored work immediately and track individual or group performances with assignment and grade reports.
- Access an instant view of student or class performances relative to learning objectives.
- Collect data and generate reports required by many accreditation organizations, such as AACSB.

### Smart Grading

When it comes to studying, time is precious. *Connect*™ *Marketing* helps students learn more efficiently by providing feedback and practice material when they need it, where they need it. When it comes to teaching, your time is also precious. The grading function enables you to:

- Have assignments scored automatically, giving students immediate feedback on their work and side-by-side comparisons with correct answers.
- Access and review each response; manually change grades or leave comments for students to review.
- Reinforce classroom concepts with practice tests and instant quizzes.

### Simple Assignment Management

With *Connect*™ *Marketing* creating assignments is easier than ever, so you can spend more time teaching and less time managing. The assignment management function enables you to:

- Create and deliver assignments easily with selectable end-of-chapter questions and test bank items.
- Streamline lesson planning, student progress reporting, and assignment grading to make classroom management more efficient than ever.
- Go paperless with eBooks and online submission and grading of student assignments.

### Instructor Library

The *Connect*™ *Marketing* Instructor Library is your repository for additional resources to improve student engagement in and out of class. You can select and use any asset that enhances your lecture. The *Connect*™ *Marketing* Instructor Library includes:

- Instructor's Manual
- PowerPoint files
- TestBank
- Videos
- eBook

### Student Study Center

The *Connect*™ *Marketing* Student Study Center is the place for students to access additional resources. This center:

- Offers students quick access to lectures, practice materials, eBooks, and more.
- Provides instant practice material and study questions, easily accessible on the go.
- Gives students access to the Personalized Learning Plan described below.

### Lecture Capture via Tegrity Campus

Increase the attention paid to lecture discussion by decreasing the attention paid to note taking. For an additional charge Lecture Capture offers new ways for students to focus on the in-class discussion, knowing they can revisit important topics later. See below for further information.

### McGraw-Hill *Connect™ Plus Marketing*

McGraw-Hill reinvents the textbook learning experience for the modern student with *Connect*™ *Plus Marketing.* A seamless integration of an eBook and *Connect*™ *Marketing, Connect*™ *Plus Marketing* provides all of the *Connect*™ *Marketing* features plus the following:

- An integrated eBook, allowing for anytime, anywhere, access to the textbook.
- Dynamic links between the problems or questions you assign to your students and the location in the eBook where that problem or question is covered.
- A powerful search function to pinpoint and connect key concepts easily.

In short, *Connect*™ *Marketing* offers you and your students powerful tools and features that will optimize your time and energies, enabling you to focus on course content, teaching, and student learning. *Connect*™ *Marketing* also offers a wealth of content resources for both instructors and students. This state-of-the-art, thoroughly tested system will support you in preparing students for the world that awaits.

For more information about Connect, go to www.mcgrawhillconnect.com, or contact your local McGraw-Hill sales representative.

## TEGRITY CAMPUS: LECTURES 24/7

Tegrity Campus is a service that makes classtime available 24/7 by automatically capturing every lecture in a searchable format for students to review when they study and complete assignments. With a simple one-click start-and-stop process, you capture all computer screens and corresponding audio. Students can replay any part of any class with easy-to-use browser-based viewing on a PC or Mac.

Educators know that the more students can see, hear, and experience class resources, the better they learn. In fact, studies prove it. With Tegrity Campus, students quickly recall key moments by using Tegrity Campus's unique search feature. This search helps students efficiently find what they need, when they need it, across an entire semester of class recordings. Help turn all your students' study time into learning moments immediately supported by your lecture.

Lecture Capture enables you to:

- Record and distribute your lecture with a click of a button.
- Record and index PowerPoint® presentations and anything shown on your computer so it is easily searchable, frame by frame.
- Offer access to lectures anytime and anywhere by computer, iPod, or mobile device.
- Increase intent listening and class participation by easing students' concerns about note taking. Lecture Capture will make it more likely you will see students' faces, not the tops of their heads.

To learn more about Tegrity watch a 2-minute Flash demo at http://tegritycampus.mhhe.com.

## ASSURANCE OF LEARNING READY

Many educational institutions today are focused on the notion of *assurance of learning,* an important element of some accreditation standards. *Advertising and Promotion: An Integrated Marketing Communications Perspective* is designed specifically to support your assurance of learning initiatives with a simple, yet powerful solution.

Each test bank question for *Advertising and Promotion: An Integrated Marketing Communications Perspective* maps to a specific chapter learning outcome/objective listed in the text. You can use our test bank software, EZ Test and EZ Test Online, or *Connect*™ *Marketing* to easily query for the learning outcomes/objectives that directly relate to the learning objectives for your course. You can then use the reporting features of EZ Test to aggregate student results in a similar fashion, making the collection and presentation of assurance of learning data simple and easy.

### AACSB Statement

The McGraw-Hill Companies is a proud corporate member of AACSB International. Understanding the importance and value of AACSB accreditation, *Advertising and Promotion: An Integrated Marketing Communications Perspective,* 9e, recognizes the curricula guidelines detailed in the AACSB standards for business accreditation by connecting selected questions (in the text and/or the test bank) to the six general knowledge and skill guidelines in the AACSB standards.

The statements contained in *Advertising and Promotion: An Integrated Marketing Communications Perspective,* 9e, are provided only as a guide for the users of this textbook. The AACSB leaves content coverage and assessment within the purview of individual schools, the mission of the school, and the faculty. While *Advertising and Promotion: An Integrated Marketing Communications Perspective,* 9e, and the teaching package make no claim of any specific AACSB qualification or evaluation, we have within *Advertising and Promotion: An Integrated Marketing Communications Perspective,* 9e, labeled selected questions according to the six general knowledge and skills areas.

## MCGRAW-HILL CUSTOMER CARE CONTACT INFORMATION

At McGraw-Hill, we understand that getting the most from new technology can be challenging. That's why our services don't stop after you purchase our products. You can e-mail our Product Specialists 24 hours a day to get product-training online. Or you can search our knowledge bank of Frequently Asked Questions on our support website. For Customer Support, call 800-331-5094, e-mail hmsupport@mcgraw-hill.com, or visit www.mhhe.com/support. One of our Technical Support Analysts will be able to assist you in a timely fashion.

### Create Mc Graw Hill create

Craft your teaching resources to match the way you teach! With McGraw-Hill Create, www.mcgrawhillcreate.com, you can easily rearrange chapters, combine material from other content sources, and quickly upload content you have written like your course syllabus or teaching notes. Find the content you need in Create by searching through thousands of leading McGraw-Hill textbooks. Arrange your book to fit your teaching style. Create even allows you to personalize your book's appearance by selecting the cover and adding your name, school, and course information. Order a Create book and you'll receive a complimentary print review copy in three to five business days or a complimentary electronic review copy (eComp) via e-mail in about one hour. Go to www.mcgrawhillcreate.com today and register. Experience how McGraw-Hill Create empowers you to teach *your* students *your* way.

## MCGRAW-HILL HIGHER EDUCATION AND BLACKBOARD HAVE TEAMED UP. WHAT DOES THIS MEAN FOR YOU?

1. **Your life, simplified.** Now you and your students can access McGraw-Hill's Connect™ and Create™ right from within your Blackboard course—all with one single sign-on. Say goodbye to the days of logging in to multiple applications.
2. **Deep integration of content and tools.** Not only do you get single sign-on with Connect™ and Create™, you also get deep integration of McGraw-Hill content and content engines right in Blackboard. Whether you're choosing a book for your course or building Connect™ assignments, all the tools you need are right where you want them—inside of Blackboard.
3. **Seamless Gradebooks.** Are you tired of keeping multiple gradebooks and manually synchronizing grades into Blackboard? We thought so. When a student completes an integrated Connect™ assignment, the grade for that assignment automatically (and instantly) feeds your Blackboard grade center.
4. **A solution for everyone.** Whether your institution is already using Blackboard or you just want to try Blackboard on your own, we have a solution for you. McGraw-Hill and Blackboard can now offer you easy access to industry leading technology and content, whether your campus hosts it, or we do. Be sure to ask your local McGraw-Hill representative for details.

## ACKNOWLEDGMENTS

While this ninth edition represents a tremendous amount of work on our part, it would not have become a reality without the assistance and support of many other people. Authors tend to think they have the best ideas, approach, examples, and organization for writing a great book. But we quickly learned that there is always room for our ideas to be improved on by others. A number of colleagues provided detailed, thoughtful reviews that were immensely helpful in making this a better book. We are very grateful to the following individuals who worked with us on earlier editions. They include

David Allen, *St. Joseph's University*
Craig Andrews, *Marquette University*
Subir Bandyopadhyay, *University of Ottawa*
Michael Barone, *Iowa State University*
Jerri Beggs, *Illinois State University*
Mike Behan, *Western Technical College and Viterbo University*
John Bennet, *University of Missouri*
Elizabeth Blair, *Ohio University*
Janice Blankenburg, *University of Wisconsin–Milwaukee*
Karen Bowman, *University of California–Riverside*
Kathy Boyle, *University of Maryland*
Terry Bristol, *Oklahoma State University*
Beverly Brockman, *University of Alabama*
Lauranne Buchanan, *University of Illinois*
Jeffrey Buchman, *Fashion Institute of Technology*
Roy Busby, *University of North Texas*
Christopher Cakebread, *Boston University*
Margaret C. Campbell, *University of Colorado–Boulder*
Les Carlson, *Clemson University*
Lindell Chew, *University of Missouri–St. Louis*
Catherine Cole, *University of Iowa*
Sherry Cook, *Missouri State University*
Robert Cutter, *Cleveland State University*
Richard M. Daily, *University of Texas–Arlington*
Don Dickinson, *Portland State University*
Robert H. Ducoffe, *Baruch College*
Roberta Elins, *Fashion Institute of Technology*
Nancy Ellis, *Suffolk Community College*
Robert Erffmeyer, *University of Wisconsin–Eau Claire*
John Faier, *Miami University*
Raymond Fisk, *Oklahoma State University*
Alan Fletcher, *Louisiana State University*
Marty Flynn, *Suffolk Community College*
Judy Foxman, *Southern Methodist University*
Amy Frank, *Wingate University*
Jon B. Freiden, *Florida State University*
Stefanie Garcia, *University of Central Florida*
Geoff Gordon, *University of Kentucky*
Norman Govoni, *Babson College*
Donald Grambois, *Indiana University*
Stephen Grove, *Clemson University*
Robert Gulonsen, *Washington University*
Bill Hauser, *University of Akron*
Ron Hill, *University of Portland*
JoAnn Hopper, *Western Carolina University*
Paul Jackson, *Ferris State College*
Karen James, *Louisiana State University–Shreveport*
Patricia Kennedy, *University of Nebraska*
Robert Kent, *University of Delaware*
Don Kirchner, *California State University–Northridge*
Paul Klein, *St. Thomas University*
Susan Kleine, *Arizona State University*

Patricia Knowles, *Clemson University*
Dr. Barbara Lafferty, *University of South Florida*
Dana Lanham, *University of North Carolina–Charlotte*
Clark Leavitt, *Ohio State University*
Lauren Lev, *Fashion Institute of Technology*
Aron Levin, *Northern Kentucky University*
Tina Lowry, *Rider University*
Karen Machleit, *University of Cincinnati*
Scott Mackenzie, *Indiana University*
Elizabeth Moore-Shay, *University of Illinois*
Joe Msylivec, *Central Michigan University*
Darrel Muehling, *Washington State University*
Barbara Mueller, *San Diego State University*
John H. Murphy II, *University of Texas–Austin*
Peter Noble, *Southern Methodist University*
Mandy H. Ortiz, *University of Alabama–Tuscaloosa*
Carol Osborne, *USF Tampa*
Charles Overstreet, *Oklahoma State University*
Notis Pagiavlas, *University of Texas–Arlington*
Paul Prabhaker, *DePaul University, Chicago*
William Pride, *Texas A&M University*
Astrid Proboll, *San Francisco State University*
Sanjay Putrevu, *Bryant University*
Sekar Raju, *University at Buffalo*
Joel Reedy, *University of South Florida*
Glen Reicken, *East Tennessee State University*
Scott Roberts, *Old Dominion University*
Michelle Rodriques, *University of Central Florida*
Herbert Jack Rotfield, *Auburn University*
Judith Sayre, *University of North Florida*
Allen D. Schaefer, *Missouri State University*
Carol Schibi, *State Fair Community College*
Denise D. Schoenbachler, *Northern Illinois University*
Lisa Sciulli, *Indiana University of Pennsylvania*
Andrea Scott, *Pepperdine University*
Elaine Scott, *Bluefield State College*
Eugene Secunda, *New York University*
Tanuja Singh, *Northern Illinois University*
Lois Smith, *University of Wisconsin*
Harlan Spotts, *Northeastern University*
Monique Stampleman, *Fashion Institute of Technology*
Mary Ann Stutts, *Southwest Texas State University*
James Swartz, *California State Polytechnic University*
Ric Sweeney, *University of Cincinnati*
Janice Taylor, *Miami University*
Robert Taylor, *Radford University*
Brian Tietje, *Cal State Polytechnic*
Frank Tobolski, *DePaul University*
Mike Weigold, *University of Florida–Gainesville*
John Weitzel, *Western Michigan University*
Kenneth C. Wilbur, *University of Southern California*
Roy Winegar, *Grand Valley State University*
Richard Wingerson, *Florida Atlantic University*
Terrence Witkowski, *California State University–Long Beach*
Merv H. Yeagle, *University of Maryland–College Park*
Elaine Young, *Champlain College*
Robert Young, *Northeastern University*

We are particularly grateful to the individuals who provided constructive comments on how to make this edition better:

Lisa Abendroth, University of Saint Thomas; Natalie Adkins, Creighton University–Omaha; Bruce Alford, Louisiana Tech University; Neil Alperstein, Loyola University Maryland; Sheila Baiers, Kalamazoo Valley Community College; Allen Bargfrede, Berklee College of Music; Elizabeth Blair, Ohio University–Athens; Janice Blankenburg, University of Wisconsin, Milwaukee; Kendrick Brunson, Liberty University; Victoria Bush, University of Mississippi; Nathaniel Calloway, University of Maryland–University College; Oscar Chilabato, Johnson & Wales University; Bob Cline, University of Iowa–Iowa City; Mary Conran, Temple University–Philadelphia; Sherry Cook, Missouri State University; Kevin Cumiskey, Oklahoma State U–Stillwater; Andrew Czaplewski, University of Colorado; Terri Faraone, Mt. San Antonio College; Theresa Flaherty, James Madison University; Debora Grossman, Suny Buffalo; Charles Gulas, Wright State University–Dayton; Holly Hapke, University of Kentucky–Lexington; Diana Haytko, Missouri State University; Yi He, California State University East Bay; Amanda Helm, University of Wisconsin, Whitewater; Christopher Joiner, George Mason University; Leslie Kendrick, Johns Hopkins University; David Koehler, University of Illinois–Chicago; Gary Kritz, Seton Hall University; Ivy Kutlu, Old Dominion University; Barbara Lafferty, University of South Florida–Tampa; Ron Lennon, Barry University; Aron Levin, Northern Kentucky University; Stacey Massey, Texas A & M University; George Meier, University of California–Irvine; Darrel Muehling, Washington State University–Pullman; Mark Neckes, Johnson & Wales University; Kathy O'Donnell, San Francisco State University; Kristen Regine, Johnson & Wales University; Herb Ritchell, DePaul University; Herb Rotfeld, Auburn University–Auburn; Hope Schau, University of Arizona; Eugene Secunda, New York University; James Swartz, California State Poly U–Pomona; Kevin Toomb, University North Carolina Charlotte; Mindy Treftz, Columbia

College–Christian County; Lisa Troy, Texas A & M University; Deb Utter, Boston University; Jim Walker, Northwest Missouri State University; Donna Wertalik, Virginia Polytechnic Institute.

We would also like to acknowledge the cooperation we received from many people in the business, advertising, and media communities. This book contains several hundred ads, illustrations, charts, and tables that have been provided by advertisers and/or their agencies, various publications, and other advertising and industry organizations. Many individuals took time from their busy schedules to provide us with requested materials and gave us permission to use them. A special thanks to all of you.

A manuscript does not become a book without a great deal of work on the part of the publisher. Various individuals at Irwin/McGraw-Hill have been involved with this project over the past several years. Our sponsoring editor on the ninth edition, Michael Ablassmeir, provided valuable guidance and was instrumental in making sure this was much more than just a token revision. A special thanks goes to Kelly Pekelder, our developmental editor, for all of her efforts and for being so great to work with. Thanks also to Dana Pauley for doing a superb job of managing the production process. We also want to acknowledge the outstanding work of Jennifer Blankenship and Margaret Marco for obtaining permissions for most of the ads that appear throughout the book. Thanks to the other members of the product team, Cara Hawthorne, Jeremy Cheshareck, Susan Lombardi, Suresh Babi, and Carol Bielski, for all their hard work on this edition.

We would like to acknowledge the support we have received from the College of Business at San Diego State University. As always, a great deal of thanks goes to our families for putting up with us while we were revising this book. Once again we look forward to returning to normal. Finally, we would like to acknowledge each other for making it through this ordeal for the ninth time! Our families and friends will be happy to know that we still get along after all this—though it is definitely getting tougher and tougher and tougher.

***George E. Belch***

***Michael A. Belch***

# Your guide through the exciting world

## Why It's a Powerful Learning Tool

The ninth edition continues to provide you with the most comprehensive and current text on the market in the area of advertising and promotion from an integrated marketing communications perspective. The following features in each chapter enhance students' understanding of the material as well as their reading enjoyment.

### CHAPTER OPENERS

**Learning Objectives** are provided at the beginning of each chapter to identify the major areas and points covered in the chapter and guide the learning effort. Each chapter also begins with a **Chapter Opening Vignette** that shows the effective use of integrated marketing communications by a company or ad agency or discusses an interesting issue that is relevant to the chapter. Some of the companies profiled in the opening vignettes include GEICO, Ford, Mountain Dew, Sony, the New York Jets, and Subway.

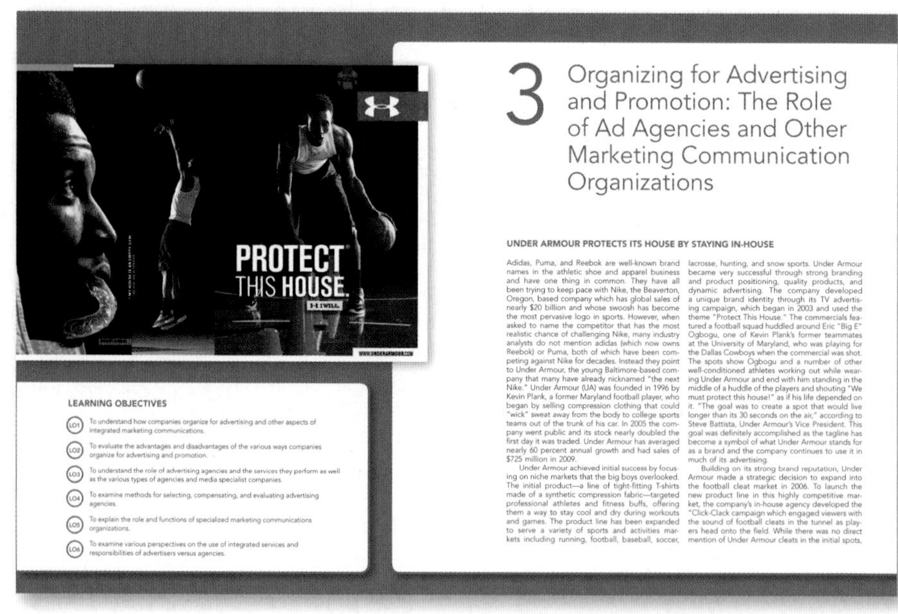


3 Organizing for Advertising and Promotion: The Role of Ad Agencies and Other Marketing Communication Organizations

LEARNING OBJECTIVES

LO1 To understand how companies organize for advertising and other aspects of integrated marketing communications.

LO2 To evaluate the advantages and disadvantages of the various ways companies organize for advertising and promotion.

LO3 To understand the role of advertising agencies and the services they perform as well as the various types of agencies and media specialist companies.

LO4 To examine methods for selecting, compensating, and evaluating advertising agencies.

LO5 To explain the role and functions of specialized marketing communications organizations.

LO6 To examine various perspectives on the use of integrated services and responsibilities of advertisers versus agencies.

UNDER ARMOUR PROTECTS ITS HOUSE BY STAYING IN-HOUSE

Adidas, Puma, and Reebok are well-known brand names in the athletic shoe and apparel business and have one thing in common. They have all been trying to keep pace with Nike, the Beaverton, Oregon, based company which has global sales of nearly $20 billion and whose swoosh has become the most pervasive logo in sports. However, when asked to name the competitor that has the most realistic chance of challenging Nike, many industry analysts do not mention adidas (which now owns Reebok) or Puma, both of which have been competing against Nike for decades. Instead they point to Under Armour, the young Baltimore-based company that many have already nicknamed "the next Nike." Under Armour (UA) was founded in 1996 by Kevin Plank, a former Maryland football player, who began by selling compression clothing that could "wick" sweat away from the body to college sports teams out of the trunk of his car. In 2005 the company went public and its stock nearly doubled the first day it was traded. Under Armour has averaged nearly 60 percent annual growth and had sales of $725 million in 2009.

Under Armour achieved initial success by focusing on niche markets that the big boys overlooked. The initial product—a line of tight-fitting T-shirts made of a synthetic compression fabric—targeted professional athletes and fitness buffs, offering them a way to stay cool and dry during workouts and games. The product line has been expanded to serve a variety of sports and activities markets including running, football, baseball, soccer, lacrosse, hunting, and snow sports. Under Armour became very successful through strong branding and product positioning, quality products, and dynamic advertising. The company developed a unique brand identity through its TV advertising campaign, which began in 2003 and used the theme "Protect This House." The commercials featured a football squad huddled around Eric "Big E" Ogbogu, one of Kevin Plank's former teammates at the University of Maryland, who was playing for the Dallas Cowboys when the commercial was shot. The spots show Ogbogu and a number of other well-conditioned athletes working out while wearing Under Armour and end with him standing in the middle of a huddle of the players and shouting "We must protect this house!" as if his life depended on it. "The goal was to create a spot that would live longer than its 30 seconds on the air," according to Steve Battista, Under Armour's Vice President. This goal was definitely accomplished as the tagline has become a symbol of what Under Armour stands for as a brand and the company continues to use it in much of its advertising.

Building on its strong brand reputation, Under Armour made a strategic decision to expand into the football cleat market in 2006. To launch the new product line in this highly competitive market, the company's in-house agency developed the "Click-Clack campaign which engaged viewers with the sound of football cleats in the tunnel as players head onto the field. While there was no direct mention of Under Armour cleats in the initial spots,

# of advertising and promotion.

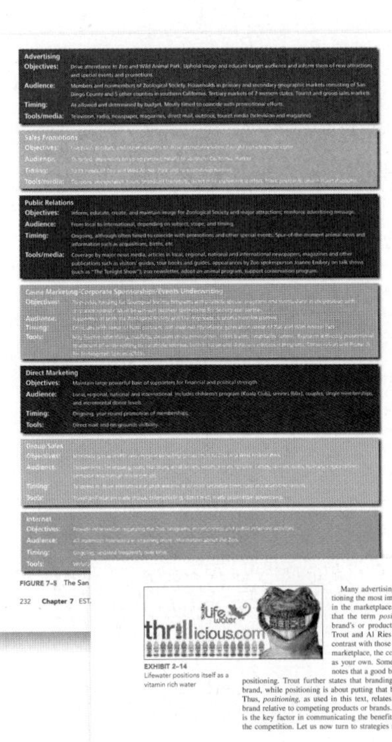


## CHAPTER PEDAGOGY

**Four-Color Visuals** throughout the book consist of photoboards, commercial shots, charts, graphs, and over 400 print ads. **Key Terms** are highlighted in boldface throughout the text and listed at the end of each chapter with a page reference. **Chapter Summaries** serve as a quick review of important topics covered and as a study guide. **Discussion Questions** tagged to learning objectives at the end of each chapter give students an opportunity to test their understanding of the material and to apply it. These questions can also serve as a basis for class discussion or assignments.

EXHIBIT 2–14
Lifewater positions itself as a vitamin rich water

Many advertising practitioners consider market positioning the most important factor in establishing a brand in the marketplace. David Aaker and John Myers note that the term *position* has been used to indicate the brand's or product's image in the marketplace.[11] Jack Trout and Al Ries suggest that this brand image must contrast with those of competitors. They say, "In today's marketplace, the competitors' image is just as important as your own. Sometimes more important."[12] Jack Trout notes that a good branding strategy cannot exist without positioning. Trout further states that branding is about the process of building a brand, while positioning is about putting that brand in the mind of the consumer.[13] Thus, *positioning*, as used in this text, relates to the image of the product and or brand relative to competing products or brands. The position of the product or brand is the key factor in communicating the benefits it offers and differentiating it from the competition. Let us now turn to strategies marketers use to position a product.

DEVELOPING A POSITIONING STRATEGY

A number of positioning strategies might be employed in developing a promotional program. David Aaker and J. Gary Shansby discuss six such strategies: positioning by product attributes, price/quality, use, product class, users, and competitor.[14] Aaker and Myers add one more approach, positioning by cultural symbols.[15]

EXHIBIT 2–15
Kohl's positions its brand as having good value for the right price

**Positioning by Product Attributes and Benefits** A common approach to positioning is setting the brand apart from competitors on the basis of the specific characteristics or benefits offered. Sometimes a product may be positioned on more than one product benefit. Marketers attempt to identify **salient attributes** (those that are important to consumers and are the basis for making a purchase decision). For example, when Apple first introduced its computers, the key benefit stressed was ease of use—an effective strategy, given the complexity of computers in the market at that time. More recently, there have been a number of new water products that enhance hydration, help the body to exert physical power, increase immunities, and so on. Sobe Lifewater also offers vitamin enhanced water (Exhibit 2–14).

**Positioning by Price/Quality** Marketers often use price/quality characteristics to position their brands. One way they do this is with ads that reflect the image of a high-quality brand where cost, while not irrelevant, is considered secondary to the quality benefits derived from using the brand. Premium brands positioned at the high end of the market use this approach to positioning.

Another way to use price/quality characteristics for positioning is to focus on the quality or value offered by the brand at a very competitive price. For example, Kohl's takes the position of a family oriented speciality store offering good value (Exhibit 2–15). Remember that although price is an important consideration, the product quality must be comparable to, or even better than, competing brands for the positioning strategy to be effective.



Chapter 2 THE ROLE OF IMC IN THE MARKETING PROCESS 55

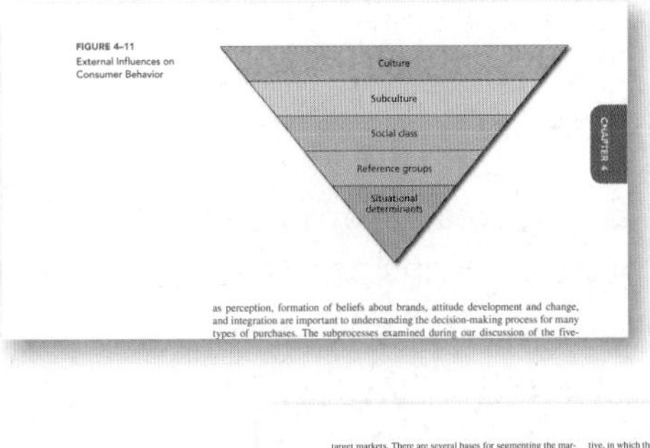

FIGURE 4–11
External Influences on Consumer Behavior



as perception, formation of beliefs about brands, attitude development and change, and integration are important to understanding the decision-making process for many types of purchases. The subprocesses examined during our discussion of the five-

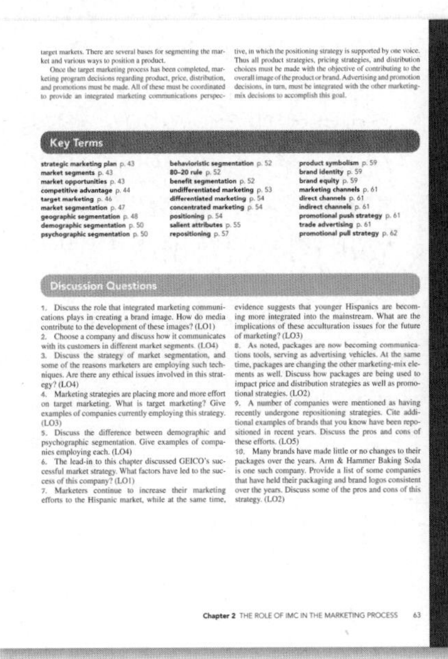

target markets. There are several bases for segmenting the market and various ways to position a product.

Once the target marketing process has been completed, marketing program decisions regarding product, price, distribution, and promotions must be made. All of these must be coordinated to provide an integrated marketing communications perspective, in which the positioning strategy is supported by one voice. Thus all product strategies, pricing strategies, and distribution choices must be made with the objective of contributing to the overall image of the product or brand. Advertising and promotion decisions, in turn, must be integrated with the other marketing-mix decisions to accomplish this goal.

**Key Terms**

**strategic marketing plan** p. 43
**market segments** p. 43
**market opportunities** p. 43
**competitive advantage** p. 44
**target marketing** p. 46
**market segmentation** p. 47
**geographic segmentation** p. 48
**demographic segmentation** p. 50
**psychographic segmentation** p. 50
**behavioristic segmentation** p. 52
**80–20 rule** p. 52
**benefit segmentation** p. 52
**undifferentiated marketing** p. 53
**differentiated marketing** p. 54
**concentrated marketing** p. 54
**positioning** p. 54
**salient attributes** p. 55
**repositioning** p. 57
**product symbolism** p. 59
**brand identity** p. 59
**brand equity** p. 59
**marketing channels** p. 61
**direct channels** p. 61
**indirect channels** p. 61
**promotional push strategy** p. 61
**trade advertising** p. 61
**promotional pull strategy** p. 62

**Discussion Questions**

1. Discuss the role that integrated marketing communications plays in creating a brand image. How do media contribute to the development of these images? (LO1)
2. Choose a company and discuss how it communicates with its customers in different market segments. (LO4)
3. Discuss the strategy of market segmentation, and some of the reasons marketers are employing such techniques. Are there any ethical issues involved in this strategy? (LO4)
4. Marketing strategies are placing more and more effort on target marketing. What is target marketing? Give examples of companies currently employing this strategy. (LO3)
5. Discuss the difference between demographic and psychographic segmentation. Give examples of companies employing each. (LO4)
6. The lead-in to this chapter discussed GEICO's successful market strategy. What factors have led to the success of this company? (LO1)
7. Marketers continue to increase their marketing efforts to the Hispanic market, while at the same time, evidence suggests that younger Hispanics are becoming more integrated into the mainstream. What are the implications of these acculturation issues for the future of marketing? (LO3)
8. As noted, packages are now becoming communications tools, serving as advertising vehicles. At the same time, packages are changing the other marketing-mix elements as well. Discuss how packages are being used to impact price and distribution strategies as well as promotional strategies. (LO2)
9. A number of companies were mentioned as having recently undergone repositioning strategies. Cite additional examples of brands that you know have been repositioned in recent years. Discuss the pros and cons of these efforts. (LO5)
10. Many brands have made little or no changes to their packages over the years. Arm & Hammer Baking Soda is one such company. Provide a list of some companies that have held their packaging and brand logos consistent over the years. Discuss some of the pros and cons of this strategy. (LO2)

Chapter 2 THE ROLE OF IMC IN THE MARKETING PROCESS 63

## REAL LIFE EXAMPLES

The authors have used many sources to find practical examples to use throughout the text. In addition to the integration of the strategy and rationale behind the ads and other types of promotion that are used for current examples of industry practice, there are special in-depth discussions highlighted in boxed sections. **IMC Perspectives** present in-depth discussion of particular issues related to the chapter material and show how companies are using integrated marketing communications. **Global Perspectives** are presented throughout the text in recognition of the increasing importance of international marketing and the challenges of advertising and promotion and the roles they play in the marketing programs of multinational marketers. **Ethical Perspectives** focus attention on important social issues and show how advertisers must take ethical considerations into account when planning and implementing advertising and promotional programs. **IMC Technology Perspectives** provide a detailed discussion of how changes and advances in technology are impacting the practice of integrated marketing communications.

## ONLINE LEARNING CENTER

## www.mhhe.com/belch9e

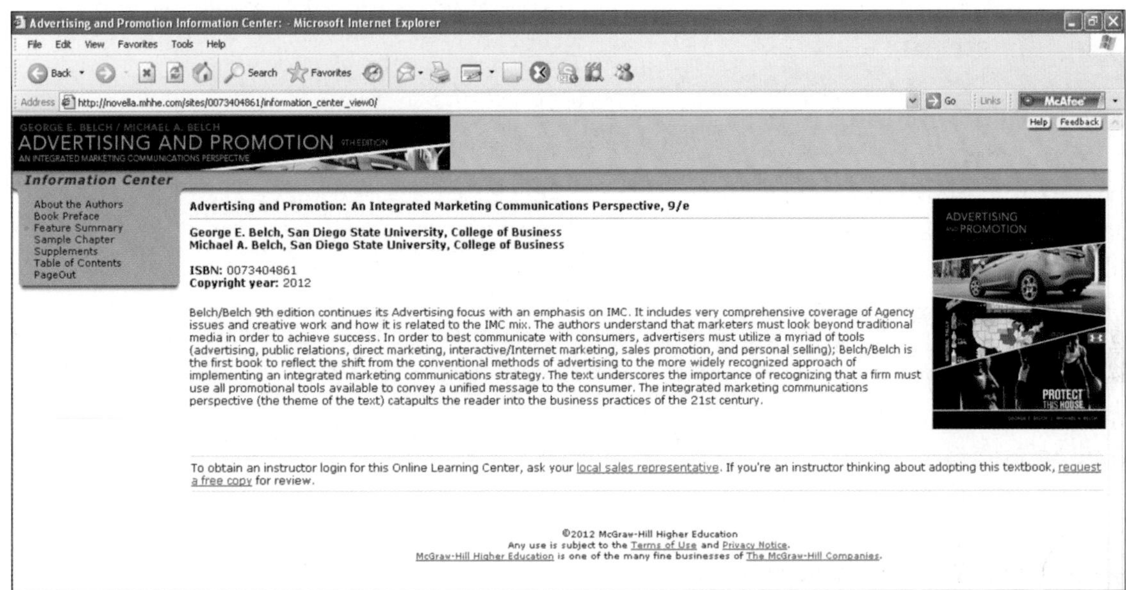


## FOR INSTRUCTORS

The resources available online for instructors include downloadable versions of the Instructor's Manual, Video Instructor's Manual, PowerPoint Presentations, Cases and case teaching notes. Instructors can access AdForum, Advertising Target Practice, and the video clips through

www.mcgrawhillconnect.com.

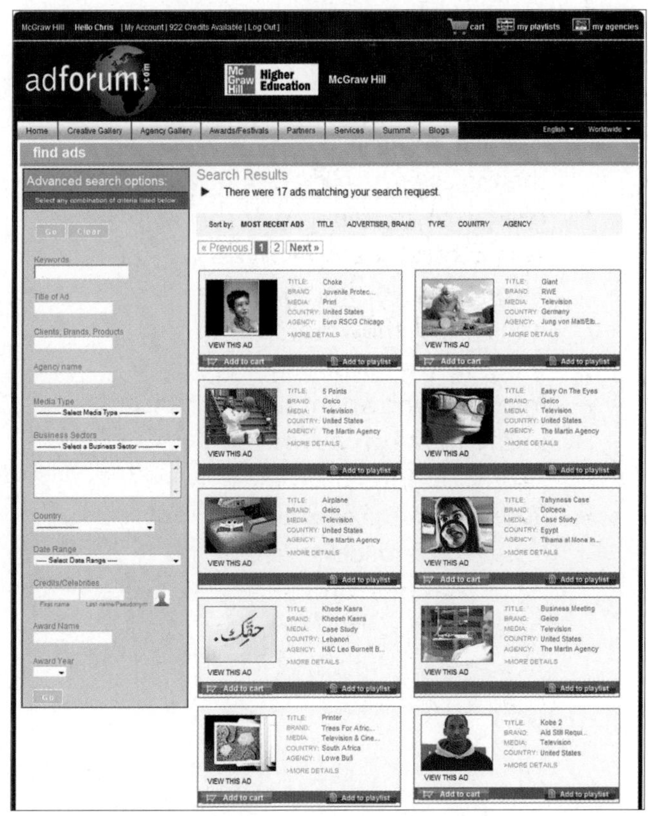


## FOR STUDENTS

A wealth of study tools is available for students at the site including self-assessing quizzes, PowerPoint Presentations, and an online Campaign Planner.

# BRIEF CONTENTS

# DETAILED CONTENTS

## Part One Introduction to Integrated Marketing Communications

## Part Two Integrated Marketing Communications Program Situation Analysis

## Part Four

## Objectives and Budgeting for Integrated Marketing Communications Programs

## Part Five

## Developing the Integrated Marketing Communications Program

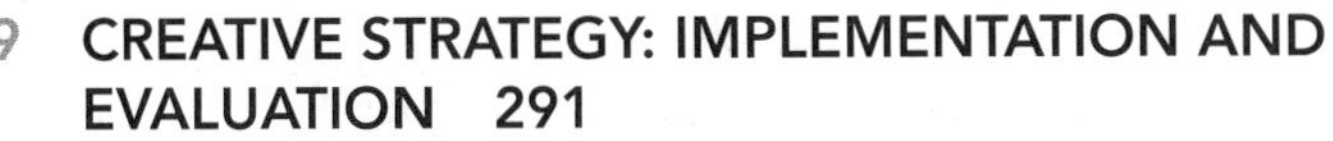

## 9 CREATIVE STRATEGY: IMPLEMENTATION AND EVALUATION 291

## 10 MEDIA PLANNING AND STRATEGY 327

## 11 EVALUATION OF MEDIA: TELEVISION AND RADIO 363

SONY
Now you can get a 7-inch window with an unobstructed view of Wall Street.
Not built to Sony guidelines

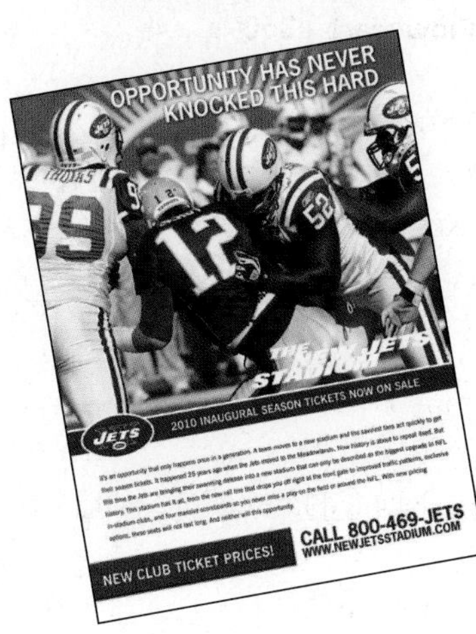
OPPORTUNITY HAS NEVER KNOCKED THIS HARD
2010 INAUGURAL SEASON TICKETS NOW ON SALE
NEW CLUB TICKET PRICES!
CALL 800-469-JETS
WWW.NEWJETSSTADIUM.COM

Lend A Paw
$100,000 donated!
Lend A Paw
Walmart ASPCA
Thanks for your support!

$5
ANY REGULAR FOOTLONG
Excludes Premium Subs.

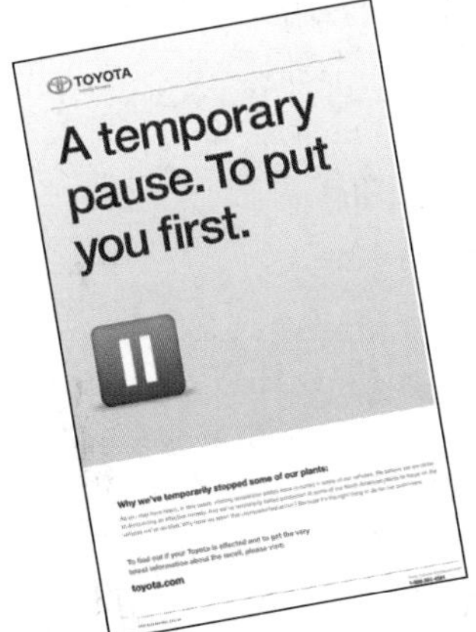




## Part Six Monitoring, Evaluation, and Control

## Part Seven Special Topics and Perspectives

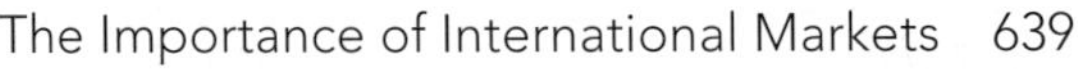

## LEARNING OBJECTIVES

LO1 To examine the marketing communication function and the growing importance of advertising and other promotional elements in the marketing programs of domestic and foreign companies.

LO2 To introduce the concept of integrated marketing communications (IMC) and consider how it has evolved.

LO3 To examine reasons for the increasing importance of the IMC perspective in planning and executing advertising and promotional programs.

LO4 To introduce the various elements of the promotional mix and consider their roles in an IMC program.

LO5 To examine the various types of contact points through which marketers communicate with their target audiences.

LO6 To examine how various marketing and promotional elements must be coordinated to communicate effectively.

LO7 To introduce a model of the IMC planning process and examine the steps in developing a marketing communications program.

# 1 An Introduction to Integrated Marketing Communications

## VOLKSWAGEN GOES AFTER THE AMERICAN AUTOMOBILE MARKET

In 2008 Volkswagen Chief Executive Officer Martin Winterkorn announced that the German company was planning on moving past Toyota to become the world's largest automaker by 2018. At the time many industry analysts questioned his intentions as Toyota was about to pass General Motors to become the global market leader and was selling 3 million more vehicles per year than Volkswagen. However, by the end of 2009 Volkswagen had closed the gap to less than 1.5 million cars and Toyota was struggling as a result of extensive negative publicity the Japanese company had received after a series of embarrassing recalls of its cars in the U.S. market. General Motors was also struggling, as the company that was the industry leader for decades had to receive bailout monies from the U.S. government to survive the global recession which had reduced demand for cars and trucks around the world.

Volkswagen's growth strategy includes going head-to-head with its major European competitors including BMW, Mercedes, Renault, and Fiat, as well as pursuing the rapidly growing markets of China, Southeast Asia, and India. However, its most ambitious plans are for the U.S. market where the company's goal is to double sales to more than 400,000 cars by 2012 and to sell 800,000 cars per year by 2018. Volkswagen of America President and CEO Stefan Jacoby convinced the company's board to build VW's first U.S. plant in Chattanooga, Tennessee, which will reduce costs and keep prices down as well as help VW overcome resistance in America's heartland to imported vehicles. The company plans to expand its product line over the next five years by introducing new compact and mid-size sedans as part of its strategy to take customers from Toyota, Honda, Ford, Hyundai, and other competitors by selling American car buyers on German engineering and styling at affordable prices.

Volkswagen recognizes that it faces a formidable marketing challenge in achieving its aggressive growth plans in the U.S. market, as nearly 80 percent of Americans are aware of the VW brand but only 2 percent buy its cars. Volkswagen of America's Vice President of Marketing Tim Ellis has noted that VW has a bigger brand than it deserves as most Americans recognize the Beetle and Jetta but draw a blank on the company's other eight models such as the Passat, Golf, GTI, Routan, Eos, Tiguan, Touareg, and the new CC sedan. He has stated that in order for the company to increase its sales volume in the U.S. market, Volkswagen has to become more relevant, and the appeal of the brand has to move beyond the base of loyal enthusiasts and captivate consumers in the mainstream market.

Volkswagen of America took its first step toward changing the perceptions of Americans and showing them that it sells more than Beetles and Jettas, when it awarded its $200 million per year advertising and marketing communications business to a new advertising agency, Deutsch LA, in October 2009. Volkswagen chose Deutsch over a number of other agencies that were competing for its business on the basis of the agency's creative ideas that include ways to extend the marketing campaign into the online space and particularly into the fast-growing realm of social media. The agency team recognized that the initial challenges they faced were to get consumers interested in Volkswagen by letting them know that the company has a car that would fit their needs and making them aware of the VW product line.

To address these challenges, Deutsch LA developed a new campaign called "Punch Dub" which was an update on the classic Punch Buggy (or Slug Bug) game that kids used to play in the heyday of the original VW Beetle, where the first person to see a Beetle would yell "Punch Bug" and playfully slug his or her friend. The campaign was launched with a 30-second commercial during the 2010 Super Bowl which was watched by more than 106 million people, surpassing the 1983 final episode of the popular sitcom "M-A-S-H" to become the most watched program in U.S. television history. The light-hearted commercial featured a variety of people in different driving situations gently slugging each other in the arm every time they spot a Volkswagen model and included cameo appearances by actor/comedian Tracy Morgan and singing legend Stevie Wonder. An online version of "Punch Dub" also debuted on the popular Facebook social network site on Super Bowl Sunday which encouraged people to dole out virtual "slugs" to friends and family for a chance to win a weekly prize (6-month leases on specific VW vehicles listed online) and the grand prize of a new Volkswagen CC sedan. Players could pick any one of thirteen VW vehicles, customize their punch, and choose a Facebook friend to punch. The more friends they punched the better their chances of winning a prize. The game was also available on the Volkswagen of America website, and an online guide to the game was also available that players could use to develop and hone their punching technique. The Punch Dub spot was one of the most popular commercials to air during the Super Bowl and within a few days had received more than 1 million online views while the game had 5,000 registered users, and nearly 30,000 punches were thrown.

As part of the campaign Volkswagen revealed that it had found the creator of the original game, Charlie "Sluggy" Patterson and made it possible for people to interact with him via a special blog and Twitter feed as well as through a series of videos on YouTube. Within a few weeks of the launch of the campaign the videos had generated more than 100,000 views on YouTube and thousands of Twitter followers. The two-month campaign included outdoor, radio, and newspaper advertising as well as an extensive public relations campaign that generated feature articles and stories in *BusinessWeek,* and *The Wall Street Journal,* as well as in local newspapers and on local television stations across the country. The campaign was also extended to Volkswagen dealerships as special point-of-sale kits were developed to promote a national sales event called "Punch Dub Days" which included special offers on various VW models.

After two months Volkswagen transitioned into the second phase of the campaign which leveraged the theme "Das Auto" which is the global tagline for Volkswagen. The Das Auto campaign continued to showcase the company's product line and define how Volkswagen is delivering German engineering at a great value in a playful, yet direct Volkswagen tone. The ads in the second phase of the campaign promoted the innovative features and benefits of modern-day Volkswagens.

In discussing the new campaign, marketing VP Tim Ellis has noted that "people think they know Volkswagen but we believe there is a bigger story to tell about our brand, our commitment to the American market, and our expansive line of affordable, German-engineered cars that are fun to drive. As an iconic brand that has achieved pop cultural status in America, people think they are familiar with all there is to know about Volkswagen. This campaign gives consumers a reason to take another look at the brand and gain a new perspective on the breadth of our vehicle offerings, quality, performance, and value." The new campaign Deutsch LA has developed for Volkswagen of America appears to be a great way for the company to show millions of Americans that VW sells more than Beetles and Jettas and help the company achieve its ambitious sales goal for the U.S. market. Watch out Toyota, VW is back!

Sources: Jean Halliday, "Hits Keep Coming from VW's Super Bowl Ads," *Automotive News,* February 12, 2010, http://www.autonews.com/apps/pbcs.dll/article?AID=/20100212/RETAIL03/100219956/1; Volkswagen of America, Inc.; "Volkswagen to Spotlight 'Punch Dub' Game in Super Bowl Ad, Online Campaign Touting Product Family" (2010, February). *Marketing Business Weekly,* p. 371. Retrieved March 2, 2010, from *ABI/INFORM Global.* (Document ID: 1954474321); David Welch, "Why VW Is the Car Giant to Watch," *Bloomberg BusinessWeek,* January 25, 2010, pp. 44–49; Jean Halliday, "How Deutsch L.A. Snared Plum VW Account, *Advertising Age,* October 26, 2009, pp. 1, 56.

The Punch Dub campaign that the Deutsch LA agency developed for Volkswagen of America illustrates the importance of having a well-planned and executed marketing communications strategy. However, it also provides an excellent example of how the roles of advertising and other forms of marketing communication are changing in the modern world of marketing. In the past, advertising was a relatively simple process as most companies relied primarily on ads run in the mass media to deliver their marketing messages to large numbers of consumers who watched television, listened to radio, and read magazines and newspapers. However, today's marketers recognize that the rapidly changing media environment is making it increasingly difficult to reach their target audiences and communicate effectively with them. The

**EXHIBIT 1–1**
Consumers can get valuable information on the Volkswagen website as well as have an entertaining interactive experience

mass media are losing their viewers, listeners, and readers to the highly fragmented but more narrowly targeted digital media that allow consumers to be more actively engaged in the communications process. Consumers are no longer passive message recipients who will sit back and receive unfiltered advertising messages dictated by marketers. They want to be in more control of the content they receive from the media and they are seeking out information, as well as entertainment, from a myriad of sources.

The various marketing communication tools used by Volkswagen of America for the Punch Dub campaign show how companies are using *integrated marketing communications* (IMC) to reach their target audiences. Volkswagen utilizes traditional mass media advertising through television, radio, magazines, newspapers, and billboards to build awareness, communicate information, and build a brand image for the company and its various models. They also use these off-line channels to influence online search behavior by driving consumers to their website (www.vw.com), which provides detailed information about the various models, prices, financing options, and local dealers and can provide an interactive experience by allowing consumers to play the Punch Dub game (Exhibit 1–1). Volkswagen is also using a variety of social media that have become an increasingly important part of the digital marketing campaigns of many companies. The humorous commercials as well as other videos created for the campaign can be viewed on YouTube, and consumers are encouraged to connect with Volkswagen through its Facebook page and on Twitter. Publicity for Volkswagen and its marketing communication campaigns is generated through press releases and other public relations activities that are designed to result in feature stories in magazines and newspapers as well as on the Internet. Volkswagen sponsors motor sports as well as professional soccer teams such as D.C. United to reach its target audience and build its brand image. Promotional efforts for Volkswagen vehicles are extended to dealerships where point-of-purchase displays and materials are provided along with training, contests, and incentives for salespeople. For example, for the campaign launch Volkswagen provided its dealers with a Punch Dub days point-of-sale and a Brand Construction kit that contained materials needed to create local advertising and to carry the advertising theme to the dealers' showrooms.

Volkswagen, along with thousands of other companies, recognizes that the way they communicate with consumers and other relevant audiences to promote their products and services is changing rapidly and they must keep pace by integrating a variety of communication tools into their marketing programs. The fragmentation of mass markets, the rapid growth of the Internet and other new digital media, the emergence of global markets, economic uncertainties, and changing lifestyles and media consumption habits of consumers are all changing the way companies develop their marketing programs—particularly advertising and promotion.[1] Developing marketing communication programs that are responsive to these changes is critical to the success of every company.

## THE GROWTH OF ADVERTISING AND PROMOTION

Advertising and promotion are an integral part of our social and economic systems. In our complex society, advertising has evolved into a vital communications system for both consumers and businesses. The ability of advertising and other promotional methods to deliver carefully prepared messages to target audiences has given them a major role in the marketing programs of most organizations. Companies ranging from large multinational corporations to small retailers increasingly rely on advertising and promotion to help them market products and services. In market-based economies, consumers have learned to rely on advertising and other forms of promotion for information they can use in making purchase decisions.

In 1980, advertising and sales promotion were the dominant forms of marketing communication used by most companies, and total expenditures in the United States across the two was just over $100 billion. Media advertising accounted for $53 billion while $49 billion was spent on sales promotion techniques such as product samples, coupons, contests, sweepstakes, premiums, rebates and trade allowances, and discounts to retailers. By 2010, total advertising and nonadvertising marketing communication expenditures in the United States were estimated to be $670 billion with $177 billion being spent on media advertising, consumer and trade sales promotion accounting for $280 billion, nearly $150 billion going to direct mail and other forms of direct marketing, and just over $30 billion spent on sponsorships and event marketing.[2]

It is particularly interesting to note the amount of marketing communication monies spent on the Internet and other nontraditional media, some of which did not even exist at the beginning of the new millennium. For example, nearly $13 billion was expected to be spent for online search and another $1 billion on online social marketing in 2010. When added to the estimated $11 billion spent on online display advertising (the graphical banner ads and towers we have become accustomed to on websites) and another $1.5 billion on online video ads, overall Internet advertising reached nearly $26 billion in 2010. Another new form of advertising, mobile marketing, whereby ads and promotions are sent directly to various types of mobile devices such as cell and smartphones, also accounted for another $1 billion in expenditures. Thus, while the traditional media and sales promotion still account for the majority of companies' marketing communication expenditures, more monies are being allocated to nontraditional media and the amount is expected to increase rapidly.[3]

Marketing communication expenditures in international markets have grown as well. Advertising expenditures outside the United States increased from $55 billion in 1980 to an estimated $270 billion in 2010.[4] Both foreign and domestic companies spent billions more on sales promotion, direct marketing, event sponsorships, and public relations as well as various forms of nontraditional media, all of which have become important parts of their marketing communications programs.

The tremendous growth in marketing communication expenditures has been impacted by the global recession that began in late 2008 as worldwide spending on advertising and promotion declined by 10 percent in 2009. U.S. spending dropped 13 percent, as many companies slashed their marketing budgets including 8 of the 10 largest advertisers led by Procter & Gamble, the world's largest advertiser, which cut spending by 16 percent.[5] Advertising and promotion spending is expected to increase over the next few years as marketers around the world recognize the value and importance of advertising and other forms of marketing communications. Integrated marketing communications play an important role in the marketing programs of companies in their efforts to communicate with and sell their products and services to consumers. To understand the role integrated marketing communications play in the marketing process, let us first examine the marketing function.

## THE ROLE OF MARKETING

Marketing has never been more important or more pervasive than it is today. Organizations ranging from large multinational corporations to small entrepreneurial companies and local businesses recognize that marketing is an important business

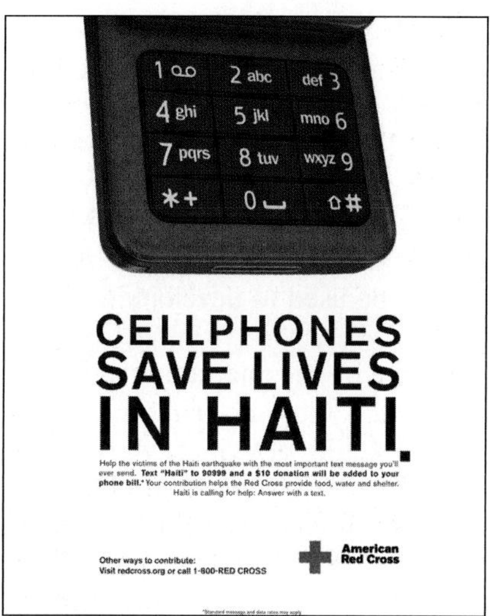


**EXHIBIT 1–2**
Nonprofit organizations use advertising to solicit contributions and support

function and plays a critical role in their ability to compete in the marketplace. For nearly two decades, the American Marketing Association (AMA), the organization that represents marketing professionals in the United States and Canada, defined marketing as *the process of planning and executing the conception, pricing, promotion, and distribution of ideas, goods, and services to create exchanges that satisfy individual and organizational objectives.*[6] This definition of marketing focused on **exchange** as a central concept in marketing and the use of the basic marketing activities to create and sustain relationships with customers.[7] For exchange to occur there must be two or more parties with something of value to one another, a desire and ability to give up that something to the other party, and a way to communicate with each other. Advertising and promotion play an important role in the exchange process by informing customers of an organization's product or service and convincing them of its ability to satisfy their needs or wants.

Not all marketing transactions involve the exchange of money for a product or service. Nonprofit organizations such as various causes, charities, religious groups, the arts, and colleges and universities (probably including the one you are attending) receive millions of dollars in donations every year. Many nonprofit organizations used ads to solicit contributions from the public such as the one shown in Exhibit 1–2 which asks for contributions to help victims of the devastating earthquake that hit Haiti in January 2010. Donors generally do not receive any material benefits for their contributions; they donate in exchange for intangible social and psychological satisfactions such as feelings of goodwill and altruism.

While many still view exchange as the core phenomenon or domain for study in marketing, there is also agreement among most academicians and practitioners that the discipline is rapidly changing. To reflect these changes, the AMA adopted a revised definition of **marketing** in 2007, which is as follows:

> Marketing is the activity, set of institutions, and processes for creating, communicating, delivering and exchanging offerings that have value for customers, clients, partners, and society at large.[8]

This revised definition is viewed as being more reflective of the role of nonmarketers to the marketing process. It also recognizes the important role marketing plays in the process of creating, communicating and delivering value to customers, as well as society at large. Today, most markets are seeking more than just a one-time exchange or transaction with customers. The focus of market-driven companies is on developing and sustaining *relationships* with their customers. Successful companies recognize that creating, communicating, and delivering *value* to their customers is extremely important. **Value** is the customer's perception of all of the benefits of a product or service weighed against all the costs of acquiring and consuming it.[9] Benefits can be functional (the performance of the product), experiential (what it feels like to use the product), and/or psychological (feelings such as self-esteem or status that result from owning a particular brand). Costs include the money paid for the product or service as well as other factors such as acquiring information about the product/service, making the purchase, learning how to use it, maintaining the product, and disposing of it.

## The Marketing Mix

Marketing facilitates the exchange process and the development of relationships by carefully examining the needs and wants of consumers, developing a product or service that satisfies these needs, offering it at a certain price, making it available through a particular place or channel of distribution, and developing a program of promotion or communication to create awareness and interest. These four Ps—product, price, place (distribution), and promotion—are elements of the **marketing mix**. The basic task of marketing is combining these four elements into a marketing program to facilitate the potential for exchange with consumers in the marketplace.

The proper marketing mix does not just happen. Marketers must be knowledgeable about the issues and options involved in each element of the mix. They must also be aware of how these elements can be combined to form an effective marketing program that delivers value to consumers. The market must be analyzed through consumer research, and the resulting information must be used to develop an overall marketing strategy and mix.

The primary focus of this book is on one element of the marketing mix: the promotional variable. However, the promotional program must be part of a viable marketing strategy and be coordinated with other marketing activities. A firm can spend large sums on advertising or sales promotion, but it stands little chance of success if the product is of poor quality, is priced improperly, or does not have adequate distribution to consumers. Marketers have long recognized the importance of combining the elements of the marketing mix into a cohesive marketing strategy. Many companies also recognize the need to integrate their various marketing communications efforts, such as media advertising, direct marketing, sales promotion, Internet marketing, event sponsorships, and public relations, to achieve more effective marketing communications.

## INTEGRATED MARKETING COMMUNICATIONS

For many years, the promotional function in most companies was dominated by mass-media advertising. Companies relied primarily on their advertising agencies for guidance in nearly all areas of marketing communication. Most marketers did use additional promotional and marketing communication tools, but sales promotion and direct-marketing agencies as well as package design firms were generally viewed as auxiliary services and often used on a per-project basis. Public relations agencies were used to manage the organization's publicity, image, and affairs with relevant publics on an ongoing basis but were not viewed as integral participants in the marketing communications process.

Many marketers built strong barriers around the various marketing and promotional functions and planned and managed them as separate practices, with different budgets, different views of the market, and different goals and objectives. These companies failed to recognize that the wide range of marketing and promotional tools must be coordinated to communicate effectively and present a consistent image to target markets.

### The Evolution of IMC

During the 1980s, many companies began taking a broader perspective of marketing communication and seeing the need for a more strategic integration of their promotional tools. The decade was characterized by the rapid development of areas such as sales promotion, direct marketing, and public relations, which began challenging advertising's role as the dominant form of marketing communication. These firms began moving toward the process of **integrated marketing communications (IMC)**, which involves coordinating the various promotional elements and other marketing activities that communicate with a firm's customers.[10] As marketers embraced the concept of integrated marketing communications, they began asking their ad agencies to coordinate the use of a variety of promotional tools rather than relying primarily on media advertising. A number of companies also began to look beyond traditional advertising agencies and use other types

**EXHIBIT 1–3**
Movado uses a variety of marketing mix elements including price, product design, brand name, and distribution strategy to create a high-quality, upscale image for its watches

of promotional specialists to develop and implement various components of their promotional plans.

Many agencies responded to the call for synergy among the promotional tools by acquiring PR, sales promotion, and direct-marketing companies and touting themselves as IMC agencies that offer one-stop shopping for all their clients' promotional needs.[11] Some agencies became involved in these nonadvertising areas to gain control over their clients' promotional programs and budgets and struggled to offer any real value beyond creating advertising. However, the advertising industry soon recognized that IMC was more than just a fad. Terms such as *new advertising, orchestration,* and *seamless communication* were used to describe the concept of integration.[12] A task force from the American Association of Advertising Agencies (the "4As") developed one of the first definitions of integrated marketing communications:

> a concept of marketing communications planning that recognizes the added value of a comprehensive plan that evaluates the strategic roles of a variety of communication disciplines—for example, general advertising, direct response, sales promotion, and public relations—and combines these disciplines to provide clarity, consistency, and maximum communications impact.[13]

The 4As' definition focuses on the process of using all forms of promotion to achieve maximum communication impact. However, advocates of the IMC concept argued for an even broader perspective that considers *all sources of brand or company contact* that a customer or prospect has with a product or service.[14] They noted that the process of integrated marketing communications calls for a "big-picture" approach to planning marketing and promotion programs and coordinating the various communication functions. It requires that firms develop a total marketing communications strategy that recognizes how all of a firm's marketing activities, not just promotion, communicate with its customers.

Consumers' perceptions of a company and/or its various brands are a synthesis of the bundle of messages they receive or contacts they have, such as media advertisements, price, package design, direct-marketing efforts, publicity, sales promotions, websites, point-of-purchase displays, and even the type of store where a product or service is sold. The integrated marketing communications approach seeks to have all of a company's marketing and promotional activities project a consistent, unified image to the marketplace. It calls for a centralized messaging function so that everything a company says and does communicates a common theme and positioning. For example, Movado uses classic design and a distinctive brand name as well as high price to position its watches as high-quality, high-status products. This upscale image is enhanced by the company's strategy of distributing its products only through boutiques, jewelry stores, and other exclusive shops. Notice how this image is reflected in the Movado ad shown in Exhibit 1–3.

Many companies have adopted this broader perspective of IMC. They see it as a way to coordinate and manage their marketing communication programs to ensure that they send customers a consistent message about the company and/or its brands. For these companies, integration represents an improvement over the traditional method of treating the various marketing and promotion elements as virtually separate activities. However, this perspective of IMC has been challenged on the basis that it focuses primarily on the tactical coordination of various communication tools with the goal of making them look and sound alike.[15] It has been criticized as an "inside-out marketing" approach that is a relatively simple matter of bundling promotional mix elements together so they have one look and speak with one voice.[16] As IMC continued to evolve, both academicians as well as practitioners recognized that a broader perspective was needed that would view the discipline from a more strategic perspective.

## A Contemporary Perspective of IMC

As marketers become more sophisticated and develop a better understanding of IMC, they are recognizing that it involves more than just coordinating the various elements of their marketing and communications programs into a "one look, one voice" approach. IMC is now recognized as a business process that helps companies identify the most appropriate and effective methods for communicating and building relationships with customers and other stakeholders. Don Schultz of Northwestern University has developed what many think is a more appropriate definition of IMC, as follows:

> Integrated marketing communication is a strategic business process used to plan, develop, execute and evaluate coordinated, measurable, persuasive brand communications programs over time with consumers, customers, prospects, employees, associates and other targeted relevant external and internal audiences. The goal is to generate both short-term financial returns and build long-term brand and shareholder value.[17]

There are several important aspects of this definition of IMC. First, it views IMC as an ongoing strategic business process rather than just tactical integration of various communication activities. It also recognizes that there are a number of relevant audiences that are an important part of the process. Externally these include customers, prospects, suppliers, investors, interest groups, and the general public. It also views internal audiences such as employees as an important part of the IMC process. Schultz also notes that this definition reflects the increasing emphasis that is being placed on the demand for accountability and measurement of the *outcomes* of marketing communication programs as well as marketing in general.

Many companies are realizing that communicating effectively with customers and other stakeholders involves more than just the tactical use of the traditional marketing communication tools. These firms, along with many advertising agencies, are embracing IMC and incorporating it into their marketing and business practices. It is true, however, that not all companies have moved beyond the stage of simply bundling promotional mix elements together and made the organization changes and investment that are needed for true integration. Moreover, some academics and practitioners have questioned whether IMC is just another "management fashion" whose influence will be transitory.[18] Critics of IMC argue that it merely reinvents and renames existing ideas and concepts and question its significance for marketing and advertising thought and practice.[19]

While the debate over the value and relevance of IMC is likely to continue, proponents of the concept far outnumber the critics. IMC is proving to be a permanent change that offers significant value to marketers in the rapidly changing communications environment they are facing in the new millennium. IMC has been described as one of the "new-generation" marketing approaches being used by companies to better focus their efforts in acquiring, retaining, and developing relationships with customers and other stakeholders.[20] We will now discuss some of the reasons for the growing importance of IMC.

## Reasons for the Growing Importance of IMC

The IMC approach to marketing communications planning and strategy is being adopted by both large and small companies and has become popular among firms marketing consumer products and services as well as business-to-business marketers. There are a number of reasons why marketers are adopting the IMC approach. A fundamental reason is that they understand the value of strategically integrating the various communications functions rather than having them operate autonomously. By coordinating their marketing communications efforts, companies can avoid duplication, take advantage of synergy among promotional tools, and develop more efficient and effective marketing communications programs. Advocates of IMC argue that it is one of the easiest ways for a company to maximize the return on its investment in marketing and promotion.[21]

The move to integrated marketing also reflects an adaptation by marketers to a changing environment, particularly with respects to consumers, technology, and media consumption behavior. For decades, reaching consumers was relatively easy as marketers could run their ads in mass media (so-named because they reach mass audiences) such as television, radio, magazines, and newspapers. The formula was really very simple as the mass media had a symbiotic relationship with mass marketers such as automotive firms, consumer packaged goods companies, and many others. The media companies would develop and deliver expensive, but high-quality content that would in turn attract large audiences. The marketers would pay large amounts of money to the television and radio networks and stations and/or magazine and newspaper publishers for access to the mass audiences who would receive the advertising messages that encouraged them to purchase the marketers' products and services. The advertising revenue that the media companies received would be used to produce the high-quality content which in turn would allow the media to continue to deliver the viewers, listeners, and readers that the marketers coveted.

Over the past decade, however, there have been major changes in the media landscape that are impacting the traditional mass media and the economic model that has supported them. There has been an evolution to *micromarketing* as the mass audience assembled by network television and augmented by other mass media is fragmenting at an accelerating rate.[22] Viewing audiences are moving from the traditional broadcast networks (ABC, CBS, NBC, and Fox) to more narrowly targeted programs on cable networks such as ESPN, VH1, and MTV, as well as to other forms of entertainment such as DVDs, video on demand (VOD), the Internet, and video games. The Internet is rapidly coming of age as an important advertising medium with online versions of nearly every television station, newspaper, and magazine in the country. The Web offers marketers tremendous opportunities for targeting based on numerous dimensions. The crude banners and pop-up ads that initially defined Internet advertising are giving way to more refined formats such as paid search, which is the fastest growing form of online advertising.

Advertisers can use the Internet in a more targeted way than traditional media. They can run their ads on websites that are narrowly targeted to consumer interests or have their ads appear on search engines such as Google and Bing which are seen when people are seeking information about a product or service. For example, Google dominates as the online search advertising marketer with its keyword-targeted advertising program called AdWords (Exhibit 1–4). Social networking sites such as MySpace, Facebook, Twitter, LinkedIn, and YouTube have become pervasive on the Internet and make it possible for people to share content, opinions, insights, and experiences as well as educate one another about companies, brands, and various issues.[23]

To respond to the media fragmentation, marketers are increasing their spending on media that are more targeted and can reach specific market segments. Many marketers are shifting more of their advertising budgets online as Internet advertising now accounts for 7 percent of the total U.S. advertising market. There appears to be no stopping the fragmentation of the consumer market as well as the proliferation of media. The success of marketing communication programs will depend on how well companies make the transition from the fading age of mass marketing to the new era of micromarketing. Most marketers are learning that it no longer makes economic sense to send an advertising message to the many in hopes of persuading the few. IMC Technology Perspective 1–1 discusses how integrated marketing communications have been impacted by technology in the first decade of the new millennium.

**EXHIBIT 1–4**

Google AdWords is the most popular program for online search advertising

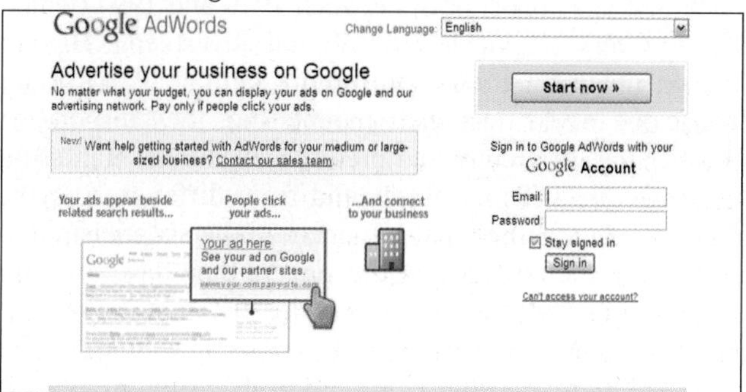

# IMC Technology Perspective 1–1 > > >

## The Technology Revolution Hits IMC

When the new millennium began 10 years ago, technology was just beginning to impact the practice of integrated marketing communications. The Internet was still constrained by technological limitations such as bandwidth problems, and most consumers were accessing the Web via dial-up telephone services such as AOL, NetZero, and EarthLink. Search engines such as Google, Yahoo, and MSN were in their infancy and products such as the Blackberry and the iPod were just being launched. In 2000 the average consumer spent less than 30 minutes online each day versus nearly four hours today. When planning a new IMC campaign for a client, advertising agencies would conceive and develop advertising primarily for mass media channels such as television, radio, and/or print. The online component would be an add-on that played a supportive role such as providing information about a company or brand, promotional offers, or a place to watch commercials or view print ads or brochures. Many experts were still pointing to the bursting of the dot-com bubble and failure of online companies as evidence that the Web was overhyped, and it would be many years before its potential would be realized.

However, by the middle of the first decade of the new millennium, the transformation of the Internet was well underway as a new version of the World Wide Web was taking shape. The term "Web 2.0" is often used to describe the changes that have taken place with the Internet which include applications that facilitate interactive information sharing and collaboration and bilateral, as opposed to unilateral, communication. On Web 2.0 sites users are not limited to the passive viewing of information and can interact with one another as well as change website content. These applications gave rise to social networking sites, video sharing sites, wikis, blogs, and online communities that have experienced explosive growth. In 2005, Facebook, Twitter, YouTube, Hulu, and LinkedIn did not even exist and MySpace was only a year old. However, by 2010 Facebook had more than 500 million members, Twitter boasted 100 million, Hulu had become a major television channel, and more than 100 million videos were viewed each day on YouTube, making it one of the most visited sites on the Internet.

The technological revolution is also impacting the two other major screens in consumers' lives—their televisions and mobile phones. The number of homes with digital video recorders (DVRs) has increased from 3.5 million in 2003 to more than 40 million in 2010, which represents more than a third of the 115 million U.S. television households. With the penetration of digital cable and direct broadcast satellite services, the average household in the United States can now receive 130 television channels versus 61 in 2000, which has led to fragmentation of television viewing audiences. The high definition flat screen televisions that are in most living rooms are now being connected to laptop computers and gaming consoles such as Sony Playstations, Microsoft Xboxes and Nintendo Wiis which is making the long predicted convergence of television and the Internet a reality. These devices make it possible to deliver custom tailored content such as movies, video games, and Web content that directly competes with television programs. Television viewers of the future are likely to be doing more fast-forwarding, pausing, and searching for content with their remote control devices, which means they may be watching fewer commercials. The advertising industry has recognized these threats and is working on ways to integrate their ads into emerging viewing behavior.

Mobile phones have become an important part of our lives as 85 percent of Americans now own one and many

In addition to the proliferation of media and fragmentation of audiences, marketers are also facing the challenge of consumers being less responsive to traditional advertising. Many consumers are turned off by advertising and other forms of marketing communication as they are tired of being bombarded with sales messages.[24] Many consumers in generation Y, the age cohort born between 1979 and 1994 (which includes most college students), are very skeptical of traditional advertising. Having grown up in an even more media-saturated and brand conscious world than their parents did, they respond to advertising differently and prefer to encounter marketing messages in different places and from different sources. Marketers recognize that to penetrate the skepticism and to capture the attention of the gen Ys they have to bring their messages to these people in different ways. For example, Ford recently introduced its new Fiesta subcompact vehicle to the U.S. market by using an aggressive social media program called the Fiesta Movement which was designed to build buzz for the new car among

**EXHIBIT 1–5**

Ford generated buzz for the new Fiesta by having agents blog on social media sites about the cars

find them an indispensible part of their lives, as evidenced by the more than 1 trillion text messages sent every year. Nearly a quarter of those with mobile devices now have smartphones such as iPhones and Blackberrys which allow them to search the Internet and also offer more than 100,000 applications (apps), many of which are designed to facilitate making purchases, such as comparison shopping, locating bars and restaurants, or having discount coupons delivered to their phones. Many marketers are developing mobile marketing programs that can deliver messages and promotional offers directly to consumers' mobile devices and can be targeted to specific locations and consumption situations. MediaFLO, a division of Qualcomm, Inc., has developed a nationwide network to broadcast television shows to mobile phones and is delivering FLO TV programming through Verizon and AT&T.

As we enter the second decade of the new millennium, yet another screen is becoming part of the lives of many consumers—the electronic reader (E-reader). The E-reader market was pioneered by Amazon (the Kindle) and Sony who introduced these devices as a way of storing and reading traditional books. However, a number of other companies such as Apple, Hewlett Packard (HP), and Dell have entered this market with versions of their own E-readers, such as tablets which make it possible to read newspapers and magazines in a format resembling the traditional paper versions and also offer a platform for textbooks. In fact, it is very likely that in the near future the traditional textbook will be obsolete and most students will purchase digital books which will be read on these devices. Many magazines and newspapers are working on developing digital versions of their publications which will include full-screen and full-color interactive ads that will be as impactful as the most compelling TV commercials.

The rapid pace of technological change that is impacting the daily lives of consumers presents a major challenge to marketers who must adapt their integrated marketing communication programs or risk having them become irrelevant. Marketing and advertising consultant Avi Dan has described the challenge very well by noting that "Ten years ago a marketer needed to know maybe 100 things to be effective: some aspects of positioning, some aspects of media, some media research, some pricing and some distribution. However, now that number is in the thousands. And whereas technology used to advance incrementally, it now evolves exponentially." It is likely that the advances in technology that occurred during the first decade of the new millennium will pale in comparison to those that will occur over the next 10 years. However, marketers will have little choice but to embrace these changes and view them as an opportunity rather than a threat.

Sources: Josh Quittner, "The Future of Reading," *Fortune,* February 11, 2010, pp.63–67; Avi Dan, "Why Brands Should Embrace Technological Change," *Advertising Age,* January 19, 2010, http:// www.adage.com/print?artic_id=141478; Brian Steinberg, "The Future of TV," *Advertising Age,* pp. 1, 18–19.

its target audience.[25] Ford chose 100 "Fiesta agents" from more than 4,000 online applicants they identified as social-media trendsetters and gave them a car to drive for six months. In exchange the agents were asked to complete monthly themed missions involving travel and social activism and post videos and update their friends and followers on YouTube, Facebook, and other social networking sites (Exhibit 1–5).

The integrated marketing communications movement is also being driven by fundamental changes in the way companies market their products and services and an ongoing marketing revolution that is changing the rules of marketing.[26] Major characteristics of this marketing revolution include:

- *A shifting of marketing expenditures from traditional media advertising to other forms of promotion as well as nontraditional media.* Many companies feel that traditional media advertising has become too expensive and is not cost effective and are shifting their monies to lower-cost, more targeted communication tools such as the Internet as well as sales promotion, event marketing, sponsorships, and various direct marketing methods. Marketers also recognize that consumers are less responsive to traditional media advertising or may even avoid it by fast-forwarding through recorded television shows or changing channels on their TV or radios during commercial breaks. This is leading many marketers to look for alternative ways to communicate with their target audiences. For example, marketers often hire product placement firms or negotiate directly with major studios to get their brands integrated into movies and television shows. For example, a Chevy Camaro played a starring role in the hit movie *Transformers 2* while a number of other brands were integrated into the film such as Budweiser, Apple, Mountain Dew, and Southwest Airlines.[27] A number of brands are integrated into popular shows such as *American Idol, Extreme Makeover: Home Edition,* and *Celebrity Apprentice.*

- *The rapid growth of the Internet and social media that is changing the nature of how companies do business and the ways they communicate and interact with consumers.* Every day more consumers are searching the Internet's World Wide Web and nearly every marketer is making the Web an integral part of their marketing communications, as well as their overall business strategy. There are now more than 1.8 billion Internet users including over 220 million in the United States. In the United States, 75 percent of the households are connected to the Internet and nearly two-thirds of these homes have broadband access.[28] We are well into the second phase of the Internet revolution (Web 2.0) which has given rise to the development and growth of social media which people use to share information, content, insight, experiences and perspectives. It is estimated that 60 percent of Americans use social media and most companies and organizations are using them as well by creating Facebook pages or posting their ads on YouTube and other sites.[29]
- *A shift in marketplace power from manufacturers to retailers.* There has been tremendous consolidation in the retail industry as many small to midsize local retailers are being replaced by regional, national, and international chains. Large retailers such as Walmart and Target are using their clout to demand more promotional fees and allowances from manufacturers, which often siphons money away from advertising. Moreover, technologies such as checkout scanners provide retailers with information on the effectiveness of manufacturers' promotional programs. This is leading many marketers to allocate more of their marketing budgets to promotional tools that can produce more immediate, short-term results, such as sales promotion.
- *The growth and development of database marketing.* Many companies now have extensive databases containing customer names; geographic, demographic, and psychographic profiles, purchase patterns; media preferences, credit and other financial information; and other relevant characteristics. Marketers are using this information to target customers through a variety of direct-marketing methods such as telemarketing, e-mail marketing, direct mail, and other direct response methods rather than relying on media advertising. These databases are an integral part of companies' customer relationship management (CRM) programs, which involve the systematic tracking of consumers' preferences and behaviors and modifying the product or service offered to meet individual needs and wants.[30]
- *Demands for greater accountability from advertising agencies and changes in the way agencies and other marketing communication firms are compensated.* Many companies are placing greater demands on their advertising agencies and holding them more accountable for measurable results. A number of marketers are using incentive-based systems whereby compensation for their advertising agencies is based, at least in part, on objective measures such as sales, market share, and profitability. Companies are also looking beyond traditional advertising agencies and turning to other marketing communication firms to work on the development and execution of their IMC programs. These include agencies that specialize in areas such as Internet and interactive marketing, direct marketing, sales promotion, public relations, and media planning and buying.

**FIGURE 1–1**
The World's 10 Most Valuable Brands

| Rank | Brand | Brand Value (billions) |
|---|---|---|
| 1 | Coca-Cola | $68.73 |
| 2 | IBM | 60.21 |
| 3 | Microsoft | 56.65 |
| 4 | General Electric | 47.78 |
| 5 | Nokia | 34.86 |
| 6 | McDonald's | 32.28 |
| 7 | Google | 31.90 |
| 8 | Toyota | 31.33 |
| 9 | Intel | 30.64 |
| 10 | Disney | 28.45 |

Source: http://www.interbrand.com/best_global_brands.aspx.



These changes and developments are affecting everyone involved in the marketing and promotional process. Companies are recognizing that they must change the ways they market and promote their products and services. They can no longer be tied to a specific communication tool (such as media advertising); rather, they should use whatever contact methods offer the best way of delivering the message to their target audiences. Ad agencies continue to reposition themselves as offering more than just advertising expertise; they strive to convince their clients that they can manage all or any part of clients' integrated communications needs. Most agencies recognize that their future success depends on their ability to understand all areas of promotion and help their clients develop and implement integrated marketing communications programs.

## The Role of IMC in Branding

One of the major reasons for the growing importance of integrated marketing communications over the past decade is that it plays a major role in the process of developing and sustaining brand identity and equity. As branding expert Kevin Keller notes, "Building and properly managing brand equity has become a priority for companies of all sizes, in all types of industries, in all types of markets."[31] With more and more products and services competing for consideration by customers who have less and less time to make choices, well-known brands have a major competitive advantage in today's marketplace. Building and maintaining brand identity and equity require the creation of well-known brands that have favorable, strong, and unique associations in the mind of the consumer.[32] Companies recognize that brand equity is as important an asset as factories, patents, and cash because strong brands have the power to command a premium price from consumers as well as investors. Figure 1–1 shows the world's most valuable brands, as measured by Interbrand, a leading brand consultancy company.

*Brand identity* is a combination of many factors, including the name, logo, symbols, design, packaging, and performance of a product or service as well as the image or type of associations that comes to mind when consumers think about a brand. It encompasses the entire spectrum of consumers' awareness, knowledge, and image of the brand as well as the company behind it. It is the sum of all points of encounter or contact that consumers have with the brand, and it extends beyond the experience or outcome of using it. These contacts can also result from various forms of integrated marketing communications activities used by a company, including mass-media

## IMC Perspective 1–1 > > >

### Building Brands in a Recession

Over the past several years the global economy has been struggling through the most difficult times since the Great Depression of the 1930s. The collapse of the housing market, followed by the implosion of the financial markets in the fall of 2008 led the economy into a deep recession from which it has been trying to recover. The recession has had a major impact on the advertising business as companies have reacted to the economic slump by slashing their marketing and advertising budgets. Global ad spending declined by 10 percent in 2009 while spending in the United States declined by 13 percent, which was the sharpest drop since the Great Depression and also marked the first time that ad spending had declined for two consecutive years.

Among the victims of the current recession are many of the brands in which companies had invested so much to build value over the years. Perhaps the most obvious impact of a weak economy is that it results in consumers spending less money, carefully scrutinizing their purchases, and rethinking their brand loyalties. Recent research conducted by the Leo Burnett Worldwide advertising agency found that 80 to 90 percent of consumers are willing to trade off or trade down. Many consumers are switching to private label brands, which have gained market share against national brands in a number of product categories. Companies in virtually every product and service category are learning that their brands are not recession proof and have been looking for ways to get consumers to pay a premium for their brands and maintain their value.

Marketing executives recognize that during a recession consumers become more price sensitive and value conscious and have been struggling with how to respond to these changes. They are balancing the temptation to pursue short-term sales gains through the use of discounts and promotions against the risk of cheapening their brands over the long haul. However, many of them must do so with smaller advertising and promotion budgets, which makes it increasingly difficult to communicate with consumers and convince them of the value of their brands. Moreover, companies are finding that an increasing number of consumers distrust not only the companies that are seen as responsible for causing the financial crisis, such as banks and other financial service firms, but business as a whole.

Many companies are recognizing that in the world of branding, trust and credibility are critical, particularly given that less than half of Americans say they trust business. However, marketers also know that they cannot gain the trust of the consuming public by running slick TV commercials or print ads. For example, McDonald's knows that many consumers still view fast food as unhealthy and has allocated a portion of its advertising budget to focus on the quality of its products and how it sources food. The company also has a section of its website called "Food, Nutrition & Fitness," which provides visitors with nutritional and other types of information and even invites them to go behind the scenes and meet suppliers of the chain's beef, vegetables, chicken, eggs, and coffee. While McDonald's value menu items have

advertising, sales promotion offers, sponsorship activities at sporting or entertainment events, websites on the Internet, and direct-mail pieces such as letters, brochures, catalogs, or videos. Consumers can also have contact with or receive information about a brand in stores at the point of sale; through articles or stories they see, hear, or read in the media; or through interactions with a company representative, such as a salesperson. For many companies, mass-media advertising has long been the cornerstone of their brand building efforts. However, as noted earlier, the global recession has led to major reductions in advertising and promotion budgets for most companies. Thus, they do not have large media budgets available to build and maintain brand awareness and identity. The recession has also impacted consumers, not only in terms of their purchasing behavior, but also in terms of how they perceive companies and the way firms market their products and services to them. IMC Perspective 1–1 discusses how marketers have changed their branding efforts in response to the recession.

Marketers recognize that in the modern world of marketing there are many different opportunities and methods for *contacting* current and prospective customers to provide them with information about a company and/or brands. The challenge is to understand how to use the various IMC tools to make such contacts and deliver the branding message effectively and efficiently. A successful IMC program requires that marketers find the right combination of communication tools and techniques, define their role and the extent to which they can or should be used, and coordinate their use. To accomplish this, the persons responsible for the company's communication efforts must have an understanding of the IMC tools that are available and the ways they can be used.

helped the company prosper during the recession, it has also been able to improve its brand image and value ratings.

Ford Motor company, which unlike General Motors and Chrysler did not ask for government bailout money to survive, is another company that has been focusing on building its credibility to win the trust of consumers. The company's advertising focuses on rational messages such as its technologies, fuel economy, quality ratings, new models, and how strong management has led to the successful turnaround of the company. The branding message appears to be resonating with consumers as Ford's market share has been increasing even though the company is spending $1,800 less on incentives per car than it did a year ago, and consumers are paying an average of $1,300 more for Ford cars and trucks.

Marketers are also finding that a way to build and maintain brand equity is by focusing on home and family and showing consumers how they can take control of their lives. For example Walmart's advertising is based around the theme "Save Money. Live Better" and in addition to touting its low prices, the ads show how the money consumers save can help improve their lives. American Express provides consumers with a set of tools that helps them better understand and manage their credit and finances which is a way of reinforcing the brand's core identity while appealing to the consumers desire to be in control.

A number of companies are using the Internet to reach out to consumers and interact with them through social networks, blogs, and other online tools. General Mills has established several of its own proprietary networks including *My Blog Spark* which engages nearly 3,000 bloggers who sign up to receive news and "sparks" of information, review new products, and participate in giveaways, surveys and events. Many brands participate in online forums devoted to specific customer segments such as *Café Mom* which is an information-sharing site aimed at mothers. Many also have Facebook pages and Twitter accounts and post their ads on the YouTube video sharing site so they can engage consumers and have them become involved in things they value.

Many economists predict that the Great Recession has led to permanent changes in buyer behavior and consumers will remain frugal and value conscious long after the economy recovers. They argue that we may never see a return to the lavish lifestyles and free spending that contributed to the collapse of the economy. Thus, marketers may have little choice but to find new ways to remain relevant to consumers and change the ways they build and maintain their brands.

Sources: Suzanne Vranica, "For Ad Industry, 2010 Promise Scant Relief," *The Wall Street Journal*, December 24, 2009, p. B5; David Kiley and Burt Helm, "The Great Trust Offensive," *BusinessWeek*, September 28, 2009, pp. 38–42; "Will the Future of Advertising Be a Blend of Old and New Media?," *Knowledge@Wharton*, http://knowledge.wharton.upenn.edu/article/2344.cfm.

## THE PROMOTIONAL MIX: THE TOOLS FOR IMC

**Promotion** has been defined as the coordination of all seller-initiated efforts to set up channels of information and persuasion in order to sell goods and services or promote an idea.[33] While implicit communication occurs through the various elements of the marketing mix, most of an organization's communications with the marketplace take place as part of a carefully planned and controlled promotional program. The basic tools used to accomplish an organization's communication objectives are often referred to as the **promotional mix** (Figure 1–2).

**FIGURE 1–2**
Elements of the Promotional Mix

| Rank | Advertiser | Ad Spending (Millions) |
|---|---|---|
| 1. | Procter & Gamble | $4,189 |
| 2. | Verizon Communications | 3,020 |
| 3. | AT&T | 2,797 |
| 4. | General Motors Co. | 2,215 |
| 5. | Pfizer | 2,097 |
| 6. | Johnson & Johnson | 2,061 |
| 7. | Walt Disney Co. | 2,004 |
| 8. | Time Warner | 1,848 |
| 9. | L'Oreal | 1,834 |
| 10. | Kraft Foods | 1,748 |
| 11. | Walmart Stores | 1,729 |
| 12. | Sears Holdings Corp. | 1,700 |
| 13. | Bank of America Corp. | 1,588 |
| 14. | General Electric Co. | 1,576 |
| 15. | Ford Motor Co. | 1,517 |
| 16. | Sprint Nextel Corp. | 1,500 |
| 17. | Anheuser-Busch InBev | 1,467 |
| 18. | GlaxoSmithKline | 1,395 |
| 19. | JPMorgan Chase & Co. | 1,341 |
| 20. | Nestle | 1,333 |
| 21. | Unilever | 1,294 |
| 22. | American Express Co. | 1,294 |
| 23. | Merck & Co. | 1,287 |
| 24. | Toyota Motor Corp. | 1,286 |
| 25. | McDonald's Corp. | 1,236 |

Source: *Advertising Age,* June 21, 2010, p. 10.

**FIGURE 1–3**

25 Leading Advertisers in the United States, 2009

Traditionally the promotional mix has included four elements: advertising, sales promotion, publicity/public relations, and personal selling. However, in this text we view direct marketing as well as interactive media as major promotional-mix elements that modern-day marketers use to communicate with their target markets. Each element of the promotional mix is viewed as an integrated marketing communications tool that plays a distinctive role in an IMC program. Each may take on a variety of forms. And each has certain advantages.

## Advertising

**Advertising** is defined as any paid form of nonpersonal communication about an organization, product, service, or idea by an identified sponsor.[34] The *paid* aspect of this definition reflects the fact that the space or time for an advertising message generally must be bought. An occasional exception to this is the public service announcement (PSA), whose advertising space or time is donated by the media.

The *nonpersonal* component means that advertising involves mass media (e.g., TV, radio, magazines, newspapers) that can transmit a message to large groups of individuals, often at the same time. The nonpersonal nature of advertising means that there is generally no opportunity for immediate feedback from the message recipient (except in direct-response advertising). Therefore, before the message is sent, the advertiser must consider how the audience will interpret and respond to it.

Advertising is the best-known and most widely discussed form of promotion, probably because of its pervasiveness. It is also a very important promotional tool, particularly for companies whose products and services are targeted at mass consumer markets such as automobile manufacturers and packaged goods and drug companies. More than 200 companies spend over $100 million on advertising and promotion in the United States each year. Figure 1–3 shows the advertising expenditures of the 25 leading national advertisers.

There are several reasons why advertising is such an important part of many marketers' IMC programs. First, media advertising is still the most cost-effective way to reach large numbers of consumers. The average 30-second commercial on the four major television networks during prime-time programming reaches nearly 5 million households. The cost per thousand households reached on network TV during prime time in 2009–10 was $22.72.[35] Popular shows such as *American Idol* and *NCIS* can reach between 15 to 20 million viewers each week. Magazines such as *Time, Sports Illustrated,* or *People* have a weekly circulation of more than 3 million and can reach more than 10 million people since there are multiple readers of each issue. Thus, for marketers who are interested in building or maintaining brand awareness and reaching the mass market with their advertising message, there is no cost effective substitute for media advertising.[36]

**EXHIBIT 1–6**
The American Advertising Federation promotes the value of advertising

Advertising is also a valuable tool for building company or brand equity as it is a powerful way to provide consumers with information as well as to influence their perceptions. Advertising can be used to create favorable and unique images and associations for a brand which can be very important for companies selling products or services that are difficult to differentiate on the basis of functional attributes. Brand image plays an important role in the purchase of many products and services, and advertising is still recognized as one of the best ways to build a brand. Exhibit 1–6 shows an ad from a campaign run by the American Advertising Federation promoting the value of advertising.

The nature and purpose of advertising differ from one industry to another and/or across situations. Companies selling products and services to the consumer market generally rely heavily on advertising to communicate with their target audiences as do retailers and other local merchants. However, advertising can also be done by an industry to stimulate demand for a product category such as beef or milk. Advertising is also used extensively by companies who compete in the business and professional markets to reach current and potential customers. For example, business-to-business marketers use advertising to perform important functions such as building awareness of the company and its products, generating leads for the sales force, reassuring customers about the purchase they have made, or helping create a favorable image of the company. Exhibit 1–7 shows an ad from the campaign for the General Electric Company's ecomagination sustainability initiative which is a companywide commitment to address global challenges such as the need for cleaner, more efficient sources of energy, reduced emissions, and abundant sources of clean water. Figure 1–4 describes the most common types of advertising.

**EXHIBIT 1–7**
Business-to-business advertisers such as General Electric use advertising to build awareness of the company and its programs

## Direct Marketing

One of the fastest-growing sectors of the U.S. economy is **direct marketing,** in which organizations communicate directly with target customers to generate a response and/or a transaction. Traditionally, direct marketing has not been considered an element of the promotional mix. However, because it has become such an integral part of the IMC program of many organizations and often involves separate objectives, budgets, and strategies, we view direct marketing as a component of the promotional mix.

Direct marketing is much more than direct mail and mail-order catalogs. It involves a variety of activities, including database management, direct selling, telemarketing,

**FIGURE 1–4**

Classifications of Advertising

**ADVERTISING TO CONSUMER MARKETS**

**National Advertising**
Advertising done by large companies on a nationwide basis or in most regions of the country. Most of the ads for well-known companies and brands that are seen on prime-time TV or in other major national or regional media are examples of national advertising. The goals of national advertisers are to inform or remind consumers of the company or brand and its features, benefits, advantages, or uses and to create or reinforce its image so that consumers will be predisposed to purchase it.

**Retail/Local Advertising**
Advertising done by retailers or local merchants to encourage consumers to shop at a specific store, use a local service, or patronize a particular establishment. Retail or local advertising tends to emphasize specific patronage motives such as price, hours of operation, service, atmosphere, image, or merchandise assortment. Retailers are concerned with building store traffic, so their promotions often take the form of direct-action advertising designed to produce immediate store traffic and sales.

**Primary- versus Selective-Demand Advertising**
Primary-demand advertising is designed to stimulate demand for the general product class or entire industry. Selective-demand advertising focuses on creating demand for a specific company's brands. Most advertising for products and services is concerned with stimulating selective demand and emphasizes reasons for purchasing a particular brand.

An advertiser might concentrate on stimulating primary demand when, for example, its brand dominates a market and will benefit the most from overall market growth. Primary-demand advertising is often used as part of a promotional strategy to help a new product gain market acceptance, since the challenge is to sell customers on the product concept as much as to sell a particular brand. Industry trade associations also try to stimulate primary demand for their members' products, among them cotton, milk, orange juice, pork, and beef.

**ADVERTISING TO BUSINESS AND PROFESSIONAL MARKETS**

**Business-to-Business Advertising**
Advertising targeted at individuals who buy or influence the purchase of industrial goods or services for their companies. Industrial goods are products that either become a physical part of another product (raw material or component parts), are used in manufacturing other goods (machinery), or are used to help a company conduct its business (e.g., office supplies, computers). Business services such as insurance, travel services, and health care are also included in this category.

**Professional Advertising**
Advertising targeted to professionals such as doctors, lawyers, dentists, engineers, or professors to encourage them to use a company's product in their business operations. It might also be used to encourage professionals to recommend or specify the use of a company's product by end-users.

**Trade Advertising**
Advertising targeted to marketing channel members such as wholesalers, distributors, and retailers. The goal is to encourage channel members to stock, promote, and resell the manufacturer's branded products to their customers.

**EXHIBIT 1–8**
Under Armour sells its product online as well as through retail channels

and direct-response ads through direct mail, the Internet, and various broadcast and print media. Some companies, such as Tupperware, Discovery Toys, and Amway, do not use any other distribution channels, relying on independent contractors to sell their products directly to consumers. Companies such as L.L. Bean, Lands' End, and J. Crew have been very successful in using direct marketing to sell their clothing products. Dell has become a market leader in the computer industry by selling a full line of personal computers through direct marketing.

One of the major tools of direct marketing is **direct-response advertising,** whereby a product is promoted through an ad that encourages the consumer to purchase directly from the manufacturer. Traditionally, direct mail has been the primary medium for direct-response advertising, although television, magazines, and the Internet have become increasingly important media. Direct-response advertising and other forms of direct marketing have become very popular over the past two decades, owing primarily to changing lifestyles, particularly the increase in two-income households. This has meant more discretionary income but less time for in-store shopping. The availability of credit cards and toll-free phone numbers has also facilitated the purchase of products from direct-response ads. More recently, the rapid growth of the Internet is fueling the growth of direct marketing. The convenience of shopping through catalogs or on a company's website and placing orders by phone or online has become very appealing to many consumers, and marketers recognize that this can be an effective way to augment their sales through traditional retail channels. For example, Under Armour, the leading company in the performance apparel market, generates a significant amount of sales through its website in addition to selling its products through sports retail stores (Exhibit 1–8).

Direct-marketing tools and techniques are also being used by companies that distribute their products through traditional distribution channels or have their own sales force. Direct marketing plays a big role in the integrated marketing communications programs of consumer-product companies and business-to-business marketers. These companies spend large amounts of money each year developing and maintaining databases containing the addresses and/or phone numbers of present and prospective customers. They use telemarketing to call customers directly and attempt to sell them products and services or qualify them as sales leads. Marketers also send out direct-mail pieces ranging from simple letters and flyers to detailed brochures, catalogs, and videotapes to give potential customers information about their products or services. Direct-marketing techniques are also used to distribute product samples.

## Interactive/Internet Marketing

Over the past decade we have been experiencing perhaps the most dynamic and revolutionary changes of any era in the history of marketing, as well as advertising and promotion. These changes are being driven by advances in technology and developments that have led to dramatic growth of communication through interactive media, particularly the Internet. **Interactive media** allow for a back-and-forth flow of information whereby users can participate in and modify the form and content of the information they receive in real time. Unlike traditional forms of marketing communications such as advertising, which are one-way in nature, the new media allow users to perform a variety of functions such as receive and alter information and images, make inquiries, respond to questions, and, of course, make purchases. In addition to the Internet, other forms of interactive media include kiosks, interactive television, and mobile phones.

The growing popularity of cell phones and other mobile devices such as smartphones along with the decisions of carriers such as Sprint Nextel, Verizon Wireless,

**EXHIBIT 1–9**
MobileVoice allows shoppers to browse product reviews before making a purchase

AT&T, and T-Mobile to open their mobile phone services to advertising and other forms of promotion has opened up a new way for marketers to connect with consumers.[37] Advertising already dominates the first two screens in most consumers' lives, television and personal computers, and more and more ads and other types of promotional messages are appearing on the "third screen" of mobile phones. Although mobile advertising is in its nascent stage, spending in the medium is expected to reach nearly $2 billion by 2012. Marketers are interested in mobile marketing as interactive messages can be delivered that are specific to a consumer's location or consumption situation. One of the major factors driving the growth of this medium is the development of mobile shopping services and applications (apps) that consumers can use to make shopping more economical, efficient, productive, and fun. Services are now available that provide consumers with mobile coupons that are sent directly to their cell phones and can be redeemed at the point-of-purchase. Other mobile applications emerging include price comparison apps, such as ShopSavvy or Red Laser which allow consumers to compare prices at a given location against nearby competitors, and social sourcing apps such as Fashism or Bazaar Voice's MobileVoice that help consumers get outside opinions and feedback on their mobile devices before making a purchase (Exhibit 1–9). Marketers are developing a number of creative ways to connect with consumers through their mobile devices by developing their own brand specific applications as well as games, videos, and ads. For example, Starbucks has developed apps for the iPhone which allow customers to share drink recipes, find the nearest Starbucks, look up nutritional information and manage their Starbucks gift cards.[38]

The Internet is actually a multifaceted promotional tool. On one hand, it is an advertising medium as many companies advertise their products and services on the websites of other companies and/or organizations or pay to link their banner ads or websites to search engines such as Google, Microsoft's Bing, and Yahoo. The Internet can also be viewed as a marketing communications tool in its own right as it is a medium that can be used to execute all of the elements of the promotional mix. In addition to advertising on the Web, marketers offer sales promotion incentives such as coupons, contests, and sweepstakes online, and they use the Internet to conduct direct marketing, personal selling, and public relations activities more effectively and efficiently.

The interactive nature of the Internet is one of its major advantages. This capability enables marketers to gather valuable personal information from customers and prospects and to adjust their offers accordingly, in some cases in real time. Unlike traditional media, which are essentially one-way forms of communication, digital media such as the Internet allow for two-way communication. Another major advantage of the Internet is that it offers the capability to more closely and precisely measure the effects of advertising and other types of promotion. There are a number of metrics that can be generated when consumers visit websites, which allow marketers to determine how consumers are responding to their campaigns and the return on investment they are getting from their promotional dollars.

Companies recognize the advantages of the Internet and the various ways it can be used. However, a number of companies are also developing campaigns that integrate their Web strategies with other aspects of their IMC programs such as media advertising. For example, General Mills launched a very creative integrated campaign to launch Wheaties Fuel, a brand extension of its popular Wheaties cereal product. Saatchi & Saatchi, the advertising agency for Wheaties Fuel, created a series of short Web videos that is posted on the Wheaties.com website and chronicles the development process for the new brand, which is positioned to help meet the nutritional needs of today's athletes.[39] The six videos featured Dr. John Ivy, a prominent sports nutritionist involved with the development of the product, interviewing a panel of star athletes including Indianapolis Colts quarterback Peyton Manning, Boston

**EXHIBIT 1–10**
General Mills used webisodes as part of the IMC launch campaign for Wheaties Fuel

Celtics forward Kevin Garnett, St. Louis Cardinals first baseman Albert Pujols, Olympic decathlon gold medalist Bryan Clay, and triathlete Hunter Kemper (Exhibit 1–10). The "webisodes" were created to be both informative and humorous by providing an entertaining behind-the-scenes look at the development of Wheaties Fuel along with discussions with the star athletes of what it takes to become a champion. Three prototypes of the new product were created and samples of each were sent to more than a 1,000 everyday athletes who were recruited online through the *Men's Health* magazine website. The volunteers had the opportunity to vote and a webisode announcing the winning formula was posted on the Wheaties website in September 2009, prior to the national rollout of the new brand in early 2010.

## Sales Promotion

The next variable in the promotional mix is **sales promotion,** which is generally defined as those marketing activities that provide extra value or incentives to the sales force, the distributors, or the ultimate consumer and can stimulate immediate sales. Sales promotion is generally broken into two major categories: consumer-oriented and trade-oriented activities.

*Consumer-oriented sales promotion* is targeted to the ultimate user of a product or service and includes couponing, sampling, premiums, rebates, contests, sweepstakes, and various point-of-purchase materials (Exhibit 1–11). These promotional tools encourage consumers to make an immediate purchase and thus can stimulate short-term sales. *Trade-oriented sales promotion* is targeted toward marketing intermediaries such as wholesalers, distributors, and retailers. Promotional and merchandising allowances, price deals, sales contests, and trade shows are some of the promotional tools used to encourage the trade to stock and promote a company's products.

Among many consumer packaged-goods companies, sales promotion is often 60 to 70 percent of the promotional budget.[40] In recent years many companies have shifted the emphasis of their promotional strategy from advertising to sales promotion. Reasons for the increased emphasis on sales promotion include declining brand loyalty and increased consumer sensitivity to promotional deals. Another major reason is that retailers have become larger and more powerful and are demanding more trade promotion support from companies.

*Promotion* and *sales promotion* are two terms that often create confusion in the advertising and marketing fields. As noted, promotion is an element of marketing

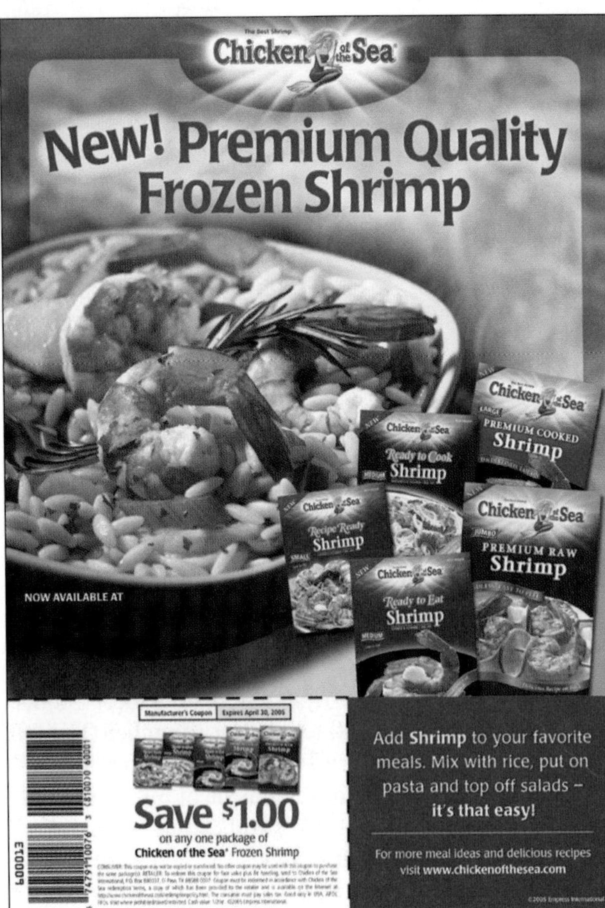


**EXHIBIT 1–11**
Coupons are a popular consumer-oriented sales promotion tool

by which firms communicate with their customers; it includes all the promotional-mix elements we have just discussed. However, many marketing and advertising practitioners use the term more narrowly to refer to sales promotion activities to either consumers or the trade (retailers, wholesalers). In this book, *promotion* is used in the broader sense to refer to the various marketing communications activities of an organization.

## Publicity/Public Relations

Another important component of an organization's promotional mix is publicity/public relations.

### Publicity

**Publicity** refers to nonpersonal communications regarding an organization, product, service, or idea not directly paid for or run under identified sponsorship. It usually comes in the form of a news story, editorial, or announcement about an organization and/or its products and services. Like advertising, publicity involves nonpersonal communication to a mass audience, but unlike advertising, publicity is not directly paid for by the company. The company or organization attempts to get the media to cover or run a favorable story on a product, service, cause, or event to affect awareness, knowledge, opinions, and/or behavior. Techniques used to gain publicity include news releases, press conferences, feature articles, photographs, films, and videotapes.

An advantage of publicity over other forms of promotion is its credibility. Consumers generally tend to be less skeptical toward favorable information about a product or service when it comes from a source they perceive as unbiased. For example, the success (or failure) of a new movie is often determined by the reviews it receives from film critics, who are viewed by many moviegoers as objective evaluators. Another advantage of publicity is its low cost, since the company is not paying for time or space in a mass medium such as TV, radio, or newspapers. While an organization may incur some costs in developing publicity items or maintaining a staff to do so, these expenses will be far less than those for the other promotional programs.

Publicity is not always under the control of an organization and is sometimes unfavorable. Negative stories about a company and/or its products can be very damaging. For example, recently the packaged food industry has received a great deal of negative publicity regarding the nutritional value of their products as well as their marketing practices, particularly to young people. Companies such as Kraft Foods', General Mills, and others have been the target of criticism by consumer activists who have argued that these companies contribute to the obesity problem in the United States by advertising unhealthy foods to children.[41] Toyota Motor Corp., the world's largest automobile manufacturer, recently had to deal with a tremendous amount of negative publicity in the U.S. market resulting from a problem with sticking gas pedals that were linked to a sudden-acceleration problem in some of its vehicles. The company issued a massive product recall and temporarily halted sales of eight of its top-selling vehicles in January 2010. The negative publicity surrounding the issue resulted in the president-CEO of the company testifying before a Congressional committee and issuing a public apology to Toyota's customers for the anxiety caused by the massive recall.[42] Toyota had to spend a significant amount of money on advertising to address the issue and restore consumer confidence in its vehicles and also increased its sales incentives to car buyers to help regain its lost market share.[43]

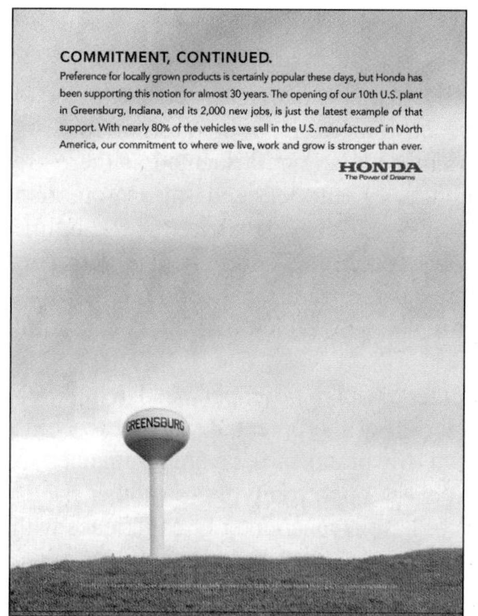

COMMITMENT, CONTINUED.
Preference for locally grown products is certainly popular these days, but Honda has been supporting this notion for almost 30 years. The opening of our 10th U.S. plant in Greensburg, Indiana, and its 2,000 new jobs, is just the latest example of that support. With nearly 80% of the vehicles we sell in the U.S. manufactured* in North America, our commitment to where we live, work and grow is stronger than ever.
HONDA
The Power of Dreams
GREENSBURG

**EXHIBIT 1–12**
Advertising is often used to enhance a company's corporate image

**Public Relations** It is important to recognize the distinction between publicity and public relations. When an organization systematically plans and distributes information in an attempt to control and manage its image and the nature of the publicity it receives, it is really engaging in a function known as public relations. **Public relations** is defined as "the management function which evaluates public attitudes, identifies the policies and procedures of an individual or organization with the public interest, and executes a program of action to earn public understanding and acceptance."[44] Public relations generally has a broader objective than publicity, as its purpose is to establish and maintain a positive image of the company among its various publics.

Public relations uses publicity and a variety of other tools—including special publications, participation in community activities, fund-raising, sponsorship of special events, and various public affairs activities—to enhance an organization's image. Companies also use advertising as a public relations tool. For example, the ad shown in Exhibit 1–12 is part of the American Honda Motor Co.'s "Value to America" campaign which publicizes how Honda has been a major contributor to the U.S. economy for over 50 years. The ad notes the opening of Honda's 10th U.S. plant in Greensburg, Indiana, which has created more than 2,000 new jobs, and also that the company now manufacturers over 80 percent of the vehicles it sells in the United States in North America.

Traditionally, publicity and public relations have been considered more supportive than primary to the marketing and promotional process. However, many firms have begun making PR an integral part of their predetermined marketing and promotional strategies. PR firms are increasingly touting public relations as a communications tool that can take over many of the functions of conventional advertising and marketing.[45]

## Personal Selling

The final element of an organization's promotional mix is **personal selling,** a form of person-to-person communication in which a seller attempts to assist and/or persuade prospective buyers to purchase the company's product or service or to act on an idea. Unlike advertising, personal selling involves direct contact between buyer and seller, either face-to-face or through some form of telecommunications such as telephone sales. This interaction gives the marketer communication flexibility; the seller can see or hear the potential buyer's reactions and modify the message accordingly. The personal, individualized communication in personal selling allows the seller to tailor the message to the customer's specific needs or situation.

Personal selling also involves more immediate and precise feedback because the impact of the sales presentation can generally be assessed from the customer's reactions. If the feedback is unfavorable, the salesperson can modify the message. Personal selling efforts can also be targeted to specific markets and customer types that are the best prospects for the company's product or service.

While personal selling is an important part of the promotional mix, it will not be covered in this text because it is not a direct part of the IMC program in most companies. Also, personal selling is managed separately in most organizations and is not under the control of the advertising or marketing communications manager. However, throughout the text we will address the many ways and situations in which various IMC tools such as media advertising and sales promotion must be coordinated with the personal selling program.

## IMC INVOLVES AUDIENCE CONTACTS

The various promotional mix elements are the major tools that marketers use to communicate with current and/or prospective customers as well as other relevant audiences. However, each of these promotional mix tools is multifaceted as there are various types of media advertising (print, broadcast, outdoor) and sales promotion as well as ways by which marketers use the Internet (websites, social media, online advertising). Moreover, there are additional ways companies communicate with current and prospective customers that extend beyond the traditional promotional mix. Figure 1–5 provides a more extensive list of the ways by which marketers can communicate with their target audiences.

Many companies are taking an *audience contact* or *touch point* perspective in developing their IMC programs whereby they consider all of the potential ways of reaching their target audience and presenting the company or brand in a favorable manner. A **contact (or touch) point** refers to each and every opportunity the customer has to see or hear about the company and/or its brands or have an encounter or experience with it. These contacts can range from simply seeing or hearing an ad for a brand to actually having the opportunity to use or experience a brand in a retail store or interacting with the company during a sales transaction or service encounter. Tom Duncan notes that there are four basic categories of contact or touch points.[46] These are as follows:

- *Company created touch points* are planned marketing communication messages created by the company such as advertisements, websites, news/press releases, packaging, brochures and collateral material, sale promotions, and point-of-purchase displays along with other types of in-store décor. Company created touch points account for a large part of an IMC program and have the advantage of being under the control of the marketer.
- *Intrinsic touch points* are interactions that occur with a company or brand during the process of buying or using the product or service such as discussions with retail sales personnel or customer service representatives. Intrinsic touch points are often not under the direct control of the marketing department or IMC program. However, Duncan notes that marketers should make suggestions regarding ways to manage and improve these interactions with customers in order to send a positive message about the company or brand. There are also

**FIGURE 1–5**
IMC Audience Contact Tools

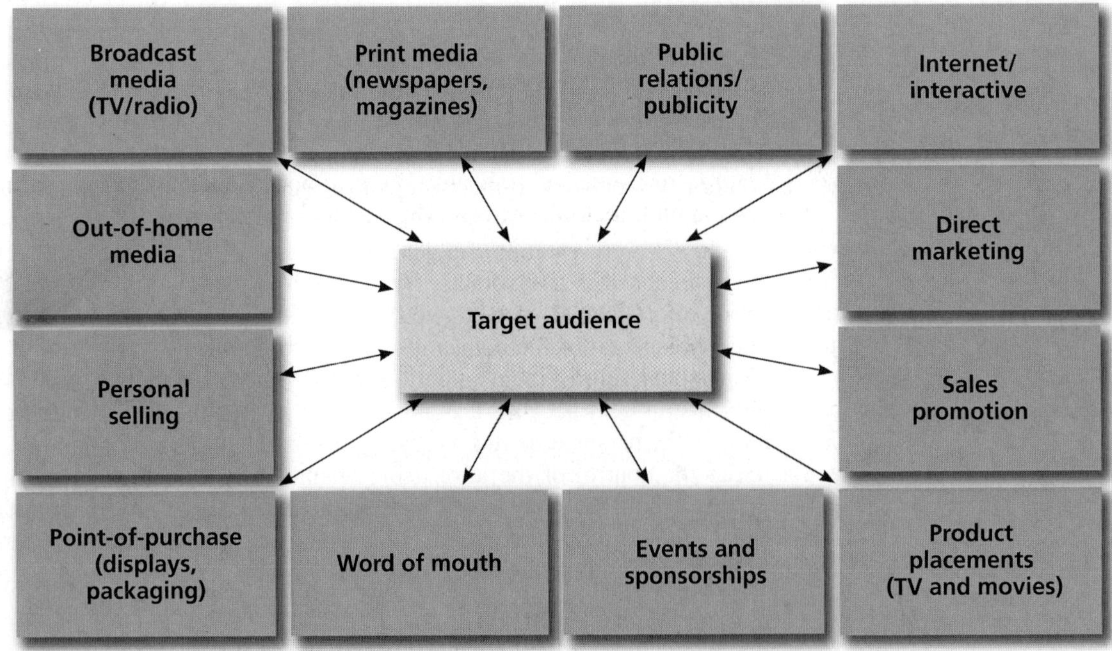

**FIGURE 1–6**

IMC Contact Points: Control vs. Impact

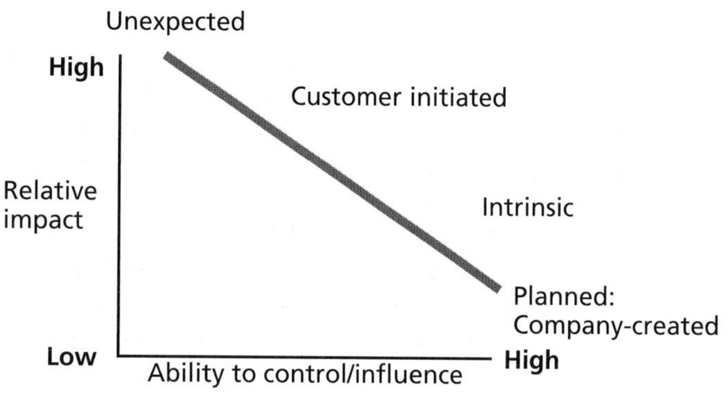




various types of intrinsic touch points that are controlled, or at least may be influenced by, the marketing or IMC manager. These include the design and functioning of the company and/or brand website, as well as the packaging, which can contain product information as well as impact the customers' experience of using a product. Marketers are also finding ways to communicate with consumers during the process of making a purchase by using some of the mobile marketing techniques discussed earlier.

- *Unexpected touch points* are unanticipated references or information about a company or brand that a customer or prospect receives that is beyond the control of the organization. Probably the most influential type of unexpected contact is a word-of-mouth message which refers to a personal communication that comes from friends, associates, neighbors, co-workers, or family members. Unexpected messages may also come from other sources such as the media which may print or broadcast stories about a company and/or its brands, as well as experts who write about products and services. Another type of unexpected point that has become very influential is websites that provide reviews of products and services. Some of these sites provide expert reviews while others give reviews from other customers. For example, CNET is widely used by consumers looking for reviews of specific brands of consumer electronic products. TripAdvisor provides more than 30 million travel related reviews and opinions each year from travelers around the world. It is important to note that information received from unexpected touch points can be either positive or negative.
- *Customer-initiated touch points* are interactions that occur whenever a customer or prospect contacts a company. Most of these contacts involve inquiries or complaints consumers might have regarding the use of a product or service and occur through calls made directly to the company, via e-mails or through specific sections of websites to which customers are directed. Many of the customer initiated contacts are handled through customer service departments although a number of companies have in-bound telemarketing departments as part of their direct sales efforts. The manner in which marketers handle customer initiated contacts has a major impact on their ability to attract and retain customers. Moreover, many companies try to differentiate themselves on the basis of customer service and promote their customer orientation in their advertising and other aspects of their IMC programs. They also encourage current or prospective customers to contact them by calling toll free 800 numbers or by putting their website addresses on packages, in ads, and in various promotional materials.

Marketers who take a contact or touch point perspective recognize that consumers' perceptions and opinions of a brand, as well as their purchase behavior, result from the information they receive, and experiences and interactions they have with the company and its products or services. They also recognize that not all touch points are equally effective and they differ in regard to a company's ability to control or influence them. Figure 1–6 plots the four categories of touch points in terms of their relative impact and the marketer's ability to control them.

As can be seen in this figure, company planned touch points are the easiest to control but are lowest in terms of impact. Marketers can control the nature and type of advertising and other forms of promotion that they send to their target audiences, but consumers often discount these messages since they receive so many of them and they recognize the persuasive intent that underlies them. At the other extreme, unexpected messages are often the most impactful but are the most difficult to control. Duncan notes than an unexpected message can be very powerful because it has the power of third party credibility since the people who provide the information are often perceived as more believable than company sources since they have no vested interest in the success or failure of the company or brand.[47] Customer initiated and intrinsic messages fall in between unexpected and company-created messages with respect to impact as well as the ability of the marketer to control them.

Marketers must determine how valuable each of these contact tools are for communicating with their current and prospective customers and how they can be combined to form an effective IMC program. This is generally done by starting with the target audience and determining which IMC tools will be most effective in reaching, informing, and persuading them and ultimately influencing their behavior. It is the responsibility of those involved in the marketing communications process to determine how the various contact tools will be used to reach the target audience and help achieve the company's marketing objectives. The IMC program is generally developed with specific goals and objectives in mind and is the end product of a detailed marketing and promotional planning process. We will now look at a model of the process that companies follow in developing and executing their IMC programs.

# THE IMC PLANNING PROCESS

In developing an integrated marketing communications strategy, a company combines the various promotional-mix elements, balancing the strengths and weaknesses of each to produce an effective communications program. **Integrated marketing communications management** involves the process of planning, executing, evaluating, and controlling the use of the various promotional-mix elements to effectively communicate with target audiences. The marketer must consider which promotional tools to use and how to integrate them to achieve marketing and communication objectives. Companies also must decide how to distribute the total marketing communications budget across the various promotional-mix elements. What percentage of the budget should be allocated to advertising, sales promotion, the Internet, sponsorships, and personal selling?

As with any business function, planning plays an important role in the development and implementation of an effective integrated marketing communications program. This process is guided by an **integrated marketing communications plan** that provides the framework for developing, implementing, and controlling the organization's IMC program. Those involved with the IMC program must decide on the role and function of the specific elements of the promotional mix, develop strategies for each element, determine how they will be integrated, plan for their implementation, and consider how to evaluate the results achieved and make any necessary adjustments. Marketing communications is but one part of, and must be integrated into, the overall marketing plan and program.

A model of the IMC planning process is shown in Figure 1–7 on page 30. The remainder of this chapter presents a brief overview of the various steps involved in this process.

## Review of the Marketing Plan

The first step in the IMC planning process is to review the marketing plan and objectives. Before developing a promotional plan, marketers must understand where the company (or the brand) has been, its current position in the market, where it intends to go, and how it plans to get there. Most of this information should be contained in the **marketing plan**, a written document that describes the overall marketing strategy and programs developed for an organization, a particular product line, or a brand. Marketing plans can take several forms but generally include five basic elements:

1. A detailed situation analysis that consists of an internal marketing audit and review and an external analysis of the market competition and environmental factors.
2. Specific marketing objectives that provide direction, a time frame for marketing activities, and a mechanism for measuring performance.
3. A marketing strategy and program that include selection of target market(s) and decisions and plans for the four elements of the marketing mix.
4. A program for implementing the marketing strategy, including determining specific tasks to be performed and responsibilities.
5. A process for monitoring and evaluating performance and providing feedback so that proper control can be maintained and any necessary changes can be made in the overall marketing strategy or tactics.

For most firms, the promotional plan is an integral part of the marketing strategy. Thus, the promotional planners must know the roles advertising and other promotional-mix elements will play in the overall marketing program. The promotional plan is developed similarly to the marketing plan and often uses its detailed information. Promotional planners focus on information in the marketing plan that is relevant to the promotional strategy.

## Promotional Program Situation Analysis

After the overall marketing plan is reviewed, the next step in developing a promotional plan is to conduct the situation analysis. In the IMC program, the situation analysis focuses on the factors that influence or are relevant to the development of a promotional strategy. Like the overall marketing situation analysis, the promotional program situation analysis includes both an internal and an external analysis.

**Internal Analysis** The **internal analysis** assesses relevant areas involving the product/service offering and the firm itself. The capabilities of the firm and its ability to develop and implement a successful promotional program, the organization of the promotional department, and the successes and failures of past programs should be reviewed. The analysis should study the relative advantages and disadvantages of performing the promotional functions in-house as opposed to hiring an external agency (or agencies). For example, the internal analysis may indicate the firm is not capable of planning, implementing, and managing certain areas of the promotional program. If this is the case, it would be wise to look for assistance from an advertising agency or some other promotional facilitator. If the organization is already using an ad agency, the focus will be on the quality of the agency's work and the results achieved by past and/or current campaigns.

In this text we will examine the functions ad agencies perform for their clients, the agency selection process, compensation, and considerations in evaluating agency performance. We will also discuss the role and function of other promotional facilitators such as sales promotion firms, direct-marketing companies, public relations agencies, digital/interactive agencies, and marketing and media research firms.

Another aspect of the internal analysis is assessing the strengths and weaknesses of the firm or the brand from an image perspective. Often the image a firm brings to the market will have a significant impact on the way the firm can advertise and promote itself as well as its various products and services. Companies or brands that are new to the market or those for whom perceptions are negative may have to concentrate on their images, not just the benefits or attributes of the specific product or service. On the

**FIGURE 1–7**

An Integrated Marketing Communications Planning Model

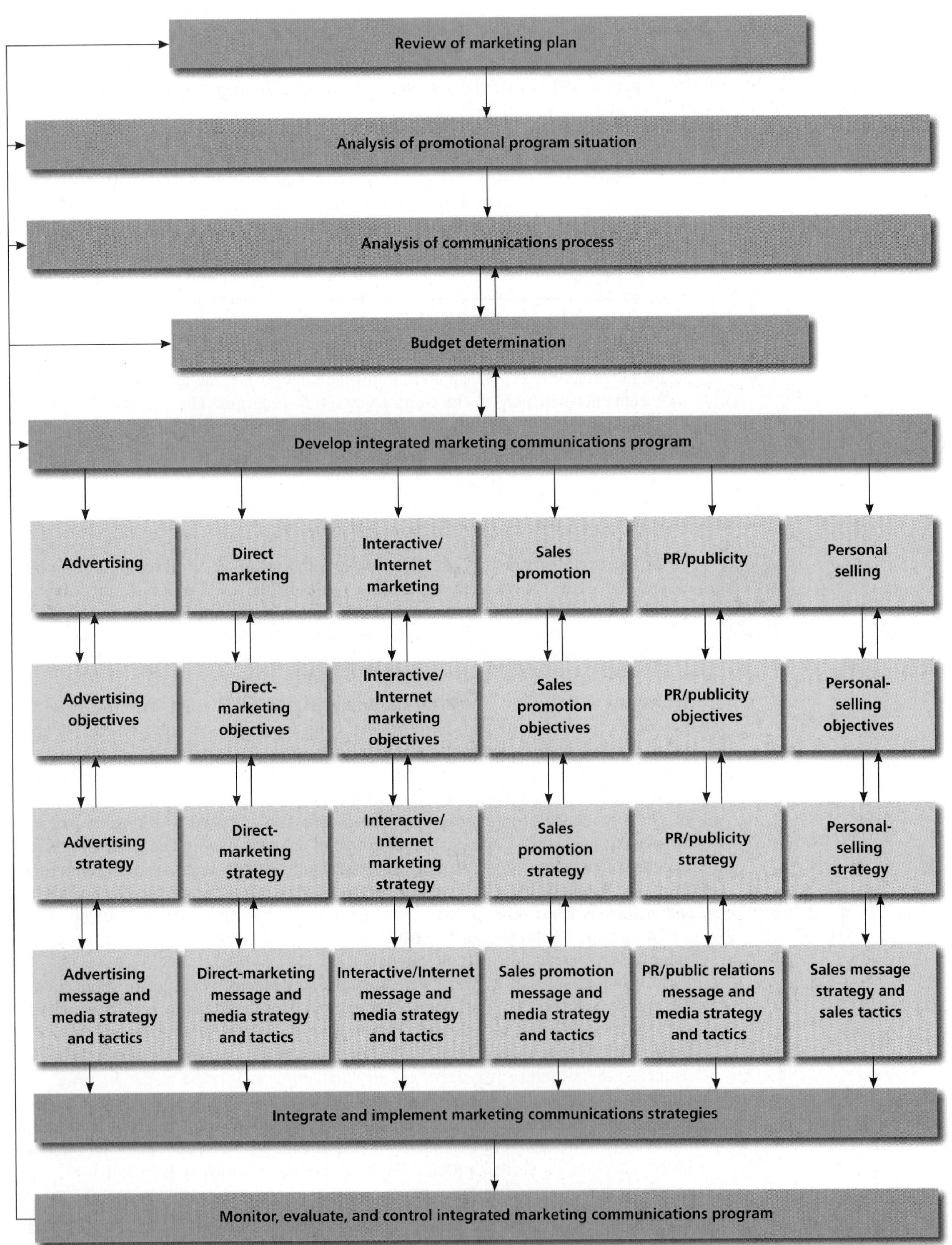

**Review of Marketing Plan**
Examine overall marketing plan and objectives
Role of advertising and promotion
Competitive analysis
Assess environmental influences

**Analysis of Promotional Program Situation**

Internal analysis
- Promotional department organization
- Firm's ability to implement promotional program
- Agency evaluation and selection
- Review of previous program results

External analysis
- Consumer behavior analysis
- Market segmentation and target marketing
- Market positioning

**Analysis of Communications Process**
Analyze receiver's response processes
Analyze source, message, channel factors
Establish communications goals and objectives

**Budget Determination**
Set tentative marketing communications budget
Allocate tentative budget

**Develop Integrated Marketing Communications Program**

Advertising
- Set advertising objectives
- Determine advertising budget
- Develop advertising message
- Develop advertising media strategy

Direct marketing
- Set direct-marketing objectives
- Determine direct-marketing budget
- Develop direct-marketing message
- Develop direct-marketing media strategy

Interactive/Internet marketing
- Set interactive/Internet marketing objectives
- Determine interactive/Internet marketing budget
- Develop interactive/Internet message
- Develop interactive/Internet media strategy

Sales promotion
- Set sales promotion objectives
- Determine sales promotion budget
- Determine sales promotion tools and develop messages
- Develop sales promotion media strategy

Public relations/publicity
- Set PR/publicity objectives
- Determine PR/publicity budget
- Develop PR/publicity messages
- Develop PR/publicity media strategy

Personal selling
- Set personal-selling and sales objectives
- Determine personal-selling/sales budget
- Develop sales message
- Develop selling roles and responsibilities

**Integrate and Implement Marketing Communications Strategies**
Integrate promotional-mix strategies
Create and produce ads
Purchase media time and space
Design and implement direct-marketing programs
Design and distribute sales promotion materials
Design and implement public relations/publicity programs
Design and implement interactive/Internet marketing programs

**Monitor, Evaluate, and Control Integrated Marketing Communications Program**
Evaluate promotional program results/effectiveness
Take measures to control and adjust promotional strategies

other hand, a firm with a strong reputation and/or image is already a step ahead when it comes to marketing its products or services. For example, Starbucks has an outstanding image that is a result of the quality of its coffee and other products as well as its reputation as a socially responsible company. The company is recognized as a good citizen in its dealings with communities, employees, suppliers, and the environment. Starbucks recognizes that being recognized as a socially responsible company is an important part of its tremendous growth and success. The company publishes a Global Responsibility Annual Report each year that describes its social, environmental, and economic impacts on the communities in which it does business (Exhibit 1–13).

The internal analysis also assesses the relative strengths and weaknesses of the product or service; its advantages and disadvantages; any unique selling points or benefits it may have; its packaging, price, and design; and so on. This information is particularly important to the creative personnel who must develop the advertising message for the brand.

Figure 1–8 is a checklist of some of the areas one might consider when performing analyses for promotional planning purposes. Addressing internal areas may require information the company does not have available internally and must gather as part of the external analysis.

STARBUCKS™ SHARED PLANET™
GLOBAL RESPONSIBILITY REPORT 2009

Year in Review: Fiscal 2009

*Starbucks has a long history of doing business in ways that are socially, environmentally, and economically responsible. Our commitment to doing the right thing has always been central to how we operate as a company. It's deeply valued by our partners (employees) and customers alike, and we believe it also makes great business sense. It hasn't always been easy; however, we've learned from our mistakes and persevered as a pioneer of innovation across the industry.*

As we've grown in size, so has our ability to drive positive change in communities around the world. In 2008 we set bold new goals in the areas where we can have the greatest impact: ethical sourcing, environmental stewardship, and community involvement. Together, we call these priorities Starbucks™ Shared Planet™.

By openly reporting on our performance, we aim to inform, inspire, and engage our partners, customers, and other stakeholders. In addition, this exercise gives us the opportunity to measure our progress and refine our strategy for the future.

In 2009 we took significant steps toward achieving our goals and also encountered challenges. Most notably, extraordinary global economic conditions forced us to make some difficult business decisions. While we adopted considerable cost-saving initiatives and invested in the customer experience to support long-term, profitable growth, we remained committed to responsible business practices.

Last year we looked beyond the boundaries of our own business structure and collaborated with external experts and organizations to find creative solutions for complex problems. This dialogue helped us gain a better understanding of the barriers we're facing and aided the development of new action plans that we've already begun to implement.

We're pleased to share our 2009 progress with you, and we hope you'll find this year's streamlined report easy to navigate. For a snapshot of year-over-year performance[1] against our Starbucks™ Shared Planet™ goals, we invite you to explore this section further. Regular updates on our broader responsible business practices are available at starbucks.com/responsibility.

As proud as we are of our accomplishments, we recognize we have a long way to go, and we welcome your input and ideas.

1 Report is based on fiscal year (October through September) performance unless otherwise indicated.

1

**EXHIBIT 1–13**
Starbucks has a very strong brand image and reputation as a socially responsible company

**External Analysis** The **external analysis** focuses on factors such as characteristics of the firm's customers, market segments, positioning strategies, and competitors, as shown in Figure 1–8. An important part of the external analysis is a detailed consideration of customers' characteristics and buying patterns, their decision processes, and factors influencing their purchase decisions. Attention must also be given to consumers' perceptions and attitudes, lifestyles, and criteria for making purchase decisions. Often, marketing research studies are needed to answer some of these questions.

A key element of the external analysis is an assessment of the market. The attractiveness of various market segments must be evaluated and the segments to target must be identified. Once the target markets are chosen, the emphasis will be on determining how the product should be positioned. What image or place should it have in consumers' minds?

This part of the promotional program situation analysis also includes an in-depth examination of both direct and indirect competitors. While competitors were analyzed in the overall marketing situation analysis, even more attention is devoted to promotional aspects at this phase. Focus is on the firm's primary competitors: their specific strengths and weaknesses; their segmentation, targeting, and positioning strategies; and the promotional strategies they employ. The size and allocation of their promotional budgets, their media strategies, and the messages they are sending to the marketplace should all be considered.

The external phase also includes an analysis of the marketing environment and current trends or developments that might affect the promotional program. For example, one of the most significant developments impacting IMC is the explosive growth of social networking sites such as Facebook which now has more than 500 million users. Marketers recognize that it is essential not only to have a Facebook page, but to find creative ways to leverage the access they provide to consumers' lives, behavior, and communications with one another.[48] For example, Naked Juice, which makes

| Internal Factors | External Factors |
|---|---|
| *Assessment of Firm's Promotional Organization and Capabilities*<br>Organization of promotional department<br>Capability of firm to develop and execute promotional programs<br>Determination of role and function of ad agency and other promotional facilitators<br>*Review of Firm's Previous Promotional Programs and Results*<br>Review previous promotional objectives<br>Review previous promotional budgets and allocations<br>Review previous promotional-mix strategies and programs<br>Review results of previous promotional programs<br>*Assessment of Firm or Brand Image and Implications for Promotion*<br>*Assessment of Relative Strengths and Weaknesses of Product or Service*<br>What are the strengths and weaknesses of product or service?<br>What are its key benefits?<br>Does it have any unique selling points?<br>Assessment of packaging, labeling, and brand image<br>How does our product or service compare with competition? | *Customer Analysis*<br>Who buys our product or service?<br>Who makes the decision to buy the product?<br>Who influences the decision to buy the product?<br>How is the purchase decision made? Who assumes what role?<br>What does the customer buy? What needs must be satisfied?<br>Why do customers buy a particular brand?<br>Where do they go or look to buy the product or service?<br>When do they buy? Any seasonality factors?<br>What are customers' attitudes toward our product or service?<br>What social factors might influence the purchase decision?<br>Do the customers' lifestyles influence their decisions?<br>How is our product or service perceived by customers?<br>How do demographic factors influence the purchase decision?<br>*Competitive Analysis*<br>Who are our direct and indirect competitors?<br>What key benefits and positioning are used by our competitors?<br>What is our position relative to the competition?<br>How big are competitors' ad budgets?<br>What message and media strategies are competitors using?<br>*Environmental Analysis*<br>Are there any current trends or developments that might affect the promotional program? |

**FIGURE 1–8**
Areas Covered in the Situation Analysis

a line of all-natural fruit juices and smoothies, worked with its interactive agency to develop a Facebook application to promote how the company had become the first nationally distributed brand to move to a recyclable polyethylene bottle (the Naked reNEWabottle). The "Naked Message in a Bottle" campaign asked Facebook users to pass virtual bottles and fun "Naked" messages along to their friends.[49] For every bottle passed Naked Juice donated five cents to Keep America Beautiful and its recycling education initiatives (Exhibit 1–14).

**EXHIBIT 1–14**
Naked Juice used a creative Facebook application to promote its new recyclable bottle

## Analysis of the Communications Process

This stage of the promotional planning process examines how the company can effectively communicate with consumers in its target markets. The promotional planner must think about the process consumers will go through in responding to marketing communications. The response process for products or services for which consumer decision making is characterized by a high level of interest is often different from that for low-involvement or routine purchase decisions. These differences will influence the promotional strategy.

Communication decisions regarding the use of various source, message, and channel factors must also be considered. The promotional planner should recognize the different effects various types of advertising messages might have on consumers and whether they are appropriate for the product or brand. Issues such as whether a celebrity spokesperson should be used and at what cost may also be studied. Preliminary discussion of media-mix options (print, TV, radio, newspaper, direct marketing, Internet) and their cost implications might also occur at this stage.

An important part of this stage of the promotional planning process is establishing communication goals and objectives. In this text, we stress the importance of distinguishing between communication and marketing objectives. **Marketing objectives** refer to what is to be accomplished by the overall marketing program. They are often stated in terms of sales, market share, or profitability.

**Communication objectives** refer to what the firm seeks to accomplish with its promotional program. They are often stated in terms of the nature of the message to be communicated or what specific communication effects are to be achieved. Communication objectives may include creating awareness or knowledge about a product and its attributes or benefits; creating an image; or developing favorable attitudes, preferences, or purchase intentions. Communication objectives should be the guiding force for development of the overall marketing communications strategy and of objectives for each promotional-mix area.

## Budget Determination

After the communication objectives are determined, attention turns to the promotional budget. Two basic questions are asked at this point: What will the promotional program cost? How will the money be allocated? Ideally, the amount a firm needs to spend on promotion should be determined by what must be done to accomplish its communication objectives. In reality, promotional budgets are often determined using a more simplistic approach, such as how much money is available or a percentage of a company's or brand's sales revenue. At this stage, the budget is often tentative. It may not be finalized until specific promotional-mix strategies are developed.

## Developing the Integrated Marketing Communications Program

Developing the IMC program is generally the most involved and detailed step of the promotional planning process. As discussed earlier, each promotional-mix element has certain advantages and limitations. At this stage of the planning process, decisions have to be made regarding the role and importance of each element and their coordination with one another. As Figure 1–7 shows, each promotional-mix element has its own set of objectives and a budget and strategy for meeting them. Decisions must be made and activities performed to implement the promotional programs. Procedures must be developed for evaluating performance and making any necessary changes.

For example, the advertising program will have its own set of objectives, usually involving the communication of some message or appeal to a target audience. A budget will be determined, providing the advertising manager and the agency with some idea of how much money is available for developing the ad campaign and purchasing media to disseminate the ad message.

Two important aspects of the advertising program are development of the message and the media strategy. Message development, often referred to as *creative strategy,* involves determining the basic appeal and message the advertiser wishes to convey to the target audience. This process, along with the ads that result, is to many students the most fascinating aspect of promotion. *Media strategy* involves determining which communication channels will be used to deliver the advertising message to the target audience. Decisions must be made regarding which types of media will be used (e.g., newspapers, magazines, radio, TV, outdoor, Internet) as well as specific media selections (e.g., a particular magazine or TV program). This task requires careful evaluation of the media options' advantages and limitations, costs, and ability to deliver the message effectively to the target market.

Once the message and media strategies have been determined, steps must be taken to implement them. Most large companies hire advertising agencies to plan and produce their messages and to evaluate and purchase the media that will carry their ads. However, most agencies work very closely with their clients as they develop the ads and select media, because it is the advertiser that ultimately approves (and pays for) the creative work and media plan.

A similar process takes place for the other elements of the IMC program as objectives are set, an overall strategy is developed, message and media strategies are determined, and steps are taken to implement them. While the marketer's advertising agencies may be used to perform some of the other IMC functions, they may also hire other communication specialists such as direct-marketing and interactive and/or sales promotion agencies, as well as public relations firms.

### Monitoring, Evaluation, and Control

The final stage of the IMC planning process is monitoring, evaluating, and controlling the promotional program. It is important to determine how well the IMC program is meeting communications objectives and helping the firm accomplish its overall marketing goals and objectives. The IMC planner wants to know not only how well the promotional program is doing but also why. For example, problems with the advertising program may lie in the nature of the message or in a media plan that does not reach the target market effectively. The manager must know the reasons for the results in order to take the right steps to correct the program.

This final stage of the process is designed to provide managers with continual feedback concerning the effectiveness of the IMC program, which in turn can be used as input into the planning process. As Figure 1–7 shows, information on the results achieved by the IMC program is used in subsequent promotional planning and strategy development.

## PERSPECTIVE AND ORGANIZATION OF THIS TEXT

Traditional approaches to teaching advertising, promotional strategy, or marketing communications courses have often treated the various elements of the promotional mix as separate functions. As a result, many people who work in advertising, sales promotion, direct marketing, interactive/Internet, or public relations tend to approach marketing communications problems from the perspective of their particular specialty. An advertising person may believe marketing communications objectives are best met through the use of media advertising; a promotional specialist argues for a sales promotion program to motivate consumer response; a public relations person advocates a PR campaign to tackle the problem. These orientations are not surprising, since each person has been trained to view marketing communications problems primarily from one perspective.

In the contemporary business world, however, individuals working in marketing, advertising, and other promotional areas are expected to understand and use a variety of marketing communications tools, not just the one in which they specialize. Ad agencies no longer confine their services to the advertising area. Many are involved in sales promotion, public relations, direct marketing, event sponsorship, Internet/interactive, and other marketing communications areas. Individuals working on the client or advertiser side of the business, such as brand, product, or promotional managers, are developing marketing programs that use a variety of marketing communications methods.

This text views advertising and promotion from an integrated marketing communications perspective. We will examine the promotional-mix elements and their roles in an organization's integrated marketing communications efforts. Although media advertising may be the most visible part of the communications program, understanding its role in contemporary marketing requires attention to other promotional areas such as the Internet and interactive marketing, direct marketing, sales promotion, and public relations. Not all the promotional-mix areas are under the direct control of the advertising or marketing communications manager. For example, as noted earlier, personal selling is typically a specialized marketing function outside the control of the advertising or promotional department. Likewise, publicity/public relations is often assigned to a separate department. All these departments should, however, communicate to coordinate all the organization's marketing communications tools.

The purpose of this book is to provide you with a thorough understanding of the field of advertising and other elements of a firm's promotional mix and show how they are combined to form an integrated marketing communications program. To plan, develop, and implement an effective IMC program, those involved must understand marketing, consumer behavior, and the communications process. The first part of this book is designed to provide this foundation by examining the roles of advertising and other forms of promotion in the marketing process. We examine the process of market segmentation and positioning and consider their part in developing an IMC strategy. We also discuss how firms organize for IMC and make decisions regarding ad agencies and other firms that provide marketing and promotional services.

We then focus on consumer behavior considerations and analyze the communications process. We discuss various communications models of value to promotional planners in developing strategies and establishing goals and objectives for advertising and other forms of promotion. We also consider how firms determine and allocate their marketing communications budget.

After laying the foundation for the development of a promotional program, this text will follow the integrated marketing communications planning model presented in Figure 1–7. We examine each of the promotional-mix variables, beginning with advertising. Our detailed examination of advertising includes a discussion of creative strategy and the process of developing the advertising message, an overview of media strategy, and an evaluation of the various media (print, broadcast, and support media). The discussion then turns to the other areas of the promotional mix: direct marketing, interactive/Internet marketing, sales promotion, and public relations/publicity. Our examination of the IMC planning process concludes with a discussion of how the program is monitored, evaluated, and controlled. Particular attention is given to measuring the effectiveness of advertising and other forms of promotion.

The final part of the text examines special topic areas and perspectives that have become increasingly important in contemporary marketing. We will examine the area of international advertising and promotion and the challenges companies face in developing IMC programs for global markets as well as various countries around the world. The text concludes with an examination of the environment in which integrated marketing communications operates, including the regulatory, social, and economic factors that influence, and in turn are influenced by, an organization's advertising and promotional program.

## Summary

Advertising and other forms of promotion are an integral part of the marketing process in most organizations. Over the past decade, the amount of money spent on advertising, sales promotion, direct marketing, and other forms of marketing communication has increased tremendously, both in the United States and in foreign markets. There has been a very large increase in the amount of monies spent on the Internet as well as various forms of nontraditional media, some of which did not exist at the beginning of the new millennium. To understand the role of advertising and promotion in a marketing program, one must understand the role and function of marketing in an organization. The basic task of marketing is to combine the four controllable elements, known as the marketing mix, into a comprehensive program that facilitates exchange with a target market. The elements of the marketing mix are the product or service, price, place (distribution), and promotion.

For many years, the promotional function in most companies was dominated by mass-media advertising. However, more and more companies are recognizing the importance of integrated marketing communications, coordinating the various marketing and promotional elements to achieve more efficient and effective communication programs. A number of factors underlie the move toward IMC by marketers as well as ad agencies and other promotional facilitators. Reasons for the growing importance of the integrated marketing communications perspective include a rapidly changing environment with respect to consumers, technology, and media. The IMC movement is also being driven by changes in the ways companies market their products and services. A shifting of marketing expenditures from traditional media advertising to other forms of promotion as well as nontraditional media, the rapid growth of the Internet and social media, a shift in marketplace power from manufacturers to retailers, the growth and development of database marketing, the demand for greater accountability from advertising agencies and other marketing communication firms, and the fragmentation of media markets, as well as changing media consumption patterns, are among the key changes taking place.

Promotion is best viewed as the communication function of marketing. It is accomplished through a promotional mix that includes advertising, personal selling, publicity/public relations, sales promotion, direct marketing, and interactive/Internet marketing. The inherent advantages and disadvantages of each of these promotional-mix elements influence the roles they play in the overall marketing program. In developing the IMC program, the marketer must decide which tools to use and how to combine them to achieve the organization's marketing and communication objectives. Many companies are taking an audience contact or touch point perspective in developing their IMC programs whereby they consider all of the potential ways of reaching their target audience and presenting the company or brand in a favorable manner. The four primary categories of contact points include company planned, intrinsic, unexpected and customer initiated. These contact points vary with respect to the impact they have on the customer and marketers' ability to control them.

Promotional management involves coordinating the promotional-mix elements to develop an integrated program of effective marketing communication. The model of the IMC planning process in Figure 1–7 contains a number of steps: a review of the marketing plan; promotional program situation analysis; analysis of the communications process; budget determination; development of an integrated marketing communications program; integration and implementation of marketing communications strategies; and monitoring, evaluation, and control of the promotional program.

## Key Terms

**exchange** p. 7
**marketing** p. 7
**value** p. 7
**marketing mix** p. 8
**integrated marketing communications (IMC)** p. 8
**promotion** p. 17
**promotional mix** p. 17
**advertising** p. 18
**direct marketing** p. 19
**direct-response advertising** p. 21
**interactive media** p. 21
**sales promotion** p. 23
**publicity** p. 24
**public relations** p. 25
**personal selling** p. 25
**contact (or touch) point** p. 26
**integrated marketing communications management** p. 28
**integrated marketing communications plan** p. 28
**marketing plan** p. 30
**internal analysis** p. 30
**external analysis** p. 32
**marketing objectives** p. 34
**communication objectives** p. 34

## Discussion Questions

1. Discuss the role of integrated marketing communications in the marketing program of automobile manufacturers such as Volkswagen. How can Volkswagen use the various IMC tools to achieve its objectives of building its brand image and increasing sales in the U.S. market? (LO5)

2. Evaluate the "PunchDub" campaign that the Deutsch LA agency developed when it took over the Volkswagen of America account. Discuss the pros and cons of the campaign and assess the way it was implemented by the agency. (LO6)

3. Discuss how integrated marketing communications differs from traditional advertising and promotion. What are some of the reasons more marketers are taking an IMC perspective to their advertising and promotional programs? (LO1)

4. Compare the new definition of integrated marketing communications developed by Don Shultz with the original definition that was developed by the American Association of Advertising Agencies. How do they differ? (LO2)

5. Identify three specific technological developments that are having an impact on the integrated marketing communications. Discuss some of the ways this technology is impacting the IMC program of various companies. (LO2)

6. Discuss the role integrated marketing communications plays in the brand building process. Find an example of a company that has been able to build and maintain its brand equity without relying primarily on mass-media advertising. (LO3)

7. Discuss the challenges companies face with respect to building and maintaining a favorable brand image during a recession such as the one the global economy has been facing for the past several years. What changes do marketers need to make in their IMC programs during a recession? (LO3)

8. Discuss the opportunities and challenges facing marketers with regard to the use of mobile marketing. Discuss the various ways marketers might send messages to consumers on their mobile phones. (LO4)

9. Why are companies such as Procter & Gamble moving away from the use of traditional mass-media advertising and looking for other contact points that can be used to connect with consumers? How can various IMC tools be used by companies such as P&G to build and maintain relationships with their customers? (LO5)

10. Why is it important for those who work in marketing to understand and appreciate all the various integrated marketing communication tools and how they can be used? (LO6)

## AdForum Exercise: "Comparing Advertising Campaigns for Volkswagen"

adforum.com

(See Advertising and Promotion Playlist, Chapter 1)

The chapter opener discusses the decision made by Volkswagen of America to move its advertising from the Crispin Porter + Bogusky agency to Deutsch LA. Your assignment is to compare some of the television commercials created by CP+B with those created by Deutsch since taking over the account. Watch four of the commercials created by each agency that are provided in the Advertising and Promotion playlist for Chapter 1 and answer the following questions.

1 How would you describe the type of ads created by CP+B for Volkswagen versus those created by Deutsch LA? How are they similar and how do they differ?

2 Do you think the type of commercials created by CP+B were effective in helping build the brand image of Volkswagen and differentiate it from competitors such as Honda, Toyota, Hyundai, and Nissan?

3 One of the objectives of the advertising created by Deutsch LA for Volkswagen of America is to increase awareness of the VW product line beyond the Bug and Jetta models. Discuss how the commercials created by Deutsch help achieve this objective.

Access to the chapter playlist is available through McGraw Hill connect™ MARKETING, www.mcgrawhillconnect.com

A proud history of savings and reliability, backed by the strength of Warren Buffett's Berkshire Hathaway Inc.
(Note: the above portrait is not Mr. Buffett.)

GEICO.
A SUBSIDIARY OF BERKSHIRE HATHAWAY INC.

## LEARNING OBJECTIVES

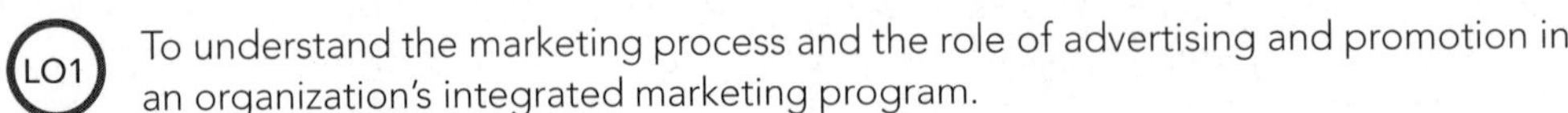

LO1 To understand the marketing process and the role of advertising and promotion in an organization's integrated marketing program.

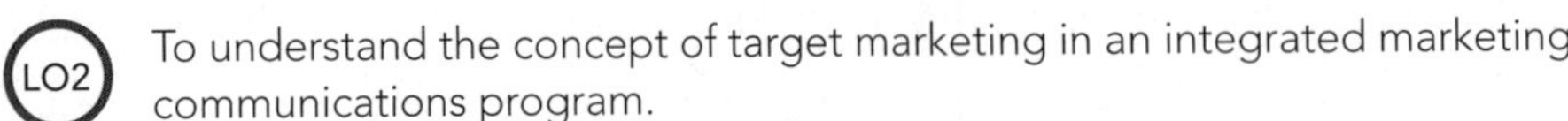

LO2 To understand the concept of target marketing in an integrated marketing communications program.

LO3 To recognize the role of market segmentation and its use in an integrated marketing communications program.

LO4 To understand the use of positioning and repositioning strategies.

LO5 To know the various decision areas under each element of the marketing mix and how they influence and interact with advertising and promotional strategy.

# 2 The Role of IMC in the Marketing Process

## GEICO: THERE'S MORE TO THE STORY THAN GECKOS AND CAVEMEN

When is the last time that you turned on the TV and didn't see a GEICO commercial? It seems like every program contains at least one GEICO 15-second spot featuring either the Gecko, the Cavemen, or a stack of money with eyes. Of course, this is not really the case, but it sure seems like it, as it shows what an over $750 million advertising budget can do to reinforce your brand.

Started in 1936 in the middle of the Great Depression by Leo Goodwin and aided by his wife, Lillian, the Government Employees Insurance Company (GEICO) pursued a direct mail marketing strategy targeting federal employees and selected enlisted military officers. By the end of the first year, the company had underwritten 3,700 policies and had a staff of 12. Ten years later an investment banker and friend of the Goodwins, Lorimer Davidson, joined the company, and in 1951 Warren Buffett purchased his first GEICO stock after an impromptu meeting with Davidson. By 1964, the company had sold its one-millionth policy, and opened up a number of sales and service offices for walk-in customers. However, the rapid expansion of the previous three decades declined significantly in the 1970s leading GEICO to pull back until 1976, when Warren Buffet again purchased stock—this time one million shares.

The company expanded its market in the 1990s, broadening its customer base through a new four-company strategy, that could meet the insurance needs of nearly every driver and by increasing its advertising budget to gain national visibility. When Buffet purchased the remaining shares of GEICO stock in 1996, the insurance company became a subsidiary of one of the most profitable organizations in the country, Berkshire Hathaway. This financial security led to an enormous increase in national television and direct-mail advertising. Sales skyrocketed, and GEICO had more than 5 million policies in force by the turn of the century. The Gecko made its first appearance during the 1999–2000 television season, and the Cavemen followed in 2004 with the powerful message that it was so easy to get a quote and buy a policy online, ". . . even a caveman could do it." The line was instantly powerful, and may become one of the most recognized messages in advertising history.

The amazing popularity of the Gecko and Cavemen campaigns was clearly instrumental in GEICO's success. The two icons have been enshrined in *Advertising Week* magazine's "Walk of Fame," and each one was voted America's favorite advertising icon—the Gecko in 2005 and the Caveman in 2008.

But the popular campaigns were not the only communications strategies that led to success. In addition to direct mail, GEICO has made extensive use of the Internet for advertising, customer service, appraisal information, and sales. The Cavemen were featured on their own interactive website, Caveman's Crib, and the company connects with the public online through a Facebook page, Twitter feeds, a Flickr site, YouTube, and the GEICO Blog. Extensive use of promotional giveaways from sun visors to ad specialties continue to be used, and the Gecko travels the country as a "spokes creature" for wildlife conservation efforts.

From its humble beginnings during the Great Depression, GEICO now has nearly ten million policyholders, and assets of more than $24 billion. Aggressive marketing communications has certainly paid off!

Sources: Bryan Sharp, "Geico Prepares to Wow Us with New Advertising Campaign," mediabane.com, July 1, 2009; "GEICO's Story from the Beginning," www.geico.com, February 9, 2010; "GEICO's Advertising Blitz: What the Lizard Won't Tell You," www.lewisandtompkins.com, 2010.

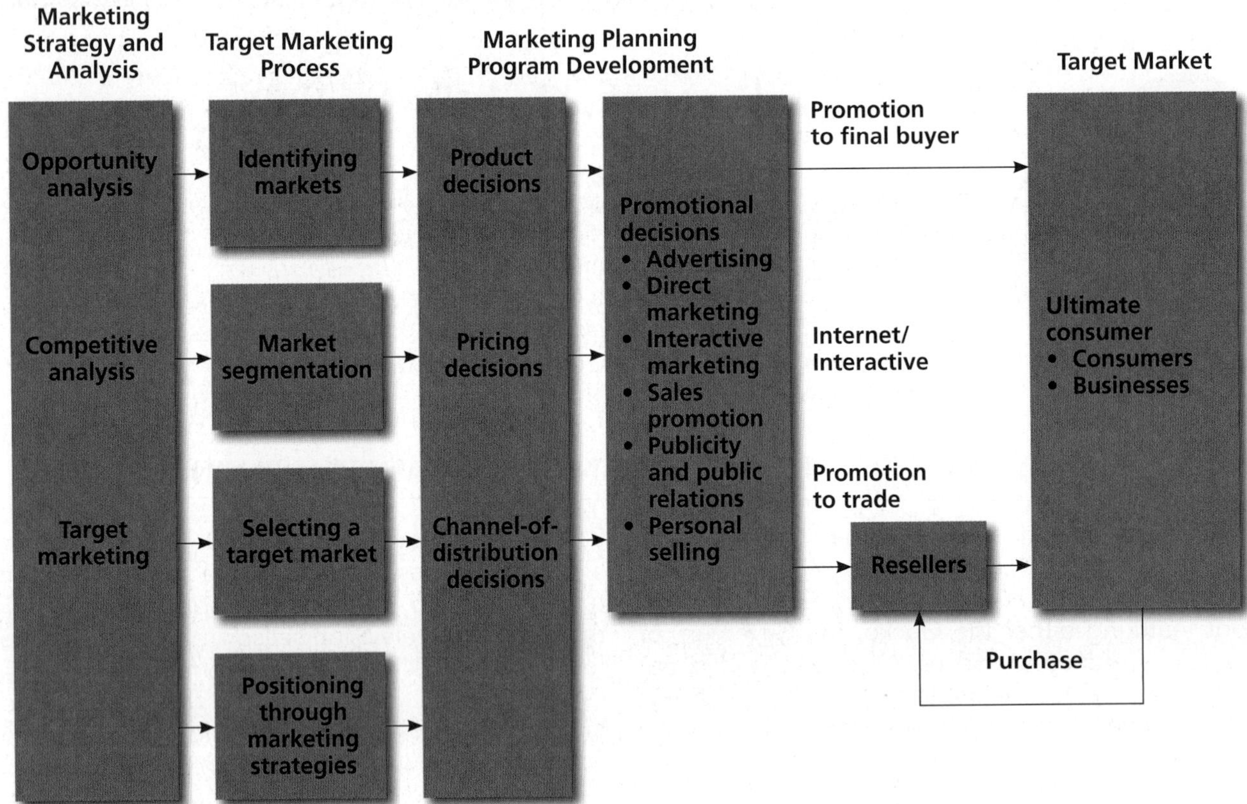


**FIGURE 2–1**

Marketing and Promotions Process Model

The GEICO success story is just one example of how companies and organizations use marketing strategies that will be discussed in this chapter. These include the identification of market opportunities, market segmentation, target marketing and positioning, and marketing program development. GEICO's recognition of the importance of a strong brand image coupled with a strong IMC program reflects the solid marketing orientation required to be successful in today's marketplace.

In this chapter, we take a closer look at how marketing strategies influence the role of promotion and how promotional decisions must be coordinated with other areas of the marketing mix. In turn, all elements of the marketing mix must be consistent in a strategic plan that results in an integrated marketing communications program. We use the model in Figure 2–1 as a framework for analyzing how promotion fits into an organization's marketing strategy and programs.

This model consists of four major components: the organization's marketing strategy and analysis, the target marketing process, the marketing planning program development (which includes the promotional mix), and the target market. As the model shows, the marketing process begins with the development of a marketing strategy and analysis in which the company decides the product or service areas and particular markets where it wants to compete. The company must then coordinate the various elements of the marketing mix into a cohesive marketing program that will reach the target market effectively. Note that a firm's promotion program is directed not only to the final buyer but also to the channel or "trade" members that distribute its products to the ultimate consumer. These channel members must be convinced there is a demand for the company's products so they will carry them and will aggressively merchandise and promote them to consumers. Promotions play an important role in the marketing program for building and maintaining demand not only among final consumers but among the trade as well.

As noted in Chapter 1, all elements of the marketing mix—price, product, distribution, and promotions—must be integrated to provide consistency and maximum communications impact. Development of a marketing plan is instrumental in achieving this goal.

As Figure 2–1 shows, development of a marketing program requires an in-depth analysis of the market. This analysis may make extensive use of marketing research as an input into the planning process. This input, in turn, provides the basis for the development of marketing strategies in regard to product, pricing, distribution, and promotion decisions. Each of these steps requires a detailed analysis, since this plan serves as the road map to follow in achieving marketing goals. Once the detailed market analysis has been completed and marketing objectives have been established, each element in the marketing mix must contribute to a comprehensive integrated marketing program. Of course, the promotional program element (the focus of this text) must be combined with all other program elements in such a way as to achieve maximum impact.

# MARKETING STRATEGY AND ANALYSIS

Any organization that wants to exchange its products or services in the marketplace successfully should have a **strategic marketing plan** to guide the allocation of its resources. A strategic marketing plan usually evolves from an organization's overall corporate strategy and serves as a guide for specific marketing programs and policies. As we noted earlier, marketing strategy is based on a situation analysis—a detailed assessment of the current marketing conditions facing the company, its product lines, or its individual brands. From this situation analysis, a firm develops an understanding of the market and the various opportunities it offers, the competition, and the **market segments** or target markets the company wishes to pursue. We examine each step of the marketing strategy and *planning* in this chapter.

**EXHIBIT 2–1**

Manischewitz sees the mainstream market as an opportunity

## Opportunity Analysis

A careful analysis of the marketplace should lead to alternative market opportunities for existing product lines in current or new markets, new products for current markets, or new products for new markets. **Market opportunities** are areas where there are favorable demand trends, where the company believes customer needs and opportunities are not being satisfied, and where it can compete effectively. The Manischewitz company—you may have heard the ad slogan "Man-O-Manischewitz! What a wine!"—a marketer of kosher foods, has revived their decades old slogan to take advantage of a new marketing opportunity. Based on research that showed that four out of five buyers of kosher foods are not traditional Jewish consumers, Manischewitz has increased its marketing efforts in an attempt to capture more of the mainstream market. Knowing that there has been an increase in interest in ethnic foods and health consciousness and that, as a result of the recession, more consumers are eating meals at home, the company hopes to reach more consumers (Exhibit 2–1). The company's new IMC program includes a multimillion dollar advertising budget, Web programs, in-store promotions, a "Cook Off," and public relations activities designed to promote its kosher food line.[1]

A company usually identifies market opportunities by carefully examining the marketplace and noting demand

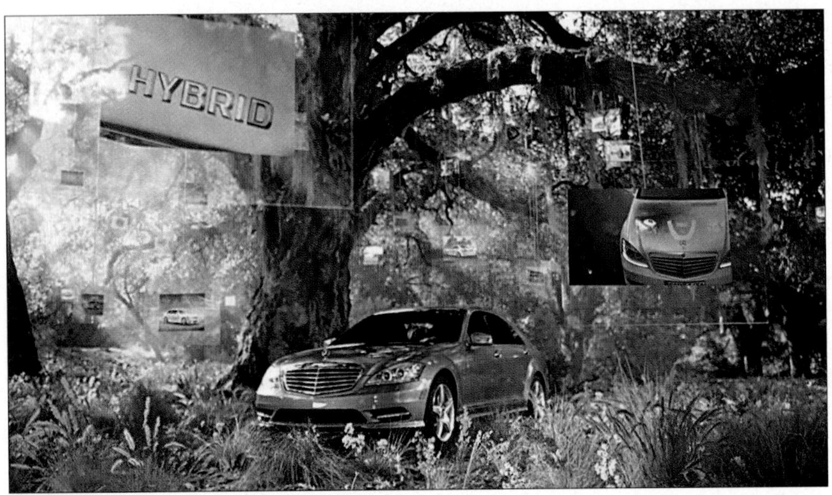


**EXHIBIT 2–2**
Many car companies now compete in the hybrid market

trends and competition in various market segments. A market can rarely be viewed as one large homogeneous group of customers; rather, it consists of many heterogeneous groups, or segments. In recent years, many companies have recognized the importance of tailoring their marketing to meet the needs and demand trends of different market segments.

For example, different market segments in the personal computer (PC) industry include the home, government, education, science, and business markets. These segments can be even further divided. The business market consists of both small companies and large corporations; the education market can range from elementary schools to colleges and universities. A company that is marketing its products in the auto industry must decide in which particular market segment or segments it wishes to compete. This decision depends on the amount and nature of competition the brand will face in a particular market. Many auto companies are now competing in the hybrid car market, offering a variety of models (Exhibit 2–2). A competitive analysis is an important part of marketing strategy development and warrants further consideration.

## Competitive Analysis

In developing the firm's marketing strategies and plans for its products and services, the manager must carefully analyze the competition to be faced in the marketplace. This may range from direct brand competition (which can also include its own brands) to more indirect forms of competition, such as product substitutes. For example, growth in the bottled water market has led numerous companies to compete in this area and offer different product varieties (Exhibit 2–3).

At a more general level, marketers must recognize they are competing for the consumer's discretionary income, so they must understand the various ways potential customers choose to spend their money. The impact of the worldwide economic downturn has made manufacturers of luxury goods brands rethink their marketing strategies. Sales of luxury products fell 2 percent in 2008, and were expected to drop another 9 percent in 2009.[2] Like consumers, luxury goods manufacturers like Versace, Chanel and others have cut back on their advertising expenditures.

An important aspect of marketing strategy development is the search for a **competitive advantage**, something special a firm does or has that gives it an edge

**EXHIBIT 2–3**
Vitaminwater offers a variety of enhanced waters

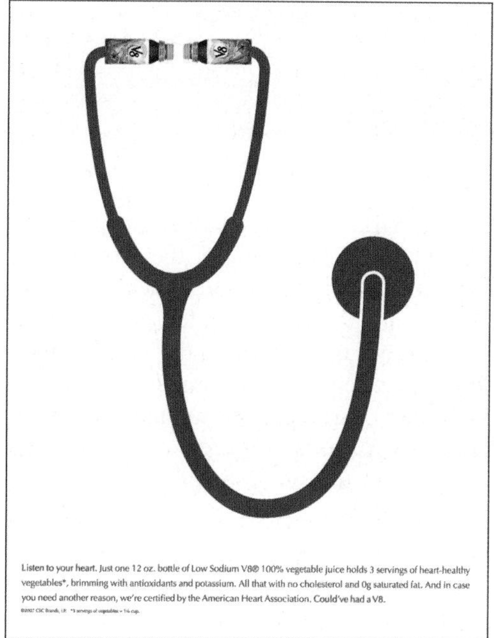


**EXHIBIT 2–4**
V-8 revitalizes its image

over competitors. Ways to achieve a competitive advantage include having quality products that command a premium price, providing superior customer service, having the lowest production costs and lower prices, or dominating channels of distribution. Competitive advantage can also be achieved through advertising that creates and maintains product differentiation and brand equity, an example of which was the long-running advertising campaign for Michelin tires, which stressed security as well as performance. The strong brand images of Colgate toothpaste, Campbell's soup, Nike shoes, BMW, and McDonald's give them a competitive advantage in their respective markets.

Recently, there has been concern that some marketers have not been spending enough money on advertising to allow leading brands to sustain their competitive edge. Advertising proponents have been calling for companies to protect their brand equity and franchises by investing more money in advertising instead of costly trade promotions. Some companies, recognizing the important competitive advantage strong brands provide, have been increasing their investments in them. Campbell's Soup Company introduced a new advertising campaign in an attempt to revitalize its 74-year-old V-8 vegetable juice brand (see Exhibit 2–4). Replicating the highly successful campaign of the 1970s in which people got bopped on the head with the catch phrase "I could've had a V8," and stressing the brand's health aspects, the company has seen a 10 percent sales increase since the new campaign began. Campbell's executives believe that as a result of their new marketing efforts, the brand is now new again.[3]

Competitors' marketing programs have a major impact on a firm's marketing strategy, so they must be analyzed and monitored. The reactions of competitors to a company's marketing and promotional strategy are also very important. Competitors may cut price, increase promotional spending, develop new brands, or attack one another through comparative advertising (Exhibit 2–5). One of the more intense competitive rivalries is the battle between Coca-Cola and Pepsi. A number of other intense competitive rivalries exist in the marketplace, including Hertz and Avis and Ford and GM among others.

**EXHIBIT 2–5**
Competitors sometimes position themselves through comparative ads

A final aspect of competition is the growing number of foreign companies penetrating the U.S. market and taking business from domestic firms. In products ranging from beer to cars to electronics, imports are becoming an increasingly strong form of competition with which U.S. firms must contend. As we now compete in a global economy, U.S. companies must not only defend their domestic markets but also learn how to compete effectively in the international marketplace.

## Target Market Selection

After evaluating the opportunities presented by various market segments, including a detailed competitive analysis, the company may select one, or more, as a target market. This target market becomes the focus of the firm's marketing effort, and goals and objectives are set according to where the company wants to be and what it hopes to accomplish in this market. As noted in Chapter 1, these goals and objectives are set in terms of specific performance variables such as sales, market share, and profitability. The selection of the target market (or markets) in which the firm will compete is an important part of its marketing strategy and has direct implications for its advertising and promotional efforts.

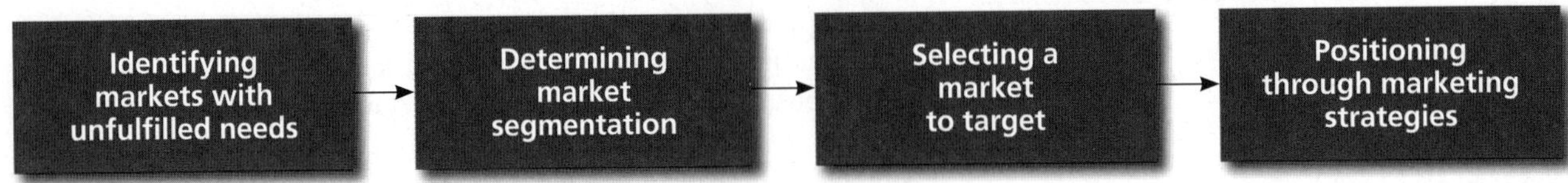


**FIGURE 2–2**

The Target Marketing Process

Recall from our discussion of the integrated marketing communications planning program that the situation analysis is conducted at the beginning of the promotional planning process. Specific objectives—both marketing and communications—are derived from the situation analysis, and the promotional-mix strategies are developed to achieve these objectives. Marketers rarely go after the entire market with one product, brand, or service offering. Rather, they pursue a number of different strategies, breaking the market into segments and targeting one or more of these segments for marketing and promotional efforts. This means different objectives may be established, different budgets may be used, and the promotional-mix strategies may vary, depending on the market approach used.

# THE TARGET MARKETING PROCESS

Because few, if any, products can satisfy the needs of all consumers, companies often develop different marketing strategies to satisfy different consumer needs. The process by which marketers do this (presented in Figure 2–2) is referred to as **target marketing** and involves four basic steps: identifying markets with unfulfilled needs, segmenting the market, targeting specific segments, and positioning one's product or service through marketing strategies.

## Identifying Markets

When employing a target marketing strategy, the marketer identifies the specific needs of groups of people (or segments), selects one or more of these segments as a target, and develops marketing programs directed to each. This approach has found increased applicability in marketing for a number of reasons, including changes in the market (consumers are becoming much more diverse in their needs, attitudes, and lifestyles); increased use of segmentation by competitors; and the fact that more managers are trained in segmentation and realize the advantages associated with this strategy. Perhaps the best explanation, however, comes back to the basic premise that you must understand as much as possible about consumers to design marketing programs that meet their needs most effectively.

Target market identification isolates consumers with similar lifestyles, needs, and the like, and increases our knowledge of their specific requirements. The more marketers can establish this common ground with consumers, the more effective they will be in addressing these requirements in their communications programs and informing and/or persuading potential consumers that the product or service offering will meet their needs.

Let's use the beer industry as an example. Years ago, beer was just beer, with little differentiation, many local distributors, and few truly national brands. The industry began consolidating; many brands were assumed by the larger brewers or ceased to exist. As the number of competitors decreased, competition among the major brewers increased. To compete more effectively, brewers began to look at different tastes, lifestyles, and so on, of beer drinkers and used this information in their marketing strategies. This process resulted in the identification of many market segments, each of which corresponds to different customers' needs, lifestyles, and other characteristics.

As you can see in Figure 2–3, the beer market now consists of 10 segments with numerous offerings available to each.[4] Most large brewers have product offerings in

**FIGURE 2–3**
The U.S. Beer Market

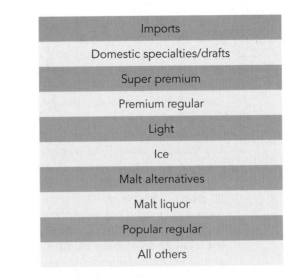

| Imports |
|---|
| Domestic specialties/drafts |
| Super premium |
| Premium regular |
| Light |
| Ice |
| Malt alternatives |
| Malt liquor |
| Popular regular |
| All others |

Source: Ted Goldammer, *The Brewer's Handbook*, 2nd ed. Apex Publishers, 2008.

each segment, competing with each other as well as smaller microbreweries (Exhibit 2–6). Each appeals to a different set of needs. Taste is certainly one; others include image, cost, and the size of one's waistline. A variety of other reasons for purchasing are also operating, including the consumer's social class, lifestyle, and economic status.

Marketers competing in nearly all product and service categories are constantly searching for ways to segment their markets in an attempt to better satisfy customers' needs. The remainder of this section discusses ways to approach this task.

## Market Segmentation

It is not possible to develop marketing strategies for every consumer. Rather, the marketer attempts to identify broad classes of buyers who have the same needs and will respond similarly to marketing actions. **Market segmentation** is "dividing

**EXHIBIT 2–6**
Miller-Coors offers a variety of beers

up a market into distinct groups that (1) have common needs and (2) will respond similarly to a marketing action.

The more marketers segment the market, the more precise is their understanding of it. But the more the market becomes divided, the fewer consumers there are in each segment. Thus, a key decision is, How far should one go in the segmentation process? Where does the process stop? As you can see by the strategy taken in the beer industry, it can go far!

In planning the promotional effort, managers consider whether the target segment is substantial enough to support individualized strategies. More specifically, they consider whether this group is accessible. Can it be reached with a communications program? For example, you will see in Chapter 10 that in some instances there are no media that can efficiently be used to reach some targeted groups. Or the promotions manager may identify a number of segments but be unable to develop the required programs to reach them. The firm may have insufficient funds to develop the required advertising campaign, inadequate sales staff to cover all areas, or other promotional deficiencies. After determining that a segmentation strategy is in order, the marketer must establish the basis on which it will address the market. The following section discusses some of the bases for segmenting markets and demonstrates examples of advertising and promotions applications.

**Bases for Segmentation** As shown in Figure 2–4, several methods are available for segmenting markets. Marketers may use one of the segmentation variables or a combination of approaches. Consider the market segmentation strategy that might be employed to market snow skis. The consumer's lifestyle—active, fun-loving, enjoys outdoor sports—is certainly important. But so are other factors, such as age (participation in downhill skiing drops off significantly at about age 30) and income (have you seen the price of a lift ticket lately?), as well as marital status. Let us review the bases for segmentation and examine some promotional strategies employed in each.

**Geographic Segmentation** In the **geographic segmentation** approach, markets are divided into different geographic units. These units may include nations, states, counties, or even neighborhoods. Consumers often have different buying habits depending on where they reside. Regional differences may exist in regard to food, drinks, attitudes toward foreign products, and the like. For example, many companies consider California a very different market from the rest of the United States and have developed specific marketing programs targeted to the consumers in that state. Other companies have developed programs targeted at specific regions. Exhibit 2–7 shows an ad for Big Red, just one of the regional soft drink "cult" brands—along with Cheerwine (the Carolinas), Vernors (Michigan), and Moxie (New England)—that have found success by marketing in regional areas (in this case, Texas). One company—Olde Brooklyn Beverage Company—even went so far as to promote a

**EXHIBIT 2–7**
Big Red markets to a specific geographic region

**FIGURE 2–4**

Some Bases for Market Segmentation

| Main Dimension | Segmentation Variables | Typical Breakdowns |
|---|---|---|
| *Customer Characteristics* | | |
| Geographic | Region | Northeast; Midwest; South; West; etc. |
| | City size | Under 10,000; 10,000–24,999; 25,000–49,999; 50,000–99,999; 100,000–249,999; 250,000–499,999; 500,000–999,999; 1,000,000 or more |
| | Metropolitan area | Metropolitan statistical area (MSAs) |
| | Density | Urban; suburban; small town; rural |
| Demographic | Gender | Male; female |
| | Age | Under 6 yrs; 6–11 yrs; 12–17 yrs; 18–24 yrs; 25–34 yrs; 35–44 yrs; 45–54 yrs; 55–64 yrs; 65–74 yrs; 75 yrs plus |
| | Race | African-American; Asian; Hispanic; White/Caucasian; etc. |
| | Life stage | Infant; preschool; child; youth; collegiate; adult; senior |
| | Birth era | Baby boomer (1946–1964); generation X (1965–1976); baby boomlet/generation Y (1977–present) |
| | Household size | 1; 2; 3–4; 5 or more |
| | Residence tenure | Own home; rent home |
| | Marital status | Never married; married; separated; divorced; widowed |
| Socioeconomic | Income | <$15,000; $15,000–$24,999; $25,000–$34,999; $35,000–$49,999; $50,000–$74,999; $75,000–$99,999; $100,000+ |
| | Education | Some high school or less; high school graduate (or GED); etc. |
| | Occupation | Managerial and professional specialty; technical, sales and administrative support; service; farming, forestry, and fishing |
| Psychographic | Personality | -Gregarious; compulsive; introverted; aggressive; ambitious |
| | Values (VALS) | Actualizers; fulfilleds; achievers; experiencers; believers; strivers; makers; strugglers |
| | Lifestyle (Claritas) | Settled in; white picket fence; and 46 other household segments |
| *Buying Situations* | | |
| Outlet type | In-store | Department; specialty; outlet; convenience; supermarket; superstore/mass merchandiser; catalog |
| | Direct | Mail order/catalog; door-to-door; direct response; Internet |
| Benefits sought | Product features | Situation specific; general |
| | Needs | Quality; service; price/value; financing; warranty; etc. |
| Usage | Usage rate | Light user; medium user; heavy user |
| | User status | Nonuser; ex-user; prospect; first-time user; regular user |
| Awareness and intentions | Product knowledge | Unaware; aware; informed; interested; intending to buy; purchaser; rejection |
| Behavior | Involvement | Minimum effort; comparison; special effort |

**EXHIBIT 2–8**
iVillage's website is targeted at women

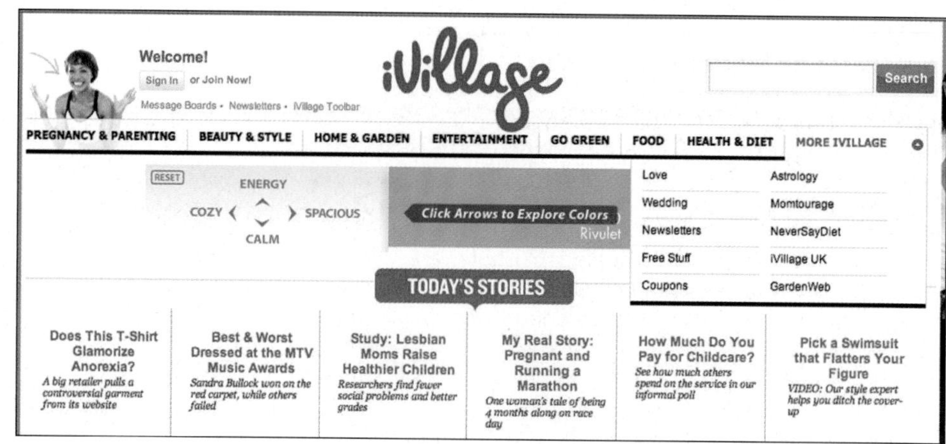


brand based on a specific section of New York City, differentiating it from bigger brands by promoting the product's "Brooklyn Attitude."

**Demographic Segmentation** Dividing the market on the basis of demographic variables such as age, sex, family size, education, income, and social class is called **demographic segmentation**. Secret deodorant and the Lady Schick shaver are products that have met with a great deal of success by using the demographic variable of sex as a basis for segmentation. iVillage, a website targeting women, may be one of the most successful websites on the Internet (Exhibit 2–8). It is interesting to note that the top 10 websites for women are further segmented by age, lifestyles, and so forth.

Although market segmentation on the basis of demographics may seem obvious, companies discover that they need to focus more attention on a specific demographic group. For example, Ikea—noting that more than 70 percent of its shoppers are women—has enhanced its store environment to be more "women friendly," as has Home Depot and Walmart. As IMC Perspective 2–1 shows, it may not be as easy as it seems. A number of companies have begun to focus more attention on the baby boomer market—those 76 million Americans born between 1946 and 1964. Given their huge spending power, this age segment has become more attractive to a number of companies including travel agencies and pharmaceutical companies among others. Recognizing their need for retirement planning, Wachovia has increased their marketing efforts to this segment.[5] *AARP,* the magazine, is targeted to the 35 percent of the population who are 50+. *Segunda Juventud* targets 50+ Hispanics (Exhibit 2–9) and has over 400,000 readers per issue.[6] This number is expected to constitute 45 percent of the U.S. population by 2015.[7]

**EXHIBIT 2–9**
*Segunda Juventud* targets the 50+ Hispanic segment

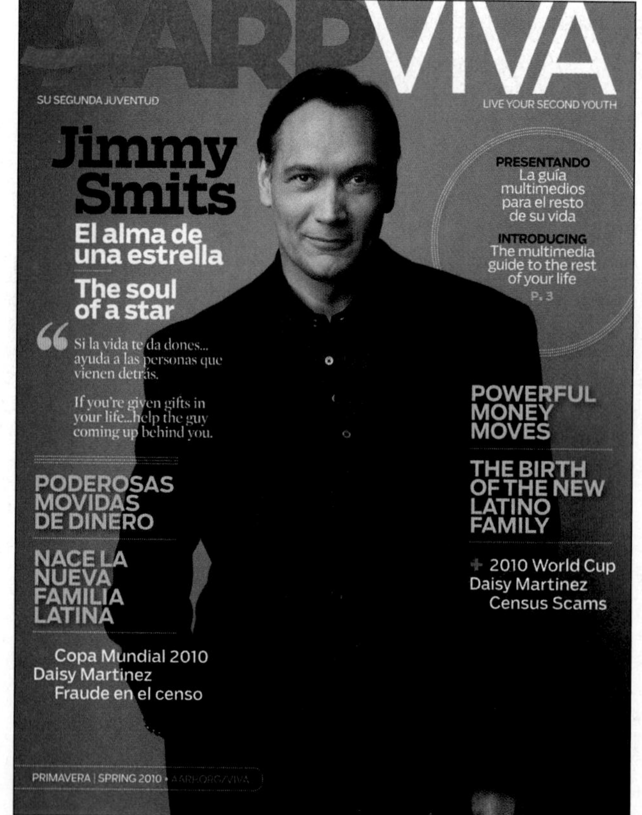


Other products that have successfully employed demographic segmentation include Dove (sex), Doan's Pills (age), Coca-Cola (race), Mercedes-Benz, Lexus, and BMW cars (income), and Banquet prepackaged dinners (family size).

While demographics may still be the most common method of segmenting markets, it is important to recognize that other factors may be the underlying basis for homogeneity and/or consumer behavior. The astute marketer will identify additional bases for segmenting and will recognize the limitations of demographics.

**Psychographic Segmentation** Dividing the market on the basis of personality and/or lifestyles is referred to as **psychographic segmentation.** While there is

# IMC Perspective 2–1 > > >

## Reaching Women Not as Easy as it Seems

While marketers have known for a long time that the women's market is a lucrative one and have targeted their marketing efforts to this segment, it's getting harder and harder to compete for the over $5 trillion in spending power (in U.S) they control. The days of reaching women through soap operas are gone forever, as the economic empowerment of women is now seen as one of the most remarkable revolutions of the past 50 years. Women now account for an estimated $55 billion in expenditures in technology products, $90 billion in consumer electronics, and control over 85 percent of household spending. The attractiveness of this segment has marketers scrambling to get their share—and sometimes they are just not very good at it.

A big part of the reason women are so hard to target is the fact that they have changed so much. In 1966, 40 percent of women who received a bachelors degree in the United States specialized in education, and 2 percent in business. In 2009 these numbers were 12 percent and 50 percent respectively. Women now earn 60 percent of college degrees in the United States and Europe, and constitute the majority of professional workers in many countries. To be successful, companies must understand the impact of these changes, and integrate them into their marketing strategies.

Consider these recent attempts:

- Procter & Gamble has recently launched a quarterly print and online *Custom Beauty* magazine in the United States and Canada, provided free to an estimated audience of 12 million women. Aided by the mommy blogger community, the magazine will be loaded with coupons and information designed to establish a long term relationship with "beauty-involved" consumers. Social media strategies will be an integral part of the marketing effort, as will a newly designed website.
- Dell Computers launched a microsite named *Della* to promote their notebooks, positioning the products as "suitably targeted to women's needs." The site provided a number of what *Advertising Age* referred to as non-technical "tech tips" including how computers can help women count calories. The homepage included three women with clothing that matched their laptops. (Both were later changed.) As noted by Teressa Iezzi, the site was yet another example of "the more that marketers do seem to be attempting to appeal directly to women, the execrable results speak to a culture that's still mired in biased, old-timey thinking."
- After extensive research conducted with women, Verizon introduced the "home phone reinvented" Hub phone in early 2009. Users could make unlimited phone calls, locate family members using GPS, text, e-mail, purchase products and services, and more. A TV commercial was developed showing a young girl sending home a picture of a dress that she liked to her mother, who then looks up the location of a dress shop on her Hub and directs her daughter there. The focus was to "connect families" as the research indicated that "women are receptive to technology, but aren't interested in how technology works."

As of the time of this writing, only one of these products is no longer on the market. Can you guess which one? If you said the Hub, you are right.

Sources: "Female Power", www.economist.com, December 30, 2009, 1–6; Jack Neff, "P&G to Launch Custom Beauty Magazine Rouge in U.S. www.Adage.com, October 7, 2009, 1–4. ; Teressa Iezzi, "Dell's Della Debacle an Example of Wrong Way to Target Women," *Advertising Age*, May 25, 2009, 2–5; Marissa Miley, "Verizon Targets Women with Hub Phone," *Advertising Age*, March 9–16, 2009, p. 18.

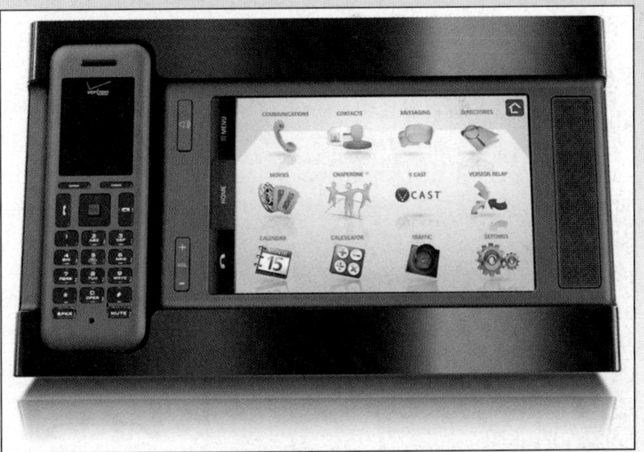

some disagreement as to whether personality is a useful basis for segmentation, lifestyle factors have been used effectively. Many consider lifestyle the most effective criterion for segmentation.

The determination of lifestyles is usually based on an analysis of the activities, interests, and opinions (AIOs) of consumers. These lifestyles are then correlated with the consumers' product, brand, and/or media usage. For many products and/or services, lifestyles may be the best discriminator between use and nonuse, accounting for differences in food, clothing, and car selections, among numerous other consumer behaviors.[8]

Psychographic segmentation has been increasingly more popular with the advent of the values and lifestyles (VALS) program. Although marketers employed lifestyle segmentation long before VALS and although a number of alternatives—for example, PRIZM—are available, VALS remains one of the more popular options. VALS 2 divides Americans into eight lifestyle segments that exhibit distinctive attitudes, behaviors, and decision-making patterns. VALS is also available for the Japan and U.K. markets (both have six lifestyle segments).[9] The VALS 2 system is an excellent predictor of consumer behaviors and a number of companies now employ lifestyle segmentation to position brands, determine value propositions, and in media selection.

**Behavioristic Segmentation** Dividing consumers into groups according to their usage, loyalties, or buying responses to a product is **behavioristic segmentation**. For example, product or brand usage, degree of use (heavy versus light), and/or brand loyalty are combined with demographic and/or psychographic criteria to develop profiles of market segments. In the case of usage, the marketer assumes that nonpurchasers of a brand or product who have the same characteristics as purchasers hold greater potential for adoption than nonusers with different characteristics. As you will see in Chapter 15, many companies target consumers through social media like Facebook based on behavioristic segmentation.

Degree of use relates to the fact that a few consumers may buy a disproportionate amount of many products or brands. Industrial marketers refer to the **80–20 rule**, meaning 20 percent of their buyers account for 80 percent of their sales volume. Again, when the characteristics of these users are identified, targeting them allows for a much greater concentration of efforts and less wasted time and money. The same heavy-half strategy is possible in the consumer market as well. The majority of purchases of many products (e.g., soaps and detergents, shampoos, cake mixes, beer, dog food, colas, bourbon, and toilet tissue—yes, toilet tissue!) are accounted for by a small proportion of the population. Perhaps you can think of some additional examples.

**Benefit Segmentation** In purchasing products, consumers are generally trying to satisfy specific needs and/or wants. They are looking for products that provide specific benefits to satisfy these needs. The grouping of consumers on the basis of attributes sought in a product is known as **benefit segmentation** and is widely used (Exhibit 2–10).

**EXHIBIT 2–10**

AT&T offers a benefit to those who wish to have worldwide coverage on their cell phones

Consider the purchase of a wristwatch. While you might buy a watch for particular benefits such as accuracy, water resistance, or stylishness, others may seek a different set of benefits. Watches are commonly given as gifts for birthdays, Christmas, and graduation. Certainly some of the same benefits are considered in the purchase of a gift, but the benefits the purchaser derives are different from those the user will obtain. Ads that portray watches as good gifts stress different criteria to consider in the purchase decision. The next time you see an ad or commercial for a watch, think about the basic appeal and the benefits it offers.

## The Process of Segmenting a Market

The segmentation process develops over time and is an integral part of the situation analysis. It is in this stage that marketers attempt to determine as much as they can about the market: What needs are not being fulfilled? What benefits are being sought? What characteristics distinguish among the various groups seeking these products and services? A number of alternative segmentation strategies may be used. Each time a specific segment is identified, additional information is gathered to help the marketer understand this group.

For example, once a specific segment is identified on the basis of benefits sought, the marketer will examine lifestyle characteristics and demographics to help characterize this group and to further its understanding of this market. Behavioristic segmentation criteria will also be examined. In

**PRIZM Social Groups**

HIGH ↑ $ ↓ LOW

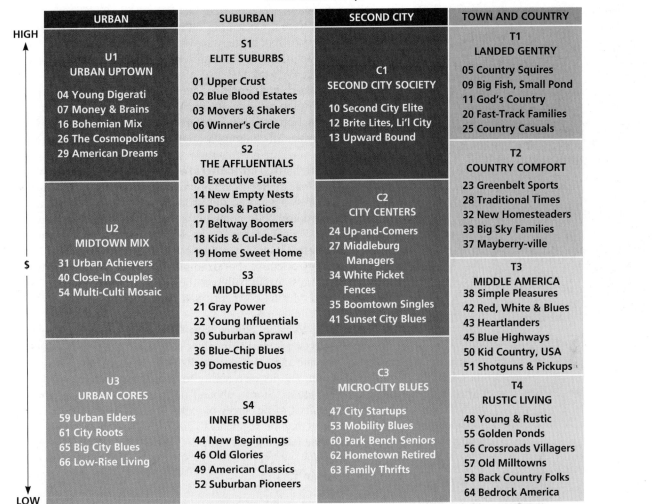

| URBAN | SUBURBAN | SECOND CITY | TOWN AND COUNTRY |
|---|---|---|---|
| U1<br>URBAN UPTOWN<br>04 Young Digerati<br>07 Money & Brains<br>16 Bohemian Mix<br>26 The Cosmopolitans<br>29 American Dreams | S1<br>ELITE SUBURBS<br>01 Upper Crust<br>02 Blue Blood Estates<br>03 Movers & Shakers<br>06 Winner's Circle | C1<br>SECOND CITY SOCIETY<br>10 Second City Elite<br>12 Brite Lites, Li'l City<br>13 Upward Bound | T1<br>LANDED GENTRY<br>05 Country Squires<br>09 Big Fish, Small Pond<br>11 God's Country<br>20 Fast-Track Families<br>25 Country Casuals |
| U2<br>MIDTOWN MIX<br>31 Urban Achievers<br>40 Close-In Couples<br>54 Multi-Culti Mosaic | S2<br>THE AFFLUENTIALS<br>08 Executive Suites<br>14 New Empty Nests<br>15 Pools & Patios<br>17 Beltway Boomers<br>18 Kids & Cul-de-Sacs<br>19 Home Sweet Home | C2<br>CITY CENTERS<br>24 Up-and-Comers<br>27 Middleburg Managers<br>34 White Picket Fences<br>35 Boomtown Singles<br>41 Sunset City Blues | T2<br>COUNTRY COMFORT<br>23 Greenbelt Sports<br>28 Traditional Times<br>32 New Homesteaders<br>33 Big Sky Families<br>37 Mayberry-ville |
| U3<br>URBAN CORES<br>59 Urban Elders<br>61 City Roots<br>65 Big City Blues<br>66 Low-Rise Living | S3<br>MIDDLEBURBS<br>21 Gray Power<br>22 Young Influentials<br>30 Suburban Sprawl<br>36 Blue-Chip Blues<br>39 Domestic Duos | C3<br>MICRO-CITY BLUES<br>47 City Startups<br>53 Mobility Blues<br>60 Park Bench Seniors<br>62 Hometown Retired<br>63 Family Thrifts | T3<br>MIDDLE AMERICA<br>38 Simple Pleasures<br>42 Red, White & Blues<br>43 Heartlanders<br>45 Blue Highways<br>50 Kid Country, USA<br>51 Shotguns & Pickups |
| | S4<br>INNER SUBURBS<br>44 New Beginnings<br>46 Old Glories<br>49 American Classics<br>52 Suburban Pioneers | | T4<br>RUSTIC LIVING<br>48 Young & Rustic<br>55 Golden Ponds<br>56 Crossroads Villagers<br>57 Old Milltowns<br>58 Back Country Folks<br>64 Bedrock America |

**EXHIBIT 2–11**
Nielsen Claritas provides cluster profiles for marketers

the purchase of ski boots, for example, specific benefits may be sought—flexibility or stiffness—depending on the type of skiing the buyer does. All this information will be combined to provide a complete profile of the skier.

A number of companies now offer research services to help marketing managers define their markets and develop strategies targeting them. The VALS and PRIZM systems discussed earlier are just a few of the services offered; others use demographic, socioeconomic, and geographic data to cluster consumer households into distinct "microgeographic" segments. One of these companies, Nielsen Claritas, provides demographic and psychographic profiles of geographic areas as small as census track, block group, or zip code +4. Users of the system include Ace Hardware, Walmart, and AOL, among others. (See Exhibit 2–11.)

## Selecting a Target Market

The outcome of the segmentation analysis will reveal the market opportunities available. The next phase in the target marketing process involves two steps: (1) determining how many segments to enter and (2) determining which segments offer the most potential.

**Determining How Many Segments to Enter** Three market coverage alternatives are available. **Undifferentiated marketing** involves ignoring segment differences and offering just one product or service to the entire market. For example,

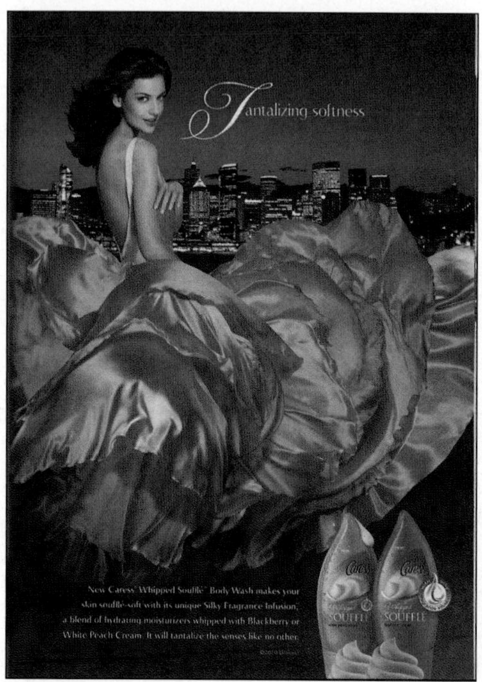


**EXHIBIT 2–12**
Positioning that focuses on the consumer

when Henry Ford brought out the first assembly-line automobile, all potential consumers were offered the same basic product: a black Ford. For many years, Coca-Cola offered only one product version. While this standardized strategy saves the company money, it does not allow the opportunity to offer different versions of the product to different markets.

**Differentiated marketing** involves marketing in a number of segments, developing separate marketing strategies for each. For example, the Marriott hotel chain offers a variety of customer services for different travelers including vacation, business, long or short stay, and so forth.

The third alternative, **concentrated marketing**, is used when the firm selects one segment and attempts to capture a large share of this market. Volkswagen used this strategy in the 1950s when it was the only major automobile company competing in the economy-car segment in the United States. While Volkswagen has now assumed a more differentiated strategy, other companies have found the concentrated strategy effective. For example, Rolls Royce has focused its automobile business exclusively on the high-income segment, while L'Oreal competes in the cosmetics and beauty segment.

**Determining Which Segments Offer Potential** The second step in selecting a market involves determining the most attractive segment. The firm must examine the sales potential of the segment, the opportunities for growth, the competition, and its own ability to compete. Then it must decide whether it can market to this group. Stories abound of companies that have entered new markets only to find their lack of resources or expertise would not allow them to compete successfully. After selecting the segments to target and determining that it can compete, the firm proceeds to the final step in Figure 2–2: the market positioning phase.

## Market Positioning

**Positioning** has been defined as "the art and science of fitting the product or service to one or more segments of the broad market in such a way as to set it meaningfully apart from competition."[10] As you can see, the position of the product, service, or even store is the image that comes to mind and the attributes consumers perceive as related to it. This communication occurs through the message itself, which explains the benefits, as well as the media strategy employed to reach the target group. Take a few moments to think about how some products are positioned and how their positions are conveyed to you. For example, what comes to mind when you hear the name Mercedes, Dr Pepper, or Apple? What about department stores such as Neiman Marcus, Sears, and JCPenney? Now think of the ads for each of these products and companies. Are their approaches different from their competitors'? When and where are these ads shown?

**EXHIBIT 2–13**
Positioning that focuses on the competition

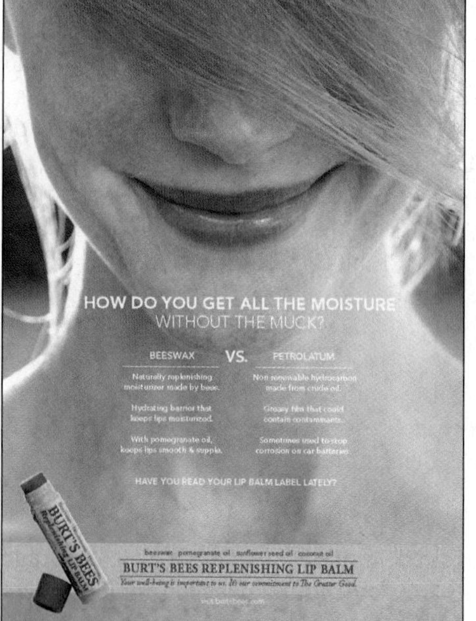


**Approaches to Positioning** Positioning strategies generally focus on either the consumer or the competition. While both approaches involve the association of product benefits with consumer needs, the former does so by linking the product with the benefits the consumer will derive or creating a favorable brand image, as shown in Exhibit 2–12. The latter approach positions the product by comparing it and the benefit it offers versus the competition. Products like Scope mouthwash (positioning itself as better tasting than Listerine) and Burt's Bees (positioned as a better value than its competitors) have employed this strategy successfully (Exhibit 2–13).

**EXHIBIT 2–14**
Lifewater positions itself as a vitamin rich water

Many advertising practitioners consider market positioning the most important factor in establishing a brand in the marketplace. David Aaker and John Myers note that the term *position* has been used to indicate the brand's or product's image in the marketplace.[11] Jack Trout and Al Ries suggest that this brand image must contrast with those of competitors. They say, "In today's marketplace, the competitors' image is just as important as your own. Sometimes more important."[12] Jack Trout notes that a good branding strategy cannot exist without positioning. Trout further states that branding is about the process of building a brand, while positioning is about putting that brand in the mind of the consumer.[13] Thus, *positioning,* as used in this text, relates to the image of the product and or brand relative to competing products or brands. The position of the product or brand is the key factor in communicating the benefits it offers and differentiating it from the competition. Let us now turn to strategies marketers use to position a product.

## DEVELOPING A POSITIONING STRATEGY

A number of positioning strategies might be employed in developing a promotional program. David Aaker and J. Gary Shansby discuss six such strategies: positioning by product attributes, price/quality, use, product class, users, and competitor.[14] Aaker and Myers add one more approach, positioning by cultural symbols.[15]

**EXHIBIT 2–15**
Kohl's positions its brand as having good value for the right price

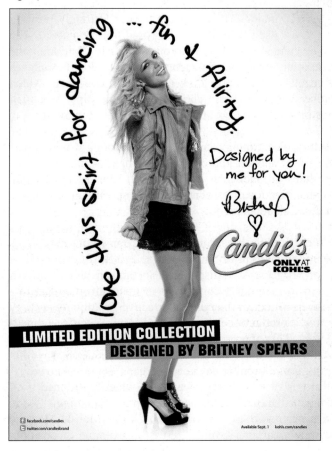

**Positioning by Product Attributes and Benefits** A common approach to positioning is setting the brand apart from competitors on the basis of the specific characteristics or benefits offered. Sometimes a product may be positioned on more than one product benefit. Marketers attempt to identify **salient attributes** (those that are important to consumers and are the basis for making a purchase decision). For example, when Apple first introduced its computers, the key benefit stressed was ease of use—an effective strategy, given the complexity of computers in the market at that time. More recently, there have been a number of new water products that enhance hydration, help the body to exert physical power, increase immunities, and so on. Sobe Lifewater also offers vitamin enhanced water (Exhibit 2–14).

**Positioning by Price/Quality** Marketers often use price/quality characteristics to position their brands. One way they do this is with ads that reflect the image of a high-quality brand where cost, while not irrelevant, is considered secondary to the quality benefits derived from using the brand. Premium brands positioned at the high end of the market use this approach to positioning.

Another way to use price/quality characteristics for positioning is to focus on the quality or value offered by the brand at a very competitive price. For example, Kohl's takes the position of a family oriented speciality store offering good value (Exhibit 2–15). Remember that although price is an important consideration, the product quality must be comparable to, or even better than, competing brands for the positioning strategy to be effective.

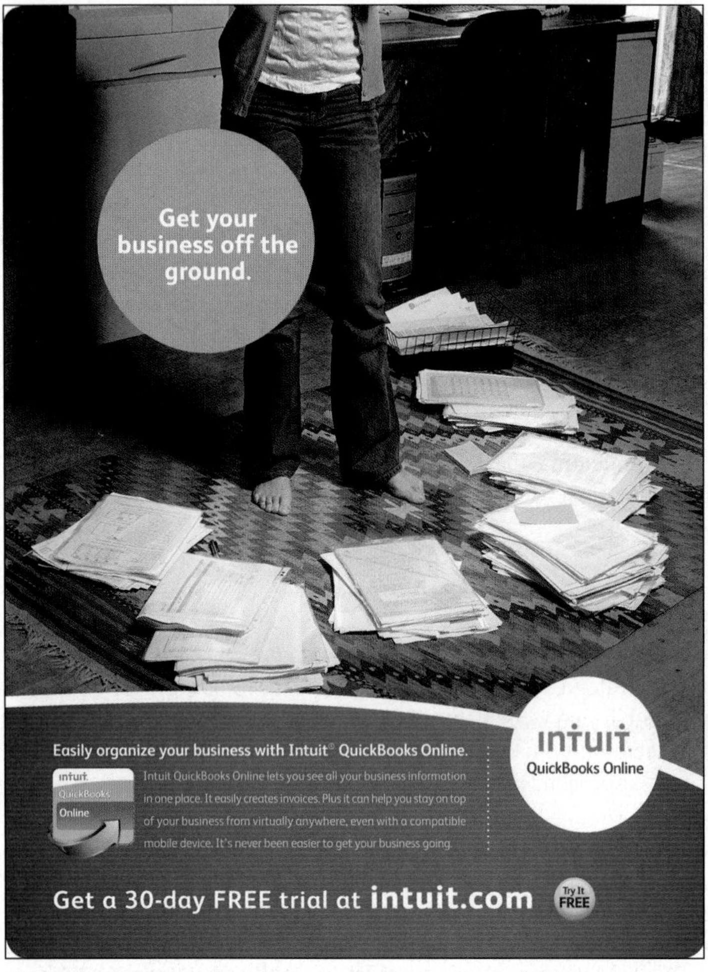


**EXHIBIT 2–16**
Intuit offers products specifically useful to small business owners

**Positioning by Use or Application** Another way to communicate a specific image or position for a brand is to associate it with a specific use or application. The Intuit ad shown in Exhibit 2–16 is specifically targeted to small business owners and/or entrepreneurs.

While this strategy is often used to enter a market on the basis of a particular use or application, it is also an effective way to expand the usage of a product. For example, Arm & Hammer baking soda has been promoted for everything from baking to relieving heartburn to eliminating odors in carpets and refrigerators (Exhibit 2–17).

**Positioning by Product Class** Often the competition for a product comes from outside the product class. For example, airlines know that while they compete with other airlines, trains and buses are also viable alternatives. Amtrak has positioned itself as an alternative to airplanes, citing cost savings, enjoyment, and other advantages. Dole fruit juices encourage consumers to "drink their fruits," claiming that 8 oz. of juice is the equivalent of two fruits. V8 promotes drinking one's vegetables. (Exhibit 2–18). Rather than positioning against another brand, an alternative strategy is to position oneself against another product category. The California Avocado Information Bureau launched a major IMC campaign to more strongly position itself as a fruit (as opposed to a vegetable). The print, radio, outdoor, and online campaign took a humorous approach, positioning the avocado as a "fun fruit," while at the same time demonstrating the healthy advantages relative to other fruits and vegetables, and providing numerous products for which it might become an alternative including cream cheese, butter, and dips. Mountain High yogurt ad positions the product as a substitute for other baking ingredients.

**EXHIBIT 2–17**
Arm & Hammer baking soda demonstrates numerous product uses

**Positioning by Product User** Positioning a product by associating it with a particular user or group of users is yet another approach. An example would be the DC Shoes ad shown in Exhibit 2–19. This ad emphasizes identification or association with a specific group, in this case, skateboarders.

**Positioning by Competitor** Competitors may be as important to positioning strategy as a firm's own product or services. Advertisers used to think it was a cardinal sin to mention a competitor in their advertising. However, in today's market, an effective positioning strategy for a product or brand may focus on specific competitors. This approach is similar to positioning by product class, although in this case the competition is within the same product category. Perhaps the best-known example of this strategy was Avis, which positioned itself against the car-rental leader, Hertz, by stating, "We're number two, so we try harder." The Malt-O-Meal ad shown earlier (Exhibit 2–5) is an example of positioning a brand against the competition. When positioning

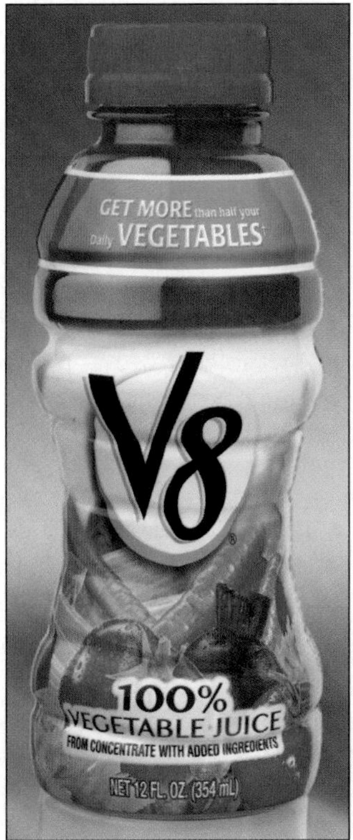


**EXHIBIT 2–18**
V8 positions itself as a drink that substitutes for vegetables

**EXHIBIT 2–19**
DC positions by product user—in this case, skateboarders

by competitor, a marketer must often employ another positioning strategy as well to differentiate the brand.

**Positioning by Cultural Symbols** Aaker and Myers include an additional positioning strategy in which cultural symbols are used to differentiate brands. By associating the brand with a meaningful symbol, the brand is easily identifiable and differentiated from others. Examples are the Jolly Green Giant, the Keebler elves, Speedy Alka-Seltzer, the Pillsbury Doughboy, the Wells Fargo stagecoach, Ronald McDonald, Chiquita Banana, and Mr. Peanut. Tony the Tiger clearly qualifies as a cultural symbol (Exhibit 2–20). Each of these symbols has successfully differentiated the product it represents from competitors'.

**Repositioning** One final positioning strategy involves altering or changing a product's or brand's position. **Repositioning** a product usually occurs because of declining or stagnant sales or because of anticipated opportunities in other market positions. Repositioning is often difficult to accomplish because of entrenched perceptions about and attitudes toward the product or brand. IMC Perspective 2–2 discusses an interesting example of a long established brand taking a new direction.

After a sales slump that began in 2008, Gatorade—once the world's most popular sports drink—changed its name to "G2," reduced the size of its lightning bolt trademark, and began to broaden its appeal to other markets (Exhibit 2–21). As noted by David Burwick, CEO of PepsiCo North America, "The functional difference is that we're going from a brand that speaks to really elite athletes to a brand that speaks for the athlete in everyone." So far, the effort has had disappointing results.[16]

**EXHIBIT 2–20**
Tony the Tiger has become a cultural symbol

**EXHIBIT 2–21**
Gatorade has made changes to appeal to a broader market

# IMC Perspective 2–2 > > >

## Repositioning MTV—The End of an Era

At the time there was nothing like it, and perhaps there never will be again. To some it is a shame that it's gone, to others it's a relief. Nevertheless, love it or hate it, one of the most powerful networks to ever hit cable television is now pretty much gone—in name certainly, and in content as well. In the first week of February 2010, MTV formally changed its logo, dropping the part that said Music Television. In fact, the MTV of today is a reality TV channel, only occasionally airing something that has to do with music.

When MTV debuted in 1981, "the channel confirmed the concept of cable niche programming, reshaped music marketing and became a symbol of youth culture" notes Bryan Reesman of *Billboard* magazine. Showing little more than music videos and DJs, music lovers tuned in in droves. By the end of its first year, MTV had over 2.1 million subscribing households. By its second year, the "I Want My MTV" ad campaign was in full force, featuring a number of rock stars including Pete Townshend, Stevie Nicks, Mick Jagger, and David Bowie, among others. Michael Jackson premiered both "Beat It" and "Thriller" on MTV in 1983. MTV had taken off, and parents everywhere were becoming concerned with their children's "addiction" to music videos.

By the mid 80s things started to change. A British sitcom was added to the programming, as was support for young comedians such as Chris Rock, Ben Stiller, and Jon Stewart. The network also started to engage in philanthropic events by airing 17 hours of the Live Aid concert, running safe sex commercials, and "Just Say No" antidrug spots. Eventually, MTV started running its own "Rock Against Drugs"—the first of many attempts to engage viewers with social programming. One of MTV's most popular shows featuring new artists, *Unplugged,* debuted in the early 1990s. By the late 1990s numerous programs were added, with less time for rock videos. The number of anti-drug and other social marketing programs also increased.

Throughout the early years of the 21st century, MTV continued to broaden both its programming and social involvement, launched new channels, and expanded internationally. The network had clearly begun to reposition itself as something other than just a music channel. Music stars like Madonna, Michael Jackson, and Britney Spears have been replaced by "Snooki" Polizzi from the reality show *Jersey Shore* and Heidi Montag from *The Hills.* As noted by Scott Collins, "MTV has evolved into a reality channel that occasionally runs programs that have to do with music." But why?

David Howe, president of SyFy (which itself used to be the Sci-Fi Channel) says that MTV—like Sci-Fi—realized that being just music television was too limiting, and current viewers don't relate to it as a music channel anymore. Instead, the programming has changed MTV, as it no longer competes with VH1 and Fuse but competes with other reality programs more, and the logo is important in communicating that fact. The fact is that MTV is no longer as central to people's lives as it was two decades ago. This may or may not be a good thing.

For the old MTV music lovers the music programming is not dead yet. In March 2010 MTV announced that as a result of a sponsorship by Starburst candies, it was bringing back (a repositioned) *Unplugged*—one of the hit musical programs of the 1990s. While eight shows will appear on cable, this time the focus will be on the Internet.

Sources: Andrew Hampp, "Unplugged to Return to MTV, Courtesy Starburst," *Advertising Age,* March 4, 2010; Scott Collins, "The Network Name Game," *Los Angeles Times,* February 13, 2010, pp. D1,12; Bryan Reesman, "Timeline: Rewinding 25 Years of MTV History," *Billboard,* September 2, 2008, pp. 36–45.

Before leaving this section, you might stop to think for a moment about the positioning (and repositioning) strategies pursued by different companies. Any successful product that comes to mind probably occupies a distinct market position.

# DEVELOPING THE MARKETING PLANNING PROGRAM

LO 02-5

The development of the marketing strategy and selection of a target market(s) tell the marketing department which customers to focus on and what needs to attempt to satisfy. The next stage of the marketing process involves combining the various elements of the marketing mix into a cohesive, effective marketing program. Each marketing-mix element is multidimensional and includes a number of decision areas.

Likewise, each must consider and contribute to the overall IMC program. We now examine product, price, and distribution channels and how each influences and interacts with the promotional program.

## Product Decisions

An organization exists because it has some product, service, or idea to offer consumers, generally in exchange for money. This offering may come in the form of a physical product (such as a soft drink, pair of jeans, or car), a service (banking, airlines, or legal assistance), a cause (Special Olympics, American Cancer Society), or even a person (a political candidate). The product is anything that can be marketed and that, when used or supported, gives satisfaction to the individual.

A *product* is not just a physical object; it is a bundle of benefits or values that satisfies the needs of consumers. The needs may be purely functional, or they may include social and psychological benefits. For example, the campaign for Michelin tires discussed earlier stresses the quality built into Michelin tires (value) as well as their performance and durability (function). The term **product symbolism** refers to what a product or brand means to consumers and what they experience in purchasing and using it.[17] For many products, strong symbolic features and social and psychological meaning may be more important than functional utility.[18] For example, designer clothing such as Versace, Gucci, and Prada is often purchased on the basis of its symbolic meaning and image, particularly by teenagers and young adults. Advertising plays an important role in developing and maintaining the image of these brands.

Product planning involves decisions not only about the item itself, such as design and quality, but also about aspects such as service and warranties as well as brand name and package design. Consumers look beyond the reality of the product and its ingredients. The product's quality, branding, packaging, and even the company standing behind it all contribute to consumers' perceptions.[19] In an effective IMC program, advertising, branding, and packaging are all designed to portray the product as more than just a bundle of attributes. All are coordinated to present an image or positioning of the product that extends well beyond its physical attributes.

### Branding

Branding is about building and maintaining a favorable identity and image of the company and/or its products or services in the mind of the consumer. The goal of branding is to (1) build and maintain brand awareness and interest, (2) develop and enhance attitudes toward the company, product, or service and (3) build and foster relationships between the consumer and the brand. The **brand identity** consists of the combination of the name, logo, symbols, design, packaging, and image of associations held by consumers. Think for a minute about the ads for Nike; the product benefits and attributes are usually not even mentioned—yet information about the brand is communicated effectively.

One important role of advertising in respect to branding strategies is creating and maintaining **brand equity**, which can be thought of as an intangible asset of added value or goodwill that results from the favorable image, impressions of differentiation, and/or the strength of consumer attachment to a company name, brand name, or trademark. Brand equity allows a brand to earn greater sales volume and/or higher margins than it could without the name, providing the company with a competitive advantage. The strong equity position a company and/or its brand enjoys is often reinforced through advertising. For example, Rolex watches command a premium price because of their high quality as well as the strong brand equity they have developed through advertising (Exhibit 2–22).

**EXHIBIT 2–22**
Rolex creates strong brand equity through advertising

### Packaging

Packaging is another aspect of product strategy that has become increasingly important. Traditionally, the package provided functional benefits such as economy, protection, and storage. However, the role and function of the package have changed because of the self-service

**EXHIBIT 2–23**
This ad for WD-40 shows just a few of the many uses for the product

emphasis of many stores and the fact that more and more buying decisions are made at the point of purchase. One study estimated that as many as two-thirds of all purchases made in the supermarket are unplanned. The package is often the consumer's first exposure to the product, so it must make a favorable first impression. A typical supermarket has more than 30,000 items competing for attention. Not only must a package attract and hold the consumer's attention, but it must also communicate information on how to use the product, divulge its composition and content, and satisfy any legal requirements regarding disclosure. Moreover, many firms design the package to carry a sales promotion message such as a contest, sweepstakes, or premium offer.

Many companies view the package as an important way to communicate with consumers and create an impression of the brand in their minds. In other instances packages can extend the brand by offering new uses (Exhibit 2–23). Design factors such as size, shape, color, and lettering all contribute to the appeal of a package and can be as important as a commercial in determining what goes from the store shelf to the consumer's shopping cart. Many companies use packaging to create a distinctive brand image and identity. The next time you walk by a perfume counter, stop to look at the many unique package designs (see Exhibit 2–24).

## Price Decisions

The *price variable* refers to what the consumer must give up to purchase a product or service. While price is discussed in terms of the dollar amount exchanged for an item, the cost of a product to the consumer includes time, mental activity, and behavioral effort.[20] The marketing manager is usually concerned with establishing a price level, developing pricing policies, and monitoring competitors' and consumers' reactions to prices in the marketplace. A firm must consider a number of factors in determining the price it charges for its product or service, including costs, demand factors, competition, and perceived value. From an IMC perspective, the price must be consistent with the perceptions of the product, as well as the communications strategy. Higher prices, of course, will communicate a higher product quality, while lower prices reflect bargain or "value" perceptions. A product positioned as highest quality but carrying a lower price than competitors would only confuse consumers. In other words, the price, the advertising, and the distribution channels must present one unified voice speaking to the product's positioning.

**EXHIBIT 2–24**
The packaging creates product image

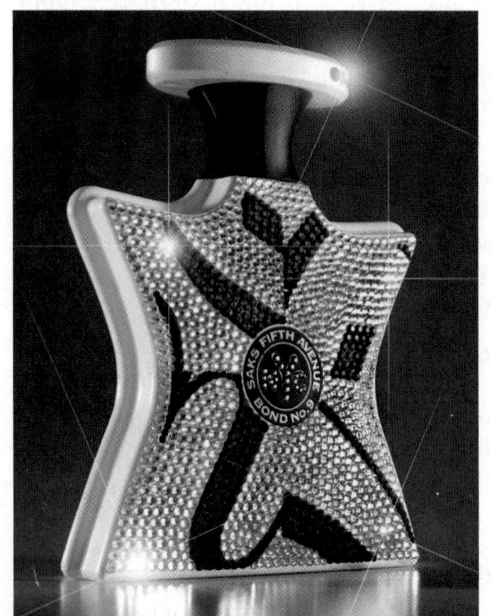


### Relating Price to Advertising and Promotion

Factors such as product quality, competition, and advertising all interact in determining what price a firm can and should charge. Studies have shown that pricing and advertising strategies go together. High relative ad expenditures should accompany premium prices, and low relative ad expenditures should be tailored to low prices. These results obviously support the IMC perspective that one voice must be conveyed. In a recent and comprehensive study, it was shown that exposure to television ads reduces consumers' tendencies to react to price changes. The study further showed that heavy users of the product category were most likely to have their sensitivities reduced.[21]

## Distribution Channel Decisions

As consumers, we generally take for granted the role of marketing intermediaries or channel members. If we want a six-pack of soda or a box of detergent, we can buy it at a supermarket, a convenience store, or even a drugstore. Manufacturers understand the value and importance of these intermediaries.



One of a marketer's most important marketing decisions involves the way it makes its products and services available for purchase. A firm can have an excellent product at a great price, but it will be of little value unless it is available where the customer wants it, when the customer wants it, and with the proper support and service. **Marketing channels**, the place element of the marketing mix, are "sets of interdependent organizations involved in the process of making a product or service available for use or consumption."[22]

The distribution strategy should take into consideration the communication objectives and the impact that the channel strategy will have on the IMC program. Stewart and colleagues discuss the need for "integrated channel management," which "reflects the blurring of the boundaries of the communications and distribution functions."[23] Consistent with the product and pricing decisions, where the product is distributed will send a communications message. Does the fact that a product is sold at Neiman Marcus or Saks convey a different message regarding its image than if it were distributed at Kmart or Walmart? If you think about it for a moment, the mere fact that the product is distributed in these channels communicates an image about it in your mind. Stewart gives examples of how channel elements contribute to communication—for example, grocery store displays, point-of-purchase merchandising, and shelf footage. The distribution channel in a well-integrated marketing program serves as a form of reminder advertising. The consumer sees the brand name and recalls the advertising. (Think about the last time you passed a McDonald's. Did it remind you of any of McDonald's ads?)

A company can choose not to use any channel intermediaries but, rather, to sell to its customers through **direct channels**. This type of channel arrangement is sometimes used in the consumer market by firms using direct-selling programs, such as Avon, Tupperware, and Mary Kay, or firms that use direct-response advertising, telemarketing, or the Internet to sell their products. Direct channels are also frequently used by manufacturers of industrial products and services, which are often selling expensive and complex products that require extensive negotiations and sales efforts, as well as service and follow-up calls after the sale.

Chapter 15 provides a discussion of the role of the Internet in an IMC program. As will be seen, the Internet is relied upon by many companies as a direct channel of distribution, since they offer products and services for sale on their websites. Amazon .com and Barnesandnoble.com are just two of the many examples of such efforts.

Most consumer-product companies distribute through **indirect channels**, usually using a network of wholesalers (institutions that sell to other resellers) and/or retailers (which sell primarily to the final consumer).

## Developing Promotional Strategies: Push or Pull?

Most of you are aware of advertising and other forms of promotion directed toward ultimate consumers or business customers. We see these ads in the media and are often part of the target audience for the promotions. In addition to developing a consumer marketing mix, a company must have a program to motivate the channel members. Programs designed to persuade the trade to stock, merchandise, and promote a manufacturer's products are part of a **promotional push strategy**. The goal of this strategy is to push the product through the channels of distribution by aggressively selling and promoting the item to the resellers, or trade.

Promotion to the trade includes all the elements of the promotional mix. Company sales representatives call on resellers to explain the product, discuss the firm's plans for building demand among ultimate consumers, and describe special programs being offered to the trade, such as introductory discounts, promotional allowances, and cooperative ad programs. The company may use **trade advertising** to interest wholesalers and retailers and motivate them to purchase its products for resale to their customers. Trade advertising usually appears in publications that serve the particular industry.

A push strategy tries to convince resellers they can make a profit on a manufacturer's product and to encourage them to order the merchandise and push it through to their customers. An alternative strategy is a **promotional pull strategy**, spending money on advertising and sales promotion efforts directed toward the ultimate consumer. The goal of a pull strategy is to create demand among consumers and encourage them to request the product from the retailer. Seeing the consumer demand, retailers will order the product from wholesalers (if they are used), which in turn will request it from the manufacturer. Thus, stimulating demand at the end-user level pulls the product through the channels of distribution.

Whether to emphasize a push or a pull strategy depends on a number of factors, including the company's relations with the trade, its promotional budget, and demand for the firm's products. Companies that have favorable channel relationships may prefer to use a push strategy and work closely with channel members to encourage them to stock and promote their products. A firm with a limited promotional budget may not have the funds for advertising and sales promotion that a pull strategy requires and may find it more cost-effective to build distribution and demand by working closely with resellers. When the demand outlook for a product is favorable because it has unique benefits, is superior to competing brands, or is very popular among consumers, a pull strategy may be appropriate. Companies often use a combination of push and pull strategies, with the emphasis changing as the product moves through its life cycle.

## THE ROLE OF ADVERTISING AND PROMOTION

As shown in the marketing model in Figure 2–1, the marketing program includes promotion both to the trade (channel members) and to the company's ultimate customers. Marketers use the various promotional-mix elements—advertising, sales promotion, direct marketing, publicity/public relations, and personal selling—to inform consumers about their products, their prices, and places where the products are available. Each promotional-mix variable helps marketers achieve their promotional objectives, and all variables must work together to achieve an integrated marketing communications program.

To this point, we have discussed the various elements of the marketing plan that serves as the basis for the IMC program. The development and implementation of an IMC program is based on a strong foundation that includes market analysis, target marketing and positioning, and coordination of the various marketing-mix elements. Throughout the following chapters of this text, we will explore the role of various IMC elements in helping to achieve marketing objectives.

## Summary

Promotion plays an important role in an organization's efforts to market its product, service, or ideas to its customers. Figure 2–1 shows a model for analyzing how promotions fit into a company's marketing program. The model includes a marketing strategy and analysis, target marketing, program development, and the target market. The marketing process begins with a marketing strategy that is based on a detailed situation analysis and guides for target market selection and development of the firm's marketing program.

In the planning process, the situation analysis requires that the marketing strategy be assumed. The promotional program is developed with this strategy as a guide. One of the key decisions to be made pertains to the target marketing process, which includes identifying, segmenting, targeting, and positioning to target markets. There are several bases for segmenting the market and various ways to position a product.

Once the target marketing process has been completed, marketing program decisions regarding product, price, distribution, and promotions must be made. All of these must be coordinated to provide an integrated marketing communications perspective, in which the positioning strategy is supported by one voice. Thus all product strategies, pricing strategies, and distribution choices must be made with the objective of contributing to the overall image of the product or brand. Advertising and promotion decisions, in turn, must be integrated with the other marketing-mix decisions to accomplish this goal.

## Key Terms

**strategic marketing plan** p. 43
**market segments** p. 43
**market opportunities** p. 43
**competitive advantage** p. 44
**target marketing** p. 46
**market segmentation** p. 47
**geographic segmentation** p. 48
**demographic segmentation** p. 50
**psychographic segmentation** p. 50
**behavioristic segmentation** p. 52
**80–20 rule** p. 52
**benefit segmentation** p. 52
**undifferentiated marketing** p. 53
**differentiated marketing** p. 54
**concentrated marketing** p. 54
**positioning** p. 54
**salient attributes** p. 55
**repositioning** p. 57
**product symbolism** p. 59
**brand identity** p. 59
**brand equity** p. 59
**marketing channels** p. 61
**direct channels** p. 61
**indirect channels** p. 61
**promotional push strategy** p. 61
**trade advertising** p. 61
**promotional pull strategy** p. 62

## Discussion Questions

1. Discuss the role that integrated marketing communications plays in creating a brand image. How do media contribute to the development of these images? (LO1)
2. Choose a company and discuss how it communicates with its customers in different market segments. (LO4)
3. Discuss the strategy of market segmentation, and some of the reasons marketers are employing such techniques. Are there any ethical issues involved in this strategy? (LO4)
4. Marketing strategies are placing more and more effort on target marketing. What is target marketing? Give examples of companies currently employing this strategy. (LO3)
5. Discuss the difference between demographic and psychographic segmentation. Give examples of companies employing each. (LO4)
6. The lead-in to this chapter discussed GEICO's successful market strategy. What factors have led to the success of this company? (LO1)
7. Marketers continue to increase their marketing efforts to the Hispanic market, while at the same time, evidence suggests that younger Hispanics are becoming more integrated into the mainstream. What are the implications of these acculturation issues for the future of marketing? (LO3)
8. As noted, packages are now becoming communications tools, serving as advertising vehicles. At the same time, packages are changing the other marketing-mix elements as well. Discuss how packages are being used to impact price and distribution strategies as well as promotional strategies. (LO2)
9. A number of companies were mentioned as having recently undergone repositioning strategies. Cite additional examples of brands that you know have been repositioned in recent years. Discuss the pros and cons of these efforts. (LO5)
10. Many brands have made little or no changes to their packages over the years. Arm & Hammer Baking Soda is one such company. Provide a list of some companies that have held their packaging and brand logos consistent over the years. Discuss some of the pros and cons of this strategy. (LO2)

## AdForum Exercise: "Understanding Market Segmentation, Target Marketing, and Positioning"

(See Advertising and Promotion Playlist, Chapter 2)

This chapter discusses how marketers use market segmentation, target marketing, and positioning to market their products and services. In the playlist are a number of commercials for a variety of food and drink products. Your assignment is to watch each of the commercials and then answer the following questions:

1 What is the primary segmentation strategy being employed by each of the products? What other segmentation strategies also might be being used?

2 Who do you think is the specific target market for each of these products?

3 Which positioning strategy is being employed by each product? Are there any others that might also be being used?

Access to the chapter playlist is available through McGraw-Hill connect™ | MARKETING, www.mcgrawhillconnect.com

## LEARNING OBJECTIVES

- LO1 To understand how companies organize for advertising and other aspects of integrated marketing communications.
- LO2 To evaluate the advantages and disadvantages of the various ways companies organize for advertising and promotion.
- LO3 To understand the role of advertising agencies and the services they perform as well as the various types of agencies and media specialist companies.
- LO4 To examine methods for selecting, compensating, and evaluating advertising agencies.
- LO5 To explain the role and functions of specialized marketing communications organizations.
- LO6 To examine various perspectives on the use of integrated services and responsibilities of advertisers versus agencies.

# 3 Organizing for Advertising and Promotion: The Role of Ad Agencies and Other Marketing Communication Organizations

## UNDER ARMOUR PROTECTS ITS HOUSE BY STAYING IN-HOUSE

Adidas, Puma, and Reebok are well-known brand names in the athletic shoe and apparel business and have one thing in common. They have all been trying to keep pace with Nike, the Beaverton, Oregon, based company which has global sales of nearly $20 billion and whose swoosh has become the most pervasive logo in sports. However, when asked to name the competitor that has the most realistic chance of challenging Nike, many industry analysts do not mention adidas (which now owns Reebok) or Puma, both of which have been competing against Nike for decades. Instead they point to Under Armour, the young Baltimore-based company that many have already nicknamed "the next Nike." Under Armour (UA) was founded in 1996 by Kevin Plank, a former Maryland football player, who began by selling compression clothing that could "wick" sweat away from the body to college sports teams out of the trunk of his car. In 2005 the company went public and its stock nearly doubled the first day it was traded. Under Armour has averaged nearly 60 percent annual growth and had sales of $725 million in 2009.

Under Armour achieved initial success by focusing on niche markets that the big boys overlooked. The initial product—a line of tight-fitting T-shirts made of a synthetic compression fabric—targeted professional athletes and fitness buffs, offering them a way to stay cool and dry during workouts and games. The product line has been expanded to serve a variety of sports and activities markets including running, football, baseball, soccer, lacrosse, hunting, and snow sports. Under Armour became very successful through strong branding and product positioning, quality products, and dynamic advertising. The company developed a unique brand identity through its TV advertising campaign, which began in 2003 and used the theme "Protect This House." The commercials featured a football squad huddled around Eric "Big E" Ogbogu, one of Kevin Plank's former teammates at the University of Maryland, who was playing for the Dallas Cowboys when the commercial was shot. The spots show Ogbogu and a number of other well-conditioned athletes working out while wearing Under Armour and end with him standing in the middle of a huddle of the players and shouting "We must protect this house!" as if his life depended on it. "The goal was to create a spot that would live longer than its 30 seconds on the air," according to Steve Battista, Under Armour's Vice President. This goal was definitely accomplished as the tagline has become a symbol of what Under Armour stands for as a brand and the company continues to use it in much of its advertising.

Building on its strong brand reputation, Under Armour made a strategic decision to expand into the football cleat market in 2006. To launch the new product line in this highly competitive market, the company's in-house agency developed the "Click-Clack campaign which engaged viewers with the sound of football cleats in the tunnel as players head onto the field. While there was no direct mention of Under Armour cleats in the initial spots, the statement "I think they hear us coming," was a message to consumers, as well as the competition, that Under Armour was entering the market.

In 2008 Under Armour moved into another segment of the athletic equipment market by launching a new line of high performance cross training shoes, its first foray into noncleated footwear. To introduce the New Proto line, Under Armour ran a commercial on the 2008 Super Bowl telecast which included nearly two dozen high profile male and female athletes and was done in its typical intense style. The New Proto shoes outperformed Nike's new SPARQ cross trainer line, which was backed by a major ad campaign that included a tagline taking a barb at Under Armour ("My better is better than your better").

Under Armour also has its sights set on running and basketball shoes which are the two largest categories of the athletic footwear market. In 2009 Under Armour launched a new line of running shoes where it competes against Nike and adidas as well as other strong brands such as New Balance, Asics, and Saucony. It is also expected that the company will soon enter the basketball shoe market as it already has Brandon Jennings, one of the up and coming stars in the NBA, wearing Under Armour shoes.

Analysts note that a major reason why Under Armour may be able to challenge Nike is because the two companies have very similar corporate cultures. Both companies are dedicated to serving athletes, have a focus on product innovation, and a strong brand mentality. An analyst at the market research firm SportsOneSource notes that "the real genius of both companies was in creating a strong brand and protecting it." While Nike is still viewed as the strongest athletic brand in the United States, Under Armour is very popular among teens and young adults indicating that the younger generation is adopting Under Armour as its own brand.

One way Under Armour differs from Nike, as well as most of its other competitors, is that rather than using an outside agency to handle its advertising and other type of integrated marketing communications, the company prefers to keep it all in-house. For more than 20 years all of Nike's advertising was handled by Wieden+Kennedy, which began as a small agency in Portland and grew with the success of its largest and best-known client. Nike still uses W+K but has expanded the roster of agencies with which it works as it looks for marketing communication firms with interactive, digital, and community building capabilities that transcend traditional media advertising.

Under Armour has chosen to go a different route as the company has its own brand team that has handled all of its creative work and media buying in-house since the company was founded. The team includes a creative director, advertising director, interactive art director, and a score of talented designers and marketing minds that help plan and create all of Under Armour's marketing communications. The company has outsourced the production work for some of its commercials and also has used the Deutsch agency to handle some of its public relations. Recently Under Amour considered hiring an outside agency to handle some of the IMC efforts for its expanding women's line and went through an agency review process.

Under Armour has definitely made it to the big leagues and now that it is there, the competition will get more intense as they battle Nike, adidas, Reebok and others for market share. However, Under Armour plans to stick to its game plan and continue to deliver its iconic message, "We Must Protect This House!" by staying in-house.

Sources: Jeremy Mullman, "Under Armour Seeks Agency to Work on Growing Women's Line," *Advertising Age,* August 31, 2009; http://adage.com/print?article_id=138703; Sean Gregory, "Under Armour's Big Step," May 26, 2008, p. 44; Terry Lefton, "The Contender, *Sports Business Journal,*" May, 5, 2008, pp. 1,18; Steve Battista, "True Confessions of a Super Bowl Ad Virgin," *Advertising Age,* February 4, 2008, p. 44.

Developing and implementing an integrated marketing communications program is usually a complex and detailed process involving the efforts of many persons. As consumers, we generally give little thought to the individuals or organizations that create the clever advertisements that capture our attention, the websites we visit, or the contests and sweepstakes we hope to win. But for those involved in the marketing process, it is important to understand the nature of the industry and the structure and functions of the organizations involved. As discussed in the first two chapters, the advertising and promotions business is changing as marketers search for better ways to communicate with their customers. These changes are impacting the way marketers organize for marketing communications, as well as their relationships with advertising agencies and other communication specialists.

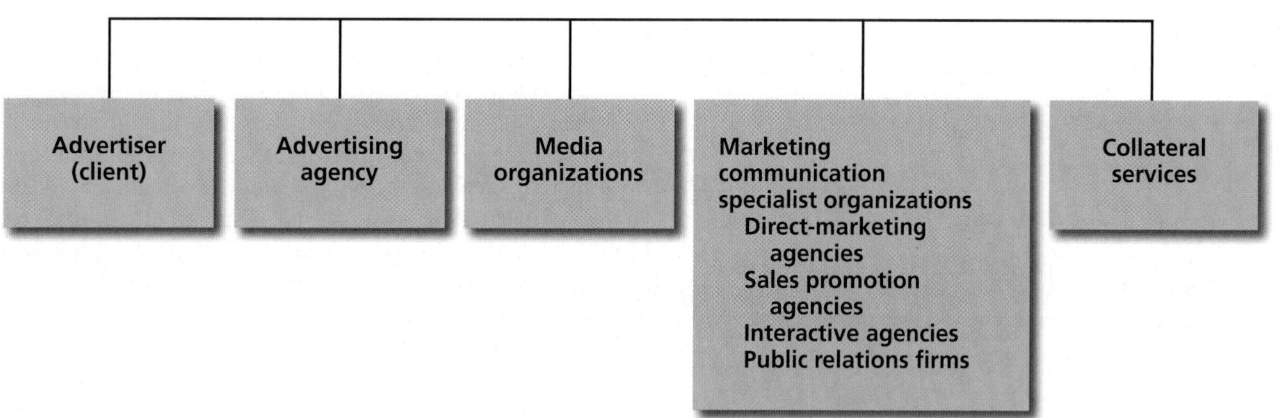


**FIGURE 3–1**
Participants in the Integrated Marketing Communications Process



This chapter examines the various organizations that participate in the IMC process, their roles and responsibilities, and their relationship to one another. We discuss how companies organize internally for advertising and promotion. For most companies, advertising is planned and executed by an outside ad agency. Many large agencies offer a variety of other IMC capabilities, including public relations, Internet/interactive, sales promotion, and direct marketing. Thus, we will devote particular attention to the ad agency's role and the overall relationship between company and agency.

Other participants in the promotional process (such as direct-marketing, sales promotion, and interactive agencies and public relations firms) are becoming increasingly important as more companies take an integrated marketing communications approach to promotion. We examine the role of these specialized marketing communications organizations in the promotional process as well. The chapter concludes with a discussion of whether marketers are best served by using the integrated services of one large agency or the separate services of a variety of communications specialists.

## PARTICIPANTS IN THE INTEGRATED MARKETING COMMUNICATIONS PROCESS: AN OVERVIEW

Before discussing the specifics of the industry, we'll provide an overview of the entire system and identify some of the players. As shown in Figure 3–1, participants in the integrated marketing communications process can be divided into five major groups: the advertiser (or client), advertising agencies, media organizations, specialized communication services, and collateral services. Each group has specific roles in the promotional process.

The advertisers, or **clients**, are the key participants in the process. They have the products, services, or causes to be marketed, and they provide the funds that pay for advertising and promotions. The advertisers also assume major responsibility for developing the marketing program and making the final decisions regarding the advertising and promotional program to be employed. The organization may perform most of these efforts itself, either through its own advertising department or by setting up an in-house agency.

However, many organizations use an **advertising agency**, an outside firm that specializes in the creation, production, and/or placement of the communications message and that may provide other services to facilitate the marketing and promotions process. Many large advertisers retain the services of a number of agencies, particularly when they market a number of products. For example, Kraft Foods uses as many as eight advertising agencies for its various brands, while Procter

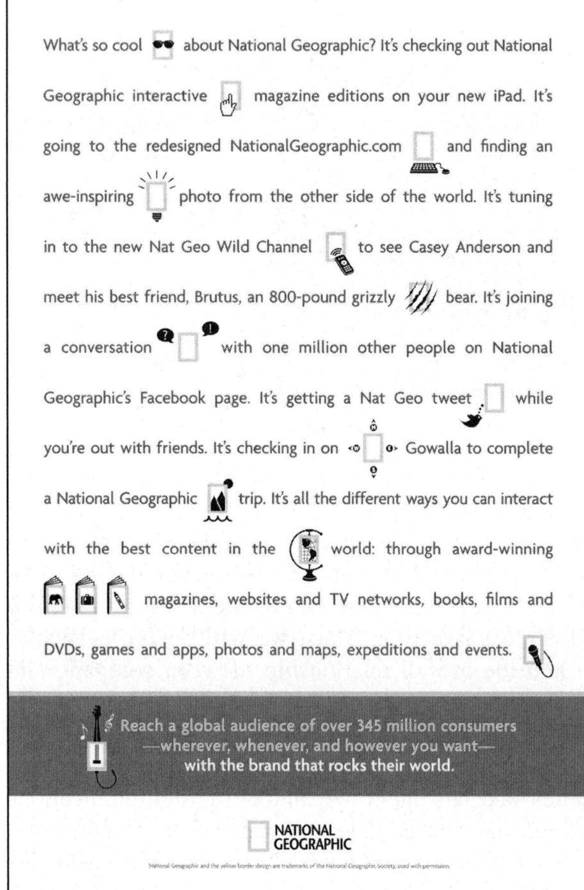

What's so cool about National Geographic? It's checking out National Geographic interactive magazine editions on your new iPad. It's going to the redesigned NationalGeographic.com and finding an awe-inspiring photo from the other side of the world. It's tuning in to the new Nat Geo Wild Channel to see Casey Anderson and meet his best friend, Brutus, an 800-pound grizzly bear. It's joining a conversation with one million other people on National Geographic's Facebook page. It's getting a Nat Geo tweet while you're out with friends. It's checking in on Gowalla to complete a National Geographic trip. It's all the different ways you can interact with the best content in the world: through award-winning magazines, websites and TV networks, books, films and DVDs, games and apps, photos and maps, expeditions and events.
Reach a global audience of over 345 million consumers
—wherever, whenever, and however you want—
with the brand that rocks their world.
NATIONAL GEOGRAPHIC

**EXHIBIT 3–1**
*National Geographic* promotes its value to advertisers

& Gamble uses eight primary ad agencies and two major media buying services companies. Many large companies often use additional agencies that specialize in creating ads for specific ethnic markets. For example, in addition to its primary agency of record, Toyota Motor Corporation uses additional agencies in the United States to create ads for the African-American, Hispanic, and Asian-American markets. More and more, ad agencies are acting as partners with advertisers and assuming more responsibility for developing the marketing and promotional programs.

**Media organizations** are another major participant in the advertising and promotions process. The primary function of most media is to provide information or entertainment to their subscribers, viewers, or readers. But from the perspective of the promotional planner, the purpose of media is to provide an environment for the firm's marketing communications message. The media must have editorial or program content that attracts consumers so that advertisers and their agencies will want to buy time or space with them. Exhibit 3–1 shows an ad run in advertising trade publications promoting the value of *National Geographic* magazine and its family of media products as a way to reach consumers around the world. While the media perform many other functions that help advertisers understand their markets and their customers, a medium's primary objective is to sell itself as a way for companies to reach their target markets with their messages effectively.

The next group of participants are organizations that provide **specialized marketing communications services**. They include direct-marketing agencies, sales promotion agencies, interactive agencies, and public relations firms. These organizations provide services in their areas of expertise. A direct-response agency develops and implements direct-marketing programs, while sales promotion agencies develop promotional programs such as contests and sweepstakes, premium offers, or sampling programs. Interactive agencies are being retained to develop websites for the Internet and help marketers as they move deeper into the realm of interactive media. Public relations firms are used to generate and manage publicity for a company and its products and services as well as to focus on its relationships and communications with its relevant publics.

The final participants shown in the promotions process of Figure 3–1 are those that provide **collateral services**, the wide range of support functions used by advertisers, agencies, media organizations, and specialized marketing communications firms. These individuals and companies perform specialized functions the other participants use in planning and executing advertising and other promotional functions. We will now examine the role of each participant in more detail. (Media organizations will be examined in Chapters 10 through 14.)

## ORGANIZING FOR ADVERTISING AND PROMOTION IN THE FIRM: THE CLIENT'S ROLE

Virtually every business organization uses some form of marketing communications. However, the way a company organizes for these efforts depends on several factors, including its size, the number of products it markets, the role of advertising and promotion in its marketing mix, the advertising and promotion budget, and its

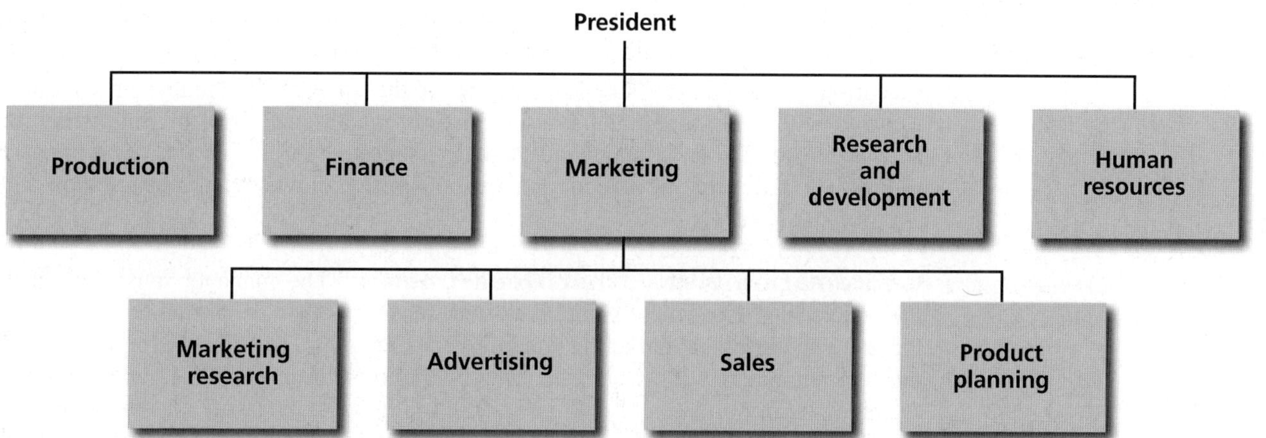


**FIGURE 3–2**
The Advertising Department under a Centralized System

marketing organization structure. Many individuals throughout the organization may be involved in the advertising and promotion decision-making process. Marketing personnel have the most direct relationship with advertising and are often involved in many aspects of the decision process, such as providing input to the campaign plan, agency selection, and evaluation of proposed programs. Top management is usually interested in how the advertising program represents the firm, and this may also mean being involved in advertising decisions even when the decisions are not part of its day-to-day responsibilities.

While many people both inside and outside the organization have some input into the advertising and promotion process, direct responsibility for administering the program must be assumed by someone within the firm. Many companies have an advertising department headed by an advertising or communications manager operating under a marketing director. An alternative used by many large multiproduct firms is a decentralized marketing (brand management) system. A third option is to form a separate agency within the firm, an in-house agency. Each of these alternatives is examined in more detail in the following sections.

## The Centralized System

In many organizations, marketing activities are divided along functional lines, with advertising placed alongside other marketing functions such as sales, marketing research, and product planning, as shown in Figure 3–2. The **advertising manager** is responsible for all promotions activities except sales (in some companies this individual has the title of marketing communications manager). In the most common example of a **centralized system**, the advertising manager controls the entire promotions operation, including budgeting, coordinating creation and production of ads, planning media schedules, and monitoring and administering the sales promotions programs for all the company's products or services.

The specific duties of the advertising or marketing communications manager depend on the size of the firm and the importance it places on promotional programs. Basic functions the manager and staff perform include the following.

**Planning and Budgeting** The advertising department is responsible for developing advertising and promotions plans that will be approved by management and recommending a promotions program based on the overall marketing plan, objectives, and budget. Formal plans are submitted annually or when a program is being changed significantly, as when a new campaign is developed. While the advertising department develops the promotional budget, the final decision on allocating funds is usually made by top management.

**Administration and Execution** The manager must organize the advertising department and supervise and control its activities. The manager also supervises the execution of the plan by subordinates and/or the advertising agency. This requires working with such departments as production, media, art, copy, digital/interactive, and sales promotion. If an outside agency is used, the advertising department is relieved of much of the executional responsibility; however, it must review and approve the agency's plans.

**Coordination with Other Departments** The manager must coordinate the advertising department's activities with those of other departments, particularly those involving other marketing functions. For example, the advertising department must communicate with marketing research and/or sales to determine which product features are important to customers and should be emphasized in the company's communications. Research may also provide profiles of product users and nonusers for the media department before it selects broadcast or print media. The advertising department may also be responsible for preparing material the sales force can use when calling on customers, such as sales promotion tools, advertising materials, and point-of-purchase displays.

**Coordination with Outside Agencies and Services** Many companies have an advertising department but still use many outside services. For example, companies may develop their advertising programs in-house while employing media buying services to place their ads and/or use collateral services agencies to develop brochures, point-of-purchase materials, and so on. The department serves as liaison between the company and any outside service providers and also determines which ones to use. Once outside services are retained, the manager will work with other marketing managers to coordinate their efforts and evaluate their performances.

A centralized organizational system is often used when companies do not have many different divisions, product or service lines, or brands to advertise. For example, airlines such as Southwest, American, and JetBlue have centralized advertising departments, as do major retailers such as Target, Walmart, and Best Buy. Many companies prefer a centralized advertising department because developing and coordinating advertising programs from one central location facilitates communication regarding the promotions program, making it easier for top management to participate in decision making. A centralized system may also result in a more efficient operation because fewer people are involved in the program decisions, and as their experience in making such decisions increases, the process becomes easier.

At the same time, problems are inherent in a centralized operation. First, it is difficult for the advertising department to understand the overall marketing strategy for the brand. The department may also be slow in responding to specific needs and problems of a product or brand. As companies become larger and develop or acquire new products, brands, or even divisions, the centralized system may become impractical.

## The Decentralized System

In large corporations with multiple divisions and many different products, it is very difficult to manage all the advertising, promotional, and other functions through a centralized department. These types of companies generally have a **decentralized system,** with separate manufacturing, research and development, sales, and marketing departments for various divisions, product lines, or businesses. Many companies that use a decentralized system, such as Procter & Gamble, Unilever, and Nestlé, assign each product or brand to a **brand manager** who is responsible for the total management of the brand, including planning, budgeting, sales, and profit performance. (The term *product manager* is also used to describe this position.) The brand manager, who may have one or more assistant brand managers, is also responsible for the planning, implementation, and control of the marketing program.[1]

**EXHIBIT 3–2**

Many of Procter & Gamble's brands compete against each other

- Corporate
  - Production
  - Finance
  - Marketing
    - Sales
    - Product management
      - Brand manager
        - Ad agency
      - Brand manager
        - Ad agency
      - Brand manager
        - Ad agency
    - Marketing services
      - Advertising department
        - Sales promotion
        - Package design
        - Merchandising
      - Marketing research
  - Research and development
  - Human resources

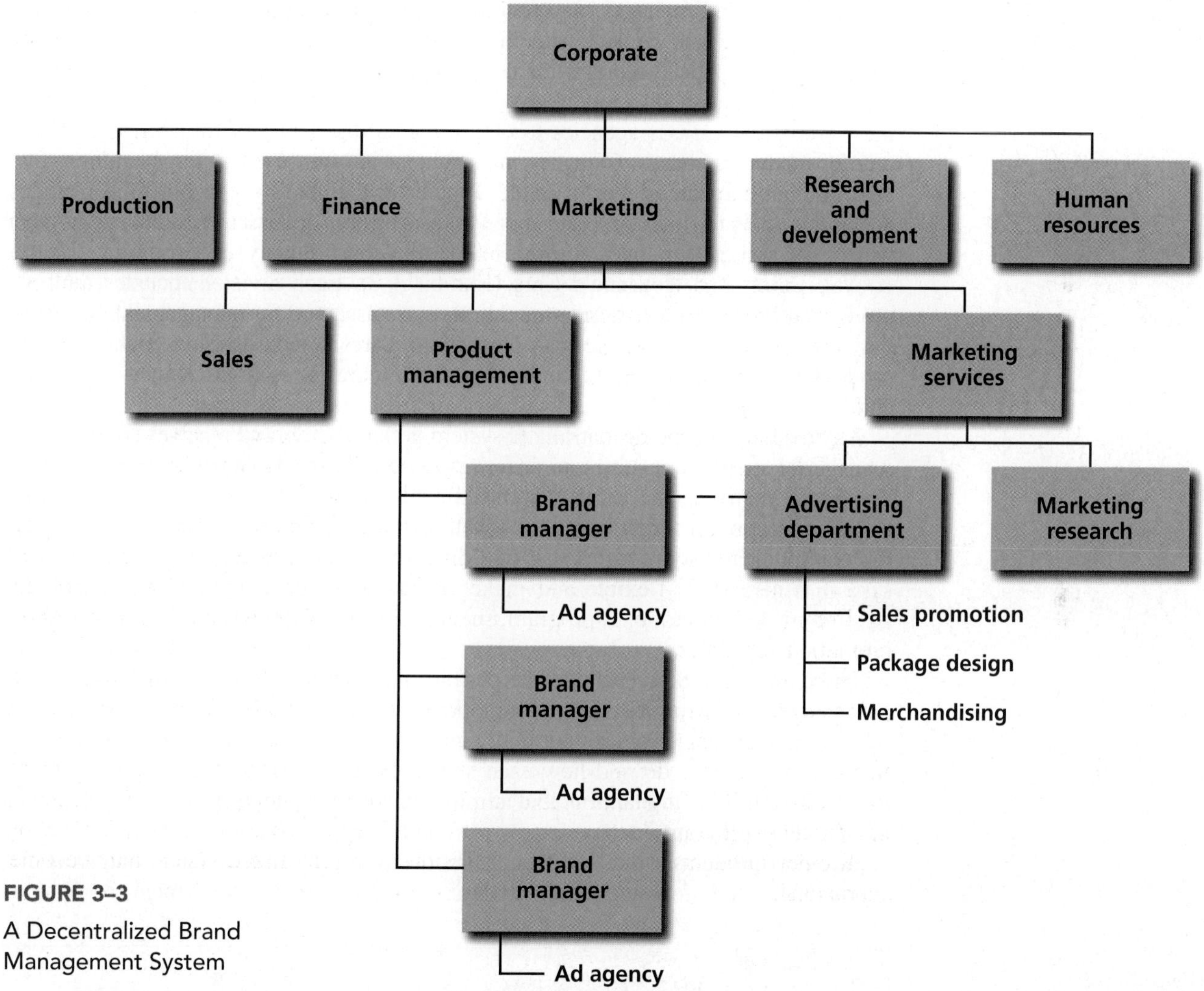

**FIGURE 3–3**

A Decentralized Brand Management System

Under this system, the responsibilities and functions associated with advertising and promotions are transferred to the brand manager, who works closely with the outside advertising agency and other marketing communications specialists as they develop the promotional program.[2] In a multiproduct firm, each brand may have its own ad agency and may compete against other brands within the company, not just against outside competitors. For example, Exhibit 3–2 shows ads for Tide and Gain, which are both Procter & Gamble products that compete for a share of the laundry detergent market.

As shown in Figure 3–3, the advertising department is part of marketing services and provides support for the brand managers. The role of marketing services is to assist the brand managers in planning and coordinating the integrated marketing communications program. In some companies, the marketing services group may include sales promotion. The brand managers may work with sales promotion people to develop budgets, define strategies, and implement tactical executions for both trade and consumer promotions. Marketing services may also provide other types of support services, such as package design and merchandising.

Some companies may have an additional layer(s) of management above the brand managers to coordinate the efforts of all the brand managers handling a related group of products. This system—generally referred to as a **category management system**—includes category managers as well as brand and advertising managers. The category manager oversees management of the entire product category and focuses on the strategic role of the various brands in order to build profits and market share.[3] Each category manager will have one or more brand managers reporting to him or her for each specific brand as well as an advertising manager.

The advertising manager may review and evaluate the various parts of the program and advise and consult with the brand managers. This person may have the authority to override the brand manager's decisions on advertising. In some multiproduct firms that spend a lot on advertising, the advertising manager may coordinate the work of the various agencies to obtain media discounts for the firm's large volume of media purchases. Category management is often used in large multiproduct or divisional companies. For example, Procter & Gamble's broad portfolio includes 86 brands (22 of which generate more than a billion dollars in revenue each year) which are assigned to one of three major divisions: Beauty & Grooming, Health & Well Being, and Household Care (Exhibit 3–3). Each division includes multiple product categories to which individual brands are assigned for management purposes. For example, the North American Household Care Brands division contains seven product categories including laundry and fabric care, household cleaners, baby and child care, batteries, paper, dishwashing, air fresheners, and paper.

An advantage of the decentralized system is that each brand receives concentrated managerial attention, resulting in faster response to both problems and opportunities. The brand managers have full responsibility for the marketing program, including the identification of target markets as well as the development of integrated marketing communications programs that will differentiate the brand.[4] The brand manager system is also more flexible and makes it easier to adjust various aspects of the advertising and promotional program, such as creative platforms and media and sales promotion schedules.[5]

There are some drawbacks to the decentralized approach. Brand managers often lack training and experience. The promotional strategy for a brand may be developed by a brand manager who does not really understand what advertising or sales promotion can and cannot do and how each should be used. Brand managers may focus too much on short-run planning and administrative tasks, neglecting the development of long-term programs.

Another problem is that individual brand managers often end up competing for management attention, marketing dollars, and other resources, which can lead to

**EXHIBIT 3–3**
P&G's broad portfolio of brands are assigned to various categories for management

unproductive rivalries and potential misallocation of funds. The manager's persuasiveness may become a bigger factor in determining budgets than the long-run profit potential of the brands. These types of problems were key factors in Procter & Gamble's decision to switch to a category management system.



Finally, the brand management system has been criticized for failing to provide brand managers with authority over the functions needed to implement and control the plans they develop.[6] Some companies have dealt with this problem by expanding the roles and responsibilities of the advertising and sales promotion managers and their staff of specialists. The staff specialists counsel the individual brand managers, and advertising or sales promotion decision making involves the advertising and/or sales promotion manager, the brand manager, and the marketing director. For example, General Motors, which is the largest advertiser in the United States, decided to drop its brand management system and give division marketing directors more control of the advertising and promotion for its various models.[7] The traditional brand management system has come under attack recently as critics argue that brand managers spend too much time on internal issues such as planning and budgeting and do not devote enough effort to external matters or to creativity and problem solving.[8] It has also been argued that this system is becoming increasingly outdated in the rapidly changing world of digital media as is discussed in IMC Technology Perspective 3–1.

LO 03-2

## In-House Agencies

Some companies, in an effort to reduce costs and maintain greater control over agency activities, have set up their own advertising agencies internally. An **in-house agency** is an advertising agency that is set up, owned, and operated by the advertiser. Some in-house agencies are little more than advertising departments, but in other companies they are given a separate identity and are responsible for the expenditure of large sums of advertising dollars. Large advertisers that use in-house agencies include Hyundai, Avon, Revlon, and Benetton. Many companies use in-house agencies exclusively; others combine in-house efforts with those of outside agencies. For example, retail giant Target has an internal creative department that handles the design of its weekly circulars, direct-mail pieces, in-store displays, promotions, and other marketing materials. However, the retailer uses outside agencies to develop most of its branding and image-oriented ads and for specific TV and print assignments. Other retailers such as Benetton and Banana Republic also have in-house advertising departments that work with outside agencies.

A major reason for using an in-house agency is to reduce advertising and promotion costs. Companies with very large advertising budgets pay a substantial amount to outside agencies in the form of media commissions. With an internal structure, these commissions go to the in-house agency. An in-house agency can also provide related work such as production of collateral materials, digital media, package design, and public relations at a lower cost than outside agencies. A study by M. Louise Ripley found that creative and media services were the most likely functions to be performed outside, while merchandising and sales promotion were the most likely to be performed in-house.[9] In-house agencies are also preferred by some companies because they keep the marketing communications function more closely tied to top management. A study by Forrester Research found that nearly 60 percent of in-house agencies report directly to the company's CEO or chief marketing officer (CMO).[10] Another reason is the stability an in-house agency provides because external agencies have much higher turnover levels which can take a toll on the client-agency relationship. In contrast, in-house agencies are known for retaining their personnel and have a turnover rate of less than 5 percent.[11]

Saving money is not the only reason companies use in-house agencies. Time savings, bad experiences with outside agencies, and the increased knowledge and understanding of the market that come from working on advertising and promotion

# IMC Technology Perspective 3–1 > > >

## How Technology Is Changing the Role of the Brand Manager

The brand management concept originated at Procter & Gamble nearly 80 years ago. A young employee working on an advertising campaign for the company's Camay soap brand became frustrated with having to compete against competing brands from Lever and Palmolive as well as P&G's own flagship Ivory soap brand. He sent a memo to P&G management which argued that more focused attention should be paid to Camay, as well as to other P&G brands, and suggested that there should be an individual or team of people responsible for overseeing all aspects of marketing each product. The idea was that each brand would be managed as if it were its own company which would result in more attention being given to it, particularly with respect to marketing. The brand management system was adopted by P&G and widely emulated in one form or another by companies throughout the world, particularly those with multiple brands competing in a product category. Marketers viewed brand management as a way to decentralize their decision making and give more autonomy to front line managers while still maintaining some centralized control over all of the individual brands in their portfolio.

The brand management system has persisted and evolved throughout the 20th century and into the new millennium. For most of this time period brand managers have focused their efforts on areas such as planning, budgeting, target marketing, and looking for ways to differentiate the products they manage. They also have worked closely with the agencies that handle the advertising, promotion, and other elements of their IMC programs. However, some critics are arguing that the traditional brand management system is becoming increasingly out-of-date in today's world of digital media where brand meaning and identity is increasingly being determined by consumers rather than marketers. In late 2009 Forrester Research, a leading technology and market research company, released a major report titled "Adaptive Brand Marketing: Rethinking Your Approach to Branding in the Digital Age" which notes that today's brand marketing organizations are ill equipped to handle the complex world of media fragmentation and "always on" marketing in the digital age. Forrester suggested that to remain relevant, marketing leaders needed to embrace what they term *adaptive brand marketing* which they describe as a more consumer-centric approach that encourages rapid response to align consumer and brand needs.

The Forester report also calls for changes in the brand management system. The authors suggest that brand managers be renamed brand "advocates" and recommend restructuring their role to better accommodate the real-time digital world. They also advocate the elimination of the formal annual budgeting process which generally includes an upfront allocation of funds for specific media, in favor of more frequently updated and spontaneous plans that can be adapted as conditions change. Forrester also recommends that market research and analytics, which they call "consumer intelligence" be given a more prominent and central role and that brand advocates should shift their emphasis from long-term external partnerships with advertising agencies to alliances with media and other content creators that can shift more rapidly.

Some of the major marketers that utilize the brand management system argue that they are already doing much of what is recommended in the Forrester report. For example, P&G recently began organizing its beauty business along gender lines rather than product category groupings and plans to organize other divisions around different customer cohorts as well. The company's global brand-building officer points to multibrand programs such as My Black Is Beautiful for African-American women and BeingGirl for teenage girls as examples of how P&G is marketing to consumer groups rather than individual brand consumers. One of the changes that P&G is making in their brand-building strategies is a greater reliance on digital media such as social networking systems. Marc Pritchard, P&G's global marketing officer, notes that "Our media strategy is pretty simple: follow the consumer. And the consumer is becoming more and more engaged in the digital world." P&G has set an explicit goal of assuring that each of its brands has a meaningful presence on Facebook by the end of 2010. The company also views Twitter as a great broadcast medium for one-to-many communications that can deliver short bursts of timely information and be a valuable listening tool that can be used to

for the product or service day-by-day are also reasons. Companies can also maintain tighter control over the process and more easily coordinate promotions with the firm's overall marketing program.

Some companies with global brands prefer an in-house shop so they can have a consistent brand image worldwide and reduce the number of marketing partners with which they work. For example, Dell has been working with the London-based WPP holding company to develop an agency dedicated exclusively to serving the company's marketing communications needs around the globe. The computer company had more than 800 agencies and marketing partners worldwide and wanted to consolidate all of its advertising and marketing communications efforts.[12] A company may also use an in-house agency because they believe it can do a better job than engage with consumers when they have a question.

P&G isn't the only company that is changing its perspective on brand-building and spending more money on digital media. Unilever, which is another consumer packaged goods giant, is also making changes. The company's CEO compares his global brand directors more to orchestra conductors than traditional managers and notes that they are more open to different types of partnerships, including those with the consumers who use the firm's products. For example, Unilever has used consumer-generated content where consumers have been invited to develop communications for products such as its Omo laundry detergents and Vaseline to complement those developed by the company and its advertising agencies. Kraft Foods has also increased its use of digital media by revamping its consumer website as well as its *Food & Family* online magazine, and targeting consumers looking for immediate cooking inspiration with e-mail newsletters. Kraft also has developed a popular app for the iPhone called iFood Assistant that has a dedicated website and provides consumers with simple recipes and food ideas, how-to videos and even built-in shopping lists.

Branding experts have noted that the traditional brand management system must change in order for managers to keep abreast of the rapidly changing world of digital media. For example, Tom Hinkes, a principal at brand consultancy company OutBranding, argues that brand managers spend too much time on internally focused skill sets such as setting and revising budgets as well as trying to improve profit margins by cutting costs. He argues that this often results in "numbers" managers who chose to compete on short-term tactics such as price and promotions rather than coming up with new or compelling things to say about their brands and ways to promote them. Lisa Braner, the principal author of the Forrester report on adaptive brand marketing, notes that much of brand managers' time is subsumed by internal management issues and much of the creative process and planning is outsourced to agencies and other parties. She argues that "brand advocates really need to be in charge of the heart and soul of what the brand stands for." For many marketers, this means that they need to begin making changes in their brand management systems to prepare for the challenges their managers will face in the rapidly changing world of digital media.

Sources: Tom Hinkes, "Our Biggest Brands Can No Longer Be Managed by Nerds," *Advertising Age*, March 17, 2010, http//adage.com/print?article_id=142841; Emily Bryson York, "Behind Kraft's Marketing Makeover: From New Ad Agencies to New Attitude," *Advertising Age*, February 8, 2010, http//adage.com/print?article_id=141943; Jack Neff, "P&G Embraces Facebook as Big Part of Its Marketing Plan," *Advertising Age*, January 25, 2010, http//adage.com/print?article_id=141733; Jack Neff, "Why It's Time to Do Away with the Brand Manager," *Advertising Age*, October 12, 2009, http//

an outside agency. They may feel they have more knowledge about the market and competitors as well as a better understanding of the intricacies and complexities of their business.

Some companies use an in-house agency simply because they believe it can do a better job than an outside agency could.[13] For example, Google launched an in-house agency in 2007 to handle its advertising. The company did very little advertising during its first 10 years in business because it relied primarily on the extensive publicity the company received and promotions done by other companies that would mention its search engine. However, as Google introduced more products and services, the company recognized the need to promote them to a broader audience and feels this can be done effectively using its own internal capabilities.[14]

**FIGURE 3–4**

Comparison of Advertising Organization Systems

| Organizational System | Advantages | Disadvantages |
|---|---|---|
| *Centralized* | ■ Facilitated communications<br>■ Fewer personnel required<br>■ Continuity in staff<br>■ Allows for more top-management involvement | ■ Less involvement with and understanding of overall marketing goals<br>■ Longer response time<br>■ Inability to handle multiple product lines |
| *Decentralized* | ■ Concentrated managerial attention<br>■ Rapid response to problems and opportunities<br>■ Increased flexibility | ■ Ineffective decision making<br>■ Internal conflicts<br>■ Misallocation of funds<br>■ Lack of authority<br>■ Internal rather than external focus |
| *In-house agencies* | ■ Cost savings<br>■ More control<br>■ Increased coordination<br>■ Stability<br>■ Access to top management | ■ Less experience<br>■ Less objectivity<br>■ Less flexibility<br>■ Less access to top creative talent |

Opponents of in-house agencies say they can give the advertiser neither the experience and objectivity of an outside agency nor the range of services. They argue that outside agencies have more highly skilled specialists and attract the best creative talent and that using an external firm gives a company a more varied perspective on its advertising problems and greater flexibility. Outside agencies also can provide greater strategic planning capabilities, outside perspectives on customers, and more creative experience with certain media such as television.[15] In-house personnel may become narrow or grow stale while working on the same product line, but outside agencies may have different people with a variety of backgrounds and ideas working on the account. Flexibility is greater because an outside agency can be dismissed if the company is not satisfied, whereas changes in an in-house agency could be slower and more disruptive.

The cost savings of an in-house agency must be evaluated against these considerations. For many companies, high-quality advertising is critical to their marketing success and should be the major criterion in determining whether to use in-house services. Companies like Rockport and Redken Laboratories have moved their in-house work to outside agencies in recent years. Redken cited the need for a "fresh look" and objectivity as the reasons, noting that management gets too close to the product to come up with different creative ideas. Companies often hire outside agencies as they grow and their advertising budgets and needs increase. For example, Best Buy, the largest electronics retailer in the United States, handled all of its advertising through its in-house agency, Best Buy Advertising, for nearly 20 years. However, in 2007 the company hired an outside agency to handle its advertising. The in-house shop was retained to work on the retailer's newspaper inserts, Hispanic, direct and local marketing, as well as local store openings and advertising for some of the company's private-label brands. Best Buy management felt that an outside agency was needed to help achieve its aggressive growth goals and better position the company as a trusted retailer in the complex and competitive technology marketplace.[16] Best Buy now uses the Crispin Porter + Bogusky agency to handle its brand-related advertising work as well as ads focusing on its Geek Squad customer-support unit.[17]

The ultimate decision as to which type of advertising organization to use depends on which arrangement works best for the company. The advantages and disadvantages of the three systems are summarized in Figure 3–4. We now turn our attention to the functions of outside agencies and their roles in the promotional process.

**FIGURE 3–5**

Top 25 Agencies Ranked by U.S. Advertising Revenue, 2009

| Rank | Agency | Headquarters | U.S. Revenue ($ millions) |
|---|---|---|---|
| 1 | McCann Erickson Worldwide (Interpublic ) | New York | $450 |
| 2 | BBDO Worldwide (Omnicom) | New York | 436 |
| 3 | JWT (WPP) | New York | 325 |
| 4 | Y&R (WPP) | New York | 286 |
| 5 | Leo Burnett Worldwide (Publicis) | Chicago | 267 |
| 6 | DDB Worldwide (Omnicom) | New York | 250 |
| 7 | Saatchi & Saatchi (Publicis) | New York | 210 |
| 8 | DraftFCB (Interpublic) | Chicago/New York | 198 |
| 9 | Euro RSCG Worldwide (Havas) | New York | 185 |
| 10 | Grey (WPP) | New York | 180 |
| 11 | Ogilvy & Mather Worldwide (WPP) | New York | 175 |
| 12 | Richards Group | Dallas | 170 |
| 13 | TBWA Worldwide (Omnicom) | New York | 168 |
| 14 | Deutsch (Interpublic) | New York | 165 |
| 14 | Publicis (Publicis) | New York/Paris | 165 |
| 16 | Campbell Ewald (Interpublic) | Warren, MI | 161 |
| 17 | Hill Holiday (Interpublic) | Boston | 160 |
| 18 | Doner | Southfield, MI | 142 |
| 19 | Crispin Porter + Bogusky (MDC Partners) | Miami/Boulder | 138 |
| 20 | Zimmerman Advertising (Omnicom) | Ft. Lauderdale, FL | 134 |
| 21 | Wieden & Kennedy | Portland, OR | 115 |
| 22 | Martin Agency (Interpublic) | Richmond, VA | 112 |
| 23 | Goodby, Silverstein & Partners (Omnicom) | San Francisco | 105 |
| 24 | RPA | Santa Monica, CA | 99 |
| 25 | Cramer-Krasselt | Chicago | 94 |

Source: *Advertising Age,* Agency Report, April 26, 2010, p. 26.

# ADVERTISING AGENCIES

Many major companies use an advertising agency to assist them in developing, preparing, and executing their promotional programs. An ad agency is a service organization that specializes in planning and executing advertising programs for its clients. More than 15,000 U.S. and international agencies are listed in the *Standard Directory of Advertising Agencies* (the "Red Book"); however, most are individually-owned small businesses employing fewer than five people. The U.S. ad agency business is highly concentrated. Nearly two-thirds of the domestic **billings** (the amount of client money agencies spend on media purchases and other equivalent activities) are handled by the top 500 agencies. In fact, just 10 U.S. agencies handle nearly 30 percent of the total volume of business done by the top 500 agencies in the United States. The top agencies also have foreign operations that generate substantial billings and income. The top 25 agencies, ranked by their U.S. gross revenue, are listed in Figure 3–5. The table shows that the advertising business is also geographically concentrated, with 13

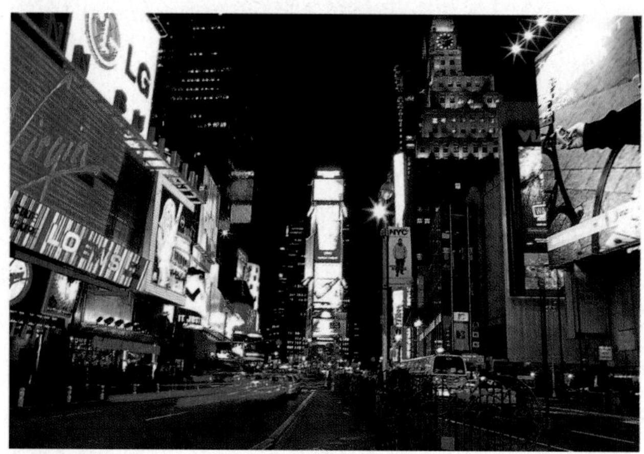


**EXHIBIT 3–4**
New York City is the center of the advertising industry in the United States

of the top 25 agencies headquartered in New York City. Nearly 40 percent of U.S. agency business is handled by New York–based agencies. Other leading advertising centers in the United States include Boston, Chicago, Los Angeles, the Detroit area, Dallas, and Minneapolis. New York City is clearly the center of the advertising industry in the United States as nearly half of the top 100 agencies are headquartered in the city or the surrounding area (Exhibit 3–4). In addition to advertising agencies, nine of the top 10 media specialist companies are based in the Big Apple as are many of the direct marketing, digital, promotion, and marketing services agencies.[18] There are several reasons why New York City is the hub of the IMC business in the United States. Many of the major companies with large advertising and promotion budgets are based in the city or the surrounding area. In 2010, 45 of the companies ranked in the Fortune 500 were headquartered in New York City while another 40 or so of the top firms were located nearby in suburbs or in cities in Connecticut or New Jersey. New York is also the world's leading media center as nearly all of the major television and radio networks are based in the city as well as many magazine and news organizations.[19]

During the late 1980s and into the 90s, the advertising industry underwent major changes as large agencies merged with or acquired other agencies and support organizations to form large advertising organizations, or superagencies. These **superagencies** were formed so that agencies could provide clients with integrated marketing communications services worldwide. Some advertisers became disenchanted with the superagencies and moved to smaller agencies that were flexible and more responsive.[20] However, during the mid-90s the agency business went through another wave of consolidation as a number of medium-size agencies were acquired and became part of large advertising organizations such as Omnicom Group, WPP Group, and the Interpublic Group of Cos. Many of the mid-size agencies were acquired by or forged alliances with larger agencies because their clients wanted an agency with international communications capabilities and their alignment with larger organizations gave them access to a network of agencies around the world. The consolidation of the agency business continued into the new millennium as large agencies such as Fallon Worldwide, Leo Burnett, Saatchi & Saatchi, and Kaplan Thaler were acquired by the giant French holding company Publicis Groupe. In 2009, the top four holding companies—WPP, Omnicom Group, Interpublic Group, and Publicis Groupe accounted for nearly half of U.S. agency revenue. Exhibit 3–5 shows the primary holdings of the top four agency holding companies. With the move toward IMC, agencies are now getting much of their revenue from more than just traditional advertising services which now account for just a third of the revenue for U.S. agencies. In 2009 agencies revenue came from other areas such as media buying (15 percent), public relations (11 percent), digital (14 percent), direct marketing (17 percent) and promotion (9 percent).[21] Many of the advertising organizations and major agencies have been acquiring companies specializing in areas such as interactive communications, public relations, direct marketing, and sales promotion so that they can offer their clients an ever-broader range of integrated marketing communication services.

## The Ad Agency's Role

The functions performed by advertising agencies might be conducted by the clients themselves through one of the designs discussed earlier in this chapter, but most large companies use outside firms. This section discusses some reasons advertisers use external agencies.

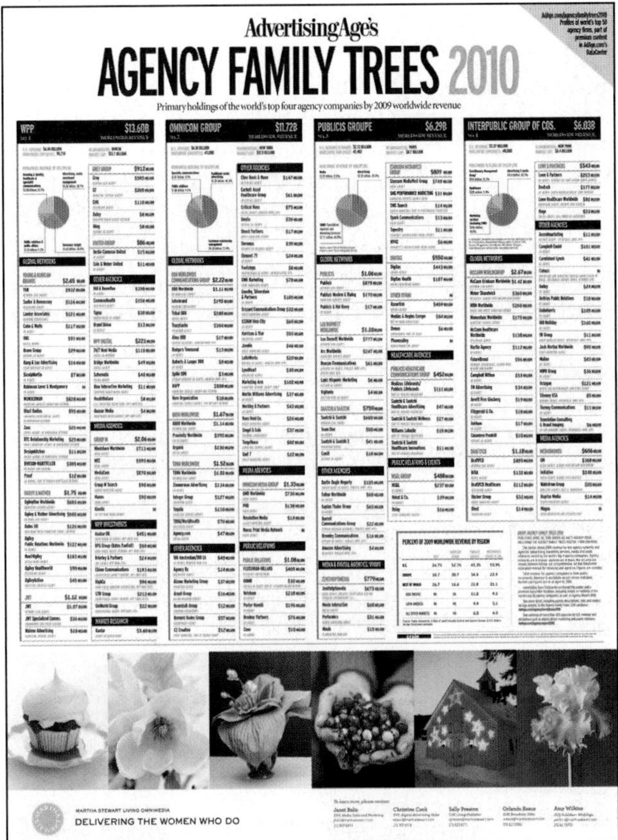


**EXHIBIT 3–5**
Primary holdings of the world's top four agency holding companies by 2009 worldwide revenue

**EXHIBIT 3–6**
Communications specializes in creating ads for high-tech companies



**Reasons for Using an Agency** Probably the main reason outside agencies are used is that they provide the client with the services of highly skilled individuals who are specialists in their chosen fields. An advertising agency staff may include artists, writers, media analysts, researchers, and others with specific skills, knowledge, and experience who can help market the client's products or services. Many agencies specialize in a particular type of business and use their knowledge of the industry to assist their clients. For example, Mentus Inc. is an agency that specializes in integrated marketing communications for the high-technology, e-commerce, and bioscience industries (Exhibit 3–6).

An outside agency can also provide an objective viewpoint of the market and its business that is not subject to internal company policies, biases, or other limitations. The agency can draw on the broad range of experience it has gained while working on a diverse set of marketing problems for various clients. For example, an ad agency that is handling a travel-related account may have individuals who have worked with airlines, cruise ship companies, travel agencies, hotels, and other travel-related industries. The agency may have experience in this area or may even have previously worked on the advertising account of one of the client's competitors. Thus, the agency can provide the client with insight into the industry (and, in some cases, the competition).

## Types of Ad Agencies

Since ad agencies can range in size from a one—or two-person operation to large organizations with over 1,000 employees, the services offered and functions performed

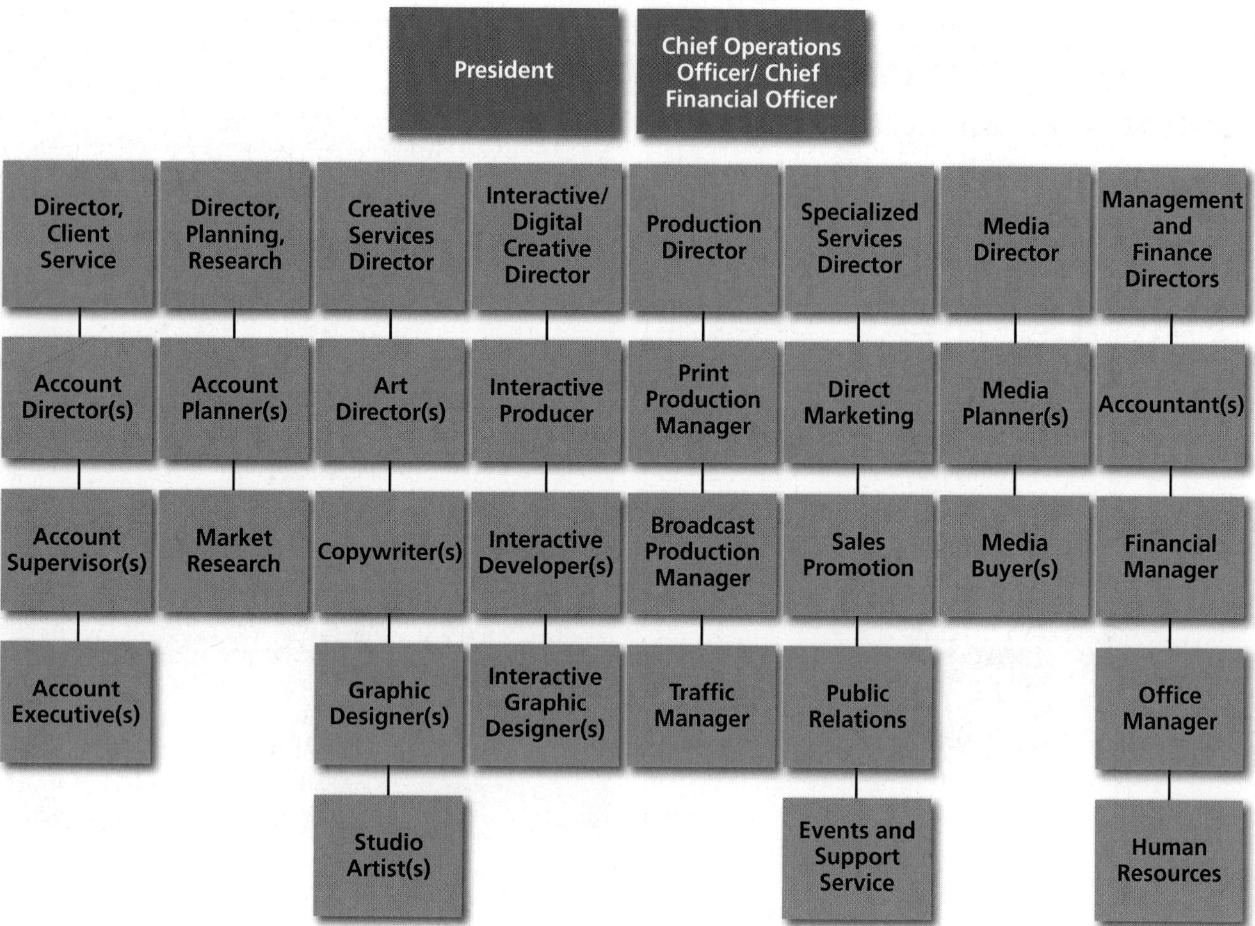


**FIGURE 3–6**
Full-Service Agency Organizational Chart

will vary. This section examines the different types of agencies, the services they perform for their clients, and how they are organized.

**Full-Service Agencies** Many companies employ what is known as a **full-service agency**, which offers its clients a full range of marketing, communications, and promotions services, including planning, creating, and producing the advertising; performing research; and selecting media. A full-service agency may also offer nonadvertising services such as strategic market planning; sales promotions, direct marketing, and interactive capabilities; package design; and public relations and publicity.

The full-service agency is made up of departments that provide the activities needed to perform the various advertising functions and serve the client, as shown in Figure 3–6.

**Account Services** Account services, or account management, is the link between the ad agency and its clients. Depending on the size of the client and its advertising budget, one or more account executives serve as liaison. The **account executive** is responsible for understanding the advertiser's marketing and promotions needs and interpreting them to agency personnel. He or she coordinates agency efforts in planning, creating, and producing ads. The account executive also presents agency recommendations and obtains client approval.

As the focal point of agency-client relationships, the account executive must know a great deal about the client's business and be able to communicate this to specialists in the agency working on the account.[22] The ideal account executive has a strong marketing background as well as a thorough understanding of all phases of the advertising process. IMC Perspective 3–1 discusses how some agencies are cutting back on their account services departments and how the role of account executives is changing.

**Marketing Services** Over the past two decades, use of marketing services has increased dramatically. One service gaining increased attention is research, as agencies realize that to communicate effectively with their clients' customers, they must have a good understanding of the target audience. As shown in Chapter 1, the advertising planning process begins with a thorough situation analysis, which is based on research and information about the target audience.



Most full-service agencies maintain a *research department* whose function is to gather, analyze, and interpret information that will be useful in developing advertising for their clients. This can be done through primary research—where a study is designed, executed, and interpreted by the research department—or through the use of secondary (previously published) sources of information. Sometimes the research department acquires studies conducted by independent syndicated research firms or consultants. The research staff then interprets these reports and passes on the information to other agency personnel working on that account. The research department may also design and conduct research to pretest the effectiveness of advertising the agency is considering. For example, copy testing is often conducted to determine how messages developed by the creative specialists are likely to be interpreted by the receiving audience.

In many large agencies, the marketing services department may include **account planners** who are individuals that gather information that is relevant to the client's product or service and can be used in the development of the creative strategy as well as other aspects of the IMC campaign. Account planners work with the client as well as other agency personnel including the account executives, creative team members, media specialists, and research department personnel to collect information that can be helpful in gaining a better understanding of the client's target audience and the best ways to communicate with them. They gather and organize information about consumers as well as developments in the marketplace that can be used to prepare the *creative brief,* which is a document that the agency's creative department uses to guide the development of advertising ideas and concepts. Account planners may also be involved in assessing consumers' reactions to the advertising and other elements of the IMC program and providing the creative staff as well as other agency personnel with feedback regarding performance.

Account planning has become a very important function in many agencies because it provides the creative team, as well as other agency personnel, with more insight into consumers and how to use advertising and other IMC tools to communicate with them.[23] However, the account planning function has also become more demanding as the number of marketing communication channels and ways of contacting consumers increases. Account planners increasingly find themselves interacting with individuals from a variety of marketing communication disciplines and have to keep up with developments that are occurring in all of these areas. John Thorpe, the director of brand strategy for the Good Silverstein & Partners, an agency which is known for its account planning, notes: "No longer can planners just be good at strategy. It's a cross-silo activity. They have to be good at a lot of things that run across advertising. Ambidexterity is required across the house."[24]

The *media department* of an agency analyzes, selects, and contracts for space or time in the media that will be used to deliver the client's advertising message. The media department is expected to develop a media plan that will reach the target market and effectively communicate the message. Since most of the client's ad budget is spent on media time and/or space, this department must develop a plan that both communicates with the right audience and is cost-effective.

Media specialists must know what audiences the media reach, their rates, and how well they match the client's target market. The media planning department reviews information on demographics, magazine and newspaper readership, radio listenership, and consumers' Internet and TV viewing patterns to develop an effective media plan. The media buyer implements the media plan by purchasing the actual time and space.

# IMC Perspective 3–1 > > >

## The Changing Role of Account Reps

Traditionally, a very important position in advertising agencies has been that of an account representative or "account rep" as they are commonly referred to in the ad business. Account reps are the liaison between the agency and client and are responsible for formulating the advertising plan, coordinating the agency's services, and representing the client's point of view to others on the agency side such as the creative team. College graduates with undergraduate and graduate degrees in marketing, advertising, and other disciplines are often hired for account executive positions and go on to have careers in account management. However, with the revolutionary changes sweeping the advertising business, the role of account reps is changing dramatically and they are struggling to remain relevant. Cost cutting by marketers has thinned the once-bloated ranks of account management personnel in agencies by as much as 30 percent over the past five years. Moreover for those who remain, the expectations and demands of the position are changing.

For many years, advertising agencies touted their extensive account-services departments and used them to build strong relationships with their clients that lasted for many years. However, as the number of account reps assigned to their business increased, clients began expressing concern over the costs associated with them and the value they provided. In fact, many years ago legendary ad man David Ogilvy questioned why account executives so often outnumbered creatives noting: "If you were a farmer, would you employ twice as many milkers as you had cows?" One of the reasons for the increase in the number of milkers was that many agencies hired additional account executives over the years as a way to justify the fees they were being paid by their clients. Many agencies were compensated based on commissions from the gross media and production spending by their clients and as media costs increased, so did the amount of money they received. However, over the past 10 years there has been a dramatic shift away from commissions to fee-based compensation and clients now want to know exactly what they are paying for and the services they are receiving from their agencies.

In addition to cutting back on the number of account executives, agencies are also changing what they are looking for in those individuals who work in their most client-facing function. Agencies want account executives that are good strategic thinkers and have broad-based business acumen, not just expertise in advertising. And as other integrated marketing communication tools such as direct, digital, and interactive media become more central, they want them to have an understanding of, and be able to coordinate activities and relationships in, these areas. One agency CEO suggests that the models that best capture the qualities of star account persons are those of entrepreneurs as they often help people see the value of a new product that has not yet been created, they raise funds, create the economic model, and must establish partnerships. He notes that "When you start to think of account people as entrepreneurs, it introduces a new level of potential into the role. They are no longer viewed

The media department is becoming an increasingly important part of the agency business. An agency's ability to negotiate prices and effectively use the vast array of media vehicles, as well as other sources of customer contact, is becoming as important as its ability to create ads. Some of the major agencies and/or their holding companies have formed independent media services companies to better serve their clients. For example, Starcom MediaVest Group is a subsidiary of the Publicis Groupe and has a network of over 100 offices in 67 countries, while McCann-Erickson Worldwide formed Universal McCann, which is now one of the primary media specialist agencies for the Interpublic Group. Other large media specialist companies include MindShare, which is owned by the WPP Group, and OMD Worldwide, which is owned by the Omnicom Group. These media specialist firms serve the media needs of the agencies that are part of their parent holding companies but may also offer media services to other clients as well.

The research and media departments perform most of the functions that full-service agencies need to plan and execute their clients' advertising programs. Some agencies offer additional marketing services to their clients to assist in other promotional areas. An agency may have a sales promotion department, or merchandising department, that specializes in developing contests, premiums, promotions, point-of-sale materials, and other sales materials. It may have direct-marketing specialists and package designers, as well as a PR/publicity department. Many agencies have developed interactive media departments to create websites for their clients. The growing popularity of integrated marketing communications has prompted many full-function as suits dutifully carrying the ideas to meetings. They become catalysts for new thinking and innovation."

While clients want account executives to be able to do more things and work across a variety of areas, finding individuals with these skills is becoming increasingly difficult. Agencies face competition for top talent from any number of higher-paying professions such as management consulting, investment banking, and financial services as well as from media companies. The competition also includes account planning in their own agencies as well as media agencies that are expanding the communications planning services they offer to clients. Many agencies feel there are not enough properly trained candidates in the talent pool who have the skills needed, which include solving complex communication problems, communicating in a mature fashion, selling the agency and its capabilities, and knowing when to push back on a client. To deal with this problem some agencies are developing client-services training programs for their account executives that are designed to educate them in a variety of areas including basic agency business issues, strategic marketing, the procurement process, and relationship building.

Account executives, like the marketing executives on the client side with whom they often work closely, also face the challenge of communicating with the creative types in advertising agencies. There is often a disconnect between the more systematic and analytical left-brain thinking of account representatives and brand managers, who often have business degrees, versus the right-brain thinking of creative types who may have degrees in design or liberal arts. Some agencies and clients are working together to address this problem by developing communication and indoctrination programs that provide agency personnel with an overview of their clients' business objectives and marketing strategy as well as their financial situation. This allows them to understand the limits within which creative solutions have to be developed.

It is unlikely that the account representative position will go away as they still play an important role in managing the relationships between agencies and their clients. However, the days of the old-school account executive in the gray wool suit are long gone as agencies look for more from those who work most closely with their clients.

Sources: Dale Buss, "Bridging the Great Divide in Marketing Thinking," *Advertising Age,* adage.com, March 26, 2007; Matthew Creamer, "The Demise of the Suit," *Advertising Age,* March 13, 2006, pp. 1, 41; Phil Johnson, "A Vision for the Future of Account Management," *Advertising Age,* March 24, 2010, http://adage.com/print?article_id=142947.



agencies to develop capabilities and offer services in these other promotional areas. Traditional advertising agencies are recognizing that they must develop integrated marketing capabilities that extend beyond media advertising.

**Creative Services** The creative services department is responsible for the creation and execution of advertisements. The individuals who conceive the ideas for the ads and write the headlines, subheads, and body copy (the words constituting the message) are known as **copywriters**. They may also be involved in determining the basic appeal or theme of the ad campaign and often prepare a rough initial visual layout of the print ad or television commercial.

While copywriters are responsible for what the message says, the *art department* is responsible for how the ad looks. For print ads, the art director and graphic designers prepare *layouts,* which are drawings that show what the ad will look like and from which the final artwork will be produced. For TV commercials, the layout is known as a *storyboard,* a sequence of frames or panels that depict the commercial in still form.

Members of the creative department work together to develop ads that will communicate the key points determined to be the basis of the creative strategy for the client's product or service. Writers and artists generally work under the direction of the agency's creative director, who oversees all the advertising produced by the organization. The director sets the creative philosophy of the department and may even become directly involved in creating ads for the agency's largest clients.

Once the copy, layout, illustrations, and mechanical specifications have been completed and approved, the ad is turned over to the *production department.* Most agencies do not actually produce finished ads; they hire printers, engravers, photographers, typographers, and other suppliers to complete the finished product. For broadcast production, the approved storyboard must be turned into a finished commercial. The production department may supervise the casting of people to appear in the ad and the setting for the scenes as well as choose an independent production studio. The department may hire an outside director to turn the creative concept into a commercial. For example, Nike has used film directors such as David Fincher and Spike Lee to direct some of its commercials; BMW has used well-known film directors such as Guy Ritchie, Ang Lee, and Tony Scott to direct some of its commercials and webisodes. Copywriters, art directors, account managers, people from research and planning, and representatives from the client side may all participate in production decisions, particularly when large sums of money are involved.

Creating an advertisement often involves many people and takes several months. In large agencies with many clients, coordinating the creative and production processes can be a major problem. A *traffic department* coordinates all phases of production to see that the ads are completed on time and that all deadlines for submitting the ads to the media are met. The traffic department may be located in the creative services area of the agency, or be part of media or account management, or be separate.

**Management and Finance** Like any other business, an advertising agency must be managed and perform basic operating and administrative functions such as accounting, finance, and human resources. It must also attempt to generate new business. Large agencies employ administrative, managerial, and clerical people to perform these functions. The bulk of an agency's income (approximately 64 percent) goes to salary and benefits for its employees. Thus, an agency must manage its personnel carefully and get maximum productivity from them.

**Agency Organization and Structure** Full-function advertising agencies must develop an organizational structure that will meet their clients' needs and serve their own internal requirements. Most medium-size and large agencies are structured under either a departmental or a group system. Under the **departmental system**, each of the agency functions shown in Figure 3–6 is set up as a separate department and is called on as needed to perform its specialty and serve all of the agency's clients. Ad layout, writing, and production are done by the creative department; marketing services is responsible for any research or media selection and purchases; and the account services department handles client contact. Some agencies prefer the departmental system because it gives employees the opportunity to develop expertise in servicing a variety of accounts.

Many large agencies use the **group system**, in which individuals from each department work together in groups to service particular accounts. Each group is headed by an account executive or supervisor and has one or more media people, including media planners and buyers; a creative team, which includes copywriters, art directors, artists, and production personnel; and one or more account executives. The group may also include individuals from other departments such as marketing research, direct marketing, or sales promotion. The size and composition of the group vary depending on the client's billings and the importance of the account to the agency. For very important accounts, the group members may be assigned exclusively to one client. In some agencies, they may serve a number of smaller clients. Many agencies prefer the group system because employees become very knowledgeable about the client's business and there is continuity in servicing the account.

## Other Types of Agencies and Services

Not every agency is a large full-service agency. Many smaller agencies expect their employees to handle a variety of jobs. For example, account executives may do their own research, work out their own media schedule, and coordinate the production

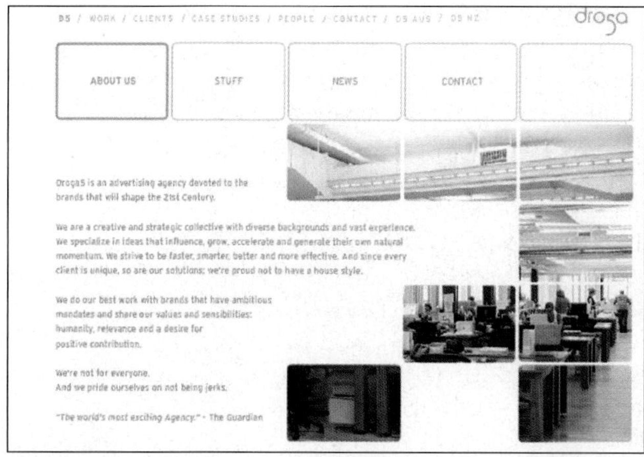


**EXHIBIT 3–7**

Droga5 is a very successful creative boutique

of ads written and designed by the creative department. Many advertisers, including some large companies, are not interested in paying for the services of a full-service agency but are interested in some of the specific services agencies have to offer. Over the past few decades, several alternatives to full-service agencies have evolved, including creative boutiques and media buying services.



**Creative Boutiques** **Creative boutiques** are small ad agencies that provide only creative services and have long been an important part of the advertising industry. These specialized agencies have creative personnel such as writers and artists on staff but do not have media, research, or account planning capabilities. Creative boutiques have developed in response to some companies' desires to use only the creative services of an outside agency while maintaining control of other marketing communication functions internally. While most creative boutiques work directly for companies, full-service agencies often subcontract work to them when they are very busy or want to avoid adding full-time employees to their payrolls. They are usually compensated on a project or hourly fee basis.

Many creative boutiques have been formed by members of the creative departments of full-service agencies who leave the firm and take with them clients who want to retain their creative talents. An advantage of these smaller agencies is their ability to turn out inventive creative work quickly and without the cumbersome bureaucracy and politics of larger agencies. Many companies also prefer working directly with a smaller creative boutique because they can get more attention and better access to creative talent than they would at a larger agency. An example of a successful creative boutique is New York–based Droga5 whose clients include Unilever's Suave shampoo brand, Puma, Rhapsody, and household cleaning products company Method. This hot agency also created the popular viral campaign for Activision featuring Tillman, the skateboarding, snowboarding, and surfing Bulldog playing the Tony Hawk RIDE video game (Exhibit 3–7).

Creative boutiques will continue to be an important part of the advertising industry. However, they face challenges as many find themselves competing against larger agencies for business, particularly when there are cutbacks in advertising spending. Moreover, many clients want the range of services that large agencies provide as they are often looking for business-building ideas rather than just creative work.[25]

**Media Specialist Companies** **Media specialist companies** are companies that specialize in the buying of media, particularly radio and television time. The task of purchasing advertising media has grown more complex as specialized media proliferate, so media buying services have found a niche by specializing in the analysis and purchase of advertising time and space. Agencies and clients usually develop their own media strategies and hire the buying service to execute them. Some media buying services do help advertisers plan their media strategies. Because media buying services purchase such large amounts of time and space, they receive large discounts and can save the small agency or client money on media purchases. Media buying services are paid a fee or commission for their work.

Media buying services have been experiencing strong growth in recent years as clients seek alternatives to full-service agency relationships. Many companies have been unbundling agency services and consolidating media buying to get more clout from their advertising budgets. Nike, Revlon, and Hyundai/Kia are among those that have switched some or all of their media buying from full-service agencies to independent media buyers. As noted earlier, many of the major agencies have formed independent media services companies that handle the media planning and buying for their clients and also offer their services separately to companies interested in a more specialized or consolidated approach to media planning, research, and/or

**EXHIBIT 3–8**
Initiative is one of the leading media specialist companies

buying. A number of large advertisers have consolidated their media buying with these large media specialist companies to save money and improve media efficiency. For example, MillerCoors consolidated its $400 million U.S. media planning and buying with Initiative which is part of the Interpublic Group while Mars-Wrigley moved its $500 million media budget to Starcom MediaVest.[26] A number of companies such as PepsiCo and Campbell Soup Co. also use media specialist companies to handle all of their global media buying which helps them achieve economies of scale and more uniform media strategies and implementation across various countries.

The rise of the independent media buying services, operating outside the structure of the traditional ad agency media department, and the divestment of these departments from the agency system are two of the most significant developments that have occurred in the advertising industry in recent years. A recent study conducted for the Association of National Advertisers found a small percentage of companies still use a "general" ad agency to handle their media planning and buying as the vast majority use a media agency specialist to handle these functions. These media specialists are often part of the same agency holding company as the primary agency that handles their creative work, particularly for large advertisers. However, about a third of the time the media specialist agency is not related to the primary agency.[27] Exhibit 3–8 shows how Initiative, which is one of the largest media specialist companies, promotes its services.

# AGENCY COMPENSATION

As you have seen, the type and amount of services an agency performs vary from one client to another. As a result, agencies use a variety of methods to get paid for their services. Agencies are typically compensated in three ways: commissions, some type of fee arrangement, or percentage charges.

## Commissions from Media

The traditional method of compensating agencies is through a **commission system**, where the agency receives a specified commission (usually 15 percent) from the media on any advertising time or space it purchases for its client. (For outdoor advertising, the commission is $16\frac{2}{3}$ percent.) This system provides a simple method of determining payments, as shown in the following example.

**FIGURE 3–7**
Example of Commission System Payment

| Media Bills Agency | | Agency Bills Advertiser | |
|---|---|---|---|
| Costs for magazine space | $100,000 | Costs for magazine space | $100,000 |
| Less 15% commission | –15,000 | Less 2% cash discount | –1,700 |
| Cost of media space | 85,000 | Advertiser pays agency | $ 98,300 |
| Less 2% cash discount | –1,700 | | |
| Agency pays media | $ 83,300 | Agency income | $ 15,000 |



Assume an agency prepares a full-page magazine ad and arranges to place the ad on the back cover of a magazine at a cost of $100,000. The agency places the order for the space and delivers the ad to the magazine. Once the ad is run, the magazine will bill the agency for $100,000, less the 15 percent ($15,000) commission. The media will also offer a 2 percent cash discount for early payment, which the agency may pass along to the client. The agency will bill the client $100,000 less the 2 percent cash discount on the net amount, or a total of $98,300, as shown in Figure 3–7. The $15,000 commission represents the agency's compensation for its services.

**Appraisal of the Commission System** While the commission system was the primary agency compensation method for many years, it has always been controversial. Critics of the commission system have long argued that it encourages agencies to recommend high-priced media to their clients to increase their commission level. The system has also been criticized on the grounds that it ties agency compensation to media costs, which have been skyrocketing over the past decade. Still others charge that the system encourages agencies to recommend mass-media advertising and avoid noncommissionable IMC tools such as direct mail, sales promotion, public relations, or event sponsorships, unless they are requested by the clients.

Defenders of the commission system argue that it is easy to administer and keeps the emphasis in agency compensation on nonprice factors such as the quality of the advertising developed for clients. Proponents of the system argue that agency services are proportional to the size of the commission, since more time and effort are devoted to the large accounts that generate high revenue for the agency. They also note that the system is more flexible than it appears as agencies often perform other services for large clients at no extra charge as a way of justifying the large commission they receive.

Companies began moving away from the commission system during the 1990s, and most companies no longer use it as the basis for compensating their agencies. The most recent study of agency compensation conducted by the Association of National Advertisers (ANA) found that only 16 percent of major advertisers still paid commissions to their agencies, down from 21 percent in 2000.[28] Among those companies that do pay commissions, most do not pay the traditional 15 percent. Many advertisers have gone to a **negotiated commission** system whereby the commissions average from 8 to 10 percent or are based on a sliding scale that becomes lower as the clients' media expenditures increase. Agencies are also relying less on media commissions for their income as their clients expand their IMC programs to include other forms of promotion and cut back on mass-media advertising. The amount of agency income coming from media commissions is declining as many companies are now using other methods of agency compensation such as fees and performance-based incentives.

## Fee, Cost, and Incentive-Based Systems

Since many believe the commission system is not equitable to all parties, many agencies and their clients have developed some type of fee arrangement or cost-plus agreement for agency compensation. Some are using incentive-based compensation, which is a combination of a commission and a fee system.

**FIGURE 3–8**

Performance Criteria Used for Incentive Plans

| | |
|---|---|
| Performance reviews | 82% |
| Sales goals | 53 |
| Brand/ad awareness | 51 |
| Achieve project objectives | 44 |
| Brand perceptions | 33 |
| Copy test results | 24 |
| Market share goals | 24 |
| Profit goals | 24 |
| Other criteria | 13 |
| *Basis for Incentives* | |
| Agency performance | 27% |
| Company performances | 13 |
| Both agency and company | 53 |

Source: Association of National Advertisers, *Trends in Agency Compensation*, 14th ed., 2007.

**Fee Arrangement** There are two basic types of fee arrangement systems. In the straight or **fixed-fee method,** the agency charges a basic monthly fee for all of its services and credits to the client any media commissions earned. Agency and client agree on the specific work to be done and the amount the agency will be paid for it. Sometimes agencies are compensated through a **fee-commission combination,** in which the media commissions received by the agency are credited against the fee. If the commissions are less than the agreed-on fee, the client must make up the difference. If the agency does much work for the client in noncommissionable media, the fee may be charged over and above the commissions received.

Both types of fee arrangements require that the agency carefully assess its costs of serving the client for the specified period, or for the project, plus its desired profit margin. To avoid any later disagreement, a fee arrangement should specify exactly what services the agency is expected to perform for the client. Fee arrangements have become the primary type of agreement used by advertisers with their agencies, accounting for 66 percent of the compensation plans in the recent ANA survey. Blended compensation plans that include fees and commissions were used by 14 percent of the companies surveyed.

**Cost-Plus Agreement** Under a **cost-plus system**, the client agrees to pay the agency a fee based on the costs of its work plus some agreed-on profit margin (often a percentage of total costs). This system requires that the agency keep detailed records of the costs it incurs in working on the client's account. Direct costs (personnel time and out-of-pocket expenses) plus an allocation for overhead and a markup for profits determine the amount the agency bills the client.

Fee agreements and cost-plus systems are commonly used in conjunction with a commission system. The fee-based system can be advantageous to both the client and the agency, depending on the size of the client, advertising budget, media used, and services required. Many clients prefer fee or cost-plus systems because they receive a detailed breakdown of where and how their advertising and promotion dollars are being spent. However, these arrangements can be difficult for the agency, as they require careful cost accounting and may be difficult to estimate when bidding for an advertiser's business. Agencies are also reluctant to let clients see their internal cost figures.

**Incentive-Based Compensation** Many clients are demanding more accountability from their agencies and tying agency compensation to performance through some type of **incentive-based system**. Recently a new variation of this system has emerged in the form of *value-based compensation* whereby agencies are compensated above their basic costs, if they achieve or exceed results as measured by agreed-upon metrics.[29] The costs are determined by the tasks that the agency is expected to perform, staffing required, and hourly rates. While there are many variations, the basic idea is that the agency's ultimate compensation level will depend on how well it meets predetermined performance goals. These goals often include objective measures such as sales or market share as well as more subjective measures such as evaluations of the quality of the agency's creative work. Companies using incentive-based systems determine agency compensation through media commissions, fees, bonuses, or some combination of these methods. The use of performance incentives varies by the size of the advertiser, with large advertisers the most likely to use them. Figure 3–8 shows the various performance criteria used along with the basis for the incentive.

Recognizing the movement toward incentive-based systems, most agencies have agreed to tie their compensation to performance. Agency executives note that pay for performance works best when the agency has complete control over a campaign.

Thus, if a campaign fails to help sell a product or service, the agency is willing to assume complete responsibility and take a reduction in compensation. On the other hand, if sales increase, the agency can receive greater compensation for its work.



## Percentage Charges

Another way to compensate an agency is by adding a markup of **percentage charges** to various services the agency purchases from outside providers. These may include market research, artwork, printing, photography, and other services or materials. Markups usually range from 17.65 to 20 percent and are added to the client's overall bill. Since suppliers of these services do not allow the agency a commission, percentage charges cover administrative costs while allowing a reasonable profit for the agency's efforts. (A markup of 17.65 percent of costs added to the initial cost would yield a 15 percent commission. For example, research costs of \$100,000 × 17.65% = \$100,000 + \$17,650 = \$117,650. The \$17,650 markup is about 15 percent of \$117,650.)

## The Future of Agency Compensation

As you can see, there is no one method of agency compensation to which everyone subscribes. Companies have continued to make significant changes in their agency compensation plans over the past decade. One of the most significant findings from the ANA survey is the rapid rise in incentive-based compensation agreements as more than half of advertisers surveyed indicated that they are using some type of performance-based system versus 38 percent in 2004 and only 13 percent in the early 1990s. Nearly 60 percent of those who use incentives feel that they result in improved agency performance and the overwhelming majority (82 percent) who use them plan to continue to do so. The ANA study concluded that the use of performance incentives as the basis for agency compensation continues to grow, and is generally gaining popularity across the board, regardless of advertiser type or size or type of agency service.[30]

As more companies adopt IMC approaches, they are reducing their reliance on traditional media advertising, and this is leading to changes in the way they compensate their agencies. For example, Procter & Gamble (P&G), which is the world's largest advertiser, no longer uses the commission system to compensate its agencies. In 2000, P&G implemented a major change in its compensation structure by moving from a commission-based system to a sales-based incentive system. P&G made the change to encourage its agencies to focus less on expensive commissionable media such as television and magazines and to make use of other IMC tools such as direct mail, event marketing, public relations, and the Internet. P&G has been very satisfied with its incentive-based compensation system and has extended it to media agencies and other marketing services providers.[31] In 2009 the Coca-Cola Company began using a "value-based" compensation model whereby agencies are guaranteed only recouped costs, with any profit coming only if certain agreed upon targets are met. The new model will encompass all of the company's advertising and media agency relationships by 2011. Coke is also encouraging the advertising industry to adopt value-based models as a standard practice.[32] A number of other major advertisers, including Colgate-Palmolive, Unilever, General Motors, Nissan, and Ford, also use some form of incentive-based compensation system. General Motors made the change to encourage its agencies to look beyond traditional mass-media advertising and to develop more creative ways of reaching automobile customers.[33]

The changes in agency compensation are also being driven by economic factors because most companies have cut their advertising and promotion budgets during the recession and are looking for ways to save money across all areas of their marketing programs. A recent survey conducted by the ANA found that 72 percent of marketers plan to reduce their advertising production budgets, 68 percent plan to challenge agencies to reduce internal expenses and/or identify cost reduction, and 48 percent

# IMC Perspective 3–2 > > >

## Agencies Face Off with Procurement Specialists

For many years Madison Avenue was a world unto itself. Advertising agencies were compensated based on a 15 percent commission on the media purchases they made for their clients: every time an ad appeared on television, played on radio, or was placed in a magazine, the cash registers rang on Madison Avenue. Agencies were dominated by "creatives" who came up with big ideas that could be translated into TV, print, radio, or billboard ads that would be run through these mass media to be seen or heard by the millions of consumers comprising the mass markets.

During the late 90s, the ad industry prospered, in large part due to the advertising frenzy driven by the Internet bubble, and many agencies were still able to get many of their clients to agree to pay them based on a percentage of their media billings. However, during the first decade of the new millennium, many major advertisers have done away with commissions entirely. The vast majority of clients now compensate their agencies by paying fees based on the agency's labor costs. To make matters more complicated, some companies now have their procurement officers negotiate contracts with their advertising agencies rather than their marketing or advertising managers. Many agencies are finding the procurement people to be much more difficult to negotiate with on issues such as their allocation of labor costs, employee salaries, overhead, and reasonable profit. The agencies argue that procurement departments really do not understand the advertising business and the role they play in brand building. Some agencies have tried to take a stand against clients who view them as vendors rather than marketing partners. However, other agencies are often willing to accept lower margins to gain new business, which has resulted in a loss of pricing power for many agencies. The intervention of procurement departments into the advertising process is also receiving a cold reception from many marketing executives who argue that the advertising process is different from sourcing raw materials for manufacturing. They note that creating ideas is different from creating widgets and also express concern over procurement executives and chief financial officers (CFOs) trying to take over the agency selection process. They argue that too much emphasis is put on policing the financial aspects of the client-agency relationship and advertising, and agency fees are viewed as an expense rather than an investment. Many marketing executives and the majority of those on the agency side feel that it is difficult to judge the value of an agency's work on the basis of the number of hours they log on a client's account but recognize that this is becoming the new model under which they must operate.

There is also a shift in the balance of power occurring within agencies. The ad industry is no longer dominated by the creatives as the media buying has become a more important and powerful area. Many of the holding companies have

plan to reduce agency compensation.[34] Most companies are also making their agencies more accountable for the fees they charge them for their services and many are now using procurement specialists to negotiate financial terms and contracts with their agencies. IMC Perspective 3–2 discusses the changes that are occurring in the agency business and how they are impacting agency compensation.

# EVALUATING AGENCIES

Given the substantial amounts of money being spent on advertising and promotion, demand for accountability of the expenditures has increased. Regular reviews of the agency's performance are necessary. The agency evaluation process usually involves two types of assessments, one financial and operational and the other more qualitative. The **financial audit** focuses on how the agency conducts its business. It is designed to verify costs and expenses, the number of personnel hours charged to an account, and payments to media and outside suppliers. The **qualitative audit** focuses on the agency's efforts in planning, developing, and implementing the client's advertising programs and considers the results achieved.

The agency evaluation is often done on a subjective, informal basis, particularly in smaller companies where ad budgets are low or advertising is not seen as the most critical factor in the firm's marketing performance. However some companies have developed formal, systematic evaluation systems, particularly when budgets are large and the advertising function receives much emphasis. The top spun off their media divisions into freestanding firms that handle only media buying. These large media-buying firms can use their size and clout to extract better media prices and cost savings for their clients. These media companies are also the major source of growth for their parent companies since clients have negotiated very thin margins in other areas.

The ascension of the media buyers into the powerful position in the advertising business is disrupting the old guard on Madison Avenue. The CEO of Carat North America, one of the largest media-buying companies, has stated, "We're getting to the point where the media plan is done first, and the creative is done behind it. This is a radical vision for the advertising business that would have been unheard of five years ago. We used to be the dorks. Now we're driving the whole advertising process." The media buyers are not immune, however, from the cost reduction pressures facing other areas of the agency business. For example, Levi Strauss & Co. held a $50 million contest for media planning and buying on its Levi's and Dockers brands whereby it sought invoices from the competing agencies that could be used to determine what their other clients were paying for national television and print media. If provided, this information could be used by Levi Strauss as leverage to negotiate similar pricing deals from the networks and publishers.

Some agencies are starting to resist the pressure from the client's procurement departments and are pushing back on efforts to reduce the fees for their services to a level where they are lower than the cost it takes to provide them. They argue that a client relationship that starts off losing money is not sustainable and that the companies need to respect the right of agencies to make a reasonable profit, just as they do. In late 2009 the JWT agency pulled out of a pitch for UPS's $200 million global advertising account citing frustration over drawn-out financial and contractual negotiations.

While agency executives may not like the changes that are occurring in the world of advertising, most recognize that they have little choice but to adapt to the changes. The involvement of clients' procurement departments is here to stay and one former agency executive's response to those who complain about it is "Welcome to the real world." He notes that most of those on the client side have had to deal with a purchasing department or hard-nosed buyer almost from the day they started work. Most clients no longer want traditional marketing approaches that rely on mass-media advertising. As a CEO of one agency notes, "Historically, agencies pushed clients. Today, clients are pushing agencies. The same-old, same-old is not being accepted."

Many persons working in the advertising industry argue that the two sides must find a way to work together. Agencies will have to continue to find ways to reduce their costs and accept smaller profit margins. However, they note that clients who continue to tighten the vise on their agencies may be cutting off their nose to spite their face as the quality of service they receive may suffer when the agency caves in to their demands.

Sources: Avi Dan, "Agencies Must Wake Up to a Different Business Model," adage.com, September 24, 2007; Chris Ingram "Time for ad world to meet the real world," *Advertising Age*, July 2, 2006, p. 14; Bradley Johnson, "Procurement, Marketing Don't See Eye to Eye," *Advertising Age*, May 9, 2005, pp. 3, 82; Rupal Parekh, "Fed-Up Shops Pitch a Fit at Procurement," *Advertising Age*, October 26, 2009, http://adage.com/print?article-id=139951; Michael Bush, "Levi's Review Asks Shops to Reveal Sensitive Price Data for Other Clients, *Advertising Age*, November 10, 2008, http://adage.com/print?article-id=132349.



management of these companies wants to be sure money is being spent efficiently and effectively. As the costs of advertising and other forms of promotion rise, more companies are adopting formal procedures for evaluating the performance of their agencies. For example, a 2009 survey conducted by the Association of National Advertisers found that 76 percent of marketers have a formal evaluation process for traditional creative agencies while 68 percent have one for traditional media agencies. The survey also found that qualitative performance is weighted more heavily than quantitative factors. Among the leading qualitative performance criteria identified in the survey were innovation, ideas, teamwork, meeting deadlines, strategy, and implementation. An interesting finding of the study was that formal reviews were much less likely to be conducted for digital, public relations, direct, and multicultural agencies.[35]

One example of a formal agency evaluation system is that used by Whirlpool, which markets a variety of consumer products. Whirlpool management meets once a year with the company's agencies to review their performance. Whirlpool managers complete an advertising agency performance evaluation, part of which is shown in Exhibit 3–9. These reports are compiled and reviewed with the agency at each annual meeting. Whirlpool's evaluation process covers six areas of performance. The company and the agency develop an action plan to correct areas of deficiency.

An important consideration in evaluating agencies is the *value* they provide to their client's business. In 2007, the American Association of Advertising Agencies and Association of National Advertisers conducted a major study to understand how both agencies and clients define value and the agency activities that provide the most value to the client's business.[36] The top seven dimensions of agency activity that

**CREATIVE SERVICES**

| Always | Often | Occasionally | Seldom | Never | NA | Marks Scored |
|---|---|---|---|---|---|---|
| 4 | 3 | 2 | 1 | 0 | | |

1. Agency produces fresh ideas and original approaches
2. Agency accurately interprets facts, strategies and objectives into usable advertisements and plans
3. Creative group is knowledgeable about company's products, markets and strategies
4. Creative group is concerned with good advertising communications and develops campaigns and ads that exhibit this concern
5. Creative group produces on time
6. Creative group performs well under pressure
7. Creative group operates in a businesslike manner to control production costs and other creative charges
8. Agency presentations are well organized with sufficient examples of proposed executions
9. Creative group participates in major campaign presentations
10. Agency presents ideas and executions not requested but felt to be good opportunities
11. Agency willingly accepts ideas generated by other locations/agency offices vs. being over-protective of its own creative product
12. Other areas not mentioned
13. Agency demonstrates commitment to client's business
14. Agency creative proposals are relevant and properly fulfill creative brief

Value—(marks)

| Rating: | | | |
|---|---|---|---|
| | Excellent | 90–100% | Total marks scored |
| | Good | 80–89% | |
| | Average | 70–79% | Total possible marks |
| | Fair | 60–69% | |
| | Poor | below 60% | Score |

**ACCOUNT REPRESENTATION & SERVICE**

| Always | Often | Occasionally | Seldom | Never | NA | Marks Scored |
|---|---|---|---|---|---|---|
| 4 | 3 | 2 | 1 | 0 | | |

1. Account representatives act with personal initiative
2. Account representatives anticipate needs in advance of direction by client (ie: are proactive)
3. Account group takes direction well
4. Agency is able to demonstrate results of programs implemented
5. Account representatives function strategically rather than as creative advisors only
6. Account representatives are knowledgeable about competitive programs and share this information along with their recommendations in a timely manner
7. Account representatives respond to client requests in a timely fashion
8. Account group operates in a business-like manner to control costs
9. Agency recommendations are founded on sound reasoning and supported factually, and appropriately fit within budget constraints
10. Agency is able to advise the client on trends and developments in technology
11. Account representatives demonstrate a high degree of professionalism in both written and oral communication
12. Agency presents ideas and executions not requested but felt to be good opportunities
13. Agency makes reasoned recommendations on allocation of budgets
14. Agency demonstrates commitment to client's business
15. There is a positive social relationship between client and agency

Value—(marks)

| Rating: | | | |
|---|---|---|---|
| | Excellent | 90–100% | Total marks scored |
| | Good | 80–89% | |
| | Average | 70–79% | Total possible marks |
| | Fair | 60–69% | |
| | Poor | below 60% | Score |

**EXHIBIT 3–9**
Whirlpool's Ad Agency Performance Evaluation

advertisers indicated add the most value to their business are shown in Figure 3–9. The study also considered how clients add value to the client-agency relationship and found that the key value drivers include understanding the brand's problems/opportunities, giving the agency the necessary time and resources to do its best work, articulating expected outcomes, giving clear direction, and providing constructive feedback.[37]

## Gaining and Losing Clients

The evaluation process described above provides valuable feedback to both the agency and the client, such as indicating changes that need to be made by the agency and/or the client to improve performance and make the relationship more productive. Many agencies have had very long-lasting relationships with their clients. For example, General Electric has been with the BBDO Worldwide agency for over 80 years. Other well-known companies or brands that have had long-lasting relationships include Marlboro/Leo Burnett (56 years), McDonald's/DDB Worldwide (43 years), and Kellogg's/Leo Burnett (68 years).

While many successful agency-client relationships go on for years, loyalty to a single agency is becoming less common as marketers seek new ways of connecting with consumers.[38] In recent years, a number of long-standing client relationships have been terminated. PepsiCo moved its Diet Pepsi account from BBDO to DDB Worldwide citing concerns over the creative work that was being done for the brand.

**FIGURE 3–9**

How Agencies Add Value to Client's Business

1. Developing and producing creative ideas that are fresh and appropriate.
2. Ensuring that agency disciplines and functions are integrated and that agency teams and divisions collaborate well on behalf of the client.
3. Working in a collaborative way with the client by creating an environment of low egos and high mutual respect.
4. Developing ideas and programs that can be integrated into multiple communication channels.
5. Assigning its best people to the client's business and making its top executives available when needed.
6. Evaluating brand drivers like awareness, consideration, and purchase intent.
7. Providing guidance and solutions in new media and technologies.

Source: "Report on the Agency-Advertiser Value Survey," American Association of Advertisers and Association of National Advertisers, August 2007.



Advertising for Diet Pepsi had been handled by BBDO since the brand was introduced in the 1960s. Although BBDO continues to handle advertising for other PepsiCo soft drink brands such as Pepsi-Cola, Mountain Dew, and Sierra Mist, the move is an example of how clients are willing to change agencies for underperforming brands. In 2010 State Farm Insurance shifted much of its creative work to DraftFCB from DDB Chicago which had handled all of the company's advertising for 70 years. DraftFCB had been handling the direct-marketing part of State Farm's IMC program over the past decade and used data-driven insights it had gained in developing a new campaign for State Farm that touts the insurers' size and competitive rates.[39]

Some companies switch agencies quite often in search of better creative work or for a variety of other reasons such as reorganizations that lead to changes in top management, changes in marketing or advertising strategy, or conflicts that might arise from mergers and acquisitions among both clients and agencies. A company may also switch agencies in order to consolidate all of its advertising and marketing efforts in one shop. A number of global marketers such as Samsung, IBM, Colgate, Microsoft, and others have reduced the number of agencies they work with in recent years as a way to gain more control over their marketing communications and create a consistent brand image worldwide.[40] IMC Perspective 3–3 discusses the decision by Hyundai Motor America to drop its highly regarded agency and move all of its advertising to an in-house agency that is a subsidiary of its parent company.

There are a number of reasons clients switch agencies. Understanding these potential problems can help the agency avoid them.[41] In addition, it is important to understand the process agencies go through in trying to win new clients.

**Why Agencies Lose Clients** Some of the more common reasons agencies lose clients follow:

- *Poor performance or service.* The client becomes dissatisfied with the quality of the advertising and/or the service provided by the agency.
- *Poor communication.* The client and agency personnel fail to develop or maintain the level of communication necessary to sustain a favorable working relationship.
- *Unrealistic demands by the client.* The client places demands on the agency that exceed the amount of compensation received and reduce the account's profitability.
- *Personality conflicts.* People working on the account on the client and agency sides do not have enough rapport to work well together.
- *Personnel changes.* A change in personnel at either the agency or the advertiser can create problems. New managers may wish to use an agency with which they have established ties. Agency personnel often take accounts with them when they switch agencies or start their own.

# IMC Perspective 3–3 > > >

## Hyundai Moves to a New Agency—Its Own

If you were to ask most consumers to name the fastest-growing automotive brand in the United States since 2000, it is likely they might mention companies such as Toyota, BMW, Mercedes, Honda, or Lexus. However, the answer is not a brand from Germany or Japan, but rather from the South Korean company Hyundai which entered the U.S. market in 1986 by offering small, affordable, entry level cars. After some initial success, Hyundai hit a speed bump as a result of some quality problems. However, the company took steps to improve the quality of its cars and started gaining traction in 1998 when it introduced the industry's first 100,000-mile warranty.

Over the past decade Hyundai Motor Co. has transformed itself from a manufacturer of low-end vehicles into a global leader in quality. In 2009 Hyundai ranked fourth best in the industry on the J.D. Powers & Associates Initial Quality Study, which serves as the industry benchmark for new vehicle quality measured after 90 days of ownership. Hyundai's focus on quality and safety, along with the introduction of new models such as the Santa Fe and Tucson SUVs, the upscale Genesis sedan and the redesigned midsize Sonata has paid off as its U.S. sales increased from 164,000 in 1999 to 435,000 in 2009, and its market share increased to 4.2 percent. While Hyundai's tremendous success in the U.S. market is a result of its focus on quality and customer satisfaction, it can also be attributed to an aggressive integrated marketing campaign that helped change the image of the brand as well as weather the worst economic crises since the Great Depression. Hyundai Motor America recognized that to continue to compete in the middle-to-upscale segment of the U.S. automotive market, the company had to develop a stronger brand image and move away from an association with low-end cars. In early 2007 Hyundai held an agency review and chose Goodby, Silverstein & Partners, San Francisco (GSP), as its new advertising agency and charged the agency with "moving the brand to a whole new place in consumers' heads."

A few months after being retained, GSP launched a new advertising campaign aimed at reframing the way U.S. consumers think about the Hyundai brand. The tagline for the campaign was "Think about It" and was designed to challenge consumers' perceptions about the brand as well as the way they think about cars in general with provocative questions and thoughts such as "Shouldn't a car have more airbags than cupholders?" and "The logo is there to tell you what the car is. Not who you are." Each ad also included the tagline "Think About It" and referred readers and viewers to a website, ThinkAboutIt.com, which provided more detailed information on the issue and presented evidence showing how Hyundai answered this challenge. In 2007 Hyundai sales reached 467,000 units, the highest since the company had entered the U.S. market.

In 2008 the U.S. economy was entering into recession and went into a tailspin in the last quarter of the year. Hyundai sales declined by 14 percent for the year and the Hyundai dealers were becoming disenchanted with Goodby's "Think about It" campaign. However, in January 2009 as the recession worsened, the company made a bold move by launching the Hyundai Assurance program which let buyers or lessees return their new vehicles if they lost their jobs. The

- *Changes in size of the client or agency.* The client may outgrow the agency or decide it needs a larger agency to handle its business. If the agency gets too large, the client may represent too small a percentage of its business to command attention.
- *Conflicts of interest.* A conflict may develop when an agency merges with another agency or when a client is part of an acquisition or merger. In the United States, an agency cannot handle two accounts that are in direct competition with each other. In some cases, even indirect competition will not be tolerated.
- *Changes in the client's corporate and/or marketing strategy.* A client may change its marketing strategy and decide that a new agency is needed to carry out the new program. As more companies adapt an integrated marketing communications approach, they are looking for agencies that have integrated capabilities and can handle more than just their media advertising.
- *Declining sales.* When sales of the client's product or service are stagnant or declining, advertising may be seen as contributing to the problem. A new agency may be sought for a new creative approach.
- *Conflicting compensation philosophies.* Disagreement may develop over the level or method of compensation. As more companies move toward incentive-based compensation systems, disagreement over compensation is becoming more commonplace.
- *Changes in policies.* Policy changes may result when either party reevaluates the importance of the relationship, the agency acquires a new (and larger) client, or either side undergoes a merger or acquisition.

program was launched with a high-profile commercial created by GSP that ran during the 2009 Super Bowl. Goodby and Hyundai's marketing team worked nonstop to develop the Assurance program, putting it all together in just 37 days from concept to running the commercial during the Super Bowl. Goodby also created a humorous commercial for the Super Bowl called "Bosses" which showed German- and Japanese-speaking automobile executives screaming at their underlings because the Hyundai Genesis had been named North American Car of the Year. Post-game surveys found that the spots significantly improved consumers' opinions of the Hyundai brand and the ads, along with the Assurance program, received extensive media coverage. Hyundai and Goodby kept the momentum going with an ad blitz during the *Academy Awards* in February and also signed a deal with Fox to place its vehicles in the hit show *24* and advertise during the show after Ford backed out. In 2009 Hyundai sales were up 8 percent even though overall industry sales were down by 21 percent as the U.S. auto market experienced one of its worst years ever. Hyundai's ability to adapt quickly to the changing economy and competitive marketplace led to the company being recognized as the 2009 Marketer of the Year by *Advertising Age*, the industry's leading trade publication.

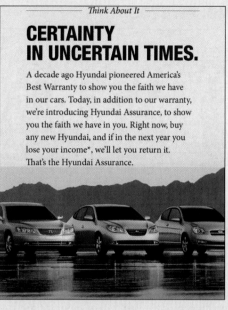

*Think About It*

**CERTAINTY IN UNCERTAIN TIMES.**

A decade ago Hyundai pioneered America's Best Warranty to show you the faith we have in our cars. Today, in addition to our warranty, we're introducing Hyundai Assurance, to show you the faith we have in you. Right now, buy any new Hyundai, and if in the next year you lose your income*, we'll let you return it. That's the Hyundai Assurance.

So one might think that Goodby, Silverstein & Partners had solidified its relationship with Hyundai Motors of America as a result of all of its hard work in helping build the Hyundai brand image and increase sales during the recession. Unfortunately this was not the case, as in April 2009 Hyundai dropped Goodby as its agency and moved all of the creative work for its national advertising, including digital, to Innocean Worldwide America. Innocean is the U.S. arm of the Seoul-based agency of the same name which is a subsidiary of the Korean parent company Hyundai Motor Group. A former Hyundai Motors of America executive said the reason for the change was that Hyundai wanted a cohesive and consistent brand image worldwide and that the home office wanted more control and influence over the marketing. While no other automakers in the United States currently have an in-house agency, the practice is common for South Korea's biggest conglomerates such as Hyundai and Samsung.

As for Goodby, the agency did what all agencies must do when they lose a major account. They began looking for new business and for another automotive account where they can utilize their market knowledge and creativity.

Sources: Kathy Jackson, "Hyundai Takes a 'Red Hot' Ride to the Top," *Advertising Age*, March 22, 2010; Jean Halliday, "Marketer of the Year: Hyundai," *Advertising Age*, November 9, 2009, pp. 1, 11; Jean Halliday, "Hyundai's In-house Agency Is Hiring But Finds Few Takers, *Advertising Age*, March 16, 2009, http://adage.com/print?article_id=155234; Jean Halliday, "Dealers Laud Hyundai Ads without Hyundais," *Advertising Age*, October 8, 2007, p.8.

- *Disagreements over marketing and/or creative strategy.* Agencies sometimes disagree with clients over the marketing strategy they want to pursue or the creative approach that might be best for the brand. For example, the Crispin Porter + Bogusky agency terminated relationships with several clients including Gateway and the Miller Brewing Co. over disagreements regarding marketing and creative strategy. The agency had developed a campaign for Miller Lite called "Man Laws" in which a group of men, including various former athletes and celebrities, came up with humorous rules for men who drink beer. However, Miller wanted to change the creative direction of the campaign to an effort more focused on the product and its attributes.[42]
- *Lack of integrated marketing capabilities.* Many clients are changing agencies in search of a shop with a broader range of capabilities across various integrated marketing communication areas or greater expertise in a particular area such as digital marketing. In some cases clients are looking for an agency that can provide more integrated marketing services under one roof. However, many marketers are moving toward an open source model whereby they hire agencies and other marketing communication partners on a project basis, based on their special talents and expertise.[43]

If the agency recognizes these warning signs, it can try to adapt its programs and policies to make sure the client is satisfied. Some of the situations discussed here are unavoidable, and others are beyond the agency's control. But to maintain the account, problems within the agency's control must be addressed.

The time may come when the agency decides it is no longer in its best interest to continue to work with the client. Personnel conflicts, changes in management philosophy, and/or insufficient financial incentives are just a few of the reasons for such a decision. Then the agency may terminate the account relationship.

**How Agencies Gain Clients** Competition for accounts in the agency business is intense, since most companies have already organized for the advertising function and only a limited number of new businesses require such services each year. While small agencies may be willing to work with a new company and grow along with it, larger agencies often do not become interested in these firms until they are able to spend at least $1 million per year on advertising. Many of the top agencies won't accept an account that spends less than $5 million per year. Once that expenditure level is reached, competition for the account intensifies.

In large agencies, most new business results from clients that already have an agency but decide to change their relationships. Thus, agencies must constantly search and compete for new clients. Some of the ways they do this follow.

**Referrals** Many good agencies obtain new clients as a result of referrals from existing clients, media representatives, and even other agencies. These agencies maintain good working relationships with their clients, the media, and outside parties that might provide business to them.

**Solicitations** One of the more common ways to gain new business is through direct solicitation. In smaller agencies, the president may solicit new accounts. In most large agencies, a new business development group seeks out and establishes contact with new clients. The group is responsible for writing solicitation letters, making cold calls, and following up on leads. The cutbacks in ad spending by many companies during the recent recession have resulted in many agencies pitching their services on an unsolicited basis to marketers who are satisfied with their agencies. Senior executives recognize that new business is the lifeblood of their agencies and are encouraging their business development teams to pursue advertisers who have not even put their accounts up for review.[44]

**Presentations** A basic goal of the new business development group is to receive an invitation from a company to make a presentation. This gives the agency the opportunity to sell itself—to describe its experience, personnel, capabilities, and operating procedures, as well as to demonstrate its previous work.

The agency may be asked to make a speculative presentation, in which it examines the client's marketing situation and proposes a tentative communications campaign. Because presentations require a great deal of time and preparation and may cost the agency a considerable amount of money without a guarantee of gaining the business, many firms refuse to participate in "creative shootouts." They argue that agencies should be selected on the basis of their experience and the services and programs they have provided for previous clients. Nevertheless, most agencies do participate in this form of solicitation, either by choice or because they must do so to gain accounts.

**EXHIBIT 3–10**
Crispin Porter + Bogusky is known for its excellent creative work for clients such as Burger King

Due in part to the emphasis on speculative presentations, a very important role has developed for *ad agency review consultants,* who specialize in helping clients choose ad agencies. These consultants are often used to bring an objective perspective to the agency review process and to assist advertisers who may lack the resources, experience, or organizational consensus needed to successfully conduct a review. The use of search consultants is increasing as studies have shown that they are used in 30 to 40 percent of the agency reviews where the ad budget for the account is worth $10 million or more.[45] Because their opinions are respected by clients, the entire agency review process may be structured according to their guidelines. However, one study found that while many companies use search consultants to help them with their reviews, they do not always have a direct influence on the final decision regarding which agency they hire.[46]

**Public Relations** Agencies also seek business through publicity/public relations efforts. They often participate in civic and social groups and work with charitable organizations pro bono (at cost, without pay) to earn respect in the community. Participation in professional associations such as the American Association of Advertising Agencies and the Advertising Research Foundation can also lead to new contacts. Successful agencies often receive free publicity throughout the industry as well as in the mass media.

**Image and Reputation** Perhaps the most effective way an agency can gain new business is through its reputation for doing excellent work for the clients it serves. Word travels fast through the advertising and marketing industry regarding the agencies that are doing outstanding creative work in advertising as well as in other areas of IMC. There are many award competitions in which advertisers may enter their work and have it recognized. For example, the Effie Awards are given each year to IMC campaigns based on the results they achieve as well as the strategy that goes into creating them. There are many other awards that recognize outstanding advertising creativity as well as work done in specific areas such as media planning and strategy, digital media, public relations and sales promotion.

The major industry publications such as *Advertising Age* and *Adweek* also recognize the top agencies based on the quality of their work.[47] One of the most recognized agencies in recent years is Crispin Porter + Bogusky which has been selected as Agency of the Year twice in the past five years by both *Advertising Age* as well as *Adweek*.[48] CP + B has been one of the hottest agencies in the business based on its outstanding creative work and the nontraditional approach to advertising and IMC that it has taken for clients such as Burger King, Coke Zero, Microsoft, and Domino's Pizza. An example of the agency's excellent creative work is the innovative campaign it created for Burger King in which CP + B worked with Microsoft to create a series of video games for the Xbox 360 (Exhibit 3–10). The games were made available for $3.99 with the purchase of a BK Value Meal and more than 3 million copies were sold, leading to significant increases in store traffic and sales.[49]

## SPECIALIZED SERVICES

Many companies assign the development and implementation of their promotional programs to an advertising agency. But several other types of organizations provide specialized services that complement the efforts of ad agencies. Direct-response

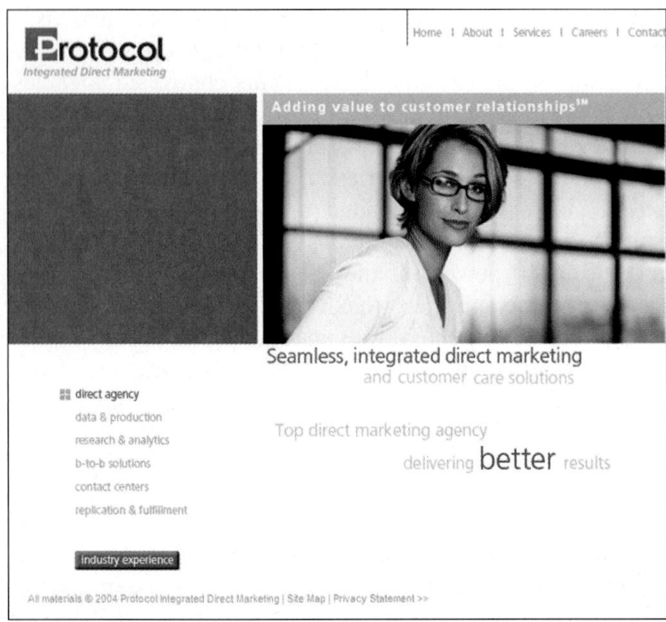


**EXHIBIT 3–11**
Protocol promotes its direct-marketing services

agencies, sales promotion agencies, and public relations firms are important to marketers in developing and executing IMC programs in the United States as well as international markets. Let us examine the functions these organizations perform.

## Direct-Marketing Agencies

One of the fastest-growing areas of IMC is direct marketing, where companies communicate with consumers through telemarketing, direct mail, television, the Internet, and other forms of direct-response advertising. As this industry has grown, numerous direct-response agencies have evolved that offer companies their specialized skills in both consumer and business markets. Many of the top direct-marketing agencies such as Rapp Collins Worldwide, Draft, Wunderman, and OgilvyOne are subsidiaries of large agency holding companies. However, there are also a number of independent direct-marketing agencies including those that serve large companies as well as smaller firms that handle the needs of local companies (Exhibit 3–11).

**Direct-marketing agencies** provide a variety of services, including database management, direct mail, research, media services, and creative and production capabilities. While direct mail is their primary weapon, many direct-response agencies are expanding their services to include such areas as infomercial production and database management. Database development and management is becoming one of the most important services provided by direct-response agencies. Many companies are using database marketing to pinpoint new customers and build relationships and loyalty among existing customers.

A typical direct-response agency is divided into three main departments: account management, creative, and media. Some agencies also have a department whose function is to develop and manage databases for their clients. The account managers work with their clients to plan direct-marketing programs and determine their role in the overall integrated marketing communications process. The creative department consists of copywriters, artists, and producers. Creative is responsible for developing the direct-response message, while the media department is concerned with its placement.

Like advertising agencies, direct-response agencies must solicit new business and have their performance reviewed by their existing clients, often through formal assessment programs. Most direct-response agencies are compensated on a fee basis.

## Sales Promotion Agencies

Developing and managing sales promotion programs such as contests, sweepstakes, refunds and rebates, premium and incentive offers, and sampling programs are very complex tasks. Most companies use a **sales promotion agency** to develop and administer these programs. Some large ad agencies have created their own sales promotion department or acquired a sales promotion firm. However, most sales promotion agencies are independent companies that specialize in providing the services needed to plan, develop, and execute a variety of sales promotion programs.

Sales promotion agencies often work in conjunction with the client's advertising and/or direct-response agencies to coordinate their efforts with the advertising and direct-marketing programs. Services provided by large sales promotion agencies include promotional planning, creative research, tie-in coordination, fulfillment, premium design and manufacturing, catalog production, and contest/sweepstakes

**EXHIBIT 3–12**
Don Jagoda Associates is one of the leading promotional agencies

management. Many sales promotion agencies are also developing direct/database marketing and telemarketing to expand their integrated marketing services capabilities. Sales promotion agencies are generally compensated on a fee basis. Exhibit 3–12 shows a page from the website of Don Jagoda Associates, one of the leading sales promotion agencies.

## Public Relations Firms

Many large companies use both an advertising agency and a PR firm. The **public relations firm** develops and implements programs to manage the organization's publicity, image, and affairs with consumers and other relevant publics, including employees, suppliers, stockholders, government, labor groups, citizen action groups, and the general public. The PR firm analyzes the relationships between the client and these various publics, determines how the client's policies and actions relate to and affect these publics, develops PR strategies and programs, implements these programs using various public relations tools, and evaluates their effectiveness.

The activities of a public relations firm include planning the PR strategy and program, generating publicity, conducting lobbying and public affairs efforts, becoming involved in community activities and events, preparing news releases and other communications, conducting research, promoting and managing special events, and managing crises. As companies adopt an IMC approach to promotional planning, they are increasingly coordinating their PR activities with advertising and other promotional areas. Many companies are integrating public relations and publicity into the marketing communications mix to increase message credibility and save media costs.[50] Public relations firms are generally compensated by retainer. We will examine their role in more detail in Chapter 17.

## Interactive Agencies

With the rapid growth of the Internet and other forms of interactive media, a new type of specialized marketing communications organization has evolved—the interactive agency. Many marketers are using **interactive agencies** that specialize in the development and strategic use of various interactive marketing tools such as websites for the Internet, banner ads, search engine optimization, mobile marketing, and social media campaigns. They recognize that the development of successful interactive marketing programs requires expertise in technology as well as areas such as creative website design, database marketing, digital media, and customer relationship management. Many traditional advertising agencies have established interactive capabilities, ranging from a few specialists within the agency to an entire interactive division. Some of the largest interactive agencies such as EuroRSCG 4D and Ogilvy Interactive are affiliates of major agencies, while others such as Agency.com, Organic, and R/GA are owned by major holding companies. Many agencies work closely with their interactive affiliates in developing integrated marketing campaigns for their clients. For example, the interactive arm of the Deutsch agency, has developed the websites and online campaigns for clients such as Volkswagen, Snapple, Almay, and the California Milk Advisory Board; the parent agency handles the off-line campaign in traditional media for these companies.

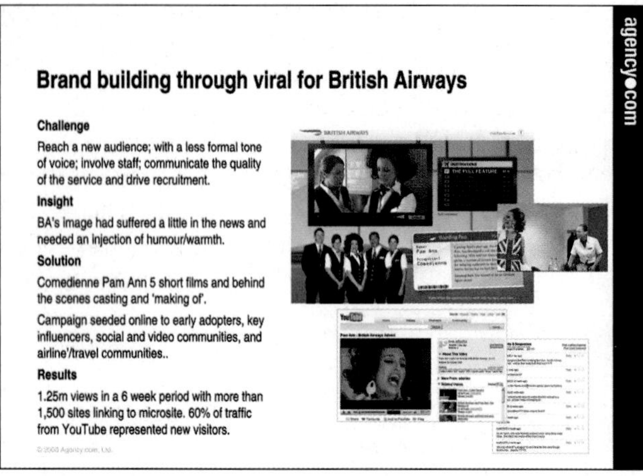

agency●com
Brand building through viral for British Airways
Challenge
Reach a new audience; with a less formal tone of voice; involve staff; communicate the quality of the service and drive recruitment.
Insight
BA's image had suffered a little in the news and needed an injection of humour/warmth.
Solution
Comedienne Pam Ann 5 short films and behind the scenes casting and 'making of'.
Campaign seeded online to early adopters, key influencers, social and video communities, and airline'/travel communities..
Results
1.25m views in a 6 week period with more than 1,500 sites linking to microsite. 60% of traffic from YouTube represented new visitors.

**EXHIBIT 3–13**
Agency.com has developed online promotions for clients such as British Airways

While many agencies have or are developing interactive capabilities, a number of marketers are turning to more specialized interactive agencies to develop websites and interactive media. They feel these companies have more expertise in designing and developing websites as well as managing and supporting them. Interactive agencies range from smaller companies that specialize in website design and creation to full-service interactive agencies that provide all the elements needed for a successful Internet/interactive marketing program. These services include strategic consulting regarding the use of the Internet and online branding, technical knowledge, systems integration, and the development of electronic commerce capabilities.

Full-service interactive agencies, such as Agency.com, have created successful Internet marketing programs for a number of companies, including Nike, MetLife, Hewlett-Packard, McDonald's, and British Airways. For example, Agency.com developed the website and various online promotions that support the global brand positioning strategy for British Airways (Exhibit 3–13). As the Internet becomes an increasingly important marketing tool, more companies will be turning to interactive agencies to help them develop successful interactive marketing programs. The growth of social media and the increase in the number of marketers using them is giving rise to companies that specialize in developing applications and campaigns for platforms such as Facebook, MySpace, and Twitter. For example, AvenueSocial is a four-year-old company that specializes in creating social media applications utilizing Facebook and has developed campaigns for a number of companies and brands such as Universal Pictures, Naked Juice, Pringles, and LG (Exhibit 3–14). The number of interactive agencies will continue to grow, as will their importance in the development and implementation of Internet-based strategies and initiatives.

**EXHIBIT 3–14**
AvenueSocial specializes in developing campaigns utilizing social media

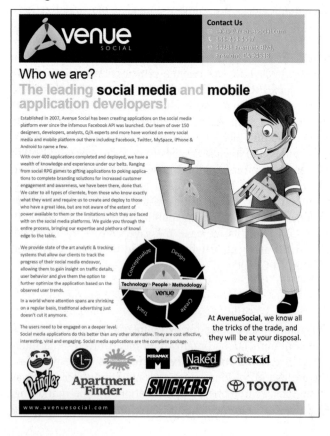

## COLLATERAL SERVICES

The final participants in the promotional process are those that provide various collateral services. They include marketing research companies, package design firms, consultants, photographers, printers, video production houses, and event marketing services companies. One of the more widely used collateral service organizations is the marketing research firm. Companies are increasingly turning to marketing research to help them understand their target audiences and to gather information that will be of value in designing and evaluating their advertising and promotions programs. Even companies with their own marketing research departments often hire outside research agencies to perform some services. Marketing research companies offer specialized services and can gather objective information that is valuable to the advertiser's promotional programs. They conduct *qualitative* research such as in-depth interviews and focus groups, as well as *quantitative* studies such as market surveys.



# INTEGRATED MARKETING COMMUNICATIONS SERVICES

You have seen that marketers can choose from a variety of specialized organizations to assist them in planning, developing, and implementing an integrated marketing communications program. But companies must decide whether to use a different organization for each marketing communications function or consolidate them with a large advertising agency that offers all of these services under one roof.

As noted previously in the chapter, during the 1980s and 90s, many of the large agencies realized that their clients were shifting their promotional dollars away from traditional advertising to other forms of promotion and began developing IMC capabilities. Some did this through mergers and acquisitions and became superagencies consisting of advertising, public relations, sales promotion, and direct-response agencies. Many large agencies are continuing to expand their IMC capabilities by acquiring specialists in various fields. All the major agency holding companies either own or have substantial investments in interactive, sales promotion, and direct-marketing agencies as well as public relations firms.

## Pros and Cons of Integrated Services

It has been argued that the concept of integrated marketing is nothing new, particularly in smaller companies and communication agencies that have been coordinating a variety of promotional tools for years. And larger advertising agencies have been trying to gain more of their clients' promotional business for over 20 years. However, in the past, the various services were run as separate profit centers. Each was motivated to push its own expertise and pursue its own goals rather than develop truly integrated marketing programs. Moreover, the creative specialists in many agencies resisted becoming involved in sales promotion or direct marketing. They preferred to concentrate on developing magazine ads or television commercials rather than designing coupons or direct-mail pieces.

Proponents of integrated marketing services contend that past problems are being solved and the various individuals in the agencies and subsidiaries are learning to work together to deliver a consistent message to the client's customers. They argue that maintaining control of the entire promotional process achieves greater synergy among each of the communications program elements. They also note that it is more convenient for the client to coordinate all of its marketing efforts—media advertising, direct mail, special events, sales promotions, and public relations—through one agency. An agency with integrated marketing capabilities can create a single image for the product or service and address everyone, from wholesalers to consumers, with one voice.

But not everyone wants to turn the entire IMC program over to one agency. Opponents say the providers become involved in political wrangling over budgets, do not communicate with each other as well and as often as they should, and do not achieve synergy. They also claim that agencies' efforts to control all aspects of the promotional program are nothing more than an attempt to hold on to business that might otherwise be lost to independent providers. They note that synergy and economies of scale, while nice in theory, have been difficult to achieve and competition and conflict among agency subsidiaries have been a major problem.[51]

Many companies use a variety of vendors for communication functions, choosing the specialist they believe is best suited for each promotional task, be it advertising, sales promotion, or public relations. While many ad agencies are working to master integration and compete against one another, they still must compete against firms that offer specialized services. As marketing consultant Jack Trout notes, "As long as there are a lot of specialized players, integrating an agency will be tricky. Specialists walk in the door and say 'this is all we do and we're good at it,' which is a hell of an argument. An agency that has all marketing operations in-house will never be perceived as the best in breed."[52]

The already complex client-agency relationship is becoming even more challenging as a result of several other factors such as the reduction in marketing budgets stemming from the recession and the accompanying desire of companies to reduce the cost of their IMC programs; and the rise of social media, mobile marketing, and other nontraditional forms of communication. A new study by Forrester Research called "The Future of Agency Relationship" suggests that one of the biggest challenges facing marketers today is knowing who to turn to when they want to change their advertising and/or IMC strategies. The study notes that many of the major agencies are trying to bundle all of the traditional and nontraditional services together and position themselves as being able to offer all of them.[53] However, the more likely scenario is that marketers will have a number of agencies from different areas working on their business and it is important that they get them to work together. They also must decide who is going to be in charge of managing and coordinating the IMC program.

## Responsibility for IMC: Agency versus Client

Surveys of advertisers and agency executives have shown that both groups believe integrated marketing is important to their organizations' success and that it will be even more important in the future.[54] However, marketers and agency executives have very different opinions regarding who should be in charge of the integrated marketing communications process. Many advertisers prefer to set strategy for and coordinate their own IMC campaigns, but some agency executives see this as their domain.

While agency executives believe their shops are capable of handling the various elements an integrated campaign requires, many marketers, particularly larger firms, disagree. Marketing executives say the biggest obstacle to implementing IMC is the lack of people with the broad perspective and skills to make it work. Internal turf battles, agency egos, and fear of budget reductions are also cited as major barriers to successful integrated marketing campaigns.[55] A study of agency and marketing executives regarding integrated marketing found that the most challenging aspect of integration is ensuring that the strategy is executed consistently in all forms along with measuring the success of different aspects of an IMC campaign. The survey also found that compensation of integrated programs is a problem as each communication discipline has a different cost structure.[56]

A study by the Corporate Executive Board's Advertising and Marketing Roundtable surveyed the heads of advertising and marketing communication departments at global companies as well as agency executives regarding the use of multiple agency partners. The study found that "the traditional, static model of a single ad agency or a fixed roster of agencies working on a brand is being supplanted by an open-source model for some marketers. Under this model, marketers hire numerous disparate marketing partners—sometimes on a project basis—to leverage their special talents and expertise as needed."[57] The CEB report notes that clients will increasingly be relegating their lead agencies to be brand stewards and coordinators of a network of specialists in various IMC areas.

Many advertising agencies do not accept the premise that they must accept a new role as stewards and coordinators of specialists. These agencies still view themselves as strategic and executional partners and are adding more resources to offer their clients a full line of services. They are expanding their agencies' capabilities in interactive and multimedia advertising, database management, direct marketing, public relations, and sales promotion. However, many marketers still want to set the strategy for their IMC campaigns and seek specialized expertise, more quality and creativity, and greater control and cost efficiency by using multiple providers. Steven Center, the Chief Marketing Officer for Honda of America, takes a position that is probably shared by most top marketing executives. He notes that "Agencies are exposed to much more than us, and they have to bring in raw ideas, market reconnaissance, and intelligence. But they will not tell us how to organize our company to accomplish our marketing mission. That responsibility should always fall entirely with the owner of the brand."[58]



## Summary

The development, execution, and administration of an advertising and promotions program involve the efforts of many individuals, both within the company and outside it. Participants in the integrated marketing communications process include the advertiser or client, ad agencies, media organizations, specialized marketing communications firms, and providers of collateral services.

Companies use three basic systems to organize internally for advertising and promotion. Centralized systems offer the advantages of facilitated communications, lower personnel requirements, continuity in staff, and more top-management involvement. Disadvantages include a lower involvement with overall marketing goals, longer response times, and difficulties in handling multiple product lines.

Decentralized systems offer the advantages of concentrated managerial attention, more rapid responses to problems, and increased flexibility, though they may be limited by ineffective decision making, internal conflicts, misallocation of funds, and a lack of authority. In-house agencies, while offering the advantages of cost savings, control, and increased coordination, have the disadvantage of less experience, objectivity, and flexibility.

Many firms use advertising agencies to help develop and execute their programs. These agencies may take on a variety of forms, including full-service agencies, creative boutiques, and media buying services. The first offers the client a full range of services (including creative, account, marketing, and financial and management services); the other two specialize in creative services and media buying, respectively. Agencies are compensated through commission systems, percentage charges, and fee—and cost-based systems. Recently, the emphasis on agency accountability has increased. Agencies are being evaluated on both financial and qualitative aspects, and some clients are using incentive-based compensation systems that tie agency compensation to performance measures such as sales and market share.

In addition to using ad agencies, marketers use the services of other marketing communication specialists, including direct-marketing agencies, sales promotion agencies, public relations firms, and interactive agencies. A marketer must decide whether to use a different specialist for each promotional function or have all of its integrated marketing communications done by an advertising agency that offers all of these services under one roof.

Recent studies have found that most marketers believe it is their responsibility, not the ad agency's, to set strategy for and coordinate IMC campaigns. The lack of a broad perspective and specialized skills in nonadvertising areas are seen as major barriers to agencies' increased involvement in integrated marketing communications.

## Key Terms

**clients** p. 69
**advertising agency** p. 69
**media organizations** p. 70
**specialized marketing communications services** p. 70
**collateral services** p. 70
**advertising manager** p. 71
**centralized system** p. 71
**decentralized system** p. 72
**brand manager** p. 72
**category management system** p. 74
**in-house agency** p. 75
**billings** p. 79
**superagencies** p. 80
**full-service agency** p. 82
**account executive** p. 82
**account planners** p. 83
**copywriters** p. 85
**departmental system** p. 86
**group system** p. 86
**creative boutique** p. 87
**media specialist companies** p. 87
**commission system** p. 88
**negotiated commission** p. 89
**fixed-fee method** p. 90
**fee-commission combination** p. 90
**cost-plus system** p. 90
**incentive-based system** p. 90
**percentage charges** p. 91
**financial audit** p. 92
**qualitative audit** p. 92
**direct-marketing agencies** p. 100
**sales promotion agency** p. 100
**public relations firm** p. 101
**interactive agencies** p. 101

## Discussion Questions

1. The opening vignette discusses how Under Armour has been able to grow its sales and build a strong brand by doing all of its advertising creative and other IMC work in-house rather than using an outside agency. Discuss why a company like Under Armour would prefer to do all of its advertising and promotion internally rather than using an outside agency. Do you think they will continue to handle all of their advertising and IMC work in-house? Why or why not? (LO1)

2. Who are the various participants in the integrated marketing communications process? Briefly discuss the roles and responsibilities of each. (LO1)

3. Discuss the various challenges faced by companies that use the brand management system when organizing for advertising and promotion. What are some of the things that marketers can do to address these problems and ensure that their brand managers are keeping abreast of external changes occurring in the market? (LO2)

4. Discuss the pros and cons of using an in-house advertising agency. What are some of the reasons why companies might change from using an in-house agency and hire an outside agency? (LO2)

5. What is an agency holding company? Discuss how the emergence of major holding companies is impacting the advertising industry as well as the entire field of integrated marketing communications. (LO3)

6. IMC Perspective 3–2 discusses the changing role of account representatives in advertising agencies. Discuss how the role of account representatives is changing and the developments that underlie these changes. Do you think account representatives will become obsolete in the future? Why or why not? (LO3)

7. Discuss the role of media specialist companies. Why are marketers likely to use a media specialist company to handle their media buying and planning versus the media department of an agency? (LO3)

8. Discuss the challenges advertising agencies face in negotiating compensation structures with their clients when the procurement department becomes involved in the process. How might an agency respond to clients who demand to see their labor costs, overhead, and profit margins as part of the negotiation process? (LO4)

9. Discuss the various criteria that might be used by an automobile company such as Ford or Honda in evaluating its advertising agencies. Which of these criteria do you think would receive the most weight and why? (LO4)

10. Discuss the reasons why advertising agencies lose accounts. Find an example of a company that changed advertising agencies and identify the factors that led them to switch to another agency. (LO4)

11. Discuss the pros and cons for a marketer having one company handle all of its integrated marketing communication needs versus using specialized marketing communication firms to handle the various components of the program. (LO5, 6)

## AdForum Exercise: "Evaluating the work of an in-house Agency"

adforum.com

(See Advertising and Promotion Playlist, Chapter 3)

IMC Perspective 3–3 discusses the decision made by Hyundai Motors of America to move all of its advertising for its Hyundai brand to an in-house agency. Innocean is the United States arm of its Seoul-based agency of the same name, which is a subsidiary of the Korean parent company Hyundai Motor group. Watch four of the commercials created by Innocean for Hyundai that are provided in the Advertising and Promotion playlist for Chapter 3 and answer the following questions.

1 How would you evaluate the quality of the commercials created by Innocean for Hyundai Motors of America? How do they compare to the quality of the ads that you see for other brands of automobiles?

2 Discuss the role television advertising plays in the marketing of automobile brands such as Hyundai? How do these commercials contribute to achieving the objectives an automotive company such as Hyundai might have for it's media advertising component of its IMC program?

3 Hyundai has been the fastest growing automobile company in the U.S. market over the past five years. Discuss how the commercials created by Innocean might be contributing to the success of Hyundai.

Access to the chapter playlist is available through Mc Graw Hill connect | MARKETING, www.mcgrawhillconnect.com

## LEARNING OBJECTIVES

LO1 To understand the role consumer behavior plays in the development and implementation of advertising and promotional programs.

LO2 To understand the consumer decision-making process and how it varies for different types of purchases.

LO3 To understand various internal psychological processes, their influence on consumer decision making, and implications for advertising and promotion.

LO4 To recognize the various approaches to studying the consumer learning process and their implications for advertising and promotion.

LO5 To recognize external factors such as culture, social class, group influences, and situational determinants and how they affect consumer behavior.

LO6 To understand alternative approaches to studying consumer behavior.

# 4 Perspectives on Consumer Behavior

## "SHOPPER MARKETING" TAKES MARKETING AND CONSUMER RESEARCH BACK TO THE STORE

Marketers never stop in their attempts to understand consumer behaviors. Using research methods including everything from surveys and focus groups to brain scans, consumer researchers continue to gather information that will allow them to better market their products. Recently, this research has resulted in marketers taking an increased focus on what they term as "shopper marketing"—that is, efforts targeted to consumers at the point of purchase.

Studies and conventional wisdom have led marketers to believe that as much as 70 to 80 percent of purchase decisions may take place in the store. However, as a result of a number of factors, including the long drawn-out recession, impulse purchases may be on the decline, (one study says as low as 40 percent) as consumers are more careful in planning how to spend their money—creating shopping lists at home, searching for bargains, and not overspending—in order to get more value for their buck. While much of the focus is on price savings, brand familiarity remains an important decision criterion. As a result, a number of companies are not quite ready to give up on "in-store" marketing efforts, and have turned to an in-store focus to help them improve the marketability of their brands. It is estimated that companies spend about $3 to $18 billion on shopper marketing, and will continue to increase these expenditures.

Colgate has achieved great success with its SoftSoap brand in the very competitive body-wash category, despite spending less than $5 million in advertising. Rekha Rako, marketing director for Colgate personal care products, attributes the success to the fact that "Our packaging is our No. 1 touch point with the consumer," and this is where much of Colgate's marketing efforts focus. Over the past four years, ConAgra has doubled its integrated-customer marketing team, which has included more shopper marketing, shopper insights, category leadership, and in-store marketing, while Proctor & Gamble has also refocused its marketing efforts to put more emphasis on in-store marketing. And, the new in-store focus is not confined to the supermarket industry. Running shoe company New Balance has shifted its focus to in-store efforts including signage, shelf talkers, and appearances by "New Balance Total Fit" specialists (who help insure that one gets the best fitting running shoe), with much success.

Along with the increase in in-store marketing efforts, has come an increase in consumer research—some of which has raised eyebrows to say the least. Take Campbell's Soup Co., for example. The company conducted traditional interviews, checked pulse and respiration rates, and used eye tracking studies in an attempt to increase the consumer's emotional response to their labels. As a result of research, they have also redesigned store shelf systems to make their soup easier to find. Kraft has utilized neuromarketing, as well as emotional studies to discover that moms have a "deep rooted psychological attachment" to its macaroni and cheese as well as to shopping for their children in general. (Kraft developed "mom cues" throughout stores to depict enjoyment, togetherness, and satisfaction, to reinforce these feelings.) Saatchi X, a worldwide advertising agency, now has a psychologist and an anthropologist on staff to assist in understanding consumers' emotional actions and reactions at the purchase site.

One research method has raised concerns among consumers as well as privacy advocates. The estimate is that over a hundred research companies now offer marketers the ability to watch buyers shop on a video camera without their knowledge. A provider of the cameras says there are now over 50,000 of them in stores throughout the world and almost every major chain including Walmart and Best Buy use them. The cameras monitor store traffic, engagement, body language, dwell time, and the selection process. They can also track how a consumer navigates through the store, observe age and gender, and just about anything else customers do while in the store. The retailers say they use the surveillance data to manage store operations and marketing and to improve overall customer satisfaction.

Privacy advocates contend that while the surveillance is not illegal, it is at the very least unethical. They note that people are being observed as though they were lab rats, and the data can be used to manipulate consumers. They are concerned that the videos will be used to identify individuals through facial recognition technologies. But mostly they don't like the fact that people are being watched without knowing it.

Nevertheless, providers of cameras and sensor systems say the surveillance industry is in its infancy, and is the research industry's "next area to explode." One way or another.

Sources: Stephanie Rosenbloom, "In Bid to Sway Sales, Cameras Track Shoppers," www.nytimes.com, March 19, 2010; Emily Bryson York, "Shopping Aisles at Cutting Edge of Consumer Research and Tech," www.adage.com, March 15, 2010; Jack Neff, "P & G Taking Its Marketing Back to the Store, www.adage.com, September 21, 2009; Jeremy Mullman, "In-store Focus Fits New Balance", www.adage.com, March 23, 2009; Jack Neff, "Trouble in Store for Shopper Marketing?", www.adage.com, March 2, 2009.

The introduction to this chapter demonstrates how much importance marketers place on consumer research to guide their marketing strategies. Marketers know that many factors may directly or indirectly influence consumers' decision making. What is important for them to know is how and why consumers' needs develop, what they are, and who is likely to use the product or service. Specifically, marketers will study consumer behaviors in an attempt to understand the many factors that lead to and impact purchase decisions. Often, in an attempt to gain insights, marketers will employ techniques borrowed from other disciplines. Research methods used in psychology, anthropology, sociology, and neuroscience are becoming more popular in businesses as managers attempt to explore consumers' purchasing motives. These motives along with consumers' attitudes, lifestyles, and decision-making processes need to be understood before effective marketing strategies can be formulated.

These are just a few of the aspects of consumer behavior that promotional planners must consider in developing integrated marketing communications programs. As you will see, consumer choice is influenced by a variety of factors.

It is beyond the scope of this text to examine consumer behavior in depth. However, promotional planners need a basic understanding of consumer decision making, factors that influence it, and how this knowledge can be used in developing promotional strategies and programs. We begin with an overview of consumer behavior.

# AN OVERVIEW OF CONSUMER BEHAVIOR

A challenge faced by all marketers is how to influence the purchase behavior of consumers in favor of the product or service they offer. For companies like Visa, this means getting consumers to charge more purchases on their credit cards. For BMW, it means getting them to purchase or lease a car; for business-to-business marketers like Xerox or FedEx, it means getting organizational buyers to purchase more of their office products or use their services. While their ultimate goal is to influence consumers' purchase behavior, most marketers understand that the actual purchase is only part of an overall process.

**Consumer behavior** can be defined as the process and activities people engage in when searching for, selecting, purchasing, using, evaluating, and disposing of products and services so as to satisfy their needs and desires. For many products and services, purchase decisions are the result of a long, detailed process that may include an extensive information search, brand comparisons and evaluations, and other activities. Other purchase decisions are more incidental and may result from

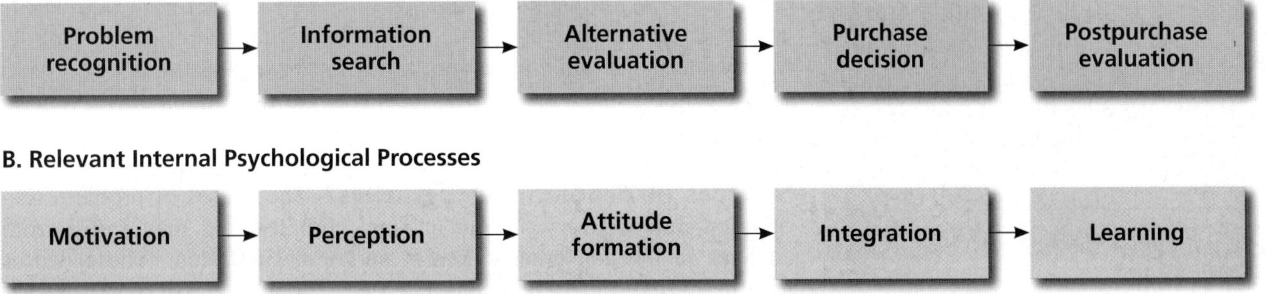


**FIGURE 4–1**
A Basic Model of Consumer Decision Making

little more than seeing a product prominently displayed at a discount price in a store. Think of how many times you have made impulse purchases while in the store.

Marketers' success in influencing purchase behavior depends in large part on how well they understand consumer behavior. Marketers need to know the specific needs customers are attempting to satisfy and how they translate into purchase criteria. They need to understand how consumers gather information regarding various alternatives and use this information to select among competing brands, and how they make purchase decisions. Where do they prefer to buy a product? How are they influenced by marketing stimuli at the point of purchase? Marketers also need to understand how the consumer decision process and reasons for purchase vary among different types of customers. For example, purchase decisions may be influenced by the personality or lifestyle of the consumer. Notice how the ad shown in Exhibit 4–1 portrays a product for the beachgoer lifestyle.

The conceptual model in Figure 4–1 will be used as a framework for analyzing the consumer decision process. We will discuss what occurs at the various stages of this model and how advertising and promotion can be used to influence decision making. We will also examine the influence of various psychological concepts, such as motivation, perception, attitudes, and integration processes. Variations in the consumer decision-making process will be explored, as will perspectives regarding consumer learning and external influences on the consumer decision process. The chapter concludes with a consideration of alternative means of studying consumer behavior.

**EXHIBIT 4–1**
Tommy Bahama appeals to the beach/island lifestyle

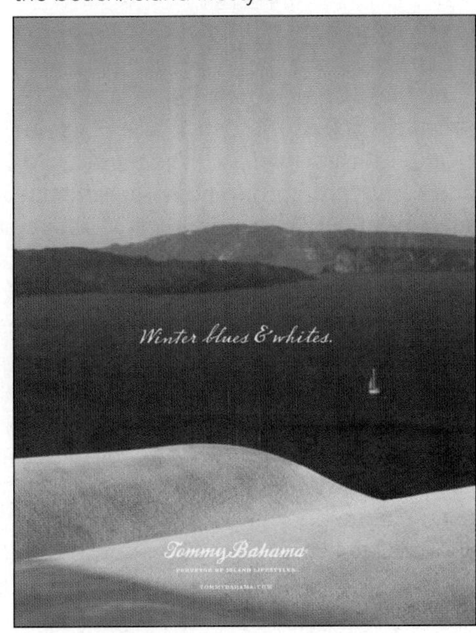


# THE CONSUMER DECISION-MAKING PROCESS

As shown in Figure 4–1, the consumer's purchase decision process is generally viewed as consisting of stages through which the buyer passes in purchasing a product or service. This model shows that decision making involves a number of internal psychological processes. Motivation, perception, attitude formation, integration, and learning are important to promotional planners, since they influence the general decision-making process of the consumer. We will examine each stage of the purchase decision model and discuss how the various subprocesses influence what occurs at this phase of the consumer behavior process. We will also discuss how promotional planners can influence this process.

## Problem Recognition

Figure 4–1 shows that the first stage in the consumer decision-making process is **problem recognition**, which occurs when the consumer perceives a need and becomes motivated to solve the problem. The problem recognition stage initiates the subsequent decision processes.

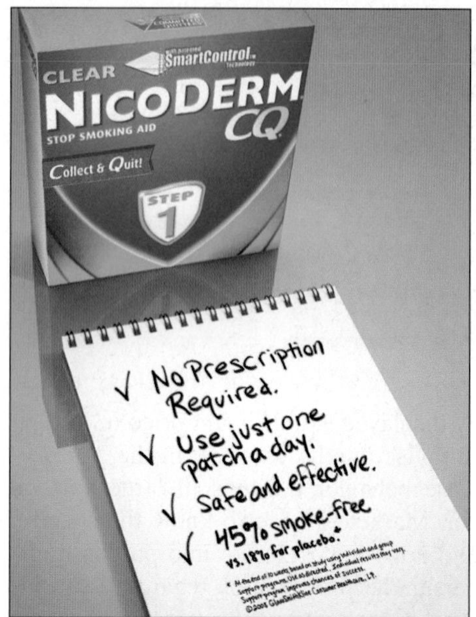


**EXHIBIT 4–2**
Nicoderm offers to help those who want to quit smoking

Problem recognition is caused by a difference between the consumer's *ideal state* and *actual state.* A discrepancy exists between what the consumer wants the situation to be like and what the situation is really like. (Note that *problem* does not always imply a negative state. A goal exists for the consumer, and this goal may be the attainment of a more positive situation.)

**Sources of Problem Recognition** The causes of problem recognition may be very simple or very complex and may result from changes in the consumer's current and/or desired state. These causes may be influenced by both internal and external factors.

**Out of Stock** Problem recognition occurs when consumers use their existing supply of a product and must replenish their stock. The purchase decision is usually simple and routine and is often resolved by choosing a familiar brand or one to which the consumer feels loyal.

**Dissatisfaction** Problem recognition is created by the consumer's dissatisfaction with the current state of affairs and/or the product or service being used. For example, a consumer may think her snow boots are no longer comfortable or stylish enough. Advertising may be used to help consumers recognize when they have a problem and/or need to make a purchase. The Nicoderm ad shown in Exhibit 4–2 offers assistance for those who may be dissatisfied with smoking and want to quit.

**New Needs/Wants** Changes in consumers' lives often result in new needs and wants. For example, changes in one's financial situation, employment status, or lifestyle may create new needs and trigger problem recognition. As you will see, when you graduate from college and begin your professional career, your new job may necessitate a change in your wardrobe. (Good-bye blue jeans and T-shirts, hello suits and ties.)

**EXHIBIT 4–3**
Splat encourages consumers to rebel by changing their hair color

Not all product purchases are based on needs. Some products or services sought by consumers are not essential but are nonetheless desired. A **want** is a desire for something one does not have. Many products sold to consumers satisfy their wants rather than their basic needs.

**Related Products/Purchases** Problem recognition can also be stimulated by the purchase of a product. For example, the purchase of a new iPod may lead to the recognition of a need for accessories, such as a dock, attachment for the car, or a carrying case. The purchase of a personal computer may prompt the need for software programs, upgrades, printers, and so on.

**Marketer-Induced Problem Recognition** Another source of problem recognition is marketers' actions that encourage consumers not to be content with their current state or situation. Ads for personal hygiene products such as mouthwash, deodorant, and foot sprays may be designed to create insecurities that consumers can resolve through the use of these products. Marketers change fashions and clothing designs and create perceptions among consumers that their wardrobes are out of style. Exhibit 4–3 shows how splat encourages one to change their hair color.

Marketers also take advantage of consumers' tendency toward *novelty-seeking behavior,* which leads them to try different brands. Consumers often try new products or brands even when they are basically satisfied with their regular brand. Marketers encourage brand switching by introducing new brands into markets that are already saturated and by using advertising and sales promotion techniques such as free samples, introductory price offers, and coupons.

CHAPTER 4

**New Products** Problem recognition can also occur when innovative products are introduced and brought to the attention of consumers. Marketers are constantly introducing new products and services and telling consumers about the types of problems they solve. For example, for many the cell phone is much more than a telephone, as more and more apps are now available to do everything from purchasing airline tickets to helping with travel directions. As more apps are added, the phones will become appealing to more consumers.

Marketers' attempts to create problem recognition among consumers are not always successful. Consumers may not see a problem or need for the product the marketer is selling. Using the cell phone example just provided, for some, all of the potential provided by apps may be considered unnecessary—they just want to be able to send and receive phone calls.

## Examining Consumer Motivations

Marketers recognize that while problem recognition is often a basic, simple process, the way a consumer perceives a problem and becomes motivated to solve it will influence the remainder of the decision process. For example, one consumer may perceive the need to purchase a new watch from a functional perspective and focus on reliable, low-priced alternatives. Another consumer may see the purchase of a watch as more of a fashion statement and focus on the design and image of various brands. To better understand the reasons underlying consumer purchases, marketers devote considerable attention to examining **motives**—that is, those factors that compel a consumer to take a particular action.

**Hierarchy of Needs** One of the most popular approaches to understanding consumer motivations is based on the classic theory of human motivation popularized many years ago by psychologist Abraham Maslow. His **hierarchy of needs** theory postulates five basic levels of human needs, arranged in a hierarchy based on their importance. As shown in Figure 4–2, the five needs are (1) *physiological*—the basic level of primary needs for things required to sustain life, such as food, shelter, clothing, and sex; (2) *safety*—the need for security and safety from physical harm; (3) *social/love and belonging*—the desire to have satisfying relationships with others and feel a sense of love, affection, belonging, and acceptance; (4) *esteem*—the need to feel a sense of accomplishment and gain recognition, status, and respect from others; and (5) *self-actualization*—the need for self-fulfillment and a desire to realize one's own potential.

According to Maslow's theory, the lower-level physiological and safety needs must be satisfied before the higher-order needs become meaningful. Once these basic needs are satisfied, the individual moves on to attempting to satisfy higher-order needs such as self-esteem. In reality, it is unlikely that people move through the needs hierarchy in a stairstep manner. Lower-level needs are an ongoing source of motivation for consumer purchase behavior. However, since basic physiological needs are met in most developed countries, marketers often sell products that fill basic physiological needs by appealing to consumers' higher-level needs. Notice how the webpage for Huggies focuses on the love between parent and child (social needs) (Exhibit 4–4).

**EXHIBIT 4–4**
Huggies appeals to needs for love

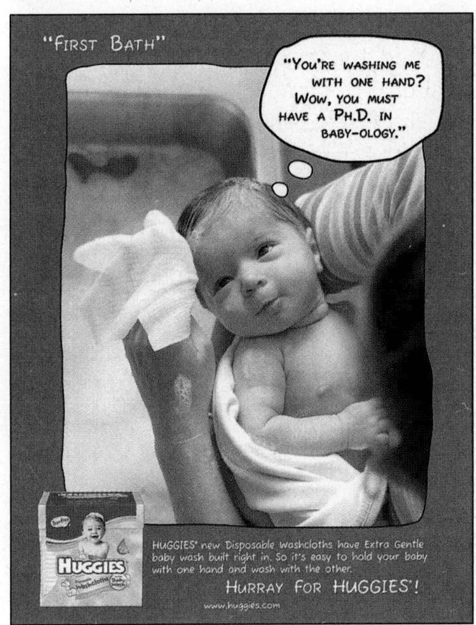

**FIGURE 4–2**
Maslow's Hierarchy of Needs

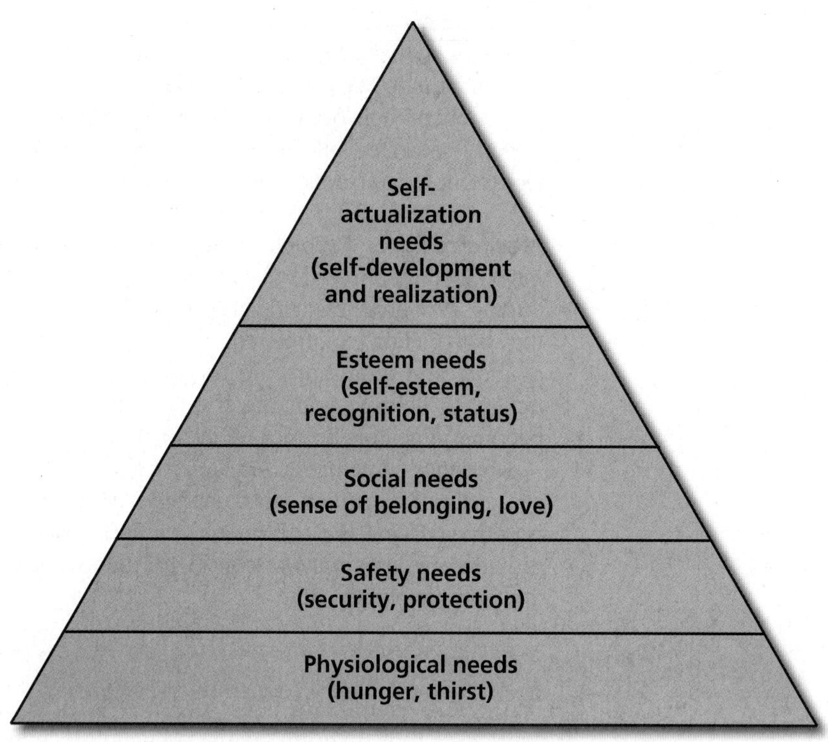


While Maslow's need hierarchy has flaws, it offers a framework for marketers to use in determining what needs they want their products and services to be shown satisfying. Advertising campaigns can then be designed to show how a brand can fulfill these needs. Marketers also recognize that different market segments emphasize different need levels. For example, a young single person may be attempting to satisfy social or self-esteem needs in purchasing a car, while a family with children will focus more on safety needs. The ad sponsored by the Consumer Healthcare Products Association in Exhibit 4–5 focuses on security needs of consumers, while the Porsche ad addresses self-actualization.

**EXHIBIT 4–5**
CHPA uses an appeal to security needs, while Porsche focuses on self-actualization

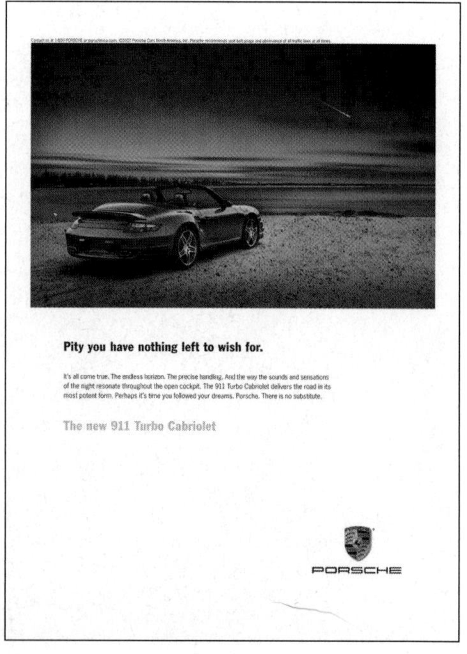

**FIGURE 4–3**

Some of the Marketing Research Methods Used to Probe the Mind of the Consumer

**In-depth interviews**
Face-to-face situations in which an interviewer asks a consumer to talk freely in an unstructured interview using specific questions designed to obtain insights into his or her motives, ideas, or opinions.

**Projective techniques**
Efforts designed to gain insights into consumers' values, motives, attitudes, or needs that are difficult to express or identify by having them project these internal states upon some external object.

**Association tests**
A technique in which an individual is asked to respond with the first thing that comes to mind when he or she is presented with a stimulus; the stimulus may be a word, picture, ad, and so on.

**Focus groups**
A small number of people with similar backgrounds and/or interests who are brought together to discuss a particular product, idea, or issue.



**Psychoanalytic Theory** A somewhat more controversial approach to the study of consumer motives is the **psychoanalytic theory** pioneered by Sigmund Freud. Although his work dealt with the structure and development of personality, Freud also studied the underlying motivations for human behavior. Psychoanalytic theory had a strong influence on the development of modern psychology and on explanations of motivation and personality. It has also been applied to the study of consumer behavior by marketers interested in probing deeply rooted motives that may underlie purchase decisions.

Those who attempt to relate psychoanalytic theory to consumer behavior believe consumers' motivations for purchasing are often very complex and unclear to the casual observer—and to the consumers themselves. Many motives for purchase and/or consumption may be driven by deep motives one can determine only by probing the subconscious.

Among the first to conduct this type of research in marketing, Ernest Dichter and James Vicary were employed by a number of major corporations to use psychoanalytic techniques to determine consumers' purchase motivations. The work of these researchers and others who continue to use this approach assumed the title of **motivation research**.

**Motivation Research in Marketing** Motivation researchers use a variety of methodologies to gain insight into the underlying causes of consumer behavior. Methods employed include in-depth interviews, projective techniques, association tests, and focus groups in which consumers are encouraged to bring out associations related to products and brands (see Figure 4–3). As one might expect, such associations often lead to interesting insights as to why people purchase. For example:

- A man's purchase of a high-priced fur for his wife proves his potency.[1]
- Consumers prefer large cars because they believe such cars protect them from the "jungle" of everyday driving.[2]
- A man buys a convertible as a substitute mistress.
- Women like to bake cakes because they feel like they are giving birth to a baby.
- Women wear perfume to "attract a man" and "glorify their existence."

- Men like frankfurters better than women do because cooking them (frankfurters, not men!) makes women feel guilty. It's an admission of laziness.
- When people shower, their sins go down the drain with the soap as they rinse.[3]

As you can see from these examples, motivation research has led to some very interesting, albeit controversial, findings and too much skepticism from marketing managers. However, major corporations and advertising agencies continue to use motivation research to help them market their products.

**Problems and Contributions of Psychoanalytic Theory and Motivation Research** Psychoanalytic theory has been criticized as being too vague, unresponsive to the external environment, and too reliant on the early development of the individual. It also uses a small sample for drawing conclusions. Because of the emphasis on the unconscious, results are difficult if not impossible to verify, leading motivation research to be criticized for both the conclusions drawn and its lack of experimental validation. Since motivation research studies typically use so few participants, there is also concern that it really discovers the idiosyncrasies of a few individuals and its findings are not generalizable to the whole population.

Still, it is difficult to ignore the psychoanalytic approach in furthering our understanding of consumer behavior. Its insights can often be used as a basis for advertising messages aimed at buyers' deeply rooted feelings, hopes, aspirations, and fears. Such strategies are often more effective than rationally based appeals.

Some corporations and advertising agencies have used motivation research to gain further insights into how consumers think. Examples include the following:

- Chrysler had consumers sit on the floor, like children, and use scissors to cut words out of magazines to describe a car.[4]
- McCann-Erickson asked women to draw and describe how they felt about roaches. The agency concluded that many women associated roaches with men who had abandoned them and that this was why women preferred roach killers that let them see the roaches die.
- Saatchi & Saatchi used psychological probes to conclude that Ronald McDonald created a more nurturing mood than did the Burger King (who was perceived as more aggressive and distant).
- Foote, Cone & Belding gave consumers stacks of photographs of faces and asked them to associate the faces with the kinds of people who might use particular products.
- The advertising agency Marcus Thomas, LLC conducted in-depth one-on-one interviews and used projective techniques to determine underlying motivations for choosing one cardiovascular care facility over another.

While often criticized, motivation research has also contributed to the marketing discipline. The qualitative nature of the research is considered important in assessing how and why consumers buy. Focus groups and in-depth interviews are valuable methods for gaining insights into consumers' feelings, and projective techniques are often the only way to get around stereotypical or socially desirable responses.

**EXHIBIT 4–6**
Joe's Jeans uses sex appeal in its advertising

**FIGURE 4–4**

Results of Survey by GfK-Roper

Source: Reprinted with permission from American Demographics, 2007. Copyright © 2007 Crain Communications.

## WHAT'S IMPORTANT IN BUYING DECISIONS

Roper's syndicated consumer research offers answers to the question: What things are most important in purchase decisions? Percent of adults who cited...

| | | RACE/ETHNICITY | | | | | TECH | | |
|---|---|---|---|---|---|---|---|---|---|
| WHAT'S IMPORTANT? | ALL ADULTS | WHITE | AFRICAN-AMERICAN | HISPANIC | "INFLUENTIALS"[1] | HAVE CHILDREN AGES 0–17 | PC IN HOME | ACCESS WEB AT HOME AND/OR OFFICE | HOME-OWNERS |
| Past experience with brand | 83% | 84% | 78% | 75% | 88% | 82% | 83% | 83% | 84% |
| How quality compares to other brands | 63 | 65 | 51 | 62 | 85 | 63 | 68 | 69 | 64 |
| Reasonably priced | 56 | 59 | 49 | 51 | 69 | 55 | 58 | 57 | 58 |
| Personal recommendation of others | 48 | 49 | 46 | 36 | 57 | 47 | 49 | 50 | 49 |
| Manufacturer's reputation for quality | 46 | 48 | 35 | 32 | 54 | 42 | 53 | 53 | 49 |
| Well-known/well-advertised | 21 | 21 | 24 | 19 | 18 | 21 | 20 | 21 | 20 |
| How rated in *Consumer Reports* | 15 | 17 | 6 | 11 | 31 | 14 | 18 | 18 | 17 |
| Manufacturer's efforts to cut pollution | 8 | 9 | 7 | 4 | 21 | 8 | 10 | 11 | 9 |
| Manufacturer's trade policies[2] | 5 | 6 | 3 | 0 | 9 | 2 | 6 | 6 | 6 |
| How manufacturer deals with union labor | 5 | 5 | 3 | 5 | 23 | 5 | 6 | 6 | 5 |

1. Consumers identified as "influentials," the 1 in 10 people who strongly influence the other nine. 2. Manufacturer trades with countries that consumer disapproves of. *Source:* GfK-Roper Consulting's syndicated research Aug.–Sept. '06, based on in-person interviews with 2,000 adults age 18+

In addition, motivation research is the forerunner of psychographics (discussed in Chapter 2).

Finally, we know that buyers are sometimes motivated by symbolic as well as functional drives in their purchase decisions. Some believe that as competition for advertisers' dollars increases, the amount and explicitness of sexual content on TV will increase as well.[5] Thus, we see the use of sexual appeals and symbols in ads like Exhibit 4–6.

## Information Search

The second stage in the consumer decision-making process is *information search.* Once consumers perceive a problem or need that can be satisfied by the purchase of a product or service, they begin to search for information needed to make a purchase decision. The initial search effort often consists of an attempt to scan information stored in memory to recall past experiences and/or knowledge regarding various purchase alternatives. This information retrieval is referred to as **internal search**. For many routine, repetitive purchases, previously acquired information that is stored in memory (such as past performance or outcomes from using a brand) is sufficient for comparing alternatives and making a choice.

If the internal search does not yield enough information, the consumer will seek additional information by engaging in **external search**. External sources of information include:

- *Personal sources,* such as friends, relatives, or co-workers.
- *Marketer-controlled (commercial) sources,* such as information from advertising, salespeople, or point-of-purchase displays and the Internet.
- *Public sources,* including articles in magazines or newspapers and reports on TV and so on.
- *Personal experience,* such as actually handling, examining, or testing the product.

Figure 4–4 shows the results of a survey conducted by GfK-Roper in regard to what is important to consumers in making a purchase decision.

Determining how much and which sources of external information to use involves several factors, including the importance of the purchase decision, the effort needed to acquire information, the amount of past experience relevant, the degree of

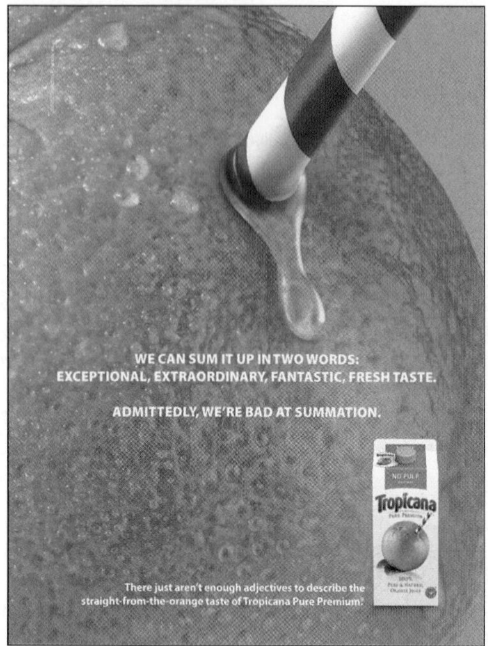


**EXHIBIT 4–7**
Tropicana uses color to focus attention on orange juice

perceived risk associated with the purchase, and the time available. For example, the selection of a movie to see on a Friday night might entail simply talking to a friend or checking the movie guide on the Internet. A more complex purchase such as a new car might use a number of information sources—perhaps a review of *Road & Track, Motortrend,* or *Consumer Reports;* discussion with family members and friends; conducting an online search; and test-driving of cars. At this point in the purchase decision, the information-providing aspects of advertising are extremely important.

## Perception

Knowledge of how consumers acquire and use information from external sources is important to marketers in formulating communication strategies. Marketers are particularly interested in (1) how consumers sense external information, (2) how they select and attend to various sources of information, and (3) how this information is interpreted and given meaning. These processes are all part of **perception**, the process by which an individual receives, selects, organizes, and interprets information to create a meaningful picture of the world. Perception is an individual process; it depends on internal factors such as a person's beliefs, experiences, needs, moods, and expectations. The perceptual process is also influenced by the characteristics of a stimulus (such as its size, color, and intensity) and the context in which it is seen or heard (Exhibit 4–7).

**Sensation** Perception involves three distinct processes. **Sensation** is the immediate, direct response of the senses (taste, smell, sight, touch, and hearing) to a stimulus such as an ad, package, brand name, or point-of-purchase display. Perception uses these senses to create a representation of the stimulus. Marketers recognize that it is important to understand consumers' physiological reactions to marketing stimuli as shown in IMC Technology Perspective 4–1. For example, the visual elements of an ad or package design must attract consumers' favorable attention.

**EXHIBIT 4–8**
This ad reminds consumers of how advertising responds to their needs

Marketers sometimes try to increase the level of sensory input so that their advertising messages will get noticed. For example, Bloomingdales' New York store sprayed Donna Karan's new perfume DKNY onto the sidewalks outside their store to introduce the perfume to consumers. Kraft Foods promoted the new DiGiorno Garlic Bread Pizza with scent strip cards in stores, while Avon uses scent strips for many products from perfumes to bubble baths in their catalogs. Scent strips have long been used in magazines, and a study of *Allure* magazine readers showed that 86 percent of readers said they had tried the scent strips, with 72 percent saying they purchased the product as a result.[6]

**Selecting Information** Sensory inputs are important but are only one part of the perceptual process. Other determinants of whether marketing stimuli will be attended to and how they will be interpreted include internal psychological factors such as the consumer's personality, needs, motives, expectations, and experiences. These psychological inputs explain why people focus attention on some things and ignore others. Two people may perceive the same stimuli in very different ways because they select, attend, and comprehend differently. An individual's perceptual processes usually focus on elements of the environment that are relevant to his or her needs and tune out irrelevant stimuli. Think about how much more attentive you are to advertising for personal computers, tires, or stereos when you are in the market for one of these products (a point that is made by the message from the American Association of Advertising Agencies in Exhibit 4–8.)

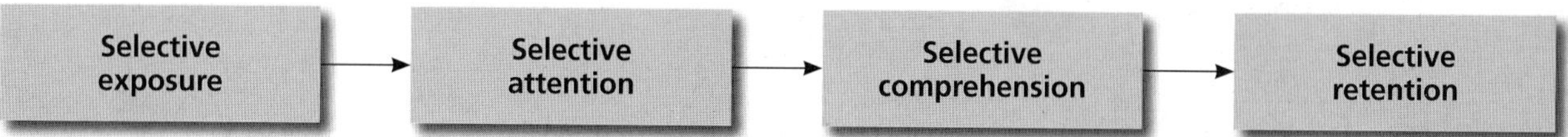


**FIGURE 4–5**
The Selective Perception Process



**Interpreting the Information** Once a consumer selects and attends to a stimulus, the perceptual process focuses on organizing, categorizing, and interpreting the incoming information. This stage of the perceptual process is very individualized and is influenced by internal psychological factors. The interpretation and meaning an individual assigns to an incoming stimulus also depend in part on the nature of the stimulus. For example, many ads are objective, and their message is clear and straightforward. Other ads are more ambiguous, and their meaning is strongly influenced by the consumer's individual interpretation.

Selectivity occurs throughout the various stages of the consumer's perceptual process. Perception may be viewed as a filtering process in which internal and external factors influence what is received and how it is processed and interpreted. The sheer number and complexity of the marketing stimuli a person is exposed to in any given day require that this filtering occur. **Selective perception** may occur at the exposure, attention, comprehension, or retention stage of perception, as shown in Figure 4–5.

**Selective Perception** **Selective exposure** occurs as consumers choose whether or not to make themselves available to information. For example, a viewer of a television show may change channels or leave the room during commercial breaks.

**Selective attention** occurs when the consumer chooses to focus attention on certain stimuli while excluding others. One study of selective attention estimated that the typical consumer is exposed to nearly 1,500 ads per day yet perceives only 76 of these messages.[7] Other estimates range as high as 4,000 exposures per day. This means advertisers must make considerable effort to get their messages noticed. Advertisers often use the creative aspects of their ads to gain consumers' attention. For example, some advertisers set their ads off from others by showing their products in color against a black-and-white background. This creative tactic has been used in advertising for many products, among them Cherry 7UP, Nuprin, Pepto-Bismol, and Tropicana. Notice how the color red is used in the ad for VO5 to attract attention while also focusing on the product line, packaging, and brand identity in Exhibit 4–9.

**EXHIBIT 4–9**
Color is used to attract attention to VO5

Even if the consumer does notice the advertiser's message, there is no guarantee it will be interpreted in the intended manner. Consumers may engage in **selective comprehension**, interpreting information on the basis of their own attitudes, beliefs, motives, and experiences. They often interpret information in a manner that supports their own position. For example, an ad that disparages a consumer's favorite brand may be seen as biased or untruthful, and its claims may not be accepted.

The final screening process shown in Figure 4–5 is **selective retention**, which means consumers do not remember all the information they see, hear, or read even after attending to and comprehending it. Advertisers attempt to make sure information will be retained in the consumer's memory so that it will be available when it is time to make a purchase. **Mnemonics** such as symbols, rhymes, associations, and images that assist in the learning and memory process are helpful. Many advertisers use telephone numbers that spell out the company name and are easy to remember (for example, 1-800-GOFEDEX).

# IMC Technology Perspective 4–1 > > >

## Mapping the Mind: Smart Marketing or Voodoo?

In their never-ending search to learn more about why consumers buy, marketers seemingly will stop at nothing. From surveys to focus groups to mind-probing interviews that put consumers in a near hypnotic state, market researchers have employed anthropologists, sociologists, economists, psychologists, and now neuroscientists to learn the "why of buy." For the most part, these efforts have been more of an art than a science—until now.

It has been estimated that by the time the average American reaches the age of 65, he or she will have been exposed to approximately 136,692,500 ads of various forms, and will have watched over 2 million television commercials. Consumers are overwhelmed by commercial messages, and advertisers know it. That's why they want to know more about which ads you see, recall, and remember, and what you think about when you see them. In an attempt to gain this understanding, marketers have turned to neuroscience, and are conducting research experiments designed to see what is happening inside of your brain.

Using technologies originally designed for the medical field such as positron emission tomography (PET) and functional magnetic resonance imaging (fMRI), the scientists have teamed up with marketers to examine physiological reactions to ads and brands through brain scan imaging. By monitoring the brain activity directly, scientists are learning how consumers make up their minds by measuring chemical activity and/or changes in the magnetic fields of the brain even though the consumers themselves may not know how or why they make these decisions. Some of these scientists believe that exposure to marketing messages may even alter the brain, just as learning to read or play the piano might.

But what is it they are looking for? In one study participants wore goggles while attached to a medical imaging scanner and watched as products such as iPods, chairs, and coffeepots and name brands such as Versace, Oakley, Evian, and Honda among others flashed in front of them inside the goggles. Two scientists observed the differences in brain activity that each product and brand evoked. Another study explored the question of what makes a product desirable, while yet another examined the price/quality relationship by examining changes in the medial orbitofrontal cortex that occurred when participants thought they were drinking a $5 glass of wine or a $45 glass (the $45 wine was more pleasurable).

Another study conducted at the Neuroimaging lab at Baylor College of Medicine repeated the Pepsi Challenge while observing participants through an fMRI. The results showed that when no brand names were known, subjects preferred Pepsi: The response was five times stronger than that of Coke. But when subjects were told which brands they were tasting, nearly all of the subjects said they preferred Coke. It was obvious that volunteers were responding to the influence of the Coke brand. Anette Asp and Steve Quartz, two researchers at Caltech, note that there are "branded brains," and that based on their neurological patterns people can be classified in broad psychological categories. At one extreme are the "cool fools" who tend to be compulsive or impulsive shoppers who respond to celebrities and "cool" brands with bursts of brain activity. At the other end are those who tend to be more anxious, apprehensive, or even neurotic and who react intensely to unstylish items. Still others purchase out of fear or anxiety that they may

**Subliminal Perception** Advertisers know consumers use selective perception to filter out irrelevant or unwanted advertising messages, so they employ various creative tactics to get their messages noticed. One controversial tactic advertisers have been accused of using is appealing to consumers' subconscious. **Subliminal perception** refers to the ability to perceive a stimulus that is below the level of conscious awareness. Psychologists generally agree it is possible to perceive things without being consciously aware of them.

As you might imagine, the possibility of using hidden persuaders such as subliminal audio messages or visual cues to influence consumers might be intriguing to advertisers but would not be welcomed by consumers. The idea of marketers influencing consumers at a subconscious level has strong ethical implications. Ethical Perspective 4–1 discusses researchers' mixed opinions as to whether motivation research and subliminal advertising are likely to be effective in influencing consumer behavior.

## Alternative Evaluation

After acquiring information during the information search stage of the decision process, the consumer moves to alternative evaluation. In this stage, the consumer compares the various brands or products and services he or she has identified as being not be seen as sufficiently stylish. Other studies have examined why people might overspend, what they are thinking about when they shop, and more.

Marketers argue that understanding the brain will help make marketing efforts more effective by improving communications, assisting in store design and layout and increasing consumer engagement. Others, however, are not so sure. Some believe the results are blown out of proportion and provide less insight than the marketers have claimed. Others have referred to the studies as "junk science." One published article claims that the studies are so methodologically flawed that half of them should be redone. April Benson, a New York psychologist who works with patients whose spending is so out of control that it ruins marriages, careers, and finances is afraid that neuroscience will be used to get consumers to shop mindlessly, when just the opposite is what they need to do—shop mindfully.

While analysts disagree over the effectiveness and value of monitoring brain activity, the research goes on as companies and their agencies continue to measure ROI. Ask the Nielsen Company—one of the world's leading audience measurement companies. Nielsen recently made a "strategic investment" in NeuroFocus—a neuromarketing company.

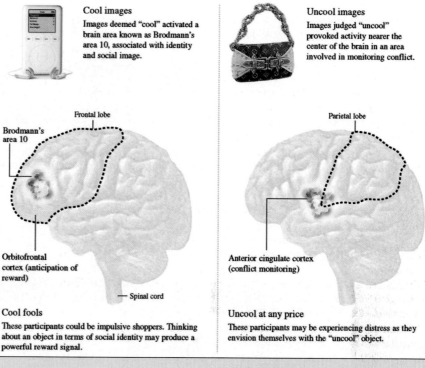

**Cool or uncool**

A team at Caltech investigated how the brain responded to designer products and celebrity faces. Study participants were shown photographs and asked to rate their "coolness." Their brains were scanned as they viewed the images. These illustrations show active brain areas.*

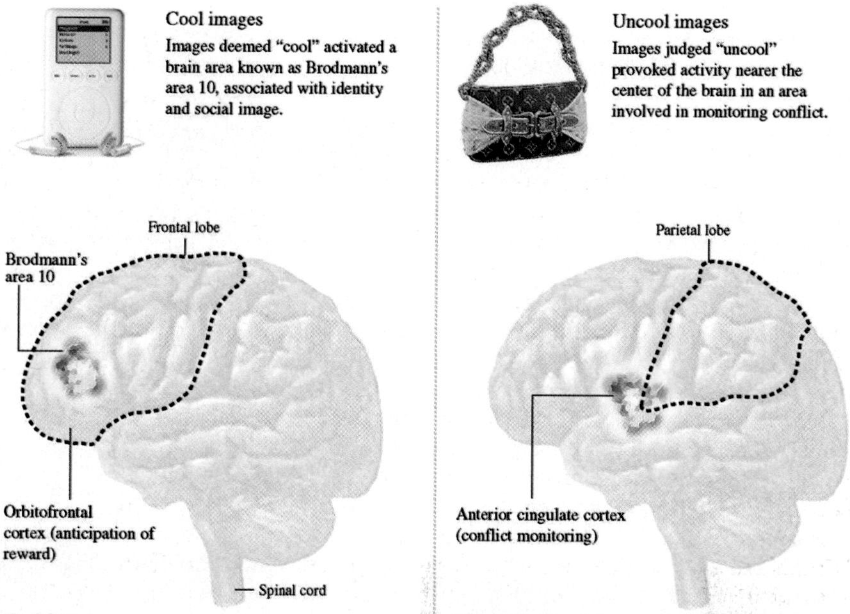

Cool images
Images deemed "cool" activated a brain area known as Brodmann's area 10, associated with identity and social image.
Uncool images
Images judged "uncool" provoked activity nearer the center of the brain in an area involved in monitoring conflict.
Frontal lobe
Brodmann's area 10
Orbitofrontal cortex (anticipation of reward)
Spinal cord
Parietal lobe
Anterior cingulate cortex (conflict monitoring)
Cool fools
These participants could be impulsive shoppers. Thinking about an object in terms of social identity may produce a powerful reward signal.
Uncool at any price
These participants may be experiencing distress as they envision themselves with the "uncool" object.

Sources: Rick Ferguson, "Neuromarketing: What the Human Brain Means to Your Campaign," www.chiefmarketer.com, October 27, 2009; Joan O'C Hamilton, "This Is Your Brain on Bargains," *Stanford Magazine*, November–December 2008, pp. 71–74; Randy Dotinga, "Advertisers Tap Brain Science," www.wired.com, May 31, 2005, pp. 1–2; Robert Lee Hotz, "Searching for the Why of Buy," *Los Angeles Times*, February 27, 2005, pp. A1, 26–27.



capable of solving the consumption problem and satisfying the needs or motives that initiated the decision process. The various brands identified as purchase options to be considered during the alternative evaluation process are referred to as the consumer's *evoked set*.

**The Evoked Set** The evoked set is generally only a subset of all the brands of which the consumer is aware. The consumer reduces the number of brands to be reviewed during the alternative evaluation stage to a manageable level. The exact size of the evoked set (sometimes referred to as the consideration threat) varies from one consumer to another and depends on such factors as the importance of the purchase and the amount of time and energy the consumer wants to spend comparing alternatives.

The goal of most advertising and promotional strategies is to increase the likelihood that a brand will be included in the consumer's evoked set and considered during alternative evaluation. Marketers use advertising to create *top-of-mind awareness* among consumers so that their brands are part of the evoked set of their target audiences. Popular brands with large advertising budgets use *reminder advertising* to maintain high awareness levels and increase the likelihood they will be considered by consumers in the market for the product. Marketers of new brands or those with a low market share need to gain awareness among consumers and break into their

# Ethical Perspective 4–1 > > >

## Subliminal Advertising—Old Story, New Results

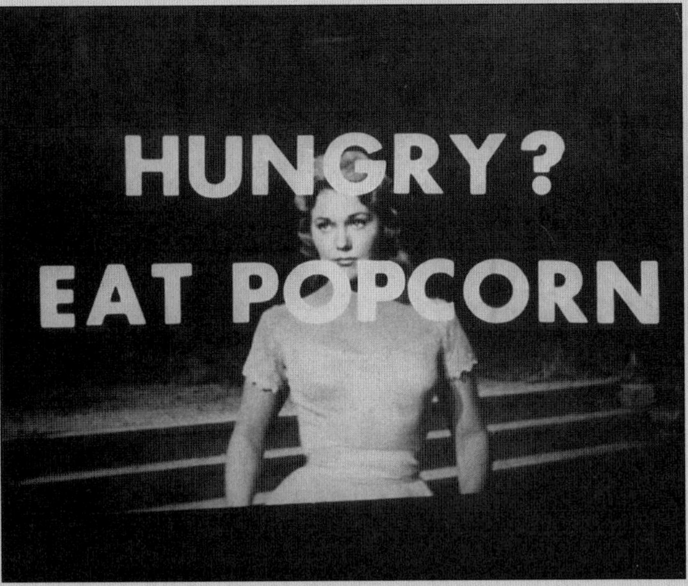


It has been half a century since Vance Packard's famous book *The Hidden Persuaders* shocked the world. In his book, Packard accused advertisers of using research techniques like "depth interviews" and "motivation research" to develop messages that appealed to consumers' subconscious. These appeals led consumers to be persuaded to make purchases without consciously being aware why they made their choices. At about the same time, James Vicary, a motivational researcher, introduced the concept of subliminal advertising, reporting that he had increased the sales of popcorn and Coke by subliminally flashing the messages "eat popcorn" and "drink Coca-Cola" across the screen. Wilson Bryant Key further fueled the fires with his books claiming that subliminal advertising was, indeed, manipulating consumer behaviors.

A rash of research studies, articles, and books designed to explore motivation research and subliminal advertising soon followed in an attempt to determine the veracity of these techniques. In a series of extensive reviews on the topic (1982, 1988), Timothy Moore concluded that there was no evidence to support the fact that subliminal messages can affect consumers' motivations, perceptions, or attitudes. For a long period of time subliminal advertising, motivation research, and the application of psychoanalytic theory to consumer behaviors seemed to go away, with members of society and academia apparently losing interest. But while the studies went away, they never really disappeared.

In the 1990s a number of studies surfaced arguing that subliminal advertising could work. Then in the 2000 Bush–Gore presidential campaign, the Republicans were accused of subliminally implanting the word *rats* into ads to attach the meaning to Al Gore. Once again, motivation research was back in the spotlight.

More recently, scientists at the University College of London in the U.K. claimed that they proved conclusively that people can perceive the emotional value of subliminal messages. Another researcher also claimed that his series of research studies proved that music, country of origin, and even product weight have subliminal influences on consumers.

This time, however, no one seems to be getting alarmed. After 50 years, consumers and researchers don't seem to be concerned that they need to worry about subliminal advertising. But they certainly haven't lost interest.

Sources: Martin Lindstrom, "How Subliminal Advertising Works," www.parade.com, January 4, 2009; "Hypnosis Reveals Ad Effects," *Adweek Asia*, January 29, 1999, p. 4; "Breaking French Connection," *Ad Age*, March 22, 1999, p. 52; Kathryn Theus, "Subliminal Advertising and the Psychology of Processing Unconscious Stimuli: A Review of Research," *Psychology & Marketing* 11, no. 3, 1994, pp. 271–90; Timothy Moore, "Subliminal Advertising: What You See Is What You Get," *Journal of Marketing* 46, no. 2 (Spring 1982), pp. 38–47; Timothy Moore, "The Case against Subliminal Manipulation," *Psychology and Marketing* 5, no. 4 (Winter 1988), pp. 297–316; Kalpana Srinivasan, "FCC Ends Probe on Republican Ad," www.individual.com, March 12, 2001, pp. 1–2; George E. Condon Jr. and Toby Eckert, "Flap over 'RATS' Latest to Plague Bush's Drive," *San Diego Tribune*, September 13, 2000, p. A1. Richard Alleyne, "Subliminal Advertising Really Does Work, Claim Scientists," www.telegraph.co.uk, September 2009.

evoked sets. The ad promoting Michigan as a better place to live and do business (Exhibit 4–10) shows this strategy being used in a different context from products and brands. The ad presents the many benefits of Michigan and encourages prospective businesses to consider it in their evoked set of places to locate or relocate.

Advertising is a valuable promotional tool for creating and maintaining brand awareness and making sure a brand is included in the evoked set. However, marketers also work to promote their brands in the actual environment where purchase decisions are made. Point-of-purchase materials and promotional techniques such as in-store sampling, end-aisle displays, or shelf tags touting special prices encourage consumers to consider brands that may not have initially been in their evoked set.

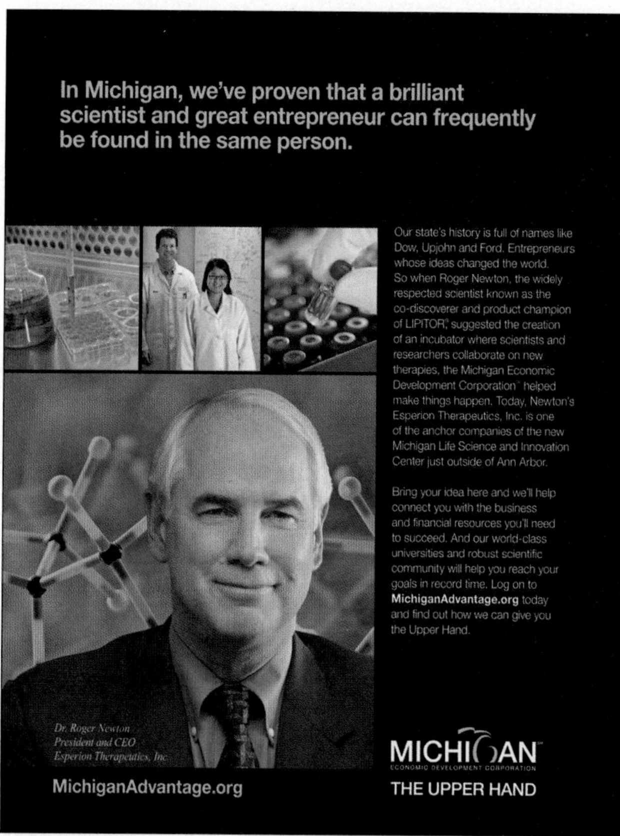

In Michigan, we've proven that a brilliant scientist and great entrepreneur can frequently be found in the same person.
Our state's history is full of names like Dow, Upjohn and Ford. Entrepreneurs whose ideas changed the world. So when Roger Newton, the widely respected scientist known as the co-discoverer and product champion of LIPITOR,® suggested the creation of an incubator where scientists and researchers collaborate on new therapies, the Michigan Economic Development Corporation℠ helped make things happen. Today, Newton's Esperion Therapeutics, Inc. is one of the anchor companies of the new Michigan Life Science and Innovation Center just outside of Ann Arbor.
Bring your idea here and we'll help connect you with the business and financial resources you'll need to succeed. And our world-class universities and robust scientific community will help you reach your goals in record time. Log on to MichiganAdvantage.org today and find out how we can give you the Upper Hand.
Dr. Roger Newton
President and CEO
Esperion Therapeutics, Inc.
MichiganAdvantage.org
MICHIGAN
ECONOMIC DEVELOPMENT CORPORATION
THE UPPER HAND

**EXHIBIT 4–10**
Michigan wants to be in the evoked set of business locations

**Evaluative Criteria and Consequences** Once consumers have identified an evoked set and have a list of alternatives, they must evaluate the various brands. This involves comparing the choice alternatives on specific criteria important to the consumer. **Evaluative criteria** are the dimensions or attributes of a product or service that are used to compare different alternatives. Evaluative criteria can be objective or subjective. For example, in buying an automobile, consumers use objective attributes such as price, warranty, and fuel economy as well as subjective factors such as image, styling, and performance.

Evaluative criteria are usually viewed as product or service attributes. Many marketers view their products or services as *bundles of attributes,* but consumers tend to think about products or services in terms of their *consequences* or *outcomes* instead. They distinguish between two broad types of consequences. **Functional consequences** are concrete outcomes of product or service usage that are tangible and directly experienced by consumers. The taste of a soft drink or a potato chip, the acceleration of a car, and the speed of the Internet service provider are examples of functional consequences. **Psychosocial consequences** are abstract outcomes that are more intangible, subjective, and personal, such as how a product makes you feel or how you think others will view you for purchasing or using it.

Product/service attributes and the consequences or outcomes consumers think they will experience from a particular brand are very important, for they are often the basis on which consumers form attitudes and purchase intentions and decide among various choice alternatives. Two subprocesses are very important during the alternative evaluation stage: (1) the process by which consumer attitudes are created, reinforced, and changed and (2) the decision rules or integration strategies consumers use to compare brands and make purchase decisions. We will examine each of these processes in more detail.

## Attitudes

Attitudes are learned predispositions to respond to an object and are some of the most heavily studied concepts in consumer behavior.[8] More recent perspectives view an attitude as a summary construct that represents an individual's overall feelings toward or evaluation of an object.[9] Consumers hold attitudes toward a variety of objects that are important to marketers, including individuals (celebrity endorsers such as Tiger Woods or Danica Patrick), brands (Cheerios, Special K), companies (Intel, Microsoft), product categories (beef, pork, tuna), retail stores (Walmart, Sears), or even advertisements (Nike ads).

Attitudes are important to marketers because they theoretically summarize a consumer's evaluation of an object (or brand or company) and represent positive or negative feelings and behavioral tendencies. Marketers' keen interest in attitudes is based on the assumption that they are related to consumers' purchase behavior. But attitudes are very important to marketers. Advertising and promotion are used to create favorable attitudes toward new products/services or brands, reinforce existing favorable attitudes, and/or change negative attitudes. An approach to studying and measuring attitudes that is particularly relevant to advertising is multiattribute attitude models.

**Multiattribute Attitude Models** Consumer researchers and marketing practitioners have been using multiattribute attitude models to study consumer attitudes for two decades. A **multiattribute attitude model** views an attitude object, such as a product or brand, as possessing a number of attributes that provide the basis on which consumers form their attitudes. According to this model, consumers have beliefs about specific brand attributes and attach different levels of importance to these attributes. Using this approach, an attitude toward a particular brand can be represented as

$$A_B = \sum_{i=1}^{a} B_i \times E_i$$

where $A_B$ = attitude toward a brand

$B_i$ = beliefs about the brand's performance on attribute $i$

$E_i$ = importance attached to attribute $i$

$n$ = number of attributes considered

For example, a consumer may have beliefs ($B_i$) about various brands of toothpaste on certain attributes. One brand may be perceived as having fluoride and thus preventing cavities, tasting good, and helping control tartar buildup. Another brand may not be perceived as having these attributes, but consumers may believe it performs well on other attributes such as freshening breath and whitening teeth.

To predict attitudes, one must know how much importance consumers attach to each of these attributes ($E_i$). For example, parents purchasing toothpaste for their children may prefer a brand that performs well on cavity prevention, a preference that leads to a more favorable attitude toward the first brand. Teenagers and young adults may prefer a brand that freshens their breath and makes their teeth white and thus prefer the second brand.

Consumers may hold a number of different beliefs about brands in any product or service category. However, not all of these beliefs are activated in forming an attitude. Beliefs concerning specific attributes or consequences that are activated and form the basis of an attitude are referred to as **salient beliefs**. Marketers should identify and understand these salient beliefs and recognize that the saliency of beliefs varies among different market segments, over time, and across different consumption situations.

**Attitude Change Strategies** Multiattribute models help marketers understand and diagnose the underlying basis of consumers' attitudes. By understanding the beliefs that underlie consumers' evaluations of a brand and the importance of various attributes or consequences, the marketer is better able to develop communication strategies for creating, changing, or reinforcing brand attitudes. The multiattribute model provides insight into several ways marketers can influence consumer attitudes, including:

- Increasing or changing the strength or belief rating of a brand on an important attribute (AT&T has the widest cell phone network).
- Changing consumers' perceptions of the importance or value of an attribute (Michelin tires emphasizing higher gas mileage and safety).
- Adding a new attribute to the attitude formation process (the fact that the product is environmentally friendly).
- Changing perceptions of belief ratings for a competing brand (GM showing their cars can compete with anyone's).

The first strategy is commonly used by advertisers. They identify an attribute or consequence that is important and remind consumers how well their brand performs on this attribute. In situations where consumers do not perceive the marketer's brand as possessing an important attribute or the belief strength is low, advertising strategies

**EXHIBIT 4–11**
Michelin stresses higher gas mileage, as well as safety, in their ads

may be targeted at changing the belief rating. Even when belief strength is high, advertising may be used to increase the rating of a brand on an important attribute. BMW's "The Ultimate Driving Machine" campaign is a good example of a strategy designed to create a belief and reinforce it through advertising.

Marketers often attempt to influence consumer attitudes by changing the relative importance of a particular attribute. This second strategy involves getting consumers to attach more importance to the attribute in forming their attitude toward the brand. Marketers using this strategy want to increase the importance of an attribute their particular brand has (Exhibit 4–11).

The third strategy for influencing consumer attitudes is to add or emphasize a new attribute that consumers can use in evaluating a brand. Marketers often do this by improving their products or focusing on additional benefits or consequences associated with using the brand.

A final strategy marketers use is to change consumer beliefs about the attributes of competing brands or product categories. This strategy has become much more common with the increase in comparative advertising, where marketers compare their brands to competitors' on specific product attributes.

## Integration Processes and Decision Rules

Another important aspect of the alternative evaluation stage is the way consumers combine information about the characteristics of brands to arrive at a purchase decision. **Integration processes** are the way product knowledge, meanings, and beliefs are combined to evaluate two or more alternatives.[10] Analysis of the integration process focuses on the different types of *decision rules* or strategies consumers use to decide among purchase alternatives.

Consumers often make purchase selections by using formal integration strategies or decision rules that require examination and comparison of alternatives on specific attributes. This process involves a very deliberate evaluation of the alternatives, attribute by attribute. When consumers apply such formal decision rules, marketers need to know which attributes are being considered so as to provide the information the consumers require.

**EXHIBIT 4–12**
Market leaders such as Levi's can appeal to consumer affect

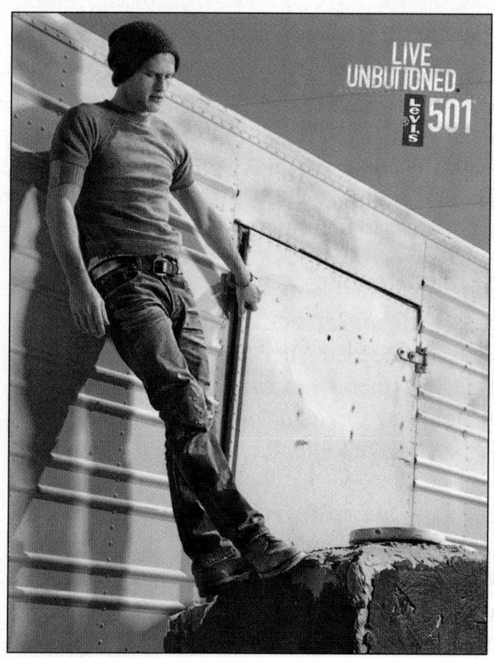


Sometimes consumers make their purchase decisions using more simplified decision rules known as **heuristics**. For familiar products that are purchased frequently, consumers may use price-based heuristics (buy the least expensive brand) or promotion-based heuristics (choose the brand for which I can get a price reduction through a coupon, rebate, or special deal).

One type of heuristic is the **affect referral decision rule**, in which consumers make a selection on the basis of an overall impression or summary evaluation of the various alternatives under consideration. This decision rule suggests that consumers have affective impressions of brands stored in memory that can be accessed at the time of purchase.

Marketers selling familiar and popular brands may appeal to an affect referral rule by stressing overall affective feelings or impressions about their products. Market leaders, whose products enjoy strong overall brand images, often use ads that promote the brand by appealing to affect. Allstate's "The Good Hands People," Rice-A-Roni's "The San Francisco Treat," Nationwide's "Nationwide is on your side," are all examples of this strategy (Exhibit 4–12).

**FIGURE 4–6**

Brands that Have the Most Brand Loyalty

| Category | Winner[a] |
|---|---|
| Airlines | Jet Blue |
| Athletic footwear | New Balance/Nike (tie) |
| Automobiles | Hyundai |
| Bank | Wells Fargo |
| Car rental | Avis |
| Clothing catalog | J. Crew |
| Computers (laptop) | Apple |
| Credit cards | American Express/Discover (tie) |
| Digital cameras | Canon/Nikon (tie) |
| DVD players | Samsung |
| Evening news show | CBS |
| HDTV | Sony/Samsung (tie) |
| Hotels (luxury) | InterContinental |
| Laundry detergent | Tide |
| Online travel | Expedia/Kayak (tie) |
| Soft drinks (reg/diet) | Pepsi/Diet Pepsi |
| Toothpaste | Tom's of Maine |
| Vodka | Grey Goose |
| Wireless phone service | AT&T Wireless |

[a] Brands listed have highest loyalty ranking in Brand Keys 2010 Customer Loyalty Engagement Index.

Source: www.brandkeys.com/awards, 2010.

## Purchase Decision

At some point in the buying process, the consumer must stop searching for and evaluating information about alternative brands in the evoked set and make a *purchase decision.* As an outcome of the alternative evaluation stage, the consumer may develop a **purchase intention** or predisposition to buy a certain brand. Purchase intentions are generally based on a matching of purchase motives with attributes or characteristics of brands under consideration. Their formation involves many of the personal subprocesses discussed in this chapter, including motivation, perception, attitude formation, and integration.

A purchase decision is not the same as an actual purchase. Once a consumer chooses which brand to buy, he or she must still implement the decision and make the actual purchase. Additional decisions may be needed, such as when to buy, where to buy, and how much money to spend. Often, there is a time delay between the formation of a purchase intention or decision and the actual purchase, particularly for highly involved and complex purchases such as automobiles, personal computers, and consumer durables.

For nondurable products, which include many low-involvement items such as consumer package goods, the time between the decision and the actual purchase may be short. Before leaving home, the consumer may make a shopping list that includes specific brand names because they have developed **brand loyalty**—a preference for a particular brand that results in its repeated purchase; of course, brand loyalty is not limited to nondurables. Consumers develop loyalties to many types of products and services. Marketers strive to develop and maintain brand loyalty among consumers. They use reminder advertising to keep their brand names in front of consumers, maintain prominent shelf positions and displays in stores, and run periodic promotions to deter consumers from switching brands.

Gaining and maintaining consumers' brand loyalty is not easy. Bank of America saw their loyalty go from number one to the bottom of the bank list in just one year. Competitors use many techniques to encourage consumers to try their brands, among them new product introductions and free samples. Figure 4–6 shows some of the brands that have achieved this goal. Marketers must continually battle to maintain their loyal consumers while replacing those who switch brands.

As seen, purchase decisions for nondurable, convenience items sometimes take place in the store, almost simultaneous with the purchase. Marketers must ensure that consumers have top-of-mind awareness of their brands so that they are quickly recognized and considered. Packaging, shelf displays, point-of-purchase materials, and promotional tools such as on-package coupons or premium offers can influence decisions made through constructive processes at the time of purchase.

## Postpurchase Evaluation

The consumer decision process does not end with the purchase. After using the product or service, the consumer compares the level of performance with expectations and is either satisfied or dissatisfied. *Satisfaction* occurs when the consumer's expectations are either met or exceeded; *dissatisfaction* results when performance is below expectations. The postpurchase evaluation process is important because the feedback acquired from actual use of a product will influence the likelihood of future purchases. Positive performance means the brand is likely to be retained in the evoked set and increases the likelihood it will be purchased again. Unfavorable outcomes may lead the consumer to form negative attitudes toward the brand, lessening the likelihood it will be purchased again or even eliminating it from the evoked set.

Another possible outcome of a purchase is **cognitive dissonance**, a feeling of psychological tension or postpurchase doubt that a consumer experiences after making a difficult purchase choice. Dissonance is more likely to occur in important decisions where the consumer must choose among close alternatives (especially if the unchosen alternative has unique or desirable features that the selected alternative does not have).

**EXHIBIT 4–13**
Some companies attempt to capitalize on consumer's dissatisfaction

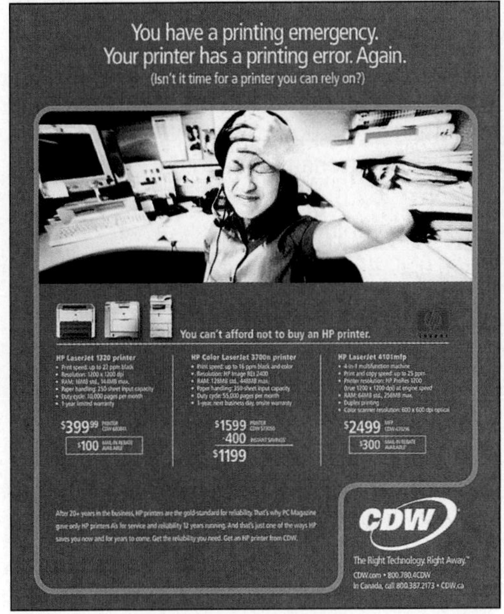


Consumers experiencing cognitive dissonance may use a number of strategies to attempt to reduce it. They may seek out reassurance and opinions from others to confirm the wisdom of their purchase decision, lower their attitudes or opinions of the unchosen alternative, deny or distort any information that does not support the choice they made, or look for information that does support their choice. An important source of supportive information is advertising as consumers tend to be more attentive to advertising for the brand they have chosen.[11] Thus, it may be important for companies to advertise to reinforce consumer decisions to purchase their brands.

Marketers have come to realize that postpurchase communication is also important. Some companies send follow-up letters and brochures to reassure buyers and reinforce the wisdom of their decision. Many companies have set up toll-free numbers or e-mail addresses for consumers to call if they need information or have a question or complaint regarding a product. Some marketers also offer liberalized return and refund policies and extended warranties and guarantees to ensure customer satisfaction. Some have used customers' postpurchase dissatisfaction as an opportunity for gaining new business, as is reflected in Exhibit 4–13.

## Variations in Consumer Decision Making

The preceding pages describe a general model of consumer decision making. But consumers do not always engage in all five steps of the purchase decision process or proceed in the sequence presented. They may minimize or even skip one or more stages if they have previous experience in purchasing the product or service or if the decision is of low personal, social, or economic significance. To develop effective promotional strategies and programs, marketers need some understanding of the problem-solving processes their target consumers use to make purchase decisions.

Many of the purchase decisions we make as consumers are based on a habitual or routine choice process. For many low-priced, frequently purchased products, the decision process consists of little more than recognizing the problem, engaging in a quick internal search, and making the purchase. The consumer spends little or no effort engaging in external search or alternative evaluation.

Marketers of products characterized by a routine response purchase process need to get and/or keep their brands in the consumer's evoked set and avoid anything that may result in their removal from consideration. Established brands that have strong market share position are likely to be in the evoked set of most consumers. Marketers of these brands want consumers to follow a routine choice process and continue to purchase their products. This means maintaining high levels of brand awareness through reminder advertising, periodic promotions, and prominent shelf positions in retail stores.

Marketers of new brands or those with a low market share face a different challenge. They must find ways to disrupt consumers' routine choice process and get them to consider different alternatives. High levels of advertising may be used to encourage trial or brand switching, along with sales promotion efforts in the form of free samples, special price offers, high-value coupons, and the like.

**EXHIBIT 4–14**
This ad for Ameriprise Financial shows how marketers can appeal to consumers engaging in extended problem solving

It's not just about where your dreams will take you.
It's where you take your dreams.
Whether your dream is to ride cross-country or write the Great American Novel, the best place to start is with someone who believes in your dreams. That's why more people come to Ameriprise for financial planning than any other company.* Our Dream > Plan > Track >® approach to financial planning begins with your dreams, not numbers. Dream > Plan > Track > is an ongoing process where, together, you and an Ameriprise financial advisor will define your dream, develop your plan and track your progress — making sure your dreams and your plans are one and the same. Get started today at ameriprise.com/plan or call 1-800-Ameriprise to schedule a conversation with one of our personal financial advisors
Financial Planning > Retirement > Investments > Insurance > Banking
The Personal Advisors of
Ameriprise Financial
To find out more about the red chair, go to ameriprise.com/redchair.
Ameriprise Financial is pleased to be using an authentic Eames DCW manufactured by Herman Miller, Courtesy Eames Office LLC, www.eamesoffice.com, www.eamesfoundation.org.
Ameriprise Financial cannot guarantee future financial results. Financial planning services and investments available through Ameriprise Financial Services, Inc., Member FINRA and SIPC.
*Based on the number of financial planning clients annually disclosed in Form ADV, Part 1A, Item 5 available at adviserinfo.sec.gov as of December 31, 2006.
© 2008 Ameriprise Financial, Inc. All rights reserved.

A more complicated decision-making process may occur when consumers have limited experience in purchasing a particular product or service and little or no knowledge of the brands available and/or the criteria to use in making a purchase decision. They may have to learn what attributes or criteria should be used in making a purchase decision and how the various alternatives perform on these dimensions. For products or services characterized by problem solving, whether limited or extensive, marketers should make information available that will help consumers decide. Advertising that provides consumers with detailed information about a brand and how it can satisfy their purchase motives and goals is important. Distribution channels should have knowledgeable salespeople available to explain the features and benefits of the company's product or service and why it is superior to competing products.

The Ameriprise Financial ad in Exhibit 4–14 is a good example of how advertising can appeal to consumers who may be engaging in extended problem solving when considering financial planning. Notice how the ad communicates with consumers who may be concerned about achieving their dreams. The ad helps the consumer by offering expert advice and planning a variety of options. The ad also makes more detailed information available by offering a toll-free number and a website.

# THE CONSUMER LEARNING PROCESS

The discussion of the decision process shows that the way consumers make a purchase varies depending on a number of factors, including the nature of the product or service, the amount of experience they have with the product, and the importance of the purchase. One factor in the level of problem solving to be employed is the consumer's *involvement* with the product or brand. Chapter 5 examines the meaning of involvement, the difference between low- and high-involvement decision making, and the implications of involvement for developing advertising and promotional strategies.



Our examination of consumer behavior thus far has looked at the decision-making process from a *cognitive orientation.* The five-stage decision process model views the consumer as a problem solver and information processor who engages in a variety of mental processes to evaluate various alternatives and determine the degree to which they might satisfy needs or purchase motives. There are, however, other perspectives regarding how consumers acquire the knowledge and experience they use in making purchase decisions. To understand these perspectives, we examine various approaches to learning and their implications for advertising and promotion.

Consumer learning has been defined as "the process by which individuals acquire the purchase and consumption knowledge and experience they apply to future related behavior."[12] Two basic approaches to learning are the behavioral approach and cognitive learning theory.

## Behavioral Learning Theory

Behavioral learning theories emphasize the role of external, environmental stimuli in causing behavior; they minimize the significance of internal psychological processes. Behavioral learning theories are based on the *stimulus–response orientation* (S–R), the premise that learning occurs as the result of responses to external stimuli in the environment. Behavioral learning theorists believe learning occurs through the connection between a stimulus and a response. We will examine the basic principles of two behavioral learning theory approaches: classical conditioning and operant conditioning.

### Classical Conditioning

**Classical conditioning** assumes that learning is an *associative process* with an already existing relationship between a stimulus and a response. Probably the best-known example of this type of learning comes from the studies done with animals by the Russian psychologist Pavlov. Pavlov noticed that at feeding times, his dogs would salivate at the sight of food. The connection between food and salivation is not taught; it is an innate reflex reaction. Because this relationship exists before the conditioning process, the food is referred to as an *unconditioned stimulus* and salivation is an *unconditioned response.* To see if salivation could be conditioned to occur in response to another neutral stimulus, Pavlov paired the ringing of a bell with the presentation of the food. After a number of trials, the dogs learned to salivate at the sound of the bell alone. Thus, the bell became a **conditioned stimulus** that elicited a **conditioned response** resembling the original unconditioned reaction.

Two factors are important for learning to occur through the associative process. The first is contiguity, which means the unconditioned stimulus and conditioned stimulus must be close in time and space. In Pavlov's experiment, the dog learns to associate the ringing of the bell with food because of the contiguous presentation of the two stimuli. The other important principle is *repetition,* or the frequency of the association. The more often the unconditioned and conditioned stimuli occur together, the stronger the association between them will be.

**FIGURE 4–7**
The Classical Conditioning Process

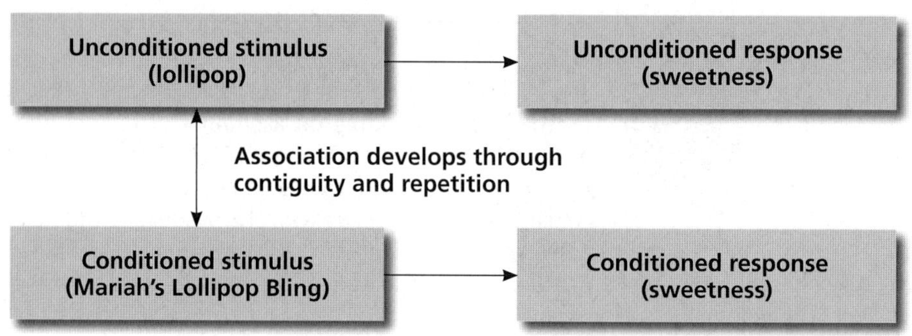


**Applying Classical Conditioning** Learning through classical conditioning plays an important role in marketing. Buyers can be conditioned to form favorable impressions and images of various brands through the associative process. Advertisers strive to associate their products and services with perceptions, images, and emotions known to evoke positive reactions from consumers. Many products are promoted through image advertising, in which the brand is shown with an unconditioned stimulus that elicits pleasant feelings. When the brand is presented simultaneously with this unconditioned stimulus, the brand itself becomes a conditioned stimulus that elicits the same favorable response.

Figure 4–7 provides a diagram of this process, and the ad for Lollipop Bling in Exhibit 4–15 shows an application of this strategy. Notice how this ad associates the product with the look and sweetness of a lollipop. The brand's positioning plays off this association.

Classical conditioning can also associate a product or service with a favorable emotional state. A study by Gerald Gorn used this approach to examine how background music in ads influences product choice.[13] He found that subjects were more likely to choose a product when it was presented against a background of music they liked rather than music they disliked. These results suggest the emotions generated by a commercial are important because they may become associated with the advertised product through classical conditioning. Other studies have shown that music that was congruent with the message enhanced both ad recall and recognition[14] and that music can be used effectively as a mnemonic device to enhance the recall of advertising slogans. Advertisers often attempt to pair a neutral product or service stimulus with an event or situation that arouses positive feelings, such as humor, an exciting sports event, or popular music.

**EXHIBIT 4–15**
Mariah Carey's new perfume associates its product with the looks and sweetness of lollipops

## Operant Conditioning

Classical conditioning views the individual as a passive participant in the learning process who simply receives stimuli. Conditioning occurs as a result of exposure to a stimulus that occurs before the response. In the **operant conditioning** approach, the individual must actively *operate* or act on some aspect of the environment for learning to occur. Operant conditioning is sometimes referred to as *instrumental conditioning* because the individual's response is instrumental in getting a positive reinforcement (reward) or negative reinforcement (a form of reward that occurs when a negative outcome is removed when the desired behavior is performed).

**Reinforcement,** the reward or favorable consequence associated with a particular response, is an important element of instrumental conditioning. Behavior that is reinforced

**FIGURE 4–8**

Instrumental Conditioning in Marketing

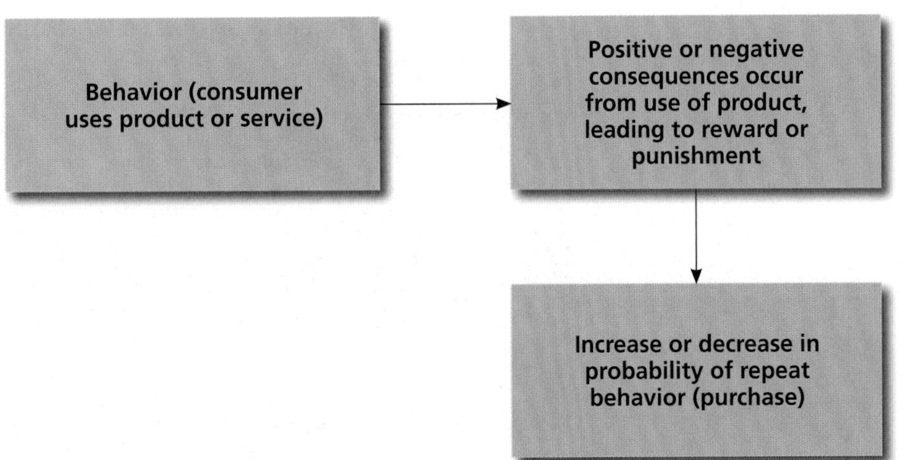


strengthens the bond between a stimulus and a response. Thus, if a consumer buys a product in response to an ad and experiences a positive outcome, the likelihood that the consumer will use this product again increases. If the outcome is not favorable, the likelihood of buying the product again decreases.

The principles of operant conditioning can be applied to marketing, as shown in Figure 4–8. Companies attempt to provide their customers with products and services that satisfy their needs and reward them to reinforce the probability of repeat purchase. Reinforcement can also be implied in advertising; many ads emphasize the benefits or rewards a consumer will receive from using a product or service. Reinforcement also occurs when an ad encourages consumers to use a particular product or brand to avoid unpleasant consequences. For example, the ad for Kyocera printers in Exhibit 4–16 shows how using this product will help avoid negative consequences—that is, the high cost of printing.

**EXHIBIT 4–16**

Kyocera shows how to avoid negative consequences

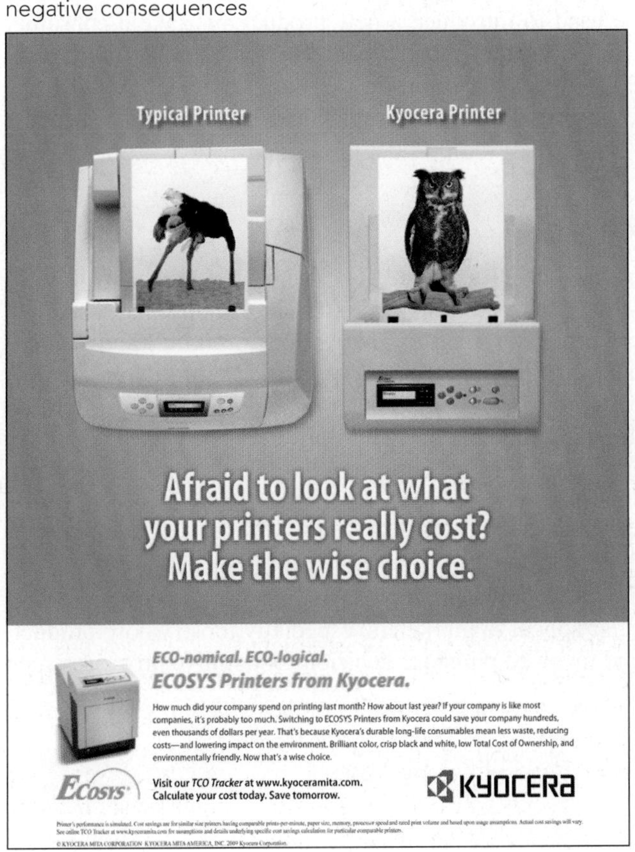


Two concepts that are particularly relevant to marketers in their use of reinforcement through promotional strategies are schedules of reinforcement and shaping. Different **schedules of reinforcement** result in varying patterns of learning and behavior. Learning occurs most rapidly under a *continuous reinforcement schedule,* in which every response is rewarded—but the behavior is likely to cease when the reinforcement stops. Marketers must provide continuous reinforcement to consumers or risk their switching to brands that do.

Learning occurs more slowly but lasts longer when a *partial* or *intermittent reinforcement schedule* is used and only some of the individual's responses are rewarded. Promotional programs have partial reinforcement schedules. A firm may offer consumers an incentive to use the company's product. The firm does not want to offer the incentive every time (continuous reinforcement), because consumers might become dependent on it and stop buying the brand when the incentive is withdrawn. A study that examined the effect of reinforcement on bus ridership found that discount coupons given as rewards for riding the bus were as effective when given on a partial schedule as when given on a continuous schedule.[15] The cost of giving the discount coupons under the partial schedule, however, was considerably less.

Reinforcement schedules can also be used to influence consumer learning and behavior through a process

FIGURE 4–9

Application of Shaping Procedures in Marketing

**Terminal Goal: Repeat Purchase Behavior**

| Approximation Sequence | Shaping Procedure | Reinforcement Applied |
|---|---|---|
| Induce product trial | Free samples distributed; large discount coupon | Product performance; coupon |
| Induce purchase with little financial obligation | Discount coupon prompts purchase with little cost; coupon good for small discount on next purchase enclosed | Product performance; coupon |
| Induce purchase with moderate financial obligation | Small discount coupon prompts purchase with moderate cost | Product performance |
| Induce purchase with full financial obligation | Purchase occurs without coupon assistance | Product performance |

known as **shaping**, the reinforcement of successive acts that lead to a desired behavior pattern or response.

In a promotional context, shaping procedures are used as part of the introductory program for new products. Figure 4–9 provides an example of how samples and discount coupons can be used to introduce a new product and take a consumer from trial to repeat purchase. Marketers must be careful in their use of shaping procedures: If they drop the incentives too soon, the consumer may not establish the desired behavior; but if they overuse them, the consumer's purchase may become contingent on the incentive rather than the product or service.

## Cognitive Learning Theory

Behavioral learning theories have been criticized for assuming a mechanistic view of the consumer that puts too much emphasis on external stimulus factors. They ignore internal psychological processes such as motivation, thinking, and perception; they assume that the external stimulus environment will elicit fairly predictable responses. Many consumer researchers and marketers disagree with the simplified explanations of behavioral learning theories and are more interested in the complex mental processes that underlie consumer decision making. The cognitive approach to studying learning and decision making has dominated the field of consumer behavior in recent years. Figure 4–10 shows how cognitive theorists view the learning process.

Since consumer behavior typically involves choices and decision making, the cognitive perspective has particular appeal to marketers, especially those whose product/service calls for important and involved purchase decisions. Cognitive processes such

FIGURE 4–10

The Cognitive Learning Process

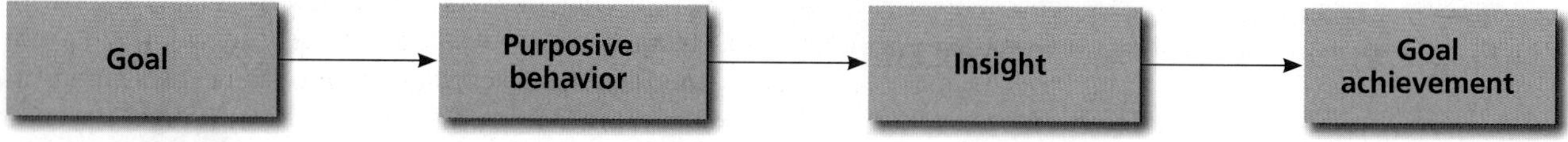

FIGURE 4–11
External Influences on Consumer Behavior

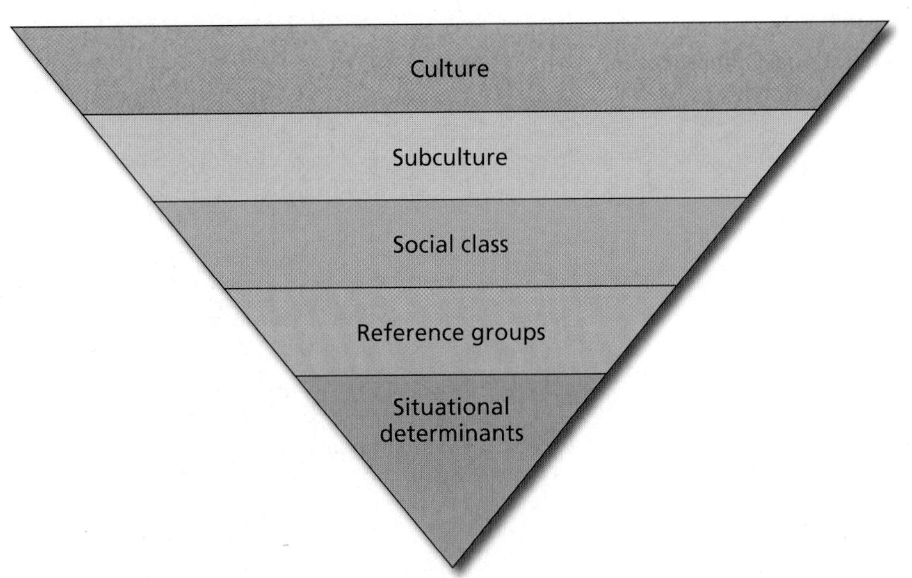


CHAPTER 4

as perception, formation of beliefs about brands, attitude development and change, and integration are important to understanding the decision-making process for many types of purchases. The subprocesses examined during our discussion of the five-stage decision process model are all relevant to a cognitive learning approach to consumer behavior.

## ENVIRONMENTAL INFLUENCES ON CONSUMER BEHAVIOR

The consumer does not make purchase decisions in isolation. A number of external factors have been identified that may influence consumer decision making. They are shown in Figure 4–11 and examined in more detail in the next sections.

### Culture

The broadest and most abstract of the external factors that influence consumer behavior is **culture**, or the complexity of learned meanings, values, norms, and customs shared by members of a society. Cultural norms and values offer direction and guidance to members of a society in all aspects of their lives, including their consumption behavior. It is becoming increasingly important to study the impact of culture on consumer behavior as marketers expand their international marketing efforts. Each country has certain cultural traditions, customs, and values that marketers must understand as they develop marketing programs.

Marketers must also be aware of changes that may be occurring in a particular culture and the implications of these changes for their advertising and promotional strategies and programs. American culture continually goes through many changes that have direct implications for advertising. Marketing researchers monitor these changes and their impact on the ways companies market their products and services.

While marketers recognize that culture exerts a demonstrable influence on consumers, they often find it difficult to respond to cultural differences in different markets. The subtleties of various cultures are often difficult to understand and appreciate, but marketers must understand the cultural context in which consumer purchase decisions are made and adapt their advertising and promotional programs accordingly.

**FIGURE 4–12**

Generational Differences in Shopping Behaviors

A generation is a group of contemporaries, all born during the same period, having shared interests and attitudes. Of interest to marketers, of course, are their shopping behaviors, some of which are shown below. While there are some variations in how different generations are defined, in general the following age groups are pretty much agreed upon:

*Greatest Generation:* *Those born prior to 1946*

With much of their behavior influenced by the Great Depression and World War II, they are frequent shoppers though they often claim they dislike shopping; heavily deal prone; use print cookbooks; spend more than other groups on ice cream, vitamins, also a lot on wine. Like to shop at smaller stores.

*Baby Boomers:* *Born: 1946–1964*

Have the highest annual spending of all groups; spend more than all other groups on wine, pet food, and carbonated beverages; deal prone; comfortable with e-mail and online shopping. Like to shop at local groceries and drugstores.

*Gen X:* *Born: 1965–1976*

Feel pressure for time; like indulgences such as lattes and coffee; spend more than other groups on hair care, cereal, and baby food; like to shop at merchandisers; love to shop at Target.

*Gen Y (Millennials)* *Born: 1977–1994*

More likely to make impulse purchases; prefer mass merchandisers and supercenters; use online coupons and shop online; will Tweet and text others about products, brands, and deals; love shopping at Target.

*Gen Z* *Born: After 1994*

We know least about this group's shopping behaviors to date, may be the hardest to reach; the most connected generation; love electronics; have video games and TVs in their rooms; use their cell phones as cameras, video recorders, and MP3 players; most technologically advanced; concerned about the environment; multitasking marvels. They tend to stay indoors more than other generations; and 80+ percent of those ages 12–17 use social networks—most daily. Communications travel quickly.

## Subcultures

Within a given culture are generally found smaller groups or segments whose beliefs, values, norms, and patterns of behavior set them apart from the larger cultural mainstream. These **subcultures** may be based on age, geographic, religious, racial, and/or ethnic differences. A number of subcultures exist within the United States. The three largest racial/ethnic subcultures are African-Americans, Hispanics, and various Asian groups. These racial/ethnic subcultures are important to marketers because of their size, growth, purchasing power, and distinct purchasing patterns. Marketers develop specific marketing programs for various products and services for these target markets. The ads in Exhibit 4–17 are just two of the many specifically designed to appeal to U.S. subcultures—in these cases, blacks and Hispanics. Many others can easily be found that target teens, generations X and Y, the elderly, and so on. Figure 4–12 demonstrates how one's generation may influence purchases.

**Social Class** Virtually all societies exhibit some form of stratification whereby individuals can be assigned to a specific social category on the basis of criteria important to members of that society. **Social class** refers to relatively homogeneous divisions in a society into which people sharing similar lifestyles, values, norms, interests, and behaviors can be grouped. While a number of methods for determining

**EXHIBIT 4–17**
Ads targeted to subcultures

social class exist, class structures in the United States are usually based on occupational status, educational attainment, and income. Sociologists generally agree there are three broad levels of social classes in the United States: the upper (14 percent), middle (70 percent), and lower (16 percent) classes.

Tropez
Your color.
Your style.
Take a look at Tropez, a line of cosmetics specially formulated for Latina skin tones. Choose from a bold spectrum of high pearl eyeshadows to enhance your eyes. Use bronzer for a sexy glow all year long. And add a touch of sheer gloss for stunning kissable lips on the go. With so many beautiful options, you can afford to create a perfect look all your own.
www.tropezbeauty.com | Bianca is wearing Opposites Attract Eyeshadow Quad in Ocean Breeze, Bronzer Deluxe in Paradise Gold, Precious Kisses Lip Gloss Quartet in Summer Fantasia and Double Dare Mascara & Primer in Midnight Black. ©2007 Markwins Beauty Products Inc.

Social class is an important concept to marketers, since consumers within each social stratum often have similar values, lifestyles, and buying behavior. Thus, the various social class groups provide a natural basis for market segmentation. Consumers in the different social classes differ in the degree to which they use various products and services and in their leisure activities, shopping patterns, and media habits. Marketers respond to these differences through the positioning of their products and services, the media strategies they use to reach different social classes, and the types of advertising appeals they develop. The ad in Exhibit 4–18 shows how a product attempts to appeal to the upper classes in both copy and illustration.

**EXHIBIT 4–18**
This Jaguar ad attempts to appeal to the upper classes

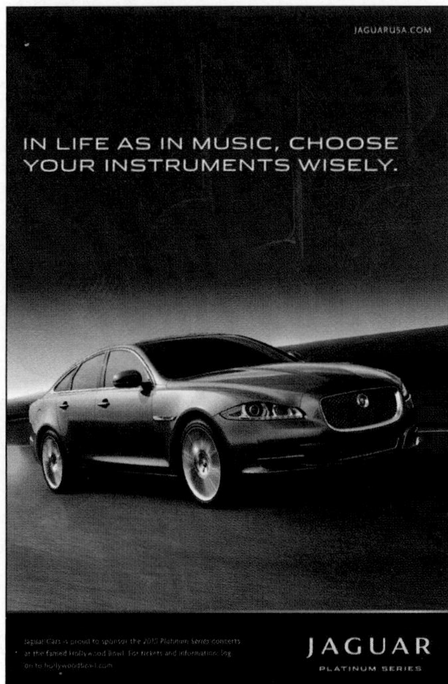

JAGUARUSA.COM
IN LIFE AS IN MUSIC, CHOOSE YOUR INSTRUMENTS WISELY.
JAGUAR
PLATINUM SERIES


## Reference Groups

Think about the last time you attended a party. As you dressed for the party, you probably asked yourself (or someone else) what others would be wearing. Your selection of attire may have been influenced by those likely to be present. This simple example reflects one form of impact that groups may exert on your behavior.

A group has been defined as "two or more individuals who share a set of norms, values, or beliefs and have certain implicitly or explicitly defined relationships to one another such that their behavior is interdependent."[16] Groups are one of the primary factors influencing learning and socialization, and group situations constitute many of our purchase decisions.

A **reference group** is "a group whose presumed perspectives or values are being used by an individual as the basis for his or her judgments, opinions, and actions." Consumers use three types of reference groups (associative, aspirational, and disassociative) as a guide to specific behaviors, even when the groups are not present. In the party example, your peers—although not present—provided a standard of dress that you

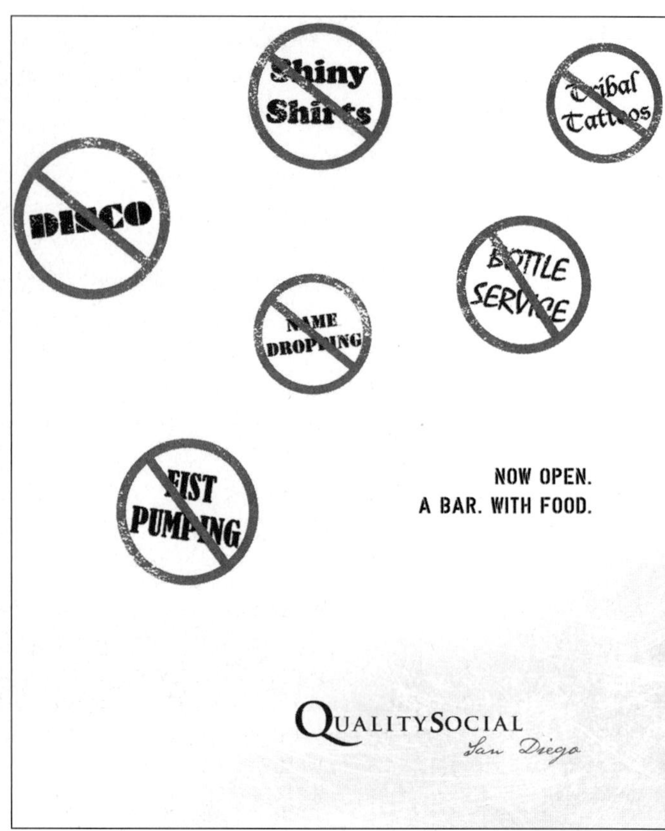


**EXHIBIT 4–19**
The ad on the left shows an aspirational reference group, the one on the right stresses a disassociative reference group

referred to in your clothing selection. Likewise, your college classmates, family, and co-workers, or even a group to which you aspire, may serve as referents, and your consumption patterns will typically conform to the expectations of the groups that are most important to you.

Marketers use reference group influences in developing advertisements and promotional strategies. The ads in Exhibit 4–19 are examples of *aspirational* reference groups (to which we might like to belong) and *disassociative* groups (to which we do not wish to belong), respectively.

**Family Decision Making: An Example of Group Influences** In some instances, the group may be involved more directly than just as a referent. Family members may serve as referents to each other, or they may actually be involved in the purchase decision process—acting as an individual buying unit. As shown in Figure 4–13, family members may assume a variety of roles in the decision-making process. Each role has implications for marketers.

First, the advertiser must determine who is responsible for the various roles in the decision-making process so messages can be targeted at that person (or those people). These roles will also dictate media strategies, since the appropriate magazines, newspapers, or TV or radio stations must be used. Second, understanding the decision-making process and the use of information by individual family members is critical to the design of messages and choice of promotional program elements. In sum, to create an effective promotional program, a marketer must have an overall understanding of how the decision process works and the role that each family member plays.

## Situational Determinants

The final external factor is the purchase and usage situation. The specific situation in which consumers plan to use the product or brand directly affects their perceptions,

**FIGURE 4–13**
Roles in the Family Decision–Making Process

**The initiator.** The person responsible for initiating the purchase decision process, for example, the mother who determines she needs a new car.

**The information provider.** The individual responsible for gathering information to be used in making the decision, for example, the teenage car buff who knows where to find product information in specific magazines or collects it from dealers.

**The influencer.** The person who exerts influence as to what criteria will be used in the selection process. All members of the family may be involved. The mother may have her criteria, whereas others may each have their own input.

**The decision maker(s).** That person(s) who actually makes the decision. In our example, it may be the mother alone or in combination with another family member.

**The purchasing agent.** The individual who performs the physical act of making the purchase. In the case of a car, a husband and wife may decide to choose it together and sign the purchase agreement.

**The consumer.** The actual user of the product. In the case of a family car, all family members are consumers. For a private car, only the mother might be the consumer.



preferences, and purchasing behaviors. Three types of **situational determinants** may have an effect: the specific usage situation, the purchase situation, and the communications situation.

*Usage* refers to the circumstance in which the product will be used. For example, purchases made for private consumption may be thought of differently from those that will be obvious to the public. The *purchase* situation more directly involves the environment operating at the time of the purchase. Time constraints, store environments, and other factors may all have an impact. The *communications* situation is the condition in which an advertising exposure occurs (in a car listening to the radio, with friends, etc.). This may be most relevant to the development of promotional strategies, because the impact on the consumer will vary according to the particular situation. For example, a consumer may pay more attention to a commercial that is heard alone at home than to one heard in the presence of friends, at work, or anywhere distractions may be present. If advertisers can isolate a particular time when the listener is likely to be attentive, they will probably earn his or her undivided attention.

In sum, situational determinants may either enhance or detract from the potential success of a message. To the degree that advertisers can assess situational influences that may be operating, they will increase the likelihood of successfully communicating with their target audiences.

## ALTERNATIVE APPROACHES TO CONSUMER BEHAVIOR

In addition to the perspectives discussed, consumer researchers complement these psychological approaches with perspectives driven from other scientific disciplines, such as economics, sociology, anthropology, philosophy, semiotics, neuroscience, or history. These cross-disciplinary perspectives have broadened the realm of methodologies used to study consumers and have provided additional insights into consumer decision processes.

### New Methodologies

Whereas psychologists often study consumer responses to advertising and other forms of communication in controlled settings, where environmental variables can be kept constant, sociologists and anthropologists study behavior in context. For this reason, they often employ qualitative methodologies such as individual interviews, participant observation studies, and/or ethnographies. These methods help capture the social, cultural, and environmental influences that may affect consumer behavior.

The humanities have also been a source of new methodologies for consumer research. Historians and semioticians focus their analyses on the advertising messages and other forms of communications themselves. These researchers examine the significance of communications from a linguistic or historical perspective. Research methods such as semiotic and structural analyses examine the symbolic meanings of advertising and different facets of consumption.

### New Insights

These alternative perspectives and methodologies provide additional insights and expand our knowledge of consumers. For example, the cultural significance of advertising messages in shaping cultures and triggering communities is now better understood. Likewise, marketers now have a better understanding of how advertising campaigns become popular and help shape our culture. Thanks to the many interpretive analyses of advertisements over recent years, we are also more aware of the influence of advertising images on society.

Some consumer researchers believe that cross-disciplinary research is better suited for the study of consumers because it takes into account their complexity and multidimensionality. When considered along with psychological research, these alternative approaches help us better understand the impact of communications.

## Summary

This chapter introduced you to the field of consumer behavior and examined its relevance to promotional strategy. Consumer behavior is best viewed as the process and activities that people engage in when searching for, selecting, purchasing, using, evaluating, and disposing of products and services to satisfy their needs and desires. A five-stage model of the consumer decision-making process consists of problem recognition, information search, alternative evaluation, purchase, and postpurchase evaluation. Internal psychological processes that influence the consumer decision-making process include motivation, perception, attitude formation and change, and integration processes.

The decision process model views consumer behavior primarily from a cognitive orientation. The chapter considered other perspectives by examining various approaches to consumer learning and their implications for advertising and promotion. Behavioral learning theories such as classical conditioning and operant (instrumental) conditioning were discussed. Problems with behavioral learning theories were noted, and the alternative perspective of cognitive learning was discussed.

The chapter also examined relevant external factors that influence consumer decision making. Culture, subculture, social class, reference groups, and situational determinants were discussed, along with their implications for the development of promotional strategies and programs. The chapter concluded with an introduction to alternative perspectives on the study of consumer behavior (also called interpretive, postmodern, or postpositivist perspectives).

## Key Terms

**consumer behavior** p. 110
**problem recognition** p. 111
**want** p. 112
**motives** p. 113
**hierarchy of needs** p. 113
**psychoanalytic theory** p. 115
**motivation research** p. 115
**internal search** p. 117
**external search** p. 117
**perception** p. 118
**sensation** p. 118
**selective perception** p. 119
**selective exposure** p. 119
**selective attention** p. 119
**selective comprehension** p. 119
**selective retention** p. 119
**mnemonics** p. 119
**subliminal perception** p. 120
**evaluative criteria** p. 123
**functional consequences** p. 123
**psychosocial consequences** p. 123
**multiattribute attitude model** p. 124
**salient beliefs** p. 124
**integration processes** p. 125
**heuristics** p. 125
**affect referral decision rule** p. 125
**purchase intention** p. 126
**brand loyalty** p. 126
**cognitive dissonance** p. 127
**classical conditioning** p. 129
**conditioned stimulus** p. 129
**conditioned response** p. 129
**operant conditioning** p. 130
**reinforcement** p. 130
**schedules of reinforcement** p. 131
**shaping** p. 132
**culture** p. 133
**subcultures** p. 134
**social class** p. 134
**reference group** p. 135
**situational determinants** p. 137

## Discussion Questions

1. Consumers experience different forms of problem recognition. Explain each type of problem recognition and give an example of a purchase of this type. (LO2)

2. The chapter discusses the role of neuroscience in understanding consumer behavior. Discuss what is meant by neuroscience and provide examples of how this field of study may be useful to consumer behavior. (LO3)

3. How might one's social class influence their consumer behaviors? Give examples of products and/or services that might be influenced by social class standing. (LO5)

4. There has been controversy over the existence and impact of subliminal advertising for quite some time. Explain why. Why do you think this topic continues to hold so much interest? (LO3)

5. Explain the process of selective perception, and the various ways in which consumers may filter information. What is the relevance of this for consumer behavior? (LO3)

6. Why is understanding consumer behavior of such importance to marketers? Give examples of how marketers apply their understanding of consumer behavior to their marketing strategies. (LO1)

7. Recently, there has been a great deal of attention paid to environmental issues resulting in a number of companies embarking on "green" campaigns. Discuss some of the reasons why companies are developing such campaigns. Do you think these campaigns will change consumers' attitudes toward the environment and/or these companies? (LO5)

8. One of the fastest growing market segments in the United States are Hispanics. Discuss how marketers have attempted to appeal to Hispanics. Do Hispanics require a different set of IMC strategies than others? Explain. (LO5)

9. Explain the differences between functional and psychosocial consequences. Give examples of advertising that focus on both types. (LO3)

10. Discuss some of the problems associated with psychoanalytic theory and its applications to understanding consumer behavior. Also, discuss some of the contributions made to our understanding of consumers. (LO3)

## AdForum Exercise: "Understanding the Use of Theory in Developing Advertising Appeals."

(See Advertising and Promotion Playlist, Chapter 4)

This chapter discussed some of the theoretical bases that have been examined in an attempt to understand consumer behaviors. The playlist for Chapter 4 contains a variety of commercials and print ads that may be based on one or more of these theories. Examine each of the ads included here, and answer the following questions:

1 Explain how each ad reflects one of the theories discussed in the chapter. Which of these theories best explains the appeal being used?

2 Are there alternative theories that could also be used to describe the appeals?

3 Discuss how three of the commercials might have created appeals employing one of the other theories as a foundation.

Access to the chapter playlist is available through 

, www.mcgrawhillconnect.com

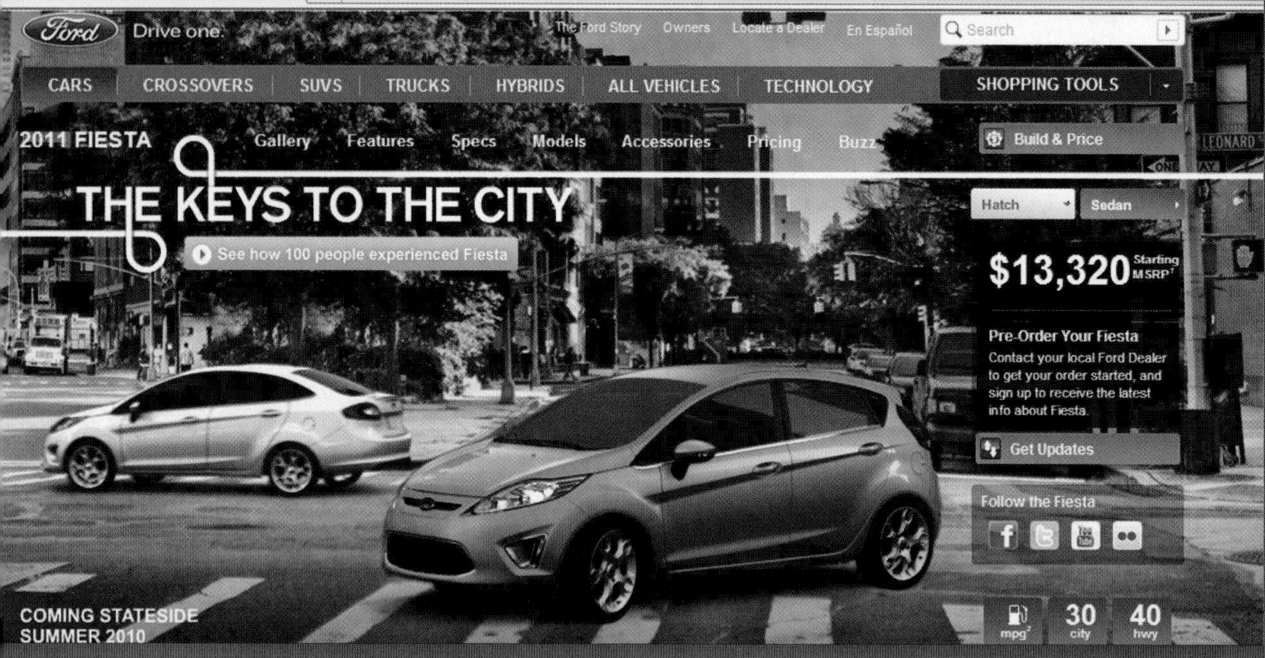


## LEARNING OBJECTIVES

LO1 To understand the basic elements of the communication process and the role of communications in marketing.

LO2 To examine various models of the communication process.

LO3 To analyze the response processes of receivers of marketing communications, including alternative response hierarchies and their implications for promotional planning and strategy.

LO4 To examine the nature of consumers' cognitive processing of marketing communications.

# 5 The Communication Process

## FORD CREATES A MOVEMENT TO LAUNCH THE FIESTA

The past two years have been very difficult for the automobile industry, as auto sales around the world have been impacted by the global recession. In the United States, sales declined from nearly 17 million units in 2008 to just under 10 million in 2009. The U.S. government had to take partial ownership in General Motors for the company to survive, and Chrysler was acquired by Italian automaker Fiat. However, Ford Motor Co., the third major U.S. automaker, managed to make it through the recession without any help and has positioned itself well for growth. A major part of Ford's strategy has been to focus on smaller, greener, more fuel efficient "global" cars that are built on a single platform which reduces costs and, with some minor modifications, can be sold in markets around the world.

One of the cars Ford is counting on to fuel its growth is the Fiesta, a global subcompact that was introduced in Europe in 1976 and has sold more than 12 million units since then. The most recent generation of the Fiesta was launched in Europe in 2008 and over 750,000 have been sold. Ford launched the Fiesta in the United States in mid-2010. However, the company recognized that it would face some challenges in marketing the Fiesta here as it is one of the smallest cars on the market and, unlike Europeans, most Americans don't like small cars. Moreover, among those who buy small cars, Ford is generally not one of the brands they consider. So rather than use a traditional marketing campaign that relied heavily on traditional media as well as the Internet, Ford took a much different and riskier approach that utilized an aggressive social media program. To gear up for their small car revolution, Ford launched the "Fiesta Movement" which involved enlisting a team of 100 special agents to test drive European Fiestas a full year before the car was available in the U.S. market. These agents participated in monthly challenges (so-called "missions") that would allow them to share interesting experiences with their friends through various forms of social media.

The idea behind the Fiesta Movement was born in the summer of 2008 when Ford's Vice President of Global Marketing Jim Farley asked the Fiesta Brand Manager Sam De La Garza what the company could do if 1,000 European Fiestas were shipped from Europe to the United States. The brainstorming included a variety of options including test drive tours, hosting events, and even dealer displays. However, Ford's marketing team recognized that the market it was targeting for the Fiesta was changing as the baby boomers and Gen Xers were being supplanted by 20-something Millenials who are more comfortable with nontraditional media such as blogs, Facebook, Twitter, and YouTube. Ford calls these new buyers "lifestreamers" as they like to constantly update their status on Facebook and text or Twitter about things going on in their life such as a song they like, things they are doing, or something that just happened such as a cool car that just drove by. Given this target audience, Ford worked with their advertising agency, Team Detroit, to brainstorm how to best put European Fiestas in the hands of consumers. Team Detroit and Ford developed the idea of the Fiesta Movement and leveraged digital think tank Undercurrent in New York to maximize what could have been just a 100 person test drive.

The 100 Fiesta agents were chosen from more than 4,000 consumers who applied by creating a YouTube video answering one simple question: "why do you want to drive a Ford Fiesta for six months?" Participants were selected based on their entrepreneurial spirit, number of social network followers or friends, social vibrancy, and creative vision and were spread among major markets across the United States. The social media trendsetters were given a new Fiesta, insurance, and gas cards and in spring 2009 began driving the cars. Ford had just one requirement for the Fiesta agents-they had to complete one "mission" or task each month, such as "drive until you run out of gas," and document their experiences behind the wheel by posting videos and updating their friends and followers on Facebook, YouTube, Twitter and other social media. The first chapter of the Fiesta Movement was about building awareness of the car and was very successful as by the end of 2009, the program had generated more than 6.2 million YouTube views, more than 750,000 Flickr views, and nearly 4 million Twitter impressions. It also set a Guinness World Record for the most attendees at a tweetup during the Fiesta Movement Awards Celebration in Hollywood in December 2009 that brought together 1,149 Fiesta Movement agents and their friends and followers.

In March 2010, chapter 2 of the Fiesta Movement began with the goal being to show more features of the new car and provide a much deeper local connection. For the second phase of the campaign 40 people were selected from more than 1,000 applicants and 20 teams comprised of 2 agents each were formed to spread the word about the Fiesta in 16 markets across the country where small cars sell well. The agent teams were given a series of missions asking them to complete challenges that were tied to people and activities in their local communities, allowing them to open the discussion about the Fiesta through social media and at the events they hosted. After completing a mission, the agents produced and placed the creative content online at www.Fiestamovement2.com, where followers could also keep up with their favorite agents. The best creative content was recognized based on online and off-line consumer interaction and consumers' opinions of the agents' work. It was also recognized through coverage in local media and events as well as through a variety of national media. Connie Fontaine, Ford's Brand Content and Alliances manager, described this as a natural progression from the first phase of the Fiesta Movement, noting that "Chapter 2 will still be rooted in social media, but this time the content will also live off-line and find its way into new mediums. Fiesta clearly needs to be the star now as the agents share their work with their communities and beyond." Buzz for the Fiesta has continued to grow, with Fiesta Movement 2 creating even more social media interactions.

The Fiesta Movement goes far beyond what any automotive marketer, or perhaps any company, has done in the past to launch a new product and was risky given that Ford put no restrictions on what their agents could say about the car. Brand manager De La Garza noted that the messages being sent by the agents were beyond Ford's control and that they had to roll with it. He noted that "For us it all rests on the quality of this product. We've all driven the Fiesta, and we feel so confident about the car that we could start this. We're going to allow people to tell the story of the Fiesta from their lives." However, Scott Monty, Ford's director–social media, acknowledged that "faith in a product or no, trusting it enough to unleash 100 to regular consumers and ask them to offer honest thoughts and reviews is a leap for most marketers. It will require a new kind of corporate responsiveness and flexibility as no matter how well you plan for something like this, something else always comes up. This is not only an experiment for Ford in terms of a marketing program, it's an experiment for us in terms of how we react to how the market picks it up."

So far the market appears to be picking up on the Fiesta Movement quite well. After the first chapter of the program more than 11,000 consumers had made reservations for the Fiesta, half of them from non-Ford customers and more than 100,000 handraisers were showing interest in the new car and requesting more information about it. The Fiesta hit the showrooms in the summer of 2010, and while Ford was using advertising and other forms of integrated marketing to introduce it, they actually spent 20 to 30 percent less on media than for a traditional new product launch.

Ford has a lot riding on the new Fiesta as it is the first of several European subcompact cars that Ford plans to bring to the U.S market. Global marketing VP Jim Farley feels that "the Fiesta can be our breakthrough product in getting people to fall back in love with Ford cars, and to do that, we have to have cars that people get emotional about and want to buy." The Fiesta Movement appears to be a great way to get young people excited about Ford cars and to tell their friends as well.

Sources: "New Set of Agents Team Up to Bring Ford Fiesta Local with Fiesta Movement Chapter 2, *PR Newswire*, March 1, 2010; Mark Rechtin, "Fiesta Viral Marketing: Chapter 2, *Automotive News*, 84 (6390) December 14, 2009, p. 6; Terry Box, "Ford Targets Young Drivers with Fiesta Movement," *McClatchy-Tribune News Service*, July 10, 2009; Michael Learmonth, "Ford's Fiesta to Party On—Without the Fiesta," *Advertising Age*, September 14, 2009, http:adage.com/print?article_id=138979; Eric Tegler, "Ford Is Counting on Army of 100 Bloggers to Launch New Fiesta," *Advertising Age*, April 20, 2009, http:adage.com/print?article_id=136045.

The function of all elements of the integrated marketing communications program is to communicate. An organization's IMC strategy is implemented through the various communications it sends to current or prospective customers as well as other relevant publics. Organizations send communications and messages in a variety of ways, such as through advertisements, brand names, logos and graphic systems, websites, press releases, package designs, promotions, and visual images. As was discussed in the chapter opener, companies such as Ford are developing more innovative ways to communicate with consumers and deliver their marketing messages as it is becoming increasingly difficult to do so through traditional media.



The way marketers communicate with their target audiences depends on many factors, including how much current and/or potential customers know and what they think about a company or brand and the image it hopes to create. Those involved in the planning and implementation of an IMC program need to understand the communication process and what it means in terms of how they create, deliver, manage, and evaluate messages about a company or brand. Developing an effective marketing communications program is far more complicated than just choosing a product feature or attribute to emphasize. Marketers must understand how consumers will perceive and interpret their messages and how these reactions will shape consumers' responses to the company and/or its product or service. And as the use of social media becomes more prevalent, it is important that marketers understand how consumers communicate with one another and how they can participate in and even influence these conversations.

This chapter reviews the fundamentals of communication and examines various perspectives and models regarding how consumers respond to advertising and promotional messages. Our goal is to demonstrate how valuable an understanding of the communication process can be in planning, implementing, and evaluating the marketing communications program.

## THE NATURE OF COMMUNICATION

**Communication** has been variously defined as the passing of information, the exchange of ideas, or the process of establishing a commonness or oneness of thought between a sender and a receiver.[1] These definitions suggest that for communication to occur, there must be some common thinking between two parties and information must be passed from one person to another (or from one group to another). As you will see in this chapter, establishing this commonality in thinking is not always as easy as it might seem; many attempts to communicate are unsuccessful.

The communication process is often very complex. Success depends on such factors as the nature of the message, the audience's interpretation of it, and the environment in which it is received. The receiver's perception of the source and the medium used to transmit the message may also affect the ability to communicate, as do many other factors. Words, pictures, sounds, and colors may have different meanings to different audiences, and people's perceptions and interpretations of them vary. For example, if you ask for a soda on the East Coast or West Coast, you'll receive a soft drink such as Coke or Pepsi. However, in parts of the Midwest and South, a soft drink is referred to as pop. If you ask for a soda, you may get a glass of pop with ice cream in it. Marketers must understand the meanings that words and symbols take on and how they influence consumers' interpretation of products and messages.

Language is one of the major barriers to effective communication, as there are different languages in different countries, different languages or dialects within a single country, and more subtle problems of linguistic nuance and vernacular. This can be particularly challenging to companies marketing their products in foreign countries, as discussed in Global Perspective 5–1. The growth of bilingual, multicultural ethnic markets in the United States is also creating challenges for domestic marketers. For example, while many marketers are recognizing the importance of appealing to the

# Global Perspective 1–1 > > >

## Communication Problems in International Marketing

Communication is a major problem facing companies that market their products and services in foreign countries. Language is one of the main barriers to effective communication, as there can be different languages or dialects within a single country, and more subtle problems of linguistic nuance and vernacular. For example, China has many languages and dialects, with differences great enough that people from different regions of the country often cannot understand each other. As another example, about 40 percent of the Canadian population does not use English as its preferred language. Of the non-English speakers, about 60 percent speak French with the balance spread among a dozen or so other languages.

Mistranslations and faulty word choices have often created problems for companies in foreign markets. International marketers must also be aware of the connotation of the words, signs, symbols, and expressions they use as brand names or logos or in various forms of promotion. Also, advertising copy, slogans, and symbols do not always transfer well into other languages. This not only impedes communication but also sometimes results in embarrassing blunders that can damage a company's or a brand's credibility or image and thereby cost it customers.

There are several widely cited examples of translation problems. For example, when Coca-Cola introduced its brand into China, the Chinese characters sounded like *Coca-Cola* but meant "bite the wax tadpole." With the help of a language specialist, the company substituted four Mandarin characters that retained the Coca-Cola sound but mean "can happy, mouth happy." KFC also encountered translation problems when the company first entered China in 1986 as its classic "Finger-lickin good" tagline was wrongly translated in Chinese to "Eat your fingers off." Then there is the classic story of when General Motors (GM) and Chevrolet introduced its Nova to Latin America: The car did not do well because "no va" means "won't go" in Spanish. However, GM denied that the name was a problem, noting that the brand did pretty well in these markets and that in grammatical terms, "no va" is *not* how a Spanish speaker would describe a dead car. However, the company did change the name of the car to the Caribe in Spanish speaking markets.

Company and brand names can also get lost in translation. Before launching *Good Housekeeping* magazine in Japan, the Hearst Corporation experimented with a number of Japanese translations of the title. The closest word in Japanese, *kaji,* means "domestic duties," which can be interpreted as work performed by servants. Hearst decided to retain the English name for the magazine, but the word *Good* appears on the cover in much larger type than the word *Housekeeping.* Mercedes-Benz also ran into a problem in 2005 when the company shortened the name of its Grand Sports Tourer to the sleek, succinct GST. However, in Canada, GST is the acronym for the widely loathed goods and services tax, which presents Canadians with the prospect of calculating the GST on the GST!

Global marketers can also encounter barriers with regard to culture and language when trying to describe characteristics of new products, such as their attributes and benefits or the way they perform, in terms that consumers in other countries can understand. The Chicago-based market research firm Synovate uses a technique for its clients called vocabulary elicitation to identify a list of attributes that consumers use to describe various product qualities in terms that are relevant to their

Hispanic market, they find that communicating with this fast-growing segment can be very challenging. They have to decide whether to use ads with a Hispanic-focused creative, dub or remake general market campaigns into Spanish, or run English-language ads and hope that they will be picked up by bilingual Hispanics. Many companies are creating ads specifically for the Hispanic market. Exhibit 5–1 shows an outdoor ad the California Milk Processor Board developed to target Hispanic consumers. Notice how the message in the ad (Family, Love and Milk) addresses commitment to family, which is a strong traditional Latino value.

# A BASIC MODEL OF COMMUNICATION

Over the years, a basic model of the various elements of the communication process has evolved, as shown in Figure 5–1 on page 148.[2] Two elements represent the major participants in the communication process, the sender and the receiver. Another two are the major communication tools, message and channel. Four others are the language and culture. One of the company's clients, a large multinational beverage company, planned to introduce a new product in Japan that had recently been introduced in North America. However, the description of some of the product attributes used in ads run in the United States and Canada lacked meaning in Japanese culture. To address the problem, Synovate conducted a vocabulary elicitation study to identify characteristics that Japanese consumers could use to evaluate the new product. For example, one of the beverage attributes was understood by consumers in North America to mean "creaminess in the mouth" but Japanese consumers lacked a corresponding descriptor for the trait. Synovate's research found that the term "milk feel" could be used to describe the product characteristic so that it would be understood by Japanese consumers in advertising as well as other marketing communications.

Companies can run into problems even when the same language is used in two countries as there may be cultural differences regarding the meaning of various words or phrases. For example, the New York–based company RecycleBank, which sets up rewards programs for individuals based on the amount they recycle, encountered an unexpected language problem when it recently expanded into England. The company was concerned and confused when the British press called the program a "scheme" in its otherwise positive coverage. However, it soon learned that the word "scheme" held no connotation of deceit in Britain, as it does in America.

Many multinational companies are trying to develop global brands that can be marketed internationally using the same brand name and advertising campaigns. However, they must be careful that brand names, advertising slogans, signs, symbols, and other forms of marketing communication don't lose something in the translation. There are several things international marketers can do to avoid joining the top 10 list of language blunders. The first line of defense is to hire a translation service to review the material and make sure there are no problems. However, experts note that relying on translators alone may not be foolproof as they may not be steeped in current slang or the subtleties of a language. The experts recommend that translated materials be read by a linguistically mixed staff as well as by contacts in the local market who know dialects and slang. For example, at the international branding consulting firm Landor Associates, new brand names or ad slogans trigger native-speaker checks in eight languages.

While the use of translators and native-speaker checks can help to identify language problems, they do not solve the problem of how well an ad campaign translates into another culture. The vice president of marketing for the direct marketing agency Infocore notes that ad campaign concepts will never translate perfectly into another culture, which is a problem that many marketers do not want to acknowledge. He cites two basic problems including multinational ad agencies being constrained by managers who do not want to surrender power to strangers in foreign markets, and the "don't mess with the creative" mantra of marketers who assume that the magic of a campaign that works in one culture can be grafted onto another.

Time and again, problems with brand names, ad slogans, and visual signs and symbols have come back to haunt even the best of marketers. As Simon Anholt, a British marketing and branding expert, notes: "Language is in many respects such a silly little thing, but it has the power to bring marketing directors to their knees. That's where the terror lies."

Sources: Mark Laswell, "Lost in Translation," *Business 2.0,* August 2004, pp. 68–70; Kevin Reagan, "In Asia, Think Globally Communicate Locally," *Marketing News,* July 19, 1999, pp. 12, 14; Yumiko Ono, "Will Good Housekeeping Translate into Japanese?" *The Wall Street Journal,* December 30, 1997, p. B1; Deborah L. Venice, "Proper Message, Design in Global Markets Require Tests," *Marketing News,* September 1, 2006, pp. 18, 24–25; Emily Maltby, "Expanding Abroad? Avoid Cultural Gaffes," *The Wall Street Journal,* January 19, 2010, p. B5.

**EXHIBIT 5–1**
This outdoor ad for milk targets Hispanic consumers by appealing to love for family

major communication functions and processes: encoding, decoding, response, and feedback. The last element, noise, refers to any extraneous factors in the system that can interfere with the process and work against effective communication.

## Source Encoding

The sender, or **source**, of a communication is the person or organization that has information to share with another person or group of people. The source may be an individual (say, a salesperson or hired spokesperson, such as a celebrity, who appears in a company's advertisements) or a nonpersonal entity (such as the corporation or organization itself). For example, the source of many ads is the company, since no specific spokesperson or source is shown. However, many companies use a spokesperson to appear in their ads and to deliver their advertising messages. In some

**FIGURE 5–1**
A Model of the Communication Process

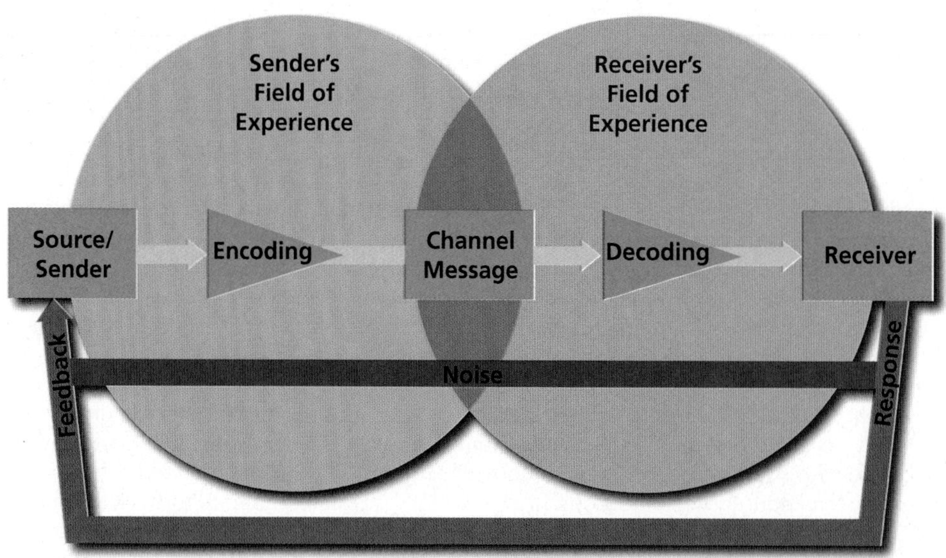


cases, a popular spokesperson can play a very important role in attracting attention to a company's advertising and delivering the message, as well as influencing how well it is received by the target audience. For example, the Citizen Watch Company has featured a variety of rising sports stars as spokespersons in the "Unstoppable" campaign for its Eco-Drive watches which was first launched in 2003. Exhibit 5–2 shows one of the ads from the campaign featuring professional golfer Paula Creamer.

Because the receiver's perceptions of the source influence how the communication is received, marketers must be careful to select a communicator the receiver believes is knowledgeable and trustworthy or with whom the receiver can identify or relate in some manner. (How these characteristics influence the receiver's responses is discussed further in Chapter 6.)

The communication process begins when the source selects words, symbols, pictures, and the like, to represent the message that will be delivered to the receiver(s). This process, known as **encoding**, involves putting thoughts, ideas, or information into a symbolic form. The sender's goal is to encode the message in such a way that it will be understood by the receiver. This means using words, signs, or symbols that are familiar to the target audience. Many symbols have universal meaning, such as the familiar circle with a line through it to denote no parking, no smoking, and so forth. Many companies also have highly recognizable symbols—such as McDonald's golden arches, Nike's swoosh, or the Coca-Cola trademark—that are known to consumers around the world.

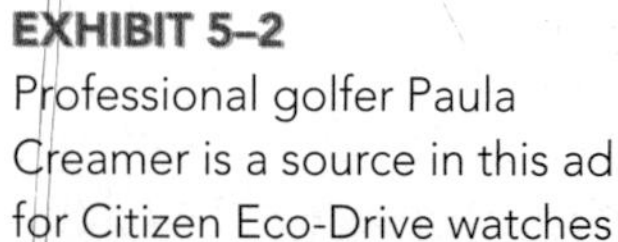

**EXHIBIT 5–2**
Professional golfer Paula Creamer is a source in this ad for Citizen Eco-Drive watches

## Message

The encoding process leads to development of a **message** that contains the information or meaning the source hopes to convey. The message may be verbal or nonverbal, oral or written, or symbolic. Messages must be put into a transmittable form that is appropriate for the channel of communication being used. In advertising, this may range from simply writing some words or copy that will be read as a radio message to producing an expensive television commercial. For many products, it is not the actual words of the message that determine its communication effectiveness but rather the impression or image the ad creates. Notice how the Coach ad shown in Exhibit 5–3 uses only a picture to deliver its message. However, the use of the brand name and picture is an effective way to communicate Coach's intended message of the eloquent simplicity as well as classic design and American style of its handbags.

Marketers must make decisions regarding the *content* of the messages they send to consumers as well as the *structure* and *design* of these messages. Content refers to the information and/or meaning contained in the

**EXHIBIT 5–3**
The image projected by an ad often communicates more than words

message while structure and design refer to the way the message is put together in order to deliver the information or intended meaning. More attention will be given to issues regarding message appeal and structure in the next chapter while message design is discussed in the chapters on creative strategy (Chapters 8 and 9).



## Channel

The **channel** is the method by which the communication travels from the source or sender to the receiver. At the broadest level, channels of communication are of two types, personal and nonpersonal. *Personal channels* of communication are direct interpersonal (face-to-face) contact with target individuals or groups. Salespeople serve as personal channels of communication when they deliver their sales message to a buyer or potential customer. Social channels of communication such as friends, neighbors, associates, co-workers, or family members are also personal channels. They often represent **word-of-mouth communication,** a powerful source of information for consumers.[3]

Many companies work hard to generate positive word-of-mouth discussion for their companies or brands using various buzz marketing techniques. **Buzz marketing** is just one of the new names for what used to be known simply as word-of-mouth communication while terms such as *consumer-generated marketing* and *viral marketing* are also used to describe the process.[4] The use of word-of-mouth marketing is really nothing new as marketers have long been handing out product samples and providing products to influential people and encouraging them to recommend the brand to others. For example, alcoholic beverage marketers have long understood the value of getting bartenders, waiters, and waitresses to hype their brands while pharmaceutical companies have always worked to encourage influential physicians to talk up their products to their peers. However, what is new is the number of companies that are now using buzz marketing, and the sophisticated ways they are going about it. Marketers use techniques such as contests that encourage consumers to create user-generated content and then use social media to disseminate it as a way to spread the word about their brands. For example, Frito Lay has sponsored "Crash the Super Bowl" competitions the past several years where consumers have been asked to create ads for its Doritos brand (Exhibit 5–4). The company actually aired four consumer-generated Doritos commercials during the 2010 Super Bowl and they were among the most popular spots shown during the game.[5]

**EXHIBIT 5–4**
Frito Lay sponsors competitions for consumer-generated commercials that have been shown during the Super Bowl

**EXHIBIT 5–5**
Vocalpoint is an online community where mothers can share information about products and various issues

Many marketers are focusing on creating viral buzz to spread the word about their brands by using online techniques such as e-mail, text messaging, blogging, and promoting them on social network sites such as MySpace, Facebook, and YouTube. For example, the advertising agency for Unilever's Dove brand created a 75-second time-lapse film of a young woman's transformation from a pretty, but ordinary, girl into a strikingly beautiful billboard model through the use of extensive makeup, hairstyling, and photoshop editing of her neck and eyes. The viral video, which ended with the comment, "No wonder our perception of beauty is distorted," generated more than 12 million hits after the agency posted it on YouTube and helped broaden awareness of Dove's Self-Esteem fund, which is part of the "Campaign for Real Beauty" IMC program that has been used over the past four years to promote the brand.[6]

Some companies are also building Web communities so customers can chat about their product experiences online. For example, in 2005 Procter & Gamble, the company that ironically is the world's largest advertiser, initiated a new word-of-mouth program to reach the most influential group of shoppers in America: moms. More than 600,000 women have enrolled in a program called Vocalpoint which is targeted to mothers between the ages of 28 to 45 who have children under the age of 19 as well as large social networks (Exhibit 5–5). These women generally speak or interact with about 25 to 30 other women during a typical day, where an average mom speaks to just five. Women who join Vocalpoint receive product samples as well as a sense of empowerment as they are asked for their opinions on a variety of issues ranging from new product ideas to the best ways to communicate with them.

While viral techniques have become a popular way to generate buzz about a brand, research conducted by the Keller Fay Group—a market research company that focuses on word-of-mouth marketing—has shown that some 90 percent of conversations about products, services, and brands take place off-line.[7] Face-to-face interaction accounts for the vast majority of word-of-mouth communications (72 percent) about a brand while phone conversations rank second (18 percent). Only 7 percent of word of mouth takes place through online channels such as e-mail/instant messages, blogs, and chat rooms. Their research also shows that nearly half the word-of-mouth conversations included references to the various IMC tools used for a brand, including print and television ads, websites, and other marketing tools such as point-of-sale displays and promotions.

These findings are very important from an integrated marketing communications perspective because they show that there can be powerful "pass-along" benefits from consumers talking favorably about a brand and referencing various elements of the IMC program. They also reinforce the importance of marketers recognizing that all of the IMC elements work in unison to impact how consumers perceive a brand and the word-of-mouth discussion that is generated about it. The finding that consumers are still influenced the most by their conversations with other people shows that marketers need to find ways to positively influence these interactions.

However, marketers must be careful about the assumptions they make when using buzz marketing techniques. For example a study conducted by David Godes and Diane Mayzlin on the effects of a word-of-mouth campaign for a chain store examined the characteristics of the most successful "agents" so that firms could better understand at whom they should target their buzz marketing efforts.[8] They found that agents who were not loyal customers of the store were more effective at generating sales through word of mouth than were loyal customers. The explanation offered for these somewhat counterintuitive findings is that loyal customers have already told their friends and acquaintances about a product and are already generating positive word of mouth. On the other hand, nonloyal customers may be more responsive to buzz marketing campaigns designed to encourage them to spread the word about a product. However, marketers still have to identify the best generators of buzz among both loyal and nonloyal customers such as those who are considered opinion leaders by their peers and "social butterflies" who have a high propensity to meet new people and connect with friends.

While the use of buzz and viral marketing campaigns is becoming more prevalent, concern has been expressed over its use and whether the person spreading the product message should disclose his or her affiliation. The Word of Mouth Marketing Association, was formed in 2004 to promote and improve the use of word-of-mouth marketing and protect consumers and the industry by providing ethical guidelines for its use. The WOMA has developed a set of rules and guidelines which mandate that marketers must make sure that people recommending products or services disclose whom they are working for. Gary Ruskin, the former executive director of Commercial Alert, a nonprofit organization dedicated to protecting consumers from commercial exploitation, notes that without such disclosures there is "a danger of the basic commercialization of human relations, where friends treat one another as advertising pawns, undercutting social trust."[9]

Experts note that buzz marketing techniques are very resistant to manipulation and marketers must be careful about how they use them. Several companies have had buzz marketing campaigns backfire when consumers recognized that the companies were artificially trying to promote buzz for their brands. Some argue that the growing popularity of buzz marketing could well spell its downfall, because when consumers recognize that everyone is trying to create a buzz for their brand, they are likely to be turned off to the technique.[10]

*Nonpersonal channels* of communication are those that carry a message without interpersonal contact between sender and receiver. Nonpersonal channels are generally referred to as the **mass media** or mass communications, since the message is sent to many individuals at one time. For example, a TV commercial broadcast on a prime-time show may be seen by 10 million households in a given evening. Nonpersonal channels of communication consist of two major types, print and broadcast. Print media include newspapers, magazines, direct mail, and billboards; broadcast media include radio and television. The Internet has characteristics of both nonpersonal as well as personal forms of communication. It has become a mass media vehicle as it now is the dominant source of information for most consumers. In many ways the Internet is nonpersonal in nature as consumers are often just consuming the information provided online and there is no personal contact between them and the companies and/or organizations that provide this information on their websites. However, the Internet is increasingly becoming a form of personal communication as consumers can interact with marketers online as well as communicate and share information with one another through the use of social media.

## Receiver/Decoding

The **receiver** is the person(s) with whom the sender shares thoughts or information. Generally, receivers are the consumers in the target market or audience who read, hear, and/or see the marketer's message and decode it. **Decoding** is the process of transforming the sender's message back into thought. This process is heavily influenced by the receiver's frame of reference or **field of experience**, which refers to the experiences, perceptions, attitudes, and values he or she brings to the communication situation.

For effective communication to occur, the message decoding process of the receiver must match the encoding of the sender. Simply put, this means the receiver understands and correctly interprets what the source is trying to communicate. As Figure 5–1 showed, the source and the receiver each have a frame of reference (the circle around each) that they bring to the communication situation. Effective communication is more likely when there is some *common ground* between the two parties.

(This is represented by the overlapping of the two circles.) The more knowledge the sender has about the receivers, the better the sender can understand their needs, empathize with them, and communicate effectively.

While this notion of common ground between sender and receiver may sound basic, it often causes great difficulty in the advertising communications process. Marketing and advertising people often have very different fields of experience from the consumers who constitute the mass markets with whom they must communicate. Most advertising and marketing people are college-educated and work and/or reside in large urban areas such as New York, Chicago, or Los Angeles. Yet they are attempting to develop commercials that will effectively communicate with millions of consumers who have never attended college, work in blue-collar occupations, and live in rural areas or small towns. The executive creative director of a large advertising agency described how advertising executives become isolated from the cultural mainstream: "We pull them in and work them to death. And then they begin moving in sushi circles and lose touch with Velveeta and the people who eat it."[11]

Another factor that can lead to problems in establishing common ground between senders and receivers is age. As the population of the United States and many other countries grows older, concern has been expressed over the potential problems that might arise because of age differences between advertising agency personnel and older consumers. A study conducted for the Association of Advertising Agencies International found that professionals who work in advertising agencies are much younger than the general population. Nearly 40 percent of agency personnel staff is between the ages of 30 to 39 while only 20 percent of the U.S. adult population is in their 30s.[12] The youth bias is particularly evident in the creative departments as many of those who work in this area are under the age of 40. The age gap has also become very prevalent in the digital/interactive area as well because these departments are dominated by younger people.

Advertisers whose agencies are unable to understand and connect with older consumers may be squandering opportunities to reach a valuable market. More than half of the nation's wealth is in the hands of people over 50, and they spend an estimated $2 trillion a year on products and services. Moreover, the 50-plus segment will increase by 23 percent over the next decade. This age group also has more discretionary income than any other age group and many of them are quite willing to spend it. Exhibit 5–6 show how the AARP promotes the various ways marketers can reach the 50+ market segment through its various media and promotional vehicles.

Critics argue that most advertising is really about the people who create it, not about the consumers who actually buy the products and services being advertised. It is important that marketers and their agencies understand the frame of reference and perspectives of the consumers in the target markets that are receiving their messages. Many companies spend a considerable amount of time and money pretesting messages to make sure consumers understand them and decode them in the manner the advertiser intended.

Advertisers spend millions of dollars every year to understand the frames of reference of the target markets who receive their messages. They also spend much time and money pretesting messages to make sure consumers understand and decode them in the manner the advertiser intended.

**EXHIBIT 5–6**
The AARP promotes its ability to reach the 50+ market

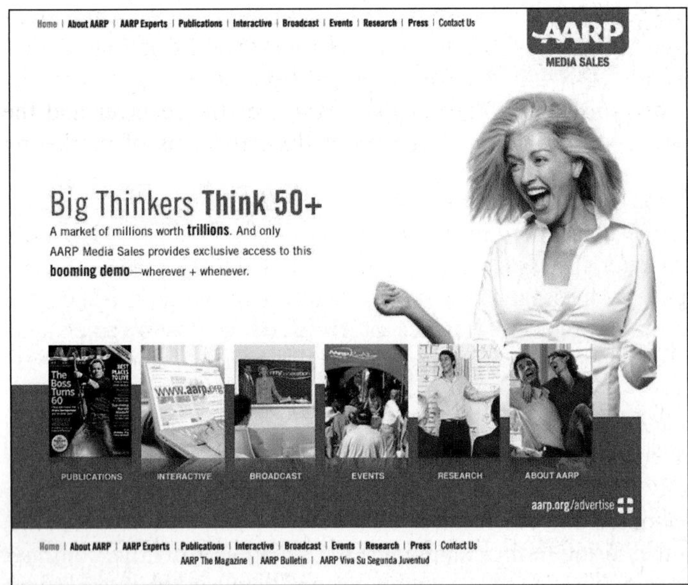


## Noise

Throughout the communication process, the message is subject to extraneous factors that can distort or interfere with its reception. This unplanned distortion or interference is known as **noise**. Errors or problems that occur in the encoding of the message, distortion in a radio or television signal, or distractions at the point of reception are examples of noise. When you are watching your favorite commercial on TV and a problem occurs in the signal transmission, it will obviously interfere with your reception, lessening the impact of the commercial.

Noise may also occur because the fields of experience of the sender and receiver don't overlap. Lack of common ground may result in improper encoding of the message—using a sign, symbol, or words that are unfamiliar or have different meaning to the receiver. The more common ground there is between the sender and the receiver, the less likely it is this type of noise will occur.



### Response/Feedback

The receiver's set of reactions after seeing, hearing, or reading the message is known as a **response**. Receivers' responses can range from nonobservable actions such as storing information in memory to immediate action such as dialing a toll-free number to order a product advertised on television. Marketers are very interested in **feedback**, that part of the receiver's response that is communicated back to the sender. Feedback, which may take a variety of forms, closes the loop in the communications flow and lets the sender monitor how the intended message is being decoded and received.

For example, in a personal-selling situation, customers may pose questions, comments, or objections or indicate their reactions through nonverbal responses such as gestures and frowns.[13] The salesperson has the advantage of receiving instant feedback through the customer's reactions. But this is generally not the case when mass media are used. Because advertisers are not in direct contact with the customers, they must use other means to determine how their messages have been received. While the ultimate form of feedback occurs through sales, it is often hard to show a direct relationship between advertising and purchase behavior. So marketers use other methods to obtain feedback, among them customer inquiries, store visits, coupon redemptions, and reply cards. Research-based feedback analyzes readership and recall of ads, message comprehension, attitude change, and other forms of response. With this information, the advertiser can determine reasons for success or failure in the communication process and make adjustments.

Successful communication is accomplished when the marketer selects an appropriate source, develops an effective message or appeal that is encoded properly, and then selects the channels or media that will best reach the target audience so that the message can be effectively decoded and delivered. In Chapter 6, we will examine the source, message, and channel decisions and see how promotional planners work with these controllable variables to develop communication strategies. Since these decisions must consider how the target audience will respond to the promotional message, the remainder of this chapter examines the receiver and the process by which consumers respond to advertising and other forms of marketing communications.

## ANALYZING THE RECEIVER

To communicate effectively with their customers, marketers must understand who the target audience is, what (if anything) it knows or feels about the company's product or service, and how to communicate with the audience to influence its decision-making process. Marketers must also know how the market is likely to respond to various sources of communication or different types of messages. Before they make decisions regarding source, message, and channel variables, promotional planners must understand the potential effects associated with each of these factors. This section focuses on the receiver of the marketing communication. It examines

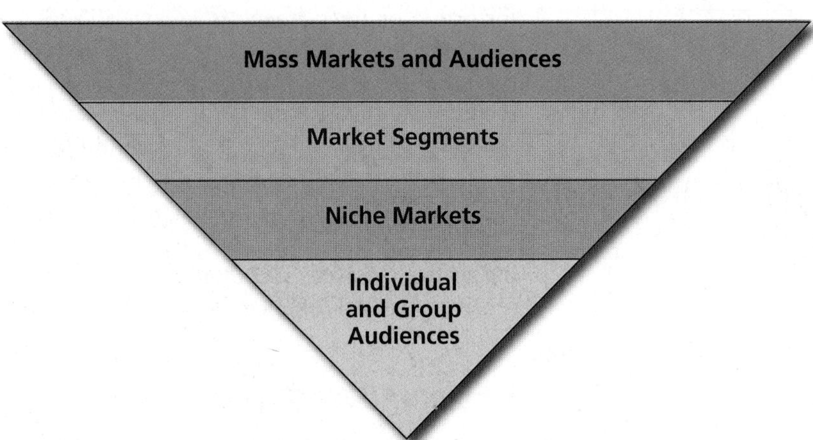


**FIGURE 5–2**
Levels of Audience Aggregation

how the audience is identified and the process it may go through in responding to a promotional message. This information serves as a foundation for evaluating the controllable communication variable decisions in the next chapter.

## Identifying the Target Audience

The marketing communication process really begins with identifying the audience that will be the focus of the firm's advertising and promotional efforts. The target audience may consist of individuals, groups, niche markets, market segments, or a general public or mass audience (Figure 5–2). Marketers approach each of these audiences differently.

The target market may consist of *individuals* who have specific needs and for whom the communication must be specifically tailored. This often requires person-to-person communication and is generally accomplished through personal selling. Other forms of communication, such as advertising, may be used to attract the audience's attention to the firm, but the detailed message is carried by a salesperson who can respond to the specific needs of the individual customer. Life insurance, financial services, and real estate are examples of products and services promoted this way.

A second level of audience aggregation is represented by the *group*. Marketers often must communicate with a group of people who make or influence the purchase decision. For example, organizational purchasing often involves buying centers or committees that vary in size and composition. Companies marketing their products and services to other businesses or organizations must understand who is on the purchase committee, what aspect of the decision each individual influences, and the criteria each member uses to evaluate a product. Advertising may be directed at each member of the buying center, and multilevel personal selling may be necessary to reach those individuals who influence or actually make decisions.

Marketers look for customers who have similar needs and wants and thus represent some type of market segment that can be reached with the same basic communication strategy. Very small, well-defined groups of customers are often referred to as *market niches*. They can usually be reached through personal-selling efforts or highly targeted media such as direct mail. The next level of audience aggregation is *market segments*, broader classes of buyers who have similar needs and can be reached with similar messages. As we saw in Chapter 2, there are various ways of segmenting markets and reaching the customers in these segments. As market segments get larger, marketers usually turn to broader-based media such as newspapers, magazines, and TV to reach them.

Marketers of most consumer products attempt to attract the attention of large numbers of present or potential customers (*mass markets*) through mass communication such as advertising or publicity. Mass communication is a one-way flow of information from the marketer to the consumer. Feedback on the audience's reactions to the message is generally indirect and difficult to measure.

| Stages | Models: AIDA model | Hierarchy of effects model | Innovation adoption model | Information processing model |
|---|---|---|---|---|
| Cognitive stage | Attention | Awareness<br>Knowledge | Awareness | Presentation<br>Attention<br>Comprehension |
| Affective stage | Interest<br>Desire | Liking<br>Preference<br>Conviction | Interest<br>Evaluation | Yielding<br>Retention |
| Behavioral stage | Action | Purchase | Trial<br>Adoption | Behavior |

**FIGURE 5–3**

Models of the Response Process



TV advertising, for example, lets the marketer send a message to millions of consumers at the same time. But this does not mean effective communication has occurred. This may be only one of several hundred messages the consumer is exposed to that day. There is no guarantee the information will be attended to, processed, comprehended, or stored in memory for later retrieval. Even if the advertising message is processed, it may not interest consumers or may be misinterpreted by them. Studies by Jacob Jacoby and Wayne D. Hoyer have shown that nearly 20 percent of all print ads and even more TV commercials are miscomprehended by readers.[14]

Unlike personal or face-to-face communications, mass communications do not offer the marketer an opportunity to explain or clarify the message to make it more effective. The marketer must enter the communication situation with knowledge of the target audience and how it is likely to react to the message. This means the receiver's response process must be understood, along with its implications for promotional planning and strategy.

# THE RESPONSE PROCESS

Perhaps the most important aspect of developing effective communication programs involves understanding the *response process* the receiver may go through in moving toward a specific behavior (like purchasing a product) and how the promotional efforts of the marketer influence consumer responses. In many instances, the marketer's only objective may be to create awareness of the company or brand name, which may trigger interest in the product. In other situations, the marketer may want to convey detailed information to change consumers' knowledge of and attitudes toward the brand and ultimately change their behavior.

## Traditional Response Hierarchy Models

A number of models have been developed to depict the stages a consumer may pass through in moving from a state of not being aware of a company, product, or brand to actual purchase behavior. Figure 5–3 shows four of the best-known

**EXHIBIT 5–7**
Sampling or demonstration programs encourage trial of new products such as disposable contact lenses

response hierarchy models. While these response models may appear similar, they were developed for different reasons.

The **AIDA model** was developed to represent the stages a salesperson must take a customer through in the personal-selling process.[15] This model depicts the buyer as passing successively through attention, interest, desire, and action. The salesperson must first get the customer's attention and then arouse some interest in the company's product or service. Strong levels of interest should create desire to own or use the product. The action stage in the AIDA model involves getting the customer to make a purchase commitment and closing the sale. To the marketer, this is the most important stage in the selling process, but it can also be the most difficult. Companies train their sales reps in closing techniques to help them complete the selling process.

Perhaps the best known of these response hierarchies is the model developed by Robert Lavidge and Gary Steiner as a paradigm for setting and measuring advertising objectives.[16] Their **hierarchy of effects model** shows the process by which advertising works; it assumes a consumer passes through a series of steps in sequential order from initial awareness of a product or service to actual purchase. A basic premise of this model is that advertising effects occur over a period of time. Advertising communication may not lead to immediate behavioral response or purchase; rather, a series of effects must occur, with each step fulfilled before the consumer can move to the next stage in the hierarchy. As we will see in Chapter 7, the hierarchy of effects model has become the foundation for objective setting and measurement of advertising effects in many companies.

**EXHIBIT 5–8**
Advertising for innovative new products such as the Sony Reader must make consumers aware of their features and benefits

SONY
"Now you can get a 7-inch window with an unobstructed view of Wall Street."
Introducing the wireless, touch screen Reader Daily Edition, by Sony. It's the premier digital reader for The Wall Street Journal, which allows you to subscribe to exclusive content and daily updates. An instant connection to the Reader Store makes getting books and news as simple as tapping the screen. To learn more, visit sony.com/reader.

The **innovation adoption model** evolved from work on the diffusion of innovations.[17] This model represents the stages a consumer passes through in adopting a new product or service. Like the other models, it says potential adopters must be moved through a series of steps before taking some action (in this case, deciding to adopt a new product). The steps preceding adoption are awareness, interest, evaluation, and trial. The challenge facing companies introducing new products is to create awareness and interest among consumers and then get them to evaluate the product favorably. The best way to evaluate a new product is through actual use so that performance can be judged. Marketers often encourage trial by using demonstration or sampling programs or allowing consumers to use a product with minimal commitment (Exhibit 5–7). After trial, consumers either adopt the product or reject it.

The innovation adoption model is especially important to companies who are using IMC tools to introduce new products to the market. These marketers recognize that there are certain types of consumers who are of particular interest to them because of their interest in new products and their ability to influence others.[18] Marketers are constantly looking for ways to identify and communicate with these early adopters and to encourage them to pass along information to other consumers. IMC Technology Perspective 5–1 discusses how marketers of high-tech products are developing profiles of digital adopters—those individuals who are among the first to use various digital products and services.

The final hierarchy model shown in Figure 5–3 is the **information processing model** of advertising effects, developed by William McGuire.[19] This model assumes the receiver in a persuasive communication situation like advertising is an information processor or problem solver. McGuire suggests that the series of steps a receiver goes through in being persuaded constitutes a response hierarchy. The stages of this

**FIGURE 5–4**
Methods of Obtaining Feedback in the Response Hierarchy

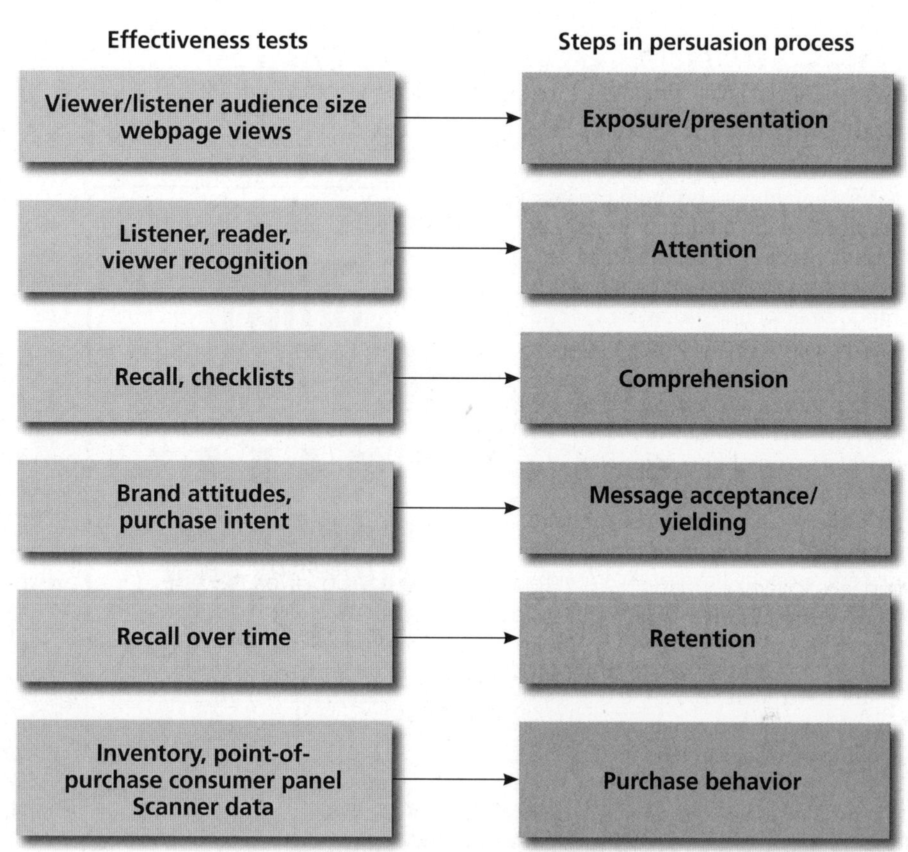




model are similar to the hierarchy of effects sequence; attention and comprehension are similar to awareness and knowledge, and yielding is synonymous with liking. McGuire's model includes a stage not found in the other models: retention, or the receiver's ability to retain that portion of the comprehended information that he or she accepts as valid or relevant. This stage is important since most promotional campaigns are designed not to motivate consumers to take immediate action but rather to provide information they will use later when making a purchase decision.

Each stage of the response hierarchy is a dependent variable that must be attained and that may serve as an objective of the communication process. As shown in Figure 5–4, each stage can be measured, providing the advertiser with feedback regarding the effectiveness of various strategies designed to move the consumer to purchase. The information processing model may be an effective framework for planning and evaluating the effects of a promotional campaign.

**Implications of the Traditional Hierarchy Models** The hierarchy models of communication response are useful to promotional planners from several perspectives. First, they delineate the series of steps potential purchasers must be taken through to move them from unawareness of a product or service to readiness to purchase it. Second, potential buyers may be at different stages in the hierarchy, so the advertiser will face different sets of communication problems. For example, a company introducing an innovative product like the Sony Reader may use media advertising to make people aware of the product along with its features and benefits (Exhibit 5–8). Sony provides product information in its ads but also encourages consumers to visit retail stores as well as its website to learn more about its electronic readers. Consumers who visit the online Reader store or go to a retail store for a product demonstration will progress through the response hierarchy and move closer to purchase than those who only see an ad. Marketers of a mature brand that enjoys customer loyalty may need only supportive or reminder advertising to reinforce positive perceptions and maintain the awareness level for the brand.

# IMC Technology Perspective 5–1 > > >

## High Tech Marketers Target Early Digital Adopters

Think for a moment about the process you went through the last time you bought a new consumer electronics product such as a computer, digital camera, smartphone, or an iPod. Chances are that you sought input from another person and took his or her input into consideration before making a purchase decision. This individual was probably someone whose opinion you value because s/he was more knowledgeable about the product and/or various brands than you were and may have been among the first group of consumers to buy it. Marketers have long recognized that there is a very important segment of consumers who are the first to purchase a new product and help bring it to the mainstream market. This influential group is commonly referred to as "early adopters" and they play a critical role in determining the success or failure of a new product because many consumers pay close attention to what they say and do. The high-tech industry is particularly interested in what are often referred to as "digital adopters" which is the group of consumers who are the first to use various new digital products and services such as smartphones, new forms of personal computers such as netbooks and tablets, electronic readers, high definition television sets, video gaming consoles, and Web browsers.

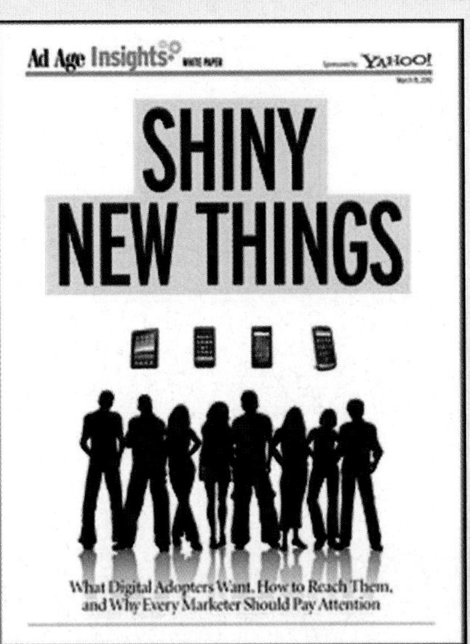


Companies marketing these new high-tech products recognize that one of the most effective ways they can launch them is to focus on the early digital adopters. This group is not only much more likely to buy new products, they also are respected for their opinions and thus can influence the purchase decisions of others who look to them for advice. A vice president of marketing and strategy for Sony Electronics notes that the company is always marketing to early adopters as they are one or two seasons of interest ahead of what's in the stores. According to Joe Bates, research director at the Consumer Electronics Association, "The early adopters are more important than they have ever been. They're the ones weeding through these products and going on product review sites like CNET or Engadget." Bates also notes that early adopters are important because they spend up to three times more money on electronic devices than the average consumer. Studies have also shown that they are two-to-five times more likely to spread the word about new products and services.

While marketers recognize the importance of targeting early adopters, they are finding that getting through to them can also be very challenging. Companies can reach early adopters through websites, blogs, and enthusiasts groups.

The hierarchy models can also be useful as intermediate measures of communication effectiveness. The marketer needs to know where audience members are on the response hierarchy. For example, research may reveal that one target segment has low awareness of the advertiser's brand, whereas another is aware of the brand and its various attributes but has a low level of liking or brand preference.

For the first segment of the market, the communication task involves increasing the awareness level for the brand. The number of ads may be increased, or a product sampling program may be used. For the second segment, where awareness is already high but liking and preference are low, the advertiser must determine the reason for the negative feelings and then attempt to address this problem in future advertising.

When research or other evidence reveals a company is perceived favorably on a particular attribute or performance criterion, the company may want to take advantage of this in its advertising.

**Evaluating Traditional Response Hierarchy Models** As you saw in Figure 5–3, the four models presented all view the response process as consisting of movement through a sequence of three basic stages. The *cognitive stage* represents what the receiver knows or perceives about the particular product or brand. This stage includes awareness that the brand exists and knowledge, information, or comprehension about its attributes, characteristics, or benefits. The *affective stage* refers to the

They use social media and their own blogs to share their knowledge and opinions about new technology, and they often attend events such as the International Consumer Electronics show held in Las Vegas each January. They also can be reached through magazines such as *Wired* (both print and online) that are very popular among technology enthusiasts as well as vertical publications targeting specific product markets. A study by the market research firm Claritas studied the media habits of digital adopters ranging in age from 45 to 64 and found that they read *The New York Times, The Wall Street Journal, The New Yorker, Fortune,* and *Esquire*. The television channels they watch include BBC America, the Sundance channel, Independent Film channel, and Showtime. They listen to National Public Radio and ESPN Radio. Claritas also studied younger digital adopters (ages 25 to 44) and found that they were not much different, although their TV preferences included IFC, VH1, and MTV.

Marquest Media & Entertainment examined the video consumed by early adopters and found that most use DVRs to watch TV on a time-shifted basis, use web video frequently, and are 14 times more likely to have the capability to deliver video content from the Internet to their television sets. A 2009 study of early adopters of technology by Nielsen found that they have a high propensity for ownership of technology products and own an average of four cross-platform devices, such as gaming consoles, computers, and mobile phones, and use them to view TV or movie content as 38 percent have their TV sets connected to their computers.

While there is a considerable amount of information available that profiles the early digital adopters, getting through to them is still not easy. A study by Forrester Research provides valuable insights as it marries their technographic profiles with psychological theories. The study found that there are three key factors that drive the behavior of early digital adopters. These include risk taking and a desire for novelty that exceeds caution and reflects openness to new products; information gathering because this group likes to mitigate risk by seeking out information to make informed decisions; and status seeking as early adopters take pride in showing off their new purchases and often choose products that represent them to the world.

Journalist Laura Rich who studies and writes about digital media notes that early adopters can be a new high tech product's best friend or worst enemy, and sometimes both. She notes that digital adopters have helped Apple quickly establish new products such as the iPhone and iPad by purchasing hundreds of thousands of these devices in the first few months after their introduction. Google usually launches its new products such as its Chrome Web browser by putting a "beta" label on them and waiting for early adopters to use them and provide feedback that can then be used to make product improvements. However, companies often have their new products rebuked by early adopters, who can use blogs and other forms of social media to do so at warp speed.

The challenges facing high tech marketers will only get greater as more and more new products are introduced each year. More than 10,000 new items were unveiled at the International Consumer Electronics show in 2010. That's a lot of new products for consumers to wade through, which makes it more important than ever for high-tech companies to market to the digital adopters and win them over.

Sources: Louis Gray, "Profiles of Digital Adopters," *Shiny New Things: Advertising Age Insights White Paper,* March 15, 2010, p. 7; "Digital Adopter Behavior," *Shiny New Things,* pp. 10–14; Laura Rich, "Shiny New Things, p.18; "Daniel B. Honigman, "Who's on First?," *Marketing News,* Vol. 41 (18), November 1, 2007, pp. 14–17.



receiver's feelings or affect level (like or dislike) for the particular brand. This stage also includes stronger levels of affect such as desire, preference, or conviction. The *conative* or *behavioral stage* refers to the consumer's action toward the brand: trial, purchase, adoption, or rejection.

All four models assume a similar ordering of these three stages. Cognitive development precedes affective reactions, which precede behavior. One might assume that consumers become aware of and knowledgeable about a brand, develop feelings toward it, form a desire or preference, and then make a purchase. While this logical progression is often accurate, the response sequence does not always operate this way.

Over the past two decades, considerable research in marketing, social psychology, and communications has led to questioning of the traditional cognitive → affective → behavioral sequence of response. Several other configurations of the response hierarchy have been theorized.

## Alternative Response Hierarchies

Michael Ray has developed a model of information processing that identifies three alternative orderings of the three stages based on perceived product differentiation and product involvement.[20] These alternative response hierarchies are the standard learning, dissonance/attribution, and low-involvement models (Figure 5–5).

**FIGURE 5–5**
Alternative Response Hierarchies. The Three-Orders Model of Information Processing

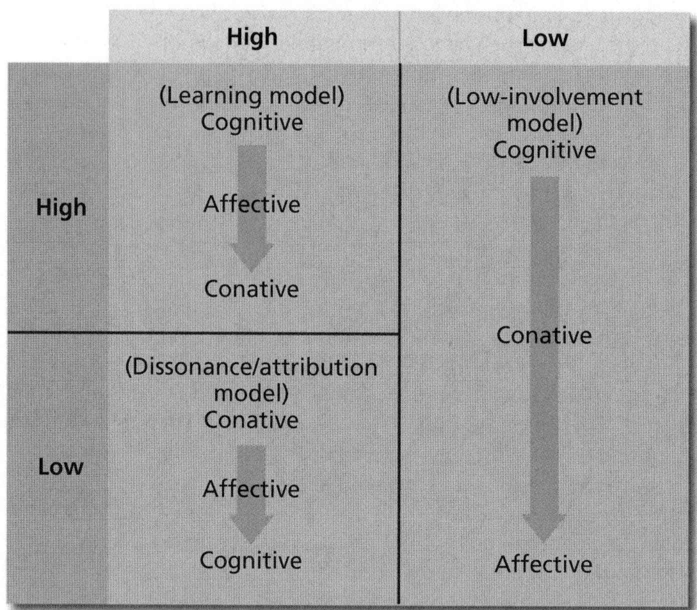


**The Standard Learning Hierarchy** In many purchase situations, the consumer will go through the response process in the sequence depicted by the traditional communication models. Ray terms this a **standard learning model**, which consists of a learn → feel → do sequence. Information and knowledge acquired or *learned* about the various brands are the basis for developing affect, or *feelings*, that guide what the consumer will *do* (e.g., actual trial or purchase). In this hierarchy, the consumer is viewed as an active participant in the communication process who gathers information through active learning.

Ray suggests the standard learning hierarchy is likely when the consumer is highly involved in the purchase process and there is much differentiation among competing brands. High-involvement purchase decisions such as those for industrial products and services and consumer durables like personal computers, printers, cameras, appliances, and cars are areas where a standard learning hierarchy response process is likely. Ads for products and services in these areas are usually very detailed and provide customers with information that can be used to evaluate brands and help them make a purchase decision. Notice how the ad for the new Acura shown in Exhibit 5–9 appeals to the cognitive and affective steps in the standard learning hierarchy.

**EXHIBIT 5–9**
This Acura ad addresses the various stages in the standard learning hierarchy

BRILLIANCE IS POWER.
THE MOST POWERFUL ACURA EVER BUILT. THE ALL-NEW TL.
ACURA
ADVANCE


**The Dissonance/Attribution Hierarchy** A second response hierarchy proposed by Ray involves situations where consumers first behave, then develop attitudes or feelings as a result of that behavior, and then learn or process information that

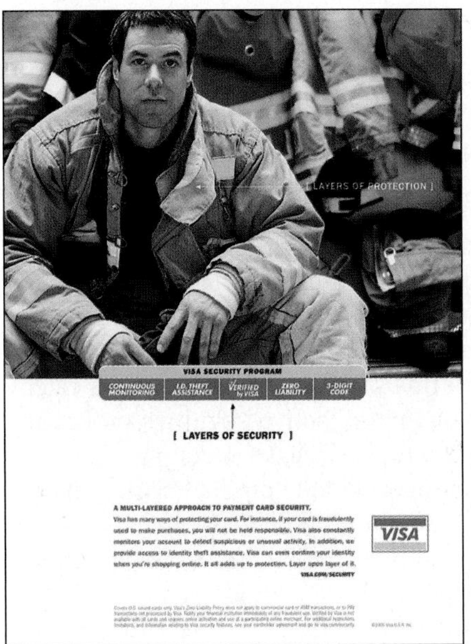


**EXHIBIT 5–10**
This ad reinforces the wisdom of the decision to use a Visa credit card

supports the behavior. This **dissonance/attribution model**, or do → feel → learn, occurs in situations where consumers must choose between two alternatives that are similar in quality but are complex and may have hidden or unknown attributes. The consumer may purchase the product on the basis of a recommendation by some nonmedia source and then attempt to support the decision by developing a positive attitude toward the brand and perhaps even developing negative feelings toward the rejected alternative(s). This reduces any *postpurchase dissonance* or anxiety the consumer may experience resulting from doubt over the purchase (as discussed in Chapter 4). Dissonance reduction involves *selective learning,* whereby the consumer seeks information that supports the choice made and avoids information that would raise doubts about the decision.

According to this model, marketers need to recognize that in some situations, attitudes develop *after* purchase, as does learning from the mass media. Ray suggests that in these situations the main effect of the mass media is not the promotion of original choice behavior and attitude change but rather the reduction of dissonance by reinforcing the wisdom of the purchase or providing supportive information. For example, the ad shown in Exhibit 5–10 reinforces consumers' decision to use a Visa credit card by reassuring them of the various layers of security the company provides to its cardholders.

As with the standard learning model, this response hierarchy is likely to occur when the consumer is involved in the purchase situation; it is particularly relevant for postpurchase situations. For example, a consumer may purchase tires recommended by a friend and then develop a favorable attitude toward the company and pay close attention to its ads to reduce dissonance.

Some marketers resist this view of the response hierarchy because they can't accept the notion that the mass media have no effect on the consumer's initial purchase decision. But the model doesn't claim the mass media have no effect—just that their major impact occurs after the purchase has been made. Marketing communications planners must be aware of the need for advertising and promotion efforts not just to encourage brand selection but to reinforce choices and ensure that a purchase pattern will continue.

**The Low-Involvement Hierarchy** Perhaps the most intriguing of the three response hierarchies proposed by Ray is the **low-involvement hierarchy**, in which the receiver is viewed as passing from cognition to behavior to attitude change. This learn → do → feel sequence is thought to characterize situations of low consumer involvement in the purchase process. Ray suggests this hierarchy tends to occur when involvement in the purchase decision is low, there are minimal differences among brand alternatives, and mass-media (especially broadcast) advertising is important.

The notion of a low-involvement hierarchy is based in large part on Herbert Krugman's theory explaining the effects of television advertising.[21] Krugman wanted to find out why TV advertising produced a strong effect on brand awareness and recall but little change in consumers' attitudes toward the product. He hypothesized that TV is basically a low-involvement medium and the viewer's perceptual defenses are reduced or even absent during commercials. In a low-involvement situation, the consumer does not compare the message with previously acquired beliefs, needs, or past experiences. The commercial results in subtle changes in the consumer's knowledge structure, particularly with repeated exposure. This change in the consumer's knowledge does not result in attitude change but is related to learning something about the advertised brand, such as a brand name, ad theme, or slogan. According to Krugman, when the consumer enters a purchase situation, this information may be sufficient to trigger a purchase. The consumer will then form an attitude toward the purchased brand as a result of experience with it. Thus, in the low-involvement situation the response sequence is as follows:

Message exposure under low involvement →
Shift in cognitive structure → Purchase →
Positive or negative experience → Attitude formation

In the low-involvement hierarchy, the consumer engages in *passive learning* and *random information catching* rather than active information seeking. The advertiser must recognize that a passive, uninterested consumer may focus more on nonmessage elements such as music, characters, symbols, and slogans or jingles than actual message content. The advertiser might capitalize on this situation by developing a catchy jingle that is stored in the consumer's mind without any active cognitive processing and becomes salient when he or she enters the actual purchase situation.

Advertisers of low-involvement products also repeat simple product claims such as a key copy point or distinctive product benefit. A study by Scott Hawkins and Stephen Hoch found that under low-involvement conditions, repetition of simple product claims increased consumers' memory of and belief in those claims.[22] They concluded that advertisers of low-involvement products might find it more profitable to pursue a heavy repetition strategy than to reach larger audiences with lengthy, more detailed messages. For example, Heinz has dominated the ketchup market for over 20 years by repeatedly telling consumers that its brand is the thickest and richest. Heinz has used a variety of advertising campaigns over the years. However, they all have communicated the same basic message that Heinz is the best and most preferred brand of ketchup (Exhibit 5–11).

Low-involvement advertising appeals prevail in much of the advertising we see for frequently purchased consumer products: Wrigley's Doublemint gum invites consumers to "Double your pleasure." Bounty paper towels claim to be the "quicker picker-upper." Oscar Mayer uses the catchy jingle, "I wish I were an Oscar Mayer wiener." Each of these appeals is designed to help consumers make an association without really attempting to formulate or change an attitude.

Another popular creative strategy used by advertisers of low-involvement products is what advertising analyst Harry McMahan calls *VIP,* or *visual image personality.*[23] Advertisers often use symbols like the Pillsbury doughboy, Morris the cat, Tony the tiger, and Mr. Clean to develop visual images that will lead consumers to identify and retain ads. Eveready began using the pink bunny in ads for its Energizer batteries in 1989, and he has helped sales of the brand keep going and going for more than 20 years. As can be seen in Exhibit 5–12, the Energizer Bunny even has his own Facebook page which has more than 40,000 fans.

**EXHIBIT 5–11**
Advertising promoting taste and quality has helped Heinz dominate the ketchup market

## Implications of the Alternative Response Models

Advertising and consumer researchers recognize that not all response sequences and behaviors are explained adequately by either the traditional or the alternative response hierarchies. Advertising is just one source of information consumers use in learning about products, forming attitudes, and/or making purchase decisions. Consumers are likely to integrate information from advertising and other forms of marketing communication as well as direct experience in forming judgments about a brand. For example, a study by Robert Smith found that advertising can lessen the negative effects of an unfavorable trial experience on brand evaluations when the ad is processed before the trial. However, when a negative trial experience precedes exposure to an ad, cognitive evaluations of the ad are more negative.[24] More recent research has also shown that advertising can affect consumers' objective sensory interpretation of their experiences with a brand and what they remember about it.[25]

**EXHIBIT 5–12**
The Energizer bunny is a popular personality symbol for the brand



The various response models offer an interesting perspective on the ways consumers respond to advertising and other forms of marketing communications. They also provide insight into promotional strategies marketers might pursue in different situations. A review of these alternative models of the response process shows that the traditional standard learning model does not always apply. The notion of a highly involved consumer who engages in active information processing and learning and acts on the basis of higher-order beliefs and a well-formed attitude may be inappropriate for some types of purchases. Sometimes consumers make a purchase decision on the basis of general awareness resulting from repetitive exposure to advertising, and attitude development occurs after the purchase, if at all. The role of advertising and other forms of promotion may be to induce trial, so consumers can develop brand preferences primarily on the basis of their direct experience with the product.

From a promotional planning perspective, it is important that marketers examine the communication situation for their product or service and determine which type of response process is most likely to occur. They should analyze involvement levels and product/service differentiation as well as consumers' use of various information sources and their levels of experience with the product or service. Once the manager has determined which response sequence is most likely to operate, the integrated marketing communications program can be designed to influence the response process in favor of the company's product or service. Several planning models have been developed that consider involvement levels as well as other factors including response processes and motives that underlie the attitude formation and subsequent brand choice.[26] These models can be of value to managers as they develop strategies for advertising and other forms of marketing communication. We will now examine a popular planning model developed by the Foote Cone & Belding advertising agency, which theorizes that advertising and other promotional tools work differently depending on the type of product involved and the decision process sequence that consumers are likely to follow.

## The FCB Planning Model

An interesting approach to analyzing the communication situation comes from the work of Richard Vaughn of the Foote Cone & Belding advertising agency. Vaughn and his associates developed an advertising planning model by building on traditional response theories such as the hierarchy of effects model and its variants and research on high and low involvement.[27] They added the dimension of thinking versus feeling processing at each involvement level by bringing in theories regarding brain specialization. The right/left brain theory suggests the left side of the brain is

**FIGURE 5–6**
The Foote Cone & Belding (FCB) Grid

| | Thinking | Feeling |
|---|---|---|
| High involvement | **1. Informative (thinker)**<br>Car–house–furnishings–new products<br>model: Learn–feel–do (economic?)<br>**Possible implications**<br>Test: Recall<br>Diagnostics<br>Media: Long copy format<br>Reflective vehicles<br>Creative: Specific information<br>Demonstration | **2. Affective (feeler)**<br>Jewelry–cosmetics–fashion apparel–motorcycles<br>model: Feel–learn–do (psychological?)<br>**Possible implications**<br>Test: Attitude change<br>Emotional arousal<br>Media: Large space<br>Image specials<br>Creative: Executional<br>Impact |
| Low involvement | **3. Habit formation (doer)**<br>Food–household items<br>model: Do–learn–feel (responsive?)<br>**Possible implications**<br>Test: Sales<br>Media: Small space ads<br>10-second I.D.s<br>Radio; POS<br>Creative: Reminder | **4. Self-satisfaction (reactor)**<br>Cigarettes–liquor–candy<br>model: Do–feel–learn (social?)<br>**Possible implications**<br>Test: Sales<br>Media: Billboards<br>Newspapers<br>POS<br>Creative: Attention |

more capable of rational, cognitive thinking, while the right side is more visual and emotional and engages more in the affective (feeling) functions. Their model, which became known as the FCB grid, delineates four primary advertising planning strategies—informative, affective, habit formation, and satisfaction—along with the most appropriate variant of the alternative response hierarchies (Figure 5–6).

Vaughn suggests that the *informative strategy* is for highly involving products and services where rational thinking and economic considerations prevail and the standard learning hierarchy is the appropriate response model. The *affective strategy* is for highly involving/feeling purchases. For these types of products, advertising should stress psychological and emotional motives such as building self-esteem or enhancing one's ego or self-image.

The *habit formation strategy* is for low-involvement/thinking products with such routinized behavior patterns that learning occurs most often after a trial purchase. The response process for these products is consistent with a behavioristic learning-by-doing model (remember our discussion of operant conditioning in Chapter 4?). The *self-satisfaction strategy* is for low-involvement/feeling products where appeals to sensory pleasures and social motives are important. Again, the do → feel or do → learn hierarchy is operating, since product experience is an important part of the learning process. Vaughn acknowledges that some minimal level of awareness (passive learning) may precede purchase of both types of low-involvement products, but deeper, active learning is not necessary. This is consistent with the low-involvement hierarchy discussed earlier (learn → do → feel).

The FCB grid provides a useful way for those involved in the advertising planning process, such as creative specialists, to analyze consumer–product relationships and develop appropriate promotional strategies. Consumer research can be used to determine how consumers perceive products or brands on the involvement and thinking/feeling dimensions.[28] This information can then be used to develop effective creative options such as using rational versus emotional appeals, increasing

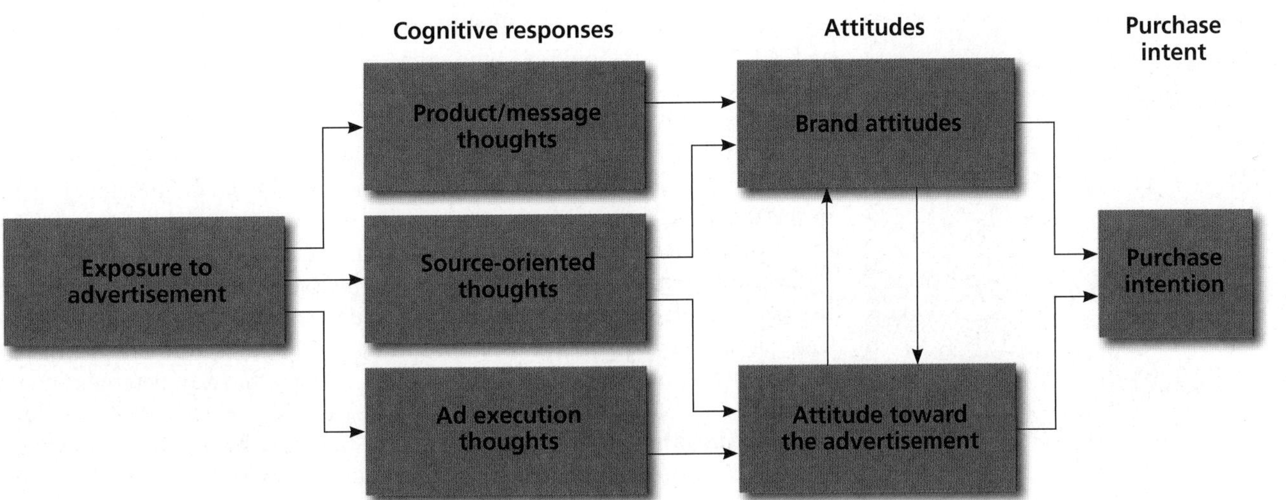


**FIGURE 5–7**

A Model of Cognitive Response

involvement levels, or even getting consumers to evaluate a think-type product on the basis of feelings. For example, in recent years appliance companies have been touting the design and image of their products as much as functionality in their advertising. These companies are capitalizing on the growth in the high-end segment of the appliances market, which has been growing at double the rate of middle and low segments.[29] LG ran an integrated marketing campaign encouraging consumers to upgrade old and unattractive appliances to the sleek LG premium line. Exhibit 5–13 shows a clever print ad from the "Upgrade" campaign.

# COGNITIVE PROCESSING OF COMMUNICATIONS

The hierarchical response models were for many years the primary focus of approaches for studying the receivers' responses to marketing communications. Attention centered on identifying relationships between specific controllable variables (such as source and message factors) and outcome or response variables (such as attention, comprehension, attitudes, and purchase intentions). This approach has been criticized on a number of fronts, including its black-box nature, since it can't explain what is causing these reactions.[30] In response to these concerns, researchers began trying to understand the nature of cognitive reactions to persuasive messages. Several approaches have been developed to examine the nature of consumers' cognitive processing of advertising messages.

**EXHIBIT 5–13**
LG encourages consumers to upgrade their appliances by focusing on product design

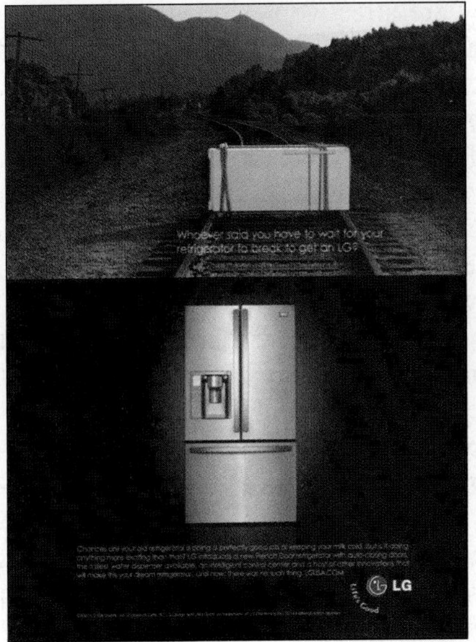


## The Cognitive Response Approach

One of the most widely used methods for examining consumers' cognitive processing of advertising messages is assessment of their **cognitive responses**, the thoughts that occur to them while reading, viewing, and/or hearing a communication.[31] These thoughts are generally measured by having consumers write down or verbally report their reactions to a message. The assumption is that these thoughts reflect the recipient's cognitive processes or reactions and help shape ultimate acceptance or rejection of the message.

The cognitive response approach has been widely used in research by both academicians and advertising practitioners. Its focus has been to determine the types of responses evoked by an advertising message and how these responses relate to attitudes toward the ad, brand attitudes, and purchase intentions. Figure 5–7 depicts the three basic categories of cognitive

CHAPTER 5

DEEP DISASTER:
Cherry Pie Packed Pleats.
DEEP CLEAN:
WHEN STAINS GET DEEP IN
ULTRA TIDE GETS THEM CLEAN OUT.


**EXHIBIT 5–14**
Consumers often generate support arguments in response to ads for quality products

responses researchers have identified—product/message, source-oriented, and ad execution thoughts—and how they may relate to attitudes and intentions.

**Product/Message Thoughts** The first category of thoughts comprises those directed at the product or service and/or the claims being made in the communication. Much attention has focused on two particular types of responses, counterarguments and support arguments.

**Counterarguments** are thoughts the recipient has that are opposed to the position taken in the message. For example, consider the ad for Ultra Tide shown in Exhibit 5–14. A consumer may express disbelief or disapproval of a claim made in an ad. ("I don't believe that any detergent could get that stain out!") Other consumers who see this ad may generate **support arguments**, or thoughts that affirm the claims made in the message. ("Ultra Tide looks like a really good product—I think I'll try it.")

The likelihood of counterarguing is greater when the message makes claims that oppose the receiver's beliefs. For example, a consumer viewing a commercial that attacks a favorite brand is likely to engage in counterarguing. Counterarguments relate negatively to message acceptance; the more the receiver counterargues, the less likely he or she is to accept the position advocated in the message.[32] Support arguments, on the other hand, relate positively to message acceptance. Thus, the marketer should develop ads or other promotional messages that minimize counterarguing and encourage support arguments.

**Source-Oriented Thoughts** A second category of cognitive responses is directed at the source of the communication. One of the most important types of responses in this category is **source derogations**, or negative thoughts about the spokesperson or organization making the claims. Such thoughts generally lead to a reduction in message acceptance. If consumers find a particular spokesperson annoying or untrustworthy, they are less likely to accept what this source has to say.

Of course, source-related thoughts are not always negative. Receivers who react favorably to the source generate favorable thoughts, or **source bolsters**. As you would expect, most advertisers attempt to hire spokespeople their target audience likes so as to carry this effect over to the message. Considerations involved in choosing an appropriate source or spokesperson will be discussed in Chapter 6.

**Ad Execution Thoughts** The third category of cognitive responses shown in Figure 5–7 consists of the individual's thoughts about the ad itself. Many of the thoughts receivers have when reading or viewing an ad do not concern the product and/or message claims directly. Rather, they are affective reactions representing the consumer's feelings toward the ad. These thoughts may include reactions to ad execution factors such as the creativity of the ad, the quality of the visual effects, colors, and voice tones. **Ad execution-related thoughts** can be either favorable or unfavorable. They are important because of their effect on attitudes toward the advertisement as well as the brand.

In recent years, much attention has focused on consumers' affective reactions to ads, especially TV commercials.[33] **Attitude toward the ad** (A → ad) represents the receivers' feelings of favorability or unfavorability toward the ad. Advertisers are interested in consumers' reactions to the ad because they know that affective reactions are an important determinant of advertising effectiveness, since these reactions may be transferred to the brand itself or directly influence purchase intentions. One study found that people who enjoy a commercial are twice as likely as those who are neutral toward it to be convinced that the brand is the best.[34]

Consumers' feelings about the ad may be just as important as their attitudes toward the brand (if not more so) in determining an ad's effectiveness.[35] The importance of affective reactions and feelings generated by the ad depends on several factors, among them the nature of the ad and the type of processing engaged in by

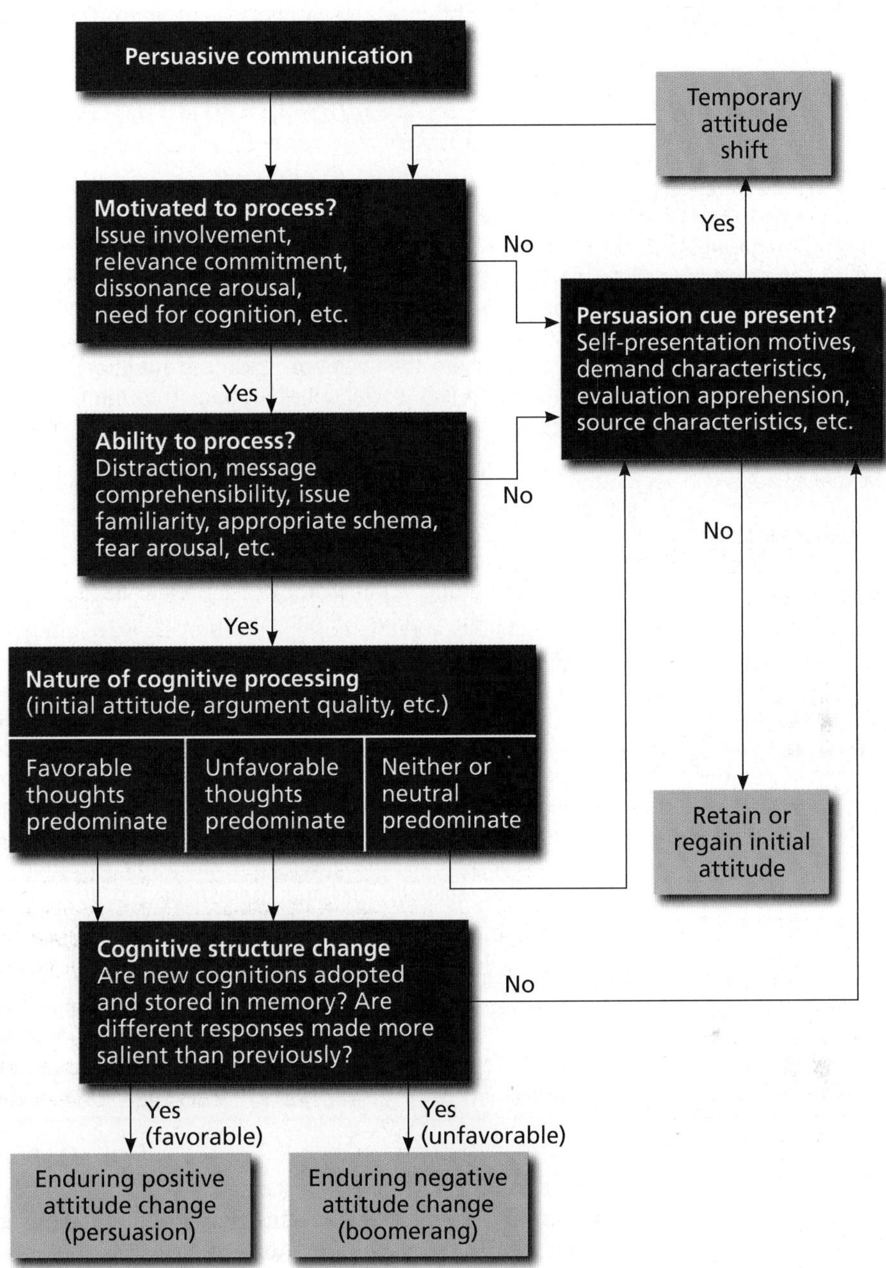


**FIGURE 5–8**

The Elaboration Likelihood Model of Persuasion



the receiver.[36] Many advertisers now use emotional ads designed to evoke feelings and affective reactions as the basis of their creative strategy. The success of this strategy depends in part on the consumers' involvement with the brand and their likelihood of attending to and processing the message. Another way marketers try to get consumers to attend to their advertising is by using sexual imagery in the visual portion of the ad. IMC Perspective 5–1 discusses the results of an interesting study that compared visual processing of ads using sexual imagery for men versus women.

We end our analysis of the receiver by examining a model that integrates some of the factors that may account for different types and levels of cognitive processing of a message.

## The Elaboration Likelihood Model

Differences in the ways consumers process and respond to persuasive messages are addressed in the **elaboration likelihood model (ELM)** of persuasion, shown in Figure 5–8.[37] The ELM was devised by Richard Petty and John Cacioppo to explain

## IMC Perspective 5–1 > > >

### Do Men and Women Process Sexy Ads Differently?

Advertisers are always looking for ways to break through the clutter of competing messages in various media such as television and magazines and draw attention to their ads. One technique sometimes used by marketers to attract consumers' attention and interest is to utilize sexually themed ads. The use of sexual appeals are quite common in the United States as well as many other countries where the societies are more liberal and accepting of them. In fact, social critic John Lahr notes that "Society drives people crazy with lust and calls it advertising."

Sexual appeals can vary in terms of their nature, content, and purpose. At one end of the spectrum are ads using decorative models whose primary role is to adorn the visual portion of the message and help attract the attention of the viewer or reader. These types of ads use physically attractive models as well as nudity or partial nudity and the model really serves no functional purpose other than to attract attention and interest. These types of appeals are often used in ads for automobiles, beer, and liquor although they are prevalent for other types of products and services as well. Of course they are also used for products where the sexual attractiveness of the model is relevant as the ad is being used to help sell a product that may have sexual connotations such as clothing, fragrances, and lingerie. At the other end of the spectrum are ads that use overt sexuality and are sexually provocative or suggestive. A number of marketers use ads that are sexually explicit and very risqué based on an assumption that these messages will attract the attention and interest of consumers and can create an image that may help sell their brands.

There is considerable debate as to whether sexual appeals, whether subtle or overt, are effective and can help sell a product. Numerous studies have been conducted by academicians as well as advertising practitioners regarding the impact of sexual messages. The findings from these studies generally show that the use of sex and nudity do increase attention to the ad but may distract consumers from attending to the brand name or advertising message. Most of these studies show consumers ads using sexual appeals and then measure their reactions by having them provide various types of cognitive and affective responses. However, a recent study conducted by an advertising research company, MediaAnalyzer Software & Research, used a different and very interesting approach to explore how men and women visually process sexually themed ads and what effect this processing might have on the ad's effectiveness.

MediaAnalyzer used its AttentionTracking software to follow the visual pattern of consumers as they looked at print ads, one sexual and one nonsexual, from each of five product categories including cigarettes, credit cards, jeans, shoes, and liquor. The software has a user move his or her computer mouse over the ad to indicate the part of the ad where he or she is looking. The company used data from the visual test to determine respondents' viewing patterns (shown by the arrows) and the percentage of time spent viewing each part of the ad.

The results of the visual tests found, as might be expected, that men tend to focus on an ad's sexual imagery (breast, legs, skin), which draws their attention away from other elements of the ad such as the logo, product shot, or headline.

the process by which persuasive communications (such as ads) lead to persuasion by influencing *attitudes*. According to this model, the attitude formation or change process depends on the amount and nature of *elaboration,* or processing, of relevant information that occurs in response to a persuasive message. High elaboration means the receiver engages in careful consideration, thinking, and evaluation of the information or arguments contained in the message. Low elaboration occurs when the receiver does not engage in active information processing or thinking but rather makes inferences about the position being advocated in the message on the basis of simple positive or negative cues.

The ELM shows that elaboration likelihood is a function of two elements, motivation and ability to process the message. *Motivation* to process the message depends on such factors as involvement, personal relevance, and individuals' needs and arousal levels. *Ability* depends on the individual's knowledge, intellectual capacity, and opportunity to process the message. For example, an individual viewing a humorous commercial or one containing an attractive model may be distracted from processing the information about the product.

According to the ELM, there are two basic routes to persuasion or attitude change. Under the **central route to persuasion**, the receiver is viewed as a very active, involved participant in the communication process whose ability and motivation to

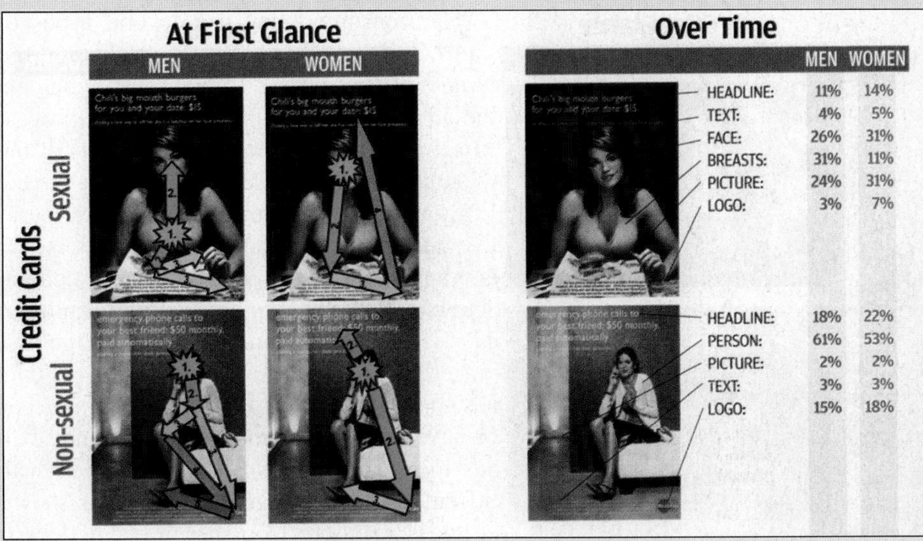


This visual pattern may explain why men's brand recall was lower for sexual ads than for the nonsexual ones. An average of 19.8 percent recalled the correct brand/product for the nonsexual ads versus only 9.8 percent for the sexual ads. MediaAnalyzer researchers call this the "vampire effect" as strong sexual imagery sucks up a lot of the attention that would have otherwise been spent on the product-related components of the advertisement. A somewhat different pattern of results was found for women as they tend to avoid looking at the sexual imagery, although their brand recall was also lower for the sexual (10.8 percent) versus the nonsexual ads (22.8 percent). MediaAnalyzer researchers hypothesized that this might be the result of a general numbing effect that sexual stimuli have on the brain.

An example of the visual processing differences between men and women can be seen in the result found for the MasterCard ads shown above. Men devoted a lot of their processing time on the sexual imagery elements of the ad, starting with the model's breasts, then moving either to her face above or the hamburger below, largely ignoring any of the text copy in the ad. Women, however, mostly avoided the sexual imagery in the ad. The differences in visual processing were not as great for the nonsexual ad, although the viewing paths did diverge. Men explored the model's body first, including her legs, before eventually reaching the logo while women almost immediately focused on the text elements of the ads.

MediaAnalyzer also measured the effectiveness of the sexual versus nonsexual ads using criteria such as liking the ad, product liking, and purchase intentions. Men indicated that they liked the sexual ads more and would be more likely to buy these products while women rated the sexual ads lower on all three criteria. Marketers are likely to continue to use sexual appeals in their advertisements. However, the results of the MediaAnalyzer study suggest that these ads may be providing men in particular with eye candy rather than an effective advertising message.

Source: Tim Nudd, "Does Sex Really Sell?" *Adweek*, October 17, 2005, pp. 14–17; Tom Reichart, "Sex in Advertising Research: A Review of Content, Effects, and Functions of Sexual Information in Consumer Advertising," *Annual Review of Sex Research* 13 (2002), pp. 242–274.

attend, comprehend, and evaluate messages are high. When central processing of an advertising message occurs, the consumer pays close attention to message content and scrutinizes the message arguments. A high level of cognitive response activity or processing occurs, and the ad's ability to persuade the receiver depends primarily on the receiver's evaluation of the quality of the arguments presented. Predominantly favorable cognitive responses (support arguments and source bolsters) lead to favorable changes in cognitive structure, which lead to positive attitude change, or persuasion.

Conversely, if the cognitive processing is predominantly unfavorable and results in counterarguments and/or source derogations, the changes in cognitive structure are unfavorable and *boomerang,* or result in negative attitude change. Attitude change that occurs through central processing is relatively enduring and should resist subsequent efforts to change it.

Under the **peripheral route to persuasion**, shown on the right side of Figure 5–8, the receiver is viewed as lacking the motivation or ability to process information and is not likely to engage in detailed cognitive processing. Rather than evaluating the information presented in the message, the receiver relies on peripheral cues that may be incidental to the main arguments. The receiver's reaction to the message depends on how he or she evaluates these peripheral cues.

**EXHIBIT 5–15**
This ad contains peripheral cues, most notably a celebrity endorser

The consumer may use several types of peripheral cues or cognitive shortcuts rather than carefully evaluating the message arguments presented in an advertisement.[38] Favorable attitudes may be formed if the endorser in the ad is viewed as an expert or is attractive and/or likable or if the consumer likes certain executional aspects of the ad such as the way it is made, the music, or the imagery. Notice how the ad in Exhibit 5–15 for Peak Long Life antifreeze contains several positive peripheral cues, including an attractive and highly relevant celebrity endorser (race car driver Danica Patrick) and appealing visual imagery that is consistent with the brand positioning. These cues might help consumers form a positive attitude toward the brand even if they do not process the message portion of the ad.

Peripheral cues can also lead to rejection of a message. For example, ads that advocate extreme positions, use endorsers who are not well liked or have credibility problems, or are not executed well (such as low-budget ads for local retailers) may be rejected without any consideration of their information or message arguments. As shown in Figure 5–8, the ELM views attitudes resulting from peripheral processing as temporary. So favorable attitudes must be maintained by continual exposure to the peripheral cues, such as through repetitive advertising.

**Implications of the ELM** The elaboration likelihood model has important implications for marketing communications, particularly with respect to involvement. For example, if the involvement level of consumers in the target audience is high, an ad or sales presentation should contain strong arguments that are difficult for the message recipient to refute or counterargue. If the involvement level of the target audience is low, peripheral cues may be more important than detailed message arguments.

An interesting test of the ELM showed that the effectiveness of a celebrity endorser in an ad depends on the receiver's involvement level.[39] When involvement was low, a celebrity endorser had a significant effect on attitudes. When the receiver's involvement was high, however, the use of a celebrity had no effect on brand attitudes; the quality of the arguments used in the ad was more important.

The explanation given for these findings was that a celebrity may serve as a peripheral cue in the low-involvement situation, allowing the receiver to develop favorable attitudes based on feelings toward the source rather than engaging in extensive processing of the message. A highly involved consumer, however, engages in more detailed central processing of the message content. The quality of the message becomes more important than the identity of the endorser.

The ELM suggests that the most effective type of message depends on the route to persuasion the consumer follows. Many marketers recognize that involvement levels are low for their product categories and consumers are not motivated to process advertising messages in any detail. That's why marketers of low-involvement products often rely on creative tactics that emphasize peripheral cues and use repetitive advertising to create and maintain favorable attitudes toward their brand.

## SUMMARIZING THE RESPONSE PROCESS AND THE EFFECTS OF ADVERTISING

As you have seen from our analysis of the receiver, the process consumers go through in responding to marketing communications can be viewed from a number of perspectives. Vakratsas and Ambler recently reviewed more than 250 journal articles and books in an effort to better understand how advertising works and affects the consumer.[40] On the basis of their review of these studies, they concluded that although effects hierarchies have been actively employed for nearly 100 years, there is little

**FIGURE 5–9**

A Framework for Studying How Advertising Works

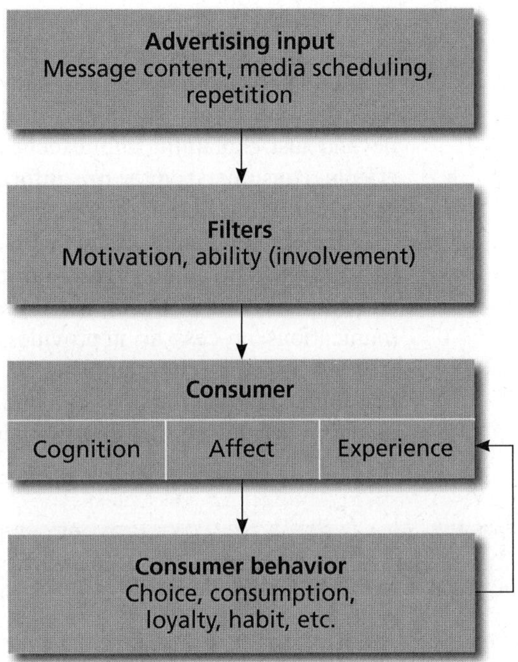




support for the concept of a hierarchy of effects in the sense of temporal sequence. They note that in trying to understand the response process and the manner in which advertising works, there are three critical intermediate effects between advertising and purchase (Figure 5–9). These include *cognition,* the "thinking" dimension of a person's response; *affect,* the "feeling" dimension; and *experience,* which is a feedback dimension based on the outcomes of product purchasing and usage. They conclude that individual responses to advertising are mediated or filtered by factors such as motivation and ability to process information, which can radically alter or change the individual's response to advertising. They suggest that the effects of advertising should be evaluated using these three dimensions, with some intermediate variables being more important than others, depending on factors such as the product category, stage of the product life cycle, target audience, competition, and impact of other marketing-mix components.

Other researchers have been critical of the hierarchy models as well. For example, Hall argues that advertisers need to move away from explicit and implicit reliance on hierarchical models of advertising effects and develop models that place affect and experience at the center of the advertising process.[41] The implication of these criticisms is that marketers should focus on cognition, affect, and experience as critical variables that advertising may affect. However, they should not assume a particular sequence of responses but, rather, engage in research and analysis to better understand how advertising and other forms of promotion may affect these intermediate variables in various product/market situations.

While a number of issues and concerns regarding hierarchy of effects models have been noted, many believe that they are of value to advertising practice and research. For example, Thomas Barry contends that despite their limitations, hierarchical models do help predict behavior. He notes that these models also provide insight into whether advertising strategies need to focus on impacting cognition, affect, and/or behavior based on audience or segmentation experiences and they provide valuable planning, training, and conceptual frameworks.[42]

Those responsible for planning the IMC program need to learn as much as possible about their target audience and how it may respond to advertising, along with other forms of marketing communication. For example, William Weilbacher has noted that marketing communications programs include more than just advertising.[43]

Consumers are continually immersed in brand-sponsored communications that include public relations, a broad range of sales promotion activities, websites, direct marketing, event sponsorships, movie and TV show product placements, and other forms of marketing communication. He argues that hierarchy models must move beyond just explaining the effects of advertising and consider how, and with what effects, consumers synthesize information from all the various integrated marketing communications activities for a brand.

The various models discussed in this chapter are important as they present the basic elements of communication and provide insight into how consumers process and respond to advertising and other IMC tools. It is vital to understand the communications process as it provides a foundation for studying and evaluating integrated marketing communications. Those involved in various aspects of IMC find that understanding the communications process helps them make better decisions in planning, implementing, and evaluating their marketing communication programs.

## Summary

The function of all elements of the IMC program is to communicate, so promotional planners must understand the communication process. This process can be very complex; successful marketing communications depend on a number of factors, including the nature of the message, the audience's interpretation of it, and the environment in which it is received. For effective communication to occur, the sender must encode a message in such a way that it will be decoded by the receiver in the intended manner. Feedback from the receiver helps the sender determine whether proper decoding has occurred or whether noise has interfered with the communication process.

Promotional planning begins with the receiver or target audience, as marketers must understand how the audience is likely to respond to various sources of communication or types of messages. For promotional planning, the receiver can be analyzed with respect to both its composition (i.e., individual, group, or mass audiences) and the response process it goes through. A number of models of the response process have been developed including the AIDA, hierarchy of effects, innovation adoption, and information processing model. Different orderings of the traditional response hierarchy include the standard learning, dissonance/attribution, and low-involvement models.

The cognitive response approach examines the thoughts evoked by a message and how they shape the receiver's ultimate acceptance or rejection of the communication. The elaboration likelihood model of attitude formation and change recognizes two forms of message processing, the central and peripheral routes to persuasion, which are a function of the receiver's motivation and ability to process a message. There are three critical intermediate effects between advertising and purchase including cognition, affect, and experience. Those responsible for planning the IMC program should learn as much as possible about their target audience and how it may respond to advertising and other forms of marketing communications.

## Key Terms

**communication** p. 145
**source** p. 147
**encoding** p. 148
**message** p. 148
**channel** p. 149
**word-of-mouth communication** p. 149
**buzz marketing** p. 149
**mass media** p. 151
**receiver** p. 151
**decoding** p. 151
**field of experience** p. 151
**noise** p. 153
**response** p. 153
**feedback** p. 153
**AIDA model** p. 156
**hierarchy of effects model** p. 156
**innovation adoption model** p. 156
**information processing model** p. 156
**standard learning model** p. 160
**dissonance/attribution model** p. 161
**low-involvement hierarchy** p. 161
**cognitive responses** p. 165
**counterarguments** p. 166
**support arguments** p. 166
**source derogations** p. 166
**source bolsters** p. 166
**ad execution-related thoughts** p. 166
**attitude toward the ad** p. 166
**elaboration likelihood model (ELM)** p. 167
**central route to persuasion** p. 168
**peripheral route to persuasion** p. 169

## Discussion Questions

1. The chapter opener discussed the Fiesta Movement social media campaign used by Ford to launch its new Fiesta subcompact car in the U.S. market. Discuss the pros and cons of this program and assess the amount of risk Ford took in allowing the agents to use social media to communicate with their friends about the car. (LO1, 2)

2. Discuss some of the ways marketers can deal with communication problems such as mistranslations when developing advertising messages in different languages. (LO1)

3. What is meant by encoding? Discuss how encoding differs for radio versus television commercials as well as for print ads. (LO2)

4. Discuss how marketers are using various techniques to generate word-of-mouth discussion and buzz for their brands. Discuss the pros and cons of these techniques. (LO2)

5. Do you think a company that recruits consumers to participate in an online brand community such as Procter & Gamble's Vocalpoint programs should encourage participants to disclose their association with the organization when discussing a product with others? Why or why not? (LO2)

6. Discuss the characteristics of early digital adopters and the role they play in the introduction of a new high-technology product. Find an example of an ad or blog for a new high-tech product that is targeting early adopters and analyze its effort to do so. (LO3)

7. Do you agree with critics who argue that many of the younger people who work in the creative departments of advertising agencies cannot develop ads that connect with older consumers because of the age gap. Do you think advertisers ignore older consumers? Evaluate both sides of this argument. (LO1)

8. Discuss how one of the consumer response models presented in Figure 5–3 could be used by a company such as Apple in planning the introduction of a new product such as the iPad. (LO3)

9. Discuss how marketers of low-involvement products such as soft drinks or paper towels would use various IMC tools differently than a marketer of a high-involvement product such as a personal computer or automobile. (LO3)

10. IMC Perspective 5–1 discusses the results of a study showing how men and women differ in their visual processing of sexual imagery in print ads. On the basis of these findings, what suggestions would you make to a marketer of hard liquor who is considering using a revealing photo of an attractive model in a print ad for the company's product? Would your answer differ for the marketer of a personal computer? (LO4)

11. Explain what is meant by a central versus peripheral route to persuasion and the factors that might determine when each might be used by consumers in response to an advertisement or other form of marketing communication. (LO4)

## AdForum Exercise: Using Communications Models to Evaluate Advertising of High Tech Products

adforum.com

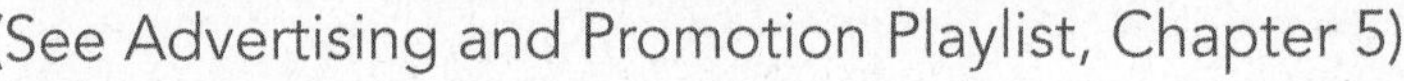

(See Advertising and Promotion Playlist, Chapter 5)

Your assignment is to use the communication models discussed in this chapter to evaluate commercials used by Apple, Amazon, and Sony to launch their new electronic reader devices. Watch the commercials for the Apple iPad ("iPad'), Sony eReader ("Speed Reading') and Amazon Kindle ("Fly Me Away") and answer the following:

1 Choose one of the models of the response process shown in Figure 5-3 and discuss how this model can be used to analyze the advertising used by each company to launch its electronic reader product. Discuss how the commercial is designed to impact various stages of the response process and evaluate how effective it is at doing so.

2 IMC Technology Perspective 5-1 discusses how marketers of high tech products try to target early digital adopters as this group plays an important role in determining the success or failure of new products such as electronic readers. Do you feel the commercials used by Apple, Sony, and Amazon are an effective way to communicate with early digital adopters? Why or why not?

3 Evaluate these three commercials using the model of the communications process shown in Figure 5-1 giving attention to source factors, encoding of the message, channel or medium used, the process by which the message might be decoded, the way the receiver might respond to the message, and the type of feedback each marketer might want to determine the effectiveness of the commercial.

Access to the chapter playlist is available through McGraw Hill connect MARKETING, www.mcgrawhillconnect.com

## LEARNING OBJECTIVES

LO1 To study the major variables in the communication system and how they influence consumers' processing of promotional messages.

LO2 To examine the considerations involved in selecting a source or communicator of a promotional message.

LO3 To examine different types of message structures and appeals that can be used to develop a promotional message.

LO4 To consider how the channel or medium used to deliver a promotional message influences the communication process.

# 6 Source, Message, and Channel Factors

## MARKETERS FACE DILEMMA OVER WHETHER TO STAND BY TIGER WOODS

Prior to Thanksgiving weekend in 2009, if you were to ask nearly any advertising or sports marketing guru to name the most impactful endorser in the history of marketing, chances are most would have responded by naming professional golfer Tiger Woods—and for good reason. Since turning professional, Woods has completely dominated golf in a manner few athletes have ever been able to do in any sport. In 13 years he has won 71 tournaments, ranking him third in all time in career wins. He also has won 14 major championships and is closing in on the record of 19 held by Jack Nicklaus. In addition to being arguably the greatest golfer of all time, Woods was also a marketer's dream as a spokesperson. As one sports executive noted: "Likeability, believability, and popularity, Nobody else has that combination. Tiger Woods delivers for his marketing partners and you can add it up." Woods's marketing partners were not the only ones who were adding it up, as Woods was making an estimated $100 million per year on his endorsement deals with numerous blue chip companies and brands including Accenture, Gillette, Tag Heuer, Gatorade, Upper Deck and, of course, Nike. For many of these companies Woods was more than an endorser, as entire brands, products, and even divisions of companies were built around him.

Nike was the first company to sign Woods to an endorsement deal when he left Stanford University and turned pro in 1996. Nike did not even sell any golf equipment at the time so Woods was primarily endorsing the company's apparel line. However, Nike's strategic plan called for using Woods to help sell more than just golf shirts and hats to golfers. In 1998 the company set up a separate business unit, Nike Golf, and began selling golf clubs as well as shoes and accessories. The decision to sign Tiger Woods to a lucrative endorsement deal has proven to be a good one as he single handedly has helped make Nike Golf one of the fastest growing brands in the golf industry with an estimated $650 million in annual sales.

Nike is not the only company that benefited from Wood's endorsement power. In 2003 Accenture, the global management consulting, technology services, and outsourcing company, made Woods the focal point of it global advertising. The company felt that as perhaps the world's ultimate symbol of high performance, Woods served as a metaphor for its commitment to helping companies become high-performance businesses. As the campaign evolved, it built on the Tiger Woods phenomenon by spelling out the ingredients for becoming a high-performance business and used the theme "We know what it takes to be a Tiger." The campaign was considered Accenture's most successful integrated marketing effort in 20 years as it helped enhance Accenture's brand identity and differentiate the company from its competitors.

Procter & Gamble's Gillette division signed Woods to an endorsement deal in 2007 along with Swiss tennis champion Roger Federer and French soccer star Thierry Henry. The three sports titans were part of the Gillette Champions program, an integrated global sport–marketing initiative being used in more than 150 countries. Another company who bet on Tiger Woods power to move the sales needle for one of its brands was PepsiCo. In 2008 the company's Gatorade division launched a new sports drink, Gatorade Tiger, marking the first time an athlete's name was licensed for use on the iconic brand.

Early in the morning of November 27, 2009, everything changed in the life of Tiger Woods after an early morning car accident outside of his home following an argument with his wife. The accident was the catalyst for intense media scrutiny of his personal life which led to revelations that the superstar, who was married with two young children, had been involved in numerous extramarital affairs. As more women came forward and claimed that they were involved with Woods, he became the lead story in not just the tabloid magazines and TV shows, but in the mainstream media as well. A few weeks after the accident Woods checked into a rehabilitation clinic to receive treatment for sexual addiction as well as addiction to pain medication. The fallout from the scandal was unprecedented in the sports industry and perhaps even in the broader world of celebrities. And while his transgressions had made a mess of Woods' personal life, they presented the companies with whom he had lucrative endorsement deals with a major problem as well as they recognized that their star endorser was now a potential liability.

One of the first companies to drop Woods as an endorser was Accenture, which ended its six-year relationship just two weeks after the public relations catastrophe began. Marketing experts noted that the company was particularly vulnerable to the negative publicity from the scandal since its ads were closely tied to the Woods image and the ad slogan was very ironic given his admitted misconduct. Shortly after the accident PepsiCo also announced that it was dropping the Gatorade drink named after Woods from its product lineup, although the company said the decision was part of an overhaul of the entire brand and was not related to the golfer's troubles. A few weeks later wireless carrier AT&T, whose logo appeared on Woods's golf bag, announced that it would no longer sponsor Woods and Swiss watchmaker Tag Heuer indicated that it would not use his image in its ads in the U.S. market for the foreseeable future.

Tiger Woods returned to the PGA Tour in April 2010 when he played in the Masters Tournament and, despite his layoff and distractions, was still able to finish in fourth place. A number of Woods' sponsors were expressing support for him upon his return including Nike, Upper Deck, NetJets TLC Eye Centers, and EA Sports. However, few of them were making him the focus of their marketing campaigns except for EA Sports which had launched a Woods themed video game and Nike, which aired a controversial commercial showing a close up of Woods's face staring blankly into a camera with a voice over of his late father Earl chastising him for his behavior. Experts note that Nike is the company most likely to support Woods as the sports giant has a history of standing by controversial athletes such as Kobe Bryant. Moreover, the brand image of Nike Golf is so closely tied to Woods that it would be difficult for the company to drop him. Surveys have also shown that attitudes toward Woods have remained favorable among the company's target demographic of male golfers.

It will be interesting to see if Tiger Woods can rebound from all of the damage to his personal brand image and regain his stature as a pitchman who marketers use to build their own brands. Despite the months of unremitting publicity, surveys show that Woods remains one of the most popular athletes in the United States along with NFL quarterbacks Peyton Manning and Brett Favre, and is still the most popular golfer, outpacing Phil Mickelson by a three-to-one margin. However, opinions of Woods are particularly negative among women, which may deter many companies from using him as a spokesperson since women either control or influence many purchase decisions. Some experts feel that Woods can still be an effective endorser, particularly if he picks up where he left off on the golf course and continues to win tournaments, particularly the majors. Others argue that Woods faces a long struggle to regain his luster and to repair his shattered image with corporate America as well as the general public. Ultimately marketers will have to decide if they think this Tiger can change his stripes.

Sources: Suzanne Vranica, "As Tiger Woods Returns to Golf, Nike, Others Embrace Their Links," *The Wall Street Journal Online,* April 8, 2010, retrieved from ABI/INFORM Global. (Document ID: 2004443411); Jeremy Mullman, "For Nike, the Tiger Woods Brand Was Too Big to Fail," *Advertising Age,* April 12, 2010, http://adage.com/print?article_id=143221; Jack Neff, Tiger Woods' Pitchman Days Are Far from Over, Study Says," *Advertising Age,* March 17, 2010, http://adage.com/print?article_id=142835; Emily Steel and Vanessa O'Connell, "Accenture Boots Tiger Off Its Team," *The Wall Street Journal,* December 13, 2009, p. B1; Rich Thomaselli, "Dream Endorser, *Advertising Age,* September 26, 2006, pp. 1, 37.

In this chapter, we analyze the major variables in the communication system: the source, the message, and the channel. We examine the characteristics of sources, how they influence reactions to promotional messages, and why one type of communicator is more effective than another. We then focus on the message itself and how structure and type of appeal influence its effectiveness. Finally, we consider how factors related to the channel or medium affect the communication process.

| Dependent variables: Steps in being persuaded | Independent variables: The communication components | | | | |
|---|---|---|---|---|---|
| | Source | Message | Channel | Receiver | Destination |
| Message presentation | | | (2) | | |
| Attention | (4) | | | | |
| Comprehension | | | | (1) | |
| Yielding | | (3) | | | |
| Retention | | | | | |
| Behavior | | | | | |

**FIGURE 6–1**
The Persuasion Matrix

# PROMOTIONAL PLANNING THROUGH THE PERSUASION MATRIX

To develop an effective advertising and promotional campaign, a firm must select the right spokesperson to deliver a compelling message through appropriate channels or media. Source, message, and channel factors are controllable elements in the communications model. The **persuasion matrix** (Figure 6–1) helps marketers see how each controllable element interacts with the consumer's response process.[1] The matrix has two sets of variables. *Independent variables* are the controllable components of the communication process, outlined in Chapter 5; *dependent variables* are the steps a receiver goes through in being persuaded. Marketers can choose the person or source who delivers the message, the type of message appeal used, and the channel or medium. And although they can't control the receiver, they can select their target audience. The destination variable is included because the initial message recipient may pass on information to others, such as friends or associates, through word of mouth.

Promotional planners need to know how decisions about each independent variable influence the stages of the response hierarchy so that they don't enhance one stage at the expense of another. A humorous message may gain attention but result in decreased comprehension if consumers fail to process its content. Many ads that use humor, sexual appeals, or celebrities capture consumers' attention but result in poor recall of the brand name or message. The following examples, which correspond to the numbers in Figure 6–1, illustrate decisions that can be evaluated with the persuasion matrix.

1. *Receiver/comprehension: Can the receiver comprehend the ad?* Marketers must know their target market to make their messages clear and understandable. A less educated person may have more difficulty interpreting a complicated message. Jargon may be unfamiliar to some receivers. The more marketers

know about the target market, the more they see which words, symbols, and expressions their customers understand.

2. *Channel/presentation: Which media will increase presentation?* A top-rated, prime-time TV program is seen by nearly 12 million households each week. Popular magazines such as *Time* and *People* reach nearly 4 million homes with each issue. But the important point is how well they reach the marketer's target audience. CNBC's financial show *Mad Money with Jim Cramer* reaches only around 200,000 viewers each weekday evening, but its audience consists mostly of upscale businesspeople who are prime prospects for expensive cars, financial services, and business-related products.
3. *Message/yielding: What type of message will create favorable attitudes or feelings?* Marketers generally try to create agreeable messages that lead to positive feelings toward the product or service. Humorous messages often put consumers in a good mood and evoke positive feelings that may become associated with the brand being advertised. Music adds emotion that makes consumers more receptive to the message. Many advertisers use explicit sexual appeals designed to arouse consumers or suggest they can enhance their attractiveness to the opposite sex. Some marketers compare their brands to the competition.
4. *Source/attention: Who will be effective in getting consumers' attention?* The large number of ads we are bombarded with every day makes it difficult for advertisers to break through the clutter. Marketers deal with this problem by using sources who will attract the target audience's attention—actors, athletes, rock stars, or attractive models.

# SOURCE FACTORS

The source component is a multifaceted concept. When Tiger Woods appears in a commercial for Nike, is the source Woods himself, the company, or some combination of the two? And, of course, consumers get information from friends, relatives, and neighbors; in fact, personal sources may be the most influential factor in a purchase decision. Word-of-mouth information transmitted from one individual to another is often perceived as more reliable and trustworthy than that received through more formal marketing channels such as advertising. As was discussed in Chapter 5, marketers are using buzz and stealth marketing methods to generate favorable word-of-mouth discussion and recommendations for their products and services.[2]

**EXHIBIT 6–1**
Actress Hayden Panettiere endorses milk

We use the term **source** to mean the person involved in communicating a marketing message, either directly or indirectly. A *direct source* is a spokesperson who delivers a message and/or endorses a product or service, like actress Hayden Panettiere who appears in an ad sponsored by The Milk Processor Education Program that promotes the nutritional value and benefits of drinking milk (Exhibit 6–1). An *indirect source,* say, a model, doesn't actually deliver a message but draws attention to and/or enhances the appearance of the ad. Some ads use neither a direct nor an indirect source; the source is the organization with the message to communicate. Since most research focuses on individuals as a message source, our examination of source factors follows this approach.

Companies are very careful when selecting individuals to deliver their selling messages. Many firms spend huge sums of money for a specific person to endorse their product or company. They also spend millions recruiting, selecting, and training salespeople to represent the company and deliver sales presentations. They recognize that the characteristics of the source affect the sales and advertising message.

**FIGURE 6–2**
Source Attributes and Receiver Processing Modes

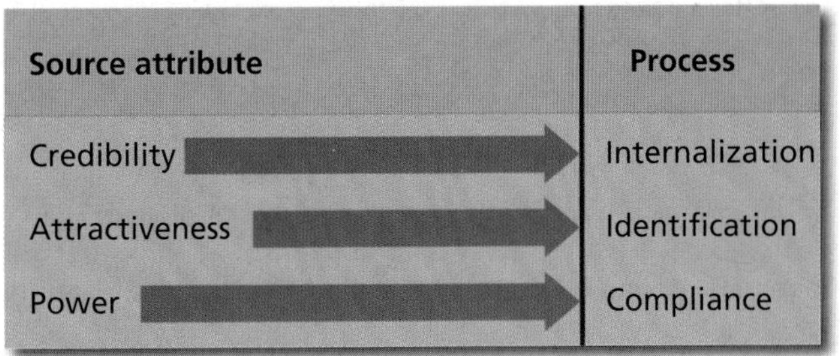




Marketers try to select individuals whose traits will maximize message influence. The source may be knowledgeable, popular, and/or physically attractive; typify the target audience; or have the power to reward or punish the receiver in some manner. Herbert Kelman developed three basic categories of source attributes: credibility, attractiveness, and power.[3] Each influences the recipient's attitude or behavior through a different process (see Figure 6–2).

## Source Credibility

**Credibility** is the extent to which the recipient sees the source as having relevant knowledge, skill, or experience and trusts the source to give unbiased, objective information. There are two important dimensions to credibility, expertise and trustworthiness.

A communicator seen as knowledgeable—someone with expertise—is more persuasive than one with less expertise. But the source also has to be trustworthy—honest, ethical, and believable. The influence of a knowledgeable source will be lessened if audience members think he or she is biased or has underlying personal motives for advocating a position (such as being paid to endorse a product).

One of the most reliable effects found in communications research is that expert and/or trustworthy sources are more persuasive than sources who are less expert or trustworthy.[4] Information from a credible source influences beliefs, opinions, attitudes, and/or behavior through a process known as **internalization**, which occurs when the receiver adopts the opinion of the credible communicator since he or she believes information from this source is accurate. Once the receiver internalizes an opinion or attitude, it becomes integrated into his or her belief system and may be maintained even after the source of the message is forgotten.

**EXHIBIT 6–2**
Dove promotes the fact that it is recommended by experts in skin care

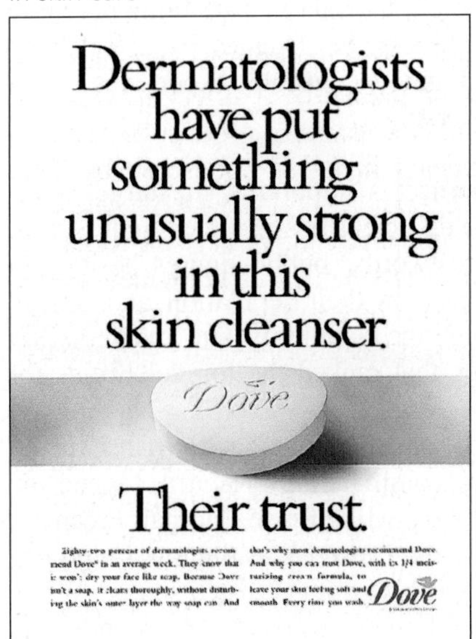


A highly credible communicator is particularly important when message recipients have a negative position toward the product, service, company, or issue being promoted, because the credible source is likely to inhibit counterarguments. As discussed in Chapter 5, reduced counterarguing should result in greater message acceptance and persuasion.

**Applying Expertise** Because attitudes and opinions developed through an internalization process become part of the individual's belief system, marketers want to use communicators with high credibility. Companies use a variety of techniques to convey source expertise. Sales personnel are trained in the product line, which increases customers' perceptions of their expertise. Marketers of highly technical products recruit sales reps with specialized technical backgrounds in engineering, computer science, and other areas to ensure their expertise.

Spokespeople are often chosen because of their knowledge, experience, and expertise in a particular product or service area. Endorsements from individuals or groups recognized as experts, such as doctors or dentists, are also common in advertising (Exhibit 6–2). The importance of using expert sources was shown in a study by Roobina Ohanian, who found that the

## Global Perspective 6–1 > > >

### Celebrities Sell Out—But Only in Japan

While many celebrities make huge sums of money endorsing products and serving as advertising spokespeople, some big stars won't appear in ads in the United States as they don't want fans to think they've sold out. There has also long been a feeling among actors and actresses that appearing in commercials might devalue their image among the powerful Hollywood producers and directors. However, this has been changing in recent years as even some of the biggest names in entertainment have decided to cash in on their celebrity and appear in commercials. For example, Nicole Kidman was paid $8 million to appear in commercials for the Chanel No. 5 fragrance line for one year while Catherine Zeta-Jones received $20 million for four years to appear for the wireless service provider T-Mobile.

While some of the A-list celebrities still resist the temptation to cash in on their fame in the United States, they are only too happy to appear in ads in foreign countries. And nowhere are ads starring American celebrities more prevalent than in Japan. Even the rich and famous have trouble saying no to Japanese advertisers who will pay them between $1 million and $3 million for a few hours' work to make 10-second spots that their Western fans across the Pacific will never see. In Japan, celebrities make more money for less work and because the commercials will never air in the United States, they think they can make the money without looking like they are selling their artistic souls.

Megastars such as Charlize Theron, Brad Pitt, Sean Connery, Kiefer Sutherland, Kevin Costner, and Harrison Ford are paid millions for appearing in Japanese commercials. Theron has appeared in an ad for Honda and for Lux bath products, while Ford received several million dollars for appearing sweaty and bare-chested in Kirin beer commercials and print ads. Pitt has appeared in ads for canned coffee and blue jeans. Actor Tommy Lee Jones endorses Boss canned coffee and his face appears on outdoor signs, subway posters, and thousands of vending machines all over Japan. Jones is a very effective endorser for the brand because the primary drinkers of canned coffee are middle-aged men who view him as

perceived expertise of celebrity endorsers was more important in explaining purchase intentions than their attractiveness or trustworthiness. She suggests that celebrity spokespeople are most effective when they are knowledgeable, experienced, and qualified to talk about the product they are endorsing.[5]

**Applying Trustworthiness** While expertise is important, the target audience must also find the source believable. Finding celebrities or other figures with a trustworthy image is often difficult. Many trustworthy public figures hesitate to endorse products because of the potential impact on their reputation and image. E-Poll Market Research, a company that gauges the popularity and marketability of public figures for clients, conducted a survey that ranked the top celebrities for trustworthiness, awareness, and appeal.[6]

Actor James Earl Jones, who has one of the most recognizable voices in the history of the entertainment industry and a very commanding presence, topped the list, which also included Tom Hanks, Michael J. Fox, Mike Rowe, Morgan Freeman, Sally Field, Ron Howard, Will Smith, Bill Cosby, and Denzel Washington. Entertainment producer and talk show host Oprah Winfrey is also a very trusted source. While nearly all of these top celebrities could command large sums of money as endorsers and spokespersons, very few of them do, often out of concern for how their image representing ruggedness, depth, character, worldliness, and strength. Sometimes celebrities are forced to change their images or personalities to suit the advertising style of Japanese companies and the tastes of audiences in Japan. Japanese commercials have a totally different feel than those in the United States and Europe and have often been described as "tacky" or "cheesy" by Western standards. For example, one ad showed actor Dennis Hopper sitting in a tub with a rubber ducky to promote a brand of shampoo and body wash while, in another, Sean Connery was shown carrying a ham into a room to a James Bond tune. Many of the commercials show a myriad of images of the celebrities during the short spots, putting even the best music video editors to shame.

There are several reasons why Japanese companies are willing to shell out huge sums of money for these stars. Many Japanese are fascinated by American culture and its celebrities, and endorsement of a brand by a star gives it a certain international cachet. Also, Japanese advertising emphasizes style and mood rather than substance; consumers expect to be entertained rather than bored by product information or testimonials. Some movie studios also encourage celebrities to do commercials in Japan because it boosts their visibility and helps the marketing of their films in Japan and other Asian markets.

In addition to their popularity, there are also some practical reasons why Japanese companies pay large sums of money to use Western movie stars in their ads. More than 80 percent of Japanese commercials are 10- or 15-second spots and around 85 percent use celebrities to capture viewers' attention. Japan's cities are also flooded with outdoor signage such as billboards, posters, and transit ads. Thus many marketers feel that an instantly recognizable Western celebrity who can attract attention and enhance the image of a brand is well worth the money.

Some celebrities cashing in on endorsement deals in Japan still try to protect their image at home and not be seen as selling their artistic souls. Many stars have nondisclosure clauses in their contracts, specifying that the ads cannot be shown, or sometimes even discussed (oops!), outside Japan. They still see their appearance in TV ads as being potentially harmful to their reputations back home, much the way Bill Murray's out-of-luck character in the Oscar-winning film *Lost in Translation* avoided making domestic ads. However, with the growth of the Internet, it is difficult to limit the viewing of the ads to one country as many of the commercials can now be found online on popular websites such as YouTube. Some celebrities have filed cease and desist orders against websites such as japander.com to stop them from showing the spots. However, if you do a Google search of "celebrities in Japanese commercials" you can see the futility of their efforts. Linda Thaler, the chief executive officer of the Kaplan Thaler Group advertising agency, notes that "the days of Brad Pitt doing a commercial in Japan that he thought no one was going to see are gone." However, she also notes that the stigma that celebrities are selling out by doing a commercial has also gone by the wayside as Hollywood snobbery toward appearing in commercials declines.

Celebrities are used to getting their way and most would probably still prefer that the knowledge of their Japanese endorsements stay across the Pacific. Sorry about that.

Sources: Sasha Haines-Stiles, "And Hello, A-Listers!," *Forbes*, July 4, 2005, p. 60; James Parsons, "Japan's Ads Are Far from Being Lost in Translation," *Campaign*, September 14, 2007, p. 21; Dave McCaughan, "The Fine Art of Matching a Celebrity with a Brand," *Advertising Age*, April 16, 2007, p. 34; Louis Story, "Seeing Stars," *The New York Times*, October 12, 2006, p. C1; Debra Lau, "Movie Stars Moonlight in Japan," Forbes .com, March 14, 2001.



might be impacted. Global Perspective 6–1 discusses how some American celebrities protect their image by endorsing products in Japan rather than in the United States.

Advertisers use various techniques to increase the perception that their sources are trustworthy. Hidden cameras are used to show that the consumer is not a paid spokesperson and is making an objective evaluation of the product. Disguised brands are compared. (Of course, the sponsor's brand always performs better than the consumer's regular brand, and he or she is always surprised.) Advertisers also use the overheard-conversation technique to enhance trustworthiness. This involves creating a situation in a commercial where a person is shown overhearing a conversation in which favorable claims are made about a product or service. Most consumers are skeptical of these techniques, so they may have limited value in enhancing perceptions of an advertiser's credibility.

Marketers can also deal with the source-trustworthiness issue by using other IMC tools such as publicity. Information received from sources such as newscasters is often very influential because these individuals are perceived as unbiased and thus more credible, even though they are often presenting stories that stem from press releases. In some situations celebrities may appear on news programs or talk shows and promote an upcoming cause or event such as the release of a new movie or music CD. With the increase in stealth marketing techniques, many consumers are becoming wary of endorsements made by celebrities on news programs and talk shows. For example, a *New York Times* article revealed that drug companies were making payments to celebrities or their favorite charities in return for the celebrities' touting the companies' pharmaceutical products on news and talk shows. As a result of the controversy from the article, CNN and the major broadcast networks announced that they would disclose any such financial deals during an interview.[7]

Concerns over potential bias in touting a product or service can involve more than celebrities. Several so-called consumer advocates and product experts have been criticized for giving favorable reviews and/or promoting specific products on local and national TV news programs and other shows without disclosing that they were being paid by the companies to mention their brands. Concern has been expressed over the practice as most television shows present the information presented by trend and fashion gurus or individuals with expertise in areas such as consumer electronics as unbiased and based solely on their expertise. However, the presentation is misleading to consumers if the experts have been paid to mention the products.[8]

**Using Corporate Leaders as Spokespeople** Another way of enhancing source credibility is to use the company president or chief executive officer as a spokesperson in the firm's advertising. Many companies believe the use of their president or CEO is the ultimate expression of the company's commitment to quality and customer service. For some firms, the use of a president or CEO in their ads can help create an identity and personality for the company and/or brand. For example, Richard Branson's irreverence and zeal for life have helped personify the image of Virgin's empire of megastores, airlines, mobile phones, and soft drinks. Branson has been used occasionally in ads for various Virgin brands. As the executive director of global brand consulting firm Enterprise IG notes: "The CEO is the absolute bottom line for a company. There's a lot of power in that."[9] There have been cases where ad campaigns featuring CEOs have not only increased sales but also helped turn the company leaders into celebrities.[10] Lee Iacocca appeared in more than 60 commercials for Chrysler Corp. and became a national business hero for guiding the successful turnaround of the company. In 2005 Chrysler brought back Iacocca to be the pitchman in ads for its "Employee Pricing Plus" program. One of the most popular corporate spokespersons ever was Dave Thomas, the founder of Wendy's fast-food restaurants. Thomas appeared in more than 800 ads for Wendy's between 1989 and early 2002 when he passed away.[11] Other well-known corporate leaders who sometimes appear in ads for their companies include Dell founder Michael Dell; August Busch IV, CEO of Anheuser-Busch; William Ford, chairman of the Ford Motor Company; and James Dyson, the inventor of high-end vacuum cleaners and other appliances, and founder of the company that bears his name. The practice of using company founders, owners, and presidents as advertising spokespersons is particularly prevalent among small and mid-size companies such as retailers and auto dealers serving local markets. For example, Exhibit 6–3 shows an ad for Jerome's Furniture featuring Jerry Navarra, the company's chairman, who has served as a very effective pitchman for the company for more than 30 years and helped grow the retailer into a multi-million dollar business.

**EXHIBIT 6–3**
Local retailers such as Jerome's Furniture often use their president or chairman as an advertising spokesperson

Many marketing and advertising experts question the strategy of using company presidents or owners in ads and note that it is often ego rather than logic that is the reason for their use.[12] The experts suggest that businesspeople should get in front of the camera only if they exude credibility and possess the intangible quality of provoking a warm, fuzzy feeling in viewers.

For example, Microsoft chairman Bill Gates appeared in several TV commercials that were designed to help build a stronger image for the company which has been taking a beating from rival Apple. Gates was paired with comedian Jerry Seinfeld in the spots which attempted to use quirky humor to get consumers to think about Microsoft in a different way. However, the ads only aired for a short time and many ad critics noted that Gates did not come across well in the ads.[13]

Another concern is that creating an image or culture around the CEO can make the corporate brand image more vulnerable if the individual becomes involved in any type of controversy such as a labor dispute, political issue, or personal problem. Critics of the practice also note that CEO spokespeople who become very popular may get more attention than their company's product/service or advertising message. And if a firm's image becomes too closely tied to a popular leader, there can be problems if that person leaves the company. For example, Wendy's has had a difficult time replacing Dave Thomas, who had become an advertising icon and was the voice and personality of the company.[14] It has also been argued that the recent financial crisis and scandals involving top executives in some companies has eroded confidence in executives which affects their ability to come across as trustworthy as they would have a few years ago. Moreover, in the new era of social media it is very easy to criticize corporate leaders who do not come across as trustworthy and believable.[15]

Major corporations are likely to continue to use their top executives in their advertising, particularly when they have celebrity value that helps enhance the firm's image. Some research suggests the use of a company president or CEO can improve attitudes and increase the likelihood that consumers will inquire about a company's product or service.[16] Defenders of the practice argue that the use of top executives or business owners in ads is an effective way of projecting an image of trust and honesty and, more important, the idea that the company isn't run by some faceless corporate monolith. As one expert notes: "These guys come into people's living rooms every night and, over the course of weeks and years, become like members of the family. It gets to the point that when you think of a certain product category, you think of the guy you see all the time on TV."[17]

**Limitations of Credible Sources** Several studies have shown that a high-credibility source is not always an asset, nor is a low-credibility source always a liability. High- and low-credibility sources are equally effective when they are arguing for a position opposing their own best interest.[18] A very credible source is more effective when message recipients are not in favor of the position advocated in the message.[19] However, a very credible source is less important when the audience has a neutral position, and such a source may even be less effective than a moderately credible source when the receiver's initial attitude is favorable.[20]

Another reason a low-credibility source may be as effective as a high-credibility source is the **sleeper effect**, whereby the persuasiveness of a message increases with the passage of time. The immediate impact of a persuasive message may be inhibited because of its association with a low-credibility source. But with time, the association of the message with the source diminishes and the receiver's attention focuses more on favorable information in the message, resulting in more support. However, many studies have failed to demonstrate the presence of a sleeper effect.[21] Many advertisers hesitate to count on the sleeper effect, since exposure to a credible source is a more reliable strategy.[22]

## Source Attractiveness

A source characteristic frequently used by advertisers is **attractiveness**, which encompasses similarity, familiarity, and likability.[23] *Similarity* is a supposed resemblance between the source and the receiver of the message, while *familiarity* refers to knowledge of the source through exposure. *Likability* is an affection for the source as a result of physical appearance, behavior, or other personal traits. Even when the sources are not athletes or movie stars, consumers often admire their physical appearance, talent, and/or personality.

Source attractiveness leads to persuasion through a process of **identification**, whereby the receiver is motivated to seek some type of relationship with the source and thus adopts similar beliefs, attitudes, preferences, or behavior. Maintaining this position depends on the source's continued support for the position as well as the receiver's continued identification with the source. If the source changes position, the receiver may also change. Unlike internalization, identification does not usually integrate information from an attractive source into the receiver's belief system. The receiver may maintain the attitudinal position or behavior only as long as it is supported by the source or the source remains attractive.

Marketers recognize that receivers of persuasive communications are more likely to attend to and identify with people they find likable or similar to themselves. Similarity and likability are the two source characteristics marketers seek when choosing a communicator.

**Applying Similarity** Marketers recognize that people are more likely to be influenced by a message coming from someone with whom they feel a sense of similarity.[24] If the communicator and receiver have similar needs, goals, interests, and lifestyles, the position advocated by the source is better understood and received. Similarity is used in various ways in marketing communications. Companies select salespeople whose characteristics match well with their customers'. A sales position for a particular region may be staffed by someone local who has background and interests in common with the customers. Global marketers often hire foreign nationals as salespeople so customers can relate more easily to them.

Companies may also try to recruit former athletes to sell sporting goods or beer, since their customers usually have a strong interest in sports. Several studies have shown that customers who perceive a salesperson as similar to themselves are more likely to be influenced by his or her message.[25]

Similarity is also used to create a situation where the consumer feels empathy for the person shown in the commercial. In a slice-of-life commercial, the advertiser usually starts by presenting a predicament with the hope of getting the consumer to think, "I can see myself in that situation." This can help establish a bond of similarity between the communicator and the receiver, increasing the source's level of persuasiveness. Many companies feel that the best way to connect with consumers is by using regular-looking, everyday people with whom the average person can easily identify. For example, some of the most popular commercials in previous years have been those from the "Whassup?" campaign for Budweiser beer. In these ads the agency cast a group of real-life friends from Philadelphia, rather than actors, who greet each other with an exaggerated "Whassup?" when they speak with one another or get together to watch a game and enjoy a Bud.

**Applying Likability: Using Celebrities** Advertisers recognize the value of using spokespeople who are admired: TV and movie stars, athletes, musicians, and other popular public figures. It is estimated that nearly 20 percent of all TV commercials feature celebrities, and advertisers pay hundreds of millions of dollars for their services.[26] A content analysis study of advertising appearing in 38 different magazines found that celebrities were used in about 15 percent of the print ads that contained a person. The use of celebrities was the highest in fashion, sports, and teen magazines and lowest in general news and business publications. With regard to product category, the use of celebrities was highest for athletic products, fashion/apparel, and cosmetics.[27]

The top celebrity endorser in recent years has been golfer Tiger Woods who, as noted in the chapter opener, was making more than $100 million per year from his various endorsement deals. Other top American athlete endorsers include golfer

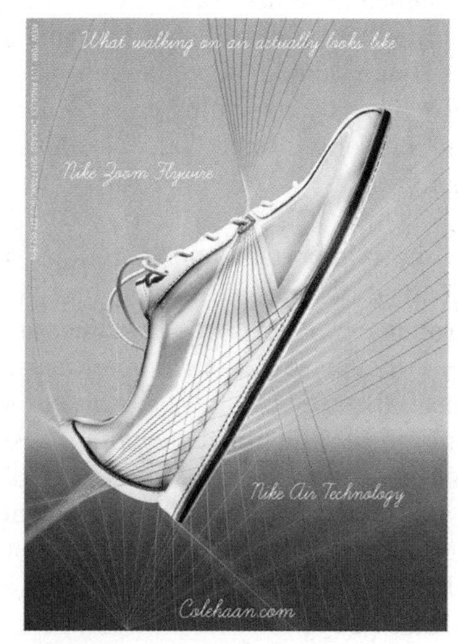

**EXHIBIT 6–4**
Maria Sharapova has endorsement contracts with a number of companies including Nike, Tiffany, Land Rover, and Cole Haan

Phil Mickelson, NBA star LeBron James, former NBA star Michael Jordan, and NASCAR driver Dale Ernhardt, Jr. The top international endorsers include soccer star David Beckham, Formula 1 race car driver Kimi Räikkönen, and tennis star Roger Federer.[28]

For women, the top endorser is tennis star Maria Sharapova, who has endorsement deals with a number of companies including Nike, Land Rover, Tiffany, and Cole Haan (Exhibit 6–4). Other top female endorsers include actress and singers Jennifer Lopez and Jessica Simpson, tennis players Venus and Serena Williams, and golfer Michele Wie.

Why do companies spend huge sums to have celebrities appear in their ads and endorse their products? They think celebrities have *stopping power.* That is, they draw attention to advertising messages in a very cluttered media environment. Marketers think a popular celebrity will favorably influence consumers' feelings, attitudes, and purchase behavior. And they believe celebrities can enhance the target audience's perceptions of the product in terms of image and/or performance. For example, a well-known athlete may convince potential buyers that the product will enhance their own performance.

A number of factors must be considered when a company decides to use a celebrity spokesperson, including the dangers of overshadowing the product and being overexposed, the target audience's receptivity, and risks to the advertiser.

**EXHIBIT 6–5**
PowerBar was one of Lance Armstrong's many endorsement deals

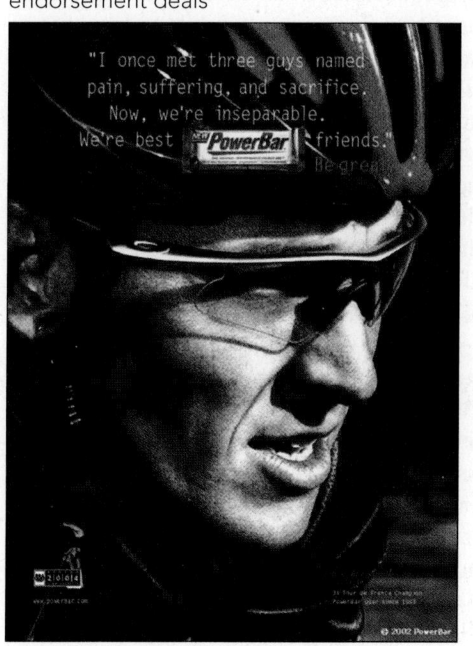


**Overshadowing the Product** How will the celebrity affect the target audience's processing of the advertising message? Consumers may focus their attention on the celebrity and fail to notice the brand. Advertisers should select a celebrity spokesperson who will attract attention and enhance the sales message, yet not overshadow the brand. For example, Chrysler Corp. chose singer Celine Dion to appear in ads for various brands including the Pacifica sport wagon, Crossfire sports coupe, and Town & Country minivan and also signed on as the sponsor of her Las Vegas show "A New Day." She starred in a number of lavish TV commercials that were part of Chrysler's "Drive & Love" campaign, which was developed to give Chrysler a more upscale image and help achieve a premium positioning for the brand. However, the campaign was not successful as it was believed that her celebrity persona overshadowed the products and did more to sell her than the cars.[29]

**Overexposure** Consumers are often skeptical of endorsements because they know the celebrities are being paid.[30] This problem is particularly pronounced when a celebrity endorses too many products or companies and becomes overexposed. For example, at one time cyclist Lance Armstrong had endorsement contracts with nearly 20 different companies, including Discovery Communications, Nike, PowerBar, General Mills, Oakley, and many others, and had to limit his endorsements so he did not become overexposed (Exhibit 6–5).[31] Advertisers can protect themselves against overexposure with an exclusivity clause limiting the number of products a celebrity can endorse. However, such clauses are usually expensive, and most celebrities agree not to endorse similar products anyway. Many celebrities, knowing their fame is fleeting, try to earn as much endorsement money as possible, yet they must be careful not to damage their credibility by endorsing too many products. For example, singer/actress Cher damaged her credibility as an advertising spokesperson by appearing in too many infomercials. When she realized that appearing in so many infomercials was devastating to her acting career as well, she ceased doing them.[32]

**Target Audiences' Receptivity** One of the most important considerations in choosing a celebrity endorser is how well the individual matches with and is received by the advertiser's target audience. Many former athletes such as Arnold Palmer and Michael Jordon are still effective endorsers because they have very favorable images among aging baby boomers and seniors. NBA star LeBron James has been an effective spokesperson for several companies since turning professional including Nike and Coca-Cola because he has tremendous name recognition and is very popular among younger consumers who are the primary target market for athletic shoes and soft drinks. In 2010 McDonald's signed James to a multiyear endorsement deal noting that his personal qualities make him a good fit for the company and that he is popular among young males who are heavy users of fast food.[33]

Consumers who are particularly knowledgeable about a product or service or have strongly established attitudes may be less influenced by a celebrity than those with little knowledge or neutral attitudes. One study found that college-age students were more likely to have a positive attitude toward a product endorsed by a celebrity than were older consumers.[34] The teenage market has generally been very receptive to celebrity endorsers, as evidenced by the frequent use of entertainers and athletes in ads targeted to this group for products such as apparel, cosmetics, and beverages. However, many marketers are finding that teenage consumers are more skeptical and cynical toward the use of celebrity endorsers and respond better to ads using humor, irony, and unvarnished truth. Some marketers targeting teenagers have responded to this by no longer using celebrities in their campaigns or by poking fun at their use.

Some companies avoid the use of celebrities entirely as they have determined that the market they are targeting is really not influenced by their endorsements. For example, New Balance became the number-two athletic footwear company behind Nike without the aid of celebrity endorsers. Its core customers are between the ages of 25 and 49 and are older and more mature than the youth and teen market that most athletic shoe companies target. Until recently, the company had an across-the-board policy against hiring athletes to endorse its products and ran several ad campaigns through the years that poke fun at its competitors for paying exorbitant amounts of money to athletes to wear their shoes. New Balance CEO Jim Davis says, "We don't see any value in paying someone $20 million to promote our shoes. We prefer to channel that money into putting out a better shoe."[35] Small companies that do not have the marketing budget to pay professionals to use their products or are opposed to doing so sometimes use this to their advantage. For example, Exhibit 6–6 shows an ad from Yes! Golf that notes how the company competes against other golf companies that pay endorsement fees based on the quality of its putters.

**EXHIBIT 6–6**
Yes! Golf promotes that it does not pay pro golfers to use its putters

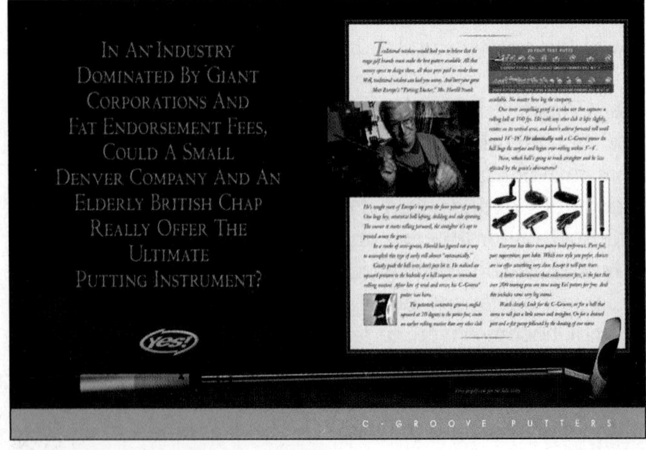


**Risk to the Advertiser** A celebrity's behavior may pose a risk to a company.[36] A number of entertainers and athletes have been involved in activities that could embarrass the companies whose products they endorsed. For example, Hertz used O. J. Simpson as its spokesperson for 20 years and lost all that equity when he was accused of murdering his ex-wife and her friend. Several companies including McDonald's, Coca-Cola, Spalding, and Nutella terminated endorsement deals with NBA superstar Kobe Bryant when he was charged with sexual assault in 2003. Other companies such as Nike and Upper Deck had long-term contracts with Bryant but limited their use of him as an endorser for a number of years. Even though the charges against Bryant were dropped, sports marketing experts noted that it would take him years to repair his image and become a marketable pitchman once again.[37] However, Bryant has been able to recover some of his status as a viable endorser by winning the NBA's Most Valuable Player award in 2008, leading the Los Angeles Lakers to world championships in 2009 and 2010 and, of course, avoiding any further controversies both on and off the court. Over the past few years several companies/brands have signed Bryant to endorsement deals including Sony, the Guitar Hero World Tour music video game, and Vitamin Water (which ironically is now owned by the Coca-Cola Company).[38]



There have been several recent cases of celebrity endorsers having their endorsement contracts canceled because of incidents involving their behavior. Swimming superstar Michael Phelps, who won seven gold medals in the 2008 Olympic Games in Beijing, lost a lucrative endorsement deal with cereal company Kellogg after he was photographed smoking marijuana through a bong at a party. Kellogg announced that it would not renew its endorsement contract with Phelps because his behavior was 'inconsistent with the company's image."[39] NFL quarterback Michael Vick lost endorsement deals worth millions of dollars after being convicted of housing a dog-fighting operation on his rural Virginia property and having a role in killing pit bulls. Among the companies terminating its deals with Vick were Nike, Reebok, AirTran Airways, and trading card companies Donruss and Upper Deck.[40]

Marketers are recognizing that the use of celebrity endorsers can be a very expensive and high-risk strategy because what the celebrities do in their personal lives can impact their image and the way they are viewed by the public. Some companies may face a dilemma in selecting celebrity endorsers: While they prefer them to be upright, they still want them to have an edge or be somewhat irreverent to be able to connect with consumers. This may be particularly true for companies marketing their products to younger consumers.

To avoid problems, companies often research a celebrity's personal life and background. Many endorsement contracts include a morals clause allowing the company to terminate the contract if a controversy arises. Several companies, including luxury brands Burberry and Chanel as well as fashion retailer H&M, canceled their contracts with supermodel Kate Moss in the wake of a British tabloid photo which showed her using cocaine.[41] However, marketers should remember that adding morals clauses to their endorsement contracts only gets them out of a problem; it does not prevent it from happening. Thus, it is important that they carefully consider the character of a celebrity as well as the potential risk associated with using him or her as a spokesperson or endorser for the company or one of its brands.[42]

**Return on Investment** Perhaps the most important factor a company must consider regarding the use of celebrity endorsers is the return on investment from using them. Marketers use celebrities to increase awareness of and attention to their company and/or brands, as well as their advertisements, and to develop strong associations between the celebrity and the brand that will result in higher purchase intentions. However, all of these factors must translate into higher sales in order for the company to get a positive return on the investment from an endorsement deal, which often does not occur. For example, General Motors used Tiger Woods as a spokesperson for its Buick brand from 1999 until the end of 2008. However, during that time period Buick sales declined from around 400,000 cars per year to under 200,000 units.[43] GM stated that Woods did help change the image of Buick as an older-person's car and attract a younger demographic to the brand.[44] However, many experts questioned GM's use of Woods and argued that he was not a good fit with Buick and might have been more effectively used for another model such as Cadillac.

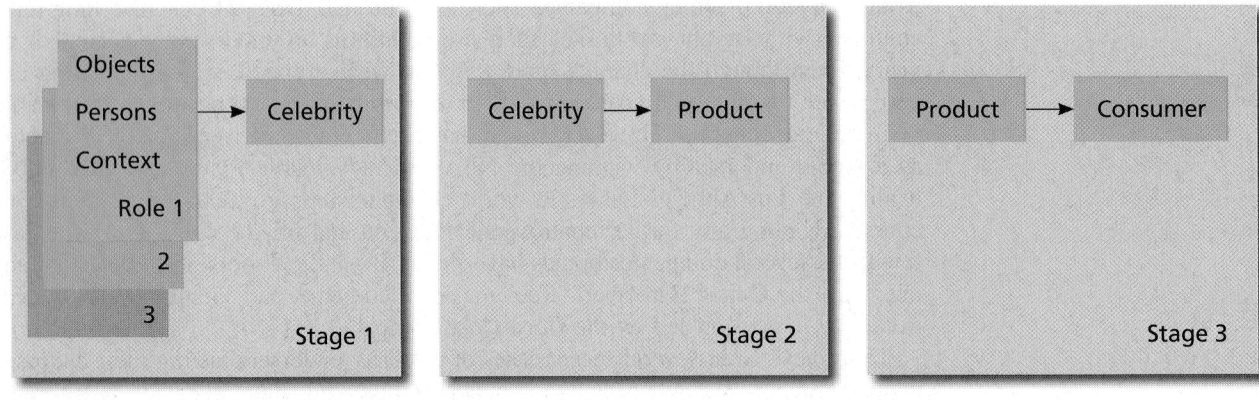


**FIGURE 6–3**

Meaning Movement and the Endorsement Process

Many companies do not reveal the increases in sales and/or market share that result from the use of celebrity endorsers. However, an interesting study was conducted by Anita Elberse and Jeroen Verleun which examined the economic impact of a sample of 347 endorsement deals for 180 athletes across six packaged goods product categories. The results of their study found that sales did increase significantly over the first six months that the athlete endorsers were used—about 4 percent. However, subsequent major achievements by the athletes did not improve the sales of the brand's studied relative to their competitors which calls into question the long term value of endorsement deals.[45]

It should be noted that there are many examples of companies that have seen sales increase, and there can be other factors that marketers consider in determining the value gained from using a celebrity endorser. Thus it is likely that many marketers will continue to use them, despite some of the drawbacks associated with their use that have been discussed.

**Understanding the Meaning of Celebrity Endorsers** Advertisers must try to match the product or company's image, the characteristics of the target market, and the personality of the celebrity.[46] The image celebrities project to consumers can be just as important as their ability to attract attention. An interesting perspective on celebrity endorsement was developed by Grant McCracken.[47] He argues that credibility and attractiveness don't sufficiently explain how and why celebrity endorsements work and offers a model based on meaning transfer (Figure 6–3).

According to this model, a celebrity's effectiveness as an endorser depends on the culturally acquired meanings he or she brings to the endorsement process. Each celebrity contains many meanings, including status, class, gender, and age as well as personality and lifestyle. In explaining stage 1 of the meaning transfer process, McCracken notes:

> Celebrities draw these powerful meanings from the roles they assume in their television, movie, military, athletic, and other careers. Each new dramatic role brings the celebrity into contact with a range of objects, persons, and contexts. Out of these objects, persons, and contexts are transferred meanings that then reside in the celebrity.[48]

Examples of celebrities who have acquired meanings include actor Bill Cosby as the perfect father (from his role on *The Cosby Show*), actor Jerry Seinfeld as the quirky comedian (from his role on the sitcom *Seinfeld*), and singer/actress Jessica Simpson as an attractive, ditzy blonde (from her MTV reality show *Newlyweds: Nick & Jessica* and the movie *The Dukes of Hazzard*). Kelly Ripa, who serves as

**EXHIBIT 6–7**

Kelly Ripa helps create the impression that Electrolux appliances are designed for the "do-it-all" woman

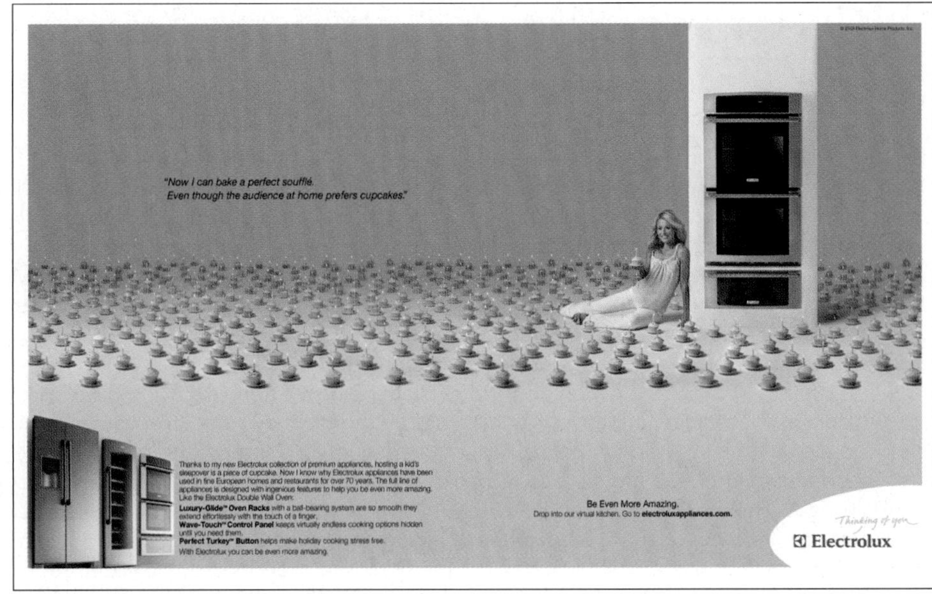




the cohost of the popular daytime show *Live with Regis and Kelly* and has also co-starred in several television shows including *All My Children* and *Hope & Faith,* has developed a very favorable image as a multitalented "do it all woman" who can balance a demanding career with her personal life.

McCracken suggests celebrity endorsers bring their meanings and image into the ad and transfer them to the product they are endorsing (stage 2 of the model in Figure 6–3). For example, Electrolux has been using Kelly Ripa in an integrated marketing campaign for its premium line of stylish, high-performance appliances that capitalizes on her image.[49] The campaign portrays Ripa as a multitalented multitasker and shows her in various roles in her busy life including scenes at work, entertaining at home, and interacting with her daughters (Exhibit 6–7). She is an effective endorser for the brand since she represents the quintessential do it all woman with an endless things-to-do list but who gets it all done.

In the final stage of McCracken's model, the meanings the celebrity has given to the product are transferred to the consumer. By using Ripa in its ads, Electrolux can deliver a powerful brand idea that its appliances are designed to help women who are already doing amazing things in their lives to be even more amazing. To help deliver this message Electrolux uses Ripa in TV and print ads and has also created an entertaining short film on its website starring her that women can watch and share with their friends. McCracken notes that this final stage is complicated and difficult to achieve. The way consumers take possession of the meaning the celebrity has transferred to a product is probably the least understood part of the process.

The meaning transfer model has some important implications for companies using celebrity endorsers. Marketers must first decide on the image or symbolic meanings important to the target audience for the particular product, service, or company. They must then determine which celebrity best represents the meaning or image to be projected. An advertising campaign must be designed that captures that meaning in the product and moves it to the consumer. Marketing and advertising personnel often rely on intuition in choosing celebrity endorsers for their companies or products, but some companies conduct research studies to determine consumers' perceptions of celebrities' meaning. For example, NBA basketball star Yao Ming has become a very effective endorser for companies trying to enter China. To help promote Yao as a pitchman, his management team commissioned a group of University of Chicago Business School students to prepare a marketing study on him. The

# IMC Perspective 6–1 > > >

## NFL Quarterbacks Sometimes Have the Image Marketers Love

Using popular athletes to serve as endorsers to pitch companies and/or their brands has become commonplace in advertising. Marketers pay several billion dollars each year to thousands of athletes in endorsement deals. Many of these athletes endorse companies and brands in the local markets where they play or products that are related to their particular sports. However, some of them have achieved notoriety and popularity that transcends their sport and makes them popular as endorsers for a variety of products and services. Among the professional athletes who are probably the most sought after for endorsement deals are the quarterbacks of National Football League teams.

One of the first NFL quarterbacks to become popular as an endorser was Joe Namath, who played for the New York Jets from 1965 to 1976. Namath is best known for leading the Jets to a win over the Baltimore Colts in the 1969 AFL–NFL World Championship game (prior to the merger of the two leagues) which later became known as the Super Bowl. The Colts were considered one of the best football teams ever while the Jets were given little chance of winning since they were from the American Football League, which was viewed as being years away from being competitive with the NFL. Namath made national headlines prior to the game when he guaranteed that the Jets would win the game, and his ability to back up his boast added to his reputation and flamboyant image.

Namath was also well known for his hedonistic lifestyle. He lived in Manhattan and was a regular in the night clubs and social scene which helped earn him the nickname "Broadway Joe." His popularity both on and off the field and brash image made him very popular on Madison Avenue as he appeared in numerous commercials.

While Joe Namath remained a popular endorser even after his playing days were over, few other NFL quarterbacks have had the same success as an endorser as Broadway Joe over the past three decades. Quarterbacks such as Joe Montana of the San Francisco 49ers and Terry Bradshaw of the Pittsburgh Steelers led their teams to multiple Super Bowl victories but both were only moderately successful as endorsers. However, recently three NFL quarterbacks, Peyton Manning, Tom Brady, and Brett Favre have become very popular as endorsers although their images are quite different as is the way they are used by advertisers.

Peyton Manning, quarterback of the Indianapolis Colts, has become the most marketable NFL player, particularly since leading his team to victory in the 2007 Super Bowl and winning the game's Most Valuable Player Award. He is

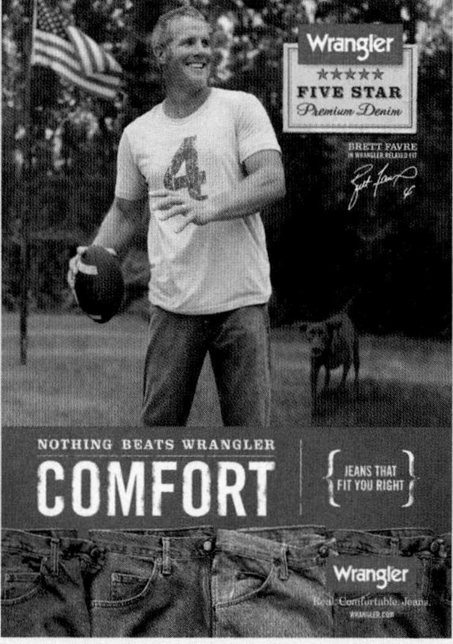

MBA students conducted extensive surveys and focus groups in five Chinese cities, including Shanghai and Beijing, to examine the core values for the 400 million urban Chinese consumers on whom they feel marketers using Yao as a spokesperson should focus. They found that attributes such as hardworking, self-confidence, respect, talent, heroism, and lightheartedness were used to describe values that are important to these Chinese urbanites and that Ming rated higher than other Chinese celebrities on these qualities.[50] IMC Perspective 6–1 discusses how NFL star quarterbacks Peyton Manning, Tom Brady, and Brett Favre have become popular spokesmen for a number a pitchman for a number of powerful brands including Reebok, Sprint, Sony, DirecTV, Gatorade, and MasterCard. Only a handful of professional athletes earn more than the $13 million he makes each year from endorsements. Manning comes from a football family. His father Archie was a star quarterback for the New Orleans Saints and his brother Eli plays the same position for the New York Giants. He has an "everyman" image with which the average person, and men in particular, can easily identify.

Manning does an excellent job of playing the football hero turned everyman in television commercials. In one memorable spot for Mastercard he can be seen cheering on everyday people and exhorting a delicatessen worker slicing cold cuts to "Cut that meat!" In another spot he begs a grocery store clerk to autograph a melon. Commercials for ESPN and DirecTV play off his sibling rivalry with brother Eli. Recently he has been appearing in ads for Sony where he stars alongside singer Justin Timberlake and a panel of celebrity experts. One of the humorous spots features Peyton and Justin playing ping pong, bantering back and forth while speaking Chinese, while ESPN reporter Erin Andrews talks about the benefits of a Sony Bravia HDTV. Marketing experts note that Manning's popularity as an endorser stems in part from his being a star quarterback on a championship team. However, they credit him for using his good-guy-next-door image, showcasing his playful sense of humor and constantly honing his acting skills. *Advertising Age* critic Bob Garfield notes that Manning "is the greatest sports endorser ever. Although Michael Jordan is the most successful, Manning's delivery, poise, and comic timing make Michael look, comparatively, like an extra on *CSI*."

New England Patriots quarterback Tom Brady is also becoming very popular as an endorser. Brady is widely regarded as one of the best quarterbacks of his era as he has led the Patriots to three Super Bowl victories, won two Super Bowl MVP awards, and in 2007 broke the NFL record for most touchdown passes in a season. Brady has a more subtle commercial image than Manning as he is known for his good looks and clean-cut sexiness. While Manning has an everyman, populist image, Brady comes across as more low key but with a quiet sense of confidence. Brady's lifestyle off the field contributes to his cachet. He has dated actresses and married a supermodel, and in 2007 topped *Esquire* magazine's "Best Dressed Men in the World" list beating out rapper Jay-Z.

While Manning is the star of the commercials in which he appears, Brady is more quiet and subdued. One of the first commercials he appeared in was for Visa and featured the Patriots offensive linemen arguing over the type of credit card protection they would provide while he quietly observed them squabbling. In 2007 he signed a multi-year deal with Coty to be the new Stetson Man and appears in print ads and commercials for the company's flagship men's fragrance brand. Brady also appears in print ads for the Movado Series 800 sports watches and recently signed a deal with Glaceau, the maker of Smartwater. Movado's chief marketing officer noted that he was chosen as an endorser because the company wanted to capture the image of an individual who conveys excellence and achievement.

The other quarterback who has become very popular as an endorser is Brett Favre who spent most of his career with the Green Bay Packers but currently plays for the Minnesota Vikings. Favre has been playing in the NFL since 1991 and has earned the reputation as a tough (he has never missed a game due to injury), blue-collar player who has a kid-like passion for the game. Favre retired in 2008 but then decided to play again and had an all-pro season in 2009 at the age of 40. Favre's endorsement deals reflect his image as he serves as a spokesperson for Wrangler jeans, a brand whose image is based on durability, quality, and comfort as well as the core values integrity and authenticity. Hyundai has used Favre in a commercial that plays off of his longevity and "Iron man" reputation to promote its 10-year, 100,000-mile warranty. The spot implies that Favre may play until he is 50 by showing him accepting the Most Valuable Player award after the 2020 football season.

NFL quarterbacks have an advantage when it comes to getting endorsement deals as they play the highest-profile position in the most popular sport in the country. However, Peyton Manning, Brett Favre, and Tom Brady show that it helps to have something extra to offer marketers when they take off their helmets and compete in the endorsement game.

Sources: Richard Sandomir, "Brady and Manning Meet in Battle of the Brands," *The New York Times*, November 4, 2007, pp. S1, 6; Greg Johnson, "He Won't Be Sold Short," *Los Angeles Times*, January 30, 2007, p. D1; "NFL QB Tom Brady Is the New Face of Stetson, promomazine.com, April 24, 2007; "Wrangler; Dale Earnhardt Jr., Brett Favre. . .and You?," *Marketing Weekly News*, October 2009, p.167; "Hyundai Super Bowl Advertising Highlights All-New Sonata and Tucson: Super Bowl Champ Brett Favre Stars in Spot Highlighting Hyundai Quality," *PR Newswire*, February 2, 2010, ProQuest Newsstand. (Document ID: 1952683111).

of major companies and brands even though they have very different images that they bring to the endorsement arena.

Marketers may also pretest ads to determine whether they transfer the proper meaning to the product. When celebrity endorsers are used, the marketer should track the campaign's effectiveness. Does the celebrity continue to be effective in communicating the proper meaning to the target audience? Celebrities who are no longer in the limelight may lose their ability to transfer any significant meanings to the product.

## CHOOSING A CELEBRITY ENDORSER

As we have seen, marketers must consider many factors when choosing a celebrity to serve as an advertising spokesperson for the company or a particular brand. Studies have shown that advertising and marketing managers take these various factors into account when choosing a celebrity endorser.[51] Among the most important factors are the celebrity's match with the target audience and the product/service or brand, the overall image of the celebrity, the cost of acquiring the celebrity, trustworthiness, the risk of controversy, and the celebrity's familiarity and likability among the target audience.

While some advertising and marketing executives rely on their own intuition and gut feeling, many turn to research that measures a celebrity's familiarity and appeal among their target audience as well as other factors. Many companies and their advertising agencies rely on Q-scores that are commercially available from the New York–based firm Marketing Evaluations, Inc. To determine its Q-scores for sport personalities, actors, actresses, and entertainers, the company surveys a representative national panel of consumers several times a year. Respondents are asked to indicate whether they have ever seen or heard of the performer or sports personality and, if they have, to rate him or her on a scale that includes one of my favorites, very good, good, fair, or poor. The *familiarity score* indicates what percentage of people has heard of the person while the *one of my favorites score* is an absolute measure of the appeal or popularity of the celebrity. The well-known *Q-score* is calculated by taking the percentage of respondents who indicate that a person is "one of my favorites" and then dividing that number by the percentage of respondents who indicate they have heard of that person. This score thus answers the question, How appealing is the person among those who do know him or her? The average Q-score for performers is generally around 18 and about 17 for sports personalities. Marketing Evaluation's Q-scores are also broken down on the basis of various demographic criteria such as a respondent's age, income, occupation, education, and race so that marketers have some idea of how a celebrity's popularity varies among different groups of consumers. Marketing Evaluations also now reports a negative Q-score which is the percentage of respondents who rate the personality as fair or poor divided by only those who are familiar with the person. Exhibit 6–8 shows a sample page from the Performer Q study. In addition to Q-scores, marketers also use information provided by a number of other research firms that provide them with data on the popularity of various celebrities and insight into how well their image might fit with their company or brand.

**Applying Likability: Decorative Models** Advertisers often draw attention to their ads by featuring a physically attractive person who serves as a passive or decorative model rather than as an active communicator. Research suggests that physically attractive communicators generally have a positive impact and generate more favorable evaluations of both ads and products than less attractive models.[52] The gender appropriateness of the model for the product being advertised and his or her relevance to the product are also important considerations.[53] Products such as cosmetics or fashionable clothing are likely to benefit from the use of an attractive model, since physical appearance is very relevant in marketing these items.

Some models draw attention to the ad but not to the product or message. Studies show that an attractive model facilitates recognition of the ad but does not enhance copy readership or message recall. Thus, advertisers must ensure that the consumer's attention will go beyond the model to the product and advertising message.[54] Marketers must also consider whether the use of highly attractive models might negatively impact advertising effectiveness. Several recent studies have shown that some women experience negative feelings when comparing themselves with beautiful models used in ads and the images of physical perfection they represent.[55]

MARKETING EVALUATIONS, INC.
PERFORMER Q STUDY

PERSONALITY NAME

| | ONE OF MY FAVORITES | VERY GOOD | GOOD | FAIR/ POOR | TOTAL FAMILIAR | POSITIVE Q SCORE | NEGATIVE Q SCORE |
|---|---|---|---|---|---|---|---|
| TOTAL SAMPLE | 9 | 18 | 30 | 25 | 83 | 11 | 31 |
| 6 - 11 YEARS | 16 | 12 | 18 | 9 | 56 | 29 | 17 |
| 12 - 17 YEARS | 11 | 21 | 30 | 23 | 86 | 13 | 27 |
| 18 - 34 YEARS | 11 | 22 | 33 | 29 | 95 | 11 | 31 |
| 35 - 49 YEARS | 11 | 20 | 34 | 26 | 90 | 12 | 29 |
| 50 AND OVER | 4 | 13 | 28 | 27 | 72 | 6 | 37 |
| 18 - 49 YEARS | 11 | 21 | 34 | 28 | 93 | 11 | 30 |
| 18 YEARS AND OVER | 8 | 18 | 32 | 27 | 85 | 10 | 32 |
| 25 - 54 YEARS | 11 | 20 | 32 | 28 | 91 | 12 | 31 |
| TOTAL MALES | | | | | | | |
| 6 AND OVER | 9 | 16 | 31 | 25 | 81 | 11 | 31 |
| 18 - 34 YEARS | 10 | 21 | 33 | 29 | 94 | 10 | 31 |
| 35 - 49 YEARS | 13 | 18 | 33 | 25 | 89 | 15 | 28 |
| 50 AND OVER | 4 | 11 | 28 | 25 | 67 | 5 | 36 |
| 18 - 49 YEARS | 11 | 20 | 33 | 27 | 91 | 13 | 30 |
| 18 YEARS AND OVER | 9 | 17 | 31 | 26 | 83 | 11 | 32 |
| 25 - 54 YEARS | 12 | 21 | 30 | 27 | 90 | 13 | 30 |
| TOTAL FEMALES | | | | | | | |
| 6 AND OVER | 10 | 19 | 30 | 26 | 84 | 12 | 31 |
| 18 - 34 YEARS | 12 | 22 | 33 | 30 | 97 | 12 | 31 |
| 35 - 49 YEARS | 8 | 21 | 35 | 27 | 91 | 9 | 30 |
| 50 AND OVER | 5 | 15 | 28 | 29 | 76 | 7 | 38 |
| 18 - 49 YEARS | 10 | 22 | 34 | 28 | 94 | 10 | 30 |
| 18 YEARS AND OVER | 8 | 19 | 32 | 29 | 87 | 9 | 33 |
| 25 - 54 YEARS | 10 | 20 | 34 | 29 | 92 | 11 | 31 |
| HOUSEHOLD INCOME | | | | | | | |
| UNDER $20,000 | 8 | 13 | 30 | 20 | 71 | 11 | 28 |
| $20,000 - $39,999 | 9 | 18 | 31 | 26 | 85 | 11 | 31 |
| $40,000 - $59,999 | 11 | 14 | 34 | 27 | 86 | 13 | 31 |
| $60,000 AND OVER | 9 | 21 | 28 | 27 | 85 | 11 | 31 |
| $75,000 AND OVER | 9 | 19 | 29 | 28 | 85 | 11 | 32 |
| EDUCATION (ADULT) | | | | | | | |
| HIGH SCHOOL GRADUATE/LESS | 10 | 19 | 30 | 23 | 80 | 12 | 28 |
| SOME COLLEGE/DEGREE | 7 | 17 | 34 | 32 | 90 | 8 | 36 |
| OCCUPATION (ADULT) | | | | | | | |
| WHITE COLLAR | 7 | 21 | 35 | 29 | 91 | 7 | 32 |
| BLUE COLLAR | 10 | 16 | 32 | 28 | 85 | 12 | 32 |
| RACE | | | | | | | |
| NON BLACK | 7 | 17 | 31 | 27 | 81 | 9 | 33 |
| BLACK | 26 | 25 | 23 | 16 | 90 | 29 | 17 |
| ETHNICITY | | | | | | | |
| HISPANIC | 12 | 17 | 37 | 23 | 89 | 13 | 26 |
| NIELSEN COUNTY SIZE | | | | | | | |
| A | 11 | 18 | 32 | 26 | 87 | 12 | 30 |
| B | 9 | 19 | 30 | 25 | 83 | 11 | 30 |
| C & D | 8 | 16 | 28 | 24 | 75 | 10 | 32 |
| REGION | | | | | | | |
| NORTHEAST | 10 | 21 | 25 | 30 | 85 | 12 | 35 |
| NORTH CENTRAL | 9 | 19 | 32 | 24 | 83 | 11 | 28 |
| SOUTH | 11 | 18 | 32 | 21 | 82 | 13 | 26 |
| WEST | 7 | 13 | 30 | 30 | 80 | 9 | 38 |

**EXHIBIT 6–8**
Sample page from Marketing Evaluations, Inc., Performer Q Study

Some companies have developed marketing campaigns that undermine the traditional approach to beauty care advertising by telling women, as well as young girls, that they're beautiful just the way they are. For example, Unilever's Dove brand has long eschewed the use of supermodels in its ads and uses everyday women and girls who resemble its typical consumers. Since 2004 the company has been running an interesting global integrated marketing campaign designed to appeal to everyday women.[56] The "Campaign for Real Beauty" includes magazine ads, extensive public relations, and a website (www.campaignforrealbeauty.com) where women can discuss beauty-related

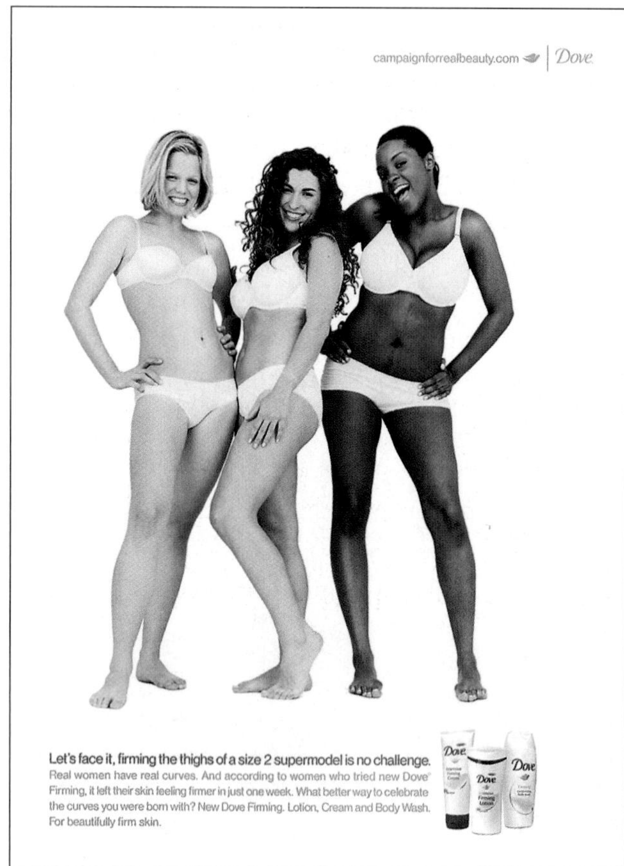

campaignforrealbeauty.com
Dove
Let's face it, firming the thighs of a size 2 supermodel is no challenge.
Real women have real curves. And according to women who tried new Dove® Firming, it left their skin feeling firmer in just one week. What better way to celebrate the curves you were born with? New Dove Firming. Lotion, Cream and Body Wash. For beautifully firm skin.
Dove
Dove
Dove

**EXHIBIT 6–9**

Dove's "Campaign for Real Beauty" uses everyday women rather than supermodels in its ads

issues (Exhibit 6–9). Dove has taken a social advocacy approach in the campaign, which it proclaims "aims to change the status quo and offer in its place a broader, healthier, more democratic view of beauty."[57]

### Source Power

The final characteristic in Kelman's classification scheme is **source power**. A source has power when he or she can actually administer rewards and punishments to the receiver. As a result of this power, the source may be able to induce another person(s) to respond to the request or position he or she is advocating. The power of the source depends on several factors. The source must be perceived as being able to administer positive or negative sanctions to the receiver *(perceived control)* and the receiver must think the source cares about whether or not the receiver conforms *(perceived concern).* The receiver's estimate of the source's ability to observe conformity is also important *(perceived scrutiny).*

When a receiver perceives a source as having power, the influence process occurs through a process known as **compliance**. The receiver accepts the persuasive influence of the source and acquiesces to his or her position in hopes of obtaining a favorable reaction or avoiding punishment. The receiver may show public agreement with the source's position but not have an internal or private commitment to this position. Persuasion induced through compliance may be superficial and last only as long as the receiver perceives that the source can administer some reward or punishment.

Power as a source characteristic is very difficult to apply in a nonpersonal influence situation such as advertising. A communicator in an ad generally cannot apply any sanctions to the receiver or determine whether compliance actually occurs. An indirect way of using power is by using an individual with an authoritative personality as a spokesperson. For example, Take Pride in America uses actor/director Clint Eastwood, whose movie roles earned him an image as a rugged tough guy, in public service campaigns commanding people not to pollute or damage public lands (Exhibit 6–10).

The use of source power applies more in situations involving personal communication and influence. For example, in a personal selling situation, the sales rep may have some power over a buyer if the latter anticipates receiving special rewards or favors for complying with the salesperson. Some companies provide their sales reps with large expense accounts to spend on customers for this very purpose. Representatives of companies whose product demand exceeds supply are often in a position of power; buyers may comply with their requests to ensure an adequate supply of the product. Sales reps must be very careful in their use of a power position, since abusing a power base to maximize short-term gains can damage long-term relationships with customers.

## MESSAGE FACTORS

The way marketing communications are presented is very important in determining their effectiveness. Promotional managers must consider not only the content of their persuasive messages but also how this information will be structured for presentation and what type of message appeal will be used. Advertising, in all media except radio, relies heavily on visual as well as verbal information. Many options are available with respect to the design and presentation of a message. This section examines the structure of messages and considers the effects of different types of appeals used in advertising.

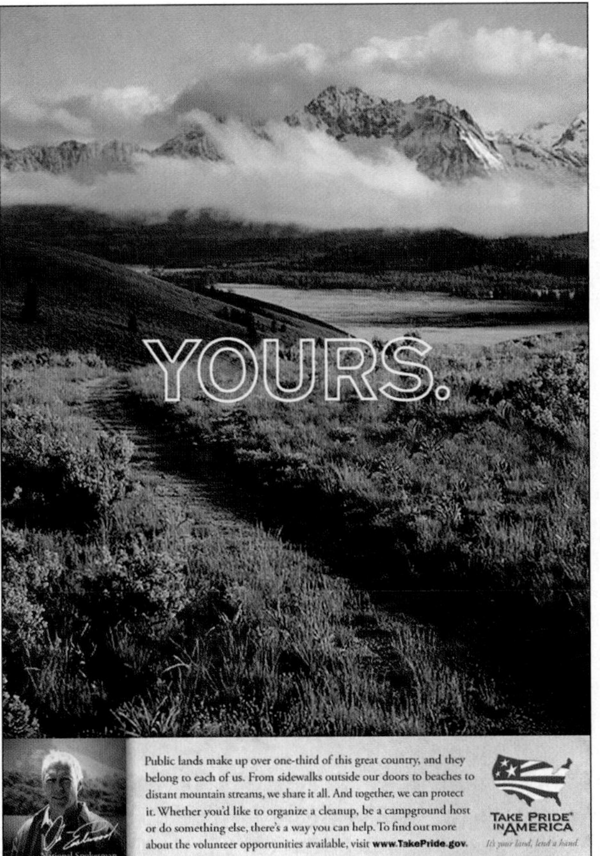


**EXHIBIT 6–10**
Actor Clint Eastwood's authoritative image makes him an effective source

## Message Structure

Marketing communications usually consist of a number of message points that the communicator wants to get across. An important aspect of message strategy is knowing the best way to communicate these points and overcome any opposing viewpoints audience members may hold. Extensive research has been conducted on how the structure of a persuasive message can influence its effectiveness, including order of presentation, conclusion drawing, message sidedness, refutation, and verbal versus visual message characteristics.

**Order of Presentation** A basic consideration in the design of a persuasive message is the arguments' order of presentation. Should the most important message points be placed at the beginning of the message, in the middle, or at the end? Research on learning and memory generally indicates that items presented first and last are remembered better than those presented in the middle (see Figure 6–4).[58] This suggests that a communicator's strongest arguments should be presented early or late in the message but never in the middle.

Presenting the strongest arguments at the beginning of the message assumes a **primacy effect** is operating, whereby information presented first is most effective. Putting the strong points at the end assumes a **recency effect**, whereby the last arguments presented are most persuasive.

Whether to place the strongest selling points at the beginning or the end of the message depends on several factors. If the target audience is opposed to the communicator's position, presenting strong points first can reduce the level of counterarguing. Putting weak arguments first might lead to such a high level of counterarguing that strong arguments that followed would not be believed. Strong arguments work best at the beginning of the message if the audience is not interested in the topic, so they can arouse interest in the message. When the target audience is predisposed toward the communicator's position or is highly interested in the issue or product, strong arguments can be saved for the end of the message. This may result in a more favorable opinion as well as better retention of the information.

The order of presentation can be critical when a long, detailed message with many arguments is being presented. Most effective sales presentations open and close with strong selling points and bury weaker arguments in the middle. For short communications, such as a 15- or 30-second TV or radio commercial, the order may be less critical. However, many product and service messages are received by consumers with low involvement and minimal interest. Thus, an advertiser may want to present the brand name and key selling points early in the message and repeat them at the end to enhance recall and retention. Order of presentation is also an important consideration in other forms of marketing communication. For example, many press releases use the "pyramid style" of writing, whereby most of the important information is presented up front to ensure that it is read since editors often cut from the end of articles.

**FIGURE 6–4**

Ad Message Recall as a Function of Order of Presentation

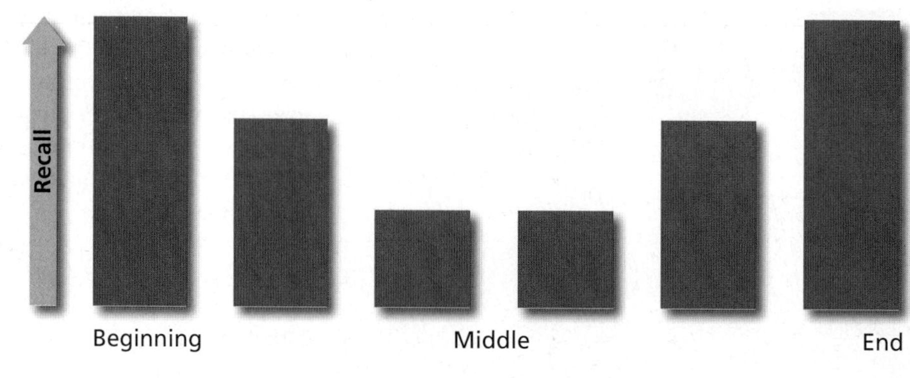


**Conclusion Drawing** Marketing communicators must decide whether their messages should explicitly draw a firm conclusion or allow receivers to draw their own conclusions. Research suggests that, in general, messages with explicit conclusions are more easily understood and effective in influencing attitudes. However, other studies have shown that the effectiveness of conclusion drawing may depend on the target audience, the type of issue or topic, and the nature of the situation.[59]

More highly educated people prefer to draw their own conclusions and may be annoyed at an attempt to explain the obvious or to draw an inference for them. But stating the conclusion may be necessary for a less educated audience, who may not draw any conclusion or may make an incorrect inference from the message. Marketers must also consider the audience's level of involvement in the topic. For highly personal or ego-involving issues, message recipients may want to make up their own minds and resent any attempts by the communicator to draw a conclusion. One study found that open-ended ads (without explicit conclusions) were more effective than closed-ended arguments that did include a specific conclusion—but only for involved audiences.[60]

Whether to draw a conclusion for the audience also depends on the complexity of the topic. Even a highly educated audience may need assistance if its knowledge level in a particular area is low. Does the marketer want the message to trigger immediate action or a more long-term effect? If immediate action is an objective, the message should draw a definite conclusion. This is a common strategy in political advertising, particularly for ads run close to election day. When immediate impact is not the objective and repeated exposure will give the audience members opportunities to draw their own conclusions, an open-ended message may be used.

**EXHIBIT 6–11**

This ad makes effective use of an open-ended approach

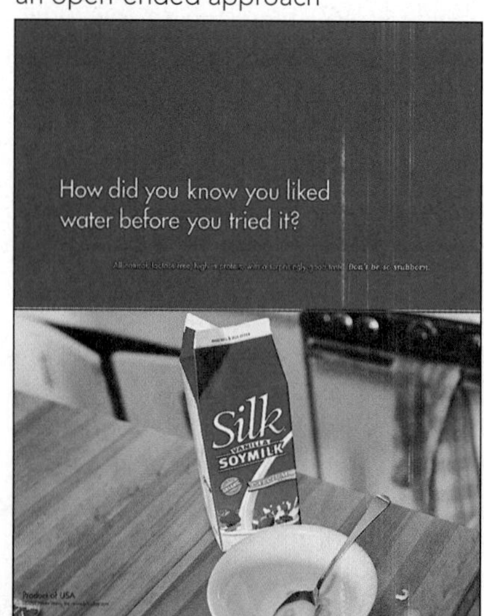

How did you know you liked water before you tried it?
Silk
SOYMILK

Drawing a conclusion in a message may make sure the target audience gets the point the marketer intended. But many advertisers believe that letting customers draw their own conclusions reinforces the points being made in the message. For example, a health services agency in Kentucky found that open-ended ads were more memorable and more effective in getting consumers to use health services than were ads stating a conclusion. Ads that posed questions about alcohol and drug abuse and left them unanswered resulted in more calls by teenagers to a help line for information than did a message offering a resolution to the problem.[61] The ad for Silk Soymilk in Exhibit 6–11 is a very good example of an open-ended message. The question in the headline encourages consumers to be open to the idea of drinking soymilk.

**Message Sidedness** Another message structure decision facing the marketer involves message sidedness. A **one-sided message** mentions only positive attributes or benefits. A **two-sided message** presents both good and bad points. One-sided messages are most effective when the target audience already holds a favorable opinion about the topic. They also work better with a less educated audience.[62]

No one said it would be easy.
Buckley's
Mixture
COUGHS & CONGESTION
It tastes awful. And it works.


EXHIBIT 6–12
Cough syrup uses a two-sided message to promote the product's effectiveness

Two-sided messages are more effective when the target audience holds an opposing opinion or is highly educated. Two-sided messages may enhance the credibility of the source.[63] A better-educated audience usually knows there are opposing arguments, so a communicator who presents both sides of an issue is likely to be seen as less biased and more objective. Martin Eisend recently conducted a meta-analysis of the research conducted on the effects of one- versus two-sided advertising messages. The results of his analysis showed that the persuasive impact of message sidedness depends on a number of factors including the amount and importance of negative information in the ad, attribute quality, placement of the negative information, the correlation between negative and positive attributes, and whether the advertiser discloses negative information voluntarily or because it is required to do so.[64]

Most advertisers use one-sided messages. They are concerned about the negative effects of acknowledging a weakness in their brand or don't want to say anything positive about their competitors. There are exceptions, however. Sometimes advertisers compare brands on several attributes and do not show their product as being the best on every one. There also may be situations in which a company feels that is best to acknowledge its shortcomings and let its customers know that it has addressed them. IMC Perspective 6–2 discusses how Domino's used a two-sided campaign that admitted there were problems with its pizza and developed a new recipe to improve its taste.

In some situations marketers may focus on a negative attribute as a way of enhancing overall perceptions of the product. For example, W. K. Buckley Limited has become one of the leading brands of cough syrup in Canada by using a blunt two-sided slogan, "Buckley's Mixture. It tastes awful. And it works." Ads for the brand poke fun at the cough syrup's terrible taste but also suggest that the taste is a reason why the product is effective (Exhibit 6–12). Buckley's is using the humorous two-sided message strategy in the U.S. market as well.[65]

**Refutation** In a special type of two-sided message known as a **refutational appeal**, the communicator presents both sides of an issue and then refutes the opposing viewpoint. Since refutational appeals tend to "inoculate" the target audience against a competitor's counterclaims, they are more effective than one-sided messages in making consumers resistant to an opposing message.[66]

EXHIBIT 6–13
A refutational appeal is used to address nutritional concerns about almonds

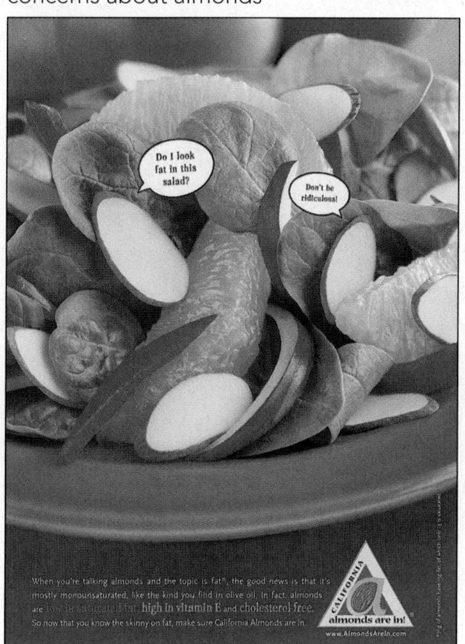


Refutational messages may be useful when marketers wish to build attitudes that resist change and must defend against attacks or criticism of their products or the company. For example, Exhibit 6–13 shows an ad used by the Almond Board of California to refute nutritional concerns about almonds regarding their fat content. Market leaders, who are often the target of comparative messages, may find that acknowledging competitors' claims and then refuting them can help build resistant attitudes and customer loyalty.

**Verbal versus Visual Messages** Thus far our discussion has focused on the information, or verbal, portion of the message. However, the nonverbal, visual elements of an ad are also very important. Many ads provide minimal amounts of information and rely on visual elements to communicate. Pictures are commonly used in advertising to convey information or reinforce copy or message claims.

Both the verbal and visual portions of an ad influence the way the advertising message is processed.[67] Consumers may develop images or impressions based on visual elements such as an illustration in an ad or the scenes in a TV commercial. In some cases, the visual portion of an ad may reduce its persuasiveness, since the processing stimulated by the picture may be less controlled and consequently less favorable than that stimulated by words.[68]

# IMC Perspective 6–2 > > >

## Domino's Mea Culpa

Marketers spend large sums of money to advertise their products and services and the general consensus is that the media time and space they buy should be used to deliver a positive message about their companies and/or brands. However, occasionally a company recognizes that perhaps the best way to win over its customers is by running ads that acknowledge its shortcomings and explain that it is committed to improving. Several companies have run ad campaigns criticizing themselves and vowing to do better. The fast-food chain Hardee's ran ads in 2004 featuring young people who looked directly into the camera and trashed the quality of its hamburgers. General Motors emerged from bankruptcy in late 2008 and shortly thereafter began running ads acknowledging that "General Motors needs to get better to get stronger." In 2009 the Chicago Bears NFL football team capped off a miserable season by taking out a full-page ad apologizing to its fans for its subpar performance and thanking fans for their support despite the teams mediocre 7 and 9 record.

While some companies have been willing to admit their flaws and make promises to improve, the Domino's pizza chain took the two-sided message strategy to a whole new level recently in an integrated marketing campaign that was very candid in acknowledging its shortcomings. In late December 2009 the pizza chain, which has nearly 9,000 stores, began airing TV commercials and posting videos on the Internet featuring company executives reading disparaging comments from consumers about the quality of its pizza. One of the spots showed a company executive grimly quoting a customer's comments saying: "Worst excuse for a pizza I ever had. Totally devoid of flavor." Another employee, who appears near tears, reads another review: "The sauce tastes like ketchup." One of the Web videos showed a clip from a focus group panel where a woman says: "Domino's pizza crust to me is like cardboard."

Domino's recognized that changes were needed after conducting focus groups with consumers which revealed that many of them had issues with the taste of its pizza.

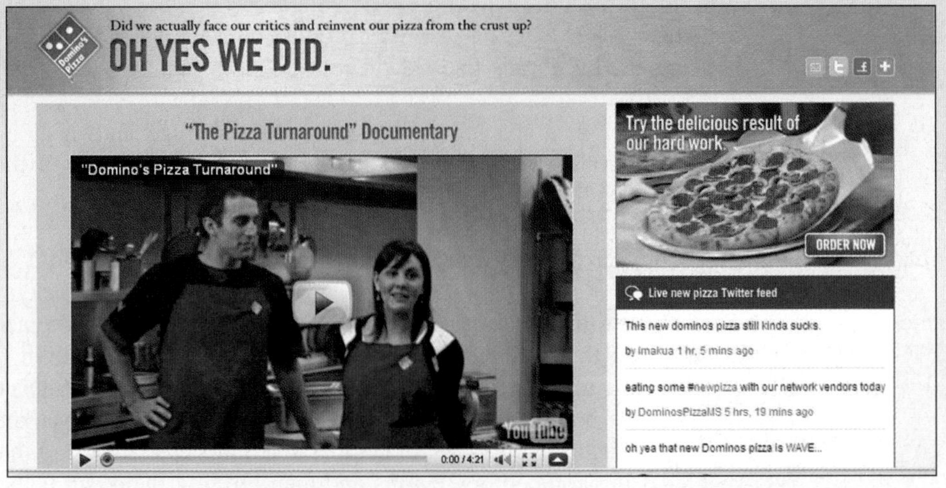


Pictures affect the way consumers process accompanying copy. A study showed that when verbal information was low in imagery value, the use of pictures providing examples increased both immediate and delayed recall of product attributes.[69] However, when the verbal information was already high in imagery value, the addition of pictures did not increase recall. Advertisers often design ads where the visual image supports the verbal appeal to create a compelling impression in the consumer's mind. Notice how the ad for Arrowhead Mountain Spring Water shown in Exhibit 6–14 uses a beautiful visual image of the mountains to communicate the key product attribute of purity.

Sometimes advertisers use a different strategy; they design ads in which the visual portion is incongruent with or contradicts the verbal information presented. The logic behind this strategy is that the use of an unexpected picture or visual image

The company's vice president of brand innovation, Brandon Solano, noted that a focus group was webcast to the executive team and they could not believe what they were hearing. According to Solano, "When somebody's saying something terrible about your pizza, you never get used to it, but for the first time all of our executives were face to face with it. We all said we can't just go to the next meeting. We have to do something about it." Solano and his team set out to make a better pizza and tested 36 different combinations of crust, cheese, and sauce. After 18 months of research and development and consumer testing, Domino's was ready to roll out its reformulated pizza which had a new cheese blend, a more robust sauce, and a garlic-heavy crust.

Once the new pizza was ready, the challenge was to find a compelling way to reintroduce it to consumers, many of whom did not like the taste of the old pizza or had heard negative comments about it. Domino's and its advertising agency, Crispin Porter + Bogusky, deliberated over how to acknowledge that there were problems with the taste of the old pizza, while telling consumers that they would like the taste of the new formulation. CP+B argued that credibility was the key and the best way to achieve it was for Domino's to acknowledge that its previous pizza could have been better. The agency's co-creative director Andrew Keller, who developed the campaign noted that: "It made sense to let people know that we knew there were issues with the old pizza, and that's why we were making changes. Honesty would create a pathway to allow for communication around the new pizza that would not be disregarded."

During the last week of December 2009 Domino's began airing 15- and 30-second commercials showing the chain's new chief executive officer, Patrick Doyle, in front of the camera admitting that he had heard what the focus groups had to say and that he took it to heart. The spots then pointed viewers to a special website (www.pizzaturnaround.com) which featured a four-minute documentary that chronicled Domino's employees' reactions to the negative comments coming from the focus groups and telling about the company's quest to make a better pizza. The website also showed both positive and negative viewer comments, as well as tweets that were linked in from Twitter.

Many marketing and advertising experts argued that Domino's took a big risk with the campaign as it could have easily backfired. Communications professor Bill Benoit noted that "Some people are going to hear only part of the message, that Domino's stinks, and not hear the part about how they're going to get better." It was also noted that apology ads can reinforce negative perceptions and raise awareness of them among people who have never tried or even heard of Domino's. Moreover, the company had been running ads for years proclaiming the great taste of its pizza which might create resentment among customers for knowingly selling an inferior product.

While Domino's and its agency knew the campaign might be risky, they moved forward with it, and the early results have been very favorable. Data from the marketing analytics firm Ace Metrics showed that the commercials were the best-scoring restaurant ads in its system which combines an ad's persuasiveness and watchability to form an overall score. A follow-up ad showing Brandon Solano and another Domino's R&D chef surprising critical focus group participants with the new pizza also received very high Ace scores. In addition to the favorable reactions to the ads, Domino's received a great deal of publicity regarding the ads, much of which praised the company for conceding the shortcomings of its product and explaining what it was doing about it.

For Domino's, the most important measure of consumer reactions to the new campaign will be its ability to move the sales needle. Initial reaction to the campaign has been very positive as Domino's profits more than doubled in the fourth quarter of 2009. Domino's CEO described market response to the new campaign as fantastic, noting that store traffic and sales showed significant increases as consumer trials of the new pizza recipe were very strong. Of course the key question is whether consumers like the new pizza which will ultimately determine if Domino's can sustain the momentum. However, it does appear that the Domino's honesty approach has earned points with consumers. CP+B's Keller explained it well by noting that "Honesty is becoming more and more valuable, because its potential is in short supply in advertising. The fact that Domino's was willing to do this says a lot about them."

Sources: Mark Brandau, "Domino's Do-Over," *Nation's Restaurant Business*, 44 (50), March 8, 2010, p. 44; Jennifer Youseff, "Domino's Profit More than Doubles on New Recipes," *Detroit News*, March 3, 2010, p. B6; Paul Lencioni, "The Power of Saying 'We Blew it', *BusinessWeek*, February 22, 2010, p. 84; Paul Farhi, "Behind Domino's Mea Culpa Ad Campaign," *The Washington Post*, January 13, 2010, p. C7.

will grab consumers' attention and get them to engage in more effortful or elaborative processing.[70] A number of studies have shown that the use of a visual that is inconsistent with the verbal content leads to more recall and greater processing of the information presented.[71]

## Message Appeals

One of the advertiser's most important creative strategy decisions involves the choice of an appropriate appeal. Some ads are designed to appeal to the rational, logical aspect of the consumer's decision-making process; others appeal to feelings in an attempt to evoke some emotional reaction. Many believe that effective advertising combines the practical reasons for purchasing a product with emotional values. In

Born Better.
Every drop of Arrowhead® 100% Mountain Spring Water comes from carefully selected mountain springs. When you start with something better, you get something better.
ArrowheadBornBetter.com
ARROWHEAD

**EXHIBIT 6–14**
Visual images are an effective way to communicate an important product attribute

this section we will examine several common types of message appeals, including comparative advertising, fear, and humor.

**Comparative Advertising** **Comparative advertising** is the practice of either directly or indirectly naming competitors in an ad and comparing one or more specific attributes.[72] This form of advertising became popular after the Federal Trade Commission (FTC) began advocating its use in 1972. The FTC reasoned that direct comparison of brands would provide better product information, giving consumers a more rational basis for making purchase decisions. Television networks cooperated with the FTC by lifting their ban on comparative ads, and the result was a flurry of comparative commercials.

Initially, the novelty of comparative ads resulted in greater attention. But since they have become so common, their attention-getting value has probably declined. Some studies show that recall is higher for comparative than noncomparative messages, but comparative ads are generally not more effective for other response variables, such as brand attitudes or purchase intentions.[73] Advertisers must also consider how comparative messages affect credibility. Users of the brand being attacked in a comparative message may be especially skeptical about the advertiser's claims.

Comparative advertising may be particularly useful for new brands, since it allows a new market entrant to position itself directly against the more established brands and to promote its distinctive advantages. Direct comparisons can help position a new brand in the evoked, or choice, set of brands the customer may be considering.

Comparative advertising is often used for brands with a small market share. They compare themselves to an established market leader in hopes of creating an association and tapping into the leader's market. For example, Savin Corp. used comparative ads for a number of years that were aimed directly at Xerox, the market leader in the copier industry. The campaign was very effective in convincing decision makers at small and mid-size companies that Savin should be considered as an alternative to Xerox as well as other copier companies. The Miller Brewing Company launched an effective comparative campaign for Miller Lite several years ago attacking the market leader. The "Good Call" campaign positioned Miller Lite as the better-tasting, low-carb alternative to Bud Light and helped increase sales of the brand to their highest level in a decade (Exhibit 6–15). Miller used the comparative campaign for several years but moved away from it when its research showed that consumers were tiring of the combative approach. However, in 2007 Miller resurrected the comparative campaign by claiming taste superiority over Bud Light.[74]

A number of other high-profile marketers have been using comparative advertising as a way to differentiate their brands in a competitive marketplace.[75] Since 2006 Apple has been running its comparative "Get a Mac" campaign, which pokes fun at problems with Microsoft's Windows operating system while promoting the user friendliness of Mac PCs. The ads feature two characters, named Mac (played by actor Justin Long) and PC (played by humorist and *New York Times Magazine* editor John Hodgman). Mac is portrayed as a laid-back, creative, and cool character while PC is usually dressed in a suit and tie and depicted as a formal, uptight, and somewhat nerdy character who is frustrated by the more laid-back Mac's capabilities (Exhibit 6–16). Apple launched the campaign to take advantage of the cool reception

ALL TOGETHER NOW...
"MORE TASTE THAN BUD LIGHT
WITH HALF THE CARBS."
Great Taste. Less Filling.
Miller
Good call.
Live Responsibly


**EXHIBIT 6–15**
Comparative ads helped Miller Lite gain market share

that Microsoft's Vista OS received from consumers and to encourage consumers to consider purchasing a Mac instead of a Windows-based PC. Microsoft launched its new Windows 7 OS in 2009 to address some of the problems with Vista, but Apple has continued to run the campaign which has helped it increase its share of the personal computer market.[76]

Market leaders often hesitate to use comparison ads, as most believe they have little to gain by featuring competitors' products in their ads. There are exceptions, of course; Coca-Cola resorted to comparative advertising in response to challenges made by Pepsi that were reducing Coke's market share. Anheuser Busch also responded to the comparative ads used by the Miller Brewing Company when its rival started gaining market share at the expense of Bud Light and other brands. Microsoft has responded to Apple's comparative campaign by running a series of ads that defended PC users and was critical of Apple for stereotyping them. Microsoft also ran a "Laptop Hunters" campaign showing consumers comparing prices of Macs versus PCs and learning that Apple's products were often priced higher.[77]

Another area where comparative messages are quite commonly used is political advertising. Political advertising is viewed as an important component of political speech and thus enjoys more First Amendment protection than commercial speech and less regulation by either government or self-policing agencies. Thus, it has become quite common for political ads to contain negative, one-sided attacks on an opposing candidate's weaknesses such as character flaws, voting record, public misstatements, broken promises, and the like.[78] The goal of these ads is to discredit the character, record, or position of an opponent and create doubt in voters' minds about his or her ability to govern effectively. A major reason why negative political ads are used successfully is that voters often tend to weight negative information more heavily than positive information when forming impressions of political candidates.[79] However, studies have shown that the use of "attack advertising" by politicians can result in negative perceptions of both candidates.[80]

**EXHIBIT 6–16**
Apple uses comparative advertising in its "Get a Mac" campaign

### Fear Appeals

Fear is an emotional response to a threat that expresses, or at least implies, some sort of danger. Ads sometimes use **fear appeals** to evoke this emotional response and arouse individuals to take steps to remove the threat. Some, like the antidrug ads used by the Partnership for a Drug-Free America, stress physical danger that can occur if behaviors are not altered. Others—like those for deodorant, mouthwash, or dandruff shampoos—threaten disapproval or social rejection.

### How Fear Operates

Before deciding to use a fear appeal–based message strategy, the advertiser should consider how fear operates, what level to use, and how different target audiences may respond. One theory suggests that the relationship between the level of fear in a message and acceptance or persuasion is curvilinear, as shown in Figure 6–5.[81] This means that message acceptance increases as the amount of fear used rises—to a point. Beyond that point, acceptance decreases as the level of fear rises.

**FIGURE 6–5**
Relationship between Fear Levels and Message Acceptance

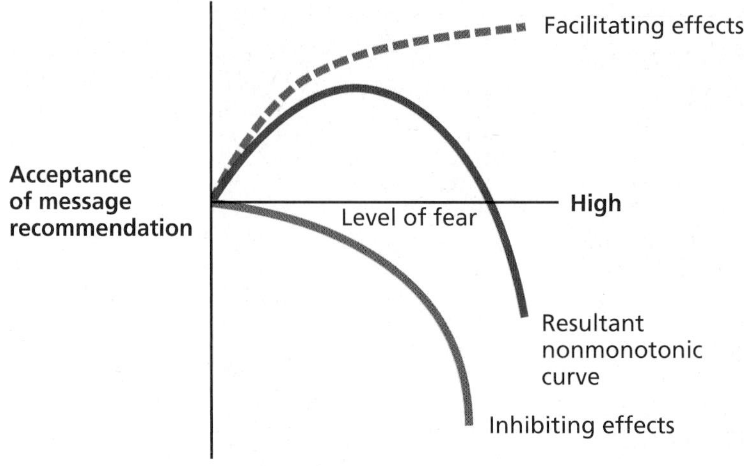


This relationship between fear and persuasion can be explained by the fact that fear appeals have both facilitating and inhibiting effects.[82] A low level of fear can have facilitating effects; it attracts attention and interest in the message and may motivate the receiver to act to resolve the threat. Thus, increasing the level of fear in a message from low to moderate can result in increased persuasion. High levels of fear, however, can produce inhibiting effects; the receiver may emotionally block the message by tuning it out, perceiving it selectively, or denying its arguments outright. Figure 6–5 illustrates how these two countereffects operate to produce the curvilinear relationship between fear and persuasion.

A study by Anand-Keller and Block provides support for this perspective on how fear operates.[83] They examined the conditions under which low- and high-fear appeals urging people to stop smoking are likely to be effective. Their study indicated that a communication using a low level of fear may be ineffective because it results in insufficient motivation to elaborate on the harmful consequences of engaging in the destructive behavior (smoking). However, an appeal arousing high levels of fear was ineffective because it resulted in too much elaboration on the harmful consequences. This led to defensive tendencies such as message avoidance and interfered with processing of recommended solutions to the problem.

Another approach to the curvilinear explanation of fear is the protection motivation model.[84] According to this theory, four cognitive appraisal processes mediate the individual's response to the threat: appraising (1) the information available regarding the severity of the perceived threat, (2) the perceived probability that the threat will occur, (3) the perceived ability of a coping behavior to remove the threat, and (4) the individual's perceived ability to carry out the coping behavior.

This model suggests that both the cognitive appraisal of the information in a fear appeal message and the emotional response mediate persuasion. An audience is more likely to continue processing threat-related information, thereby increasing the likelihood that a coping behavior will occur.

The protection motivation model suggests that ads using fear appeals should give the target audience information about the severity of the threat, the probability of its occurrence, the effectiveness of a coping response, and the ease with which the response can be implemented.[85] For example, the ad shown in Exhibit 6–17 uses a

**EXHIBIT 6–17**
Seagate uses a mild fear appeal that alerts consumers to a problem and offers a solution

State 1

State 2

State 3

State 4

State 5

State 6

**EXHIBIT 6–18**
This clever ad is an example of how humor can be executed in print media

mild fear appeal for Seagate Technology's Replica product which is used to backup computer hard drives. The ad uses playful illustrations in a graphic style to communicate the message of what can happen if your computer crashes and all of the files are lost. Notice how the ad also offers a solution to the threat by showing the ease of using the Replica product and the resulting peace of mind.

It is also important to consider how the target audience may respond. Fear appeals are more effective when the message recipient is self-confident and prefers to cope with dangers rather than avoid them.[86] They are also more effective among nonusers of a product than among users. Thus, a fear appeal may be better at keeping nonsmokers from starting than persuading smokers to stop.

In reviewing research on fear appeals, Herbert Rotfeld has argued that some of the studies may be confusing different types of threats and the level of potential harm portrayed in the message with fear, which is an emotional response.[87] He concludes that the relationship between the emotional responses of fear or arousal and persuasion is not curvilinear but rather is monotonic and positive, meaning that higher levels of fear do result in greater persuasion. However, Rotfeld notes that not all fear messages are equally effective, because different people fear different things. Thus they will respond differently to the same threat, so the strongest threats are not always the most persuasive. This suggests that marketers using fear appeals must consider the emotional responses generated by the message and how they will affect reactions to the message.

**Humor Appeals** Humorous ads are often the best known and best remembered of all advertising messages. Many advertisers, including FedEx, GEICO, Pepsi, and Budweiser, have used humor appeals effectively. Humor is usually presented through radio and TV commercials as these media lend themselves to the execution of humorous messages. However, humor is occasionally used in print ads as well. The clever ad shown in Exhibit 6–18 is a good example of how humor can be used effectively in print. The ad is used by the Australasian New Car Assessment Program (ANCAP) which provides consumers in Australia and New Zealand with information on the level of occupant protection provided by vehicles in front and side crashes.

Advertisers use humor for many reasons. Humorous messages attract and hold consumers' attention. They enhance effectiveness by putting consumers in a positive mood, increasing their liking of the ad itself and their feeling toward the product or service. And humor can distract the receiver from counterarguing against the message.[88]

Critics argue that funny ads draw people to the humorous situation but distract them from the brand and its attributes. Also, effective humor can be difficult to produce and some attempts are too subtle for mass audiences. And, there is concern that humorous ads may wear out faster than serious appeals. **Wearout** refers to the tendency of a television or radio commercial to lose its effectiveness when it is seen and/or heard repeatedly.[89] Wearout may occur if consumers no longer pay attention to a commercial after several exposures or become annoyed at seeing or hearing an ad multiple times. Some experts argue that humorous ads wear out faster than other formats because once the consumer gets the joke, the ad becomes boring. However, advocates of humor argue that funny ads are effective longer as consumers will respond more favorably to a well-executed humorous ad than a serious message.[90] IMC Perspective 6–3 discusses why marketers often run the same ads repeatedly and how humor and other techniques may be used to deal with the problem of wearout.

Clearly, there are valid reasons both for and against the use of humor in advertising. Not every product or service lends itself to a humorous approach. A number of studies have found that the effectiveness of humor depends on several factors, including the type of product and audience characteristics.[91] For example, humor has been more prevalent and more effective with low-involvement, feeling products than high-involvement, thinking products.[92] A recent study examined how audience involvement moderates the effects of humorous ads. The researchers found that for products that are not intrinsically humorous, the use of humor in an advertising message is more effective when involvement is relatively low rather than high. These findings support the idea that high-involvement products may not be as well suited for advertising humor as low-involvement products.[93] An interesting study surveyed the research and creative directors of the top 150 advertising agencies.[94] They were asked to name which communications objectives are facilitated through the appropriate situational use of humor in terms of media, product, and audience factors. The general conclusions of this study are shown in Figure 6–6.

# CHANNEL FACTORS

The final controllable variable of the communication process is the channel, or medium, used to deliver the message to the target audience. While a variety of methods are available to transmit marketing communications, as noted in Chapter 5 they can be classified into two broad categories, personal and nonpersonal media.

## Personal versus Nonpersonal Channels

There are a number of basic differences between personal and nonpersonal communications channels. Information received from personal influence channels is generally more persuasive than information received via the mass media. Reasons for the differences are summarized in the following comparison of advertising and personal selling:

> From the standpoint of persuasion, a sales message is far more flexible, personal, and powerful than an advertisement. An advertisement is normally prepared by persons having minimal personal contact with customers. The message is designed to appeal to a large number of persons. By contrast, the message in a good sales presentation is not determined in advance. The salesman has a tremendous store of knowledge about his product or service and selects appropriate items as the interview progresses. Thus, the salesman can adapt this to the thinking and needs of the customer or prospect at the time of the sales call. Furthermore, as objections arise and are voiced by the buyer, the salesman can treat the objections in an appropriate manner. This is not possible in advertising.[95]

Personal channels are used in several ways in an IMC program. As was discussed in Chapter 5, many marketers are recognizing the importance of word-of-mouth communications which is becoming more prevalent with the growth of social media. The more traditional use of personal communications is through sales programs

**FIGURE 6–6**

Summary of Top Ad Agency Research and Creative Directors' Opinions Regarding Humor

- Humor does aid awareness and attention, which are the objectives best achieved by its use.
  - Humor may harm recall and comprehension in general.
  - Humor may aid name and simple copy registration.
  - Humor may harm complex copy registration.
  - Humor may aid retention.
- Humor does not aid persuasion in general.
  - Humor may aid persuasion to switch brands.
  - Humor creates a positive mood that enhances persuasion.
- Humor does not aid source credibility.
- Humor is generally not very effective in bringing about action/sales.
- Creatives are more positive on the use of humor to fulfill all the above objectives than research directors are.
- Radio and TV are the best media in which to use humor; direct mail and newspapers are least suited.
- Consumer nondurables and business services are best suited to humor; corporate advertising and industrial products are least suited.
- Humor should be related to the product.
- Humor should not be used with sensitive goods or services.
- Audiences that are younger, better educated, upscale, male, and professional are best suited to humor; older, less educated, and downscale groups are least suited to humor appeals.



which are implemented through a company's sales force as well as at the point-of-purchase through retail sales personnel. However, the advertising and promotion programs for most marketers rely heavily on media advertising as well as the Internet. Thus, we will discuss some of the important factors that marketers must consider with respect to the mass media.

## Effects of Alternative Mass Media

The various mass media that advertisers use to transmit their messages differ in many ways, including the number and type of people they reach, costs, information processing requirements, and qualitative factors. The mass media's costs and efficiency in exposing a target audience to a communication will be evaluated in Chapters 10 through 12. However, we should recognize differences in how information is processed and how communications are influenced by context or environment.

**Differences in Information Processing** There are basic differences in the manner and rate at which information from various forms of media is transmitted and can be processed. Information from ads in print media, such as newspapers, magazines, or direct mail, as well as the Internet is *self-paced;* readers process the ad at their own rate and can study it as long as they desire. In contrast, information from the broadcast media of radio and television is *externally paced;* the transmission rate is controlled by the medium.

The difference in the processing rate for print and broadcast media has some obvious implications for advertisers. Self-paced print media make it easier for the message recipient to process a long, complex message. Advertisers often use print ads when they want to present a detailed message with a lot of information. Broadcast media are more effective for transmitting shorter messages or, in the case of TV, presenting pictorial information along with words.

While there are limits to the length and complexity of broadcast messages, advertisers can deal with this problem. One strategy is to use a radio or TV ad to get consumers' attention and direct them to specific print media for a more detailed message. For example, home builders use radio ads to draw attention to new developments and direct listeners to the real estate section of the newspaper for more details. Some advertisers develop broadcast and print versions of the same message. The copy portion is similar in both media, but the print ad can be processed at a rate comfortable to the receiver.

# IMC Perspective 6–3 > > >

## Why Do We Have to Watch Some Ads So Many Times?

If you watch television regularly, or even on a limited basis, at some point it is likely that you have become annoyed at seeing the same commercial being shown over and over. An issue that is always of concern to advertisers is the problem of commercial wearout, or the tendency of a message to lose its effectiveness when it is seen or heard repeatedly. Wearout may occur for several reasons. One is inattention as consumers may no longer pay attention to a TV or radio commercial after watching or listening to it several times, because it no longer is novel and/or interesting. Another reason is when the same ad airs too often, consumers become bored, annoyed, or even irate as advertisers can drive them crazy by subjecting them to the same spot over and over. Having to endure the same ad multiple times can be particularly annoying during sporting events such as football, baseball, and basketball games which last for several hours. The problem can also be compounded when multiple games or events are shown during a concentrated period, such as the summer and winter Olympics, the NCAA "March Madness" college basketball tournament, the college football bowl games, or the playoffs for various professional sports. Some marketers will air the same ad multiple times during a single game and hundreds of times over the duration of a major event or playoffs, which can be very irritating to people who are heavy viewers.

The problem of advertising wearout has intrigued advertising practitioners as well as academic researchers for decades. Studies suggest that TV commercials can be viewed anywhere from 4 to 25 times before losing their effectiveness, although a 2003 study by the Publicis Groupe's Starcom MediaVest Group found that ads with storylines wore out more slowly than hard sell ads with an aggressive call to action. The study also found that pairing humor and music together helped reduce wearout, and ads that went off the air for at least 12 weeks could start up again and retain their effectiveness. However, Kate Sirkin, who is the global research director at Starcom, recently noted that consumers have become much more sensitive to multiple showings of the same commercial and that a TV ad can reach a wearout point after only 8 showings, versus

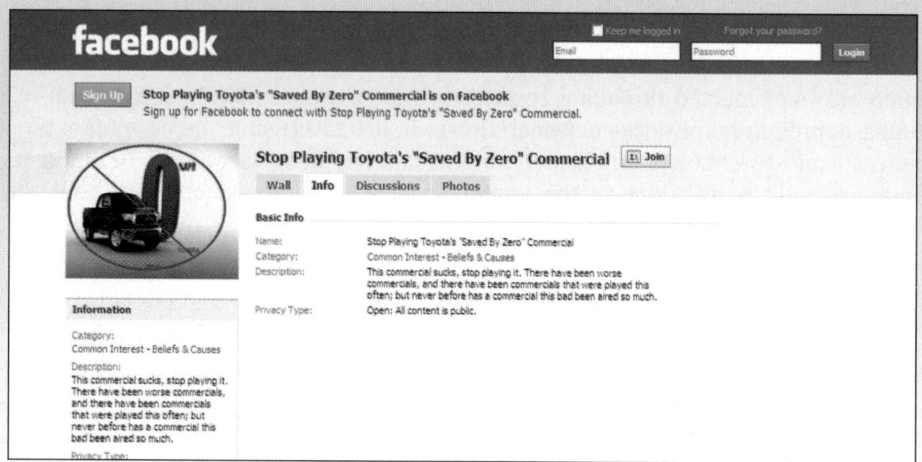


### Effects of Context and Environment

Interpretation of an advertising message can be influenced by the context or environment in which the ad appears. Communication theorist Marshall McLuhan's thesis, "The medium is the message," implies that the medium communicates an image that is independent of any message it contains.[96] A **qualitative media effect** is the influence the medium has on a message. The image of the media vehicle can affect reactions to the message. For example, an ad for a high-quality men's clothing line might have more of an impact in a fashion magazine like *GQ* than in *Sports Afield*. Airlines, destination resorts, and travel-related services advertise in publications such as *Travel & Leisure* partly because the articles, pictures, and other ads help to excite readers about travel (Exhibit 6–19).

A media environment can also be created by the nature of the program in which a commercial appears. One study found that consumers reacted more positively to commercials seen during a happy TV program than a sad one.[97] Advertisers pay premium dollars to advertise on popular programs that create positive moods, like the Olympic Games and Christmas specials. Conversely, advertisers tend to avoid programs that create a negative mood among viewers or may be detrimental to the

the 15 to 20 found in the 2003 study. She notes that consumers are more aware of a greater range of entertainment options and are "all multitasking, less patient, and don't like to have their time wasted."

There are several ways that marketers can deal with the wearout problem. One of the ways is to develop multiple executions that can be rotated so no one ad airs incessantly. Large advertisers often create a pool of commercials as part of a campaign that is updated regularly. An excellent example of this is the "Real Men of Genius" radio campaign for Bud Light beer which has been running since 1999 and features sappy rock music, a bombastic announcer, and outlandish tributes to and spoofs of trivial achievements or unsung heroes such as "Mr. Footlong Hotdog Inventor" or "Mr. Really Bad Toupee Wearer." More than 100 different ads have been created over the past 10 years which has helped make it one of the best radio campaigns of all time. Advertisers can also use certain creative techniques that may make a commercial tolerable for a longer time such as appeals that tap into consumer emotions rather than hard sell approaches. As noted above, the original Starcom study found that utilizing humor or popular music can be helpful in staving off viewer fatigue. However, some industry experts argue that humorous ads can wear out at the same rate as other types of ads because once consumers see the ad a few times, the hilarity loses its impact.

While marketers, agency executives, and media buyers recognize that wearout is a problem, many companies still bombard their target audiences repeatedly with the same commercial which begs the question of why they continue to do so. One reason is that companies do not have large budgets to create multiple ads for a campaign and often may rely on only one or two executions. The average production costs for a high quality TV commercial is nearly $400,000 and many ads cost much more to produce. Smaller advertisers such as local retailers, automobile dealers, banks, and other companies are particularly likely to have a limited budget for their TV creative work and often end up producing one TV spot that airs repeatedly. Another reason is that television has become a much more complex medium to buy. The fragmentation of the media market has resulted in the top shows delivering much smaller audiences than in the past, which means that marketers must run the same ad more often to reach the millions of people they want to attract. Also contributing to the problem is the increasing penetration of DVRs which allow consumers to fast-forward through commercials when they playback recorded shows and thus make it difficult for marketers to achieve their desired levels of reach and frequency.

In some cases it is likely that marketers know that they are saturating the airways with their ads and actually do so intentionally. For example, in late 2008 and early 2009, Toyota created an ad based on the 1983 hit song "Saved by Zero" by the group Fixx that promoted the company's no-interest payment option that was run so often that it resulted in the creation of a Facebook group with nearly 9,000 fans who organized to try to get the company to stop running the ad. However, a company spokesperson noted that Toyota intentionally ran the ad repeatedly to counter all the media reports that credit was not available for new car buyers. Advertisers can also get better rates on TV advertising time when they purchase large numbers of spots which leads to media efficiencies.

It is unlikely that many of the advertisers whose media plans include heavy repetition of their commercials are going to change any time soon. However, the more astute marketers may want to consider whether they are doing more harm than good by bombarding consumers with the same commercial over and over and over.

Sources: Jean Halliday, "New Ram Truck Spot to Air 190 Times Tonight," *Advertising Age*, November 4, 2009, http://adage.com/print?article_id=140320; Brian Steinberg, "Ad Nauseam: Repetition of TV Spots Risks Driving Consumers Away," *Advertising Age*, December 1, 2008, http://adage.com/print?article_id=132884; George Anders, "Marketers Get Creative to Stave Off Ad Fatigue, *The Wall Street Journal*, October 1, 2007, p B5.

company or its products. Many companies won't advertise on programs with excessive violence or sexual content. Coca-Cola never advertises on TV news programs because it thinks bad news is inconsistent with Coke's image as an upbeat, fun product. A study by Andrew Aylesworth and Scott MacKenzie found that commercials placed in programs that induce negative moods are processed less systematically than ads placed in programs that put viewers in positive moods.[98] They suggest that media buyers might be well advised to follow the conventional wisdom of placing their ads during "feel-good" programming, especially if the message is intended to work through a central route to persuasion. However, messages intended to operate through a peripheral route to persuasion might be more effective if they are shown during more negative programs, where presumably viewers will not analyze the ad in detail because of their negative mood state.

## Clutter

Another aspect of the media environment, which is important to advertisers, is the problem of **clutter**, which has been defined as the amount of advertising in a medium.[99] However, for television, clutter is often viewed as including all the

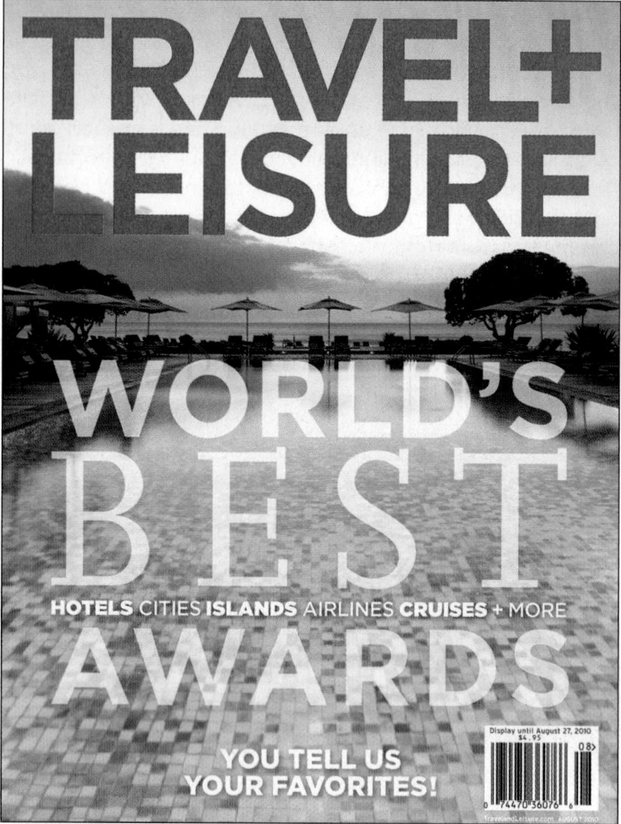


**EXHIBIT 6–19**
*Travel & Leisure* magazine creates an excellent reception environment for travel-related ads

nonprogram material that appears in the broadcast environment—commercials, promotional messages for shows, public service announcements (PSAs), and the like. Clutter is of increasing concern to advertisers since there are so many messages in various media competing for the consumer's attention. Half of the average magazine's pages contain ads and in some publications the ratio of ads to editorial content is even higher. On average, around a quarter of a broadcast hour on TV is devoted to commercials, while most radio stations carry an average of 10 to 12 minutes of commercial time per hour. The high level of advertising often annoys consumers and makes it difficult for ads to communicate effectively.

Clutter has become a major concern among television advertisers as a result of increases in nonprogram time and the trend toward shorter commercials. While the 30-second commercial replaced 60-second spots as the industry standard in the 1970s, many advertisers are now using 15-second spots. The advertising industry continues to express concern over the highly cluttered viewing environment on TV, as the amount of clutter increased as much as 30 percent during the 1990s and another 8 percent since 2000. However, the four major networks have kept their clutter levels relatively flat in recent years but are still running an average of around 15 minutes of nonprogram time per hour in prime time.[100] A study found that the average length of a commercial break during prime time on the major networks is just over three minutes. Thus, a viewer watching three hours of prime-time programs on the major networks would be subjected to as many as 100 commercials, programming promotions, and public service announcements (PSAs).[101] Clutter levels are even higher on many cable networks and during daytime programs. The problem is also greater during popular shows, to which the networks add more commercials because they can charge more. And, of course, advertisers and their agencies perpetuate the problem by pressuring the networks to squeeze their ads into top-rated shows with the largest audiences.

Advertisers and agencies want the networks to commit to a minimum amount of program time and then manage the nonprogram portion however they see fit. If the networks wanted to add more commercials, it would come out of their promos, PSAs, or program credit time. The problem is not likely to go away, however, and advertisers will continue to search for ways to break through the clutter, such as using humor, celebrity spokespeople, or novel, creative approaches.[102]

## Summary

This chapter focused on the controllable variables that are part of the communication process—source, message, and channel factors. Decisions regarding each of these variables should consider their impact on the various steps of the response hierarchy the message receiver passes through. The persuasion matrix helps assess the effect of controllable communication decisions on the consumer's response process.

Selection of the appropriate source or communicator to deliver a message is an important aspect of communications strategy. Three important attributes are source credibility, attractiveness, and power. Marketers enhance message effectiveness by hiring communicators who are experts in a particular area and/or have a trustworthy image. The use of celebrities to deliver advertising messages has become very popular; advertisers hope they will catch the receivers' attention and influence their attitudes or behavior through an identification process. The chapter discusses the meaning a celebrity brings to the endorsement process and the importance of matching the image of the celebrity with that of the company or brand.

The design of the advertising message is a critical part of the communication process. There are various options regarding message structure, including order of presentation of message arguments, conclusion drawing, message sidedness, refutation, and verbal versus visual traits. The advantages and disadvantages of different message appeal strategies were considered, including comparative messages and emotional appeals such as fear and humor.

Finally, the channel or medium used to deliver the message was considered. Differences between personal and nonpersonal channels of communication were discussed. Alternative mass media can have an effect on the communication process as a result of information processing and qualitative factors. The context in which an ad appears and the reception environment are important factors to consider in the selection of mass media. Clutter has become a serious problem for advertisers, particularly on TV, where commercials have become shorter and more numerous.

## Key Terms

**persuasion matrix** p. 179
**source** p. 180
**credibility** p. 181
**internalization** p. 181
**sleeper effect** p. 185
**attractiveness** p. 185
**identification** p. 186
**source power** p. 196
**compliance** p. 196
**primacy effect** p. 197
**recency effect** p. 197
**one-sided message** p. 198
**two-sided message** p. 198
**refutational appeal** p. 199
**comparative advertising** p. 202
**fear appeals** p. 203
**wearout** p. 206
**qualitative media effect** p. 208
**clutter** p. 209

## Discussion Questions

1. The chapter opener discusses the negative publicity Tiger Woods has had resulting from the extensive media scrutiny of his extramarital affairs. Choose one of the companies or brands that Woods is still endorsing and discuss the pros and cons of retaining him as a spokesperson. Do you think this company will renew its contract with him when it expires? Why or why not? (LO2)
2. Discuss how marketers can use the persuasion matrix shown in Figure 6–1 to plan their integrated marketing communication programs. Choose a TV commercial or print ad and use the persuasion matrix to evaluate how it might influence consumers' response process. (LO1)
3. Discuss the three primary source attributes noted by Herbert Kelman and the different processes by which they can influence attitude and/or behavior change. Find an example of an advertisement or other type of promotional message that utilizes each attribute. (LO2)
4. Discuss the pros and cons of a company using one of its top executives such as the founder, CEO or president as an advertising spokesperson. Find an example of a corporate executive who you feel is a good spokesperson and discuss the reasons s/he is effective. (LO2)
5. IMC Perspective 6–1 discusses how NFL quarterbacks Peyton Manning, Tom Brady, and Brett Favre have become popular endorsers. Compare Manning, Brady, and Favre as advertising spokesmen. Why might a company choose to use one versus the other as an endorser? (LO2)
6. Do you agree with the Coca-Cola Company's decision to use NBA star Kobe Bryant as an advertising spokesperson for its Vitamin Water brand? Discuss the pros and cons of using him. (LO2)
7. Find a celebrity who is currently appearing in an ad for a particular company or brand and use McCracken's meaning transfer model (shown in Figure 6–4) to analyze the use of this individual as a spokesperson. (LO2)
8. Evaluate Domino's decision to run an advertising campaign acknowledging the problems with the taste of its pizza as a way to promote its new recipe. Do you think this strategy was an effective way to promote its reformulated product? (LO3)
9. Discuss the factors that lead to commercial wearout giving attention to some of the reasons marketers often run the same ad repeatedly. What are some strategies for delaying or even avoiding wearout? (LO4)
10. Discuss what is meant by clutter in the context of television advertising. Watch a one-hour television program and assess the amount of clutter that appears during the show. How might advertisers deal with the clutter problem. (LO4)
11. What is meant by a qualitative media effect? Select a magazine and discuss the nature of the media environment in that publication. (LO4)

## AdForum Exercise: Using Celebrities as Advertising Spokespersons

adforum.com

(See Advertising and Promotion Playlist, Chapter 6)

### PART 1

Your assignment is to evaluate the use of three celebrities as advertising spokespersons with respect to their source characteristics as well as their cultural meaning. Watch the television commercials for Peak Long Life Antifreeze featuring Danica Patrick; the Electrolux appliance ad featuring Kelly Ripa; and the Priceline.com spot with William Shatner and answer the following:

**1** Evaluate the use of this celebrity as an advertising spokesperson for this company/brand using the source attributes shown in Figure 6-2.
**2** Analyze the use of this celebrity using McCracken's Meaning Transfer Model, which is shown in Exhibit 6-3. Your analysis should address the cultural meaning of the celebrity and how it was acquired, what type of meaning the celebrity is transferring to the company or brand, and how consumers might take possession of the meaning the celebrity is attempting to transfer to the brand.
**3** Discuss whether you feel this celebrity is an effective spokesperson for the company/brand they are endorsing and defend your position.

### PART 2

IMC Perspective 6-1 discusses how NFL quarterbacks Peyton Manning, Brett Favre, and Tom Brady have become popular advertising spokesmen for various companies. Watch the MasterCard commercials featuring Manning, the Hyundai, and Wrangler commercials featuring Favre, and the Sirius and VISA commercials featuring Brady and answer the following:

**1** How would you describe the image of each of these star NFL quarterbacks and their attributes as advertising spokesmen?
**2** Analyze the way Manning, Favre, and Brady are used in the commercials for the companies/brands they are endorsing.
**3** Discuss whether you feel these quarterbacks are effective spokesmen for the company/brands they are endorsing and defend your position.

Access to the chapter playlist is available through McGraw-Hill connect™ MARKETING, www.mcgrawhillconnect.com

## LEARNING OBJECTIVES

LO1 To recognize the importance and value of setting specific objectives for advertising and promotion.

LO2 To understand the role objectives play in the IMC planning process and the relationship of promotional objectives to marketing objectives.

LO3 To know the differences between sales and communications objectives and the issues regarding the use of each.

LO4 To recognize some problems marketers encounter in setting objectives for their IMC programs.

LO5 To understand the process of budgeting for IMC.

LO6 To understand theoretical issues involved in budget setting.

LO7 To know various methods of budget setting.

# 7 Establishing Objectives and Budgeting for the Promotional Program

## THE CONSUMER PURCHASE FUNNEL: DEAD, OR ALIVE AND PREGNANT?

Discussions of consumer response hierarchies have appeared in the marketing literature for over a half century, and have had probably as many opponents as proponents regarding their usefulness in developing marketing and communications strategies. Nevertheless, a number of large companies including Sprint, Honda, and General Motors, have employed their own hierarchies, typically referring to them as purchase funnels. These purchase funnels have been used as a planning guide to move consumers from awareness to final purchase. They are referred to as funnels, as the number of consumers who continue through the stages of the funnel decreases, with fewer actually making a purchase than are actually aware of the product or brand. While consumer purchase funnels have their advocates, there are still some nonbelievers out there.

For example, a study published in the *McKinsey Quarterly* proclaimed the purchase funnel as dead, arguing that consumers do not make decisions in a linear fashion and have changed the way they go about making purchase decisions. Relying on a study of five industries on three continents, the report states that decision making has become more complex and dynamic, and the stages have become interdependent. Consumers no longer determine a consideration set, weigh options, and make a decision, but can be influenced at any time during the process. The study also concludes that because of these changes, marketers must focus more attention on reaching consumers at the precise moment that most influences their decision—something marketers have failed to do. According to McKinsey, marketers must employ touch points including advertising, news reports, product experiences, and such, throughout the buying process to have maximum impact.

Sue Unerman, chief strategy officer at MediaCom, claims that the purchasing funnel is not dead, but alive and pregnant. She contends that the traditional model is being threatened by new media and that marketers must adapt. Ms. Unerman notes that the traditional funnel shape is being replaced by one which shows the traditional narrowing at the consideration stage, but then bulges when the known and trusted brands are joined by those found on Internet searches, blogs, Facebook, and other new media. Like the McKinsey report, she argues that media planners must focus on touch points, switching much of their focus to reaching consumers through PlayStations, Wiis, and the Internet. The new media buyer must know more than how to buy in traditional media, and "will need to know an awful lot about everything."

Like Unerman, Joseph Jaffe, president of Crayon, doesn't think the purchase funnel is dead. He thinks it needs to be flipped! According to Jaffe, the traditional funnel is outmoded, as marketers spend too much money trying to funnel the consumer universe (many of whom don't care about the product or service) down to a handful. He says monies should be spent on this handful so as to get more out of them, resulting in a more efficient, effective, and profitable strategy. By focusing on establishing a strong relationship with customers after the sale, companies can take advantage of the new viral world as consumers interact with many other consumers, each of whom may make multiple transactions. By keeping customers happy and engaged with the product or brand, they essentially do the work for you, at a much reduced cost. Of course, flipping the funnel will also result in changing the way we buy media, which media we buy, and even the structure of the company. No small task, indeed.

However, not everyone is convinced that we need to bury the funnel, impregnate it, or flip it. In a study designed to determine if the purchase funnel works or not, the Television Bureau of Advertising (TVB) was more interested in how media impacts consumers in the decision making process. Yankelovich (a research company) and TVB took a slightly different approach to studying the purchase funnel. Instead of looking at how consumers move through the funnel, this study examined the effect of various media at each stage, and how these media interact to influence the purchase decision process across 15 product categories. The study examined how 3,002 consumers employed traditional and new media at each step in the process. The results indicated that media had an influence on 80 percent of the consumers at the awareness phase, declining to 53 percent at the transaction stage, and that the impact varied depending upon the product category. Television (the traditional medium) was considered to be the most impactful at the awareness, consideration, preference, and purchase levels, with the Internet second at each. Interestingly, the survey dispelled popular thinking that traditional media (particularly TV) would have the most impact at the top of the funnel, with interactive media being more effective near the bottom, as both TV and the Internet showed the most impact *throughout* the process.

So what can we conclude about all of these perspectives? While some feel the funnel is dead and the focus must shift to new media, others feel it needs only to be tweaked, flipped, or left alone. The one thing that is certain is, that no one is certain!

Sources: Sue Unerman, "The Year Ahead for. . .Media Planning," *Campaign*, January 8, 2010, p. 19; Martin Bihl, "Marketing to the Masses? Here's Why You Shouldn't," www.adage.com, March 23, 2010; Jon Lafayette, "Study Shows TV's Impact on Consumer Purchasing Behavior," www.tvweek.com, April 15, 2009; David Court, Dave Elzinga, Susan Mulder, Ole Jorgen Vetvik, "The Consumer Decision Journey," *The McKinsey Quarterly*, New York; 2009, pg. 96.

The lead-in to this chapter discusses the value of using a consumer purchase funnel to set communications objectives. As you can see, while many large companies have been using these purchase decision models for a number of years, and continue to do so, not everyone agrees with their use or their validity, arguing that the models are either outdated or should never have been used in the first place. As this chapter will demonstrate, the success of a program can and should be measured by both marketing and communications objectives. This chapter will examine how the goals for the integrated marketing communications program follow the company's overall marketing strategy and how these goals determine and are determined by the promotional budget.

Unfortunately, many companies have difficulty with the most critical step in the promotional planning process—setting realistic objectives that will guide the development of the IMC program. Complex marketing situations, conflicting perspectives regarding what advertising and other promotional mix elements are expected to accomplish, and uncertainty over resources make the setting of marketing communications objectives "a job of creating order out of chaos." While the task of setting objectives can be complex and difficult, it must be done properly, because specific goals and objectives are the foundation on which all other promotional decisions are made. Budgeting for advertising and other promotional areas, as well as creative and media strategies and tactics, evolves from these objectives. They also provide a standard against which performance can be measured.

Setting specific objectives should be an integral part of the planning process. However, many companies either fail to use specific marketing communications objectives or set ones that are inadequate for guiding the development of the promotional plan or measuring its effectiveness. Many marketers are uncertain as to what integrated marketing communications should be expected to contribute to the marketing program. The goal of their company's advertising and promotional program is simple: to generate sales. They fail to recognize the specific tasks that advertising and other promotional mix variables must perform in preparing customers to buy a particular product or service.

As we know, advertising and promotion are not the only marketing activities involved in generating sales. Moreover, it is not always possible or necessary to measure the effects of advertising in terms of sales. For example, the Standard Bank ad shown in Exhibit 7–1 has a goal beyond just supporting its bank. The ad appeared in a special advertising section of *Fortune* magazine supporting the All for Africa Organization.

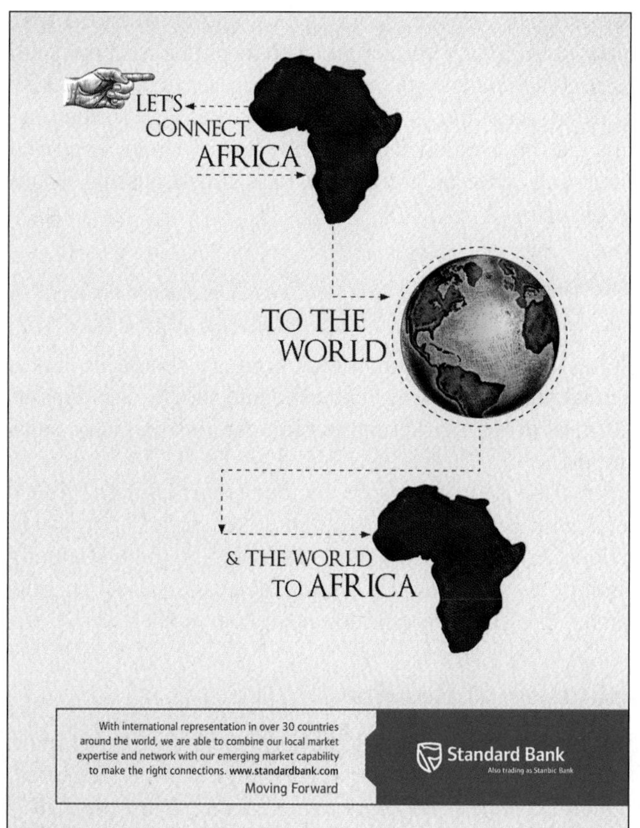


**EXHIBIT 7–1**
The objective of this ad is to demonstrate the Standard Bank's support for Africa

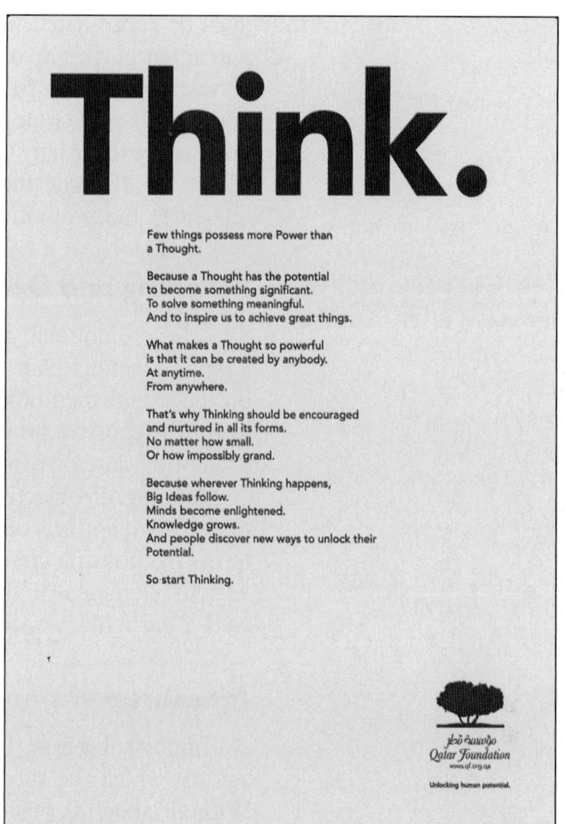


**EXHIBIT 7–2**
The Qatar Foundation's objectives for this ad may be other than generating sales

Consider the Qatar Foundation ad shown in Exhibit 7–2. What objectives might the company have for this ad? How might its effectiveness be measured?

This chapter examines the nature and purpose of objectives and the role they play in guiding the development, implementation, and evaluation of an IMC program. Attention is given to the various types of objectives appropriate for different situations. We will also examine the budget-setting process and the interdependence of objective setting and budgeting.

## THE VALUE OF OBJECTIVES

Perhaps one reason many companies fail to set specific objectives for their integrated marketing communications programs is that they don't recognize the value of doing so. Another may be disagreement as to what the specific objectives should be. Advertising and promotional objectives are needed for several reasons, including the functions they serve in communications, planning and decision making, and measurement and evaluation.

### Communications

Specific objectives for the IMC program facilitate coordination of the various groups working on the campaign. Many people are involved in the planning and development of an integrated marketing communications program on the client side as well as in the various promotional agencies. The advertising and promotional program must be coordinated within the company, inside the ad agency, and between the two. Any other parties involved in the promotional campaign, such as public relations and/or sales promotion firms, research specialists, or media buying services, must also know what the company hopes to accomplish through its marketing communications program. Many problems can be avoided if all parties have written, approved objectives to guide their actions and serve as a common base for discussing issues related to the promotional program.

### Planning and Decision Making

Specific promotional objectives also guide development of the integrated marketing communications plan. All phases of a firm's promotional strategy should be based on the established objectives, including budgeting, creative, and media decisions as well as supportive programs such as direct marketing, public relations/publicity, sales promotion, and/or reseller support.

Meaningful objectives can also be a useful guide for decision making. Promotional planners are often faced with a number of strategic and tactical options in terms of choosing creative options, selecting media, and allocating the budget among various elements of the promotional mix. Choices should be made based on how well a particular strategy matches the firm's promotional objectives.

### Measurement and Evaluation of Results

An important reason for setting specific objectives is that they provide a benchmark against which the success or failure of the promotional campaign can be measured. Without specific objectives, it is extremely difficult to determine what the firm's advertising and promotion efforts accomplished. One characteristic of good objectives is that they are *measurable;* they specify a method and criteria for determining how well the promotional program is working. By setting specific and meaningful objectives, the promotional planner provides a measure(s) that can be used to evaluate the effectiveness of the marketing communications program. Most organizations are concerned about the return on their promotional investment, and comparing actual performance against measurable objectives is the best way to determine if the return justifies the expense.

## DETERMINING INTEGRATED MARKETING COMMUNICATIONS OBJECTIVES

Integrated marketing communications objectives should be based on a thorough situation analysis that identifies the marketing and promotional issues facing the company or a brand. The situation analysis is the foundation on which marketing objectives are determined and the marketing plan is developed. IMC objectives evolve from the company's overall marketing plan and are rooted in its marketing objectives. Advertising and promotion objectives are not the same as marketing objectives (although many firms tend to treat them as synonymous).

### Marketing versus Communications Objectives

**Marketing objectives** are generally stated in the firm's marketing plan and are statements of what is to be accomplished by the overall marketing program within a given time period. Marketing objectives are usually defined in terms of specific, measurable outcomes such as sales volume, market share, profits, or return on investment. Good marketing objectives are *quantifiable;* they delineate the target market and note the time frame for accomplishing the goal (often one year). For example, a copy machine company may have as its marketing objective "to increase sales by 10 percent in the small-business segment of the market during the next 12 months." To be effective, objectives must also be *realistic* and *attainable*.

A company with a very high market share may seek to increase its sales volume by stimulating growth in the product category. It might accomplish this by increasing consumption by current users or encouraging nonusers to use the product. Some firms have as their marketing objectives expanding distribution and sales of their product in certain market areas. Companies often have secondary marketing objectives that are related to actions they must take to solve specific problems and thus achieve their primary objectives.

Once the marketing communications manager has reviewed the marketing plan, he or she should understand where the company hopes to go with its marketing program, how it intends to get there, and the role advertising and promotion will play. Marketing goals defined in terms of sales, profit, or market share increases are usually not appropriate promotional objectives. They are objectives for the entire marketing program, and achieving them depends on the proper coordination and execution of all the marketing-mix elements, including not just promotion but product planning and production, pricing, and distribution. For example, a company may be very successful in its promotional program, creating interest and/or trial for a product. But what if the product is unavailable when the consumer goes to buy it, or what if, once in the store, the consumer feels the product is overpriced and decides not to buy? Should the promotional program be blamed when the product's poor performance is due to other marketing strategies or tactics?

**Integrated marketing communications objectives** are statements of what various aspects of the IMC program will accomplish. They should be based on the particular communications tasks required to deliver the appropriate messages to the target audience. Managers must be able to translate general marketing goals into communications goals and specific promotional objectives.

Sometimes companies do not have a formal marketing plan, and the information needed may not be readily available. In this case, the promotional planner must attempt to gather as much information as possible about the product and its markets from sources both inside and outside the company.

After reviewing all the information, the promotional planner should see how integrated marketing communications fits into the marketing program and what the firm hopes to achieve through advertising and other promotional elements. The next step is to set objectives in terms of specific communications goals or tasks.

Many planners approach promotion from a communications perspective and believe the objective of advertising and other promotional mix elements is usually to communicate information or a selling message about a product or service. Other managers argue that sales or some related measure, such as market share, is the only meaningful goal for advertising and promotion and should be the basis for setting objectives. These two perspectives have been the topic of considerable debate and are worth examining further.

CHAPTER 7

## SALES VERSUS COMMUNICATIONS OBJECTIVES

### Sales-Oriented Objectives

To many managers, the only meaningful objective for their promotional program is sales. They take the position that the basic reason a firm spends money on advertising and promotion is to sell its product or service. Promotional spending represents an investment of a firm's resources that requires an economic justification. Managers generally compare investment options on a common financial basis, such as return on investment (ROI). However, determining the specific return on advertising and promotional dollars is often quite a difficult task. At the same time, many managers believe that monies spent on advertising and other forms of promotion should produce measurable results, such as increasing sales volume by a certain percentage or dollar amount or increasing the brand's market share. They believe objectives (as well as the success or failure of the campaign) should be based on the achievement of sales results.

As a result, many managers have increased their efforts to make agencies more accountable for their performances. In turn, some agencies have developed their own tools to attempt to provide more ROI information in regard to how their integrated communications programs are performing. These agencies often attempt to differentiate themselves from others on this premise.

Some managers prefer sales-oriented objectives to make the individuals involved in advertising and promotion think in terms of how the promotional program will influence sales. For example, GEICO, once ranked fourth behind State Farm, Allstate, and Progressive insurance companies, increased its advertising budget by 75 percent—nearly double that of its competitors, and broadened its media placements. As a result, GEICO is now the number one insurance company in new customer acquisitions.[1] Likewise, Heinz doubled its IMC budget, resulting in a 19 percent sales increase.[2] The success of these advertising and promotional campaigns was judged by attainment of these goals.

**Problems with Sales Objectives** It appears that increases in advertising expenditures seemed to work for GEICO and Heinz as both experienced sales increases. Does this mean that these results can be attributed directly to the increased advertising budgets? Not necessarily. It might help to compare this situation to a football game and think of advertising as a quarterback. The quarterback is one of the most important players on the team but can be effective only with support from the other players. If the team loses, is it fair to blame the loss entirely on the quarterback? Of course not. Just as the quarterback is but one of the players on the football team, promotion is but one element of the marketing program, and there are many other reasons why the targeted sales level was not reached. The quarterback can lead his team to victory only if the linemen block, the receivers catch his passes, and the running backs help the offense establish a balanced attack of running and passing. Even if the quarterback plays an outstanding game, the team can still lose if the defense gives up too many points.

In the business world, sales results can be due to any of the other marketing-mix variables, including product design or quality, packaging, distribution, or pricing. Advertising can make consumers aware of and interested in the brand, but it can't make them buy it, particularly if it is not readily available or is priced higher than a competing brand. As shown in Figure 7–1, sales are a function of many factors, not just advertising and promotion. There is an adage in marketing that states, "Nothing will kill a poor product faster than good advertising." Taken with the other factors shown in Figure 7–1, this adage demonstrates that all the marketing elements must work together if a successful plan is to be implemented.

Another problem with sales objectives is that the effects of advertising often occur over an extended period. Many experts recognize that advertising has a lagged or **carryover effect**; monies spent on advertising do not necessarily have an immediate impact on sales.[3] Advertising may create awareness, interest, and/or favorable attitudes toward a brand, but these feelings will not result in an actual purchase until the consumer enters the market for the product, which may occur later. A review of econometric studies that examined the duration of cumulative advertising effects found that for mature, frequently purchased, low-priced products, advertising's effect on sales lasts up to nine months.[4] Models have been developed to account for the carryover effect of advertising and to help determine the long-term effect of advertising on sales.[5] The carryover effect adds to the difficulty of determining the precise relationship between advertising and sales.

FIGURE 7–1
Factors Influencing Sales

Another problem with sales objectives is that they offer little guidance to those responsible for planning and developing the promotional program. The creative and media people working on the account need some direction as to the nature of the advertising message the company hopes to communicate, the intended audience, and the particular effect or response sought. As you will see shortly, communications objectives are recommended because they provide operational guidelines for those involved in planning, developing, and executing the advertising and promotional program.

**Where Sales Objectives Are Appropriate** While there can be many problems in attempting to use sales as objectives for a promotional campaign, there are situations where sales objectives are appropriate. Certain types of promotion efforts are direct action in nature; they attempt to induce an immediate behavioral response from the prospective customer. A major objective of most sales promotion programs is to generate short-term increases in sales. At the same time, short-term strategies hopefully will lead to longer term gains as well. A good example is that of Kayem Foods of Chelsea, Massachusetts. To celebrate their 100th anniversary, Kayem changed the design of their frankfurter package. After consumer research suggested changing the copy and label on the package, the product was reintroduced. In the first 12 weeks Kayem saw sales rise by 15.7 percent (Exhibit 7–3), and the regional company planned for a national rollout.[6]

EXHIBIT 7–3
Kayem Foods' marketing strategy led to sales increases

Direct-response advertising is one type of advertising that evaluates its effectiveness on the basis of sales. Merchandise is advertised in material mailed to customers, in newspapers and magazines, through the Internet, or on television. The consumer purchases the merchandise by mail, on the Internet, or by calling a toll-free number. The direct-response advertiser generally sets objectives and measures success in terms of the sales response generated by the ad. For example, objectives for and the evaluation of a direct-response ad on TV are based on the number of orders received each time a station broadcasts the commercial. Because advertising is really the only form of communication and promotion used in this situation

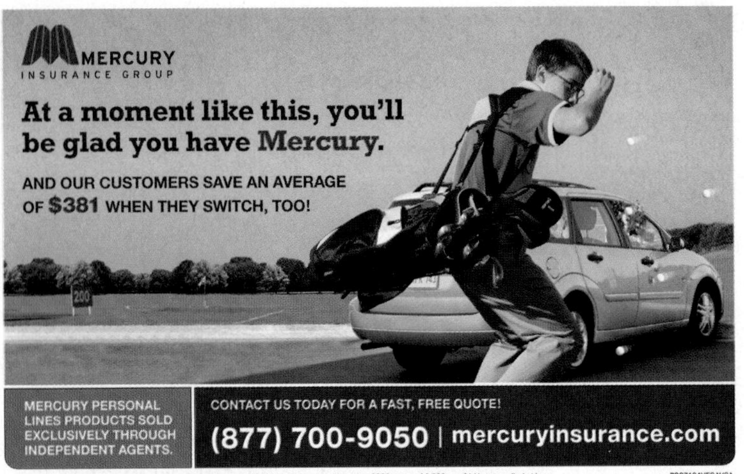

MERCURY
INSURANCE GROUP
At a moment like this, you'll be glad you have Mercury.
AND OUR CUSTOMERS SAVE AN AVERAGE OF $381 WHEN THEY SWITCH, TOO!
MERCURY PERSONAL LINES PRODUCTS SOLD EXCLUSIVELY THROUGH INDEPENDENT AGENTS.
CONTACT US TODAY FOR A FAST, FREE QUOTE!
(877) 700-9050 | mercuryinsurance.com


**EXHIBIT 7–4**
Mercury Insurance Group uses direct-response advertising to sell products and services

and response is generally immediate, setting objectives in terms of sales is appropriate. The Mercury Insurance Group ad shown in Exhibit 7–4 is an example of a product sold through direct-response advertising.

Retail advertising, which accounts for a significant percentage of all advertising expenditures, is another area where the advertiser often seeks an immediate response, particularly when sales or special events are being promoted. The ad for JCPenney's 60 percent off sale shown in Exhibit 7–5 is designed to attract consumers to stores during the sales period (and to generate sales volume). JCPenney's management can determine the effectiveness of its promotional effort by analyzing store traffic and sales volume during the sale and comparing them to figures for nonsale days. But retailers may also allocate advertising and promotional dollars to image-building campaigns designed to create and enhance favorable perceptions of their stores. For example, after a period of declining sales, Domino's Pizza made significant changes to their product. To announce these changes, Domino's introduced a new advertising campaign that included television commercials showing participants from their focus groups denigrating the pizza and then being delivered the new product formulation. The campaign was clearly a risky strategy for a company that has been in the pizza business since the 1960s with over 8,000 stores worldwide. In this case using sales-oriented objectives alone would not be appropriate; the effectiveness of the campaign would be based on its ability to create or change consumers' image of the brand, as well.

Sales-oriented objectives are also used when advertising plays a dominant role in a firm's marketing program and other factors are relatively stable. For example, many packaged-goods companies compete in mature markets with established channels of distribution, stable competitive prices and promotional budgets, and products of similar quality. They view advertising and sales promotion as the key determinants of a brand's sales or market share, so it may be possible to isolate the effects of these promotional mix variables. Many companies have accumulated enough market knowledge with their advertising, sales promotion, and direct-marketing programs to have considerable insight into the sales levels that should result from their promotional efforts. Mark Baynes, vice president of Kellogg's Morning Foods Division, attributed a turnabout in sales to effective advertising, brand repositioning, and more emotional appeals that generate interest.[7] Thus, many companies believe it is reasonable to set objectives and evaluate the success of their promotional efforts in terms of sales results.

**EXHIBIT 7–5**
JCPenney seeks sales from this ad

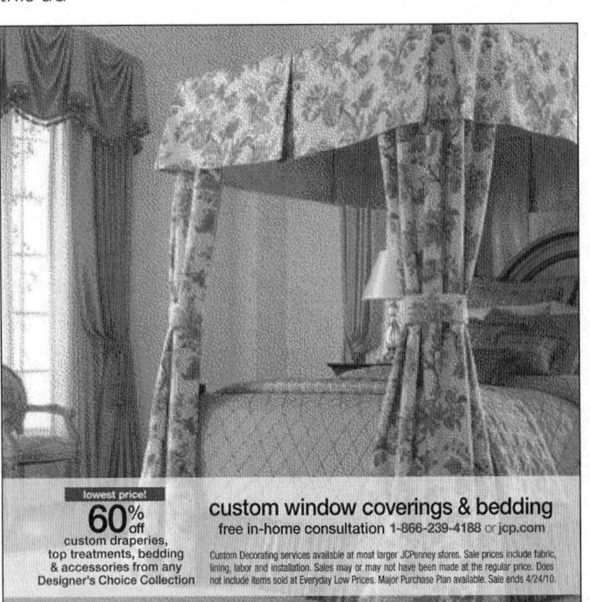

lowest price!
60% off
custom draperies, top treatments, bedding & accessories from any Designer's Choice Collection
custom window coverings & bedding
free in-home consultation 1-866-239-4188 or jcp.com


Advertising and promotional programs tend to be evaluated in terms of sales, particularly when expectations are not being met. Marketing and brand managers under pressure to show sales results often take a short-term perspective in evaluating advertising and sales promotion programs. They are often looking for a quick fix for declining sales or loss of market share. They ignore the pitfalls of making direct links between advertising and sales, and campaigns, as well as ad agencies, may be changed if sales expectations are not being met. As discussed in Chapter 3, many companies want their agencies to accept incentive-based compensation systems tied to sales performance. Thus, while sales may not be an appropriate objective in many advertising and promotional situations, managers are inclined to keep a close eye on sales and market share figures and make changes in the promotional program when these numbers become stagnant, or decline.

## Communications Objectives

Some marketers do recognize the problems associated with sales-oriented objectives. They recognize that the primary role of an IMC program is to communicate and that planning should be based on communications objectives. Advertising and other promotional efforts are designed to achieve such communications as brand knowledge and interest, favorable attitudes and image, and purchase intentions. Consumers are not expected to respond immediately; rather, advertisers realize they must provide relevant information and create favorable predispositions toward the brand before purchase behavior will occur.

For example, the ad in Exhibit 7–6 is designed to inform consumers of the company's focus on building for the future. While there is no call for immediate action, the ad creates favorable impressions about the company by using pictures of children alongside Con Ed workers in action to create a distinct image of the company. Viewers will consider this image when they think about Consolidated Edison.

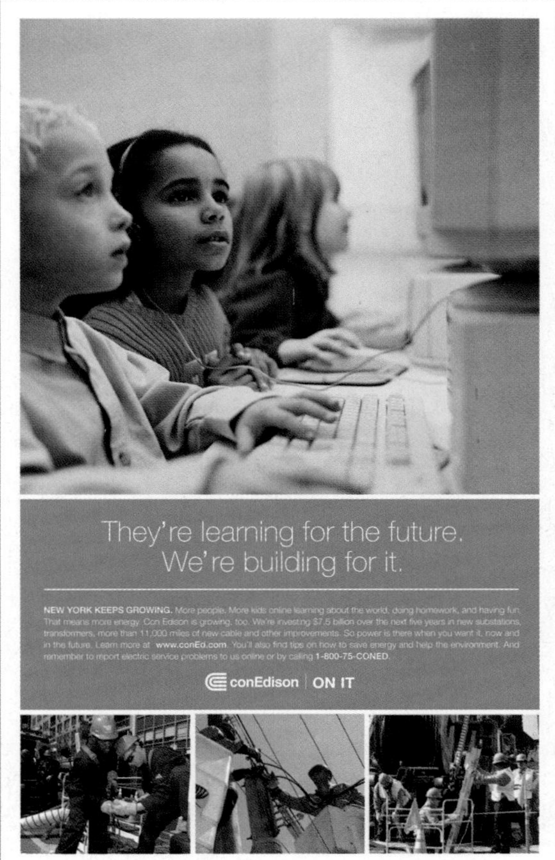


**EXHIBIT 7–6**
Consolidated Edison creates an image of its company

Advocates of communications-based objectives generally use some form of the hierarchical models discussed in Chapter 5 and the opening vignette when setting advertising and promotion objectives. In all these models, consumers pass through three successive stages: cognitive (thinking), affective (feeling), and conative (behavioral). As consumers proceed through the three stages, they move closer to making a purchase.

### Communications Effects Pyramid

Advertising and promotion perform communications tasks in the same way that a pyramid is built, by first accomplishing lower-level objectives such as awareness and knowledge or comprehension. Subsequent tasks involve moving consumers who are aware of or knowledgeable about the product or service to higher levels in the pyramid (Figure 7–2). The initial stages, at the base of the pyramid, are easier to accomplish than those toward the top, such as trial and repurchase or regular use. Thus, the percentage of prospective customers will decline as they move up the pyramid (or down the funnel). Global Perspective 7–1 shows how two companies had different strategies to move consumers through the various stages.

The communications pyramid can also be used to determine promotional objectives for an established brand. The promotional planner must determine where the target audience lies with respect to the various blocks in the pyramid. If awareness levels for a brand and knowledge of its features and benefits are low, the communications objective should be to increase them. If these blocks of the pyramid are already in place, but liking or preference is low, the advertising goal may be to change the target markets' image of the brand and move consumers through to purchase. For example, Caribou Coffee, a regional brand in fifteen Eastern and Midwestern states, while a distant number two to Starbucks, has a very favorable brand image among its customers, and has been ranked number one in quality by *Consumer Reports*. In 2010, the company decided to pursue a national presence and rebranded itself, in part by changing its logo and increasing advertising expenditures[8] (Exhibit 7–7). Using the communications pyramid, you can see that the objectives would change

**FIGURE 7–2**
Communications Effects Pyramid

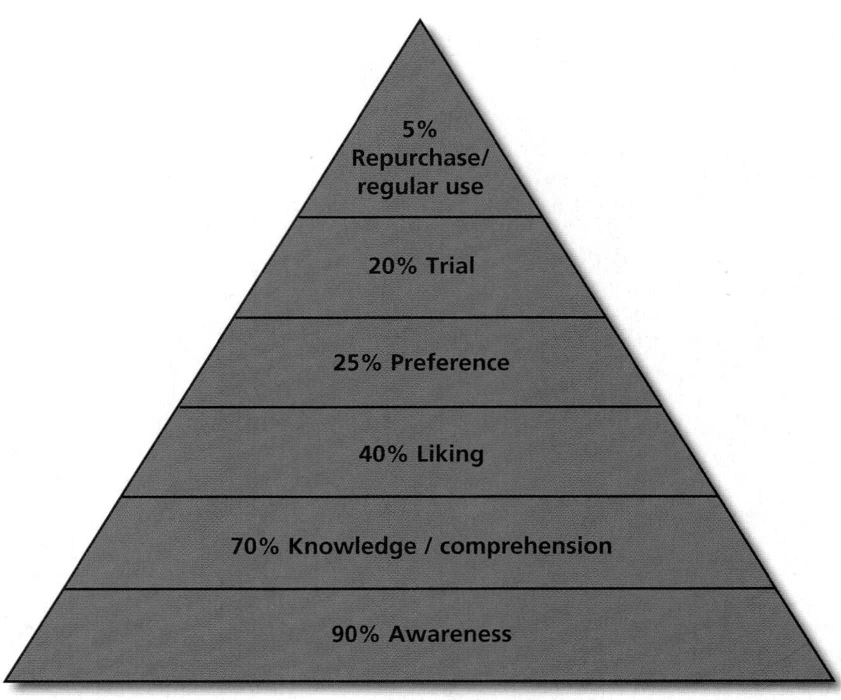


for different geographic areas, with a focus on creating awareness and knowledge in new markets, while reinforcing and maintaining the current brand image in the East and Midwest. Ultimately, of course, the goal would be to move everyone in the target market to trial and purchase.

**Problems with Communications Objectives** Not all marketing and advertising managers accept communications objectives; some say it is too difficult to translate a sales goal into a specific communications objective. But at some point a sales goal must be transformed into a communications objective. If the marketing plan for an established brand has an objective of increasing sales by 10 percent, the promotional planner will eventually have to think in terms of the message that will be communicated to the target audience to achieve this. Possible objectives include the following:

- Increasing the percentage of consumers in the target market who associate specific features, benefits, or advantages with our brand.
- Increasing the number of consumers in the target audience who prefer our product over the competition's.
- Encouraging current users of the product to use it more frequently or in more situations.
- Encouraging consumers who have never used our brand to try it.

**EXHIBIT 7–7**
Caribou Coffee must set different objectives for different target markets

In some situations, promotional planners may gain insight into communications objectives' relationship to sales from industry research. Figure 7–3 provides an example of the GfK International purchase funnel used by many in the automobile industry as a diagnostic model of consumer decision making.

In attempting to translate sales goals into specific communications objectives, promotional planners often are not sure what constitutes adequate levels of awareness, knowledge, liking, preference, or conviction. There are no formulas to provide this information. The promotional manager will have to use his or her personal experience and that of the brand or product managers, as well as the marketing history of this and similar brands. Average scores on various communications measures

# Global Perspective 7–1 > > >

## How Two Companies in Different Countries Use a Funnel

*The Zain Group*—Mobile Telecommunications (MTC), a little known company operating in the Middle East, wants to be the next AT&T or Verizon. Started in 1983 in Kuwait, the company reshaped itself into a regional powerhouse starting in 2002 through acquisitions in Jordan, Lebanon, Sudan, and Bahrain. In 2007, MTC acquired the African telecom company Celtel International, expanding its market to 20 countries. While the expansion put them on the path to become a giant, one problem remained—the acquisitions resulted in a number of different brand names, without a unified identification.

To remedy this problem, MTC conducted research to arrive at a new brand name—"The Zain Group." Zain, which means "beautiful," "good," and "wonderful" in Arabic, was thought to have an uplifting image for an area currently undergoing numerous hardships. Creating awareness of the new name was not easy, however, given the numerous cultures and operational issues existing in 20 different countries. In addition, Zain also needed to go beyond creating awareness and make consumers think of the brand as a "global family that improves lives through communication." To do this, Zain held a simultaneous launch in four different countries (see insert). The successful event served as the model for the subsequent African launch which had over 100,000 attendees. While the company may not yet be AT&T, their customer base has now grown from 600,000 in 2002 to over 64.7 million by 2009.

**EVENT AT A GLANCE**

Objective: **Support efforts to become a top-10 global telecommunications provider by rolling out a unified brand.**

Strategy: **Build awareness and understanding of the brand with four simultaneous launch events in four Middle Eastern countries.**

Tactics: **Coordinate live, simultaneous rollout events with a satellite presentation between site managers and the Zain Group CEO to demonstrate the unity of a boundary-free global brand.**

Results: **Zain successfully executed the events for 12,000 attendees, and paved the way for a 14-country African launch 11 months later. The company's 2009 first-quarter revenues were up 25 percent over first quarter 2008 to $1.96 billion.**

Sources: Christopher Nelson, "Branding without Borders," Corporate Event, Winter 2009, pp. 30–35; Whitney Archibald, "Seven Degrees of Socialization," Corporate Event, Winter, 2009, pp. 42–47.

*Sun Microsystem's Java 1*—A U.S company, Sun Microsystems, had a different problem, and took a different approach. Sun (now Oracle Corp) has held an annual JavaOne Conference each year to reach software developers for the purpose of developing new ideas and to create new products and technologies. After the JavaOne event's inception in 1995, the software developers who use Java (Sun's computer software platform), formed a community through social networks such as Facebook and LinkedIn. The community offered assistance to others, and spurred new ideas and concepts, growing in size each year. Sun wanted to be a part of this community, but not just be a member. Specifically, the company wanted to get themselves and others involved by increasing registration and attendance at the conferences, gathering feedback, and offering support to others who might need it. It was determined that the best way to accomplish this goal was to make extensive use of social networking media (see insert 2). For the 2008 conference, Sun developed a seven part social media campaign that used YouTube, blogs, and Second Life, as well as Facebook and a variety of promotional activities that included a pre-event competition for a free JavaOne pass. In 2009, Sun also added Blogtalk Radio to the social networking toolbox, adding 47 *i*Pod episodes.

The results: While the conference continues to be held each year, the social community has grown significantly, and communicates 365 days a year, not just during the conference. Sun has developed a new sense of loyalty and stronger relationships with its clients and the software community.

**EVENT AT A GLANCE**

Objective: **Promote the annual JavaOne conference, gather customer feedback, foster community among attendees, and extend event content to developers who could not attend the live event in person.**

Strategy: **Develop a multifaceted social-media campaign comprising Twitter, YouTube, Second Life, Facebook, LinkedIn, Ustream, and blogs.**

Tactics: **Aggregate blog posts about JavaOne, stream real-time event footage online, post behind-the-scenes videos and interviews, host virtual parties, and encourage the production of user-generated marketing materials.**

Results: **Netted more than 6,000 JavaOne-related blog posts, 2,700 Twitter followers, approximately 100,000 video views on YouTube and Ustream, and thousands of Facebook friends and fans.**

**FIGURE 7–3**
GfK Purchase Funnel

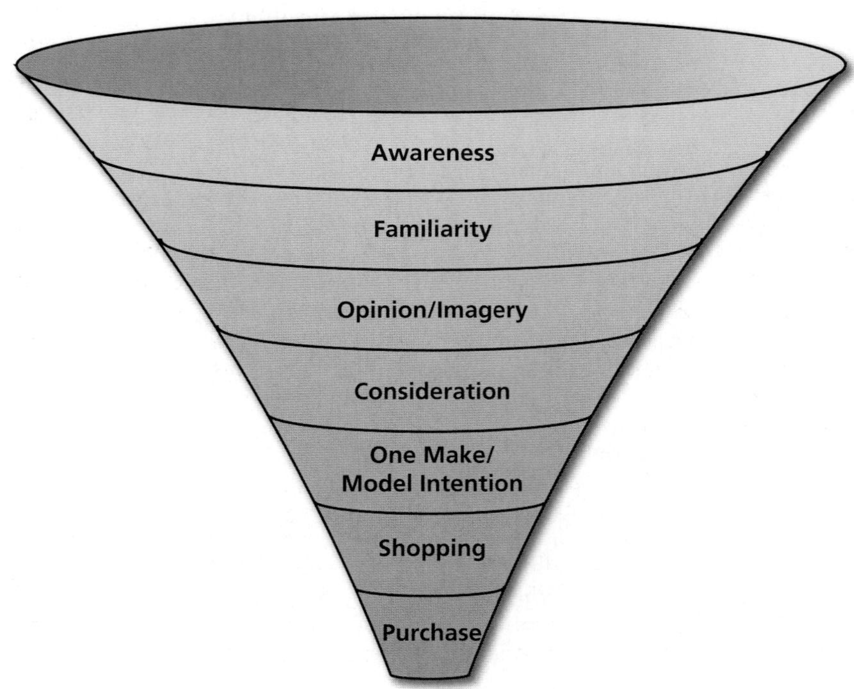


for this and similar products should be considered, along with the levels achieved by competitors' products. This information can be related to the amount of money and time spent building these levels as well as the resulting sales or market share figures. However, at some point, sales-oriented objectives must be translated into what the company hopes to communicate and to whom it hopes to communicate it.

Many marketing and promotional managers recognize the value of setting specific communications objectives and their important role as operational guidelines to the planning, execution, and evaluation of the promotional program. Communications objectives are the criteria used in the DAGMAR approach to setting advertising goals and objectives, which has become one of the most influential approaches to the advertising planning process.

## DAGMAR: AN APPROACH TO SETTING OBJECTIVES

In 1961, Russell Colley prepared a report for the Association of National Advertisers titled *Defining Advertising Goals for Measured Advertising Results* (DAGMAR).[9] In it, Colley developed a model for setting advertising objectives and measuring the results of an ad campaign. The major thesis of the **DAGMAR** model is that communications effects are the logical basis for advertising goals and objectives against which success or failure should be measured.

Under the DAGMAR approach, an advertising goal involves a **communications task** that is specific and measurable. A communications task, as opposed to a marketing task, can be performed by, and attributed to, advertising rather than to a combination of several marketing factors. Colley proposed that the communications task be based on a hierarchical model of the communications process with four stages:

- *Awareness*—making the consumer aware of the existence of the brand or company.
- *Comprehension*—developing an understanding of what the product is and what it will do for the consumer.

- *Conviction*—developing a mental disposition in the consumer to buy the product.
- *Action*—getting the consumer to purchase the product.

As discussed earlier, other hierarchical models of advertising effects can be used as a basis for analyzing the communications response process. Some advertising theorists prefer the Lavidge and Steiner hierarchy of effects model, since it is more specific and provides a better way to establish and measure results.[10]

While the hierarchical model of advertising effects was the basic model of the communications response process used in DAGMAR, Colley also studied other specific tasks that advertising might be expected to perform in leading to the ultimate objective of a sale. He developed a checklist of 52 advertising tasks to characterize the contribution of advertising and serve as a starting point for establishing objectives.



## Characteristics of Objectives

A second major contribution of DAGMAR to the advertising planning process was its definition of what constitutes a good objective. Colley argued that advertising objectives should be stated in terms of concrete and measurable communications tasks, specify a target audience, indicate a benchmark starting point and the degree of change sought, and specify a time period for accomplishing the objective(s).

**Concrete, Measurable Tasks** The communications task specified in the objective should be a precise statement of what appeal or message the advertiser wants to communicate to the target audience. Advertisers generally use a copy platform to describe their basic message. The objective or copy platform statement should be specific and clear enough to guide the creative specialists who develop the advertising message. For example, Hyundai, after years of being at or near the bottom of the list of automobiles in customer satisfaction ratings, focused their attention on increasing the quality, as well as improving consumers' perceptions, of their cars. The result, as noted in Chapter 4, is that Hyundai is now at the very top of the list in customer satisfaction (Exhibit 7–8). According to DAGMAR, the objective must also be measurable. As can be seen in Exhibit 7–8, the various awards won along the way provided a measure of Hyundai's success.

**EXHIBIT 7–8**
Hyundai has moved to the top of the list in customer satisfaction

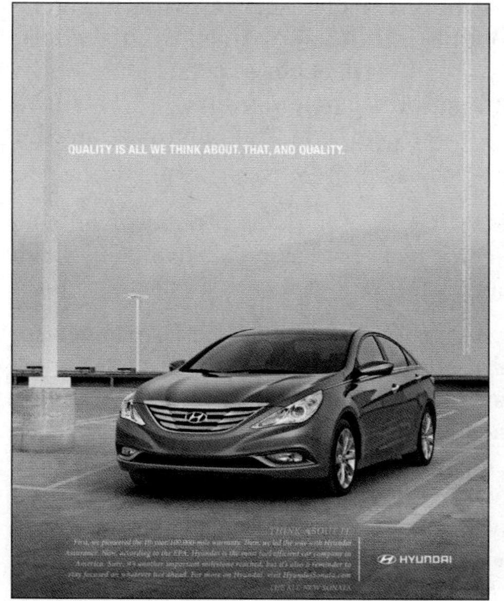


**Target Audience** Another important characteristic of good objectives is a well-defined target audience. The primary target audience for a company's product or service is described in the situation analysis. It may be based on descriptive variables such as geography, demographics, and psychographics (on which advertising media selection decisions are based) as well as on behavioral variables such as usage rate or benefits sought.

**Benchmark and Degree of Change Sought** To set objectives, one must know the target audience's present status concerning response hierarchy variables such as awareness, knowledge, image, attitudes, and intentions and then determine the degree to which consumers must be changed by the campaign. Determining the target market's present position regarding the various response stages requires **benchmark measures**. Often a marketing research study must be conducted to determine prevailing levels of the response hierarchy. In the case of a new product or service, the starting conditions are generally at or near zero for all the variables, so no initial research is needed.

Establishing benchmark measures gives the promotional planner a basis for determining what communications tasks need to be accomplished and for specifying particular objectives. For example, a preliminary study for a brand may reveal that awareness is high but consumer

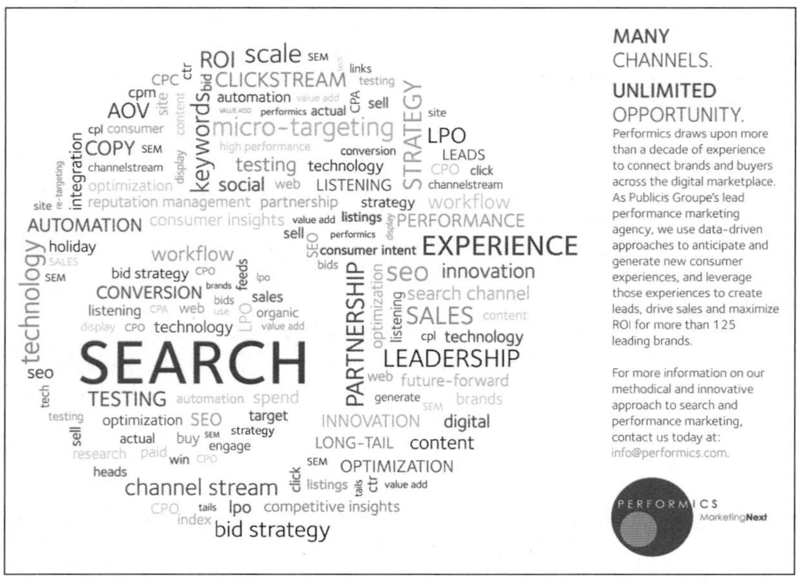

SEARCH
EXPERIENCE
MANY
CHANNELS.
UNLIMITED
OPPORTUNITY.
Performics draws upon more than a decade of experience to connect brands and buyers across the digital marketplace. As Publicis Groupe's lead performance marketing agency, we use data-driven approaches to anticipate and generate new consumer experiences, and leverage those experiences to create leads, drive sales and maximize ROI for more than 125 leading brands.
For more information on our methodical and innovative approach to search and performance marketing, contact us today at: info@performics.com.
PERFORMICS
MarketingNext

**EXHIBIT 7–9**
Performics suggests that consumers go through a marketing spiral

perceptions and attitudes are negative. The objective for the campaign must then be to change the target audience's perceptions of and attitudes toward the brand.

Quantitative benchmarks are not only valuable in establishing communications goals and objectives but essential for determining whether the campaign was successful. Objectives provide the standard against which the success or failure of a campaign is measured. An ad campaign that results in a 90 percent awareness level for a brand among its target audience cannot really be judged effective unless one knows what percentage of the consumers were aware of the brand before the campaign began. A 70 percent precampaign awareness level would lead to a different interpretation of the campaign's success than would a 30 percent level.

**Specified Time Period** A final consideration in setting advertising objectives is specifying the time period in which they must be accomplished. Appropriate time periods can range from a few days to a year or more. Most ad campaigns specify time periods from a few months to a year, depending on the situation facing the advertiser and the type of response being sought. For example, awareness levels for a brand can be created or increased fairly quickly through an intensive media schedule of widespread, repetitive advertising to the target audience. Repositioning of a product requires a change in consumers' perceptions and takes much more time.

## Assessment of DAGMAR

The DAGMAR approach to setting objectives has had considerable influence on the advertising planning process. Many promotional planners use this model as a basis for setting objectives and assessing the effectiveness of their promotional campaigns. DAGMAR also focused advertisers' attention on the value of using communications-based rather than sales-based objectives to measure advertising effectiveness and encouraged the measurement of stages in the response hierarchy to assess a campaign's impact. Colley's work has led to improvements in the advertising and promotional planning process by providing a better understanding of the goals and objectives toward which planners' efforts should be directed. This usually results in less subjectivity and leads to better communication and relationships between client and agency.

**Criticisms of DAGMAR** While DAGMAR has contributed to the advertising planning process, it has not been totally accepted by everyone in the advertising field. A number of problems have led to questions regarding its value as a planning tool:[11]

- *Problems with the response hierarchy.* A major criticism of the DAGMAR approach is its reliance on the hierarchy of effects model. The fact that consumers do not always go through this sequence of communications effects before making a purchase has been recognized, and alternative response models have been developed. As indicated in the lead in to this chapter, much of the criticism stems from the argument that the World Wide Web has significantly changed the consumer's decision making process from a linear one to one in which consumers can enter or leave at any stage, resulting in a more circular process (Exhibit 7–9). DAGMAR MOD II recognizes that the appropriate response model depends on the situation and emphasizes identifying the sequence of decision-making steps that apply in a buying situation.[12]

- *Sales objectives.* Another objection to DAGMAR comes from those who argue that the only relevant measure of advertising objectives is sales. They have little tolerance for ad campaigns that achieve communications objectives but fail to increase sales. Advertising is seen as effective only if it induces consumers to make a purchase. The problems with this logic were addressed in our discussion of communications objectives.
- *Practicality and costs.* Another criticism of DAGMAR concerns the difficulties involved in implementing it. Money must be spent on research to establish quantitative benchmarks and measure changes in the response hierarchy. This is costly and time-consuming and can lead to considerable disagreement over method, criteria, measures, and so forth. Many critics argue that DAGMAR is practical only for large companies with big advertising and research budgets. Many firms do not want to spend the money needed to use DAGMAR effectively.
- *Inhibition of creativity.* A final criticism of DAGMAR is that it inhibits advertising creativity by imposing too much structure on the people responsible for developing the advertising. Many creative personnel think the DAGMAR approach is too concerned with quantitative assessment of a campaign's impact on awareness, brand-name recall, or specific persuasion measures. The emphasis is on passing the numbers test rather than developing a message that is truly creative and contributes to brand equity.



## PROBLEMS IN SETTING OBJECTIVES

Although the DAGMAR model suggests a logical process for advertising and promotion planning, most advertisers and their agencies fail to follow these basic principles. They fail to set specific objectives for their campaigns and/or do not have the proper evidence to determine the success of their promotional programs. Many advertising agencies do not state appropriate objectives for determining success and thus can't demonstrate whether a supposedly successful campaign was really a success. Even though these campaigns may be doing something right, they generally did not know what it is.

One study examined the advertising practices of business-to-business marketers to determine whether their ads used advertising objectives that met Colley's four DAGMAR criteria.[13] Entries from the annual Business/Professional Advertising Association Gold Key Awards competition, which solicits the best marketing communications efforts from business-to-business advertisers, were evaluated with respect to their campaigns' objectives and summaries of results. Most of these advertisers did not set concrete advertising objectives, specify objective tasks, measure results in terms of stages of a hierarchy of effects, or match objectives to evaluation measures.

### Improving Promotional Planners' Use of Objectives

As we have seen, it is important that advertisers and their agencies pay close attention to the objectives they set for their campaigns. They should strive to set specific and measurable objectives that not only guide promotional planning and decision making but also can be used as a standard for evaluating performance. Unfortunately, many companies do not set appropriate objectives for their integrated marketing communications programs.

Many companies fail to set appropriate objectives because top management has only an abstract idea of what the firm's IMC program is supposed to be doing.

**FIGURE 7–4**

Traditional Advertising-Based View of Marketing Communications

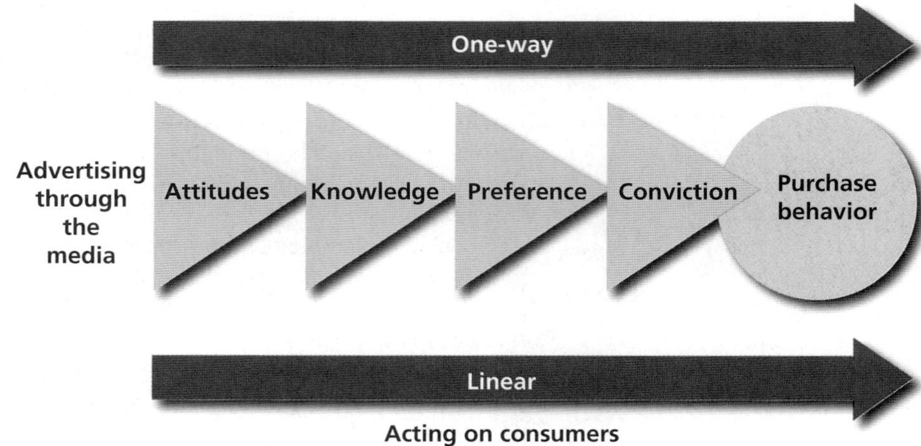


In a study by the American Business Press that measured the attitudes of chairs, presidents, and other senior managers of business-to-business advertising companies, more than half of the 427 respondents said they did not know whether their advertising was working and less than 10 percent thought it was working well.[14] This study showed overwhelmingly that top management did not even know what the company's advertising was supposed to do, much less how to measure it.

Few firms will set objectives that meet all the criteria set forth in DAGMAR. However, promotional planners should set objectives that are specific and measurable and go beyond basic sales goals. Even if specific communications response elements are not always measured, meeting the other criteria will sharpen the focus and improve the quality of the IMC planning process.

## Setting Objectives for the IMC Program

One reason so much attention is given to advertising objectives is that for many companies advertising has traditionally been the major way of communicating with target audiences. Other promotional mix elements such as sales promotion, direct marketing, and publicity are used intermittently to support and complement the advertising program.

Another reason is that traditional advertising-based views of marketing communications planning, such as DAGMAR, have dominated the field for so long. These approaches are based on a hierarchical response model and consider how marketers can develop and disseminate advertising messages to move consumers along an effects path. This approach, shown in Figure 7–4, is what professor Don Schultz calls *inside-out planning.* He says, "It focuses on what the marketer wants to say, when the marketer wants to say it, about things the marketer believes are important about his or her brand, and in the media forms the marketer wants to use."[15]

Schultz advocates an *outside-in planning* process for IMC that starts with the customer and builds backward to the brand. This means that promotional planners study the various media customers and prospects use, when the marketer's messages might be most relevant to customers, and when they are likely to be most receptive to the message.

A similar approach is suggested by Professor Tom Duncan, who argues that IMC should use **zero-based communications planning**, which involves determining what tasks need to be done and which marketing communications functions should be used and to what extent.[16] This approach focuses on the task to be done and searches for the best ideas and media to accomplish it. Duncan suggests that an effective IMC program should lead with the marketing communications function that

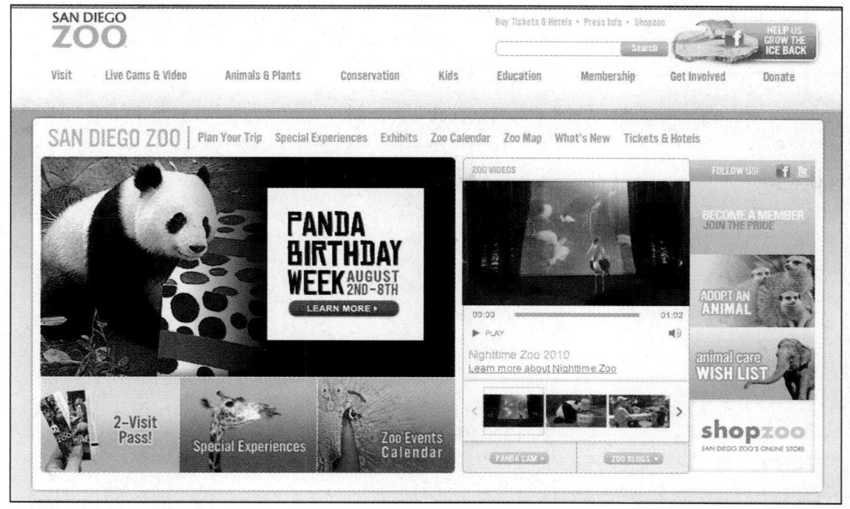


**EXHIBIT 7–10**
The San Diego Zoo attempts to attract visitors through a variety of media

most effectively addresses the company's main problem or opportunity and should use a promotional mix that draws on the strengths of whichever communications functions relate best to the particular situation.

Many of the considerations for determining advertising objectives are relevant to setting goals for other elements of the integrated marketing communications program. The promotional planner should determine what role various sales promotion techniques, publicity and public relations, direct marketing, the Internet, and personal selling will play in the overall marketing program and how they will interact with advertising as well as with one another.



For example, the marketing communications program for the San Diego Zoological Society has a number of objectives. First, it must provide funding for the society's programs and maintain a large and powerful base of supporters for financial and political strength. The program must educate the public about the society's various programs and maintain a favorable image on a local, regional, national, and even international level. A major objective of the IMC program is drawing visitors to the two attractions (Exhibit 7–10).

To achieve these objectives, the San Diego Zoological Society and its advertising agency developed an IMC program. As can be seen in Figure 7–5, this program employed a variety of integrated marketing communication tools. When setting objectives for these promotional elements, planners must consider what the firm hopes to communicate through the use of this element, among what target audience, and during what time period. As with advertising, results should be measured and evaluated against the original objectives, and attempts should be made to isolate the effects of each promotional element. Objectives for marketing communications elements other than advertising are discussed more thoroughly in Part Five of the text.

## ESTABLISHING AND ALLOCATING THE PROMOTIONAL BUDGET

If you take a minute to look back at Figure 1–4 in Chapter 1, you will see that while the arrows from the review of the marketing plan and the promotional situation analysis to analysis of the communications process are *unidirectional,* the flow between the communications analysis and budget determination is a *two-way interaction.* What this means is that while establishing objectives is an important part of the planning process, the limitations of the budget are important too. No organization has an unlimited budget, so objectives must be set with the budget in mind.

Often when we think of promotional expenditures of firms, we think only about the huge amounts being spent. We don't usually take the time to think about how these monies are being allocated and about the recipients of these dollars. The budgeting decisions have a significant impact not only on the firm itself but also on numerous others involved either directly or indirectly. The remainder of this chapter provides insight into some underlying theory with respect to budget setting, discusses how companies budget for promotional efforts, and demonstrates the inherent strengths and weaknesses associated with these approaches. Essentially, we focus on two primary budgeting decisions: establishing a budget amount and allocating the budget.

**Advertising**

**Objectives:** Drive attendance to Zoo and Wild Animal Park. Uphold image and educate target audience and inform them of new attractions and special events and promotions.

**Audience:** Members and nonmembers of Zoological Society. Households in primary and secondary geographic markets consisting of San Diego County and 5 other counties in southern California. Tertiary markets of 7 western states. Tourist and group sales markets.

**Timing:** As allowed and determined by budget. Mostly timed to coincide with promotional efforts.

**Tools/media:** Television, radio, newspaper, magazines, direct mail, outdoor, tourist media (television and magazine).

**Sales Promotions**

**Objectives:** Use price, product, and other variables to drive attendance when it might not otherwise come.

**Audience:** Targeted, depending on co-op partner, mostly to southern California market.

**Timing:** To fit needs of Zoo and Wild Animal Park and co-sponsoring partner.

**Tools/media:** Coupons, sweepstakes, tours, broadcast tradeouts, direct mail: statement stuffers, fliers, postcards, online ticket discounts.

**Public Relations**

**Objectives:** Inform, educate, create, and maintain image for Zoological Society and major attractions; reinforce advertising message.

**Audience:** From local to international, depending on subject, scope, and timing.

**Timing:** Ongoing, although often timed to coincide with promotions and other special events. Spur-of-the-moment animal news and information such as acquisitions, births, etc.

**Tools/media:** Coverage by major news media, articles in local, regional, national and international newspapers, magazines and other publications such as visitors' guides, tour books and guides, appearances by Zoo spokesperson Joanne Embery on talk shows (such as "The Tonight Show"), zoo newsletter, adopt an animal program, support conservation program.

**Cause Marketing/Corporate Sponsorships/Events Underwriting**

**Objectives:** To provide funding for Zoological Society programs and promote special programs and events done in cooperation with corporate sponsor. Must be win-win business partnership for Society and partner.

**Audience:** Supporters of both the Zoological Society and the corporate or product/service partner.

**Timing:** Coincides with needs of both partners, and seasonal attendance generation needs of Zoo and Wild Animal Park.

**Tools:** May involve advertising, publicity, discount co-op promotions, ticket trades, hospitality centers. Exposure is directly proportional to amount of underwriting by corporate sponsor, both in scope and duration, education programs, Conservation and Research for Endangered Species (CRES).

**Direct Marketing**

**Objectives:** Maintain large powerful base of supporters for financial and political strength.

**Audience:** Local, regional, national and international. Includes children's program (Koala Club), seniors (60+), couples, single memberships, and incremental donor levels.

**Timing:** Ongoing, year-round promotion of memberships.

**Tools:** Direct mail and on-grounds visibility.

**Group Sales**

**Objectives:** Maximize group traffic and revenue by selling group tours to Zoo and Wild Animal Park.

**Audience:** Conventions, incentive groups, bus tours, associations, youth, scouts, schools, camps, seniors, clubs, military, organizations, domestic and foreign travel groups.

**Timing:** Targeted to drive attendance in peak seasons or at most probable times such as convention season.

**Tools:** Travel and tourism trade shows, telemarketing, direct mail, trade publication advertising.

**Internet**

**Objectives:** Provide information regarding the Zoo, programs, memberships and public relations activities.

**Audience:** All audiences interested in acquiring more information about the Zoo.

**Timing:** Ongoing, updated frequently over time.

**Tools:** Website, Zoo blog, including videos, shop Zoo and Zoo e-newsletter calendar, Facebook, Twitter.

**FIGURE 7–5** The San Diego Zoo Sets Objectives for Various Promotional Elements

**FIGURE 7–6**

Conclusions on Research of Advertising in a Recession

- Advertising is strongly related to economic cycles across major world economies.
- The single most compelling reason for cutting back advertising during a recession is that sales during a recession are likely to be lower than they would be during an expansion.
- There is strong, consistent evidence that cutting back on advertising can hurt sales during and after a recesssion.
- Not cutting back on advertising during a recession could increase sales during and after the recession.
- Firms that increased advertising during a recession experienced higher sales, market share, or earnings during or after the recession.
- Most firms tend to cut back on advertising during a recession, reducing noise and increasing the effectiveness of advertising of the firm that advertises.

Source: G. Tellis and K. Tellis, "Research on Advertising in a Recession." *Journal of Advertising Research*, 49(3), 2009, pp. 304–327.



## Establishing the Budget

The size of a firm's advertising and promotions budget can vary from a few thousand dollars to more than a billion. When companies like Procter & Gamble and Verizon spend more than $2 billion per year to promote their products, they expect such expenditures to accomplish their stated objectives. The budget decision is no less critical to a firm spending only a few thousand dollars; its ultimate success or failure may depend on the monies spent. One of the most critical decisions facing the marketing manager is how much to spend on the promotional effort.

**EXHIBIT 7–11**

The AAAA promotes the continued use of advertising in a recession

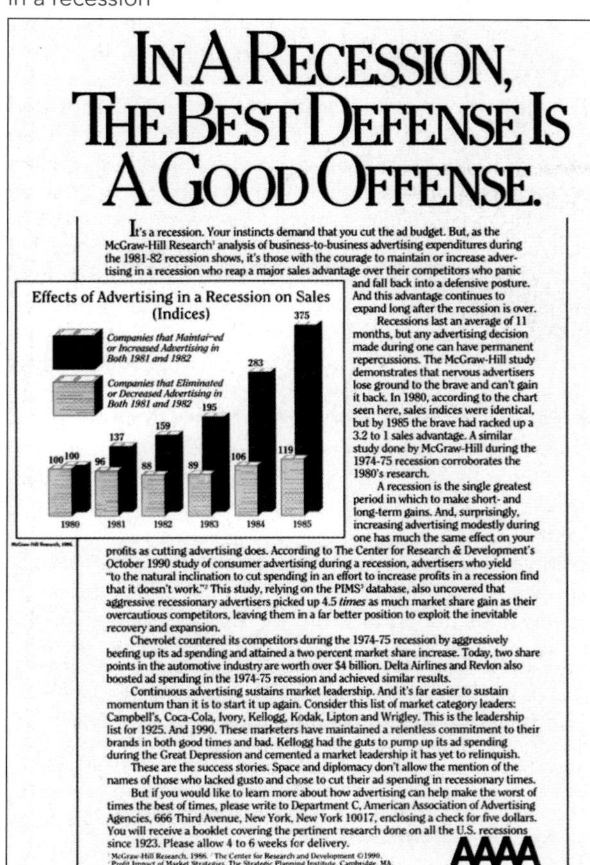


Unfortunately, many managers fail to realize the value of advertising and promotion. They treat the communications budget as an expense rather than an investment. Instead of viewing the dollars spent as contributing to additional sales and market share, they see budget expenses as cutting into profits. As a result, when times get tough, the advertising and promotional budget is the first to be cut—even though there is strong evidence that exactly the opposite should occur, as Exhibit 7–11 argues. Figure 7–6 shows the results of an extensive review of research involving advertising during a recession. The review covers 40 studies in the United States from 1926 to 2009. As can be seen, the argument for continuing to advertise during an economic downturn outweighs that of decreasing ad expenditures.[17] As shown in IMC Perspective 7–1, a number of successful companies agree, as indicated by their ad expenditures. Moreover, the decision is not a one-time responsibility. A new budget is formulated every year, each time a new product is introduced, or when either internal or external factors necessitate a change to maintain competitiveness.

While it is one of the most critical decisions, budgeting has perhaps been the most resistant to change. A comparison of advertising and promotional texts over the past 10 years would reveal the same methods for establishing budgets. The theoretical basis for this process remains rooted in economic theory and marginal analysis. (Advertisers also use an approach based on **contribution margin**—the difference between the total revenue generated by a brand and its total variable costs. But, as Robert Steiner says, *marginal analysis* and *contribution margin* are essentially synonymous terms.)[18] We begin our discussion of budgeting with an examination of these theoretical approaches.

# IMC Perspective 7–1 > > >

## Companies Look for Edge in a Recession by Spending More

For most companies, a downturn in the economy leads to spending cutbacks. Unfortunately, one of the first areas to feel the pain of these cutbacks is marketing—particularly advertising. Indeed, in a survey conducted by the Association of National Advertisers in 2009, a staggering 77 percent of marketers indicated that they had plans to reduce their advertising media budgets in the upcoming months. Seventy-two percent planned to reduce their production budgets, 48 percent were considering reducing agency compensation, and 68 percent said they would challenge their agencies to find ways to cut costs. Clearly, these companies were looking at ways to save money. But were they doing the right thing? It appears that some of the leading advertisers don't agree with this strategy.

Fix that thirst but good...here's your
real thirst-quencher!
7up
Nothing does it like Seven-Up!
You like it... it likes you!

One of these is *7Up*. The soft drink brand now owned by Dr Pepper Snapple Group has never fully recovered from its elimination from the soft drink line of PepsiCo and being replaced by Sierra Mist. Sales in 2008 were off by 8.1 percent, and in the first six months of 2009, they declined by another 7.7 percent. To make things worse, the overall soft drink category was in a decline, with lemon-lime flavors among the hardest hit. *7-Up*'s plans for 2010 were pretty ambitious, including the first new advertising campaign in three years, new positioning, product line extensions, and an in-store facelift. The new budget was significantly increased over the $21 million (not including online) spent in 2008. When asked "Why spend now?," David Falk, director of *7Up* and flavors at the Dr Pepper Snapple Group had a simple response: "Brands that advertise during economic lulls come out of those times a lot stronger."

Similar thinking is apparent at Burger King. The fast food company announced a double digit (20–25 percent) increase in ad spending over its $294 million in 2008, beginning in late 2009, with a big boost in the summer of 2010, the biggest season for fast food sales. Interestingly, not only is Burger King going against the grain in spending, but the largest increases were targeted for television ads as opposed to those in digital media. As noted by Russ Klein, Burger King's chief marketing officer, "There is no way to replace television," underscoring the medium's broad reach. Mr. Klein also noted, "With the economic downturn, it's important for us to be front and center with value messaging, innovation and strategy," and "There is strong historical evidence about companies that step up with their innovation and advertising and their ability to move through economic downturns and then emerge with stronger brands on the other end."

Another reason for increased ad spending comes from General Mills. As the recession lingers on, General Mills research indicated that more Americans were eating at home due to uncertainty about their fortunes in the years ahead. After a 25 percent increase in ad spending in the first quarter of 2009, the cereal company announced another high single digit increase later in the year, believing that "the reinvestment is fueling net sales growth." (General Mills's retail sales increased 12 percent and operating profits were up 30 percent even with the increased ad spending.) The General Mills 2008 ad budget (defined as advertising, promotions, and other initiatives) was $688.8 million. The Hispanic market would continue to be much of the focus of the spending, with a push on Honey Nut Cheerios, as well as more messages about the health benefits targeted to the health conscious baby boomer market.

A number of other retailers also bucked the cutback trend in an attempt to increase Christmas Holiday sales in 2009. Kmart, Walmart, and JCPenney all doubled their advertising spending from the previous year, while Home Depot and Lowe's were up by 50 percent. Gap increased its spending by $25 million in the third quarter and by $45 million in the fourth. Gap also went back to television advertising for the first time in two years. According to a Walmart spokesperson, the world's number one retailer has always believed in maintaining spending even during a recession, noting that it benefits from media cost deflation. Best Buy, while maintaining their budget, shifted some of the allocations to lower cost alternatives, including Twitter and Facebook. Procter & Gamble and Coca-Cola also continued to spend during the economic downturn, shifting dollars to what they considered "more efficient and innovative" media buys. P&G announced an increase in expenditures in mid-2010.

Looking at the names on this list of companies that are not cutting—and some of whom are even increasing—advertising expenditures during a downturn, one wonders if maybe they know something the other 77 percent don't know.

Sources: Kenneth Hein, "To Counter Downward Sales Trend, 7UP Ups Ad Spend," *Brandweek*, October 12, 2009, p. 5; Suzanne Vranica, " Retailers Boost Spending on Holiday Advertising," www.wsj.com, Nov. 9, 2009; Emily Bryson York, "Burger King to Boost Ad Spending," www.adage.com, April 17, 2009; David Goetzl, "General Mills To Increase Ad Spending," www.mediapost.com, July 6, 2009; ____ "Coca-Cola, P&G to Keep Spending," www.warc.com., April 23, 2009.

**FIGURE 7–7**
Marginal Analysis

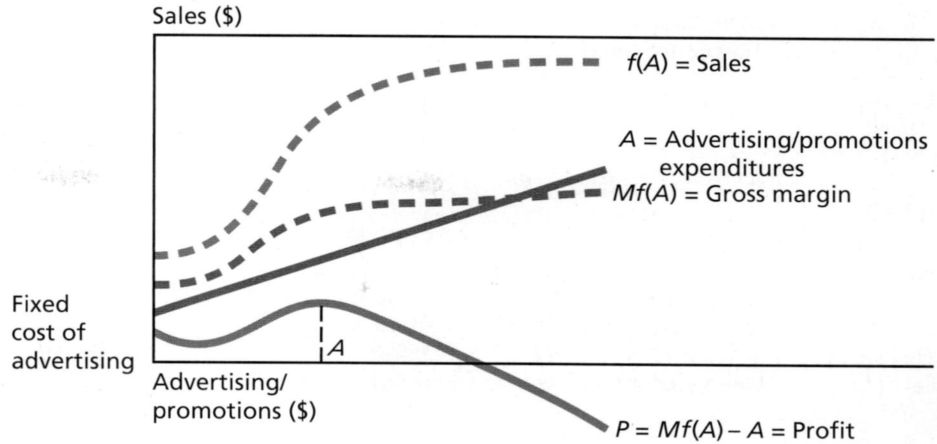

**Theoretical Issues in Budget Setting** Most of the models used to establish advertising budgets can be categorized as taking an economic or a sales response perspective.

**Marginal Analysis** Figure 7–7 graphically represents the concept of **marginal analysis**. As advertising/promotional expenditures increase, sales and gross margins also increase to a point, but then they level off. Profits are shown to be a result of the gross margin minus advertising expenditures. Using this theory to establish its budget, a firm would continue to spend advertising/promotional dollars as long as the marginal revenues created by these expenditures exceeded the incremental advertising/promotional costs. As shown on the graph, the optimal expenditure level is the point where marginal costs equal the marginal revenues they generate (point *A*). If the sum of the advertising/promotional expenditures exceeded the revenues they generated, one would conclude the appropriations were too high and scale down the budget. If revenues were higher, a higher budget might be in order. (We will see later in this chapter that this approach can also be applied to the allocation decision.)

While marginal analysis seems logical intuitively, certain weaknesses limit its usefulness. These weaknesses include the assumptions that (1) sales are a direct result of advertising and promotional expenditures and this effect can be measured and (2) advertising and promotion are solely responsible for sales. Let us examine each of these assumptions in more detail.

1. *Assumption that sales are a direct measure of advertising and promotions efforts.* Earlier in this chapter we discussed the fact that the advertiser needs to set communications objectives that contribute to accomplishing overall marketing objectives but at the same time are separate. One reason for this strategy is that it is often difficult, if not impossible, to demonstrate the effects of advertising and promotions on sales. In studies using sales as a direct measure, it has been almost impossible to establish the contribution of advertising and promotion. In the words of David Aaker and James Carman, "Looking for the relationship between advertising and sales is somewhat worse than looking for a needle in a haystack."[19] Thus, to try to show that the size of the budget will directly affect sales of the product is misleading. A more logical approach would be to examine the impact of various budgets on the attainment of communications objectives.

   As we saw in the discussion of communications objectives, sales are not the only goal of the promotional effort. Awareness, interest, attitude change, and other communications objectives are often sought, and while the bottom line may be to sell the product, these objectives may serve as the basis on which the promotional program is developed.

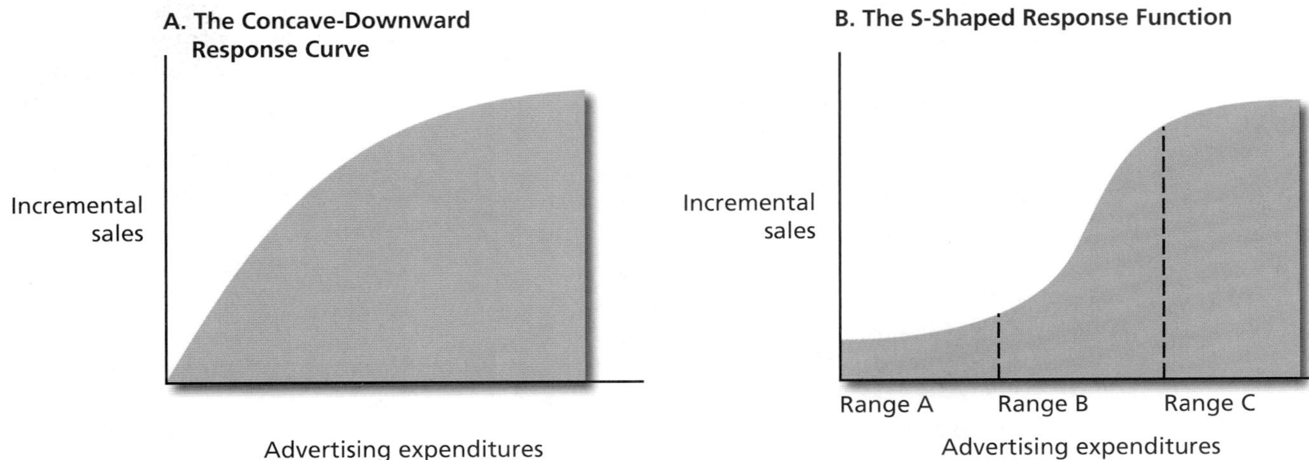


**FIGURE 7–8**
Advertising Sales/Response Functions

2. *Assumption that sales are determined solely by advertising and promotion.* This assumption ignores the remaining elements of the marketing mix—price, product, and distribution—which do contribute to a company's success. Environmental factors may also affect the promotional program, leading the marketing manager to assume the advertising was or was not effective when some other factor may have helped or hindered the accomplishment of the desired objectives.

Overall, you can see that while the economic approach to the budgeting process is a logical one, the difficulties associated with determining the effects of the promotional effort on sales and revenues limit its applicability. Marginal analysis is seldom used as a basis for budgeting (except for direct-response advertising).

**Sales Response Models** You may have wondered why the sales curve in Figure 7–7 shows sales leveling off even though advertising and promotions efforts continue to increase. The relationship between advertising and sales has been the topic of much research and discussion designed to determine the shape of the response curve.

Almost all advertisers subscribe to one of two models of the advertising/sales response function: the concave-downward function or the S-shaped response curve.

- *The concave-downward function.* After reviewing more than 100 studies of the effects of advertising on sales, Julian Simon and Johan Arndt concluded that the effects of advertising budgets follow the microeconomic law of diminishing returns.[20] That is, as the amount of advertising increases, its incremental value decreases. The logic is that those with the greatest potential to buy will likely act on the first (or earliest) exposures, while those less likely to buy are not likely to change as a result of the advertising. For those who may be potential buyers, each additional ad will supply little or no new information that will affect their decision. Thus, according to the **concave-downward function model,** the effects of advertising quickly begin to diminish, as shown in Figure 7–8A. Budgeting under this model suggests that fewer advertising dollars may be needed to create the optimal influence on sales.
- *The S-shaped response function.* Many advertising managers assume the **S-shaped response curve** (Figure 7–8B), which projects an S-shaped response function to the budget outlay (again measured in sales). Initial outlays of the advertising budget have little impact (as indicated by the essentially flat sales curve in range A). After a certain budget level has been reached (the beginning of range B), advertising and promotional efforts begin to have an effect, as additional increments of expenditures result in increased sales. This incremental gain continues only to a point, however, because at the beginning

of range C additional expenditures begin to return little or nothing in the way of sales. This model suggests a small advertising budget is likely to have no impact beyond the sales that may have been generated through other means (for example, word of mouth). At the other extreme, more does not necessarily mean better: Additional dollars spent beyond range B have no additional impact on sales and for the most part can be considered wasted. As with marginal analysis, one would attempt to operate at that point on the curve in area B where the maximum return for the money is attained.

Weaknesses in these sales response models render them of limited use to practitioners for direct applications. Many of the problems seen earlier—the use of sales as a dependent variable, measurement problems, and so on—limit the usefulness of these models. At the same time, keep in mind the purpose of discussing such models. Even though marginal analysis and the sales response curves may not apply directly, they give managers some insight into a theoretical basis of how the budgeting process should work. There's some empirical evidence indicating the models may have validity.



The studies discussed in earlier chapters on learning and the hierarchy of effects also demonstrate the importance of repetition on gaining awareness and on subsequent higher-order objectives such as adoption. Thus, while these models may not provide a tool for setting the advertising and promotional budget directly, we can use them to guide our appropriations strategy from a theoretical basis. As you will see later in this chapter, such a theoretical basis has advantages over many of the methods currently being used for budget setting and allocation.

### Additional Factors in Budget Setting

While the theoretical bases just discussed should be considered in establishing the budget appropriation, a number of other issues must also be considered. A weakness in attempting to use sales as a *direct* measure of response to advertising is that various situational factors may have an effect. Some of the factors that have been shown to affect the advertising/sales ratio

**FIGURE 7–9**
Factors Influencing Advertising Budgets

| Factor | Relationship of Advertising/Sales |
|---|---|
| ***Product Factors*** | |
| Basis for differentiation | + |
| Hidden product qualities | + |
| Emotional buying motives | + |
| Durability | — |
| Large dollar purchase | — |
| Purchase frequency | Curvilinear |
| ***Market Factors*** | |
| Stage of product life cycle: | |
| Introductory | + |
| Growth | + |
| Maturity | — |
| Decline | — |
| Inelastic demand | + |
| Market share | — |
| Competition: | |
| Active | + |
| Concentrated | + |
| Pioneer in market | — |
| ***Customer Factors*** | |
| Industrial products users | — |
| Concentration of users | + |
| ***Strategy Factors*** | |
| Regional markets | — |
| Early stage of brand life cycle | + |
| High margins in channels | — |
| Long channels of distribution | + |
| High prices | + |
| High quality | + |
| Media strategy | + |
| Creative strategy | + |
| Promotional strategy | + |
| ***Cost Factors*** | |
| High profit margins | + |

Note: + relationship means the factor leads to a positive effect of advertising on sales; — relationship indicates little or no effect of advertising on sales.

**FIGURE 7–10**

Factors Considered in Budget Setting

| | |
|---|---|
| Changes in advertising strategy and/or creative approach | 51% |
| Competitive activity and/or spending levels | 47 |
| Profit contribution goal or other financial target | 43 |
| Level of previous year's spending, with adjustment | 17 |
| Senior management dollar allocation or set limit | 11 |
| Volume share projections | 8 |
| Projections/assumptions on media cost increases | 25 |
| Modifications in media strategy and/or buying techniques | 17 |

are shown in Figure 7–9. For a product characterized by emotional buying motives, hidden product qualities, and/or a strong basis for differentiation, advertising would have a noticeable impact on sales. Products characterized as large-dollar purchases and those in the maturity or decline stages of the product would be less likely to benefit.

As we will see later in this chapter, the percentage-of-sales method of budgeting has inherent weaknesses in that the advertising and sales effects may be reversed. So we cannot be sure whether the situation actually led to the advertising/sales relationship or vice versa. Thus, while these factors should be considered in the budget appropriation decision, they should not be the sole determinants of where and when to increase or decrease expenditures.

The *Advertising Age* Editorial Sounding Board consists of 92 executives of the top 200 advertising companies in the United States (representing the client side) and 130 executives of the 200 largest advertising agencies and 11 advertising consultants (representing the agency side). A survey of the board yielded the factors shown in Figure 7–10 that are important in budget setting.

Overall, the responses of these two groups reflect in part their perceptions as to factors of importance in how budgets are set. To understand the differences in the relative importance of these factors, it is important to understand the approaches currently employed in budget setting. The next section examines these approaches.

## Budgeting Approaches

The theoretical approaches to establishing the promotional budget are seldom employed. In smaller firms, they may never be used. Instead, a number of methods developed through practice and experience are implemented. This section reviews some of the more traditional methods of setting budgets and the relative advantages and disadvantages of each. First, you must understand two things: (1) Many firms employ more than one method, and (2) budgeting approaches vary according to the size and sophistication of the firm.

### Top-Down Approaches

The approaches discussed in this section may be referred to as **top-down approaches** because a budgetary amount is established (usually at an executive level) and then the monies are passed down to the various departments (as shown in Figure 7–11). These budgets are essentially predetermined and have no true theoretical basis. Top-down methods include the affordable method, arbitrary allocation, percentage of sales, competitive parity, and return on investment (ROI).

**The Affordable Method** In the **affordable method** (often referred to as the "all-you-can-afford method"), the firm determines the amount to be spent in various areas such as production and operations. Then it allocates what's left to advertising and promotion, considering this to be the amount it can afford. The task to be performed by the advertising/ promotions function is not considered, and the

**FIGURE 7–11**

Top-Down versus Bottom-Up Approaches to Budget Setting

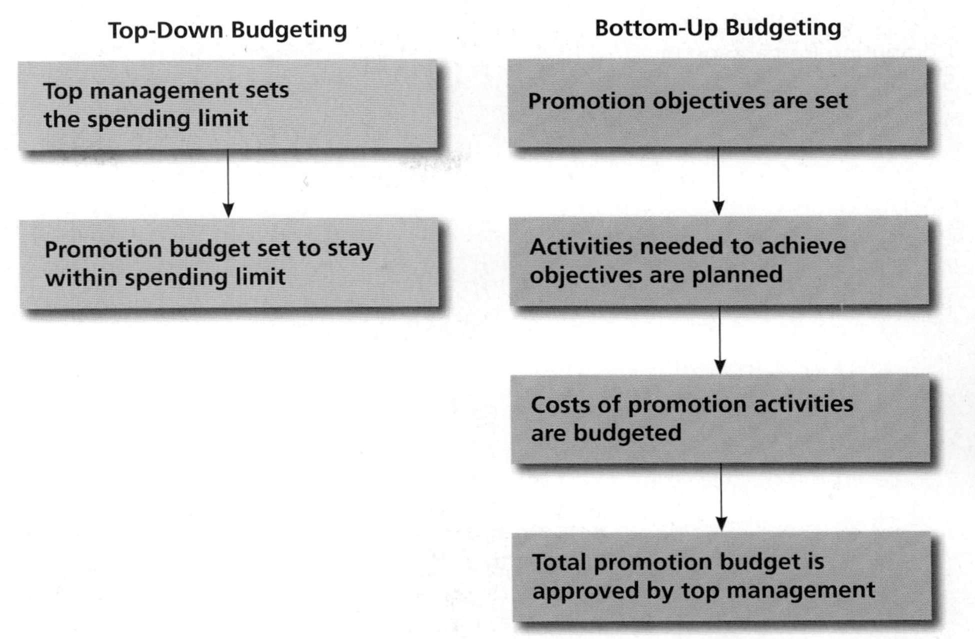
Top-Down Budgeting
Top management sets the spending limit
Promotion budget set to stay within spending limit
Bottom-Up Budgeting
Promotion objectives are set
Activities needed to achieve objectives are planned
Costs of promotion activities are budgeted
Total promotion budget is approved by top management

likelihood of under- or overspending is high, as no guidelines for measuring the effects of various budgets are established.

Strange as it may seem, this approach is common among small firms. Unfortunately, it is also used in large firms, particularly those that are not marketing-driven and do not understand the role of advertising and promotion. For example, many high-tech firms focus on new product development and engineering and assume that the product, if good enough, will sell itself. In these companies, little money may be left for performing the advertising and promotions tasks.

The logic for this approach stems from "We can't be hurt with this method" thinking. That is, if we know what we can afford and we do not exceed it, we will not get into financial problems. While this may be true in a strictly accounting sense, it does not reflect sound managerial decision making from a marketing perspective. Often this method does not allocate enough money to get the product off the ground and into the market. In terms of the S-shaped sales response model, the firm is operating in range A. Or the firm may be spending more than necessary, operating in range C. When the market gets tough and sales and/or profits begin to fall, this method is likely to lead to budget cuts at a time when the budget should be increased.

**Arbitrary Allocation** Perhaps an even weaker method than the affordable method for establishing a budget is **arbitrary allocation**, in which virtually no theoretical basis is considered and the budgetary amount is often set by fiat. That is, the budget is determined by management solely on the basis of what is felt to be necessary. In a discussion of how managers set advertising budgets, Melvin Salveson reported that these decisions may reflect "as much upon the managers' psychological profile as they do economic criteria."[21] While Salveson was referring to larger corporations, the approach is no less common in small firms and nonprofit organizations.

The arbitrary allocation approach has no obvious advantages. No systematic thinking has occurred, no objectives have been budgeted for, and the concept and purpose of advertising and promotion have been largely ignored. Other than the fact that the manager believes some monies must be spent on advertising and promotion and then picks a number, there is no good explanation why this approach continues to be used. Yet budgets continue to be set this way, and our purpose in discussing this method is to point out only that it is used—not recommended.

**FIGURE 7–12**

Alternative Methods for Computing Percentage of Sales

| METHOD 1: STRAIGHT PERCENTAGE OF SALES | | |
|---|---|---|
| 2011 | Total dollar sales | $1,000,000 |
| | Straight % of sales at 10% | $100,000 |
| 2012 | Advertising budget | $100,000 |
| **METHOD 2: PERCENTAGE OF UNIT COST** | | |
| 2011 | Cost per bottle to manufacturer | $4.00 |
| | Unit cost allocated to advertising | 1.00 |
| 2012 | Forecasted sales, 100,000 units | |
| 2012 | Advertising budget (100,000 × $1) | $100,000 |

**Percentage of Sales** Perhaps the most commonly used method for budget setting (particularly in large firms) is the **percentage-of-sales method,** in which the advertising and promotions budget is based on sales of the product. Management determines the amount by either (1) taking a percentage of the sales dollars or (2) assigning a fixed amount of the unit product cost to promotion and multiplying this amount by the number of units sold. These two methods are shown in Figure 7–12.

A variation on the percentage-of-sales method uses a percentage of projected future sales as a base. This method also uses either a straight percentage of projected sales or a unit cost projection. In the straight-percentage method, sales are projected for the coming year based on the marketing manager's estimates. The budget is a percentage of these sales, often an industry standard percentage like those presented in Figure 7–13.

One advantage of using future sales as a base is that the budget is not based on last year's sales. As the market changes, management must factor the effect of these changes on sales into next year's forecast rather than relying on past data. The resulting budget is more likely to reflect current conditions and be more appropriate.

Figure 7–13 reveals that the percentage allocated varies from one industry to the next. Some firms budget a very small percentage (for example, 0.2 percent in construction machinery and equipment), and others spend a much higher proportional amount (15.6 percent on distilled and blended liquors). Actual dollar amounts spent vary markedly according to the company's total sales figure. Thus, a smaller percentage of sales in the construction machinery industry may actually result in significantly more advertising dollars being spent.

Proponents of the percentage-of-sales method cite a number of advantages. It is financially safe and keeps ad spending within reasonable limits, as it bases spending on the past year's sales or what the firm expects to sell in the upcoming year. Thus, there will be sufficient monies to cover this budget, with increases in sales leading to budget increases and sales decreases resulting in advertising decreases. The percentage-of-sales method is simple, straightforward, and easy to implement. Regardless of which basis—past or future sales—is employed, the calculations used to arrive at a budget are not difficult. Finally, this budgeting approach is generally stable. While the budget may vary with increases and decreases in sales, as long as these changes are not drastic the manager will have a reasonable idea of the parameters of the budget.

At the same time, the percentage-of-sales method has some serious disadvantages, including the basic premise on which the budget is established: sales. Letting the level of sales determine the amount of advertising and promotions dollars to be spent reverses the cause-and-effect relationship between advertising and sales. It treats advertising as an expense associated with making a sale rather than an investment.

**FIGURE 7–13** Advertising-to-Sales Ratios by Industry Sector

| Industry | SIC | Ad as % Sales | Ad as % Margin | Annual Ad % Growth | Industry | SIC | Ad as % Sales | Ad as % Margin | Annual Ad % Growth |
|---|---|---|---|---|---|---|---|---|---|
| ABRASIVE, ASBESTOS, MISC MINRL | 3290 | 5.2 | 21.8 | 11.3 | DRUG & PROPRIETARY STORES | 5912 | 0.7 | 3.6 | 6.9 |
| ACCIDENT & HEALTH INSURANCE | 6321 | 1.3 | 7.4 | 11.6 | DRUGS AND PROPRIETARY-WHSL | 5122 | 0 | 0.7 | 9.1 |
| ADVERTISING | 7310 | 1.1 | 2.5 | 13 | DURABLE GOODS-WHOLESALE | 5000 | 0.5 | 2.2 | 13.4 |
| ADVERTISING AGENCIES | 7311 | 0.3 | 0.7 | −10.7 | EATING PLACES | 5812 | 3.1 | 11.8 | 7 |
| AGRICULTURAL CHEMICALS | 2870 | 1.7 | 4.7 | 5.7 | EDUCATIONAL SERVICES | 8200 | 11.3 | 24 | 8.9 |
| AGRICULTURE PRODUCTION-CROPS | 100 | 0.7 | 5.9 | 47.4 | ELEC MEAS & TEST INSTRUMENTS | 3825 | 0.6 | 1 | −9.5 |
| AIR COURIER SERVICES | 4513 | 0.8 | 3.6 | 8.6 | ELECTR, OTH ELEC EQ, EX CMP | 3600 | 2.1 | 6.3 | 4.6 |
| AIR TRANSPORT, SCHEDULED | 4512 | 0.9 | 4.3 | 7.1 | ELECTRIC & OTHER SERV COMB | 4931 | 0.4 | 4.7 | −5.9 |
| AIR-COND, HEATING, REFRIG EQ | 3585 | 1.2 | 4.5 | 5.3 | ELECTRIC HOUSEWARES AND FANS | 3634 | 2 | 6.8 | −1.2 |
| AIRCRAFT | 3721 | 0.1 | 0.6 | 12.1 | ELECTRIC LIGHTING, WIRING EQ | 3640 | 0.8 | 2.4 | 7.3 |
| AMUSEMENT & RECREATION SVCS | 7900 | 4.8 | 21.6 | 6.6 | ELECTROMEDICAL APPARATUS | 3845 | 0.9 | 1.3 | 10.1 |
| AMUSEMENT PARKS | 7996 | 7 | 14.3 | −6 | ELECTRONIC COMPONENTS, NEC | 3679 | 0.5 | 1.7 | 7.6 |
| APPAREL & OTHER FINISHED PDS | 2300 | 5.1 | 11.1 | 8.9 | ELECTRONIC COMPUTERS | 3571 | 1.2 | 4.3 | 9 |
| APPAREL AND ACCESSORY STORES | 5600 | 4.5 | 9.9 | 5.2 | EMPLOYMENT AGENCIES | 7361 | 2.4 | 7.4 | −1.7 |
| AUTO AND HOME SUPPLY STORES | 5531 | 2.2 | 4.7 | 10 | ENGINEERING SERVICES | 8711 | 0.3 | 1.4 | 16.3 |
| AUTO DEALERS, GAS STATIONS | 5500 | 0.8 | 5.6 | 5.4 | ENGINES AND TURBINES | 3510 | 1.6 | 6.5 | 16 |
| AUTO RENT & LEASE, NO DRIVERS | 7510 | 1.9 | 5.2 | 5.5 | EQUIP RENTAL & LEASING, NEC | 7359 | 1.8 | 2.9 | 6.6 |
| AUTO REPAIR, SERVICES, PARKING | 7500 | 3.8 | 15.7 | −2.2 | FABRICATED RUBBER PDS, NEC | 3060 | 9 | 27.4 | 13.8 |
| BEVERAGES | 2080 | 7.3 | 11.6 | 8.6 | FAMILY CLOTHING STORES | 5651 | 2 | 5.6 | 4.7 |
| BIOLOGICAL PDS, EX DIAGNSTICS | 2836 | 1.7 | 2.2 | 11 | FARM MACHINERY AND EQUIPMENT | 3523 | 0.7 | 2.4 | 3.2 |
| BLANKBOOKS, BINDERS, BOOKBIND | 2780 | 5 | 10.8 | 9.8 | FINANCE LESSORS | 6172 | 1.4 | 2 | 7.3 |
| BLDG MATL, HARDWR, GARDEN-RETL | 5200 | 2.2 | 6.7 | 8.5 | FIRE, MARINE, CASUALTY INS | 6331 | 0.9 | 9.7 | 10.9 |
| BOOKS: PUBG, PUBG & PRINTING | 2731 | 11.7 | 22.1 | −1.4 | FOOD AND KINDRED PRODUCTS | 2000 | 10 | 22.1 | −5 |
| BTLD & CAN SOFT DRINKS, WATER | 2086 | 3 | 6.3 | 9 | FOOTWEAR, EXCEPT RUBBER | 3140 | 3.8 | 8.8 | 9.7 |
| BUSINESS SERVICES, NEC | 7389 | 0.4 | 1.1 | 6.5 | FUNCTIONS REL TO DEP BKG, NEC | 6099 | 7.6 | 18.8 | 4.8 |
| CABLE AND OTHER PAY TV SVCS | 4841 | 7.4 | 13.4 | 6.3 | FURNITURE STORES | 5712 | 8.5 | 22.8 | 10.8 |
| CAN FRUIT, VEG, PRESRV, JAM, JEL | 2033 | 1.9 | 6.2 | 9.2 | GAMES, TOYS, CHLD VEH, EX DOLLS | 3944 | 10.7 | 20.9 | −1.9 |
| CAN, FROZN, PRESRV FRUIT & VEG | 2030 | 4.6 | 12 | 0.2 | GENERAL INDUSTRIAL MACH & EQ | 3560 | 0.6 | 1.8 | 7.8 |
| CATALOG, MAIL-ORDER HOUSES | 5961 | 3.3 | 12.4 | 13.3 | GRAIN MILL PRODUCTS | 2040 | 2.6 | 10.4 | 5.7 |
| CEMENT, HYDRAULIC | 3241 | 0.5 | 1.4 | 8.8 | GROCERIES & RELATED PDS-WHSL | 5140 | 0.8 | 3.8 | 4.3 |
| CHEMICALS & ALLIED PDS-WHSL | 5160 | 0.9 | 5.1 | −6 | GROCERIES, GENERAL LINE-WHSL | 5141 | 0.7 | 6.2 | 5.4 |
| CHEMICALS & ALLIED PRODUCTS | 2800 | 5.5 | 9.7 | 6.6 | GROCERY STORES | 5411 | 0.9 | 3.2 | 2.7 |
| CIGARETTES | 2111 | 2.2 | 4.2 | 2.6 | HELP SUPPLY SERVICES | 7363 | 0.4 | 1.9 | 5.6 |
| CMP INTEGRATED SYS DESIGN | 7373 | 1.4 | 3.3 | 10.9 | HOBBY, TOY, AND GAME SHOPS | 5945 | 3.8 | 10.9 | 7.1 |
| CMP PROCESSING, DATA PREP SVC | 7374 | 2 | 5.7 | 2.5 | HOME FURNITURE & EQUIP STORE | 5700 | 5.4 | 14.3 | 9.5 |
| CMP PROGRAMMING, DATA PROCESS | 7370 | 3.7 | 8 | 8.2 | HOME HEALTH CARE SERVICES | 8082 | 1.5 | 3.3 | 13.1 |
| COMMERCIAL PRINTING | 2750 | 7.4 | 35.6 | 0.9 | HOSPITAL & MEDICAL SVC PLANS | 6324 | 0.4 | 1.6 | 29 |
| COMMUNICATIONS EQUIP, NEC | 3669 | 3.7 | 8.5 | 1.5 | HOTELS AND MOTELS | 7011 | 1.6 | 8 | 6.6 |
| COMMUNICATIONS SERVICES, NEC | 4899 | 8.5 | 19.6 | 14.9 | HOUSEHOLD APPLIANCES | 3630 | 2.4 | 12.2 | 3.2 |
| COMPUTER & OFFICE EQUIPMENT | 3570 | 0.7 | 2.8 | −14.3 | HOUSEHOLD AUDIO & VIDEO EQ | 3651 | 5.3 | 41.8 | 0.5 |
| COMPUTER COMMUNICATION EQUIP | 3576 | 0.3 | 0.5 | 5.9 | HOUSEHOLD FURNITURE | 2510 | 5.2 | 17.4 | 5.7 |
| COMPUTER PERIPHERAL EQ, NEC | 3577 | 2.9 | 6.3 | 4.8 | IN VITRO, IN VIVO DIAGNOSTICS | 2835 | 3.7 | 6.1 | 13.6 |
| COMPUTER STORAGE DEVICES | 3572 | 0.3 | 0.8 | 12.3 | INDL INORGANIC CHEMICALS | 2810 | 0.3 | 0.9 | 8.8 |
| CONCRETE, GYPSUM, PLASTER PDS | 3270 | 0.6 | 2 | 4 | INDUSTRIAL MACH & EQ-WHSL | 5084 | 1.5 | 3.1 | 11.7 |
| CONGLOMERATE | 9997 | 0.5 | 2.1 | 9.6 | INDUSTRIAL ORGANIC CHEMICALS | 2860 | 0.1 | 0.4 | 14.2 |
| CONSTRUCTION MACHINERY & EQ | 3531 | 0.2 | 0.8 | 11.7 | INS AGENTS, BROKERS & SERVICE | 6411 | 0.3 | 2.1 | 5.8 |
| CONVRT PAPR, PAPRBRD, EX BOXES | 2670 | 1.4 | 3.5 | 4.2 | INVESTMENT ADVICE | 6282 | 1.5 | 2.1 | 9.5 |
| CREDIT REPORTING AGENCIES | 7320 | 2.1 | 3.8 | 23.1 | JEWELRY STORES | 5944 | 8.2 | 21.7 | 10.5 |
| CUTLERY, HANDTOOLS, GEN HRDWR | 3420 | 1.4 | 3.5 | 8.4 | KNITTING MILLS | 2250 | 4.3 | 12.3 | −1.7 |
| DAIRY PRODUCTS | 2020 | 1.4 | 6.3 | 4.7 | LAB ANALYTICAL INSTRUMENTS | 3826 | 1.2 | 2.1 | 10.3 |
| DENTAL EQUIPMENT & SUPPLIES | 3843 | 3.9 | 6.8 | 10.5 | LEATHER AND LEATHER PRODUCTS | 3100 | 3.7 | 5.5 | 12.7 |
| DEPARTMENT STORES | 5311 | 4.7 | 12.2 | 9.2 | LIFE INSURANCE | 6311 | 1.2 | 6.6 | 7.7 |
| DISTILLED AND BLENDED LIQUOR | 2085 | 15.6 | 25.9 | 18.2 | LUMBER & OTH BLDG MATL-RETL | 5211 | 1.6 | 4.9 | 12.5 |
| DOLLS AND STUFFED TOYS | 3942 | 10.2 | 21.6 | 5 | LUMBER AND WOOD PDS, EX FURN | 2400 | 0.6 | 4.3 | 13.2 |

NOTE: Advertising Ratios & Budgets covers over 300 industries. The 200 industries listed here were selected as the industries with the largest dollar volume of advertising based on estimated 2007 spending. For information about other industries, contact Schonfeld & Associates, Inc. SIC 5 Standard Industrial Classification number; Ad $ as % Sales 5 Advertising / Net Sales; Ad $ as % Margin 5 Advertising Expense/(Net Sales-Cost of Goods Sold); Annual Ad Growth Rate % 5 Average Annual Compound Growth Rate in Ad Spending. Source: Advertising Ratios & Budgets, 31st Edition, 202 pages. Published by Schonfeld & Associates, Inc., 1931 Lynn Circle Libertyville, IL 60048. Phone 800-205-0030. Price $395 US for book, book with database $ 495 US. For more information, visit www.saiBooks.com

FIGURE 7–14

Investments Pay Off in Later Years

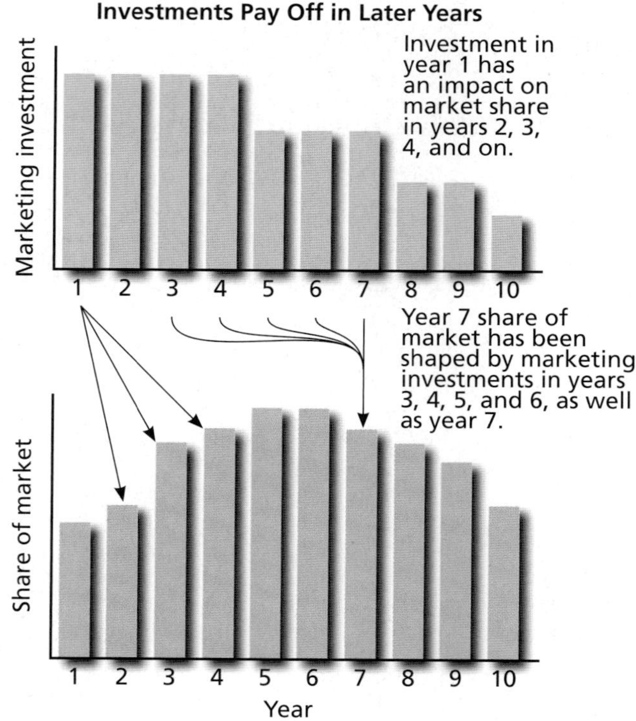

Investments Pay Off in Later Years
Marketing investment
Investment in year 1 has an impact on market share in years 2, 3, 4, and on.
1 2 3 4 5 6 7 8 9 10
Year 7 share of market has been shaped by marketing investments in years 3, 4, 5, and 6, as well as year 7.
Share of market
1 2 3 4 5 6 7 8 9 10
Year

As shown in Figure 7–14, companies that consider promotional expenditures an investment reap the rewards.

A second problem with this approach was actually cited as an advantage earlier: stability. Proponents say that if all firms use a similar percentage, that will bring stability to the marketplace. But what happens if someone varies from this standard percentage? The problem is that this method does not allow for changes in strategy either internally or from competitors. An aggressive firm may wish to allocate more monies to the advertising and promotions budget, a strategy that is not possible with a percentage-of-sales method unless the manager is willing to deviate from industry standards.

The percentage-of-sales method of budgeting may result in severe misappropriation of funds. If advertising and promotion have a role to perform in marketing a product, then allocating more monies to advertising will, as shown in the S-shaped curve, generate incremental sales (to a point). If products with low sales have smaller promotion budgets, this will hinder sales progress. At the other extreme, very successful products may have excess budgets, some of which may be better appropriated elsewhere.

The percentage-of-sales method is also difficult to employ for new product introductions. If no sales histories are available, there is no basis for establishing the budget. Projections of future sales may be difficult, particularly if the product is highly innovative and/or has fluctuating sales patterns.

Finally, if the budget is contingent on sales, decreases in sales will lead to decreases in budgets when they most need to be increased. Continuing to cut the advertising and promotion budgets may just add impetus to the downward sales trend. On the other hand, some of the more successful companies have allocated additional funds during hard times or downturns in the cycle of sales as shown earlier. Companies that maintain or increase their ad expenditures during recessions achieve increased visibility and higher growth in both sales and market share (compared to those that reduce advertising outlays).

While the percentage-of-future-sales method has been proposed as a remedy for some of the problems discussed here, the reality is that problems with forecasting, cyclical growth, and uncontrollable factors limit its effectiveness.

FIGURE 7–15

Competitors' Advertising Outlays Do Not Always Hurt

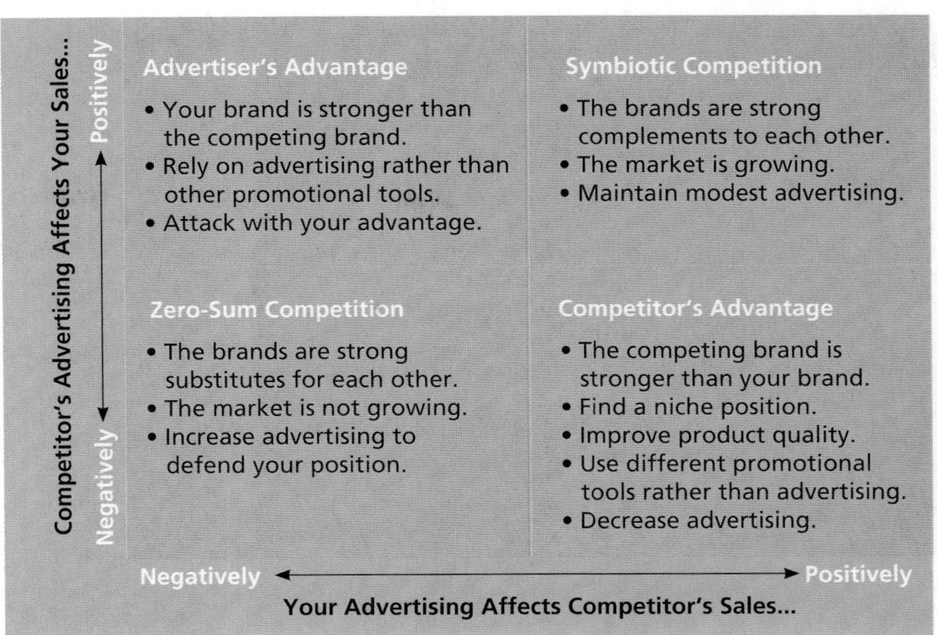




**Competitive Parity** If you asked marketing managers if they ever set their advertising and promotions budgets on the basis of what their competitors allocate, they would probably deny it. Yet if you examined the advertising expenditures of these companies, both as a percentage of sales and in respect to the media where they are allocated, you would see little variation in the percentage-of-sales figures for firms within a given industry. Such results do not happen by chance alone. Companies that provide competitive advertising information, trade associations, and other advertising industry periodicals are sources for competitors' expenditures. Larger corporations often subscribe to services such as Competitive Media Reporting, which estimates the top 1,000 companies' advertising in 10 media and in total. Smaller companies often use a **clipping service**, which clips competitors' ads from local print media, allowing the company to work backward to determine the cumulative costs of the ads placed.

In the **competitive parity method**, managers establish budget amounts by matching the competition's percentage-of-sales expenditures. The argument is that setting budgets in this fashion takes advantage of the collective wisdom of the industry. It also takes the competition into consideration, which leads to stability in the marketplace by minimizing marketing warfare. If companies know that competitors are unlikely to match their increases in promotional spending, they are less likely to take an aggressive posture to attempt to gain market share. This minimizes unusual or unrealistic ad expenditures.

The competitive parity method has a number of disadvantages, however. For one, it ignores the fact that advertising and promotions are designed to accomplish specific objectives by addressing certain problems and opportunities. Second, it assumes that because firms have similar expenditures, their programs will be equally effective. This assumption ignores the contributions of creative executions and/or media allocations, as well as the success or failure of various promotions. Further, it ignores possible advantages of the firm itself; some companies simply make better products than others. A study by Yoo and Mandhachitara indicates that a competitive parity strategy must consider the fact that a competitor's advertising can actually benefit one's own firm, and that one competitor's gain is not always the other's loss. As shown in Figure 7–15 there are four different situations to determine how the competitive budgets may impact sales—only one of which involved the zero-sum scenario.[22]

| Medium | The Measurement Challenge | ROI Measurability |
|---|---|---|
| Direct Response | Direct mail, telemarketing, and other forms are the most measurable of media listed here. Direct can have a synergistic effect, especially for pharma, telecom, and financial services. | 5 |
| Sales Promotion | Offers such as coupons and discounts generate a lot of consumer response and therefore a bounty of data. The data lend themselves to measurement, especially for package goods via syndicated scanner data. Free-standing inserts generate much valuable data. | 5 |
| Internet | The Internet can be very influential for big-ticket purchases like cars. Very measurable, with the cautionary note that "Internet is a very broad net," ranging from search engines to ads in content to websites such as in the auto market, where such marques as Saab get lots of hits, and all should be looked at separately. The goal is to understand how the consumer is interacting online with the brand. | 5 |
| TV | While promotions have very pronounced, short-term effects that allow precise measurement, TV has a more subtle and gradual effect that may show greater variability. But ROI can be measured with a high degree of accuracy, and there's no excuse for TV not to show a measurable effect. MMA clients have been using a lot more analysis to create a better mix between :15s and :30s, and better allocation across dayparts. | 4.5 |
| Print | The experts can slice and dice print by weekly vs. monthly publications, by targeted vs. general market, by promotional ads vs. equity-building. Print promotional materials, like free-standing inserts, are a separate—and much more measurable—matter. As with all other media, accuracy and timing of the data are crucial in determining how measurable the medium is. Print can play a strong role in expanding the reach of the media mix. | 4.5 |
| Public Relations | There are companies that specialize in the measurement of PR campaigns' quality; they can measure the number of impressions delivered—via positive or negative PR—for a brand name or category. PR can have a measurable impact on sales (think trans fats in food). The problem: Many marketers aren't buying these PR data. | 4 |
| Video Games | Whether the game is played online or off-line is crucial. An ad embedded in a game cartridge is very hard to measure because there's no way to know how often it's played, though there's no denying "True Crime's" Nick Kang is a big hit. With online games, there are great data available through the Internet. | Online<br>Off-line |

Scale: 5 = Best

**FIGURE 7–16**

Aegis Rated ROI of Various Media

Also, there is no guarantee that competitors will continue to pursue their existing strategies. Since competitive parity figures are determined by examination of competitors' previous years' promotional expenditures (short of corporate espionage), changes in market emphasis and/or spending may not be recognized until the competition has already established an advantage. Further, there is no guarantee that a competitor will not increase or decrease its own expenditures, regardless of what other companies do. Finally, competitive parity may not avoid promotional wars. Coke versus Pepsi and AT&T versus Verizon have been notorious for their spending wars, each responding to the other's increased outlays.

In summary, few firms employ the competitive parity method as a sole means of establishing the promotional budget. This method is typically used in conjunction with the percentage-of-sales or other methods. It is never wise to ignore the competition; managers must always be aware of what competitors are doing. But they should not just emulate them in setting goals and developing strategies.

**Return on Investment (ROI)** In the percentage-of-sales method, sales dictate the level of advertising appropriations. But advertising causes sales. In the marginal

| Medium | The Measurement Challenge | ROI Measurability |
|---|---|---|
| Radio | The available data typically aren't as strong as those for its traditional-media colleagues of TV and print, and this hampers radio. | 3 |
| Cinema | Movie advertising can be measured by the number of impressions delivered, much like outdoor or kiosk advertising would be measured. | 3 |
| Sponsored Events | Measurability depends on whether sponsorship is likely to spark short-term effect. A major recurring event like the Olympics is very measurable. Others can be difficult to measure short term. Measurement can be complex because events have so many pieces, including how the event is advertised, the PR buzz, signage, and the recollection of the event itself. | 3 |
| Product Placement | There are companies that measure quality of placement as well as the quantity of exposures. Treated much like TV advertising, with the caveat that not every product placement is the same. Fox's *American Idol* is a great example: AT&T Wireless's tie-in, which involved voting by text message, is interactive—even part of the entertainment—while Paula Abdul drinking from a Coke cup is not. (P.S. AT&T Wireless, now owned by Cingular, isn't an MMA client.) So the question becomes: How do you score the quality of placement? | 3 |
| Outdoor | Available data are limited due to the nature of outdoor advertising; there's no syndicated vendor that sells the needed data on outdoor. And outdoor lacks "variance"—the billboard is up X number of months and seen by an unchanging X number of people each day. | 2 |
| Guerrilla Marketing | Hard to measure if the variable you're using is sales. If 10,000 people at an event get free T-shirts, it's difficult to measure the effect on the 400,000 people living in that market. Because guerrilla can encompass so many different kinds of tactics, getting useful data can be a problem—it depends on how measurable the response is. Marketers' ROI expectations for guerrilla are lower than for other media, so the urgency to measure is less. Not to mention they spend a lot less on guerrilla than on traditional media like TV. | 1 |

Scale: 5 = Best

**FIGURE 7–16**
(Concluded)

analysis and S-shaped curve approaches, incremental investments in advertising and promotions lead to increases in sales. The key word here is *investment.* In the **ROI budgeting method**, advertising and promotions are considered investments, like plant and equipment. Thus, the budgetary appropriation (investment) leads to certain returns. Like other aspects of the firm's efforts, advertising and promotion are expected to earn a certain return. Over the years, ROI has received a great deal of attention by practitioners over the past few years, with many still disagreeing as to how it should be measured. Figure 7–16 reports the results of *Advertising Age*'s report of the Aegis Group rating of how various media perform under this criterion (5 = best).

While the ROI method looks good on paper, the reality is that it is rarely possible to assess the returns provided by the promotional effort—at least as long as sales continue to be the basis for evaluation. Thus, while managers are certain to ask how much return they are getting for such expenditures, the question remains unanswered and, as shown in the chapter introduction, depends on the criteria used to determine effectiveness. ROI remains a difficult method to employ.

**Summary of Top-Down Budgeting Methods** You are probably asking yourself why we even discussed these budgeting methods if they are not recommended for use or have severe disadvantages that limit their effectiveness. But you must understand the various methods used in order to recognize their limitations, especially since these flawed methods are commonly employed by marketers. Research conducted over a number of years by various researchers indicates that the affordable, competitive parity, percentage of sales, and objective and task methods are the most

**FIGURE 7–17**

The Objective and Task Method

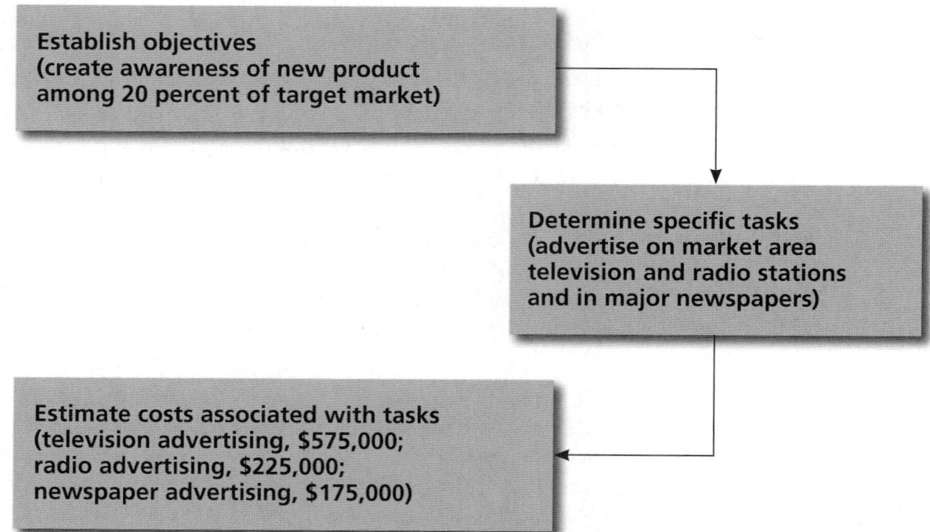


commonly employed budgeting methods. As noted, the emphasis on ROI has dramatically increased over the past few years.[23,24,25,26,27] Tradition and top management's desire for control are probably the major reasons why top-down methods continue to be popular.

**Build-Up Approaches** The major flaw associated with the top-down methods is that these judgmental approaches lead to predetermined budget appropriations often not linked to objectives and the strategies designed to accomplish them. A more effective budgeting strategy would be to consider the firm's communications objectives and budget what is deemed necessary to attain these goals. As noted earlier, the promotional planning model shows the budget decision as an interactive process, with the communications objectives on one hand and the promotional mix alternatives on the other. The idea is to budget so these promotional mix strategies can be implemented to achieve the stated objectives.

**Objective and Task Method** It is important that objective setting and budgeting go hand in hand rather than sequentially. It is difficult to establish a budget without specific objectives in mind, and setting objectives without regard to how much money is available makes no sense. For example, a company may wish to create awareness among *X* percent of its target market. A minimal budget amount will be required to accomplish this goal, and the firm must be willing to spend this amount.

The **objective and task method** of budget setting uses a **buildup approach** consisting of three steps: (1) defining the communications objectives to be accomplished, (2) determining the specific strategies and tasks needed to attain them, and (3) estimating the costs associated with performance of these strategies and tasks. The total budget is based on the accumulation of these costs.

Implementing the objective and task approach is somewhat more involved. The manager must monitor this process throughout and change strategies depending on how well objectives are attained. As shown in Figure 7–17, this process involves several steps:

1. *Isolate objectives.* When the promotional planning model is presented, a company will have two sets of objectives to accomplish—the marketing objectives for the product and the communications objectives. After the former are established, the task involves determining what specific communications objectives will be designed to accomplish these goals. Communications objectives must be specific, attainable, and measurable, as well as time limited.

2. *Determine tasks required.* A number of elements are involved in the strategic plan designed to attain the objectives established. (These strategies constitute the remaining chapters in this text.) These tasks may include advertising in various media, sales promotions, and/or other elements of the promotional mix, each with its own role to perform.
3. *Estimate required expenditures.* Buildup analysis requires determining the estimated costs associated with the tasks developed in the previous step. For example, it involves costs for developing awareness through advertising, trial through sampling, and so forth.
4. *Monitor.* As you will see in Chapter 19 on measuring effectiveness, there are ways to determine how well one is attaining established objectives. Performance should be monitored and evaluated in light of the budget appropriated.
5. *Reevaluate objectives.* Once specific objectives have been attained, monies may be better spent on new goals. Thus, if one has achieved the level of consumer awareness sought, the budget should be altered to stress a higher-order objective such as evaluation or trial.



The major advantage of the objective and task method is that the budget is driven by the objectives to be attained. The managers closest to the marketing effort will have specific strategies and input into the budget-setting process.

The major disadvantage of this method is the difficulty of determining which tasks will be required and the costs associated with each. For example, specifically what tasks are needed to attain awareness among 50 percent of the target market? How much will it cost to perform these tasks? While these decisions are easier to determine for certain objectives—for example, estimating the costs of sampling required to stimulate trial in a defined market area—it is not always possible to know exactly what is required and/or how much it will cost to complete the job. This process is easier if there is past experience to use as a guide, with either the existing product or a similar one in the same product category. But it is especially difficult for new product introductions. As a result, budget setting using this method is not as easy to perform or as stable as some of the methods discussed earlier. Given this disadvantage, many marketing managers have stayed with those top-down approaches for setting the total expenditure amount.

The objective and task method offers advantages over methods discussed earlier but is more difficult to implement when there is no track record for the product. The following section addresses the problem of budgeting for new product introductions.

**Payout Planning** The first months of a new product's introduction typically require heavier-than-normal advertising and promotion appropriations to stimulate higher levels of awareness and subsequent trial. After studying more than 40 years of Nielsen figures, James O. Peckham estimated that the average share of advertising to sales ratio necessary to launch a new product successfully is approximately 1.5:2.0.[28] This means that a new entry should be spending at approximately twice the desired market share, as shown in the two examples in Figure 7–18. For example, in the food industry, brand 101 gained a 12.6 percent market share by spending 34 percent of the total advertising dollars in this category. Likewise, brand 401 in the toiletry industry had a 30 percent share of advertising dollars to gain 19.5 percent of sales.

To determine how much to spend, marketers often develop a **payout plan** that determines the investment value of the advertising and promotion appropriation. The basic idea is to project the revenues the product will generate, as well as the costs it will incur, over two to three years. Based on an expected rate of return, the payout plan will assist in determining how much advertising and promotions expenditure will be necessary and when the return might be expected. A three-year payout plan is shown in Figure 7–19. The product would lose money in year 1, almost break even in year 2, and finally begin to show substantial profits by the end of year 3.

**FIGURE 7–18**

Share of Advertising Sales Relationship (Two-Year Summary)

**A. New Brands of Food Products**

| Brand | Average share of advertising | Attained share of sales | Ratio of share of advertising to share of sales |
|---|---|---|---|
| 101 | 34% | 12.6% | 2.7 |
| 102 | 16 | 10.0 | 1.6 |
| 103 | 8 | 7.6 | 1.1 |
| 104 | 4 | 2.6 | 1.5 |
| 105 | 3 | 2.1 | 1.4 |

**B. New Brands of Toiletry Products**

| Brand | Average share of advertising | Attained share of sales | Ratio of share of advertising to share of sales |
|---|---|---|---|
| 401 | 30% | 19.5% | 1.5 |
| 402 | 25 | 16.5 | 1.5 |
| 403 | 20 | 16.2 | 1.2 |
| 404 | 12 | 9.4 | 1.3 |
| 405 | 16 | 8.7 | 1.8 |
| 406 | 19 | 7.3 | 2.6 |
| 407 | 14 | 7.2 | 1.9 |
| 408 | 10 | 6.0 | 1.7 |
| 409 | 7 | 6.0 | 1.2 |
| 410 | 6 | 5.9 | 1.0 |
| 411 | 10 | 5.9 | 1.7 |
| 412 | 6 | 5.2 | 1.2 |

The advertising and promotion figures are highest in year 1 and decline in years 2 and 3. This appropriation is consistent with Peckham's findings and reflects the additional outlays needed to make as rapid an impact as possible. (Keep in mind that shelf space is limited, and store owners are not likely to wait around for a product to become successful.) The budget also reflects the firm's guidelines for new product expenditures, since companies generally have established deadlines by which the product must begin to show a profit. Finally, keep in mind that building market share may be more difficult than maintaining it—thus the substantial dropoff in expenditures in later years.

**FIGURE 7–19**

Example of Three-Year Payout Plan ($ Millions)

| | Year 1 | Year 2 | Year 3 |
|---|---|---|---|
| Product sales | 15.0 | 35.50 | 60.75 |
| Profit contribution (@ $0.50/case) | 7.5 | 17.75 | 30.38 |
| Advertising/promotions | 15.0 | 10.50 | 8.50 |
| Profit (loss) | (7.5) | 7.25 | 21.88 |
| Cumulative profit (loss) | (7.5) | (0.25) | 21.63 |

**FIGURE 7–20**

How Advertising and Promotions Budgets Are Set

*The Nature of the Decision Process*

- Managers develop overall marketing objectives for the brand.
- Financial projections are made on the basis of the objectives and forecasts.
- Advertising and promotions budgets are set on the basis of quantitative models and managerial judgment.
- The budget is presented to senior management, which approves and adjusts the budgets.
- The plan is implemented (changes are often made during implementation).
- The plan is evaluated by comparing the achieved results with objectives.

*Factors Affecting Budget Allocations*

- The extent to which risk taking is encouraged and/or tolerated.
- Sophistication regarding the use of marketing information.
- Managerial judgment.
- Use of quantitative tools.
- Brand differentiation strategies.
- Brand equity.
- The strength of the creative message.
- Retailer power.
- Short- versus long-term focus.
- Top-down influences.
- Political sales force influences.
- Historical inertia.
- Ad hoc changes.



While the payout plan is not always perfect, it does guide the manager in establishing the budget. When used in conjunction with the objective and task method, it provides a much more logical approach to budget setting than the top-down approaches previously discussed. Yet on the basis of the studies reported on earlier, payout planning does not seem to be a widely employed method.

**Quantitative Models** Attempts to apply *quantitative models* to budgeting have met with limited success. For the most part, these methods employ **computer simulation models** involving statistical techniques such as multiple regression analysis to determine the relative contribution of the advertising budget to sales. Because of problems associated with these methods, their acceptance has been limited, and quantitative models have yet to reach their potential. As requirements for accountability continue to increase, more sophisticated models may be forthcoming. Specific discussion of these models is beyond the scope of this text, however. Such methods do have merit but may need more refinement before achieving widespread success.

**Summary of Budgeting Methods** There is no universally accepted method of setting a budget figure. Weaknesses in each method may make it unfeasible or inappropriate. As earlier studies have shown, the use of the objective and task method continues to stay high, whereas less sophisticated methods vary in their rates of adoption. More advertisers are also employing the payout planning approach.

In a study of how managers make decisions regarding advertising and promotion budgeting decisions, George Low and Jakki Mohr interviewed 21 managers in eight consumer-product firms. Their research focused on the decision processes and procedures used to set spending levels on the factors that influence the allocation of advertising and promotion dollars.

On the basis of their results (shown in Figure 7–20), the authors concluded that the budget-setting process is still a perplexing issue to many managers and that institutional pressures led to a greater proportion of dollars being spent on sales promotions than managers would have preferred. In addition, the authors concluded that to successfully develop and implement the budget, managers must (1) employ a

**FIGURE 7–21**

U.S. Media Expenditures, 2008–2009

| **PERCENT CHANGE IN MEASURED AD SPENDING** | |
|---|---|
| **MEDIA SECTOR** | **Full Year 2009 vs. 2008** |
| *Television Media* | *−9.5%* |
| ■ Network TV | −7.6 |
| ■ Cable TV | −1.4 |
| ■ Spot TV | −23.7 |
| ■ Spanish-language TV | −8.9 |
| ■ Syndication-National | −4.9 |
| *Magazine Media* | *−17.4* |
| ■ Consumer magazines | −16.6 |
| ■ B-to-B magazines | −26.2 |
| ■ Sunday magazines | −11.0 |
| ■ Local magazines | −27.7 |
| ■ Spanish-language magazines | −21.6 |
| *Newspaper Media* | *−19.7%* |
| ■ Newspapers (local) | −20.0 |
| ■ National newspapers | −17.8 |
| ■ Spanish-language newspapers | −16.4 |
| *Internet (display ads only)* | *7.3* |
| *Radio Media* | *−20.3* |
| ■ Local radio | −20.6 |
| ■ National spot radio | −24.6 |
| ■ Network radio | −8.7 |
| *Outdoor* | *−13.2%* |
| *FSIs* | *3.0%* |
| **TOTAL** | **−12.3%** |

Source: Reprinted with permission from *Advertising Age*. Copyright © 2010 Crain Communications.

comprehensive strategy to guide the process, avoiding the piecemeal approach often employed, (2) develop a strategic planning framework that employs an integrated marketing communications philosophy, (3) build in contingency plans, (4) focus on long-term objectives, and (5) consistently evaluate the effectiveness of programs.[29]

By using these approaches in combination with the percentage-of-sales methods, these advertisers are likely to arrive at a more useful, accurate budget. For example, many firms now start the budgeting process by establishing the objectives they need to accomplish and then limit the budget by applying a percentage-of-sales or another method to decide whether or not it is affordable. Competitors' budgets may also influence this decision.

## Allocating the Budget

Once the budget has been appropriated, the next step is to allocate it. The allocation decision involves determining which markets, products, and/or promotional elements will receive which amounts of the funds appropriated.

**Allocating to IMC Elements** As noted earlier, many advertisers are shifting some of their budget dollars away from traditional advertising media and into sales promotions targeted at both the consumer and the trade. Figure 7–21 shows that for most traditional media, ad spending went down from 2008 to 2009, with radio and some magazines hit the hardest. The only media showing increases during that period were for the Internet (display advertising only) and free standing inserts (FSIs).

Some marketers have also used the allocation decision to stretch their advertising dollar and get more impact from the same amount of money. Companies have taken a number of steps including consolidating and cutting division expenditures, reducing agency fees, producing less campaigns, and relying more on targeted media. As noted earlier, P&G and Coca-Cola have made efforts to become more innovative and efficient as well as allocating significant portions of their budgets from traditional to nontraditional media.

**Client/Agency Policies** Another factor that may influence budget allocation is the individual policy of the company or the advertising agency. The agency may discourage the allocation of monies to sales promotion, preferring to spend them on the advertising area. The agency may take the position that these monies are harder to track in terms of effectiveness and may be used improperly if not under its control. (In many cases commissions are not made on this area, and this fact may contribute to the agency's reluctance.)

The orientation of the agency or the firm may also directly influence where monies are spent. Many ad agencies are managed by officers who have ascended through the creative ranks and are inclined to emphasize the creative budget. Others may have preferences for specific media. For example, some agencies position themselves as experts in nontraditional media and often spend more client money in this medium. Others tend to spend more monies on the Internet. Both the agency and the client may favor certain aspects of the promotional program, perhaps on the basis of past successes, that will substantially influence where dollars are spent.



**Market Size** While the budget should be allocated according to the specific promotional tools needed to accomplish the stated objectives, the *size* of the market will affect the decision. In smaller markets, it is often easier and less expensive to reach the target market. Too much of an expenditure in these markets will lead to saturation and a lack of effective spending. In larger markets, the target group may be more dispersed and thus more expensive to reach. Think about the cost of purchasing media in Chicago or New York City versus a smaller market like Columbus, Ohio, or Birmingham, Alabama. The former would be much more costly and would require a higher budget appropriation.

**Market Potential** For a variety of reasons, some markets hold more potential than others. Marketers of snow skis would find greater returns on their expenditures in Denver, Colorado, than in Fort Lauderdale, Florida. Imported Mexican beers sell better in the border states (Texas, Arizona, California) than in the Midwest. A disproportionate number of imported cars are sold in California and New England. When particular markets hold higher potential, the marketing manager may decide to allocate additional monies to them. (Keep in mind that just because a market does not have high sales does not mean it should be ignored. The key is *potential*—and a market with low sales but high potential may be a candidate for additional appropriations.)

**Market Share Goals** Two studies in the *Harvard Business Review* discussed advertising spending with the goal of maintaining and increasing market share.[30] John Jones compared the brand's share of market with its share of advertising voice (the total value of the main media exposure in the product category). Jones classified the brands as "profit taking brands, or underspenders" and "investment brands, those whose share of voice is clearly above their share of market." His study indicated that for those brands with small market shares, profit takers are in the minority; however, as the brands increase their market share, nearly three out of five have a proportionately smaller share of voice.

Jones noted that three factors can be cited to explain this change. First, new brands generally receive higher-than-average advertising support. Second, older, more mature brands are often "milked"—that is, when they reach the maturity

**FIGURE 7–22**

The Share of Voice (SOV) Effect and Ad Spending: Priorities in Individual Markets

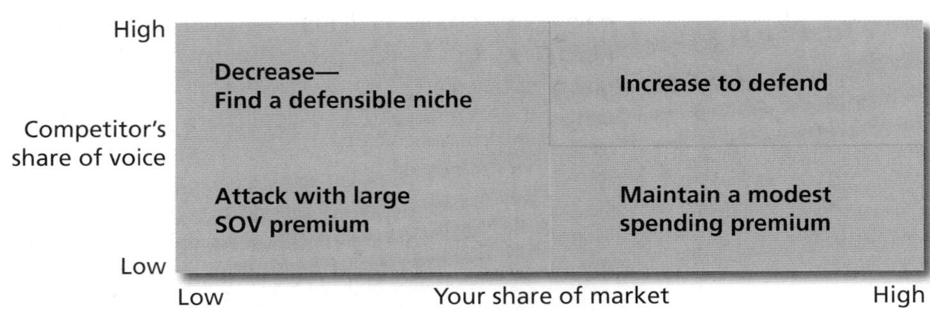


stage, advertising support is reduced. Third, there's an advertising economy of scale whereby advertising works harder for well-established brands, so a lower expenditure is required. Jones concluded that for larger brands, it may be possible to reduce advertising expenditures and still maintain market share. Smaller brands, on the other hand, have to continue to maintain a large share of voice.

James Schroer addressed the advertising budget in a situation where the marketer wishes to increase market share. His analysis suggests that marketers should:

- Segment markets, focusing on those markets where competition is weak and/or underspending instead of on a national advertising effort.
- Determine their competitors' cost positions (how long the competition can continue to spend at the current or increased rate).
- Resist the lure of short-term profits that result from ad budget cuts.
- Consider niching strategies as opposed to long-term wars.

Figure 7–22 shows Schroer's suggestions for spending priorities in various markets.

**Economies of Scale in Advertising** Some studies have presented evidence that firms and/or brands maintaining a large share of the market have an advantage over smaller competitors and thus can spend less money on advertising and realize a better return.[31] Larger advertisers can maintain advertising shares that are smaller than their market shares because they get better advertising rates, have declining average costs of production, and accrue the advantages of advertising several products jointly. In addition, they are likely to enjoy more favorable time and space positions, cooperation of middlepeople, and favorable publicity. These advantages are known as **economies of scale**.

Reviewing the studies in support of this position and then conducting research over a variety of small package products, Kent Lancaster found that this situation did not hold true and that in fact larger brand share products might actually be at a disadvantage.[32] His results indicated that leading brands spend an average of 2.5 percentage points more than their brand share on advertising. More specifically, his study concluded:

1. There is no evidence that larger firms can support their brands with lower relative advertising costs than smaller firms.
2. There is no evidence that the leading brand in a product group enjoys lower advertising costs per sales dollar than do other brands.
3. There is no evidence of a static relationship between advertising costs per dollar of sales and the size of the advertiser.

The results of this and other studies suggest there really are no economies of scale to be accrued from the size of the firm or the market share of the brand.[33]

**Organizational Characteristics** In a review of the literature on how allocation decisions are made between advertising and sales promotion, George Low and Jakki Mohr concluded that organizational factors play an important role in determining how communications dollars are spent.[34] The authors note that the following factors influence the allocation decision. These factors vary from one organization to another, and each influences the relative amounts assigned to advertising and promotion:

- The organization's structure—centralized versus decentralized, formalization, and complexity.
- Power and politics in the organizational hierarchy.
- The use of expert opinions (for example, consultants).
- Characteristics of the decision maker (preferences and experience).
- Approval and negotiation channels.
- Pressure on senior managers to arrive at the optimal budget.

One example of how these factors might influence allocations relates to the level of interaction between marketing and other functional departments, such as accounting and operations. The authors note that the relative importance of advertising versus sales promotion might vary from department to department. Accountants, being dollars-and-cents minded, would argue for the sales impact of promotions, while operations would argue against sales promotions because the sudden surges in demand that might result would throw off production schedules. The marketing department might be influenced by the thinking of either of these groups in making its decision.

The use of outside consultants to provide expert opinions might also affect the allocation decision. Trade journals, academic journals, and even books might also be valuable inputs into the decision maker's thinking. In sum, it seems obvious that many factors must be taken into account in the budget allocation decision. Market size and potential, specific objectives sought, and previous company and/or agency policies and preferences all influence this decision.

## Summary

This chapter has examined the role of objectives in the planning and evaluation of the IMC program and how firms budget in an attempt to achieve these objectives. Specific objectives are needed to guide the development of the promotional program, as well as to provide a benchmark against which performance can be measured and evaluated. Objectives serve important functions as communications devices, as a guide to planning the IMC program and deciding on various alternatives, and for measurement and evaluation.

Objectives for IMC evolve from the organization's overall marketing plan and are based on the roles various promotional mix elements play in the marketing program. Many managers use sales or a related measure such as market share as the basis for setting objectives. However, many promotional planners believe the role of advertising and other promotional mix elements is to communicate because of the various problems associated with sales-based objectives. They use communications-based objectives like those in the response hierarchy as the basis for setting goals.

Much of the emphasis in setting objectives has been on traditional advertising-based views of marketing communications. However, many companies are moving toward zero-based communications planning, which focuses on what tasks need to be done, which marketing communication functions should be used, and to what extent. Many of the principles used in setting advertising objectives can be applied to other elements in the promotional mix.

As you have probably concluded, the budget decision is not typically based on supporting experiences or strong theoretical foundations. Nor is it one of the more soundly established elements of the promotional program. The budgeting methods used now have some major problems. Economic models are limited, often try to demonstrate the effects on sales directly, and ignore other elements of the marketing mix. Some of the methods discussed have no theoretical basis and ignore the roles advertising and promotion are meant to perform.

One possible way to improve the budget appropriation is to tie the measures of effectiveness to communications objectives rather than to the broader-based marketing objectives. Using the objective and task approach with communications objectives may not be the ultimate solution to the budgeting problem, but it is an improvement over the top-down methods. Marketers often find it advantageous to employ a combination of methods.

As with determining the budget, managers must consider a number of factors when allocating advertising and promotions dollars. Market size and potential, agency policies, and the preferences of management itself may influence the allocation decision.

## Key Terms

**marketing objectives** p. 218
**integrated marketing communications objectives** p. 219
**carryover effect** p. 220
**DAGMAR** p. 226
**communications task** p. 226
**benchmark measures** p. 227
**zero-based communications planning** p. 230
**contribution margin** p. 233
**marginal analysis** p. 235
**concave-downward function model** p. 236
**S-shaped response curve** p. 236
**top-down approaches** p. 238
**affordable method** p. 238
**arbitrary allocation** p. 239
**percentage-of-sales method** p. 240
**clipping service** p. 243
**competitive parity method** p. 243
**ROI budgeting method** p. 245
**objective and task method** p. 246
**buildup approach** p. 246
**payout plan** p. 247
**computer simulation models** p. 249
**economies of scale** p. 252

## Discussion Questions

1. Why is it important for marketers to set specific objectives for advertising and promotion: What criteria must these objectives meet to be valid? (LO1)
2. What are some of the problems associated with setting communications objectives? How can marketers overcome these problems? Cite examples. (LO4)
3. What are the values associated with setting objectives for IMC? How can marketers improve their communications programs by establishing specific objectives? (LO1)
4. What are the two key issues that marketers must make in regard to budgeting? Explain the differences, and give examples of each. (LO5)
5. Explain the S-shaped response curve and the concave downward curve as they relate to budget setting. What are the differences in these two curves? Give examples of how each might be more appropriate for different products. (LO6)
6. There have always been attempts to directly measure the effects of advertising on sales. At the same time, there are many who believe that this is rarely possible. Why is it so difficult to establish a relationship between advertising and sales? (LO3)
7. Explain the difference between the S-shaped response model and the rapidly diminishing returns model. Some believe that the former of these may be best suited for low involvement products, and the latter for high involvement products. Do you agree or disagree with this position? Explain. (LO6)
8. Hierarchy of effects models have been adopted by a number of firms (though sometimes under different titles, for example, funnel models). Discuss the value of using hierarchy of effects models for establishing communications objectives. Are there any weaknesses associated with these models? (LO4)
9. In periods of downturns in the economy, many companies slash their advertising and promotions budgets. Explain why this is not always the best strategy to pursue. (LO7)
10. As noted in the chapter, there is an increased emphasis on the determination of ROI. Discuss some of the reasons leading to this increase in attention. Why is it so difficult to measure ROI? (LO7)

## AdForum Exercise: Using Advertising to Move Consumers through the Purchase Funnel to Set Objectives

adforum.com

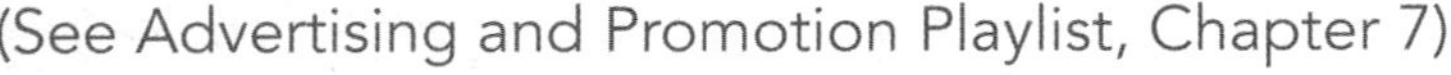


As discussed in the chapter, many companies use purchase funnels to guide their communications objectives. The playlist for Chapter 7 includes a variety of commercials. Review these commercials and answer the following questions:

1 What goal do you think this commercial is attempting to achieve?

2 At what stage of the consumer funnel do you think each commercial will be most likely to be effective? Explain your answer.

3 Do you think the commercial is attempting to achieve communications or sales oriented goals, or both? Explain your answer.

Access to the chapter playlist is available through 

, www.mcgrawhillconnect.com

## LEARNING OBJECTIVES

LO1 To discuss what is meant by advertising creativity and examine the role of creative strategy in advertising.

LO2 To consider the process that guides the creation of advertising messages and the research inputs into the stages of the creative process.

LO3 To examine creative strategy development and the roles of various client and agency personnel involved in it.

LO4 To examine various approaches used for determining major selling ideas that form the basis of an advertising campaign.

# 8 Creative Strategy: Planning and Development

## CREATIVE ADVERTISING REJUVENATES OLD SPICE

For generations, young men would bathe or shower using a bar of soap such as Ivory, Safeguard, Zest, Irish Spring, Coast, or one of many other brands. However, over the past seven years the body cleansing category has been changing dramatically, as males who were heavy users of bar soap have been converting to body washes. Young men who were once pouf-averse, and preferred to use traditional bar soaps that sell at lower price points, have become increasingly willing to experiment with more involved shower products and many have switched to body washes with more complex, benefit-driven features.

Procter & Gamble was one of the first major U.S. brands to enter the body-wash market when it launched its Old Spice Hair & Body wash products in 2003. Old Spice was a prominent brand of male grooming products marketed by the Shulton Company since 1938 using a nautical theme and sailing ships as its trademark. P&G purchased Old Spice from Shulton in 1990 and slowly began repositioning the venerable brand toward the 13- to 34-year old male market. P&G launched a number of new products under the Old Spice brand that became market leaders, such as its men's deodorant line which is the market leader in the United States. However, the company has been facing stiff competition from Unilever's Axe brand which had been a market leader in Europe and Latin America before entering the U.S. market in 2003. Over a span of several years, Axe launched a number of grooming and body-wash products that were supported with irreverent and often risqué ads filled with sexy women and suggestive taglines.

In 2006 P&G decided to switch advertising agencies and named Wieden + Kennedy as its global agency for the Old Spice brand. One of the reasons P&G cited for moving its account to W+K was the agency's impressive brand-building track record, particularly with brands targeted to men such as Nike and ESPN. After taking over the Old Spice account, W+K conducted focus groups and quantitative market research studies which revealed that the target 13- to 34-year old males were confused by the array of body cleansing products on the store shelves and were hesitant to spend much time sorting through the options, most of which they described as too complicated, overly feminine, or just "not for me." The research also revealed that although Old Spice Hair & Body Wash had been on the market for several years, most young men were not aware of the brand. Armed with this information W+K set out to position Old Spice as a simple, manly choice for no-nonsense guys in the increasingly complicated body product category.

To bring the new positioning strategy to life W+K set out to find the big idea on which the advertising creative strategy and execution could be built. The creative team recognized that rather than trying to move away from the image of Old Spice as a grandfatherly brand, its heritage and inherent knowledge of all things manly were assets that could be embraced and used to position it as "helping guys navigate the seas of manhood." One of the first campaigns W+K developed for Old Spice Hair & Body products used humor to celebrate the diversity of men and their ability to grow hair in strange and wondrous places. Dozens of "hair archetypes," each highlighting a different hair and body combination, were created and a print and digital campaign was developed to illustrate them and encourage young men to visit a website (oshairbodymetrics.com). Once there, they could use an interactive, pseudo-scientific tool to depict their current hair situation and analyze their hair/body profile. The TV commercials developed for the campaign spoofed pharmaceutical ads such as those for male enhancement drugs and used humor to deliver the message that Old Spice Hair & Body Wash works for all types of men, with all types of hair. The "Is Old Spice Hair & Body Wash Right for Me?" campaign launched in early 2008 and helped increase sales by 70 percent from the previous year in the first few months. It also won a 2009 Silver Effie, one of the awards given each year to the most effective advertising and marketing communication campaigns.

In early 2010 Wieden + Kennedy developed another highly popular creative campaign for Old Spice After Hours, one of the many brands in the product line, that has struck a responsive chord with consumers. The campaign is built around a commercial that has become known as "The man your man could smell like" and stars Isaiah Mustafa a former NFL wide receiver and obscure, but suave, actor who has a magnetic presence to go along with his six-pack abs. The spot, which is a Cannes Lions Grand Prix award winner, opens with him stepping out of the shower with a towel around his waist brandishing a bottle of Old Spice body wash and saying: "Hello ladies, look at your man. Now back to me. Now back at your man. Now back to me. Sadly it isn't me. But if he stopped using lady-scented body wash and switched to Old Spice, he could smell like me." The 30-second spot goes on to show Mustafa on a boat wielding an oyster filled with "tickets to that thing you like" as it changes to a handful of diamonds. The commercial ends with the camera pulling back revealing the shirtless Mustafa on horseback as he redundantly says what has become the signature line from the spot: "I'm on a horse."

The brand manager for Old Spice, James Moorhead, notes that the brand hadn't really targeted women directly in recent memory so the goal of the spot was to find a way to reach out to them through an ad that men and women would enjoy together. The ad ran in theaters on Valentine's Day and before airing on television was released to Old Spice's Facebook page where a quarter of the fans are female. Within two months of its launch, the "smell like a man" spot became a viral sensation on the Internet as it logged more than 8 million hits on YouTube making it one of the most watched videos on the site. It also generated over 7,000 comments on Old Spice's Facebook page. The commercial also became a public relations bonanza for Old Spice as Mustafa appeared on numerous talk shows including the *Ellen DeGeneres Show* and *Oprah* and also has made the rounds on all the major morning news shows.

W+K is building an integrated campaign around the spot that includes a Web application on its Facebook page called "My Perpetual Love" which includes a video where Mustafa offers men the opportunity to be more like him by e-mailing their females and tweeting them a continual string of humorous virtual love notes. Procter & Gamble plans to develop additional humorous commercials featuring Mustafa, although they also will monitor whether the popularity of the campaign translates into sales for Old Spice body wash. However, brand manager Moorhead notes that the P&G feels that the new campaign has tremendous potential and is going to lead to strong business results as the humor is a great way to spark interest and create a deeper connection with the brand.

Sources; Jack Neff, "Meet the Man Your Man Could Smell Like," *Advertising Age,* March 29, 2010, pp. 2, 3; Barbara Lipert, "Man, This Man Can Sell," *Adweek,* March 1, 2010, p. 9; Jack Neff, "How Body Wash Finally Beat the Bar in Battle of the Bathing Products," *Advertising Age,* February 15, 2010, p. 9; "Is Old Spice Hair & Body Wash Right for Me?" 2009 Silver Effie Winner, Effie Awards Showcase, http://www.effie.org/winners/showcase/2009/328.

One of the most important components of an integrated marketing communications program is the advertising message. While the fundamental role of an advertising message is to communicate information, it does much more. The commercials we watch on TV or hear on radio, the print ads we see in magazines and newspapers, and the banner ads and other forms of advertising on the Internet are a source of entertainment, motivation, fascination, fantasy, and sometimes irritation as well as information. Ads and commercials appeal to, and often create or shape, consumers' problems, desires, and goals. From the marketer's perspective, the advertising message is a way to tell consumers how the product or service can solve a problem or help satisfy desires or achieve goals. Advertising can also be used to create images

JOY IS IN GOOD COMPANY.
JOY IS THE BMW 3 SERIES COUPE AND CONVERTIBLE.
BMW EfficientDynamics

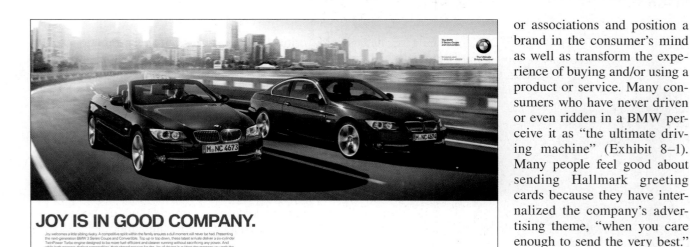

**EXHIBIT 8–1**
Excellent advertising helps create an image for BMW automobiles as "the ultimate driving machine"

or associations and position a brand in the consumer's mind as well as transform the experience of buying and/or using a product or service. Many consumers who have never driven or even ridden in a BMW perceive it as "the ultimate driving machine" (Exhibit 8–1). Many people feel good about sending Hallmark greeting cards because they have internalized the company's advertising theme, "when you care enough to send the very best."

One need only watch an evening of commercials or peruse a few magazines to realize there are a myriad of ways to convey an advertising message. Underlying all of these messages, however, are a **creative strategy** that determines what the advertising message will say or communicate and **creative tactics** for how the message strategy will be executed. In this chapter, we focus on advertising creative strategy. We consider what is meant by creativity, particularly as it relates to advertising, and examine a well-known approach to creativity in advertising.



We also examine the creative strategy development process and various approaches to determining the *big idea* that will be used as the central theme of the advertising campaign and translated into attention-getting, distinctive, and memorable messages. Creative specialists are finding it more and more difficult to come up with big ideas that will break through the clutter and still satisfy the concerns of their risk-averse clients. Yet their clients are continually challenging them to find the creative message that will strike a responsive chord with their target audience.

Some of you may not be directly involved in the design and creation of ads; you may choose to work in another agency department or on the client side of the business. However, because creative strategy is often so crucial to the success of the firm's IMC effort, everyone involved in the promotional process should understand the creative strategy and tactics that underlie the development of advertising campaigns and messages, as well as the creative options available to the advertiser. Also, individuals on the client side as well as agency people outside the creative department must work with the creative specialists in developing the advertising campaign, implementing it, and evaluating its effectiveness. Thus, marketing and product managers, account representatives, researchers, and media personnel must appreciate the creative process and develop a productive relationship with creative personnel.

## THE IMPORTANCE OF CREATIVITY IN ADVERTISING

For many students, as well as many advertising and marketing practitioners, the most interesting aspect of advertising is the creative side. We have all at one time or another been intrigued by an ad and admired the creative insight that went into it. A great ad is a joy to behold and often an epic to create, as the cost of producing a TV commercial can exceed $1 million. Many companies see this as money well spent. They realize that the manner in which the advertising message is developed

**EXHIBIT 8–2**
Advertising for Altoids won creative awards but did not increase sales

and executed is often critical to the success of the promotional program, which in turn can influence the effectiveness of the entire marketing program. Major advertisers such as Procter & Gamble, Verizon, AT&T, Unilever, Ford Motor Co., Nike, McDonald's, Coca-Cola, and many other companies spend millions of dollars each year to develop advertising messages that will win the hearts and minds of consumers. They also spend hundreds of millions of dollars more to purchase media time and space to run these messages. While these companies make excellent products, they realize creative advertising is also an important part of their marketing success.

Good creative strategy and execution can often be central to determining the success of a product or service or reversing the fortunes of a struggling brand. Conversely, an advertising campaign that is poorly conceived or executed can be a liability. Many companies have solid marketing and promotional plans and spend substantial amounts of money on advertising, yet have difficulty coming up with a creative campaign that will differentiate them from their competitors. However, just because an ad or commercial is creative or popular does not mean it will increase sales or revive a declining brand. Many ads have won awards for creativity but failed to increase sales. In some instances, the failure to generate sales has cost the agency the account. For example, many advertising people believe some of the best ads of all time were those done for Alka-Seltzer in the 1960s and 70s, including the classic "Mama Mia! That's a spicy meatball!" and "I can't believe I ate the whole thing." While the commercials won numerous creative awards, Alka-Seltzer sales still declined and the agencies lost the account.[1] More recently, the Leo Burnett agency handled the advertising for Altoids breath mints for 13 years and the "Curiously Strong" campaign they created for the brand won numerous creative awards (Exhibit 8–2). However, Altoids sales declined and the brand lost its position as the market leader in the breath-freshener category, which led to the decision by the Wm. Wrigley Jr. Co. to change agencies and move to a new creative approach.[2]

Many advertising and marketing people have become ambivalent toward, and in some cases even critical of, advertising awards.[3] They argue that agency creative people are often more concerned with creating ads that win awards than ones that sell their clients' products. Other advertising people believe awards are a good way to recognize creativity that often does result in effective advertising. Global Perspective 8–1 discusses how the emphasis on creative awards has shifted to the international arena with awards like the Cannes Lions.

As we saw in Chapter 7, the success of an ad campaign cannot always be judged in terms of sales. However, many advertising and marketing personnel, particularly those on the client side, believe advertising must ultimately lead the consumer to purchase the product or service. Finding a balance between creative advertising and effective advertising is difficult. To better understand this dilemma, we turn to the issue of creativity and its role in advertising.

# ADVERTISING CREATIVITY

## What Is Creativity?

*Creativity* is probably one of the most commonly used terms in advertising. Ads are often called creative. The people who develop ads and commercials are known as creative types. And advertising agencies develop reputations for their creativity. Perhaps so much attention is focused on the concept of creativity because many people view the specific challenge given to those who develop an advertising message as being creative. It is their job to turn all of the information regarding product features and benefits, marketing plans, consumer research, and communication objectives into a creative concept that will bring the advertising message to life. This begs the question: What is meant by *creativity* in advertising?

## Different Perspectives on Advertising Creativity

Perspectives on what constitutes creativity in advertising differ. At one extreme are people who argue that advertising is creative only if it sells the product. An advertising message's or campaign's impact on sales counts more than whether it is innovative or wins awards. At the other end of the continuum are those who judge the creativity of an ad in terms of its artistic or aesthetic value and originality. They contend creative ads can break through the competitive clutter, grab the consumer's attention, and have some impact.

As you might expect, perspectives on advertising creativity often depend on one's role. A study by Elizabeth Hirschman examined the perceptions of various individuals involved in the creation and production of TV commercials, including management types (brand managers and account executives) and creatives (art director, copywriter, commercial director, and producer).[4] She found that product managers and account executives view ads as promotional tools whose primary purpose is to communicate favorable impressions to the marketplace. They believe a commercial should be evaluated in terms of whether it fulfills the client's marketing and communicative objectives. The perspective of those on the creative side was much more self-serving, as Hirschman noted:

> In direct contrast to this client orientation, the art director, copywriter, and commercial director viewed the advertisement as a communication vehicle for promoting their own aesthetic viewpoints and personal career objectives. Both the copywriter and art director made this point explicitly, noting that a desirable commercial from their standpoint was one which communicated their unique creative talents and thereby permitted them to obtain "better" jobs at an increased salary.[5]

In her interviews, Hirschman also found that brand managers were much more risk-averse and wanted a more conservative commercial than the creative people, who wanted to maximize the impact of the message.

What constitutes creativity in advertising is probably somewhere between the two extremes. To break through the clutter and make an impression on the target audience, an ad often must be unique and entertaining. As noted in Chapter 5, research has shown that a major determinant of whether a commercial will be successful in changing brand preferences is its "likability," or the viewer's overall reaction.[6] TV commercials and print ads that are well designed and executed and generate emotional responses can create positive feelings that are transferred to the product or service being advertised. Many creative people believe this type of advertising can come about only if they are given considerable latitude in developing advertising messages. But ads that are creative only for the sake of being creative often fail to communicate a relevant or meaningful message that will lead consumers to purchase the product or service.

Everyone involved in planning and developing an advertising campaign must understand the importance of balancing the "it's not creative unless it sells" perspective with the novelty/uniqueness and impact position. Marketing and brand managers or account executives must recognize that imposing too many sales- and marketing-oriented communications objectives on the creative team can result in mediocre advertising, which is often ineffective in today's competitive, cluttered media environment. At the same time, the creative specialists must recognize that the goal of advertising is to assist in selling the product or service and good advertising must communicate in a manner that helps the client achieve this goal.

# Global Perspective 8–1 > > >

## Cannes Festival—The Olympic Games of Advertising

For many years the most coveted prize for creativity in advertising was a Clio award. However, the Clios lost much of their prestige after financial problems resulted in cancellation of the 1992 awards ceremony. And although the Clio Festival is becoming an increasingly popular awards competition, the Clios have not quite regained their former status as the advertising industry's premier award for creative excellence. There are a number of other popular and well-recognized U.S.-based advertising award competitions that recognize outstanding creative work. These include the Kelley Awards given by the Magazine Publishers of America, the Effies, which were founded by the New York chapter of the American Marketing Association, but recently assigned the rights to a new entity named Effie Worldwide, and the Creative Excellence in Business Advertising (CEBA) Awards which are sponsored by American Business Media.

While these contests remain very popular in the United States, on a global level the Cannes Lions International Advertising Festival is now widely considered the most prestigious advertising award competition. Inspired by the movie industry's more famous Cannes Film Festival, the Cannes Lions is considered by many to be the "Olympics of Advertising." The Cannes competition receives entries from agencies around the world hoping to win Lions (the name of the awards) in each of the major categories—film (television, cinema and Web film ads), press and poster (print and outdoor ads), Cyber (online marketing and ads for websites) advertising, media planning/buying, and direct marketing. The competition recently added several new awards—the Titanium Lion, which is given for innovative work across integrated media, along with the Radio Lion and Public Relations Lion.

While the awards given each year at the Cannes ad festival receive a great deal of attention, the annual meeting on the French Riviera has also become an important forum where many of the world's largest advertisers and agencies meet to discuss the future of advertising and integrated marketing communications. During the 2009 meeting, senior executives from top agencies and corporations discussed issues such as the increasing importance of digital media, the future role of television advertising, the impact of the global recession, and client/agency relationships.

The awards given each year at the festival also provide insight into the changing world of marketing communications. For example, in 2009 the top awards were given to campaigns that engage consumers in ways other than through traditional media advertising. The Grand Prix award, which is the highest award given at the world's largest and most revered advertising competition, was given to an interactive film produced for the Philips Electronics new movie theater–proportioned 21:9 LCD television by the agency Tribal DDB, Amsterdam. The 2 minute and 19 second film, which is shown through a special website created for the new product, was shot in one continuous tracking shot, and offers an exploration into the world of movies, seeing the cinema screen

## Determinants of Creativity

**Advertising creativity** is the ability to generate fresh, unique, and appropriate or relevant ideas that can be used as solutions to communication problems. Those who study as well as work in advertising generally agree on these two central determinants of creativity which are often viewed in terms of divergence and relevance.[7] **Divergence** refers to the extent to which an ad contains elements that are novel, different, or unusual. Robert Smith and his colleagues have identified five factors that could account for the ways divergence can be achieved in advertising, which they describe as follows[8]:

1. *Originality* Ads that contain elements that are rare, surprising, or move away from the obvious and commonplace.
2. *Flexibility* Ads that contain different ideas or switch from one perspective to another.
3. *Elaboration* Ads that contain unexpected details or finish and extend basic ideas so they become more intricate, complicated, or sophisticated.
4. *Synthesis* Ads that combine, connect, or blend normally unrelated objects or ideas.
5. *Artistic value* Ads that contain artistic verbal impressions or attractive shapes and colors

The second major determinant of creativity is **relevance** which reflects the degree to which the various elements of the ad are meaningful, useful, or valuable to the through the eyes of the director and the special effects and lighting experts. During playback of the movie, viewers have interactive touch points in which they can access additional content and feature demonstrations.

Another big winner at the 2009 competition was the Obama for America 2008 presidential campaign which won both the Titanium award for work across integrated media as well as the top award in the Integrated category. The campaign was recognized for its digital-savvy, grass-roots success in community building and its willingness to allow the Obama brand message to be created by consumers rather than traditional top-down political mandates. The award was given to the GMMB agency along with David Plouffe who was the campaign manager for the Obama/Biden presidential bid. The Obama campaign was the first high-level political campaign to use social media such as YouTube, Twitter, Facebook, MySpace, LinkedIn and numerous other Web 2.0 tools, in order to bypass traditional media and meet and inform potential voters on their own turf and connect directly with supporters. Cannes juror Richard Silverstein, of the Goodby, Silverstein & Partners agency, has noted that "There will never be a political campaign that doesn't use what they started."

The Grand Prix award for film at the 2010 Cannes Lions International Advertising Festival was awarded to the Old Spice "Man Your Man Could Smell Like" commercial discussed in the chapter opener. The President of the Cannes jury noted that the commercial showed "the power of creativity to ignite a sleeping giant." The Portland office of Wieden + Kennedy, which created the Old Spice commercial, also won two other Grand Prix awards for Nike in the cyber and integrated categories. W+K's award in the integrated category was for Nike's "Chalkbot" campaign which was developed to help promote Lance Armstrong's Livestrong foundation's fight against cancer and included events, outdoor, online, and web films.

Sources: Laurel Wentz, "Old Spice's Manly Body Wash TV Spot Takes Film Grand Prix," *Advertising Age*, June 26, 2010, http://adage.com/print?article_id=144688; ______________, "Cannes Swept by PR, Integrated, Internet Winners," *Advertising Age*, June 29, 2009, http://adage.com/print?article_id+137630; Matthew Creamer, "Yes We Cannes: Obama Campaign Takes Titanium and Integrated Grand Prix," *Advertising Age*, June 27, 2009, http://adage.com/print?article_id+1376333.

consumer.[9] Smith et al. suggest that relevance can be achieved in two ways. *Ad-to-consumer relevance* refers to situations where the ad contains execution elements that are meaningful to consumers. For example, advertisers may use celebrities with whom consumers identify with, music that they like, or visual images and other execution techniques that capture their interest and attention. *Brand-to-consumer relevance* refers to situations where the advertised brand of a product or service is of personal interest to consumers. Relevance or appropriateness can also be viewed in terms of the degree to which an advertisement provides information or an image that is pertinent to the brand. Ads for many products such as fashionable clothing, jewelry, cosmetics, and liquor often rely on visual images to deliver their message rather than providing specific product information. However, these images are important to consumers in forming impressions and attitudes toward these brands and deciding whether to selection one brand over another.

The ad for Absolut vodka shown in Exhibit 8–3 is a good example of a creative advertising that relies primarily on thought-provoking imagery. The ad is part of the integrated global campaign which uses the tagline "In an Absolut World" and plays off of the brand name to illustrate a whimsical, imagined world where everything is as ideal as Absolut vodka.[10] This particular ad features New York's Times Square adorned with famous works of art rather than billboards and is designed to show media clutter as a means to share the world's artistic treasures. The creative strategy calls for the advertising and other components of the IMC program to be inspiring,

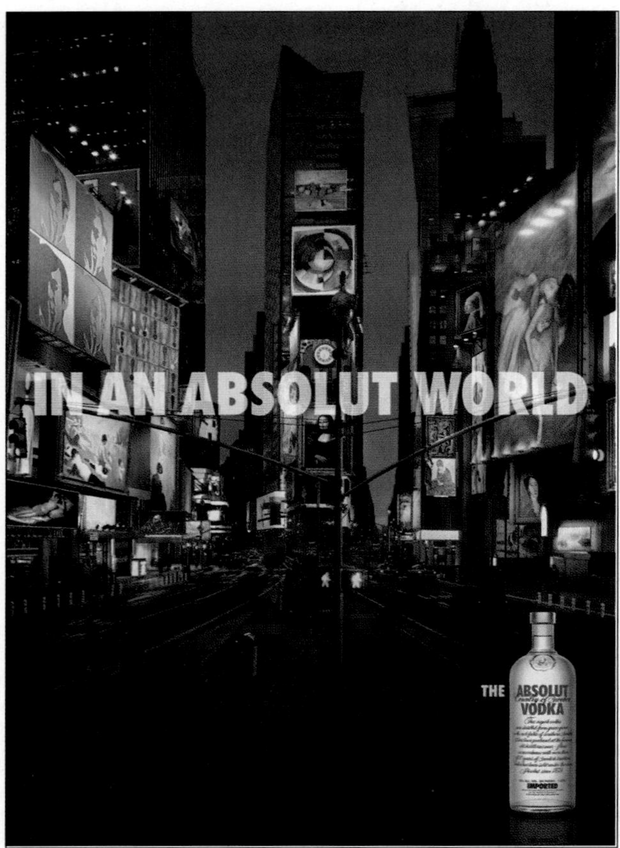


**EXHIBIT 8–3**
Creative advertising has helped make Absolut vodka an iconic brand

humorous, and thought-provoking by encouraging consumers to think about what an Absolut world might look like, as well as to challenge them to reflect on their own visions of the world. Absolut is a brand that views itself as being on the leading edge of popular culture and the ultimate goal of the campaign is to maintain the brand as a cultural icon.

A number of studies have been conducted showing that advertising creativity impacts consumers' responses to advertising messages across various stages of the response hierarchy including cognitive, affective, and behavioral responses.[11] For example, advertising that is more novel has been shown to require consumer processing time, resulting in longer exposure and greater attention. Studies have also shown that creative ads draw more attention to the advertised brand, higher levels of recall, greater motivation to process the information, and deeper levels of processing.[12] In addition to these cognitive outcomes, studies have also shown that creative advertising positively impacts emotional reactions including attitudes and purchase intentions.[13] Several of these studies have shown that novelty in terms of divergence is a particularly important component of advertising creativity. However, clients often favor relevance over divergence as they want their agencies to create ads that communicate pertinent information such as specific product features and benefits. Smith and his colleagues suggest that clients should be less resistant to divergent approaches and note that there is a fundamental need for divergent thinkers in the ad development process.[14] Considering that most advertising messages are seen and/or heard in a very cluttered media environment where marketers must compete for the attention of consumers, it is important that attention be given to creating ads that are novel and divergent as well as relevant and meaningful.

Those who work in agencies, particularly in the creative departments, recognize the importance of developing advertising messages that are novel and unique but still communicate relevant information to the target audience. Figure 8–1 shows the guidelines for developing creative advertising that the former D'Arcy Masius Benton & Bowles agency developed to guide its creative efforts and help achieve superior creative work. The agency views a creative advertising message as one that is built around a core or power idea (which will be discussed later in this chapter) and uses excellent design and execution to communicate information that is relevant to the target audience. The agency used these principles to develop outstanding creative work for clients such as Procter & Gamble's Charmin and Pampers brands, Norelco, Budweiser, and many other popular brands. The agency was integrated into the Publicis Groupe in 2002 but these Universal Advertising Standards are still used by the various agencies that are part of the Publicis's agency family.

# PLANNING CREATIVE STRATEGY

## The Creative Challenge

Those who work on the creative side of advertising often face a real challenge. They must take all the research, creative briefs, strategy statements, communications objectives, and other input and transform them into an advertising message. Their job is to write copy, design layouts and illustrations, or produce commercials that

**FIGURE 8–1**

D'Arcy Masius Benton & Bowles's Universal Advertising Standards

Source: Reprinted with permission.

1. *Does this advertising position the product simply and with unmistakable clarity?*

   The target audience for the advertised product or service must be able to see and sense in a flash *what* the product is for, *whom* it is for, and *why* they should be interested in it.

   Creating this clear vision of how the product or service fits into their lives is the first job of advertising. Without a simple, clear, focused positioning, no creative work can begin.

2. *Does this advertising bolt the brand to a clinching benefit?*

   Our advertising should be built on the most compelling and persuasive consumer benefit—not some unique-but-insignificant peripheral feature.

   Before you worry about how to say it, you must be sure you are saying *the right thing.* If you don't know what the most compelling benefit is, you've got to find out before you do anything else.

3. *Does this advertising contain a Power Idea?*

   The Power Idea is the vehicle that transforms the strategy into a dynamic, creative communications concept. It is the core creative idea that sets the stage for brilliant executions to come. The ideal Power Idea should:

   - Be describable in a simple word, phrase, or sentence without reference to any final execution.
   - Be likely to attract the prospect's attention.
   - Revolve around the clinching benefit.
   - Allow you to brand the advertising.
   - Make it easy for the prospect to vividly experience our client's product or service.

4. *Does this advertising design in Brand Personality?*

   The great brands tend to have something in common: the extra edge of having a Brand Personality. This is something beyond merely identifying what the brand does for the consumer; all brands *do* something, but the great brands also *are* something.

   A brand can be whatever its designers want it to be—and it can be so from day one.

5. *Is this advertising unexpected?*

   Why should our clients pay good money to wind up with advertising that looks and sounds like everybody else's in the category? They shouldn't.

   We must dare to be different, because sameness is suicide. We can't be outstanding unless we first stand out.

   The thing is not to *emulate* the competition but to *annihilate* them.

6. *Is this advertising single-minded?*

   If you have determined the right thing to say and have created a way to say it uncommonly well, why waste time saying anything else?

   If we want people to remember one big thing from a given piece of advertising, let's not make it more difficult than it already is in an overcommunicated world.

   The advertising should be all about that one big thing.

7. *Does this advertising reward the prospect?*

   Let's give our audience something that makes it easy—even pleasurable—for our message to penetrate: a tear, a smile, a laugh. An emotional stimulus is that special something that makes them want to see the advertising again and again.

8. *Is this advertising visually arresting?*

   Great advertising you remember—and can play back in your mind—is unusual to look at: compelling, riveting, a nourishing feast for the eyes. If you need a reason to strive for arresting work, go no further than Webster: "Catching or holding the attention, thought, or feelings. Gripping. Striking. Interesting."

9. *Does this advertising exhibit painstaking craftsmanship?*

   You want writing that is really written. Visuals that are designed. Music that is composed.

   Lighting, casting, wardrobe, direction—all the components of the art of advertising are every bit as important as the science of it. It is a sin to nickel-and-dime a great advertising idea to death.

   Why settle for good, when there's great? We should go for the absolute best in concept, design, and execution.

   This is our craft—the work should sparkle.

   "Our creative standards are not a gimmick. They're not even revolutionary. Instead, they are an explicit articulation of a fundamental refocusing on our company's only reason for being.

   "D'Arcy's universal advertising standards are the operating link between our vision today—and its coming reality."

effectively communicate the central theme on which the campaign is based. Rather than simply stating the features or benefits of a product or service, they must put the advertising message into a form that will engage the audience's interest and make the ads memorable.[15]

The job of the creative team is challenging because every marketing situation is different and each campaign or advertisement may require a different creative approach. Numerous guidelines have been developed for creating effective advertising,[16] but there is no magic formula. As copywriter Hank Sneiden notes in his book *Advertising Pure and Simple:*

> Rules lead to dull stereotyped advertising, and they stifle creativity, inspiration, initiative, and progress. The only hard and fast rule that I know of in advertising is that there are no rules. No formulas. No right way. Given the same problem, a dozen creative talents would solve it a dozen different ways. If there were a sure-fire formula for successful advertising, everyone would use it. Then there'd be no need for creative people. We would simply program robots to create our ads and commercials and they'd sell loads of product—to other robots.[17]

## Taking Creative Risks

Many creative people follow proven formulas when creating ads because they are safe. Clients often feel uncomfortable with advertising that is too different. Bill Tragos, former chair of TBWA, the advertising agency noted for its excellent creative work for Absolut vodka, Evian, and many other clients, says, "Very few clients realize that the reason that their work is so bad is that they are the ones who commandeered it and directed it to be that way. I think that at least 50 percent of an agency's successful work resides in the client."[18]

Many creative people say it is important for clients to take some risks if they want breakthrough advertising that gets noticed. One agency that has been successful in getting its clients to take risks is Wieden + Kennedy, best known for its excellent creative work for companies such as Nike, Microsoft, and ESPN (see Exhibit 8–4). The agency's founders believe a key element in its success has been a steadfast belief in taking risks when most agencies and their clients have been retrenching and becoming more conservative.[19] The agency can develop great advertising partly because clients like Nike are willing to take risks and go along with the agency's priority system, which places the creative work first and the client–agency relationship second. The agency has even terminated relationships with large clients like Gallo when they interfered too much with the creative process. Several major advertisers including Procter & Gamble and Coca-Cola have added Wieden + Kennedy to their agency roster in efforts to increase the creativity of their advertising.[20] The Old Spice campaign discussed in the chapter opener is an example of the excellent creative work being done by W+K.

**EXHIBIT 8–4**
Wieden + Kennedy's belief in taking risks has led to creative advertising for clients such as Nike

An example of a company that has been taking more of a creative risk with its advertising is Marriott International as can be seen in the advertising for its Residence Inn chain. A highly evocative campaign was created to showcase Residence Inn's new "Innfusion" décor which redefines the extended-stay experience with distinctive zones that meet the living needs of the extended stay guest—cooking, dining, working, relaxing, and sleeping. The ads use theatrical performers to show guests how to master, not just survive a long trip. In one spot showcasing Residence's in-room grocery service, a performer flips upside down and lands on the kitchen counter and balances an apple on her toes (see Exhibit 8–5). In other ads a trapeze artist glides across the chain's newly designed rooms, a plate spinner twirls four plates to highlight the full kitchen in each unit,

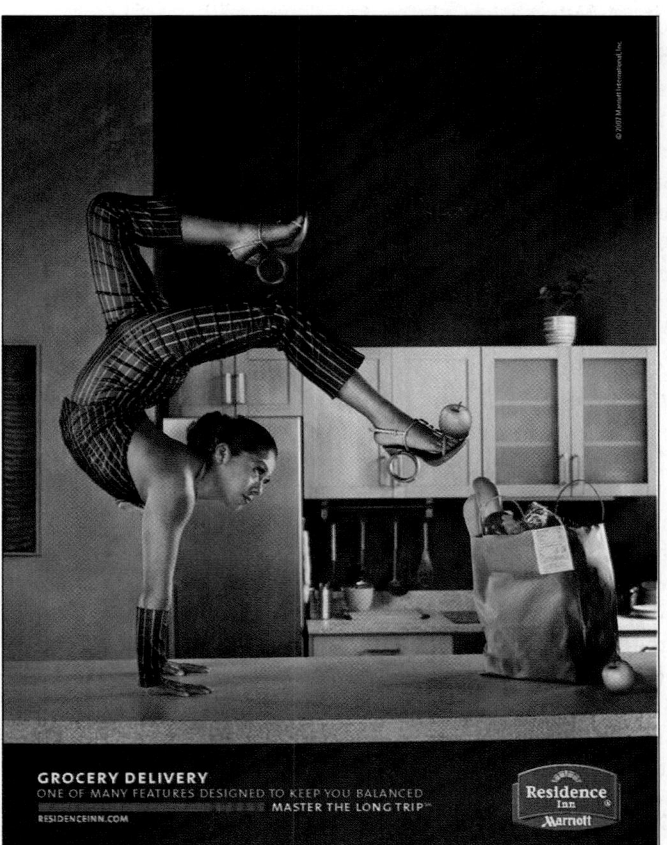


**EXHIBIT 8–5**
Residence Inn takes a very creative approach with its new ads

and a fire breather/juggler performs at an outdoor fire pit to showcase the new look of Residence properties. The television spots are part of an integrated campaign that includes print and online components such as a website (masterthelongtrip.com) that engages visitors with a virtual tour of the new Residence Inn designs.[21]

Not all companies or agencies agree that advertising has to be risky to be effective, however. Many marketing managers are more comfortable with advertising that simply communicates product or service features and benefits and gives the consumer a reason to buy. They see their ad campaigns as multimillion-dollar investments whose goal is to sell the product rather than finance the whims of their agency's creative staff. They argue that some creative people have lost sight of advertising's bottom line: Does it sell? There has been an ongoing debate over the artsy, image-oriented approach to advertising taken by many creative types versus the more hard-sell approach that many clients prefer.



## The Perpetual Debate: Creative versus Hard-Sell Advertising

For decades there has been a perpetual battle over the role of advertising in the marketing process. The war for the soul of advertising has been endlessly fought between those who believe ads should move people and those who just want to move product. On one side are the "suits" or "rationalists" who argue that advertising must sell the product or service, and that the more selling points or information in an ad, the better its chance of moving the consumer to purchase. On the other side are the "poets" or proponents of creativity who argue that advertising has to build an emotional bond between consumers and brands or companies that goes beyond product advertising. The debate over the effectiveness of creative or artsy advertising is not new. The rationalists have taken great delight in pointing to long lists of creative and award-winning campaigns over the years that have failed in the marketplace. Some note that even legendary adman David Ogilvy, who many consider the greatest copywriter of all time, once said: "If it doesn't sell, it's not creative."[22]

The "poets" argue that the most important thing good advertising does is make an emotional connection with consumers. They note that consumers do not want to be bombarded by ads; they want to be entertained and inspired. Indeed a recent survey of regular TV viewers found that 64 percent look for ways to avoid commercials rather than watch them.[23] Thus, advertising has to be creative and enjoyable enough that consumers will not zap it, yet still be able to help sell a product or service. It is the second part of this mandate that causes concern among the "suits." They note that there are many examples of creative campaigns that moved consumers' emotions, but were terminated because they did not increase sales and/or market share and put accounts and reputations on the line. A number of major advertisers have dismissed agencies that earned critical acclaim and awards for their creative work but failed to move the sales needle including Levi Strauss, Norwegian Cruise Lines, Miller Brewing Co., Gateway, and many others.[24]

Most of the "poets" who support advertising that connects on an emotional level insist that selling product is as much a priority for them as it is for those on the rational side of the debate. One top agency executive notes that "we've proven that this kind of advertising works, otherwise we wouldn't be in business, us or the agencies that practice the craft at this level." However, Brent Bouchez, former executive creative director at the Bozzell agency, argues the poets are losing sight of the fact that advertising is about selling things and being really creative in advertising means solving problems and building interesting brands that people want to buy. He notes, "It's time we stopped teaching young creative people to consider it a victory if the logo in an ad is hard to find, or if the product doesn't appear in the commercial at all. It's time we stopped using "break through the clutter" as an excuse to say nothing about what it is we're selling or why you should buy it."[25]

The issue of how much latitude creative people should be given and how much risk the client should be willing to take is open to considerable debate. However, clients and agency personnel generally agree that the ability to develop novel yet appropriate approaches to communicating with the customer makes the creative specialist valuable—and often hard to find.

## Creative Personnel

The image of the creative advertising person perpetuated in novels, movies, and TV shows is often one of a freewheeling, freethinking, eccentric personality. The educational background of creative personnel is often in nonbusiness areas such as art, literature, music, humanities, or journalism, so their interests and perspectives tend to differ from those of managers with a business education or background. Creative people tend to be more abstract and less structured, organized, or conventional in their approach to a problem, relying on intuition more often than logic. For example, Arthur Kover conducted a study of advertising copywriters and found that they work without guidance from any formal theories of communication. However, those interviewed in his study did have similar informal, implicit theories that guide them in creating ads. These theories are based on finding ways to break through the ad clutter, open the consciousness of consumers, and connect with them to deliver the message.[26]

Advertising creatives are sometimes stereotyped as odd, perhaps because they dress differently and do not always work the conventional 9-to-5 schedule. Of course, from the perspective of the creatives, it is the marketing or brand managers and account executives (the "suits") who are strange. In many agencies, you can't tell the creative personnel from the executives by their dress or demeanor. Yet the differences between creative and managerial personalities and perspectives must be recognized and tolerated so that creative people can do their best work and all those involved in the advertising process can cooperate.

It is important to note that creativity is not the exclusive domain of those who work in the creative department of ad agencies. Integrated marketing communications requires creative thinking from everyone involved in the planning and execution of IMC programs. Personnel from other parts of the agency such as account services and planning, media planners, digital media specialists and researchers, as well as those on the client side, such as marketing and brand managers, must all seek creative solutions to challenges faced in planning developing, and executing an IMC campaign. For example, awards are given each year for creativity in areas such as media planning, sales promotion, and digital and interactive media. Exhibit 8–6 shows an ad congratulating Media Storm for

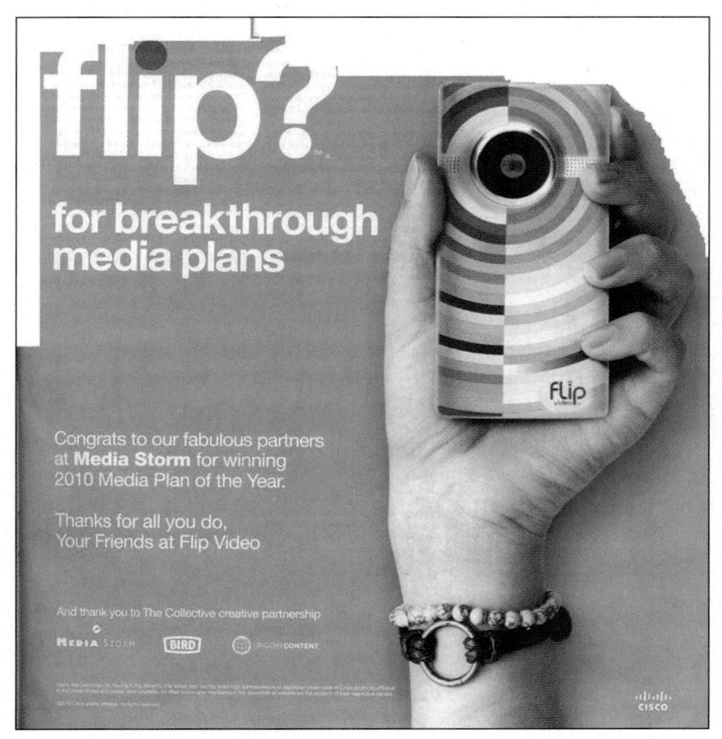


**EXHIBIT 8–6**
Awards for creativity are given for media planning as well as other components of an IMC program

winning *Mediaweek*'s 2010 Media Plan of the Year Award for its work on Cisco System's Flip pocket-size camcorder.

It is also important that those working on the client side do not create a relationship with their agencies that inhibits the creative processes required to produce good advertising. Shelia Sasser and Scott Koslow point out that the most highly-skilled creatives aspire to work with open-minded clients who are receptive to new ideas. They also note some of the best creative work developed by agencies does not get used because clients are resistant to taking creative risks, unless they are under pressure to perform.[27] Advertising agencies, as well as other IMC specialist organizations thrive on creativity as it is at the heart of what they do. Thus, agencies, as well as clients, must create an environment that fosters the development of creative thinking and creative advertising. Clients must also understand the differences between the perspectives of the creative personnel and marketing and product managers. While the client has ultimate approval of the advertising, the opinions of creative specialists must be respected when advertising ideas and content are evaluated. (Evaluation of the creatives' ideas and work is discussed in more detail in Chapter 9.)



# THE CREATIVE PROCESS

Some advertising people say creativity in advertising is best viewed as a process and creative success is most likely when some organized approach is followed. This does not mean there is an infallible blueprint to follow to create effective advertising; as we saw earlier, many advertising people reject attempts to standardize creativity or develop rules. However, most do follow a process when developing an ad.

One of the most popular approaches to creativity in advertising was developed by James Webb Young, a former creative vice president at the J. Walter Thompson agency. Young said, "The production of ideas is just as definite a process as the production of Fords; the production of ideas, too, runs an assembly line; in this production the mind follows an operative technique which can be learned and controlled; and that its effective use is just as much a matter of practice in the technique as in the effective use of any tool."[28] Young's model of the creative process contains five steps:

1. *Immersion.* Gathering raw material and information through background research and immersing yourself in the problem.
2. *Digestion.* Taking the information, working it over, and wrestling with it in the mind.
3. *Incubation.* Putting the problems out of your conscious mind and turning the information over to the subconscious to do the work.
4. *Illumination.* The birth of an idea—the "Eureka! I have it!" phenomenon.
5. *Reality or verification.* Studying the idea to see if it still looks good or solves the problem; then shaping the idea to practical usefulness.

Young's process of creativity is similar to a four-step approach outlined much earlier by English sociologist Graham Wallas in his classic book *The Art of Thought.*[29]

1. *Preparation.* Gathering background information needed to solve the problem through research and study.
2. *Incubation.* Getting away and letting ideas develop.
3. *Illumination.* Seeing the light or solution.
4. *Verification.* Refining and polishing the idea and seeing if it is an appropriate solution.

Models of the creative process are valuable to those working in the creative area of advertising, since they offer an organized way to approach an advertising problem. Preparation or gathering of background information is the first step in the creative process. As we saw in earlier chapters, the advertiser and agency start by developing a thorough understanding of the product or service, the target market, and the competition. They also focus on the role of advertising in the marketing and promotional program.

These models do not say much about how this information will be synthesized and used by the creative specialist because this part of the process is unique to the individual. In many ways, it's what sets apart the great creative minds and strategists in advertising. However, many agencies are now using a process called *account planning* to gather information and help creative specialists as they go through the creative process of developing advertising.

## Account Planning

To facilitate the creative process, many agencies now use **account planning**, which is a process that involves conducting research and gathering all relevant information about a client's product or service, brand, and consumers in the target audience. Account planning began in Great Britain during the 1960s and 70s and has spread to agencies in the United States as well as throughout Europe and Asia. The concept has become very popular in recent years as many agencies have seen the successful campaigns developed by agencies that are strong advocates of account planning.[30] One such agency is Goodby, Silverstein & Partners, which has used account planning to develop highly successful campaigns for clients such as Saturn, Hewlett-Packard, Sega, and Nike, as well as the popular "Got milk?" ads for the California Milk Processor Board.

Jon Steel, a former vice president and director of account planning at the agency's San Francisco office, has written an excellent book on the process titled *Truth, Lies & Advertising: The Art of Account Planning.*[31] He notes that the account planner's job is to provide the key decision makers with all the information they require to make an intelligent decision. According to Steel, "Planners may have to work very hard to influence the way that the advertising turns out, carefully laying out a strategic foundation with the client, handing over tidbits of information to creative people when, in their judgment, that information will have the greatest impact, giving feedback on ideas, and hopefully adding some ideas of their own."

Account planning plays an important role during creative strategy development by driving the process from the customers' point of view. Planners will work with the client as well as other agency personnel, such as the creative team and media specialists. They discuss how the knowledge and information they have gathered can be used in the development of the creative strategy as well as other aspects of the advertising campaign. Account planners are usually responsible for all the research (both qualitative and quantitative) conducted during the creative strategy development process. In the following section we examine how various types of research and information can provide input to the creative process of advertising. This information can be gathered by account planners or others whose job it is to provide input to the process.

## Inputs to the Creative Process: Preparation, Incubation, Illumination

**Background Research** Only the most foolish creative person or team would approach an assignment without first learning as much as possible about the client's product or service, the target market, the competition, and any other relevant background information. The creative specialist should also be knowledgeable about general trends, conditions, and developments in the marketplace, as well as research on specific advertising approaches or techniques that might be effective. The creative specialist can acquire background information in numerous ways. Some informal fact-finding techniques have been noted by Sandra Moriarty:

- Reading anything related to the product or market—books, trade publications, general interest articles, research reports, and the like.
- Asking everyone involved with the product for information—designers, engineers, salespeople, and consumers.
- Listening to what people are talking about. Visits to stores, malls, restaurants, and even the agency cafeteria can be informative. Listening to the client can be particularly valuable, since he or she often knows the product and market best.
- Using the product or service and becoming familiar with it. The more you use a product, the more you know and can say about it.
- Working in and learning about the client's business to understand better the people you're trying to reach.[32]



To assist in the preparation, incubation, and illumination stages, many agencies provide creative people with both general and product-specific preplanning input. **General preplanning input** can include books, periodicals, trade publications, scholarly journals, pictures, and clipping services, which gather and organize magazine and newspaper articles on the product, the market, and the competition, including the latter's ads. This input can also come from research studies conducted by the client, the agency, the media, or other sources.

Another useful general preplanning input concerns trends, developments, and happenings in the marketplace. Information is available from a variety of sources, including local, state, and federal governments, secondary research suppliers, and various industry trade associations, as well as advertising and media organizations. For example, advertising industry groups like the American Association of Advertising Agencies and media organizations like the National Association of Broadcasters (NAB) and Magazine Publishers of America (MPA) publish research reports and newsletters that provide information on market trends and developments and how they might affect consumers. Those involved in developing creative strategy can also gather relevant and timely information by reading publications like *Adweek, Advertising Age, Brandweek,* and *The Wall Street Journal* (see Exhibit 8–7).

**EXHIBIT 8–7**
Advertising industry publications are excellent sources of information on market trends

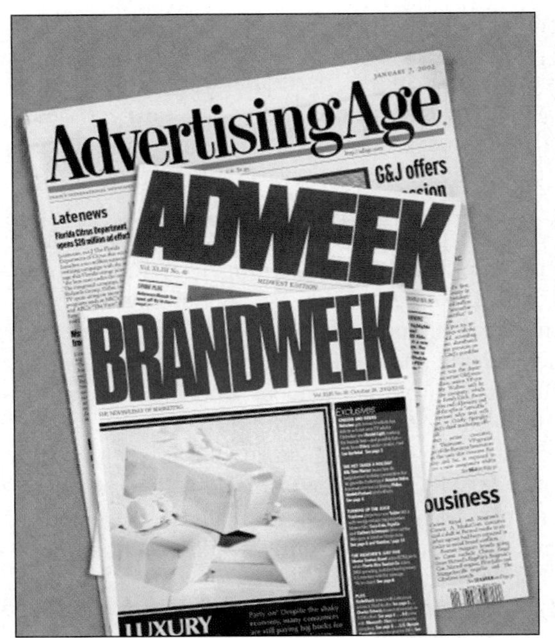


### Product/Service-Specific Research

In addition to getting general background research and preplanning input, creative people receive **product/service-specific preplanning input**. This information generally comes in the form of specific studies conducted on the product or service, the target audience, or a combination of the two. Quantitative and qualitative consumer research such as attitude studies, market structure, and positioning studies such as perceptual mapping and lifestyle research, focus group interviews, and demographic and psychographic profiles of users of a particular product, service, or brand are examples of product-specific preplanning input.

Many product- or service-specific studies helpful to the creative team are conducted by the client or the agency. A number of years ago, the BBDO ad agency developed an approach called **problem detection** for finding ideas around which creative strategies could be based.[33] This research technique involves asking consumers familiar with a product (or service) to generate an exhaustive list of things that bother them or problems they encounter when using it. The consumers rate these problems in order of importance and evaluate various brands in terms of their association with each problem. A problem detection study can provide valuable input for product improvements, reformulations, or new products. It can also give the creative people ideas regarding attributes or features to emphasize and guidelines for positioning new or existing brands.

Some agencies conduct psychographic studies annually and construct detailed psychographic or lifestyle profiles of product

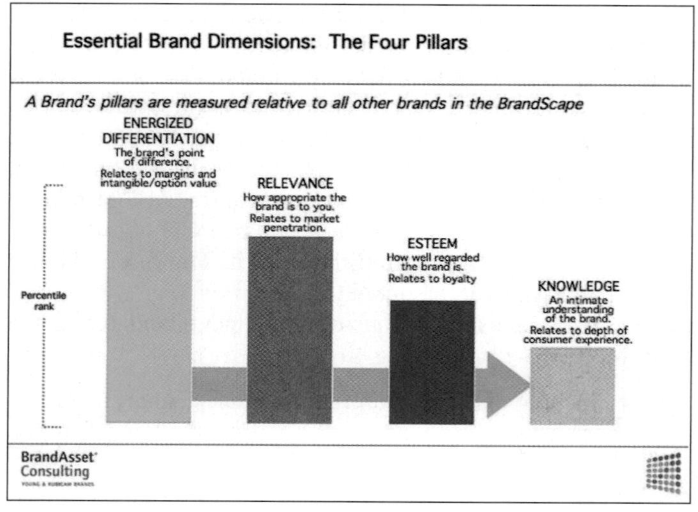


**EXHIBIT 8–8**

BrandAsset Valuator is used by Young & Rubicam to manage brands

Source: Reprinted with permission of BrandAsset Consulting.

or service users. DDB Worldwide conducts a large-scale psychographic study each year that taps into the minds of 4,000 consumers to measure their activities, interests, opinions, and attitudes as well as their usage of a wide range of products and services. The information is used to construct a psychographic profile of the target audiences for whom they are developing ads as well as to gain insight into general consumer trends.

A number of advertising agencies conduct branding research to help better identify clients' customers and how they connect to their brands. For example, Young & Rubicam has developed a proprietary tool, BAV$^{TM}$ for building and managing a brand. The model uses four pillars: energized differentiation, relevance, esteem, and knowledge. These pillars identify cores issues for the brand and evaluate current and future financial performance and potential (Exhibit 8–8). The Leo Burnett agency relies on its Brand Belief System to guide its global brand building philosophy and practice. This system focuses on the development of the brand believer bond, which is at the core of the relationship between a brand and its believers and considers four fundamental questions.

Nearly all of the major agencies are conducting branding research and/or developing models or systems that they can use to gain better insight into consumers and develop more effective campaigns for their clients. The importance of building and maintaining strong brands is likely to become even greater in the future. This will put even more pressure on agencies to develop new and better tools and techniques that can be used to guide their clients' advertising campaigns.

### Qualitative Research Input

Many agencies, particularly larger ones with strong research departments, have their own research programs and specific techniques they use to assist in the development of creative strategy and provide input to the creative process. In addition to the various quantitative research studies, qualitative research techniques such as in-depth interviews or focus groups can provide the creative team with valuable insight at the early stages of the creative process. **Focus groups** are a research method whereby consumers (usually 10 to 12 people) from the target market are led through a discussion regarding a particular topic. Focus groups give insight as to why and how consumers use a product or service, what is important to them in choosing a particular brand, what they like and don't like about various products or services, and any special needs they might have that aren't being satisfied. A focus group session might also include a discussion of types of ad appeals to use or evaluation of the advertising of various companies.

Focus group interviews bring the creative people and others involved in creative strategy development into contact with the customers. Listening to a focus group gives copywriters, art directors, and other creative specialists a better sense of who the target audience is, what the audience is like, and who the creatives need to write, design, or direct to in creating an advertising message. Focus groups can also be used to evaluate the viability of different creative approaches under consideration and suggest the best direction to pursue.[34] Many marketers are now conducting focus groups online using groups of consumers who are part of an online community, as well as Internet research panels of 80 to 100 consumers organized by research firms such as Greenfield Online and Invoke Solutions. Concepts can be presented to these panels using instant-message and chatroom styles, and detailed feedback can be gathered and processed in a few hours versus several weeks that are needed to get comparable results from traditional focus groups.[35]

Agency creative personnel have long expressed concern over the idea of having their ideas and work critiqued by consumers. Many creatives insist that good ideas don't need to be tested and that testing can often weaken a creative execution. Moreover, they argue that it interferes with the creative process and limits their ability to develop innovative and breakthrough advertising messages.[36] Those critical of focus groups note that highly successful campaigns such as the one featuring the Aflac duck would never have made it on the air if the company had heeded the responses of focus group participants. While many participants found the duck funny, others found it insulting. The duck survived only after executives from the Kaplan Thaler Group convinced the company to allow the Ipso-ASI research firm to test the ad along with four others it created and four spots from other agencies competing for the account.[37] The recall score of the spot featuring the duck was the highest score Ipsos-ASI had seen in the insurance category at the time. Kaplan Thaler won the account and the award-winning campaign featuring the duck debuted in late 1999 and has been running ever since (Exhibit 8–9). It also has helped increase raise awareness of Aflac and led to significant increases in sales for the supplemental insurance provider.

CHAPTER 8

While many creative personnel may be opposed to having their ideas scrutinized in a focus group, there are, of course, numerous examples of situations where input from focus groups have proven to be very valuable and insightful. Creative personnel must recognize that companies want to ensure that the ads that are being developed for their brands have the best possible chance of evoking favorable reactions from consumers and encouraging them to purchase their product and/or services. Joe Plummer, the former chief research officer of the Advertising Research Foundation, explains their position pretty well by noting that "Any creative director worth his salt who really thinks a client is going to lay down $100 million without a high level of confidence of success is naïve."[38]

**EXHIBIT 8–9**
The Aflac duck did not test well in focus groups but has been the basis for a very successful campaign

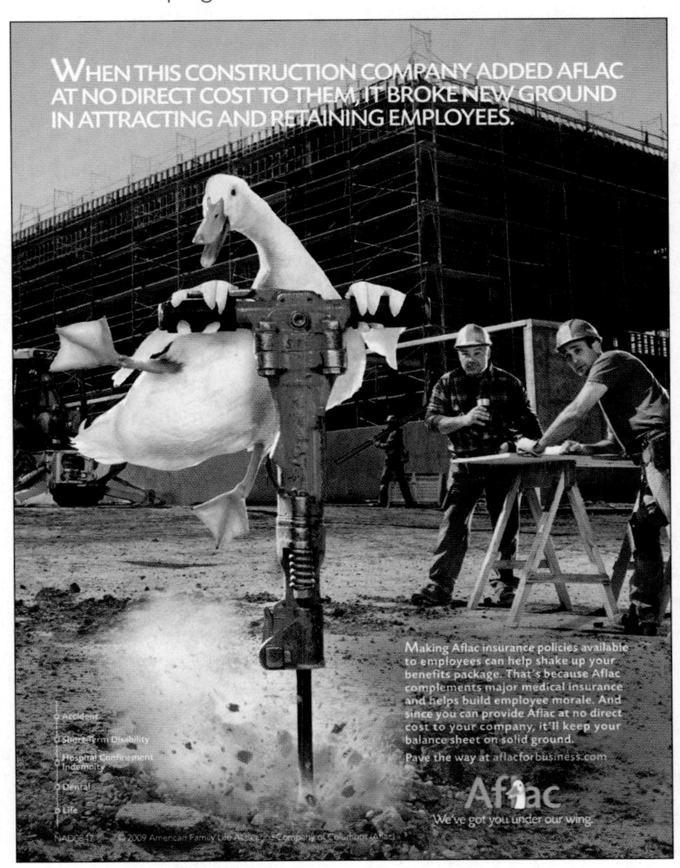


Another form of qualitative input that has become popular among advertising agencies is **ethnographic research**, which involves observing consumers in their natural environment.[39] Some agencies send anthropologists or trained researchers into the field to study and observe consumers in their homes, at work, or at play. For example, the Ogilvy & Mather agency has a research unit called the Discovery Group, which moves into consumers' homes, follows consumers in their leisure pursuits, or trails them as they move through their daily lives. For Ogilvy client Miller Brewing Co., Discovery staffers traveled around the country filming Miller drinkers, as well as those drinking competitive brands. They used the tapes to study group dynamics and how the dynamics changed while people were drinking. The agency used the insights gained from the study to help develop a new advertising campaign for Miller Lite beer. Many marketing and agency researchers prefer ethnographic research over the use of focus groups, as the latter technique has a number of limitations. Strong personalities can often wield undue influence in focus groups, and participants often will not admit, or may not even recognize, their behavior patterns and motivations. However, ethnographic studies can cost more to conduct and are more difficult to administer.

Generally, creative people are open to any research or information that will help them understand the client's target market better and assist in generating

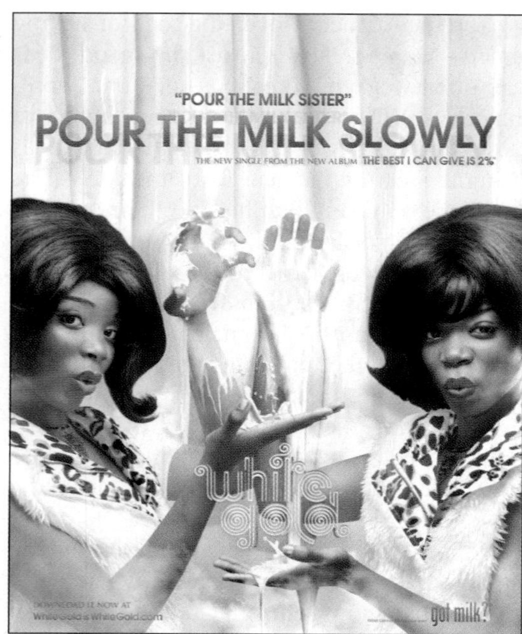


**EXHIBIT 8–10**
Research played an important role in the development of this Ogilvy award-winning campaign

creative ideas. The advertising industry is recognizing the importance of using research to guide the creative process. The Advertising Research Foundation initiated the David Ogilvy Awards, named after the advertising legend who founded Ogilvy & Mather. These awards are presented to teams of advertising agencies, client companies, and research companies in recognition of research that has been used successfully to determine the strategy and effectiveness of ad campaigns.

The Goodby, Silverstein & Partners agency won an Ogilvy award in 2010 for a research driven campaign created for the California Milk Fluid Processor Board to target teens and increase their milk consumption. Research showed that freshly liberated teens living away from home (such as college students) were drinking less milk, particularly when they were around their friends, as they preferred beverages with a cooler image such as Red Bull, Vitamin Water, or Starbucks's teas and coffee. The agency used both qualitative and quantitative research as the basis for a social media-based campaign that repositioned milk to teens as a *vessel of health and hotness*. The agency invented a fictitious band called White Gold that was named after its lead singer and guitarist and backed up by the Calcium Twins Wholena and Skimberly (Exhibit 8–10). The agency wrote and recorded humorous songs about milk and its transformative superpowers and even produced full-length music videos of some of the songs. To give the band a social media networking presence band pages were created for MySpace and Facebook and a special website was created for the campaign. Television and rock-poster style print ads were used to tell the story of the band and drive teens to the website and social media pages. The campaign has been very successful in changing teens' perceptions of milk on its key image attributes, elevating its social acceptability, and increasing consumption among teens in California.[40]

## Inputs to the Creative Process: Verification, Revision

The verification and revision stage of the creative process evaluates ideas generated during the illumination stage, rejects inappropriate ones, refines and polishes those that remain, and gives them final expression. Techniques used at this stage include directed focus groups to evaluate creative concepts, ideas, or themes; message communication studies; portfolio tests; and evaluation measures such as viewer reaction profiles.

At this stage of the creative process, members of the target audience may be asked to evaluate rough creative layouts and to indicate what meaning they get from the ad, what they think of its execution, or how they react to a slogan or theme. The creative team can gain insight into how a TV commercial might communicate its message by having members of the target market evaluate the ad in storyboard form. A **storyboard** is a series of drawings used to present the visual plan or layout of a proposed commercial. It contains a series of sketches of key frames or scenes along with the copy or audio portion for each scene (see Exhibit 8–11).

Testing a commercial in storyboard form can be difficult because storyboards are too abstract for many consumers to understand. To make the creative layout more realistic and easier to evaluate, the agency may produce an **animatic**, a videotape of the storyboard along with an audio soundtrack. Storyboards and animatics are useful for research purposes as well as for presenting the creative idea to other agency personnel or to the client for discussion and approval.

At this stage of the process, the creative team is attempting to find the best creative approach or execution style before moving ahead with the campaign themes and going into actual production of the ad. The verification/revision process may

**EXHIBIT 8–11**
Marketers can gain insight into consumers' reactions to a commercial by showing them a storyboard

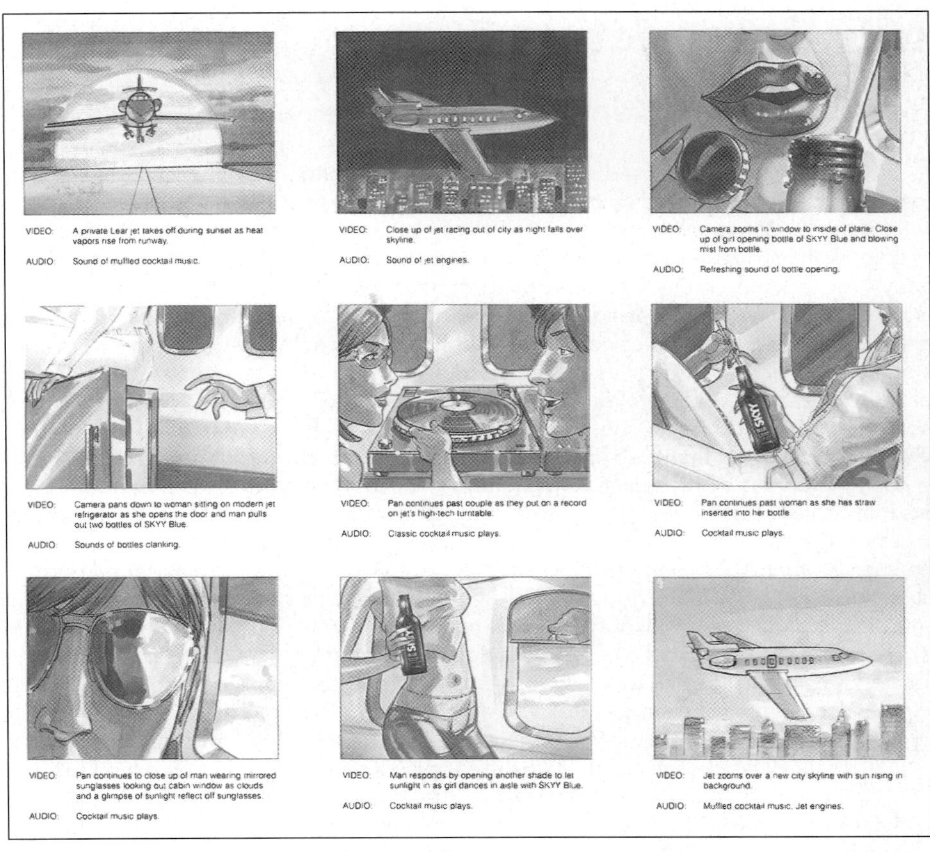




include more formal, extensive pretesting of the ad before a final decision is made. Pretesting and related procedures are examined in detail in Chapter 19.

# CREATIVE STRATEGY DEVELOPMENT

## Advertising Campaigns

Most ads are part of a series of messages that make up an IMC or **advertising campaign**, which is a set of interrelated and coordinated marketing communication activities that center on a single theme or idea that appears in different media across a specified time period. Determining the unifying theme around which the campaign will be built is a critical part of the creative process, as it sets the tone for the individual ads and other forms of marketing communications that will be used. A **campaign theme** should be a strong idea, as it is the central message that will be communicated in all the advertising and other promotional activities. The theme for the advertising campaign is usually expressed through a **slogan** or **tagline** that reduces the key idea into a few words or a brief statement. The advertising slogan should serve as a summation line that succinctly expresses the company or brand's positioning, as well as the message it is trying to deliver to the target audience.[41] The slogan usually appears in every advertisement and is often used in other forms of marketing communications to serve as a reminder of, and to reinforce, the marketer's branding message.

Advertising campaign plans are short-term in nature and, like marketing and IMC plans, are done on an annual basis. However, the campaign themes are usually developed with the intention of being used for a longer time period. Unfortunately, many campaign themes last only a short time, usually because they are ineffective

# IMC Perspective 8–1 > > >

## Creating More Effective Ad Slogans

We as consumers are exposed to hundreds of advertising messages as we go through our daily media consumption routines of reading newspapers and magazines, listening to radio, watching television, and surfing the Internet. And nearly every advertisement that we see and/or hear contains a slogan or tagline that is designed to serve as a summation line that quickly and succinctly expresses the company or brand's positioning as well as the message it is trying to deliver to the target audience. Stop and think for a moment about Nike's "Just do it" tagline, which has been used in its advertising for more than two decades and is recognized by nearly everyone. The tagline is designed to encourage personal athletic achievement, whether through playing a sport or engaging in some type of exercise or workout routine such as running, biking, aerobics, or even walking. Of course Nike wants us all to do it while wearing its shoes or exercise apparel, which millions of consumers around the world proudly do. Even when we see a Nike ad that does not contain the slogan, the famous "swoosh" trademark often prompts consumers to rehearse the "Just do it" line in their minds.

Nike's tagline was chosen as one of the top five ad slogans of all time and has even been enshrined in the Smithsonian Institution. Some of the other top taglines that effectively communicate the benefits or unique feature of a company or brand include "M&M's: Melts in your mouth, not in your hands," McDonald's "I'm Lovin' It," Allstate Insurance's "You're in Good Hands with Allstate," and Kay Jewelers' "Every kiss begins with Kay." And while there are many other examples of good taglines, there are probably many more examples of very poor slogans that are vague and mean absolutely nothing. Communication professor Stephen Winzenburg notes that many major companies do a poor job of communicating their identities by using meaningless phrases in their taglines. Examples of slogans that he cites as generic and bland include JCPenney's "Every day matters," Sears's "Where it begins," Kohl's "Expect great things," and Radio Shack's "Do stuff." Winzenburg argues these slogans are meaningless and fail to give the consumer a sense of what these companies are about. He also notes that these slogans are interchangeable and do little, if anything, to differentiate these companies from their competitors.

Marketing experts note that a good tagline must break through the advertising clutter, differentiate the company or brand and be memorable. John Mathes, director of brand services at Bancography, a bank branding and positioning consulting company, notes that "The tagline is a hardworking collection of words that should give you that 'aha' moment every time you see or hear it." He reminds marketers that a tagline is your brand's sound bite and is often all you can expect consumers to remember. Mathes suggests that a good tagline starts with the brand positioning statement, which should be well articulated and truly differentiating, and he offers a helpful guideline: A brand's positioning can be expressed verbatim as a tagline (think BMW and "Ultimate Driving Machine"), but a tagline is not usually the brand positioning unless it is a direct lift from the positioning statement.

Long-time marketing executive Steve Cone argues that creating strong slogans is a marketer's most important job but today is a forgotten part of marketing planning. He suggests that advertising messages should contain "powerlines," or powerful taglines, which he describes as "words that are well chosen and have the power to awe, inspire, motivate, alienate, subjugate, and in a marketing context, change the buying habits of consumers." He argues that since we are

or market conditions and/or competitive developments in the marketplace change. IMC Perspective 8–1 discusses some of the reasons why many advertising slogans do a poor job of communicating a distinctive identity for a company or brand and offers some guidelines for developing more effective taglines.

While some marketers change their campaign themes often, a successful campaign theme may last for decades. Philip Morris has been using the "Marlboro country" campaign for over 50 years, General Mills has positioned Wheaties cereal as the "Breakfast of Champions" for decades, and BMW has used the "ultimate driving machine" theme since 1974. Even though BMW has changed agencies several times over the past three decades, the classic tagline has been retained. Figure 8–2 lists some of the advertising slogans currently being used by marketers that are recognized as being very effective because they are memorable and communicate a unique message for the company or brand.

Like any other area of the marketing and promotional process, the creative aspect of advertising and the development of the campaign theme is guided by specific goals and objectives. A creative strategy that focuses on what must be communicated will guide the selection of the campaign theme and the development of all messages bombarded by so many advertising messages, a powerline can do the heavy lifting and break through all of the sensory overload. Cone offers the slogan used in ads for the Las Vegas Convention and Visitors' Authority—"What happens here stays here"—as an example of an effective tagline. He notes that consumers remember the thought and essence of the message, which is that people go to Las Vegas to cut loose, have fun, and do things they wouldn't do back home.

One factor marketers must consider is how long they can use a tagline before it becomes wallpaper to the target audience. Mathes suggests that taglines should be reviewed every two to three years and that ongoing brand awareness and attribute-tracking studies can provide the benchmarks needed to determine whether a slogan is doing its job or is wearing out. Cone cautions against changing advertising slogans too often and argues that the more things change, the more taglines should not, particularly if they are a special promise or claim that a competitor cannot easily duplicate.

Steve Cone offers four basic guidelines for creating a compelling tagline that will get noticed and stand the test of time. He suggests that a good tagline should say why the company or brand is different and not use common words; it should have real attitude and bypass wishy-washy phrases; appear at all customer touch points and ideally be the headline of every marketing promotion; and marketers should recognize that creating good taglines is an art, as the best ones come from flashes of inspirations by great copywriters who see clear and compelling brand promises and make them come to life.

The next time you see an ad, pay attention to the tagline and evaluate it against these four guidelines. If Cone is correct, 98 percent of the time the tagline will fail to communicate anything unique or relevant, nor will it contribute to the image of the company or brand. However, those that have a powerline can help make a company or brand's marketing message more memorable and effective and give it a leg up on the competition.

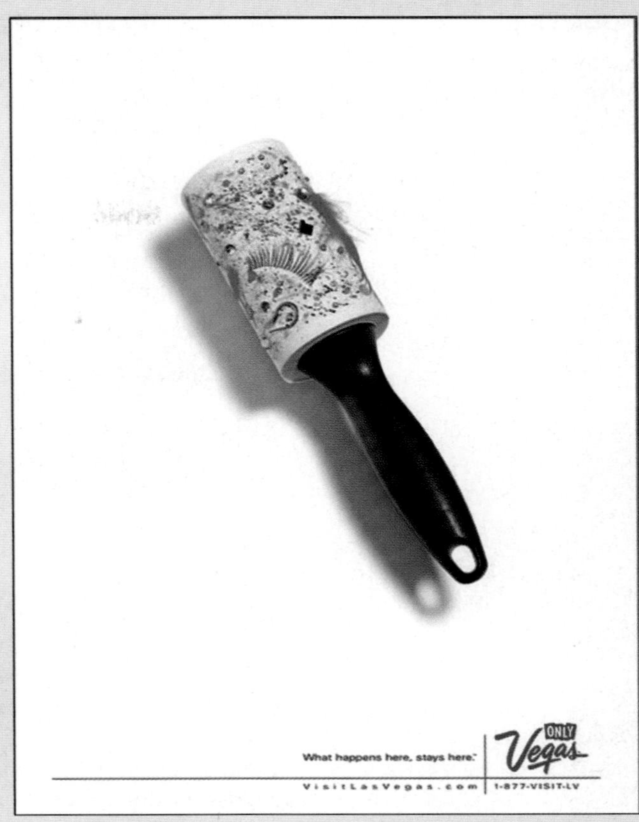


Sources: Steve Cone, "Help Taglines Regain Lost Glory," *Advertising Age*, April 14, 2008, http://adage.com/print?article_id=126290; Stephen Winzenburg, "Your Advertising Slogans Are Crummy. Can't You Do Better," *Advertising Age*, January 14, 2008, p.15; John Mathes, "Taglines That Stick; Here's How to Create an Effective Brand Summation Line. How Long Should It Be? Is It the Same as Your Brand Positioning? How Often Do You Need to Refresh It?," *ABA Bank Marketing*, December 1, 2008, pp. 22–25.

used in the ad campaign. The creative strategy is based on several factors, including identification of the target audience; the basic problem, issue, or opportunity the advertising must address; the major selling idea or key benefit the message needs to communicate; and any supportive information that needs to be included in the ad. Once these factors are determined, a creative strategy statement should describe the message appeal and execution style that will be used. Many ad agencies outline these elements in a document known as the copy or creative platform.

## Creative Brief

The written **creative brief** specifies the basic elements of the creative strategy. Different agencies may call this document a *creative platform* or *work plan, creative blueprint,* or *creative contract.* The account representative or manager assigned to the account usually prepares the creative brief. In larger agencies, an individual from research or the strategic account planning department may write it. People from the agency team or group assigned to the account, including creative personnel as well as representatives from media and research, have input. The advertising manager

**FIGURE 8–2**
Examples of Effective Advertising Slogans

| Company or brand | Slogan |
|---|---|
| 1. Nike | Just do it |
| 2. Home Depot | You can do it. We can help. |
| 3. Gillette | The Best a Man Can Get |
| 4. McDonald's | I'm Lovin It! |
| 5. De Beers | A Diamond is Forever |
| 6. Southwest Airlines | A symbol of freedom |
| 7. adidas | Impossible is nothing |
| 8. Lexus | The Pursuit of Perfection |
| 9. Under Armour | We Must Protect This House. I Will. |
| 10. Macy's | The magic of Macy's |

and/or the marketing and brand managers from the client side ultimately approve the creative brief. Figure 8–3 shows a sample copy platform outline that can be used to guide the creative process. Just as there are different names for the creative brief, there are variations in the outline and format used and in the level of detail included.

Several components of the creative brief were discussed in previous chapters. For example, Chapter 7 examined the DAGMAR model and showed how the setting of advertising objectives requires specifying a well-defined target audience and developing a communication task statement that spells out what message must be communicated to this audience. Determining what problem the product or service will solve or what issue must be addressed in the ad helps in establishing communication objectives for the campaign to accomplish. Two critical components of the brief are the development of the major selling idea and creative strategy development. These two steps are often the responsibility of the creative team or specialist and form the basis of the advertising campaign theme.

Many creative briefs also include supporting information and requirements (brand identifications, disclaimers, and the like) that should appear in any advertising message. This information may be important in ensuring uniformity across various executions of the ads used in a campaign or in meeting any legal requirements. Exhibits 8–12A and B show an example of a creative brief used by the Lambesis agency to create a print campaign for Tacori, a fine jewelry company that has experienced strong sales growth over the past several years, and an ad that was created based on the brief. As noted in the brief, the primary objective of the advertising for Tacori is to establish the Tacori collection as a more accessible fashion jewelry line.

Obtaining information regarding customers, the product or service, and the market that can be used in developing the creative brief is an important part of the creative planning process. While it is important that this basic information is provided to agency creatives, this may not always occur due to breakdowns in communication

**FIGURE 8–3**
Creative Brief Outline

1. Basic problem or issue the advertising must address.
2. Advertising and communications objectives.
3. Target audience.
4. Major selling idea or key benefits to communicate.
5. Creative strategy statement (campaign theme, appeal, and execution technique to be used).
6. Supporting information and requirements.

Lambesis

2800 Roosevelt Street, Carlsbad California, 92008 Main 760.547.2333 Fax 760.547.2331 lambesis.com

Creative Brief

Client: Tacori

Assignment

Develop new print concepts for the launch of the 18K925 line by Tacori

Objectives

- Support the long-term goal of growing 18K925 to become 50% of Tacori's business by clearly establishing the new Tacori collection as a more accessible, fashion jewelry line

Target

- Women, Age 25-49, HHI $75K+, Urban dwellers, Brand driven consumers, in market for fashion jewelry for self or as a gift for someone special.
- *What do they currently think?*
  I know and love Tacori as a high-end jewelry brand that's gifted for special occasions (=expressions of love)
- *What do we want them to think?*
  Tacori is also a brand with bold, statement-making, accessible designs that still have that distinctly artisanal Tacori touch (=expressions of style)

Product positioning

Tacori's 18K925 designer jewelry line is the ultimate expression of passion, with modern, accessible style and lasting quality.

Reasons to believe

- Accessible price points between $400 - $3000
- Bold, fun, wearable designs fuse colorful gemstones and gold+silver metals, with classic Tacori design cues
- Distinct Tacori brand name and image

Tonality

Modern meets heirloom, bold, aspirational, unique

Creative considerations

- Develop concepts within the Iconic Passion campaign
- Creative requirements:
  - Demonstrate aspirational, yet attainable luxury
  - Accommodate a variety of product imagery including necklaces, bracelets and/or rings to showcase the range of jewelry
  - Use the Tacori logo
- Other considerations that need be addressed:
  - Concepts must be able to work for print and horizontal OOH and B&W newspaper
  - Concepts need to ensure that retailer tags added to the bottom of the ad are legible

**EXHIBIT 8–12A**

Creative brief for Tacori jewelry

**EXHIBIT 8–12B**

Print ad created based on creative brief to establish Tacori as an accessible fashion jewelry line

on the client as well as the agency side or between the two. John Sutherland, Lisa Duke, and Avery Abernethy developed a model of the flow of marketing information from clients to the agency creative staff, shown in Figure 8–4.[42] The model shows that there are five major communication interfaces and decision points where gatekeepers can impede the flow of information to agency creatives.

A great deal of attention has been paid to the client–agency communication interface that occurs between the brand manager and/or advertising manager on the client side and the account manager on the agency side. Communication problems can occur between clients and their agencies, which can make the job of the creative staff much more difficult. However, this model shows that there are four other potential communication interface failure points, including (1) the client or client gatekeeper lacking knowledge of some or all of the information needed for effective advertising, (2) the client deciding not to share with the agency all of the available information that is relevant to creating effective advertising, (3) the agency gatekeeper(s) deciding not to share with creative staffers all of the client information they receive, and (4) internal agency communication failures which may result in the creative staff not receiving all of the relevant information received from the client.

Sutherland, Duke, and Abernethy conducted an extensive survey of agency creative directors, copywriters, and art directors on the specific types of marketing information that is made available to them for use in developing and executing a creative strategy. They identified six specific types of marketing information including the demographic profile of the target audience, customer product usage information, client's product performance information, competitors' product performance information, marketing strategy information, and the main selling point supplied by the client. Their study showed that agency creative personnel often lack the information needed to effectively design and execute creative strategies. They found that information in these specific categories was provided to creatives only around one-half to two-thirds

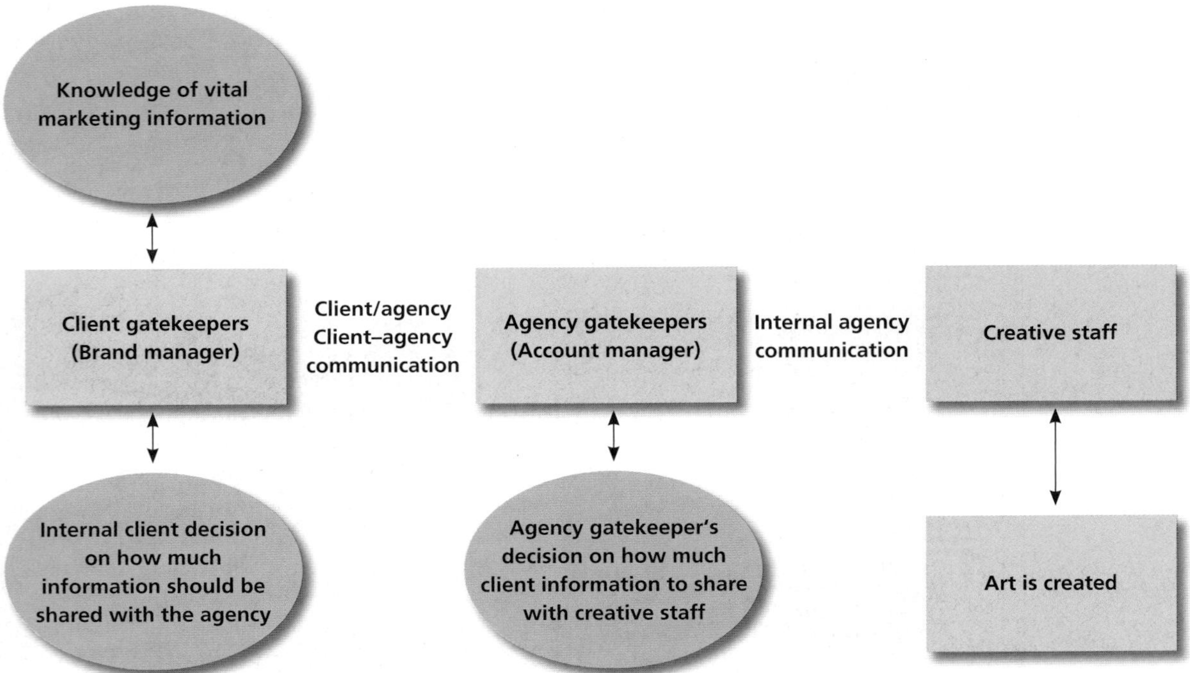


**FIGURE 8–4**

Model of Marketing Information Flow from the Marketing Manager to the Creative Staff

Source: John Sutherland, Lisa Duke, and Avery Abernethy, "A Model of Marketing Information Flow," *Journal of Advertising* 33, No. 4 (Winter 2004), p. 42. Copyright © 2004 by American Academy of Advertising. Reprinted with permission of M. E. Sharpe, Inc. All rights reserved. Not for reproduction.

of the time. Even the most basic target demographic profile was not provided 30 percent of the time. This study indicates that there is a gap in the information that creative personnel need to develop effective advertising and what they are being provided and points to the need for better communication between clients and agencies.

The information contained in the copy platform provides the creative staff with important background information and the basic elements of the overall advertising strategy. The next step in the creative process is the development of the message strategy and begins with the search for the *big idea* that will build on the strategy and bring it to life. One of the major challenges for the creative team is determining the major selling idea that will be used as the basis of the campaign. We will examine some approaches often used for determining the major selling idea and campaign theme.

## The Search for the Major Selling Idea

An important part of creative strategy is determining the central theme that will become the **major selling idea** of the ad campaign. As A. Jerome Jeweler states in his book *Creative Strategy in Advertising:*

> The major selling idea should emerge as the strongest singular thing you can say about your product or service. This should be the claim with the broadest and most meaningful appeal to your target audience. Once you determine this message, be certain you can live with it; be sure it stands strong enough to remain the central issue in every ad and commercial in the campaign.[43]

Some advertising experts argue that for an ad campaign to be effective it must contain a big idea that attracts the consumer's attention, gets a reaction, and sets the advertiser's product or service apart from the competition's. Well-known adman John O'Toole describes the *big idea* as "that flash of insight that synthesizes the purpose of the strategy, joins the product benefit with consumer desire in a fresh, involving way, brings the subject to life, and makes the reader or audience stop, look, and listen."[44]

Of course, the real challenge to the creative team is coming up with the big idea to use in the ad. Many products and services offer virtually nothing unique, and it can be difficult to find something interesting to say about them. The late David Ogilvy, generally considered one of the most creative advertising copywriters ever to work in the business, has stated:

> I doubt if more than one campaign in a hundred contains a big idea. I am supposed to be one of the more fertile inventors of big ideas, but in my long career as a copywriter I have not had more than 20, if that.[45]

While really great ideas in advertising are difficult to come by, there are many big ideas that became the basis of very creative, successful advertising campaigns. Classic examples include "We try harder," which positioned Avis as the underdog car-rental company that provided better service than Hertz; the "Pepsi generation" theme and subsequent variations like "the taste of a new generation" and "GenerationNext"; the "Be all you can be" theme used in recruitment ads for the U.S. Army; and Wendy's "Where's the beef?" which featured the late, gravelly voiced Clara Peller delivering the classic line that helped make the fast-food chain a household name. More recent big ideas that have resulted in effective advertising campaigns include the "Intel inside" campaign for Intel microprocessors that go in personal computers; Nike's "Just do it"; the "Got milk" and milk moustache themes used to promote milk consumption; the "I'm Lovin' It!" theme for McDonald's and Apple's "Think Different" campaign. Some of the big ideas that are used in the IMC campaign of companies are no longer being developed for execution through traditional mass media. As discussed in IMC Technology Perspective 8–1, many companies are taking advantage of the expanded creative opportunities that are available on the Internet and are integrating traditional media with online elements and using a new genre of advertising known as *advertainment.*

Big ideas are important in business-to-business advertising as well. For example, United Technologies Corporation (UTC) is a diversified company whose products include Carrier heating and air conditioning, Hamilton Sundstrand aerospace systems and industrial products, Otis elevators and escalators, Pratt & Whitney aircraft engines and Sikorsky helicopters, UTC Fire & Security systems and UTC Power fuel cells. The company launched an integrated marketing campaign to give the business and investment community a better understanding of its products and business achievements. The campaign uses the theme "You can see everything from here" and is designed to deliver a richer, deeper message about UTC and make the target audience curious to learn more about the company and its innovative products. One of the initial print ads used in the campaign showed intricately detailed cross-section views of a Sikorsky helicopter and a Pratt & Whitney aircraft engine (Exhibit 8–13). These ads have been very effective in building familiarity and favorability among the investor target audience, cutting through the clutter of corporate advertising in business publications such as *The Wall Street Journal, Barrons, Forbes,* and *BusinessWeek.*

**EXHIBIT 8–13**
This United Technologies Corporation ad is an example of a big idea in business-to-business advertising

## Developing the Major Selling Idea

It is difficult to pinpoint the inspiration for a big idea or teach advertising creatives an easy way to find one. As noted earlier, Arthur Kover conducted a study of advertising copywriters to understand how they approach the creative process and search for big

# IMC Technology Perspective 8–1 > > >

## Many Creative Campaigns Are Moving Online

Traditionally, when planning a new campaign for a client, most agencies would have their creative teams conceive and develop advertising for mass media channels such as television, radio, and/or print. The online component would be an add-on that played a supportive role such as providing additional information about a brand, promotional offers, or a place to watch commercials. However, the online component is increasingly becoming the centerpiece or starting point of a campaign as many marketers are creating short films, or *webisodes,* that are designed to entertain viewers while delivering a branding message. These webisodes often involve a series of films and can cost several million dollars to produce, depending on their level of sophistication, the number of episodes, and the types of talent who appear in them.

Many in the advertising industry point to the webisode series created by Fallon Worldwide for BMW in 2001 as the milestone event that launched a new genre of advertising known as *advertainment.* Fallon worked with the Hollywood production company Anonymous Content to create a series of short films called "The Hire" which featured British actor Clive Owen as a James Bond–type driver who takes costars such as Madonna, Mickey Rourke, and Stellan Skarsgaard for the ride of their lives in a BMW. A special website, BMW Films.com, was created to show the films and they were also distributed on DVDs by BMW dealers. A number of other companies/brands were among the first to use the advertainment genre to promote their products including SKYY Spirits, Levi's, Mini-Cooper, and American Express.

There are a number of reasons why marketers are making webisodes the focal point of their IMC campaigns. First, they recognize that consumers are spending more time on the Internet than they are with traditional media. Surveys show that younger consumers in particular are spending more time online than watching television or reading newspapers and magazines. Moreover, many of them are now watching TV shows, movies, and videos online rather than on television. The second major reason is that there are more creative opportunities available through webisodes and other forms of online advertising versus traditional media. Unlike TV commercials, webisodes are not limited to the traditional 30- or 15-second spots, because films created for viewing online can be any length. There are also very few rules or restrictions for webisodes as networks cannot censor what is shown or said and marketers do not have to worry as much about various regulatory or media watchdog groups policing their short films. Webisodes and other forms of online videos are also becoming increasingly popular because they provide consumers with the opportunity to interact or even create the message. For example, athletic shoe brand Converse created an award-winning campaign that was built around the Converse Gallery website which featured 50 24-second films that were created by consumers about the sneakers.

The type of webisodes agencies are creating for marketers is changing as they are evolving from short-story focused films and documentaries to new genres that include interviews, live events, and behind-the-scenes perspectives on various issues. For example, in 2009 the Coca-Cola Company launched *The Style Series Presented by Diet Coke* which is an online site that contains entertainment and lifestyle webisodes featuring interviews with celebrity guests such as Rihanna, singer/songwriter Michelle Branch, actor Edward Norton, and others who discuss keys to their success as well as the tools needed to enjoy a healthy, active, and enriched life. *The Style Series* is part of a broader online effort by Diet Coke to attract a younger, broader demographic beyond the 30- to 40-year-old females that comprise its core market. The webisodes have helped the brand achieve its goal as the median age of visitors to DietCoke.com, which is the main hub for *The Style Series,* has gone from the mid-40s to 26 in just a year while generating more than 25 million views of the webisodes.

Several other companies are using new types of webisodes to connect with their customers. Upscale retailer Nordstrom, Inc., used a series of online videos starring singer Michael Buble in connection with his 2010 "Crazy Love

ideas. He found that they view the purpose of a big idea as breaking through the advertising clutter and delivering a message.[46] Advertising professor John Rossiter argues most copywriters focus on communicating the *key benefit claim* which refers to the benefit thought by the copywriter to be the key to selling the advertised product. He notes that most creative ideas are based on finding ways to dramatically and effectively convey the key benefit claim.[47] As noted earlier, the key benefit claim is often explicit in the tagline that is used as the basis for the advertising campaign such as the "I'm Lovin It!" theme for McDonald's. However, the creative team must still work to develop effective ways to communicate this message in the executions of the advertising and other components of the IMC program.

Tour" for which Nordstrom was the exclusive sponsor. The humorous online videos are titled "80 Suits" and highlight Buble's relationship with Nordstrom stores through the eyes of Buble's truck driver, who is responsible for delivering his tour wardrobe to each concert venue. Jim Beam Bourbon is partnering with the cable sports network ESPN to launch *The Next Round Served Up by Jim Beam* Web series which is hosted by ESPN personality and award-winning journalist Scoop Jackson. The series features a range of guests including actors, athletes, media personalities, and comedians discussing the news and other relevant topics with a focus on sports and pop-culture. *The Next Round* is being featured across several ESPN properties and has its own custom page on ESPN.com that contains videos of the show, video podcasts, pictures, and links and which serves as the hub for fan–social media interaction.

A number of business-to-business marketers are also using the Internet to deliver their messages. For example, General Electric uses webisodes as part of its "Ecoimagination" campaign which is designed to show what the company is doing to solve global environmental challenges and problems. The campaign includes a series of webisodes showing GE's efforts in areas such as clean coal technology, harnessing wind and solar power, and producing greener jet engines with lower emissions. The webisodes can be seen on a micro website created for the campaign (ecoimagination.com) and also have run on other sites such as AOL, MSNBC, and Yahoo. Hitachi America, Ltd., made webisodes an integral part of a recent brand building campaign. The integrated campaign included webisodes entitled "Hitachi/True Stories" which are set in small towns across North America and showcase how Hitachi is enhancing the lives of everyday people through its advanced medical technology, information and telecommunications, and consumer electronics.

As more companies integrate the Internet into their IMC campaigns, greater attention is being given to how to do so successfully. Those creating webisodes and other online content note that the best interactive work should engage its audience without demanding too much for it, be viral, tie back to the brand promise, and be something consumers will actually seek out. It must also give the consumer the feeling s/he is discovering his or her own entertainment experience. With technology becoming increasingly able to handle more creative forms, marketers will be developing online campaigns that use various types of online video and other integrated digital technologies such as social media, smartphones, and podcasts. Marketers are demanding more out of the box thinking from their agencies when it comes to creativity. This may mean moving beyond the TV screen and onto the PC or mobile device screen.

Sources: Stuart Elliott, "Old and New Media Coexisting Nicely, Thank You," *The New York Times*, March 19, 2010, p. B4; "Nordstrom Launches Webisodes Starring Michael Buble: Retailer Sponsors 2010 U.S. 'Crazy Love Tour'," *PR Newswire*, March 23, 2010; Andrew Hampp, "Diet Coke Brings Back 'The Style Series'," *Advertising Age*, September 25, 2009, http://adage.com/print?article_id=139278; "Hitachi Unveils Online North America Branding Campaign to Boost Awareness, Connections," *Business Wire*, November 9, 2006; Kris Oser, "Web Wizards Take the Lead in Creative Process," *Advertising Age*, December 6, 2004, p. 6; Michael McCarthy, "Ads Go Hollywood with Short Films," *USA Today*, June 20, 2002, p. 3b.



There are myriad ways that creative personnel can approach the search for big ideas and how to execute them. However, over the years several dominant approaches have emerged that can guide the creative team's search for a major selling idea and the development of effective advertising. Among the four best-known approaches are the following:

- Using a unique selling proposition.
- Creating a brand image.
- Finding the inherent drama.
- Positioning.

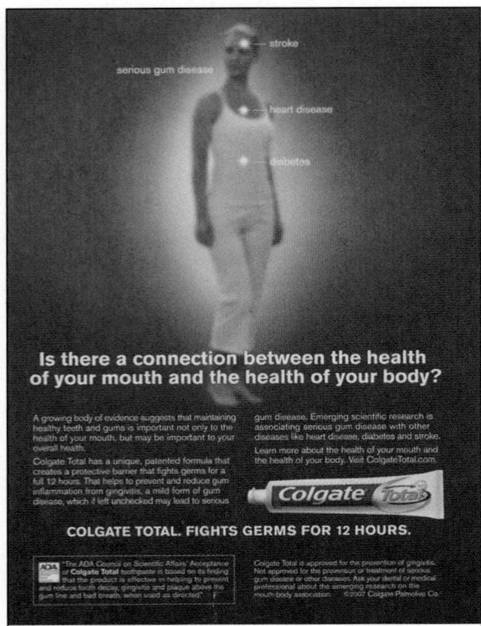


**EXHIBIT 8–14**
This Colgate Total ad uses a unique selling proposition

**Unique Selling Proposition** The concept of the **unique selling proposition (USP)** was developed by Rosser Reeves, former chair of the Ted Bates agency, and is described in his influential book *Reality in Advertising.* Reeves noted three characteristics of unique selling propositions:

1. Each advertisement must make a proposition to the consumer. Not just words, not just product puffery, not just show-window advertising. Each advertisement must say to each reader: "Buy this product and you will get this benefit."
2. The proposition must be one that the competition either cannot or does not offer. It must be unique either in the brand or in the claim.
3. The proposition must be strong enough to move the mass millions, that is, pull over new customers to your brand.[48]

Reeves said the attribute claim or benefit that forms the basis of the USP should dominate the ad and be emphasized through repetitive advertising. An example of advertising based on a USP is the campaign for Colgate's Total toothpaste (Exhibit 8–14). The brand has a unique, patented formula that creates a protective barrier that fights germs for 12 hours which helps reduce and prevent gum disease.

For Reeves's approach to work, there must be a truly unique product or service attribute, benefit, or inherent advantage that can be used in the claim. The approach may require considerable research on the product and consumers, not only to determine the USP but also to document the claim. As we shall see in Chapter 21, the Federal Trade Commission objects to advertisers' making claims of superiority or uniqueness without providing supporting data. Also, some companies have sued their competitors for making unsubstantiated uniqueness claims.[49]

Advertisers must also consider whether the unique selling proposition affords them a *sustainable competitive advantage* that competitors cannot easily copy. In the packaged-goods field in particular, companies quickly match a brand feature for feature, so advertising based on USPs becomes obsolete. For example, in 2008 the Miller Brewing Co. introduced MGD 64, a 64-calorie version of its Miller Genuine Draft brand and the lowest-calorie domestic beer on the market. However, within a year its major rival Anheuser Busch launched Bud Select 55, which contained only 55 calories, after noting the success Miller had with its ultra-low calorie beer.[50]

**Creating a Brand Image** In many product and service categories, competing brands are so similar that it is very difficult to find or create a unique attribute or benefit to use as the major selling idea. Many of the packaged-goods products that account for most of the advertising dollars spent in the United States are difficult to differentiate on a functional or performance basis. The creative strategy used to sell these products is based on the development of a strong, memorable identity for the brand through **image advertising**.

David Ogilvy popularized the idea of brand image in his famous book *Confessions of an Advertising Man.* Ogilvy said that with image advertising, "every advertisement should be thought of as a contribution to the complex symbol which is the brand image." He argued that the image or personality of the brand is particularly important when brands are similar:

> The greater the similarity between brands, the less part reason plays in brand selection. There isn't any significant difference between the various brands of whiskey, or cigarettes, or beer. They are all about the same. And so are the cake mixes and the detergents and the margarines. The manufacturer who dedicates his advertising to building the most sharply defined personality for his brand will get the largest share of the market at the highest profit. By the same token, the manufacturers who will find themselves up the creek are those shortsighted opportunists who siphon off their advertising funds for promotions.[51]

**EXHIBIT 8–15**
bebe uses advertising to build an image as a sexy and stylish brand

Image advertising has become increasingly popular and is used as the main selling idea for a variety of products and services, including soft drinks, liquor, cigarettes, cars, airlines, financial services, perfume/colognes, and clothing. Many consumers wear designer jeans or Ralph Lauren polo shirts or drink certain brands of beer or soft drinks because of the image of these brands. The key to successful image advertising is developing an image that will appeal to product users. This is often done by associating a brand with certain symbols or artifacts that have cultural meaning. For example, Marlboro became the leading brand of cigarettes by using advertising that associates the brand with the cowboy, who is perceived as rugged, individualistic, and a symbol of freedom and independence. Many fashion brands build an image by using ads that feature attractive models and visual appeals that convey psychosocial associations and feelings such as sexy, stylish, glamorous, and sophisticated. Advertising for bebe embodies many of these image characteristics as a way of building an emotional connection with young women who are interested in style and fashion (Exhibit 8–15).



**Finding the Inherent Drama** Another approach to determining the major selling idea is finding the **inherent drama** or characteristic of the product that makes the consumer purchase it. The inherent drama approach expresses the advertising philosophy of Leo Burnett, founder of the Leo Burnett agency in Chicago. Burnett said inherent drama "is often hard to find but it is always there, and once found it is the most interesting and believable of all advertising appeals."[52] He believed advertising should be based on a foundation of consumer benefits with an emphasis on the dramatic element in expressing those benefits.

Burnett advocated a down-home type of advertising that presents the message in a warm and realistic way. Some of the more famous ads developed by his agency using the inherent-drama approach are for McDonald's, Maytag appliances, Kellogg cereals, and Hallmark cards. For example, during the recent recession Burnett developed an emotion-based campaign for Hallmark, touting a greeting card as "The biggest little thing you can do." The ads emphasized the gratitude and appreciation that can come from a small gesture such as sending a card and promoted the 99-cent line of cards Hallmark had been selling for many years. The campaign featured a series of 15-second TV commercials which showed how spouses, children, and mentors respond to unexpected cards and used John Mayer's "Say What You Need to Say" as a musical backdrop for the message. The campaign also used rich media Internet banner ads, such as the one shown in Exhibit 8–16 which when clicked on and opened allowed the consumer to choose the card that is given to the person in the ad and then sit back and view the different reactions by the person who receives it.[53]

**EXHIBIT 8–16**
Advertising for Hallmark often uses inherent drama

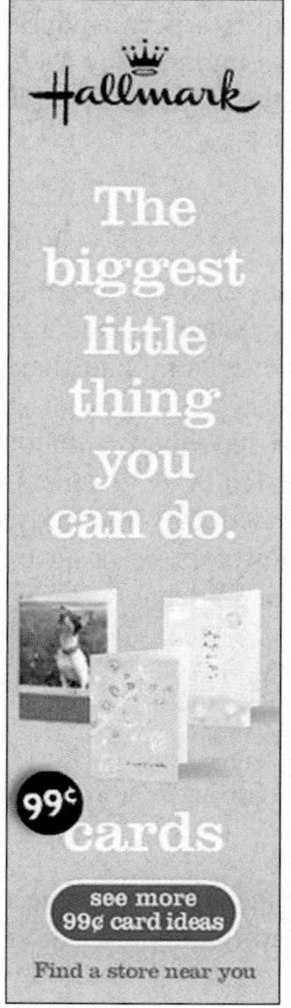


**Positioning** The concept of *positioning* as a basis for advertising strategy was introduced by Jack Trout and Al Ries in the early 1970s and has become a popular basis of creative development.[54] The basic idea is that advertising is used to establish or "position" the product or service in a particular place in the consumer's mind. Positioning is done for companies as well as for brands. Many of the top brands in various product and service categories have retained their market leadership because they have established and maintained a strong position or identity in the minds of consumers.[55] For example, Crest has built and maintained the success of its toothpaste based on the position of cavity prevention while BMW's positioning of its car as the "ultimate driving machine" transcends and helps to differentiate its entire product line.

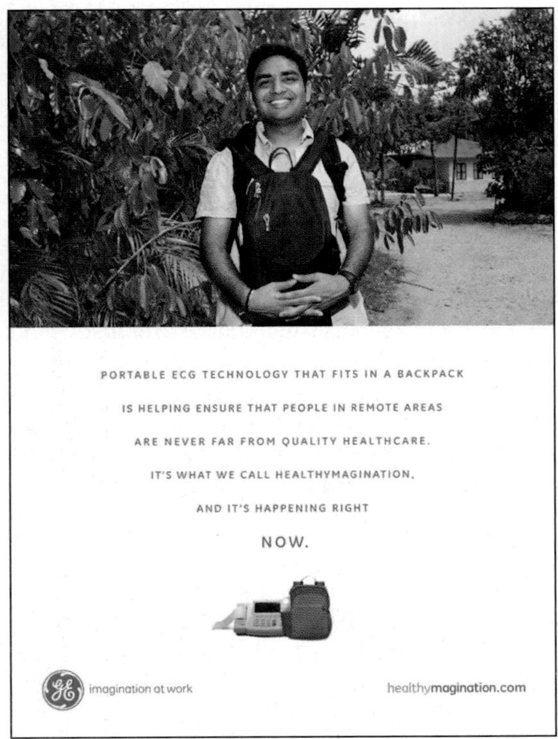


**EXHIBIT 8–17**
General Electric positions itself as an innovative company in areas such as health care

Positioning is also done for entire companies as well as various divisions of large corporations. For example, General Electric positions itself as an innovative and imaginative company that is making a difference in the world by building the energy, health, transportation, and technology infrastructure for the new millennium. Exhibit 8–17 shows an ad from GE's Healthyimagination campaign which focuses on how the company is changing health care delivery in more than 100 countries by focusing on early diagnosis, intervention, and prevention of illness.

Trout and Ries originally described positioning as the image consumers had of the brand in relation to competing brands in the product or service category, but the concept has been expanded beyond direct competitive positioning. As discussed in Chapter 2, products can be positioned on the basis of product attributes, price/quality, usage or application, product users, or product class. Any of these can spark a major selling idea that becomes the basis of the creative strategy and results in the brand's occupying a particular place in the minds of the target audience. Since positioning can be done on the basis of a distinctive attribute, the positioning and unique selling proposition approaches can overlap. Positioning approaches have been used as the foundation for a number of successful creative strategies.

Positioning is often the basis of a firm's creative strategy when it has multiple brands competing in the same market. For example, the two top-selling brands of motor oil, Pennzoil and Quaker State, became part of the same company following a merger a few years ago and are now owned by the Shell Oil Company. The company creates separate identities for the two brands by positioning them differently and targeting a slightly different group of motor oil consumers for each.[56] Pennzoil is positioned as a brand that stands for protection and is targeted at the "Active Specifier" or person who will most likely pay to have their oil changed. Quaker State/Q uses a performance positioning and targets the "Enthusiast" segment that is involved in maintaining their car and will most likely purchase their own oil and install it themselves. Exhibit 8–18 shows ads for each brand reflecting these positioning themes.

## Contemporary Approaches to the Big Idea

The USP, brand image, inherent-drama, and positioning approaches are often used as the basis of the creative strategy for ad campaigns. These creative styles have become associated with some of the most successful creative minds in advertising and their agencies.[57] However, many other creative approaches are available.

Some of the more contemporary advertising visionaries who have had a major influence on modern-day advertising include Hal Riney of Hal Riney & Partners, Lee Clow and Jay Chiat of TBWA/Chiat/Day, Dan Wieden of Wieden + Kennedy, and Jeff Goodby and Rich Silverstein of Goodby, Silverstein & Partners. In describing today's creative leaders, Anthony Vagnoni of *Advertising Age* writes:

> The modern creative kings don't write books, rarely give interviews or lay out their theories on advertising. They've endorsed no set of rules, professed no simple maxims like Mr. Ogilvy's famous "When you don't have anything to say, sing it." If pronouncements and books are out the window, what's replaced them is a conscious desire to lift the intelligence level of advertising. Today's leaders see advertising as an uplifting social force, as a way to inspire and entertain.[58]

Goodby and Silverstein note: "Advertising works best when it sneaks into people's lives, when it doesn't look or feel like advertising. It's about treating people at their

**EXHIBIT 8–18**
Advertising for Pennzoil and Quaker State positions the brands differently

best, as opposed to dealing with them at their lowest common denominator." They describe their creative formula as doing intelligent work that the public likes to see and that, at the same time, has a sales pitch.[59] Lee Clow says, "No rule book will tell you how to target the masses anymore. The best of us understand the sociocultural realities of people and how they interact with the media. If we didn't, we couldn't make the kinds of messages that people would be able to connect with."[60]

Specific agencies are by no means limited to any one creative approach. For example, the famous "Marlboro country" campaign, a classic example of image advertising, was developed by Leo Burnett Co. Many different agencies have followed the unique selling proposition approach advocated by Rosser Reeves at Ted Bates. The challenge to the creative specialist or team is to find a major selling idea—whether it is based on a unique selling proposition, brand image, inherent drama, position in the market, or some other approach—and use it as a guide in developing an effective creative strategy.

Advertisers are facing major challenges in their search for the big idea in the new world of integrated marketing communications. They are faced with the challenge of developing creative ideas that can differentiate their brands and extend beyond traditional mass media. Most marketers and their agencies recognize that they must come up with big ideas that can be used across a variety of media and can engage consumers and enter into a dialogue with them.[61] The problem facing advertisers was noted recently by Jeff Goodby, co-chair of Goodby, Silverstein & Partners, San Francisco, which was selected as Agency of the Year by the trade publication *Adweek* for its excellent creative work for clients such as Hyundai, Sprint, and Hewlett-Packard.

In explaining the success of the agency and its ability to adapt, Goodby stated that "the company has changed more in the last two years than it did in the first 23. It's a necessary change and the whole business is going to have to change to exist. Nobody knows what advertising is anymore and the change in our company is a reaction to that."[62]

## Summary

The creative development and execution of the advertising message are crucial parts of a firm's integrated marketing communications program and are often the key to the success of a marketing campaign. Marketers generally turn to ad agencies to develop, prepare, and implement their creative strategy since these agencies are specialists in the creative function of advertising. The creative specialist or team is responsible for developing an effective way to communicate the marketer's message to the customer. Other individuals on both the client and the agency sides work with the creative specialists to develop the creative strategy, implement it, and evaluate its effectiveness.

The challenge facing the writers, artists, and others who develop ads is to be creative and come up with fresh, unique, and appropriate ideas that can be used as solutions to communications problems. Creativity in advertising is a process of several stages, including preparation, incubation, illumination, verification, and revision. Various sources of information are available to help the creative specialists determine the best campaign theme, appeal, or execution style.

Creative strategy development is guided by specific goals and objectives and is based on a number of factors, including the target audience, the basic problem the advertising must address, the objectives the message seeks to accomplish, and the major selling idea or key benefit the advertiser wants to communicate. These factors are generally stated in a copy platform, which is a work plan used to guide development of the ad campaign. An important part of creative strategy is determining the major selling idea that will become the central theme of the campaign. There are several approaches to doing this, including using a unique selling proposition, creating a brand image, looking for inherent drama in the brand, and positioning.

## Key Terms

**creative strategy** p. 259
**creative tactics** p. 259
**advertising creativity** p. 262
**divergence** p. 262
**relevance** p. 262
**account planning** p. 270
**general preplanning input** p. 271
**product/service-specific preplanning input** p. 271
**problem detection** p. 271
**focus groups** p. 272
**ethnographic research** p. 273
**storyboard** p. 274
**animatic** p. 274
**advertising campaign** p. 275
**campaign theme** p. 275
**slogan (tagline)** p. 275
**creative brief** p. 277
**major selling idea** p. 280
**unique selling proposition (USP)** p. 284
**image advertising** p. 284
**inherent drama** p. 285

## Discussion Questions

1. The chapter opener discusses the popular "The man your man could smell like" commercial the Wieden + Kennedy agency has created for Old Spice body wash. Analyze this commercial from an advertising creativity perspective and discuss some of the reasons it has become so popular. Do you view it as an effective way to sell the product? Why or why not? (LO1)

2. Advertising creativity is viewed as the ability to generate unique and appropriate ideas that can be used as solutions to communication problems. This definition suggests that a creative ad is one that is novel but also relevant or appropriate. Find an example of an advertisement (either a print ad or TV commercial) that is novel but not necessarily relevant to the product or service. Discuss why the client would have approved this ad. (LO1)

3. Discuss the various factors that account for the way divergence can be achieved in advertising creativity. Find

an example of an advertisement that reflects these various characteristics and explain how it does so. (LO1)

4. What is your opinion of advertising awards, such as the Cannes Lions, that are based solely on creativity? If you were a marketer, would you take these creative awards into consideration in your agency evaluation process? Why or why not? (LO1)

5. Evaluate the debate over creative versus hard-sell advertising. Discuss the arguments for and against each perspective. Who should be responsible for judging the creativity of an ad—clients or agency creative personnel? (LO1)

6. Many advertising creative personnel are opposed to focus group research as they argue that they may inhibit the creative process. Discuss the problems, as well as the value, of using focus groups to evaluate advertising creative work. (LO2)

7. Assume that you have been hired as an account planner by an advertising agency and assigned to work on the advertising campaign for a new brand of bottled water. Describe the various types of general and product-specific preplanning input you might provide to the creative team. (LO2)

8. Discuss the role an advertising slogan plays in the development of an advertising campaign as well as some of the factors that should be considered in developing an effective tagline. Find an example of a good tagline as well as one that does not communicate effectively. Discuss the reasons why you view these as either good or bad examples of advertising slogans. (LO3)

9. Briefly describe the five major communication interfaces and decision points in the model of marketing information flow shown in Figure 8–4. Discuss how breakdowns in communication can occur at each interface and how this might negatively impact the creative process. (LO3)

10. Discuss the key characteristics of a unique selling proposition. What are some of the factors an advertiser must consider in developing an advertising campaign that uses a USP as the basis for the major selling idea? (LO4)

11. Find an example of an ad or campaign that you think reflects one of the approaches used to develop a major selling idea such as unique selling proposition, brand image, inherent drama, or positioning. Discuss how the major selling idea is reflected in this ad or campaign. (LO4)

## AdForum Exercise: Analyzing Award Winning Campaigns and Commercials

(See Advertising and Promotion Playlist, Chapter 8)

### PART I: INTEGRATED CAMPAIGNS

The AdForum Playlist for this chapter contains the three campaigns that received Grand Prix awards in the Integrated Marketing category at the 2010 Cannes Lions Advertising Festival including "Replay" for Gatorade, "Chalkbot" for Nike Livestrong apparel, and "Choose a Different Ending" for the London Metropolitan Police Service. Answer the following for each of these campaigns:

1 Analyze each award winning campaign from an integrated marketing communications perspective giving attention to the way various IMC tools are used.

2 Discuss the major selling idea behind each campaign and discuss how it is reflected in the way the campaign is implemented.

3 Assume you are a judge at the Cannes Advertising Festival and are asked to write a short summary describing why this campaign should be considered for a Grand Prix award in the Integrated category. What would you say in your summary?

### PART II: FILM AWARDS

The playlist for this chapter also includes the Old Spice commercial that won the 2010 Grand Prix award for film along with four other commercials that won Cannes Lions awards in the film category. Watch each of these commercials and address the following:

1 Analyze each commercial in terms of the two major determinants of creativity (divergence and relevance) discussed in the chapter.

2 Why do you think this ad was selected as a Cannes Lion award winner in the film category?

3 Evaluate this award winning commercial with respect to its effectiveness in helping sell the product or service being advertised. Do you think this commercial has an appropriate balance between creativity and delivering an effective sales message for the brand?

Access to the chapter playlist is available through 

, www.mcgrawhillconnect.com

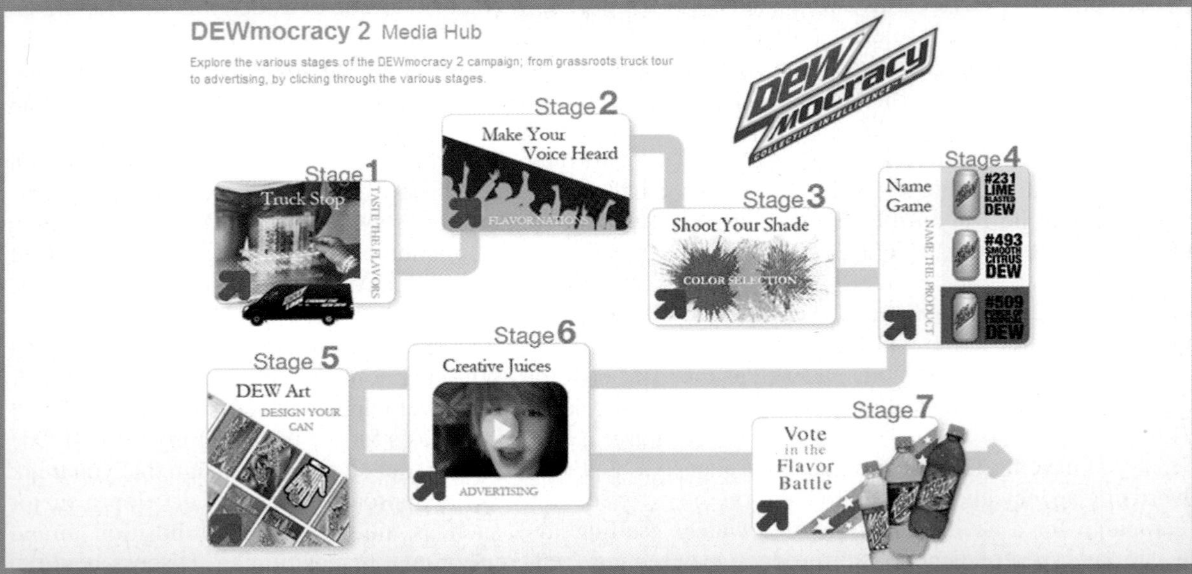


## LEARNING OBJECTIVES

LO1 To analyze various types of appeals that can be used in the development and implementation of an advertising message.

LO2 To analyze the various creative execution styles that advertisers can use and the advertising situations where they are most appropriate.

LO3 To analyze various tactical issues involved in the creation of print advertising and TV commercials.

LO4 To consider how clients evaluate the creative work of their agencies and discuss guidelines for the evaluation and approval process.

# 9 Creative Strategy: Implementation and Evaluation

## MOUNTAIN DEW USES DEWMOCRACY TO CREATE A NEW FLAVOR

From its initial creation by the Hartman Beverage Company in Tennessee in the late 1940s, Mountain Dew has always been known as the soft drink that provides a little extra. The drink was initially used as a mixer for liquor and the founders named the product after an old-time Appalachian folk song that told of the pleasure of "mountain dew" moonshine whiskey. The bright yellow-green citrus flavored drink came in a green bottle and contained more sugar and caffeine, and less carbonation so it could be chugged quickly and provide the drinker with a rush. Mountain Dew evolved into a stand-alone soft drink with a bit of a renegade attitude as the initial advertising featured a comic hillbilly character named Willy. Over the next two decades the popularity of Mountain Dew spread beyond the Appalachian region and the drink became a favorite along the Eastern seaboard and into the Midwest.

PepsiCo noticed the growing popularity of Mountain Dew and purchased the brand in 1964 to add a non-cola, flavored soft drink to its product line. The company kept the hillbilly character, renamed him Clem, and put him in animated ads linked to the brand's backwoods heritage that used the tagline "Yahoo! Mountain Dew!" and proclaimed that "Thar's a bang in ever' bottle." In 1973 PepsiCo began working with BBDO on the advertising for Mountain Dew, and over the next two decades various campaigns were used to create a national identity for the brand that went beyond rural areas and into the major metropolitan markets as well. The advertising toned down the energizing effects of the extra sugar and caffeine and began positioning Mountain Dew as a refreshing part of an active, country lifestyle and expanding the target market to include suburban teenagers. A new campaign called "Country Cool" ran for a few years but soon gave way to a new creative approach built around daredevil athletic stunts involving alternative sports such as skateboarding, snowboarding, windsurfing, rollerblading, and BMX biking, which were becoming increasingly popular among urban teens.

By 1992 Mountain Dew had become a national brand, but distribution of the diet version of the product was still limited to rural markets where the brand was the strongest. To expand the market for Diet Mountain Dew, a campaign was created using the tagline "Do Diet Dew" and featured the "Dew Dudes"—four young slacker type guys who live in a world in which only extreme stunts and Mountain Dew matter and who witness and/or participate in all of the stunts. Although originally developed for the diet product, the Dew Dudes helped solidify the association with action sports, as well as irreverence, and became the basis of the advertising for the entire Mountain Dew brand. The tagline evolved into "Do the Dew", which served as an umbrella theme for the Mountain Dew brand and ads featuring the Dew Dudes were the basis of one of the best known advertising campaigns of the past two decades.

Mountain Dew continued to build on its image as an irreverent brand that stands for individuality by continuing to embrace all things edgy including extreme sports, video gaming, and other activities. In 2005 Mountain Dew began sponsoring the Dew Tour which has become a premier action sports tour and helps keep the brand connected to the action sports community. However, as the beverage market became more competitive with the myriad of new drinks competing for consumers' attention, Mountain Dew looked for additional ways to connect with its loyal consumers, most of whom are males between the ages of 18 and 39 and are very active online.

In 2007 the Mountain Dew brand team gave its highly loyal customer base a way to become more involved with the brand through an initiative called DEWmocracy. The goal of this program was to open up the product development process and have the brand's passionate fans create and choose a new Mountain Dew flavor. More than 1 million people participated in a series of interactive games on the DEWmocracy.com website to develop every aspect of three alternatives for the new line extension, including color, flavor, graphics, and name. The three consumer-created flavors were made available in stores across the country for a limited time and approximately 500,000 votes were cast. The winner was Mountain Dew Voltage, a citrus flavor charged with raspberry and ginseng that was launched in January 2009 and became the first Mountain Dew made by fans for fans.

With one user-created beverage successfully launched, the Mountain Dew brand team decided to launch a second DEWmocracy initiative that takes the "crowd-sourcing" model several steps further and gives passionate fans even more control by taking advantage of the growing power of social media. DEWmocracy 2 kicked off in July 2009 with a tiered grassroots campaign that included a mobile tour that created 222,712 sampling experiences and a contest which rewarded 50 Dew fanatics with home-tasting kits of seven potential flavors. Recipients of the kits were selected from fans who submitted video clips of up to 12 seconds explaining why they deserved a kit. The home tasters were given video cameras and encouraged to upload videos about their tasting experiences to Facebook and YouTube. Three finalist flavors emerged from the grassroots voting and feedback from brand fanatics.

Once the flavors were selected, DEW Labs, a brand community composed of Mountain Dew's 4,000 most passionate fans, was created. Each member received samples of the three final flavors, chose a favorite, and joined the corresponding "Flavor Nation" which was charged with developing names, package designs, and colors for each. Consumers were asked to participate in the development of the products as well. Colors were selected via a live UStream event on Facebook, where Mountain Dew had half-million fans at the time. Consumers cast more than 7,000 votes and the brand team devised a clever visual way to demonstrate the vote count that fit well with the culture of Mountain Dew's irreverent fans—the votes triggered paint balls in the voters' preferred color to be shot at volunteers during a live event. To name their beverage, Flavor Nation members submitted lists of suggestions then chose their three favorites. Once PepsiCo's legal department had vetted the name, the final names were picked via a "Twitter race" where each name was assigned a Twitter account and the one that attracted the most followers won. The three winners were Mtn Dew Typhoon, Mtn Dew Distortion, and Mtn Dew White Out.

Mountain Dew also turned over the selection of a creative agency to fans, as agencies and individuals were invited to submit 12-second videos via 12seconds.tv outlining their ideas for marketing the three new flavor options. More than 200 ads were submitted, many by advertising agencies, and six finalists were selected by consumers who cast more than 15,000 votes. The finalists created short pitch videos for the Flavor Nations and three were selected to work closely with the DEW brand team and the Flavor Nations to create television spots for each flavor. They began airing nationally in April 2010 and marked the first use of traditional media for the campaign in 10 months of activity.

The final phase of DEWmocracy involved having the Flavor Nations fight for the allegiance of DEW fans when their products hit the store shelves and rallying consumers around the country to vote for their products. Each nation had its own Facebook page and Twitter account to get the word out during the eight week period that the products were available at retail.

Voting ran until early June and the flavor receiving the most votes was Mtn Dew White Out. The DEW online community was once again engaged to help develop the launch plan for the new brand which debuted as a permanent member of the Mountain Dew family in October of 2010. DEWmocracy prevailed and Mtn Dew White Out became the second flavor of Mountain Dew created entirely by DEW drinkers for DEW drinkers.

Sources: Natalie Zmuda, "Why Mtn Dew Let Skater Dudes Take Control of Its Marketing," *Advertising Age*, February 22, 2010, http://adage.com/print?article_id=14220 ; Natalie Zmuda, "New Pepsi 'Dewmocracy' Push Threatens to Crowd Out Shops, *Advertising Age*, November 2, 2009, http://adage.com/print?article_id=140120; "Dewmocracy Campaign Overview," www.dewmocracymediahub.com.

In Chapter 8, we discussed the importance of advertising creativity and examined the various steps in the creative process. We focused on determining what the advertising message should communicate. This chapter focuses on *how* the message will be executed. It examines various appeals and execution styles that can be used to develop the ad and tactical issues involved in the design and production of effective advertising messages. We conclude by presenting some guidelines clients can use to evaluate the creative work of their agencies.

# APPEALS AND EXECUTION STYLES

The **advertising appeal** refers to the approach used to attract the attention of consumers and/or to influence their feelings toward the product, service, or cause. An advertising appeal can also be viewed as "something that moves people, speaks to their wants or needs, and excites their interest."[1] The **creative execution style** is the way a particular appeal is turned into an advertising message presented to the consumer. According to William Weilbacher:

> The appeal can be said to form the underlying content of the advertisement, and the execution the way in which that content is presented. Advertising appeals and executions are usually independent of each other; that is, a particular appeal can be executed in a variety of ways and a particular means of execution can be applied to a variety of advertising appeals. Advertising appeals tend to adapt themselves to all media, whereas some kinds of executional devices are more adaptable to some media than others.[2]

## Advertising Appeals

Many different appeals can be used as the basis for advertising messages. At the broadest level, these approaches are generally broken into two categories: informational/rational appeals and emotional appeals. In this section, we focus on ways to use rational and emotional appeals as part of a creative strategy. We also consider how rational and emotional appeals can be combined in developing the advertising message.

### Informational/Rational Appeals

**Informational/rational appeals** focus on the consumer's practical, functional, or utilitarian need for the product or service and emphasize features of a product or service and/or the benefits or reasons for owning or using a particular brand. The content of these messages emphasizes facts, learning, and the logic of persuasion.[3] Rational-based appeals tend to be informative, and advertisers using them generally attempt to convince consumers that their product or service has a particular attribute(s) or provides a specific benefit that satisfies their needs. Their objective is to persuade the target audience to buy the brand because it is the best available or does a better job of meeting consumers' needs. For example, the Acura ad shown in Exhibit 9–1 uses a rational appeal focusing on how the Advanced Compatibility Engineering™ body structure in the Acura TL automobile is an innovative safety feature.

**EXHIBIT 9–1**
A rational appeal is used to promote the safety features of the Acura TL

Pound your fist here.

Many rational motives can be used as the basis for advertising appeals, including comfort, convenience, economy, health, and sensory benefits such as touch, taste, and smell. Other rational motives or purchase criteria commonly used in advertising include quality, dependability, durability, efficiency, efficacy, and performance. The particular features, benefits, or evaluative criteria that are important to consumers and can serve as the basis of an informational/rational appeal vary from one product or service category to another as well as among various market segments.

Weilbacher identified several types of advertising appeals that fall under the category of rational approaches, among them feature, competitive advantage, favorable price, news, and product/service popularity appeals.

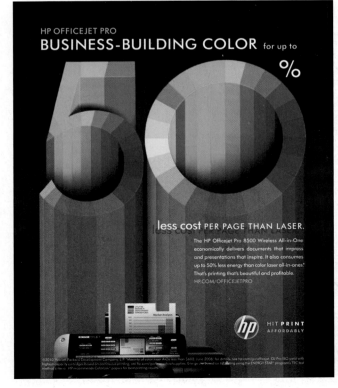

Ads that use a *feature appeal* focus on the dominant traits of the product or service. These ads tend to be highly informative and present the customer with a number of important product attributes or features that will lead to favorable attitudes and can be used as the basis for a rational purchase decision. Technical and high-involvement products such as automobiles often use this type of advertising appeal. However, a feature appeal can be used for a variety of products and services. These types of appeals often show how product attributes can result in specific benefits for consumers. For example, Exhibit 9–2 shows an ad for Red Bull that focuses on the various ingredients contained in the energy drink and the benefits they provide such as enhanced performance, endurance, and concentration. This particular ad is targeted to students, who are an important target market for energy drinks, and suggests that Red Bull can help you stay awake and alert when studying for exams.

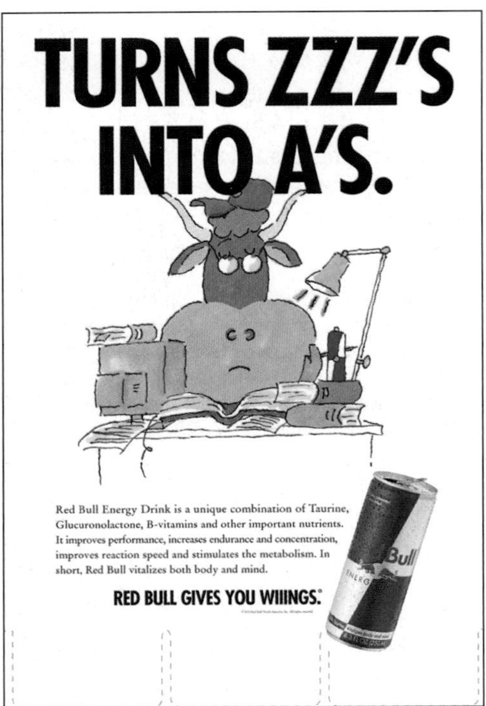


**EXHIBIT 9–2**
Red Bull uses a feature appeal to promote its product benefits to students

When a *competitive advantage appeal* is used, the advertiser makes either a direct or an indirect comparison to another brand (or brands) and usually claims superiority on one or more attributes. This type of appeal was discussed in Chapter 6 under "Comparative Advertising."

A *favorable price appeal* makes the price offer the dominant point of the message. Price appeal advertising is used most often by retailers to announce sales, special offers, or low everyday prices. Price appeal ads are often used by national advertisers during recessionary times. Many fast-food chains have made price an important part of their marketing strategy through promotional deals and "value menus" or lower overall prices, and their advertising strategy is designed to communicate this. Many other types of advertisers use price appeals as well, such as airlines and car-rental companies. Price-based appeals are also often used by business-to-business marketers to advertise products and/or services and promote their value or affordability. For example, the Hewlett-Packard advertisement shown in Exhibit 9–3 promotes the affordability of the HP Officejet Pro printer for business use. The ad copy explains how it can print in color at a cost that is up to 50 percent less per page than a laser printer and consumes less energy. The visual portion of the ad also uses very vivid colors to represent the number 50 and deliver a message regarding the quality of the color printing capabilities of the Officejet Pro.

**EXHIBIT 9–3**
HP advertises the affordability of color printing to businesses that use the Officejet Pro

HP OFFICEJET PRO
BUSINESS-BUILDING COLOR for up to 50%
less cost PER PAGE THAN LASER.
The HP Officejet Pro 8500 Wireless All-in-One economically delivers documents that impress and presentations that inspire. It also consumes up to 50% less energy than color laser all-in-ones.* That's printing that's beautiful and profitable.
HP.COM/OFFICEJETPRO
HIT PRINT AFFORDABLY

*News appeals* are those in which some type of news or announcement about the product, service, or company dominates the ad. This type of appeal can be used for a new product or service or to inform consumers of significant modifications or improvements. This appeal works best when a company has important news it wants to communicate to its target market. For example, airlines sometimes use news appeals when they begin offering service to new cities or opening new routes as a way of informing consumers as well as generating media interest that can result in publicity for them.

*Product/service popularity appeals* stress the popularity of a product or service by pointing out the number of consumers who use the brand, the number who have switched to it, the number of experts who recommend

**FIGURE 9–1**
Bases for Emotional Appeals

| Personal States or Feelings | | Social-Based Feelings |
|---|---|---|
| Safety | Arousal/stimulation | Recognition |
| Security | Sorrow/grief | Status |
| Fear | Pride | Respect |
| Love | Achievement/accomplishment | Involvement |
| Affection | Self-esteem | Embarrassment |
| Happiness | Actualization | Affiliation/belonging |
| Joy | Pleasure | Rejection |
| Nostalgia | Ambition | Acceptance |
| Sentiment | Comfort | Approval |
| Excitement | | |

it, or its leadership position in the market. The main point of this advertising appeal is that the wide use of the brand proves its quality or value and other customers should consider using it. The ad shown in Exhibit 9–4 uses a popularity appeal by noting how TaylorMade drivers are used by more PGA Tour professionals than its leading competitors combined. Ads such as this are used to implement TaylorMade's marketing strategy which focuses on innovation, the technological superiority of its golf equipment, and the popularity and use of its clubs by tour professionals who exert a strong influence on the purchase decisions of amateur golfers.

**Emotional Appeals** **Emotional appeals** relate to the customers' social and/or psychological needs for purchasing a product or service. Many consumers' motives for their purchase decisions are emotional, and their feelings about a brand can be more important than knowledge of its features or attributes. Advertisers for many products and services view rational, information-based appeals as dull. Many advertisers believe appeals to consumers' emotions work better at selling brands that do not differ markedly from competing brands, since rational differentiation of them is difficult.[4]

Many feelings or needs can serve as the basis for advertising appeals designed to influence consumers on an emotional level, as shown in Figure 9–1. These appeals are based on the psychological states or feelings directed to the self (such as pleasure or excitement), as well as those with a more social orientation (such as status or recognition). The ad shown in Exhibit 9–5, featuring actress Amanda Bynes, appeals to emotional motives such as self-esteem and pride and is part of the "Body by Milk" integrated marketing campaign created by America's Milk Processors. The ads are targeted at teens and designed to educate them about the nutritional benefits of milk and how it can help them look their best.

Advertisers can use emotional appeals in many ways in their creative strategy. Kamp and Macinnis note that commercials often rely on the concept

**EXHIBIT 9–4**
TaylorMade promotes the popularity of its drivers among professional golfers

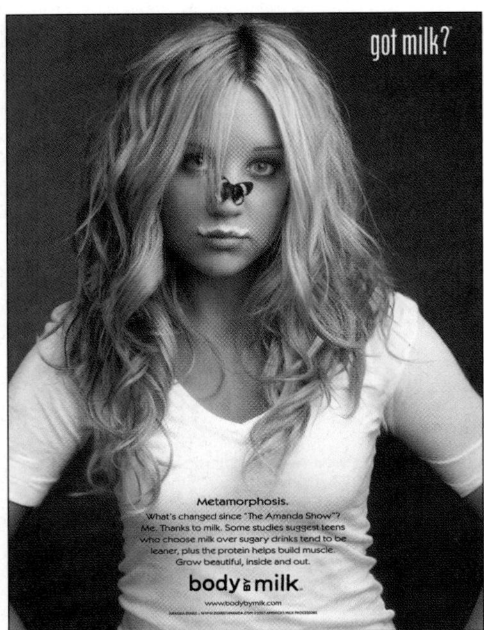


**EXHIBIT 9–5**
This milk ad appeals to emotional motives such as self-esteem and pride

of *emotional integration,* whereby they portray the characters in the ad as experiencing an emotional benefit or outcome from using a product or service.[5] Ads using humor, sex, and other appeals that are very entertaining, arousing, upbeat, and/or exciting can affect the emotions of consumers and put them in a favorable frame of mind. Many TV advertisers use poignant ads that bring a lump to viewers' throats. Hallmark, Nike, Kodak, and McDonald's often create commercials that evoke feelings of warmth, nostalgia, and/or sentiment. Marketers use emotional appeals in hopes that the positive feeling they evoke will transfer to the brand and/or company. Research shows that positive mood states and feelings created by advertising can have a favorable effect on consumers' evaluations of a brand.[6] Studies also show that emotional advertising is better remembered than nonemotional messages.[7]

The effectiveness of emotion-based appeals has also been documented in research conducted by Hamish Pringle and Peter Field and is discussed in their new book *Brand Immortality.*[8] Pringle and Field analyzed 880 case studies of successful advertising campaigns submitted for the United Kingdom–based Institute of Practitioners in Advertising Effectiveness Award competition over the past three decades and included campaigns from the U.K as well as international competitions. Their analysis compared advertising campaigns that relied primarily on emotional appeals versus those that used rational persuasion and information. A key finding from their study is that advertising campaigns with purely emotional content are nearly twice as likely to generate large profit gains than campaigns using only rational content. The emotional only campaigns were also more effective than those that used a combination of emotional and rational content. Their research also showed that one of the reasons why emotional campaigns work so well is that they reduce price sensitivity and strengthen the ability of brands to charge a price premium which contributes to profitability. They also found that emotional campaigns continue to work well during economic downturns such as the recent global recession.[9]

Many successful companies and brands rely on emotional appeals as the basis for their advertising campaigns. For example, McDonald's changed its advertising strategy in 2003 and began putting more of an emotional emphasis into its commercials to evoke more of a feel-good connection with consumers. McDonald's believes the emotional ads take advantage of the chain's unique bond with consumers, which is a significant point of differentiation in the highly competitive fast-food business. In 2003, McDonald's began using the "I'm Lovin It" theme which has been the basis for a global IMC campaign that is designed to enhance consumers' emotional attachment to the fast-food chain. The campaign has been very successful and has helped the company achieve strong sales growth over the past several years.[10] McDonald's recently announced that after a year of consumer research and creative brainstorming that it was continuing with the "I'm Lovin It' campaign, which is its most successful and longest-running ad campaign ever. The company plans to integrate even more emotion into the campaign by focusing more on family bonding and fun with food as well as celebrating uniquely McDonald's moments in its ads.[11]

Another reason for using emotional appeals is to influence consumers' interpretations of their product usage experience. One way of doing this is through what is known as transformational advertising. A **transformational ad** is defined as "one which associates the experience of using (consuming) the advertised brand with a unique set of psychological characteristics which would not typically be associated with the brand experience to the same degree without exposure to the advertisement."[12]

Transformational ads create feelings, images, meanings, and beliefs about the product or service that may be activated when consumers use it, transforming their interpretation of the usage experience. Christopher Puto and William Wells note that a transformational ad has two characteristics:

1. It must make the experience of using the product richer, warmer, more exciting, and/or more enjoyable than that obtained solely from an objective description of the advertised brand.
2. It must connect the experience of the advertisement so tightly with the experience of using the brand that consumers cannot remember the brand without recalling the experience generated by the advertisement.[13]

Transformational advertising can help differentiate a product or service by making the consumption experience more enjoyable by suggesting the type of experiences consumers might have when they consume the product or service. This type of advertising is often used by companies in the travel industry to help consumers envision the experience or feeling they might have when they take a trip such as a cruise or visit a particular destination.

Image advertising, which is designed to give a company or brand a unique association or personality, is often transformational in nature. It is designed to create a certain feeling or mood that is activated when a consumer uses a particular product or service. For example, the Lambesis agency has created a unique image for SKYY vodka by creating ads that associate the brand with cinematic-inspired cocktail moments (see Exhibit 9–6). The high-impact ads do not contain any copy but rather rely on stylish, seductive visuals that set up various story lines but leave the interpretation of the actual scenarios up to the mind of the viewer. All of the ads feature SKYY's distinctive cobalt blue and showcase the brand as a catalyst for a great cocktail moment. The ads have helped SKYY achieve a deep emotional connection with the style-conscious trendsetters that the brand targets.[14]



**Combining Rational and Emotional Appeals** In many advertising situations, the decision facing the creative specialist is not whether to choose an emotional or a rational appeal but, rather, determining how to combine the two approaches. As noted copywriters David Ogilvy and Joel Raphaelson have stated:

> Few purchases of any kind are made for entirely rational reasons. Even a purely functional product such as laundry detergent may offer what is now called an emotional benefit—say, the satisfaction of seeing one's children in bright, clean clothes. In some product categories the rational element is small. These include soft drinks, beer, cosmetics, certain personal care products, and most old-fashioned products. And who hasn't experienced the surge of joy that accompanies the purchase of a new car?[15]

Consumer purchase decisions are often made on the basis of both emotional and rational motives, and attention must be given to both elements in developing effective advertising. For example, in the personal computer market, design and

**EXHIBIT 9–6**
Advertising for SKYY vodka uses a cinematic theme to create an image for the brand

FIGURE 9–2

Levels of Relationships with Brands

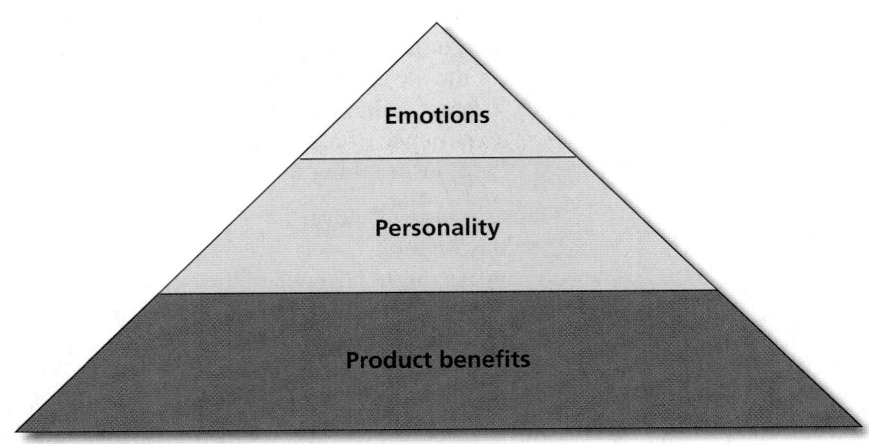


style have become very important to many consumers in choosing a brand in addition to technical features. Companies such as Dell are now focusing a great deal of attention to the design of their computers and are also changing the way they advertise them. Purchase decisions regarding services can also be based on both rational and emotional motives. For example, many consumers choose an airline based on factors such as price, availability, arrival and/or departure time, and the ability to earn miles or points for their travel. However, airlines recognize that it is also important to appeal to emotional factors in competing for passengers. Frequent flyers in particular often become loyal to one airline based on emotional as well as rational motives, and some airlines use ads that are designed to connect to these travelers on an emotional level. For example, American Airlines has been running its "We Know Why You Fly" campaign since 2004, which was created to demonstrate that American has a genuine understanding of the frequent flyer with respect to how and why they fly. The TV commercials and print ads used in the campaign are designed to illustrate how American can better help flyers navigate through their entire travel experience (Exhibit 9–7). The award-winning campaign has helped American connect emotionally with its most valuable customers and increase their brand loyalty.[16]

EXHIBIT 9–7

Advertising for American Airlines often appeals to emotional as well as rational motives

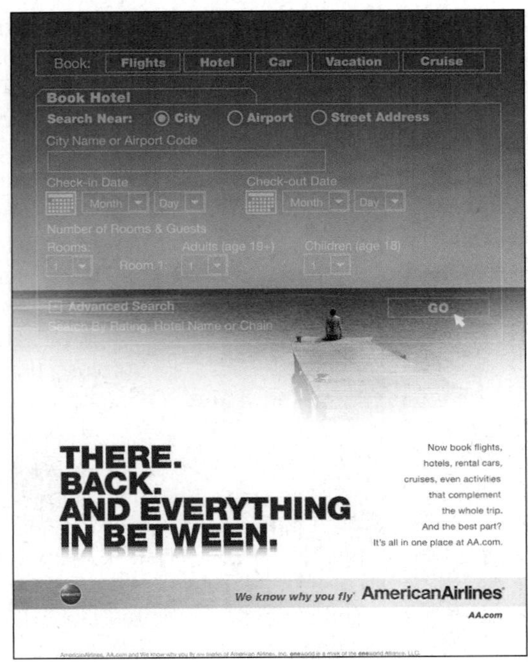


Advertising researchers and agencies have given considerable thought to the relationship between rational and emotional motives in consumer decision making and how advertising influences both. McCann-Erickson Worldwide, in conjunction with advertising professor Michael Ray, developed a proprietary research technique known as *emotional bonding.* This technique evaluates how consumers feel about brands and the nature of any emotional rapport they have with a brand compared to the ideal emotional state they associate with the product category.[17]

The basic concept of emotional bonding is that consumers develop three levels of relationships with brands, as shown in Figure 9–2. The most basic relationship indicates how consumers *think* about brands in respect to product benefits. This occurs, for the most part, through a rational learning process and can be measured by how well advertising communicates product information. Consumers at this stage are not very brand loyal, and brand switching is common.

At the next stage, the consumer assigns a *personality* to a brand. For example, a brand may be thought of as self-assured, aggressive, and adventurous, as opposed to compliant and timid. The consumer's judgment of the brand has moved beyond its attributes or delivery of product/service benefits. In most instances, consumers

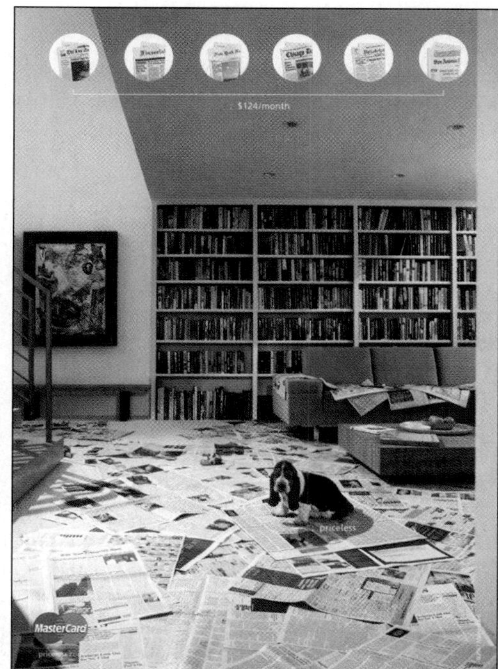


EXHIBIT 9–8
MasterCard's "Priceless" campaign creates an emotional bond with consumers

judge the personality of a brand on the basis of an assessment of overt or covert cues found in its advertising.

McCann-Erickson researchers believe the strongest relationship that develops between a brand and the consumer is based on feelings or emotional attachments to the brand. Consumers develop *emotional bonds* with certain brands, which result in positive psychological movement toward them. The marketer's goal is to develop the greatest emotional linkage between its brand and the consumer. McCann-Erickson believes advertising can develop and enrich emotional bonding between consumers and brands. McCann and its subsidiary agencies use emotional bonding research to provide strategic input into the creative process and determine how well advertising is communicating with consumers. McCann-Erickson used emotional bonding research as the basis for the "Priceless" campaign for MasterCard International, which has been extremely successful. When the agency took over the account in the late '90s, MasterCard had become the third card in the consumer's wallet behind Visa and American Express. The challenge was to reposition the brand and create an emotional bond between consumers and MasterCard while retaining the brand's functional appeal. The idea behind the campaign is that good spenders use credit cards to acquire things that are important to them and enrich their daily lives. The creative execution involves showing a shopping list of items that could be purchased for a certain dollar amount and one key item that could not and thus was deemed "Priceless." The tagline "There are some things money can't buy. For everything else there's MasterCard," positions the card as the way to pay for everything that matters. An entire integrated marketing campaign has been built around the "Priceless" campaign theme that includes sponsorships with Major League Baseball, the National Hockey League, and the PGA golf tour. Contests and sweepstakes have also been part of the campaign. The campaign now runs in 80 countries and has won numerous creative awards. Exhibit 9–8 shows one of the recent print ads from the campaign.

EXHIBIT 9–9
This clever ad reminds golfers to carry Nature Valley Granola Bars

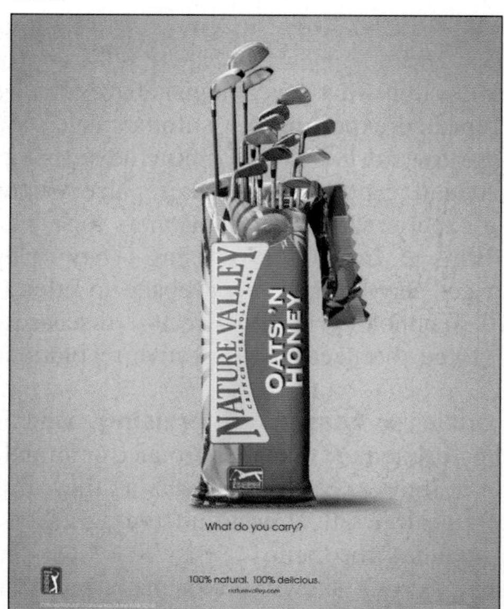


**Additional Types of Appeals** Not every ad fits neatly into the categories of rational or emotional appeals. For example, ads for some brands can be classified as **reminder advertising**, which has the objective of building brand awareness and/or keeping the brand name in front of consumers. Well-known brands and market leaders often use reminder advertising to maintain top-of-mind awareness among consumers in their target markets. For example, Nature Valley runs clever ads such as the one shown in Exhibit 9–9 in golf magazines to remind golfers to carry its granola bars in their bags. Many golfers consume granola and energy bars during a round and this ad uses a golf metaphor (What do you carry?) to encourage them to add Nature Valley bars to the clubs and other accessories in their bags. Products and services that have a seasonal pattern to their consumption also use reminder advertising, particularly around the appropriate period. For example, marketers of candy products often increase their media budgets and run reminder advertising around Halloween, Valentine's Day, Christmas, and Easter.

Online ads often serve as a form of reminder advertising. Many of the banner ads that are pervasive on Internet websites have very low click-through rates but still can be effective and serve a valuable function by fostering familiarity, even though most consumers may never click through to the source of the ads. Research into the psychology of online advertising has shown that repeated exposure to banner advertising can enhance familiarity with and generate positive feelings toward a

# IMC Technology Perspective 9–1 > > >

## The Need for a Creative Revolution in Online Advertising

Before reading this page, take a moment to click on the home page of a popular website such as YouTube.com, ESPN.com, or MSN.com, spend a minute or so on the site as you might normally do, and then close the site. Now answer this simple question: do you recall the name of any company or brand that was advertised in a banner ad on the site or through some other type of message such as a commercial video? Chances are that few, if any, of the products or services being advertised on this website caught your attention and it is extremely unlikely that you clicked on a banner ad or watched an entire commercial video. While a great deal of attention has been given to advertising creativity over the years, much of the focus has been on traditional forms of advertising such as print, television, or outdoor. However, as marketers move large amounts of their media budgets to the online space, more attention needs to be given to creativity for Internet advertising as well.

It has been noted recently that those creating online advertising need to step up their creative game. Getting consumers to pay attention to, not to mention engage with an online ad is very difficult since doing so takes them away from the content on the website. Television and radio ads air during commercial breaks and do not compete for viewers' attention during a program, while print ads often appear on separate pages of a magazine or newspaper and can easily be attended to or ignored by simply turning the page. However, online ads often interrupt our viewing sessions and unless they are providing relevant information that gives consumers something they really need, it is likely they will be ignored.

Critics argue that one of the major problems with Internet advertising is that it has been too focused on ubiquitous banner ads as well as the targeting and measurement of them in terms of click through rates. A great deal of effort focuses on optimizing media placement and measuring the effects of online advertising campaigns, but less attention is given to creative considerations. Randall Rothenberg, CEO of the Interactive Advertising Bureau, argues that advertising on the Internet has been "an unthinking hostage to a direct-marketing culture and tradition that devalues creativity and its long-term effect on brands" and has called for a "creative renaissance" for online advertising. Rothenberg is not alone in his criticism of online advertising. Shaw Riegsecker, founder and CEO of Centro, a company that facilitates the buying and selling of online media, notes that too many marketers are trying to build a favorable brand identity by simply buying massive amounts of banner ads across a myriad of websites. He argues that marketers have been enticed by the idea of cheap banner impressions and spent most of their resources on quantitative analysis, predictive measurement, and audience targeting while ignoring the fundamentals of great advertising.

Creativity for Internet advertising is beginning to receive more attention. One of the firms that is leading the way in this effort is Dynamic Logic, an online advertising research group that is owned by Millward Brown, a leading marketing and advertising research company. Dynamic Logic conducted an extensive study of Internet advertising and factors that determine its effectiveness by analyzing the highest and lowest performers from its data base of more than 170,000 online ads. The study found that creative factors such as persistent branding, strong calls to action, and the use of human faces result in better ad recall, brand awareness, and

brand.[18] These favorable feelings often occur through what psychologists have identified as the *mere exposure effect,* whereby repeated exposure to a stimulus (such as a brand name) can result in favorable feelings toward it.[19] While online advertising may have positive effects through the incidental exposure that takes place when consumers visit a website, many advertising experts argue that consumers tune out most of the banner ads, as well as other forms of Internet advertising. They note that it is becoming increasingly difficult to get people visiting a website to attend to, let alone engage with, online ads.[20] IMC Technology Perspective 9–1 discusses how many in the advertising industry have noted the need for a creative revolution in online advertising.

Advertisers introducing a new product often use **teaser advertising**, which is designed to build curiosity, interest, and/or excitement about a product or brand by talking about it but not actually showing it. Teasers, or *mystery ads* as they are sometimes called, are also used by marketers to draw attention to upcoming advertising campaigns and generate interest and publicity for them.

Teaser ads also are often used for new movies or TV shows and for major product launches. They are especially popular among automotive advertisers for introducing purchase intentions rather than highly targeted or high-profile online ad placements. The results of the study support past research conducted by the company which has shown that creative quality accounts for 50 to 75 percent of the success or failure of online advertising while factors such as ad size, technology, and targeting make up the remainder.

Dynamic Logic's research manager for custom solutions notes that while the finding that good creative makes for better advertising borders on the obvious, the firm still sees a "shockingly large percentage of creative that falls short of its potential." This, of course, leads to the question of why there are so many problems with the creative quality of online advertising. Rei Inamoto, chief creative officer at digital agency AKQA, feels that creative quality suffers because publisher-determined online ad formats are limiting, while the myriad of banner sizes requires creative that has to be constantly reformatted to fit into ad constraints that vary from one website to another. He notes that "unlike TV or, to some extent print, where formats are fairly consistent, online ads suffer from numerous formats. Agencies have to create so many of the same things. Thus the creative becomes somewhat generic and standards are all over the place."

Another problem that impacts online advertising is the overreliance on large size ad formats such as horizontally oriented leaderboards (a 728×90 pixel ad unit that stretches across a webpage) or skyscrapers (120×600 or 160×600 pixel–wide version) that are vertically oriented and give advertisers the ability to place an ad adjacent to the website content. The Dynamic Logic study analyzed results from 4,800 online campaigns and found that the best-performing ad unit in terms of metrics such as brand awareness, recall, and purchase intent was the traditional 180×150 pixel rectangular banner ad. Ken Mallon, a senior vice president for the company, notes that ads surrounding content, such as well-worn skyscraper and leaderboard units, are the least effective, as people have developed "banner blindness." Mallon says: "It's like going into an art gallery—if I found you later and asked what color the frame on such-and-such a painting was, you'll have no clue because you're trained to block out the frame. But you could probably answer questions about the painting."

Traditional rectangular banner ads are thought to be more effective because they are often closer to, and interrupt the content, which means that as you read the information on the site, your eye naturally has to roll over the ad. However, ads that cover content are also among the most annoying online advertising formats. Dynamic Logic suggests that online ads should never cover the content a user is trying to find and should not be so busy that they are annoying. A study conducted in a Harris interactive poll reinforces these points as the survey found that ads that cover content or do not have a "skip" or "close' button are the most annoying online advertising formats.

Marketers are likely to continue to move more of their advertising to the Internet as they know that their target audiences are spending more time online. Moreover, many marketers feel that the targeting and measurement capabilities of the Internet more than make up for the creative limitations of online advertising. However, it is also important for marketers to challenge their agencies to develop online ads that are entertaining and engaging rather than continuing to bombard consumers with more leaderboards, skyscrapers, banner ads, and/or video buttons to click. Most industry experts agree that online advertising will work even better if there is an interactive creative revolution.

Sources: "Online Advertising Needs a Different Kind of Creativity," editorial—*Advertising Age*, October 26, 2009, http://adage.com/print?article_id=139931; Kunur Patel, "Online Ads Not Working for You? Blame the Creative," *Advertising Age*, October 20, 2009, http://adage.com/print?article_id=139795; Hernan Lopez, "Why Interactive Advertising Needs a Creative Revolution, *Advertising Age*, June 15, 2009, http://adage.com/print?article_id=137246.

CHAPTER 9

a new model or announcing significant changes in a vehicle. For example, teasers ads were used to generate curiosity during the initial phase of the "Think About It" campaign for Hyundai discussed in Chapter 3. Exhibit 9–10 shows one of the teaser ads used as part of the campaign. Teaser campaigns can generate interest in a new product, but advertisers must be careful not to extend them too long or they will lose their effectiveness. As one advertising executive says, "Contrary to what we think, consumers don't hold seminars about advertising. You have to give consumers enough information about the product in teaser ads to make them feel they're in on the joke."[21]

Another form of advertising that is becoming increasingly popular is **user-generated content** whereby ads are created by consumers rather than by the company and/or its agency.[22] A number of marketers have developed contests that involve having consumers create ads and submit them for consideration. For example, Frito-Lay was one of the first marketers to use UGC on a major level when it sponsored a "Crash the Super Bowl" creative competition and ran a user-generated ad that was entirely conceived and produced by amateurs rather than advertising professionals. The winning spot was aired during the 2008 Super Bowl and topped

**EXHIBIT 9–10**
Hyundai used teaser ads as part of the "Think About It" campaign

*USA Today's* Ad Meter as the most liked commercial on the big game telecast.[23] The DEWmocracy campaign discussed in the chapter opener is also an example of the use of user-generated content as the various aspects of the marketing program for the three new Mountain Dew flavor options were created by consumers. The increasing use of interactive and social media such as YouTube and Facebook is likely to result in greater use of user-generated content by marketers as a way of getting consumers more involved with their brands.[24]

Many ads are not designed to sell a product or service but rather to enhance the image of the company or meet other corporate goals such as soliciting investment or recruiting employees. These are generally referred to as corporate image advertising and are discussed in detail in Chapter 17.

## Advertising Execution

LO 09-2

Once the specific advertising appeal that will be used as the basis for the advertising message has been determined, the creative specialist or team begins its execution. *Creative execution* is the way an advertising appeal is presented. While it is obviously important for an ad to have a meaningful appeal or message to communicate to the consumer, the manner in which the ad is executed is also important.

One of the best-known advocates of the importance of creative execution in advertising was William Bernbach, founder of the Doyle Dane Bernbach agency. In his famous book on the advertising industry, *Madison Avenue,* Martin Mayer notes Bernbach's reply to David Ogilvy's rule for copywriters that "what you say in advertising is more important than how you say it." Bernbach replied, "Execution can become content, it can be just as important as what you say. A sick guy can utter some words and nothing happens; a healthy vital guy says them and they rock the world."[25] Bernbach was one of the revolutionaries of his time who changed advertising creativity on a fundamental level by redefining how headlines and visuals were used, how art directors and copywriters worked together, and how advertising could be used to arouse feelings and emotions.

An advertising message can be presented or executed in numerous ways:

- Straight sell or factual message
- Scientific/technical evidence
- Demonstration
- Comparison
- Testimonial
- Slice of life
- Animation
- Personality symbol
- Imagery
- Dramatization
- Humor
- Combinations

We now examine these formats and considerations involved in their use.

### Straight-Sell or Factual Message

One of the most basic types of creative executions is the straight sell or factual message. This type of ad relies on a straightforward presentation of information concerning the product or service. This execution is often used with informational/rational appeals, where the focus of the message is the product or service and its specific attributes and/or benefits.

Straight-sell executions are commonly used in print ads. A picture of the product or service occupies part of the ad, and the factual copy takes up the rest of the space. They are also used in TV advertising, with an announcer generally delivering

**EXHIBIT 9–11**
Ford uses a straight-sell execution in this ad for the new Fiesta

the sales message while the product/service is shown on the screen. Ads for high-involvement consumer products as well as industrial and other business-to-business products generally use this format. The ad for the Ford Fiesta shown in Exhibit 9–11 is an excellent example of a straight-sell execution. The creative layout uses a picture of the new Fiesta while the ad copy discusses the various high-end technology features available on the car. This print ad was part of the "It's a Pretty Big Deal" IMC campaign used to launch the new Fiesta in the United States market.

**Scientific/Technical Evidence** In a variation of the straight sell, scientific or technical evidence is presented in the ad. Advertisers often cite technical information, results of scientific or laboratory studies, or endorsements by scientific bodies or agencies to support their advertising claims. For example, an endorsement from the American Council on Dental Therapeutics on how fluoride helps prevent cavities was the basis of the campaign that made Crest the leading brand of toothpaste. The ad for Kinerase anti-aging skin care treatment shown in Exhibit 9–12 uses this execution style by noting how the product has been clinically proven to reduce signs of aging.

**Demonstration** Demonstration advertising is designed to illustrate the key advantages of the product/service by showing it in actual use or in some staged situation. Demonstration executions can be very effective in convincing consumers of a product's utility or quality and of the benefits of owning or using the brand. TV is particularly well suited for demonstration executions, since the benefits or advantages of the product can be shown right on the screen. Although perhaps a little less dramatic than TV, demonstration ads can also work in print. The ad for Samsung's new LED 9000 high-definition TV shown in Exhibit 9–13 is an excellent example of the use of this technique. The image showing a side view of the television being held between two fingers is a very effective way to demonstrate the ultra thin feature of the TV as well as its elegant design.

**Comparison** Brand comparisons can also be the basis for the advertising execution. The comparison execution approach is increasingly popular among advertisers, since it offers a direct way of communicating a brand's particular advantage over its competitors or positioning a new or lesser-known brand with industry leaders. Comparison executions are often used to execute competitive advantage appeals, as discussed earlier.

**EXHIBIT 9–12**
Kinerase promotes how clinical tests results support the product performance claim

**Testimonial** Many advertisers prefer to have their messages presented by way of a testimonial, where a person praises the product or service on the basis of his or her personal experience with it. Testimonial executions can have ordinary satisfied customers discuss their own experiences with the brand and the benefits of using it. This approach can be very effective when the person delivering the testimonial is someone with whom the target audience can identify or who has an interesting story to tell. The

**EXHIBIT 9–13**

This ad is an effective way to demonstrate the ultra thin feature of Samsung's new LED TV

**EXHIBIT 9–14**

Jenny Craig uses testimonials to advertise its weight loss program

testimonial must be based on actual use of the product or service to avoid legal problems, and the spokesperson must be credible.

A number of marketers, such as weight loss companies, use testimonials to advertise their products, services, and programs. For example, Jenny Craig uses television commercials and print ads featuring ordinary consumers as well as celebrities discussing how they have been able to lose weight by following the company's programs. Exhibit 9–14 shows an ad showing a person who lost weight using the Jenny Craig program.

A related execution technique is the *endorsement,* where a well-known or respected individual such as a celebrity or expert in the product or service area speaks on behalf of the company or the brand. When endorsers promote a company or its products or services, the message is not necessarily based on their personal experiences.

**Slice of Life** A widely used advertising format, particularly for packaged-goods products, is the slice-of-life execution, which is generally based on a problem/solution approach. This type of ad portrays a problem or conflict that consumers might face in their daily lives. The ad then shows how the advertiser's product or service can resolve the problem.

Slice-of-life executions are often criticized for being unrealistic and irritating to watch because they are often used to remind consumers of problems of a personal nature, such as dandruff, bad breath, body odor, and laundry problems. Often these ads come across as contrived, silly, phony, or even offensive to consumers. However, many advertisers still prefer this style because they believe it is effective at presenting a situation to which most consumers can relate and at registering the product feature or benefit that helps sell the brand. For many years, Procter & Gamble was known for its reliance on slice-of-life advertising executions as many of the company's commercials used either the slice-of-life or testimonial format. However, P&G has begun using humor, animation, and other less traditional execution styles and now relies less on slice-of-life or testimonials.[26]

Slice-of-life or problem/solution execution approaches are not limited to consumer-product advertising. Many business-to-business marketers use this type of advertising to demonstrate how their products and services can be used to solve business problems.[27]

Some business-to-business marketers use a variation of the problem/solution execution that is sometimes referred to as *slice-of-death advertising.*[28] This execution style is used in conjunction with a fear appeal, as the focus is on the negative consequences that result when businesspeople make the wrong decision in choosing a supplier or service provider. For example, FedEx has used this type of advertising for nearly three decades through humorous, but to-the-point commercials that show what might happen when important packages and documents aren't received on time.

Execution is critical in using the technique effectively as these ads are designed to be dramatizations of a supposedly real-life situation that consumers might encounter. Getting viewers to identify with the situation and/or characters depicted in the ad can be very challenging. Since the success of slice-of-life ads often depends on how well the actors come across and execute their roles, professional

**EXHIBIT 9–15**
Listerine uses a slice-of-life execution to introduce a new flavor

actors are often used to achieve credibility and to ensure that the commercial is of high quality. Smaller companies and local advertisers often do not have ad budgets large enough to hire the talent or to pay for the production quality needed to effectively create slice-of-life spots. Thus, this execution technique is more likely to be used by companies with ad budgets that are large enough to fund the use of professional talent and production of quality commercials.

Many marketers like to use the slice-of-life genre as they believe it can be an effective way of addressing a problem or issue and offering a solution. For example, Listerine used a slice-of-life commercial effectively to introduce a new Natural Citrus flavor of the popular mouthwash.[29] The spot was designed to address the problem that some consumers have with the intense taste of the original flavor of the product. The spot opens with a mother returning home from the store with two surprises: danish and Listerine. However, when her husband and two kids see the mouthwash they run and hide. The mother then tells them it is Natural Citrus Listerine, which tastes less intense. The humorous spot ends with the father coming out of a kitchen cupboard and pots and pans dangling as one of the boys climbs down from the top of the kitchen island as the voiceover says, "You can handle it. Germs can't" (see Exhibit 9–15).

**Animation** An advertising execution approach that has become popular in recent years is animation. With this technique, animated scenes are drawn by artists or created on the computer, and cartoons, puppets, or other types of fictional characters may be used. Cartoon animation is especially popular for commercials targeted at children. Animated cartoon characters have also been used in many campaigns including Green Giant vegetables (the Jolly Green Giant) and Keebler cookies (the Keebler elves).

The use of animation as an execution style may increase as creative specialists discover the possibilities of computer-generated graphics and other technological innovations. For example, an interesting form of animation has been used recently by Charles Schwab & Co. in television commercials promoting its financial services. The commercials use a technique known as *rotoscoping,* which involves shooting live-action digital videos of actors and then using a special software to paint over the screen images on a computer to make them look animated.[30] The technique has been effective in drawing attention to the ads and creating an image of the company as being candid and real (Exhibit 9–16).

**Personality Symbol** Another type of advertising execution involves developing a central character or personality symbol that can deliver the advertising message and with which the product or service can be identified. This character can be a person, like Mr. Whipple, who asked shoppers, "Please don't squeeze the Charmin," or the Maytag repairman, who sits anxiously by the phone but is never needed because the company's appliances are so reliable.

**EXHIBIT 9–16**
An animated technique known as rotoscoping was used to create this Charles Schwab commercial

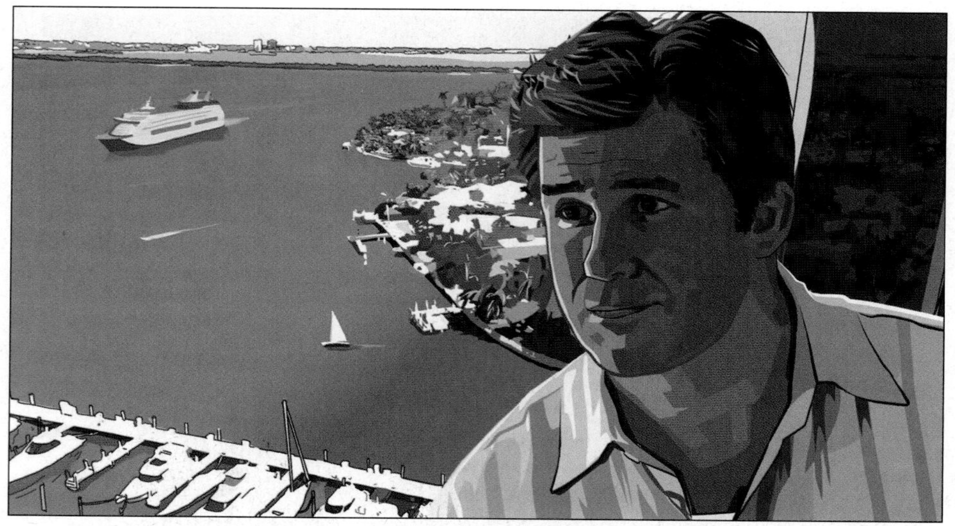

Personality figures can also be built around animated characters and animals. As discussed in Chapter 5, personality symbols such as Morris the cat, Tony the tiger, and Charlie the tuna have been used for decades to promote 9-Lives cat food, Kellogg's Frosted Flakes, and Star-Kist tuna, respectively. Other popular personality symbols that have been used more recently include the Energizer bunny, GEICO insurance's gecko, and the Burger King character.

One of the most popular and effective advertising personality symbols has been the Aflac duck which has been very successful in raising awareness, as well as sales, for the supplemental insurance company over the past five years.[31] Aflac has even integrated the duck into the company's redesigned corporate logo to take advantage of the tremendous equity that has resulted from the ads featuring the character (Exhibit 9–17).

**EXHIBIT 9–17**
The Aflac Duck is a very popular advertising personality symbol for the company

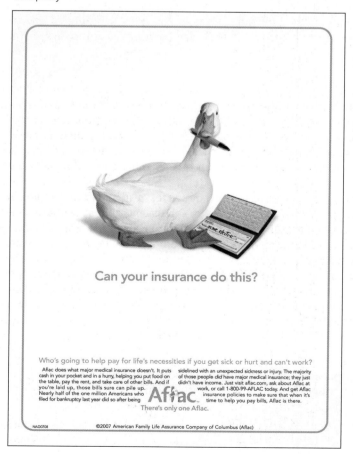

Can your insurance do this?

Who's going to help pay for life's necessities if you get sick or hurt and can't work?

Aflac does what major medical insurance doesn't. It puts cash in your pocket and in a hurry, helping you put food on the table, pay the rent, and take care of other bills. And if you're laid up, those bills sure can pile up. Nearly half of the one million Americans who filed for bankruptcy last year did so after being sidelined with an unexpected sickness or injury. The majority of those people *did* have major medical insurance; they just didn't have income. Just visit aflac.com, ask about Aflac at work, or call 1-800-99-AFLAC today. And get Aflac insurance policies to make sure that when it's time to help you pay bills, Aflac is there.

Aflac

There's only one Aflac.

NAD0708

©2007 American Family Life Assurance Company of Columbus (Aflac)

IMC Perspective 9–1 discusses how the advertising agency for Dos Equis, one of the leading brands of imported beer, has created a very effective integrated marketing campaign around a personality character developed for the brand who is portrayed as "The Most Interesting Man in the World."

**Imagery** You have probably noticed that some ads contain little or no information about the brand or company and are almost totally visual. These advertisements use imagery executions whereby the ad consists primarily of visual elements such as pictures, illustrations, and/or symbols rather than information. An imagery execution is used when the goal is to encourage consumers to associate the brand with the symbols, characters, and/or situation shown in the ad. Imagery ads are often the basis for emotional appeals that are used to advertise products or services where differentiation based on physical characteristics is difficult, such as soft drinks, liquor, designer clothing, and cosmetics. However, image is important for all types of products and services as marketers want the target audience to hold a favorable set of psychosocial associations for their company or brand.

An imagery execution may be based on *usage imagery* by showing how a brand is used or performs

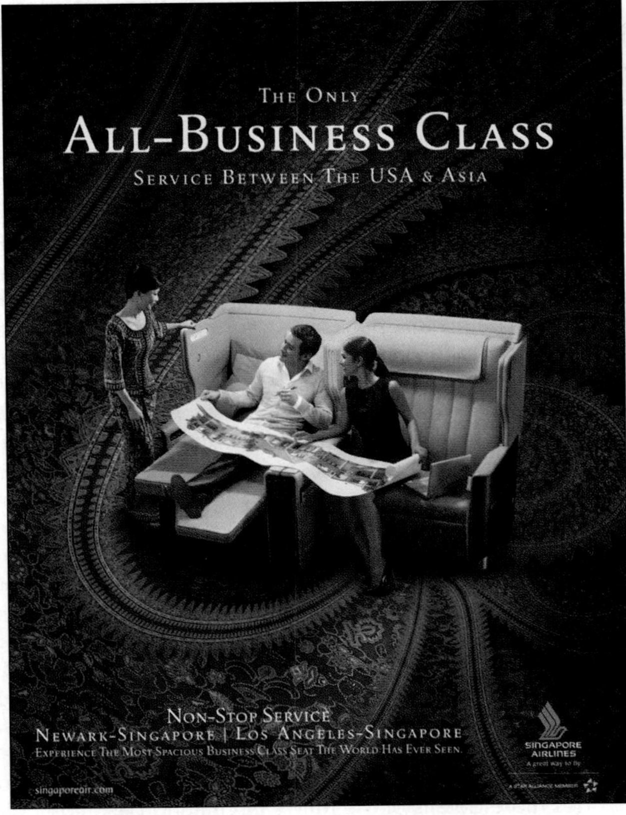


**EXHIBIT 9–18**
Singapore Airlines utilizes usage imagery by communicating the spaciousness of its business class seats

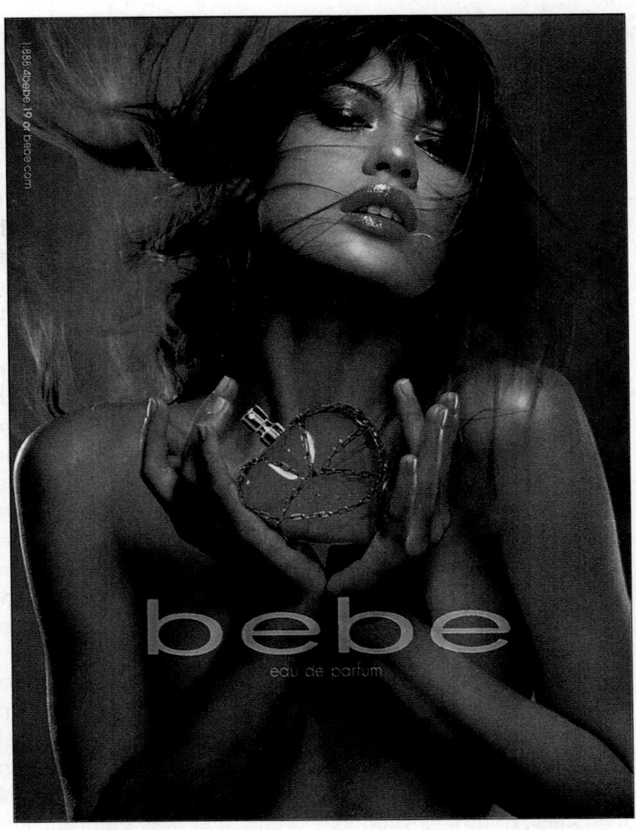


**EXHIBIT 9–19**
This bebe ad uses an attractive model to create a favorable image for the brand



and the situation in which it is used. For example, advertising for trucks and SUVs often shows the vehicles navigating tough terrain or in challenging situations such as towing a heavy load. Usage imagery executions are also often used in the marketing of services to show favorable images related to the use of a company's service offering. An excellent example of this is the ad shown in Exhibit 9–18 for Singapore Airlines all-business class service between the United States and Asia. The visual image used in the ad is a very effective way for Singapore Airlines to promote this service by communicating the message that it has the most spacious business class seats of any airline. This type of execution can also be based on *user imagery* where the focus is on the type of person who uses the brand. Ads for cosmetics, jewelry, and designer clothing brands often use very attractive models in the hope of getting consumers to associate his or her physical attractiveness with the brand (see Exhibit 9–19). Image executions rely heavily on visual elements such as photography, color, tonality, and design to communicate the desired image to the consumer. Marketers who rely on image executions have to be sure that the usage or user imagery with which they associate their brand evokes the right feelings and reactions from the target audience.

**Dramatization** Another execution technique particularly well suited to television is dramatization, where the focus is on telling a short story with the product or service as the star. Dramatization is somewhat akin to slice-of-life execution in that it often relies on the problem/solution approach, but it uses more excitement and suspense in telling the story. The purpose of using drama is to draw the viewer



heads are often used to enhance the readability of the message by breaking up large amounts of body copy and highlighting key sales points. Their content reinforces the headline and advertising slogan or theme. The ad for GEICO auto insurance shown



product to the company, the role of advertising in the marketing program, and the

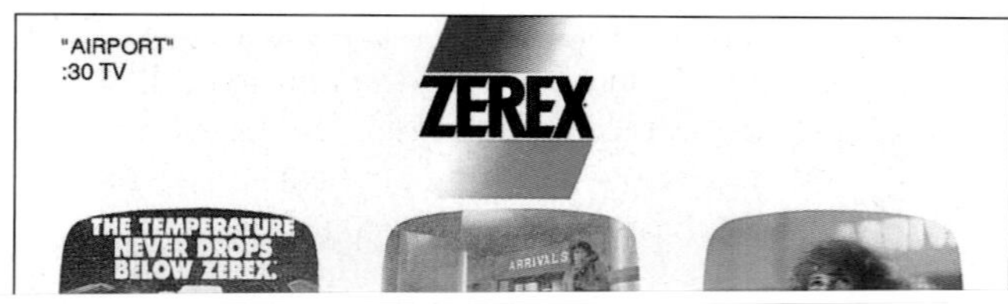


**Humor** Like comparisons, humor was discussed in Chapter 6 as a type of advertising appeal, but this technique can also be used as a way of presenting other advertising appeals. Humorous executions are particularly well suited to television or radio, although some print ads attempt to use this style. The pros and cons of

**FIGURE 9–4**
Production Costs for a 30-second Television

Big Time Productions
1234 Production Place
Santa Monica, CA 90404

| Bid Date 3/25/10 | Firm Bid (x) Cost Plus Fixed Fee ( ) |
| --- | --- |

**EXHIBIT 9–26**
Apple's famous "1984" commercial almost never made it to television

advertising approach being recommended. For example, the Chiat/Day agency had to convince Apple's board of directors to air the famous "1984" commercial used to introduce the Macintosh personal computer. Apple's board thought the commercial, which was based on the concept of Big Brother from George Orwell's classic novel *1984,* was too controversial and might be detrimental to its image, particularly in the business market. The spot used stark images of Orwell's dystopia, and a dramatic scene of a young woman throwing a mallet through a movie screen to destroy a controlling force, purportedly symbolizing its major competitor IBM (see Exhibit 9–26). The agency convinced Apple's board to run the commercial during the 1984 Super Bowl, which is the only time it ever appeared as a commercial on TV, and the impact was tremendous. The spot was the focus of attention in the media and was the talk of the marketing and advertising industries. A few years ago, *TV Guide* named the "1984" spot the greatest television commercial of all time.

Earlier in this chapter, we noted that Procter & Gamble has been moving away from testimonials and slice-of-life advertising executions to somewhat riskier and more lively forms of advertising. But the company remains conservative and has been slow to adopt the avant-garde ads used by many of its competitors. Agencies that do the advertising for various P&G brands recognize that quirky executions that challenge the company's subdued corporate culture are not likely to be approved.[50]

In many cases, top management is involved in selecting an ad agency and must approve the theme and creative strategy for the campaign. Evaluation and approval of the individual ads proposed by the agency often rest with the advertising and product managers who are primarily responsible for the brand. The account executive and a member of the creative team present the creative concept to the client's advertising and product and/or marketing managers for their approval before beginning production. A careful evaluation should be made before the ad actually enters production, since this stage requires considerable time and money as suppliers are hired to perform the various functions required to produce the actual ad.

The client's evaluation of the print layout or commercial storyboard can be difficult, since the advertising or brand manager is generally not a creative expert and must be careful not to reject viable creative approaches or accept ideas that will result in inferior advertising. However, personnel on the client side can use the guidelines discussed next to judge the efficacy of creative approaches suggested by the agency.

## Guidelines for Evaluating Creative Output

Advertisers use numerous criteria to evaluate the creative approach suggested by the ad agency. In some instances, the client may want to have the rough layout storyboard or animatic pretested to get quantitative information to assist in the evaluation. (Various methods for pretesting print ads and TV commercials will be discussed in Chapter 18.) However, the evaluation process is usually more subjective; the advertising or brand manager relies on qualitative considerations. Basic criteria for evaluating creative approaches are discussed next:

- *Is the creative approach consistent with the brand's marketing and advertising objectives?* One of the most important factors the client must consider is whether the creative appeal and execution style recommended by the agency are consistent with the marketing strategy for the brand and the role advertising and promotion have been assigned in the overall marketing program. This means the creative approach must be compatible with the image of the brand and the way it is positioned in the marketplace and should contribute to the marketing and advertising objectives. For example, SKYY Spirits recently extended its product line by introducing an all natural, infused super-premium vodka to capitalize on the growth in the flavored segment of the vodka market. Advertising for the new SKYY Infusions line uses bold creative featuring strong visual images that communicate the natural flavor ingredients, as well as the brand's distinctive cobalt blue bottle (Exhibit 9–27). These ads are consistent with the core brand equity base of SKYY, from which several new product lines have been launched. The SKYY Infusions line extension also contributes to the equity of the core SKYY brand, which helps build the strength and value of the overall brand franchise.
- *Is the creative approach consistent with the creative strategy and objectives? Does it communicate what it is supposed to?* The advertising appeal and execution must meet the communications objectives laid out in the copy platform, and the ad must say what the advertising strategy calls for it to say. Creative specialists can lose sight of what the advertising message is supposed to be and come up with an approach that fails to execute the advertising strategy. Individuals responsible for approving the ad should ask the creative specialists to explain how the appeal or execution style adheres to the creative strategy and helps meet communications objectives.
- *Is the creative approach appropriate for the target audience?* Generally, much time has been spent defining, locating, and attempting to understand the target audience for the advertiser's product or service. Careful consideration should be given to whether the ad appeal or execution recommended will appeal to, be understood by, and communicate effectively with the target audience. This involves studying all elements of the ad and how the audience will respond to them. Advertisers do not want to approve advertising that they believe will receive a negative reaction from the target audience. For example, it has been suggested that advertising targeted to older consumers should use models who are 10 years younger than the average age of the target audience, since most people feel younger than their chronological age.[51] Advertisers also face a considerable challenge developing ads for the teen market because teenagers' styles, fashions, language, and values change so rapidly. They may find they are using an advertising approach, a spokesperson, or even an expression that is no longer popular among teens.
- *Does the creative approach communicate a clear and convincing message to the customer?* Most ads are supposed to communicate a message that will help sell the brand. Many ads fail to communicate a clear and convincing message that motivates consumers to use a brand. While creativity is important in advertising, it is also important that the advertising communicate information attributes, features and benefits, and/or images that give consumers a reason to buy the brand. The Golf Pride ad shown in Exhibit 9–28 is an example of how advertising can be creative yet still communicate important product benefits. The ad uses a humorous appeal by

**EXHIBIT 9–27**

Advertising for SKYY Infusions builds off of the core brand equity base and is consistent with marketing objectives

showing a snowman staring at a golfer as he gets ready to eat breakfast. *Snowman* is a term used by golfers for a score of an eight on a hole (which is very bad) in reference to the character's resemblance to the shape of the number 8. The visual image is likely to attract the attention of golfers while the copy explains how they can improve their performance by regripping their clubs with Golf Pride grips.

- *Does the creative execution keep from overwhelming the message?* A common criticism of advertising, and TV commercials in particular, is that so much emphasis is placed on creative execution that the advertiser's message gets overshadowed. Many creative, entertaining commercials have failed to register the brand name and/or selling points effectively. For example, Aflac had to modify the commercials using its iconic duck character after several research studies showed that many consumers were not exactly sure what Aflac insurance was. Consumers indicated that the advertising didn't explain what supplemental insurance is and what Aflac does, so recent ads focus more attention on explaining the product and the company.[52]

  With the increasing amount of clutter in most advertising media, it may be necessary to use a novel creative approach to gain the viewer's or reader's attention. However, the creative execution cannot overwhelm the message. Clients must walk a fine line: Make sure the sales message is not lost, but be careful not to stifle the efforts of the creative specialists and force them into producing dull, boring advertising.

- *Is the creative approach appropriate for the media environment in which it is likely to be seen?* Each media vehicle has its own specific climate that results from the nature of its editorial content, the type of reader or viewer it attracts, and the nature of the ads it contains. Consideration should be given to how well the ad fits into the media environment in which it will be shown. For example, the Super Bowl has become a showcase for commercials. People who care very little about advertising know how much a 30-second commercial costs and pay as much attention to the ads as to the game itself, so many advertisers feel compelled to develop new ads for the Super Bowl or to save new commercials for the game.

**EXHIBIT 9–28**
This humorous Golf Pride ad is creative and communicates an important product benefit

- *Is the ad truthful and tasteful?* Marketers also have to consider whether an ad is truthful, as well as whether it might offend consumers. For example, household cleaner marketer Method recently had to pull the "Shiny Suds" online commercial for its organic bathroom tile cleaning product. The video began by showing a woman appearing in a commercial featuring the friendly bubble creatures who are similar to those shown in the ads for rival SC Johnson's Scrubbing Bubbles brand. However, when the woman takes a shower the next day, the bubble creatures are still there and turn into leering perverts who make sexually suggestive comments while the woman is cleansing her body. The commercial was intended to be a parody of advertising for traditional household cleaner advertising and support the Household Product Labeling Acts, which would require disclosure of ingredients in household cleaners. However, the spot evoked negative reactions from some consumers who felt that the spot was degrading to women and threatened to boycott Method products. Although Method indicated that most of the comments it received about the spot were positive, it removed the spot from its website.[53]

  The ultimate responsibility for determining whether an ad deceives or offends the target audience lies with

the client. It is the job of the advertising or brand manager to evaluate the approach suggested by the creative specialists against company standards. The firm's legal department may be asked to review the ad to determine whether the creative appeal, message content, or execution could cause any problems for the company. It is much better to catch any potential legal problems before the ad is shown to the public.

The advertising manager, brand manager, or other personnel on the client side can use these basic guidelines in reviewing, evaluating, and approving the ideas offered by the creative specialists. There may be other factors specific to the firm's advertising and marketing situation. Also, there may be situations where it is acceptable to deviate from the standards the firm usually uses in judging creative output. As we shall see in Chapter 18, the client may want to move beyond these subjective criteria and use more sophisticated pretesting methods to determine the effectiveness of a particular approach suggested by the creative specialist or team.

## Summary

In this chapter, we examined how the advertising message is implemented and executed. Once the creative strategy that will guide the ad campaign has been determined, attention turns to the specific type of advertising appeal and execution format to carry out the creative plan. The appeal is the central message used in the ad to elicit some response from consumers or influence their feelings. Appeals can be broken into two broad categories, rational and emotional. Rational appeals focus on consumers' practical, functional, or utilitarian need for the product or service; emotional appeals relate to social and/or psychological reasons for purchasing a product or service. Numerous types of appeals are available to advertisers within each category.

The creative execution style is the way the advertising appeal is presented in the message. A number of common execution techniques were examined in the chapter, along with considerations for their use. Attention was also given to tactical issues involved in creating print and TV advertising. The components of a print ad include headlines, body copy, illustrations, and layout. We also examined the video and audio components of TV commercials and various considerations involved in the planning and production of commercials.

Creative specialists are responsible for determining the advertising appeal and execution style as well as the tactical aspects of creating ads. However, the client must review, evaluate, and approve the creative approach before any ads are produced or run. A number of criteria can be used by advertising, product, or brand managers and others involved in the promotional process to evaluate the advertising messages before approving final production.

## Key Terms

**advertising appeal** p. 293
**creative execution style** p. 293
**informational/rational appeals** p. 293
**emotional appeals** p. 295
**transformational ad** p. 296
**reminder advertising** p. 299
**teaser advertising** p. 300
**user-generated content** p. 301
**headline** p. 310
**direct headlines** p. 311
**indirect headlines** p. 311
**subheads** p. 311
**body copy** p. 312
**layout** p. 313
**voiceover** p. 314
**needledrop** p. 314
**jingles** p. 315
**script** p. 318

## Discussion Questions

1. The chapter opener discusses the DEWmocracy social media campaign used by PepsiCo to select a new flavor to add to the Mountain Dew product line. Discuss the pros and cons of using social media and consumer-generated content to select an addition to the Mountain Dew product line. How might Mountain Dew's ad agency react to having do the creative work for the brand? (LO1, 2)

2. Some advertising creatives argue that the distinction between rational and emotional advertising is irrelevant since nearly all advertising includes aspects of both. Evaluate this argument. (LO1)

3. Find an example of an advertisement that uses a feature appeal and analyze it giving attention to the type of product or service attributes discussed in the ad and the benefits they provide to consumers in the target audience. What is your opinion of the effectiveness of the ad you have selected? (LO1)
4. IMC Technology Perspective 9–1 discusses the need for a creative revolution in online advertising. Discuss how online advertising differs from the type of advertising done in traditional media such as print or television and the challenges marketers face when advertising on Internet websites. (LO1)
5. What is meant by the mere exposure effect? Discuss how banner ads that appear on various websites might take advantage of the mere exposure effect. (LO1)
6. What is meant by transformational advertising? Analyze the cinematic-themed ad for Skyy vodka shown in Exhibit 9–6 from a transformational advertising perspective. (LO1)
7. Discuss the use of slice-of-life execution techniques in advertising. For what types of products and services might this execution technique work best? (LO2)
8. IMC Perspective 9–1 discusses how "The Most Interesting Man in the World" campaign was able to increase sales for Dos Equis imported beer. Discuss the reasons for the success of this campaign giving attention to the advertising as well as other components of the IMC program. (LO2)
9. Discuss the role of headlines in a print advertisement. What is the difference between a direct headline and an indirect headline and when might each type be used. (LO3)
10. Discuss the role of music in advertising. Find an example of a television commercial that is using a song and discuss the role the music plays in delivering the message. (LO3)
11. Choose a current advertising campaign and analyze it with respect to the creative guidelines discussed in the last section of the chapter. Identify any areas where you feel the campaign does not meet the guidelines and discuss why this is so. (LO4)

## AdForum Exercise: Analyzing Advertising Appeals and Execution Styles

adforum.com

(see Advertising and Promotion Playlist, Chapter 9)

### PART I: MCDONALD'S

The playlist for this chapter contains three commercials for McDonald's. Watch these three spots and answer the following:

1 Analyze the type of advertising appeal used in each commercial.
2 What type of creative advertising execution technique is being used for each spot?
3 Discuss the target audience for each commercial and whether you feel the ad is an effective way to communicate with this market segment.

### PART II: TIDE LAUNDRY DETERGENT

The playlist for this chapter also includes three TV commercials for Tide laundry detergent.

1 Analyze the type of advertising appeal and creative execution technique used for each ad and discuss why the agency may have chosen to use it.
2 Why do you think Procter & Gamble is using different advertising execution methods to advertise Tide? Discuss the role each ad plays in the marketing of Tide laundry detergent.

Access to the chapter playlist is available through Mc Graw Hill connect™ |MARKETING, www.mcgrawhillconnect.com

## LEARNING OBJECTIVES

LO1 To understand the key terminology used in media planning.

LO2 To know how a media plan is developed.

LO3 To know what constitutes media objectives.

LO4 To know the process of developing and implementing media strategies.

LO5 To be familiar with various characteristics of media.

# 10 Media Planning and Strategy

## THE CHANGING MEDIA LANDSCAPE—WILL ADVERTISING SURVIVE?

If you have anything to do with advertising at all, or just casually read or listen to business news, you have to know that the media landscape is undergoing significant changes. Besides the fact that the economic downturn has led to significant cutbacks in media spending, there have also been significant changes in the media environment itself that have forever altered the way marketers will communicate in the future. While there seem to be as many views on this subject as there are marketers, most seem to agree upon a few predictions: (1) Media budgets will not increase significantly in the next few years; (2) Traditional media will be forced to take on a different role and will lose media dollars to a variety of new media; and (3) How consumers use media will never be the same.

Numerous forecasts are consistent in projections that newer forms of media such as mobile, social, e-mail, search, Internet display, and alternative will see increases in their shares of companies' media budgets, while traditional broadcast and print will continue to see decreases. Forecasts for direct media vary. To many, traditional media are dying—if not already dead.

But are they? Will we see the end of advertising on TV? Will we have to pay for radio due to a lack of commercials? Will all magazines be online only? There is still a lot of support for traditional media according to a number of academic and business research studies, and forecasts of their impending doom may be greatly exaggerated. Studies have shown that TV is still an effective advertising medium, DVRs may not have as negative an impact as originally assumed, newspapers are being read by more people than previously thought (they are just passed on more), and direct marketing has increased in effectiveness over the past few years. In addition, all of these media have been proven to drive consumers to the Internet and search, influence the final sale, and contribute substantially to word-of-mouth advertising about brands.

One thing everyone does agree on is the fact that the media landscape of today will not mirror the one of the future. Changes in viewers' media consumption, technology changes and inventions, and so forth will create havoc for media planners and everyone else looking for the holy grail of the optimal advertising media mix. So what is a marketer to do?

Professor Jerry Wind of the University of Pennsylvania, and the director of the SEI Center for Advanced Studies in Management's *Future of Advertising Project* (a project where academics and industry professionals contribute articles and research study), envisions a "portfolio model" in which advertisers will develop a combination of traditional and new media much like investors develop financial portfolios. This new model would consider synergism between media, resulting in an optimal and effective media mix. Others participating in the project have provided additional interesting insights, noting that while technological changes have created the most unsettling period in advertising since the advent of TV in the 1950s, replacing traditional media with new media is overly simplistic and an unrealistic solution. A number of studies made so far call for a complete review of our existing media system, including the review and understanding of all media, reorganization of advertising agencies to eliminate media "silos," and the incorporation of social change strategies into the business message.

Wind, as well as many other experts, cites a global advertising campaign for Unilever's laundry detergents as the perfect example for the future of advertising. Marketed as Omo in Asia, and Skip in France, as well as other names in other countries, the "Dirt is Good" campaign sends the social message that "Every child has a right to play and explore." Supported by a multimedia campaign that included TV, promotions, support media, and online, the campaign shows images of children splashing around in mud with the social message that "Every child has a right to play and explore" (and, of course, the Unilever detergent will get their clothes clean). Besides being successful in selling detergent, the advertising also is credited with pushing the country of Singapore to increase its recess time in its academic heavy schools. It is this kind of message that will promote social change as well as renew consumers' faith in business, they say. And in the new world of advertising, it is what will be required to be successful.

If advertisers start sending messages that promote social change and sell products, that will be a new media landscape!

Sources: Steven Kurutz, "Sea Change," www.whartonmagazine.com., January 29, 2010, 9; ____, "Will the Future of Advertising Be a Blend of Old and New Media?," www.knowledg.@wharton.upenn.edu, September. 30, 2009, pp. 1–3; Kenneth Hein, "TV Ads More Effective Than Ever," www.adweek, February 25, 2009, pp. 1–3.

The discussion in this chapter's opening vignette demonstrates the many changes taking place in the media environment. Perhaps at no other time in history have so many changes taken place that significantly alter the media decision process. As a result, media planning has become more complex than ever before. As you will see in the following chapters, these changes offer the marketer opportunities not previously available, but they also require in-depth knowledge of all the alternatives. Integrated marketing communications programs are no longer a luxury; they are a necessity. Media planners must now consider multiple new options as well as recognize the changes that are occurring in traditional sources. New and evolving media contribute to the already difficult task of media planning. Planning when, where, and how the advertising message will be delivered is a complex and involved process. The primary objective of the media plan is to develop a framework that will deliver the message to the target audience in the most efficient, cost-effective manner possible—that will communicate what the product, brand, and/or service can do.

This chapter presents the various methods of message delivery available to marketers, examines some key considerations in making media decisions, and discusses the development of media strategies and plans. Later chapters will explore the relative advantages and disadvantages of the various media and examine each in more detail.

It should be noted that while new media often use their own terms and concepts, many also use the more traditional metrics as well. Much of the focus in this chapter will be on traditional concepts, with subsequent chapters dealing with media specific terminology. For example, in social media, a medium would be user generated video, YouTube a platform, and a channel would be www.60secondmarketer.com.[1]

## AN OVERVIEW OF MEDIA PLANNING

The media planning process is not an easy one. Options include mass media such as television, newspapers, radio, and magazines (and the choices available within each of these categories) as well as out-of-the-home media such as outdoor advertising, transit advertising, and electronic billboards. A variety of other media such as direct marketing, the Internet, promotional products, and others such as sales promotions, and in-store point-of-purchase options must also be considered. A proliferation of new media, including branded entertainment, wireless, and interactive media, has also provided the marketer with many options to consider.

While at first glance the choices among these alternatives might seem relatively straightforward, this is rarely the case. Part of the reason media selection becomes so involved is the nature of the media themselves. TV combines both sight and sound, an advantage not offered by most other media. Magazines can convey more information and may keep the message available to the potential buyer for a much longer time.

**EXHIBIT 10–1**
The Honda Accord appeared in the TV show *Chuck* along with the actors

Newspapers also offer their own advantages, as do outdoor, direct media, and each of the others. The Internet offers many of the advantages of other media but is also limited in its capabilities. The characteristics of each alternative must be considered, along with many other factors. This process becomes even more complicated when the manager has to choose between alternatives within the same medium—for example, between *Time* and *Newsweek* or between *The Good Wife* and *CSI,* or Facebook and MySpace.

Many companies, large and small, have come to realize the importance of a sound media strategy. They are focusing additional attention on the integration of creative work and media, as well as the use of multiple media vehicles to achieve the optimal impact. For example, ads that have been shown on TV now appear for viewing on the company's Internet site. Some commercials now feature the television program's actors and actresses in commercials shown during the program. In a commercial that appeared to be part of the episode, NBC used the actors in *Chuck* to promote the 2010 Winter Olympics and the Honda Crosstour (Exhibit 10–1).



The product and/or service being advertised affects the media planning process. As demonstrated in Figure 10–1, firms have found some media more useful than others in conveying their messages to specific target audiences. For example, Verizon, AT&T, and Procter & Gamble spend heavily on broadcast media, while others like GM and Bank of America, while still spending on TV, allocate higher percentages of the budget to the Internet. The result is placement of advertising dollars in these preferred media—and significantly different media strategies.

## Some Basic Terms and Concepts

Before beginning our discussion of media planning, we review some basic terms and concepts used in the media planning and strategy process.

**Media planning** is the series of decisions involved in delivering the promotional message to the prospective purchasers and/or users of the product or brand. Media planning is a process, which means a number of decisions are made, each of which may be altered or abandoned as the plan develops.

The media plan is the guide for media selection. It requires development of specific **media objectives** and specific **media strategies** (plans of action) designed to attain these objectives. Once the decisions have been made and the objectives and strategies formulated, this information is organized into the media plan.

The **medium** is the general category of available delivery systems, which includes broadcast media (like TV and radio), print media (like newspapers and magazines), direct marketing, outdoor advertising, and other support media. The **media vehicle** is the specific carrier within a medium category. For example, *Time* and *Newsweek* are print vehicles; *The Good Wife* and *60 Minutes* are broadcast vehicles. As you will see in later chapters, each vehicle has its own characteristics as well as its own relative advantages and disadvantages. Specific decisions must be made as to the value of each in delivering the message.

**Reach** is a measure of the number of different audience members exposed at least once to a media vehicle in a given period of time. **Coverage** refers to the potential audience that might receive the message through a vehicle. Coverage relates to potential audience; reach refers to the actual audience delivered. (The importance of this distinction will become clearer later in this chapter.) Finally, **frequency** refers to the number of times the receiver is exposed to the media vehicle in a specified period. While there are numerous more media planning terms that are important and

**FIGURE 10–1** Leading National Advertisers, Ranked by Total U.S. Advertising Spending, 2008—$ Millions

| Rank | | | | Total U.S. Spending | | Estimated | Measured | U.S. Measured Media Spending Breakout in 2009 | | | | | |
|---|---|---|---|---|---|---|---|---|---|---|---|---|---|
| 2009 | 2008 | Marketer | Headquarters | 2009 | % Chg | Unmeasured | Media | Magazine | Newspaper | Outdoor | Tv | Radio | Internet |
| **1** | 1 | **Procter & Gamble Co.** | Cincinnati | $4,188.9 | –13.4 | $1,351.2 | $2,837.7 | $949.3 | $187.7 | $0.5 | $1,582.3 | $17.6 | $100.3 |
| **2** | 2 | **Verizon Communications** | New York | 3,020.0 | –8.0 | 779.0 | 2,241.0 | 98.8 | 475.5 | 78.9 | 1,182.8 | 162.7 | 242.2 |
| **3** | 3 | **AT&T** | Dallas | 2,797.0 | –9.0 | 886.7 | 1,910.3 | 40.6 | 257.9 | 42.1 | 1,289.8 | 131.6 | 148.2 |
| **4** | 4 | **General Motors Co.** | Detroit | 2,214.9 | –21.6 | 0.0 | 2,214.9 | 274.2 | 632.0 | 19.4 | 1,013.9 | 66.6 | 208.9 |
| **5** | 10 | **Pfizer** | New York | 2,097.0 | 10.0 | 579.2 | 1,517.8 | 317.8 | 77.4 | 3.0 | 1,004.0 | 41.1 | 74.6 |
| **6** | 5 | **Johnson & Johnson** | New Brunswick, NJ | 2,060.9 | –18.5 | 764.7 | 1,296.3 | 323.3 | 48.2 | 2.3 | 851.5 | 11.6 | 59.5 |
| **7** | 6 | **Walt Disney Co.** | Burbank, CA | 2,003.8 | –9.6 | 909.1 | 1,094.7 | 150.7 | 113.4 | 36.2 | 643.2 | 48.4 | 102.8 |
| **8** | 8 | **Time Warner** | New York | 1,848.1 | –10.7 | 643.6 | 1,204.5 | 242.4 | 108.7 | 49.6 | 726.0 | 34.9 | 42.8 |
| **9** | 14 | **L'Oréal** | Clichy, France | 1,833.6 | –0.4 | 943.7 | 889.9 | 387.9 | 40.0 | 0.2 | 455.2 | 0.8 | 5.8 |
| **10** | 16 | **Kraft Foods** | Northfield, IL | 1,748.4 | 3.6 | 957.2 | 791.2 | 301.1 | 53.5 | 2.0 | 397.8 | 15.6 | 21.3 |
| **11** | 21 | **Walmart Stores** | Bentonville, AR | 1,729.5 | 14.2 | 555.2 | 1,174.3 | 231.7 | 41.8 | 3.1 | 796.3 | 51.2 | 50.2 |
| **12** | 11 | **Sears Holdings Corp.** | Hoffman Estates, IL | 1,700.3 | –8.8 | 1,004.2 | 696.1 | 44.3 | 168.3 | 0.7 | 434.0 | 25.0 | 23.8 |
| **13** | 7 | **Bank of America Corp.** | Charlotte, NC | 1,587.8 | –24.8 | 1,123.4 | 464.4 | 52.8 | 105.5 | 3.2 | 150.9 | 19.6 | 132.5 |
| **14** | 9 | **General Electric Co.** | Fairfield, CT | 1,575.7 | –22.0 | 647.0 | 928.7 | 89.1 | 120.5 | 26.3 | 563.7 | 60.3 | 68.8 |
| **15** | 13 | **Ford Motor Co.** | Dearborn, MI | 1,516.8 | –17.7 | 418.5 | 1,098.2 | 175.8 | 28.5 | 3.4 | 711.6 | 36.6 | 142.2 |
| **16** | 22 | **Sprint Nextel Corp.** | Overland Park, KS | 1,500.0 | 0.0 | 254.7 | 1,245.3 | 106.8 | 107.7 | 32.5 | 639.8 | 33.1 | 325.5 |
| **17** | 18 | **Anheuser-Busch InBev** | Leuven, Belgium/St. Louis | 1,467.2 | –7.6 | 931.8 | 535.4 | 49.9 | 4.0 | 37.0 | 412.3 | 25.7 | 6.5 |
| **18** | 15 | **GlaxoSmithKline** | Brentford, Middlesex, U.K. | 1,394.9 | –23.6 | 597.3 | 797.7 | 188.9 | 18.9 | 0.1 | 544.9 | 13.1 | 31.8 |
| **19** | 12 | **JPMorgan Chase & Co.** | New York | 1,341.0 | –27.6 | 998.0 | 342.9 | 26.7 | 67.0 | 23.4 | 154.1 | 40.6 | 31.2 |
| **20** | 35 | **Nestlé** | Vevey, Switzerland | 1,332.6 | 17.0 | 488.2 | 844.4 | 227.5 | 55.7 | 4.2 | 489.5 | 23.2 | 44.2 |
| **21** | 29 | **Unilever** | Rotterdam/London | 1,294.3 | 6.7 | 430.2 | 864.1 | 300.2 | 31.3 | 0.2 | 490.8 | 8.9 | 32.7 |
| **22** | 17 | **American Express Co.** | New York | 1,294.2 | –22.0 | 909.6 | 384.7 | 40.7 | 111.5 | 12.7 | 138.8 | 27.6 | 53.3 |
| **23** | 20 | **Merck & Co.** | Whitehouse Station, NJ | 1,286.5 | –17.0 | 587.7 | 698.7 | 247.0 | 51.2 | 0.7 | 366.9 | 1.6 | 31.3 |
| **24** | 19 | **Toyota Motor Corp.** | Toyota City, Japan | 1,286.3 | –18.2 | 450.1 | 836.1 | 108.2 | 21.3 | 16.8 | 629.9 | 8.0 | 51.9 |
| **25** | 30 | **McDonald's Corp.** | Oak Brook, IL | 1,236.4 | 2.9 | 362.8 | 873.6 | 43.2 | 4.1 | 58.9 | 675.8 | 65.0 | 26.7 |

Source: *Advertising Age*. Copyright © 2010 Crain Communications.

commonly used (for a useful reference see *Advertising Media A to Z*),[2] we will begin our discussion with these as they are critical to your understanding of the planning process.

## The Media Plan

The media plan determines the best way to get the advertiser's message to the market. In a basic sense, the goal of the media plan is to find that combination of media that enables the marketer to communicate the message in the most effective manner to the largest number of potential customers at the lowest cost.

The activities involved in developing the media plan and the purposes of each are presented in Figure 10–2. As you can see, a number of decisions must be made throughout this process. As the plan evolves, events may occur that necessitate changes. Many advertisers find it necessary to alter and update their objectives and strategies frequently.

## Problems in Media Planning

CHAPTER 10

Unfortunately, the media strategy decision has not become a standardized task. A number of problems contribute to the difficulty of establishing the plan and reduce its effectiveness. These problems include insufficient information, inconsistent terminologies, time pressures, and difficulty measuring effectiveness.

**Insufficient Information** While a great deal of information about markets and the media exists, media planners often require more than is available. Some data are just not measured, either because they cannot be or because measuring them would be too expensive. For example, continuous measures of radio listenership exist, but only periodic listenership studies are reported due to sample size and cost constraints. There are problems with some measures of audience size in other media as well.

The timing of measurements is also a problem; some audience measures are taken only at specific times of the year. (For example, **sweeps periods** in February, May, July, and November are used for measuring TV audiences and setting advertising rates.) This information is then generalized to succeeding months, so future planning decisions must be made on past data that may not reflect current behaviors. (In the largest 56 TV markets meters are used to provide information.) Think about planning for TV advertising for the fall season. There are no data on the audiences of new shows, and audience information taken on existing programs during the summer may not indicate how these programs will do in the fall because summer viewership is generally much lower. While the advertisers can review these programs before they air, all markets do not have actual audience figures.

The lack of information is even more of a problem for small advertisers, or smaller markets, who may not be able to afford to purchase the information they require. As a result, their decisions are based on limited or out-of-date data that were provided by the media themselves, or no data at all.

**Inconsistent Terminologies** Problems arise because the cost bases used by different media often vary and the standards of measurement used to establish these costs are not always consistent. For example, print media may present cost data in terms of the cost to reach a thousand people (cost per thousand, or CPM), broadcast media use the cost per ratings point (CPRP), and outdoor media use the number of showings. The advent of the Internet brought about a whole new lexicon of terminologies. Audience information that is used as a basis for these costs has also been collected by different methods. Finally, terms that actually mean something different (such as *reach* and *coverage*) may be used synonymously, by some adding to the confusion.

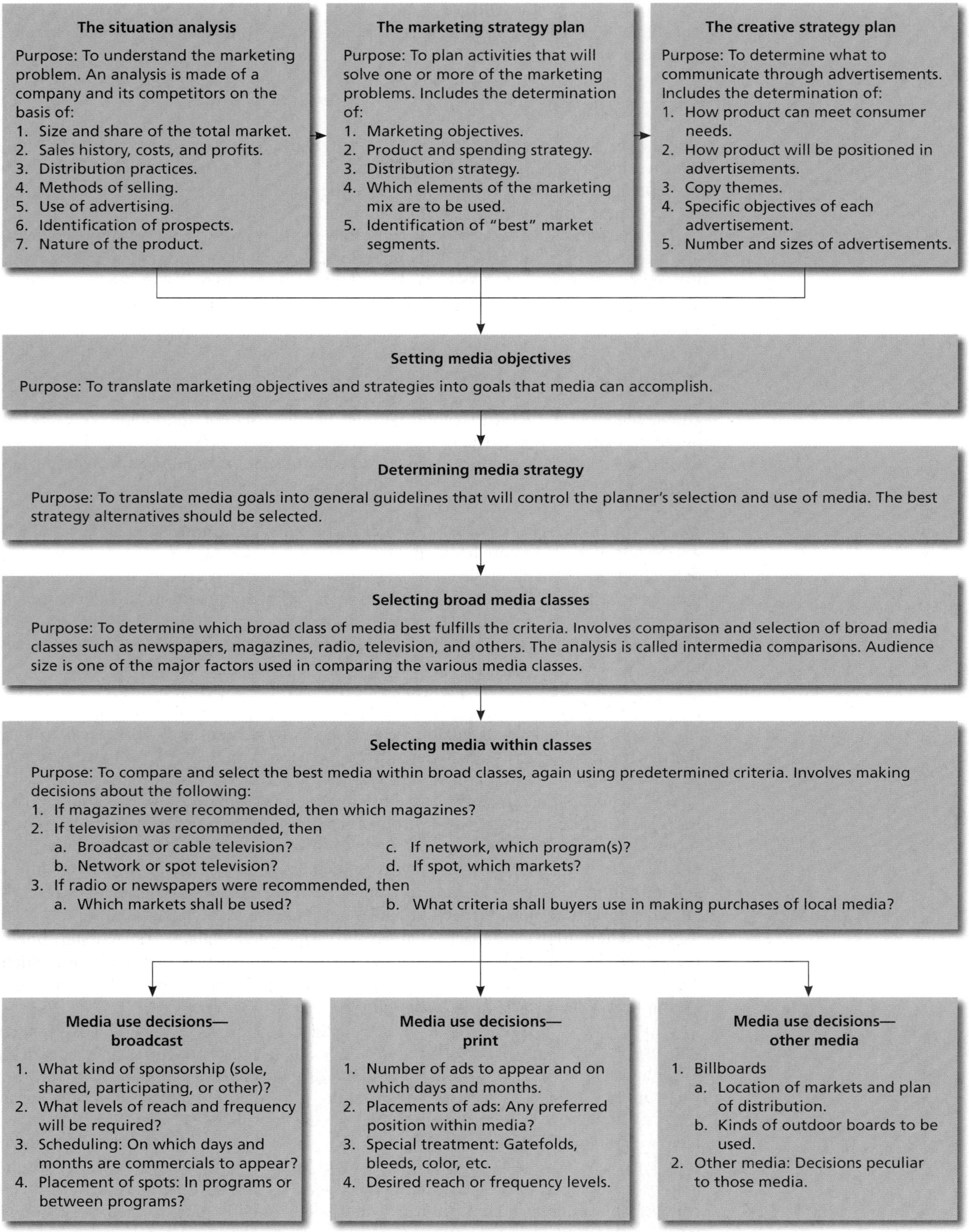

**The situation analysis**

Purpose: To understand the marketing problem. An analysis is made of a company and its competitors on the basis of:

1. Size and share of the total market.
2. Sales history, costs, and profits.
3. Distribution practices.
4. Methods of selling.
5. Use of advertising.
6. Identification of prospects.
7. Nature of the product.

**The marketing strategy plan**

Purpose: To plan activities that will solve one or more of the marketing problems. Includes the determination of:

1. Marketing objectives.
2. Product and spending strategy.
3. Distribution strategy.
4. Which elements of the marketing mix are to be used.
5. Identification of "best" market segments.

**The creative strategy plan**

Purpose: To determine what to communicate through advertisements. Includes the determination of:

1. How product can meet consumer needs.
2. How product will be positioned in advertisements.
3. Copy themes.
4. Specific objectives of each advertisement.
5. Number and sizes of advertisements.

**Setting media objectives**

Purpose: To translate marketing objectives and strategies into goals that media can accomplish.

**Determining media strategy**

Purpose: To translate media goals into general guidelines that will control the planner's selection and use of media. The best strategy alternatives should be selected.

**Selecting broad media classes**

Purpose: To determine which broad class of media best fulfills the criteria. Involves comparison and selection of broad media classes such as newspapers, magazines, radio, television, and others. The analysis is called intermedia comparisons. Audience size is one of the major factors used in comparing the various media classes.

**Selecting media within classes**

Purpose: To compare and select the best media within broad classes, again using predetermined criteria. Involves making decisions about the following:

1. If magazines were recommended, then which magazines?
2. If television was recommended, then
   a. Broadcast or cable television?
   b. Network or spot television?
   c. If network, which program(s)?
   d. If spot, which markets?
3. If radio or newspapers were recommended, then
   a. Which markets shall be used?
   b. What criteria shall buyers use in making purchases of local media?

**Media use decisions—broadcast**

1. What kind of sponsorship (sole, shared, participating, or other)?
2. What levels of reach and frequency will be required?
3. Scheduling: On which days and months are commercials to appear?
4. Placement of spots: In programs or between programs?

**Media use decisions—print**

1. Number of ads to appear and on which days and months.
2. Placements of ads: Any preferred position within media?
3. Special treatment: Gatefolds, bleeds, color, etc.
4. Desired reach or frequency levels.

**Media use decisions—other media**

1. Billboards
   a. Location of markets and plan of distribution.
   b. Kinds of outdoor boards to be used.
2. Other media: Decisions peculiar to those media.

**FIGURE 10–2** Activities Involved in Developing the Media Plan

**FIGURE 10–3**

The Top Five Most Engaging TV Shows

1. *One Tree Hill*
2. *90210*
3. *John and Kate Plus 8*
4. *Desperate Housewives*
5. *So You Think You Can Dance*

Source: LiveHive Systems. Reported in: Amy Hotz, "*One Tree Hill*" has TV's most socially engaged viewers, www.starnewsonline.com, August 27, 2009, pp. 1–2. Reprinted with permission.

In 2005, a joint task force composed of members of the National Association of Advertisers (AAAA) and the Advertising Research Foundation (ARF) launched an initiative to determine a better way to measure consumer exposure to an advertisement. The group unveiled an initiative that would significantly change the way exposure was measured, essentially replacing the use of frequency (the number of exposures to an ad) with engagement, a measure they said would better reflect the growing number of media choices available to consumers. Although the committee agreed on backing the new term, others were not so willing, asking for a more precise definition of *engagement*. The committee agreed to further examine and validate the concept.[3]

At the same time, the importance of engagement has been recognized by marketers. The Nielsen Company, which provides ratings data, recently purchased IAG Research—one of many firms now providing engagement data, while Toyota struck a deal with NBC that guaranteed that their ads would appear only in shows with high audience engagement.[4] Other companies also provide engagement data (Figure 10–3).

**Time Pressures** It seems that advertisers are always in a hurry—sometimes because they need to be; other times because they think they need to be. Actions by a competitor—for example, the cutting of airfares by one carrier—require immediate response. But sometimes a false sense of urgency dictates time pressures. In either situation, media selection decisions may be made without proper planning and analysis of the markets and/or media.

**Difficulty Measuring Effectiveness** Because it is so hard to measure the effectiveness of advertising and promotions in general, it is also difficult to determine the relative effectiveness of various media or media vehicles. (Recall the discussion of ROI from Chapter 7.) While progress is being made in this regard, the media planner may have little more than an estimate of or a good guess at the impact of these alternatives.

Because of these problems, not all media decisions are quantitatively determined. Sometimes managers have to assume the image of a medium in a market with which they are not familiar, anticipate the impact of recent events, or make judgments without full knowledge of all the available alternatives.

While these problems complicate the media decision process, they do not render it an entirely subjective exercise. The remainder of this chapter explores in more detail how media strategies are developed and ways to increase their effectiveness.

# DEVELOPING THE MEDIA PLAN

The promotional planning model in Chapter 1 discussed the process of identifying target markets, establishing objectives, and formulating strategies for attaining them. The development of the media plan and strategies follows a similar path, except that the

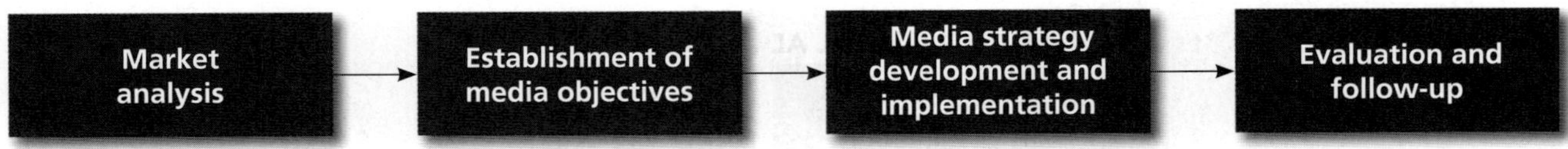


**FIGURE 10–4**
Developing the Media Plan

focus is more specifically keyed to determining the best way to deliver the message. The process, shown in Figure 10–4, involves a series of stages: (1) market analysis, (2) establishment of media objectives, (3) media strategy development and implementation, and (4) evaluation and follow-up. Each of these is discussed in turn, with specific examples. The website for this text contains an actual media plan, which we refer to throughout the remainder of the chapter to exemplify each phase further.

# MARKET ANALYSIS AND TARGET MARKET IDENTIFICATION

The situation analysis stage of the overall promotional planning process involves a complete review of internal and external factors, competitive strategies, and the like. In the development of a media strategy, a market analysis is again performed, although this time the focus is on the media and delivering the message. The key questions at this stage are these: To whom shall we advertise (who is the target market)? What internal and external factors may influence the media plan? Where (geographically) and when should we focus our efforts?

## To Whom Shall We Advertise?

While a number of target markets might be derived from the situation analysis, to decide which specific groups to go after, the media planner may work with the client, account representative, marketing department, and creative directors. A variety of factors can assist media planners in this decision. Some will require primary research, whereas others will be available from published (secondary) sources.

Experian Simmons, formerly the Simmons Market Research Bureau (SMRB), provides information through their annual *Experian National Consumer Study*. The study provides information regarding traditional media usage (English and Spanish languages), product, brands and services used, and demographic and psychographic characteristics. Experian also provides a *New Media Study* providing insights into Americans' use of mobile phones, social networking, and dozens of other new emerging technologies. The company's competitor *GfK-Mediamark Research, Inc.* (GfK MRI), also provides consumer information and media usage characteristics of the population.

Media planners are often more concerned with the percentage figures and index numbers than with the raw numbers. This is largely due to the fact that they may have their own data from other sources, both primary and secondary; the numbers provided may not be specific enough for their needs; or they question the numbers provided because of the methods by which they were collected. The total (raw) numbers provided by Experian and GfK MRI are used in combination with the media planner's own figures.

On the other hand, the **index number** is considered a good indicator of the potential of the market. This number is derived from the formula

$$\text{Index} = \frac{\text{Percentage of users in a demographic segment}}{\text{Percentage of population in the same segment}} \times 100$$

An index number over 100 means use of the product is proportionately greater in that segment than in one that is average (100) or less than 100. For example, the GfK MRI data in Figure 10–5 show that people in the age groups 18–24 and 25–34, respectively,

**FALL 2009 PRODUCT: BEVERAGES**
**ENERGY DRINKS DRANK IN LAST 6 MONTHS—TOTAL ADULTS**

| | Total '000 | Proj '000 | Pct Across | Pct Down | Index |
|---|---|---|---|---|---|
| Total | 225887 | 37773 | 16.7 | 100 | 100 |
| Educ: graduated college plus | 60806 | 7865 | 12.9 | 20.8 | 77 |
| Educ: attended college | 63023 | 12270 | 19.5 | 32.5 | 116 |
| Educ: graduated high school | 69801 | 11069 | 15.9 | 29.3 | 95 |
| Educ: did not graduate HS | 32257 | 6569 | 20.4 | 17.4 | 122 |
| Educ: postgraduate | 20290 | 1804 | 8.9 | 4.8 | 53 |
| Educ: no college | 102058 | 17638 | 17.3 | 46.7 | 103 |
| Age 18–24 | 28537 | 10756 | 37.7 | 28.5 | 225 |
| Age 25–34 | 40349 | 10766 | 26.7 | 28.5 | 160 |
| Age 35–44 | 42375 | 7937 | 18.7 | 21 | 112 |
| Age 45–54 | 44155 | 4952 | 11.2 | 13.1 | 67 |
| Age 55–64 | 33466 | 1831 | 5.5 | 4.8 | 33 |
| Age 65+ | 37006 | 1531 | 4.1 | 4.1 | 25 |
| Adults 18–34 | 68885 | 21522 | 31.2 | 57 | 187 |
| Adults 18–49 | 134084 | 32198 | 24 | 85.2 | 144 |
| Adults 25–54 | 126879 | 23655 | 18.6 | 62.6 | 111 |
| Men 18–34 | 34689 | 13460 | 38.8 | 35.6 | 232 |
| Men 18–49 | 66843 | 20561 | 30.8 | 54.4 | 184 |
| Men 25–54 | 62815 | 14895 | 23.7 | 39.4 | 142 |
| Women 18–34 | 34196 | 8062 | 23.6 | 21.3 | 141 |
| Women 18–49 | 67241 | 11637 | 17.3 | 30.8 | 103 |
| Women 25–54 | 64064 | 8760 | 13.7 | 23.2 | 82 |
| Occupation: professional and related occupations | 30311 | 4277 | 14.1 | 11.3 | 84 |
| Occupation: management, business, finance | 21717 | 2882 | 13.3 | 7.6 | 79 |
| Occupation: sales and office occupations | 33214 | 6831 | 20.6 | 18.1 | 123 |
| Occupation: natural resources, construction, maintenance | 13444 | 3812 | 28.4 | 10.1 | 170 |
| Occupation: other employed | 39994 | 8856 | 21.1 | 23.4 | 132 |
| HHI $150,00+ | 23605 | 3657 | 15.5 | 9.7 | 93 |
| HHI $75,000–149,999 | 64718 | 10284 | 15.9 | 27.2 | 95 |
| HHI $60,000–74,999 | 24815 | 4517 | 18.2 | 12 | 109 |
| HHI $50,000–59,999 | 18294 | 3193 | 16.9 | 8.5 | 101 |
| HHI $40,000–49,999 | 20241 | 3364 | 16.6 | 8.9 | 99 |
| HHI $30,000–39,999 | 21328 | 3743 | 17.5 | 9.9 | 105 |

**FIGURE 10–5**

GfK MRI Report on Energy Drink Consumers

Source: Mediamark Research, GfK MRI. Reprinted with permission.

are more likely to drink energy drinks than those in the other age segments, while those employed in professional or managerial occupations are the least likely to consume them. Depending on their overall strategy, marketers may wish to use this information to determine which groups are now using the product and target them or to identify a group that is currently using the product less and attempt to develop that segment. Figure 10–6 provides more instruction on how to read a GfK MRI report. (There is also an instructional video on YouTube—Google GfK MRI-PLUS.)

While the index is helpful, it should not be used alone. Percentages and product usage figures are also needed to get an accurate picture of the market. Just because the index for a particular segment of the population is very high, that doesn't always mean it is an attractive segment to target. The high index may be a result of a low denominator (a very small proportion of the population in this segment). In Figure 10–7, the 18- to 24-year-old age segment has the highest index, but it also has both the lowest product usage and the lowest population percentage. A marketer who relied solely on the index would be ignoring a full 82 percent of product users.

**FIGURE 10–6**

How to Read an Internet Reporter Report

## How to Read an Internet Reporter Report

Below is a screen capture of a Reporter Report, complete with explanations of key numbers. Please note that the numbers are based on the 2002 Fall MRI study, and that the projected numbers (000) are expressed in thousands.

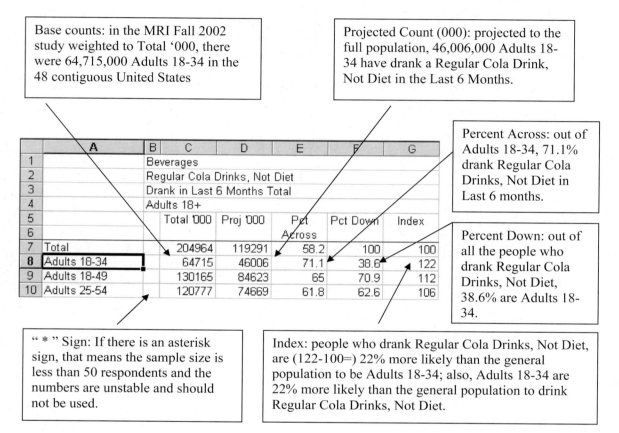

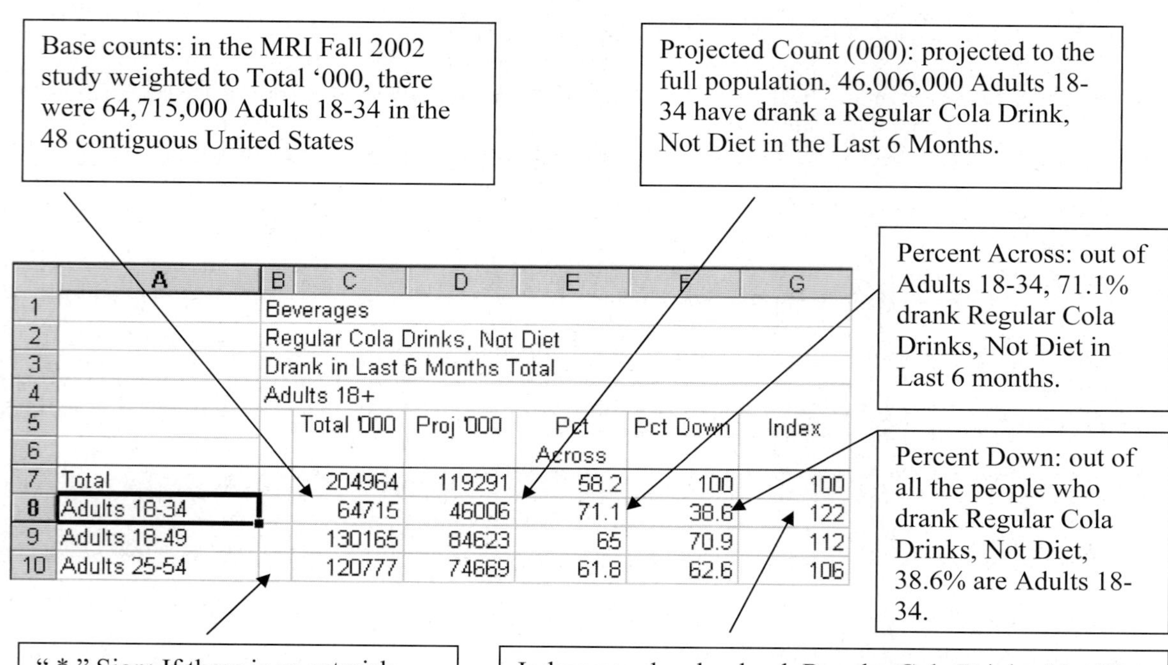

Base counts: in the MRI Fall 2002 study weighted to Total '000, there were 64,715,000 Adults 18-34 in the 48 contiguous United States
Projected Count (000): projected to the full population, 46,006,000 Adults 18-34 have drank a Regular Cola Drink, Not Diet in the Last 6 Months.
Percent Across: out of Adults 18-34, 71.1% drank Regular Cola Drinks, Not Diet in Last 6 months.
Percent Down: out of all the people who drank Regular Cola Drinks, Not Diet, 38.6% are Adults 18-34.

| | A | B | C | D | E | F | G |
|---|---|---|---|---|---|---|---|
| 1 | | Beverages | | | | | |
| 2 | | Regular Cola Drinks, Not Diet | | | | | |
| 3 | | Drank in Last 6 Months Total | | | | | |
| 4 | | Adults 18+ | | | | | |
| 5 | | | Total '000 | Proj '000 | Pct | Pct Down | Index |
| 6 | | | | | Across | | |
| 7 | Total | | 204964 | 119291 | 58.2 | 100 | 100 |
| 8 | Adults 18-34 | | 64715 | 46006 | 71.1 | 38.6 | 122 |
| 9 | Adults 18-49 | | 130165 | 84623 | 65 | 70.9 | 112 |
| 10 | Adults 25-54 | | 120777 | 74669 | 61.8 | 62.6 | 106 |

"*" Sign: If there is an asterisk sign, that means the sample size is less than 50 respondents and the numbers are unstable and should not be used.

Index: people who drank Regular Cola Drinks, Not Diet, are (122-100=) 22% more likely than the general population to be Adults 18-34; also, Adults 18-34 are 22% more likely than the general population to drink Regular Cola Drinks, Not Diet.

| How the Numbers are Derived | |
|---|---|
| **Pct. Across= 71.1** | The percent calculated by dividing the Proj '000 value in the row by the Total '000 value in the base column=46006/64715=71.1%. |
| **Pct. Down= 38.6** | The percent calculated by dividing the Proj' 000 value in the row by the Proj. '000 value in the base row=46006/119291=38.6%. |
| **Index=122** | The percent calculated by dividing the Pct. Across in the row by the Pct. Across in the base row (71.1/58.2). |

Source: Mediamark Research & Intelligence, LLC (GfK MRI). Reprinted with permission.

Keep in mind that while Experian and GfK MRI provide demographic, geographic, and some psychographic information, other factors may also be useful in defining specific markets and media usage. IMC Perspective 10–1 shows how other factors may have an impact.[4]

### What Internal and External Factors Are Operating?

Media strategies are influenced by both internal and external factors operating at any given time. *Internal factors* may involve the size of the media budget, managerial and administrative capabilities, or the organization of the agency. *External factors* may

# IMC Perspective 10–1 > > >

## Can Personality Predict What Media Someone Uses?

For as long as anyone can remember, media purchasing has relied heavily on demographics. For example, the most sought after age group for buyers of TV time is the 18–49 year old female (which, in itself, is a little scary to assume that there are no differences between 18- and 49-year-old females!). GfK MRI and Experian (SMRB) focus attention on demographics, as does virtually every media kit. Over the years, numerous articles have appeared in the literature espousing the position that demographics may not be the optimal way to make media purchase decisions, but little (if anything) has changed. But now more evidence has been found to support the fact that other factors may be responsible for one's media usage beyond age, income, and so forth.

A recent study conducted by the Entertainment Technology Center at the University of Southern California, the Hallmark Channel, and E-Poll Market Research concludes that a better predictor of media usage is the user's lifestyle. Identifying eight lifestyle groups (teens, college students, recent graduates, single, no kids, new nesters, established families, married couples with no children, and empty nesters), the researchers concluded that while cohorts of these groups may have similar demographic profiles, they may have different attitudes and media usage habits. For example, new nesters rate the importance of family relationships as more important than do childless couples (70 percent versus 56 percent). New nesters also watch more TV than other groups, and place high value on devices that filter content, like DVRs, video on demand services, and DVD players, so as to display family appropriate programming. Childless couples, on the other hand, tend to be engaged more outside of the home, relying less on TV, and when they do watch TV, they prefer drama to family programming. Differences also exist in regard to other media, for example, social networking. New nesters use social networks to stay in touch with friends and family, and are the most satisfied with the technology. Childless couples are less satisfied, primarily using the networking sites for professional purposes. The conclusion of the study is that there are clear and distinct differences between these groups that offer media buyers an advantage over demographics.

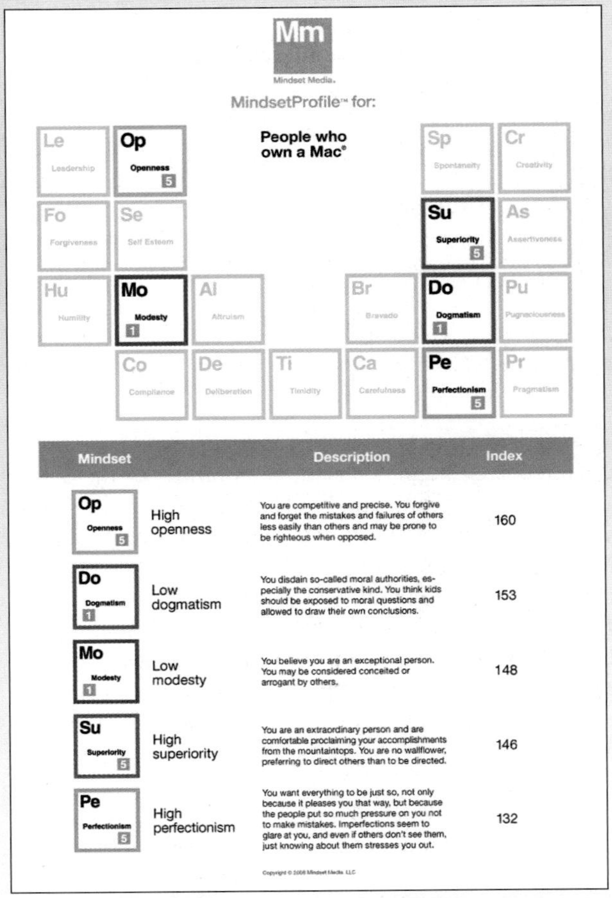

Another study, conducted by the psychographic research company Mindset Media, provided similar findings. Examining both demographic data and personalities, this study concluded that younger people use new media more than their elders; older generations prefer print; and women read magazines more than men. Not much new there. But the study also concluded that the more exciting findings are related to the influence of one's personality on media usage. For example, while almost everyone uses the Internet for a variety of reasons, the heaviest users tend to be high in openness and bravado, while low level users are high in dogmatism, socially conservative, and religious. Liberals are most likely to have the Internet as their most consumed medium. Newspaper readers are more likely to be optimists, recycle, purchase a luxury car, and are dynamic and leaders. Magazine readers are also dynamic, but are more open than newspaper readers. They are comfortable with their emotions, like the movies, and have music collections. Introverts and those low in self-motivation are less likely to read magazines. On the other hand, dynamic people don't watch TV, nor do those who exhibit high openness and leadership. Those high in bravado, and risk takers are TV watchers, as are those who score low on openness and leadership, and are less likely to plan. Finally, there are the radio listeners. The most dynamic of media users, they watch very little TV and always have the radio on in the car or at home. Introverts use almost no radio, are most likely to watch TV for five or more hours a day, and rarely plan. They also discourage their children from using the Internet. Overall, the study concludes, personality may be a better predictor of media usage than are age, gender, and income, and researchers may be better off using a personality test rather than focus groups and demographic data to determine media usage.

It all seems to make sense. So long as you have a personality.

Mm
Mindset Media.
MindsetProfile™ for:
People who own a Mac®

Le Leadership · Op Openness 5 · Sp Spontaneity · Cr Creativity
Fo Forgiveness · Se Self Esteem · Su Superiority 5 · As Assertiveness
Hu Humility · Mo Modesty 1 · Al Altruism · Br Bravado · Do Dogmatism 1 · Pu Pugnaciousness
Co Compliance · De Deliberation · Ti Timidity · Ca Carefulness · Pe Perfectionism 5 · Pr Pragmatism

| Mindset | | Description | Index |
|---|---|---|---|
| Op Openness 5 | High openness | You are competitive and precise. You forgive and forget the mistakes and failures of others less easily than others and may be prone to be righteous when opposed. | 160 |
| Do Dogmatism 1 | Low dogmatism | You disdain so-called moral authorities, especially the conservative kind. You think kids should be exposed to moral questions and allowed to draw their own conclusions. | 153 |
| Mo Modesty 1 | Low modesty | You believe you are an exceptional person. You may be considered conceited or arrogant by others. | 148 |
| Su Superiority 5 | High superiority | You are an extraordinary person and are comfortable proclaiming your accomplishments from the mountaintops. You are no wallflower, preferring to direct others than to be directed. | 146 |
| Pe Perfectionism 5 | High perfectionism | You want everything to be just so, not only because it pleases you that way, but because the people put so much pressure on you not to make mistakes. Imperfections seem to glare at you, and even if others don't see them, just knowing about them stresses you out. | 132 |

Copyright © 2008 Mindset Media, LLC

Sources: Steve McClellan, "Are Demographics Dead?," www.adweek.com, February 23, 2010, pp. 1–2; Beth Snyder Bulik, "How Personality Can Predict Media Usage," www.adage.com, May 4, 2009, pp. 1–4.

**FIGURE 10–7**

How High Indexes Can Be Misleading

| Age Segment | Population in Segment (%) | Product Use in Segment (%) | Index |
|---|---|---|---|
| 18–24 | 15.1 | 18.0 | 119 |
| 25–34 | 25.1 | 25.0 | 100 |
| 35–44 | 20.6 | 21.0 | 102 |
| 45+ | 39.3 | 36.0 | 91 |

include the economy (the rising costs of media), changes in technology (the availability of new media), competitive factors, and the like. While some of this information may require primary research, much information is available through secondary sources, including magazines, syndicated services, and even the daily newspaper.

One service's competitive information was shown in Figure 10–1. The Competitive Media Reporting Service provides media spending figures for various brands competing in the same market. Competitive information is also available from many other sources.

## Where to Promote?

The question of where to promote relates to geographic considerations. As noted in Chapter 7, companies often find that sales are stronger in one area of the country or the world than another and may allocate advertising expenditures according to the market potential of an area. For example, the Mexican beer Pacifico has a much greater brand share of the beer market in the Pacific census region than in the Midwest census region. The question is, where will the ad dollars be more wisely spent? Should Pacifico allocate additional promotional monies to those markets where the brand is already among the leaders to maintain market share, or does more potential exist in those markets where the firm is not doing as well and there is more room to grow? Perhaps the best answer is that the firm should spend advertising and promotion dollars where they will be the most effective—that is, in those markets where they will achieve the desired objectives. Unfortunately, as we have seen so often, it is not always possible to measure directly the impact of promotional efforts. At the same time, certain tactics can assist the planner in making this determination.

**Using Indexes to Determine Where to Promote** In addition to the indexes from Simmons and GfK MRI, three other indexes may also be useful:

1. The **survey of buying power index** is conducted for every major metropolitan market in the United States and is based on a number of factors, including population, effective buying income, and total retail sales in the area. Each of these factors is individually weighted to drive a buying power index that charts the potential of a particular metro area, county, or city relative to the United States as a whole. The resulting index gives media planners insight into the relative value of that market, as shown in Figure 10–8. When used in combination with other market information, the survey of buying power index helps the marketer determine which geographic areas to target.
2. The **brand development index (BDI)** helps marketers factor the rate of product usage by geographic area into the decision process.

$$\text{BDI} = \frac{\text{Percentage of brand to total U.S. sales in the market}}{\text{Percentage of total U.S. population in the market}} \times 100$$

**FIGURE 10–8**

Survey of Buying Power Index

| DMA | Total Population | Households | Asian / Pacific Islander | African-American Pop. | Hispanic Pop. | Population by Age Group | | | | | | |
|---|---|---|---|---|---|---|---|---|---|---|---|---|
| | | | | | | 2 - 11 | 12 - 17 | 18 - 24 | 25 - 34 | 35 - 49 | 50+ |
| Ft. Myers-Naples, FL | 1,217,708 | 508,145 | 15,343 | 84,084 | 247,548 | 141,863 | 80,224 | 85,712 | 149,848 | 222,580 | 508,015 |
| Gainesville, FL | 322,150 | 129,627 | 12,118 | 55,007 | 22,018 | 34,805 | 22,127 | 59,388 | 47,021 | 57,414 | 93,993 |
| Jacksonville, FL | 1,758,602 | 680,711 | 44,550 | 384,062 | 99,011 | 240,379 | 142,160 | 158,680 | 235,808 | 379,557 | 552,285 |
| Miami-Ft. Lauderdale, FL | 4,300,579 | 1,561,568 | 90,165 | 886,325 | 1,979,958 | 542,344 | 334,111 | 384,710 | 502,057 | 984,256 | 1,443,731 |
| Orlando-Daytona Beach-Melbourne, FL | 3,723,526 | 1,464,418 | 105,286 | 488,912 | 640,945 | 457,847 | 276,477 | 323,235 | 493,413 | 775,064 | 1,304,938 |
| Panama City, FL | 368,863 | 148,310 | 4,522 | 50,011 | 12,953 | 43,900 | 26,555 | 31,351 | 51,089 | 76,883 | 129,719 |
| Tallahassee-Thomasville, FL-GA | 725,699 | 281,591 | 10,361 | 230,056 | 36,005 | 92,149 | 54,215 | 95,867 | 106,825 | 142,844 | 213,904 |
| Tampa-St.Petersburg (Sarasota), FL | 4,368,468 | 1,821,660 | 98,189 | 464,796 | 620,598 | 519,526 | 310,946 | 343,185 | 531,163 | 867,935 | 1,691,454 |
| West Palm Beach-Ft. Pierce, FL | 1,905,978 | 786,561 | 37,615 | 272,071 | 318,530 | 223,654 | 134,638 | 144,177 | 218,045 | 372,294 | 768,673 |

| DMA | Total EBI | Retail Sales | Buying Power Index |
|---|---|---|---|
| Ft. Myers-Naples, FL | 31,562,042,500 | 21,286,463,216 | 0.4633 |
| Gainesville, FL | 5,844,027,500 | 4,651,926,011 | 0.0968 |
| Jacksonville, FL | 37,164,647,500 | 28,725,730,663 | 0.5906 |
| Miami-Ft. Lauderdale, FL | 89,188,970,000 | 75,015,224,126 | 1.4625 |
| Orlando-Daytona Beach-Melbourne, FL | 77,523,552,500 | 59,556,677,892 | 1.2333 |
| Panama City, FL | 7,087,285,000 | 5,238,076,874 | 0.1133 |
| Tallahassee-Thomasville, FL-GA | 12,952,682,500 | 10,535,214,913 | 0.2166 |
| Tampa-St.Petersburg (Sarasota), FL | 96,233,265,000 | 65,492,720,766 | 1.4595 |
| West Palm Beach-Ft. Pierce, FL | 51,014,940,000 | 35,632,927,152 | 0.7529 |

Source: Copyright © 2009 by Nielsen Claritas Inc., a part of the Nielsen Company, and/or infoUSA, Inc. (as applicable): This product contains proprietary and confidential property of Nielsen Claritas Inc. and/or infoUSA, Inc. (as applicable). Unauthorized use, including copying of the product is expressly prohibited.

**FIGURE 10–9**
Calculating BDI

$$\text{BDI} = \frac{\text{Percentage of brand sales in South Atlantic region}}{\text{Percentage of U.S. population in South Atlantic region}} \times 100$$
$$= \frac{50\%}{16\%} \times 100$$
$$= 312$$

The BDI compares the percentage of the brand's total U.S. sales in a given market area with the percentage of the total population in the market to determine the sales potential for that brand in that market area. An example of this calculation is shown in Figure 10–9. The higher the index number, the more market potential exists. In this case, the index number indicates this market has high potential for brand development.

**FIGURE 10–10**
Using CDI and BDI to Determine Market Potential

$$\text{CDI} = \frac{\text{Percentage of product category sales in Utah/Idaho}}{\text{Percentage of total U.S. population in Utah/Idaho}} \times 100$$
$$= \frac{1\%}{1\%} \times 100$$
$$= 100$$

$$\text{BDI} = \frac{\text{Percentage of total brand sales in Utah/Idaho}}{\text{Percentage of total U.S. population in Utah/Idaho}} \times 100$$
$$= \frac{2\%}{1\%} \times 100$$
$$= 20$$

3. The **category development index (CDI)** is computed in the same manner as the BDI, except it uses information regarding the product category (as opposed to the brand) in the numerator:

$$\text{CDI} = \frac{\text{Percentage of product category total sales in market}}{\text{Percentage of total U.S. population in market}} \times 10$$

The CDI provides information on the potential for development of the total product category rather than specific brands. When this information is combined with the BDI, a much more insightful promotional strategy may be developed. For example, consider the market potential for coffee in the United States. One might first look at how well the product category does in a specific market area. In Utah and Idaho, for example, the category potential is low (see Figure 10–10). The marketer analyzes the BDI to find how the brand is doing relative to other brands in this area. This information can then be used in determining how well a particular product category and a particular brand are performing and figuring what media weight (or quantity of advertising) would be required to gain additional market share, as shown in Figure 10–11.

While these indexes provide important insights into the market potential for the firm's products and/or brands, this information is supplemental to the overall strategy determined earlier in the promotional decision-making process. In fact, much of this information may have already been provided to the media planner. Since it may be used more specifically to determine the media weights to assign to each area, this decision ultimately affects the budget allocated to each area as well as other factors such as reach, frequency, and scheduling.

**FIGURE 10–11**
Using BDI and CDI Indexes

| | High BDI | Low BDI |
|---|---|---|
| High CDI | High market share<br>Good market potential | Low market share<br>Good market potential |
| Low CDI | High market share<br>Monitor for sales decline | Low market share<br>Poor market potential |

| | |
|---|---|
| High BDI and high CDI | This market usually represents good sales potential for both the product category and the brand. |
| High BDI and low CDI | The category is not selling well, but the brand is; probably a good market to advertise in but should be monitored for declining sales. |
| Low BDI and high CDI | The product category shows high potential but the brand is not doing well; the reasons should be determined. |
| Low BDI and low CDI | Both the product category and the brand are doing poorly; not likely to be a good place for advertising. |



## ESTABLISHING MEDIA OBJECTIVES

Just as the situation analysis leads to establishment of marketing and communications objectives, the media situation analysis should lead to determination of specific media objectives. The media objectives are not ends in themselves. Rather, they are designed to lead to the attainment of communications and marketing objectives. Media objectives are the goals for the media program and should be limited to those that can be accomplished through media strategies. An example of media objectives is this: Create awareness in the target market through the following:

- Use broadcast media to provide coverage of 80 percent of the target market over a six-month period.
- Reach 60 percent of the target audience at least three times over the same six-month period.
- Create a positive brand image through mood and creativity.

## DEVELOPING AND IMPLEMENTING MEDIA STRATEGIES

Having determined what is to be accomplished, media planners consider how to achieve these objectives. That is, they develop and implement media strategies, which evolve directly from the actions required to meet objectives and involve the criteria in Figure 10–12.

- The media mix
- Target market coverage
- Geographic coverage
- Scheduling
- Reach and frequency
- Recency
- Creative aspects and mood
- Flexibility
- Budget considerations

**FIGURE 10–12**
Criteria Considered in the Development of Media Plans

### The Media Mix

A wide variety of media and media vehicles are available to advertisers. While it is possible that only one medium and/or vehicle might be employed, it is much more likely that a number of alternatives will be used. The objectives sought, the characteristics of the product or service, the size of the budget, and individual

**FIGURE 10–13**
Marketing Coverage Possibilities

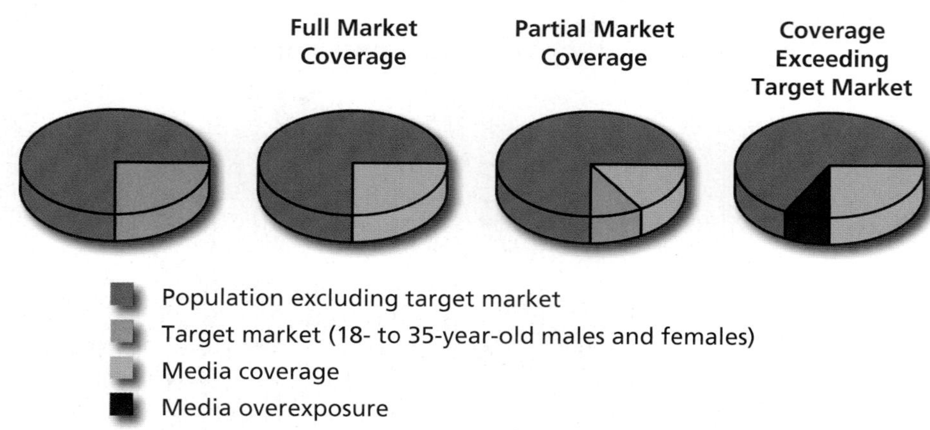


preferences are just some of the factors that determine what combination of media will be used.

As an example, consider a promotional situation in which a product requires a visual demonstration to be communicated effectively. In this case, TV may be the most effective medium. If the promotional strategy calls for coupons to stimulate trial, print media may be necessary. (Some companies also provide the capability to print coupons from their websites.) For in-depth information, the Internet may be best.

By employing a media mix, advertisers can add more versatility to their media strategies, since each medium contributes its own distinct advantages (as demonstrated in later chapters). By combining media, marketers can increase coverage, reach, and frequency levels while improving the likelihood of achieving overall communications and marketing goals.

## Target Market Coverage

The media planner determines which target markets should receive the most media emphasis. Developing media strategies involves matching the most appropriate media to this market by asking, "Through which media and media vehicles can I best get my message to prospective buyers?" The issue here is to get coverage of the market, as shown in Figure 10–13. The optimal goal is full market coverage, shown in the second pie chart. But this is a very optimistic scenario. More realistically, conditions shown in the third and fourth charts are most likely to occur. In the third chart, the coverage of the media does not allow for coverage of the entire market, leaving some potential customers without exposure to the message. In the fourth chart, the marketer is faced with a problem of overexposure (also called **waste coverage**), in which the media coverage exceeds the targeted audience. If media coverage reaches people who are not sought as buyers and are not potential users, then it is wasted. (This term is used for coverage that reaches people who are not potential buyers and/or users. Consumers may not be part of the intended target market but may still be considered as potential—for example, those who buy the product as a gift for someone else.)

The goal of the media planner is to extend media coverage to as many of the members of the target audience as possible while minimizing the amount of waste coverage. The situation usually involves trade-offs. Sometimes one has to live with less coverage than desired; other times, the most effective media expose people not sought. In this instance, waste coverage is justified because the media employed are likely to be the most effective means of delivery available and the cost of the waste coverage is exceeded by the value gained from their use.

**FALL 2009 PRODUCT: BEVERAGES**
**ENERGY DRINKS DRANK IN LAST 6 MONTHS—TOTAL ADULTS**

| | | Total '000 | Proj '000 | Pct Across | Pct Down | Index |
|---|---|---|---|---|---|---|
| **Total** | | 163435 | 31134 | 16 | 100 | 100 |
| *Cooking Light* average audience | | 11436 | 1329 | 11.6 | 3.5 | 70 |
| *Cooking with Paula Deen* average audience | | 6772 | 790 | 11.7 | 2.1 | 70 |
| *Cosmopolitan* average audience | | 18208 | 4226 | 23.2 | 11.2 | 139 |
| *Country Living* average audience | | 11560 | 1279 | 11.1 | 3.4 | 66 |
| *Country Sampler* average audience | * | 1790 | 154 | 8.6 | 0.4 | 52 |
| *Cycle World* average audience | | 3047 | 779 | 25.6 | 2.1 | 153 |
| *Diabetes Forecast* average audience | | 4970 | 654 | 13.2 | 1.7 | 79 |
| *Dirt Rider* average audience | | 1898 | 666 | 35.1 | 1.8 | 210 |
| *Discover* average audience | | 7140 | 1735 | 24.3 | 4.6 | 145 |
| *Ducks Unlimited* average audience | | 2352 | 566 | 24 | 1.5 | 144 |
| *Ebony* average audience | | 10055 | 2051 | 20.4 | 5.4 | 122 |
| *The Economist* average audience | | 2850 | 474 | 16.6 | 1.3 | 100 |
| *Elle* average audience | | 5942 | 1324 | 22.3 | 3.5 | 133 |
| *Elle Decor* average audience | * | 1928 | 285 | 14.8 | 0.8 | 88 |
| *Entertainment Weekly* average audience | | 10650 | 2765 | 26 | 7.3 | 155 |
| *Entrepreneur* average audience | | 2736 | 726 | 26.5 | 1.9 | 159 |
| *ESPN The Magazine* average audience | | 14621 | 5043 | 34.5 | 13.4 | 206 |
| *Esquire* average audience | | 3238 | 643 | 19.8 | 1.7 | 119 |
| *Essence* average audience | | 7491 | 1485 | 19.8 | 3.9 | 119 |
| *Every Day with Rachael Ray* average audience | | 6393 | 992 | 15.5 | 2.6 | 93 |
| *Everyday Food* average audience | | 4228 | 717 | 17 | 1.9 | 101 |
| *Family Circle* average audience | | 19553 | 1779 | 9.1 | 4.7 | 54 |
| *Family Handyman* average audience | | 4577 | 672 | 14.7 | 1.8 | 88 |

**FIGURE 10–14**

GfK MRI Provides Media Usage of Energy Drink Users

Source: Mediamark Research, GfK MRI. Reprinted with permission.

CHAPTER 10

When watching football games on TV, you may have noticed commercials for stock brokerage firms such as Charles Schwab, Ameritrade, and E*Trade. Not all viewers are candidates for stock market services, but a very high percentage of potential customers can be reached with this strategy. So football programs are considered a good media buy because the ability to generate market coverage outweighs the disadvantages of high waste coverage.

Figure 10–14 shows how information provided by GfK MRI can be used to match media to target markets. It profiles magazines read and TV shows watched by the energy drink users identified in Figure 10–5. (You can practice using index numbers here.) From Figure 10–14, you can see that *Dirt Rider, Cycle World* and *ESPN The Magazine* would likely be wise selections, whereas *Country Sampler, Country Living*, and *Family Circle* would be less likely to lead to the desired exposures.

## Geographic Coverage

Snow skiing is much more popular in some areas of the country than in others. It would not be the wisest of strategies to promote skis in those areas where interest is not high, unless you could generate an increase in interest. It may be possible to promote an interest in skiing in the Southeast, but a notable increase in sales of ski equipment is not very likely, given the market's distance from snow. The objective of weighting certain geographic areas more than others makes sense, and the strategy of exerting more promotional efforts and dollars in those areas follows naturally.

**FIGURE 10–15**
Three Methods of Promotional Scheduling

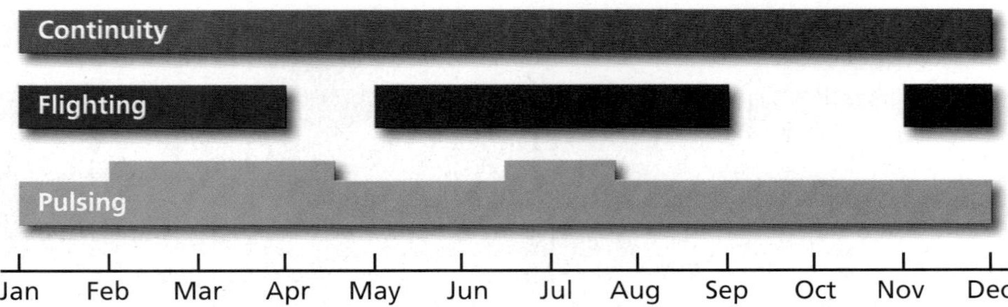


## Scheduling

Obviously, companies would like to keep their advertising in front of consumers at all times as a constant reminder of the product and/or brand name. In reality, this is not possible for a variety of reasons (not the least of which is the budget). Nor is it necessary. The primary objective of *scheduling* is to time promotional efforts so that they will coincide with the highest potential buying times. For some products these times are not easy to identify; for others they are very obvious. Three scheduling methods available to the media planner—continuity, flighting, and pulsing—are shown in Figure 10–15.

**Continuity** refers to a continuous pattern of advertising, which may mean every day, every week, or every month. The key is that a regular (continuous) pattern is developed without gaps or nonadvertising periods. Such strategies might be used for advertising for food products, laundry detergents, or other products consumed on an ongoing basis without regard for seasonality.

A second method, **flighting**, employs a less regular schedule, with intermittent periods of advertising and nonadvertising. At some time periods there are heavier promotional expenditures, and at others there may be no advertising. Many banks, for example, spend no money on advertising in the summer but maintain advertising throughout the rest of the year. Snow skis are advertised heavily between October and April; less in May, August, and September; and not at all in June and July.

**Pulsing** is actually a combination of the first two methods. In a pulsing strategy, continuity is maintained, but at certain times promotional efforts are stepped up. In the beer industry, advertising continues throughout the year but may increase at holiday periods such as Memorial Day, Labor Day, or the Fourth of July. The scheduling strategy depends on the objectives, buying cycles, and budget, among other factors. There are certain advantages and disadvantages to each scheduling method, as shown in Figure 10–16. One recent and comprehensive study (acclaimed by many in the TV research community as "the most comprehensive study ever to shed light on scheduling") indicates that continuity is more effective than flighting. On the basis of the idea that it is important to get exposure to the message as close as possible to when the consumer is going to make the purchase, the study concludes that advertisers should continue weekly schedules as long as possible.[5] The key here may be the "as long as possible" qualification. Given a significant budget, continuity may be more of an option than it is for those with more limited budgets.

## Reach versus Frequency

Since advertisers have a variety of objectives and face budget constraints, they usually must trade off reach and frequency. They must decide whether to have the message be seen or heard by more people (reach) or by fewer people more often (frequency).

**FIGURE 10–16**
Characteristics of Scheduling Methods

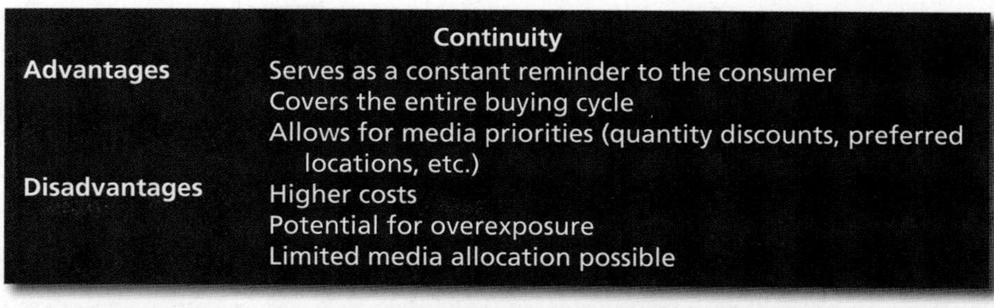

| | Continuity |
|---|---|
| **Advantages** | Serves as a constant reminder to the consumer<br>Covers the entire buying cycle<br>Allows for media priorities (quantity discounts, preferred locations, etc.) |
| **Disadvantages** | Higher costs<br>Potential for overexposure<br>Limited media allocation possible |

| | Flighting |
|---|---|
| **Advantages** | Cost efficiency of advertising only during purchase cycles<br>May allow for inclusion of more than one medium or vehicle with limited budgets |
| **Disadvantages** | Weighting may offer more exposure and advantage over competitors<br>Increased likelihood of wearout<br>Lack of awareness, interest, retention of promotional message during nonscheduled times<br>Vulnerability to competitive efforts during nonscheduled periods |

| | Pulsing |
|---|---|
| **Advantages** | All of the same as the previous two methods |
| **Disadvantages** | Not required for seasonal products (or other cyclical products) |



**How Much Reach Is Necessary?** Thinking back to the hierarchies discussed in Chapter 5, you will recall that the first stage of each model requires awareness of the product and/or brand. The more people are aware, the more are likely to move to each subsequent stage. Achieving awareness requires reach—that is, exposing potential buyers to the message. New brands or products need a very high level of reach, since the objective is to make all potential buyers aware of the new entry. High reach is also desired at later stages of the hierarchy. For example, at the trial stage of the adoption hierarchy, a promotional strategy might use cents-off coupons or free samples. An objective of the marketer is to reach a larger number of people with these samples, in an attempt to make them learn of the product, try it, and develop favorable attitudes toward it. (In turn, these attitudes may lead to purchase.)

The problem arises because there is no known way of determining how much reach is required to achieve levels of awareness, attitude change, or buying intentions, nor can we be sure an ad placed in a vehicle will actually reach the intended audience. (There has been some research on the first problem, which will be discussed in the section below on effective reach.)

If you buy advertising time on *60 Minutes,* will everyone who is tuned to the program see the ad? No. Many viewers will leave the room, be distracted during the commercial, and so on, as shown in Figure 10–17 (which also provides a good example of the difference between reach and coverage). If I expose everyone in my target group to the message once, will this be sufficient to create a 100 percent level of awareness? The answer again is no. This leads to the next question: What frequency of exposure is necessary for the ad to be seen and to have an impact?

How many viewers actually watch a commercial? R. D. Percy & Co. reports that its advanced people meters, equipped with heat sensors that detect viewers present, indicate that spots retain, on average, 82 percent of the average-minute ratings for the quarter hour. During early morning news programs, "commercial efficiency" (as Percy calls it) is lower because so many people are bustling about, out of the room (blue), but the rate rises at night.

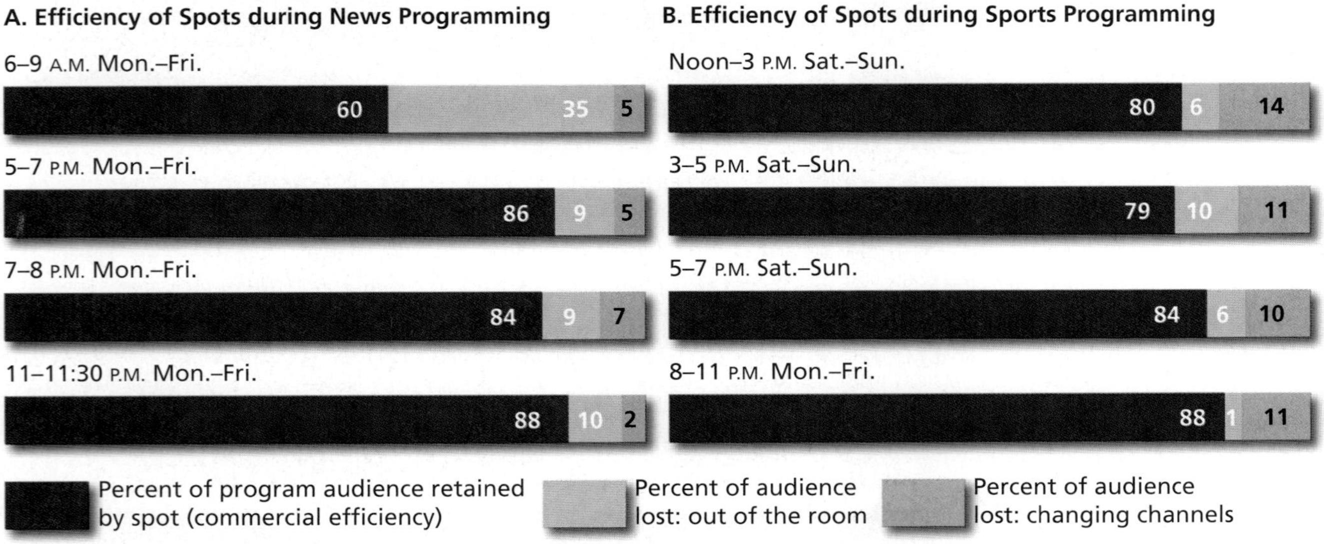

**A. Efficiency of Spots during News Programming**

| Time | Retained | Out of room | Changing channels |
|---|---|---|---|
| 6–9 A.M. Mon.–Fri. | 60 | 35 | 5 |
| 5–7 P.M. Mon.–Fri. | 86 | 9 | 5 |
| 7–8 P.M. Mon.–Fri. | 84 | 9 | 7 |
| 11–11:30 P.M. Mon.–Fri. | 88 | 10 | 2 |

**B. Efficiency of Spots during Sports Programming**

| Time | Retained | Out of room | Changing channels |
|---|---|---|---|
| Noon–3 P.M. Sat.–Sun. | 80 | 6 | 14 |
| 3–5 P.M. Sat.–Sun. | 79 | 10 | 11 |
| 5–7 P.M. Sat.–Sun. | 84 | 6 | 10 |
| 8–11 P.M. Mon.–Fri. | 88 | 1 | 11 |

Percent of program audience retained by spot (commercial efficiency)

Percent of audience lost: out of the room

Percent of audience lost: changing channels

**FIGURE 10–17**

Who's Still There to Watch the Ads?

**What Frequency Level Is Needed?** With respect to media planning, *frequency* carries a slightly different meaning. (Remember when we said one of the problems in media planning is that terms often take on different meanings?) Here frequency is the number of times one is exposed to the media vehicle in a specified time period (usually 13 weeks), not necessarily to the ad itself. Figure 10–17 demonstrates that depending on the program, this number may range from 12 to 40 percent. Marketers have always known that everyone that is watching a program is not going to stay in the room to watch the commercials. Given the rise in the number of people able to skip ads, one can be sure the number of those not exposed to the ad is on the increase. As noted, marketers continue to seek ways to increase engagement, hoping to reduce the number leaving the room during commercial breaks.

Most advertisers do agree that a 1:1 exposure ratio does not exist. So while your ad may be placed in a certain vehicle, the fact that a consumer has been exposed to that vehicle does not ensure that your ad has been seen. As a result, the frequency level expressed in the media plan overstates the actual level of exposure to the ad. This overstatement has led some media buyers to refer to the reach of the media vehicle as "opportunities to see" an ad rather than actual exposure to it.

Because the advertiser has no sure way of knowing whether exposure to a vehicle results in exposure to the ad, the media and advertisers have adopted a compromise: One exposure to the vehicle constitutes reach, given that this exposure must occur for the viewer even to have an opportunity to see the ad. Thus, the exposure figure is used to calculate reach and frequency levels. But this compromise does not help determine the frequency required to make an impact. The creativity of the ad, the involvement of the receiver, noise, and many other intervening factors confound any attempts to make a precise determination.

At this point, you may be thinking, "If nobody knows this stuff, how do they make these decisions?" That's a good question, and the truth is that the decisions are not always made on hard data. Says Joseph Ostrow, executive vice president/director of communications services with Young and Rubicam, "Establishing frequency goals for an advertising campaign is a mix of art and science but with a definite bias toward art."[6] Let us first examine the process involved in setting reach and frequency objectives and then discuss the logic of each.

**FIGURE 10–18**

Representation of Reach and Frequency

A. Reach of One TV Program

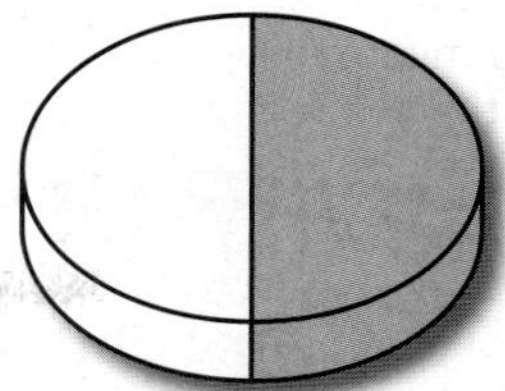

Total market audience reached

B. Reach of Two Programs

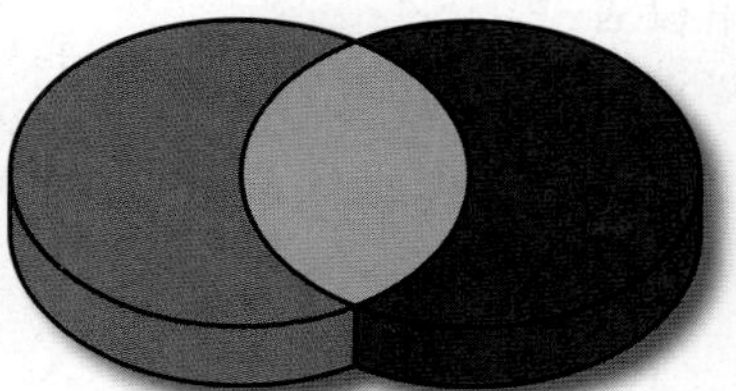

Total market audience reached

C. Duplicated Reach

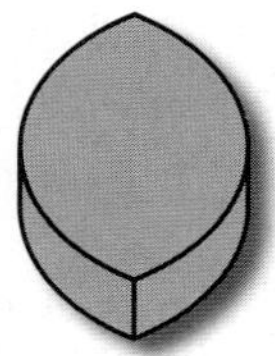

Total market reached with both shows

D. Unduplicated Reach

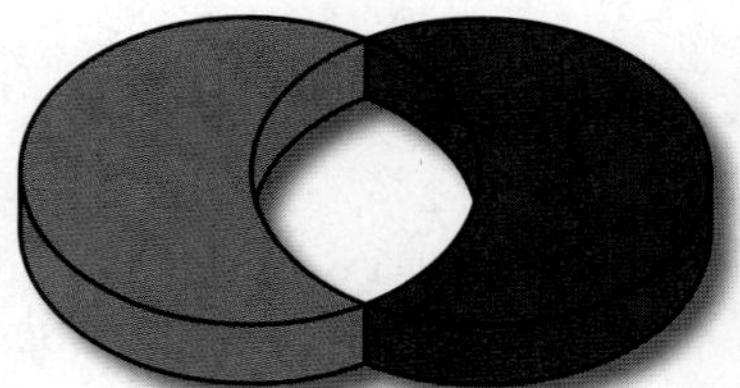

Total reach less duplicated reach

CHAPTER 10

**Establishing Reach and Frequency Objectives** It is possible to be exposed to more than one media vehicle with an ad, resulting in repetition (frequency). If one ad is placed on one TV show one time, the number of people exposed is the reach. If the ad is placed on two shows, the total number exposed once is **unduplicated reach**. Some people will see the ad twice. The reach of the two shows, as depicted in Figure 10–18, includes a number of people who were reached by both shows (C). This overlap is referred to as **duplicated reach**.

Both unduplicated and duplicated reach figures are important. Unduplicated reach indicates potential new exposures, while duplicated reach provides an estimate of frequency. Most media buys include both forms of reach. Let us consider an example.

A measure of potential reach in the broadcast industry is the TV (or radio) **program rating**. This number is expressed as a percentage. For an estimate of the total number of homes reached, multiply this percentage times the number of homes with TV sets. For example, if there are 114.9 million homes with TV sets in the United States and the program has a rating of 30, then the calculation is 0.30 times 114.9, or 34.47 million homes. (We go into much more detail on ratings and other broadcast terms in Chapter 11.)

**Using Gross Ratings Points** To determine how much advertising volume or weight is necessary to accomplish advertiser's objectives, marketers rely on ratings (the number of people reached) and frequency (the average number of times exposed) figures. A summary measure that combines the program rating and the average number of times the home is reached during this period (frequency of exposure) is a commonly used reference point known as **gross ratings points (GRPs)**:

$$\text{GRP} = \text{Reach} \times \text{Frequency}$$

GRPs are based on the total audience the media schedule may reach using a duplicated reach estimate. **Target ratings points (TRPs)** refer to the number of people in the primary target audience the media buy will reach—and the number of times. Unlike GRP, TRP does not include waste coverage.

Given that GRPs do not measure actual reach, the advertiser must ask: How many GRPs are needed to attain a certain reach? How do these GRPs translate into effective reach? For example, how many GRPs must one purchase to attain an

**FIGURE 10–19**

Estimates of Reach for Network TRPs

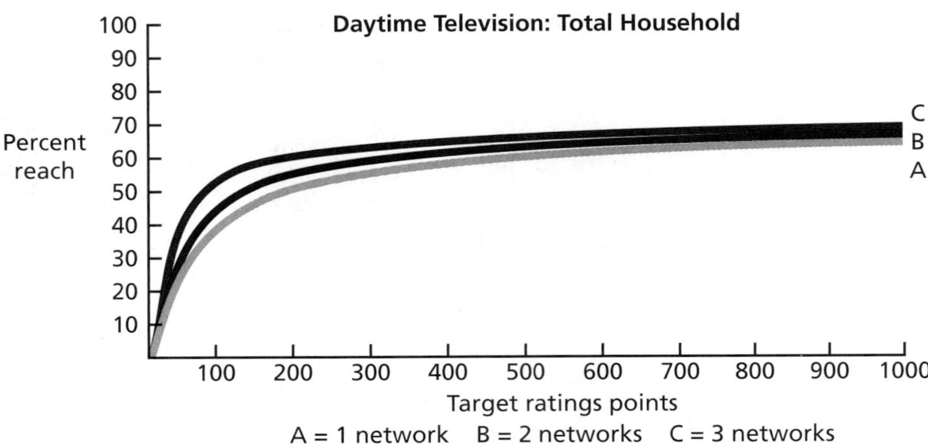


unduplicated reach of 50 percent, and what frequency of exposure will this schedule deliver? The following example may help you to understand how this process works.

First you must know what these ratings points represent. A purchase of 100 GRPs could mean 100 percent of the market is exposed once or 50 percent of the market is exposed twice or 25 percent of the market is exposed four times, and so on. As you can see, this information must be more specific for the marketer to use it effectively. To know how many GRPs are necessary, the manager needs to know how many members of the intended audience the schedule actually reaches. The graph in Figure 10–19 helps make this determination.

In Figure 10–19, a purchase of 100 TRPs on one network would yield an estimated reach of 32 percent of the total households in the target market. This figure would climb to 37.2 percent if two networks were used and 44.5 percent with three. Working backward through the formula for GRPs, the estimate of frequency of exposure—3.125, 2.688, and 2.247, respectively—demonstrates the trade-off between reach and frequency.

An interesting example of the use of GRPs is provided by the race to be the Republican candidate for California governor in 2010. With the election to be held in June, the advertising schedule for March for the leading candidate Meg Whitman consisted of 1,000 GRPs per week in 11 California media markets. This buy was expected to yield a frequency of approximately 10 exposures per week to the average TV watcher in the largest markets, and approximately 6 per week in the smaller ones. The opposing candidate spent an estimated 15–50 percent of this amount, depending on the specific market.[7] Whitman won the race.

The overriding question is, how many GRPs are necessary to achieve our objectives? According to Scott Walker, most advertisers prefer to get 500–700 GRPs to be sure their message is seen and seen often.[8] A number of researchers have explored this issue. David Berger, vice president and director of research at Foote, Cone & Belding, has determined that 2,500 GRPs are likely to lead to roughly a 70 percent probability of high awareness, 1,000 to 2,500 would yield about a 33 percent probability, and less than 1,000 would probably result in almost no awareness.[9] David Olson obtained similar results and further showed that as awareness increased, trial of the product would also increase, although at a significantly slower rate.[10] In both cases, it was evident that high numbers of GRPs were required to make an impact.

Figure 10–20 summarizes the effects that can be expected at different levels of exposure, on the basis of research in this area. A number of factors may be operating, and direct relationships may be difficult to establish. In addition to the results shown in Figure 10–20, Joseph Ostrow has shown that while the number of repetitions increases awareness rapidly, it has much less impact on attitudinal and behavioral responses.[11]

You can imagine how expensive it was for the candidate mentioned earlier to purchase 1,000 GRPs per week in 11 markets well before the election. To spend at

**FIGURE 10–20**
The Effects of Reach and Frequency

1. One exposure of an ad to a target group within a purchase cycle has little or no effect in most circumstances.
2. Since one exposure is usually ineffective, the central goal of productive media planning should be to enhance frequency rather than reach.
3. The evidence suggests strongly that an exposure frequency of two within a purchase cycle is an effective level.
4. Beyond three exposures within a brand purchase cycle or over a period of four or even eight weeks, increasing frequency continues to build advertising effectiveness at a decreasing rate but with no evidence of decline.
5. Although there are general principles with respect to frequency of exposure and its relationship to advertising effectiveness, differential effects by brand are equally important.
6. Nothing we have seen suggests that frequency response principles or generalizations vary by medium.
7. The data strongly suggest that wearout is not a function of too much frequency; it is more of a creative or copy problem.



that level for an extended period of time could result in overexposure (not to mention a major hit on the pocketbook), as viewers might get tired of the ads.

**Determining Effective Reach** Since marketers have budget constraints, they must decide whether to increase reach at the expense of frequency or increase the frequency of exposure but to a smaller audience. A number of factors influence this decision. For example, a new product or brand introduction will attempt to maximize reach, particularly unduplicated reach, to create awareness in as many people as possible as quickly as possible. At the same time, for a high-involvement product or one whose benefits are not obvious, a certain level of frequency is needed to achieve effective reach.

**Effective reach** represents the percentage of a vehicle's audience reached at each effective frequency increment. This concept is based on the assumption that one exposure to an ad may not be enough to convey the desired message. As we saw earlier, no one knows the exact number of exposures necessary for an ad to make an impact, although advertisers have settled on three as the minimum. Effective reach (exposure) is shown in the shaded area in Figure 10–21 in the range of 3 to 10 exposures. Fewer than 3 exposures is considered insufficient reach, while more than 10 is considered overexposure and thus ineffective reach. This exposure level is no guarantee of effective communication; different messages may require more or fewer exposures. For example, Jack Myers, president of Myers Reports, argues that the three-exposure theory was valid in the 1970s when consumers were exposed to approximately 1,000 ads per day. Now that they are exposed to 3,000 to 5,000 per day, three exposures may not be enough. Adding in the fragmentation of television, the proliferation of magazines, and the advent of a variety of alternative media leads Myers to believe that 12 exposures may be the *minimum* level of frequency required. Also, Jim Surmanek, president/CEO of Media Analysis Plus, contends that the complexity of the message, message length, and recency of exposure also impact this figure.[12]

Since they do not know how many times the viewer will actually be exposed, advertisers typically purchase GRPs that lead to more than three exposures to increase the likelihood of effective reach and frequency. Surmanek also argues that effective reach can be as low as one exposure, if the exposure is very recent or close to the purchase occasion (thus, recency is more important than frequency). He contends that more exposures are necessary when the message is complex and requires several exposures to be understood.[13]

Erwin Ephron, an expert in media planning, disagrees. Ephron notes that while increasing reach at minimum frequency was popular in the 1990s, it is no longer

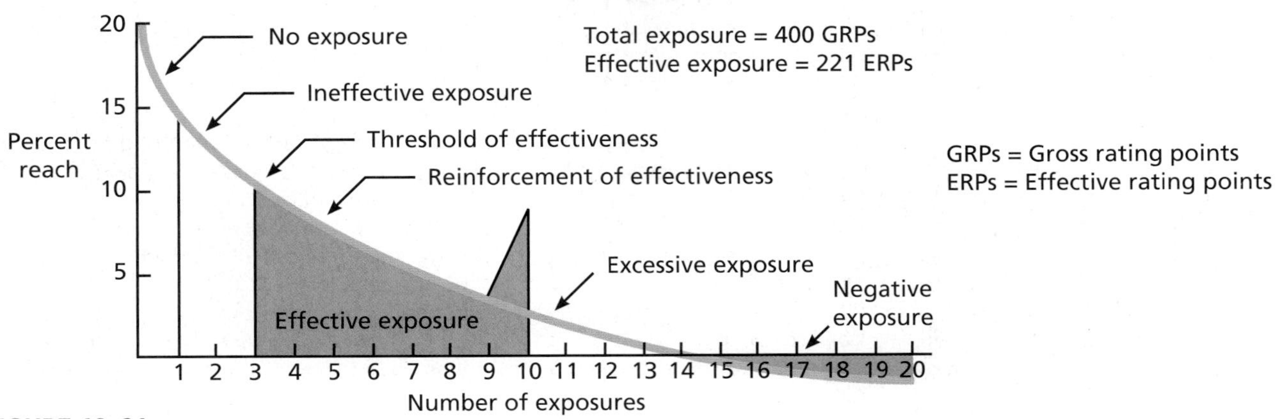


**FIGURE 10–21**

Graph of Effective Reach

a viable strategy as changes in the marketplace (commercial avoidance, multitasking, and technological innovations like the DVR) have made it more difficult to get exposure to an ad. As a result, it is important to create plans that value both reach and frequency to insure that the ad gets seen and has an impact. In other words, higher frequency results in higher reach.[14] Determining effective reach is further complicated by the fact that when calculating GRPs, advertisers use a figure that they call **average frequency**, or the average number of times the target audience reached by a media schedule is exposed to the vehicle over a specified period. The problem with this figure is revealed in the following scenario:

Consider a media buy in which:

> 50 percent of audience is reached 1 time.
> 30 percent of audience is reached 5 times.
> 20 percent of audience is reached 10 times.
> Average frequency = 4

In this media buy, the average frequency is 4, which is slightly more than the number established as effective. Yet a full 50 percent of the audience receives only one exposure. Thus, the average-frequency number can be misleading, and using it to calculate GRPs might result in underexposing the audience.

Although GRPs have their problems, they can provide useful information to the marketer. A certain level of GRPs is necessary to achieve awareness, and increases in GRPs are likely to lead to more exposures and/or more repetitions—both of which are necessary to have an effect on higher-order objectives. Perhaps the best advice for purchasing GRPs is offered by Ostrow, who recommends the following strategies:[15]

1. Instead of using average frequency, the marketer should decide what minimum frequency goal is needed to reach the advertising objectives effectively and then maximize reach at that frequency level.
2. To determine effective frequency, one must consider marketing factors, message factors, and media factors. (See Figure 10–22.)

In summary, the reach-versus-frequency decision, while critical, is very difficult to make. A number of factors must be considered, and concrete rules do not always apply. The decision is often more of an art than a science.

**Recency** As noted by Ephron, the idea that one exposure to an ad had a greater impact than additional exposures did if it was shown in the week preceding a purchase, led many advertisers to focus more attention on reach, less on frequency,

**FIGURE 10–22**

Factors Important in Determining Frequency Levels

*Marketing Factors*

- *Brand history.* Is the brand new or established? New brands generally require higher frequency levels.
- *Brand share.* An inverse relationship exists between brand share and frequency. The higher the brand share, the lower the frequency level required.
- *Brand loyalty.* An inverse relationship exists between loyalty and frequency. The higher the loyalty, the lower the frequency level required.
- *Purchase cycles.* Shorter purchasing cycles require higher frequency levels to maintain top-of-mind awareness.
- *Usage cycle.* Products used daily or more often need to be replaced quickly, so a higher level of frequency is desired.
- *Competitive share of voice.* Higher frequency levels are required when a lot of competitive noise exists and when the goal is to meet or beat competitors.
- *Target group.* The ability of the target group to learn and to retain messages has a direct effect on frequency.

*Message or Creative Factors*

- *Message complexity.* The simpler the message, the less frequency required.
- *Message uniqueness.* The more unique the message, the lower the frequency level required.
- *New versus continuing campaigns.* New campaigns require higher levels of frequency to register the message.
- *Image versus product sell.* Creating an image requires higher levels of frequency than does a specific product sell.
- *Message variation.* A single message requires less frequency; a variety of messages requires more.
- *Wearout.* Higher frequency may lead to wearout. This effect must be tracked and used to evaluate frequency levels.
- *Advertising units.* Larger units of advertising require less frequency than smaller ones to get the message across.

*Media Factors*

- *Clutter.* The more advertising that appears in the media used, the more frequency is needed to break through the clutter.
- *Editorial environment.* The more consistent the ad is with the editorial environment, the less frequency is needed.
- *Attentiveness.* The higher the level of attention achieved by the media vehicle, the less frequency is required. Low-attention-getting media require more repetitions.
- *Scheduling.* Continuous scheduling requires less frequency than does flighting or pulsing.
- *Number of media used.* The fewer media used, the lower the level of frequency required.
- *Repeat exposures.* Media that allow for more repeat exposures (for example, monthly magazines) require less frequency.



and an emphasis on **recency**. Campaigns employed **recency planning**—focusing on short interval reach at minimum frequency levels as close to the purchase decision as possible. Rather than focusing on a four-week planning period for reach, recency planning calls for a continuous schedule over a one week period, and less targeting so as to gain exposure to reach as many potential consumers as possible.[16] While one might argue that many of the exposures are then wasted, Ephron would disagree, noting that people are in the market at different times, and that awareness and image building also can benefit by the exposures.[17] Both Ephron and Krugman suggest that advertising needs to act like a brand and that "Advertising needs to be like a product sitting on the shelf, because you never know when the consumer is going to be looking for you, so advertising has to rent the shelf-space all the time."

## Creative Aspects and Mood

The context of the medium in which the ad is placed may also affect viewers' perceptions. A specific creative strategy may require certain media. Because TV provides both sight and sound, it may be more effective in generating emotions than other media; magazines may create different perceptions from newspapers. In developing a media strategy, marketers must consider both creativity and mood factors. Let us examine each in more detail.

**Creative Aspects** It is possible to increase the success of a product significantly through a strong creative campaign. But to implement this creativity, you must employ a medium that will support such a strategy. For example, the campaign for Lancome moisturizer shown in Chapter 4 used print media to communicate the message effectively. Hallmark, among many others, has effectively used TV to create emotional appeals. In some situations, the media strategy to be pursued may be the driving force behind the creative strategy, as the media and creative departments work closely together to achieve the greatest impact with the audience of the specific media.

**Mood** Certain media enhance the creativity of a message because they create a mood that carries over to the communication. For example, think about the moods created by the following magazines: *Gourmet, Skiing, Travel and Leisure,* and *House Beautiful.* Each of these special-interest vehicles puts the reader in a particular mood. The promotion of fine wines, ski boots, luggage, and home products is enhanced by this mood. What different images might be created for your product if you advertised it in the following media?

*The New York Times* versus the *National Enquirer*
*Architectural Digest* versus *Reader's Digest*
A highly rated prime-time TV show versus an old rerun
Television versus the Internet

The message may require a specific medium and a certain media vehicle to achieve its objectives. Likewise, certain media and vehicles have images that may carry over to the perceptions of messages placed within them.

## Flexibility

An effective media strategy requires a degree of flexibility. Because of the rapidly changing marketing environment, strategies may need to be modified. If the plan has not built in some flexibility, opportunities may be lost and/or the company may not be able to address new threats. Flexibility may be needed to address the following:

1. *Market opportunities.* Sometimes a market opportunity arises that the advertiser wishes to take advantage of. For example, wine companies have attempted to capitalize on the increasing interest in this drink created by changing trends in the U.S. marketplace. The development of a new advertising medium may offer an opportunity that was not previously available.
2. *Market threats.* Internal or external factors may pose a threat to the firm, and a change in media strategy is dictated. For example, a competitor may alter its media strategy to gain an edge. Failure to respond to this challenge could create problems for the firm.
3. *Availability of media.* Sometimes a desired medium (or vehicle) is not available to the marketer. Perhaps the medium does not reach a particular target segment or has no time or space available. There are still some geographic areas that certain media do not reach. Even when the media are available, limited advertising time or space may have already been sold or cutoff dates for entry may have passed. Alternative vehicles or media must then be considered.

**FIGURE 10–23**

Cost per Thousand Computations: *Time* versus *Newsweek*

| | *Time* | *Newsweek* |
|---|---|---|
| Per-page cost | $287,440 | $165,000 |
| Circulation | 3.25 million | 1.5 million |
| Calculation of CPM | 287,440 × 1,000 | 165,000 × 1,000 |
| | 3,250,000 | 1,500,000 |
| CPM | $88.44 | $110 |

4. *Changes in media or media vehicles.* A change in the medium or in a particular vehicle may require a change in the media strategy. For example, the advent of cable TV opened up new opportunities for message delivery, as will the introduction of interactive media. The Internet has led many consumer companies to adopt this medium while a number of new technologies have provided additional options. New special-interest magazines, mobile phone, social network, and videogame ads are just a few. Likewise, a drop in ratings or a change in editorial format may lead the advertiser to use different alternatives.

Fluctuations in these factors mean the media strategy must be developed with enough flexibility to allow the manager to adapt to specific market situations.



## Budget Considerations

One of the more important decisions in the development of media strategy is cost estimating. The value of any strategy can be determined by how well it delivers the message to the audience with the lowest cost and the least waste. We have already explored a number of factors, such as reach, frequency, and availability that affect this decision. The marketer tries to arrive at the optimal delivery by balancing cost with each of these. As the following discussion shows, understanding cost figures may not be as easy as it seems.

Advertising and promotional costs can be categorized in two ways. The **absolute cost** of the medium or vehicle is the actual total cost required to place the message. For example, a full-page four-color ad in *Newsweek* magazine costs about $165,000. **Relative cost** refers to the relationship between the price paid for advertising time or space and the size of the audience delivered; it is used to compare media vehicles. Relative costs are important because the manager must try to optimize audience delivery within budget constraints. Since a number of alternatives are available for delivering the message, the advertiser must evaluate the relative costs associated with these choices. The way media costs are provided and problems in comparing these costs across media often make such evaluations difficult.

### Determining Relative Costs of Media

To evaluate alternatives, advertisers must compare the relative costs of media as well as vehicles within these media. Unfortunately, the broadcast, print, and out-of-home media do not always provide the same cost breakdowns, nor necessarily do vehicles within the print media. Following are the cost bases used:

1. **Cost per thousand (CPM).** For years the magazine industry has provided cost breakdowns on the basis of cost per thousand people reached. The formula for this computation is

$$\text{CPM} = \frac{\text{Cost of ad space (absolute cost)}}{\text{Circulation}} \times 1{,}000$$

Figure 10–23 provides an example of this computation for two vehicles in the same medium—*Time* and *Newsweek*—and shows that (all other things being

**FIGURE 10–24**

Comparison of Cost per Ratings Point: *CSI* versus *Survivor* in a Local TV Market

| | *CSI* | *Survivor* |
|---|---|---|
| Cost per spot ad | $10,000 | $7,500 |
| Rating | 18 | 17 |
| Reach (households) | 197,100 | 186,150 |
| Calculation | $10,000/18 | $7,500/17 |
| CPRP (CPP) | $555 | $441 |

equal) *Time* is a more cost-effective buy, even though its absolute cost is higher. (We will come back to "all other things being equal" in a moment.)

2. **Cost per ratings point (CPRP).** The broadcast media provide a different comparative cost figure, referred to as cost per ratings point or *cost per point (CPP),* based on the following formula:

$$\text{CPRP} = \frac{\text{Cost of commercial time}}{\text{Program rating}}$$

**FIGURE 10–25**

Comparative Costs in Newspaper Advertising

| | *Pittsburgh Post Gazette* | *Cleveland Plain Dealer* |
|---|---|---|
| Cost per page | $20,969 | $59,598 |
| Cost per inch | 303.90 | 473 |
| Circulation | 184,234 | 271,180 |
| Calculation | $\text{CPM} = \frac{\text{Page cost} \times 1{,}000}{\text{Circulation}}$ | |
| | $\frac{\$2{,}969 \times 1{,}000}{189{,}234}$ | $\frac{\$59{,}598 \times 1{,}000}{271{,}180}$ |
| | $113.81 | $219.77 |

An example of this calculation for a spot ad in a local TV market is shown in Figure 10–24. It indicates that *Survivor* would be more cost-effective than *CSI.*

3. **Daily inch rate.** For newspapers, cost effectiveness is based on the daily inch rate, which is the cost per column inch of the paper. Like magazines, newspapers now use the cost-per-thousand formula discussed earlier to determine relative costs. As shown in Figure 10–25, the *Pittsburgh Post Gazette* costs significantly more to advertise in than does the *Cleveland Plain Dealer* (again, all other things being equal).

As you can see, it is difficult to make comparisons across various media. What is the broadcast equivalent of cost per thousand or the column inch rate? In an attempt to standardize relative costing procedures, the broadcast and newspaper media have begun to provide costs per thousand, using the following formulas:

$$\text{Television: } \frac{\text{Cost of 1 unit of time} \times 1{,}000}{\text{Program rating}} \qquad \text{Newspapers: } \frac{\text{Cost of ad space} \times 1{,}000}{\text{Circulation}}$$

While the comparison of media on a cost-per-thousand basis is important, intermedia comparisons can be misleading. The ability of TV to provide both sight and sound, the longevity of magazines, and other characteristics of each medium make

**FIGURE 10–26**
Cost-per-Thousand Estimates

| *Scenario A: Overestimation of Efficiency* | |
|---|---|
| Target market | 18–49 |
| Magazine circulation | 3,250,000 |
| Circulation to target market | 65% (2,112,500) |
| Cost per page | $287,440 |

$$\text{CPM} = \frac{\$287{,}480}{3{,}250.00} = \frac{\$88.40}{\$287{,}480}$$

$$\text{CPM (actual target audience)} = \frac{\$287{,}440 \times 1{,}000}{2{,}112{,}500} = \$136.07$$

| *Scenario B: Underestimation of Efficiency* | |
|---|---|
| Target market | All age groups, male and female |
| Magazine circulation | 3,250,000 |
| Cost per page | $287,440 |
| Pass-along rate | 3* (33% of households) |

$$\text{CPM (based on readers per copy)} = \frac{\text{Page cost} \times 1{,}000}{\text{Circulation} + 3(1{,}072{,}500)} = \frac{(287{,}440 \times 1{,}000)}{4{,}322{,}500} = \$66.50$$

*Assuming pass-along was valid.

CHAPTER 10

direct comparisons difficult. The media planner should use the cost-per-thousand numbers but must also consider the specific characteristics of each medium and each media vehicle in the decision.

The cost per thousand may overestimate or underestimate the actual cost effectiveness. Consider a situation where some waste coverage is inevitable. The circulation (using the *Time* magazine figures to demonstrate our point) exceeds the target market. If the people reached by this message are not potential buyers of the product, then having to pay to reach them results in too low a cost per thousand, as shown in scenario A of Figure 10–26. We must use the potential reach to the target market—the destination sought—rather than the overall circulation figure. A medium with a much higher cost per thousand may be a wiser buy if it is reaching more potential receivers. (Most media buyers rely on **target CPM**, or **TCPM**, which calculates CPMs based on the target audience, not the overall audience.)

CPM may also underestimate cost efficiency. Magazine advertising space sellers have argued for years that because more than one person may read an issue, the actual reach is underestimated. They want to use the number of **readers per copy** as the true circulation. This would include a **pass-along rate**, estimating the number of people who read the magazine without buying it. Scenario B in Figure 10–26 shows how this underestimates cost efficiency. Consider a family in which a father, mother, and two teenagers read each issue of *Time.* Assume such families constitute 33 percent of *Time*'s circulation base. While the circulation figure includes only one magazine, in reality there are four potential exposures in these households, increasing the total reach to 4.32 million.

While the number of readers per copy makes intuitive sense, it has the potential to be extremely inaccurate. The actual number of times the magazine changes hands is difficult to determine. How many people in a fraternity read each issue of *Sports Illustrated* or *Maxim* that is delivered? How many people in a sorority or on a dorm floor read each issue of *Cosmopolitan* or *Vanity Fair?* How many of either group read each issue of *BusinessWeek?* While research is conducted to make these

**FIGURE 10–27**
Media Characteristics

| Media | Advantages | Disadvantages |
|---|---|---|
| Television | Mass coverage<br>High reach<br>Impact of sight, sound, and motion<br>High prestige<br>Low cost per exposure<br>Attention getting<br>Favorable image | Low selectivity<br>Short message life<br>High absolute cost<br>High production costs<br>Clutter |
| Radio | Local coverage<br>Low cost<br>High frequency<br>Flexible<br>Low production costs<br>Well-segmented audiences | Audio only<br>Clutter<br>Low attention getting<br>Fleeting message |
| Magazines | Segmentation potential<br>Quality reproduction<br>High information content<br>Longevity<br>Multiple readers | Long lead time for ad placement<br>Visual only<br>Lack of flexibility |
| Newspapers | High coverage<br>Low cost<br>Short lead time for placing ads<br>Ads can be placed in interest sections<br>Timely (current ads)<br>Reader controls exposure<br>Can be used for coupons | Short life<br>Clutter<br>Low attention-getting capabilities<br>Poor reproduction quality<br>Selective reader exposure |
| Outdoor | Location specific<br>High repetition<br>Easily noticed | Short exposure time requires short ad<br>Poor image<br>Local restrictions |
| Direct mail | High selectivity<br>Reader controls exposure<br>High information content<br>Opportunities for repeat exposures | High cost/contact<br>Poor image (junk mail)<br>Clutter |
| Internet and interactive media | User selects product information<br>User attention and involvement<br>Interactive relationship<br>Direct selling potential<br>Flexible message platform | Limited creative capabilities<br>Websnarl (crowded access)<br>Technology limitations<br>Few valid measurement techniques<br>Limited reach |

determinations, pass-along estimates are very subjective and using them to estimate reach is speculative. These figures are regularly provided by the media, but managers are selective about using them. At the same time, the art of media buying enters, for many magazines' managers have a good idea how much greater the reach is than their circulation figures provided.

In addition to the potential for over- or underestimation of cost efficiencies, CPMs are limited in that they make only *quantitative* estimates of the value of media. While they may be good for comparing very similar vehicles (such as *Time* and *Newsweek*), they are less valuable in making intermedia comparisons, for example, CPM for magazines versus Internet banner ads. We have already noted some differences among media that preclude direct comparisons.

You can see that the development of a media strategy involves many factors. Ostrow may be right when he calls this process an art rather than a science, as so much of it requires going beyond the numbers.

# EVALUATION AND FOLLOW-UP

All plans require some evaluation to assess their performance. The media plan is no exception.

In outlining the planning process, we stated that objectives are established and strategies developed for them. Having implemented these strategies, marketers need to know whether or not they were successful. Measures of effectiveness must consider two factors: (1) How well did these strategies achieve the media objectives? (2) How well did this media plan contribute to attaining the overall marketing and communications objectives? If the strategies were successful, they should be used in future plans. If not, their flaws should be analyzed.

The problem with measuring the effectiveness of media strategies is probably obvious to you at this point. At the outset of this chapter, we suggested the planning process was limited by problems with measurements and lack of consistent terminology (among others). While these problems limit the degree to which we can assess the relative effectiveness of various strategies, it is not impossible to make such determinations. Sometimes it is possible to show that a plan has worked. Even if the evaluation procedure is not foolproof, it is better than no attempt. We will discuss more about measuring effectiveness in Chapter 19.



# CHARACTERISTICS OF MEDIA

To this point, we have discussed the elements involved in the development of media strategy. One of the most basic elements in this process is the matching of media to markets. In the following chapters, you will see that each medium has its own characteristics that make it better or worse for attaining specific objectives. First, Figure 10–27 provides an overall comparison of media and some of the characteristics by which they are evaluated. This is a very general comparison, and the various media options must be analyzed for each situation. Nevertheless, it is a good starting point and serves as a lead-in to subsequent chapters.

## Summary

This chapter has presented an overview of the determination of media objectives, development of the media strategy, and formalization of objectives and strategy in the form of a media plan. Sources of media information, characteristics of media, and key media decisions were also discussed.

The media strategy must be designed to supplement and support the overall marketing and communications objectives. The objectives of this plan are designed to deliver the message the program has developed.

The basic task involved in the development of media strategy is to determine the best matching of media to the target market, given the constraints of the budget. The media planner attempts to balance reach and frequency and to deliver the message to the intended audience with a minimum of waste coverage. At the same time, a number of additional factors affect the media decision. Media strategy development has been called more of an art than a science because while many quantitative data are available, the planner also relies on creativity and nonquantifiable factors.

This chapter discussed many factors, including developing a proper media mix, determining target market and geographic coverage, scheduling, and balancing reach and frequency. Creative aspects, budget considerations, the need for flexibility in the schedule, and the use of computers in the media planning process were also considered.

The chapter also introduced a number of resources available to the media planner. A summary chart of advantages and disadvantages of various media was provided.

## Key Terms

**media planning** p. 329
**media objectives** p. 329
**media strategies** p. 329
**medium** p. 329
**media vehicle** p. 329
**reach** p. 329
**coverage** p. 329
**frequency** p. 329
**sweeps periods** p. 331
**index number** p. 334
**survey of buying power index** p. 338
**brand development index (BDI)** p. 338
**category development index (CDI)** p. 340
**waste coverage** p. 342
**continuity** p. 344
**flighting** p. 344
**pulsing** p. 344
**unduplicated reach** p. 347
**duplicated reach** p. 347
**program rating** p. 347
**gross ratings points (GRPs)** p. 347
**target ratings points (TRPs)** p. 347
**effective reach** p. 349
**average frequency** p. 350
**recency** p. 351
**recency planning** p. 351
**absolute cost** p. 353
**relative cost** p. 353
**cost per thousand (CPM)** p. 353
**cost per ratings point (CPRP)** p. 354
**daily inch rate** p. 354
**target CPM (TCPM)** p. 355
**readers per copy** p. 355
**pass-along rate** p. 355

## Discussion Questions

1. One well-known media planner has noted that media buying is a combination of art and science with a definite bias toward art. Explain what this means and give examples of circumstances of situations in which this might be the case. (LO4)

2. GfK MRI and Experian Simons both provide indexes to describe profiles of product users. Using the index provided in Figure 10–5, describe the profile of the energy drink user. Who is least likely to drink this product? (LO2)

3. What does it mean for a company when they discover that their product has a High BDI but low CDI? What about a Low CDI and Low BDI? (LO2)

4. As the media landscape continues to change, and advertisers shift more and more of their monies into new media, there are those who predict that some traditional media like TV and newspapers may not survive—at least in their present forms. Discuss whether you think this is an accurate statement and why or why not. (LO5)

5. Some media claim that advertisers should focus more attention to Readers per Dollar than CPM as a relative cost figure. Explain why they feel this way, and discuss some of the advantages and disadvantages with the use of both of these measures. (LO2)

6. What is meant by engagement (in media terms)? Explain the relevance of engagement to media planners. (LO1)

7. A criticism of the current rating system for TV is that the numbers are based on sweeps periods. Some argue that a more accurate picture is provided by the meter system. Discuss some of the advantages and disadvantages of each method. (LO1)

8. Some marketers estimate that the average consumer may be exposed to as many as 3,000 to 5,000 ads per day. Current estimates of effective frequency are based on 1,500 exposures per day. Discuss how, if at all, more exposures to advertising may necessitate changes in effective frequency. (LO3)

9. Some business to business advertisers (for example, copy machine companies) advertise on NFL Sunday and/or Monday Night football games. As might be expected, such a buy would lead to a high level of waste coverage. Explain what is meant by waste coverage. Discuss whether this might or might not be a good media buy. (LO1)

10. Explain what is meant by BDI and CDI. How do advertisers use these indices in their media planning? (LO2)

## AdForum Exercise: Analyzing Advertising Appeals and Execution Styles

(See Advertising and Promotion Playlist, Chapter 9)

### PART I: MCDONALD'S

The playlist for this chapter contains three commercials for McDonald's. Watch these three spots and answer the following:

1 Analyze the type of advertising appeal used in each commercial.

2 What type of creative advertising execution technique is being used for each spot?

3 Discuss the target audience for each commercial and whether you feel the ad is an effective way to communicate with this market segment.

### PART II: TIDE LAUNDRY DETERGENT

The playlist for this chapter also includes three TV commercials for Tide laundry detergent.

1 Analyze the type of advertising appeal and creative execution technique used for each ad and discuss why the agency may have chosen to use it.

2 Why do you think Procter & Gamble is using different advertising execution methods to advertise Tide? Discuss the role each ad plays in the marketing of Tide laundry detergent.

Access to the chapter playlist is available through McGraw Hill connect™ MARKETING, www.mcgrawhillconnect.com

# ASICS America 2009 Summary Flowchart

| | January | | | | February | | | | March | | | | | April | | | | May | | | | June | | |
|---|---|---|---|---|---|---|---|---|---|---|---|---|---|---|---|---|---|---|---|---|---|---|---|---|
| | 29 | 5 | 12 | 19 | 26 | 2 | 9 | 16 | 23 | 2 | 9 | 16 | 23 | 30 | 6 | 13 | 20 | 27 | 4 | 11 | 18 | 25 | 1 | 8 |
| **Global/Branding** | | | | | | | | | | | | | | | | | | | | | | | | |
| TV | | | | | | | | | | | ■ | ■ | ■ | ■ | ■ | | | | | | | | | |
| Hulu-online TV | | | | | | | | | | | | | | ■ | ■ | ■ | ■ | | | | | | | |
| **Performance Running** | | | | | | | | | | | | | | | | | | | | | | | | |
| Print | | | | | | | | | ■ | ■ | ■ | ■ | ■ | ■ | ■ | ■ | ■ | ■ | ■ | ■ | ■ | ■ | ■ | ■ |
| Online | | | | | | | | | | | | | | ■ | ■ | ■ | ■ | ■ | ■ | ■ | ■ | ■ | ■ | ■ |
| **Onitsuka Tiger** | | | | | | | | | | | | | | | | | | | | | | | | |
| Print | | | | | | | | | ■ | ■ | ■ | ■ | ■ | ■ | ■ | ■ | ■ | ■ | ■ | ■ | ■ | ■ | ■ | ■ |
| Online | | | | | | | | | | | | | | | | | | | | | | | | |
| **NYC Marathon** | | | | | | | | | | | | | | | | | | | | | | | | |
| Outdoor/Online/TV | | | | | | | | | | | | | | | | | | | | | | | | |
| **Trade** | | | | | | | | | | | | | | | | | | | | | | | | |
| Print | ■ | ■ | ■ | ■ | | | | | | | | | | | | | | | | | | | | |

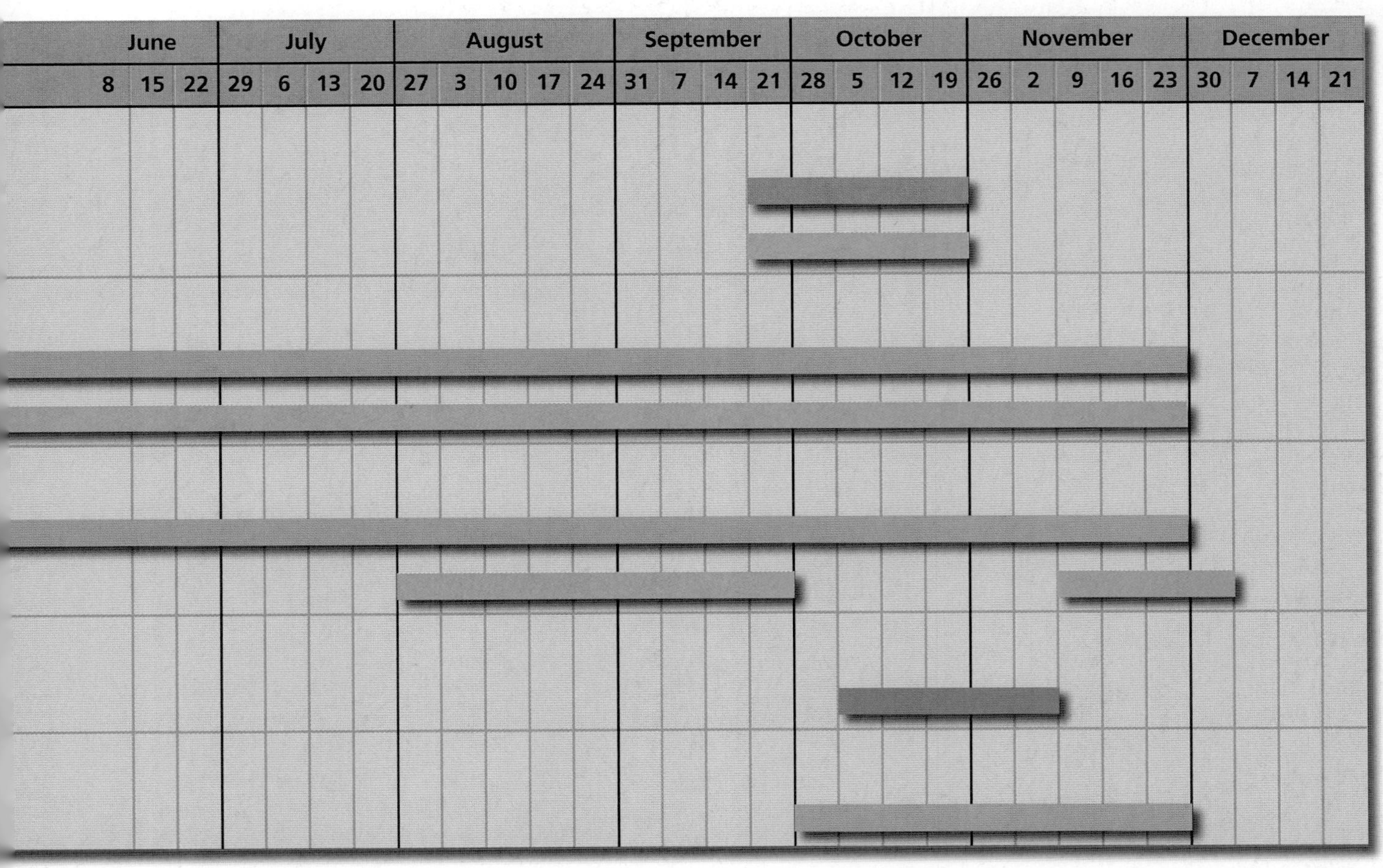
June
July
August
September
October
November
December
8 15 22 29 6 13 20 27 3 10 17 24 31 7 14 21 28 5 12 19 26 2 9 16 23 30 7 14 21

## LEARNING OBJECTIVES

LO1 To examine the structure of the television and radio industries and the role of each medium in the advertising program.

LO2 To consider the advantages and limitations of TV and radio as advertising media.

LO3 To explain how advertising time is purchased for the broadcast media, how audiences are measured, and how rates are determined.

LO4 To consider future trends in TV and radio and how they will influence the use of these media in advertising.

# 11 Evaluation of Media: Television and Radio

## THE MORE TELEVISION CHANGES, THE MORE IT STAYS THE SAME

Television has been the dominant form of entertainment in most households for more than half a century and advertising has been the lifeblood of the industry for nearly as long. Ever since Bulova ran the first TV ad in 1941 at a cost of ten dollars, the commercial has been considered the quintessential form of advertising for many marketers. Television advertising has gone through many changes over the past 60 years. For decades it was dominated by three major broadcast networks (ABC, CBS, and NBC), which could deliver more than 90 percent of the prime time viewing audience on any given evening. However, with the growth of cable and direct broadcast satellite services, most television households can now receive more than 100 channels that offer various types of shows, news, sports, music, information, and other entertainment genres. The devices that deliver all of these into our homes have evolved as well as the squat cubes are rapidly being replaced by larger flat panels that offer sharper and brighter digital images along with high-quality sound. Moreover, these flatscreen TVs in our living rooms are being joined by other devices including digital video recorders (DVRs), gaming consoles, and computers, while the cable and satellite companies that deliver the signals also offer access to movies, sports, and other forms of entertainment through their on-demand services. And many experts argue that it is only a matter of time before all of this content is delivered to TV sets online via the Internet.

The changes that have been occurring in the television industry are challenging its role as an advertising medium, particularly the technological developments of the past decade. One of the most significant developments was TiVo Inc.'s introduction of the first DVR at the beginning of the new millennium as these devices allow users to record many hours of programming and easily fast-forward through content when playing back a recorded show. The penetration of DVRs has been much slower than expected as just under a third of U.S. households now have them and the vast majority of TV shows are still watched when the broadcasters air them. However, changes in the measurement of television viewing audiences have already been made by Nielsen Research to account for recorded shows that are played back on DVRs. And as penetration of the devices increases, additional changes may be needed for measuring viewing audiences, as well as finding ways to get consumers not to fast-forward through the commercials or to send them some type of advertising message as they do so.

In addition to DVRs, there are many other developments impacting television and threatening its role as the king of advertising media, as well as its basic business model which is based on delivering large numbers of viewers of its programs to advertisers. One of the most significant factors is the continued fragmentation of the viewing audience that is occurring with the increase in channels available through digital cable and satellite systems. Total viewership of the four major networks (which now include Fox) has declined by more than 42 percent over the past 15 years and collectively they account for only 25 percent of the prime time viewing audience. The top rated shows used to be watched by at least 20 percent of all TV households. However, it is rare for the most popular TV shows such as *American Idol* or *NCIS* to reach this many people and most top 10 shows struggle to get double digit ratings. While the number of prime time viewers has declined, many of these viewers are being lost to cable channels that offer programs that appeal to very narrow audiences that are interested in news, sports, fashion, music, cooking, entertainment, and many other specialized areas.

Television viewing patterns are also being impacted by technologies that provide access to other forms of entertainment that are delivered on our TV screens. Video on demand was used in 42 percent of American households in 2009 and this figure is expected to reach nearly two-thirds of all households by 2014. Many households have video game consoles such as a Sony Playstation, Nintendo Wii, or Microsoft Xbox connected to their TV sets which allow them to play games, access the Internet, or watch movies on demand from sources such as Netflix. Television viewing is also being impacted by the number of people who are now watching shows through online video streams on platforms such as YouTube, Hulu, Fancast, and the TV networks' own websites.

Predictions of television's imminent demise as a major advertising medium have come and gone through the years like fast-forwarded commercial breaks. Media experts have argued that all of the technological developments would lead to the demise of TV's traditional advertising based business model, as consumers want to watch what they want and when they want, and this does not include commercials. And while consumers continue to gain more control over television, their viewing behavior is still not supporting the dire predictions of the so called experts. The average household is still watching an average of more than seven hours a day of television, and the traditional image of the family gathered together to watch TV is still an accurate depiction of how most people watch television. Studies by the Kaiser Family Foundation have shown that total media consumption among young people continues to rise as they now spend nearly 11 hours each day with some form of media. And while more of this time is being spent surfing the Internet, playing video games, or with social media, the amount of time spent watching television has increased over the past five years to more than four hours a day.

Efforts to change and improve the way people watch television will continue and new technologies will be developed that offer ways to improve the TV viewing experience and allow more control over it. The television networks recognize that they must continue to adapt to these changes and the impact they are having on TV as an advertising medium. For example, David Polltrack, the chief research officer for CBS, already envisions selling advertising in a new way that involves multiple platforms including the episode of the show that airs in its scheduled time slot as well as all streams of the show online for one week. There is also discussion of the networks and cable operators offering addressable advertising, a technology that could send different commercials to a household based on their product usage or predefined demographic characteristics.

Television has always been the medium of choice for marketers who want to reach large audiences and deliver an impactful message. However, changes are well under way that are impacting the way we watch TV and will challenge its role as the quintessential advertising medium. But these changes may occur more slowly than many experts predict as TV viewing habits are very entrenched and will not change easily. The comment of an industry executive sums it up pretty well as he notes, "The killer application on television turns out to be television."

Sources: "Changing the Channel: A Special Report on Television," *The Economist,* May 1, 2010, pp. 3–10; Brian Steinberg, "The Future of TV," *Advertising Age,* November 30, 2009, pp. 1, 3; Burt Helm, "TV Commercials: Who Needs Them," *BusinessWeek,* May 25, 2009, p. 24.

The changes that are occurring in the television industry are important as they are having a profound impact on the primary form of entertainment in most households as well as the largest advertising medium. TV has virtually saturated households throughout the United States and most other countries and has become a mainstay in the lives of most people. The average American household watches over eight hours of TV a day, and the tube has become the predominant source of news and entertainment for many people. Over 80 percent of the TV households in the United States have a DVD player, while many have entertainment centers with big-screen TVs, DVRs, and surround sound. On any given evening during the prime-time hours of 8 to 11 P.M., more than 100 million people are watching TV. Popular shows like *NCIS* and *American Idol* can draw more than 20 million viewers. The large numbers of people who watch television are important to the TV networks and stations because they can sell time on these programs to marketers who want to reach that audience with their advertising messages. Moreover, the qualities that make TV a great medium for news and entertainment also encourage creative ads that can have a strong impact on customers.

Radio is also an integral part of our lives. Many of us wake up to clock radios in the morning and rely on radio programs to inform and/or entertain us while we drive to work or school. For many people, radio is a constant companion in their cars, at home, even at work. The average American listens to the radio nearly three hours each day.[1] Like TV viewers, radio listeners are an important audience for marketers.

In this chapter, we examine the broadcast media of TV and radio, including the general characteristics of each as well as their specific advantages and disadvantages. We examine how advertisers use TV and radio as part of their advertising and media strategies, how they buy TV and radio time, and how audiences are measured and evaluated for each medium. We also examine the factors that are changing the role of TV and radio as advertising media.

# TELEVISION

It has often been said that television is the ideal advertising medium. Its ability to combine visual images, sound, motion, and color presents the advertiser with the opportunity to develop the most creative and imaginative appeals of any medium. However, TV does have certain problems that limit or even prevent its use by many advertisers.

## Advantages of Television

TV has numerous advantages over other media, including creativity and impact, coverage and cost effectiveness, captivity and attention, and selectivity and flexibility.

**Creativity and Impact** Perhaps the greatest advantage of TV is the opportunity it provides for presenting the advertising message. The interaction of sight and sound offers tremendous creative flexibility and makes possible dramatic, lifelike representations of products and services. TV commercials can be used to convey a mood or image for a brand as well as to develop emotional or entertaining appeals that help make a dull product appear interesting.

Television is also an excellent medium for demonstrating a product or service. For example, print ads are effective for showing a product such as a high-definition television and communicating information regarding its features. However, a TV commercial like the acclaimed "Power Unleashed" spot for the Hitachi UltraVision plasma set shown in Exhibit 11–1 is a very effective way to communicate its rich color, vivid detail, and lifelike picture.

**EXHIBIT 11–1**
A television ad is an effective way to communicate the picture quality of this Hitachi plasma TV

**FIGURE 11–1**

Top 10 Network TV Advertisers, 2006

| Rank | Company | Measured TV Advertising (millions) |
|---|---|---|
| 1 | AT&T | $762.7 |
| 2 | Pfizer | 605.2 |
| 3 | General Motors | 544.2 |
| 4 | Verizon Communications | 510.1 |
| 5 | Ford Motor Co. | 509.5 |
| 6 | Procter & Gamble | 496.4 |
| 7 | Sprint Nextel Corp. | 442.4 |
| 8 | Time Warner | 396.9 |
| 9 | Toyota Motor Corp. | 340.4 |
| 10 | Walmart Stores | 329.6 |

Source: "100 Leading National Advertisers," *Advertising Age,* June 21, 2010, p. 14. Copyright © 2010 Crain Communications.

**Coverage and Cost Effectiveness** Television advertising makes it possible to reach large audiences. Nearly everyone, regardless of age, sex, income, or educational level, watches at least some TV. Most people do so on a regular basis. According to Nielsen Media Research estimates, nearly 280 million people age 2 or older live in the nation's 114.9 million TV households, nearly 77 percent of whom are 18 or older.[2]

Marketers selling products and services that appeal to broad target audiences find that TV lets them reach mass markets, often very cost efficiently. The average prime-time TV show reaches 5 million homes; a top-rated show like *American Idol* may reach nearly 12 million homes and almost twice that many viewers. In 2009, the average cost per thousand (CPM) homes reached was nearly $27 for network evening shows and $7.35 for daytime weekly shows.[3]

Because of its ability to reach large audiences in a cost-efficient manner, TV is a popular medium among companies selling mass-consumption products. Companies with widespread distribution and availability of their products and services use TV to reach the mass market and deliver their advertising messages at a very low cost per thousand. Television has become indispensable to large consumer packaged-goods marketers, telecommunication companies, carmakers, and major retailers. Companies like AT&T and Procter & Gamble spend nearly two-thirds of their media budgets on various forms of TV—network, spot, cable, and syndicated programs—while PepsiCo and Coca-Cola spend more than 40 percent. Figure 11–1 shows the top 10 network television advertisers and their expenditures. IMC Perspective 11–1 discusses the Super Bowl, which is the television program that delivers the largest viewing audience each year. We discuss how many advertisers are turning their involvement with the big game into an integrated marketing opportunity by using the Internet to expand the life of their commercials.

**Captivity and Attention** Television is basically intrusive in that commercials impose themselves on viewers as they watch their favorite programs. Unless we make a special effort to avoid commercials, most of us are exposed to thousands of them each year. The increase in viewing options and the penetration of DVDs, DVRs, remote controls, and other automatic devices have made it easier for TV viewers to avoid commercial messages.[4] However, the remaining viewers are likely to devote some attention to many advertising messages. As discussed in Chapter 5,

**EXHIBIT 11–2**
Oxygen promotes its ability to reach young, upscale women

the low-involvement nature of consumer learning and response processes may mean TV ads have an effect on consumers simply through heavy repetition and exposure to catchy slogans and jingles.

**Selectivity and Flexibility** Television has often been criticized for being a nonselective medium, since it is difficult to reach a precisely defined market segment through the use of TV advertising. But some selectivity is possible due to variations in the composition of audiences as a result of program content, broadcast time, and geographic coverage. For example, Saturday morning TV caters to children; Saturday and Sunday afternoon programs are geared to the sports-oriented male; and weekday daytime shows appeal heavily to homemakers.

With the growth of cable TV, advertisers refine their coverage further by appealing to groups with specific interests such as sports, news, history, the arts, or music, as well as specific demographic groups. Exhibit 11–2 shows an ad promoting the Oxygen cable network and how it reaches young, upscale women who like to try new products, as well as recommend them to others.

Advertisers can also adjust their media strategies to take advantage of different geographic markets through local or spot ads in specific market areas. Ads can be scheduled to run repeatedly or to take advantage of special occasions. For example, companies such as Miller/Coors, Anheuser-Busch and Gillette are often major sponsors during sporting events such as major league baseball or NFL football games, which allows them to advertise heavily to men who constitute the primary market for their products.

## Limitations of Television

Although television is unsurpassed from a creative perspective, the medium has several disadvantages that limit or preclude its use by many advertisers. These problems include high costs, the lack of selectivity, the fleeting nature of a television message, commercial clutter, limited viewer attention, and distrust of TV ads.

**Costs** Despite the efficiency of TV in reaching large audiences, it is an expensive medium in which to advertise. The high cost of TV stems not only from the expense of buying airtime but also from the costs of producing a quality commercial. Production costs for a national brand 30-second spot average nearly $400,000 and can reach over a million for more elaborate commercials.[5] Many advertisers also develop commercials specifically for certain ethnic markets such as African-Americans and Hispanics.[6] More advertisers are using media-driven creative strategies that require production of a variety of commercials, which drive up their costs. Even local ads can be expensive to produce and often are not of high quality. The high costs of producing and airing commercials often price small- and medium-size advertisers out of the market.

**Lack of Selectivity** Some selectivity is available in television through variations in programs and cable TV. But advertisers who are seeking a very specific, often small, target audience find the coverage of TV often extends beyond their market, reducing its cost effectiveness (as discussed in Chapter 10). Geographic selectivity can be a problem for local advertisers such as retailers, since a station bases its rates on the total market area it reaches. For example, stations in Pittsburgh, Pennsylvania, reach viewers in western and central Pennsylvania, eastern Ohio, northern West Virginia, and even parts of Maryland. The small company

## IMC Perspective 11–1 > > >

### Marketers Go Online to Expand Their Super Bowl Playbook

America loves its football, and Super Bowl Sunday has become an unofficial national holiday. The game always draws the largest TV viewing audience of the year, and its appeal spans various age groups, sexes, and regions of the country. The game has even developed a global appeal; it is now seen in more than 80 countries. While most consumers think about the Super Bowl as the biggest football game of the year, many marketers view it as the premier marketing event as well. The Super Bowl has become the most important advertising showcase of the year, particularly for marketers willing to spend nearly $3 million for a 30-second commercial. Despite the high costs of advertising on the Super Bowl, many companies think it is well worth the money. They point out that the big game is usually the most-watched program of the year and delivers more than 90 million viewers in the United States and millions more abroad. For example, more than 106 million people watched the 2010 Super Bowl, making it the most watched telecast in U.S. television history. Advertisers also note that the Super Bowl is one occasion where as much attention is paid to the commercials as to the program. Many consumers actually wait to see the new ads that often debut during the telecast, and the spots often receive a considerable amount of hype and publicity prior to, as well as after, the game.

While the large and attentive viewing audience is a major reason why companies advertise on the Super Bowl, many also view their involvement with the game as an excellent integrated marketing opportunity. Marketers use a variety of other IMC tools to accompany the ads they run on Super Bowl Sunday including user-generated ad contests, sweepstakes, video-sharing sites, blogs, mobile advertising, and webisodes. They also use pre- and postgame public relations efforts to maximize the value of their multimillion-dollar ad buys as many tout their Super Bowl ads with leaks to the press and partial reviews of their spots.

The goal of many marketers in hyping their Super Bowl ads is to generate buzz about them leading up to the big game and to prolong the shelf life of the campaign well beyond the game. One of the primary ways companies are doing this is through ongoing online efforts that utilize social media as well as paid-search advertising. More than 90 percent of the companies or brands that advertised on the last two Super Bowls had their ads posed on YouTube while more than a quarter of them used social networks to drive additional comments and conversations. Marketers' efforts to extend the exposure to their ads are also being facilitated by numerous online video-sharing sites that have been developed around the Super Bowl commercials. For example, YouTube hosted all 65 of the ads from the 2010 Super Bowl on its AdBlitz site and promoted it as a place where consumers could go to vote for their favorite commercials and share them with others. Break.com has also created an online channel around the Super Bowl ads and various media such as *USA Today, Advertising Age,* and *Forbes,* as well as the major TV networks that host the game each year also have micro sites that host all of the Super Bowl spots.

Marketers are also purchasing ads on search engines such as Google, Microsoft Bing, and Yahoo to draw more attention to their ads online. While only 21 percent of the advertisers invested in paid search around their Super Bowl

---

whose market is limited to the immediate Pittsburgh area may find TV an inefficient media buy, since the stations cover a larger geographic area than the merchant's trade area.

Audience selectivity is improving as advertisers target certain groups of consumers through the type of program or day and/or time when they choose to advertise. However, TV still does not offer as much audience selectivity as radio, magazines, newspapers, or direct mail for reaching precise segments of the market.

**Fleeting Message** TV commercials usually last only 30 seconds or less and leave nothing tangible for the viewer to examine or consider. Commercials have become shorter and shorter as the demand for a limited amount of broadcast time has intensified and advertisers try to get more impressions from their media budgets. Thirty-second commercials became the norm in the mid-1970s, and in September 1986, the three major networks began accepting 15-second spots across their full schedules (except during children's viewing time). Since 1987, these shorter spots have been accounting for a little more than a third of all network commercials and up to 14 percent of nonnetwork commercial activity. Thirty-second spots remain the dominant commercial length, accounting for 51 percent of network spots and nearly 70 percent of nonnetwork ads.[7]

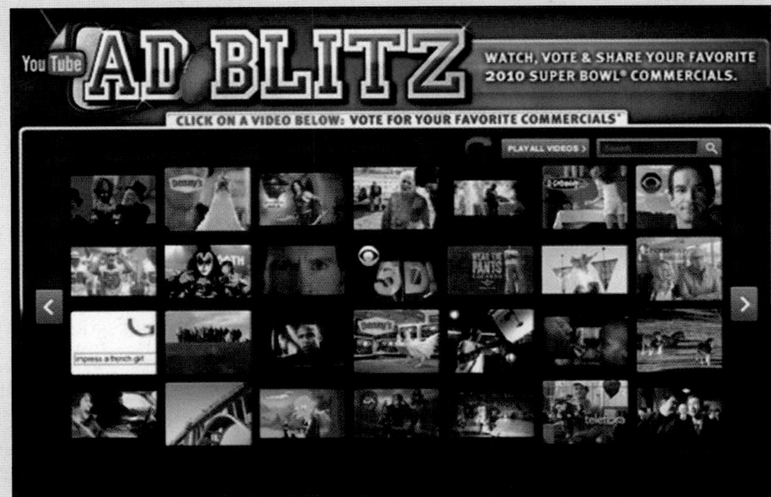


ads in 2005, the number tripled to nearly 70 percent in 2010. According to Google, online searches for the term "Super Bowl commercials" start increasing about a week before the game at a rate of 10 to 20 percent per day leading up to the game and peak the following Monday. Marketers recognize that many consumers, as well as the media, want a sneak preview of their Super Bowl commercials and will post them online. For example, E-Trade, the online brokerage firm that has advertised on several of the past Super Bowls, developed a pregame strategy that included releasing outtakes from its humorous talking toddlers campaign several days before the game. They also took over the YouTube home page on Thursday before the game to promote their Super Bowl ads, bought search terms on primary search engines, and set up a Facebook page and Twitter account to promote the ads.

Despite the concerns expressed by some advertising and media experts, the Super Bowl is likely to continue to be a popular media buy among companies who can afford it and for good reason. In terms of cost per thousand (the cost to reach a thousand viewers) the Super Bowl is a very efficient media buy and is still the only time advertisers can reach pretty much everyone who is watching TV on a given day. Moreover, Super Bowl ads may receive nearly the same number of views online as they do during the game. According to Visible Measures, a company that tallies viral video metrics, during the week following the 2010 Super Bowl, the 10 most-watched videos online were all Super Bowl commercials and collectively racked up nearly 45 million views. The four commercials for Frito-Lay's Doritos brand that aired during the game had nearly 18 million views, with one of the commercials garnering over 9 million views alone, while the E-Trade toddler spot "Girlfriend" had 3.4 million views.

The Super Bowl is likely to remain advertising's premier event, particularly for companies with large budgets who can pay the high price for a 30-second spot as well as smaller companies who feel they can generate millions of dollars worth of additional free exposure from the media attention that often accompanies Super Bowl ads. It is also likely that marketers will continue to find creative ways to get consumers involved with Super Bowl ads, both before and after the game, to get the most out of their investment.

Sources: Michael Learmonth, "Doritos, Google Super Bowl Ads Storm Chart," *Advertising Age,* February 18, 2010, http://adage.com/print?article_id=142151; Abbey Klassen, "How to Boost Your Super Bowl ROI,' *Advertising Age,* December 7, 2009, http://adage.com/print?article_id=140896; Keith Darce, "Web Tie-ins Part of Super Bowl Advertising Playbook," *San Diego Union-Tribune,* January 31, 2008, pp. A1.10.



An important factor in the decline in commercial length has been the spiraling inflation in media costs over the past decade. With the average cost of a prime-time spot reaching nearly $100,000, many advertisers see shorter commercials as the only way to keep their media costs in line. A 15-second spot typically sells for half the price of a 30-second spot. By using 15- or even 10-second commercials, advertisers think they can run additional spots to reinforce the message or reach a larger audience. Many advertisers believe shorter commercials can deliver a message just as effectively as longer spots for much less money.

Several years ago, many advertising people predicted 15-second spots would become the dominant commercial unit. However, the use of 15-second commercials has settled at around 38 percent since 2003. This may be due to several factors, including creative considerations, lower prices for network time, and a desire by the networks to restrict clutter.[8]

**Clutter** The problems of fleeting messages and shorter commercials are compounded by the fact that the advertiser's message is only one of many spots and other nonprogramming material seen during a commercial break, so it may have trouble being noticed. One of advertisers' greatest concerns with TV advertising is the potential decline in effectiveness because of such *clutter.*

The next time you watch TV, count the number of commercials, promotions for the news or upcoming programs, or public service announcements that appear during a station break and you will appreciate why clutter is a major concern. With all of these messages competing for our attention, it is easy to understand why the viewer comes away confused or even annoyed and unable to remember or properly identify the product or service advertised.

While the use of shorter commercials by advertisers has contributed to the problem, clutter also increases when the networks and individual stations run promotional announcements for their shows, make more time available for commercials, and redistribute time to popular programs. For many years, the amount of time available for commercials was restricted by the Code Authority of the National Association of Broadcasters to 9.5 minutes per hour during prime time and 12 minutes during nonprime time. The Justice Department suspended the code in 1982 on the grounds that it violated antitrust law. At first the networks did not alter their time standards, but over the past two decades they have increased the number of commercial minutes in their schedules. The networks argue that they must increase commercial inventory or raise their already steep rates. Advertisers and agencies have been pressuring the networks to cut back on the commercials and other sources of clutter.

**Limited Viewer Attention** When advertisers buy time on a TV program, they are not purchasing guaranteed exposure but rather the opportunity to communicate a message to large numbers of consumers. But there is increasing evidence that the size of the viewing audience shrinks during a commercial break. People leave the room to go to the bathroom or to get something to eat or drink, or they are distracted in some other way during commercials.

Getting consumers to pay attention to commercials has become an even greater challenge in recent years as most homes have the ability to record programs with a VCR or DVR. Moreover, most households have either cable or satellite service and receive an average of more than 100 channels, which means there are more viewing options available. These factors have contributed to the problems of zipping and zapping. **Zipping** occurs when viewers fast-forward through commercials as they play back a previously recorded program. With the increased penetration of DVRs, more people are watching recorded shows and fast-forwarding through the commercials. The problem is being compounded by the fact that many of the networks schedule their most popular shows against one another on the same nights (usually Wednesday and Thursday) and in the same time slots. Thus, the most popular shows also end up being the most recorded. Moreover, the audience for these shows is comprised of upscale viewers in the 18-to-49 age group that are highly coveted by many advertisers.[9]

**EXHIBIT 11–3**
TiVo tracks the viewing patterns of its subscribers

TiVo, the company that is the leading provider of digital video recorders, sells advertisers second-by-second ratings of programs and commercials based on the viewing habits of its subscribers. The service is called Stop/Watch, and in addition to the commercial ratings data, it includes demographic information as well as the opportunity for marketers to survey a panel of 20,000 TiVo subscribers to better understand their viewing habits and why they might skip ads (Exhibit 11–3). Nielsen Media Research also has conducted studies of those who fast-forward through ads and have found that men and women between the ages of 18 and 34 skip more commercials and older women tend to skip fewer ads than younger women.[10]

**Zapping** refers to changing channels to avoid commercials. Nearly all television sets come with remote controls, which enable viewers to switch channels easily. An observational study conducted by John Cronin found as much as a third of program audiences may be lost to electronic zapping when commercials appear.[11] A Nielsen study found that most commercial zapping occurs at the beginning and, to a lesser extent, the end of a program. Zapping at these points is likely to occur because commercial breaks are so long and predictable. Zapping has also been fueled by the emergence of 24-hour continuous-format programming on cable channels such as CNN, MTV2, and ESPN. Viewers can switch over for a few news headlines, sports scores, or a music video and then switch back to the program. Research shows that young adults zap more than older adults and that men are more likely to zap than women.[12]

Character
These are the different qualities our communications and actions take on as we engage key audiences.
Up for It
Means
Energetic, always looking for fun; spontaneous, challenging, surprising, inviting and lively.
It matters because
GSN should always be ready and waiting to have a great time.
Casual
Means
Easy to learn and simple to play.
It matters because
People need to trust that they can come and go as they please and still easily engage and enjoy.
Open to Everyone
Means
Democracy; everyone treated well and treated fairly. It provides a welcome respite for all.
It matters because
All are reflected and all are treated the same. All are welcome, all are invited.
Trusted
Means
Well thought out, everything is there for a reason; reliable and safe.
It matters because
It brings a sense of quality, fairness, diversity, excellence and dignity to a realm that can be cluttered and messy.
Light & Bright
Means
Happy and optimistic. Surprising and unexpected.
It matters because
At GSN, no one is a loser and humiliation is against the rules. It's a positive, fun and rewarding world where all are welcome.
6

**EXHIBIT 11–4**
GSN promotes the engagement level of its viewers

Studies conducted on zapping behavior among television viewers have found that people stop viewing TV during a commercial break because they have a reason to stop watching television altogether or they want to find out what is being shown on other channels. The number of people zapping in and out was not related to the type of product being advertised or by specific characteristics of the commercials.[13] Research has also shown that zappers recalled fewer of the brands advertised than nonzappers and that most of the brands that were recalled by zappers were placed near the end of the commercial break, which is when viewers would be likely to return to a program.[14]

As more consumers become turned off by advertising and the number of channels available to them increases, the level of zapping is likely to increase. Thus, the challenge facing the networks, as well as advertisers, is how to discourage viewers from changing channels during commercial breaks and may be more receptive to the advertising. Exhibit 11–4 shows an ad for the GSN Games Network promoting how higher engagement with its programming increases the engagement level of its viewers, which in turn leads to greater receptivity to advertising messages and higher purchase intentions.

The networks are also finding ways to address the problem by partnering with advertisers to devise ways to retain people during ad breaks. For example, the CW network teamed up with Clairol to create commercial breaks designed to look like a minishow built around products. These two-minute "content wraps," aired during programs such as *America's Top Model,* and featured products being shown as part of consumer makeovers and styling tips.[15] NBC is working with advertisers by developing a new "hybrid" pod commercial break that is part show promotion and part ad. The network has worked with advertisers such as Sprint and American Express to tie the content of ads into the surrounding programs. The network also is putting these spots at the beginning of the commercial break, which is when viewers are most likely to be watching.[16] A study by IAG Research found that hybrid ads generate about 30 percent higher recall than traditional ads for the same product.[17] However, tweaking ads for every program in which it airs can become very expensive. Thus, advertisers will continue to look for other ways to address the problem.

Some advertisers believe that producing different executions of a campaign theme is one way to maintain viewers' attention. Others think the ultimate way to zap-proof commercials is to produce creative advertising messages that will attract and hold viewers' attention. However, this is easier said than done, as many consumers just do not want to watch commercials.

Advances in technology are likely to continue to lead to changes in television viewing habits, which will impact the number of consumers who watch TV commercials. As noted in the opening vignette, DVRs are becoming a major threat to the television industry. In addition to DVRs, television viewing patterns are also being impacted by the availability of another time-shifting technology, video on demand (VOD), which is being offered by cable operators as well as by some satellite television services. More than 43 million households have access to VOD and usage has been growing rapidly. VOD systems allow users to select and watch programs interactively and pause, fast-forward, or rewind the program just as they might on a VCR or DVR. Thus, they can avoid commercials altogether.

Most VOD services require viewers to pay a fee of around 99 cents per episode to watch a program. The shows have not contained any ads and the networks have made a limited number of shows available because they have been reluctant to allow viewers access to shows without commercials since they are concerned that they might become accustomed to that type of viewing experience. However, in 2007 the Walt Disney Co., which owns the two major TV networks ABC and ESPN, negotiated a deal with Cox Communications, a major cable operator, to offer hit shows and football games on demand for free but under the condition that Cox disable the fast-forward feature that allows viewers to skip the commercials. ABC and ESPN can sell ad time on the shows although viewers will not necessarily see the same number of commercials they would if they watched the original broadcast of the program or game.[18]

It is likely that consumers' interest in watching TV shows in alternative ways and on their own schedule will increase as more homes acquire DVRs and services such as video on demand. More people are also watching TV shows on the Internet through sites such as Hulu and Fancast, and the networks, and local TV stations are making more shows available on their websites.[19] The challenge facing the TV industry is how to accommodate the demand for these alternative viewing methods and capture revenue from them while protecting their traditional advertising business model.

**Distrust and Negative Evaluation** To many critics of advertising, TV commercials personify everything that is wrong with the industry. Critics often single out TV commercials because of their pervasiveness and the intrusive nature of the medium. Consumers are seen as defenseless against the barrage of TV ads, since they cannot control the transmission of the message and what appears on their screens. Viewers dislike TV advertising when they believe it is offensive, uninformative, or shown too frequently or when they do not like its content.[20] Studies have shown that of the various forms of advertising, distrust is generally the highest for TV commercials.[21] Also, concern has been raised about the effects of TV advertising on specific groups, such as children or the elderly.[22]

## BUYING TELEVISION TIME

A number of options are available to advertisers that choose to use TV as part of their media mix. They can purchase time in a variety of program formats that appeal to various types and sizes of audiences. They can purchase time on a national, regional, or local basis. Or they can sponsor an entire program, participate in the sponsorship, or use spot announcements during or between programs.

The purchase of TV advertising time is a highly specialized phase of the advertising business, particularly for large companies spending huge sums of money. Large advertisers that do a lot of TV advertising generally use agency media specialists or specialized media buying services to arrange the media schedule and purchase TV time. Decisions have to be made regarding national or network versus local or spot purchases, selection of specific stations, sponsorship versus participation, different classes of time, and appropriate programs. Local advertisers may not have to deal with the first decision, but they do face all the others.

**EXHIBIT 11–5**
The CW Network has a number of popular shows such as *America's Next Top Model*

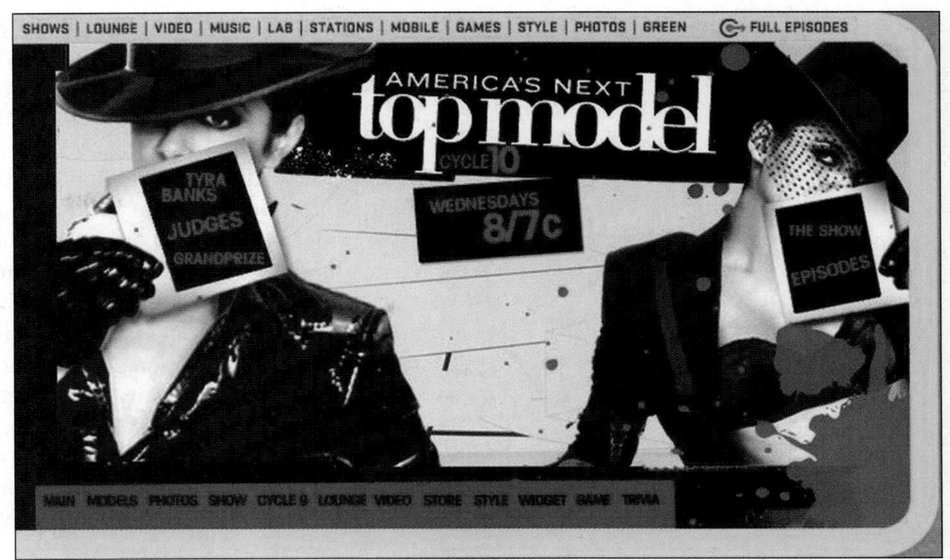




## Network versus Spot

A basic decision for all advertisers is allocating their TV media budgets to network versus local or spot announcements. Most national advertisers use network schedules to provide national coverage and supplement this with regional or local spot purchases to reach markets where additional coverage is desired.

**Network Advertising** A common way advertisers disseminate their messages is by purchasing airtime from a **television network**. A network assembles a series of affiliated local TV stations, or **affiliates**, to which it supplies programming and services. These affiliates, most of which are independently owned, contractually agree to preempt time during specified hours for programming provided by the networks and to carry the national advertising within the program. The networks share the advertising revenue they receive during these time periods with the affiliates. The affiliates are also free to sell commercial time in nonnetwork periods and during station breaks in the preempted periods to both national and local advertisers.

The three traditional major networks are NBC, ABC, and CBS. The Fox Broadcasting Co. broadcasts its programs over a group of affiliated independent stations and has become the fourth major network. A number of Fox's prime-time programs, such as *Family Guy, American Idol, House,* and *Glee,* have become very popular, particularly among the 18-to-49 age group that is often targeted by advertisers. Fox has also become a major player in sports programming with its contracts to broadcast sporting events such as NFL football and Major League Baseball.

The other television network in the United States is CW, which was formed in 2006 when two 11-year-old networks, WB and UPN, decided to merge.[23] The CW Network is co-owned by CBS/Viacom and Warner Bros., which is part of the Time Warner media conglomerate. Both WB and UPN targeted younger viewers with their shows and CBS and Warner Bros. hope that by combining the two networks' programming and affiliates they can eventually make CW the fifth major broadcast network. The CW Network still targets the 18-to-49 demographic but does not offer a full prime-time schedule. It airs 15 hours of prime-time programming over six days, with only a morning cartoon block on Saturdays. The new network has a number of popular programs including *America's Next Top Model, Supernatural,* and *Gossip Girl* (Exhibit 11–5). In addition to CW and the four major networks, there are also several Spanish-language networks in the United States.[24] Spanish-language television networks such

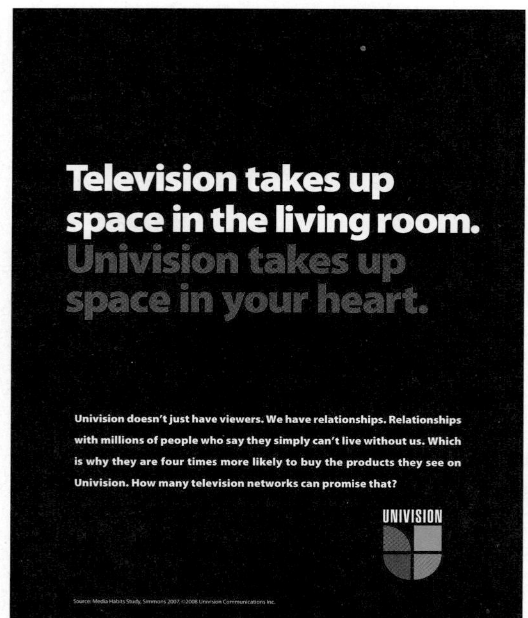


**EXHIBIT 11–6**
Univision is the leading Spanish-language network

as Univision and Telemundo are becoming increasingly popular and provide advertisers a way to reach the fast-growing Hispanic market (Exhibit 11–6).

The networks have affiliates throughout the nation for almost complete national coverage. When an advertiser purchases airtime from one of these four national networks, the commercial is transmitted across the nation through the affiliate station network. Network advertising truly represents a mass medium, as the advertiser can broadcast its message simultaneously throughout the country.

A major advantage of network advertising is the simplification of the purchase process. The advertiser has to deal with only one party or media representative to air a commercial nationwide. The networks also offer many of the most popular and widely watched programs, particularly during prime time. Advertisers interested in reaching large national audiences generally buy commercials on shows that air during the prime-time viewing hours of 8 to 11 P.M. (7 to 10 P.M. in the Central and Mountain time zones).

While network advertising is an effective way to reach large audiences, the cost of advertising on prime time shows is much higher because of the number of viewers they reach. Many of the popular prime time shows such as *Grey's Anatomy, Two and a Half Men, NCIS* and *The Office* can charge well over $200,000 for a 30-second spot.[25] TV shows that do well among viewers in the 18–49 age group can often charge a premium since this demographic segment is very important to many advertisers. The most expensive program for the past five television seasons has been *American Idol,* which airs from January to May and has been the number one show for the past six years among total viewers as well as the 18–49 demographic. During the past several seasons Idol averaged nearly 25 million viewers each week and was able to charge nearly $1 million for ads airing during the show's late May finale.[26]

Availability of time can also be a problem as more advertisers turn to network advertising to reach mass markets. Traditionally, most prime-time commercial spots, particularly on the popular shows, are sold during the **up-front market**, a buying period that occurs before the TV season begins. Advertisers hoping to use prime-time network advertising must plan their media schedules and often purchase TV time as much as a year in advance. Demands from large clients who are heavy TV advertisers force the biggest agencies to participate in the up-front market. However, TV time is also purchased during the **scatter market** that runs through the TV season. Some key incentives for buying up front, such as cancellation options and lower prices, are becoming more available in the quarterly scatter market. Network TV can also be purchased on a regional basis, so an advertiser's message can be aired in certain sections of the country with one media purchase.

Recently the major networks as well as their cable counterparts have been reserving at least 10 percent or more of their inventory of advertising time rather than offering all of it for sale during the up-front market. This is done when sales during the up-front buying period are weak in hopes of being able to sell the advertising time at higher prices on the scatter market.[27] Networks can also get higher prices for commercial time on the scatter market for new shows that end up attracting large audiences over the course of the television season. Fluctuations in supply and demand for network time can also work to the benefit of advertisers as often they can take advantage of weak demand for ad time on certain programs and purchase it at lower rates on the scatter market.

### Spot and Local Advertising

**Spot advertising** refers to commercials shown on local TV stations, with time negotiated and purchased directly from the individual stations. All nonnetwork advertising done by a national advertiser is known as **national spot advertising**; airtime sold to local firms such as retailers, restaurants, banks, and auto dealers is known as **local advertising**. Local advertisers want media whose coverage is limited to the geographic markets in which they do business. This may be difficult to accomplish with TV, but many local businesses are large enough to make efficient use of TV advertising.

Spot advertising offers the national advertiser flexibility in adjusting to local market conditions. The advertiser can concentrate commercials in areas where market potential is greatest or where additional support is needed. This appeals to advertisers with uneven distribution or limited advertising budgets, as well as those interested in test marketing or introducing a product in limited market areas. National advertisers often use spot television advertising through local retailers or dealers as part of their cooperative advertising programs and to provide local dealer support.

A major problem for national advertisers is that spot advertising can be more difficult to acquire, since the time must be purchased from a number of local stations. Moreover, there are more variations in the pricing policies and discount structure of individual stations than of the networks. However, this problem has been reduced somewhat by the use of **station reps**, individuals who act as sales representatives for a number of local stations in dealings with national advertisers.

Spot ads are subject to more commercial clutter, since local stations can sell time on network-originated shows only during station breaks between programs, except when network advertisers have not purchased all the available time. Viewership generally declines during station breaks, as people may leave the room, zap to another channel, attend to other tasks, or stop watching TV.

While spot advertising is mostly confined to station breaks between programs on network-originated shows, local stations sell time on their own programs, which consist of news, movies, syndicated shows, or locally originated programs. Most cities have independent stations that spot advertisers use. Local advertisers find the independent stations attractive because they generally have lower rates than the major network affiliates.

The decision facing most national advertisers is how to combine network and spot advertising to make effective use of their TV advertising budget. Another factor that makes spot advertising attractive to national advertisers is the growth in syndication.



**Syndication** Advertisers may also reach TV viewers by advertising on **syndicated programs**, shows that are sold or distributed on a station-by-station, market-by-market basis. A syndicator seeks to sell its program to one station in every market. There are several types of syndicated programming. *Off-network syndication* refers to reruns of network shows that are bought by individual stations. Shows that are popular in off-network syndication include *Two and a Half Men* and *Family Guy*. The FCC prime-time access rule forbids large-market network affiliates from carrying these shows from 7 to 8 P.M., but independent stations are not affected by this restriction. A show must have a minimum number of episodes before it is eligible for syndication, and there are limits on network involvement in the financing or production of syndicated shows.

Off-network syndication shows are very important to local stations because they provide quality programming with an established audience. The syndication market is also very important to the studios that produce programs and sell them to the networks. Most prime-time network shows initially lose money for the studios, since the licensing fee paid by the networks does not cover production costs. Over four years (the time it takes to produce the number of episodes needed to break into syndication), half-hour situation comedies often run up a deficit of millions, and losses on a one-hour drama show are even higher. However, the producers recoup their money when they sell the show to syndication.

*First-run syndication* refers to shows produced specifically for the syndication market. The first-run syndication market is made up of a variety of shows, including some that did not make it as network shows. Examples of popular first-run

**FIGURE 11–2**
Top 10 Regularly Scheduled Syndicated Programs for 2009–2010 Season

| Rank | Program | Household Rating |
|---|---|---|
| 1 | *Wheel of Fortune* | 6.6 |
| 2 | *Jeopardy* | 5.6 |
| 3 | *Two and a Half Men* | 4.8 |
| 4 | *Judge Judy* | 4.5 |
| 5 | *Oprah Winfrey Show* | 4.4 |
| 6 | *Entertainment Tonight* | 4.2 |
| 7 | *Family Guy* | 3.4 |
| 8 | *CSI New York* | 3.3 |
| 9 | *Inside Edition* | 3.0 |
| 10 | *Wheel of Fortune* (weekend) | 3.0 |

Source: The Nielsen Company

syndication shows include talk shows such as *Live with Regis & Kelly* and *The Jerry Springer Show,* entertainment shows such as *Inside Edition* and *Entertainment Tonight,* and court shows such as *Judge Judy.*

*Advertiser-supported* or *barter syndication* is the practice of selling shows to stations in return for a portion of the commercial time in the show, rather than (or in addition to) cash. The commercial time from all stations carrying the show is packaged into national units and sold to national advertisers. The station sells the remaining time to local and spot advertisers. Both off-network and first-run syndicated programs are offered through barter syndication. Usually, more than half of the advertising time is presold, and the remainder is available for sale by the local advertiser. Barter syndication allows national advertisers to participate in the syndication market with the convenience of a network-type media buy, while local stations get free programming and can sell the remainder of the time to local or spot advertisers. Recently, the straight barter deal has given way to more barter/cash arrangements, where the station pays for a program at a reduced rate and accepts a number of preplaced bartered ads. Top-rated barter syndicated programs include *Wheel of Fortune, Jeopardy,* and *The Oprah Winfrey Show.*

Syndication now accounts for more than a third of the national broadcast audience and has become a very big business, generating ad revenue comparable to any of the big-four networks. Syndicated shows have become more popular than network shows in certain dayparts, such as daytime, early prime time, and late fringe. In some markets, syndicated shows like *Wheel of Fortune* draw a larger audience than the network news.

Many national advertisers use syndicated shows to broaden their reach, save money, and target certain audiences. For example, off-network syndication shows such as *Two and a Half Men, Family Guy,* and *CSI* are popular with advertisers because they reach the highly sought after, and often difficult to reach, young-adult audience (ages 18 to 34) and are lower on a cost-per-thousand basis than network shows. Figure 11–2 shows the top 10 syndicated programs in 2009–2010. Syndication continues to gain in popularity, and more advertisers are making syndicated shows part of their television media schedules. Exhibit 11–7 shows a page from the website of the Syndicated Network Television Association (SNTA) promoting the advantages of syndication.

Syndication has certain disadvantages. The audience for some syndicated shows is often older and more rural, and syndicators do not supply as much research information as the networks do. Syndication also creates more problems for media buyers, since a syndicated show may not be seen in a particular market or may be aired during an undesirable time period. Thus, media buyers have to look at each market and check airtimes and other factors to put together a syndication schedule.

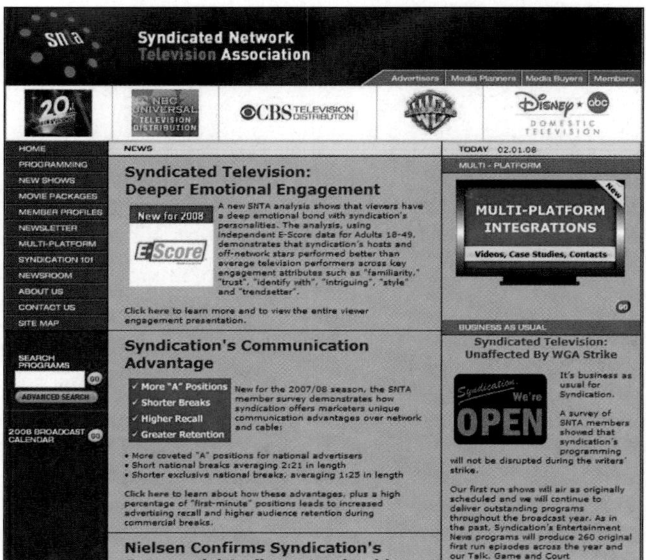


**EXHIBIT 11–7**
The SNTA promotes the advantages of syndication

## Methods of Buying Time

In addition to deciding whether to use network versus spot advertising, advertisers must decide whether to sponsor an entire program, participate in a program, or use spot announcements between programs. Sponsorship of a program and participations are available on either a network or a local market basis, whereas spot announcements are available only from local stations.

**Sponsorship** Under a **sponsorship** arrangement, an advertiser assumes responsibility for the production and usually the content of the program as well as the advertising that appears within it. In the early days of TV, most programs were produced and sponsored by corporations and were identified by their name, for example, *Texaco Star Theater* and *The Colgate Comedy Hour.* Today most shows are produced by either the networks or independent production companies that sell them to a network.

Some companies are still involved in the production business. For example, Procter & Gamble, which has been producing soap operas since 1950, entered into an agreement with Paramount Television Groups to develop shows for network TV and first-run syndication. Several major companies have been sponsoring special programs for many years, such as the *Kraft Theater* and *Hallmark Hall of Fame* dramatic series. Sole sponsorship of programs is usually limited to specials and has been declining. However, some companies, including Ford, AT&T, General Electric, and IBM, do still use program sponsorships occasionally.

A company might choose to sponsor a program for several reasons. Sponsorship allows the firm to capitalize on the prestige of a high-quality program, enhancing the image of the company and its products. Traditionally, commercial-free sponsorships have been rare, particularly on the major networks, as sponsoring an entire show can be very costly; it requires buying out all of the national time as well as the local minutes from network affiliates. However, recently a number of companies have paid for shows to run commercial free as part of a larger package involving placements of their products in the program. For example, the Ford Motor Company sponsored commercial-free season premieres of the drama show *24* on Fox for several seasons in exchange for having its vehicles featured in the program. Cable network FX has often used commercial-free sponsorship deals in exchange for product placement guarantees for premieres of such shows as *Nip/Tuck* and *Rescue Me.*[28]

Companies also sponsor programs to gain more control over the shows carrying their commercials including the number, placement, and content of commercials. Commercials can be of any length as long as the total amount of commercial time does not exceed network or station regulations. Advertisers introducing new products or brands sometimes sponsor a program and run commercials that are several minutes long to launch them. While these factors make sponsorship attractive to some companies, the high costs of sole sponsorship limit this option to large firms. Most commercial time is purchased through other methods, such as participations.

**Participations** Most advertisers either cannot afford the costs of sponsorship or want greater flexibility than sole sponsorship permits. Nearly 90 percent of network advertising time is sold as **participations**, with several advertisers buying

**FIGURE 11–3**
Common Television Dayparts

| | | |
|---|---|---|
| Early morning | 5:00 A.M.–9:00 A.M. | Monday through Friday |
| Daytime | 9:00 A.M.–3:00 P.M. | Monday through Friday |
| Early fringe | 3:00 P.M.–5:00 P.M. | Monday through Friday |
| Early news | 5:00 P.M.–7:00 P.M. | Monday through Saturday |
| Prime access | 7:00 P.M.–8:00 P.M. | Monday through Saturday |
| Prime | 8:00 P.M.–11:00 P.M.<br>7:00 P.M.–11:00 P.M. | Monday through Saturday and<br>Sunday |
| Late news | 11:00 P.M.-11:30 P.M. | Sunday through Saturday |
| Late fringe | 11:30 P.M.–2:00 A.M. | Monday through Friday |
| Overnight | 2:00 A.M. – 5:00 A.M. | Monday through Friday |

Times shown are for Eastern and Pacific time zones. Times may vary by market and station.

commercial time or spots on a particular program. An advertiser can participate in a certain program once or several times on a regular or irregular basis. Participating advertisers have no financial responsibility for production of the program; this is assumed by the network or individual station that sells and controls the commercial time.

There are several advantages to participations. First, the advertiser has no long-term commitment to a program, and expenditures can be adjusted to buy whatever number of participation spots fits within the budget. This is particularly important to small advertisers with a limited budget. The second advantage is that the TV budget can be spread over a number of programs, thereby providing for greater reach in the media schedule.

The disadvantage of participations is that the advertiser has little control over the placement of ads, and there may also be problems with availability. Preference is given to advertisers willing to commit to numerous spots, and the firm trying to buy single spots in more than one program may find that time is unavailable in certain shows, especially during prime time.

**Spot Announcements** As discussed previously, spot announcements are bought from the local stations and generally appear during time periods adjacent to network programs (hence the term **adjacencies**), rather than within them. Spot announcements are most often used by purely local advertisers but are also bought by companies with no network schedule (because of spotty or limited distribution) and by large advertisers that use both network and spot advertising.

## Selecting Time Periods and Programs

Another consideration in buying TV time is selecting the right period and program for the advertiser's commercial messages. The cost of TV advertising time varies depending on the time of day and the particular program, since audience size varies as a function of these two factors. TV time periods are divided into **dayparts**, which are specific segments of a broadcast day.

The time segments that make up the programming day vary from station to station. However, a typical classification of dayparts for a weekday is shown in Figure 11–3. The various daypart segments attract different audiences in both size and nature, so advertising rates vary accordingly. Prime time draws the largest audiences, with 8:30 to 9 P.M. being the most watched half-hour time period and Sunday the most popular night for television. Since firms that advertise during prime time must pay premium rates, this daypart is dominated by the large national advertisers.

The various dayparts are important to advertisers since they attract different demographic groups. For example, daytime TV generally attracts women; early morning attracts women and children. The late-fringe (late-night) daypart period has become popular among advertisers trying to reach young adults who tune in to *The Late Show with David Letterman* on CBS and NBC's *The Tonight Show with Jay Leno.* Audience size and demographic composition also vary depending on the type of program.

## Cable Television

**The Growth of Cable** Perhaps the most significant development in the television industry has been the expansion of **cable television**. Cable, or CATV (community antenna television), which delivers TV signals through fiber or coaxial wire rather than the airways, was developed to provide reception to remote areas that couldn't receive broadcast signals. Cable then expanded to metropolitan areas and grew rapidly due to the improved reception and wider selection of stations it offered subscribers. Cable has experienced substantial growth during the past two decades. In 1975, only 13 percent of TV households had cable. By 2010, cable penetration reached 91 percent of the nation's 114.9 million households either through wired cable or through alternative delivery systems such as direct broadcast satellite (DBS).

Cable subscribers pay a monthly fee for which they receive an average of more than 100 channels, including the local network affiliates and independent stations, various cable networks, superstations, and local cable system channels. Cable networks and channels have a dual revenue stream; they are supported by both subscriber fees and ad revenue. Cable operators also offer programming that is not supported by commercial sponsorship and is available only to households willing to pay a fee beyond the monthly subscription charge. These premium channels include HBO, Showtime, and The Movie Channel.

Cable TV broadens the program options available to the viewer as well as the advertiser by offering specialty channels, including all-news, pop music, country music, sports, weather, educational, and cultural channels as well as children's programming. Figure 11–4 shows the most popular cable channels along with the types of programming they carry. Many cable systems also carry **superstations**, independent local stations that send their signals nationally via satellite to cable operators to make their programs available to subscribers. Programming on superstations such as TBS and WGN generally consists of sports, movies, and reruns of network shows. The superstations do carry national advertising and are a relatively inexpensive option for cable households across the country.

Cable has had a considerable influence on the nature of television as an advertising medium. First, the expanded viewing options have led to considerable audience fragmentation. Much of the growth in cable audiences has come at the expense of the four major networks. Cable channels now have more of the prime-time viewing audience than the major networks. Many cable stations have become very popular among consumers, leading advertisers to re-evaluate their media plans and the prices they are willing to pay for network and spot commercials on network affiliate stations. The networks, recognizing the growing popularity of cable, have become involved with the cable industry. ABC purchased ESPN, while NBC launched the Consumer News and Business Channel (CNBC) in 1989—and in 1996 entered in a joint venture with Microsoft to launch MSNBC, a 24-hour news channel.[29] In 2004, NBC joined with Vivendi Universal Entertainment to form NBC Universal, which owns and operates a motion picture company, television stations, and 10 different cable networks including CNBC, MSNBC, Bravo, USA Network, Sci Fi Channel, and mun2, which targets young Hispanics. In addition to the networks, major cable operators also own cable networks. For example, Comcast, the largest cable operator, owns several networks including E! Entertainment Television, the Golf Channel, and

| Network | Type of Programming |
|---|---|
| ABC Family | Family/general/original |
| A&E Network | Biographies/dramas/movies/documentaries |
| Adult Swim | Young adult entertainment/programs |
| AMC | Movies/documentaries |
| Animal Planet | Wildlife and nature documentaries/adventure/children's entertainment |
| BBC America | Drama/comedy/news/arts |
| BET | Entertainment/information for African-Americans |
| Big 10 Network | College Sports |
| BIO | Biographies, drama |
| Bloomberg Television | Business and financial news |
| Bravo | Drama/movies/reality shows |
| Cartoon Network | Cartoons |
| CMT: Country Music Television | Country music video/concert/specials |
| CNBC | Financial and business news/interviews and discussions |
| CNN | News/information |
| CNN Espanol | News/information (Spanish language) |
| CNN/HLN | News/information |
| Comedy Central | Comedy programs/original |
| Court TV | Court/legal |
| Discovery Channel | Family/health/technology/science |
| E! Entertainment Television | Entertainment/celebrities/pop culture |
| ESPN | Sports/specials/events |
| ESPN 2 | Sports |
| ESPN Sports Classics | Sports history/biographies |
| ESPN Deportes | Sports (Spanish language) |
| ESPNEWS | Sports news |
| Food Network | Food/cooking/entertainment |
| Fox Business Network | Business news |
| FOX News Channel | News/information |
| Fox Soccer Channel | Soccer/sports |
| FSN | Sports |
| Fuse | Music/concerts |
| FX | Entertainment/original programs |
| GAC: Great American Country | Country music/concerts |
| Galavision | Programming/entertainment for Hispanics |
| GSN: Games Network | Game shows |
| Golf Channel | Golf |
| Hallmark Channel | Original movies/miniseries |
| HGTV | Decorating/gardening |
| History Channel | Historical documentaries/ movies |
| Lifetime Networks | News/information/women's interests |
| MLB Network | Major league baseball |
| MSNBC | News/information |
| MTV | Music/reality shows/drama |
| MTV 2 | Music/videos/popular culture |
| mun2 Television | Bilingual programming for Hispanics/Latino youth culture |
| NGC (National Geographic Channel) | Adventure/exploration/science/culture |
| NFL Network | NFL football |
| Nickelodeon/Nick at Nite | Youth interest/cartoons/comedy/game shows |
| Oxygen | Movies/news/comedy/women's interests |
| SOAPnet | Soap operas/drama |
| Syfy Channel | Science fiction |
| Speed | Motor sports/automotive |
| Spike TV | Original programming/sports/entertainment for men |
| Superstation WGN | Movies/dramas/sports/sitcoms/reality-based programs |
| TBS | Entertainment/movies/sports |
| Tennis Channel | Tennis/health and fitness/lifestyle |
| TLC (Learning Channel) | Science/history/adventure/behavior |
| TNT | Movies/general entertainment/sports |
| Travel Channel | Travel information |
| TV Guide Channel | Television entertainment information |
| USA Network | Entertainment/movies/sports |
| VH1 | Music videos/movies/concerts/documentaries |
| Versus | Sports/outdoor/nature |
| Weather Channel | Weather |
| WGN | Entertainment/sports/movies |
| WE tv | Women's entertainment/fashion/health |

**FIGURE 11–4**

Major Cable Networks

Versus (formerly known as the Outdoor Life Network). Comcast has been positioning Versus as a mainstream sports network to take on industry leader ESPN. In 2005 the network acquired the rights to broadcast National Hockey League games (Exhibit 11–8) and in 2007 it began broadcasting some collegiate football and basketball games.[30] Versus also broadcasts the annual Tour de France cycling race that takes place for several weeks every summer.

**EXHIBIT 11–8**
Versus is becoming a major cable sports network

**Advertising on Cable** Cable advertising revenues have increased steadily since the mid-1980s and exceeded $25 billion in 2010. Much of this growth has come from advertising on the national cable networks such as ESPN, USA, TNT, MTV, and VH1. However, many national advertisers have been shifting some of their advertising budgets to spot cable and purchasing through local operators as well as the national cable networks. Over the past four years, spot cable revenues have also grown, reaching nearly $6 billion in 2010.

Like broadcast TV, cable time can be purchased on a national, regional, or local (spot) level. Many large marketers advertise on cable networks to reach large numbers of viewers across the country with a single media buy. Regional advertising on cable is available primarily through sports and news channels that cover a certain geographic area.

Many national advertisers are turning to spot advertising on local cable systems to reach specific geographic markets. Spot cable affords them more precision in reaching specific markets, and they can save money by using a number of small, targeted media purchases rather than making one network buy. The growth in spot cable advertising is also being facilitated by the use of **interconnects**, where a number of cable systems and networks in a geographic area are joined for advertising purposes. These interconnects increase the size of the audience an advertiser can reach with a spot cable buy. For example, the Comcast Spotlight interconnect in Chicago reaches more than 2.3 million cable TV households in the greater Chicago metropolitan area; the ADLINK Digital Interconnect delivers 3 million cable subscribers in Los Angeles and four surrounding counties. New York Interconnect reaches 3.5 million households in the largest market area in the country and offers advertisers targeting capabilities on 60 different networks (Exhibit 11–9). More sophisticated interconnect systems are developing that will pool large numbers of cable systems and allow spot advertisers to reach more viewers. These new systems will also allow local advertisers to make more selective cable buys, since they can purchase the entire interconnect or one of several zones within the system.

While spot cable is becoming very popular among national advertisers, it has some of the same problems as spot advertising on broadcast TV. The purchasing process is very complicated and time-consuming; media buyers must contact hundreds of cable systems to put together a media schedule consisting of spot cable buys. Local cable systems also do not provide advertisers with strong support or much information on demographics, lifestyle, or viewership patterns.

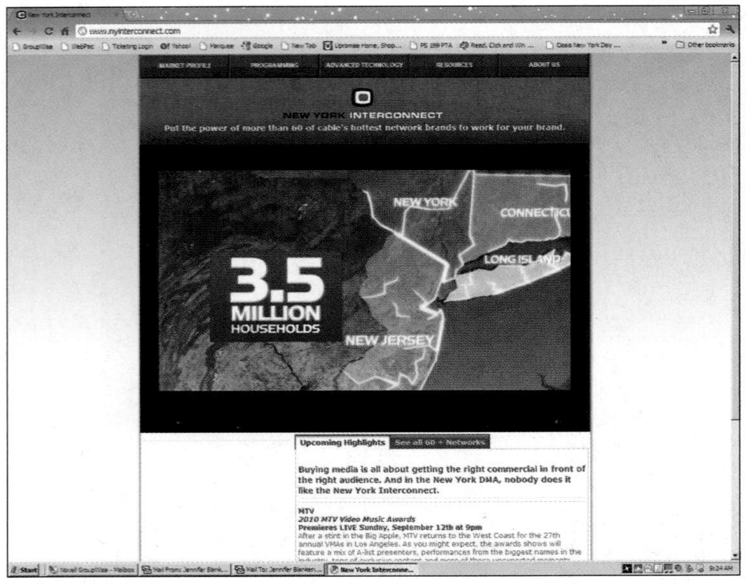


**EXHIBIT 11–9**
New York interconnect promotes its targeting potential to advertisers

### Advantages of Cable

Cable TV has experienced tremendous growth as an advertising medium because it has some important advantages. A primary one is selectivity. Cable subscribers tend to be younger, more affluent, and better educated than nonsubscribers and have greater purchasing power. Moreover, the specialized programming on the various cable networks reaches very specific target markets.

Many advertisers have turned to cable because of the opportunities it offers for **narrowcasting**, or reaching very specialized markets. For example, MTV is used by advertisers in the United States and many other countries to reach teenagers and young adults. CNBC is now the worldwide leader in business news and reaches a highly educated and affluent audience (Exhibit 11–10). ESPN has become synonymous with sports and is very popular among advertisers who want to target men of all ages. As discussed in IMC Perspective 11–2, ESPN has become more than just a 24-hour sports network as it has changed the way sports are covered and played a major role in making sports programming very popular and lucrative.

Advertisers are also interested in cable because of its low cost and flexibility. Advertising rates on cable programs are much lower than those for the shows on the major networks. Advertising time on network shows can cost two to three times as much on a cost-per-thousand basis in some time periods. Spot advertising is also considerably cheaper on most cable stations, while local cable is the most affordable television advertising vehicle available. This makes TV a much more viable media option for smaller advertisers with limited budgets and those interested in targeting their commercials to a well-defined target audience. Also, cable advertisers generally do not have to make the large up-front commitments, which may be as much as a year in advance, the networks require.

**EXHIBIT 11–10**
CNBC has become the leader in business news and has a very affluent viewing audience

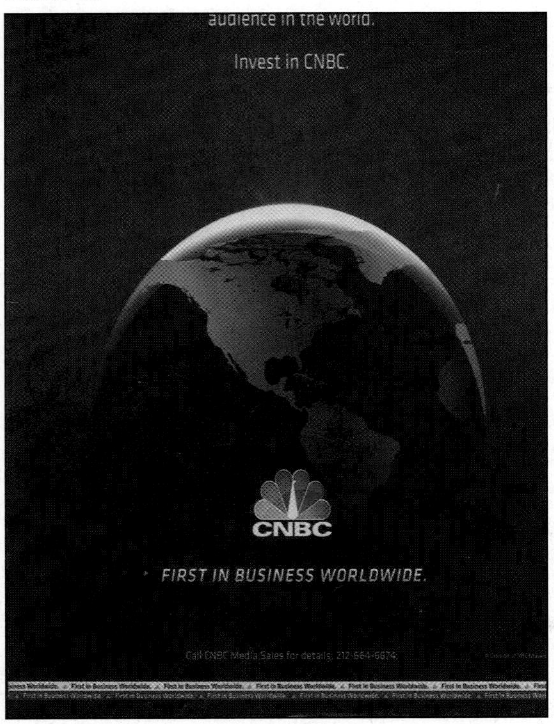


The low costs of cable make it a very popular advertising medium among local advertisers. Car dealers, furniture stores, restaurants, and many other merchants are switching advertising spending from traditional media such as radio, newspapers, and even magazines to take advantage of the low rates of local cable channels. Local cable advertising is one of the fastest growing segments of the advertising market, and cable systems are increasing the percentage of revenue they earn from local advertising.

### Limitations of Cable

While cable has become increasingly popular among national, regional, and local advertisers, it still has some drawbacks. One major problem is that cable is still somewhat overshadowed by the major networks, as households with basic cable service still watch considerably more network and syndicated programming than cable shows. This stems from the fact that cable generally has less popular programming than broadcast TV.

Another drawback of cable is audience fragmentation. Although cable's share of the TV viewing audience has increased significantly, the viewers are spread out among the large number of channels available to cable subscribers. The number of viewers who watch any one cable channel is generally quite low. Even

MTV, ESPN, and CNN have prime-time ratings of only about 1 or 2 for their regular programming. The large number of cable stations has fragmented audiences and made buying procedures more difficult, since numerous stations must be contacted to reach the majority of the cable audience in a market. There are also problems with the quality and availability of local ratings for cable stations as well as research on audience characteristics.

Cable also still lacks total penetration, especially in some major markets. In 2010, overall cable penetration from both wired and alternative delivery systems such as satellite was 86 percent in the Los Angeles–designated market area (DMA), 82 percent in Houston, and 84 percent in the Dallas–Ft. Worth DMA. In some designated market areas, wired cable penetration is low as many households receive cable programming from alternative delivery systems that do not offer local advertising. For example, penetration of wired cable is under 60 percent in some major DMAs such as Los Angeles, Denver, and Dallas–Ft. Worth. Thus, local advertisers in these markets would not be able to reach a significant number of households by advertising on local cable networks.

**The Future of Cable** Cable TV should continue to experience strong growth as its audience share increases and advertisers spend more money to reach cable viewers. However, the cable industry faces several challenges: increases in the number of channels, leading to fragmentation of the audience, changes in government regulations, and competition in the programming distribution business from other telecommunications companies and direct broadcast satellite services. Advances in technology such as digital video compression and fiber optics, coupled with massive investments in system upgrades, are making it possible for cable operators to offer more channels and thus subject existing cable channels to greater competition. Increases in the number of channels available lead to further fragmentation of the cable audience and make it more difficult for cable networks to charge the ad rates needed to finance original programming. Some of the growth in cable channels will come from **multiplexing**, or transmitting multiple channels from one network. Several major cable networks, including A&E Television Networks, ESPN, and the Discovery Communications, own several channels.

**EXHIBIT 11–11**
*Mad Men* is an example of the high quality programs now shown on cable networks

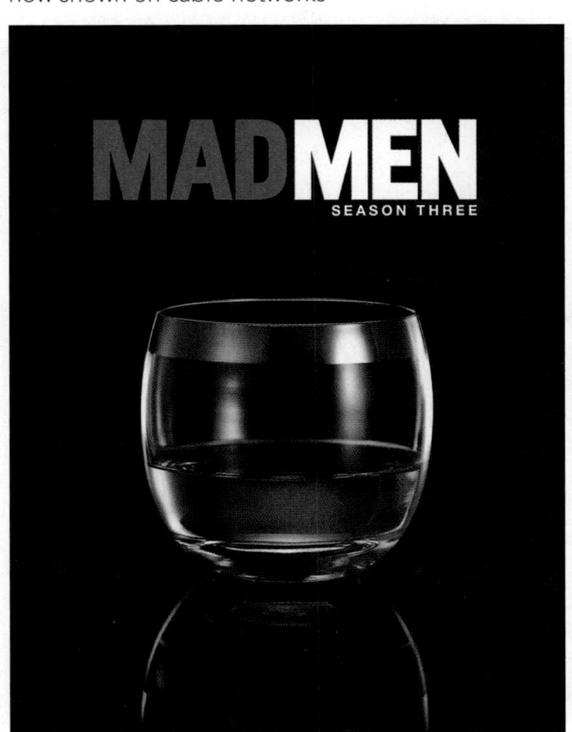


The future of cable as an advertising medium will ultimately depend on the size and quality of the audiences cable stations can reach with their programs. This in turn will depend on cable's ability to offer programs that attract viewers and subscribers. Cable's image as a stepchild in program development and acquisition has changed. Cable networks such as VH1, E!, TBS, ESPN, and others have been creating original films, documentaries, and other programs that draw significant ratings. Networks like A&E, the Discovery Channel, the National Geographic Channel, and the History Channel provide outstanding cultural and educational programming.

Many advertising and media experts note that many people, and particularly children and young adults under the age of 35, really do not differentiate between cable and traditional broadcast television.[31] Cable programs generally cannot deliver the broad reach and mass audiences of popular network shows such as *American Idol* or *NCIS*. However, cable networks have been developing high quality and critically acclaimed programs such as AMC's *Mad Men,* a drama show that follows the lives of highly competitive men and women working on Madison Avenue during the glory days of advertising in the 1960s (Exhibit 11–11). The critically acclaimed show has won numerous awards including an Emmy for Outstanding Drama Series and two Golden Globe Awards for Best Television Drama

## IMC Perspective 11–2 > > >

### Sports and Television—A Great Love Affair

For many years, TV sports programming consisted primarily of football, baseball, and, to a lesser extent, basketball, shown primarily on weekends on network television. Hardcore sports fans had to wait until the weekend to see major sporting events such as NFL or college football games, and sports news coverage was limited to five-minute sportscasts on the 11 P.M. news on the local network affiliate. However, on September 7, 1979, a small cable network called ESPN began broadcasting from a trailer in a swampy industrial park in Bristol, Connecticut, showing Hartford Whalers ice-hockey games. The network was the idea of Bill Rasmussen, a former sportscaster whose original concept was for it to be a sports network for Connecticut, but who discovered that it would cost no more to offer the first cable network devoted entirely to sports.

When ESPN was launched, the critics declared that "All the good sports are already on the three networks" and ridiculed the network for broadcasting such sports as stock car racing, which was described as "two hours of left turns." To help fill 24 hours a day of programming, ESPN aired sports that the major broadcast networks did not cover such as Australian rules football, professional wrestling, boxing, and replays of college football and basketball games. However, no one is laughing at ESPN today, as the cable network that markets itself as "The Worldwide Leader in Sports," has become the world's largest sports media brand. In addition to reaching nearly 99 million homes in the United States, ESPN also operates 46 TV networks outside of the country. Its media franchise also includes six other U.S. channels, a radio network, ESPN.com which is the most popular sport site on the Internet, and *ESPN The Magazine*.

ESPN has clearly changed the way sports are covered as well as the consumption of sports by TV viewers. The tremendous success of ESPN over the past three decades has led to the major TV networks spending more money for sports programming as well as the creation of several rival cable sports networks such as FSN and Versus. There are also many cable networks that focus on specific sports such as the Golf Channel, Tennis Channel, Fox Soccer Channel, and NFL Network, as well as several that are dedicated to college sports such as CBS College Sports and the Big Ten Network. The increased coverage of sports has been very lucrative for professional sports leagues and individual teams as well. Over the past five years the major networks of CBS, NBC, Fox, and ESPN have paid a combined $20 billion for the rights to broadcast National Football League (NFL) games while the National Basketball Association (NBA) teams receive nearly $1 billion each year for their broadcast rights.

College sports has also been a beneficiary of the marriage between sports and television, particularly those schools who have popular Division 1 football and basketball teams that play in conferences such as the Big Ten, Big East, Big 12, Pacific 10, Atlantic Coast, and Southeastern Conferences. While these teams receive revenue for broadcast rights to their games, additional revenue is also received by the NCAA (National Collegiate Athletic Association) which governs all of college sports. For example, in 2010 the NCAA signed a 14-year $10.8 billion contract with CBS and Turner

Series. Other quality shows on cable networks include AMC's *Breaking Bad,* TNT's *The Closer,* and Lifetime's *Army Wives.*

Cable TV will continue to be a popular source of sports programming and is very important to advertisers interested in reaching the male market. There are a number of regional sports networks (RSNs) that provide sports programming to local markets. The most important programming on these RSNs is live broadcasts of professional and college sports events such as football, basketball, and baseball. Many of these regional networks are associated with Fox Sports Net or Comcast SportsNet. Thus, advertisers purchase ads in multiple regions with one media buy. Deals by ESPN for Monday night coverage of National Football League and Major League Baseball games, along with its six-year deal to broadcast National Basketball Association games, have proved that cable networks can compete with the major networks in a sports bidding war.[32]

As cable penetration increases, its programming improves, and more advertisers discover its efficiency and ability to reach targeted market segments, cable's popularity as an advertising medium should continue to grow. Many agencies and media specialist companies have developed specialists to examine the use of cable in their clients' media schedules.

Broadcasting to televise its men's basketball tournament. The deal will funnel at least $740 million annually to NCAA member colleges which is much needed revenue for athletic programs that have been experiencing major budget cuts. Revenue from TV broadcast rights helps fund college athletic programs including many minor sports and women's sports.

There are a number of reasons why media companies are willing to pay so much for sports broadcast rights. First, these rights are often very unique as there are a limited number of NFL, NBA, or major college football and basketball teams and they play each other only a limited number of times each year. Second, sporting events are nearly always watched live on TV which reduces the number of people who record the games and fast-forward through the commercials. Third, popular sporting events can still deliver good ratings which is very important as television viewing audiences become more fragmented and it has become more difficult to attract large viewing audiences.

Advertisers are also willing to pay more for sporting events because they are a good way to reach young men who are a valuable, and elusive, target audience for advertisers. Young men tend to spend less time watching television than most people—unless they are into sports. Media research studies have shown that the average sports fan consumes almost 10 hours of media in an average day, versus just over 5 hours for other young men. And while they spend more time consuming all types of media—including radio, surfing the Internet, and even reading newspapers—the avid sports fan is more likely to watch television with much of this view time being focused on sports programming.

Sports programming including various games and events and news shows, such as ESPN's signature show *SportsCenter,* have become a major part of the sports fan's daily media diet. Some experts argue that the airways are becoming oversaturated with sports programs, and networks and cable channels must be careful not to overpay for sports rights. However, ESPN turns over more than $6 billion in revenue each year to Disney, which owns 80 percent of the company. The first words ever spoken on ESPN by host Lee Leonard were "If you're a fan, what you'll see in the next minutes, hours, and days to follow may convince you that you've gone to sports heaven." More than 30 years later, most sport fans indeed feel they are in sports heaven with all of the sport programs airing on their TV sets.

Sources: "The Killer App" in "Changing The Channel: A Special Report on Television," *The Economist,* May 1, 2010, pp. 10–11; Andrew Hampp, "How ESPN Became the World's Biggest Sports-Media Brand," *Advertising Age,* August 31, 2009, http://adagec.om/print?article_id=13871111.



## Measuring the TV Audience

One of the most important considerations in TV advertising is the size and composition of the viewing audience. Audience measurement is critical to advertisers as well as to the networks and stations. Advertisers want to know the size and characteristics of the audience they are reaching when they purchase time on a particular program. And since the rates they pay are a function of audience size, advertisers want to be sure audience measurements are accurate.

Audience size and composition are also important to the network or station, since they determine the amount it can charge for commercial time. Shows are frequently canceled because they fail to attract enough viewers to make their commercial time attractive to potential advertisers. Determining audience size is not an exact science and has been the subject of considerable controversy through the years. In this section, we examine how audiences are measured and how advertisers use this information in planning their media schedules.

**Audience Measures** The size and composition of television audiences are measured by ratings services. The sole source of network TV and local audience information is Nielsen Media Research. For many years local audience information was also available from the Arbitron Co., but Arbitron exited the local TV ratings business at the end of 1993 due to steep financial losses.[33] Nielsen gathers viewership information from a sample of TV homes and then projects this information to the total viewing area. The techniques used to gather audience measurement information include diaries, electronic meters or recorders, and personal interviews. Nielsen provides various types of information that can be used to measure and evaluate a station's audience. These measures are important to media planners as they weigh the value of buying commercial time on a program.

**Television Households** The number of households in the market that own a TV is sometimes referred to as the *universe estimate (UE).* Nielsen estimates that 114.9 million U.S. households owned at least one TV set as of the 2009–2010 television season. Since over 98 percent of U.S. households own a TV set, **television households** generally correspond to the number of households in a given market.

**Program Rating** Probably the best known of all audience measurement figures is the **program rating**, the percentage of TV households in an area that are tuned to a specific program during a specific time period. The program rating is calculated by dividing the number of households tuned to a particular show by the total number of households in the area. For example, if 10 million households (HH) watched *American Idol,* the national rating would be 8.7, calculated as follows:

$$\text{Rating} = \frac{\text{HH tuned to show}}{\text{Total U.S. HH}} = \frac{10{,}000{,}000}{114{,}900{,}000} = 8.7$$

A **ratings point** represents 1 percent of all the television households in a particular area tuned to a specific program. On a national level, 1 ratings point represents 1,149,000 households. Thus, if a top-rated program like *American Idol* averages a rating of 9, it would reach 10.3 million households each week (9 × 1,149,000).

The program rating is the key number to the stations, since the amount of money they can charge for commercial time is based on it. Ratings points are very important to the networks as well as to individual stations. A 1 percent change in a program's ratings over the course of a viewing season can gain or lose millions of dollars in advertising revenue. Advertisers also follow ratings closely, since they are the key measure for audience size and commercial rates.

**Households Using Television** The percentage of homes in a given area where TV is being watched during a specific time period is called **households using television (HUT)**. This figure, sometimes referred to as *sets in use,* is always expressed as a percentage. For example, if 70 million of the U.S. TV households have their sets turned on at 9 P.M. on a Thursday night, the HUT figure is 61 percent (70 million out of 114.9 million). Television usage varies widely depending on the time of day and season of the year.

**Share of Audience** Another important audience measurement figure is the **share of audience**, which is the percentage of households using TV in a specified time period that are tuned to a specific program. This figure considers variations in the number of sets in use and the total size of the potential audience, since it is based only on those households that have their sets turned on. Audience share is calculated by dividing the number of households (HH) tuned to a show by the number of households using television (HUT). Thus, if 70 million U.S. households had their sets turned on during the 9 P.M. time slot when *American Idol* is shown, the share of audience would be 14.3, calculated as follows:

$$\text{Share} = \frac{\text{HH tuned to show}}{\text{U.S. households using TV}} = \frac{10{,}000{,}000}{70{,}000{,}000} = 14.3$$

**EXHIBIT 11–12**
Nielsen uses the people meter to measure national TV audiences

Audience share is always higher than the program rating unless all the households have their sets turned on (in which case they would be equal). Share figures are important since they reveal how well a program does with the available viewing audience. For example, late at night the size of the viewing audience drops substantially, so the best way to assess the popularity of a late-night program is to examine the share of the available audience it attracts relative to competing programs.

Ratings services also provide an audience statistic known as **total audience**, the total number of homes viewing any five-minute part of a telecast. This number can be broken down to provide audience composition figures that are based on the distribution of the audience into demographic categories.

**National Audience Information** Nielsen Media Research has a national TV ratings service known as the **Nielsen Television Index** which provides daily and weekly estimates of the size and composition of the national viewing audiences for programs aired on the broadcast and major cable networks. To measure the viewing audience, Nielsen uses a national sample of approximately 10,000 homes carefully selected to be representative of the population of U.S households. The widely cited Nielsen ratings are based on the viewing patterns of this cross section of homes, which are measured using an electronic metering technology. The **people meter** is an electronic measuring device that incorporates the technology of the old-style audimeter in a system that records not only what is being watched but also by whom in 10,000 households. The actual device is a small box with eight buttons—six for the family and two for visitors—that can be placed on the top of the TV set (Exhibit 11–12). A remote control unit permits electronic entries from anywhere in the room. Each member of the sample household is assigned a button that indicates his or her presence as a viewer. The device is also equipped with a sonar sensor to remind viewers entering or leaving the room to log in or out on the meter.

The viewership information the people meter collects from the household is stored in the home system until it is retrieved by Nielsen's computers. Data collected include when the set is turned on, which channel is viewed, when the channel is changed, and when the set is off, in addition to who is viewing. The demographic characteristics of the viewers are also in the system, and viewership can be matched to these traits. Nielsen's operation center processes all this information each week for release to the TV and advertising industries. Nielsen uses a sample of metered households in 55 markets across the country to provide overnight viewing results.

**Local Audience Information** Information on local audiences is important to both local advertisers and firms making national spot buys. Nielsen Media Research's local market measurement service is called Nielsen Station Index (NSI), which measures viewing audiences in 210 local markets known as **designated market areas (DMAs)**. DMAs are nonoverlapping areas used for planning, buying, and evaluating TV audiences and are generally a group of counties in which stations located in a metropolitan or central area achieve the largest audience share. NSI reports information on viewing by time periods and programs and includes audience size and estimates of viewing over a range of demographic categories for each DMA.

In addition to the national audience measurement, Nielsen also measures the largest local markets using electronic Local People Meter (LPM) technology. Local People Meters are currently used in the top 20 markets and Nielsen plans to expand their use to the top 56 markets by 2011. In large to mid-size local markets, viewing information is gathered from 400 to 500 households using electronic set meters that only capture the channel to which the TV set is tuned. This information is augmented at least four times a year with demographic data that are collected from separate samples of households who fill out seven-day paper viewing diaries (or eight-day diaries in homes with DVRs). Smaller markets (DMAs ranked over 60) are currently

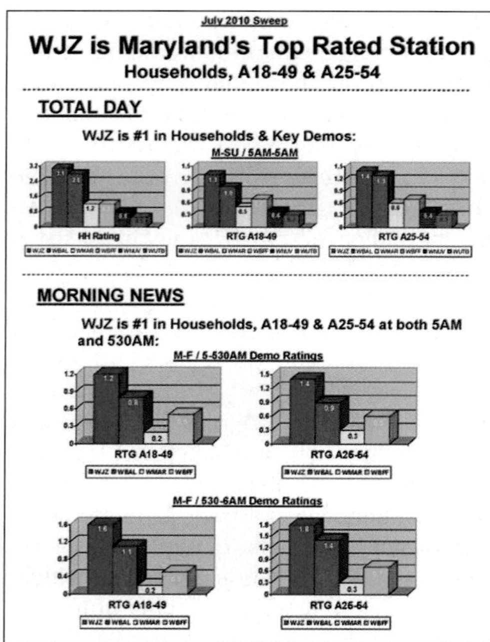


**EXHIBIT 11–13**

WJZ promotes its dominance of the sweeps rating period for local news

measured using paper diaries only, although Nielsen plans to extend electronic measurement to these markets as well.

Nielsen measures viewing audiences in every local television market at least four times a year during rating periods known as **sweeps**. The term dates back to the 1950s, when Nielsen began mailing diaries to households and reporting the results, beginning with the East Coast markets before *sweeping* across the country. Sweeps rating periods are held in November, February, May, and July. In some of the larger markets, diaries provide viewer information for up to three additional sweeps months. The viewing information gathered during the sweeps periods are used for program scheduling decisions by local television stations and cable systems and are a basis for pricing and selling advertising time. Exhibit 11–13 shows how WJZ, the CBS affiliate in Baltimore, promotes its dominance of the sweeps ratings in various categories.

Many advertising executives and media buyers are skeptical of the local audience estimates gathered during the sweeps periods. They argue that special programming and promotion efforts are often used by the networks and their local affiliates to bolster their ratings during the sweeps and that the numbers gathered during these periods are not indicative of audience size for the remaining weeks of the year.[34]

Much of the concern over the measurement system used by Nielsen involves the use of the paper diaries to measure viewing in local markets. The system requires households in the sample to keep a tally of what is being watched and by whom. With so many channels now available, along with the increase in viewing through DVRs and video on demand, it has become very challenging for the Nielsen panelists to accurately record all of their television viewing in the diaries. Many homes do not return completed diaries and many of those that are returned are often not filled out. Nielsen has acknowledged the problems with its measurement system for local markets and is working to correct them.[35] It is expanding the use of Local People Meters and hopes to extend full electronic measurement to all local markets over the next three years.

**Developments in Audience Measurement** For years the advertising industry has been calling for changes in the way TV viewing audiences are measured, at both the local and national levels. They have argued that new digital technologies are leading to major changes with regard to when, where, and how people watch television. They also argue that the Nielsen measurement system is being overwhelmed by the explosion in the number of TV sets, delivery systems, and program options available. Advertisers and media planners note that these developments must be carefully monitored as they are having a major impact on audience size and composition and on the way advertisers use and should pay for TV as an advertising medium.

One of the major concerns of advertisers has been the need to measure ratings for television commercials, not just for programs. In 2007 Nielsen began providing **commercial ratings** data, known as "C3," which includes measures of the average viewership of the commercials both live and up to three days after the ads are played back on a DVR.[36] The new ratings do not track individual ads or specific time slots, but rather offer an average viewership of all the national commercial minutes in a program. Many advertisers now pay for advertising time on network shows based on Nielsen measures of how many viewers watched commercials live and on DVR-recorded playback within three days of the airing of the show, rather than simply on the traditional program ratings.

While advertisers view the availability of commercial ratings as a significant improvement over program ratings, there is still concern over how viewing audiences are measured. While expanded use of the people meter is seen as an improvement over the use of paper diaries, critics note that these devices still require cooperation on an ongoing basis from people in the metered homes. Panelists in the Nielsen households, including children, must enter a preassigned number on the remote control device every time they start or stop watching. Media researchers argue that children in particular often forget and adults tire of the task over the two years they are in the Nielsen sample. There has been a call for the use of more passive measurement systems that require less involvement by people in the metered homes and can produce more accurate measures of the program, as well as commercial, viewing audiences.[37] IMC Technology Perspective 11–1 discusses the ongoing battle between the television networks and advertisers over the measurement of TV viewing audiences.

Nielsen Media Research is working to address the ongoing challenges of audience measurement. In 2006 the company announced a major initiative known as *Anytime Anywhere Media Measurement* (A2/M2), which includes a number of improvements designed to respond to changes in the way people watch television. The initiative includes the introduction of electronic measurement in all local markets, the addition of Internet and out-of-home measurement in Nielsen's People Meter sample, as well as the development of passive measurement devices.[38] As part of the initiative, Nielsen has begun measuring the television viewing patterns of college students. In 2007, for the first time ever, Nielsen Media Research's national ratings included information on the TV viewing patterns of students who live in households that are part of its national sample but live away at college. Nielsen's Extended Home study used people meters installed in dormitories and common areas, sorority and fraternity houses, and off-campus houses at college across the country to track the viewing patterns of about 150 students.

One of more interesting findings from the Extended Home study was that college students watch as much television as other 18 to 24 year olds. Students watch the tube up to 30 hours per week and they also watch a lot of late night TV (after 11 P.M.). As might be expected MTV ranked first among the networks watched by college students followed by Turners Adult Swim, TBS, ESPN, and Comedy Central. The ratings showed that that Comedy Central's *South Park,* was the number one cable program among male college students between the ages of 18 to 24 (Exhibit 11–14). The results also showed that animated TV programming is very popular among college students and that the number of women watching sports is higher than media experts expected.[39] In 2010 Nielsen also released its first quarterly report on away-from home viewing by measuring viewing audiences for 10 major networks including at health clubs, hotels, bars and restaurants, and transit locations. The initial study found that the 10 away-from-home networks generate 237 million monthly exposures with nearly half of them coming from the highly coveted 18-to-34 demographic segment.[40]

**EXHIBIT 11–14**
*South Park* is one of the most widely watched TV shows by male college students

The A2/M2 initiative also includes the development of new metrics for measuring viewer engagement in television programming. **Engagement** can be defined as the focused mental and emotional connection between a consumer, a media vehicle, and a brand's message. This will address the concern of media experts who argue that consideration must be given to measuring media involvement and determining when consumers are most tuned into television programs and open to receiving advertisements and other types of marketing messages.[41] Current audience measurement methods are often criticized for only reporting the sizes of viewing audiences and not distinguishing among them in terms of the intensity of their relationships with television programs. These limitations have prompted researchers to investigate the qualitative distinctions among viewers who may

# IMC Technology Perspective 11–1 > > >

## TV Networks and Advertisers Battle over Viewers

Television programs have always been shown in time-slots, with viewers watching whatever is on at that particular time. Advertisers are used to this world of synchronous viewing and have traditionally bought TV ad time based on measures of how many people watch various programs at scheduled times. However, with the growing popularity of digital video recorders (DVRs), more and more television viewers are able to record programs and watch them on their own schedule. And much to the disdain of advertisers, many of these viewers fast-forward through the commercials during the playback.

TiVo Inc. introduced the first digital video recorder in 1999 and is still a market leader with 2.38 million subscribers as of October 2010. However, there are other companies making DVRs and cable operators now integrate digital recording technology into their set-top boxes, and satellite television operators provide DVRs to subscribers who agree to pay a monthly service fee. In 2010 nearly 30 percent of U.S. homes had DVRs and this figure is expected to increase to 42 percent by 2014, although DVR penetration has not increased as rapidly as expected.

As DVRs become more popular, the television networks and stations are facing challenges from advertisers who do not want to pay for viewers who change channels during a commercial break or fast-forward through ads when watching a recorded show. They point to studies showing that up to 20 percent of viewers switch channels during the breaks and that more than a third of the commercials are skipped when a prime-time program is viewed played back on a DVR. However, the television networks argue that nearly 90 percent of prime-time viewing still occurs live and 60 percent of the shows that are recorded are viewed within a day. Moreover, they note that DVRs increase the number of people who see a television program and insist that they get paid for those who watch the shows, and sometimes the ads, after they originally air.

The two sides reached a compromise in 2007 when Nielsen Media Research began making commercial ratings available rather than program ratings. For decades Nielsen had provided the number of TV viewers per half-hour for programs, and prices for advertising time were based on the average viewership of the programs they interrupted. However, commercial ratings take into account how many viewers bail out during a commercial break by changing channels or fast-forwarding through the ads if they are watching a recorded show. Nielsen's new commercial-ratings data, known as "C3," includes measures of the average viewership of the commercials both live and up to three days after the ads are played back on a DVR.

The commercial rating data were used for the first time during the 2007 upfront ad negotiations, which is the time period when much of the network advertising time for the upcoming season is sold. The initial commercial-ratings data released by Nielsen confirmed what advertising executive and media buyers have long suspected—that about 3 to 15 percent of an audience changes the channel during commercials or fast-forwards through them when watching a prerecorded show. The results also showed that teens and older people tend to skip commercials slightly less than viewers ages 18 to 34 and that the closer viewers watch a show to its original airtime, the more likely they are to watch the ads.

Television networks use rating data from Nielsen Media Research to set prices for television advertising time and changes in that data can have a major impact on the prices advertisers ultimately pay. Nielsen's new C3 ratings mean the networks now have to negotiate with advertisers on the basis of smaller live viewing audience numbers. However, in exchange for letting Madison Avenue have its commercial ratings, the networks are now paid for the DVR-enabled viewers who may watch the programs and the ads at a later time. They note that the Nielsen data refutes the myth that nearly all DVR viewers skips the ads when they play back a show and that those who watch the ads raise the program's total commercial audience. However, many advertising and media executives still disagree with the networks over the

all be counted as "watching" a TV program but have very different levels of attention, attitudes, and even behaviors related to the show. Researchers Cristel Russell, Andrew Norman, and Susan Heckler have introduced the concept of audience *connectedness* to capture the fact that some television viewers build relationships, loyalty, and connections with certain TV shows, with the characters portrayed in these programs, and with fellow audience members.[42] These connected viewers are very different from viewers who are less involved with a program. They may be more attentive to advertising and product placements and more likely to engage in behaviors such as visiting a program's website or purchasing brands that are associated with the show. Nielsen has begun measuring engagement levels with its IAG rankings which measure viewers recollection of and reaction to programs, product placements promotions and commercials.[43]

value of the DVR viewers. They point to research showing that while the viewing audience may grow over time, viewership of commercials still lags significantly behind viewership of programs.

While Nielsen's current C3 ratings are seen as an improvement over the old measurement system, many are still dissatisfied with the system since it is based on an average of all national commercial minutes in a program. Marketers argue that payment should be based on the viewership of *each* individual commercial rather than an average across all the commercial minutes. They argue that there is a substantial amount of research data available showing that viewership of commercials during a break depends on the position, as the first or second commercial may have more viewers than spots aired during the middle of a two- or three-minute pod. The advertising director for State Farm Insurance has expressed the position of many advertisers noting that: "As marketers who are under more and more scrutiny concerning what our plans truly deliver, actual commercial ratings for any specific ad in a specific pod position will give me an even truer idea of the value for the price paid. This is where we need to be."

While marketers may be clamoring for more precise commercial ratings, Nielsen questions whether they are willing to pay for it as encoding each ad so that it can be tracked requires a substantial investment in technology. Nielsen notes that it is open to discussing individual commercial ratings but a cost-benefit analysis is needed to determine whether the benefits would warrant the investment. While there is little argument that a company like McDonald's might want to know how many TV viewers watched one of its commercials in real time, there is still concern over whether they would be willing to pay more for this level of precision or are content to live with the average commercial minute ratings.

While Nielsen has resolved some of the concerns marketers have regarding issues such as viewership of commercials and the impact of DVRs, other issues will arise as media consumption patterns continue to change. For example, the number of people who are watching TV shows online using YouTube or Hulu as well as various TV-network run websites continues to increase. However, Nielsen recently took steps to address this issue as the company is taking data from online viewing of TV programs and merging it with standard TV audience data to generate a single combined national television rating. The new report will include online views of shows that have the same program and national commercial content that aired on television. Online shows that do not run the same ads as the traditional programs will not be included in the new measure.

Technology will continue to change the way consumers watch television and present challenges for measuring viewing audiences. As penetration of DVRs increases, more TV viewers will be watching playbacks of recorded shows and fast forwarding through the commercials or going to various websites to view their favorite programs. Thus marketers will continue to look for ways to adapt their advertising messages to changes in viewer behavior. It may not be long before we see sponsorships of fast-forwards and rewinds or full motion ads that pop up when viewers pause a show and that are contextual to the content.

Sources: Brian Steinberg, "New Nielsen Ratings Combine Shows' TV and Online Views. *Advertising Age,* January 22, 2010, http://adage.com/print?article_id=141675; Brian Steinberg, Marketers Demanding Ratings for Each TV Ad," *Advertising Age,* February 23, 2009, http://adage.com/print?article_id=134785; Stephanie Kang, "Looking at Data through a DVR," *The Wall Street Journal,* January 4, 2008, p. B5.

CHAPTER 11

# RADIO

Television has often been referred to as the ideal advertising medium, and to many people it personifies the glamour and excitement of the industry. Radio, on the other hand, has been called the Rodney Dangerfield of media because it gets no respect from many advertisers. Dominated by network programming and national advertisers before the growth of TV, radio has evolved into a primarily local advertising medium. Network advertising generally accounts for less than 5 percent of radio's revenue. Radio has also become a medium characterized by highly specialized programming appealing to very narrow segments of the population.

The importance of radio to advertisers is best demonstrated by the numbers, as it is a pervasive medium. There are more than 10,600 commercial radio stations in

**EXHIBIT 11–15**
The Radio Advertising Bureau promotes the value of radio to advertisers

the United States. There are over 576 million radios in use, which is an average of 5.6 per household. Radio reaches 71 percent of all Americans over the age of 12 each day and has grown into a ubiquitous background to many activities, among them reading, driving, running, working, and socializing. The average American listens to radio nearly 3 hours every weekday and 5 hours every weekend.[44] The pervasiveness of this medium has not gone unnoticed by advertisers; radio advertising revenue grew from $8.8 billion in 1990 to over $16 billion in 2009.

Radio plays an integral role in the lifestyle of consumers and has the power to reach and influence their purchase behavior. It has survived and flourished as an advertising medium because it has a number of advantages that make it an effective way for marketers to communicate with consumers. The radio industry promotes these advantages to advertisers to encourage use of the medium (Exhibit 11–15).

## Advantages of Radio

Radio has many advantages over other media, including cost and efficiency, selectivity, flexibility, mental imagery, and integrated marketing opportunities.

**Cost and Efficiency** One of the main strengths of radio as an advertising medium is its low cost. Radio commercials are very inexpensive to produce. They require only a script of the commercial to be read by the radio announcer or a copy of a prerecorded message that can be broadcast by the station. The cost for radio time is also low. A minute on network radio may cost only $5,000, which translates into a cost per thousand of only $3 to $4. Local advertising on radio is lower on a cost-per-thousand basis, compared to local TV advertising. The low relative costs of radio make it one of the most efficient of all advertising media, and the low absolute cost means the budget needed for an effective radio campaign is often lower than that for other media.

The low cost of radio means advertisers can build more reach and frequency into their media schedule within a certain budget. They can use different stations to broaden the reach of their messages and multiple spots to ensure adequate frequency. Advertisers can use radio as a fast and relatively inexpensive way to get their names known. Radio commercials can be produced more quickly than TV spots, and the companies can run them more often. Many national advertisers also recognize the cost efficiency of radio and use it as part of their media strategy.

**Receptivity** Radio often provides advertisers with a very receptive environment for their advertising messages. The Radio Advertising Bureau has conducted studies in conjunction with the research firm Harris Interactive which show that consumers perceive radio advertising to be more personally relevant to them than ads on television or the Internet.[45] The study found that radio listeners have a unique relationship with radio as a medium because they often are more emotionally connected to the radio stations to which they listen. This emotional connection can make consumers more receptive to radio ads when the message is designed and placed properly. Figure 11–5 shows how consumers rate their emotional connection with radio versus other media. The study also found that consumers perceive radio advertising as being more personally relevant to them. This may be due to the nature of radio ads usually being targeted to the demographics and psychographic characteristics of the listeners of particular stations as discussed below.

**FIGURE 11–5**
Rating of Emotional Attributes for Radio

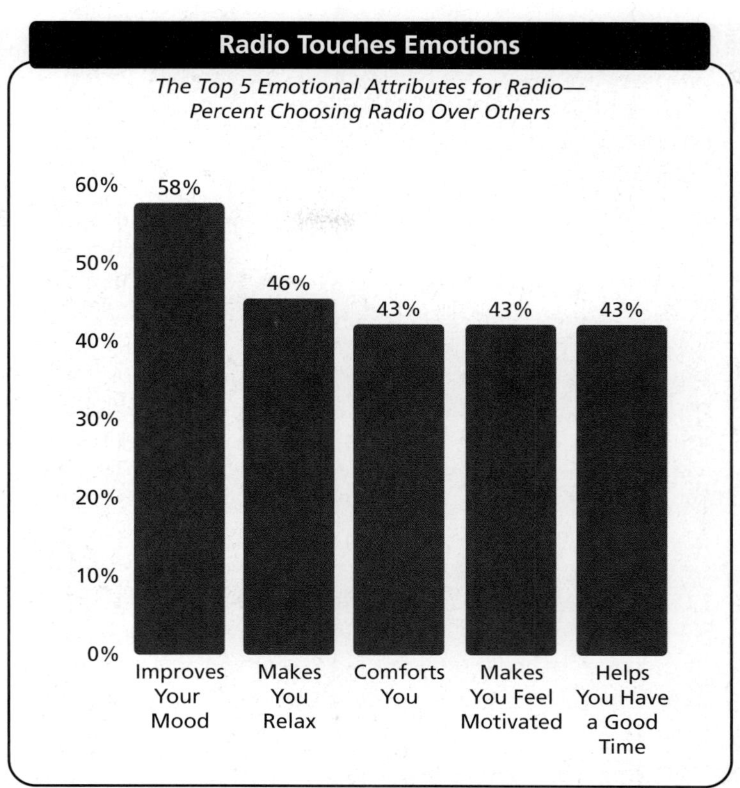


CHAPTER 11

**Selectivity** Another major advantage of radio is the high degree of audience selectivity available through the various program formats and geographic coverage of the numerous stations. Radio lets companies focus their advertising on specialized audiences such as certain demographic and lifestyle groups. Most areas have radio stations with formats such as adult contemporary, easy listening, classical music, country, news/talk shows, jazz, and all news, to name a few. Figure 11–6 shows the percentage of the radio listening audience captured by various radio formats for the 18–24 and 25–34 age groups. As can be seen in these numbers, contemporary hits radio gets nearly two-thirds of its listeners from these two demographic groups while formats such as news/talk and easy listening get a very small percentage from the young adults. Elusive consumers like teenagers, college students, and working adults can be reached more easily through radio than most other media.

Radio can reach consumers other media can't. Light television viewers spend considerably more time with radio than with TV and are generally an upscale market in terms of income and education level. Light readers of magazines and newspapers also spend more time listening to radio. Radio has become a popular way to reach specific non-English-speaking ethnic markets. Los Angeles, New York City, Dallas, and Miami have several radio stations that broadcast in Spanish and reach these areas' large Hispanic markets. As mass marketing gives way to market segmentation and regional marketing, radio will continue to grow in importance.

**Flexibility** Radio is probably the most flexible of all the advertising media because it has a very short closing period, which means advertisers can change their message almost up to the time it goes on the air. Radio commercials can usually be produced and scheduled on very short notice. Radio advertisers can easily adjust their messages to local market conditions and marketing situations.

**Mental Imagery** A potential advantage of radio that is often overlooked is that it encourages listeners to use their imagination when processing a commercial message. While the creative options of radio are limited, many advertisers take advantage

| ADULTS 18–24 | | ADULTS 25–34 | |
|---|---|---|---|
| **Format** | **18+ Audience in 18–24 Demo. (%)** | **Format** | **18+ Audience in 25–34 Demo. (%)** |
| Contemporary hit radio (CHR, Top 40) | 31.8% | Contemporary hit radio (CHR, Top 40) | 31.6% |
| Urban | 28.2 | Alternative | 30.4 |
| Alternative | 25.8 | Hispanic | 29.6 |
| Rock | 22.8 | Rock | 28.0 |
| Hispanic | 19.5 | Urban | 26.7 |
| Adult hits ("Jack," etc) | 15.3 | Adult hits ("Jack," etc) | 23.3 |
| Classic rock | 14.3 | Adult contemporary | 22.8 |
| Country | 14.0 | Classic rock | 19.9 |
| Adult contemporary | 13.5 | Country | 19.4 |
| Classic hits | 11.8 | All sports | 18.5 |
| Soft AC/lite rock | 10.8 | Classic hits | 17.3 |
| Gospel | 10.3 | Soft AC/lite rock | 17.3 |
| Religious | 10.0 | All talk | 16.5 |
| Oldies | 9.3 | Religious | 16.3 |
| All talk | 8.1 | Gospel | 15.1 |
| Ethnic | 7.8 | Ethnic | 12.9 |
| Jazz | 7.5 | Oldies | 12.5 |
| Classical | 7.1 | Jazz | 11.7 |
| All sports | 6.4 | Classical | 11.3 |
| Easy listening | 4.1 | All news | 10.4 |
| Adult standards | 3.6 | News/talk | 10.1 |
| News/talk | 3.6 | Easy listening | 6.1 |
| All news | 3.0 | Adult standards | 5.5 |

Note: 31.8% of CHR Radio's 18+ audience is in the 18–24 demographic.
Numbers based on Media Mark Research & Intelligence LLC, DoubleBase 2009, Adults 18+ Audience Distribution by Age Cell—Total Week Cume.
Source: *Radio Advertising Bureau Marketing Guide 2010.*

**FIGURE 11–6**

Radio Format Audience Shares by Age Group

of the absence of a visual element to let consumers create their own picture of what is happening in a radio message.

Radio may also reinforce television messages through a technique called **image transfer**, where the images of a TV commercial are implanted into a radio spot.[46] First the marketer establishes the video image of a TV commercial. Then it uses a similar, or even the same, audio portion (spoken words and/or jingle) as the basis for the radio counterpart. The idea is that when consumers hear the radio message, they will make the connection to the TV commercial, reinforcing its video images. Image transfer offers advertisers a way to make radio and TV ads work together synergistically. This promotional piece put out by the Radio Advertising Bureau shows how the image transfer process works (Exhibit 11–16).

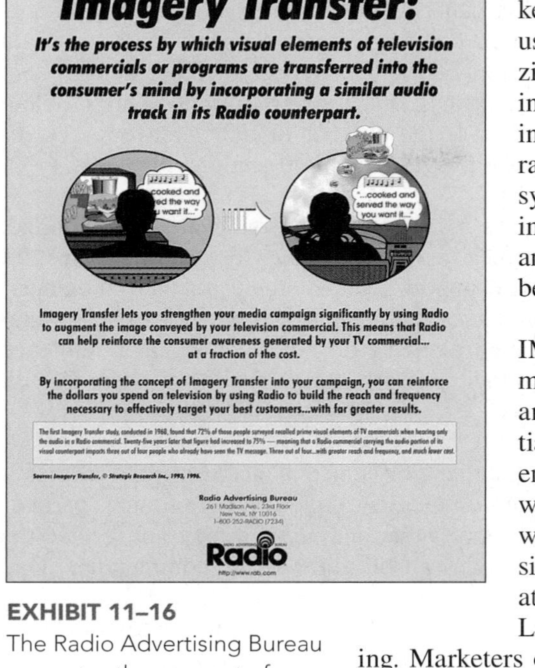
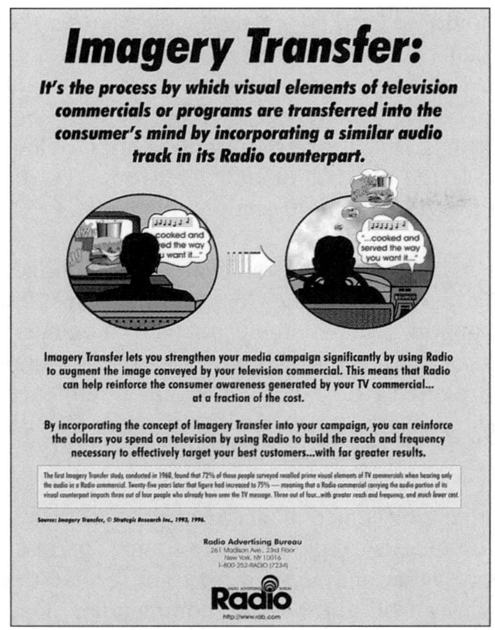


**EXHIBIT 11–16**
The Radio Advertising Bureau promotes the concept of imagery transfer

**Integrated Marketing Opportunities** Radio provides marketers with a variety of integrated marketing opportunities. It can be used in combination with other media including television, magazines, and newspapers to provide advertisers with synergistic effects in generating awareness and communicating their message. The radio industry recently sponsored a major research study to determine how radio works in combination with other media. The study found that the synergistic use of radio with television and newspapers had a positive impact on brand awareness and brand selection.[47] Exhibit 11–17 shows an ad run by the Radio Advertising Bureau promoting the synergy between radio and newspaper advertising.

Radio can also be used in conjunction with a variety of other IMC tools such as sales promotion, event marketing, and cause-related marketing. Radio stations are an integral part of many communities and the deejays and program hosts are often popular and influential figures. Advertisers often use radio stations and personalities to enhance their involvement with a local market and to gain influence with local retailers. Radio also works very effectively in conjunction with place-based/point-of-purchase promotions. Retailers often use on-site radio broadcasts combined with special sales or promotions to attract consumers to their stores and get them to make a purchase. Live radio broadcasts are also used in conjunction with event marketing. Marketers often sponsor live broadcast promotions at beaches, sporting events, and festivals, setting up product booths for sampling and giveaways.

## Limitations of Radio

Several factors limit the effectiveness of radio as an advertising medium, among them creative limitations, fragmentation, chaotic buying procedures, limited research data, limited listener attention, and clutter. The media planner must consider them in determining the role the medium will play in the advertising program.

**EXHIBIT 11–17**
The radio industry promotes findings from a study showing the synergistic effects of radio

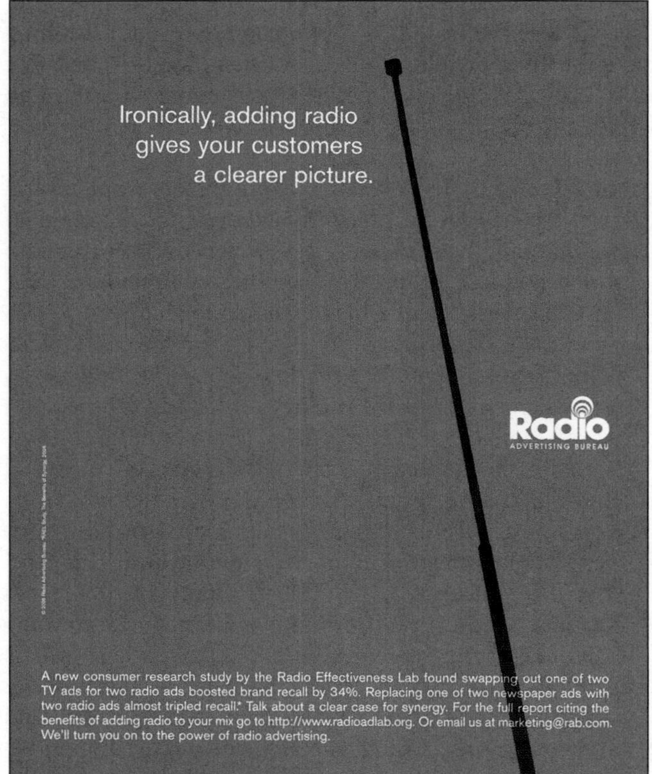


**Creative Limitations** A major drawback of radio as an advertising medium is the absence of a visual image. The radio advertiser cannot show the product, demonstrate it, or use any type of visual appeal or information. A radio commercial is, like a TV ad, a short-lived and fleeting message that is externally paced and does not allow the receiver to control the rate at which it is processed. Because of these creative limitations many companies tend to ignore radio, and agencies often assign junior people to the development of radio commercials.

**Fragmentation** Another problem with radio is the high level of audience fragmentation due to the large number of stations. The percentage of the market tuned to any particular station is usually very small. The top-rated radio station in many major metropolitan areas with a number of AM and FM stations may attract less than 10 percent of the total listening audience. Advertisers that want a broad reach in their radio advertising media schedule have to buy time on a number of stations to cover even a local market.

LO 11-2

**Chaotic Buying Procedures** It should be readily apparent how chaotic the media planning and purchasing process can become for the advertiser that wants to use radio on a nationwide spot basis. Acquiring information and evaluating and contracting for time with even a fraction of the 10,600 commercial stations that operate across the country can be very difficult and time-consuming. This problem has diminished somewhat in recent years as the number of radio networks and of syndicated programs offering a package of several hundred stations increases.

**Limited Research Data** Audience research data on radio are often limited, particularly compared with TV, magazines, or newspapers. Most radio stations are small operations and lack the revenue to support detailed studies of their audiences. And most users of radio are local companies that cannot support research on radio listenership in their markets. Thus, media planners do not have as much audience information available to guide them in their purchase of radio time as they do with other media.

**Limited Listener Attention** Another problem that plagues radio is that it is difficult to retain listener attention to commercials. Radio programming, particularly music, is often the background to some other activity and may not receive the listeners' full attention. Thus they may miss all or some of the commercials. One environment where radio has a more captive audience is in cars. But getting listeners to pay attention to commercials can still be difficult. Most people preprogram their car radio and change stations during commercial breaks. A study by Avery Abernethy found large differences between exposure to radio programs versus advertising for listeners in cars. They were exposed to only half of the advertising broadcast and changed stations frequently to avoid commercials.[48] However, a study by the companies Arbitron Inc. and Coleman Research analyzed the audience retained during commercial breaks by comparing the audience level for each minute of a commercial break to the audience for the minute before the commercials began.[49] The study found that on average 92 percent of the lead-in audience was retained during commercial breaks. Nearly the entire audience was retained during one-minute commercial pods (Exhibit 11–18). Another factor that is detracting from radio listening in motor vehicles is the rapid growth of cellular phones. A recent study found that half of commuters surveyed who own a cell phone reported listening to less radio than they did a year earlier.[50]

**Competition from Digital Media** Radio is also facing threats from several digital-based technologies that are impacting the listening audience for commercial radio. A major threat to conventional broadcast radio is the growth of satellite radio which bounces signals off satellites stationed over the East and West coasts and back down to receivers, which encode the signals digitally. The primary target for satellite radio is currently vehicle owners who purchase a receiver for about $100 and pay a monthly subscription fee of around $13 for virtually commercial-free digital radio that includes nearly 100 channels of music, news, talk, sports, and children's programming. Sirius paid $500 million to lure shock jock Howard Stern away from terrestrial radio by signing him to a five-year deal that began in 2006 (Exhibit 11–19). Both XM and Sirius also spent large amounts to acquire the broadcast rights for professional and college sports as well as NASCAR. They have also been adding more locally tailored programming such as traffic and weather reports, which makes them more competitive against terrestrial stations in local markets. In 2008 the

**EXHIBIT 11–18**
Radio promotes audience retention during commercial breaks

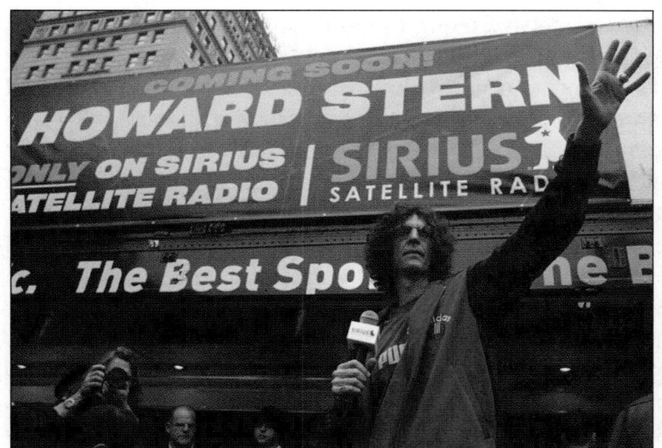


**EXHIBIT 11–19**
Satellite radio now competes against traditional broadcast stations for listeners

two rival satellite radio companies merged to form one major satellite radio firm, Sirius XM, which currently has around 19 million subscribers. The merger was approved on the grounds that the new company would have lower costs and be better positioned to compete against conventional terrestrial radio stations as well as fast-growing audio alternatives including HD radio, MP3 players, and online listening via the Internet. However, the new company has been facing financial problems as the dramatic decline in automobile sales over the past two years have resulted in fewer new-car buyers who activate the satellite radio receivers installed in their cars and account for a large part of the company's subscriber base.[51]

In addition to satellite, terrestrial radio is also being significantly impacted by the growing popularity of MP3 players such as Apple's iPod as well as music services that are becoming available over the Internet such as Pandora and Yahoo! Music. One such digital technology that threatens radio is the growth of podcasting, which is a method of distributing audio content via the Internet. Podcasting enables independent producers to create their own radio shows and bypass the traditional entry barriers such as licenses, airwave frequencies, and transmission.[52]



**Clutter** Clutter is just as much a problem with radio as with other advertising media. Most radio stations carry an average of nearly 10 minutes of commercials every hour. During the popular morning and evening rush hours, the amount of commercial time may exceed 12 minutes. Also contributing to the clutter problem is the practice of some stations to offer "commercial-free" blocks of music to attract listeners. This practice results in more commercials being aired in a short time period and may also result in listeners switching to another station rather than listening through a long block of ads. Advertisers must create commercials that break through the clutter or use heavy repetition to make sure their messages reach consumers. In a study of radio listeners conducted by Edison Research, perceptions of increased ad clutter were cited by participants as a reason for spending less time listening to radio.[53]

A number of radio stations have begun to address the clutter problem by reducing the number of commercials. Clear Channel Communications, which owns more than 1,200 radio stations across 300 markets in the United States, cut back on the number of minutes of commercials its stations run per hour to entice both listeners and advertisers. Other large companies that own radio stations including Viacom and Entercom Communications have also reduced the frequency of commercials as have some individual stations in many markets.[54]

The radio industry is looking for other ways to make radio advertising more valuable to marketers. In 2010 Clear Channel began offering advertisers a new service known as contextual radio ads that can automatically insert radio commercials immediately after specific programming or certain kinds of content, including other ads.[55] A number of companies have been using the service to better target their radio advertising messages. For example, Walmart ran ads for AC/DC's *Black Ice* album, which was sold exclusively at its stores, on various rock stations owned by Clear Channel immediately after songs by the group were played. GEICO also used the service to air commercials with its "Save 15 percent on insurance" after ads for cars, motorcycles, or RVs aired.

## Buying Radio Time

The purchase of radio time is similar to that of television, as advertisers can make either network, spot, or local buys. Since these options were reviewed in the section on buying TV time, they are discussed here only briefly.

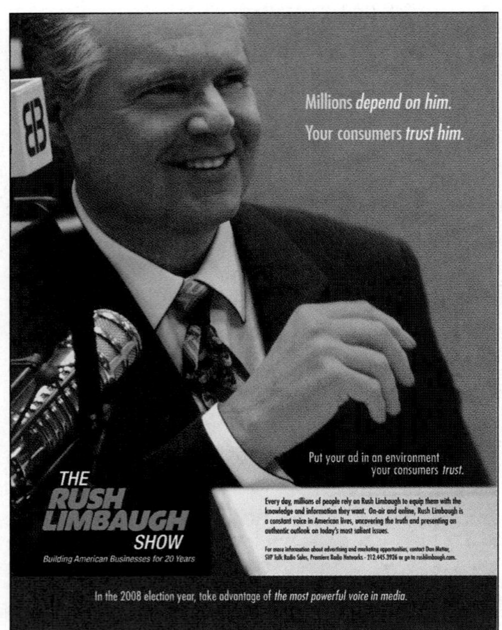


**EXHIBIT 11–20**
Limbaugh's talk radio show is syndicated nationally

**Network Radio** Advertising time on radio can be purchased on a network basis using one of the national networks. There are currently seven major national radio networks such as Westwood One, Citadel Media, and Premiere. There are also more than 100 regional radio networks across the country. Using networks minimizes the amount of negotiation and administrative work needed to get national or regional coverage, and the costs are lower than those for individual stations. However, the number of affiliated stations on the network roster and the types of audiences they reach can vary considerably, so the use of network radio reduces advertisers' flexibility in selecting stations.

An important trend in radio is the increasing number of radio networks and syndicated programs that offer advertisers a package of several hundred stations. For example, conservative Rush Limbaugh's radio show is syndicated nationally and is carried on nearly 600 stations, reaching nearly 20 million people weekly (Exhibit 11–20). Syndication reduces audience fragmentation and purchasing problems and increases radio's appeal to national advertisers.

**Spot Radio** National advertisers can also use spot radio to purchase airtime on individual stations in various markets. The purchase of spot radio provides greater flexibility in selecting markets, individual stations, and airtime and adjusting the message for local market conditions. Spot radio accounts for about 20 percent of radio time sold.

**Local Radio** By far the heaviest users of radio are local advertisers; nearly 79 percent of radio advertising time is purchased from individual stations by local companies. Auto dealers, retailers, restaurants, and financial institutions are among the heaviest users of local radio advertising. But a number of radio advertisers are switching to local cable TV because the rates are comparable and there is the added advantage of TV's visual impact.

## Time Classifications

As with television, the broadcast day for radio is divided into various time periods or dayparts, as shown in Figure 11–7. The size of the radio listening audience varies widely across the dayparts, and advertising rates follow accordingly. The largest radio audiences (and thus the highest rates) occur during the early morning and late afternoon drive times. Radio rates also vary according to the number of spots or type of audience plan purchased, the supply and demand of time available in the local market, and the ratings of the individual station. Rate information is available directly from the stations and is summarized in SRDS's Radio Advertising Source, which provides spot radio rates and data for both local stations and radio networks. Some stations issue rate cards showing their ad rates across various dayparts. However, many stations do not adhere strictly to rate cards and the rates published in SRDS. Their rates are negotiable and depend on factors such as availability, time period, and number of spots purchased.

## Audience Information

One problem with radio is the lack of audience information. Because there are so many radio stations and thus many small, fragmented audiences, the stations cannot support the expense of detailed audience measurement. Also, owing to the nature of radio as incidental or background entertainment, it is difficult to develop precise measures of who listens at various time periods and for how long. The major radio ratings services are owned by Arbitron, which provides audience information for local stations and network audiences.

**FIGURE 11–7**
Dayparts for Radio

| | |
|---|---|
| Morning drive time | 6:00–10:00 A.M. |
| Daytime | 10:00 A.M.–3:00 P.M. |
| Afternoon/evening drive time | 3:00–7:00 P.M. |
| Nighttime | 7:00 P.M.–12:00 A.M. |
| All night | 12:00–6:00 A.M. |

**Arbitron** Arbitron covers 286 local radio markets with one to four ratings reports per year. Arbitron has a sample of representative listeners in each market maintain a diary of their radio listening for seven days. Audience estimates for the market are based on these diary records and reported by time period and selected demographics in the Arbitron Radio Market Report, to which clients subscribe. Figure 11–8 provides a sample page from the Arbitron ratings report for people in the 18-to-49 age target audience across the various dayparts. The three basic estimates in the Arbitron report are

- Person estimates—the estimated number of people listening.
- Rating—the percentage of listeners in the survey area population.
- Share—the percentage of the total estimated listening audience.

These three estimates are further defined by using quarter-hour and cume figures. The **average quarter-hour (AQH) figure** expresses the average number of people estimated to have listened to a station for a minimum of five minutes during any quarter-hour in a time period. For example, station KCBQ has an average quarter-hour listenership of 2,500 during the weekday 6 to 10 A.M. daypart. This means that any weekday, for any 15-minute period during this time period, an average of 2,500 people between the ages of 18 and 49 are tuned to this station. This figure helps to determine the audience and cost of a spot schedule within a particular time period.

**Cume** stands for "cumulative audience," the estimated total number of different people who listened to a station for at least five minutes in a quarter-hour period within a reported daypart. In Figure 11–8, the cumulative audience of people 18 to 49 for station KCBQ during the weekday morning daypart is 26,300. Cume estimates the reach potential of a radio station.

The **average quarter-hour rating (AQH RTG)** expresses the estimated number of listeners as a percentage of the survey area population. The **average quarter-hour share (AQH SHR)** is the percentage of the total listening audience tuned to each station. It shows the share of listeners each station captures out of the total listening audience in the survey area. The average quarter-hour rating of station KCBQ during the weekday 6 to 10 A.M. daypart is 0.2, while the average quarter-hour share is 0.8.

Arbitron is conducting market trials of its portable people meter (PPM) device for use in measuring radio audiences. The **Portable People Meter** is a wearable pager–sized device that electronically tracks what consumers listen to on the radio by detecting inaudible identification codes that are embedded in the programming. The radio industry and advertisers have called on Arbitron to provide more detailed and accurate measures of radio audiences. They view the new PPM technology as a more valid audience measurement system.[56] Arbitron had been using the new system to measure radio audiences in Houston and Philadelphia, and expanded it to other markets in 2008 including New York, Los Angeles, Chicago, and Dallas. The company plans to have the PPM in the top 50 markets, by the end of 2010. The radio industry feels that the PPM system will demonstrate that more people are listening to

**FIGURE 11–8**
Partial Sample Page from Arbitron Radio Ratings Report

| | TARGET AUDIENCE, PERSONS 18–49 | | | | | | | |
|---|---|---|---|---|---|---|---|---|
| | MONDAY–FRIDAY 6–10 A.M. | | | | MONDAY–FRIDAY 10 A.M.–3 P.M. | | | |
| | AQH (00) | CUME (00) | AQH RTG | AQH SHR | AQH (00) | CUME (00) | AQH RTG | AQH SHR |
| KCBQ | | | | | | | | |
| METRO | 25 | 263 | .2 | .8 | 40 | 365 | .3 | 1.3 |
| TSA | 25 | 263 | | | 40 | 365 | | |
| KCBQ-FM | | | | | | | | |
| METRO | 101 | 684 | .7 | 3.1 | 117 | 768 | .9 | 3.7 |
| TSA | 101 | 684 | | | 117 | 768 | | |
| KCEO | | | | | | | | |
| METRO | 11 | 110 | .1 | .3 | 8 | 81 | .1 | .3 |
| TSA | 11 | 110 | | | 8 | 81 | | |
| KFMB | | | | | | | | |
| METRO | 171 | 790 | 1.3 | 5.3 | 106 | 678 | .8 | 3.3 |
| TSA | 171 | 790 | | | 106 | 678 | | |

radio, which in turn will encourage advertisers to buy more commercial time. Exhibit 11–21 shows an ad from Arbitron promoting the value of the personal people meter.

Arbitron also recently began measuring listenership to webcasts. Arbitron Online Radio Ratings is an audience measurement service that measures Internet audio and video tuning across all webcasting sources. However, this service is still in a pilot testing phase. Arbitron's research has found that 30 percent of online users have listened to Internet radio stations and the number continues to grow. This will make the measurement of radio listening over the Internet a very important area in the future.

**EXHIBIT 11–21**
Arbitron promotes its Portable People Meter

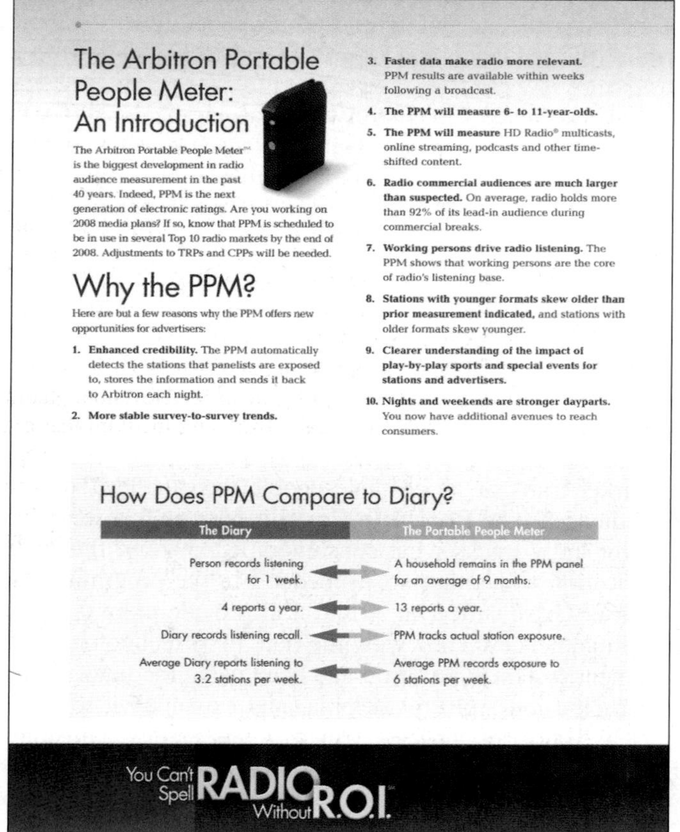


**RADAR** Another rating service that is now owned by Arbitron is RADAR (Radio's All Dimension Audience Research), which is supported by radio networks, media services companies, and advertisers. RADAR measurements are based on information collected throughout the year by means of diary interviews from a probability sample of 200,000 respondents age 12 and older who live in telephone households. Respondents are instructed to record all radio listening as well as the day of the week, time of day, and location for a one-week period. Demographic information is also collected in the diaries.

RADAR reports are issued four times a year and provide network audience measures, along with estimates of audience and various segments. The audience estimates are time-period measurements for the various dayparts. RADAR also provides estimates of network audiences for all commercials and commercials within various programs.

As with TV, media planners must use the audience measurement information to evaluate the value of various radio stations in reaching the advertiser's target audience and their relative cost. The media buyer responsible for the purchase of radio time works with information on target audience coverage, rates, time schedules, and availability to optimize the advertiser's radio media budget.

| | TARGET AUDIENCE, PERSONS 18–49 | | | | | | | | | | | |
|---|---|---|---|---|---|---|---|---|---|---|---|---|
| | MONDAY–FRIDAY 3–7 P.M. | | | | MONDAY–FRIDAY 7 P.M.–MID. | | | | WEEKEND 10 A.M.–7 P.M. | | | |
| | AQH (00) | CUME (00) | AQH RTG | AQH SHR | AQH (00) | CUME (00) | AQH RTG | AQH SHR | AQH (00) | CUME (00) | AQH RTG | AQH SHR |
| KCBQ | | | | | | | | | | | | |
| METRO | 36 | 340 | .3 | 1.4 | 6 | 138 | .5 | 51 | 356 | .4 | 2.4 | |
| TSA | 36 | 340 | | | 6 | 138 | | | 51 | 356 | | |
| KCBQ-FM | | | | | | | | | | | | |
| METRO | 83 | 736 | .6 | 3.2 | 23 | 354 | .2 | 2.1 | 67 | 616 | .5 | 3.2 |
| TSA | 83 | 736 | | | 23 | 354 | | | 67 | 616 | | |
| KCEO | | | | | | | | | | | | |
| METRO | 10 | 95 | .1 | .4 | | 8 | | | 1 | 8 | | |
| TSA | 10 | 95 | | | | 8 | | | 1 | 8 | | |
| KFMB | | | | | | | | | | | | |
| METRO | 141 | 1092 | 1.0 | 5.4 | 87 | 827 | .6 | 7.9 | 92 | 567 | .7 | 4.4 |
| TSA | 141 | 1092 | | | 87 | 827 | | | 92 | 567 | | |

## Summary

Television and radio, or the broadcast media, are the most pervasive media in most consumers' daily lives and offer advertisers the opportunity to reach vast audiences. Both broadcast media are time- rather than space-oriented and organized similarly in that they use a system of affiliated stations belonging to a network, as well as individual stations, to broadcast their programs and commercial messages. Advertising on radio or TV can be done on national or regional network programs or purchased in spots from local stations.

TV has grown faster than any other advertising medium in history and has become the leading medium for national advertisers. No other medium offers its creative capabilities; the combination of sight, sound, and movement gives the advertiser a vast number of options for presenting a commercial message with high impact. Television also offers advertisers mass coverage at a low relative cost. Variations in programming and audience composition, along with the growth of cable, are helping TV offer more audience selectivity to advertisers. While television is often viewed as the ultimate advertising medium, it has several limitations, including the high cost of producing and airing commercials, a lack of selectivity relative to other media, the fleeting nature of the message, and the problem of commercial clutter. The latter two problems have been compounded in recent years by the trend toward shorter commercials.

Information regarding the size and composition of national and local TV audiences is provided by Nielsen Media Research. The amount of money networks or stations can charge for commercial time on their programs is based on its audience measurement figures. This information is also important to media planners, as it is used to determine the combination of shows needed to attain specific levels of reach and frequency with the advertiser's target market.

Future trends in television include the continued growth of cable, competition to local cable operators from direct broadcast satellite systems, and a resulting increase in channels available to television households. Changes are also likely to occur in the measurement of viewing audiences—for example, continuous measurement of audiences.

The role of radio as an entertainment and advertising medium has changed with the rapid growth of television. Radio has evolved into a primarily local advertising medium that offers highly specialized programming appealing to narrow segments of the market. Radio offers advertisers the opportunity to build high reach and frequency into their media schedules and to reach selective audiences at a very efficient cost. It also offers opportunities for integrated marketing programs such as place-based promotions and event sponsorships.

The major drawback of radio is its creative limitations owing to the absence of a visual image. The short and fleeting nature of the radio commercial, the highly fragmented nature of the radio audience, and clutter are also problems.

As with TV, the rate structure for radio advertising time varies with the size of the audience delivered. The primary sources of audience information are Arbitron for local radio and its RADAR studies for network audiences.

## Key Terms

**zipping** p. 370
**zapping** p. 370
**television network** p. 373
**affiliates** p. 373
**up-front market** p. 374
**scatter market** p. 374
**spot advertising** p. 374
**national spot advertising** p. 375
**local advertising** p. 375
**station reps** p. 375
**syndicated programs** p. 375
**sponsorship** p. 377
**participations** p. 377
**adjacencies** p. 378
**dayparts** p. 378
**cable television** p. 379
**superstations** p. 379
**interconnects** p. 381
**narrowcasting** p. 382
**multiplexing** p. 383
**television households** p. 386
**program rating** p. 386
**ratings point** p. 386
**households using television (HUT)** p. 386
**share of audience** p. 386
**total audience** p. 387
**Nielsen Television Index** p. 387
**people meter** p. 387
**designated market areas (DMAs)** p. 387
**sweeps** p. 388
**commercial ratings** p. 388
**engagement** p. 389
**image transfer** p. 394
**average quarter-hour (AQH) figure** p. 399
**cume** p. 399
**average quarter-hour rating (AQH RTG)** p. 399
**average quarter-hour share (AQH SHR)** p. 399
**Portable People Meter** p. 399

## Discussion Questions

1. The opening vignette discusses how various technological changes have been impacting the television industry and TV's role as a major advertising medium. Discuss the key developments that have impacted television over the past two decades and other factors that are likely to affect it in the future. (LO1, 4)
2. Discuss the advantages and limitations of television as an advertising medium and how these factors affect its use by both major national advertisers as well as smaller local companies. (LO2)
3 Discuss some of the ways companies that advertise on the Super Bowl are using it as an integrated marketing opportunity and leveraging their involvement with the game both leading up to and after Super Bowl Sunday. (LO2)
4. The most popular form of television commercials is the 30-second spot. Discuss why 30-second spots are so popular among advertisers. When might a marketer be able to effectively use a 10- or 15-second commercial? (LO2)
5. What are the various options available to advertisers for purchasing advertising time on television? How does the use of these options differ for national versus local advertisers? (LO3)
6. Discuss the reasons for the growing popularity of sports programming on television. What are some of the ways advertisers can capitalize on the popularity of sports programs as a media vehicle. (LO2)
7. IMC Technology Perspective 11–1 discusses the debate between the television networks and advertisers over the measurement of TV viewing audiences. Evaluate the changes that have been made to provide advertisers with better measures of TV viewing audiences as well as commercials. (LO3)
8. Evaluate the use of sweeps rating periods as a method for measuring local television viewing audiences. Do you think sweeps ratings provide reliable and valid estimates of local television viewing audiences? How might they be improved? (LO3)
9. What is a commercial rating and how does this measure differ from a program rating? Discuss why advertisers and media planners prefer commercial ratings rather than program ratings. (LO3)
10. Discuss the advantages and disadvantages of advertising on radio. Discuss how radio advertising can be used by national versus local advertisers. (LO2)
11. Discuss how radio stations, as well as advertisers, can deal with the clutter problem on radio and draw attention to their commercials. Provide an example of an advertiser who might be able to benefit from the contextual programming service offered by Clear Channel. (LO3, 4)

## AdForum Exercise: Advertising on Major Sporting Events

(see Advertising and Promotion Playlist, Chapter 11)

### PART I: 2010 FIFA WORLD CUP

The playlist for this chapter contains five of the most popular commercials from the 2010 FIFA World Cup soccer tournament that was played in South Africa. Watch these five spots and answer the following:

**1** Analyze the type of appeal used in each commercial and discuss why this type of advertising worked well during the World Cup.
**2** Discuss why this commercial was selected as one of the top ads aired during the 2010 World Cup or 2010. What makes the ad memorable and distinctive?
**3** Discuss the specific objectives that each marketer might have for each commercial and discuss how effective the ad was in achieving these goals.

### PART II: 2010 SUPER BOWL

The playlist for this chapter also includes five of the most popular TV commercials from the 2010 Super Bowl based on the results from the 22nd Annual Super Bowl Ad Meter study conducted by the newspaper *USA TODAY.* The Ad Meter study is conducted by recruiting 250 consumers and electronically charting their second-by-second reactions to ads shown during the Super Bowl. Watch these five spots and answer the following:

**1** Analyze the type of advertising appeal and creative execution technique used for each ad and discuss why you think it was used for the Super Bowl spot.
**2** Why do you think this commercial was rated highly among consumers on the Ad Meter panel? What are the characteristics of the ad that make it so likeable?
**3** Discuss the specific objectives that each marketer might have for each commercial. Do you feel this ad can be used to achieve these objectives when aired during regular programming? What particular TV shows would be a good place to run these commercials?

Access to the chapter playlist is available through McGraw Hill connect™ |MARKETING, www.mcgrawhillconnect.com

## LEARNING OBJECTIVES

- **LO1** To examine the various types of magazines and newspapers and the value of each as an advertising medium.
- **LO2** To analyze the advantages and limitations of magazines and newspapers as advertising media.
- **LO3** To discuss how advertising space is purchased in magazines and newspapers, how readership is measured, and how rates are determined.
- **LO4** To consider future developments in magazines and newspapers and how these trends will influence their use as advertising media.

# 12 Evaluation of Print Media

## MAGAZINES AND NEWSPAPERS FACE TOUGH TIMES

The past few years have not been kind to the traditional media of magazines and newspapers as they have been facing major challenges on a number of fronts. Both of these print media have been hit hard by the recession which has led many companies to reduce their advertising budgets and shift more of the monies they are spending to nontraditional media and the Internet in particular. Advertising revenue for magazines declined from nearly $25 billion in 2007 to just under $20 billion in 2009, while the total number of advertising pages has dropped by nearly 25 percent over the past two years. Total advertising spending in newspapers declined by 40 percent from $42 billion in 2007 to $25 billion in 2009. Revenue from advertising is the primary source of income for both magazines and newspapers so the impact on publishers is obvious. However, advertising revenue is dependent upon the number of readers that magazines and newspapers can deliver to advertising and both mediums have been struggling to retain readers.

In 2009 average weekday readership of newspapers declined by 10.6 percent and among the 25 largest papers, 15 reported double-digit declines in circulation while only one, *The Wall Street Journal,* reported a gain. Magazines have also been experiencing declines in readership, with single copy sales which occur at newsstands particularly hard hit, as they declined by nearly 10 percent each of the past two years. While single-copy sales account for a small percentage of circulation for most magazines, it is considered the best measure of a magazine's appeal to consumers since unlike subscriptions, they cannot be artificially inflated by deep discounts or the distribution of free copies. Newsweeklies and business magazines have been experiencing particularly large declines in newsstand sales as publications such as *Newsweek, Time, The Economist, BusinessWeek,* and *Fortune* have experienced major drops in single-copy sales. In May 2010 the Washington Post Co., which owns *Newsweek,* put the venerable publication up for sale after suffering several years of losses resulting from declines in circulation and advertising revenue. McGraw-Hill also sold *BusinessWeek* in late 2009 to Bloomberg LP for less than $5 million while *TV Guide* was sold to a private equity company for a whopping $1, which is less than the price of a single issue of the magazine.

One of the major problems facing magazines and newspapers is that more consumers are now going online to get their news as well as to read the magazines and newspapers that they are longer willing to purchase. Nearly all of the major publications now offer online versions, but the problem is that consumers are used to getting this Internet content for free and are not willing to pay for it. *The Wall Street Journal* is one of the few publications that has been able to charge consumers for online content, although other newspapers and magazines continue to look for ways to monetize their websites such as by making certain articles available only to people who pay for a subscription. While the publishers can sell banners and other forms of online advertising to marketers, the ad rates they can charge on the Web cannot match their levels in print and generate enough revenue to make up for the losses they are incurring. Moreover, since online ad revenue is fueled by page views, publications that attempt to charge for access run the risk of reducing Web traffic which would be self-defeating.

Most media experts remain extremely skeptical regarding consumers' willingness to pay for access to online publications because categories such as sports, business, national, and international news have become commoditized and consumers do not perceive enough differences to pay for something they can get for free. Thus, publishers are going to have to continue to find ways to charge marketers more money for various forms of online advertising. One development that may help them is the growing popularity of electronic readers such as Sony's Reader Daily Edition, Apple's iPad, and other tablet computers that are being introduced. These devices have full color touch screens that offer video viewing capabilities as well as interactive ads that can grab the reader's attention or be skipped with the swipe of a finger. They also are network connected to virtual newsstands and stores from which magazines and newspapers can be easily downloaded. A number of newspapers such as *The Wall Street Journal* and *The New York Times* are already offering digital versions of their publications for Sony's Reader Daily Edition and the Apple iPad. Major magazines have also begun publishing offering digital versions of their publications including *Time, Men's Health, Sports Illustrated,* and *Popular Science.* The digital versions of these publications will be able to offer full-screen ads that can deliver the best of both the old world and the new because they can offer the same impact as magazine spreads or TV commercials while also offering the same analytics as the Internet to measure viewership and other metrics.

While e-readers and other forms of tablet PCs may be the publishing industry's digital life preserver, the costs of these devices are still high and it will take time for them to cross the technology chasm and achieve mass market adoption. Thus, in the short term magazines and newspapers have to continue to search for ways to attract and retain current readers as well as the advertising pages and revenue that accompanies them.

Sources: Josh Quittner, "The Future of Reading," *Fortune,* May 1, 2010, pp. 63–70; Nat Ives, "Washington Post Puts Newsweek on the Block," *Advertising Age,* May 5, 2010, http://adage.com/print?article_id=143702; Russell Adams, "Magazine Sales Continue to Slip," *The Wall Street Journal,* February 9, 2010, http://online.wsj.com; Al DiGuido, "E-Readers; Publishing's Digital Life Preserver?," *Advertising Age,* December 29, 2009, http://adage.com/print?article_id=141230.

Magazines and newspapers have been advertising media for more than two centuries; for many years, they were the only major media available to advertisers. With the growth of the broadcast media, particularly television, reading habits declined. More consumers turned to TV viewing not only as their primary source of entertainment but also for news and information. But despite the competition from the broadcast media, newspapers and magazines remained important media vehicles to both consumers and advertisers.

Thousands of magazines are published in the United States and throughout the world. They appeal to nearly every specific consumer interest and lifestyle, as well as to thousands of businesses and occupations. By becoming a highly specialized medium that reaches specific target audiences, the magazine industry has prospered. Newspapers are still the primary advertising medium in terms of both ad revenue and number of advertisers. Newspapers are particularly important as a local advertising medium for hundreds of thousands of retail businesses and are often used by large national advertisers as well.

Magazines and newspapers are an important part of our lives. For many consumers, newspapers are their primary source of product information. They would not think of going shopping without checking to see who is having a sale or clipping coupons from the weekly food section or Sunday inserts. Many people read a number of different magazines each week or month to become better informed or simply entertained. Individuals employed in various occupations rely on business magazines to keep them current about trends and developments in their industries as well as in business in general.

While most of us are very involved with the print media, it is important to keep in mind that few newspapers or magazines could survive without the support of advertising revenue. Consumer magazines generate an average of 54 percent of their revenues from advertising; business publications receive nearly 73 percent. Newspapers generate 70 percent of their total revenue from advertising. In many cities, the number of daily newspapers has declined because they could not attract enough advertising revenue to support their operations. The print media must be able to attract large numbers of readers or a very specialized audience to be of interest to advertisers.

As discussed in the chapter opener, both magazines and newspapers are facing significant challenges from the Internet which is impacting the number of people who read the traditional version of each medium and is also attracting an increasingly larger amount of marketers' advertising budgets each year. Despite the challenges they face, magazines and newspapers are still very important media vehicles for most advertisers and it is important to understand their role in the media plan, as well as the overall IMC program.[1]

# THE ROLE OF MAGAZINES AND NEWSPAPERS

The role of magazines and newspapers in the advertiser's media plan differs from that of the broadcast media because they allow the presentation of detailed information that can be processed at the reader's own pace. The print media are not intrusive like radio and TV, and they generally require some effort on the part of the reader for the advertising message to have an impact. For this reason, newspapers and magazines are often referred to as *high-involvement media*.[2] Magazine readership has remained strong despite the growth of new media options as 80 percent of adults 18+ read magazines and they read an average of 11 issues per month.[3]



Newspapers are received in nearly two-thirds of American households daily. Most magazines, however, reach a very selective audience. Like radio, they can be valuable in reaching specific types of consumers and market segments. While both magazines and newspapers are print media, the advantages and disadvantages of the two are quite different, as are the types of advertising each attracts. This chapter focuses on these two major forms of print media. It examines the specific advantages and limitations of each, along with factors that are important in determining when and how to use newspapers and magazines in the media plan.

**EXHIBIT 12–1**
Magazines targeted to a specific industry or profession

## MAGAZINES

Over the past several decades, magazines have grown rapidly to serve the educational, informational, and entertainment needs of a wide range of readers in both the consumer and business markets. Magazines are the most specialized of all advertising media. While some magazines—such as *Reader's Digest, Time,* and *Newsweek*—are general mass-appeal publications, most are targeted to a very specific audience. There is a magazine designed to appeal to nearly every type of consumer in terms of demographics, lifestyle, activities, interests, or fascination. Numerous magazines are targeted toward specific businesses and industries as well as toward individuals engaged in various professions (Exhibit 12–1).

The wide variety makes magazines an appealing medium to a vast number of advertisers. Although TV accounts for the largest dollar amount of advertising expenditures among national advertisers, more companies advertise in magazines than in any other medium. Users of magazine ads range from large consumer-product companies such as Kraft Foods and General Motors, which spend over $400 million a year on magazine advertising, to a small company advertising scuba equipment in *Skin Diver* magazine.

| By Subscriptions | | | By Single-Copy Sales | | |
|---|---|---|---|---|---|
| 1. | *AARP The Magazine** | 24,462,726 | 1. | *Cosmopolitan* | 1,685,138 |
| 2. | *AARP Bulletin** | 24,174,159 | 2. | *People* | 1,322,399 |
| 3. | *Better Homes and Garden* | 7,434,849 | 3. | *Woman's World* | 1,172,254 |
| 4. | *Reader's Digest* | 7,377,684 | 4. | *First* | 1,053,589 |
| 5. | *National Geographic* | 4,436,244 | 5. | *US Weekly* | 827,784 |
| 6. | *Good Housekeeping* | 4,209,676 | 6. | *In Touch Weekly* | 746,048 |
| 7. | *AAA Westways** | 3,831,215 | 7. | *Family Circle* | 695,533 |
| 8. | *Game Informer Magazine* | 3,691,124 | 8. | *O, The Oprah Magazine* | 677,679 |
| 9. | *Ladies Home Journal* | 3,645,046 | 9. | *In Style* | 657,647 |
| 10. | *Woman's Day* | 3,511,374 | 10. | *Glamour* | 588,671 |

Note: Figures are averages for total paid and verified circulation for 2009 based on Audit Bureau of Circulation statements.

* High proportion of title's circulation attributed to membership benefits.

Source: The Association of Magazine Media, *Fact Sheets and Trends*, March 2010, www.magazine.org. Reprinted with permission.

**FIGURE 12–1**
Magazines by Subscriptions and Single-Copy Sales

## Classifications of Magazines

To gain some perspective on the various types of magazines available and the advertisers that use them, consider the way magazines are generally classified. The media research company SRDS, the primary reference source on periodicals for media planners, divides magazines into three broad categories based on the audience to which they are directed: consumer (which include farm), health care, and business publications. Each category is then further classified according to the magazine's editorial content and audience appeal.

**Consumer Magazines** Consumer magazines are bought by the general public for information and/or entertainment. SRDS divides 2,700 domestic consumer magazines into 77 classifications, among them general editorial, sports, travel, and women's. Another way of classifying consumer magazines is by distribution: They can be sold through subscription or circulation, store distribution, or both. *Time* and *Newsweek* are sold both through subscription and in stores; *Woman's World* is sold primarily through stores. Figure 12–1 shows the top 10 magazines in terms of subscriptions and single-copy sales, respectively. Magazines can also be classified by frequency; weekly, monthly, and bimonthly are the most common.

Consumer magazines represent the major portion of the magazine industry, accounting for nearly two-thirds of all advertising dollars spent in magazines. Consumer magazines are best suited to marketers interested in reaching general consumers of products and services as well as to companies trying to reach a specific target market. The most frequently advertised categories in consumer magazines are automotive, telecommunications, direct response, toiletries and cosmetics, computers, office equipment and stationery, and business and consumer services. Marketers of tobacco products spend most of their media budget in magazines, since they are prohibited from advertising in the broadcast media.

While large national advertisers tend to dominate consumer magazine advertising in terms of expenditures, the 2,700 consumer magazines are also important to smaller companies selling products that appeal to specialized markets. Special-interest magazines assemble consumers with similar lifestyles or interests and offer marketers an efficient way to reach these people with little wasted coverage or circulation. For example, a manufacturer of ski or snowboarding equipment such as K2, Rossignol, or Salomon might find *Powder* the best vehicle for advertising to skiers or snowboarders.

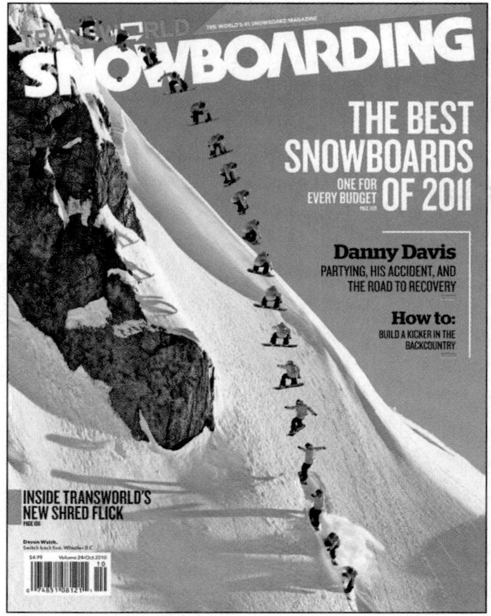


**EXHIBIT 12–2**
*Transworld Snowboarding* magazine is an excellent medium for reaching the serious snowboarder

Not only are these specialty magazines of value to firms interested in reaching a specific market segment, but their editorial content often creates a very favorable advertising environment for relevant products and services. For example, avid skiers and snowboarders cannot wait for the first snowfall after reading the season's first issues of *Transworld Snowboarding* or *Skiing* magazine and may be quite receptive to the ads they carry for skiing and snowboarding products and destination ski resorts (Exhibit 12–2).

**Farm Publications** The consumer SRDS category also consists of all the magazines directed to farmers and their families. About 300 publications are tailored to nearly every possible type of farming or agricultural interest. SRDS breaks farm publications into 9 classifications, ranging from general-interest magazines aimed at all types of farmers (e.g., *Farm Journal, Successful Farming, Progressive Farmer*) to those in specialized agricultural areas such as poultry (*Gobbles*), hog farming (*National Hog Farmer*), or cattle raising (*Beef*—see Exhibit 12–3). A number of farm publications are directed at farmers in specific states or regions, such as *Nebraska Farmer* or *Montana Farmer Stockman.* Farm publications are not classified with business publications because historically farms were not perceived as businesses.

**Business Publications** Business publications are those magazines or trade journals published for specific businesses, industries, or occupations. Standard Rate and Data Service breaks down over 9,300 U.S. magazines and trade journals into more than 220 market classifications. The major classifications include:

**EXHIBIT 12–3**
*Beef* magazine is read by many cattle ranchers

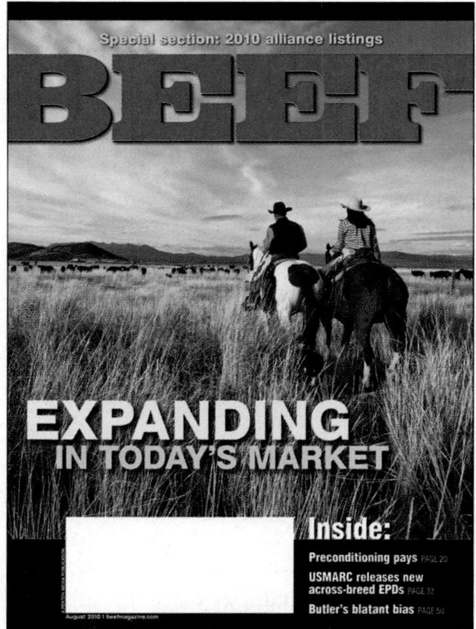


1. Magazines directed at specific professional groups, such as *National Law Review* for lawyers and *Architectural Forum* for architects.
2. Industrial magazines directed at businesspeople in various manufacturing and production industries—for example, *Iron and Steelmaker, Chemical Week,* and *Industrial Engineering.*
3. Trade magazines targeted to wholesalers, dealers, distributors, and retailers, among them *Progressive Grocer, Drug Store News, Women's Wear Daily,* and *Restaurant Business.*
4. General business magazines aimed at executives in all areas of business, such as *Forbes, Fortune,* and *BusinessWeek.* (General business publications are also included in SRDS's consumer publications edition.)
5. Health care publications targeted to various areas including dental, medical and surgical, nursing, biotechnological sciences, and hospital administration.

The numerous business publications reach specific types of professional people with particular interests and give them important information relevant to their industry, occupation, and/or careers. Business publications are important to advertisers because they provide an efficient way of reaching the specific types of individuals who constitute their target market. Much marketing occurs at the trade and business-to-business level, where one company sells its products or services directly to another.

## Advantages of Magazines

Magazines have a number of characteristics that make them attractive as an advertising medium. Strengths of magazines include their selectivity, excellent reproduction quality, creative flexibility, permanence, prestige, readers' high receptivity and involvement, and services they offer to advertisers.

25
25 most notable launches of the last 25 years


**EXHIBIT 12–4**
Magazine expert Samir Husni's 30 most notable magazine launches of the past 2 years

**Selectivity** One of the main advantages of using magazines as an advertising medium is their **selectivity**, or ability to reach a specific target audience. Magazines are the most selective of all media except direct mail. Most magazines are published for special-interest groups. The thousands of magazines published in the United States reach all types of consumers and businesses and allow advertisers to target their advertising to segments of the population who buy their products. For example, *PC World* is targeted toward computer buffs, *Spin* reaches those with an avid interest in music, and *Ebony* focuses on the upscale African-American market. Many new magazines are introduced each year targeting new interests and trends. According to Dr. Samir Husni, who has been tracking magazine launches since 1985, an average of 64 new publications were launched each month in 2009.[4] New consumer magazines are continually being introduced to meet the changing needs, interests, and passions of the public in areas such as sports/recreation, entertainment/celebrity, travel, fashion/apparel, and beauty/grooming. New business publications are also frequently launched to respond to developments in business and industry. Exhibit 12–4 shows the most notable magazine launches of the past 25 years as chosen by Dr. Husni.

In addition to providing selectivity based on interests, magazines can provide advertisers with high demographic and geographic selectivity. *Demographic selectivity,* or the ability to reach specific demographic groups, is available in two ways. First, most magazines are, as a result of editorial content, aimed at fairly well-defined demographic segments. *Ladies' Home Journal, Ms., Self,* and *Cosmopolitan* are read predominantly by women; *Esquire, Playboy,* and *Sports Illustrated* are read mostly by men. Older consumers can be reached through publications like *Modern Maturity.* IMC Perspective 12–1 discusses how celebrity-focused magazines, which are read primarily by women, have become extremely popular in recent years.

A second way magazines offer demographic selectivity is through special editions. Even magazines that appeal to broader audiences, such as *Reader's Digest, Time,* or *Newsweek,* can provide a high degree of demographic selectivity through their special demographic editions. Most of the top consumer magazines publish different editions targeted at different demographic markets.

*Geographic selectivity* lets an advertiser focus ads in certain cities or regions. One way to achieve geographic selectivity is by using a magazine that is targeted toward a particular area. Magazines devoted to regional interests include *Yankee* (New England), *Southern Living* (South), *Sunset* (West), and *Texas Monthly* (guess where?), among many others. One of the more successful media developments of recent years has been the growth of city magazines in most major American cities. *Los Angeles Magazine, Philadelphia,* and *Boston,* to name a few, provide residents of these areas with articles concerning lifestyle, events, and the like, in these cities and

**EXHIBIT 12–5**
City magazines offer advertisers high geographic selectivity

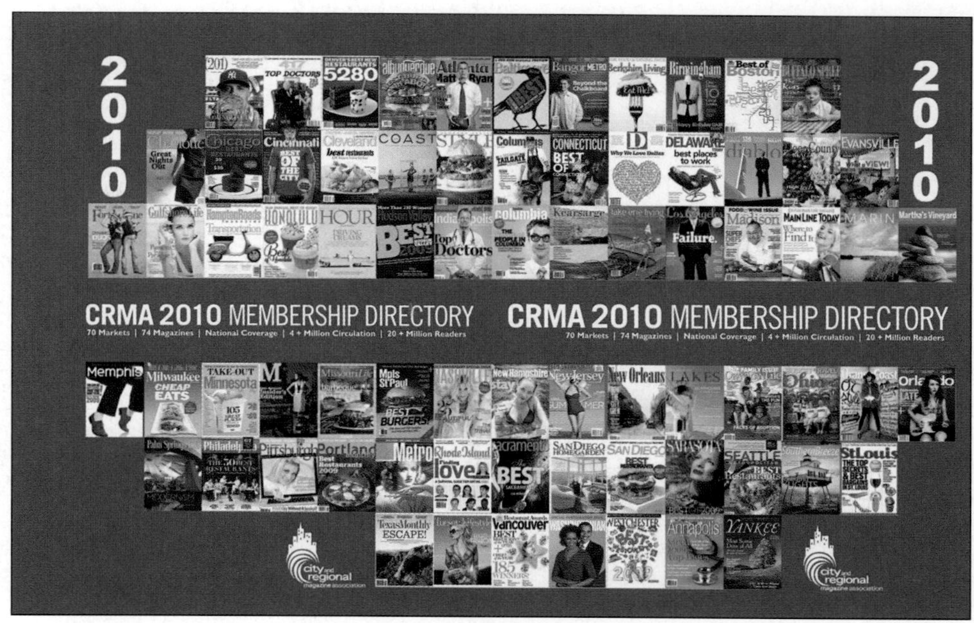




their surrounding metropolitan areas. City and regional magazines make it possible for advertisers to focus on specific local markets that may be of interest to them. They also have a readership profile that appeals to marketers of upscale brands: high income, college educated, loyal, and influential in their communities. Most of these publications belong to the City and Regional Magazine Association which represents magazines in 73 different markets (Exhibit 12–5). An advertiser can run an ad in all of the magazines that belong to the association with one media buy.

Another way to achieve geographic selectivity in magazines is through purchasing ad space in specific geographic editions of national or regional magazines. A number of publications divide their circulation into groupings based on regions or major metropolitan areas and offer advertisers the option of concentrating their ads in these editions. A magazine may break the United States into geographic areas and offer regional editions for each, and/or offer advertisers their choice of editions directed to specific states or metropolitan areas. Many magazines allow advertisers to combine regional or metropolitan editions to best match the geographic market of interest to them.

SRDS lists more than 350 consumer magazines offering geographic and/or demographic editions. Regional advertisers can purchase space in editions that reach only areas where they have distribution, yet still enjoy the prestige of advertising in a major national magazine. National advertisers can use the geographic editions to focus their advertising on areas with the greatest potential or those needing more promotional support. They can also use regional editions to test-market products or alternative promotional campaigns in various regions of the country.

Ads in regional editions can also list the names of retailers or distributors in various markets, thus encouraging greater local support from the trade. The trend toward regional marketing is increasing the importance of having regional media available to marketers. The availability of regional and demographic editions can also reduce the cost per thousand for reaching desired audiences.

**Reproduction Quality** One of the most valued attributes of magazine advertising is the reproduction quality of the ads. Magazines are generally printed on high-quality paper stock and use printing processes that provide excellent reproduction in black and white or color. Since magazines are a visual medium where illustrations

# IMC Perspective 12–1 > > >

## Celebrity Magazines Are Hot

The American public has always been fascinated by celebrities. However, in recent years the interest in celebrities has become an obsession, and magazines that focus on the rich and famous, and sometimes even the infamous, are exploding in popularity. The number of magazines devoted to providing news, information, gossip, and, most important, pictures of celebrities such as Jessica Simpson, Sandra Bullock, Miley Cyrus, Britney Spears, Brad Pitt, Angelina Jolie, and other stars is growing as is their circulation. Magazines such as *US Weekly, In Touch, Star, OK!,* and *Life & Style Weekly* are attracting more readers as well as advertising pages, which translates into more revenue for their publishers.

A number of factors are fueling the growth in the popularity of star-obsessed magazines. Robert Thompson, a professor of popular culture and television at Syracuse University, notes that because our society has no aristocracy, Americans have always been obsessed with celebrity. However, for many years, there were few outlets which served the public's desire for celebrity news and gossip. Television exposure for celebrities was limited to late-night talk shows and an occasional network show such as *The Barbara Walters Special.* Only a few magazines, such as *People,* chronicled the lives of celebrities, as the stars were mostly covered in tabloids such as *The National Enquirer* or *Star.* Although the tabloids were fun to read, many people only scanned them in the supermarket checkout lines and were embarrassed if they were caught actually reading them. However, the growth of cable television and syndication gave rise to numerous programs that focus on celebrities, including *Access Hollywood, Entertainment Tonight, Extra!, Inside Edition,* and *TMZ.*

Magazine industry experts note the growth in the number of celebrity-focused magazines began in 2000 when *US* was transformed from a monthly publication to a weekly. It took a few years for *US Weekly* to connect with its sharply defined target audience of women, but the magazine has found its way to a younger and wealthier audience. Noting the success of *US Weekly,* a number of other celebrity-focused magazines were introduced including *In Touch* in 2002, *Life & Style Weekly* in 2004 , and *OK!,* a celebrity-drenched weekly magazine from the United Kingdom, which was launched in 2005. Several magazines also repositioned themselves to focus more on celebrities. For example, *Star* was transformed from a supermarket tabloid that competed against the *National Enquirer* to an entertainment and celebrity magazine with a glossy format while *TV Guide* also got into the act with a new larger, full-color format and more stories about television shows and the stars who appear in them.

Although celebrity magazines remain very popular, the category's red hot growth has been cooling down over the past several years. In late 2009 *Ok!* magazine cut its circulation guarantee by 100,000 copies or 11 percent of its total. The move followed similar cuts at *Star* and *In Touch Weekly,* and reduced the category's combined paid-circulation guarantee to its lowest point since 2005 and 900,000 copies below its peak in 2007. However,

---

are often a dominant part of an ad, this is a very important property. The reproduction quality of most magazines is far superior to that offered by the other major print medium of newspapers, particularly when color is needed. The use of color has become a virtual necessity in most product categories, and more than two-thirds of all magazine ads now use color. The excellent reproduction quality of magazines provides the opportunity for innovative creative work by agencies. For example, Exhibit 12–6 shows a creative ad created by the GSD&M Idea City agency as part of the campaign used to launch the all-new BMW 1 Series in the North American market.

**Creative Flexibility** In addition to their excellent reproduction capabilities, magazines also offer advertisers a great deal of flexibility in terms of the type, size, and placement of the advertising material. Some magazines offer (often at extra charge) a variety of special options that can enhance the creative appeal of the ad and increase attention and readership. Examples include gatefolds, bleed pages, inserts, and creative space buys.

**Gatefolds** enable an advertiser to make a striking presentation by using a third page that folds out and gives the ad an extra-large spread. Gatefolds are often found at the inside cover of large consumer magazines or on some inside pages. Advertisers use gatefolds to make a very strong impression, especially on special occasions such

the celebrity weeklies held their ground better than most other magazines as their decline in circulation was lower than the drop for women's titles, entertainment magazines, and sports publications. Recently several of the celebrity weeklies have increased their circulation guarantees including *US Weekly* and *Life & Style Weekly.*

While many celebrity weeklies are struggling to maintain circulation numbers, they are finding other ways to reach consumers, and consumers are finding other ways to reach them. Nearly all of the publications now have websites, Facebook pages, and Twitter feeds. For example, Time Inc.'s *People,* which is the category leader with a circulation of 3.6 million, attracts more than 9 million unique visitors each month to its website (People.com) while its Twitter feed has nearly 1.5 million followers. *People* has even created a spin off site, PeoplePets.com whose Twitter account has nearly 800,000 followers. *People* has moved even further into the digital age by launching a Celebrity Tracker app for the Apple iPhone and iPod Touch which brings up the latest news as well as photos and celebrity biographies.

Although celebrity magazines remain popular, industry experts question whether the economics of the business can sustain growth in the category. Unlike other publications which are supported by subscriptions, most celebrity magazines live and die by their newsstand sales. The magazines essentially pay rent to be displayed in racks at grocery stores with other publications and have to pay for the "pockets" even if they do not sell the forecasted number of copies. Magazine newsstand sales have been hit particularly hard during the recession as prices for single copies are generally much higher than subscription based prices.

Many in the magazine industry wonder how long our insatiable appetite for pictures, stories, and gossip about celebrities will continue. Where there are plenty of celebrities to show and write about, there are only a few megastars—such as Jennifer Aniston, Sandra Bullock, Brad Pitt, and Angelia Jolie—who can really move magazines. However, the increased media focus on celebrities seems to make people want to know even more about them. And as long as our celebrity-obsessed society continues to ask for more news about the status of Brad and Angelina's or Sandra Bullock's marriages, Mylie Cyrus' love life, or Jennifer Aniston's future husband, the magazines will be there to make sure we get it.

Sources: Nat Ives, "People Is No. 5 on Ad Age's Magazine A-List," *Advertising Age,* October 19, 2009, http://adage.com/print?article_id-139692; Nat Ives, "Ok Latest Celeb Weekly to Cut Rate Base," *Advertising Age,* September 3, 2009, http://adage.com/print?article_id-138783; Nat Ives, "Going Ga-Ga Over Gossip, *Advertising Age,* February 12, 2007, pp. 4, 29.

as the introduction of a new product or brand. For example, automobile advertisers often use gatefolds to introduce new versions of their cars each model year. Not all magazines offer gatefolds, however, and they must be reserved well in advance and are sold at a premium.

**Bleed pages** are those where the advertisement extends all the way to the end of the page, with no margin of white space around the ad. Bleeds give the ad an impression of being larger and make a more dramatic impact. Many magazines charge an extra 10 to 20 percent for bleeds.

In addition to gatefolds and bleed pages, creative options available through magazines include unusual page sizes and shapes. Some advertisers have grabbed readers' attention by developing three-dimensional pop-up ads that jump off the page. Various other *inserts* are used in many magazines. These include return cards, recipe booklets, coupons, records, and even product samples. Cosmetic companies use scratch-and-sniff inserts to introduce new fragrances, and some companies use them to promote deodorants, laundry detergents, or other products whose scent is important. Inserts are also used in conjunction with direct-response ads and as part of sales promotion strategies.

Scented ads, pop-ups, singing ads, heavy card stock, stickers, and CD-ROMs are among the types of inserts used by advertisers in magazines. Advertisers sometimes

**EXHIBIT 12–6**
This BMW ad utilizes the excellent reproduction quality available through magazines

use special inserts to break through the clutter in magazines and to capture readers' attention. For example, the CW Network also used a very creative insert to promote its new drama show *Supernatural.* The insert appeared in *US Weekly* and *Rolling Stone.* As the insert is opened, a high-quality sound chip is triggered. The illustration of a 1967 Impala comes to life as the headlights illuminate and begin to flicker. And, as a haunting Dave Matthews tune sets the mood, the lead character's dialogue brings their supernatural story to life (Exhibit 12–7). Many magazine publishers are willing to work with advertisers who want to use creative inserts because they are eager to show that magazines can compete with new media as a way to showcase products. While the inserts pose challenges to production staff and printers, these costs along with any extra postage fees are generally passed onto the advertisers. The total cost of manufacturing inserts varies depending on the complexity, weight, assembly requirements, and other factors. Some of the very elaborate inserts can cost advertisers as much as several million dollars.[5]

There has been some backlash against various types of *printaculars.* Critics argue that they alter the appearance and feel of a magazine and the reader's relationship to it. Advertisers do not want to run regular ads that have to compete against heavy inserts, pop-ups, talking ads, or other distractions. Some advertisers and agencies are even asking publishers to notify them when they plan to run any spectacular inserts so that they can decide whether to pull their regular ads from the issue.[6]

*Creative space buys* are another option of magazines. Some magazines let advertisers purchase space units in certain combinations to increase the impact of their media budget. For example, WD-40, an all-purpose lubrication product, uses half- or quarter-page ads on consecutive pages of several magazines, mentioning a different use for the product on each page, as shown in Exhibit 12–8. This strategy gives the company greater impact for its media dollars and is helpful in promoting the product's variety of uses.

**EXHIBIT 12–7**
The CW Network used a creative insert to promote its new drama show *Supernatural*

**Permanence** Another distinctive advantage offered by magazines is their long life span. TV and radio are characterized by fleeting messages that have a very short life span; newspapers are generally discarded soon after being read. Magazines, however, are generally read over several days and are often kept for reference. They are retained in the home longer than any other medium and are generally referred to on several occasions. A study of magazine audiences found that readers devote nearly an hour over a period of two or three days to reading an average magazine.[7] Studies have also found that nearly 75 percent of consumers retain magazines for future reference.[8] One benefit of the longer life of magazines is that reading occurs at a less hurried pace and there is more opportunity to examine ads in considerable detail. This means ads can use longer and more detailed copy, which can be very important for high-involvement and complex products or services. The permanence of magazines also means readers can be exposed to ads on multiple occasions and can pass magazines along to other readers.

**Prestige** Another positive feature of magazine advertising is the prestige the product or service

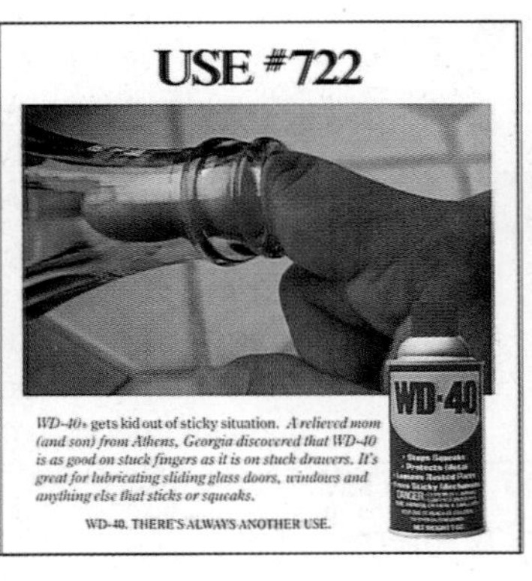


**EXHIBIT 12–8**

WD-40 uses quarter-page ads to get greater impact from its media budget

may gain from advertising in publications with a favorable image. Companies whose products rely heavily on perceived quality, reputation, and/or image often buy space in prestigious publications with high-quality editorial content whose consumers have a high level of interest in the advertising pages. For example, *Esquire* and *GQ* cover men's fashions in a very favorable environment, and a clothing manufacturer may advertise its products in these magazines to enhance the prestige of its lines. *Architectural Digest* provides an impressive editorial environment that includes high-quality photography and artwork. The magazine's upscale readers are likely to have a favorable image of the publication that may transfer to the products advertised on its pages. *Good Housekeeping* has a unique consumer policy which states that if a product bearing its famous seal proves to be defective within two years of purchase, the magazine will replace the product or refund the purchase price. The research division of the company, now known as the Good Housekeeping Research Institute, has been evaluating products for more than a century. The seal may be used only by products whose ads have been reviewed and accepted for publication in *Good Housekeeping*. The seal can increase consumer confidence in a particular brand and reduce the amount of perceived risk associated with a purchase since it really is a money-back guarantee (Exhibit 12–9).[9]

While most media planners recognize that the environment created by a publication is important, it can be difficult to determine the image a magazine provides. Subjective estimates based on media planners' experience are often used to assess a magazine's prestige, as are objective measures such as reader opinion surveys.[10]

**EXHIBIT 12–9**

The *Good Housekeeping* seal gives consumers confidence in products advertised in the magazine

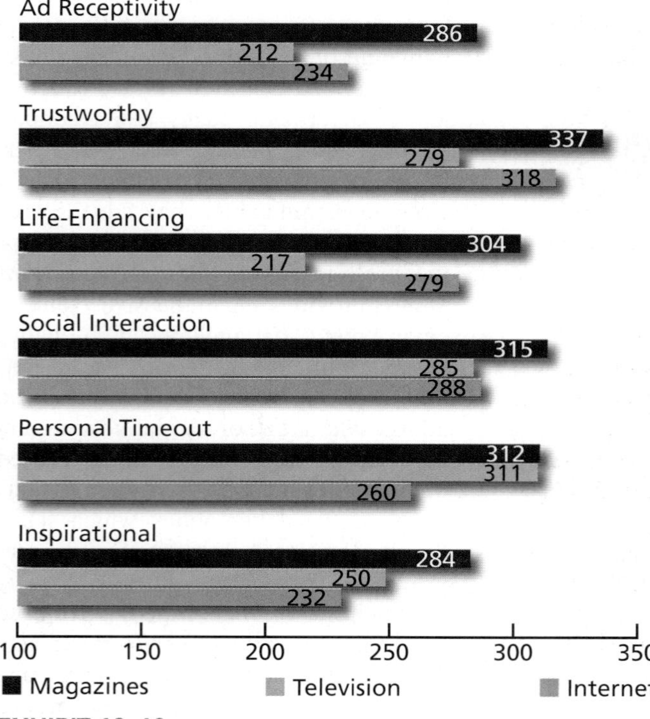


**EXHIBIT 12–10**

Magazines score more favorably than TV or the Internet in consumer engagement

Source: Reprinted with permission from Experian Simmons Multi-Media Engagement Study, 2008 Full-year study.

## Consumer Receptivity and Engagement

With the exception of newspapers, consumers are more receptive to advertising in magazines than in any other medium. Magazines are generally purchased because the information they contain interests the reader, and ads provide additional information that may be of value in making a purchase decision. Studies have shown that magazines are consumers' primary source of information for a variety of products and services, including automobiles, beauty and grooming, clothing and fashion, financial planning, and personal and business travel.[11]

Media planners recognize that one of the major advantages of advertising in magazines is the ability of the medium to engage readers and hold their attention. Numerous studies have shown that consumers become involved with magazines when they read them and are also more likely to find ads acceptable, enjoyable, and even a valuable part of a publication. Intrusive media such as television, radio, and the Internet struggle with problems such as inattention and consumers trying to avoid advertising messages. And as advertisers try harder to get their commercials seen and heard in these media, the more consumers search for ways to tune them out. However, magazine readers recognize that they control the rate and duration of their exposure to editorial content as well as advertisements and view ads as less disruptive to their media consumption experience.

Exhibit 12–10 shows the results of a Multi-Media Engagement study conducted by Simmons which found that magazines score significantly higher than television or the Internet in ad receptivity and other engagement dimensions. Research has shown that engagement with an advertising medium is important because it is directly related to increased advertising recall and specific actions taken such as searching for additional information about an advertiser's brand, visiting its website, saving an ad for future reference, and purchasing a product or service, as well as recommending it to others.

**Services** A final advantage of magazines is the special services some publications offer advertisers. Some magazines have merchandising staffs that call on trade intermediaries like retailers to let them know a product is being advertised in their publication and to encourage them to display or promote the item. Another service offered by magazines (usually the larger ones) is research studies that they conduct on consumers. These studies may deal with general consumer trends, changing purchase patterns, and media usage or may be relevant to a specific product or industry.

An important service offered by some magazines is **split runs**, where two or more versions of an ad are printed in alternate copies of a particular issue of a magazine. This service is used to conduct a split-run test, which allows the advertiser to determine which ad generates the most responses or inquiries, providing some evidence as to their effectiveness. Technological developments have also made it possible for magazines to offer advertisers the opportunity to deliver personalized messages to tightly targeted audiences through selective binding and ink-jet imaging. **Selective binding** is a computerized production process that allows the creation of hundreds of copies of a magazine in one continuous sequence. Selective binding enables magazines to target and address specific groups within a magazine's circulation base. The magazine publishers can then send different editorial or advertising messages to various groups of subscribers within the same issue of a publication. **Ink-jet imaging** reproduces a message by projecting ink onto paper rather than using mechanical plates. This process makes it possible to personalize an advertising message. Many publishers believe selective binding and ink-jet imaging will let advertisers target their messages more finely and let magazines compete more effectively with direct mail and other direct-marketing vehicles.

## Disadvantages of Magazines

Although the advantages offered by magazines are considerable, they have certain drawbacks too. These include the costs of advertising, their limited reach and frequency, the long lead time required in placing an ad, and the problem of clutter and heavy advertising competition.

**Costs** The costs of advertising in magazines vary according to the size of the audience they reach and their selectivity. Advertising in large mass-circulation magazines like *Time, Reader's Digest,* or *Better Homes and Gardens* can be very expensive. For example, a full-page, four-color ad in *Time* magazine's national edition (circulation 3.3 million) cost $287,000 in 2010. Popular positions such as the back cover cost nearly $400,000.

Like any medium, magazines must be considered not only from an absolute cost perspective but also in terms of relative costs. Most magazines emphasize their effectiveness in reaching specific target audiences at a low cost per thousand. Also, an increasing number of magazines are offering demographic and geographic editions, which helps lower their costs. Media planners generally focus on the relative costs of a publication in reaching their target audience. However, they may recommend a magazine with a high cost per thousand because of its ability to reach a small, specialized market segment. Of course, advertisers with limited budgets will be interested in the absolute costs of space in a magazine and the costs of producing quality ads for these publications.

CHAPTER 12

**Limited Reach and Frequency** Magazines are generally not as effective as other media in offering reach and frequency. While nearly 90 percent of adults in the United States read one or more consumer magazines each month, the percentage of adults reading any individual publication tends to be much smaller, so magazines have a thin penetration of households. For example, *Reader's Digest* has the third-highest circulation of any magazine, at 7.6 million, but this represents only 7 percent of the 115 million households in the United States.

As shown in Figure 12–2, only 39 magazines had a paid circulation over 2 million in 2009. Thus, advertisers seeking broad reach must make media buys in a number of magazines, which means more negotiations and transactions. For a broad-reach strategy, magazines are used in conjunction with other media. Since most magazines are monthly or at best weekly publications, the opportunity for building frequency through the use of the same publication is limited. Using multiple ads in the same issue of a publication is an inefficient way to build frequency. Most advertisers try to achieve frequency by adding other magazines with similar audiences to the media schedule.

**Long Lead Time** Another drawback of magazines is the long lead time needed to place an ad. Most major publications have a 30- to 60-day lead time, which means space must be purchased and the ad must be prepared well in advance of the actual publication date. No changes in the art or copy of the ad can be made after the closing date. This long lead time means magazine ads cannot be as timely as other media, such as radio or newspapers, in responding to current events or changing market conditions.

**FIGURE 12–2**

Top 50 Magazines in Average Paid Circulation

| 2009 Rank | Publication Name | 2009 Total Paid & Verified |
|---|---|---|
| 1 | *AARP The Magazine** | 24,463,228 |
| 2 | *AARP Bulletin** | 24,174,159 |
| 3 | *Reader's Digest* | 7,629,105 |
| 4 | *Better Homes And Gardens* | 7,627,992 |
| 5 | *Good Housekeeping* | 4,641,651 |
| 6 | *National Geographic* | 4,602,119 |
| 7 | *Woman's Day* | 3,949,248 |
| 8 | *Family Circle* | 3,874,240 |
| 9 | *Ladies Home Journal* | 3,850,782 |
| 10 | *AAA Westways** | 3,831,215 |
| 11 | *Game Informer Magazine* | 3,703,120 |
| 12 | *People* | 3,614,861 |
| 13 | *Time* | 3,350,415 |
| 14 | *Taste Of Home* | 3,258,915 |
| 15 | *Sports Illustrated* | 3,227,409 |
| 16 | *Prevention* | 3,106,409 |
| 17 | *Cosmopolitan* | 2,954,665 |
| 18 | *Southern Living* | 2,848,107 |
| 19 | *AAA Via** | 2,775,449 |
| 20 | *TV Guide Magazine* | 2,682,799 |
| 21 | *Maxim* | 2,525,432 |
| 22 | *AAA Living* | 2,459,874 |
| 23 | *O, The Oprah Magazine* | 2,438,710 |
| 24 | *AAA Going Places** | 2,438,377 |
| 25 | *Glamour* | 2,419,017 |
| 26 | *Newsweek* | 2,316,590 |
| 27 | *American Legion Magazine** | 2,287,971 |
| 28 | *Remedy/Remedy MD* | 2,275,882 |
| 29 | *Playboy* | 2,275,882 |
| 30 | *Redbook* | 2,224,448 |
| 31 | *Parenting* | 2,186,320 |
| 32 | *FamilyFun* | 2,175,670 |
| 33 | *AAA World** | 2,103,343 |
| 34 | *Seventeen* | 2,075,401 |
| 35 | *ESPN The Magazine* | 2,070,363 |
| 36 | *Parents* | 2,064,249 |
| 37 | *Martha Stewart Living* | 2,061,226 |
| 38 | *Guideposts* | 2,055,606 |
| 39 | *Smithsonian* | 2,023,786 |
| 40 | *Real Simple* | 1,995,625 |
| 41 | *Money* | 1,926,070 |
| 42 | *US Weekly* | 1,924,093 |
| 43 | *Men's Health* | 1,862,937 |
| 44 | *Endless Vacation* | 1,838,685 |
| 45 | *Every Day With Rachael Ray* | 1,801,034 |
| 46 | *Entertainment Weekly* | 1,788,799 |
| 47 | *Cooking Light* | 1,772,793 |
| 48 | *In Style* | 1,763,475 |
| 49 | *Birds & Blooms* | 1,747,499 |
| 50 | *Golf Digest* | 1,676,068 |

*High proportion of title's circulation attributed to membership benefits.

Averages calculated by the MPA from Audit Bureau of Circulations statements for the first and second six months of each year. Domestic titles audited by ABC; annuals, international editions, and comics have been excluded. Totals may not add exactly, due to rounding of averaged numbers.

Source: The Association of Magazine Media, Fact Sheet, www.magazine.org. Reprinted with permission.

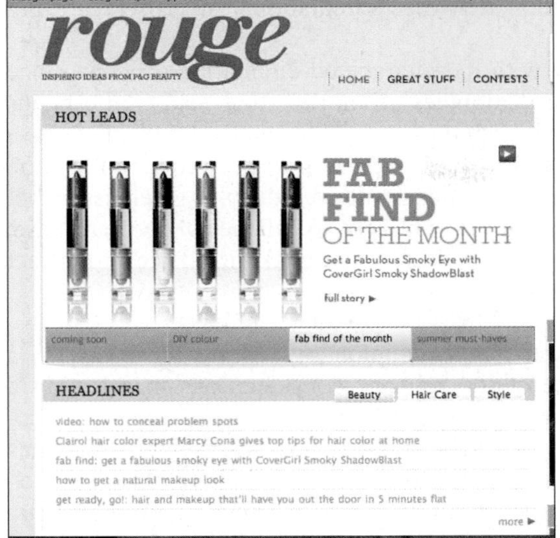


**EXHIBIT 12–11**
*Rouge* is a custom magazine published by Procter & Gamble

**Clutter and Competition** While the problem of advertising clutter is generally discussed in reference to the broadcast media, magazines also have this drawback. The clutter problem for magazines is something of a paradox: The more successful a magazine becomes, the more advertising pages it attracts, and this leads to greater clutter. In fact, magazines generally gauge their success in terms of the number of advertising pages they sell.

Magazine publishers do attempt to control the clutter problem by maintaining a reasonable balance of editorial pages to advertising. According to the Association of Magazine Media, the average consumer magazine contains 47 percent advertising and 53 percent editorial.[12] However, many magazines contain ads on more than half of their pages. This clutter makes it difficult for an advertiser to gain readers' attention and draw them into the ad. Thus, many print ads use strong visual images, catchy headlines, or some of the creative techniques discussed earlier to grab the interest of magazine readers. Some advertisers create their own custom magazines to sidestep the advertising clutter problem as well as to have control over editorial content. A number of companies have also been publishing their own magazines to build relationships with their customers. For example, Farmer's Insurance sends its customers a magazine called *The Friendly Review* that contains useful articles on a variety of topics. Custom-published magazines have also become very popular among tobacco companies, such as Philip Morris, which direct-mail them to their customer base.[13] Some companies have begun offering online versions of their custom magazines. For example, Procter & Gamble began publishing *HomeMadeSimple* several years ago and the custom publication branched into a program on the TLC Network and shopper marketing programs. In late 2009 P&G launched *Rouge* in the U.S. market, a custom published magazine that has been available in Canada since 2005.[14] *Rouge* focuses on beauty and fashion tips and trends and is targeted toward consumers identified as "beauty evolved" who are active in buying beauty products. The magazine publishes a quarterly print edition and is also available online at rougemag.com (Exhibit 12–11). Kraft Foods also publishes an online magazine called *Kraft Food & Family* and the success of the online version led the company to begin offering a print version, which is sent to more than 3 million consumers.[15]

Clutter is not as serious an issue for the print media as for radio or TV, since consumers tend to be more receptive and tolerant of print advertising. They can also control their exposure to a magazine ad simply by turning the page.

## Magazine Circulation and Readership

Two of the most important considerations in deciding whether to use a magazine in the advertising media plan are the size and characteristics of the audience it reaches. Media buyers evaluate magazines on the basis of their ability to deliver the advertiser's message to as many people as possible in the target audience. To do this, they must consider the circulation of the publication as well as its total readership and match these figures against the audience they are attempting to reach.

**Circulation** Circulation figures represent the number of individuals who receive a publication through either subscription or store purchase. The number of copies distributed to these original subscribers or purchasers is known as *primary circulation* and is the basis for the magazine's rate structure. Circulation fluctuates from issue to issue, particularly for magazines that rely heavily on retail or newsstand sales. Many publications base their rates on *guaranteed circulation* and give advertisers a rebate if the number of delivered magazines falls below the guarantee. To minimize rebating, most guaranteed circulation figures are conservative; that is, they are set safely below the average actual delivered circulation. Advertisers are not charged for any excess circulation.

Many publishers became unhappy with the guaranteed circulation concept, since it requires them to provide refunds if guarantees are not met but results in a bonus for advertisers when circulation exceeds the guarantee. Thus, many publications have gone to a circulation rate base system. Rates are based on a set average circulation that is nearly always below the actual circulation delivered by a given issue but carries no guarantee. However, circulation is unlikely to fall below the rate base, since this would reflect negatively on the publication and make it difficult to attract advertisers at prevailing rates.

**Circulation Verification** Given that circulation figures are the basis for a magazine's advertising rates and one of the primary considerations in selecting a publication, the credibility of circulation figures is important. Most major publications are audited by one of the circulation verification services. Consumer magazines and farm publications are audited by the Audit Bureau of Circulations (ABC), which was organized in 1914 and is sponsored by advertisers, agencies, and publishers. ABC collects and evaluates information regarding the subscriptions and sales of magazines and newspapers to verify their circulation figures. Only publications with 70 percent or more paid circulation are eligible for verification audits by ABC. In 2002 the ABC approved new guidelines for counting magazine circulation and sales. The changes did away with the long-standing "50 percent rule," in which copies that sold for less than half of the basic price of a magazine could not be counted as paid circulation. Under the new rules copies sold at any price may be counted, but the magazine must disclose sales and prices in its circulation statements.[16] More than 2,000 business publications are audited by the Business Publications Audit (BPA) of Circulation. Many of these are published on a **controlled-circulation basis**, meaning copies are sent (usually free) to individuals the publisher believes can influence the company's purchases.

Circulation verification services provide media planners with reliable figures regarding the size and distribution of a magazine's circulation that help them evaluate its worth as a media vehicle. The ABC statement also provides other important information. It shows how a magazine is distributed by state and size, as well as percentage of the circulation sold at less than full value and percentage arrears (how many subscriptions are being given away). Many advertisers believe that subscribers who pay for a magazine are more likely to read it than are those who get it at a discount or for free.

Circulation verification has come under very close scrutiny over the past two years as circulation scandals emerged at several high-profile magazines and newspapers. *PC Magazine,* for example, was discovered to have misclassified 320,000 subscriptions as "paid," which resulted in the publication overestimating its rate base by as much as 21 percent.[17] Disclosure regarding overstatements of circulation contributed to the demise of *YM* magazine, which ceased publication at the end of 2004. Problems have also been found in the newsstand sales reported by other magazines, which have led advertisers to more closely scrutinize the circulation numbers used by magazines.[18]

Media buyers are generally skeptical about publications whose circulation figures are not audited by one of the verification services, and some companies will not advertise in unaudited publications. Circulation data, along with the auditing source, are available from SRDS or from the publication itself. Exhibit 12–12 shows a sample magazine publisher's statement, which is subject to audit by the Audit Bureau of Circulations.

**Readership and Total Audience** Advertisers are often interested in the number of people a publication reaches as a result of secondary, or pass-along, readership. **Pass-along readership** can occur when the primary subscriber or purchaser gives a

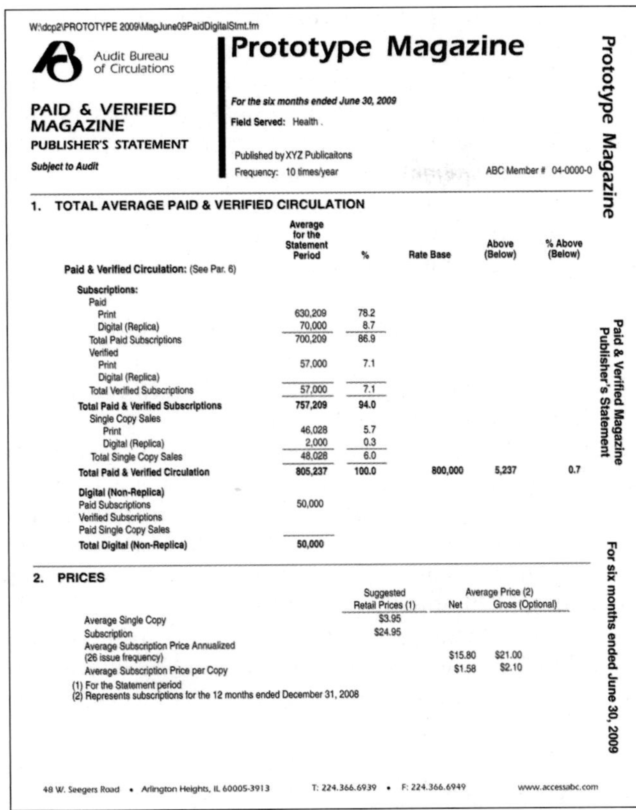

W:\dcp2\PROTOTYPE 2009\MagJune09PaidDigitalStmt.fm

Audit Bureau of Circulations

**PAID & VERIFIED MAGAZINE**
**PUBLISHER'S STATEMENT**
*Subject to Audit*

# Prototype Magazine

***For the six months ended June 30, 2009***

**Field Served:** Health .

Published by XYZ Publicaitons
Frequency: 10 times/year

ABC Member # 04-0000-0

Prototype Magazine

**1. TOTAL AVERAGE PAID & VERIFIED CIRCULATION**

| | Average for the Statement Period | % | Rate Base | Above (Below) | % Above (Below) |
|---|---|---|---|---|---|
| **Paid & Verified Circulation:** (See Par. 6) | | | | | |
| **Subscriptions:** | | | | | |
| Paid | | | | | |
| Print | 630,209 | 78.2 | | | |
| Digital (Replica) | 70,000 | 8.7 | | | |
| Total Paid Subscriptions | 700,209 | 86.9 | | | |
| Verified | | | | | |
| Print | 57,000 | 7.1 | | | |
| Digital (Replica) | | | | | |
| Total Verified Subscriptions | 57,000 | 7.1 | | | |
| **Total Paid & Verified Subscriptions** | **757,209** | **94.0** | | | |
| Single Copy Sales | | | | | |
| Print | 46,028 | 5.7 | | | |
| Digital (Replica) | 2,000 | 0.3 | | | |
| Total Single Copy Sales | 48,028 | 6.0 | | | |
| **Total Paid & Verified Circulation** | **805,237** | **100.0** | **800,000** | **5,237** | **0.7** |
| **Digital (Non-Replica)** | | | | | |
| Paid Subscriptions | 50,000 | | | | |
| Verified Subscriptions | | | | | |
| Paid Single Copy Sales | | | | | |
| **Total Digital (Non-Replica)** | **50,000** | | | | |

Paid & Verified Magazine
Publisher's Statement

**2. PRICES**

| | Suggested Retail Prices (1) | Average Price (2) Net | Gross (Optional) |
|---|---|---|---|
| Average Single Copy | $3.95 | | |
| Subscription | $24.95 | | |
| Average Subscription Price Annualized (26 issue frequency) | | $15.80 | $21.00 |
| Average Subscription Price per Copy | | $1.58 | $2.10 |

(1) For the Statement period
(2) Represents subscriptions for the 12 months ended December 31, 2008

For six months ended June 30, 2009

48 W. Seegers Road • Arlington Heights, IL 60005-3913 T: 224.366.6939 • F: 224.366.6949 www.accessabc.com

**3. PAID & VERIFIED CIRCULATION BY ISSUE OF PRINT AND DIGITAL REPLICA**

| Issue | Paid Subscriptions: Print | Digital (Replica) | Total Paid Subscriptions | Verified Subscriptions: Print | Digital (Replica) | Total Verified Subscriptions | Total Paid & Verified Subscriptions | Single Copy Sales: Print | Digital (Replica) | Total Single Copy Sales | Total Paid & Verified Circulation Print | Total Paid & Verified Circulation Digital (Replica) | Total Paid & Verified Circulation |
|---|---|---|---|---|---|---|---|---|---|---|---|---|---|
| Jan. | 632,381 | 70,000 | 702,381 | 57,000 | | 57,000 | 759,381 | 44,228 | 2,000 | 46,228 | 733,609 | 72,000 | 805,609 |
| Feb. | 631,848 | 70,000 | 701,848 | 57,000 | | 57,000 | 758,848 | 44,601 | 2,000 | 46,601 | 733,449 | 72,000 | 805,449 |
| Mar. | 629,100 | 70,000 | 699,100 | 57,000 | | 57,000 | 756,100 | 46,436 | 2,000 | 48,436 | 732,536 | 72,000 | 804,536 |
| Apr. | 626,899 | 70,000 | 696,899 | 57,000 | | 57,000 | 753,899 | 49,602 | 2,000 | 51,602 | 733,501 | 72,000 | 805,501 |
| May/June | 630,818 | 70,000 | 700,818 | 57,000 | | 57,000 | 757,818 | 45,273 | 2,000 | 47,273 | 733,091 | 72,000 | 805,091 |

**3A. PAID & VERIFIED CIRCULATION BY MONTH OF DIGITAL NON-REPLICA**

| Issue | Paid Subscriptions | Verified Subscriptions | Total Paid & Verified Subscriptions | Single Copy Sales | Total Paid & Verified Circulation |
|---|---|---|---|---|---|
| Jan. | 40,000 | | 40,000 | | 40,000 |
| Feb. | 40,000 | | 40,000 | | 40,000 |
| Mar. | 40,000 | | 40,000 | | 40,000 |
| Apr. | 60,000 | | 60,000 | | 60,000 |
| May | 60,000 | | 60,000 | | 60,000 |
| June | 60,000 | | 60,000 | | 60,000 |

**4. AVERAGE CIRCULATION BY REGIONAL, METRO & DEMOGRAPHIC EDITIONS**

| Edition | Number of Issues | Paid Subscriptions: Print | Digital (Replica) | Total Paid Sub-scriptions | Verified Subscriptions: Print | Digital (Replica) | Total Verified Subscrip-tions | Total Paid & Verified Subscrip-tions | Single Copy Sales: Print | Digital (Replica) | Total Single Copy Sales | Total Paid & Verified Circulation (Print) | Total Paid & Verified Circulation Digital (Replica) | Total Paid & Verified Circulation | Rate Base |
|---|---|---|---|---|---|---|---|---|---|---|---|---|---|---|---|
| South | 5 | 130,200 | | 130,200 | | | | 130,200 | | | | 130,200 | | 130,200 | |
| Northeast | 5 | 170,100 | | 170,100 | | | | 170,100 | | | | 170,100 | | 170,100 | |

**5. TREND ANALYSIS**

| | 2003 | % | 2004 | % | 2005 | % | 2006 | % | 2007 | % |
|---|---|---|---|---|---|---|---|---|---|---|
| **Subscriptions:** | | | | | | | | | | |
| Paid | 750,211 | 94.9 | 755,025 | 95.0 | 755,312 | 94.9 | 750,105 | 93.7 | 757,212 | 94.0 |
| Verified | | | | | | | | | | |
| **Total Paid & Verified Subscriptions** | **750,211** | **94.9** | **755,025** | **95.0** | **755,312** | **94.9** | **750,105** | **93.7** | **757,212** | **94.0** |
| Single Copy Sales | 40,101 | 5.1 | 40,210 | 5.0 | 45,311 | 5.1 | 50,101 | 6.3 | 48,211 | 6.0 |
| **Total Paid & Verified Circulation** | **790,312** | **100.0** | **795,235** | **100.0** | **800,623** | **100.0** | **800,206** | **100.0** | **805,423** | **100.0** |
| Year Over Year Percent of Change | | 0.5 | | 0.6 | | 0.7 | | 0.0 | | 0.7 |
| Avg. Annualized Subscription Price | $15.90 | | $15.40 | | $15.75 | | $15.23 | | $15.80 | |

Page 2 of 6 - Prototype Magazine (04-0000-0)
Copyright © 2009 Audit Bureau of Circulations. All rights reserved.

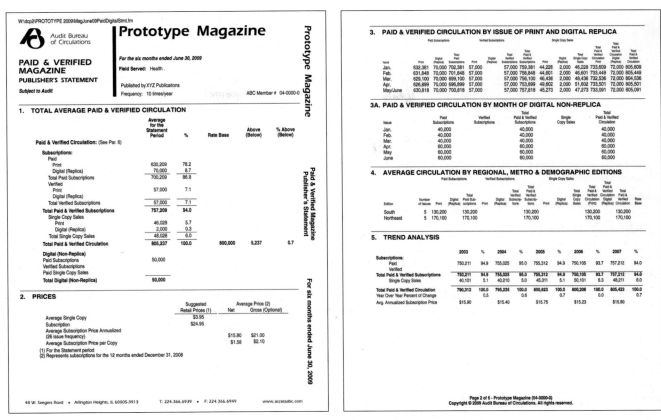

**EXHIBIT 12–12**
Example of an Audit Bureau of Circulations publisher's statement
Source: Reprinted with permission of Audit Bureau of Circulations.

CHAPTER 12

magazine to another person or when the publication is read in doctors' waiting rooms or beauty salons, on airplanes, and so forth.

Advertisers generally attach greater value to the primary in-home reader than the pass-along reader or out-of-home reader, as the former generally spends more time with the publication, picks it up more often, and receives greater satisfaction from it. Thus, this reader is more likely to be attentive and responsive to ads. However, the value of pass-along readers should not be discounted. They can greatly expand a magazine's readership. *People* magazine commissioned a media research study to determine that its out-of-home audience spends as much time reading the publication as do its primary in-home readers.

You can calculate the **total audience**, or **readership**, of a magazine by multiplying the readers per copy (the total number of primary and pass-along readers) by the circulation of an average issue. For example, a magazine such as *Time* may have a circulation base of 3.3 million but an audience of over 19 million readers since it has a high pass-along rate that yields up to six readers per copy. However, rate structures are generally based on the more verifiable primary circulation figures, and many media planners devalue pass-along readers by as much as 50 percent. Total readership estimates are reported by major syndicated magazine research services (discussed next), but media buyers view these numbers with suspicion.

## Audience Information and Research for Magazines

A very valuable source for information on magazines is SRDS, whose print and online service provides complete planning information on domestic and international consumer magazines as well as business and health care trade publications. The SRDS Media Solutions proprietary database contains standardized ad rates, circulation figures, dates, general requirements, contact information, and links to online media kits, websites, and audit statements that provide additional information on readership and positioning. Exhibit 12–13 shows an example of a profile for *Fitness* magazine from SRDS.

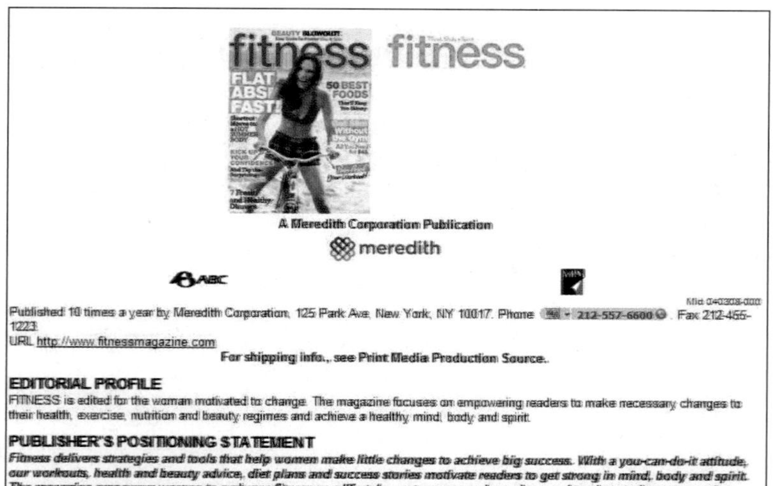

fitness

A Meredith Corporation Publication

meredith

Mid 040308-000

Published 10 times a year by Meredith Corporation, 125 Park Ave, New York, NY 10017. Phone 212-557-6600. Fax 212-455-1223

URL http://www.fitnessmagazine.com

For shipping info., see Print Media Production Source.

**EDITORIAL PROFILE**

FITNESS is edited for the woman motivated to change. The magazine focuses on empowering readers to make necessary changes to their health, exercise, nutrition and beauty regimes and achieve a healthy mind, body and spirit.

**PUBLISHER'S POSITIONING STATEMENT**

*Fitness delivers strategies and tools that help women make little changes to achieve big success. With a you-can-do-it attitude, our workouts, health and beauty advice, diet plans and success stories motivate readers to get strong in mind, body and spirit. The magazine empowers women to embrace fitness as a lifestyle – not an age or dress size – and to change the conversation from "skinny" to "healthy."*

**EXHIBIT 12–13**
Information about magazines is available from SRDS

While circulation and total audience size are important in selecting a media vehicle, the media planner is also interested in the match between the magazine's readers and the advertiser's target audience. Information on readers is available from several sources, including the publication's own research and syndicated studies. Most magazines provide media planners with reports detailing readers' demographics, financial profile, lifestyle, and product usage characteristics. The larger the publication, the more detailed and comprehensive the information it usually can supply about its readers.

Syndicated research studies are also available. For consumer magazines, primary sources of information are Experian Simmons and the studies of Mediamark Research Inc. (MRI). These studies provide a broad range of information on the audiences of major national and regional magazines, including demographics, lifestyle characteristics, and product purchase and usage data. Most large ad agencies and media buying services also conduct ongoing research on the media habits of consumers. All this information helps determine the value of various magazines in reaching particular types of product users.

Audience information is generally more limited for business publications than for consumer magazines. The widely dispersed readership and nature of business publication readers make audience research more difficult. Media planners generally rely on information provided by the publication or by sources such as Business Publication Audits, which provide the titles of individuals who receive the publication and the type of industry in which they work. This information can be of value in understanding the audiences reached by various business magazines.

## Purchasing Magazine Advertising Space

**Cost Elements** Magazine rates are primarily a function of circulation. Other variables include the size of the ad, its position in the publication, the particular editions (geographic, demographic) chosen, any special mechanical or production requirements, and the number and frequency of insertions.

Advertising space is generally sold on the basis of space units such as full page, half page, and quarter page, although some publications quote rates on the basis of column inches. The larger the ad, the greater the cost. However, many advertisers use full-page ads since they result in more attention and readership. Studies have found that full-page ads generated 30 percent more readership than half-page ads.[19]

Ads can be produced or run using black and white, black and white plus one color, or four colors. The more color used in the ad, the greater the expense because of the increased printing costs. On average, a four-color ad costs 30 percent more than a black-and-white ad. Advertisers generally prefer color ads because they have greater visual impact and are superior for attracting and holding attention.[20] Roper Starch Worldwide analyzed the effect of various factors on the readership of magazine ads. The "noted" scores (the percentage of readers who remember seeing the ad in a publication they read) are anywhere from 6 to 59 percent higher for a four-color full-page ad than for a black-and-white ad, depending on the product category. "Read-most" scores (the percentage who say they read more than half of the copy of an ad) are also higher for four-color versus black-and-white ads, by about 25 percent on average.[21] Other studies have examined the impact of size and color and found

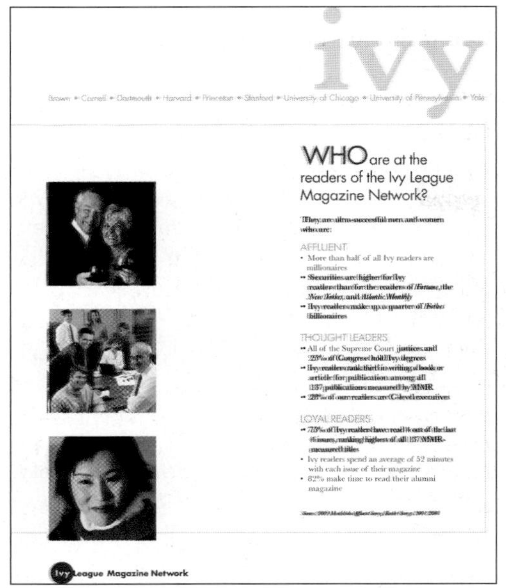


**EXHIBIT 12–14**
Advertisers can reach alumni of Ivy League schools through the Ivy League Network

that a four-color spread (two facing pages) outperforms a one-page color ad by 30 percent and a black-and-white spread by 35 percent in terms of ad recall.[22] Ads requiring special mechanical production such as bleed pages or inserts may also cost extra.

Rates for magazine ad space can also vary according to the number of times an ad runs and the amount of money spent during a specific period. The more often an advertiser contracts to run an ad, the lower are the space charges. Volume discounts are based on the total space purchased within a contract year, measured in dollars. Advertisers can also save money by purchasing advertising in magazine combinations, or networks.

**Magazine networks** offer the advertiser the opportunity to buy space in a group of publications as a package deal. The publisher usually has a variety of magazines that reach audiences with similar characteristics. Networks can also be publishers of a group of magazines with diversified audiences or independent networks that sell space in groups of magazines published by different companies. For example, the News Network sells space in a group of news-oriented publications such as *Time, Newsweek,* and *U.S. News & World Report.* The Ivy League Magazine Network is a consortium of alumni magazines of Ivy League schools and two non-Ivies, Stanford University and the University of Chicago. Advertisers can purchase ad space and reach the well-educated, affluent alumni of all nine schools with one media purchase through the network (Exhibit 12–14).

## The Future for Magazines

Like other major advertising media, magazines are strongly impacted by the economy and the increases and decreases in ad spending that occur with changes in economic situations. The past several years have been very difficult for the magazine industry; many publications experienced reductions in revenue as advertisers cut back on spending due to the recession.[23] Many publications saw their number of advertising pages decline and found it difficult to raise their rates to offset the reduction in ad pages. And while advertising revenue has been decreasing, publishers' other major revenue stream, circulation, has also been declining.

A number of magazines that have been published for many years have gone out of business recently including *Gourmet* (68 years), *I.D. Magazine* (55 years), *Metropolitan Home* (28 years), *Vibe* (17 years), and *Blender* (8 years).[24] Several other magazines have also ceased publishing their print editions and now offer their magazines online. For example, *Teen People* shut down its print edition in 2007 and is now published only online, while a sharp decline in advertising pages led Ziff Davis to end *PC Magazine*'s 27 years in print in 2009 and make it a digital publication.[25]

While the health of the economy has a major impact on the magazine industry, there are a number of other important issues facing the industry. The costs of paper and ink continue to rise, and the industry has had to weather several significant increases in postal rates in recent years, which have had a major impact on their cost structure.[26] Magazines are also facing strong competition from other media such as television, the Internet, and direct mail. Ethical Perspective 12–1 discusses how many magazines are facing pressure from advertisers to offer them the opportunity for more creative ways to promote their products, some of which threaten the traditional church-and-state divide between editorial versus advertising. Publishers are looking at a number of ways to improve their position—including stronger editorial platforms, better circulation management, cross-magazine and media deals, database marketing, technological advances, and electronic delivery methods—to make advertising in magazines more appealing to marketers.

# Ethical Perspective 12–1 > > >

## Should Ads Be on the Cover of a Magazine?

As it becomes increasingly difficult to reach consumers with traditional advertising messages, many marketers have been turning to alternative ways to promote their products and services. Product placement is very common in movies and TV shows and brands have seeped into video games, websites, and even the plots of novels. Marketers also have been finding ways to more effectively integrate advertising messages and content in magazines such as by running ads next to magazine stories about the same product or service, getting products mentioned in stories, creating contests linked to magazines, and running ads that look like magazine layouts. However, recently marketers have begun taking their efforts to make an impact in print to a new level by making their ads part of the cover of a magazine.

The front cover of a magazine has always been considered sacred editorial space and off limits to advertisers. Over the past few years a number of publications have allowed marketers to use techniques such as putting tabs on the front cover that readers could pull to reveal inserts or ads tucked inside. However, in April 2009, *ESPN The Magazine* published an issue with a cover that was half-obscured by a blank flap that said "You Wouldn't Settle for an Incomplete Cover." Opening the flap revealed the remainder of the cover along with a Gatorade ad that finished the thought: "Then Don't Settle for an Incomplete Drink." A cover of *Scholastic Parent & Child* magazine published that same month went all the way and published an ad directly on its cover and has been running cover ads for various brands such as Juicy Juice, SunnyD Smoothies, and PediaSure almost every month since then.

Magazine publishers have become more open to running ads on their covers as many have been experiencing a reduction in ad pages because of the recession, which has taken a chunk out of many companies' advertising budgets, along with competition from digital and other media. Advertisers using cover ads argue that they are trying to break through the clutter and come up with more creative media solutions for magazines just like they are doing in other media. However, critics argue that they are threatening one of the most important assets of a magazine—its relationship with readers.

The church-and-state divide of editorial versus advertising has always been important; magazine and newspaper publishers regard the separation as essential to their independence and credibility. For years the American Society of Magazine Editors (ASME) has maintained guidelines upholding that separation. ASME Guidelines state that ad pages should not be related to editorial material in a manner that implies editorial endorsement, "including advertising that features the same celebrity or product image as the cover image." The guidelines also state that no ad or promotional contest may be promoted on the cover or in the table of contents, including cover stickers and other inserts; ad pages should look distinctly different than editorial pages, and if they don't they must be "clearly and conspicuously identified as a message paid for by advertisers." Although the ASME has no formal means to enforce its guidelines, it does preside over the annual National Magazine awards which are highly valued in the magazine industry. A magazine that violates the guidelines risks being declared ineligible for the awards or expelled from the society.

Some industry experts point out that these are limited sanctions and there is really very little the ASME can do to prevent breaches of its guidelines. However, the society has reaffirmed its position by publishing a new statement on its website that reads: *The front cover and spine are editorial space. Companies and products should appear on covers only in an editorial context and not in a way that sug-*

**EXHIBIT 12–15**
ESPN The Magazine has been very successful in attracting the male audience

**Stronger Editorial Platforms** Magazines with strong editorial platforms that appeal to the interests, lifestyles, and changing demographics of consumers as well as business and market trends are in the best position to attract readers and advertisers. For example, general news publications such as *Time* and *Newsweek,* as well as broadly focused business magazines such as *Forbes, Fortune,* and *BusinessWeek,* have been struggling during the recession and have experienced declines in circulation as well as advertising pages.[27] However, fashion and lifestyle magazines targeted to women such as *Vogue, Glamour,* and *Women's Health* have done well as have well-targeted men's publications such as *Esquire, Men's Journal* and *ESPN The Magazine*[28] (Exhibit 12–15).

**Circulation Management** One of the major challenges facing magazine publishers is trying to increase or even maintain their circulation bases. Circulation is the second major source of revenue for most publications, and publishers must carefully manage the costs of attracting and maintaining additional readers or subscribers. The cost of acquiring subscriptions has increased dramatically over the past decade. At the same time, there has been a decline in the prices consumers pay for subscriptions for many magazines.[29] Thus, publishers have

*gests advertisement.* The statement notes that the cover is the most important editorial page as well as a brand statement and says: "Advertising on the cover suggests editorial endorsement of advertised products, indicates that editorial coverage is for sale, and threatens editorial independence."

The magazine industry recognizes that it is important to adhere to the ASME standards to maintain the integrity of their publications. However, while publishers recognize that they must maintain the separation, they are increasingly been pressured by some advertisers to break down or breach the advertising/editorial divide. Marketers argue that they need more creative media solutions and have to be able to prove that magazine advertising can increase brand recognition or help boost sales. And research shows that cover ads work very well and often outperform magazines' other premium positions such as back covers and gatefolds. Studies conducted on three *Scholastic Parent & Child* covers showed that on average, they generated some action among 73 percent of readers such as saving the ad for future reference, visiting a website or store, or buying the product or service. This figure exceeds the magazine's average action scores for other premium positions over the past three years such as 66 percent for either the back cover or the inside front cover, and 65 percent for the inside back cover. The front cover ads also averaged a 78 percent total recall score which was the best of any premium position in the magazine and nearly 10 points higher than ads on the back cover and on the page opposite the table of contents.

The pressure on magazines to respond to the demands of marketers to allow a mixing of advertising with content is getting greater, particularly since some publications are facing declines in circulation. Industry executives argue that magazines will have to adapt to remain competitive and need more flexibility to compete with other media. For example, nearly all of the major newspapers have been selling ads on their front pages for several years, despite decades of concern that advertising there would damage their journalistic integrity. Critics will continue to argue that the church-and-state division lies at the heart of what magazines sell to their readers, as well as the advertisers themselves. However, what the advertisers really want is for magazine readers to notice their ads, and when they are on the cover there is little doubt people will do so.

Source: Nat Ives, "Cover Ads Often Outperform Magazines' Other Premium Spots," *Advertising Age*, February 10, 2010, http://adage.com/print?article_id=142035; Nat Ives, "ASME Calls ESPN, EW on the Carpet over Covers," *Advertising Age*, April 10, 2009, http://adage.com/print?article_id=135911; Nat Ives, "Magazines Eager to Do 'Creative' Covers for Advertisers," *Advertising Age*, April 1, 2009, http://adage.com/print?article_id=135726; "Ads on Covers? ASME Says No," April 8, 2009, http://www.magazine.org/asme/statement-on-cover.aspx.



to pay more to maintain their rate bases (the circulation level guaranteed to advertisers), but they make less money on each subscription sold.

Publishers are also facing a drop in sweepstakes-generated circulation as a result of the controversy that developed over consumer confidence in the sweepstakes-related subscription offers. Agents such as Publishers Clearing House have been going through changes, both self-imposed and externally dictated, that have greatly reduced the number of subscriptions they generate for publishers. To compensate for losses from sweepstakes agents, publishers are looking to other methods of generating subscribers, such as making subscriptions available through websites, offering free trial copies online, conducting special promotions, or using other agents such as school-related subscription services.[30] Some publications such as *InStyle* have begun selling magazine subscriptions on Facebook by allowing users of the social media site to expand blurbs of magazine content that are common in news feeds into full articles that contain ads as well as options to subscribe.[31]

Many magazines are also focusing more attention on managing their circulation bases. For many years, magazines focused on increasing their circulation under the assumption that higher circulation meant higher advertising rates. However, publishers are now realizing that the cost of attracting and maintaining the last 10 to 15 percent of their circulation base is often greater than the additional revenue generated, since these subscribers require numerous direct-mail solicitations, premium offers, or discount subscriptions.

# IMC Perspective 12–2 > > >

## Magazine Publishers Take on the Internet

Media experts recognize that one of the major advantages of advertising in magazines is the ability of the medium to engage readers and hold their attention. Numerous studies have shown that consumers become involved with magazines when they read them and are also more likely to find ads acceptable, enjoyable, and even a valuable part of the publication. Intrusive media such as television and radio struggle with problems such as inattention and consumers trying to avoid the advertising messages they contain, while consumers often ignore the banner ads that are prevalent on the Internet and rarely click on them. And as advertisers try harder to get their commercials and/or banner ads seen and heard, the more consumers search for ways to tune them out. However, magazine readers recognize that they control the rate and duration of their exposure to editorial content as well as advertisements and view ads as less disruptive to their media consumption experience.

While magazine publishers have always promoted these inherent advantages of magazines as an advertising medium, they recently decided that it was time to go on the offensive and promote them more extensively. In 2010, five leading magazine publishers including Conde Nast, Hearst Magazines, Meredith Corporation, Time Inc., and Wenner Media joined forces and launched one of the largest print campaigns ever created to promote the value of magazines as an advertising medium. The tagline for the campaign is "Magazines, The Power of Print" and was created by Y&R New York and is supported by the Association of Magazine Media, the industry association that represents consumer magazines and works closely with them to represent their interests.

The campaign targets the marketing and advertising community including advertisers, media decision makers, and other industry influencers, as well as consumers and seeks to reshape the image of magazines and challenge misperceptions about the medium's relevance and longevity as well as to reinforce their cultural role. The impetus for the campaign was a "manifesto" written in 2009 by Jann Wenner of Wenner Media, whose publications include *Rolling Stone, US Weekly,* and *Men's Journal.* Wenner noted that just as TV did not kill magazines, the Internet was a threat only to publications that lost focus on what makes magazines unique. He argued that "Magazines have enduring value for readers and advertisers that have gotten a little neglected and misunderstood in the era of Internet instant buzz and chatter. Magazines are beloved and powerful in people's lives for very good reasons that need to be remembered and reinforced."

The primary goal of the campaign is to promote the vitality of magazines and the idea that they remain an effective advertising medium in the age of the Internet because of the depth and lasting quality of print compared with the fleeting nature of much of the Web's content. The campaign is also designed to remind people that many of the popular digital brands are rooted in print publications which have tremendous cultural and commercial influence. The campaign debuted with four-

A number of magazines have reduced their circulation base in recent years. Many publishers believe they can pass on price increases more easily to their core readers or subscribers and offer advertisers a more loyal and focused audience. Many advertisers welcome the improvement in circulation management. They would rather reach a few hundred thousand fewer subscribers than pay for inefficient circulation and be hit with advertising rate increases each year. Many magazines are also using the monies saved on the circulation side to improve the editorial content of their publications, which should attract more readers—and advertisers.

While magazine publishers are working to manage their circulation, some publishers are moving beyond circulation guarantees and taking steps to ensure advertisers that ads run in their publications will work. For example, Time Inc. is collaborating with one of the largest buyers of advertising space in its publications, Starcom MediaVest Group, to develop guarantees that certain numbers of consumers will remember ads run in its magazines and/or take action on them. The effort is being called the Alliance for Magazine Accountability and will use performance data from outside companies such as Affinity's Vista Service and Mediamark Research as part of the effort.[32]

**Online Delivery Methods** Many magazines are keeping pace with the digital revolution and the continuing consumer interest in technology by making their publications available online. According to the Association of Magazine Media, there were 15,204 magazines with websites in 2009 including nearly 7,500 consumer magazine websites.[33] The number of consumer and business magazine websites has color spreads prominently placed in the front one-fifth of the publishers' top magazines that use iconic images lifted from the pages of the best known publications. For example, the first ad in the campaign featured a photo of swimmer Michael Phelps from *ESPN The Magazine* with the headline "We Surf the Internet. We Swim in Magazines." The ad is accompanied by copy discussing the appeal of magazines. The second phase of the campaign uses ads that embed multiple cover images from widely recognized publications into the ad's text to convey key phrases. The campaign includes three other essay-type ads as well as three that are more light-hearted. A special "Magazines" logo was also created for the campaign by combining the distinctive typographies of multiple magazine logos: "M" from *Time*, "A" from *Vanity Fair*, "G" from *Rolling Stone*, "A" from *Entertainment Weekly*, "Z" from *Harper's Bazaar*, "I" from *Marie Claire*, "N" from *Fortune*, and "ES" from *Esquire*.

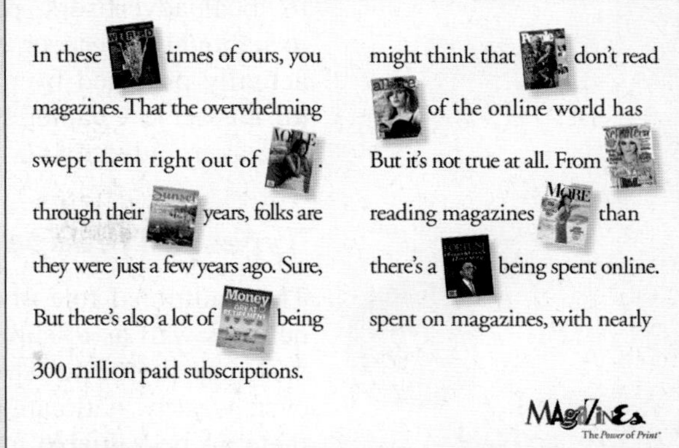


The magazine industry will continue to be challenged by the Internet as marketers continue to shift more of their advertising budgets away from traditional media. However, advertising has begun creeping back into magazines after a two-year drought which provides the industry with more ammunition to persuade readers and advertisers that the industry is not dying. The publishers cite other metrics in support of the campaign's message such as the fact that magazine readership has increased by 4.3 percent over the past five years, the number of average paid subscriptions reached nearly 300 million in 2009, and magazine effectiveness is growing as ad recall has increased 13 percent over the past five years. Hearst Magazines president Cathie Black notes that "Magazines are the most cost effective and consistent medium at both ends of the purchase funnel. They drive consumer attitudes and intended behavior more effectively and efficiently than television advertising alone or when TV is combined with online advertising."

In his message to his fellow publishers, Wenner argued that the industry sat back for way too long and listened to criticism that magazines were losing their relevance without doing anything about it. His colleagues are definitely heeding his call to action as the five magazine publishers are devoting advertising space valued at more than $90 million to the "Power of Print" campaign. Wenner notes that magazines sit on top of one of the greatest mediums and they plan to tell everyone that they remain relevant, even in the Internet age.

Sources: Russell Adams and Shira Ovide, "Magazine Team Up to Tout 'Power of Print'," *The Wall Street Journal*, March 1, 2010, p. B4; "Magazine Publishers Unite & Unveil Industry-Wide Ad Campaign Promotion Strength of and Consumer Commitment to Magazines," *PRNewswire*, March 1, 2010, http://multivu.prnewswire.com/mnr/magazines/42679.



nearly doubled over the past five years. Online versions of magazines offer the many advantages of the Internet to publishers as well as advertisers. They provide advertisers with the opportunity for sponsorships as well as running video and banner ads and promotions on the online versions of the magazines. More and more people are becoming comfortable with reading magazines online rather than in traditional print form, which is leading many publications to expand beyond their basic print publications. A number of publishers are extending their magazine brands to include online, social networking, mobile, and user-generated content, which provides increasing readership as well as advertising reach opportunities. While most magazines are developing online versions of their publications, the magazine industry has also been promoting the value of traditional print publications. IMC Perspective 12–2 discusses a campaign developed by five of the major magazine publishers to promote the vitality of magazines and how they remain an effective advertising medium in the new digital age.

# NEWSPAPERS

Newspapers, the second major form of print media, are the largest of all advertising media in terms of total dollar volume. In 2009, nearly $25 billion was spent on newspaper advertising, or about 18 percent of the total advertising expenditures in the United States. Newspapers are an especially important advertising medium to local advertisers, particularly retailers. However, newspapers are also valuable to national advertisers. Many of the advertising dollars spent by local retailers are actually provided by national advertisers through cooperative advertising programs (discussed in Chapter 16). Newspapers vary in terms of their characteristics and their role as an advertising medium.

## Types of Newspapers

The traditional role of newspapers has been to deliver prompt, detailed coverage of news as well as to supply other information and features that appeal to readers. The vast majority of newspapers are daily publications serving a local community. However, weekly, national, and special-audience newspapers have special characteristics that can be valuable to advertisers.

**Daily Newspapers** Daily newspapers, which are published each weekday, are found in cities and larger towns across the country. Many areas have more than one daily paper. Daily newspapers are read by nearly 50 percent of adults each weekday and by 55 percent on Sundays.[34] They provide detailed coverage of news, events, and issues concerning the local area as well as business, sports, and other relevant information and entertainment. Daily newspapers can further be classified as morning, evening, or Sunday publications. In 2009 (the latest year for which figures are available), there were 1,408 daily newspapers in the United States; of these, 38 percent were evening papers and 62 percent morning. There were also 902 Sunday newspapers, most of which were published by daily newspapers.

**Weekly Newspapers** Most weekly newspapers originate in small towns or suburbs where the volume of news and advertising cannot support a daily newspaper. These papers focus primarily on news, sports, and events relevant to the local area and usually ignore national and world news, sports, and financial and business news. There are 6,700 weekly newspapers published in the United States, and they have an average circulation of close to 7,500. Weeklies appeal primarily to local advertisers because of their geographic focus and lower absolute cost. Most national advertisers avoid weekly newspapers because of their duplicate circulation with daily or Sunday papers in the large metropolitan areas and problems in contracting for and placing ads in these publications. However, the contracting and scheduling problems associated with these papers have been reduced by the emergence of syndicates that publish them in a number of areas and sell ad space in all of their local newspapers through one office.

**EXHIBIT 12–16**
*The Wall Street Journal* is the leading national newspaper and reaches a very affluent audience

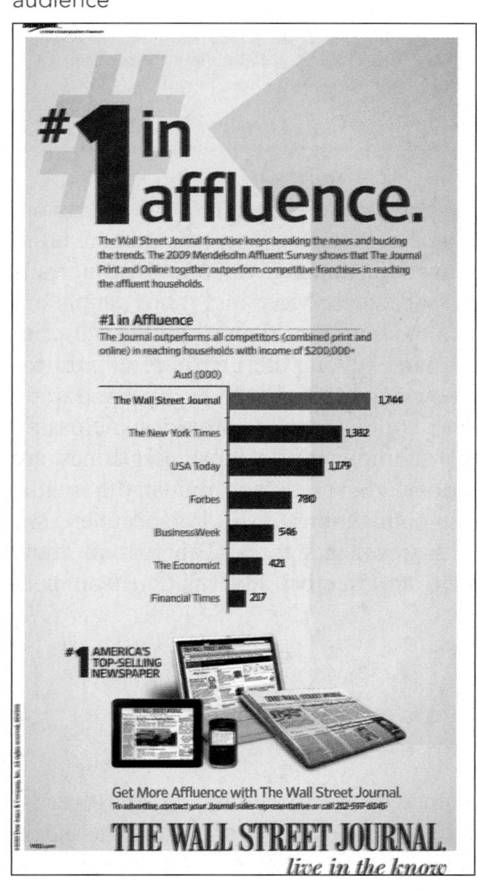


**National Newspapers** Newspapers in the United States with national circulation include *USA Today, The Wall Street Journal,* and *The New York Times.* All three are daily publications and have editorial content with a nationwide appeal. *The Wall Street Journal* has the largest circulation of any newspaper in the country with just over 2 million readers and has recently passed *USA Today* to become the nation's leading paper.[35] The *Journal* includes online readers in its circulation figures as it charges them a subscription fee to read its online edition, while most newspapers have not been successful at doing so and only count print subscriptions and newsstand sales. *The Wall Street Journal* is an excellent media vehicle for reaching businesspeople and also has a very affluent readership base as shown in the ad in Exhibit 12–16. The second most popular national newspaper is *USA Today,* which positions itself as "the nation's newspaper." *USA Today* has become a very popular daily newspaper, particularly among business and leisure travelers, with its coverage of national news as well as its money, sports, lifestyle, and entertainment sections. National newspapers appeal primarily to large national advertisers and to regional advertisers that use specific geographic editions of these publications. For example, *The Wall Street Journal* has three geographic editions covering 18 regions in which ads can be placed, while *USA Today* offers advertisers the opportunity to run ads in its national edition or any of 25 regionals.

In 1999, *The New York Times* was classified as a national newspaper rather than a regional publication by Competitive Media Reporting, which has developed a new policy on how it defines national newspapers.[36] This policy states that a paper must publish at least five times a week and have no more than 67 percent of its distribution in any one area. More than 33 percent of its display advertising must come from national advertising categories, and more than 50 percent of its advertising must come from national advertisers. Designation as a national newspaper is important to major newspapers in attracting national advertisers.[37]

*The Christian Science Monitor* is also considered a national newspaper although in late 2008 the publication, which was founded in 1908, dropped its daily print edition to focus on publishing online. The paper now offers a print edition only on weekends. The *Monitor*'s print circulation had fallen to only 50,000 while its online traffic had increased to nearly 5 million page views per month.[38]

**Special-Audience Newspapers** A variety of papers offer specialized editorial content and are published for particular groups, including labor unions, professional organizations, industries, and hobbyists. Many people working in advertising read *Advertising Age,* while those in the marketing area read *Marketing News.* Specialized newspapers are also published in areas with large foreign-language-speaking ethnic groups, among them Polish, Chinese, Hispanics, Vietnamese, and Filipinos. In the United States, there are newspapers printed in more than 40 languages.

Newspapers targeted at various religious groups compose another large class of special-interest papers. For example, more than 140 Catholic newspapers are published across the United States. Another type of special-audience newspaper is one most of you probably read regularly during the school year, the college newspaper. More than 1,300 colleges and universities publish newspapers and, as discussed at the beginning of the chapter, offer advertisers an excellent medium for reaching college students. IMC Perspective 12–3 discusses how college newspapers have become very popular among advertisers as a way of reaching college students who are a difficult target audience for marketers.

**EXHIBIT 12–17**
*Parade* is a popular Sunday supplement

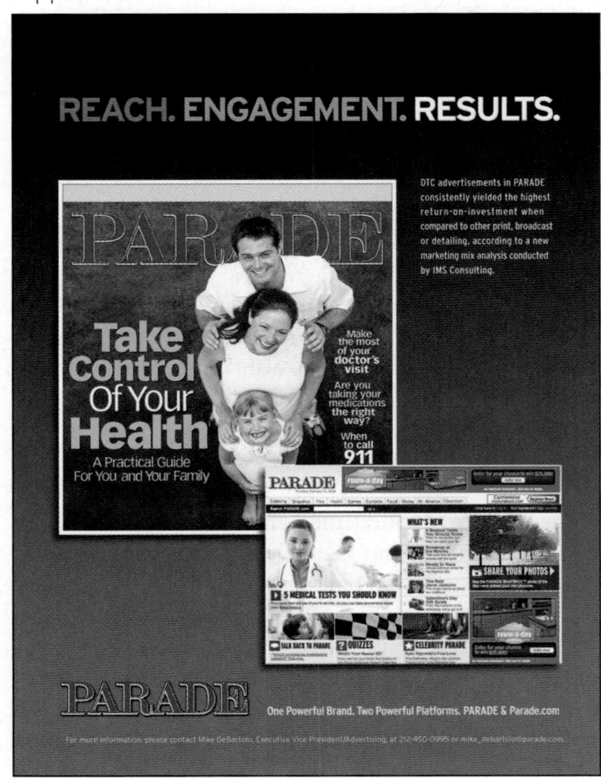


**Newspaper Supplements** Although not a category of newspapers per se, many papers include magazine-type supplements, primarily in their Sunday editions. Sunday supplements have been part of most newspapers for many years and come in various forms. One type is the syndicated Sunday magazine, such as *Parade* or *USA Weekend,* distributed in hundreds of papers throughout the country. *Parade* is distributed through more than 500 newspapers and reaches 72 million readers (Exhibit 12–17); *USA Weekend* is carried by more than 700 newspapers and seen by 48 million readers every weekend. These publications are similar to national magazines and carry both national and regional advertising.

Some large newspapers publish local Sunday supplements distributed by the parent paper. These supplements contain stories of local interest, and both local and national advertisers buy ad space. *The New York Times Sunday Magazine*

CHAPTER 12

# IMC Perspective 12–3 > > >

## College Newspapers Attract Readers and Advertisers

It is likely that you have read a newspaper today although it probably is not the paper that serves the local city, town, or community where you are living or a national publication such as *USA Today* or *The Wall Street Journal*. It is much more likely that you read the student-run newspaper that serves the college you are attending. While many mainstream newspapers are facing declining circulation and shrinking advertising revenue, college newspapers are more popular than ever. Most college newspapers have a mission to inform the university community and provide a training ground for future journalists and marketers. And while a college newspaper may not have the high-powered columnists or staff of most major daily papers, students see their school paper as hip, local, and relevant. Many see them as the best way to get the local campus news, read about entertainment options, or see what is happening with the school's athletic teams.

While most urban newspapers are trying to attract younger readers, college papers have a ready-made audience that is interested in and willing to read news about what is happening on campus. A survey by the marketing research firm Student Monitor, which tracks the buying habits, concerns, and activities of college students, found that 76 percent of the 6 million full-time college undergraduates read at least one of the last five issues of their school newspaper. The popularity of college newspapers is also being driven by the explosive growth of the Internet as more than 600 schools now publish online editions of their papers. Studies show that 38 percent of students regularly read an online edition of their campus paper and spend an average of 19 minutes doing so.

College newspapers have become very popular with advertisers who view them as an excellent way to reach a very coveted but elusive target market. More than 17 million full- and part-time students are enrolled in U.S. colleges, the largest number in history, and they spend an estimated $182 billion a year. Moreover college students are a very attractive demographic group that spends a lot of money for various products and services including computers, mobile phones, as well as entertainment. A number of major companies are advertising in college newspapers or are using online ads to reach these students including Apple, Microsoft, Samsung, and Dell, as well as retailers such as Walmart. For example, Walmart runs ads promoting back-to-school products such as school and dorm room supplies.

Another reason marketers are interested in college students is that many of them are making first-time purchase decisions for major items such as cars, consumer electronics, banking, and insurance. National advertisers such as Ford Motor Co., General Motors, and GEICO, as well as national and local banks, view this as an opportunity to introduce students to their products and services and hopefully build brand loyalty at an early age. They also recognize that they need multiple touch points to get inside the college bubble and campus newspapers complement their other media such as online and broadcast.

The ability of student newspapers to attract advertising revenue has been noticed by a number of major media companies who want to get in on the action. For example, in 2006 Viacom's MTV unit, which already runs a 24-hour online network (mtvU) targeted at college students,

is the best-known local supplement. The *Washington Post, San Francisco Examiner,* and *Los Angeles Times* have their own Sunday magazines.

In some areas, papers have begun carrying regional supplements as well as specialized weekday supplements that cover specific topics such as food, sports, or entertainment. Supplements are valuable to advertisers that want to use the newspaper yet get four-color reproduction quality in their ads.

### Types of Newspaper Advertising

The ads appearing in newspapers can also be divided into different categories. The major types of newspaper advertising are display and classified. Other special types of ads and preprinted inserts also appear in newspapers.

**Display Advertising** **Display advertising** is found throughout the newspaper and generally uses illustrations, headlines, white space, and other visual devices in addition to the copy text. Display ads account for approximately 70 percent of the advertising revenue of the average newspaper. The two types of display advertising in newspapers are local and national (general).

purchased Y2M: Youth Media & Market networks, a company that hosts the websites for over 500 campus papers. The purchase also included Y2M's College Publisher Unit which serves as an advertising agency, placing national ads on the paper's websites in exchange for a share of the revenue. In explaining the acquisition the general manager of mtvU noted that "College newspapers are the most relevant brand on any campus. It immediately gives our advertisers another visceral connection with this audience." mtvU now owns and operates the College Media network, which is the largest interactive network of college newspapers in the United States, as well as RateMyProfessors.com, the largest online listing of collegiate professor ratings.

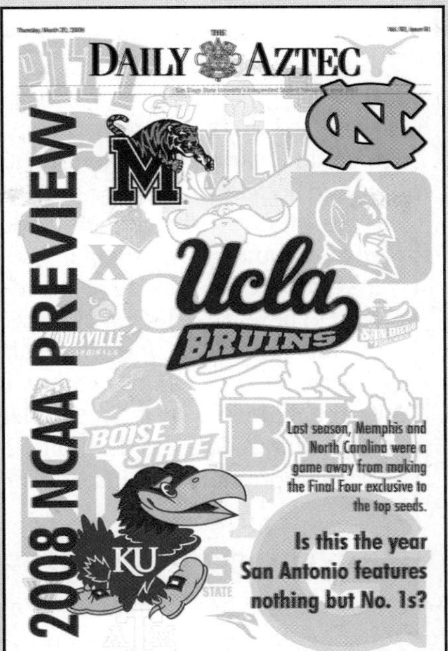
THE DAILY AZTEC

2008 NCAA PREVIEW

Last season, Memphis and North Carolina were a game away from making the Final Four exclusive to the top seeds.

Is this the year San Antonio features nothing but No. 1s?

Major newspaper publishers are also looking at college newspapers as a source of growth as circulation drops at their mainstream papers. *The Tallahassee Democrat,* which is owned by the Gannett Co., the nation's largest newspaper chain, recently acquired Florida State University's *FS View & Florida Flambeau.* The paper is one of few for-profit college newspapers and has an annual budget and sales volume estimated to be in the top 5 percent of college newspapers.

While college newspapers have become very popular, just like other types of newspapers they have been impacted by the recession and have seen a decline in advertising revenue. Much of the decline has come from reductions in national advertising including recruitment ads by major companies as well as ads placed by various college departments and associations that have been experiencing large budget cuts. Many student-run papers have also suffered reductions in subsidies they receive from their universities so they can provide free papers to students. Some college papers have responded by dropping a publication day to cut costs and by looking for new ways to attract more advertising revenue. College newspapers are also trying to attract more readers to their online versions although the vast majority of students still prefer to read the print edition.

Most college newspapers are nonprofit organizations and funnel their advertising revenue back into the operation to support the paper and their staff. And while the weak economy has created some challenges for them, they are likely to continue to have a steady revenue stream as picking up a copy of the campus paper or reading it online has become part of their daily routine for most college students. And as long as college papers can draw readers, they will attract the attention of the advertisers who want to reach them.

Bryan Murley, "College Newspapers Finally Hit by Economic Downturn," *MediaShift,* January 28, 2009, http://www.pbs.org/mediashift/2009/01/college-newspapers-finally-hit-by-economic-downturn028.html; Nick Madigan, "College Papers Deliver; While the Mainstream Press Struggles, Corporations and Advertisers Latch onto Profitable Campus Publications," *The Baltimore Sun,* November 20, 2006, p. 1.C; Emily Steel, "Big Media on Campus," *The Wall Street Journal,* August 9, 2006, pp. B1, 3.



*Local advertising* refers to ads placed by local organizations, businesses, and individuals who want to communicate with consumers in the market area served by the newspaper. Supermarkets and department stores are among the leading local display advertisers, along with numerous other retailers and service operations such as banks and travel agents. Local advertising is sometimes referred to as retail advertising because retailers account for 85 percent of local display ads.

*National* or *general advertising* refers to newspaper display advertising done by marketers of branded products or services that are sold on a national or regional level. These ads are designed to create and maintain demand for a company's product or service and to complement the efforts of local retailers that stock and promote the advertiser's products. Major retail chains, automakers, and airlines are heavy users of newspaper advertising.

**Classified Advertising** **Classified advertising** also provides newspapers with a substantial amount of revenue. These ads are arranged under subheads according to the product, service, or offering being advertised. Employment, real estate, and automotive are the three major categories of classified advertising. While most classified ads are just text set in small type, some newspapers also accept classified

**EXHIBIT 12–18**
Newspaper inserts are used to reach target markets

display advertising. These ads are run in the classified section of the paper but use illustrations, larger type sizes, white space, borders, and even color to stand out.

**Special Ads and Inserts** Special advertisements in newspapers include a variety of government and financial reports and notices and public notices of changes in business and personal relationships. Other types of advertising in newspapers include political or special-interest ads promoting a particular candidate, issue, or cause. **Preprinted inserts** are another type of advertising distributed through newspapers. These ads do not appear in the paper itself; they are printed by the advertiser and then taken to the newspaper to be inserted before delivery. Many retailers use inserts such as circulars, catalogs, or brochures in specific circulation zones to reach shoppers in their particular trade areas. Exhibit 12–18 shows how the *San Diego Union-Tribune* promotes its insert distribution service to advertisers.

## Advantages of Newspapers

Newspapers have a number of characteristics that make them popular among both local and national advertisers. These include their extensive penetration of local markets, flexibility, geographic selectivity, reader involvement, and special services.

**Extensive Penetration** One of the primary advantages of newspapers is the high degree of market coverage, or penetration, they offer an advertiser. In most areas, 50 percent or more of households read a daily newspaper, and the reach figure may exceed 70 percent among households with higher incomes and education levels. Most areas are served by one or two daily newspapers, and often the same company owns both, publishing a morning and an evening edition. By making one space buy, the advertiser can achieve a high level of overall reach in a particular market.

The extensive penetration of newspapers makes them a truly mass medium and provides advertisers with an excellent opportunity for reaching all segments of the population with their message. Also, since many newspapers are published and read daily, the advertiser can build a high level of frequency into the media schedule.

**EXHIBIT 12–19**
Bridgestone Golf used a newspaper ad for a timely salute to professional golfer Fred Couples

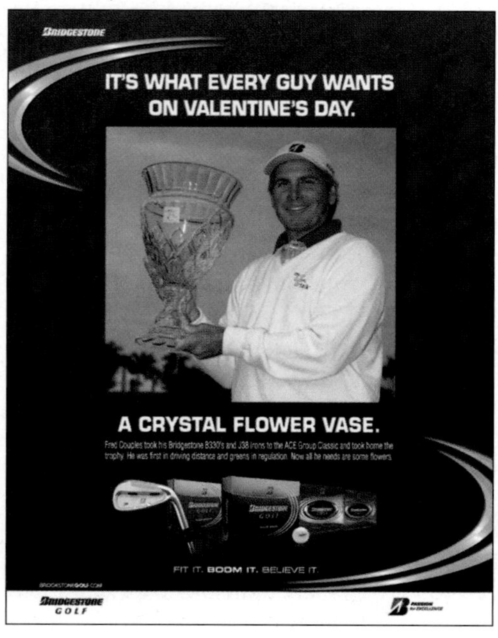


**Flexibility** Another advantage of newspapers is the flexibility they offer advertisers. First, they are flexible in terms of requirements for producing and running the ads. Newspaper ads can be written, laid out, and prepared in a matter of hours. For most dailies, the closing time by which the ad must be received is usually only 24 hours before publication (although closing dates for special ads, such as those using color, and Sunday supplements are longer). The short production time and closing dates make newspapers an excellent medium for responding to current events or presenting timely information to consumers. For example, Bridgestone Golf ran a newspaper ad congratulating professional golfer Fred Couples on his victory at the Ace Group Classic a few days after the tournament. Couples is a member of the Bridgestone Golf team and the newspaper ad was a very timely way to acknowledge his accomplishment and promote his use of Bridgestone golf clubs and balls (Exhibit 12–19).

A second dimension of newspapers' flexibility stems from the creative options they make available to advertisers. Newspaper ads can be produced and run in various sizes, shapes, and formats; they can use color or special inserts to gain the interest of readers. Ads can be run in Sunday magazines or other supplements, and a variety of scheduling options are possible, depending on the advertiser's purpose.

**EXHIBIT 12–20**

The *Chicago Tribune* offers advertisers combinations of different circulation area zones

**Geographic Selectivity** Newspapers generally offer advertisers more geographic or territorial selectivity than any other medium except direct mail. Advertisers can vary their coverage by choosing a paper—or combination of papers—that reaches the areas with the greatest sales potential. National advertisers take advantage of the geographic selectivity of newspapers to concentrate their advertising in specific areas they can't reach with other media or to take advantage of strong sales potential in a particular area. For example, BMW, Mercedes, and Volvo use heavy newspaper media schedules in California and New York/New Jersey to capitalize on the high sales potential for luxury import cars in these markets.

A number of companies use newspapers in their regional marketing strategies. Newspaper advertising lets them feature products on a market-by-market basis, respond and adapt campaigns to local market conditions, and tie into more retailer promotions, fostering more support from the trade.

Local advertisers like retailers are interested in geographic selectivity or flexibility within a specific market or trade area. Their media goal is to concentrate their advertising on the areas where most of their customers are. Many newspapers now offer advertisers various geographic areas or zones for this purpose. For example, the *Chicago Tribune* offers advertisers eight different circulation area zones as shown in Exhibit 12–20.

**Reader Involvement and Acceptance** Another important feature of newspapers is consumers' level of acceptance and involvement with papers and the ads they contain. The typical daily newspaper reader spends time each day reading the weekday newspaper and even more time reading the Sunday paper. Most consumers rely heavily on newspapers not only for news, information, and entertainment but also for assistance with consumption decisions.

Many consumers actually purchase a newspaper *because* of the advertising it contains. Consumers use retail ads to determine product prices and availability and to see who is having a sale. One aspect of newspapers that is helpful to advertisers is readers' knowledge about particular sections of the paper. Most of us know that ads for automotive products and sporting goods are generally found in the sports section, while ads for financial services are found in the business section. The weekly food section in many newspapers is popular for recipe and menu ideas as well as for the grocery store ads and coupons offered by many stores and companies.

The value of newspaper advertising as a source of information has been shown in several studies. One study found that consumers look forward to ads in newspapers more than in other media. In another study, 80 percent of consumers said newspaper ads were most helpful to them in doing their weekly shopping. Newspaper advertising has also been rated the most believable form of advertising in numerous studies.

**Services Offered** The special services newspapers offer can be valuable to advertisers. For example, many newspapers offer merchandising services and programs to manufacturers that make the trade aware of ads being run for the company's product and help convince local retailers they should stock, display, and promote the item.

Many newspapers are also excellent sources of local market information through their knowledge of market conditions and research like readership studies and consumer surveys. For example, the publisher of the *San Diego Union-Tribune,* the major daily newspaper in San Diego, provides information on the local market

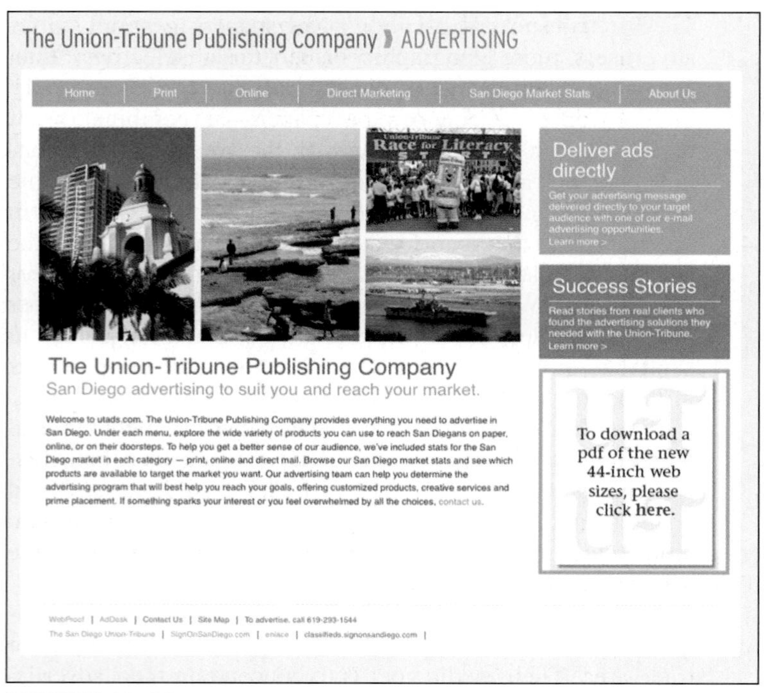

The Union-Tribune Publishing Company ❯ ADVERTISING
Home | Print | Online | Direct Marketing | San Diego Market Stats | About Us
Race for Literacy
Deliver ads directly
Get your advertising message delivered directly to your target audience with one of our e-mail advertising opportunities.
Learn more >
Success Stories
Read stories from real clients who found the advertising solutions they needed with the Union-Tribune.
Learn more >
The Union-Tribune Publishing Company
San Diego advertising to suit you and reach your market.
Welcome to utads.com. The Union-Tribune Publishing Company provides everything you need to advertise in San Diego. Under each menu, explore the wide variety of products you can use to reach San Diegans on paper, online, or on their doorsteps. To help you get a better sense of our audience, we've included stats for the San Diego market in each category — print, online and direct mail. Browse our San Diego market stats and see which products are available to target the market you want. Our advertising team can help you determine the advertising program that will best help you reach your goals, offering customized products, creative services and prime placement. If something sparks your interest or you feel overwhelmed by all the choices, contact us.
To download a pdf of the new 44-inch web sizes, please click here.


**EXHIBIT 12–21**

Newspaper publishers are often an excellent source for information on local markets

through various reports and market studies (Exhibit 12–21).

Newspapers can also assist small companies through free copywriting and art services. Small advertisers without an agency or advertising department often rely on the newspaper to help them write and produce their ads.

## Limitations of Newspapers

While newspapers have many advantages, like all media they also have disadvantages that media planners must consider. The limitations of newspapers include their reproduction problems, short life span, lack of selectivity, and clutter.

**Poor Reproduction** One of the greatest limitations of newspapers as an advertising medium is their poor reproduction quality. The coarse paper stock used for newspapers, the absence of color, and the lack of time papers have available to achieve high-quality reproduction limit the quality of most newspaper ads. Newspapers have improved their reproduction quality in recent years, and color reproduction has become more available. Also, advertisers desiring high-quality color in newspaper ads can turn to such alternatives as freestanding inserts or Sunday supplements. However, these are more costly and may not be desirable to many advertisers. As a general rule, if the visual appearance of the product is important, the advertiser will not rely on newspaper ads. Ads for food products and fashions generally use magazines to capitalize on their superior reproduction quality and color.

**Short Life Span** Unlike magazines, which may be retained around the house for several weeks, a daily newspaper is generally kept less than a day. So an ad is unlikely to have any impact beyond the day of publication, and repeat exposure is very unlikely. Compounding this problem are the short amount of time many consumers spend with the newspaper and the possibility they may not even open certain sections of the paper. Media planners can offset these problems somewhat by using high frequency in the newspaper schedule and advertising in a section where consumers who are in the market for a particular product or service are likely to look. Figure 12–3 on page 436 shows readership figures for various sections of newspapers by age group.

**Lack of Selectivity** While newspapers can offer advertisers geographic selectivity, they are not a selective medium in terms of demographics or lifestyle characteristics. Most newspapers reach broad and very diverse groups of consumers, which makes it difficult for marketers to focus on narrowly defined market segments. For example, manufacturers of fishing rods and reels will find newspapers very inefficient because of the wasted circulation that results from reaching all the newspaper readers who don't fish. Thus, they are more likely to use special-interest magazines such as *Field & Stream* or *Fishing World.* Any newspaper ads for their products will be done through cooperative plans whereby retailers share the costs or spread them over a number of sporting goods featured in the ad.

**Clutter** Newspapers, like most other advertising media, suffer from clutter. Because 64 percent of the average daily newspaper in the United States is devoted to advertising, the advertiser's message must compete with numerous other ads for

**EXHIBIT 12–22**
The *Los Angeles Times* promotes the innovative advertising shapes it now offers

consumers' attention and interest. Moreover, the creative options in newspapers are limited by the fact that most ads are black and white. Thus, it can be difficult for a newspaper advertiser to break through the clutter without using costly measures such as large space buys or color.

Many newspapers are now offering advertisers the opportunity to use innovative shape-based ads that utilize unconventional sizes and formats such as stairsteps, bookends, U-shapes, island ads, spadea ads, and half-page spreads. Many newspapers are also now accepting ads on the front page of their publications as well as on the first page of various sections of the paper. The use of these innovative formats makes it possible for advertisers to more easily attract the attention of readers and increase recall of their advertising message. Exhibit 12–22 shows a page from the media kit for the *Los Angeles Times* promoting several of the innovative ad forms that the paper now offers advertisers.

## The Newspaper Audience



As with any medium, the media planner must understand the nature and size of the audience reached by a newspaper in considering its value in the media plan. Since newspapers as a class of media do an excellent job of penetrating their market, the typical daily newspaper gives advertisers the opportunity to reach most of the households in a market. But, while local advertisers aim to cover a particular market or trade area, national advertisers want to reach broad regions or even the entire country. They must purchase space in a number of papers to achieve the desired level of coverage.

The basic sources of information concerning the audience size of newspapers come from the circulation figures available through rate cards, publishers' statements, or SRDS's *Newspaper Advertising Source*. Circulation figures for many newspapers are verified by the Audit Bureau of Circulation, which was discussed earlier. Advertisers that use a number of papers in their media plan generally find SRDS the most convenient source.

Newspaper circulation figures are generally broken down into three categories: the city zone, the retail trading zone, and all other areas. The **city zone** is a market area composed of the city where the paper is published and contiguous areas similar in character to the city. The **retail trading zone** is the market outside the city zone whose residents regularly trade with merchants within the city zone. The "all other" category covers all circulation not included in the city or retail trade zone.

Sometimes circulation figures are provided only for the primary market, which is the city and retail trade zones combined, and the other area. Both local and national advertisers consider the circulation patterns across the various categories in evaluating and selecting newspapers.

National advertisers often buy newspaper space on the basis of the size of the market area they cover. For example, General Motors might decide to purchase advertising in the top 10 markets, the top 50 markets, the top 100 markets, and so on. A national advertiser gets different levels of market coverage depending on the number of market areas purchased.

**Audience Information** Circulation figures provide the media planner with the basic data for assessing the value of newspapers and their ability to cover various market areas. However, the media planner also wants to match the characteristics of a newspaper's readers with those of the advertiser's target audience. Data on

| Daily Newspaper Sections Read | 18–24 | 25–34 | 35–44 | 45–54 | 55–64 | 65+ |
|---|---|---|---|---|---|---|
| Main news/front page | 75% | 80% | 85% | 89% | 92% | 93% |
| International national news | 32 | 43 | 49 | 57 | 65 | 63 |
| Local news | 66 | 79 | 85 | 86 | 90 | 92 |
| Business/finance | 23 | 31 | 41 | 47 | 51 | 47 |
| Comics | 43 | 31 | 32 | 33 | 42 | 51 |
| Editorial page | 12 | 21 | 32 | 42 | 55 | 60 |
| Entertainment/lifestyle | 33 | 42 | 42 | 49 | 54 | 45 |
| Fashion | 21 | 15 | 17 | 20 | 26 | 25 |
| Food/cooking | 22 | 25 | 33 | 41 | 49 | 46 |
| Home design/furnishings/gardening | 10 | 16 | 24 | 29 | 36 | 32 |
| Movie listings and reviews | 39 | 30 | 31 | 33 | 39 | 33 |
| Science and technology | 18 | 21 | 25 | 29 | 34 | 28 |
| Sports | 55 | 53 | 55 | 55 | 52 | 56 |
| Travel | 12 | 20 | 25 | 31 | 39 | 34 |
| TV listings | 18 | 21 | 24 | 29 | 37 | 45 |
| Advertisements | 25 | 29 | 34 | 38 | 43 | 41 |
| Circulars/inserts/fliers | 15 | 29 | 40 | 41 | 46 | 41 |
| Classified advertising | 45 | 44 | 41 | 39 | 37 | 29 |
| Any advertising | 56% | 61% | 64% | 64% | 65% | 59% |
| Average weekday audience (000) | 7,686 | 12,423 | 17,037 | 20,347 | 15,910 | 21,870 |

Source: Newspaper Association of America: Newspaper Daily Section Readership, 2008, www.naa.org.

**FIGURE 12–3**

Newspaper Daily Section Readership by Age

newspaper audience size and characteristics are available from studies conducted by the papers as well as from commercial research services. As for magazines, a very valuable source for information on newspapers is the SRDS, whose print and online service provides complete planning information on daily papers, newspaper groups, ethnic newspapers, college newspapers, comics, and newspaper-distributed magazines. The SRDS *Newspaper Advertising Source* data contain standardized ad rates, circulation figures, dates, general requirements, contact information, and other valuable information for media.

Companies such as Experian Simmons and Mediamark Research Inc. provide syndicated research studies on lifestyles, media behavior, and product/brand preferences that include information on newspapers. These studies can be valuable for comparing newspapers with other media vehicles.

Many newspapers commission their own audience studies to provide current and potential advertisers with information on readership and characteristics of readers such as demographics, shopping habits, and lifestyles. These studies are often designed to promote the effectiveness of the newspaper in reaching various types of consumers. Since they are sponsored by the paper itself, many advertisers are skeptical of their results. Careful attention must be given to the research methods used and conclusions drawn by these studies.

## Purchasing Newspaper Space

Advertisers are faced with a number of options and pricing structures when purchasing newspaper space. The cost of advertising space depends not only on the newspaper's circulation but also on factors such as premium charges for color or special sections as well as discounts available. The purchase process and the rates paid for newspaper space differ for general and local advertisers.

**General versus Local Rates** Newspapers have different rate structures for general or national advertisers and local or retail advertisers. **General advertising rates** apply to display advertisers outside the newspaper's designated market area (DMA) and to any classification deemed by the publisher to be "general" in nature. This includes ads run by national advertisers such as automotive, tobacco, packaged-goods, and pharmaceutical companies. **Retail** or **local advertising rates** apply to advertisers that conduct business or sell goods or services within the DMA. The rates paid by general advertisers are, on average, 75 percent higher than those paid by local advertisers. Newspaper publishers claim the rate differential is justified for several reasons. First, they argue it costs more to handle general advertising since ad agencies get a 15 percent commission and commissions must also be paid to the independent sales reps who solicit nonlocal advertising. Second, they note that general advertising is less dependable than local advertising; general advertisers usually don't use newspapers on a continual basis like local advertisers do. Finally, newspaper publishers contend that demand for general advertising is inelastic—it will not increase if rates are lowered or decrease if rates are raised. This means there is no incentive to lower the national advertisers' rates.

National advertisers do not view these arguments as valid justification for the rate differential. They argue that the costs are not greater for handling national advertising than for local business and that many national advertisers use newspapers on a regular basis. Since they use an agency to prepare their ads, national advertisers are less likely to request special services. The large and costly staff maintained by many newspapers to assist in the design and preparation of advertising is used mostly by local advertisers.

**EXHIBIT 12–23**
The Newspaper National Network encourages national advertisers to run their ads in newspapers

The differential rate structure for national versus local advertising has been the source of considerable controversy. Some newspapers are making efforts to narrow the rate differential, as is the Newspaper Association of America (NAA). In 1993, the NAA created the Newspaper National Network (NNN) to target national advertisers in six low-use categories: automotive, cosmetics and toiletries, food, household products, liquor and beverages, and drugs and remedies.[39] The network's goal is to attract more advertising dollars from national advertisers in these categories by promoting the strategic use of newspapers and facilitating the purchase of newspaper space with their one order/one bill model. Exhibit 12–23 shows an ad encouraging national advertisers to place their ads in newspapers through the NNN.

Many marketers sidestep the national advertiser label and the higher rates by channeling their newspaper ads through special category plans, cooperative advertising deals with retailers, and local dealers and distributors that pay local rates. However, the rate differential does keep many national advertisers from making newspapers a larger part of their media mix.

## Newspaper Rates

Traditionally, newspaper space for national advertisers has been sold by the agate line. The problem is that newspapers use columns of varying width. Some have six columns per page, while others have eight or nine, which affects the size, shape, and costs of an ad. This results in a complicated production and buying process for national advertisers purchasing space in a number of newspapers.

To address this problem and make newspapers more comparable to other media that sell space and time in standard units, the newspaper industry switched to **standard advertising units (SAUs)** in 1984. All newspapers under this system use column widths 2-1/16 inches wide, with tabloid-size papers five columns wide and standard or broadcast papers six columns. The column inch is the unit of measurement to create the standard broadsheet or tabloid ad size.

A national advertiser can prepare one ad in a particular SAU, and it will fit every newspaper in the country that uses that format size. Rates are quoted on that basis. Since most daily newspapers use the SAU system, the purchase and production process has been simplified tremendously for national advertisers.

Newspaper rates for local advertisers continue to be based on the column inch, which is 1 inch deep by 1 column wide. Advertising rates for local advertisers are quoted per column inch, and media planners calculate total space costs by multiplying the ad's number of column inches by the cost per inch.

**Rate Structures** While the column inch and SAU are used to determine basic newspaper advertising rates, the media planner must consider other options and factors. Many newspapers charge **flat rates**, which means they offer no discount for quantity or repeated space buys. Others have an **open-rate structure**, which means various discounts are available. These discounts are generally based on frequency or bulk purchases of space and depend on the number of column inches purchased in a year.

Newspaper space rates also vary with an advertiser's special requests, such as preferred position or color. The basic rates quoted by a newspaper are **run of paper (ROP)**, which means the paper can place the ad on any page or in any position it desires. While most newspapers try to place an ad in a requested position, the advertiser can ensure a specific section and/or position on a page by paying a higher **preferred position rate**. Color advertising is also available in many newspapers on an ROP basis or through preprinted inserts or Sunday supplements.

Advertisers can also buy newspaper space based on **combination rates**, where they get a discount for using several newspapers as a group. Typically, a combination rate occurs when a publisher owns both a morning and an evening newspaper in a market and offers a reduced single rate for running the same ad in both newspapers, generally within a 24-hour period. Combination discounts are also available when the advertiser buys space in several newspapers owned by the publisher in a number of markets or in multiple newspapers affiliated in a syndicate or newspaper group.

## The Future for Newspapers

Newspapers remain the largest advertising medium in terms of total advertising volume, but as noted at the beginning of the chapter, advertising revenue for traditional print papers has declined dramatically over the past several years. Newspapers generate most of their advertising revenue from local advertisers, particularly retailers who use display ads to advertise their products and services and inform consumers of sales and other types of promotions. Newspapers account for less than 5 percent of advertising expenditures for national advertisers so they are very dependent on regional and local marketers for their advertising revenue.

Newspapers' major strength lies in their role as a medium that can be used effectively by local advertisers on a continual basis. It is unlikely that newspapers' importance to local advertisers will change in the near future. However, there are a number of problems and issues newspapers must address to maintain their strong position as a dominant local advertising medium and to gain more national advertising. These include competition from other advertising media, maintaining and managing circulation, cross-media opportunities, and declining readership.

**Competition from Other Media** The newspaper industry's battle to increase its share of national advertising volume has been difficult. In addition to the problems of reproduction quality and rate differentials, newspapers face competition from other media for both national and local advertisers' budgets.

The intermedia battle that newspapers find themselves involved in is no longer limited to national advertising. Many companies are investigating the Internet as a marketing tool and a place to invest advertising dollars that might otherwise go to newspapers. Local radio and TV stations (particularly cable stations), as well as the expanding number of Yellow Pages publishers, are aggressively pursuing local advertisers. Newspapers will have to fight harder to retain those advertisers.

Newspapers are also facing new competition from various online sites for classified and employment advertising, which have long been important major profit centers. Classified advertising revenue for U.S. newspapers has declined steadily since 2000, while help-wanted advertising revenue is less than half of what it was at that time. Newspapers must now compete against online employment sites such as Monster.com and Job.com for job listings. Websites such as eBay and Craigslist have become very popular ways for selling a variety of merchandise that traditionally was sold through classified ads in local newspapers. Craigslist, which began as a type of counterculture message board for young people in the San Francisco area, has now expanded to most major cities and has become popular among people under 30. The online site includes sections for selling merchandise, apartment rentals, services, personals, and job listings. Some newspapers are recognizing that it is very difficult to compete against online sites for classified ads and are responding by offering free classified ads for merchandise under certain price points as a way to grow readership.[40]

Newspapers are doing a number of other things to respond to the challenges from other media. Many papers have expanded their marketing capabilities and are making efforts to develop and sustain relationships with their advertisers. Some have created sophisticated databases and direct-mail capabilities, which they offer as value-added services. Others are increasing their marketing research departments, preparing comprehensive market studies for major customers, and, in some cases, serving as media advisors and marketing partners.

**Circulation** The newspaper industry has been struggling for years to reverse declining circulation.[41] Many of the major newspapers in the United States have been experiencing a decline in circulation and are seeking ways to respond to the problem, such as by emphasizing readership measures and developing online versions of their papers. Like magazines, many newspapers are taking a closer look at their circulation and analyzing whether the cost of getting additional circulation is justified by the advertising revenue it generates. Many papers are raising newsstand and home delivery rates, and circulation revenue is accounting for more of their total revenue.

Several major metropolitan newspapers have found that advertisers use newspapers to reach consumers within specific geographic areas and do not want to pay for readers in outlying areas. Thus, some papers are eliminating what has been called "ego circulation" and focusing more on regional editions in their immediate trade area.

Newspapers have found that it is more cost-effective to focus on retaining subscribers rather than spending large sums of money to acquire new ones. The cancellation rate for newspaper subscribers has declined significantly from 55 percent in 2000 to 32 percent in 2009 according to statistics from the Newspaper Association of America. These numbers reflect the fact that many newspapers are focusing more on retention of their core readers and offering programs such as discounts for automatic renewal payment plans.[42]

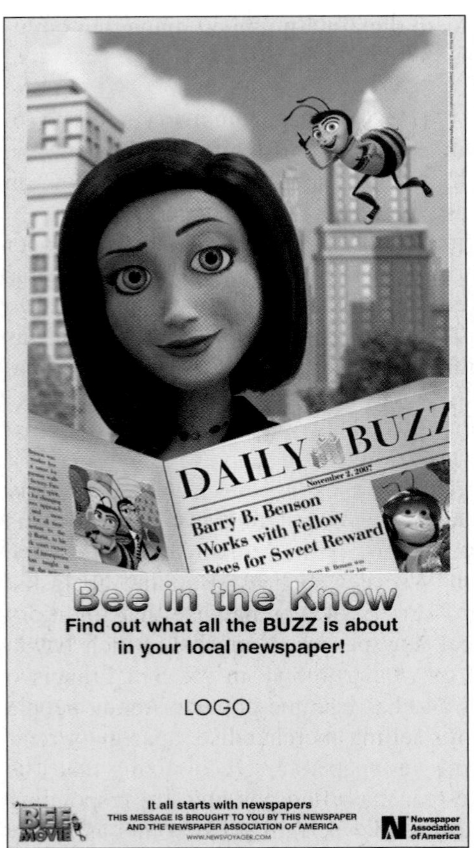


**EXHIBIT 12–24**
This ad is part of a campaign encouraging young people to read newspapers

**Attracting and Retaining Readers** The growth of newspapers as an advertising medium may be limited by the reduced popularity of the medium itself. Newspaper readership has been on a steady decline for the past two decades. The percentage of the adult population reading a newspaper on the average weekday has declined from 78 percent in 1970 to 48 percent more recently. The percentage of U.S. households receiving a daily newspaper has declined from 77 percent in 1980 to 60 percent. The decline in newspaper readership can be attributed to several factors, including the fast-paced, time-poor lifestyle of the modern dual-income household and the increase in viewing options of TV, and of course, competition from the Internet.

A number of newspapers have been redesigned to be more interesting and easier and faster to read. Changes include the increased use of color and graphics as well as expanded coverage of sports and entertainment. Some papers have begun providing short summaries of articles in each section of the paper so readers can skim them and decide what they want to read.

Of particular concern to publishers is the decline in newspaper readership among important market segments such as women and young adults. Surveys show that the percentage of women who read a newspaper on a typical day declined from 67 percent in 1981 to 46 percent recently.[43] Newspapers and advertisers are concerned because women are far more likely than men to make buying decisions. Many newspapers are introducing new women's sections and revising old ones to make them more appealing to modern women. This means including articles on such issues as health, parenting, and careers—for example, how women with children and jobs manage their time.

Newspapers are also concerned about where their future readers will come from, since many young people are heavy TV viewers and also are spending more and more time surfing the Internet. However, a recent study found that newspaper readership is high among teens, and many papers are making special efforts to attract teenagers in hopes they will become and remain regular readers. The newspaper industry is also taking steps to maintain readership among young people. For example, the Newspaper Association of America (NAA) sponsors advertising that encourages young people to read the newspaper (Exhibit 12–24).[44] For the past several years the NAA has been running a campaign featuring familiar characters from children's entertainment to promote literacy through newspaper readership. The ad shown in Exhibit 12–24 features characters from the animated film *The Bee Movie* reading a copy of the "Daily Buzz."

## Online Delivery

The growth of the Internet and online services is another factor that may erode traditional print version newspaper readership. As penetration of the Internet into households increases, newspapers and magazines are among the most threatened of the major media. A survey conducted for *Advertising Age* found that consumers with home Internet access are less likely to use magazines or newspapers as a primary information source when shopping for a car, financial services, travel, or fashion. The study also found that consumers from teens to seniors are comfortable with the idea of using the Internet in the future to read books, magazines, and newspapers.[45]

Newspaper publishers are addressing this threat by making their papers available online. Nearly every major newspaper has established a website, and many publishers now make their papers available online. The number of U.S. newspapers available online has increased from less than 100 in 1995 to more than 1,500. From January 2005 to the fourth quarter of 2007, the digital newspaper

**EXHIBIT 12–25**
The *San Diego Union-Tribune* promotes its online newspaper

audience increased by 60 percent to over 70 million unique users.[46] Most dailies now offer online versions of their newspapers and thus are capturing readers who prefer to get their news from websites. Studies have shown that people who use online newspapers are highly engaged and are an upscale audience—they spend more time online, are better educated, and have higher incomes than online audiences in general. They are also more likely to make purchases online and to use the Internet to help them decide what to buy.[47] Many newspapers are using this information to promote their online editions to advertisers. Exhibit 12–25 shows a promotional piece for SignOnSanDiego.com, the online newspaper/website of the *San Diego Union-Tribune* newspaper.

Many newspapers are working to attract advertising dollars from both local and national advertisers. Networks are also forming to help local newspapers sell online ads on their websites to national advertisers. For example, the National Newspaper Network provides national advertisers with access to newspaper websites across the country and facilitates the purchase of online ads in the same way it does with traditional print ads. While newspaper publishers are focusing more attention on the sale of online advertising, they are also facing strong competition from the major Internet search players such as Google, Yahoo, and Local.com because these companies have made it inexpensive and easy for local companies to run ads with them. Many newspapers are forming alliances with these Internet search competitors whereby they can use their technology to sell more sophisticated ad offerings, such as behaviorally targeted ads.[48]

## Summary

Magazines and newspapers, the two major forms of print media, play an important role in the media plans and strategy of many advertisers. Magazines are a very selective medium and are very valuable for reaching specific types of customers and market segments. The three broad categories of magazines are consumer, farm, and business publications. Each of these categories can be further classified according to the publication's editorial content and audience appeal.

In addition to their selectivity, the advantages of magazines include their excellent reproduction quality, creative flexibility, long life, prestige, and readers' high receptivity to magazine advertising, as well as the services they offer to advertisers. Disadvantages of magazines include their high cost, limited reach and frequency, long lead time, and the advertising clutter in most publications.

Advertising space rates in magazines vary according to a number of factors, among them the size of the ad, position in the publication, particular editions purchased, use of color, and number and frequency of insertions. Rates for magazines are compared on the basis of the cost per thousand, although other factors such as the editorial content of the publication and its ability to reach specific target audiences must also be considered.

Newspapers represent the largest advertising medium in terms of total volume, receiving nearly a fourth of all advertising dollars. Newspapers are a very important medium to local advertisers, especially retailers. They are also used by national advertisers, although the differential rate structure for national versus local advertisers is a source of controversy. Newspapers are a broad-based medium that reaches a large percentage of households in a particular area. Newspapers' other advantages include flexibility, geographic selectivity, reader involvement, and special services. Drawbacks of newspapers include their lack of high-quality ad reproduction, short life span, lack of audience selectivity, and clutter.

Trends toward market segmentation and regional marketing are prompting many advertisers to make more use of newspapers and magazines. However, both magazines and newspapers face increasing competition from such other media as radio, cable TV, direct marketing, and the Internet. Both magazines and newspapers are working to improve the quality of their circulation bases, offer database marketing services, and initiate cross-media deals. Rising costs and declining readership are problems for many magazines and newspapers. Both magazines and newspapers are making their publications available online, as a way to retain readers and grow advertising revenue.

## Key Terms

**selectivity** p. 410
**gatefolds** p. 412
**bleed pages** p. 413
**split runs** p. 416
**selective binding** p. 416
**ink-jet imaging** p. 417
**controlled-circulation basis** p. 420
**pass-along readership** p. 420
**total audience/readership** p. 421
**magazine networks** p. 423
**display advertising** p. 430
**classified advertising** p. 431
**preprinted inserts** p. 432
**city zone** p. 435
**retail trading zone** p. 435
**general advertising rates** p. 437
**retail or local advertising rates** p. 437
**standard advertising units (SAUs)** p. 438
**flat rates** p. 438
**open-rate structure** p. 438
**run of paper (ROP)** p. 438
**preferred position rate** p. 438
**combination rates** p. 438

## Discussion Questions

1. Discuss some of the developments that are impacting the traditional print media of magazines and newspapers. What are some of the ways magazine and newspaper publishers can respond to these changes and retain advertisers? (LO1)
2. Discuss how technological developments such as electronic readers, the iPad, and tablet PCs will impact the role of magazines and newspapers as advertising media vehicles. How long do you think it will take for these devices to achieve mass market penetration? (LO1, 2)
3. Discuss the role of magazines as part of an advertiser's media strategy. What are the advantages and limitations of magazines? (LO1, 2)
4. What is meant by selectivity with regard to the purchase of advertising media? Discuss the various ways magazines offer selectivity to advertisers. (LO2)
5. IMC Perspective 12–1 examines the growing popularity of celebrity magazines. Discuss some of the reasons why celebrity magazines have become so popular. What types of companies might choose to advertise in these magazines? (LO1, 2)
6. Discuss the decision by magazines and newspapers to allow advertising on the covers of their publications. Do you think it is appropriate for ads to appear on the covers of these publications? (LO2)
7. Evaluate the "Power of Print" advertising campaign being run by the five major magazine publishers to promote the vitality of magazines to advertisers. Do you feel this campaign will be effective? Why or why not. (LO1)
8. If you were purchasing print advertising space for a manufacturer of golf clubs such as Callaway or TaylorMade, what factors would you consider? Would your selection of magazines be limited to golf publications? Why or why not? (LO3)
9. IMC Perspective 12–3 discusses the growing popularity of college newspapers. Discuss some of the reasons why marketers would want to advertise in a college newspaper. Analyze the types of companies that advertise in the newspaper published by your university. (LO1)
10. More magazines and newspaper publishers are now making their publications available online. Discuss how the availability of online magazines and newspapers is impacting the traditional print versions. How can publishers use online magazines and newspapers to attract more advertising revenue? (LO4)
11. What are the major challenges facing the newspaper industry and the use of newspapers as an advertising medium? How can newspapers respond to these challenges? (LO4)

## AdForum Exercise: Selecting Magazines for Automotive Ads

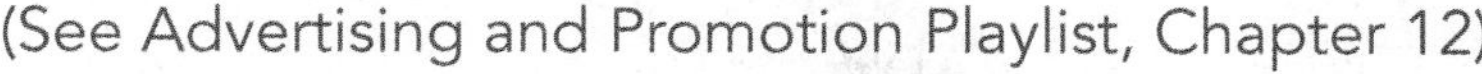

(See Advertising and Promotion Playlist, Chapter 12)

The playlist for this chapter contains a collection of print ads for three popular automotive brands including BMW, Honda, and Chevrolet. Review each ad and answer the following questions:

1 Discuss the target audience this ad is intended for based on the type of message used.

2 Create a list of magazines in which each ad might be run by the company based on the target audience and the message contained in the advertisement. Discuss why this magazine is a good fit for this particular ad.

You can find a list of various magazines published in the United States by category at:

http://en.wikipedia.org/wiki/List_of_United_States_magazines

Many of these publications also have online media kits that can be accessed to gain insight into their editorial content as well as a profile of their readers.

Access to the chapter playlist is available through McGraw-Hill connect™ MARKETING, www.mcgrawhillconnect.com

## LEARNING OBJECTIVES

LO1 To examine the role of support media in the IMC program.

LO2 To recognize the various traditional and nontraditional support media available to the marketer in developing an IMC program.

LO3 To develop an understanding of the advantages and disadvantages of support media.

LO4 To know how audiences for support media are measured.

# 13 Support Media

## LADY GAGA: TOPPING THE CHARTS IN MUSIC AND PRODUCT PLACEMENT

The pop music world hasn't seen anything like it in years. Lady Gaga, the biggest rock artist superstar since Madonna, has hit the world with a bang! With appearances on the *Grammy's*, the *American Music Awards,* and *American Idol,* concerts around the globe and an exclusive interview with Barbara Walters, the sometimes controversial rock star is about as popular as popular can get. Her online videos have had over a billion hits, with her "Bad Romance" video the most watched of all times—even more than Michael Jackson's "Thriller".

But Lady Gaga is more than just a talented musician—she is a star marketer as well. A quick glance at the "Bad Romance" and "Telephone" videos also shows that Lady Gaga may also be at the top for the number of product placements in music videos. The nine-minute music video "Telephone" had nine including: Heartbeats earphones, Virgin Mobile, Diet Coke, HP Envy laptop, Polaroid, Wonder Bread, Miracle Whip, and the PlentyOfFish dating website (Polaroid and Virgin Mobile appeared twice), while "Bad Romance" included placements for Parrot, Nemiroff vodka, Heartbeats earphones, Burberry trench coats, Nintendo Wii, HP Envy, Alexander McQueen clothes, and White Safari Carrera sunglasses. Gaga has also signed on as creative director for Polaroid cameras, and has branding deals with Heartbeats and HP, and Verizon sponsored her Monster Ball Tour. Indeed, Lady Gaga has become a brand, with trademarks that cover (among other things) "caps, visors, boxer shorts, headbands, sneakers, swimwear, bras, scarves, hosiery, pajamas, robes, and sweatpants".

Not everyone is so impressed with Gaga's marketing skills, however. Song artist M.I.A. (who licenses her own songs for Honda Civic commercials) slams her for being too commercial, while others claim she is a shill for products and is associating her name with too many, and some unfavorable brands. There are criticisms that she may be stretching herself too thin. Almost as soon as the "Telephone" video appeared, articles appeared on the Web from the *Guardian, Jezebel, Rolling Stone,* and *Interview* magazine, commenting on the placements.

So is it shrewd marketing or crass commercialism? For one thing, it has generated a lot of publicity—albeit not all of which is positive. Andrew Hampp of *Advertising Age* says that both the artist and advertiser win in such arrangements—particularly when there seems to be a commitment to authenticity on both sides (more about this later). The advertiser capitalizes on the relationship with Lady Gaga, as well as access to her millions of fans around the world. Lady Gaga, her label, and the video director get some cash to offset the continually rising costs of creating videos. (The "Telephone" video had a budget of $300,000–$400,000!) Consider the case of Miracle Whip. Justin Parnell, the brand manager of the age old brand, notes that the target market for the newly relaunched mayonnaise—18–35 year olds—is a perfect match with Gaga's audience. New creative and an association with the rock star can't hurt, he says. PlentyOfFish says they have noticed a massive jump in brand awareness after the video placements, as well as a 15 percent increase in searches—and the numbers continue to climb.

But back to the authenticity issue. Are the relationships real, or will Lady Gaga's marketing team accept all offers? Consider these placements: Wonder Bread was free. Diet Coke was free (homage to Gaga's mother who used it to curl her hair). Miracle

Whip was a paid placement, while Virgin Mobile and Polaroid were there as an acknowledgement of their Monster Tour sponsorship. So at least with "Telephone," authenticity seems to be a more appropriate word than shill.

When it comes to product placements, they may not always be what they seem. Most viewers think they are paid for, like buying a commercial. Some are paid for, some are not. While many are strategic, others appear for a variety of unsuspected reasons. Lady Gaga again sets an example!

Sources: Andrew Hampp and Emily Bryson York, "How Miracle Whip, Plenty of Fish Tapped Lady Gaga's 'Telephone,'" www.adage.com, March 13, 2010; Evann Gastaldo, "Lady Gaga Video Has Lots of. . . Product Placement," www.newser.com, March 15, 2010, 1p.; ____, "The Lady's Gaga For Product Placement in Her New *Telephone* Music Video," www. X17online.com, May 10, 2010; Abe Sauer, "Lady Gaga's Next Hit: 'Shiller'," www.brandchannel.com, April 15, 2010.

The Lady Gaga example demonstrates how pervasive product placements have become, appearing everywhere from movies to television to videos and videogames. Given the increasing concern with consumers' abilities to avoid advertising, advertisers have turned to other ways to get their messages in front of prospective buyers. The result of this is increased attention to getting exposure, which, in turn, has led to significant changes in the media industry. Over the past few years there has been significant growth in the use of support media—both traditional and new media forms. In many ways, the consumers' efforts to avoid commercial exposure may have had an opposite effect, as it seems ads now appear in many places not previously home to such messages.

Ads have appeared on manhole covers, inside restroom stalls, on bus shelters, in grocery stores, on hubcaps, on cell phones, and even on people's bodies. In this chapter, we review a number of support media, some that are new to the marketplace and others that have been around a while. We discuss the relative advantages and disadvantages, how they are used, and audience measurement of each. We refer to them as **support media** because the media described in the previous chapters dominate the media strategies of large advertisers, particularly national advertisers. Support media are used to reach those people in the target market the primary media may not have effectively reached and to reinforce, or support, their messages. It is important to remember that some of these media are not used only for support, but for some companies may be the primary or sole medium used.

You may be surprised at how many different ways there are to deliver the message and how often you are exposed to them. Let's begin by examining the scope of the support media industry and some of the many alternatives available to marketers.

## THE SCOPE OF THE SUPPORT MEDIA INDUSTRY

Support media are referred to by several titles, among them **alternative media**, **below-the-line media**, **nonmeasured media**, and **nontraditional media**. These terms describe a vast variety of channels used to deliver communications and to promote products and services. In this chapter we will discuss many of these media (though, as you might imagine, it would be impossible for us to discuss them all).

Many advertisers, as well as the top 100 advertising agencies, have increased their use of support media, and as new alternatives are developed, this use will continue to grow. Given the rapid emergence of a variety of new media, we will further divide support media into *traditional* and *nontraditional* support media categories. There is no particular necessity for this further distinction other than to demonstrate that many of the various forms of support media have been around for quite some time, while others have surfaced only recently. Let us examine some of these in more detail.

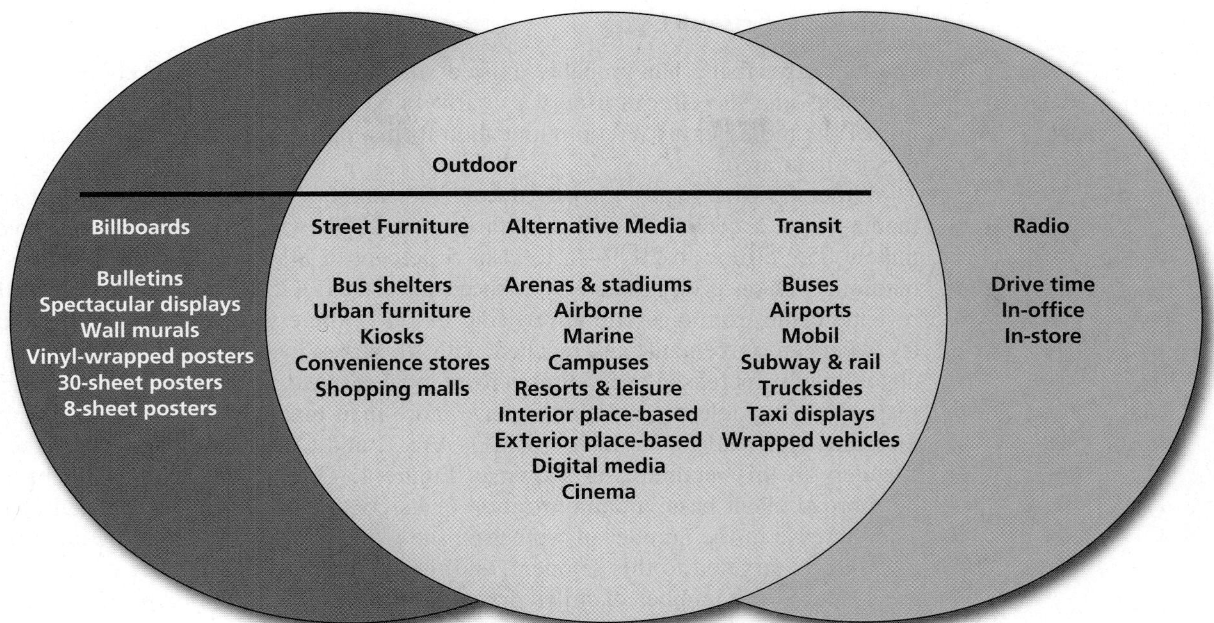


**FIGURE 13–1**

Out-of-Home Media: A Diverse Cross Section of Formats Comprise Outdoor Advertising Today

Source: Reprinted with permission of Outdoor Advertising Association of America, Inc.

CHAPTER 13

# TRADITIONAL SUPPORT MEDIA

**Out-of-home advertising** media encompass many advertising forms (see Figure 13–1). As can be seen, the Outdoor Advertising Association of America, Inc. (OAAA) categorizes these media as outdoor—including billboards, street furniture, alternative media, and transit—as well as specific forms of radio. As shown in Figure 13–2, billboards and street furniture together constitute 71 percent of the outdoor billings. Given the similarity of these forms, we will discuss them together while addressing transit and alternative media subsequently.

**FIGURE 13–2**

Four Major Product Categories, 2009
Total OOH Revenue: $5,900.7

Notes: Figures in millions.

Digital OOH advertising (billboards, cinema and place-based) accounted for $1.1 billion in 2009.

Source: Outdoor Advertising Association of America, Inc.

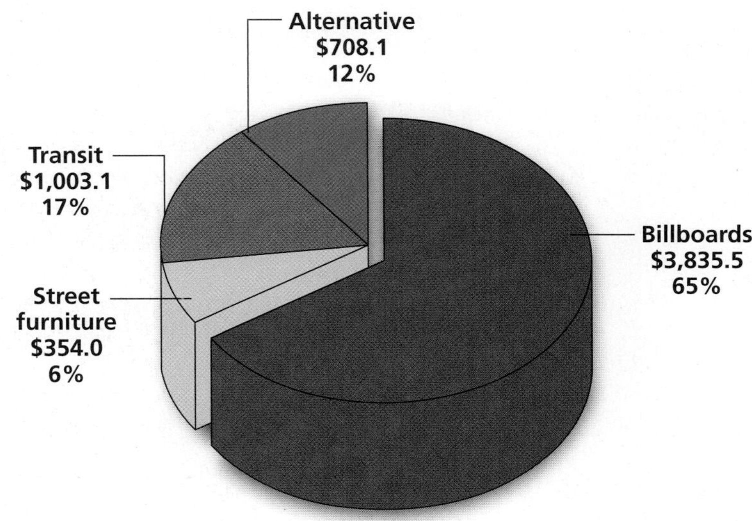

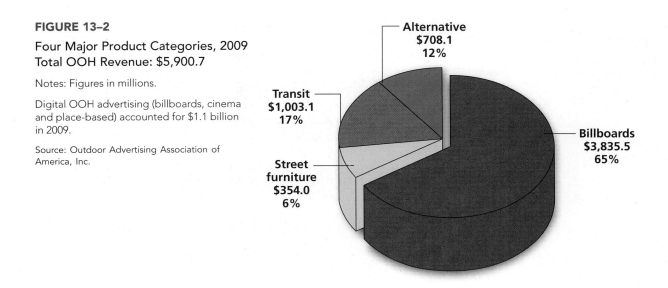

## Outdoor Advertising

Outdoor advertising has probably existed since the days of cave dwellers. Both the Egyptians and the Greeks used it as early as 5,000 years ago. Outdoor is certainly one of the more pervasive communication forms, particularly if you live in an urban or suburban area.

While showing steady growth since 2000, outdoor advertising—like most other media—saw a decline in billings starting in 2008, with expenditures of approximately \$5.9 billion in 2009—a total of 5 percent of all advertising dollars.[1] As the medium was once dominated by tobacco advertisers (25 percent of its \$1.5 billion revenue came from cigarette advertising in 1991), there were concerns in the industry when an agreement was reached with 46 states in November 1998 to ban all cigarette ads. Increased expenditures from local services and amusements, insurance, real estate, and telecom companies have more than made up for the losses. Companies like McDonald's, Verizon, GEICO, AT&T, and Coca-Cola are some of the top spenders in this medium. As shown in Figure 13–3, outdoor continues to be used by a broad client base, a demonstration of its continued acceptance in the industry. The increase in the number of women in the work force has led to more advertising of products targeted to this segment, and the increases in the number of vehicles on the road and the number of miles driven have led to increased expenditures by gas companies, food and lodging providers, and other media.

A major reason for the continued success of outdoor is its ability to remain innovative through technology. As Exhibit 13–1 shows, billboards are no longer limited to standard sizes and two dimensions; 3-D forms and extensions are now used to attract attention. Digital outdoor media have also contributed to the success. Digital messages on billboards, transit signs, and in stores have allowed more advertisers to participate as messages can be changed quickly and often. In addition, it allows outdoor advertising to appear in places previously unavailable, and in a timely fashion (Exhibit 13–2). You probably have been exposed to either signboards or electronic billboards at sports stadiums, in supermarkets, in the campus bookstores and dining halls, in shopping malls, on the freeways, or on the sides of buildings, from neon signs on skyscrapers in New York City to Mail Pouch Tobacco signs painted on the sides of barns in the Midwest. This is truly a pervasive medium.

Outdoor advertising, particularly billboards, does have its critics. Ever since Lady Bird Johnson tried to rid the interstate highways of billboard advertising during her husband's presidency with the Highway Beautification Act of 1965, there has been

**FIGURE 13–3**
Top 10 Outdoor Advertising Categories (based on 2009 year-end outdoor expenditures)

| | |
|---|---|
| 1. | Miscellaneous services and amusements |
| 2. | Insurance and real estate |
| 3. | Communications |
| 4. | Public transportation, hotels and resorts |
| 5. | Media and advertising |
| 6. | Retail |
| 7. | Restaurants |
| 8. | Financial |
| 9. | Automotive dealers and services |
| 10. | Automotive, auto accessories and equipment |

Source: Outdoor Advertising Association of America, 2010.

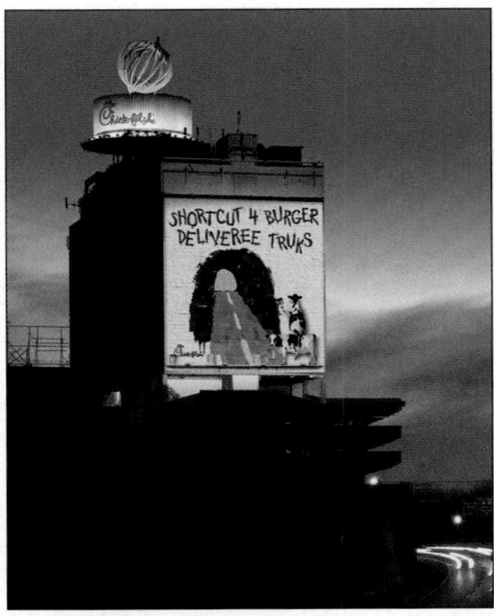


**EXHIBIT 13–1**
Billboards can be attention-getting

**EXHIBIT 13–2**
Toshiba promotes through a billboard on Times Square



controversy regarding its use. As previously noted, legislation has passed in 46 states banning the advertising of cigarettes on billboards. In addition, a number of cities and states in the United States and internationally have banned or restricted the use of billboards.

**Digital Outdoor** One of the fastest growing outdoor industries is that of **digital out-of-home media**. Digital outdoor media take three forms: (1) video advertising networks, which include digital video screens that appear in offices, stores, theaters, inside transit networks, and entertainment venues such as health clubs, sporting arenas, bars, and restaurants; and (2) digital billboards, or screens which transmit in LED (light emitting diodes) or LCD (liquid crystal display) technologies. Digital billboards include large boards found at sports and entertainment venues, retail locations (like malls), in transit locations (terminals, etc.) and at roadsides or large traffic locations. Ambient advertising, which is not a purely digital out-of-home medium, often uses digital technology to send its messages. These typically include smaller signs that appear in restrooms, stairs, personal vehicles, and on specialty items. The digital out-of-home media segment now accounts for over $1.9 billion in advertising revenues, due to its ability to be creative, attract attention, and engage the consumer (see IMC Technology Perspective 13–1).

## Alternative Out-of-Home Media

Several other forms of outdoor advertising are also available including aerial advertising, place-based, mobile boards, and more. The OAAA classifies these as alternative media. Let's examine a few of these.

**Aerial Advertising** Airplanes pulling banners, skywriting (in letters as high as 1,200 feet), and blimps all constitute another form of outdoor advertising available to the marketer: **aerial advertising**. Generally these media are not expensive in absolute terms and can be useful for reaching specific target markets. For example, Coppertone has often used skywriting over beach areas to promote its tanning lotions, beer companies (among others) commonly employ aerial advertising

# IMC Technology Perspective 13–1 > > >

## Digital Out-of-Home Media Is Changing the Way We Look at (and Interact with) Signs

It has always been hard to ignore billboards, whether you want to or not, which is part of the reason the industry has not been as hard-hit as some other media during the economic downturn. Now due to technology, it may be even harder to ignore them. The growth of digital billboards (and other out-of-home advertising vehicles) may actually lead to consumers wanting to see—and even to interact with—a medium that many would like to see go away. Digital billboards are attracting attention around the world, for a variety of products, services, and causes.

Beck's Brewery is one such example of supporting a cause—contemporary music and art. In a highly integrated campaign, Beck's, along with its creative and media agencies, placed 12 digital billboards on highly trafficked Clear Channel outdoor locations throughout London. The "Music Inspired Art" billboards encouraged viewers to plug in and play songs from their MP3 players through a socket attached to the billboard. Through a Flash-based application, the billboards interpreted the song into art, immediately displaying it on the board while they watched. When finished, the art images were uploaded to a Flickr gallery on the Beck's website, where the "artist" could go to see the work. In two weeks, over 10,000 images were uploaded, and a lot more people knew that Beck's supported the arts.

NEC, a Japanese electronics company, has developed a digital billboard with a camera inside that can identify a shopper's age and gender as they walk by in a store. The facial recognition system can then offer them a product they might like based on their demographics—accurate to within 10 years of their age. The longer they stand in front of the billboard, the more accurate the data. NEC says the technology would enable advertisers to better target customers in public venues such as airports and shopping malls. While not available in the United States yet, NEC says they have received a lot of interest from U.S. companies.

The FBI is also using the new billboard technology. As a result of a free public service provided by Clear Channel Outdoor, a 30 × 40 digital billboard in Times Square displays fugitives wanted for crimes in the New York area, resulting in thousands of exposures. The billboard—announced on the *Today Show,* and seen by millions of viewers—can also be used to help rescue kidnap victims, and provide high-security messages. Unlike traditional billboards, the messages can be posted or changed at a moment's notice—often right after the event occurs. Three other organizations have joined the effort, resulting in now over 1,500 billboards in 40 states, that have already led to the solving of at least 30 cases. Digital is clearly changing the outdoor landscape.

Sources: Andrew Hough, "'Minority Report' Digital Billboard Watches Consumers Shop," www.telegraph.co.uk, March 10, 2010; ____ "Big Apple Joins National Initiative," www.fbi.gov, Jan. 15, 2010; ___ ,"Beck's Music Inspired Art Interactive Installations," www.blog.electrolyte.co.uk, October 6, 2009.

at sporting events, and local advertisers promote special events, sales, and the like. Exhibit 13–3 shows one of the many products, services, and/or events that have used this medium.

**Mobile Billboards** Another outdoor medium is **mobile billboards**. Some companies paint their cars with ads; others paint trucks and vans. Still others put ads on small billboards, mount them on trailers, and drive around and/or park in the geographic areas being targeted (Exhibit 13–4). Costs depend on the area and the mobile board company's fees, though even small and large organizations have found the medium affordable. A number of studies have shown that mobile billboards can lead to a high number of impressions, while a study conducted by the Product

**FIGURE 13–4**
Out-of-Home Displays

Source: Outdoor Advertising Association of America (OAAA). 2010

| Number of Out of Home Displays (2010) | | | | |
|---|---|---|---|---|
| **Billboards** | **Street Furniture** | **Transit** | **Alternative** | **Cinema** |
| **Bulletins**<br>148,868 faces | **Bus Shelters**<br>49,082 displays | **Buses**<br>205,426 faces | **Digital Place-Based**<br>101,805 screens | **Cinema**<br>17,800 |
| **Digital Bulletins**<br>2,000 faces | **Urban Furniture, i.e.**<br>Phone Kiosks<br>Newsracks | **Airports**<br>68,560 faces | **Arena & Stadiums**<br>1,352 | |
| **Posters**<br>146,606 faces | **Shopping Malls**<br>30,532 displays | **Subway & Rail**<br>184,078 faces | **Interior Place-Based, i.e.**<br>Convenience Stores<br>Health Clubs<br>Restaurants/Bars | |
| **Junior Posters**<br>23,336 faces | | **Truckside/Mobile**<br>10,593 vehicles | **Exterior Place-Based, i.e.**<br>Airborne<br>Marine<br>Resorts & Leisure | |
| **Walls/Spectaculars**<br>1,133 faces | | **Taxis/**<br>**Wrapped Vehicles**<br>46,194 vehicles | | |

Acceptance and Research Organization indicate that mobile ads lead to high levels of recall and readership, and were likely to have an impact on sales.[2]

A number of companies including McDonald's, Saab, and Sprint PCS are frequent users of mobile ads.

## In-Store Media

Advertisers use **in-store media** such as in-store ads, aisle displays, store leaflets, shopping cart signage, and in-store TV to reach shoppers at the place where they buy. A study by MEC Sensor and BMRB International revealed that one-third of shoppers say in-store ads influence them to make a purchase decision, 44 percent say they notice such ads, and 75 percent of those who noticed the ads said they are likely to purchase the advertised brand.[3]

Much of the attraction of point-of-purchase media is based on figures from the Point of Purchase Advertising Institute (POPAI) that states that approximately two-thirds of consumers' purchase decisions are made in the store; some impulse categories demonstrate an 80 percent rate.[4] Many advertisers are spending more of their dollars where decisions are made now that they can reach consumers at the point of purchase, providing additional product information while reducing their overall marketing efforts.

**EXHIBIT 13–3**
A variety of companies use blimps as an advertising medium

## Miscellaneous Outdoor Media

As shown in Figure 13–4, there are numerous outdoor media available, adding to the pervasiveness of this medium. The next time you are out, take a few moments to observe how many different forms of outdoor advertising you are exposed to.

## Transit Advertising

Another form of out-of-home advertising is **transit advertising**. Transit is targeted at the millions of people who are exposed to commercial transportation facilities, including buses, taxis, commuter trains, trolleys, airplanes, and subways.

Transit advertising has been around for a long time, but recent years have seen a renewed interest in this medium. Due in part to the increased number of women in the work force (they can be reached on their way to

**EXHIBIT 13–4**
An interesting and unusual example of a mobile billboard in an international setting

Trucks often serve as mobile billboards

work more easily than at home), audience segmentation, and the fact that many people spend more time outside of the home than inside, transit continues to be a popular medium. McDonald's, Sprint, Frito-Lay, the United Way, and numerous state lotteries, and others, like transit's lower costs, frequency of exposures, flexibility, and point of sale presence. Kellogg's has found transit to be an effective medium for marketing Nutri-Grain, while the California Beef Council found that 42 percent of rail commuters in Northern California saw their beef ads inside terminals in just one month, and as a result developed more positive attitudes toward beef.[5]

**Types of Transit Advertising** There are actually three forms of transit advertising: (1) inside cards, (2) outside posters, and (3) station, platform, or terminal posters.

**Inside Cards** If you have ever ridden a commuter bus, you have probably noticed the **inside cards** placed above the seats and luggage area advertising restaurants, TV or radio stations, or a myriad of other products and services. As noted earlier, companies now advertise on digital screens in transit vehicles, which deliver news, video ads, restaurant information, and so forth. The ability to change the message and the visibility provide the advertiser with a more attention-getting medium.

Transit cards can be controversial. For example, in the New York subway system, many of the ads for chewing gum, soup, and Smokey the Bear have given way to public service announcements about AIDS, unwanted pregnancies, rape, and infant mortality. While subway riders may agree that such issues are important, many of them complain that the ads are depressing and intrusive.

**Outside Posters** Advertisers use various forms of outdoor transit posters to promote products and services. These **outside posters** may appear on the sides, backs, and/or roofs of buses, taxis, trains, and subway and trolley cars.

The increasing sophistication of this medium is demonstrated by a technology, developed by Vert, Inc. (a division of Clear Channel), that transforms ads on top of taxicabs into real-time animated electronic billboards. A Web server that communicates with a global positioning satellite (GPS) is built into the taxi-top screen. The GPS determines the taxi's location and sends it to the local server, which then delivers the relevant ads for a particular area. A taxi traveling through a Hispanic community can have a message in Spanish, stock quotes could appear in the financial district, and so on. The message can also be changed by time of day—for example,

**EXHIBIT 13–5**
Electronic outside posters often appear on taxicabs

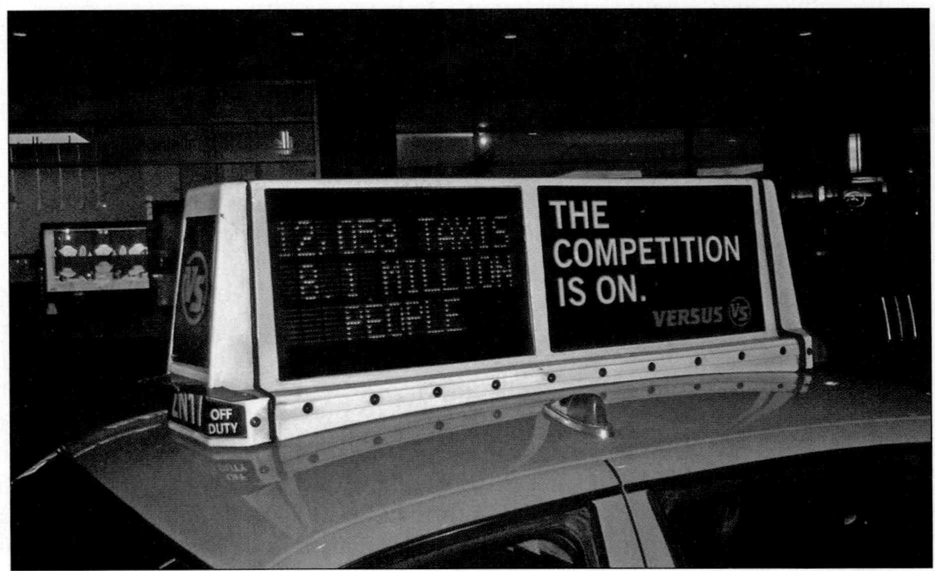


to advertise coffee in the mornings and dinner specials later in the day. The ads appear in color in a format similar to banner ads, at 10 times the brightness of a TV screen. (See Exhibit 13–5).

**Station, Platform, and Terminal Posters** Floor displays, island showcases, electronic signs, and other forms of advertising that appear in train or subway stations, airline terminals, and the like are all forms of transit advertising. As Exhibit 13–6 shows, **terminal posters** can be very attractive and attention-getting. Bus shelters often provide the advertiser with expanded coverage where other outdoor boards may be restricted. Digital signs on subway platforms have become a common sight.

CHAPTER 13

**Advantages and Disadvantages of Outdoor Advertising** Outdoor advertising offers a number of advantages:

LO 13-3

1. *Wide coverage of local markets.* With proper placement, a broad base of exposure is possible in local markets, with both day and night presence. Think about the millions of people exposed to billboards in Times Square!

**EXHIBIT 13–6**
Terminal posters can be used to attract attention

2. *Frequency.* Because purchase cycles are typically for 30-day periods, consumers are usually exposed a number of times, resulting in high levels of frequency.
3. *Geographic flexibility.* Outdoor can be placed along highways, near stores, or on mobile billboards, almost anywhere that laws permit. For local advertisers, outdoor can reach people in specific geographic and/or demographic areas. Local, regional, or even national markets may be covered.
4. *Creativity.* As shown earlier, outdoor ads can be very creative. Large print, colors, and other elements like digital signs attract attention.
5. *Ability to create awareness.* Because of its impact (and the need for a simple message), outdoor can lead to a high level of awareness.
6. *Efficiency.* Outdoor usually has a very competitive CPM when compared to other media. The average CPM of outdoor is often one-half of radio and far less than that of TV, magazines, and newspapers. Transit is one of the least expensive media in both relative and absolute costs.
7. *Effectiveness.* Outdoor advertising can be effective, as demonstrated by the California Beef example. In a study reported by BBDO advertising, 35 percent of consumers surveyed said they had called a phone number they saw on an out-of-home ad.[6] A study reported by Mukesh Bhargava and Naveen Donthu showed that outdoor advertising can have a significant effect on sales, particularly when combined with a promotion.[7]
8. *Production capabilities.* Modern technologies have reduced production times for outdoor advertising to allow for rapid turnaround time, and digital messages can be changed in minutes.
9. *Timeliness.* Many outdoor ads appear in or near shopping areas or on or in the vehicles taking customers there, thus resulting in timely exposures.

At the same time, however, there are limitations to outdoor, many of them related to its advantages:

1. *Waste coverage.* While it is possible to reach very specific audiences, in many cases the purchase of outdoor results in a high degree of waste coverage. It is not likely that everyone driving past a billboard is part of the target market.
2. *Limited message capabilities.* Because of the speed with which most people pass by outdoor ads, exposure time is short, so messages are limited to a few words and/or an illustration. Lengthy appeals are not likely to be effective. Some transit forms are not conducive to creative messages.
3. *Wearout.* Because of the high frequency of exposures, outdoor may lead to a quick wearout. People are likely to get tired of seeing the same ad every day.
4. *Cost.* Because of the decreasing signage available and the higher cost associated with inflatables, outdoor advertising can be expensive in both an absolute and a relative sense.
5. *Measurement problems.* One of the more difficult problems of outdoor advertising lies in the accuracy of measuring reach, frequency, and other effects. (As you will see in the measurement discussion, this problem is currently being addressed, though it has not been resolved.)
6. *Image problems.* Outdoor advertising has suffered some image problems as well as some disregard among consumers.

In sum, outdoor advertising has both advantages and disadvantages for marketers. Some of these problems can be avoided with other forms of out-of-home advertising.

**Advantages and Disadvantages of Transit Advertising** In addition to sharing some of the advantages and disadvantages of other outdoor media, transit has a few more specific to this medium. Advantages of using transit advertising include the following:

1. *Exposure.* Long length of exposure to an ad is one major advantage of indoor transit forms. The average ride on mass transit is 45 minutes, allowing for plenty of exposure time. As with airline tickets, the audience is essentially a captive one, with nowhere else to go and nothing much to do. As a result, riders are likely to read the ads—more than once. A second form of exposure transit advertising provides is the absolute number of people exposed. About 9 million people ride mass transit every week, and over 10.5 billion rides were taken in 2008, providing a substantial number of potential viewers.[8]
2. *Frequency.* Because our daily routines are standard, those who ride buses, subways, and the like are exposed to the ads repeatedly. If you rode the same subway to work and back every day, in one month you would have the opportunity to see the ad 20 to 40 times. The locations of station and shelter signs also afford high frequency of exposure.

Some disadvantages are also associated with transit:

1. *Reach.* While an advantage of transit advertising is the ability to provide exposure to a large number of people, this audience may have certain lifestyles and/or behavioral characteristics that are not true of the target market as a whole. For example, in rural or suburban areas, mass transit is limited or nonexistent, so the medium is not very effective for reaching these people.
2. *Mood of the audience.* Sitting or standing on a crowded subway may not be conducive to reading advertising, let alone experiencing the mood the advertiser would like to create. Controversial ad messages may contribute to this less than positive feeling. Likewise, hurrying through an airport may create anxieties that limit the effectiveness of the ads placed there.



## Measurement in Out-of-Home Media

In 2010 the OAAA announced a new audience measurement system that had been in development for the past five years. Eyes On is considered to be an improvement over the traditional measure of opportunity to see, with a "likely to see" metric that can also provide demographic and ethnographic data. The new data is a combination of eye tracking, circulation, and travel survey data all combined into one rating by a coalition of research companies.[9]

A number of other sources of audience measurement and information are available:

- Competitive Media Reports (formerly BAR/LNA) provides information on expenditures on outdoor media by major advertisers.
- Simmons Market Research Bureau conducts research annually for the Institute of Outdoor Advertising, providing demographic data, exposures, and the like. Mediamark Research Inc. (MRI) provides similar data.

- The Point of Purchase Advertising Institute is a trade organization of point-of-purchase advertisers collecting statistical and other market information on POP advertising.
- The Outdoor Advertising Association of America (OAAA) is the primary trade association of the industry. It assists members with research, creative ideas, and more effective use of the medium and has a website at www.oaa.org.
- The Traffic Audit Bureau (TAB) is the auditing arm of the transit industry. TAB conducts traffic counts on which the published rates are based.
- Scarborough publishes local market studies providing demographic data, product usage, and outdoor media usage.
- The American Public Transportation Association (APTA) provides ridership statistics, studies, and other transit usage information.

# PROMOTIONAL PRODUCTS MARKETING

According to the Promotional Products Association International (PPA), **promotional products marketing** is "the advertising or promotional medium or method that uses promotional products, such as ad specialties, premiums, business gifts, awards, prizes, or commemoratives." Promotional products marketing is the more up-to-date name for what used to be called specialty advertising. **Specialty advertising** has now been provided with a new definition:

> A medium of advertising, sales promotion, and motivational communication employing imprinted, useful, or decorative products called advertising specialties, a subset of promotional products.
>
> Unlike premiums, with which they are sometimes confused (called advertising specialties), these articles are always distributed free—recipients don't have to earn the specialty by making a purchase or contribution.[10]

As you can see from these descriptions, specialty advertising is often considered both an advertising and a sales promotion medium. In our discussion, we treat it as a supportive advertising medium in the IMC program.

There are thousands of *advertising specialty* items, including ballpoint pens, coffee mugs, key rings, calendars, T-shirts, and matchbooks. Unconventional specialties such as plant holders, wall plaques, and gloves with the advertiser's name printed on them are also used to promote a company or its product; so are glassware, trophies, awards, and vinyl products. In fact, advertisers spend over $18.1 billion per year on specialty advertising items (Figure 13–5).[11]

If you stop reading for a moment and look around your desk (or bed or beach blanket), you'll probably find some specialty advertising item nearby. It may be the pen you are using, a matchbook, or even a book cover with the campus bookstore name on it. Specialty items are used for many promotional purposes: to thank a customer for patronage, keep the name of the company in front of consumers, introduce new products, or reinforce the name of an existing company, product, or service. Advertising specialties are often used to support other forms of product promotions.

## Advantages and Disadvantages of Promotional Products Marketing

Like any other advertising medium, promotional products marketing offers the marketer both advantages and disadvantages. Advantages include the following:

1. *Selectivity.* Because specialty advertising items are generally distributed directly to target customers, the medium offers a high degree of selectivity. The communication is distributed to the desired recipient, reducing waste coverage.
2. *Flexibility.* As the variety of specialty items in Figure 13–5 demonstrates, this medium offers a high degree of flexibility. A message as simple as a logo or as long as is necessary can be distributed through a number of means. Both small and large companies can employ this medium for a variety of objectives limited only by their own creativity.
3. *Frequency.* Most forms of specialty advertising are designed for retention. Key chains, calendars, and pens remain with the potential customer for a long time, providing repeat exposures to the advertising message at no additional cost.
4. *Cost.* Some specialty items are rather expensive (for example, leather goods), but most are affordable to almost any size organization. While they are costly on a CPM basis when compared with other media, the high number of repeat exposures drives down the relative cost per exposure of this advertising medium.

FIGURE 13–5

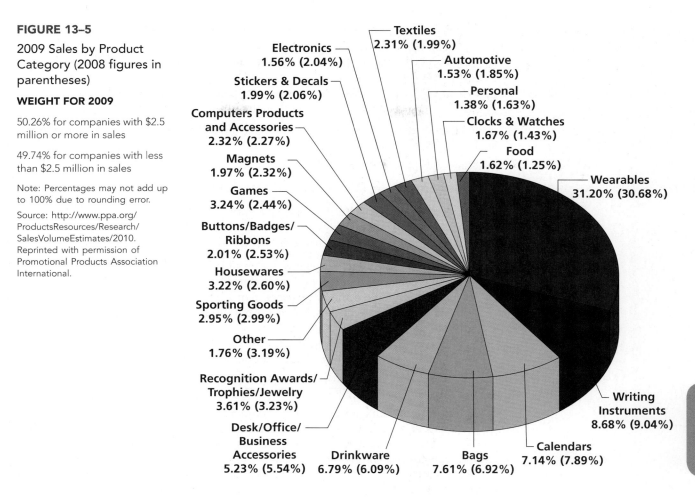

2009 Sales by Product Category (2008 figures in parentheses)

**WEIGHT FOR 2009**

50.26% for companies with $2.5 million or more in sales

49.74% for companies with less than $2.5 million in sales

Note: Percentages may not add up to 100% due to rounding error.

Source: http://www.ppa.org/ProductsResources/Research/SalesVolumeEstimates/2010. Reprinted with permission of Promotional Products Association International.

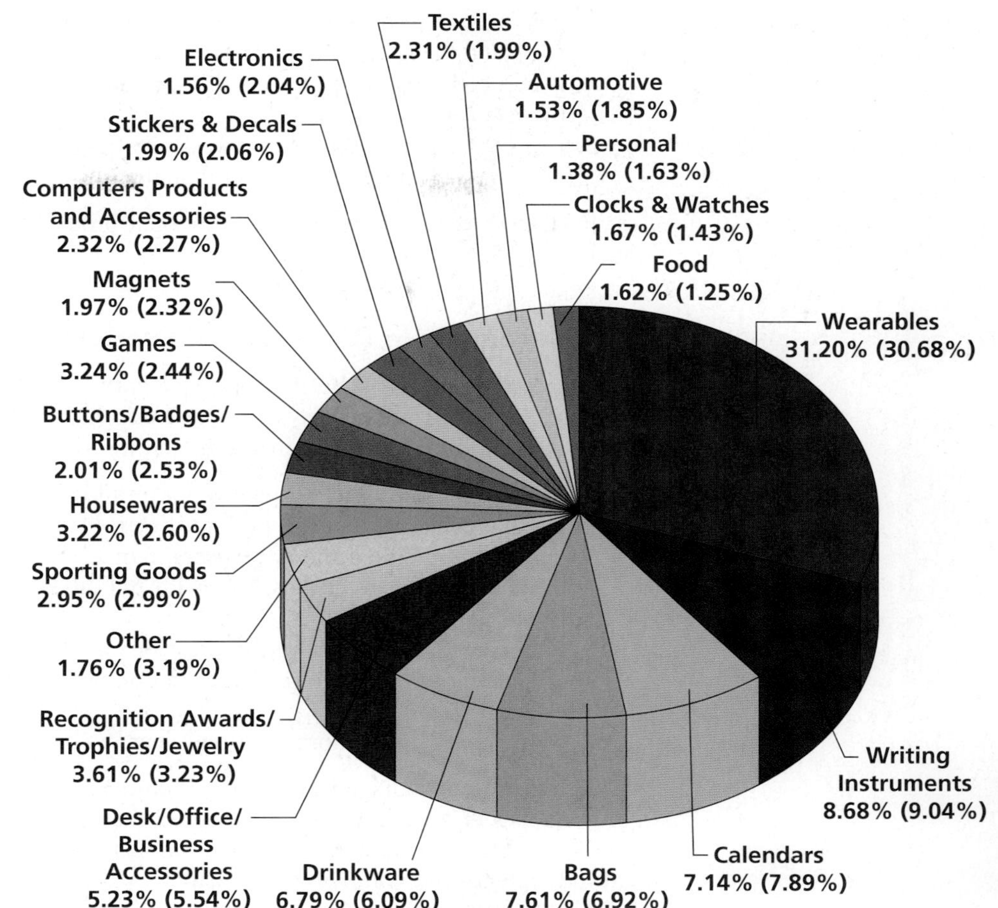


5. *Goodwill.* Promotional products are perhaps the only medium that generates goodwill in the receiver. Because people like to receive gifts and many of the products are functional (key chains, calendars, etc.), consumers are grateful to receive them. The products also lead to a favorable impression of the advertiser.
6. *High recall.* Specialties lead to high recall of both the advertisers' name and message.
7. *Supplementing other media.* A major advantage of promotional products marketing is its ability to supplement other media. Because of its low cost and repeat exposures, the simplest message can reinforce the appeal or information provided through other forms.

Promotional products have also been used to support trade shows, motivate dealers, recognize employees, and promote consumer and sales force contests.

Disadvantages of promotional products marketing include the following:

1. *Image.* While most forms of specialty advertising are received as friendly reminders of the store or company name, the firm must be careful choosing the specialty item. The company image may be cheapened by a chintzy or poorly designed advertising form.
2. *Saturation.* With so many organizations now using this advertising medium, the marketplace may become saturated. While you can always use another ballpoint

pen or book of matches, the value to the receiver declines if replacement is too easy, and the likelihood that you will retain the item or even notice the message is reduced. The more unusual the specialty, the more value it is likely to have to the receiver.

3. *Lead time.* The lead time required to put together a promotional products message is significantly longer than that for most other media.

Even with its disadvantages, promotional products marketing can be an effective medium.

## Measurement in Promotional Products Marketing

Owing to the nature of the industry, specialty advertising has no established ongoing audience measurement system. Research has been conducted in an attempt to determine the impact of this medium leading to the following results:

LO 13-4

- 71 percent report having received a promotional product in the last 12 months.
- 33.7 percent still had the item on them.
- 76 percent recalled the advertiser's name.
- 52 percent conducted business with the advertiser after receiving the promotional item.
- 52.1 percent had improved impressions of the company.
- 73 percent of those using the promotion used it once a week, 45.2 percent once a day.
- 55 percent kept it more than one year.[12]

A second study conducted by Georgia Southern University showed that 71.6 percent of attendees at a trade show remembered the name of the company that gave them the specialty; 65.5 percent thought it was useful; and 76.3 percent had a favorable attitude toward the company as a result.[13]

The Promotional Products Association International (www.ppai.org) is the trade organization of the field. The PPAI helps marketers develop and use specialty advertising forms. It also provides promotional and public relations support for specialty advertising and disseminates statistical and educational information.

## Yellow Pages Advertising

When we think of advertising media, many of us overlook one of the most popular forms in existence—the **Yellow Pages**. While most of us use them frequently, we tend to forget they are advertising. The Yellow Pages account for over $31 billion worldwide ($13 billion in the United States) in advertising expenditures in the print and online versions.[14]

The Yellow Pages are often referred to as a **directional medium** because the ads do not create awareness or demand for products or services; rather, once consumers have decided to buy, the Yellow Pages point them in the direction where their purchases can be made (Exhibit 13–7). Eighty percent of all people who referenced the Yellow Pages (print or online) either made a purchase or said they were likely to do so. In addition, 38 percent of people who referenced the Yellow Pages were new customers to the business they chose.[15] The Yellow Pages are thus considered the final link in the buying cycle.

### Advantages and Disadvantages of Yellow Pages

The Yellow Pages offer the following advantages to advertisers:

LO 13-3

1. *Wide availability.* A variety of directories are published. According to the Yellow Pages Publishers Association, consumers refer to the Yellow Pages more than 13.4 billion times yearly.[16]

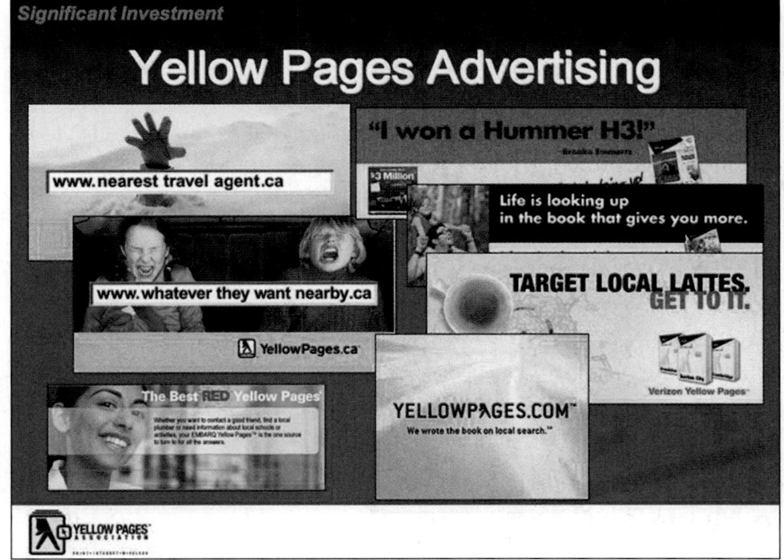


**EXHIBIT 13–7**
The Yellow Pages are the final ink in the buying cycle

2. *Action orientation.* Consumers use the Yellow Pages when they are considering, or have decided to take, action. The YPPA reports that 20.4 percent say their purchase was influenced by the Yellow Pages.[17]
3. *Costs.* Ad space and production costs are relatively low compared to other media.
4. *Frequency.* Because of their longevity (print Yellow Pages are published yearly), consumers return to the directories time and again.
5. *Nonintrusiveness.* Because consumers choose to use the Yellow Pages, they are not considered an intrusion. Studies show that most consumers rate the Yellow Pages very favorably. Among users, 79 percent agree that the Yellow Pages are an important source of information, 76 percent report that the books are helpful for learning about new products, and 70 percent use the information to assist in their buying decisions.[18]
6. *Trust.* A 2009 study showed that 67 percent of consumers trusted the Yellow Pages more than a computer search for local information.[19]



Disadvantages of the Yellow Pages include the following:

1. *Market fragmentation.* Since Yellow Pages are essentially local media, they tend to be very localized. Add to this the increasing number of specialized directories, and the net result is a very specific offering.
2. *Timeliness.* Because print Yellow Pages are printed only once a year, they become outdated. Companies may relocate, go out of business, or change phone numbers in the period between editions. (This problem is greatly reduced with the Internet pages.)
3. *Lack of creativity.* While the Yellow Pages are somewhat flexible, their creative aspects are limited, though the use of four-color processes is increasing.
4. *Lead times.* Printing schedules require that ads be placed a long time before the publications appear. It is impossible to get an ad in after the deadline, and advertisers need to wait a long time before the next edition.
5. *Clutter.* A study by Avery Abernethy indicated that the Yellow Pages (like other media) experience problems with clutter. (Though the Yellow Pages trade organization offers research evidence to contradict this conclusion.)[20]
6. *Size requirements.* Response to Yellow Pages ads is directly tied to the size of the ad. Thus to get noticed, one may have to pay more.

As noted, many of these disadvantages will be reduced or eliminated with the Internet.

**Audience Measurement in the Yellow Pages** A number of forms of audience measurement are employed in the Yellow Pages industry. As with other print media, *circulation* is counted as the number of either individuals or households possessing a particular directory. But Yellow Pages advertisers have resisted the use of circulation figures for evaluating audience size, arguing that this number represents only *potential* exposures to an ad. Given that households may possess more than one directory, advertisers argued for a figure based on *usage.* The National Yellow Pages Monitor (NYPM) now provides Yellow Pages directory ratings and usage behavior by market. Using a diary method similar to that used for broadcast media, this ratings method allows advertisers to determine both the absolute and relative costs of advertising in different directories. NYPM has developed a strategic alliance with Media Metrix to measure online Yellow Pages usage. Statistical Research Inc. (SRI) also conducts national studies to measure Yellow Pages usage. Simmons and MRI provide demographic and usage information.

The trade association for the Yellow Pages, the Yellow Pages Integrated Media Association (www.yellowpagesima.org and www.yppa.org), provides industry information, rates, educational materials, and assistance to advertisers and potential advertisers. The YPPA also disseminates educational and statistical information.

# OTHER TRADITIONAL SUPPORT MEDIA

There are numerous other traditional ways to promote products. Some are reviewed here.

## Advertising in Movie Theaters

Another method of delivering a message that is increasing quickly (to the dismay of many) is the use of movie theaters to promote products and/or services. Commercials shown before the film and previews, with both local and national sponsorships, are now regularly shown in movie theaters. In addition, ads in theater lobbies, at kiosks, and on popcorn tubs and drink cups are used. Automotive, food, and package good companies and regional and local companies are just some of the product categories that find this medium attractive. At least one study has estimated that more than one-half of all theaters show ads before the films. The growth rate has increased steadily since the 1980s, resulting in a $500 million industry.

Consumer reaction to ads in movie theaters is mixed. A number of earlier studies have shown that most people think these ads are annoying or very annoying although now people may be becoming more used to them. The Cinema Advertising Council (CAC) reported that 63 percent of moviegoers say they do not mind ads before the movie starts.[21] On the other hand, many consumers complain that having paid for a ticket, they shouldn't have to sit through ads and/or commercials. A Portland, Oregon, group called Captive Motion Picture Audiences of America (CMPAA) recruited over 3,000 people to sign a petition against the ads.[22]

Nevertheless, a number of products and brands have used this advertising medium including Allstate, BMW, Cadillac, Kmart, Old Navy, and Taco Bell among others. In addition, a research study commissioned by one in-theater advertising broker showed that the ads were three times more likely to be remembered than TV ads.[23]

**Advantages of Movie Theater Advertising** Movies provide a number of advantages to advertisers, including the following:

1. *Exposure.* The number of people attending movies is substantial: over 1.6 billion tickets were sold in 2009.[24] Ticket sales are over $9.8 billion per year.
2. *Emotional attachment.* A 2010 report found that 41.5 percent of movie goers say they become emotionally attached to cinema ads and brands—more than the ads on the broadcasts of the *Super Bowl, Summer Olympics, World Series,* or the *Oscars.*[25]

3. *Cost.* The cost of advertising in a theater varies from one setting to the next. However, it is low in terms of both absolute and relative costs per exposure.
4. *Attention.* Movie watchers pay attention to the ads shown in theaters, as research indicates that cinema ads reach many consumers who say they are usually ad avoiders. These consumers are 157 percent more likely to see an ad in a movie than any other medium.[26]
5. *Clutter.* Lack of clutter is another advantage offered by advertising in movie theaters. Most theaters limit the number of ads.

6. *Proximity.* Since many theaters are located in or adjacent to shopping malls, potential customers are "right next door." (Of moviegoers, 74 percent combine the activity with dining out.[27])
7. *Segmentation.* A key advantage of movie advertising is the ability to target specific demographic segments. The profile of the moviegoer is above-average in education and affluence. The movie titles and ratings enable advertisements to reach specific groups.

**Disadvantages of Movie Theater Advertising** Some of the disadvantages associated with movie theaters as advertising media follow:

1. *Irritation.* Perhaps the major disadvantage is that many people do not wish to see advertising in these media. A number of studies suggest these ads may create a high degree of annoyance. If true, this dissatisfaction may carry over to the product itself, to the movies, or to the theaters.
2. *Cost.* While the cost of advertising in local theaters has been cited as an advantage because of the low rates charged, ads exposed nationally are often as much as 20 percent higher than an equal exposure on television. CPMs also tend to be higher than in other media.

While viewers seemingly either like or dislike cinema ads, it seems they are here to stay.



# NONTRADITIONAL SUPPORT MEDIA

## Branded Entertainment

Perhaps the major change that has occurred in the area of integrated marketing communications over the past few years is the enormous growth associated with **branded entertainment**. Branded entertainment is a form of advertising that blends marketing and entertainment through television, film, music talent, and technology. Essentially, the goal is to use entertainment media to gain consumers' attention and exposure to products and/or brands. It is extremely difficult to place a dollar amount on branded entertainment, but there is no doubt that its use continues to increase yearly.

Let's take a look at the ways companies use branded entertainment.

LO 13-2

**Product Placements** While **product placements** account for only a small portion of major advertisers' budgets, the use of this medium has increased tremendously in recent years. Estimates are that in 2009 placements on broadcast TV were up 3 percent, and on cable up 5 percent.[28] It should be noted, however, that it is difficult to assess the accuracy of these figures. As many product placements are free or provided in exchange for trade. Product placement agencies contend that as much as 70 to 95 percent of their placements are for trade.[29] An in-depth study of the product placement industry by Russell and Belch supports this contention.[30] Industry analysts expect this trend to continue as placements move from traditional media to alternative media, as personal video recorder growth sales continue (allowing for increased avoidance of commercials), and as consumers' lifestyles change. Placements are also starting to catch on in Europe.

Interestingly, product placements are not a new phenomenon as placements are known to have existed as early as the 1930s and were commonly employed via soap operas in the 1950s. However, it was not until the turn of the century that the number of placements skyrocketed. Today, product placements are used to gain exposure by numerous companies large and small (Exhibit 13–8) and are a very important part of the IMC strategy for companies like BMW, Apple Computers, PepsiCo, and

**EXHIBIT 13–8**
Audi's Spyder was a hit in *Ironman 2*

Anheuser Busch (just to name a few). Much of the logic behind product placement is that since the placement is embedded in the script or program setting, it cannot be avoided, thereby increasing exposure. Given the lack of intrusiveness of the placement, consumers may not have the same negative reactions to it as they may to a commercial. Further, research has demonstrated that association with a program or movie—or particularly with a celebrity—may enhance the image of the product and, in some instances, lead to increased sales.[31,32]

Given the intense growth in the number of product placements, some marketers are concerned that placements may be becoming too common. It is very rare to watch a movie or TV show without being exposed to one or more placements. Given the obvious attempt to gain exposure in many of these, placements may be becoming more obvious; consumers may perceive them more like ads and, as a result, they may have less impact on the viewer.[33] Some industry watchdogs have called for more regulation of placements, contending that they blur the lines between advertising and programming and therefore may be deceptive. The FCC is currently considering this possibility.

As of this time, however, product placements continue to increase both in number and in dollar amounts. In addition, placements are appearing in media and situations never before imagined including music videos, video games and books (see the lead-in to this chapter).

**Product Integration** A more involved form of product placements actually leads to the placement being integrated throughout the program content and/or script. In **product integrations** the product is woven throughout the program or becomes the program itself. Like product placements, product integrations are on the increase as the networks continue to search for new program content, and the proliferation of cable media channels affords marketers with numerous integration opportunities. For example, on a recent episode of *Modern Family,* much of the show was devoted to the family's bumbling of the father's request for an Apple iPad for his birthday and their frantic efforts to find one. When the family actually obtained one, the program ended with the father sitting on the couch with the iPad in his lap, enjoying the product.[34] In another instance, GEICO was able to get TNT's NBA All-Star Game's classic "shoot out" changed from h-o-r-s-e to G-E-I-C-O. *America's Hottest Mom* (Restylane) and *America's Next Top Model* (Cover Girl) have also successfully employed integrations, as have others.

**Advertainment** The creation of video and/or music content by an advertiser in an attempt to entertain viewers while advertising their products is known as advertainment. For example, Coca-Cola developed a long-form advertainment to reach TiVo viewers. The program included 25 minutes of interviews, music videos, behind-the-scenes footage, and live performances with recording artists Sting, Mary J. Blige, Ashanti, and Leona Ness. Coca-Cola ads were tagged so that TiVo users could see them and then click on an icon to download the program. Nike and SKYY Vodka have also produced ad films, as has BMW. The automaker had one of the first series of such films called *The Hire,* and is now developing a new set of episodes. While initially shown only on the Internet, the advertainments have now made their way to a few cable and satellite channels.

**Content Sponsorship** Rather than developing their own content, some advertisers agree to sponsor specific programs, receiving product placements, integration, and promotions in return. For example, P&G has collaborated with the Discovery Health Channel on a *National Body Challenge* 12-week weight loss program. TNT and Fox introduced content-sponsored programs, as has NBC. Advertiser content has also been used on *Ugly Betty,* among others.[35] Interestingly, the content exchange seems to be going the other direction as well. ABC has worked with Sprint to develop commercials on *Desperate Housewives* that feature vignettes reflecting the program's content. Sprint's Palm Pre plays a central role in seven such vignettes in which a couple finds that the product helps them learn more about infidelity, betrayal, and justice than they may ever have imagined—essentially reflecting the content of the program. NBC had pioneered the technique on shows like *30 Rock* and *Heroes.*[36]

**Ad-Supported Video on Demand (VOD)** VODs are specialized content programs offered through cable TV networks that are developed by advertisers and provided to the cable operators for free. For example, General Motors produced a short feature on the history of the Corvette to be shown on CNN through Time Warner and Comcast's VOD channels. MTV launched a series called the *How to Show* in which musicians, athletes, and celebrities offer the "tricks of their trades" (the U.S. Air Force was the first advertiser). ESPN and ABC have offered VODs of college football games 12 hours after they were played. A number of TV shows have been made available as well; the San Diego Zoo provides a video tour to San Diego cable subscribers. On some VODs advertisers can buy placements, commercials, and/or virtual signage or sponsor specific segments.

CHAPTER 13

**Others** While other forms of branded entertainment continue to develop through wireless, mobile, and "branded locations," space does not allow us to discuss each in detail. Suffice it to say that the use of branded entertainment continues to increase and will continue to do so as more and more technological innovations provide opportunities.

**Advantages of Branded Entertainment** A number of advantages of branded entertainment have been suggested:

LO 13-3

1. *Exposure.* In regard to product placements, a large number of people see movies each year (over 1.6 billion admissions per year). The average film is estimated to have a life span of three and one-half years (with 75 million exposures), and most moviegoers are very attentive audience members. When this is combined with the home video rental market and network and cable TV (including HBO, Showtime, the Movie Channel), the potential exposure for a product placed in a movie or on television is enormous. And this form of exposure is not subject to zapping, at least not in the theater.

   High exposure numbers are also offered for TV placements, based on the ratings and the possibility to direct the ad to a defined target market.
2. *Frequency.* Depending on how the product is used in the movie (or program), there may be ample opportunity for repeated exposures (many, for those who like to watch a program or movie more than once). For example, if you are a regular watcher of the programs containing placements and/or integrations, you

will be exposed to the products placed therein a number of times. Syndication will result in additional exposures.

3. *Support for other media.* Branded entertainment supports other promotional tools. A trend is to have the client that is placing the product cross-promote the product and movie tie-in in multiple media venues. As noted, the tie-ins reinforce and are reinforced by ads and commercials.
4. *Source association.* In Chapter 6 we discussed the advantages of source identification. When consumers see their favorite TV celebrities or movie stars using certain brands, the association may lead to a favorable product image or even to sales. In one study of 524 eight- to fourteen-year-olds, 75 percent stated that they notice when brands are placed on their favorite shows, and 72 percent said that seeing a favorite character using a brand makes them want to purchase that brand.[37] Another study among adults showed that one-third of viewers said they try a product after seeing it on a TV show or movie.[38]
5. *Cost.* While the cost of branded entertainment may range from free samples to millions, the latter is an extreme. The CPM for this form of advertising can be very low, owing to the high volume of exposures it generates. For many products, like the Apple iPad in the *Modern Family* episode, the placements may be free, except for the cost of the products.
6. *Recall.* A number of firms have measured the impact of product placements on next-day recall. Results ranged, but most show recall is higher than for TV commercials.
7. *Bypassing regulations.* In the United States as well as many foreign countries, some products are not permitted to advertise on television or to specific market segments. Product placements and integrations have allowed the cigarette and liquor industries to have their products exposed, circumventing these restrictions. Recently there have been attempts to control the bypassing of regulations. The Marin Institute, an alcohol industry watchdog group, has filed suit against Budweiser for their tie-ins to the movie *The Wedding Crasher,* arguing that the movie encouraged underage drinking. Spirits manufacturers Diageo, Bacardi USA, and Brown-Forman have also been named in lawsuits for similar reasons.[39]
8. *Acceptance.* Studies have shown that viewers are accepting of product placements and in general evaluate them positively, though some products (alcohol, guns, cigarettes) are perceived as less acceptable. Other studies report similar results, with one showing that as many as 80 percent of consumers say they have a positive attitude toward placements.[40] In a study conducted with tweens, 43 percent said they found placements to be funny, 39 percent found them to be informative, and 35 percent found them entertaining and interesting.[41] A 2006 study by eMarketer reported similar results.[42]
9. *Targeting.* Content sponsorships and VOD may effectively reach potential customers with a strong interest in the subject matter (i.e., fashion, football).

**Disadvantages of Product Placements** Some disadvantages are also associated with product placements:

1. *High absolute cost.* While the CPM may be very low for various forms of branded entertainment, the absolute costs may be very high, pricing some advertisers out of the market. The increased demand for branded entertainment, coupled with the rising emphasis by the studios for cross-promotions, drives costs up considerably. A study conducted by the National Association of Advertisers indicated that 79 percent of advertisers believe that the costs of branded entertainment deals were too high.[43] Some companies have ceased using this form of promotion citing the rising costs.
2. *Time of exposure.* While the way some products are exposed to the audience has an impact, there is no guarantee viewers will notice the product. Some product

placements are more conspicuous than others. When the product is not featured prominently, the advertiser runs the risk of not being seen (although, of course, the same risk is present in all forms of media advertising).

3. *Limited appeal.* The appeal that can be made in some of these media forms is limited. There is no potential for discussing product benefits or providing detailed information. Rather, appeals are limited to source association, use, and enjoyment. The endorsement of the product is indirect, and the flexibility for product demonstration is subject to its use in the medium.
4. *Lack of control.* In many movies, the advertiser has no say over when and how often the product will be shown. Many companies have found that their placements in movies did not work as well as expected. Fabergé developed an entire Christmas campaign around its Brut cologne and its movie placement, only to find the movie was delayed until February. Others have had their placements cut from the script.
5. *Public reaction.* Many TV viewers and moviegoers are incensed at the idea of placing ads in programs or movies. These viewers want to maintain the barrier between program content and commercials. If the placement is too intrusive, they may develop negative attitudes toward the brand. The increased use of placements and integrations has led many consumers to be annoyed by what they consider to be crass commercialization. The FTC has explored options for limiting placements without consumer notification, though they have not sought increased regulation to date. Still others are upset about programs such as *Undercover Boss* in which a CEO goes undercover in his/her own company to see how his employees work. Critics contend that these shows are nothing more than public relations disguised as programming.
6. *Competition.* The appeal of branded entertainment has led to increased competition to get one's product placed, increasing demand and costs.
7. *Negative placements.* Some products may appear in movie scenes that are disliked by the audience or create a less than favorable mood. For example, in the movie *Missing,* a very good, loyal father takes comfort in a bottle of Coke, while a Pepsi machine appears in a stadium where torturing and murders take place—not a good placement for Pepsi. Emerson—the manufacturer of the garbage disposal brand In-Sink-Erator—has sued NBC for showing a cheerleader getting her hand mangled in the program *Heroes.* NBC never received permission from Emerson to show their brand.
8. *Clutter.* The rapid growth of branded entertainment tie-ins has led to an overwhelming number of placements and integrations as noted previously. Like other forms of advertising, too many placements and integrations will eventually lead to clutter and loss of effectiveness.

**Measurement in Branded Entertainment** With the rapid growth in branded entertainment have come a number of research studies and companies attempting to monitor and measure the impact of this media form. At this time, there is no one accepted standard used by advertisers or industry members.[44] However, a number of high-profile companies now offer services in this area including those listed below.

- *Nielsen Media Research.* The TV ratings company currently tracks product placements on network television. The company has plans to track cable programs in the near future.
- *Nielsen-IAG Research.* IAG maintains a panel where an average of 5,000 daily viewers take an online quiz about the previous night's prime-time programs, the commercials, and product placements therein. The information is used to determine which ads work best; what shows, spots, and placements are being remembered; and viewers' attitudes toward the same.

- *Deutsch/iTVX.* The advertising agency and product integration valuation company have combined efforts to measure Results-Oriented-Integration. The method values the quality of each hundredth of a second of an integration, and then translates them into a Product Placement/Commercial Cost Ratio to value the integration by comparing it to the value of a commercial.
- *Brand Advisors.* The company attempts to value brand integration in feature films. A number of other companies have begun to offer various services including NextMedium, Delivery Agent, IEG, Image Impact, and others. As noted, however, none of these has received universal acceptance in the industry or among advertisers.

In addition to the studies reported earlier, research has provided evidence that an aura of glamour is added to products associated with celebrities.

## Guerrilla Marketing

In addition to branded entertainment another nontraditional way that advertisers are now attempting to reach consumers is referred to by a variety of names including guerrilla marketing, stealth, street, buzz, ambush, or viral marketing. Whatever it is called, there seems to be no end in sight to where advertisers will attempt to reach you. While previously targeted primarily to college students and others of the same age group, these efforts have now been expanded to reach additional audiences as well.[45] In addition, larger portions of the communications budgets (while still small) are being allocated to this media form, and the size of the various projects is also getting larger.[46] Guerilla marketing has benefited by technology in that they can be even more creative, as well as the fact that cell phones now have cameras, allowing viewers to send their pictures to others.

The most successful guerilla campaigns most often have an unusual idea, an irreverent execution, and the element of surprise. For example, Blu Dot, a Minneapolis furniture store left its $129 "Real Good Chair" at various curbsides in New York City. Concealed within each chair was a GPS device to track the chairs to the chairs' "rescuers" homes, and a Google map was posted on the company's website, and Twitter feeds were provided to follow their paths. Street teams were later dispatched to the homes, and those who agreed to chat were given a second chair free.[47] Also in New York in Times Square, Scholastic Media promoted the introduction of its first interactive console game by having an elementary school teacher carve pumpkins on Halloween in an attempt to break his own record of 50 in one hour (he did). Approximately 3,200 smiling viewers stayed for 20 minutes to watch him do so.[48] Other examples include showing projected pictures on empty buildings, giveaways, and many other unconventional ideas too numerous to mention.

## Miscellaneous Other Media

The variety of options for placing ads appears endless. Obviously, we have reported on only a few of these. Chapter 15 will discuss a few more, specifically online vehicles. Before leaving this chapter, however, we would like to mention a few of the faster growing and more widely used options.

- *Videogame ads.* As the number of videogamers and the time they spend playing these games continues to increase, advertising in this medium is expected to grow right along with it. Companies such as Orbitz and T-Mobile have found videogame ads to be successful, as have Nike, Coca-Cola, Nokia, Levi Strauss & Company, and others. A Barack Obama ad appeared in a X-Box game promoting his campaign website, www.voteforchange.com. An estimated 68 percent of American households play computer or video games, 40 percent of whom are female.[49]

EXHIBIT 13–9
Advertising on people's bodies is becoming more common

- *Parking lot ads.* An out-of-home medium showing increased growth is that of parking lot signage. From signs on cart docks to painting the walls of indoor parking garages, more companies are finding this medium attractive—particularly for point-of-purchase items. The ads reach a variety of demographics, depending on where they are placed. PepsiCo is just one of a number of companies employing this medium.
- *Gas station pump ads.* Screens appearing on gas pumps now reach an estimated 150 consumers monthly in over 125 markets. A study conducted by Nielsen shows that the ads have high recall and engagement rates, consumers enjoy them and find them entertaining and say that they would watch them again on their next visit.[50]
- *Place-based media.* The idea of bringing the advertising medium to the consumers wherever they may be underlies the strategy behind place-based media. TV monitors and magazine racks have appeared in classrooms, doctors' offices, and health clubs, among a variety of other locations. PRN (the Premiere Retail Network) has TV channels in more than 10,000 locations, including Walmart, Costco, Best Buy, Circuit City, and Sam's Clubs in the United States reaching an estimated 237 million consumers a month.[51] Place-based media have become a profitable venture and an attractive alternative for media buyers. Many advertisers, particularly pharmaceutical companies, have found place-based media an effective way to reach their markets, and Nielsen now provides quarterly audience reports.
- *Others.* Just a few other examples of the use of support media: Coca-Cola installed 1,000 feet of light boxes in the Atlanta subway to show motion picture ads for Dasani; Muzak, a provider of background music, has teamed with Tyme ATMs to broadcast ads at bank ATM sites; ads now appear on luggage conveyors at some airports, on hubcaps, in elevators, and on fruit. People are even allowing ads to be placed on their bodies (Exhibit 13–9). There are many other examples, as is well demonstrated in Exhibit 13–10 (at least he earned something from the fight!). Ethical Perspective 13–1 shows that ads are now appearing in unexpected places to serve other purposes.

EXHIBIT 13–10
Ads often appear in the strangest places

# Ethical Perspective 13–1

## The Uncomfortable Tie between Advertising and the Public Sector

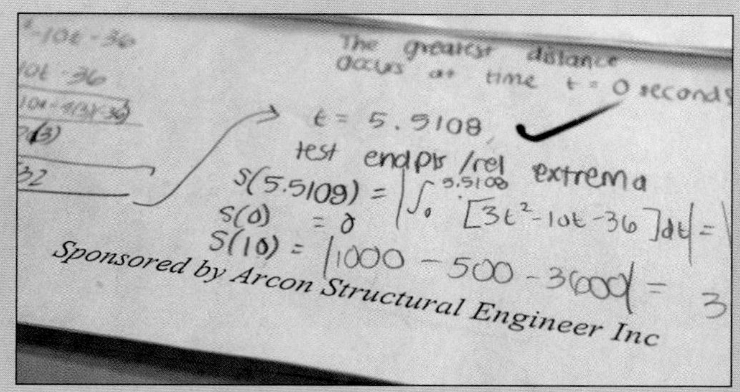


While there are many critics of the increasing amounts of advertising we see, as well as the increasing intrusiveness, there are many in the public sector that are seeking even more. As the economic downturn continues to drag on, budgets for a variety of services continue to decrease, leaving managers to seek out alternative means of financing. One of these is to find advertisers to help allay the costs of a number of services. Consider some of the following:

After his school cut its materials and supplies budget by 30 percent to save jobs, a high school teacher in San Diego, California started offering an opportunity to advertise on his students' quizzes and exams. Quizzes cost $10, chapter tests $20, and a semester final $30, with the ads appearing on the first page only. Most of the ads have come from small store owners, parents, and well wishers, and most students are receptive, knowing the financial situation. So far, the idea raised enough money to cover the teacher's deficit, with some extra left over for others in the math department.

Also in California, the state has considered offering advertisers the opportunity to place messages on digital signs on freeways that were installed for Amber Alerts and other emergencies. The ads would be allowed to appear when the signs are not in use, with the monies going to the state highway fund. While proponents argue that the money is sorely needed and that the signage would be improved, opponents say that's not what the 674 signs are intended for, and that it would create an environmental blight while distracting motorists.

A high school in Houston, near the George Bush Intercontinental Airport is offering its roof, parking lot, stadium, and even the bottom of its swimming pool to advertisers to raise money. Chicago is taking offers from advertisers to allow them to name individual station stops on its "L" line. Brooklyn, New York, has proposed selling ads on city trash cans and on construction scaffolding. A number of cities are considering selling ads on the outsides of school buses. In Los Angeles, New York, and Philadelphia, 200 Domino's logos have been stenciled into ecofriendly images into the street grime to promote its new American Legends pizza while also helping clean the streets. KFC is helping tackle the pothole problem in Louisville, Kentucky. KFC fills the potholes in exchange for the permission to stamp "Refreshed by KFC" on each one repaired. (The chalky stencils will fade away with the next rainstorm.) Toyota has donated 17 new 4WD-drive vehicles to the city of Huntington Beach, California, for lifeguards to use while patrolling the beaches, while Toyota claims the moniker "The Official Vehicle of Huntington Beach." More public sector–advertiser deals are in the works.

While municipalities desperately need the money and other contributions (the Toyota deal saved Huntington Beach $500,000), not everyone thinks this type of advertising is such a good idea. As noted, in California there was a lot of resistance to using safety alert signs for ads. Others argue that the reason they pay taxes is for public services, and towns should not have to rely on private citizens. Still others contend the ads everywhere idea will contribute to visual pollution. It is the equivalent of selling our souls, they say.

For now, it seems everything is for sale. At least until the recession ends.

Sources: Emily Bryson York, "Need a Pothole Filled in Your City? Call KFC," www.adage.com, March 25, 2009; Elana Glowatz, "Domino's Ads Pop Up on City Sidewalks," www.brandweek.com, July 10, 2009; Linda Lou, "Funds Sliced, Teacher Sells Ads on Tests," The *San Diego Union Tribune*, November 22, 2008, pp. NC 1–3; Patrick McGreevy, "Ads between Amber Alerts?" *Los Angeles Times*, September 24, 2008, pp. B1, 5; Robert Klara, "Cities for Sale," *Adweek Media*, March 9, 2009, pp. 6–8.

**Advantages and Disadvantages of Miscellaneous Alternative Media** Advantages of alternative media include the following:

- *Awareness and attention.* Perhaps the major advantage of these tactics is their ability to attract attention. Given their novelty and the nontraditional locations in which they appear, they are likely to create awareness and gain attention.
- *Cost efficiencies.* Because of the nontraditional nature of alternative media, many advertisers are using media not previously used for advertising, or that, in general, do not require high expenditures. As such, the absolute and relative costs are not yet that high.

- *Targeting.* Depending on the tactic used, the campaign can be very targeted. It can be exposed only to a specific event, location, age, or interest group.

Disadvantages of alternative media include the following:

- *Irritation.* Unless the advertiser is careful, advertising placed in the wrong medium may have a negative impact, resulting in irritation, negative attitudes toward the advertiser, or even opportunities for the competitor. When Microsoft logos were painted on sidewalks, the city and consumers were not impressed and Microsoft was fined. One of their competitors gained significant public relations benefits when the company announced it would be happy to remove the paintings. The City of New York was not very happy with Snapple when the company's giant popsicle started to melt and created a flood in Union Square.
- *Wearout.* For now, many of these campaigns are novel and unique and are attracting consumer interest. As the number of efforts increases, however, there is the potential to lose the uniqueness associated with them.

## Summary

This chapter introduced you to the vast number of support media available to marketers. These media, also referred to as nontraditional or alternative media, are just a few of the many ways advertisers attempt to reach their target markets. We have barely scratched the surface here. Support media include out-of-home advertising (outdoor, in-store, and transit), promotional products, and in-flight advertising, among many others. The fastest growing area is that of branded entertainment including product placements, product integrations, and others.

Support media offer a variety of advantages. Cost, ability to reach the target market, and flexibility are just a few of those cited in this chapter. In addition, many of the media discussed here have effectively demonstrated the power of their specific medium to get results.

But each of these support media has disadvantages. Perhaps the major weakness with most is the lack of audience measurement and verification. Unlike many of the media discussed earlier in this text, most nontraditional media do not provide audience measurement figures. So the advertiser is forced to make decisions without hard data or based on information provided by the media.

As the number and variety of support media continue to grow, it is likely the major weaknesses will be overcome. When that occurs, these media may no longer be considered nontraditional or alternative.

## Key Terms

**support media** p. 446
**alternative media** p. 446
**below the line media** p. 446
**nonmeasured media** p. 446
**nontraditional media** p. 446
**out-of-home advertising** p. 447
**digital out-of-home media** p. 449
**aerial advertising** p. 449
**mobile billboards** p. 450
**in-store media** p. 451
**transit advertising** p. 451
**inside cards** p. 452
**outside posters** p. 452
**terminal posters** p. 453
**promotional products marketing** p. 456
**specialty advertising** p. 456
**Yellow Pages** p. 458
**directional medium** p. 458
**branded entertainment** p. 461
**product placements** p. 461
**product integrations** p. 462

## Discussion Questions

1. Digital out-of-home media have been experiencing rapid growth. Give examples of some of these new media forms and why they have an advantage over existing traditional out of home media. (LO2)

2. Promotional products, often referred to as advertising specialties, constitute a multi-billion-dollar industry. Explain some of the various forms of promotional products, and how they might be used. (LO2)

3. Traditional out-of-home advertising such as billboards, transit, etc. have recently experienced growth in years when other media forms have seen their business decline. Why is this so? Give examples as to when outdoor may be more attractive to advertisers than other media. (LO3)

4. Discuss some of the advantages and disadvantages of branded entertainment. Do you see business in this area increasing or decreasing in the future? Explain your answer. (LO3)

5. In the lead-in to the chapter, there was a discussion of Lady Gaga's extensive use of product placements. There have already been reports that Gaga has sold out. Discuss whether you agree or disagree with these comments. Explain your answer. (LO1)

6. Recently there has been an increase in the showing of commercials before movies. Discuss some of the advantages and disadvantages of this practice, and some of the reasons there has been an increase in the use of this medium. (LO3)

7. It seems that guerrilla marketers are becoming more and more aggressive. One agency, while not revealing the client, said that the client actually asked him to break the law so as to get some publicity. Others seemingly have already broken the law by defacing property and other means. Discuss some of the potentially unethical or illegal practices of guerrilla marketers. What should be done to curb these activities? (LO1)

8. Discuss some recent examples of product placements and/or integrations. Describe the context in which they were used, and how they intended to reach their target markets. Do you think these placements/integrations were successful? Why or why not? (LO4)

9. Advertising in video games is becoming more popular. Discuss some of the reasons this medium is attractive. Do you see any downside to advertising through video games?

10. Over the past few years there has been enormous growth in the use of product placements. Explain some of the reasons for this growth. Do you think this growth will likely continue into the future? Why or why not? (LO2)

## AdForum Exercise: Examining the Objectives of Airline Media Usage

(see Advertising and Promotion Playlist, Chapter 13)

In Chapter 13 a number of support media were explored. In the playlist for Chapter 13 are several ads for airline companies that have used a variety of media to deliver their messages from cinema advertising to posters. Review these ads and then answer the following questions:

1 What is the objective being sought with each ad?

2 Is this the best medium the airline could have used to accomplish this objective?

3 What other media could be used to accomplish this objective?

4 Are there other objectives that might be achieved by these media?

Access to the chapter playlist is available through 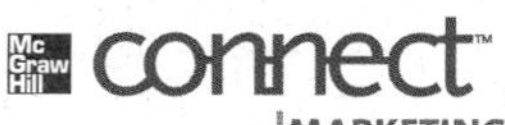 , www.mcgrawhillconnect.com

OPPORTUNITY HAS NEVER KNOCKED THIS HARD
THE NEW JETS STADIUM
JETS
2010 INAUGURAL SEASON TICKETS NOW ON SALE
It's an opportunity that only happens once in a generation. A team moves to a new stadium and the savviest fans act quickly to get their season tickets. It happened 25 years ago when the Jets moved to the Meadowlands. Now history is about to repeat itself. But this time the Jets are bringing their swarming defense into a new stadium that can only be described as the biggest upgrade in NFL history. This stadium has it all, from the new rail line that drops you off right at the front gate to improved traffic patterns, exclusive in-stadium clubs, and four massive scoreboards so you never miss a play on the field or around the NFL. With new pricing options, these seats will not last long. And neither will this opportunity.
NEW CLUB TICKET PRICES!
CALL 800-469-JETS
WWW.NEWJETSSTADIUM.COM

## LEARNING OBJECTIVES

- LO1 To recognize the area of direct marketing as a communications tool.
- LO2 To know the strategies and tactics involved in direct marketing.
- LO3 To demonstrate the use of direct-marketing media.
- LO4 To determine the scope and effectiveness of direct marketing.

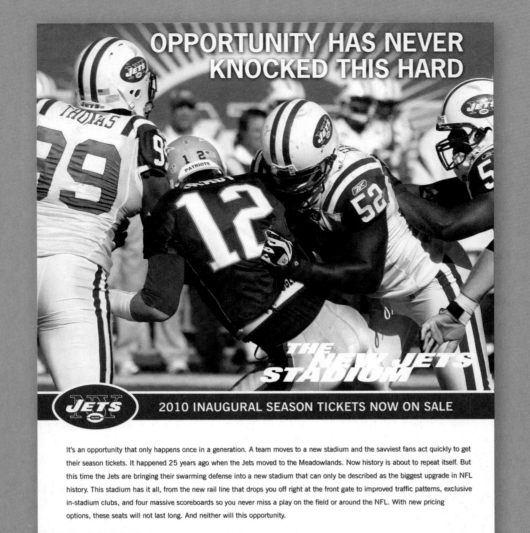

# 14 Direct Marketing

## THE NEW YORK JETS TURN TO DIRECT MARKETING TO FILL THE STADIUM

The New York Jets football team has never had a home of their own. Even though the franchise has been around for 50 years, they have never had their own stadium. Starting as the New York Titans in the original American Football League in 1960, the team played their first game in the Polo Grounds. In 1964 they moved to Shea Stadium—a venue built for baseball and the home of the New York Mets. After 20 years, the Jets moved to the Meadowlands in New Jersey—as a tenant. To make matters worse, the team shared the stadium with their crosstown rival New York Giants in—of all things—Giants Stadium. While the team was the first AFL team to defeat the NFL champions with Joe Namath at quarterback (1969) prior to the merging of the AFL and NFL leagues, in the 1970s, '80s and '90s they were not as competitive, and had troubles drawing fans. But by the turn of the century, the Jets once again began to compete for the division title and fill the stadium for almost every home game. Season tickets could not be bought for years, and it got so bad, fans gave up on trying to do so. So the Jets built a new facility—for the first time ever—their own stadium!

Good news, bad news! With the new Jets stadium set to open in Fall 2010, marketing of season tickets started in 2008—right in the middle of the recession. While new season tickets had not been available for decades, the new stadium would hold 82,500 people, many of whom were unaware of ticket availability. The Jets hired a Manhattan advertising agency to coordinate the IMC campaign, which included advertising, an interactive microwebsite, support media, public relations, and a heavy emphasis on direct marketing. The campaign was called "Opportunity Knocks," and the initial theme line was "Finally, we're the home team." A three-pronged approach was taken with phase 1 focusing on branding and awareness and accompanied with call-to-action direct response media. Existing ticket holders were invited to tour the new stadium when completed, and received glossy brochures to encourage them to buy seats in the new venue. Finally, follow-up phone calls, e-mails, and direct mail pieces were used to close the deal. Existing ticket holders were offered the best seating options based on their seniority, but good seats were still available.

While the season ticket holders responded well, seats remained. After the existing ticket holders had their chance, the unsold seats (including club seats) were made available to the general public—with a "Ticket for everybody" program that included a wide variety of price options and a 15-year financing program for the more expensive seats. All of the media efforts including the TV spot, a print campaign, direct mail, Web advertising, and e-mails again included a specific call to action.

One of the benefits of using direct response, according to Jessica Ciccone, the team's director of corporate communications, was its measurability. Ciccone notes that the Jets' marketing office was able to track what respondents wanted, and by what source buyers came to them, allowing them to be flexible and adapt the promotional message as needed. She notes that each phase of the campaign provided enough ROI to cover the implementation.

While all of the seats are not yet sold, the Jets consider the two-year campaign a success and believe that without it, many more tickets would have gone unsold. They believe that as more fans become aware of the opportunity to see the games and to purchase good seats, the team will have no problems playing in front of packed houses. Now it's time for the Jets to do their part!

Sources: Thomas Haire, "Jets Audible into Direct Response," *Response*, January 2010, pp. 26–32; ____"New York Jets Engage Ad Agency Fly Communications to Help Market New Jets Stadium Scheduled to Open in August 2010," *Business Wire*, September 3, 2008, pp. 1–3.

The discussion of the New York Jets' marketing program in this chapter's opening demonstrates just one of the means of effectively utilizing direct marketing. The team's use of various direct-response media, when combined with other IMC elements led to successful marketing of the new stadium seats. It is important to realize that there are numerous direct marketing tools that can be used to reach one's target market. This chapter will discuss these direct media.

# DIRECT MARKETING

While many companies rely on a variety of promotional mix elements to move their products and services through intermediaries, an increasing number are going directly to the consumer. These companies believe that while promotional mix tools such as advertising, sales promotion, support media, and personal selling are effective in creating brand image, conveying information, and/or creating awareness, going direct can generate an immediate behavioral response. Direct marketing is a valuable tool in the integrated communications program, though it usually seeks somewhat different objectives.

In this chapter, we discuss direct marketing and its role as a communications tool. For many companies and organizations, direct marketing is a key element in their IMC program, and for some marketers it has become the medium of choice for reaching consumers. We begin by defining direct marketing and then examine direct-marketing media and their use in the overall communications strategy. The section concludes with a basis for evaluating the direct-marketing program and a discussion of the advantages and disadvantages of this marketing tool.

## Defining Direct Marketing

As noted in Chapter 1, **direct marketing** is a system of marketing by which organizations communicate directly with target customers to generate a response or transaction. This response may take the form of an inquiry, a purchase, or even a vote. The Direct Marketing Association (DMA) defines direct marketing as

> . . . an interactive system of marketing which uses one or more advertising media to effect a measurable response and/or transaction at any location.[1]

First we must distinguish between direct marketing and direct-marketing media. As you can see in Figure 14–1, direct marketing is an aspect of total marketing—that is, it involves marketing research, segmentation, evaluation, and the like, just as our planning model in Chapter 1 did. Direct marketing uses a set of **direct-response media**, including direct mail, telemarketing, interactive TV, print, the Internet, and other media. These media are the tools by which direct marketers implement the communications process.

The purchases of products and services through direct-response advertising currently exceed $1.7 trillion and are projected to reach $2.22 trillion by the year 2014.[2] Firms that use this marketing method range from major retailers such as the Gap, Restoration Hardware, and Victoria's Secret to airline companies to financial services and local companies. Business-to-business and industrial marketers have also significantly increased their direct-marketing efforts, with an estimated $998 billion in sales forecast by 2014.[3]

## The Growth of Direct Marketing

Direct marketing has been around since the invention of the printing press in the 15th century. Ben Franklin was a very successful direct marketer in the early 1700s, and Warren Sears and Montgomery Ward were using this medium in the 1880s.

The major impetus behind the growth of direct marketing may have been the development and expansion of the U.S. Postal Service, which made catalogs available

**FIGURE 14–1** DM Advertising Expenditures by Medium and Market (in billions of dollars)

| | | | | | | COMPOUND ANNUAL GROWTH | |
|---|---|---|---|---|---|---|---|
| **CHANNEL / MARKET** | **2004** | **2008** | **2009** | **2010** | **2014** | **2004–09** | **2009–14** |
| **Direct Mail (catalog)** | **17.9** | **18.9** | **15.1** | **15.6** | **18.6** | **−3.3%** | **4.3%** |
| Business | 6.8 | 7.4 | 5.8 | 6.0 | 7.5 | −3.1% | 5.1% |
| Consumer | 11.1 | 11.5 | 9.3 | 9.5 | 11.1 | −3.5% | 3.7% |
| **Direct Mail (noncatalog)** | **28.9** | **33.6** | **29.3** | **29.9** | **34.5** | **0.3%** | **3.3%** |
| Business | 10.9 | 13.0 | 11.2 | 11.5 | 13.4 | 0.6% | 3.7% |
| Consumer | 18.0 | 20.6 | 18.1 | 18.4 | 21.1 | 0.1% | 3.1% |
| **Commercial E-mail** | **0.3** | **0.6** | **0.6** | **0.7** | **01.1** | **18.8%** | **13.1%** |
| Business | 0.1 | 0.3 | 0.3 | 0.4 | 0.6 | 18.7% | 13.1% |
| Consumer | 0.1 | 0.3 | 0.3 | 0.3 | 0.5 | 19.0% | 13.1% |
| **Internet Display** | **3.6** | **7.3** | **7.2** | **7.8** | **10.9** | **14.7%** | **8.7%** |
| Business | 2.0 | 4.1 | 4.0 | 4.3 | 6.0 | 14.6% | 8.7% |
| Consumer | 1.6 | 3.2 | 3.2 | 3.5 | 4.9 | 14.9% | 8.6% |
| **Insert Media** | **0.8** | **0.9** | **0.8** | **0.8** | **1.1** | **0.4%** | **5.3%** |
| Business | 0.3 | 0.3 | 0.3 | 0.3 | 0.4 | 0.9% | 5.8% |
| Consumer | 0.5 | 0.6 | 0.5 | 0.5 | 0.7 | 0.2% | 5.0% |
| **Internet Other** | **0.8** | **3.6** | **3.6** | **4.2** | **6.7** | **34.6%** | **13.2%** |
| Business | 0.5 | 2.0 | 2.0 | 2.3 | 3.7 | 34.5% | 13.2% |
| Consumer | 0.4 | 1.6 | 1.6 | 1.9 | 3.0 | 34.8% | 13.2% |
| **Internet Search** | **4.9** | **10.8** | **11.2** | **12.2** | **18.5** | **17.7%** | **10.6%** |
| Business | 2.7 | 6.0 | 6.2 | 6.7 | 10.2 | 17.6% | 10.6% |
| Consumer | 2.2 | 4.7 | 5.0 | 5.5 | 8.2 | 17.9% | 10.6% |
| **DR Magazine** | **7.8** | **8.2** | **6.7** | **6.6** | **7.7** | **−3.1%** | **3.0%** |
| Business | 4.0 | 4.2 | 3.4 | 3.4 | 4.1 | −3.3% | 4.0% |
| Consumer | 3.8 | 3.9 | 3.3 | 3.2 | 3.6 | −2.9% | 2.0% |
| **DR Newspaper** | **15.4** | **11.9** | **8.9** | **8.4** | **7.6** | **−10.4%** | **−3.0%** |
| Business | 5.7 | 4.5 | 3.4 | 3.2 | 3.0 | −10.2% | −2.4% |
| Consumer | 9.6 | 7.3 | 5.5 | 5.2 | 4.6 | −10.6% | −3.5% |
| **Other** | **2.5** | **2.7** | **2.4** | **2.6** | **3.4** | **−0.8%** | **6.8%** |
| Business | 1.1 | 1.2 | 1.0 | 1.1 | 1.5 | −0.7% | 7.8% |
| Consumer | 1.4 | 1.5 | 1.4 | 1.5 | 1.8 | −1.0% | 6.0% |
| **DR Radio** | **4.8** | **4.3** | **3.3** | **3.3** | **4.1** | **−6.9%** | **4.4%** |
| Business | 2.4 | 2.1 | 1.7 | 1.6 | 2.1 | −6.7% | 5.1% |
| Consumer | 2.4 | 2.1 | 1.7 | 1.7 | 2.0 | −7.1% | 3.6% |
| **Telephone Marketing** | **45.0** | **41.8** | **39.4** | **39.5** | **41.5** | **−2.6%** | **1.0%** |
| Business | 27.2 | 25.4 | 23.8 | 23.9 | 25.6 | −2.7% | 1.4% |
| Consumer | 17.7 | 16.4 | 15.6 | 15.6 | 15.9 | −2.5% | 0.4% |
| **DR Television** | **20.0** | **22.2** | **19.4** | **20.3** | **26.9** | **−0.6%** | **6.8%** |
| Business | 8.9 | 10.1 | 8.8 | 9.2 | 12.6 | −0.3% | 7.5% |
| Consumer | 11.1 | 12.2 | 10.7 | 11.1 | 14.3 | −0.8% | 6.1% |
| **Mobile** | **0.0** | **0.2** | **0.2** | **0.3** | **0.8** | n/a | **29.1%** |
| Business | 0.0 | 0.1 | 0.1 | 0.1 | 0.3 | n/a | 24.2% |
| Consumer | 0.0 | 0.1 | 0.2 | 0.2 | 0.6 | n/a | 31.6% |
| **Social Networking** | **0.0** | **1.2** | **1.2** | **1.3** | **2.3** | n/a | **14.7** |
| Business | 0.0 | 0.5 | 0.5 | 0.6 | 1.0 | n/a | 14.7% |
| Consumer | 0.0 | 0.7 | 0.6 | 0.7 | 1.3 | n/a | 14.7% |
| **Total** | **152.7** | **168.1** | **149.3** | **153.3** | **185.7** | **−0.4%** | **4.5%** |
| Business | 72.7 | 81.4 | 72.5 | 74.6 | 92.1 | −0.1% | 4.9% |
| Consumer | 79.9 | 86.7 | 76.8 | 78.7 | 93.5 | −0.8% | 4.0% |

Source: From The Power of Direct Marketing, 2009–2010. Reprinted with permission of Direct Marketing Association.

to both urban and rural dwellers. Catalogs revolutionized America's buying habits; consumers could now shop without ever leaving their homes.

But catalogs alone do not account for the rapid growth of direct marketing. A number of factors in American society have led to the increased attractiveness of this medium for both buyer and seller:

- *Consumer credit cards.* There are now more than 1 billion credit cards—bank, oil company, retail, and so on—in circulation in the United States. This makes it feasible for consumers to purchase both low- and high-ticket items through direct-response channels and assures sellers that they will be paid. It is estimated that over $1.79 trillion are charged on credit cards each year. Of course, not all of this was through direct marketing, but a high percentage of direct purchases do use this method of payment, and companies such as American Express, Diners Club, MasterCard, and Visa are among the heaviest direct advertisers.
- *The changing structure of American society and the market.* One of the major factors contributing to the success of direct marketing is that so many Americans are now "money-rich and time-poor." The rapid increase in dual-income families has meant more income. (It is estimated that in 2010 women made up about 46.5 percent of the labor force.)[4] At the same time, the increased popularity of physical fitness, do-it-yourself crafts and repairs, and home entertainment has reduced the time available for shopping and has increased the attractiveness of direct purchases.
- *Technological advances.* The rapid technological advancement of the electronic media and the Internet has made it easier for consumers to shop and for marketers to be successful in reaching the desired target markets. Well over 110 million television homes receive home shopping programs. Virtually 100 percent of those homes are connected to cable and satellite.
- *Miscellaneous factors.* A number of other factors have contributed to the increased effectiveness of direct marketing, including changing values, more sophisticated marketing techniques, and the industry's improved image. These factors will also ensure the success of direct marketing in the future. The variety of companies employing direct marketing demonstrates its potential.

While some organizations rely on direct marketing solely to generate a behavioral response, for many others direct marketing is an integral part of the IMC program. They use direct marketing to achieve other than sales goals and integrate it with other program elements. We first examine the role of direct marketing in the IMC program and then consider its more *traditional* role.

**EXHIBIT 14–1**
Bose uses multiple methods to promote its products

Bose® SoundDock® Portable digital music system
Compare it to any other sound system for the iPod. Portable or not.
Order by June 26, 2010, and save 10%.
1-XXX-XXX-XXXX, ext. xxxxx | Bose.com/SoundDock
BOSE
Better sound through research.


## The Role of Direct Marketing in the IMC Program

Long the stepchild of the promotional mix, direct marketing has now become an important component in the integrated marketing programs of many organizations. In fact, direct-marketing activities support and are supported by other elements of the promotional mix.

### Combining Direct Marketing with Advertising

Obviously, direct marketing is in itself a form of advertising. Whether through mail, print, or TV, the direct-response offer is an ad. It usually contains a toll-free or 900 number or a form that requests mailing information. Sometimes the ad supports the direct-selling effort. For example, Victoria's Secret runs image ads and commercials to support its store and catalog sales. Bose Audio also markets through stores and online, supporting its efforts through advertising (Exhibit 14–1). Direct-response ads or infomercials are also referred to in retail outlet displays. Sometimes an advertisement will be sent through direct mail.

### Combining Direct Marketing with Public Relations

As you will see later in this text, public relations activities often employ

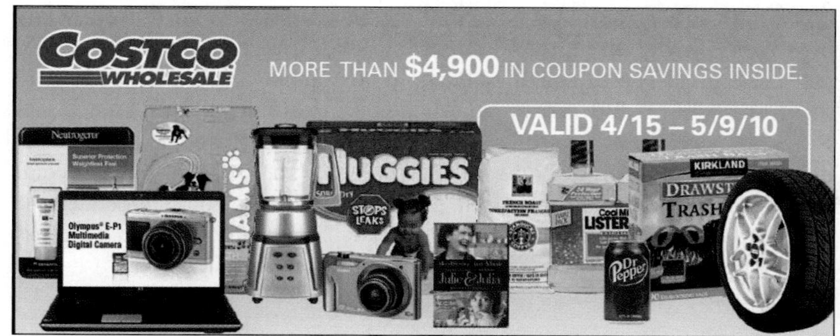


EXHIBIT 14–2
Costco sends promotional offers through the mail

direct-response techniques. Private companies may use telemarketing activities to solicit funds for charities or co-sponsor charities that use these and other direct-response techniques to solicit funds. Likewise, corporations and/or organizations engaging in public relations activities may include toll-free numbers or website URLs in their ads or promotional materials. The DMA Nonprofit Federation has worked with numerous organizations and small and large companies in support of those affected by the earthquake in Haiti, and the Gulf oil spill off the coast of Louisiana.

**Combining Direct Marketing with Personal Selling** Telemarketing and direct selling are two methods of personal selling used to generate sales. Nonprofit organizations like charities often use telemarketing to solicit funds. As you will see, for-profit companies are also using telemarketing with much greater frequency to screen and qualify prospects (which reduces selling costs) and to generate leads. Direct-mail pieces are often used to invite prospective customers to visit auto showrooms to test-drive new cars; the salesperson then assumes responsibility for the selling effort. Automobile manufacturers and their dealers have both made effective use of this approach.

**Combining Direct Marketing with Sales Promotions** How many times have you received a direct-mail piece notifying you of a sales promotion or event or inviting you to participate in a contest or sweepstakes? Ski shops regularly mail announcements of special end-of-season sales. Airlines send out mailers or e-mails announcing promotional airfares. Nordstom and other retail outlets call their existing customers to notify them of special sales promotions. Each of these is an example of a company using direct-marketing tools to inform customers of sales promotions (Exhibit 14–2). In turn, the sales promotion event may support the direct-marketing effort. A 2007 study conducted by Vertis indicated that marketers could increase the effectiveness of their direct-mail campaigns by offering exclusive deals and/or coupons. Seventy-two percent of adults surveyed said they had responded to a direct-mail offering of a buy-one-get-one-free offer, and 63 percent said they had responded to an offer of a percentage discount on merchandise. Both of these numbers had increased since the previous study conducted in 2005.[5] Databases are often built from the names and addresses acquired from a promotion, and direct mail and/or telemarketing calls follow.

**Combining Direct Marketing with Support Media** Adding a promotional product to a direct mailer has proven to increase response rates. One company included a promotional product in half of its 10,000 mailers and not in the other half. The former generated 65 percent more orders. 3M used a promotional product as an incentive for people responding to a direct-mail offer. The incentive generated a 23 percent response rate versus only 9 percent for the regular mailer.

To successfully implement direct-marketing programs, companies must make a number of decisions. As in other marketing programs, they must determine (1) what the program's objectives will be, (2) which markets to target (through the use of a list or marketing database), (3) what direct-marketing strategies will be employed, and (4) how to evaluate the effectiveness of the program.

## Direct-Marketing Objectives

The direct marketer usually seeks a direct response. The objectives of the program are normally behaviors—for example, test drives, votes, contributions, and/or sales. A typical objective is defined through a set response, perhaps a 2 to 3 percent response rate.

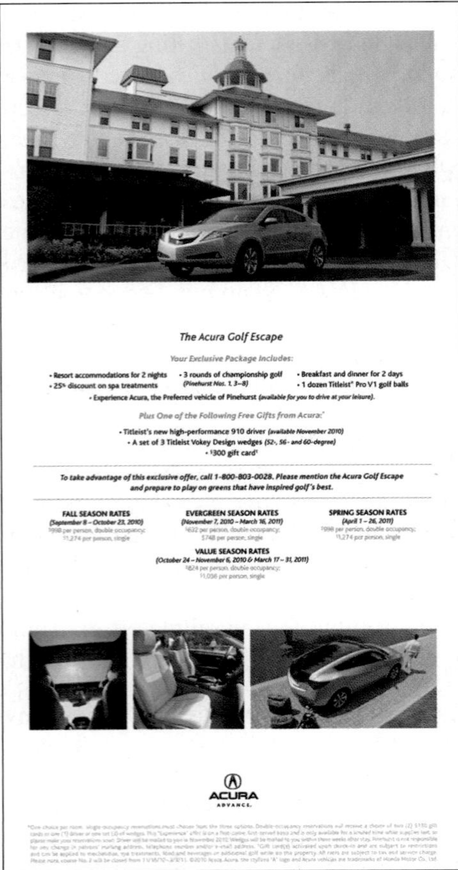


**EXHIBIT 14–3**
Acura and Pinehurst Golf Resort partner on a direct-mail program

Not all direct marketing seeks a behavioral response, however. Many organizations use direct marketing to build an image, maintain customer satisfaction, and inform and/or educate customers in an attempt to lead to future actions. Exhibit 14–3 provides an example of how Acura and Pinehurst Golf Resort partnered to offer consumers a special three hour use of an Acura—the "Preferred Vehicle of Pinehurst"—and a special package price for their vacation getaway. The two companies believe that they share a common target market profile and similar business philosophies of offering only the highest quality product.

## Developing a Database

As we have discussed throughout this text, market segmentation and targeting are critical components of any promotional program. Direct-marketing programs employ these principles even more than others, since the success of a direct-marketing program is in large part tied to the ability to do *one-to-one marketing.* To segment and target their markets, direct marketers use a **database**, a listing of customers and/or potential customers. This database is a tool for **database marketing**—the use of specific information about individual customers and/or prospects to implement more effective and efficient marketing communications.

Figure 14–2 demonstrates how database marketing works. As you can see, the database marketing effort must be an integral part of the overall IMC program. At the very least, this list contains names, addresses, and Zip codes; more sophisticated databases include information on demographics and psychographics, purchase transactions and payments, personal facts, neighborhood data, and even credit histories (see Figure 14–3). This database serves as the foundation from which the direct-marketing programs evolve. Databases are used to perform the following functions:[6]

- *Improving the selection of market segments.* Some consumers are more likely to be potential purchasers, users, voters, and so on than others. By analyzing the characteristics of the database, a marketer can target a greater potential

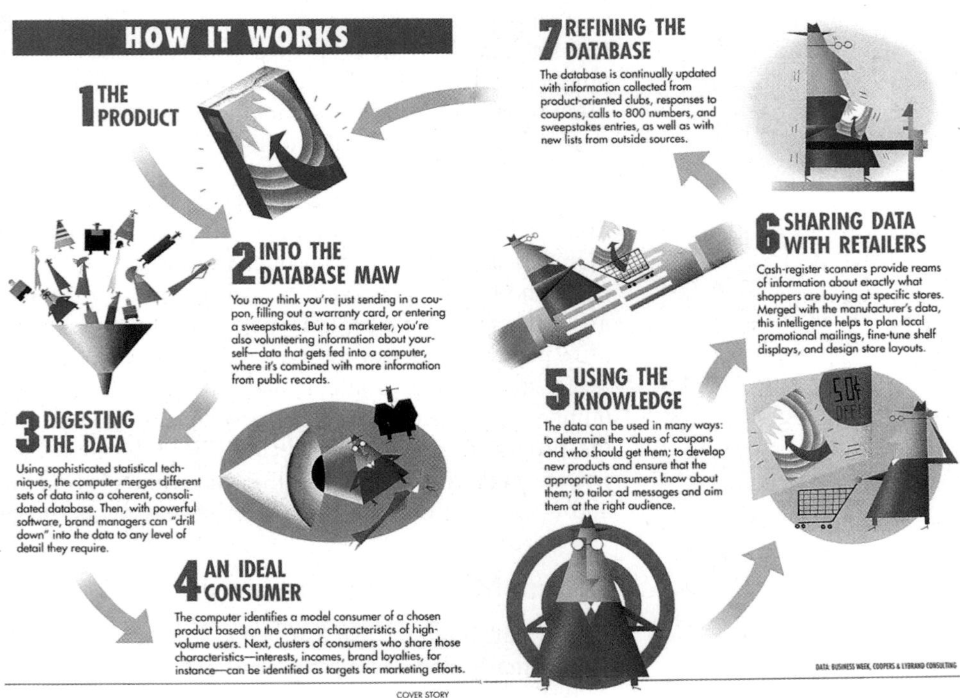


**FIGURE 14–2**
How Database Marketing Works

audience. For example, catalog companies have become very specialized. Companies such as Lands' End, Lilly's Kids, and Johnson & Murphy have culled their lists and become much more efficient, targeting only those who are most likely to purchase their products.

- *Stimulate repeat purchases.* Once a purchase has been made, the customer's name and other information are entered into the database. These people are proven direct-marketing users who offer high potential for repurchase and a greater likelihood of responding to an offer. Direct marketers often lose money on lists of prospects purchased, but generally find those based on their own database to be profitable. Companies from window cleaners to carpet cleaners to car dealers build a base of customers and contact them when they are "due" to repurchase.
- *Cross-sell.* Customers who demonstrate a specific interest also constitute strong potential for other products of the same nature. For example, the National Geographic Society has successfully sold globes, maps, videos, travel magazines, and an assortment of other products to subscribers who obviously have an interest in geography and/or travel. Likewise, Victoria's Secret has expanded its clothing lines primarily through sales to existing customers, and Kraft–GF has successfully cross-sold products in its varied food line. American Airlines uses mailers like the one shown in Exhibit 14–4, to cross promote a variety of products and services (Exhibit 14–5).
- *Customer relationship management.* Customer relationship management (CRM), which is described in more detail in Chapter 16, requires that the marketer develop and maintain a significant amount of information about its clients. The aim of CRM is to establish a relationship with one's customers through affinities, personalized communications, and product/service offerings.



**FIGURE 14–3**
Contents for a Comprehensive Database

| Consumer Database | Business-to-Business Database |
|---|---|
| Name | Name of company/contact/decision maker(s) |
| Address/Zip code | Title of contact |
| Telephone number | Telephone number |
| Length of residence | Source of order/inquiry or referral |
| Age | Credit history |
| Gender | Industrial classification |
| Marital status | Size of business |
| Family data (number of children, etc.) | Revenues |
| Education | Number of employees |
| Income | Time in business |
| Occupation | Headquarters location |
| Transaction history | Multiple locations |
| Promotion history | Purchase history |
| Inquiring history | Promotion history |
| Unique identifier | Inquiry history |
| | Unique identifier |

**EXHIBIT 14–4**
American Airlines uses mailers to cross-promote

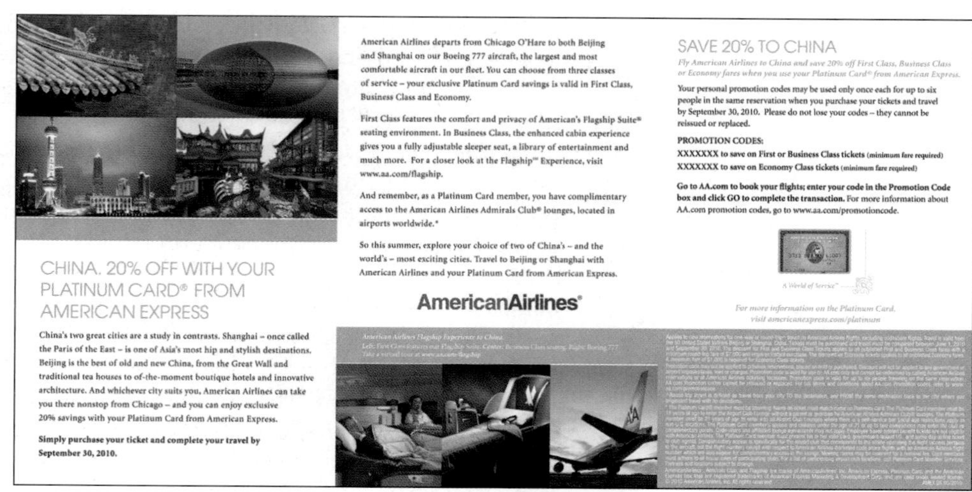


For CRM to work effectively, a database is required. While CRM relies on technology specifically designed for managing customer relationships, there are overlapping characteristics of CRM and database marketing. Suffice it to say at this point that many of the techniques employed in database marketing are necessary to develop an effective CRM program.

Numerous other companies have established comprehensive databases on existing and potential customers both in the United States and internationally. To many automobile manufacturers, the CRM program is a major part of their overall marketing efforts. Database marketing has become so ubiquitous that many people are concerned about invasion of privacy. Direct marketers are concerned as well. The Direct Marketing Association (DMA) has asked its members to adhere to ethical rules of conduct in their marketing efforts. It points out that if the industry does not police itself, the government will.

**Sources of Database Information** There are many sources of information for direct-marketing databases:

- *The U.S. Census Bureau.* Census data provide information on almost every household in the United States. Data include household size, demographics, income, and other information.
- *The U.S. Postal Service.* Postal Zip codes and the extended four-digit code provide information on both household and business locations. Typically people residing in the same Zip code have similar demographics.
- *List Brokers.* Many providers of lists are available. The accuracy and timeliness of the lists vary.
- *Standard Rate and Data Service.* SRDS provides information regarding both consumer and business lists. Published in two volumes, *Direct Mail List Rates and Data* contains over 50,000 list selections in hundreds of classifications.
- *Experian Simmons Market Research Bureau.* SMRB conducts an annual study of customers who buy at home via mail, telephone, or Internet. GfK MRI provides these data as well. It compiles information on total orders placed, types of products purchased, demographics, and purchase satisfaction, among others.

**EXHIBIT 14–5**
American Airlines promotes a variety of products and services

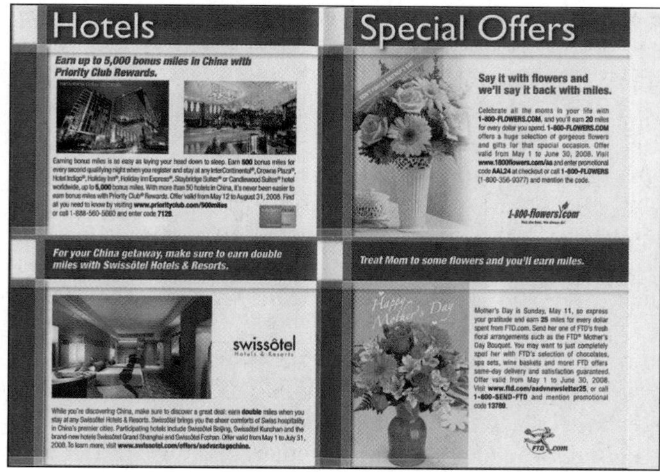

- *Direct Marketing Association.* The direct marketers' trade organization promotes direct marketing and provides statistical information on direct-marketing use. The DMA's *Fact Book of Direct Marketing* contains information regarding use, attitudes toward direct marketing, rules and regulations, and so forth.

Consumer-goods manufacturers, banks, credit bureaus, retailers, charitable organizations, and other business operations also rent lists and other selected information. Companies can build their own databases through completed warranty cards, surveys, and so on.

**Determining the Effectiveness of the Database** While many companies maintain a database, many do not use them effectively. Collecting names and information is not enough; the list must be kept current, purged of old and/or inactive customers, and updated frequently. The more information about customers that can be contained in the database, the more effective it will be. A commonly employed method for this purpose is the **RFM scoring method**. *RFM* stands for the recency, frequency, and monetary transactions between the company and the customer. More specifically, data need to be entered each time there is a transaction so the company can track how recently purchases have been made, how often they are made, and what amounts of money are being spent. In addition, tracking which products and/or services are used increases the ability to conduct the activities previously mentioned. By analyzing the database on a regular basis, the company or organization can identify trends and buying patterns that will help it establish a better relationship with its customers by more effectively meeting their needs.

## Direct-Marketing Strategies and Media

As with all other communications programs discussed in this text, marketers must decide the message to be conveyed, the size of the budget, and so on. Perhaps the major difference between direct-marketing programs and other promotional mix programs regards the use of media.

As shown in Figure 14–1, direct marketing employs a number of media, including direct mail, telemarketing, direct-response broadcasting, the Internet, and print. Each medium is used to perform specific functions, although they all generally follow a one- or two-step approach.

In the **one-step approach**, the medium is used directly to obtain an order. You've probably seen TV commercials for products like wrench sets, workout equipment, or magazine subscriptions in which the viewer is urged to phone a toll-free number to place an order immediately. Their goal is to generate an immediate sale when the ad is shown.

The **two-step approach** may involve the use of more than one medium. The first effort is designed to screen, or qualify, potential buyers. The second effort generates the response (e.g., the order). For example, many companies use telemarketing to screen on the basis of interest, and then follow up to interested parties with more information designed to achieve an order or use personal selling to close the sale.

**Direct Mail** Direct mail is often called "junk mail"—the unsolicited mail you receive. More advertising dollars continue to be spent in direct mail than in almost any other advertising medium—an estimated $44 billion in 2009.[7] Direct mail is not restricted to small companies seeking our business. Respected large companies and organizations in the retail financial services, and fund-raising sectors (among others) commonly employ this medium. In 2009, the average household in the United States received 25 direct-mail pieces per week.[8]

Many advertisers shied away from direct mail in the past, fearful of the image it might create or harboring the belief that direct mail was useful only for low-cost products. But this is no longer the case. For example, Porsche Cars North America, Inc., uses direct mail to target high-income, upscale consumers who are most likely

**EXHIBIT 14–6**
Maserati used direct mail to introduce its new GranTurismo and Quattroporte Sport GT S

to purchase its expensive sports cars. In one example, Porsche developed a direct-mail piece that was sent to a precisely defined target market: physicians in specialties with the highest income levels. This list was screened to match the demographics of Porsche buyers and narrowed further to specific geographic areas. The direct-mail piece was an X-ray of a Porsche 911 Carrera 4 written in the language of the medical audience. This creative campaign generated one of the highest response rates of any mailing Porsche has done in recent years. The piece shown in Exhibit 14–6 is just one sent by Maserati to market its new Gran Turismo and Quattroporte Sport GTS automobile. Exhibit 14–7 shows how direct mail can be used throughout the purchase funnel.

Keys to the success of direct mail are the **mailing list**, which constitutes the database from which names are generated, and the ability to segment markets and, of course the offer. Lists have become more current and more selective, eliminating waste coverage. Segmentation on the basis of geography (usually through Zip codes), demographics, and lifestyles has led to increased effectiveness. The most commonly used lists are of individuals who have already purchased direct-mail products.

The importance of the list has led to a business of its own. It has been estimated that there are over 38 billion names on lists, and many companies have found it profitable to sell the names of purchasers of their products and/or services to list firms. Companies like A. B. Zeller, Experian, and Nielsen Business Media (Exhibit 14–8) provide such lists on a national level, and in most metropolitan areas there are firms providing the same service locally.

While direct mail continues to be a favorite medium of many advertisers, and projections are that the market will grow, this medium has been seriously threatened by the Internet. The lower cost of e-mail and the convenience of the Internet have raised concerns among traditional direct-mail marketers. Interestingly, the Internet is both a threat and an opportunity, as Internet companies have increased their expenditures in direct mail to drive potential customers to their sites. Nevertheless, the direct-mail business has experienced lower response rates from many consumers who see the offer first through direct mail then go online to order. Many companies, particularly in the business-to-business market, have shifted from print to online catalogs, saving money and keeping more current.

**EXHIBIT 14–7**
Direct mail can be used to move consumers through the purchase funnel.

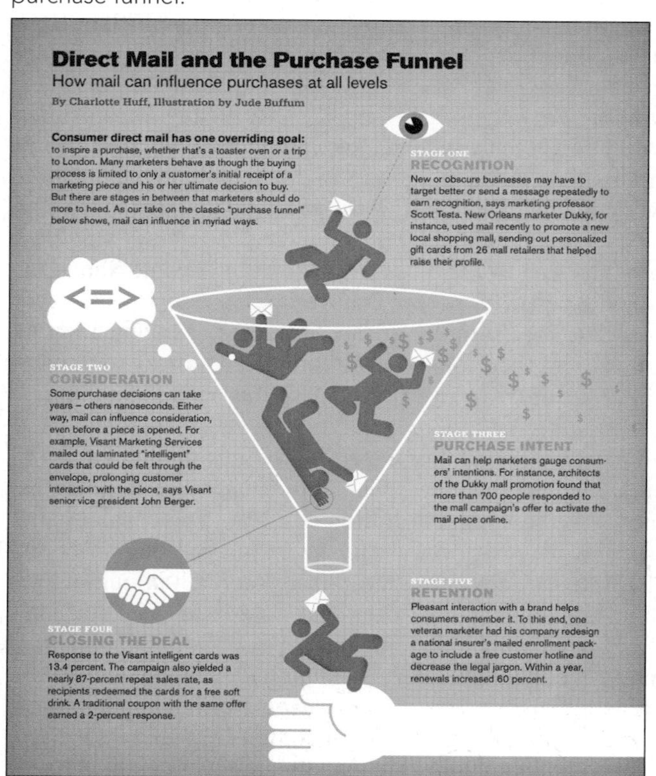


**Catalogs** Major participants in the direct-marketing business include catalog companies. The number of catalogs mailed and the number of catalog shoppers have increased significantly since 1984, with an estimated 13.5 billion catalogs mailed in 2009.[9] While some predicted that catalogs would cease to exist with more use of the Internet, just the opposite is true. The emotional appeal of the traditional catalog exceeds that of online catalogs, and ultimately is one of the best ways to drive consumers online.[10]

Many companies use catalogs in conjunction with their more traditional sales and promotional strategies. For example, companies like Pottery Barn, Bloomingdales, Nordstrom, and Illuminations sell directly through catalogs but also use them to inform consumers

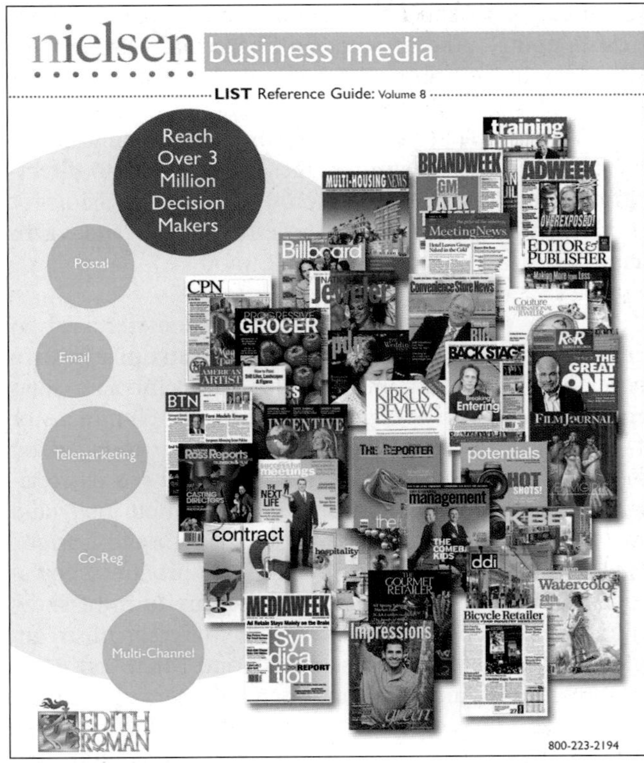


**EXHIBIT 14–8**
Nielsen Business Media provides lists for purchase

of product offerings available in the stores. Some companies (for example, Oriental Trading Company) rely solely on catalog sales. Others that started out exclusively as catalog companies have branched into retail outlets, among them Road Runner Sports, Eddie Bauer, Banana Republic, and Illuminations (Exhibit 14–9). The products being offered through this medium have reached new heights as well. The 2009 Neiman Marcus Christmas catalog featured:

- His & Hers gift package, $250,000: An ICON A5 sport aircraft with custom trailer and sport pilot license training for two.
- A 2010 Supercharged Jaguar XJL, Neiman Marcus edition, $105,000
- HALL artisan wine and art experience, $20,000

Of course these products were designed to attract publicity more than anything else!

In addition to the traditional hard copies, catalogs are now available on the Internet for both consumer and business-to-business customers. In some instances in the consumer market the catalog merchandise is available in retail stores as well. In others, the catalog and retail divisions are treated as separate entities. For example, if you purchase through the Eddie Bauer catalog, you can exchange or return the merchandise to the retail stores. Victoria's Secret products must be returned to the catalog department. At the Gap, the catalog is used to supplement the inventory in stock, and phone orders for different sizes and so on can be made from the store and shipped for free.



**Broadcast Media** The success of direct marketing in the broadcast industry has been truly remarkable; as far back as 1996 over 77 percent of the U.S. population reported that they had viewed a direct-response appeal on TV.[11] Direct-response TV is estimated to have generated more than $5.3 billion in advertising billings in 2009.[12]

Two broadcast media are available to direct marketers: television and radio. While radio was used quite extensively in the 1950s, its use and effectiveness have dwindled substantially in recent years. Thus, the majority of direct-marketing broadcast advertising now occurs on TV, which receives the bulk of our attention here. It should be pointed out, however, that the two-step approach is still very common on the radio, particularly with local companies.

**EXHIBIT 14–9**
Road Runner Sports is one of many successful catalog companies now in retail

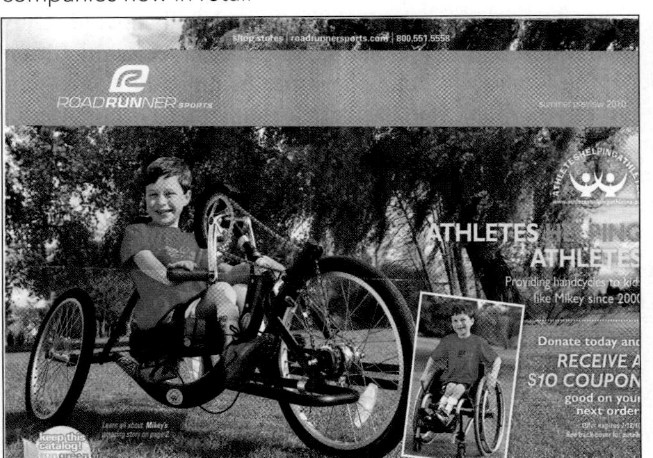


Direct marketing in the broadcast industry involves both direct-response advertising and support advertising. In **direct-response advertising**, the product or service is offered and a sales response is solicited, through either the one- or two-step approach previously discussed. Examples include ads for apparel, exercise equipment, and collectables, and so on. Toll-free phone numbers are included so that the receiver can immediately call to order. **Support advertising** is designed to do exactly that—support other forms of advertising. Ads for Publishers Clearing House or *Reader's Digest* or other companies telling you to look in your mailbox for a sweepstakes entry are examples of support advertising.

Direct-response TV encompasses a number of media, including direct-response TV spots like those

**EXHIBIT 14–10**
Bentley has successfully used an infomercial to attract buyers

just mentioned, infomercials, and home shopping shows (teleshopping). And as noted in Chapter 10, Internet TV has recently been introduced.

**TV Spots** Referred to in the direct-marketing industry as *short-form programs,* these spots include direct-response commercials commonly seen on television for products such as drugs and toiletries, audio and video supplies, household products, and more.

**Infomercials** The lower cost of commercials on cable and satellite channels has led advertisers to a new form of advertising. An **infomercial** is a long commercial that is designed to fit into a 30-minute or 1-hour time slot. Many infomercials are produced by the advertisers and are designed to be viewed as regular TV shows. Today's infomercials use both one- and two-step approaches. Programs such as "Liquid Luster," "Amazing Discoveries," and "Stainerator" (the so-called miracle-product shows) were the most common form of infomercial in the 1980s. While this form of show is still popular, the infomercial industry has been adopted by many large, mainstream marketers including Coca Cola, Braun, Disney, Nissan, Apple, and Microsoft. (See Exhibit 14–10.) Both Hillary Clinton and Barack Obama used infomercials in their presidential campaigns in 2008.

As to their effectiveness, IMC Perspective 14–1 proves that infomercials are watched and sell products. The demographics of the infomercial shopper reflect a married female, mean age of 45, Caucasian, working full time with a household income of $55,000$^+$ per year.[13] This advertising medium is indeed effective with a broad demographic base, not significantly different from the infomercial nonshopper in age, education, income, or gender. Retail stores are benefiting from infomercials as well, as brand awareness leads to increased in-store purchases. For example, a $500,000 print campaign combined with an infomercial for the George Foreman grill led to more sales at retail stores than through Direct TV.[14]

The popularity of the infomercial has led companies to expand into the more frequently watched daytime TV market and the creation of infomercial networks. GM's OnStar system has offered a daytime version of the infomercial called "Tales from the Road," it refers to as a "documercial," and an infomercial network called ExpoTV has been launched and now claims to reach 25 million households.[15,16]

However, some people are not sold on the idea of ads disguised as programs. For example, infomercials disguised as "ultrahip" TV shows have been targeted at teenagers, raising fears that kids under the age of 13 will be susceptible to their lure. Consumer complaints are on the rise, and the FTC has already levied fines for deceptive endorsements against infomercial sponsors, and has taken legal action against those engaging in deceptive practices. Four consumer groups (the Consumer Federation of America, Center for the Study of Commercialism, Center for Media Education, and Telecommunications Research and Action Center) have asked the FCC to require all infomercials to display a symbol that indicates a "paid ad" or "sponsored by" so that viewers won't confuse them with regular programming.

**Homeshopping** The development of toll-free telephone numbers, combined with the widespread use of credit cards, has led to a dramatic increase in the number of people who shop via their TV sets through home shopping channels. Jewelry, kitchenware, fitness products, insurance, household products, and a variety of items are now promoted (and sold) this way. The major shopping channel in the United States (QVC) offers about 1,150 products a week for sale, broadcasting 24 hours/day and online. While Internet e-commerce sales have hurt the TV home shopping channels, in the

# IMC Perspective 14–1 > > >

## What Makes Infomercials Work?

Did you ever ask yourself why someone would sit down to watch an infomercial? Well, besides the fact that these programs usually air when there is nothing else on worth watching, the fact is that they can be very entertaining and quite often sell products that offer benefits we never even imagined we needed. Besides, many of these products are not available in stores, so if we want to buy them, then we have to have seen them on TV. Remember the Ronco Vegematic, Spray on Hair, the George Foreman Grill, The Clapper, and Ginsu Knives? If you Google "Top 10 Infomercials," you will find a variety of sources providing their own best (or worst) infomercial programs. Following are a few that seem to appear on everyone's list:

- *The Magic Bullet*—Developed and sold by Homeland Housewares, the blender is smaller than a regular blender and can also be used as a juicer or a food processor. It comes with a number of attachments that can be used for chopping foods or crushing ice. The Magic Bullet can be used to make personal-size drinks, chop food for storage, and prepare products for the microwave. Cost: $99.99.
- *The Snuggie*—Essentially a blanket with sleeves that you can "snuggle up" in while watching TV, laying in bed, or wherever, the Snuggie has sold over 7 million ($150 million dollars) worth of product and developed a cult following on Facebook.
- *The Chia Pet*—You probably have one of these ceramic seed covered heads that you just add water to and it grows. The popularity of the product led to its appearance in offices, kids' rooms, and kitchens everywhere. Since its introduction in 1977, over 500,000 Chia Pets have been sold. Now there is a Chia President (President Obama's likeness) which has perhaps led to more controversy than sales.

There are probably an equal number of infomercials that have met with less success—the Wearable Towel, Exercise with Richard Simmons, Get a Grip, and the Potty Putter (really!) to name a few. But the incredible success of the infomercial (a $150 billion dollar industry) has led marketers and academics to study this phenomenon.

One such study, conducted by *Consumer Reports* and Martin Lindstrom, an advertising expert, and author of *Buyology: Truth and Lies about Why We Buy,* says that the secret lies in neuroscience. Based on a study of 2,000 consumers, Lindstrom says that the infomercials are carefully scripted to pump up dopamine levels in the brain, taking the viewer on a " psychological roller-coaster ride." As he explains, "The fun starts with dramatizations of a problem you didn't know you had, followed by the incredible solution, then a series of ever more amazing product benefits, bonuses, and giveaways, all leading to the final thrilling plunge of an unbelievably low price." The call to action tells you to buy in the next three minutes (the dopamine high only lasts about six minutes). So, I guess the infomercial takes control of our brains!

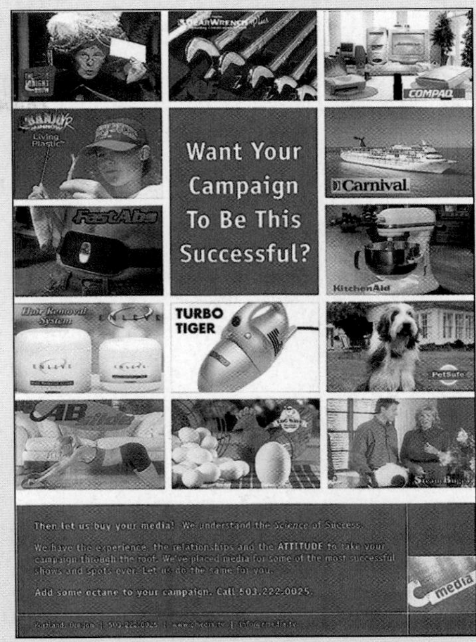


So why do so many people buy, and are they getting as good a deal as promised? Christian Holiday, CEO of Global Media Marketing and an infomercial producer says that the magic of TV can make any product look good. Larry Nusbaum, CEO of Ronco, a successful company selling on infomercials, says that "About half of infomercials deliver on their promises, 30 percent do what they say, but are expensive, and the rest are junk." I wish I had known that before I bought the Shake Weight for Men Workout. I never did lose those 14 pounds!

Sources: ____ "The 25 Worst Infomercials Ever," www.businesspundit.com, February 8, 2010; ____ "Signaling in Retail Sales—Snuggie Edition," www.liberalorder.com, January 7, 2010; Darren Rovell, "Infomercials Bloom Amid Economic Drought," www.msnbc.com, April 22, 2009.

first quarter of 2010 both QVC and HSN realized significant growth.[17] The success of home shopping networks has led to a proliferation of shopping channels including Shop@homeTV, Shop NBC, and the Liquidation Channel to name just a few. As the demographics of shopping channel buyers continue to move upscale, the products offered on these channels continue to move upscale as well. In 2010 HSN started carrying the Sally Hershberger line of hair care products. (Hershberger is known for charging up to $800 for a haircut.)

**Print Media** Magazines and newspapers are difficult media to use for direct marketing. Because these ads have to compete with the clutter of other ads and because the space is relatively expensive, response rates and profits may be lower than in other media. Exhibit 14–11 shows a direct ad that appeared in a magazine. You can find many more in specific interest areas like financial newspapers or sports, sex, or hobby magazines.

**Telemarketing** If you have a telephone, you probably do not have to be told about **telemarketing**, or sales by telephone. Both profit and charitable organizations have employed this medium effectively in both one- and two-step approaches. Combined telemarketing sales (consumer and business-to-business), continuing to decrease since 2004, totaled over $334 billion in 2010.[18] Telemarketing is still a very big industry.

**EXHIBIT 14–11**
Cutco is one of many companies using direct selling

In recent years, the telemarketing industry has suffered from a decline due to a number of factors. Problems associated with telemarketing include its potential for fraud and deception and its potential for annoyance. These developments have led to the development of a Do Not Call list for both landline and cell phones.

Those in the telemarketing and telemedia industry have responded to public criticisms, while Dial-a-Porn and its ilk hold a diminishing share of 800, 900, and 976 offerings.

## DIRECT SELLING

An additional element of the direct-marketing program is **direct selling**, the direct, personal presentation, demonstration, and sales of products and services to consumers in their homes. Amway, Avon, Cutco, Mary Kay, Inc., and Tupperware are some of the best-known direct-selling companies in the United States and have now extended these programs overseas (Exhibit 14–12). Close to 16.1 million people engage in direct selling throughout the United States and 65 million worldwide; 99 percent of them are independent contractors (not employees of the firm they represent). Direct selling generates over $28.33 billion in sales.[19]

The three forms of direct selling are

1. *Repetitive person-to-person selling.* The salesperson visits the buyer's home, job site, or other location to sell frequently purchased products or services (for example, Amway). Mary Kay has given away over 100,000 Cadillacs—the company's symbol of sales success.
2. *Nonrepetitive person-to-person selling.* The salesperson visits the buyer's home, job site, or other location to sell infrequently purchased products or services (for example, *World Book Encyclopedia*).
3. *Party plans.* The salesperson offers products or services to groups of people through home or office parties and demonstrations (for example, Tupperware and PartyLite Gifts).

FIGURE 14–4

Sales Strategy (methods used to generate sales, reported as a percent of sales dollars)

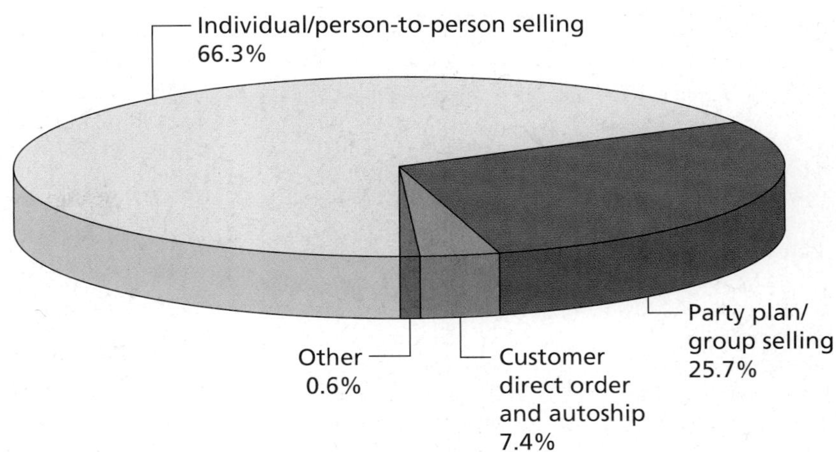


While a number of products and services are sold through direct selling, home and family durables, weight-loss and wellness products, and personal care products are the most popular. The "typical" direct-selling representative is female (over 80 percent), married (77 percent), and between 35 and 54 years of age. For most of the representatives, direct selling is not a full-time job but an opportunity to earn additional income and a way to get the product at a discount for themselves. Over half of those in this industry spend fewer than 10 hours a week selling, and the vast majority spend less than 30 hours a week selling. Figure 14–4 reflects the means by which they sell.



# EVALUATING THE EFFECTIVENESS OF DIRECT MARKETING

Because they generate a direct response, measuring the effectiveness of direct-marketing programs is not difficult. Using the **cost per order (CPO)**, advertisers can evaluate the relative effectiveness of an ad in only a few minutes based on the number of calls generated. By running the same ad on different stations, a direct marketer can determine the relative effectiveness of the medium itself. For example, if the advertiser targets a $5 return per order and a broadcast commercial (production and print) costs $2,500, the ad is considered effective if it generates more than 500 orders. Similar measures have been developed for print and direct-mail ads.

For direct-marketing programs that do not have an objective of generating a behavioral response, traditional measures of effectiveness can be applied. (We discuss these measures in Chapter 18.)

## Advantages and Disadvantages of Direct Marketing

Many of the advantages of direct marketing have already been presented. A review of these and some additions follow:

1. *Selective reach.* Direct marketing lets the advertiser reach a large number of people and reduces or eliminates waste coverage. Intensive coverage may be obtained through broadcast advertising or through the mail. While not everyone drives on highways where there are billboards or pays attention to TV commercials, virtually everyone receives mail. A good list allows for minimal waste, as only those consumers with the highest potential are targeted. For example, a political candidate can direct a message at a very select group of people (those living in a certain Zip code or members of the Sierra Club, say); a book club can target recent purchasers or avid readers.

# Ethical Perspective 14–1 > > >

## A Few Bad Apples Impact Direct Marketing's Image

In so many ways, direct marketers are among the most sophisticated in the industry. When it comes to targeting, no one does it better. When it comes to measuring effectiveness, they are among the best. Their organizations support a number of causes, including a strong and positive relationship with education. So why is it that to some, the mention of direct marketing conjures up a less than positive image?

People refer to direct mail as "junk mail." They get on a "Do Not Call list" to avoid telemarketers. Even though the success of infomercials speaks for itself, some consumers are reluctant to admit that they watch, and enjoy, them. Part of the reason for this less-than-positive image may be a carryover from the past, when people were being deluged by telemarketers. Another may be that consumers feel direct marketing is intrusive. But a major cause of the image problem may come from just a few bad apples—and the publicity they generate. Consider just a few examples:

- Home shopping channel QVC had to pay $7.5 million for making false claims for health products. The products were weight-loss pills, weight-loss food bars and shakes, energy supplements and a cellulite target lotion. The $7.5 million included a payment of $6 million to reimburse consumers who had bought the products, and a $1.5 million civil penalty. The director of the FTC Bureau of Consumer Protection said the claims were unsubstantiated.
- *The wonder products*—These are the companies that promise you that if you will use their products you will lose weight, improve your health, grow hair, even be more attractive to the opposite sex—among a seemingly endless array of other claims. Some of these companies have been forced to cease making unsubstantiated claims (for example, the ephedra products), others have been forced out of business completely, and still more have had legal actions taken against them for deceptive practices. Some of those that remain make claims that consumers consider questionable at best.
- *Environmental consciousness*—A number of companies were recently pointed out as not being concerned (or concerned enough) about the environment. Sears, Neiman Marcus, and Eddie Bauer along with financial companies Capital One, Chase Bank, Citi, and American Express were all cited (along with others) by environmental agency Forest Ethics for their lack of a green effort. The organization chastised the companies for the cutting down of trees, not recycling, and not trying to cut down on their use of paper (most of which went into their shares of the 100 billion pieces of direct mail distributed in 2008).
- *Telemarketing*—While telemarketers may be annoying, most of them are legitimate. However, every now and then, some scam artists come along, and the industry suffers. Recently, a group operating out of Toronto, Can-

2. *Segmentation capabilities.* Marketers can rent lists of recent product purchasers, car buyers, bank-card holders, and so on. These lists may allow segmentation on the basis of geographic area, occupation, demographics, and job title, to mention a few. Combining this information with the geocoding capabilities of Prizm or VALS (discussed in Chapter 2), marketers can develop effective segmentation strategies.
3. *Frequency.* Depending on the medium used, it may be possible to build frequency levels. The program vehicles used for direct-response TV advertising are usually the most inexpensive available, so the marketer can afford to purchase repeat times. Frequency may not be so easily accomplished through the mail, since consumers may be annoyed to receive the same mail repeatedly.
4. *Testing.* Direct marketing allows for a strong ability to test the effectiveness of the overall program as well as specific elements.
5. *Timing.* While many media require long-range planning and have long closing dates, direct-response advertising can be much more timely. Direct mail, for example, can be put together very quickly and distributed to the target population. TV programs typically used for direct-response advertising are older, less sought programs that are likely to appear on the station's list of available spots. Another common strategy is to purchase available time at the last possible moment to get the best price.
6. *Personalization.* No other advertising medium can personalize the message as well as direct media. Parents with children at different age levels can

ada, and India worked together to call a list of World War II veterans, retired schoolteachers, and thousands of other elderly citizens posing as government and insurance workers updating their files. The callers had purchased their names from a database company in the United States. The list, compiled by InfoUSA, was advertised as "Elderly Opportunity Seekers," "Suffering Seniors," and "Oldies but Goodies" likely as a result of the fact that they had entered sweepstakes or lotteries, gambled, or engaged in other activities that made them "gullible." After tricking them into revealing their banking information, they raided their accounts leaving some of them penniless.

According to the FTC, despite the Do Not Call lists, telemarketing fraud has been on the increase—due in large part to the fact that the elderly do not get on the list. In addition, they are often at home to receive calls, rely on deliveries, and desire companionship. The FTC estimates that the elderly account for as much as 30 percent of telemarketing sales, and that as many as 11 percent of those over 55 have been victims of consumer fraud.

- *Infomercials*—Those long-form programs you see on TV promising you that you can lose 20 pounds in 30 days, that there are miracle creams that stop aging, or herbs that will provide a medical cure, sound too good to be true. It's probably because they are too good to be true. As noted by Terry Rindfleisch of the *La Crosse Tribune*, if the infomercial claims to "detoxify," "purify," "balance," or "revitalize" or if it "rejuvenates" various organs or "supports" vital organs, be careful, and when in doubt, don't buy the product. Likewise, if they call into question physicians or dieticians because "they don't want you to be cured" be skeptical as well.

One high-profile example is that of Kevin Trudeau. In 2007, the FTC expanded its campaign against Direct Marketing Concepts, Inc., for marketing Kevin Trudeau's book, *Weight Loss Cures "They" Don't Want You to Know About* and the accompanying infomercial. The infomercial promotes educational materials and natural dietary supplements touting their health benefits. The FTC said that the book and the infomercials made misleading claims regarding the ease of weight loss. The FTC has been in a legal battle to suppress Trudeau's opinions on weight loss and alternative medicines as well as his criticisms of government agencies. Trudeau claims his First Amendment rights have been violated.

The above are just a few examples of how "bad apples" make it difficult for direct marketers to improve on their images. While some of the perpetrators are caught and their practices stopped (two Philadelphia executives who cheated consumers by selling computer parts that were never delivered ended up getting prison sentences), others sometimes get away with it. But even if they don't, it is the good apples that suffer as a result—and there are a lot more of them.

Sources: Michael Bush, "Sears, Capital One, AmEx Make Watchdog's 'Naughty' List of Direct Mailers," *Advertising Age*, December 16, 2008, p. 1–3; UPI, "QVC to Pay for False Claims," www.backchannelmedia.com, March 23, 2009; Charles Duhigg, "Telemarketing Swindlers Buy Info on Elderly," *San Diego Union-Tribune*, May 20, 2007, pp. A1, 9; John Shiffman, "Infomercial Fraud Nets Year in Jail," *The Philadelphia Inquirer*, January 31, 2007, p. 1; Terry Rindfleisch, "Searching for the Truth in All Those Infomercials," *La Crosse Tribune*, September 20, 2006, p. 1.



be approached, with their child's name included in the appeal. Car owners are mailed letters congratulating them on their new purchase and offering accessories. Computer purchasers are sent software solicitations. College students receive very personalized information that recognizes their specific needs and offers solutions, as well as college loan offers.

7. *Costs.* While the CPM for direct mail may be very high on an absolute and a relative basis, its ability to specifically target the audience and eliminate waste coverage reduces the actual CPM. While costs may be higher than in other media, direct methods may be more profitable. The ads used on TV are often among the lowest-priced available. As you will see, direct mail via the Internet is extremely inexpensive.

   A second factor contributing to the cost effectiveness of direct-response advertising is the cost per customer purchasing. Because of the low cost of media, each sale generated is very inexpensive.
8. *Measures of effectiveness.* No other medium can measure the effectiveness of its efforts as well as direct response. Feedback is often immediate and always accurate.

Disadvantages of direct marketing include the following:

1. *Image factors.* As we noted earlier, the mail segment of this industry is often referred to as junk mail. Many people believe unsolicited mail promotes junk products, and others dislike being solicited. Even some senders of direct mail,

including Motorola, GM, and Air Products & Chemicals, say they throw out most of the junk mail they receive. This problem is particularly relevant given the increased volume of mail being sent. (One study estimates the typical American receives 14 pieces of junk mail per week.)[20] Another estimates consumers receive over 3,900 junk e-mails per year.[21] In 2009, more than 200 billion pieces of mail were sent in the United States to over 134 million addresses.[22]

Likewise, direct-response ads on TV are often low-budget ads for lower-priced products, which contributes to the image that something less than the best products are marketed in this way. (Some of this image is being overcome by the home shopping channels, which promote some very expensive products.) Telemarketing is found to be irritating to many consumers, as is "spam" or Internet junk mail. Other factors have also created image problems for the direct-marketing industry.

2. *Accuracy.* One of the advantages cited for direct mail and telemarketing was targeting potential customers specifically. But the effectiveness of these methods depends on the accuracy of the lists used. People move, change occupations, and so on, and if the lists are not kept current, selectivity will decrease. Computerization has greatly improved the currency of lists and reduced the incidence of bad names; however, the ability to generate lists is becoming a problem. The cost of generating a lead can range from a few dollars to as much as hundreds depending on its quality.
3. *Content support.* In our discussion of media strategy objectives in Chapter 10, we said the ability of magazines to create mood contributes to the overall effectiveness of the ads they carry. In direct-response advertising, mood creation is limited to the surrounding program and/or editorial content. Direct-mail and online services are unlikely to create a desirable mood.
4. *Rising costs.* As postal rates increase, direct-mail profits are immediately and directly impacted. The same is true for print costs, which drives up the costs of mailers and catalogs. The low cost of e-mail has led many companies to switch to this medium.
5. *Do Not Contact lists.* Do Not Call lists now exist for both land and cell phones. A "Do Not Contact" list in which consumers can choose not to receive "junk mail" is under consideration by the FTC.

Ethical Perspective 14–1 provides some other issues impacting direct marketing.

## Summary

This chapter introduced you to the rapidly growing field of direct marketing, which involves a variety of methods and media beyond direct mail and telemarketing. The versatility of direct marketing offers many different types of companies and organizations a powerful promotional and selling tool.

Direct marketing continues to outpace other advertising and promotional areas in growth; many of the Fortune 500 companies now use sophisticated direct-marketing strategies. Database marketing has become a critical component of many marketing programs.

Advantages of direct marketing include its selective reach, segmentation, frequency, flexibility, and timing. Personalized and custom messages, low costs, and the ability to measure program effectiveness are also advantages of direct-marketing programs.

At the same time, a number of disadvantages are associated with the use of direct marketing. Image problems, the proliferating sale and use of databases (some of them based on inaccurate lists), lack of content support, and the intrusive nature of the medium make some marketers hesitant to use direct-marketing tools. However, self-policing of the industry and involvement by large, sophisticated companies have led to significant improvements. As a result, the use of direct marketing will continue to increase.

## Key Terms

**direct marketing** p. 474
**direct-response media** p. 474
**database** p. 478
**database marketing** p. 478
**RFM scoring method** p. 481
**one-step approach** p. 481
**two-step approach** p. 481
**mailing list** p. 482
**direct-response advertising** p. 483
**support advertising** p. 483
**infomercial** p. 484
**telemarketing** p. 486
**direct selling** p. 486
**cost per order (CPO)** p. 487

## Discussion Questions

1. As noted in the text, a number of home shopping channels now offer a variety of upscale products. Discuss reasons why you think this will work to their advantage. Are there any disadvantages to this strategy? (LO1)
2. What is customer relationship management? Discuss how direct marketing can be employed to improve customer relationship management. (LO1)
3. What is an infomercial? What are some of the reasons that infomercials have been so successful? Which types of products and services do you think are likely to be candidates for successful infomercials? (LO3)
4. Direct marketers are very good at determining the effectiveness of their programs. Many direct marketers now measure the impact of the program on the consumer funnel. Explain how direct marketers measure effectiveness, and how they now use the consumer funnel for this purpose. (LO4)
5. As the Internet continues to grow in popularity, some marketers predict that the print catalogs will cease to exist, replaced by Internet catalogs. Others disagree. Explain some of the reasons why this situation may or may not occur. (LO1), (LO2)
6. The number of telemarketing centers in the United States has decreased in the past few years. Why has this occurred? (LO3)
7. Explain why direct marketing has been so successful. Do you see this trend continuing into the future? (LO1)
8. Discuss some of the factors that contribute to the negative impact of direct marketing. What can be done to improve direct marketing's image? (LO1)
9. Direct marketers are some of the most successful when it comes to measuring effectiveness of their programs. Give reasons why this may be true. (LO4)
10. Explain how companies use database marketing. Name some of the companies that may have your information in their database. Explain how this information is used to reach you. (LO2)

## AdForum Exercise: "Direct Marketers Use of Other IMC Media"

(See Advertising and Promotion Playlist, Chapter 14)

Some of the largest users of direct marketing also employ television commercials and other media to market their products. Go to the AdForum playlist and answer the following questions:

1 What is the objective(s) that the advertisement is trying to achieve?

2 Does the advertisement support the direct marketing effort, or is it supported by direct marketing?

3 Is this ad an effective use of IMC? Explain why or why not.

4 How could these media be combined with others to market the product?

Access to the chapter playlist is available through McGraw Hill connect MARKETING, www.mcgrawhillconnect.com

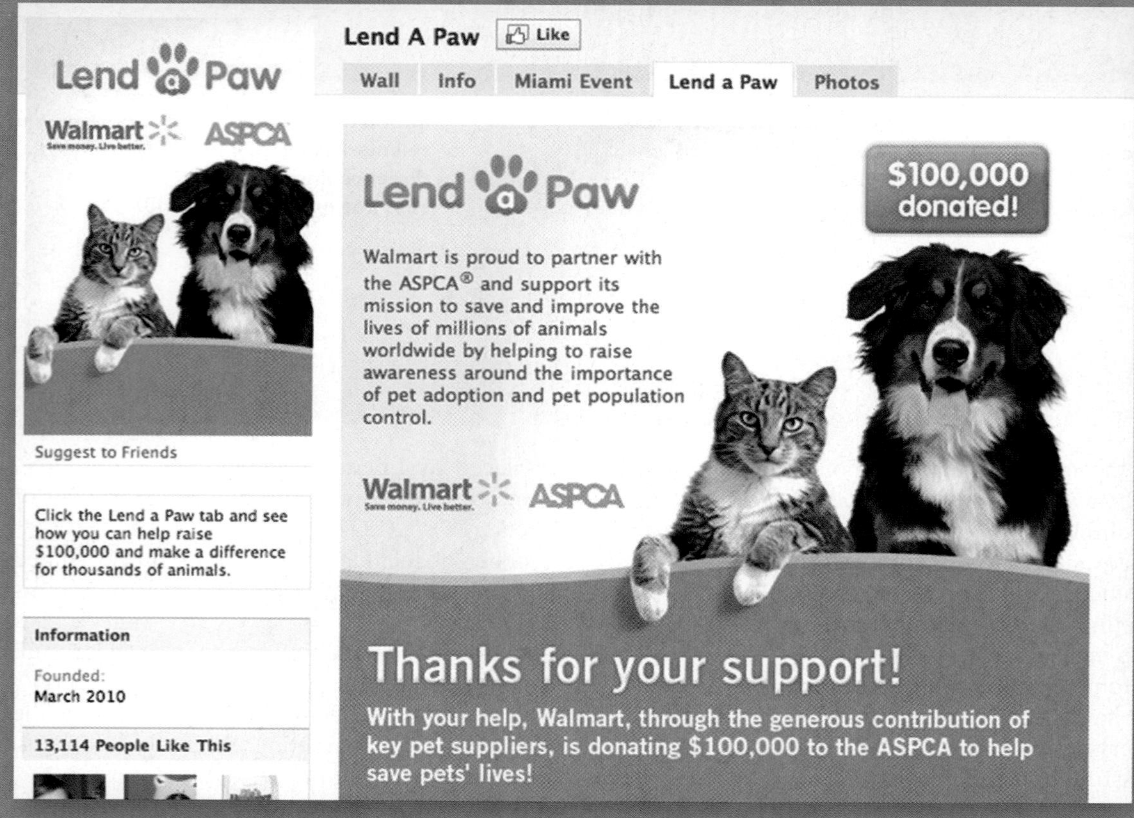


## LEARNING OBJECTIVES

- **LO1** To understand the role of the Internet and interactive media in an IMC program.
- **LO2** To understand the use of Web 1.0 and Web 2.0 media platforms in the IMC process.
- **LO3** To understand how to evaluate the effectiveness of communications through the Internet.
- **LO4** To know the advantages and disadvantages of the Internet and interactive media.
- **LO5** To examine the role of additional online media.

# 15 The Internet and Interactive Media

## SOCIAL MEDIA HAVE CHANGED THE ADVERTISING ENVIRONMENT FOREVER

It's not that marketers were caught by surprise by the fact that the Internet would change the way they did business, but the degree to which things would change could not be imagined in their wildest dreams. While the Internet recently had its 40th birthday celebration, it is only in the last 10 years that the world changed so dramatically with the introduction of social media—the Facebook, MySpace, Twitter, and LinkedIns of the world (to name just a few).

Consider just Facebook. Since the site was launched in 2004 by two students in a Harvard dorm room as a way for Ivy Leaguers to keep in touch, the website has now officially logged its 500 millionth active member worldwide. If Facebook were a country it would have the world's third largest population. Seventy percent of Facebook users are from outside the United States, and one in every four people who uses the Internet now has a Facebook account. While membership is free, the company is expected to generate over $1 billion in revenue in 2010 by selling advertisements on the site—176 billion banner ads were placed in the first quarter of 2010 alone! The ability to target audiences based on users' social activities (and now, their friends) is considered to be a major advantage over other media forms, attracting marketers enough to make Facebook the world's largest advertising website.

Perhaps the most amazing thing about this is that Facebook is just one of many social media websites now attracting advertisers' attention. While Facebook added 117 million unique visitors in March 2010, others added millions as well, including MySpace (42 million), Twitter (20 million), and LinkedIn (14 million)—and these are just a few of scores of social sites out there.

What is also interesting is the versatility of social media for advertising uses. Small companies instantly recognize their capabilities of reaching potentially large audiences around the world on a very small budget. But most of the advertising giants have recognized social media's potential as well. In 2010, for the first time in 23 years, Pepsi did not have a spot during the Super Bowl, instead opting for a $20 million digital campaign. Pepsi believes that the new-age consumer is more interested in the two way dialog, storytelling, and word of mouth that social networks provide more than celebrities like Britney Spears and Cindy Crawford (used in previous Super Bowl spots). They also believe that social networks will be more effective than Internet searches or banner ads in developing connections with the brand. Walmart and the American Society for the Prevention of Cruelty to Animals (ASPCA), have teamed up with a "Lend a Paw" promotional effort on Facebook, in which users click on a button at the site, triggering a donation from Walmart's pet suppliers. All donations go to helping homeless animals.

Procter and Gamble (P&G) also believes in Facebook as a "must have" for digital advertising and brand building. P&G believes that social media are where consumers are spending more and more of their time, and that they need to be there to engage them in their brands. P&G is so convinced that this is the place to be, they have opened up an office in Silicon Valley to help develop their social-networking and digital marketing capabilities. (Interestingly, P&G does not consider Twitter as valuable as Google or Facebook, considering it too much of a one-way medium like television!)

Others do see the value of tweeting, however. Brands ranging from ESPN to Starbucks to Dell support active accounts boasting tens of thousands of followers. Whole Foods has over 300,000 followers enabling them to communicate instantly on a variety of topics including recipes, lifestyles, promotions, and other news. Southwest Airlines recently used Twitter to steal a traveler by seeing and responding to a complaint about JetBlue, and JetBlue, in turn, has also been able to save customers by responding quickly to negative comments posted. Many other companies now carefully monitor social networks to see what trends may be developing, what consumers are saying about them and their competitors, and so forth.

Another interesting aspect of social networks that appeals to marketers is that these sites are not just the playgrounds for young people. LinkedIn's greatest appeal is in the business community, Twitter is used less by teens than older adults, and 28 percent of Facebook's membership now consists of those over 34 years old—and it is their fastest growing segment.

With over $1 billion in advertising being spent on Facebook alone, social networks seem to have a very rosy future. Who would have dreamed?

Sources: Dan Fletcher, "Friends without Borders," *Time*, May 31, 2010, pp. 32–38; Jack Neff, "P&G Embraces Facebook as Big Part of Its Marketing Plan," www.adage.com, January 25, 2010; Sarah Mahoney, "Walmart, ASPCA Launch Facebook Effort," www.mediapost.com, April 16, 2010; David Gelles, "Pepsi Pushes Harnesses Facebook Potential," www.ft.com; January 31, 2010, pp. 1–2; Jonathan Paisner and Bill Westcott, "To Tweet or Not to Tweet? How Twitter Can Further Your Brand," www.printthis.clickability.com, April 21, 2009.

As you can see from the lead-in to this chapter, social networks have certainly had a major impact on the media landscape and the way that marketers communicate with their existing and potential customers. While the Internet itself has required marketers to rethink their IMC programs, the advent of Web 2.0, which led to even more capabilities, has altered the environment forever.

This chapter will examine the role of the Internet as well as other interactive media. We will examine the history of the Internet, its role in an IMC program, and some of the advantages and disadvantages associated with this medium. We will also discuss the various new media options that have resulted from the Internet and their roles in an IMC program. The chapter will conclude with a discussion of the measurement of these media.

# THE GROWTH OF THE INTERNET

## Why the Rapid Adoption of the Internet?

The unprecedented growth of the Internet—the digital revolution—has led to changes in the marketing environment forcing marketers to rethink almost everything they do. As the World Wide Web evolves, so too do marketing communications programs. As can be seen in Figure 15–1, there are now close to two billion Internet users worldwide, and the growth since the year 2000 is staggering. A number of reasons can be cited as to why this growth has been so rapid. One is consumers' increased desire for information that they are now able to obtain easily. The speed and convenience of acquiring this information, as well as the ability to control what and how much is received, has had great appeal. The ability to conduct e-commerce through one's personal computer is also very attractive as it now seems there is almost nothing that one can't find or buy on the Web. It is as though the Internet has no bounds, as every day one can find something new there.

Like the consumers', marketers' adoption of this medium has also soared. The ability to target customers effectively through the Net is attractive to marketers. The increased attention for accountability on the part of businesses has led to a view of the Internet as a medium that would provide more direct feedback on the value of marketing expenditures, customer satisfaction, trends, and the competition. As was true of direct marketing, companies liked the fact that, unlike traditional media, it was often easier to account for the ROI of their expenditures. In fact, in its earliest stages, a number of marketing companies perceived the Internet as a direct-response medium. While a large component of the Web is still that of e-commerce, today's marketers now employ the medium for numerous other communications and

**FIGURE 15–1**

The Worldwide Growth of the Internet

| TOP 20 COUNTRIES WITH THE HIGHEST NUMBER OF INTERNET USERS | | | | | | | |
|---|---|---|---|---|---|---|---|
| # | Country or Region | Population, 2010 Est. | Users Latest Data | % Population (Penetration) | Growth 2000–2010 | % of World Users |
| 1 | China | 1,330,141,295 | 420,00,00 | 31.6% | 1,766.7% | 21.4% |
| 2 | United States | 310,232,863 | 239,893,600 | 77.3% | 151.6% | 12.2% |
| 3 | Japan | 126,804,433 | 99,143,700 | 78.2% | 110.6% | 5.0% |
| 4 | India | 1,173,108,018 | 81,000,000 | 6.9% | 1,520.0% | 4.1% |
| 5 | Brazil | 201,103,330 | 75,943,600 | 37.8% | 1,418.9% | 3.9% |
| 6 | Germany | 82,282,988 | 65,123,800 | 79.1% | 171.3% | 3.3% |
| 7 | United Kingdom | 62,348,447 | 51,442,100 | 82.5% | 234.0% | 2.6% |
| 8 | Russia | 139,390,205 | 59,700,000 | 42.8% | 1,825.8% | 3.0% |
| 9 | France | 64,768,389 | 44,625,300 | 68.9% | 425.0% | 2.3% |
| 10 | Korea South | 48,636,068 | 39,440,000 | 81.1% | 107.1% | 2.0% |
| 11 | Iran | 76,923,300 | 33,200,00 | 43.2% | 13,180.0% | 1.7% |
| 12 | Italy | 58,090,681 | 30,026,400 | 51.7% | 127.5% | 1.5% |
| 13 | Indonesia | 242,968,342 | 30,000,000 | 12.3% | 1,400.0% | 1.5% |
| 14 | Spain | 46,505,963 | 29,093,984 | 62.6% | 440.0% | 1.5% |
| 15 | Mexico | 112,468,855 | 30,600,000 | 27.2% | 1,028.2% | 1.6% |
| 16 | Turkey | 77,804,122 | 35,000,000 | 45.0% | 1,650.0% | 1.8% |
| 17 | Canada | 33,759,742 | 26,224,900 | 77.7% | 106.5% | 1.3% |
| 18 | Philippines | 99,900,177 | 29,700,00 | 29.7% | 1,385.0% | 1.5% |
| 19 | Vietnam | 89,571,130 | 24,269,083 | 27.1% | 12,034.5% | 1.2% |
| 20 | Poland | 38,463,699 | 22,450,600 | 58.4% | 701.8% | 1.1% |
| | Top 20 Countries | 4,415,272,037 | 1,466,877,067 | 33.2% | 408.9% | 74.6% |
| | Rest of the World | 2,430,337,923 | 499,637,749 | 20.6% | 586.7% | 25.4% |
| | Total World Users | 6,845,609,960 | 1,966,514,816 | 28.7% | 444.8% | 100.0% |

NOTES: (1) World Internet User Statistics were updated for June 30, 2010.



marketing objectives (as we will discuss shortly). Other factors that have contributed to marketers' increased attention on the Internet include the increase in high-speed Internet connections which has led users to spend more time online, and has increased use of new media options that attract attention and involvement, and new ways to advertise, technologies that allow for tracking consumers' interests and purchase behaviors, and an increased ability to reach many more potential buyers.

Today's World Wide Web has evolved into a different medium than anyone could have expected 10 years ago. Unlike other media, which are essentially unidirectional

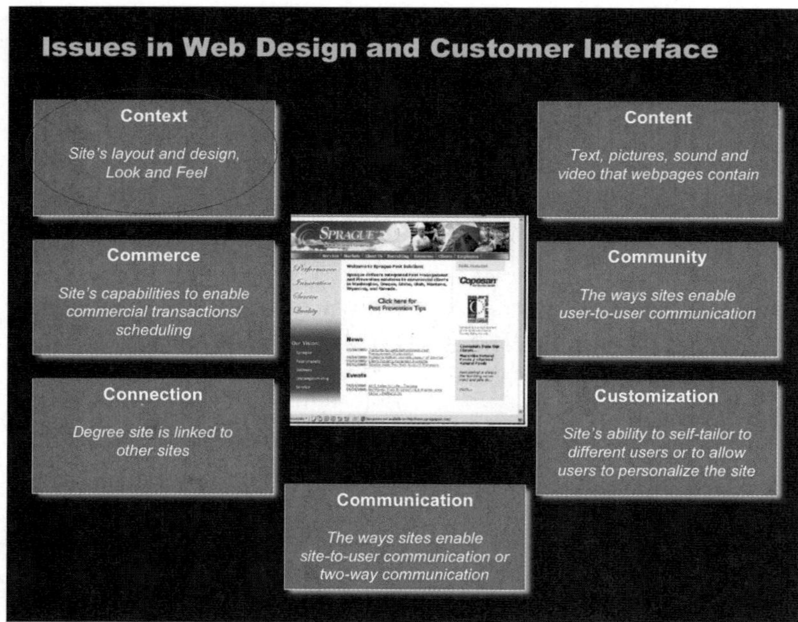


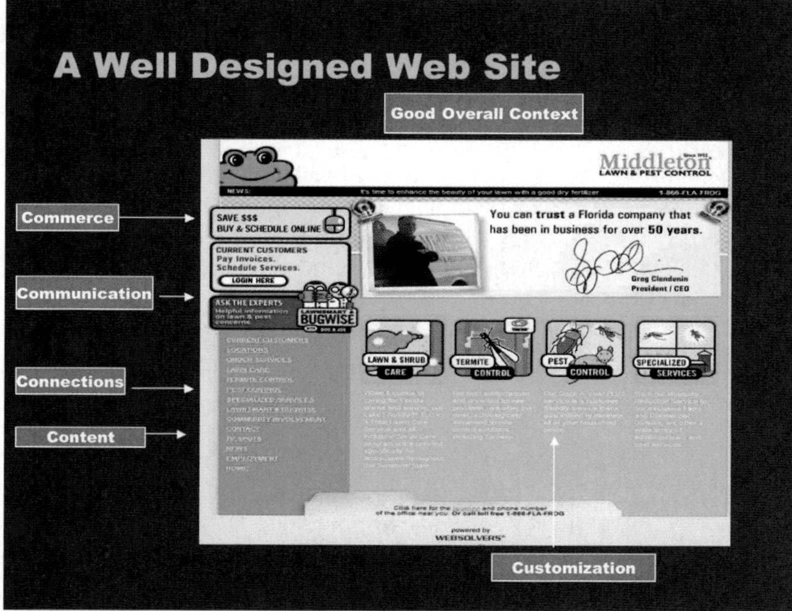


**EXHIBIT 15–1**
Factors that lead to an effective website

and responsible for the content provided and products and services offered for sale, the Internet is interactive, allowing for a two-way flow. Consumers not only control when and which messages and content they are exposed to, but now provide their own content, offer their own goods and services for sale, and provide feedback on the same as provided by others. As you will see, both marketers and consumers use the Internet in a variety of ways to provide and collect information as well as make transactions.

## Web Objectives

When major corporations first began to conduct business on the Internet, they put up websites primarily for information purposes and a one-way flow of information resulted. Companies like Kmart and Maytag had sites that were really not much more than online catalogs, while those of other companies were designed for information purposes only. The role of the website quickly changed, however, as sites are now designed to accomplish a number of objectives and have become much more creative, by promoting brand images, positioning, and offering promotions, product information, and products and services for sale with many allowing interactivity. With the introduction of Java, it became possible to create fancier graphics, audio, and animation online. This resulted in marketers utilizing the Internet in an entirely new way, moving beyond the purely informational role. As you will see, the objective of disseminating information and selling products remains, but additional communications and sales objectives are also being pursued.

## Developing and Maintaining a Website

Before we discuss marketers' Web objectives in detail, it is important that you understand the role of the **website**—the place where providers make information available to users of the Internet. Developing and maintaining a successful website require significant time and effort. To attract visitors to the site and have them return to it require a combination of creativity, effective marketing, and continual updating of the site. In addition, the site must be integrated with other media in regard to objectives, appearance, and other factors.

Exhibit 15–1 demonstrates the factors that contribute to an effective website. Making a site work and having one work successfully are not the same thing, however, and whether a site is effective is determined by what it is that management hopes to achieve. As already noted, some sites are offered for informational

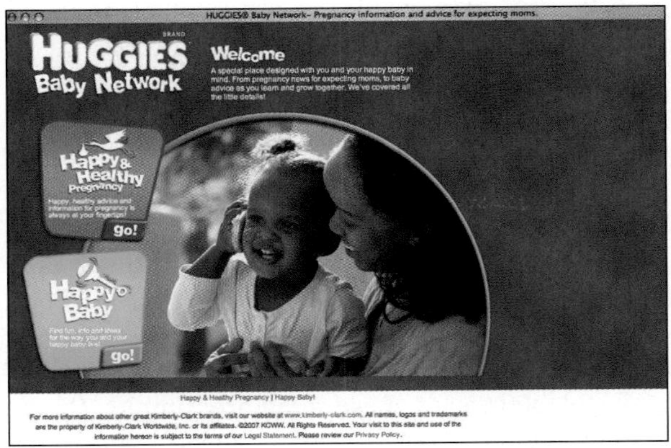


**EXHIBIT 15–2**
The HUGGIES website provides information on babies and parenting

purposes only (though this has become more of the exception than the rule and is more common in the business-to-business market than in the consumer market), while others approach the market much more aggressively. For example, Kimberly-Clark Corporation, the manufacturer of HUGGIES brand of diapers, Pull-Ups training pants, and Little Swimmers swim pants, has been extremely successful in its Internet marketing efforts. The HUGGIES homepage (Exhibit 15–2) goes well beyond providing information. The site has additional objectives, such as developing a long-term relationship with parents, establishing a brand image for the products, and supporting sales. The HUGGIES site provides expectant mothers with encouragement and ideas as to how to maintain a happy and healthy pregnancy. By clicking onto this part of the site, the expectant mother is provided with informative articles on what to expect, tips on healthy eating, other valuable information, and the opportunity to personalize the site to her personal needs. The site also provides information to be used once the baby has been born. Tips on how to create a nursery, games to play with the baby, and more information from experts are just part of this section of the site. The site is designed to develop one-on-one relationships by offering very useful information, as well as product samples, a rewards program, coupons, giveaways, and more.[1] Thousands of people have become members providing Kimberly-Clark with an enormous database the company can use for future marketing efforts. Finally, to support sales, the site directs customers to the nearest retail store that sells HUGGIES brands, or the visitor can buy online.

As the HUGGIES example demonstrates, a website can be an effective tool for the marketer, depending on the nature of one's business and one's marketing objectives. A website can range from a very simple source of information about the company and its products to a powerful tool for developing a brand image, sampling, loyalty, and even generating sales.

## Communications Objectives

Unlike other media discussed thus far in the text, the Internet is actually a hybrid of media. In part, it is a communications medium, allowing companies to create awareness, provide information, and influence attitudes, as well as pursue other communications objectives. But for some it is also a direct-response medium, allowing the user to both purchase and sell products through e-commerce. Thus, we will discuss two sets of objectives pursued by companies that use the Internet. Let's first look at some of the communications objectives these companies want to achieve.

**Create Awareness** Advertising on the Web can be useful in creating awareness of an organization as well as its specific product and service offerings. For small companies with limited budgets, the Web offers the opportunity to create awareness well beyond what might be achieved through traditional media. For example, a start-up company like the one shown in Exhibit 15–3, can almost immediately gain worldwide exposure at a reasonable cost—something that was not possible before the Internet. While a valuable tool for creating awareness—particularly for smaller companies that may have limited advertising budgets—the Internet is not likely to be the most effective of the IMC elements for achieving this objective for larger companies. Mass-media advertising may be more useful for this purpose, given its larger reach and lower cost per exposure (as the TV people will be glad to remind you!). Studies have demonstrated the effectiveness of TV to drive visitors to websites.

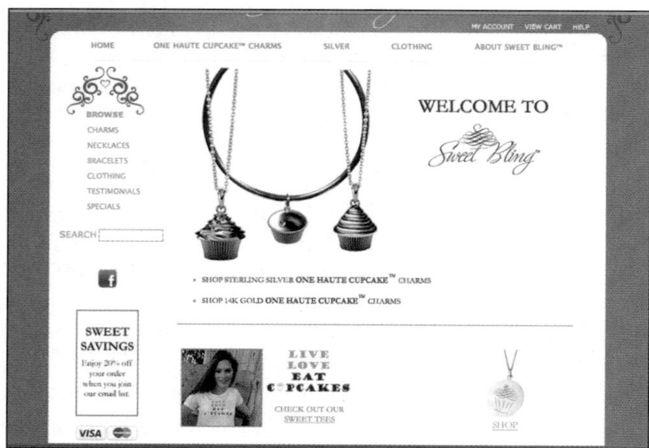


**EXHIBIT 15–3**
Start-up company SweetBling.com has benefited from the use of the Internet

**Generate Interest** A visit to Pepsi.com will quickly demonstrate how a site can be used to generate interest. The site provides news, downloads, clips from TV commercials, current promotions, and more. In addition, visitors can purchase concert tickets, purchase Pepsi merchandise, and so on. The Red Bull website shown in Exhibit 15–4 also provides information on events, photos, sports information, Red Bull TV, and more, giving visitors a reason to return. An information center, games, product information, sales items, and even an opportunity to personalize the site are all available. The objectives of these sites are simple: Create interest that will bring visitors back to learn more about the products—and, of course, to sell stuff.

**Disseminate Information** One of the primary objectives for using the Web is to provide in-depth information about a company's products and services. In business-to-business markets, having a website has become a necessity, as more and more buyers expect that a company will have a site providing them with detailed information about its offerings. In the government sector, contracts are often put out to bid on the Internet. Information regarding requirements, specifications, submission dates, and so on, is disseminated more quickly, to more potential candidates, and at a much lower cost via the Net than it is through other media. For consumer companies, their websites serve as a means of communicating more information about their products and services, philanthropic efforts, and the company itself.

**Create an Image** Many websites are designed to reflect the image a company wants to portray. For example, check out the consumer site at www.olukai.com (Exhibit 15–5). The site is an excellent example of a website used for image building. Interestingly, one of the difficulties traditional marketers have experienced is that of creating a brand image on the Internet. While some of these companies have been successful, others have not fared as well and have come to realize that branding and image-creating strategies must be specifically adapted to this medium.

**Create a Strong Brand** The Internet—as part of an integrated marketing communications program—can be a useful tool for branding. Unfortunately, many companies have not yet figured out how to successfully brand through this medium. Successful branding does not take place overnight. Unfortunately, many marketers aren't willing, or feel that they can't afford, to wait. These marketers may view the Internet as a quick fix that will allow them to establish their brands instantly. When they discover that they do not achieve this objective in the short run, they may quickly return to their focus on ROI or the bottom line. Cutting advertising and brand identity efforts on the Internet will immediately reflect cost savings.

**EXHIBIT 15–4**
RedBull.com offers a number of reasons to visit its website

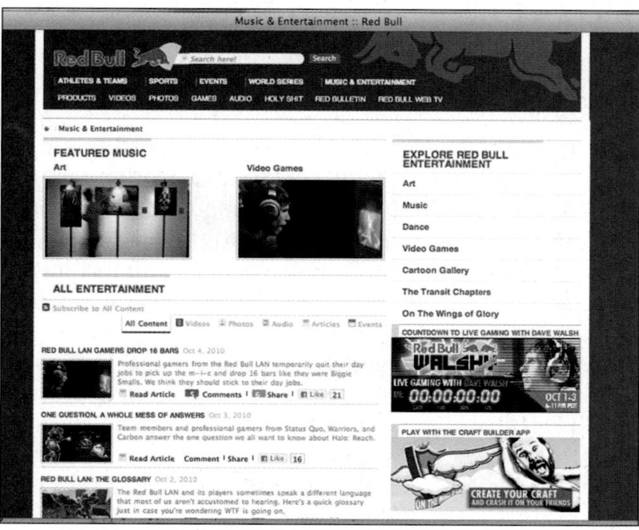


**Stimulate Trial** Many marketers have found the Internet to be an effective medium for stimulating trial of their products or services. Often websites offer electronic coupons in an attempt to stimulate trial of their products. Others offer samples, promotions, and sweepstakes designed to encourage trial. Music sites, like iTunes.com, allow for a "sampling" of songs before you purchase, while some business-to-business sites allow you to test their software online.

**EXHIBIT 15–5**
A website used for image building

**Create Buzz** One of the many advantages of the Web is the ability to create buzz. The viral nature of social networking and other sites make them attractive to marketers intending to spread the word.

**Gain Consideration** Many marketers believe that the Internet is an effective medium for achieving communications objectives such as consideration and/or evaluation. Blogs and discussion boards are considered particularly useful for providing information useful in evaluating products and brands.

### E-Commerce

The Internet also offers the opportunity to sell directly to customers in both the consumer market and the business-to-business market. This direct selling of goods and services has been labeled **e-commerce**. Sales through e-commerce were expected to reach $151.2 billion in the United States in 2010, with the profile of the online shopper reflecting that of the nation as a whole (Exhibit 15–6).[2] Many of the sites already mentioned in this chapter have a sales component—as either a primary or secondary goal.

Many companies maintain their existing "brick and mortar" stores while also selling through the Internet. Ann Taylor, Macy's, and Nordstrom are placing more emphasis on online sales, often by adding kiosks inside their stores. Barnes & Noble has increased its online efforts in an attempt to regain business lost to Amazon.com.[3]

We will discuss more about e-commerce and strategies employed in this area a little later in the chapter. Before we do, let's have a look at how the Internet can be used as part of an IMC program.



## THE INTERNET AND INTEGRATED MARKETING COMMUNICATIONS

Up to this point, we have mentioned the need for using the Internet as part of an IMC program. In this section, we discuss how the Web can be used with other program elements.

**WEB 1.0 and 2.0** Wikipedia, among other sources, makes a distinction between Web 1.0 and Web 2.0. Web 1.0 is generally referred to as the first decade or so of the World Wide Web, ending with the "bursting of the dot-com bubble".[4] For the most part, Web 1.0 consisted mainly of static sites resulting in a one-way flow of communication. Web 2.0 has led to dramatic changes in the World Wide Web, primarily as a result of decentralization of content and interactivity, with information provided by users as contributors, as well as the Web 1.0 participants (Figure 15–2). For purposes of this chapter, we are not concerned with the technical changes that have taken place, but rather the resulting impact on marketing communications. Everything we have discussed to this point still constitutes the way marketers use the Web; however, Web 2.0 has added some key components that have had a drastic impact on how the Internet is used in an IMC program, so we will discuss them separately.

**EXHIBIT 15–6**
eBay is one of the most popular e-commerce sites

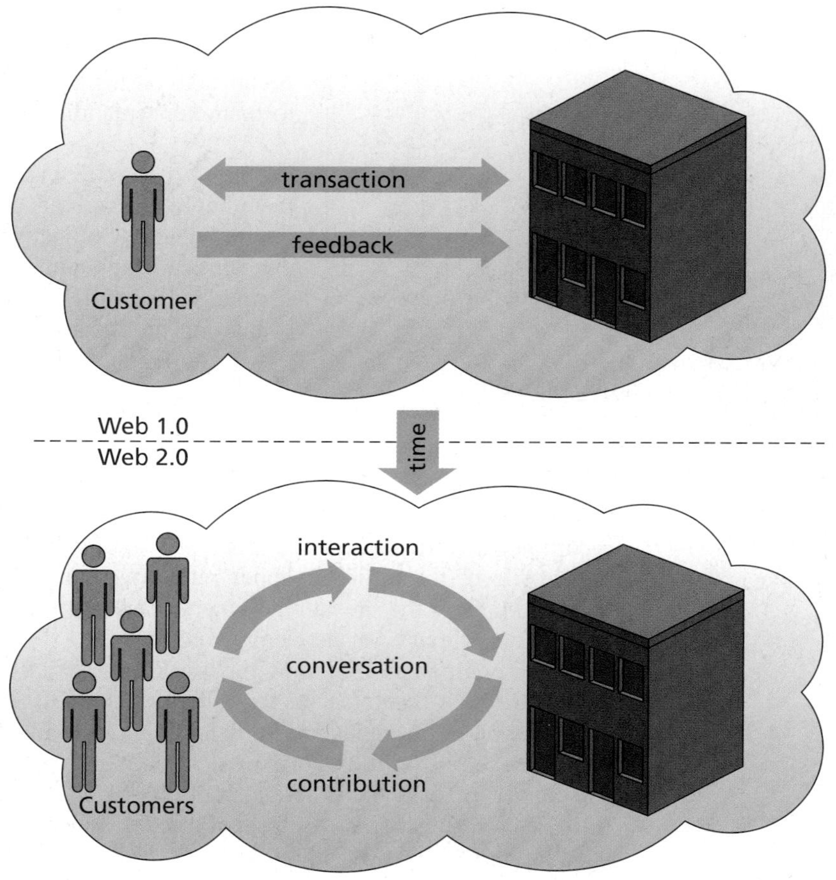


**FIGURE 15–2**
Differences in the Way Organizations Have Interacted with Customers on the Web

## Advertising on the Internet

Like broadcast or print, the Internet is an advertising medium. Companies and organizations working to promote their products and services must consider this medium as they would television, magazines, outdoor, and so on. Advertising on the Internet employs a variety of forms, including banners, sponsorships, pop-ups and pop-unders, interstitials, push technologies, links, paid searches, behavior targeting, contextual ads, and rich media.

**Banners** The most common form of advertising on the Web is **banner ads**. Banner ads may be used for creating awareness or recognition, entering viewers into contests and sweepstakes, or direct-marketing objectives. Banner ads may take on a variety of forms, as shown in Exhibit 15–7, as well as a number of names such as *side panels, skyscrapers,* or *verticals.* Initially banner ads constituted the vast majority of advertising on the Net, but studies indicating their questionable effectiveness have led to a decline in usage. Reports on click-through rates vary, but most studies indicate a less than 1 percent response rate.[5] At the same time, a number of studies have shown that while viewers may not click through the banners, they can still be effective in driving consumers to search or visit the ad's website.[6,7] A study reported in the *Journal of Consumer Research* showed evidence that even with low click-through rates, banner ads may still create a favorable attitude toward the ads through repeated exposures.[8]

**Sponsorships** Another common form of advertising is **sponsorships**. There are two types of sponsorships. *Regular sponsorships* occur when a company pays to sponsor a section of a site, for example, a *House Beautiful* magazine or *Cosmopolitan* magazine sponsorship on iVillage.com, or a corporate sponsorship of a page on Forbes.com. A more involved agreement is the **content sponsorship**, in which the sponsor not

**EXHIBIT 15–7**
Banner ad formats

only provides dollars in return for name association but participates in providing the content itself. In some cases, the site is responsible for providing content and having it approved by the sponsor; in other instances, the sponsor may contribute all or part of the content.

### Pop-Ups/Pop-Unders

When you access the Internet, you no doubt have seen a window or a creature of some sort appear on your screen in an attempt to get your attention. These advertisements are known as **pop-ups**, and they often appear when you access certain sites. Pop-ups are usually larger than banner ads but smaller than a full screen.

**Pop-unders** are ads that appear underneath the webpage and become visible only when the user leaves the site. For example, if you have ever visited a travel website, you probably were hit with a pop-under ad for Orbitz, one of the heaviest users of this form of Web advertising. Go to the *Los Angeles Times* website and when you leave, you will almost certainly see an example of pop-under advertising.

While some companies believe that pop-ups and pop-unders are effective forms of advertising, others disagree. Consumer complaints have led some sites to no longer accept these advertising forms. A study conducted by TNS revealed that 93 percent of respondents found pop-up ads annoying or very annoying.[9] The frequency and effectiveness of pop-ups and pop-unders have been greatly reduced given the opportunity for Internet users to purchase pop-up screeners, which will screen out the ads before they appear on your screen.

### Interstitials

**Interstitials** are ads that appear on your screen while you are waiting for a site's content to download. Although some advertisers believe that interstitials are irritating and more of a nuisance than a benefit, a study conducted by Grey Advertising found that only 15 percent of those surveyed felt that the ads were irritating and that 47 percent liked the ads. Perhaps more important, while ad recall of banner ads was approximately 51 percent, recall of interstitials was much higher, at 76 percent.[10] Acura introduced its Integra Type R model using an interstitial; Coca-Cola, TriStar, and Macy's have also employed this advertising form. Unfortunately for advertisers who may want to employ this medium, however, interstitials can also be blocked by pop-up blockers.

CHAPTER 15

### Links

While considered by some as not a type of advertising, **links** serve many of the same purposes as are served by the types discussed above. For example, a visitor to one site may click on a link that provides additional information and/or related materials at another site. At the bottom of the homepage at Forbes.com are sponsored links to other sites that may offer information of interest to the visitor.

**EXHIBIT 15–8**
Results of a Google search for flowers

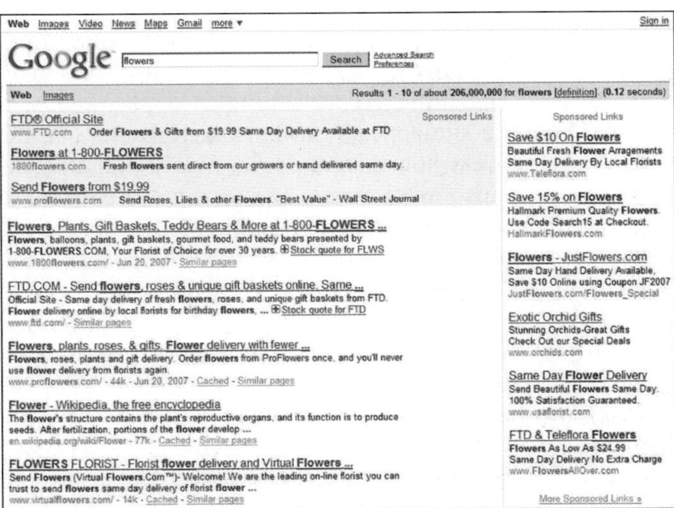


### Paid Search

One of the most used forms of advertising on the Internet is that of **paid search**, or search engine advertising, in which advertisers pay only when a consumer clicks on their ad or link from a search engine page. A report by the Search Engine Marketing Professional Organization (SEMPO) indicated that 70 percent of marketers now report that they use paid search strategies.[11] Search now constitutes over 45 percent of all online spending. While there are a number of search engines offering their services, Google (Exhibit 15–8) is by far the dominant provider, accounting for two out of every three searches (see IMC Technology Perspective 15–1). In an effort to more specifically target customers that

# IMC Technology Perspective 15–1 > > >

## Google—The World's Largest Search Engine—Reshapes the Advertising World

Rarely has a company grown so fast and in so many ways as Google, the company whose mission is to "organize the world's information and make it universally accessible and useful." Since its founding in 1998, Google has grown into a company with annual revenues exceeding $23 billion and was ranked as "the most powerful brand" in the world in a 2007 study by the leading global market research and consulting firm Millward Brown, with an estimated brand value of $66.4 billion. Very few, if any, companies have achieved such great success and reached iconic status as quickly as Google.

Google was cofounded by Sergey Brin and Larry Page in 1998 while they were graduate students at Stanford University working on the problem of trying to improve the online search process. The system they developed delivered relevant search results by favoring pages that were referenced or linked to by other websites. Consumers fell in love with the simplicity of Google's search engine as well as the speedy, accurate results it provided. The Google search engine attracted a loyal following among the growing number of Internet users and quickly became the number 1 gateway to the vast amount of information available online. Now, two out of three online searches are done using Google and the company's name has become a generic term for conducting online searches on the Internet.

While Google provides Internet users with a much better way to find information online, almost all the company's revenue comes from selling advertisements associated with search keywords. In 2000 Google launched a keyword-targeted advertising program called AdWords that uses short text-only ads to maintain an uncluttered page design and to maximize page loading speed. These text ads are identified as "sponsored links" that appear at the top or far right side of the search results page and are separated for clear user distinction. Online advertisers compete for the privilege of having their ads displayed with the results of a particular keyword search in a higher position than their competitors' ads. Advertisers pay only when an ad is clicked (called cost-per-click or CPC), which in turn takes the Web surfer to the advertiser's website. AdWords runs a specialized auction to decide which ads to show on the basis of (1) each advertiser's CPC bid and (2) the advertiser's *quality score*, which is a measure of the *relevance* of how well an ad matches a user's search query. The AdWords pricing system is designed to reward more relevant ads and keywords by showing them higher in the search results. Google does this by decreasing the amount that relevant ads must bid per click to beat their competition. This means that Google can display the advertisements that are the most targeted and relevant to a Google user's *search query*, which draws more users and click-throughs and thus generates more revenue for Google.

In 2003 Google expanded beyond search-related advertising by launching contextual paid listings which appear on other Google content pages (like Gmail and Google Maps) or on the websites of companies with whom Google partners via the Google AdSense program. *Site-targeted* campaigns (ads that are designed to appear on particular websites) can be used to generate sales, but can also be designed to assist in the branding process by increasing awareness of a company or brand, while not necessarily generating clicks or traffic. Site-targeted campaigns are priced on the basis of the more traditional cost-per-thousand-impressions (CPM) model rather than CPC. Advertisers set the maximum price they are willing

may be interested in their offerings, advertisers employ **search engine optimization (SEO)**. SEO is the process of improving the volume of traffic driven to one's site by a search engine through unpaid (organic) results as opposed to paid inclusions. The belief is that the higher a site appears on the search results list, the more visitors it will receive. SEO considers how search engines work and edits its HTML and coding to increase its relevance to keywords and to remove barriers to the indexing activities of search engines.[12] SEO has now become an integral part of the Internet marketing strategy of companies and organizations of all sizes.

**Behavioral Targeting** Another Internet advertising strategy that has seen rapid growth is **behavioral targeting**. Behavioral targeting is based on advertisers' targeting consumers by tracking their website surfing behaviors, such as which websites they have visited and/or searches they have made. By compiling clickstream data and Internet protocol (IP) information, segments of potential buyers can be identified and ads directed specifically to them. For example, by tracking an individual's visits to

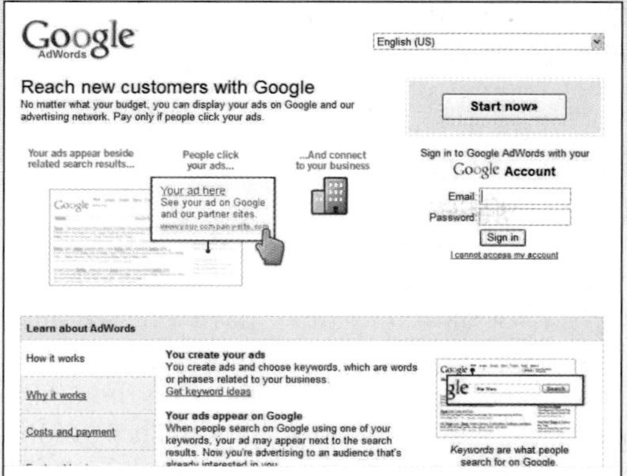


to pay for every thousand impressions their ads accrue on the sites where they are displayed, regardless of whether a user clicks on the ad.

Google has revolutionized the online advertising industry as well as the practice of marketing. The company has refined the concept of targeted advertising and taken it well beyond what conventional media can offèr. Never before could you make your add appear at the moment a potential customer was searching for your product. The simple text-only format used by AdWords allows marketers to try a myriad of variations and measure the results. They can see how many Web surfers click a text ad to get to their website, and then use Google Analytics to determine how many of those clicks result in sales or other *conversions,* as well as discern other useful information about visitors. This helps them assess the effectiveness of their ads and determine return on investment for ad spending—something that is very difficult to do with traditional media advertising. Moreover, many small businesses that could not afford to advertise nationally or globally can now do so by using search advertising. The vast majority of companies are now allocating at least part of their marketing budget to online advertising, which has become the fastest-growing category among advertising media. And no company is profiting more form the increased spending for online advertising than Google, which has a 29 percent share of the market for U.S. on line advertising revenue.

Google also offers an online platform for buying, selling, measuring, and delivering television commercials, and has begun experimenting with new varieties of online ads such as a click-to-call service that allows people to initiate a phone call to an advertiser when a telephone icon appearing next to a text ad is clicked. Google has also begun experimenting with "pay-per-action" advertising: pay-per-action is a new pricing model that allows advertisers to pay only when specific actions that they define (such as making a purchase) are completed by a user on their site. This has been the dream of advertisers for ages: to only pay for the advertising that works.

In addition to its advertising-related products, Google offers a variety of other popular Web-based applications and services including Gmail and Google Earth. Gmail is a free Web-based e-mail service that generates revenue by displaying text ads from the AdWords service that are tailored to the content of the e-mail messages displayed on the screen. Google Earth is an interactive mapping program that uses satellite and aerial imagery that covers most of the planet.

As marketers develop their advertising plans, many are meeting with Google to consider the various options the company provides for reaching consumers. Moreover, many traditional media, marketing, and technology companies are recognizing that they must now compete against the Google juggernaut. As noted in one *BusinessWeek* article, "Google is ground zero in a battle among traditional media and tech industry leaders and start-ups alike for the hearts and minds of the world's consumers—or at least their eyeballs and wallets." Perhaps even more telling is the comment made by a marketing executive who noted: "It's Google's world. We just live in it."

Sources: "2010 Financial Tables," www.google.com; Robert D. Hof, "Is Google Too Powerful?" *BusinessWeek*, April 9, 2007, pp. 47–54; David Kiley, "Google: Searching for an Edge in Ads," *BusinessWeek*, January 30, 2006, pp. 81–82. Kevin J. Delaney, "Google Tests New Ad Offerings—but Will Advertisers Follow?" *The Wall Street Journal*, December 14, 2006, pp. #1, 3.



a number of automobile websites, an ad for cars or a dealership could be served to that individual in real time. As will be seen later in this chapter, behavioral targeting has been shown to be an effective, albeit controversial strategy.

**Contextual Ads** Advertisers who target their ads based on the content of the webpage are using **contextual advertising**. Whereas behavioral advertising tracks surfing behaviors, contextual ads are determined by the content on the webpage. For example, an advertiser may place an airline ad on a travel site, or a golf club ad on a golf site, or even in or near a story about golf on another site. For example, Google's AdSense targets ads to match the content of a publisher's site. The ads come in a variety of formats including images and video ads and can be targeted to geographic or local markets.

**Rich Media** The increased penetration of broadband into households has increased the attention given to streaming video. **Rich media**, as defined by *Wikipedia,* are "a broad range of interactive digital media that exhibit dynamic motion, taking advantage of enhanced sensory features such as video, audio and animation."[13] Others state that rich media include all content that is created in flash.[14] The successful adoption of music videos, sports clips, news, and more has led advertisers to create a variety of forms of streaming video advertising content.

Types of rich media include the following.

**Online Commercials** The equivalent of traditional television commercials, online commercials are appearing on the Net. Some companies have created their own Web commercials, while others run the same spots they show on TV. A number of companies have been successful in blending the two media, showing the commercial on TV and then directing interested viewers to the Web if they wish to see it again or to view longer versions. Online advertising spending continues to rise, with forecasts that it will constitute 17 percent of total U.S. ad spending in 2010.[15] Likewise, consumer acceptance of these ads is increasing.

**Video on Demand** As described in Chapter 13, video clips of various entertainment activities (which include ads or are sponsored) are also available through the Internet. College basketball games, FIFA World Cup highlights, and demonstrations on how to use the Apple iPhone are just a few of the many options available.

**Webisodes** Short featured films created by the advertiser such as those created by Skyy Vodka and BMW, are examples of Webisodes, in which companies create their own content to advertise their products. Target, Hitachi, and Honda are just a few of the companies that have employed Webisodes, but the range of these efforts also includes small jewelers, baking companies, and others.

**Other Forms of Rich Media Advertising** Advertising Interactive banner ads, expandable ads, and rich media ads placed in video games, instant messaging, podcasts, and video ads within blogs are additional ways that rich media are currently employed.

LO 15-2

**Web 2.0** As noted earlier in the chapter, after the "dot-com bust" at the turn of the century, the World Wide Web underwent significant changes. These changes led to the adoption of the new Web as "Web 2.0." As defined in Wikipedia:

> "The term **Web 2.0** is commonly associated with Web applications that facilitate interactive information sharing, interoperability, user-centered design, and collaboration on the World Wide Web. A Web 2.0 site allows its users to interact with each other as contributors to the website's content, in contrast to websites where users are limited to the passive viewing of information that is provided to them.[16]

Among the examples provided along with the definition were social networking sites, video-sharing sites, wikis, and blogs, among others (Figure 15–3). Marketers were quick to adopt the new Web. As space does not allow us to discuss all, we will provide examples of those used most often to date (no doubt, this will change by the time you read this book!).

**Social Networking** Social networking sites allow users to share ideas, activities, events, and interests within their individual networks.[17] Examples of such sites include, MySpace, Facebook, Friendster, Bebo, Twitter, and LinkedIn, to mention just a few. As seen in the lead-in to this chapter, marketers have become enamored with the potential provided by these sites as a result of their target marketing capabilities, low costs, and the high levels of engagement of their members. Essentially, marketers like the idea that the viral aspects of the networks will spread the word for them. Smaller businesses also like the fact that they can now reach large audiences for small financial outlays. Figure 15–4 provides a number of examples as to how companies and organizations have used social media in their IMC programs.

**FIGURE 15–3**

Web 2.0 is a Multi-Faceted Version of the Internet

Source: Gary Hayes and Laurel Papworth, 2008

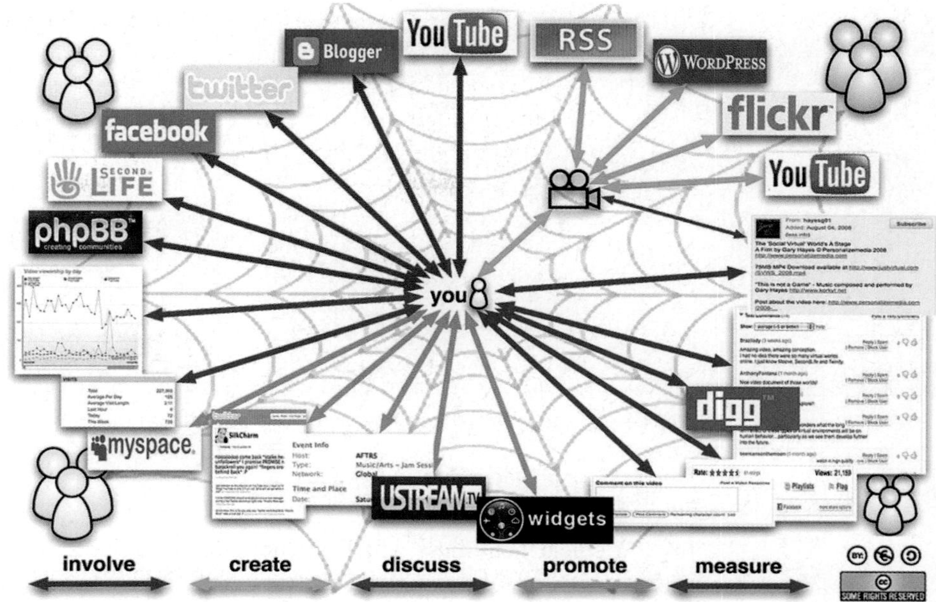


**User-Generated Video Sharing** User-generated sites mostly offer free services whereby users can upload video clips, music videos, video blogs, and other content and share it with the masses.[18] Larger organizations such as CBS, the BBC, and Vevo (among others) have now begun to post commercials and other forms of information (such as product assembly instructions, trouble shooting guides, and so on) on YouTube and other sites. A number of companies have also used this medium to encourage consumers to create and upload commercials of their own through

**FIGURE 15–4**

Some Examples of How Marketers Use Social Media Networks

| Site | Example |
|---|---|
| *Facebook* | *Sharpie*—The 45 year old marker company known more for the use of its product to mark cardboard boxes (Sharpie enjoys 97% brand awareness) than its creativity, unveiled a campaign to "Uncap What's Inside," designed to encourage consumers to uncap their creativity and individuality by using a variety of Sharpie products—some of which they had little or no awareness—to decorate anything from surfboards to sneakers. A key component of the campaign was the use of community websites from Facebook to Flickr to showcase the user generated creations.<br>Others: Mountain Dew employed Facebook to have consumers select a new Mt. Dew flavor; Dr. Scholls placed an ad with a free sample of an insole in *Shape* magazine. Once the insole was removed from the page, readers were instructed to go to Facebook and sign up for a free sample.<br>As of 2009, 97% of large charities used some form of social media—93% on Facebook. |
| *Twitter* | *Land Rover*—Land Rover became the first national brand to execute a nationwide Twitter campaign to promote its newest models. By using hashtags (words used in tweets to make it easier to follow an ongoing conversation via online searches) on billboards, taxi TVs, and other out-of-home media, as well as auto blogs and 4,500 compensated and heavily followed Twitter users, more than 300,000 Tweets about the new models were sent.<br>Others: The Oscars employed Twitter and Facebook to create buzz and excitement for the 2010 awards show; Eminem used Twitter to increase fan engagement; Wheat Thins created TV commercials featuring consumers who tweeted positively about the band. 90% of charities say they tweet. |
| *LinkedIn* | *Ernst & Young* and *EMC Corp*—both firms use LinkedIn to highlight their companies, recruit new candidates, and target specific interest groups. Other business-to-business companies including SAP and Microsoft allow members to view the profiles of others with whom they are communicating.<br>Others: Numerous companies have used LinkedIn to develop sales leads. 36% of charities employ LinkedIn. |

| Site | Example |
|---|---|
| *YouTube* | *Carl's Junior*—As part of their effort to introduce the new Portobello Mushroom Six-Dollar Burger to Young men, the fast food company hired nine popular YouTube video creators to participate in an the campaign by putting a spin on the CKE brand's infamous Paris Hilton eating-a-burger commercial by showing how they would do it. The creators were instructed to mention the burger by name, and were paid a flat fee for the videos. While not marked as ads on the YouTube network, each carried a notice that they were paid for by Carl's Jr. The "personal endorsements" were expected to generate about 10 million viewings. Many other companies now place commercials on YouTube.<br>Others: Retail stores like JCPenney, American Eagle and Forever 21 have employed "haul videos" in which teens post "look at what I got at the store" videos in an effort to create buzz for their stores. The teens are compensated or provided with gift certificates to buy the merchandise, often without revealing this fact. An estimated 150,000 hauler videos are now on YouTube, with tens of millions of viewers. |
| *Bebo* | *Open Media*—Owned by Bebo, Open Media is a platform of channels offering free content. Any media company (MTV, CBS, Sky, BBC) can keep complete control over their content on the channel as well as 100% of any advertising revenues generated there. The result for the media companies is exposure to 40 million-plus Bebo customers. In return, Bebo hopes to attract even more visitors.<br>Others: A number of rock bands like the Jonas Brothers have promoted themselves through videos on the site; Samsung has placed ads, as have numerous others. |

**FIGURE 15–5**
Examples of How Marketers Use User-Generated Video Networks

contests—GM and Doritos selected the best entries to appear on the Super Bowl with their developers in attendance. Examples of video sharing sites include: Flickr, Hulu, and YouTube. (See Figure 15–5).

**Podcasting** **Podcasting** is a medium that uses the Internet to distribute radiolike files for downloading into iPods and other MP3 players. As the market for iPods and MP3 players grows, the attractiveness of this medium does as well. Radio stations, including Clear Channel Communications and National Public Radio, and television programs, such as *60 Minutes,* now podcast. As noted by Paul Verna, author of the report *Podcasting: Into the Mainstream,* this shift has resulted in the evolution of podcasting from a long tail medium to a Web 2.0 extension of popular, traditional media.[19] Traditional advertisers are adopting the medium, while others find it useful as well (Exhibit 15–9). For example, Durex, a condom manufacturer, has purchased product placements in podcasts—in part to reach young listeners with risque marketing messages while skirting FCC decency rules.

**EXHIBIT 15–9**
Podcasts have become popular with a number of advertisers

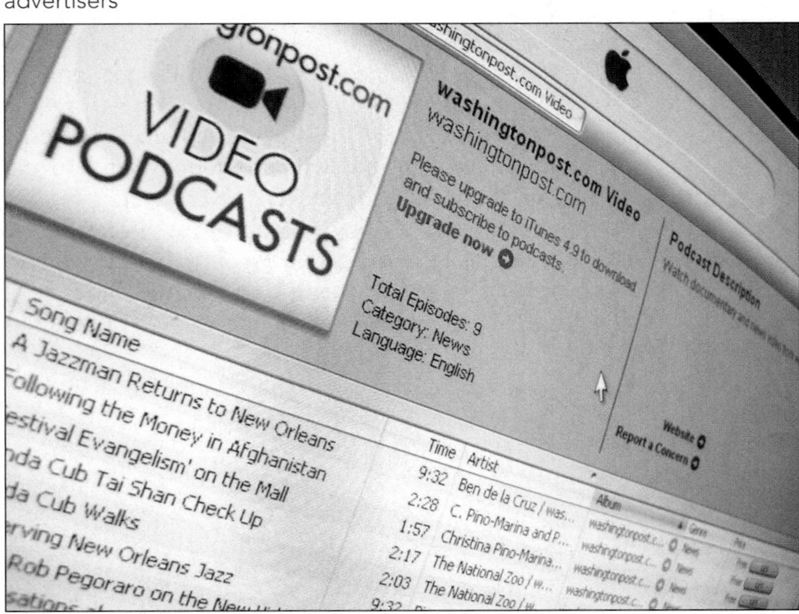


**RSS** **Really Simple Syndication (RSS)** is a specification that uses XML to organize and format Web-based content in a standard way. Content owners create an RSS feed, which usually consists of titles and brief descriptions of about 10 articles elsewhere on the site. The difference between Web content and an RSS feed is that the latter can send out notifications whenever new material is available.[20] Because the alerts can be customized to the viewers' preferences, advertisers have found it useful for disseminating information to those who may be most interested. For example, the *Washington Post* allows for advertising in its RSS feeds, and companies like American Express, Continental Airlines, and Verizon have all run ads through RSS feeds.

| | |
|---|---|
| *Widgets* | a common feature on many websites and Facebook, widgets or buttons, allow users to share a piece of content by posting it to a news feed for dissemination to others. |
| *Virtual reality* | a term that applies to computer-simulated environments that can simulate places in the real world, as well as in imaginary worlds. For example, Second Life.com. Volvo launched a new car campaign on MyTown; H&M, the apparel chain, and MTV have also employed this medium. |
| *Augmented reality* | is a term for a view of a physical real-world environment whose elements are **augmented** by virtual computer-generated imagery. |
| *QR codes* | A user, who has a camera phone, smart phone or quick response QR reader app can take a photo of a barcode, where it gets scanned and directed to the URL assigned to the QR Code. The code has the ability to display text, contact information, connect to a wireless network, or open a webpage in the phone's browser. Special K put a weight loss video accessible from the barcodes on their cereal boxes; wine importer Lion Nathan Wine Group places the codes on bottles of wine. |

**FIGURE 15–6**
Other Web 2.0 Media Commonly Used to Reach Consumers

**Blogs** A **blog** (or Weblog) is a Web-based publication consisting primarily of periodic articles, normally presented in reverse chronological order. As noted, blogs may reflect the writings of an individual, a community, a political organization, or a corporation, and they offer advertisers a new way to reach their target audiences. For example, there are blogs about beer, current events, sports, raising children, and so on. In 2009 there were an estimated 126 million blogs on the Internet. (This information came from a blog!)[21] Some marketers are excited about the potential of blogs to reach large audiences at a small cost. As a result, these marketers attempt to keep the bloggers happy by feeding them exclusives, releasing product news to them before it hits the mainstream, and so on. Others are a bit more skeptical, noting that there are a number of problems with the use of blogs, including the potential for deception and limited reach (see Ethical Perspective 15–1).



**Other 2.0 Media Forms** There are numerous other 2.0 media forms also available to marketers including the use of widgets, virtual and augmented reality, and QR codes (see Figure 15–6). Unfortunately, space limitations do not permit their discussion at this time.

## Sales Promotion on the Internet

Companies have found the Internet to be a very effective medium for disseminating sales promotions. As noted earlier, HUGGIES ties in the use of sales promotions with its website as do many others (Exhibit 15–10). Numerous companies now print online coupons. Other examples include the use of trivia games, contests, sweepstakes, instant win promotions, and so on. Kellogg teamed up with Disney/Pixar to promote *Toy Story 3* by providing point codes inside cereal boxes redeemable on line for *Toy Story 3* characters. McDonald's offered a "Healthy Diet Shrek" promotion for kids to go along with the release of *Shrek the Third.*

**EXHIBIT 15–10**
Sales promotions are common on websites

## Personal Selling on the Internet

The Internet has been both a benefit and a detriment to many of those involved in personal selling—particularly those in the business-to-business market. For some, the Internet has been a threat that might take away job opportunities. Companies have

# Ethical Perspective 15–1 > > >

## Promises and Pitfalls of the Internet in the IMC Program: Is It Time to Tame the Beast?

As promising as the Internet is to both marketers and to consumers, it is not without its perils. Often referred to as the "Wild, Wild West" given its relative lack of controls and regulations compared to traditional media, the freedom of the Internet constitutes a large part of its attractiveness. However, like the West, there seems to be a rising constituency who think it's time to tame the Beast. Some of the practices raising concern include the following:

- *Deception.* Let's start with blogs. While the vast majority of blogs are legitimate, they also offer the potential for deception. For example, if someone comments on a product or brand—either positively or negatively—does anyone know the objectivity of the blogger? The opportunity exists for companies to anonymously promote their brands through positive comments. Likewise, competitive brand bashing can also be done anonymously. Can one really believe what's being said. A study by *PQ Media* indicated that spending for "sponsored conversations," in which bloggers and social media users are compensated (often in free goods) for discussing brands' products, rose to $46 million in 2009, and is likely to continue to do so in coming years. In addition to social networking friends, celebrities have also been paid to mention brands (it is reported that Kim Kardashian has been paid over $10,000 to tweet on behalf of advertisers). A similar practice involves the identification of social network "influencers," or opinion leaders in certain product categories who are promoting products, brands, or services without disclosing that they are being compensated.
- *Behavioral Targeting.* By tracking Internet sites visited, or through social networks and personal and lifestyle details, companies have become more able to match Web users with products and services that may be of interest to them. For example, if you surf websites for vacation details, don't be surprised if you start seeing an increase in hotel and airline ads. This form of electronic eavesdropping is on the increase, as marketers attempt to gather more and more data about your life without you knowing it. Most marketers see no ethical implications in collecting reams of data, arguing that they can then offer consumers relevant information that they can use—not wasting their time with things they are not interested in.
- *Privacy.* As noted, behavioral targeting is considered a form of privacy invasion to some. By extending the practice to social networks in other forms ("Like" buttons), Facebook has raised the ire of its members as well as the FTC and other regulators, as well as trade organizations such as the AAAA and the Association of National Advertisers, the Interactive Advertising Bureau, and the DMA. In 2007 Facebook introduced such a program called "Beacon." Complaints by members and others led to a modification of the program. In 2010 a second program was introduced to gain even more personal information. Again, members complained about the "opt out" process and the long and complicated privacy policy. Some threatened to boycott or drop their membership, and, once again Facebook made changes. Nevertheless, Facebook, among others continue to collect information about their members and their friends.

These actions, plus some others not discussed, have led concerned parties to get involved. In 2009, the FTC—the agency that protects consumers from fraud or deceptive business practices—voted to update its rules governing endorsements. The new guidelines require bloggers to clearly disclose any "material connection" to an advertiser, including payments for endorsements. For the first time, these rules have been extended to include social media. In Spring 2010, the IAB announced a new plan for dealing with behavioral targeting in which advertisers place notices alongside banner ads that enable users to find out more information about where the ad came from, and even opt out of receiving similar behavior-based ads in the future. A *Data Usage & Control Primer: Best Practices & Definitions,* guide was also made available for advertisers explaining what constitutes appropriate practices in this area.

For their part, consumers either don't know about or seem to be all that bothered by the practices. While some boycotts have taken place, and some have dropped their memberships in social networks, for the most part it just doesn't seem to matter to people that much. As one consumer stated, "As long as the ads are of interest to me, it is better than having to see those that aren't!"

Sources: Maria Aaron, "IAB Increases Transparency in the Use of Data in the Interactive Advertising Industry; Releases 'Data Usage & Control Primer: Best Practices & Definitions," www.iab.net, May 3, 2010; Michael Bush, "Bloggers Be Warned: FTC May Monitor What You Say," www.adage.com, April 13, 2009; Michael Learmouth, "FTC Cracks Down on Blogger Payola, Celebrity Tweets," www.adage.com, October 5, 2009.

found that they can remain effective, or even increase effectiveness, by building a strong Web presence. The high-cost and poor-reach disadvantages of personal selling are allowing these companies to reduce new hires and even cut back on their existing sales forces.

On the positive side, websites have been used quite effectively to enhance and support the selling effort. As noted earlier, the Web has become a primary source of information for millions of customers in the consumer and business-to-business markets. Visitors to websites can gain volumes of information about a company's products and services. In return, the visitors become a valuable resource for leads that both internal and external salespersons can follow up, and they become part of a prospect database. Not only can potential customers learn about the company's offerings, but the selling organization can serve and qualify prospects more cost-effectively.

The Web can also be used to stimulate trial. For many companies, personal salespersons can reach only a fraction of the potential customer base. Through trial demonstrations or samples offered online, customers can determine if the offering satisfies their needs and, if so, request a personal sales call. In such cases both parties benefit from time and cost savings.

Some companies have used the Internet to improve their one-on-one relationships with customers. By providing more information in a more timely and efficient manner, a company enables customers to learn more about what it has to offer. This increases the opportunity for cross-selling and customer retention. Twitter has become a powerful tool for consumers to voice their opinions of companies or complaints, while also allowing the involved company to respond quickly.

In a well-designed IMC program, the Internet and personal selling are designed to be complementary tools, working together to increase sales. It appears that more and more companies are coming to this realization.



## Public Relations on the Internet

The Internet is a useful medium for conducting public relations activities. Many sites devote a portion of their content to public relations activities, including the provision of information about the company, its philanthropic activities, annual reports, and more.

Companies, nonprofit organizations, and political parties have become quite adept at using the Internet for public relations purposes. An excellent example of the use of public relations on the Internet is provided by Chrysler (Exhibit 15–11). The site provides up-to-date news stories and other forms of content, photo images, and cross-references to other sites or media as well as press kits and a calendar of upcoming events. It also provides information about Chrysler automobiles and the corporation itself and allows for customer feedback and registration for updates. In addition, Daimler-Chrysler's homepage contains many of the articles written about the corporation, including awards won and philanthropic efforts achieved such as its concern for the environment and their support for numerous causes.

**EXHIBIT 15–11**
Chrysler uses its website for public relations purposes

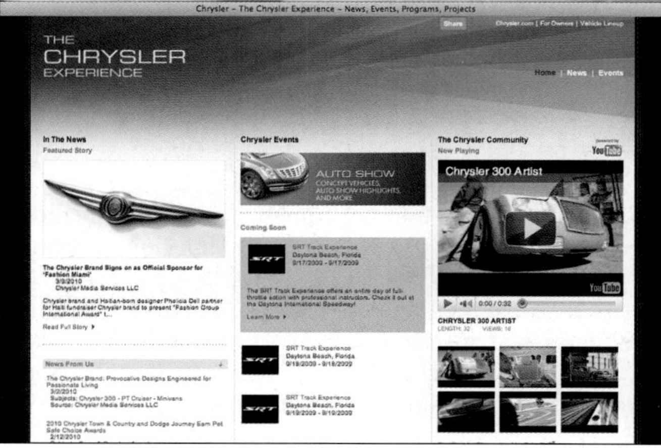


Other examples of the effective use of public relations activities on the Internet are also available, as you will see in the chapter on public relations. The Web is a useful medium for conducting public relations activities, and its use for this function is on the increase.

At the same time, many philanthropic and nonprofit organizations have found the Internet to be a useful way to generate funds. As noted earlier, charitable organizations have also formed sites to handle public relations activities, provide information regarding the causes the charity supports, collect contributions, and so on. In an example of integrating the Internet with public relations and television, companies have found the Internet to be extremely useful for providing information in times of a crisis, and for gathering feedback about their products and services and about themselves (particularly through blogs and RSS feeds).

### Direct Marketing on the Internet

Our discussion of direct marketing and the Internet will approach the topic from two perspectives: the use of direct-marketing tools for communications objectives (as discussed in Chapter 14) and e-commerce. As we stated previously, many direct-marketing tools like direct mail, infomercials, and the like, have been adapted to the Internet. At the same time, e-commerce—selling directly to the consumer via the Internet—has become an industry all its own.

**Direct Mail** Direct mail on the Internet **(e-mail)** is essentially an electronic version of regular mail. Like regular mail it is highly targeted, relies heavily on lists, and attempts to reach consumers with specific needs through targeted messages. The Direct Marketing Association estimates that e-mail volume may reach as much as $2.7 trillion by 2007 and continue to increase through 2011.[22]

Sometimes users may also receive less-targeted and unwanted e-mails. The electronic equivalent of junk mail, these messages are referred to as **spam**.[23] Because of the high volumes of spam and the fact that many consumers consider it a nuisance, the U.S. government has passed laws regulating its use. In addition, antispam software like that created to screen pop-ups viruses has been developed.

While many consumers don't like spam or other forms of e-mail, studies have shown the effectiveness of e-mails, and, as we have noted, all indications are that the end of this form of marketing is not in sight.

**Infomercials** Even the infomercial has discovered the Net. Travelzoo, an online travel company, promotes destinations and carriers through infomercials. The same people who brought you "Amazing Discoveries" infomercials on television has produced infomercials for the Internet (and they are not alone). One such infomercial was produced by iMall, a company based in Provo, Utah, which has run marketing seminars on how to make money on the Internet. There is even a website called the Infomercial Index.com which serves as a listing of infomercials—many of which are shown on the Net.

**Home-Shopping Channels** In the direct-marketing chapter, we mentioned that QVC has taken its home-shopping TV channel to the Internet as have HSN, Shop NBC, and others. HSN also has an Internet shopping channel, as does buy.com. Amazon and eBay, while they are not purely home-shopping channels, nevertheless, sell a lot of products online.

## MEASURING EFFECTIVENESS OF THE INTERNET

Companies measuring the effectiveness of the Internet employ a variety of methods, most of which can be done electronically. As you will see, a number of companies provide Internet measures as part of a package; that is, they provide audience measurement information (demographics, psychographics, etc.) as "up-front" information, as well as some of the effectiveness measures described below. First, we will discuss some of the measures used to determine the effectiveness of a website. Then, we will discuss some of the companies providing these measures.

| |
|---|
| Clicks |
| Post-click conversions |
| Cost per conversion |
| Unique visitors |
| Average frequency |
| Frequency to conversion ratios |
| Advertising exposure time |
| Ad interaction rate |
| View-through rate |
| Visits |
| Webpage eye tracking |
| Offline sales lift |
| Cross-media models |

**FIGURE 15–7**

Measures of Internet Effectiveness

Source: IAB.net.

## Audience Measures and Measures of Effectiveness

When the Internet industry first developed its own measures of effectiveness, problems with these measures led to a slower rate of adoption by traditional media buyers. In an attempt to respond to criticism of the audience metrics employed, as well as to standardize some of the measures used to gauge effectiveness of the Internet, the Interactive Advertising Bureau (IAB)—the largest and most influential trade group—formed a task force in November 2004, consisting of major global corporations involved in advertising and research. The task force was created to examine and create standardized measures to measure advertising impact that could be used to assess the impact of ads and to eliminate confusion. The three key points of the new recommendations are detailed in a 20-page report available from the IAB.net. Industry experts believe that the adoption of these guidelines, along with objective auditing, would make the Internet a more attractive medium for many of those who advertise in traditional media. The guidelines have the support of major online publishers, as well as the nearly 40 major proprietary online ad-server technologies and major associations worldwide.[24]

### Measures of Effectiveness

**Internet-Specific Measures** One of the perceived advantages of the Internet is a company's ability to measure commercial effectiveness, due in part to its ability to measure activity in real time. Figure 15–7 shows some of the measures that are currently used by companies. These measures include those specific to the Internet and interactive industry, as well as more traditional measures such as ad recall, brand awareness, and purchase intentions. (For a detailed explanation of each of these terms, visit www.IAB.net.)

**Traditional Measures** In addition to the Internet-specific measures, companies employ a number of traditional marketing and communications measures. Some of these include the following.

- *Recall and retention.* A number of companies use traditional measures of recall and retention to test their Internet ads. These same measures have been used to pretest online commercials as well.
- *Surveys.* Survey research, conducted both online and through traditional methods, is employed to determine everything from site usage to attitudes toward a site.
- *Sales.* For the e-commerce marketers, a prime indicator of effectiveness is the volume of sales generated. Adding information regarding demographics, user behaviors, and so on, can increase the effectiveness of this measure.
- *Tracking.* Some companies now offer more traditional tracking measures such as brand awareness, ad recall, message association, and purchase intent.
- *ROI.* A study conducted by ComScore, MySpace, and Dunnhumby measured the ROI of online sales generated by a $1 million campaign on MySpace.[25]

The aforementioned measures reveal that the Internet has its own set of criteria for measuring effectiveness and is also borrowing from traditional measures; for example, brand recall has become a major area of focus. The Association of Advertising Agencies and the Association of National Advertisers uses a system called Advertising Digital Identification (Ad-Id). Ad-Id assigns advertising across all media a specific media code to facilitate cross-media buys. In 2008 Ad-Id became the official media coding standard.[26] The goal of the coalition is to develop cross-media standards employing impression comparisons that include the Internet. Many of the companies that provide research information in traditional media (Nielsen, Ipsos-ASI) are now extending their reach into the Internet world. Others (Insights

.com, Forrester) have developed measures specifically for online users. Two of the commonly used Internet advertising effectiveness measurement companies used are Comscore and MediaMetrix. These companies offer a combination of effectiveness measures for marketers to use. Academics are also beginning to publish articles related to measuring effectiveness on the Internet. Studies on consumers' attitudes toward a site, response variations in e-mail surveys, and similarities between brick-and-mortar retailing and e-commerce are just a few of the many articles being published in academic journals to advance the measurement of Internet use.

Unfortunately, not all of the methods used to measure Internet activity and effectiveness are accurate. We discuss some of these problems later in this chapter, when considering disadvantages of the Internet.

## ADVANTAGES AND DISADVANTAGES OF THE INTERNET

A number of advantages of the Internet can be cited:

1. *Target marketing.* A major advantage of the Web is the ability to target very specific groups of individuals with a minimum of waste coverage. For those in the business-to-business market, the Internet resembles a combination trade magazine and trade show, as only those most interested in the products and/or services a site has to offer will visit the site (others have little or no reason to do so). In the consumer market, through personalization and other targeting techniques, sites are becoming more tailored to meet one's needs and wants.
2. *Message tailoring.* As a result of precise targeting, messages can be designed to appeal to the specific needs and wants of the target audience, much of which comes from behavior tracking. The interactive capabilities of the Net make it possible to carry on one-to-one marketing with increased success in both the business and the consumer markets.
3. *Interactive capabilities.* Because the Internet is interactive, it provides strong potential for increasing customer involvement and satisfaction and almost immediate feedback for buyers and sellers.
4. *Information access.* Perhaps the greatest advantage of the Internet is its availability as an information source. Internet users can find a plethora of information about almost any topic of their choosing merely by conducting a search. Once they have visited a particular site, users can garner a wealth of information regarding product specifications, costs, purchase information, and so on. Links will direct them to even more information if it is desired.
5. *Sales potential.* The numbers provided previously in this chapter demonstrate the incredible sales numbers being generated in both the business-to-business and the consumer segments. Forecasts are for continued growth in the future. In addition, the number of persons who shop online and then purchase offline has continued to increase.
6. *Creativity.* Creatively designed sites can enhance a company's image, lead to repeat visits, and positively position the company or organization in the consumer's mind. Visit some of the sites mentioned earlier to see what we mean.
7. *Exposure.* For many smaller companies, with limited budgets, the World Wide Web enables them to gain exposure to potential customers that heretofore would have been impossible. For a fraction of the investment that would be required using traditional media, companies can gain national and even international exposure in a timely manner.
8. *Speed.* For those requesting information on a company, its products, and/or its service offerings, the Internet is the quickest means of acquiring this information.

9. *Complement to IMC.* The Net both complements and is complemented by other IMC media. As such, it serves as a vital link in the integrative process. In a study conducted by eMarketer, business managers perceive the ability for the Internet to enhance and complement other media to be its major advantage.

While it is a potentially effective medium, the Internet also has its disadvantages, including the following:

1. *Measurement problems.* One of the greatest disadvantages of the Internet is the lack of reliability of the research numbers generated. A quick review of forecasts, audience profiles, and other statistics offered by research providers will demonstrate a great deal of variance—leading to a serious lack of validity and reliability. One company mentioned earlier, eMarketer, has attempted to reconcile such differences and explain the reasoning for the discrepancies (differences in methodologies employed), but the problem still exists. The actions taken by the IAB to standardize metrics will help in reducing some of this problem. But due to difficulties involved in both measuring and forecasting in this medium, it remains necessary to proceed with caution when using these numbers. In a study of 410 marketing executives published by McKinsey, the primary reason cited for not investing online was the lack of sufficient metrics.[27]
2. *Clutter.* As the number of ads proliferates, the likelihood of one's ad being noticed drops accordingly. The result is that some ads may not get noticed, and some consumers may become irritated by the clutter. Some studies already show that banner ads have lost effectiveness for this very reason, while others show consistently declining click-through rates.
3. *Potential for deception.* The Center for Media Education has referred to the Web as "a web of deceit" in regard to advertisers' attempts to target children with subtle advertising messages. The Center, among others, has asked the government to regulate the Internet. In addition, data collection without consumers' knowledge and permission, hacking, and credit card theft are among the problems confronting Internet users. Ethical Perspective 15–1 addressed this issue.
4. *Privacy.* One of the many issues of concern for Internet users is that of privacy. While many younger users seem to be less worried, actions taken by websites like Facebook, among others, have led to user boycotts as well as calls for more regulation. The IAB has issued a policy on privacy to which it asks companies to adhere (see www.iab.net).
5. *Irritation.* Numerous studies have reported on the irritating aspects of some Web tactics. These studies have shown consumers' discontent with clutter, e-mail SPAM, and pop-ups and pop-unders. These irritating aspects can deter visitors from coming to and or returning to the sites, or result in negative attributes toward the advertiser.

Overall, the Internet offers marketers some very definite advantages over traditional media. At the same time, disadvantages and limitations render this medium as less than a one-stop solution. However, as part of an IMC program, the Internet is a very valuable tool.



# ADDITIONAL INTERACTIVE MEDIA

While the Internet has captured most of the attention of marketers, additional interactive media are also available and can be used as a contributor to an IMC program. A variety of digital media such as interactive CD-ROMS, kiosks, and interactive phones have been used by marketers to provide information to their audiences. Agency

**EXHIBIT 15–12**
Google introduces Google TV

executives note that the most important capability of these media was their ability to be linked with traditional marketing projects.

One of the more attention-getting and promising of the new interactive media is interactive TV. **Interactive TV**, or iTV (Exhibit 15–12), allows the viewer of a television program to interact with the program and the ads, essentially merging television and the Internet. Many marketers, including Logitech, Sony, and Intel, are betting that future computer users will access the Internet through their television sets. Multitasking allows television viewers to watch an event—for example, a football game—and to pull up information on players, history of the matchups between the teams, and other statistics without ever leaving the couch or the game through a small picture in a picture box within the main screen. Nike, in what some consider to be the largest iTV campaign ever, teamed with the Dish Network to offer 20 minutes of "Quick Is Deadly" content on its Zoom training shoes. Dish users with DVRs were able to click onto 30- and 60-second TV spots starring fleet-footed Nike athletes, and had the option of watching the entire workout of football star LaDainian Tomlinson. In addition, viewers were able to access a store locator listing stores that carry the shoes with a click of the button.[28]

In May 2010, Google introduced a new platform called Google TV. Sony, Intel, and Logitech are making hardware that will run the platform and promises to change interactive TV forever, by for example, integrating search and discussions through Twitter while watching programs, and other options such as accessing websites and viewing content on a large screen (Exhibit 15–12).[29]

While many marketers believe that the rapid adoption of iTV is just around the corner, others regard it as a very large corner, given that the promise of iTV has not yet been fulfilled though the technology has been around for quite some time. One of the most recent attempts, Apple's "Apple TV" launched in 2007 but has had limited success. In Europe, iTV has been more rapidly adopted than in the United States. On Rupert Murdoch's BSkyB satellite service in the United Kingdom, viewers can make home-shopping purchases, play games, and even change camera angles during soccer matches. Apparently these options are more attractive to the European market than to the current U.S. viewer.

Nevertheless, some companies have demonstrated successful interactive campaigns, and as more consumers purchase broadband access, the marketing potential of the medium is likely to increase. As for now, it may just be that when viewers are watching TV, they just want to watch TV. We will wait to see.

**EXHIBIT 15–13**
Cell phone users in Asia have been able to use their cell phones in various ways

## Mobile

What's the fastest growing medium in the United States? If you said the Internet, you were close, but actually it is **mobile**. The existing installed base of cell phone users (over 80 percent), and the rapid adoption of smartphones like the iPhone, Blackberry, and Droid have created a wealth of new advertising opportunities. No other medium is as personal or interactive and constantly with the viewer as is the cell phone. In addition, the variety of applications seems endless. There are apps for games, entertainment, finance, lifestyle, and social networking to mention just a few. Mobile ads can be delivered in the form of messages, banners, and full page ads, mobile search ads, and mobile videos. It is also now possible to offer mobile coupons.[30]

One of the most attractive characteristics of mobile for advertisers is the ability to target customers. Marketers can determine the user's location, behavioral and demographic information, frequency of use, reach, and usage contexts. For example, certain mobile users have been shown to be interested in travel-related information and apps. As a result, travel-related industries like hotels, airlines, and rental car agencies have increased their advertising expenditures in this area. Ace Hardware ran a mobile campaign in the week leading up to Memorial Day, and found that those who saw the ad were 30 percent more likely to have visited an Ace store for the sale.[31]

Adoption of wireless technology in Asia has outpaced that in the United States as it is common for Asian cell phone users to send e-mails, buy music, and surf the Web, all the while being exposed to banner ads, branded contests, and coupons (Exhibit 15–13). The U.S. market may be catching up.

# Summary

This chapter introduced you to the Internet and interactive media. It explained some of the objectives for these media and how they can be used in an IMC program.

The discussion of the Internet focused on understanding the growth of the Internet, the objectives sought when using the Internet, and Internet communications strategies. In addition, we discussed the role of the Internet in an IMC program, explaining how all the IMC program elements can be used with the Internet.

The chapter discussed a number of new online tools including paid search, behavioral targeting, contextual ads, rich media, and a number of Web 2.0 platforms including social networks, user-generated content, blogs, RSS, and podcasting. We noted advantages of the Internet—including targeting markets, using interactive capabilities, and building relationships. In addition, we reviewed disadvantages—including high costs, unreliable measurements and statistics, and relatively low reach (compared to that of traditional media).

The Internet has been the most rapidly adopted medium of our time (until mobile). It holds great potential for both business-to-business and consumer marketers. However, contrary to popular belief, the Internet is not a stand-alone medium. Its role in an integrated marketing communications program strengthens the overall program as well as the effectiveness of the Internet itself.

Some interactive media like interactive TV have not yet fulfilled their promise. While still in its infancy, the medium has not received the level of acceptance and use expected. On the other hand, mobile advertising is experiencing incredible growth, and wireless communication is starting to experience growth, particularly in Asia.

## Key Terms



## Discussion Questions

1. The growth of Facebook has had a major impact on the way advertisers attempt to reach their customers. Discuss how Facebook has changed the media environment, citing examples. (LO2)
2. Discuss why mobile has become an attractive medium for advertisers. Provide examples of how companies have used mobile. (LO2)
3. There are indications that the popularity of blogs may have already reached the maturity stage. Take a position as to whether this is true or not, providing examples to support your opinion. (LO1)
4. A trend among advertisers is to make more use of consumer generated commercials to be placed on YouTube and similar sites. Discuss some of the advantages and disadvantages of employing this strategy. (LO4)
5. Some marketers have argued that the strength of the Internet in an IMC program is at the mid stage of the consumer funnel (knowledge consideration, etc.). Discuss whether you agree or disagree with this position, and support your position with examples. (LO1)
6. The Internet has changed the advertising environment forever. Discuss the impact the Internet has had on advertising and discuss what this has meant for traditional media. (LO1)
7. One of the fastest-growing mediums in regard to advertising expenditures is mobile. Explain why mobile has become so attractive to advertisers. (LO5)
8 The chapter notes that while the Internet has some distinct advantages over other media, some traditional media have characteristics that make them more useful for achieving communications objectives. Provide examples and discuss. (LO1)
9. Explain how the Internet has changed the practice of public relations. Pick a website as an example of this change. (LO1)
10. Exhibit 15–1 demonstrates the factors that are essential to an effective website. Discuss each of these factors, and provide examples of websites that demonstrate them in practice. (LO3)

## AdForum Exercise: "Internet Advertising"

(See Advertising and Promotion Playlist, Chapter 15)

Many large companies have increased their advertising expenditures on the Internet and Interactive media. At the same time, Internet Service Providers have also employed traditional media in their marketing efforts. Visit the AdForum playlist and answer the following questions:

1 What is the nature of the business of the advertiser?
2 What objective(s) do you think that the advertiser is trying to accomplish? Are there any additional objectives of the ad?
3 What other media might be employed to achieve the objectives sought in these ads?
4 Do you think the ad is likely to be effective? Why or why not?

Access to the chapter playlist is available through , www.mcgrawhillconnect.com

## LEARNING OBJECTIVES

LO1 To understand the role of sales promotion in a company's integrated marketing communications program and to examine why it is increasingly important.

LO2 To examine the various objectives of sales promotion programs.

LO3 To examine the types of consumer- and trade-oriented sales promotion tools and the factors to consider in using them.

LO4 To understand how sales promotion is coordinated with advertising.

LO5 To consider potential problems and abuse by companies in their use of sales promotion.

# 16 Sales Promotion

## SUBWAY STRIKES GOLD WITH THE $5 FOOTLONG PROMOTION

Six years ago Stuart Frankel, the owner of two small Subway sandwich shops located in Miami's Jackson Memorial Hospital, was looking for ways to increase his sales which generally dropped off on weekends. He came up with a relatively simple idea of offering every footlong sandwich on Saturday and Sunday for $5, which was about a dollar less than the usual price. Frankel says he chose the $5 price because he likes round numbers and it soon became apparent that consumers liked the number as well as sales quickly rose by double digits, and his stores had lines out the door. Frankel kept the promotion going for more than a year and sales kept increasing. In 2007, Steve Sager, the Subway market development agent who oversaw 225 franchises across South Florida heard about the success of Frankel's $5 deal and decided to try it in a struggling store in Ft. Lauderdale that was located on a busy street with numerous strip malls. On the first day of the promotion sales doubled, and the store ran out of bread and meat, leading Sager to call Subway cofounder Fred DeLuca who lived in the area and share the good news. Other stores in South Florida began running the deal with similar success and soon other franchisees in other cities ranging from Chicago to Washington D.C. were onboard.

During the time that the $5 footlong promotion was gaining momentum, Subway's marketing team was looking for ideas for a new national advertising campaign. The company had been running a campaign for several years that featured spokesman Jared Fogle, who had lost more than 200 pounds by eating Subway six-inch subs for lunch and dinner. However, Jeff Moody, the CEO of Subway's franchise-owned advertising and marketing arm, had noticed the success of the dollar value menus being used by McDonald's and along with other top executives in the company, he wanted a value offering of their own. At the end of 2008 the Subway board voted to take the $5 footlong promotion national even though the company had no formal marketing research to back up the idea.

After deciding to move forward with the campaign Subway began working with advertising agency, MMB of Boston, which decided to keep the ads that would be used to publicize the campaign relatively simple and as straightforward as possible. The creative team devised a simple hand gesture to convey both the price (five fingers) and the size of the sandwich (which was shown by people in the commercials who spread their hands about a foot apart). Keeping with the simplicity theme, MMB creatives decided that they did not want anyone babbling in the commercials, so the best way to communicate the $5 price was to mention it as often as possible in a jingle. To make sure no one would forget it, the price was embedded three times in the catchy jingle ("Five. Five dollar. Five dollar footlong,") that was used in the Subway commercial that promoted the offer. The national campaign was launched in March 2008, which was excellent timing because the recession was tightening its grip on the economy around the same time. Over the first two weeks of the campaign Subway franchisees reported a 25 percent average increase in sales, and consumers became intrigued by the simple commercials with the catchy jingle and hand gestures. Within a few weeks, more than 3,600 videos of people performing the jingle and gestures appeared on YouTube and the $5 footlongs were being mentioned on TV shows, on websites and in the media. The North Carolina State Fair even held an *American Idol* type $5 Footlong Song Challenge event.

When the $5 footlong promotion began, the company really had no idea that what started out as a short-term promotion would evolve into a national phenomenon that would not only ignite Subway's sales, but change the entire fast food industry. Over the past two years the $5 footlong has generated more than $4 billion in sales for Subway which alone would place the sandwich among the top

10 fast-food brands. The promotion has helped lift Subway's U.S. sales 17 percent during a time period when most restaurant chains have been struggling to stay even. The chain now has over 23,400 locations in the United States and another 10,000 in other countries and will soon pass McDonald's to become the world's largest fast food chain based on number of locations.

The success of the $5 Footlong promotion and the appeal of round numbers has not gone unnoticed by Subway's competitors such as Quiznos, Domino's, Pizza Hut, and others. Domino's recently launched a $5 toasted sub, Quiznos has a $4 sandwich, Pizza Hut launched a $5 calzone while other fast-food chains promote value meals at the critical $5 point which has become the reference price point that everyone is trying to meet or beat.

Industry analysts and marketing experts keep speculating as to how long the $5 Footlong promotion might be sustainable, and the managing partner at MMB admits that the issue of when it will run out of steam keeps him up at night. However, Subway's Chief Marketing Officer Tony Pace has stated that the $5 footlong will remain "as long as it makes economic sense" and perhaps sums it all up quite well with a rhetorical question: "If you had a brand that represented nearly $4 billion in sales, would you plan an exit strategy for it?" The answer should be obvious.

Sources: "Matthew Boyle, "The Accidental Hero," *BusinessWeek,* November 16, 2009, pp. 58–61; Emily Bryson York, "Subway Set to Overtake McD's in Omnipresence," *Advertising Age,* September 21, 2009, http://adage.com/print?article_id=139145; _____; "Subway's $5 Footlong Becomes Yardstick for Fast-Food Deals," *Advertising Age,* June 8, 2009, http://adage.com/print?article_id=137119.

As discussed in the opening vignette, marketers recognize that advertising alone is not always enough to move their products off store shelves and into the hands of consumers. They are using a variety of sales promotion methods targeted at both consumers and the wholesalers and retailers that distribute their products to stimulate demand. Most companies' IMC programs include consumer and trade promotions that are coordinated with their advertising, direct marketing, publicity/publications, and online/Web-related marketing as well as their personal selling efforts.

This chapter focuses on the role of sales promotion in a firm's IMC program. We examine how marketers use both consumer- and trade-oriented promotions to influence the purchase behavior of consumers as well as wholesalers and retailers. We explore the objectives of sales promotion programs and the various types of sales promotion tools that can be used at both the consumer and trade level. We also consider how sales promotion can be integrated with other elements of the promotional mix and look at problems that can arise when marketers become overly dependent on consumer and trade promotions, especially the latter.

# THE SCOPE AND ROLE OF SALES PROMOTION

**Sales promotion** has been defined as "a direct inducement that offers an extra value or incentive for the product to the sales force, distributors, or the ultimate consumer with the primary objective of creating an immediate sale."[1] Keep in mind several important aspects of sales promotion as you read this chapter.

First, sales promotion involves some type of inducement that provides an *extra incentive* to buy. This incentive is usually the key element in a promotional program; it may be a coupon or price reduction, the opportunity to enter a contest or sweepstakes, a money-back refund or rebate, or an extra amount of a product. The incentive may also be a free sample of the product, given in hopes of generating a future purchase or a premium such as the free movie DVD mail-in offer used by Kellogg's Corn Flakes (Exhibit 16–1). The Kellogg Company used this promotion to improve purchase frequency and build long-term brand loyalty for its group of all-family and adult cereals. With DVD penetration at over 80 percent of households and the average household buying 18 new movies each year, the free movie offer

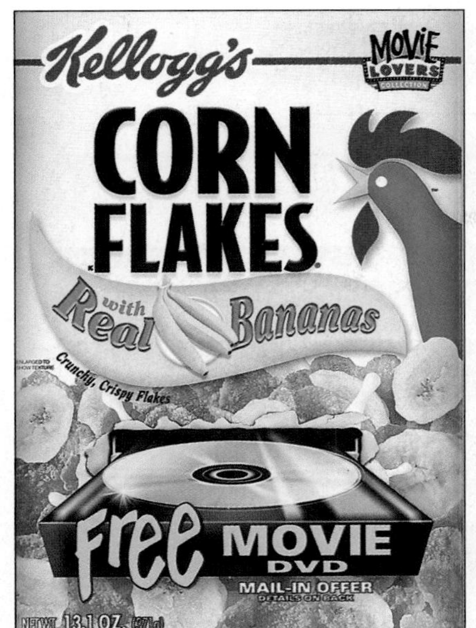


**EXHIBIT 16–1**
A premium offer is used to provide extra incentive to purchase Kellogg's Corn Flakes

was an ideal premium for broad family appeal. Consumers could receive a free movie with five proofs of product purchase. Over a two-year period, the promotion produced more than 2 million DVD redemptions and helped generate 10 million units of cereal purchases for the participating brands.[2] Most sales promotion offers attempt to add some value to the product or service. While advertising appeals to the mind and emotions to give the consumer a reason to buy, sales promotion appeals more to the pocketbook and provides an incentive for purchasing a brand.

Sales promotion can also provide an inducement to marketing intermediaries such as wholesalers and retailers. A trade allowance or discount gives retailers a financial incentive to stock and promote a manufacturer's products. A trade contest directed toward wholesalers or retail personnel gives them extra incentive to perform certain tasks or meet sales goals.

A second point is that sales promotion is essentially an *acceleration tool,* designed to speed up the selling process and maximize sales volume.[3] By providing an extra incentive, sales promotion techniques can motivate consumers to purchase a larger quantity of a brand or shorten the purchase cycle of the trade or consumers by encouraging them to take more immediate action.

Companies also use limited-time offers such as price-off deals to retailers or a coupon with an expiration date to accelerate the purchase process.[4] Sales promotion attempts to maximize sales volume by motivating customers who have not responded to advertising. The ideal sales promotion program generates sales that would not be achieved by other means. However, as we shall see later, many sales promotion offers end up being used by current users of a brand rather than attracting new users.

A final point regarding sales promotion activities is that they can be *targeted to different parties* in the marketing channel. As shown in Figure 16–1, sales promotion can be broken into two major categories: consumer-oriented and trade-oriented promotions. Activities involved in **consumer-oriented sales promotion** include sampling, couponing, premiums, contests and sweepstakes, refunds and rebates, bonus packs, price-offs, frequency programs, and event marketing. These promotions are directed at consumers, the end purchasers of goods and services, and are designed to induce them to purchase the marketer's brand.

As discussed in Chapter 2, consumer-oriented promotions are part of a promotional pull strategy; they work along with advertising to encourage consumers to purchase a particular brand and thus create demand for it. Consumer promotions are also used by retailers to encourage consumers to shop in their particular stores. Many grocery stores use their own coupons or sponsor contests and other promotions to increase store patronage.

**Trade-oriented sales promotion** includes dealer contests and incentives, trade allowances, point-of-purchase displays, sales training programs, trade shows, cooperative advertising, and other programs designed to motivate distributors and retailers to carry a product and make an extra effort to push it to their customers. Many marketing programs include both trade- and consumer-oriented promotions, since motivating both groups maximizes the effectiveness of the promotional program.



## THE GROWTH OF SALES PROMOTION

While sales promotion has been part of the marketing process for a long time, its role and importance in a company's integrated marketing communications program have increased dramatically over the past decade. Consumer sales promotion–related spending increased from $56 billion in 1991 to nearly $350 billion in 2009.[5] Marketers also spend an estimated $150 billion each year on promotions targeted at

**FIGURE 16–1**
Types of Sales Promotion Activities

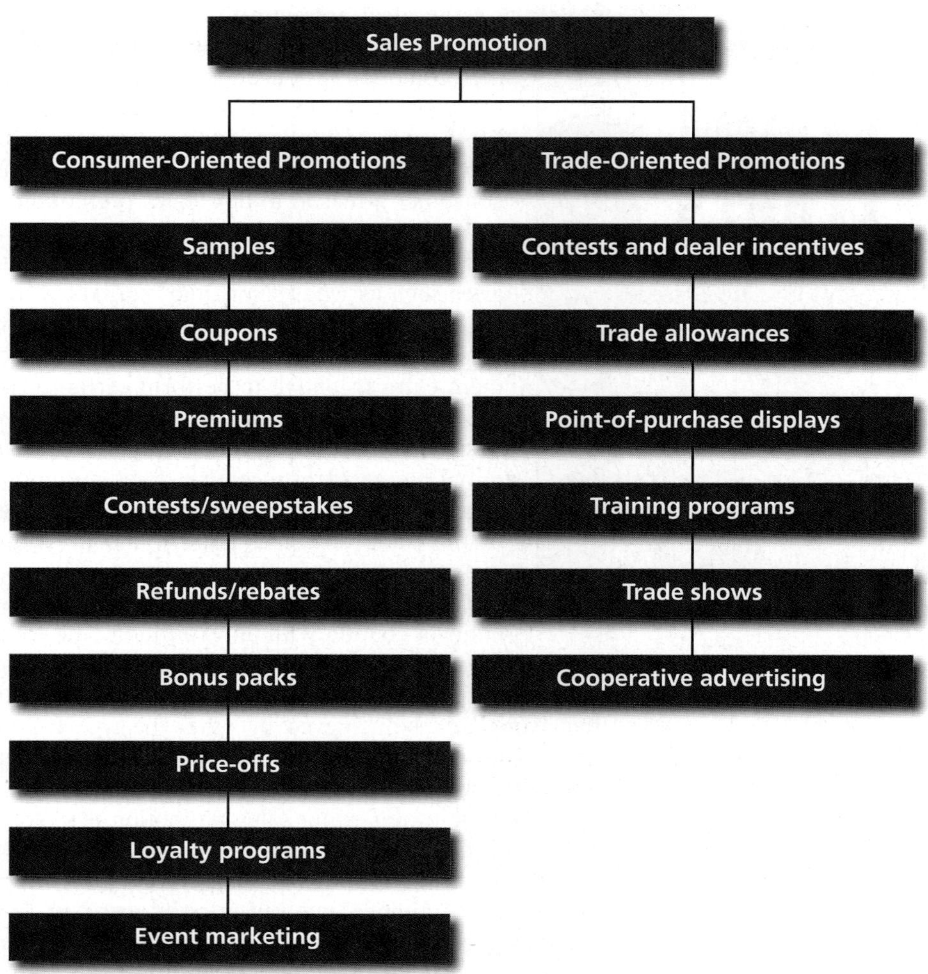


retailers and wholesalers. Consumer packaged goods firms continue to be the core users of sales promotion programs and tools. However, sales promotion activity is also increasing in other categories, including health care, computer hardware and software, consumer electronics, and service industries.

Not only has the total amount of money spent on sales promotion increased, but the percentage of marketers' budgets allocated to promotion has grown as well. For many years advertising was the major component in the promotional mix of most consumer-product companies. Until the 1980s, nearly half of marketers' promotional dollars was spent on advertising campaigns designed to create or reinforce brand awareness and build long-term loyalty. However by the mid- to late 80s, a fundamental change had occurred in the way most consumer-product companies were marketing their products. The proportion of the marketing budget allocated to sales promotion rose sharply, while the amount spent on media advertising declined. The increase in spending on sales promotion at the expense of media advertising continued throughout the decade of the 90s and into the new millennium. Currently, estimates are that marketers spend between 60 and 75 percent of their promotional budgets on sales promotion, with the remainder being allocated to media advertising.[6]

Allocation of marketing budgets among consumer promotions, trade promotions, and media advertising varies by industry and company. For example, trade promotion accounts for nearly 50 percent of the budget for consumer packaged-goods companies, with 27 percent going to consumer promotion and 24 percent to media advertising.[7] Moreover, a significant amount of the monies that marketers allocate to media advertising is spent on ads that deliver promotional messages regarding

**EXHIBIT 16–2**
Advertisements often use promotions such as sweepstakes to draw attention

contests, games, sweepstakes, and rebate offers.[8] Surveys have shown that marketers devote about 17 percent of their ad budgets to promotional messages.[9] Promotional messages are also used to help attract attention to image-building ads. For example, the ad shown in Exhibit 16–2 shows how ChannelLock uses a sweepstakes promotion to help draw attention to an ad promoting the quality of its tools.

## Reasons for the Increase in Sales Promotion

The reallocation of the marketing budget concerned many marketers who still viewed media advertising as the primary tool for brand building and saw sales promotion programs as little more than gimmicks that contributed little to brand equity. However, most have recognized that consumers may love certain brands but often want an extra incentive to buy them. Marketers also know they must partner effectively with trade accounts, and this often means providing them with an additional incentive to stock and promote their brands and participate in various promotional programs.

A major reason for the increase in spending on sales promotion is that the promotion industry has matured over the past several decades. Increased sophistication and a more strategic role and focus have elevated the discipline and its role in the IMC program of many companies. In the past, sales promotion specialists would be brought in after key strategic branding decisions were made. Promotional agencies were viewed primarily as tacticians whose role was to develop a promotional program such as a contest or sweepstakes or a coupon or sampling program that could create a short-term increase in sales. However, many companies are now making promotional specialists part of their strategic brand-building team, a move that puts sales promotion on par with media advertising. Many promotional agencies have expanded their capabilities and expertise and now offer clients a variety of integrated marketing services that extend beyond just sales promotion. For example, Exhibit 16–3 shows how Aspen Marketing Services, one of the largest providers of integrated marketing and promotional services, promotes its capabilities which include a variety of IMC tools.

There are also a number of other factors that have led to the increase in the importance of sales promotion and the shift in marketing dollars from media advertising to consumer and trade promotions. Among them are the growing power of retailers, declining brand loyalty, increased promotional sensitivity, brand proliferation, fragmentation of the consumer market, the short-term focus of many marketers, increased accountability, competition, and clutter.

**EXHIBIT 16–3**
Aspen Marketing Services touts its IMC capabilities

**The Growing Power of Retailers** One reason for the increase in sales promotion is the power shift in the marketplace from manufacturers to retailers. For many years, manufacturers of national brands had the power and influence; retailers were just passive distributors of their products. Consumer-product manufacturers created consumer demand for their brands by using heavy advertising and some consumer-oriented promotions, such as samples, coupons, and premiums, and exerted pressure on retailers to carry the products. Retailers did very little research and sales analysis; they relied on manufacturers for information regarding the sales performance of individual brands.

In recent years, however, several developments have helped to transfer power from the manufacturers to the retailers. With the advent of optical checkout scanners and sophisticated in-store computer systems, retailers gained access to data concerning how quickly products turn over, which sales promotions are working, and which products make money.[10] Retailers use this information to analyze sales of manufacturers' products and then demand discounts and other promotional support from manufacturers of lagging brands. Companies that fail to comply with retailers' demands for more trade support often have their shelf space reduced or even their product dropped.

Another factor that has increased the power of retailers is the consolidation of the grocery store industry, which has resulted in larger chains with greater buying power and clout. These large chains have become accustomed to trade promotions and can pressure manufacturers to provide deals, discounts, and allowances. Consolidation has also given large retailers more money for advancing already strong private label initiatives, and sales promotion is the next step in the marketing evolution of private label brands. Private label brands in various packaged-good categories such as foods, drugs, and health and beauty care products are giving national brands more competition for retail shelf space and increasing their own marketing, including the use of traditional sales promotion tools. Well-marketed private label products are forcing national brand leaders, as well as second-tier brands, to develop more innovative promotional programs and to be more price-competitive.[11]

One of the most significant developments among retailers is the tremendous growth of Walmart, which has become the largest company in the world as well as the most powerful retailer.[12] Walmart operates nearly 8,500 stores in 15 countries including more than 4,200 in the United States and had sales of $405 billion in fiscal 2010. It controls 20 percent of dry grocery, 29 percent of nonfood grocery, 30 percent of health and beauty aids, and 45 percent of general merchandise sales in the United States. Walmart accounts for a large share of the business done by every major U.S. consumer-products company and can use its power to influence the way marketers use sales promotions. Like many large retailers, Walmart often asks for account-specific promotions that are designed for and offered only through its stores. The company has been known to mandate that marketers forego promotional offers and use the monies to reduce prices.[13]

**Declining Brand Loyalty** Another major reason for the increase in sales promotion is that consumers have become less brand loyal and are purchasing more on the basis of price, value, and convenience. Some consumers are always willing to buy their preferred brand at full price without any type of promotional offer. However, many consumers are loyal coupon users and/or are conditioned to look for deals when they shop. They may switch back and forth among a set of brands they view as essentially equal. These brands are all perceived as being satisfactory and interchangeable, and consumers purchase whatever brand is on a special sale or for which they have a coupon.

**Increased Promotional Sensitivity** Marketers are making greater use of sales promotion in their marketing programs because consumers respond favorably to the incentives it provides. A major research project completed by Promotion Decisions, Inc., tracked the purchase behavior of over 33,000 consumers and their response to both consumer and trade promotions. The results showed that 42 percent of the total unit volume of the 12 packaged-good products analyzed was purchased with some type of incentive while 58 percent was purchased at full price. Coupons were particularly popular among consumers, as 24 percent of the sales volume involved the use of a coupon.[14]

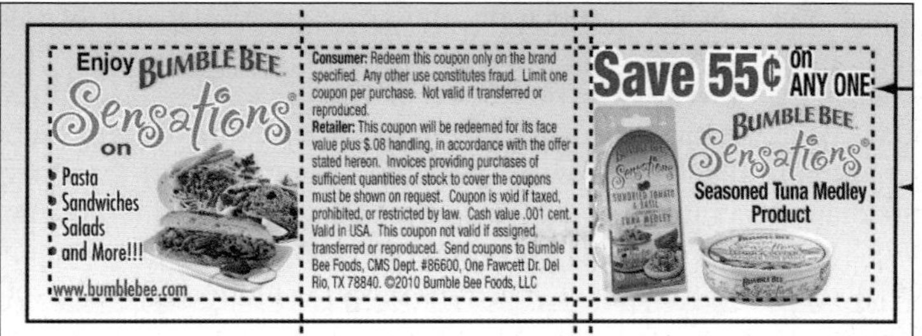


**EXHIBIT 16–4**

Sales promotion tools such as coupons are often used to encourage trial of a new brand

An obvious reason for consumers' increased sensitivity to sales promotion offers is that they save money. Another reason is that many purchase decisions are made at the point of purchase by consumers who are increasingly time-sensitive and facing too many choices. Some studies have found that up to 70 percent of purchase decisions are made in the store, where people are very likely to respond to promotional deals.[15] Buying a brand that is on special or being displayed can simplify the decision-making process and solve the problem of overchoice. Professor Leigh McAlister has described this process:

> As consumers go down the supermarket aisle they spend 3 to 10 seconds in each product category. They often don't know the regular price of the chosen product. However, they do have a sense of whether or not that product is on promotion. As they go down the aisle, they are trying to pensively fill their baskets with good products without tiresome calculations. They see a "good deal" and it goes in the cart.[16]

**Brand Proliferation** A major aspect of many firms' marketing strategies over the past decade has been the development of new products. Companies are launching nearly 20,000 new products each year, according to the research firm Marketing Intelligence Service (compared with only 2,689 in 1980).[17] The market has become saturated with new brands, which often lack any significant advantages that can be used as the basis of an advertising campaign. Thus, companies increasingly depend on sales promotion to encourage consumers to try these brands. In Chapter 4, we saw how sales promotion techniques can be used as part of the shaping process to lead the consumer from initial trial to repeat purchase at full price. Marketers are relying more on samples, coupons, rebates, premiums, and other innovative promotional tools to achieve trial usage of their new brands and encourage repeat purchase (Exhibit 16–4).

Promotions are also important in getting retailers to allocate some of their precious shelf space to new brands. The competition for shelf space for new products in stores is enormous. Supermarkets carry an average of 30,000 products (compared with 13,067 in 1982). Retailers favor new brands with strong sales promotion support that will bring in more customers and boost their sales and profits. Many retailers require special discounts or allowances from manufacturers just to handle a new product. These slotting fees or allowances, which are discussed later in the chapter, can make it expensive for a manufacturer to introduce a new product.

**Fragmentation of the Consumer Market** As the consumer market becomes more fragmented and traditional mass-media–based advertising less effective, marketers are turning to more segmented, highly targeted approaches. Many companies are tailoring their promotional efforts to specific regional markets. Sales promotion tools have become one of the primary vehicles for doing this, through programs tied into local flavor, themes, or events. For example, fast-food restaurants and take-out pizza chains such as Domino's spend a high percentage of their marketing budget on local tie-ins and promotions designed to build traffic and generate sales from their trade areas.

Marketers are also shifting more of their promotional efforts to direct marketing, which often includes some form of sales promotion incentive. Many marketers use information they get from premium offers, trackable coupons, rebates, and sweepstakes to build databases for future direct-marketing efforts. As marketers continue to shift from media advertising to direct marketing, promotional offers will probably be used even more to help build databases. The technology is already in place to enable marketers to communicate individually with target consumers and transform mass promotional tools into ways of doing one-to-one marketing.[18]

**Short-Term Focus** Many businesspeople believe the increase in sales promotion is motivated by marketing plans and reward systems geared to short-term performance and the immediate generation of sales volume as discussed in the opening vignette to the chapter. Some think the packaged-goods brand management system has contributed to marketers' increased dependence on sales promotion. Brand managers use sales promotions routinely, not only to introduce new products or defend against the competition but also to meet quarterly or yearly sales and market share goals.[19] The sales force, too, may have short-term quotas or goals to meet and may also receive requests from retailers and wholesalers for promotions. Thus, reps may pressure marketing or brand managers to use promotions to help them move the products into the retailers' stores.

Many managers view consumer and trade promotions as the most dependable way to generate short-term sales, particularly when they are price-related. The reliance on sales promotion is particularly high in mature and slow-growth markets, where it is difficult to stimulate consumer demand through advertising. This has led to concern that managers have become too dependent on the quick sales fix that can result from a promotion and that the brand franchise may be eroded by too many deals.

**Increased Accountability** In addition to pressuring their marketing or brand managers and sales force to produce short-term results, many companies are demanding to know what they are getting for their promotional expenditures. Results from sales promotion programs are generally easier to measure than those from advertising. Many companies are demanding measurable, accountable ways to relate promotional expenditures to sales and profitability. For example, some companies use computerized sales information from checkout scanners in determining compensation for marketing personnel. Part of the pay managers receive depends on the sales a promotion generates relative to its costs.

Managers who are being held accountable to produce results often use price discounts or coupons, since they produce a quick and easily measured jump in sales. It takes longer for an ad campaign to show some impact and the effects are more difficult to measure. Marketers are also feeling pressure from the trade as powerful retailers demand sales performance from their brands. Real-time data available from computerized checkout scanners make it possible for retailers to monitor promotions and track the results they generate on a daily basis.

**Competition** Another factor that led to the increase in sales promotion is manufacturers' reliance on trade and consumer promotions to gain or maintain competitive advantage. The markets for many products are mature and stagnant, and it is increasingly difficult to boost sales through advertising. Exciting, breakthrough creative ideas are difficult to come by, and consumers' attention to mass-media advertising continues to decline. Rather than allocating large amounts of money to run dull ads, many marketers have turned to sales promotion.

Many companies are tailoring their trade promotions to key retail accounts and developing strategic alliances with retailers that include both trade and consumer promotional programs. A major development in recent years is **account-specific marketing** (also referred to as *comarketing*), whereby a manufacturer collaborates with an individual retailer to create a customized promotion that accomplishes mutual objectives. For example, when Unilever launched its new Sunsilk hair spray line the company developed 14 different account-specific promotions to get retailers to stock and promote the brand (Exhibit 16–5). For Shoppers Mart, they published 600,000 copies of a minimagazine called *Hairapy* that was made available in the store and sent out with *Glow,* the retailer's in-house magazine. For Walmart, Sunsilk

**EXHIBIT 16–5**

Unilever developed a number of account-specific promotions to launch Sunsilk

"Hairapy guys" appeared in stores as part of a retailtainment initiative, which was supported by cinema ads designed to drive traffic to the retailer.[20]

Estimates are that marketers will soon be spending more than half of their promotion budgets on account-specific marketing. A number of companies are developing promotional programs for major retail accounts such as supermarket chains, mass merchandisers, and convenience stores.

Retailers may use a promotional deal with one company as leverage to seek an equal or better deal with its competitors. Consumer and trade promotions are easily matched by competitors, and many marketers find themselves in a promotional trap where they must continue using promotions or be at a competitive disadvantage. (We discuss this problem in more detail later in the chapter.)

**Clutter** A promotional offer in an ad can break through the clutter that is prevalent in most media today. A premium offer may help attract consumers' attention to an ad, as will a contest or sweepstakes. Some studies have shown that readership scores are higher for print ads with coupons than for ads without them.[21] However, more recent studies by Starch INRA Hooper suggest that magazine ads with coupons do not generate higher readership.[22] Promotional messages are prevalent in both magazine and newspaper ads, particularly the latter. Sweepstakes, games, and contests are often advertised in magazine ads, while coupons and sales offers are common in newspaper advertising.

## Concerns about the Increased Role of Sales Promotion

Many factors have contributed to the increased use of sales promotion by consumer-product manufacturers. Marketing and advertising executives are concerned about how this shift in the allocation of the promotional budget affects brand equity. As noted in Chapter 2, *brand equity,* or consumer franchise, is an intangible asset of added value or goodwill that results from consumers' favorable image, impressions of differentiation, and/or strength of attachment to a brand.

Some critics argue that sales promotion increases come at the expense of brand equity and every dollar that goes into promotion rather than advertising devalues the brand.[23] They say trade promotions in particular contribute to the destruction of brand franchises and equity as they encourage consumers to purchase primarily on the basis of price.

Proponents of advertising argue that marketers must maintain strong franchises if they want to differentiate their brands and charge a premium price for them. They say advertising is still the most effective way to build the long-term franchise of a brand: It informs consumers of a brand's features and benefits, creates an image, and helps build and maintain brand loyalty. However, many marketers are not investing in their brands as they take monies away from media advertising to fund short-term promotions.

Marketing experts generally agree that advertising plays an important role in building and maintaining a brand's image and position, which are core components of its equity. As discussed in IMC Perspective 16–1, many are concerned that if the trend toward spending more on sales promotion at the expense of media advertising continues, brands may lose the equity that advertising helped create and be forced to compete primarily on the basis of price. Many of these concerns are justified, but not all sales promotion activities detract from the value of a brand. It is important to distinguish between consumer franchise-building and nonfranchise-building promotions.

## IMC Perspective 16–1 > > >

### Sales Promotion and Brand Building Often Clash

Marketers often struggle with problem of determining the extent to which they should use promotions to help generate sales for their brands or drive traffic to their retail stores versus relying on brand image as a way of avoiding price competition. Given a choice, many companies would prefer to minimize their reliance on promotions and discounts and compete on the basis of product quality and/or brand image. However, most companies have found that it can be very difficult to avoid using promotions, particularly when consumers have become accustomed to them. For example, a few years ago Macy's, which is one of the nation's premier retailers with over 800 stores, embarked on a new strategy designed to wean consumers off of the 15 to 20 percent coupons as well as the "One-day sales" which it had relied on to drive store traffic. The new strategy also called for more advertising to let consumers know about Macy's makeover and build a strong brand image for the chain. A highly regarded and seasoned new chief marketing officer with extensive brand-building experience was hired to lead the new initiative to turn Macy's into a destination retailer.

Macy's implemented its new strategy but soon found that it was backfiring, as consumers across the country turned their back on Macy's, and sales dropped for four consecutive months. While some customers cited the merchandising changes as the reason they were no longer shopping at Macy's, it became clear to the company that its strategy of abruptly curtailing discounts and coupons was the primary factor. Macy's had to backtrack on its plan and revert to the previous strategy which relied heavily on various forms of discounts as well as one-day and short-term sales. And after just 13 months on the job, the chief marketing officer hired to lead the new strategy was replaced. For the past several years the retailer has been locally focused with a merchandising and marketing program called "My Macy's" that involves tailoring each of its store's product and promotions to local markets.

Macy's, like many other companies, learned the hard way that it had violated a basic law of human nature when it comes to marketing: consumers love a deal. Moreover, retailers, like many other marketers, often train consumers to wait for discounts through sales, special offers, and coupons, which make it very difficult to sell their merchandise at full price. Surveys have shown that consumers are 50 percent more price sensitive than they were 25 years ago and for good reason. Marketers issue more than 300 billion coupons each year, or nearly 1,000 per person, an increase of 15 percent over the past five years. They also use rebates, buy one get one free offers, special sales events, price-off deals, and other discounts to attract price-sensitive consumers. Retailers also contribute to the increased price sensitivity of shoppers by issuing their own rebates and coupons, or sometimes doubling those of the manufacturer, offering guaranteed lowest prices, or price matching, and constantly running sales and specials. Consumers are not naïve; they know manufacturers and/or retailers will offer some type of promotion, which encourages them to wait for the next deal rather than purchase a product at full price.

The extensive use of discounts and promotional offers by marketers and retailers is creating a problem for companies as it is undermining their ability to build and maintain brand equity. Wharton Business School marketing professor Leonard Lodish and Carl Mela, a marketing professor at Fuqua School of Business at Duke University, have conducted research which suggests that many companies are damaging their brands by investing too much in short-term price promotions and too

## Consumer Franchise-Building versus Nonfranchise-Building Promotions

Sales promotion activities that communicate distinctive brand attributes and contribute to the development and reinforcement of brand identity are **consumer franchise-building (CFB) promotions**.[24] Consumer sales promotion efforts cannot make consumers loyal to a brand that is of little value or does not provide them with a specific benefit. But they can make consumers aware of a brand and, by communicating its specific features and benefits, contribute to the development of a favorable brand image. Consumer franchise-building promotions are designed to build long-term brand preference and help the company achieve the ultimate goal of full-price purchases that do not depend on a promotional offer.

For years, franchise or image building was viewed as the exclusive realm of advertising, and sales promotion was used only to generate short-term sales increases. But now marketers are recognizing the image-building potential of sales promotion

little in long-term brand building. They note that while many consumer products companies blame the problem on the emergence of big-box discount retailers such as Walmart, there are several factors that are contributing to the weakening of once-powerful brands. These include the increased availability of weekly, or even hourly, scanner data, which show the relationship between discounts and increases in sales; the difficulty of measuring the effects of media advertising, new-product development, and distribution strategy—all of which can contribute to the long-term health of a brand; the short tenure of most brand managers; and the short-term orientation of financial analysts.

Lodish and Mela note that the profusion of scanner data allows brand and marketing managers, as well as retailers, to see how sales often spike in response to promotional discounts. They argue that managers became enamored with these short-term increases in sales, which resulted in the allocation of the majority of their marketing budgets to consumer and trade promotions. This reallocation has occurred largely at the expense of advertising, whose impact plays out over a longer time period and is thus more difficult to measure. They also argue that many companies are paying less attention to the long-term effects of their distribution and new-product strategies. Many of these companies have aligned themselves with mass merchandisers and discount retailers, which has resulted in short-term sales increases but also the brands losing their cache.

Another problem Lodish and Mela note is that many brand managers stay in their positions for a short time period, which motivates them to focus more on the use of promotional tactics that can have more of an immediate impact. They often view investing in advertising or product development as benefiting the performance of subsequent managers rather than their own. When asked why they take a short-term perspective, marketing and brand managers point out that they are judged on quarterly sales because investors focus on these numbers, and the link between promotion and sales is obvious.

Many marketers and retailers have created a dilemma from which there is no easy escape. They know that discounts will increase sales in the short term, but the more a manufacturer or retailer uses promotions and discounts, the more consumers learn to purchase an item when it is on sale or they have a coupon. Lodish and Mela suggest that managers need to develop and arm themselves with long-term measures of brand performance and use them to make smarter marketing decisions that will not undermine brand equity. Of course, the temptation to look for the quick fix and sales spike from a promotion will always be there. And it is likely that many marketers will continue to yield to the temptation rather than try to sell their brands at full price.

Sources: Natalie Zmuda, "Macy's Takes Marketing Local, Cuts Jobs Nationwide," *Advertising Age*, February 2, 2009, http://adage.com/print?article_id=143271; Michael Barbaro, Karen Ann Cullotta, and Christopher Maag, "Given Fewer Coupons to Clip, Bargain Hunters Snub Macy's," *The New York Times*, September 29, 2007, p. A1; Leonard M. Lodish and Carl F. Mela, "If Brands Are Built over Years, Why Are They Managed over Quarters?" *Harvard Business Review*, July–August 2007, pp. 104–112; Lisa Sanders, "Brand vs. Street: The Classic Clash Fells Macy's CEO," *Advertising Age*, June 4, 2007, pp. 1, 2.



and paying attention to its CFB value. Surveys have found that nearly 90 percent of senior marketing executives believe consumer promotions can help build brand equity while nearly 60 percent think trade promotions can contribute.[25] Marketers recognize that the value of sales promotion extends well beyond quick-fix tactics such as price-off deals. Most sales promotion agencies recognize the importance of developing consumer and trade promotions that can help build brand equity. For example, Exhibit 16–6 shows a classic ad for Ryan Partnership that stresses how the agency develops trade promotions that help build brand equity.

Companies can use sales promotion techniques in a number of ways to contribute to franchise building. Rather than using a one-time offer, many companies are developing frequency programs that encourage repeat purchases and long-term patronage. Many credit cards have loyalty programs where consumers earn bonus points every time they use their card to charge a purchase. These points can then be redeemed for various items. Most airlines and many hotel chains offer frequent-flyer or guest programs to encourage repeat patronage. Many retail

**EXHIBIT 16–6**
This promotion agency ad stresses the importance of using trade promotions to build brand equity

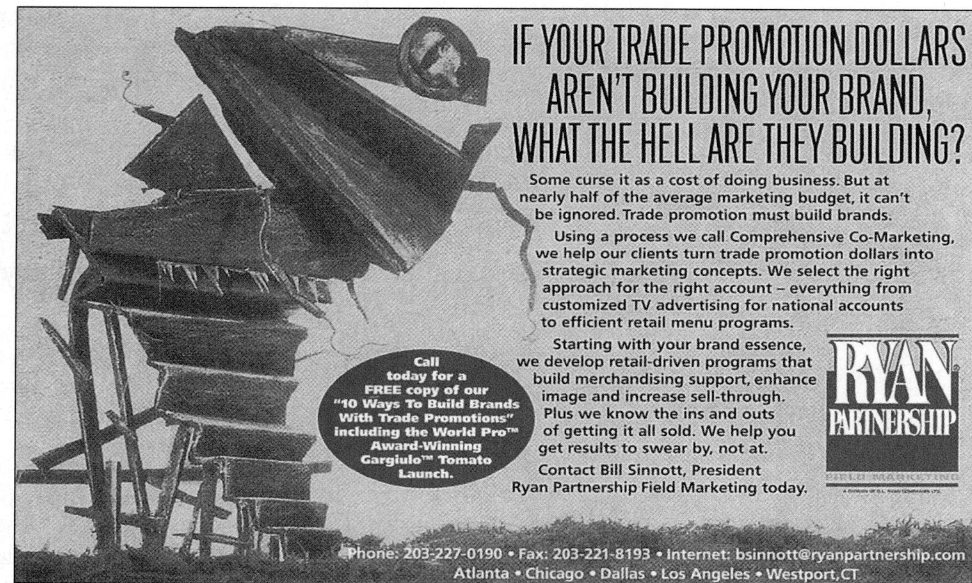


stores have also begun using frequency programs to build loyalty and encourage repeat purchases.[26]

**Nonfranchise-building (non-FB) promotions** are designed to accelerate the purchase decision process and generate an immediate increase in sales. These activities do not communicate information about a brand's unique features or the benefits of using it, so they do not contribute to the building of brand identity and image. Price-off deals, bonus packs, and rebates or refunds are examples of non-FB sales promotion techniques. Trade promotions receive the most criticism for being nonfranchise building—for good reason. First, many of the promotional discounts and allowances given to the trade are never passed on to consumers. Most trade promotions that are forwarded through the channels reach consumers in the form of lower prices or special deals and lead them to buy on the basis of price rather than brand equity.

Many specialists in the promotional area stress the need for marketers to use sales promotion tools to build a franchise and create long-term continuity in their promotional programs. Whereas non-FB promotions merely borrow customers from other brands, well-planned CFB activities can convert consumers to loyal customers. Short-term non-FB promotions have their place in a firm's promotional mix, particularly when competitive developments call for them. But their limitations must be recognized when a long-term marketing strategy for a brand is developed.

# CONSUMER-ORIENTED SALES PROMOTION

Marketers have been using various types of sales promotion for more than a hundred years and have found a variety of ways to give consumers an extra incentive to purchase their products and services. In this section, we examine the various sales promotion tools and techniques marketers can use to influence consumers. We study the consumer-oriented promotions shown in Figure 16–1 and discuss their advantages and limitations. First, we consider some objectives marketers have for sales promotion programs targeted to the consumer market.

## Objectives of Consumer-Oriented Sales Promotion

As the use of sales promotion techniques continues to increase, companies must consider what they hope to accomplish through their consumer promotions and how they interact with other promotional activities such as advertising, direct marketing, and personal selling. Not all sales promotion activities are designed to achieve the same objectives. As with any promotional mix element, marketers must plan consumer promotions by conducting a situation analysis and determining sales promotion's specific role in the integrated marketing communications program. They must decide what the promotion is designed to accomplish and to whom it should be targeted. Setting clearly defined objectives and measurable goals for their sales promotion programs forces managers to think beyond the short-term sales fix (although this can be one goal).

While the basic goal of most consumer-oriented sales promotion programs is to induce purchase of a brand, the marketer may have a number of different objectives for both new and established brands—for example, obtaining trial and repurchase, increasing consumption of an established brand, defending current customers, targeting a specific market segment, or enhancing advertising and marketing efforts.

**Obtaining Trial and Repurchase** One of the most important uses of sales promotion techniques is to encourage consumers to try a new product or service. While thousands of new products are introduced to the market every year, as many as 90 percent of them fail within the first year. Many of these failures are due to the fact that the new product or brand lacks the promotional support needed either to encourage initial trial by enough consumers or to induce enough of those trying the brand to repurchase it. Many new brands are merely new versions of an existing product without unique benefits, so advertising alone cannot induce trial. Sales promotion tools have become an important part of new brand introduction strategies; the level of initial trial can be increased through techniques such as sampling, couponing, and refund offers. The success of a new brand depends not only on getting initial trial but also on inducing a reasonable percentage of people who try the brand to repurchase it and establish ongoing purchase patterns. Promotional incentives such as coupons or refund offers are often included with a sample to encourage repeat purchase after trial.

**Increasing Consumption of an Established Brand** Many marketing managers are responsible for established brands competing in mature markets, against established competitors, where consumer purchase patterns are often well set. Awareness of an established brand is generally high as a result of cumulative advertising effects, and many consumers have probably tried the brand. These factors can create a challenging situation for the brand manager. Sales promotion can generate some new interest in an established brand to help increase sales or defend market share against competitors.

**EXHIBIT 16–7**
Arm & Hammer used this FSI to promote a specific use for the product

Marketers attempt to increase sales for an established brand in several ways, and sales promotion can play an important role in each. One way to increase product consumption is by identifying new uses for the brand. Sales promotion tools like recipe books or calendars that show various ways of using the product often can accomplish this. One of the best examples of a brand that has found new uses is Arm & Hammer baking soda. Exhibit 16–7 shows a clever freestanding insert (FSI) that promotes the brand's new fridge-freezer pack, which absorbs more odors in refrigerators and freezers.

Another strategy for increasing sales of an established brand is to use promotions that attract nonusers of the product category or users of a competing brand. Attracting nonusers of the product category can be very difficult, as consumers may not see a need for the product. Sales promotions can appeal to nonusers by providing them with an extra incentive to try the product, but a more common strategy for increasing sales of an established brand is to attract consumers who

CHAPTER 16

use a competing brand. This can be done by giving them an incentive to switch, such as a coupon, premium offer, bonus pack, or price deal. Marketers can also get users of a competitor to try their brand through sampling or other types of promotional programs.

For example, the Miller Brewing Company used a Taste Challenge promotion recently to help regain market share for its flagship brand, Miller Lite, which had lost its category leadership to Bud Light. A key component of this integrated campaign was an interactive, on-premise promotion in bars, restaurants, and night clubs where consumers were given the opportunity to compare the taste of Miller Lite against Bud Light. Mobile computer tablets were used to track responses to the comparisons and national TV commercials were run showing the outcome of several of the blind taste tests. An additional phase of the promotion featured a "Make the Call for More" in which Miller Lite promotion specialists dressed as football referees approached consumers who were drinking competitive brands and challenged them to a football-themed Taste Challenge that showed why Miller Lite offers more (Exhibit 16–8). Over 400,000 consumers were engaged with the Taste Challenge and the promotion helped increase sales and market share by an average of 13 percent in markets where the challenge was conducted and over 11 percent overall.[27]

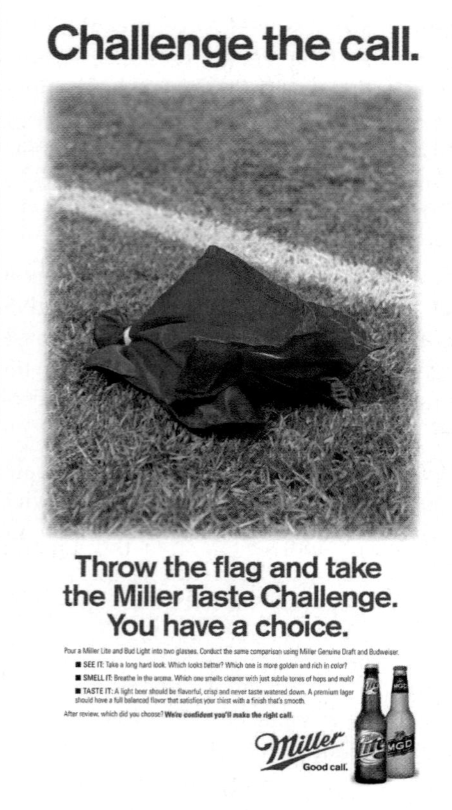

Challenge the call.
Throw the flag and take the Miller Taste Challenge. You have a choice.
Pour a Miller Lite and Bud Light into two glasses. Conduct the same comparison using Miller Genuine Draft and Budweiser.
SEE IT: Take a long hard look. Which looks better? Which one is more golden and rich in color?
SMELL IT: Breathe in the aroma. Which one smells cleaner with just subtle tones of hops and malt?
TASTE IT: A light beer should be flavorful, crisp and never taste watered down. A premium lager should have a full balanced flavor that satisfies your thirst with a finish that's smooth.
After review, which did you choose? We're confident you'll make the right call.
Miller
Good call.
Lite
MGD

**EXHIBIT 16–8**
Miller Lite's Taste Challenge was a very successful promotion for attracting users of competing brands

**Defending Current Customers** With more new brands entering the market every day and competitors attempting to take away their customers through aggressive advertising and sales promotion efforts, many companies are turning to sales promotion programs to hold present customers and defend their market share. A company can use sales promotion techniques in several ways to retain its current customer base. One way is to load them with the product, taking them out of the market for a certain time. Special price promotions, coupons, or bonus packs can encourage consumers to stock up on the brand. This not only keeps them using the company's brand but also reduces the likelihood they will switch brands in response to a competitor's promotion.

**Targeting a Specific Market Segment** Most companies focus their marketing efforts on specific market segments and are always looking for ways to reach their target audiences. Many marketers are finding that sales promotion tools such as contests and sweepstakes, events, coupons, and samplings are very effective ways to reach specific geographic, demographic, psychographic, and ethnic markets. Sales promotion programs can also be targeted to specific user-status groups such as nonusers or light versus heavy users.

In addition, promotions programs can be developed to coincide with peak sales periods for certain products and services. For example, candy companies such as Mars and Hershey often develop sales promotions that are run right before Halloween while clothing and school supply companies targeting children and teens run promotions in late summer when most of the back-to-school shopping occurs.

**Enhancing Integrated Marketing Communications and Building Brand Equity** A final objective for consumer-oriented promotions is to enhance or support the integrated marketing communications effort for a brand or company. While building and/or maintaining brand equity was traditionally viewed as something that was done through media advertising, it has also become an important goal for marketers as they develop their sales promotion programs. Companies are asking their promotion agencies to think strategically and develop promotional programs that can do more than simply generate short-term sales. They want promotions that require consumers to become more involved with their brands and offer a way

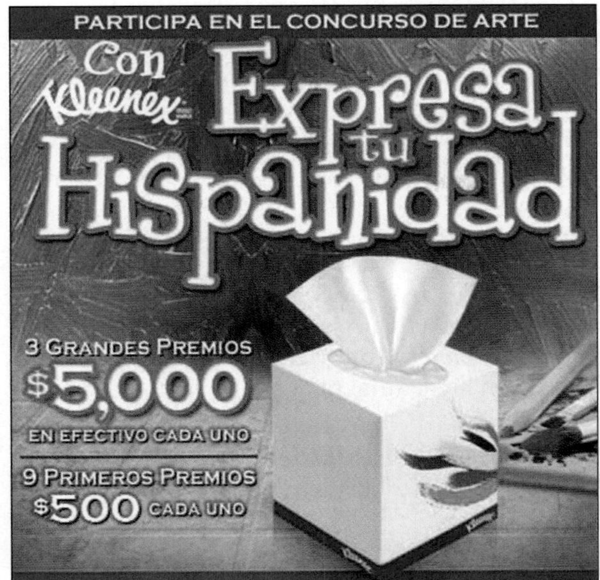


**EXHIBIT 16–9**
Kimberly Clark used a contest targeted to Hispanic consumers to increase their involvement and connection to Kleenex

of presenting the brand essence in an engaging way. Many marketers are recognizing that a well-designed and executed promotion can be a very effective way to engage consumers and to differentiate their brands. Sales promotion techniques such as contests or sweepstakes and premium offers are often used to draw attention to an advertising campaign, to increase involvement with the message and product or service, and to help build relationships with consumers.

A number of marketers are recognizing the value of contests to create interest and excitement in their brands that can get consumers to become more involved with them. For example, MASS Hispanic, the promotional agency for Kimberly Clark's Kleenex brand of facial tissues, created an award winning promotion whose objective was to increase the relevance of the brand and build a better connection with the Hispanic market. Another important goal of the promotion was to leverage the importance of package aesthetics to Hispanics, who are much more likely to purchase on the basis of package color and design than the general population.

The agency created a promotion called "Con Kleenex Express Tu Hispanidad" (Express Your Hispanic Pride with Kleenex) where Hispanic consumers were invited to express their traditions and cultural pride through an art contest (Exhibit 16–9). The contest called on aspiring amateur Hispanic artists and consumers around the country to submit an original design expressing their Latino pride for the opportunity to win $5,000 plus the privilege of having the artwork appear on a boutique-sized Kleenex tissue carton during Hispanic Heritage month. The back end of the promotion included a chance for consumers to participate in selecting a "People's Choice" winner and to purchase special cartons of Kleenex that were displayed in retail stores during Hispanic Heritage month. Over 30,000 consumers voted online to pick the best design and 18 of Kimberly Clark's key retail accounts provided special retail displays of the winning cartons which led to a 476 percent increase in Kleenex sales in the stores during the promotional period.[28]



## CONSUMER-ORIENTED SALES PROMOTION TECHNIQUES

LO 16-3

### Sampling

Marketers use a variety of consumer-oriented sales promotion tools to accomplish the objectives just discussed. We will discuss how these various sales promotion tools are used and factors marketers must consider in using them, beginning with sampling.

**Sampling** involves a variety of procedures whereby consumers are given some quantity of a product for no charge to induce trial. Sampling is generally considered the most effective way to generate trial, although it is also the most expensive. As a sales promotion technique, sampling is often used to introduce a new product or brand to the market. However, sampling is also used for established products as well. Some companies do not use sampling for established products, reasoning that samples may not induce satisfied users of a competing brand to switch and may just go to the firm's current customers, who would buy the product anyway. This may not be true when significant changes (new and improved) are made in a brand.

Manufacturers of packaged-goods products such as food, health care items, cosmetics, and toiletries are heavy users of sampling since their products meet the three criteria for an effective sampling program:

1. The products are of relatively low unit value, so samples do not cost too much.
2. The products are divisible, which means they can be broken into small sample sizes that are adequate for demonstrating the brand's features and benefits to the user.
3. The purchase cycle is relatively short, so the consumer will consider an immediate purchase or will not forget about the brand before the next purchase occasion.

**Benefits and Limitations of Sampling** Samples are an excellent way to induce trial as they provide consumers with a risk-free way to try new products. A major study conducted by the Promotion Marketing Association found that the vast majority of consumers receiving a sample either use it right away or save it to use sometime later.[29] Sampling generates much higher trial rates than advertising or other sales promotion techniques.

Getting people to try a product leads to a second benefit of sampling: Consumers experience the brand directly, gaining a greater appreciation for its benefits. This can be particularly important when a product's features and benefits are difficult to describe through advertising. Many foods, beverages, and cosmetics have subtle features that are most appreciated when experienced directly. Thus, marketers in these industries often use samples as a way to introduce consumers to their new products. For example, Jack in the Box, one of the major fast-food restaurant chains in the Western region of the United States, used a "Free Fryday" promotion to give consumers the opportunity to sample its new French fries (Exhibit 16–10). Nearly 70 percent of the respondents in the PMA survey indicated they have purchased a product they did not normally use after trying a free sample. The study also found that samples are even more likely to lead to purchase when they are accompanied by a coupon.

While samples are an effective way to induce trial, the brand must have some unique or superior benefits for a sampling program to be worthwhile. Otherwise, the sampled consumers revert back to other brands and do not become repeat purchasers. The costs of a sampling program can be recovered only if it gets a number of consumers to become regular users of the brand at full retail price.

Another possible limitation to sampling is that the benefits of some products are difficult to gauge immediately, and the learning period required to appreciate the brand may require supplying the consumer with larger amounts of the brand than are affordable. An example would be an expensive skin cream that is promoted as preventing or reducing wrinkles but has to be used for an extended period before any effects are seen.

**EXHIBIT 16–10**
Jack in the Box's "Free Fryday" promotion was an effective way to encourage consumers to try its new French fries

**Sampling Methods** One basic decision the sales promotion or brand manager must make is how the sample will be distributed. The sampling method chosen is important not only in terms of costs but also because it influences the type of consumer who receives the sample. The best sampling method gets the product to the best prospects for trial and subsequent repurchase. Some basic distribution methods include door-to-door, direct-mail, in-store, and on-package approaches.

*Door-to-door sampling,* in which the product is delivered directly to the prospect's residence, is used when it is important to control where the sample is delivered. This distribution method is very expensive because of labor costs, but it can be cost-effective if the marketer has information that helps define the target market and/or if the prospects are located in a well-defined geographic area. Some companies have samples delivered directly to consumers' homes by including them with newspapers. Sunday papers have become an increasingly attractive way of mass distributing samples. However, there are also a number of newspapers that can now distribute a sample into a subscriber segment as small as 250 households with little increase in costs to marketers. Many

**EXHIBIT 16–11**
Armor All uses on-package samples for related products

newspapers distribute samples through polybags, which are plastic bags that serve as covers for the paper and deliver a promotional message along with the sample.

*Sampling through the mail* is common for small, lightweight, nonperishable products. A major advantage of this method is that the marketer has control over where and when the product will be distributed and can target the sample to specific market areas. Many marketers are using information from geodemographic target marketing programs such as Claritas's Prizm to better target their sample mailings. The main drawbacks to mail sampling are postal restrictions and increasing postal rates.

*In-store sampling* is increasingly popular, especially for food products. The marketer hires temporary demonstrators who set up a table or booth, prepare small samples of the product, and pass them out to shoppers. The in-store sampling approach can be very effective for food products, since consumers get to taste the item and the demonstrator can give them more information about the product while it is being sampled. Demonstrators may also give consumers a cents-off coupon for the sampled item to encourage immediate trial purchase. While this sampling method can be very effective, it can also be expensive and requires a great deal of planning, as well as the cooperation of retailers.

*On-package sampling,* where a sample of a product is attached to another item, is another common sampling method (see Exhibit 16–11). This procedure can be very cost-effective, particularly for multiproduct firms that attach a sample of a new product to an existing brand's package. A drawback is that since the sample is distributed only to consumers who purchase the item to which it is attached, the sample will not reach nonusers of the carrier brand. Marketers can expand this sampling method by attaching the sample to multiple carrier brands and including samples with products not made by their company.

*Event sampling* has become one of the fastest-growing and most popular ways of distributing samples. Many marketers are using sampling programs that are part of integrated marketing programs that feature events, media tie-ins, and other activities that provide consumers with a total sense of a brand rather than just a few tastes of a food or beverage or a trial size of a packaged-goods product. Event sampling can take place in stores as well as at a variety of other venues such as concerts, sporting events, and other places.

**EXHIBIT 16–12**
Consumers can request samples from websites such as StartSampling.com

### Other Methods of Sampling

The four sampling methods just discussed are the most common, but several other methods are also used. Marketers may insert packets in magazines or newspapers (particularly Sunday supplements). Some tobacco and cereal companies send samples to consumers who call toll-free numbers to request them or mail in sample request forms. As discussed in Chapter 14, these sampling methods are becoming popular because they can help marketers build a database for direct marketing.

Many companies also use specialized sample distribution service companies. These firms help the company identify consumers who are nonusers of a product or users of a competing brand and develop appropriate procedures for distributing a sample to them. Many college students receive sample packs at the beginning of the semester that contain trial sizes of such products as mouthwash, toothpaste, headache remedies, and deodorant.

The Internet is yet another way companies are making it possible for consumers to sample their products, and it is adding a whole new level of targeting to the mix by giving consumers the opportunity to choose the samples they want. Several companies offer websites where consumers can register to receive free samples for products that interest them including StartSampling, Eversave, and MyTownOffers. Exhibit 16–12 shows the homepage from the website of StartSampling.com promoting the samples and offers it makes available to consumers. The service asks consumers qualifying questions on product usage that can be used by marketers to target their samples and other promotional offers more effectively.

Marketers are also starting to use various forms of social media as a way to distribute samples. For example, Splenda used Facebook to distribute samples of a pocket-size spray form of its sweetener. The company used engagement ads to direct consumer to the Splenda Mist page where they could sign up for a "first look" at the new product and provide the company with information about themselves. Splenda also used its Facebook page to solicit valuable feedback from consumers who received the samples.[30]

## Couponing

The oldest, most widely used, and most effective sales promotion tool is the cents-off coupon. Coupons have been around since 1895, when the C. W. Post Co. started using the penny-off coupon to sell its new Grape-Nuts cereal. In recent years, coupons have become increasingly popular with consumers, which may explain their explosive growth among manufacturers and retailers that use them as sales promotion incentives. Coupons are the most popular sales promotion technique as they are used by nearly all the packaged-goods firms.

Coupon distribution rose dramatically over the past 30 years. The number of coupons distributed by consumer packaged-goods (CPG) marketers increased from 16 billion in 1968 to a peak of 310 billion in 1994. However, for the next seven years, coupon distribution declined steadily and dropped to 239 billion in 2001. Over the past five years, coupon distribution has rebounded reaching nearly 311 billion in 2009, an 11% increase over the prior year and the largest single year quantity ever recorded. According to NCH Marketing Services, a company that tracks coupon distribution and redemption patterns, 88 percent of consumers in the United States use coupons and 21 percent say they always use them when they shop. The average face value of coupons distributed increased from 21 cents in 1981 to $1.37 in 2009. The average face value of the 3.3 billion coupons that were redeemed in 2009 was $1.09.[31]

Adding additional fuel to the coupon explosion of the past several decades has been the vast number of coupons distributed through retailers that are not even included in these figures. In most markets, a number of grocery stores make manufacturers' coupons even more attractive to consumers by doubling the face value.

**Advantages and Limitations of Coupons** Coupons have a number of advantages that make them popular sales promotion tools for both new and established products. First, coupons make it possible to offer a price reduction only to those consumers who are price-sensitive. Such consumers generally purchase *because* of coupons, while those who are not as concerned about price buy the brand at full value. Coupons also make it possible to reduce the retail price of a product without relying on retailers for cooperation, which can often be a problem. Coupons are generally regarded as second only to sampling as a promotional technique for generating trial. Since a coupon lowers the price of a product, it reduces the consumer's perceived risk associated with trial of a new brand. Coupons can encourage repurchase after initial trial. Many new products include a cents-off coupon inside the package to encourage repeat purchase.

Coupons can also be useful promotional devices for established products. They can encourage nonusers to try a brand, encourage repeat purchase among current users, and get users to try a new, improved version of a brand. Coupons may also help coax users of a product to trade up to more expensive brands. The product category where coupons are used most is disposable diapers, followed by cereal, detergent, and deodorant. Some of the product categories where coupons are used the least are carbonated beverages, candy, and gum.

But there are a number of problems with coupons. First, it can be difficult to estimate how many consumers will use a coupon and when. Response to a coupon is rarely immediate; it typically takes anywhere from two to six months to redeem one. A study of coupon redemption patterns by Inman and McAlister found that many coupons are redeemed just before the expiration date rather than in the period following the initial coupon drop.[32] Many marketers are attempting to expedite redemption by shortening the time period before expiration. The average length of time from issue date to expiration date for coupons in 2009 was 2.5 months for consumer packaged goods. However, coupons remain less effective than sampling for inducing initial product trial in a short period.

A problem associated with using coupons to attract new users to an established brand is that it is difficult to prevent the coupons from being used by consumers who already use the brand. Rather than attracting new users, coupons can end up reducing the company's profit margins among consumers who would probably purchase the product anyway.

Other problems with coupons include low redemption rates and high costs. Couponing program expenses include the face value of the coupon redeemed plus costs for production, distribution, and handling of the coupons. Figure 16–2 shows the calculations used to determine the costs of a couponing program using an FSI (free-standing insert) in the Sunday newspaper and a coupon with a face value of $1.00. As can be seen from these figures, the cost of a couponing program can be very high. Former Procter & Gamble chairman Durk Jager, who led efforts to rein in the company's use of coupons in the late 90s, has argued that they are extremely inefficient. He contends that it may cost as much as $50 to move a case of goods with coupons that may generate only $10 to $12 in gross profit.[33] Marketers should track coupon costs very carefully to ensure their use is economically feasible.

Another problem with coupon promotions is misredemption, or the cashing of a coupon without purchase of the brand. Coupon misredemption or fraud occurs in a number of ways, including:

- Redemption of coupons by consumers for a product or size not specified on the coupon.
- Redemption of coupons by salesclerks in exchange for cash.



**FIGURE 16–2**
Calculating Couponing Costs

| COST PER COUPON REDEEMED: AN ILLUSTRATION | |
|---|---|
| 1. Distribution cost<br>55,000,000 circulation × $6.25/M | $343,750 |
| 2. Redemptions at 1.5% | 825,000 |
| 3. Redemption cost<br>825,000 redemptions × $1.00 face value | $825,000 |
| 4. Retailer handling cost and processor fees<br>25,000 redemptions × $.10 | $82,5008 |
| 5. Creative costs | $1,500 |
| 6. Total program cost<br>Items 1 + 3 + 4 + 5 | $1,252,750 |
| Cost per coupon redeemed<br>Cost divided by redemption | $1.52 |
| 7. Actual product sold on redemption<br>(misredemption estimated at 20%)<br>825,000 × 80% | 660,000 |
| 8. Cost per product moved<br>Program cost divided by amount of product sold | $1.90 |

- Gathering and redemption of coupons by store managers or owners without the accompanying sale of the product.
- Gathering or printing of coupons by criminals who sell them to unethical merchants, who, in turn, redeem them.
- Web-source coupon fraud, whereby phony coupons are produced and distributed online.

Coupon fraud and misredemption cost manufacturers an estimated $500 million a year in the United States alone. However, with the surge in Internet-related coupon fraud in recent years, this number is considered low. In 2007 the largest coupon clearinghouse in the United States was indicted for an alleged nine-year $250 million fraud against package-goods marketers. Consumers have also taken advantage of flaws in bar codes to fraudulently use coupons. However, a new bar coding system is being developed by the industry that will be harder to exploit and will simplify the use of coupons.[34]

Many manufacturers hold firm in their policy to not pay retailers for questionable amounts or suspicious types of coupon submissions. However, some companies are less aggressive, and this affects their profit margins. Marketers must allow a certain percentage for misredemption when estimating the costs of a couponing program. Ways to identify and control coupon misredemption, such as improved coding, are being developed, but it still remains a problem. Many retailers are tightening their policies regarding Internet coupons. For example, Walmart will not accept Internet coupons unless they have a valid expiration date, remit address, and bar code.

**Coupon Distribution** Coupons can be disseminated to consumers by a number of means, including freestanding inserts in Sunday newspapers, direct mail, newspapers (either in individual ads or as a group of coupons in a cooperative format), magazines, and packages. Distribution through newspaper *freestanding inserts* is by far the most popular method for delivering coupons to consumers, accounting for 86 percent of all coupons distributed. This growth has come at the expense of vehicles such as manufacturers' ads in newspapers (newspaper ROP), newspaper co-op ads, and magazines.

There are a number of reasons why FSIs are the most popular way of delivering coupons, including their high-quality four-color graphics, competitive distribution costs, national same-day circulation, market selectivity, and the fact that they can be competition-free due to category exclusivity (by the FSI company). Prices for a full-page FSI are currently about $6 to $7 per thousand, which makes FSI promotions very efficient and affordable. Because of their consumer popularity and predictable distribution, coupons distributed in FSIs are also a strong selling point with the retail trade.

The increased distribution of coupons through FSIs has, however, led to a clutter problem. Consumers are being bombarded with too many coupons, and although each FSI publisher offers product exclusivity in its insert, this advantage may be negated when there are three inserts in a Sunday paper. Redemption rates of FSI coupons have declined from 4 percent to only 1 percent and even lower for some products (Figure 16–3). These problems are leading many marketers to look at ways of delivering coupons that will result in less clutter and higher redemption rates, such as direct mail.

*Direct mail* accounts for about 2 percent of all coupons distributed. Most are sent by local retailers or through co-op mailings where a packet of coupons for many different products is sent to a household. These couponing programs include Metromail's Red Letter Day, Advo System's Super Coups, and Cox Target Media's Valpak. Cox Target Media redesigned the familiar Valpak blue envelope that delivers billions of coupons each year and uses advertising to improve the image of the direct-mail piece and increase consumers' use of the coupons distributed inside (Exhibit 16–13).

Direct-mail couponing has several advantages. First, the mailing can be sent to a broad audience or targeted to specific geographic or demographic markets such as teenagers, senior citizens, Hispanics, and other market segments. Firms that mail

**FIGURE 16–3**
Coupon Redemption Rates by Media Type

| Media | Grocery Products | Health and Beauty Products |
|---|---|---|
| FSI | 1.0% | 0.5% |
| Newspaper | 0.8 | 0.4 |
| Magazine | 1.1 | 0.6 |
| Direct mail | 3.4 | 2.0 |
| Regular in-pack | 5.6 | 2.5 |
| Regular on-pack | 6.0 | 12.9 |
| In-pack cross-ruff | 2.9 | 3.8 |
| On-pack cross-ruff | 3.8 | 8.0 |
| Instant on-pack | 20.6 | 21.5 |
| Instant on-pack cross-ruff | 8.3 | 12.9 |
| Handout electronically dispensed | 7.9 | 8.1 |
| On-shelf distributed | 7.9 | 7.6 |
| All other handouts in store | 3.6 | 2.0 |
| All other handouts away from store | 2.7 | 2.3 |
| Internet | 17.3 | 9.8 |

Source: NCH Marketing Services, *2010 Coupon Facts.*

CHAPTER 16

their own coupons can be quite selective about recipients. Another advantage of direct-mail couponing is a redemption rate that is higher than that for FSIs. Direct-mail couponing can also be combined with a sample, which makes it a very effective way to gain the attention of consumers.

**EXHIBIT 16–13**
Valpak uses advertising to promote the value of the coupons inside

The major disadvantage of direct-mail coupon delivery is the expense relative to other distribution methods. The cost per thousand for distributing coupons through co-op mailings ranges from $10 to $15, and more targeted promotions can cost $20 to $25 or even more. Also, the higher redemption rate of mail-delivered coupons may result from the fact that many recipients are already users of the brand who take advantage of the coupons sent directly to them.

The use of *newspapers* and *magazines* as couponing vehicles has declined dramatically since the introduction of FSIs as only 1 percent of coupons are distributed via newspapers. The advantages of newspapers as a couponing vehicle include market selectivity, shorter lead times with timing to the day, cooperative advertising opportunities that can lead to cost efficiencies, and promotional tie-ins with retailers. Other advantages of newspaper-delivered coupons are the broad exposure and consumer receptivity. Many consumers actively search the newspaper for coupons, especially on Sundays or "food day" (when grocery stores advertise their specials). This enhances the likelihood of the consumer at least noticing the coupon. Problems with newspapers as couponing vehicles include higher distribution costs, poor reproduction quality, clutter, and declining readership of newspapers; all contribute to low redemption rates.

**EXHIBIT 16–14**
Kellogg Company uses an on-package coupon to encourage repurchase

The use of magazines as a couponing vehicle has also declined steadily since the introduction of FSIs. Magazines now account for around 2 percent of the total number of coupons distributed each year. Distribution of coupons through magazines can take advantage of the selectivity of the publication to reach specific target audiences, along with enhanced production capabilities and extended copy life in the home. However, the cost of distributing coupons through magazines is very high and redemption rates are low (just under 1 percent).

Placing coupons either *inside* or on the *outside* of the *package* is a distribution method that accounts for just over 1 percent of the coupons distributed. The in/on-package coupon has virtually no distribution costs and a much higher redemption rate than other couponing methods, averaging from 3 to 20 percent. An in/on-pack coupon that is redeemable for the next purchase of the same brand is known as a **bounce-back coupon**. This type of coupon gives consumers an inducement to repurchase the brand.

Bounce-back coupons are often used with product samples to encourage the consumer to purchase the product after sampling. They may be included in or on the package during the early phases of a brand's life cycle to encourage repeat purchase, or they may be a defensive maneuver for a mature brand that is facing competitive pressure and wants to retain its current users. The main limitation of bounce-back coupons is that they go only to purchasers of the brand and thus do not attract nonusers. A bounce-back coupon placed on the package for Kellogg Company's Nutri-Grain bars is shown in Exhibit 16–14.

Another type of in/on-pack coupon is the **cross-ruff coupon**, which is redeemable on the purchase of a different product, usually one made by the same company but occasionally through a tie-in with another manufacturer. Cross-ruff coupons have a redemption rate of 3 to 13 percent and can be effective in encouraging consumers to try other products or brands. Companies with wide product lines, such as cereal manufacturers, often use these coupons.

Yet another type of package coupon is the **instant coupon**, which is attached to the outside of the package so the consumer can rip it off and redeem it immediately at the time of purchase. Instant coupons have the highest redemption levels of all types of coupons, averaging around 21 percent for grocery products and for health and beauty items. However, the redemption level is much lower for instant cross-ruff coupons, as it averages around 10 percent. Instant coupons give consumers an immediate point-of-purchase incentive, and can be selectively placed in terms of promotion timing and market region. Exhibit 16–15 shows an instant cross-ruff coupon used by the California Milk Advisory Board for Real California Cheese as part of a promotional tie-in with Tia Rosa Tortillas. These types of coupons are often used to promote the purchase of complementary products. Some companies prefer instant coupons to price-off deals because the latter require more cooperation from retailers and can be more expensive, since every package must be reduced in price.

**EXHIBIT 16–15**
An instant cross-ruff coupon is used to promote the purchase of complementary products

DO NOT DOUBLE
SAVE 45¢
On any Real California Cheese (must carry this seal) with this purchase of Tia Rosa® Tortillas
Great Cheese comes from Happy Cows, Happy Cows come from California.
REAL CALIFORNIA CHEESE
PEEL HERE


Another distribution method that has experienced strong growth over the past 10 years or so is **in-store couponing**, which includes all co-op couponing programs distributed in a retail store environment. This medium now accounts for around 6 percent of total coupon distribution. Coupons are distributed to consumers in stores in several ways, including tear-off pads, handouts in the store (sometimes as part of a sampling demonstration), on-shelf dispensers, and electronic dispensers.

Most of the coupons distributed in stores are through instant coupon machines. These coupon dispensers are mounted on the shelf in front of the product being promoted and have blinking red lights to draw consumers' attention to the savings opportunity. These in-store coupons have several advantages: They can reach consumers when they are ready to make a purchase, increase brand awareness on the shelf, generate impulse buying, and encourage product trial. They also provide category exclusivity. In-store couponing removes the need for consumers to clip coupons from FSIs or print ads and then remember to bring them to the store. Redemption rates for coupons distributed by the instant coupon machine average about 8 percent.

Another popular way to distribute in-store coupons is through electronic devices such as kiosks or at the checkout counter. Some electronically dispensed coupons, such as Catalina Marketing Corp.'s Checkout Coupon, are tied to scanner data at each grocery store checkout. When the specified product, such as a competitive brand, is purchased, the consumer receives a coupon at the checkout for the company's brand. Companies also use this system to link purchases of products that are related. For example, a consumer who purchases a caffeine-free cola might be issued a coupon for a decaffeinated coffee.

Major advantages of electronically dispensed checkout coupons are that they are cost-effective and can be targeted to specific categories of consumers, such as users of competitive or complementary products. Since 65 to 85 percent of a manufacturer's coupons are used by current customers, marketers want to target their coupons to users of competitive brands. Redemption rates for electronically dispensed coupons average around 7 to 8 percent.

**Couponing Trends** In 2009 consumers used more coupons than ever before as 3.3 billion coupons were redeemed for packaged goods products, which represented a 27 percent increase over the 2.6 billion redeemed in 2008, and the first time in 17 years that consumers used more coupons than in the previous year. The increase in coupon use is primarily a result of the difficult economic times that many households are experiencing as a result of the recession. However, the increase also reflects the fact that more coupons were distributed by marketers who are using them as a way to compete against lower priced competitors as well as private label store brands.[35] While consumers are using more coupons, there are still a number of problems marketers are faced with in using them. The average U.S. household is still barraged with nearly 3,000 coupons per year and consumers redeem less than 2 percent of the hundreds of billions of coupons distributed.

Concerns over the cost and effectiveness of coupons have led some marketers to cut back on their use and/or change the way they use them. For example, marketers have reduced the duration period, with expiration dates of three months or less becoming more common. Marketers are also moving to greater use of multiple-item purchase requirements for coupons, particularly for grocery products where nearly 40 percent of the coupons use this tactic. The percentage of multiple purchase requirement coupons for health and beauty products has been declining and is now around 8 percent.[36] Critics argue that coupons cost too much to print, distribute, and process and that they do not benefit enough consumers. Former Procter & Gamble CEO Durk Jager echoed the sentiment of many consumer-product companies when he said, "Who can argue for a practice that fails 98 percent of the time?"[37]

Despite the growing sentiment among major marketers that coupons are inefficient and costly, very few companies, including Procter & Gamble, are likely to abandon them entirely. Although most coupons never get used, consumers use some of them and have come to expect them. More than 80 percent of consumers use coupons and nearly one-quarter say they use them every time they shop. With so many consumers eager for coupons, marketers will continue to accommodate them. However, companies as well as the coupon industry are looking for ways to improve on their use. For example, General Mills, Kellogg Company, and Post Cereals replaced brand-specific coupons with universal coupons good for any of their cereal brands. To make its couponing spending more efficient, Post began using universal coupons worth $1.50 off two boxes (matching the average cereal-coupon discount of 75 cents) and cut coupon distribution in half.

Some marketers are broadening their use of account-specific direct-mail couponing, in which coupons are co-branded with individual retailers but can be used by consumers at any retail store. Procter & Gamble began using account-specific couponing with Tide detergent and has broadened the program to include mailings for a number of other brands.[38] P&G also has expanded its use of coupons through its BrandSaver coupon booklet that is distributed in Sunday newspapers.[39]

Some marketers and retailers are looking to the Internet as a medium for distributing coupons. Several companies now offer online couponing services. Catalina Marketing started Valupage.com as a way for marketers to reach consumers at home with promotions traditionally offered in-store, including coupons. Consumers can log on to the website, type in their Zip code, and choose from a list of participating grocery stores in their area and download manufacturer- and retailer-sponsored coupons. A number of retailers, particularly supermarkets, are also using the Internet to distribute coupons to encourage consumers to shop at their stores. Cox Target Media also offers consumers the opportunity to access coupons online, through Valpak.com. The website makes the same coupons and offers available to consumers that come in the Valpak direct-mail envelope.

Another way to distribute coupons that is growing rapidly is mobile couponing whereby coupons are sent directly to mobile phones. A number of marketers are working with Cellfire, a company that distributes coupons to mobile devices of consumers who sign up for its service.[40] Cellfire also has been partnering with a number of major grocery stores to offer mobile grocery coupons (Exhibit 16–16). Marketers are also using various social media channels, such as Facebook and Twitter, to deliver coupons. For example, Burger King ran a "Whopper Sacrifice" promotion on Facebook in which consumers were given a coupon for a free whopper in exchange for deleting 10 friends. Facebook eventually shut down the promotion noting that it was a violation of the site's privacy policy, but not before nearly 24,000 coupons were awarded and 240,000 people were "unfriended."[41] IMC Technology Perspective 16–1 discusses a new form of couponing that is becoming popular that utilizes the growing popularity of social media and the power of group purchasing.

## Premiums

Premiums are a sales promotion device used by many marketers. A **premium** is an offer of an item of merchandise or service either free or at a low price that is an extra incentive for purchasers. Many marketers are eliminating toys and gimmicks in favor of value-added premiums that reflect the quality of the product and are consistent with its image and positioning in the market. Marketers spend over $4 billion a year on value-added premium incentives targeted at the consumer market. The two basic types of offers are the free premium and the self-liquidating premium.

**EXHIBIT 16–16**
Cellfire distributes coupons to mobile phones

**Free Premiums** Free premiums are usually small gifts or merchandise included in the product package or sent to consumers who mail in a request along with a proof of purchase. In/on-package free premiums include toys, balls, trading cards, or other items included in cereal packages, as well

**EXHIBIT 16–17**
McDonald's Happy Meals use toys to help attract children

as samples of one product included with another. Surveys have shown that in/on-package premiums are consumers' favorite type of promotion.[42]

Package-carried premiums have high impulse value and can provide an extra incentive to buy the product. However, several problems are associated with their use. First, there is the cost factor, which results from the premium itself as well as from extra packaging that may be needed. Finding desirable premiums at reasonable costs can be difficult, particularly for adult markets, and using a poor premium may do more harm than good.

Another problem with these premiums is possible restrictions from regulatory agencies such as the Federal Trade Commission and the Food and Drug Administration or from industry codes regarding the type of premium used. The National Association of Broadcasters has strict guidelines regarding the advertising of premium offers to children. There is concern that premium offers will entice children to request a brand to get the promoted item and then never consume the product. The networks' policy on children's advertising is that a premium offer cannot exceed 15 seconds of a 30-second spot, and the emphasis must be on the product, not the premium.

Since most free mail-in premium offers require the consumer to send in more than one proof of purchase, they encourage repeat purchase and reward brand loyalty. But a major drawback of mail-in premiums is that they do not offer immediate reinforcement or reward to the purchaser, so they may not provide enough incentive to purchase the brand. Few consumers take advantage of mail-in premium offers; the average redemption rate is only 2 to 4 percent.[43]

Free premiums have become very popular in the restaurant industry, particularly among fast-food chains such as McDonald's and Burger King, which use premium offers in their kids' meals to attract children. McDonald's has become the world's largest toymaker on a unit basis, commissioning about 750 million toys per year for its Happy Meals (Exhibit 16–17). Many of the premium offers used by the fast-food giants have cross-promotional tie-ins with popular movies and can be very effective at generating incremental sales. McDonald's negotiates movie tie-in deals with a number of studios, including DreamWorks Animation SKG and Pixar Animation Studios, as well as Disney. McDonald's uses movie tie-ins as the basis for many of its Happy Meal promotions.

**EXHIBIT 16–18**
American Airlines promotes the value of AAdvantage miles as a purchase incentive

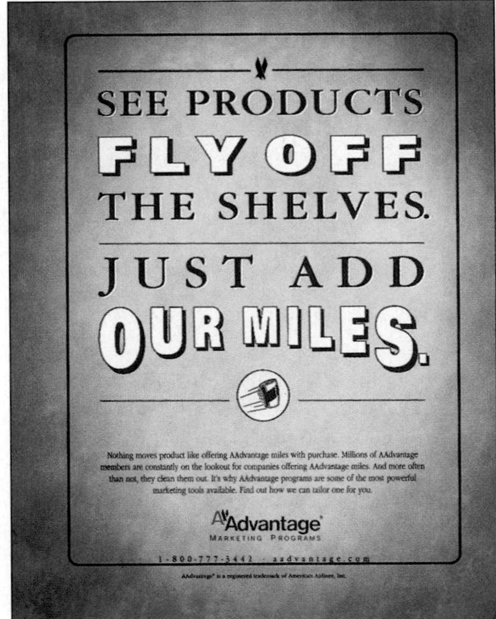


One of the fastest-growing types of incentive offers being used by marketers is airline miles, which have literally become a promotional currency. U.S. airlines make more than an estimated $2 billion each year selling miles to other marketers. Consumers are now choosing credit-card services, phone services, hotels, and many other products and services on the basis of mileage premiums for major frequent-flyer programs such as American Airlines' AAdvantage program or United Airlines' Mileage Plus program. Exhibit 16–18 shows a trade ad run by American Airlines promoting the value of AAdvantage miles as a promotional incentive that companies can offer their customers to help generate sales.

**Self-Liquidating Premiums** **Self-liquidating premiums** require the consumer to pay some or all of the cost of the premium plus handling and mailing costs. The marketer usually purchases items used as self-liquidating premiums in large quantities and offers them to consumers at lower-than-retail prices. The goal is not to make a

# IMC Technology Perspective 16–1 > > >

## Coupons Go Social with Groupon

Marketers have been bombarding consumers with coupons and other types of promotional discounts and offers for decades with the vast majority of the more than 300 billion coupons being distributed through traditional methods such as FSIs in Sunday newspapers and direct mail packets sent directly to consumers' homes. However, marketers have recognized that most of these coupon offers end up in the recycling bin of the more digitally-oriented millennials who spend more time online, particularly on social media sites, than they do reading newspapers or sorting through direct mail pieces. Thus, in recent years a number of companies have emerged that make coupons available to consumers online as well as through other methods such as sending them directly to mobile devices.

While these online and mobile couponing methods provide marketers with a good way to reach tech-savvy consumers, a new spin on couponing is gaining popularity among the Facebook and Twitter generation that capitalizes on the growing popularity of social media, as well as the power of group purchasing. The best known company competing in this new promotional space is Groupon which was founded in late 2008 in Chicago and is rapidly expanding throughout world, currently operating in North America, Latin America, Europe, Russia, and Japan. The company offers a single deal per day on its website, Groupon.com, and the item must be purchased that day to take advantage of the discount. The offer is valid only if a certain number of people agree to use it within 24 hours. If the deal falls short of its target, the deal is "off" and the credit card of those who purchased it are not charged. Consumers can join the site for free and, once registered, they receive email notifications of discounted deals being offered in their market area each day.

The basis of Groupon's business model is that it uses collective buying power to offer deep discounts and provides a win-win for businesses as well as consumers. Consumers save money by shopping en masse and can learn about new businesses in their local markets, while businesses are exposed to a larger audience and gain new customers by offering discounts to people who might otherwise not purchase from them. Under the arrangement, Groupon makes money by having businesses who participate in the program pay them a percentage of their deal sales, which can range from 30 to 50%. One of the key aspects of the program is that the deal works only if it attracts a critical mass and the threshold varies by advertiser as some deals require only 5 consumers to buy, while others may require 500. Thus, there is an incentive for consumers to spread the word and generate support for the deals among their friends and associates with various forms of social media such as Facebook and Twitter often being the best way to do so.

The concept of trying to leverage the purchasing power of groups to get deep discounts from companies is not exactly new. A company called OnlineChoice launched a group-purchasing site in the late 1990s but was one of the many Internet businesses that fell victim to the dot.com bust at the beginning of the new millen-

profit on the premium item but rather just to cover costs and offer a value to the consumer.

In addition to cost savings, self-liquidating premiums offer several advantages to marketers. Offering values to consumers through the premium products can create interest in the brand and goodwill that enhances the brand's image. These premiums can also encourage trade support and gain in-store displays for the brand and the premium offer. Self-liquidating premiums are often tied directly to the advertising campaign, so they extend the advertising message and contribute to consumer franchise building for a brand. For example, Philip Morris offers Western wear, outdoor items, and other types of Marlboro gear through its Marlboro Country catalog, which reinforces the cigarette brand's positioning theme.

Self-liquidating premium offers have the same basic limitation as mail-in premiums: a very low redemption rate. Fewer than 10 percent of U.S. households have ever sent for a premium, and fewer than 1 percent of self-liquidating offers are actually redeemed.[44] Low redemption rates can leave the marketer with a large supply of items with a logo or some other brand identification that makes them hard to dispose of. Thus, it is important to test consumers' reaction to a premium incentive and determine whether they perceive the offer as a value. Another option is to use premiums with no brand identification, but that detracts from their consumer franchise-building value.

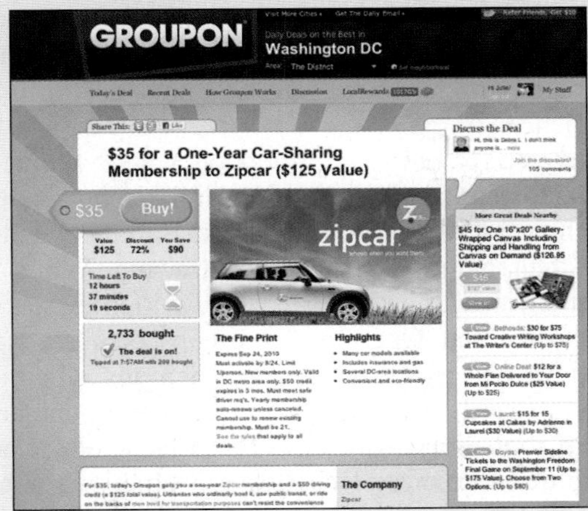


nium. However, experts argue that the new generation of start-up companies that include Groupon, as well as others such as LivingSocial, BuyWithMe, and NimbleBuy, have a much better chance of succeeding in today's new world of Web 2.0. Social network sites such as Facebook and Twitter have become extremely popular and provide consumers with a vehicle to spread the word about the deals and help make the quota thresholds. Moreover, consumers are much more comfortable with using the Internet and are more prone to share information online than they were 10 years ago.

The evidence suggests that the group couponing phenomenon is gaining traction among consumers. Groupon has more than 19 million subscribers and continues to add millions of new members each month as it expands into new cities. The company also has begun offering discounts from major companies and brands such as Gap, Zipcar, the National Basketball Association, and Jamba Juice to add to its stable of local businesses that offer discounts on their products and services. Marketers are also finding that Groupon can be an effective way to expand their customer base. For example, Zipcar used Groupon to gain nearly 1,500 new members in seven cities in late 2009 and is expanding its use to other cities. While more large companies are turning to Groupon and its competitors as a way of offering deals to consumers, the bulk of the offers are coming from small, local businesses such as retailers, restaurants, health and beauty clubs, and entertainment options.

Groupon and other services are learning that it is important to provide consumers with good offers and to make sure that consumers understand the terms and conditions of the deals as well. For example, Groupon experienced some backlash when it offered a free six-week trial for Blockbuster's DVD mail service that required consumers to opt-out on their own in order to avoid getting billed. The company's site offers a comment section for each deal and consumers do not hesitate to note which offers they like and dislike. Business owners are also recognizing that they have to offer consumers attractive deals and be capable of handling a potential surge in business if the offer strikes a responsive chord with consumers. However, for most companies this is a problem they will be more than happy to find ways to handle.

Sources: Jennifer Youssef, "Group Deals Pump Up Sales Online: Groupon.com Comes to Detroit, Works to Lure New Customers with Discounts," *Detroit News*, April 27, 2010, p. B6; Sarah E. Needleman, "Corporate News: Services Combine Social Media, Marketing," *Wall Street Journal*, February 23, 2010, p. B7; Kunur Patel, "Groupon Takes Coupons into the Social-Media Age," *Advertising Age*, December 21, 2009, http://adage.com/print?article_id=141172.



## Contests and Sweepstakes

Contests and sweepstakes are an increasingly popular consumer-oriented promotion. Marketers spent nearly $2 billion on these promotions in 2009. These promotions seem to have an appeal and glamour that such tools as cents-off coupons lack. Contests and sweepstakes are exciting because, as one expert has noted, many consumers have a "pot of gold at the end of the rainbow mentality" and think they can win the big prizes being offered.[45] The lure of sweepstakes and promotions has also been influenced by the "instant-millionaire syndrome" that has derived from huge cash prizes given by many state lotteries in recent years. Marketers are attracted to contests and sweepstakes as a way of generating attention and interest among a large number of consumers.

There are differences between contests and sweepstakes. A **contest** is a promotion where consumers compete for prizes or money on the basis of skills or ability. The company determines winners by judging the entries or ascertaining which entry comes closest to some predetermined criteria (e.g., picking the winning teams and total number of points in the Super Bowl or NCAA basketball tournament). Contests usually provide a purchase incentive by requiring a proof of purchase to enter or an entry form that is available from a dealer or advertisement. Some contests require consumers to read an ad or package or visit a store display to gather information

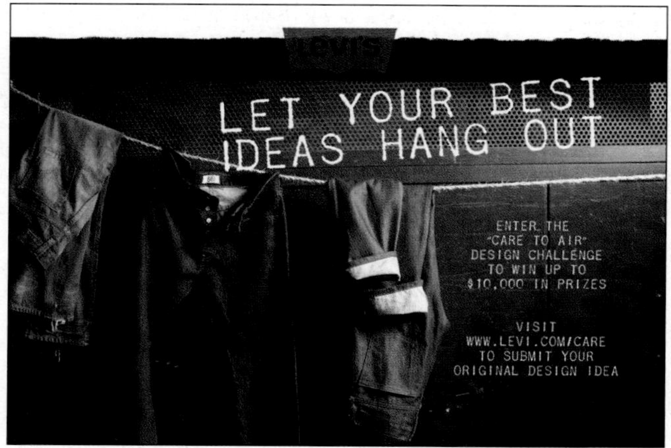


**EXHIBIT 16–19**
Levi's "Care to Air" Contest ties in well to the product and the interests of the target market

needed to enter. Marketers must be careful not to make their contests too difficult to enter, as doing so might discourage participation among key prospects in the target audience.

A **sweepstakes** is a promotion where winners are determined purely by chance; it cannot require a proof of purchase as a condition for entry. Entrants need only submit their names for the prize drawing. While there is often an official entry form, handwritten entries must also be permitted. One form of sweepstakes is a **game**, which also has a chance element or odds of winning. Scratch-off cards with instant winners are a popular promotional tool. Some games occur over a longer period and require more involvement by consumers. Promotions where consumers must collect game pieces are popular among retailers and fast-food chains as a way to build store traffic and repeat purchases.

Because they are easier to enter, sweepstakes attract more entries than contests. They are also easier and less expensive to administer, since every entry does not have to be checked or judged. Choosing the winning entry in a sweepstakes requires only the random selection of a winner from the pool of entries or generation of a number to match those held by sweepstakes entrants. Experts note that the costs of mounting a sweepstakes are also very predictable. Companies can buy insurance to indemnify them and protect against the expense of awarding a big prize. In general, sweepstakes present marketers with a fixed cost, which is a major advantage when budgeting for a promotion.

Contests and sweepstakes can involve consumers with a brand by making the promotion product relevant or by connecting the prizes to the lifestyle, needs, or interests of the target audience. For example, Levi Strauss & Co. recently ran an innovative contest called the "Care to Air Challenge" which sought the world's most innovative, covetable, and sustainable air-drying solution for clothing (Exhibit 16–19). The contest was designed to address an important environmental issue by informing consumers that nearly 60 percent of the climate impact of owning a pair of jeans over their life cycle comes from the energy intensive methods used for drying them. The contest offered consumers the chance to win $10,000 in prize money by submitting a photo and description of how they use clothesline designs or other innovative air drying solutions that are better for the environment and help reduce the carbon footprint.

The nature of contests and sweepstakes, as well as the way they are deployed, is changing as many companies are delivering them online rather than through traditional entry forms that are submitted via the mail or dropped in an entry box. Marketers are using the Internet for their contests and sweepstakes because of its cost efficiency, immediate data collection capabilities, and ability to keep consumers engaged. Promotions are being designed to ensure an engaging consumer experience by making them more entertaining and interactive and also developing prizes that are not only larger, but more customized and experiential-based.[46] A number of companies are also integrating user-generated content into their contests. For example, as noted in Chapter 11, Frito-Lay used "Crash the Super Bowl" promotions for the past several years for its Doritos brand whereby consumers created their own TV commercials for the brand as well as songs.[47]

**Problems with Contests and Sweepstakes** While the use of contests and sweepstakes continues to increase, there are some problems associated with these types of promotions. Many sweepstakes and/or contest promotions do little to contribute to consumer franchise building for a product or service and may even detract from it. The sweepstakes or contest often becomes the dominant focus rather than the brand, and little is accomplished other than giving away substantial amounts of money and/or prizes. Many promotional experts question the effectiveness of contests and sweepstakes. Some companies have cut back or even stopped using them because of concern over their effectiveness and fears that consumers might become dependent on them.

Another problem with contests and sweepstakes is the participation in them by hobbyists who submit entries but have no real interest in the product or service. Because most states make it illegal to require a purchase as a qualification for a sweepstakes entry, consumers can enter as many times as they wish. Entrants may enter a sweepstakes numerous times, depending on the nature of the prizes and the number of entries allowed. There are numerous websites on the Internet such as sweepstakes advantage.com that inform consumers of all of the contests and sweepstakes being held, the entry dates, estimated probabilities of winning, how to enter, and solutions to any puzzles or other information that might be needed. The presence of the professional entrants not only defeats the purpose of the promotion but also may discourage entries from consumers who feel that their chances of winning are limited.

Numerous legal considerations affect the design and administration of contests and sweepstakes.[48] These promotions are regulated by several federal agencies, and each of the 50 states has its own rules. The regulation of contests and sweepstakes has helped clean up the abuses that plagued the industry for many years and has improved consumers' perceptions of these promotions. But companies must still be careful in designing a contest or sweepstakes and awarding prizes. Most firms use consultants that specialize in the design and administration of contests and sweepstakes to avoid any legal problems, but they may still run into problems with promotions, as discussed in IMC Perspective 16–2.

## Refunds and Rebates

**Refunds** (also known as *rebates*) are offers by the manufacturer to return a portion of the product purchase price, usually after the consumer supplies some proof of purchase. Consumers are generally very responsive to rebate offers, particularly as the size of the savings increases. Rebates are used by makers of all types of products, ranging from packaged goods to major appliances, cars, and computer software.

Packaged-goods marketers often use refund offers to induce trial of a new product or encourage users of another brand to switch. Consumers may perceive the savings offered through a cash refund as an immediate value that lowers the cost of the item, even though those savings are realized only if the consumer redeems the refund or rebate offer. Redemption rates for refund offers typically range from 1 to 3 percent for print and point-of-purchase offers and 5 percent for in/on-package offers.

**EXHIBIT 16–20**
Pennzoil uses a refund offer that is tied to a future purchase

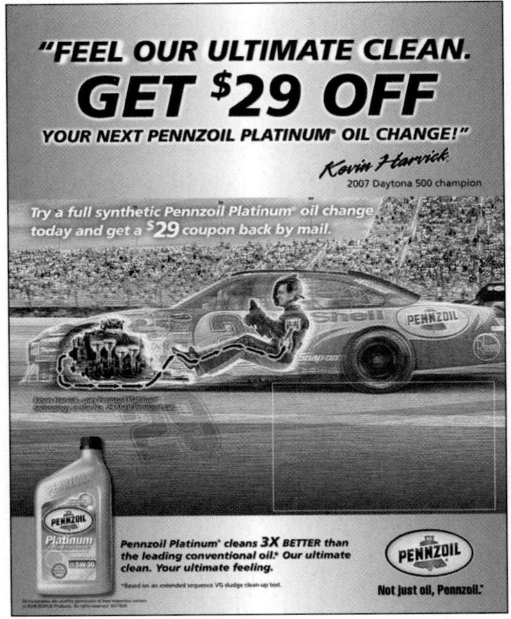


Refund offers can also encourage repeat purchase. Many offers require consumers to send in multiple proofs of purchase. The size of the refund offer may even increase as the number of purchases gets larger. Some packaged-goods companies are switching away from cash refund offers to coupons or cash/coupon combinations. Using coupons in the refund offer enhances the likelihood of repeat purchase of the brand. For example, Exhibit 16–20 shows a coupon refund offer used by Pennzoil that can be redeemed on the next oil change.

### Evaluating Refunds and Rebates

Rebates can help create new users and encourage brand switching or repeat purchase behavior, or they can be a way to offer a temporary price reduction. This offer can influence purchase even if the consumer fails to realize the savings, so the marketer can reduce price for much less than if it used a direct price-off deal.

# IMC Perspective 16–2 > > >

## Marketers and Consumers Learn the Perils of Promotions

Contests, sweepstakes, and premium offers are often used by marketers to give consumers an extra incentive to purchase their products. However, when these promotions don't go as planned, they can embarrass a company or even create legal problems. A number of high-profile companies known for their marketing excellence have experienced problems with promotions over the years. These botched promotions were embarrassing for the companies and resulted in the loss of goodwill as well as money.

Kraft was one of the first to learn how expensive it can be when a promotion goes awry. In 1989, a printing error resulted in the printing of too many winning game pieces for a match-and-win game promotion. Kraft canceled the promotion but still had to spend nearly $4 million to compensate the winners—versus the $36,000 budgeted for prizes. The snafu gave birth to the "Kraft clause," a disclaimer stating that a marketer reserves the right to cancel a promotion if there are problems and hold a random drawing if there are more winners than prizes.

A few years later, PepsiCo had a major problem when a bottle-cap promotion offering a grand prize of 1 million pesos (about $36,000) went wrong in the Philippines. Due to a computer glitch, the winning number appeared on more than 500,000 bottle caps, which would have made the company liable for more than $18 billion in prize money. When the error was discovered, Pepsi announced that there was a problem and quickly offered to pay $19 for each winning cap, which ended up costing the company nearly $10 million. The furor caused by the botched promotion prompted anti-Pepsi rallies, death threats against Pepsi executives, and attacks on Pepsi trucks and bottling plants.

Harrah's Entertainment, Inc., made a major couponing error that ended up costing the company nearly $6 million. A mailing sent to its Total Rewards cardholders in its loyalty program included a coupon that members could redeem at Harrah's Joliet Casino near Chicago. Only a small number of the coupons were supposed to be worth $525 each; however, a printing error resulted in 11,000 coupons worth $525 being sent out. The coupons were barcoded but most of the codes did not match the $525 printed on the coupon's face value and casino staff initially refused to honor the coupons when the bar codes did not match the face value. However, the Illinois gaming board ordered Harrah's to honor all of the coupons and most were eventually redeemed.

McDonald's also ran into a major problem when winning game pieces were embezzled from its popular Monopoly game promotion. McDonald's ran its first Monopoly game promotion in 1987 and began running it annually in 1991. However, in August 2001 the Federal Bureau of Investigation arrested eight people for embezzling winning game pieces from the Monopoly game as well as the company's "Who Wants to Be a Millionaire" sweepstakes in order to divert nearly $24 million worth of prizes to co-conspirators.

Fifty-one people were indicted in the case, nearly all of whom either pleaded guilty or were convicted following trial. Among those pleading guilty was the director of security for McDonald's promotional agency, Simon Marketing, who stole the winning tickets and conspired with the others to distribute them to a network of recruiters who solicited individuals to falsely claim they were legitimate game winners. Following the arrests McDonald's immediately fired Simon Marketing, as did several other of the agency's clients. The company also

Some problems are associated with refunds and rebates. Many consumers are not motivated by a refund offer because of the delay and the effort required to obtain the savings. They do not want to be bothered saving cash register receipts and proofs of purchase, filling out forms, and mailing in the offer.[49] A study of consumer perceptions found a negative relationship between the use of rebates and the perceived difficulties associated with the redemption process.[50] The study also found that consumers perceive manufacturers as offering rebates to sell products that are not faring well. Nonusers of rebates were particularly likely to perceive the redemption process as too complicated and to suspect manufacturers' motives. This implies that companies using rebates must simplify the redemption process and use other promotional elements such as advertising to retain consumer confidence in the brand.

When small refunds are being offered, marketers may find other promotional incentives such as coupons or bonus packs more effective. They must be careful created an independent task force comprised of anti-fraud and game security experts to review procedures for future promotions. McDonald's began running the Monopoly promotion again in 2003, and it has again become very popular among consumers.

A recent example of a well intended sales promotion tactic going awry involved an online coupon promotion that KFC was running in China in April 2010 in conjunction with Taobao.com, China's largest e-commerce site. KFC, which is China's largest fast food chain with 2,000 outlets, planned to distribute coupons for three different menu items with each offering a 50 percent discount. The coupons could be downloaded on KFC's online store on Taobao.com at specific time periods. However, a problem arose when news of the discounts circulated around the Internet and the coupons were republished on other sites, where they were downloaded and redeemed at restaurants, far surpassing the volume anticipated by KFC. Store employees began refusing coupons arguing that they were illegally produced from unauthorized sites, but the explanations varied from store to store, which added to the problem. Many consumers reacted, and some became violent, and police had to rush to some restaurants to restore order. KFC issued an apology for the problem, but the company's failure to honor the coupons damaged the brand's relationship with thousands of consumers, many of whom criticized KFC on blogs and social media sites in many cities around China.

Marketers are not the only ones who encounter problems with promotions as consumers who win contests and sweepstakes often learn that there may be unexpected tax consequences because the prizes are treated as income by the Internal Revenue Service. For example, in 2004, 276 audience members on *The Oprah Winfrey Show* each won a Pontiac G6 automobile valued at $28,500. Winners could decline the prize, accept the car and pay the taxes, or immediately sell the car and get the difference in cash and pay taxes on that amount.

A winner of a recent American Airlines "We know why you fly" contest faced even greater tax liability as the grand prize was 12 round-trip restricted coach tickets for two to anywhere in the world the airline flies. The contest's official rules explained that winners must pay federal and state income taxes, where applicable, on American's approximated retail value of the 24 tickets, which the airline valued at $2,200 per ticket or $52,800. The New York resident who won the contest was facing taxes on the tickets that could amount to nearly $19,000 and so declined the prize. However, airline promotions offering free travel remain very popular. In January 2008, American launched its DealFinder Travel the World Sweepstakes to build awareness for its online tool, which searches for discounted fares on the airline. The sweepstakes directed people to a special website to register for a chance to win first-class air travel for two around the world and a $25,000 MasterCard gift card. American had to temporarily remove the sweepstakes from its website because so many people tried to register for the promotion causing technical problems with the microsite.

While marketers continue to use contests, sweepstakes, and games, they are taking precautions to safeguard them in an attempt to avoid the problems these companies encountered. Consumers who enter these promotions might also be well-advised to read the fine print to understand the tax liability associated with the prize and make sure they can really afford to win.

Sources: Normandy Madden, "KFC Gets Burned by Digital Coupon Promotion," *Advertising Age*, April 14, 210, http://adage.com/print?article_id=143283; Amy Johannes, "American Airlines Pulls Promotion after Big Response Clogs Site," promomagazine.com, January 15, 2008; Kate McArthur, "McSwindle," *Advertising Age*, August 27, 2002, pp. 1, 22; Betsy Spethmann, "The Perils of Promotion," *Promo*, November 1996, pp. 22, 134; Melanie Trottman and Ron Lieber, "Contest Winner Declines 'Free' Airline Tickets," *The Wall Street Journal*, July 6, 2005; Betsy Spethmann, "Harrah's Coupon Error to Cost $2.8 Billion," promomagazine.com, November 23, 2005.



not to overuse rebate offers and confuse consumers about the real price and value of a product or service. Also, consumers can become dependent on rebates and delay their purchases or purchase only brands for which a rebate is available. Many retailers have become disenchanted with rebates and the burden and expense of administering them.[51] However, as discussed in Ethical Perspective 16–1, the use of rebates is on the rise and many companies factor the redemption rates into their pricing structure.

## Bonus Packs

**Bonus packs** offer the consumer an extra amount of a product at the regular price by providing larger containers or extra units (Exhibit 16–21). Bonus packs result in a lower cost per unit for the consumer and provide extra value as well as more product

## Ethical Perspective 16–1 > > >

### Rebates: Marketers Love Them but Consumers Often Loathe Them

If you are like most consumers, the chances are pretty good that one of the factors that influenced your recent purchase of a product was the availability of a rebate. The use of rebates as a sales promotion tool has been proliferating as numerous companies ranging from consumer electronics firms such as Dell, Hewlett-Packard, TiVo, and Sony to packaged goods marketers and retailers such as Unilever and Rite-Aid use them. Consumer products marketers pioneered rebates in the 1970s as a way to advertise small discounts without actually marking the product down. Their popularity soared in the 1990s as computer electronics companies began using them to move piles of products such as personal computers, cell phones, and TV sets before they became obsolete. Today, nearly one-third of all computers are sold with some form of rebate, along with more than 20 percent of camcorders and LCD televisions, according to the market research firm NPD Group Inc.

So why have rebates become the rage among marketers and retailers? One reason is that, like other sales promotion tools, they give consumers an extra incentive to make a purchase. However, critics argue that the use of rebates has also skyrocketed because the industry knows that 40 percent of all rebates never get redeemed, which translates into extra revenue for manufacturers and retailers. Rebates get consumers to focus on the discounted price of the product taking into account the rebate, then purchase it at full price. Consumers believe they will redeem the rebates but often do not end up doing so, thus paying more for items than they expected. As the director of retail research at the consulting firm Aberdeen Group Inc. notes, "the game is obviously that anything less than 100 percent redemption is free money."

Critics of rebates have noted that even for expensive items with rebates worth $50, the redemption rate is often below 50 percent. In fact one rebate fulfillment company published a "Rebate Redemption Guide" for its customers which cited low redemption rates they could expect such as 10 percent for a $10 rebate on a $100 product and just 35 percent for a $50 rebate on a $200 product. There are many reasons why rebates end up not being redeemed. Critics argue that companies design the terms and conditions to keep redemption rates low, citing problems such as complex rules, short filing periods, repeated requests for copies of receipts, and long delays in sending out checks that discourage consumers from attempting to retrieve the money they are owed. They also note that in some cases, even when the checks arrive, they get tossed in the trash because they look like junk mail or they get misplaced and never end up being cashed.

However, according to Tim Silk, a marketing professor at the University of British Columbia who has done extensive research on consumers' perceptions and use of rebates, it is not always the manufacturers and retailers offering the rebates that are creating the problem. He notes that consumers' tendency to procrastinate and their inability to fol-

---

**EXHIBIT 16–21**
Bonus packs provide more value for consumers

for the money. There are several advantages to bonus pack promotions. First, they give marketers a direct way to provide extra value without having to get involved with complicated coupons or refund offers. The additional value of a bonus pack is generally obvious to the consumer and can have a strong impact on the purchase decision at the time of purchase.

Bonus packs can also be an effective defensive maneuver against a competitor's promotion or introduction of a new brand. By loading current users with large amounts of its product, a marketer can often remove these consumers from the market and make them less susceptible to a competitor's promotional efforts. Bonus packs may result in larger purchase orders and favorable display space in the store if relationships with retailers are good. They do, however, usually require additional shelf space without providing any extra profit margins for the retailer, so the marketer can encounter problems with bonus packs if trade relationships are not good. Another problem is that bonus packs may appeal primarily to current users who probably would have purchased the brand anyway or to promotion-sensitive consumers who may not become loyal to the brand.

### Price-Off Deals

Another consumer-oriented promotion technique is the direct **price-off deal**, which reduces the price of the brand. Price-off reductions are typically offered right on low directions are a reason why many rebates go unfulfilled. Silk conducted experiments giving participants different lengths of time to redeem their rebates and found that those given only a day were more than 20 percent more likely to send them in versus those given three weeks—a result he attributes to procrastination.

A recent survey conducted by *Consumer Reports* using a nationally representative sample found the primary reason people cited for ignoring rebate offers was the work involved in redeeming them, such as completing the forms, providing receipts and UPC labels, and sending all of this by a certain deadline. The survey also found that of those who did not apply for a rebate, 26 percent said they doubted they would receive it, a skepticism that may be justified since 21 percent of those who applied did not receive the rebate or were turned down because of a technicality. The *Consumer Reports* study also found that low-income people (making less than $50,000 per year) for whom rebates could be most useful were least likely to apply for them.

While failure to redeem rebates may be the customers' own fault, there is growing resentment toward marketers and retailers offering the rebates. Complaints to the Better Business Bureau have increased by 350 percent since 2002 to almost 4,500 per year. Regulators are also intensifying their scrutiny of the industry and taking steps to force companies to fulfill rebate requests more quickly and be more receptive to customer questions and complaints. Texas recently enacted legislation requiring companies to pay rebates within 30 days unless they specify a different time period. A new law went into effect in North Carolina in October 2007 that requires companies to offer consumers at least 30 days to submit their rebate and some states are considering giving consumers as much as a year to turn in their forms.

Marketers are unlikely to eliminate the use of rebates because they are too effective to do away with, despite the consumer complaints. A well-promoted, high-value rebate can increase sales as much as 500 percent on some products, and eliminating them can have a negative impact on sales in many product categories where consumers have come to expect them, such as consumer electronics. Marketers recognize that they can accomplish a perceived price reduction among consumers who plan to redeem the rebates but never do so and build this into their pricing structure. Thus, consumers' love/hate relationship with rebates is likely to continue.

Sources: "Rebates: Get What You Deserve," *Consumer Reports*, September 2009, p. 7; Kimberly Palmer, "Why Shoppers Love to Hate Rebates," www.usnews.com, January 18, 2008; Brian Grow and Rishi Chhatwai, "The Great Rebate Runaround," *BusinessWeek*, December 5, 2005, pp. 34–38.

**EXHIBIT 16–22**
Examples of price-off packages

the package through specially marked price packs, as shown in Exhibit 16–22. Typically, price-offs range from 10 to 25 percent off the regular price, with the reduction coming out of the manufacturer's profit margin, not the retailer's. Keeping the retailer's margin during a price-off promotion maintains its support and cooperation.

Marketers use price-off promotions for several reasons. First, since price-offs are controlled by the manufacturer, it can make sure the promotional discount reaches the consumer rather than being kept by the trade. Like bonus packs, price-off deals usually present a readily apparent value to shoppers, especially when they have a reference price point for the brand and thus recognize the value of the discount.[52] So price-offs can be a strong influence at the point of purchase when price comparisons are being made. Price-off promotions can also encourage consumers to purchase larger quantities, preempting competitors' promotions and leading to greater trade support.

Price-off promotions may not be favorably received by retailers, since they can create pricing and inventory problems. Most retailers will not accept packages with a specific price shown, so the familiar *X* amount off the regular price must be used. Also, like bonus packs, price-off deals appeal primarily to regular users instead of attracting nonusers. Finally, the Federal Trade Commission has regulations regarding the conditions that price-off labels must meet and the frequency and timing of their use.

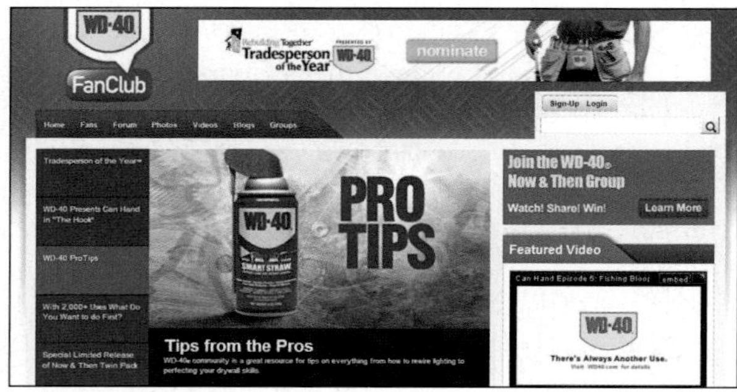


**EXHIBIT 16–23**
The WD-40 Fan Club is a popular customer loyalty program

## Loyalty Programs

One of the fastest-growing areas of sales promotion is the use of **loyalty programs** (also referred to as *continuity* or *frequency programs*). American Airlines was one of the first major companies to use loyalty programs when it introduced its AAdvantage frequent-flyer program in 1981. Since then frequency programs have become commonplace in a number of product and service categories, particularly travel and hospitality, as well as among retailers. Virtually every airline, car rental company, and hotel chain has some type of frequency program. American Airlines has more than 50 million members in its AAdvantage program, while Marriott International has enlisted more than 20 million business travelers into its Rewards program.

Many packaged-goods companies are also developing loyalty programs. Pillsbury, Nestlé, Kraft, and others have recently introduced continuity programs that offer consumers the opportunity to accumulate points for continuing to purchase their brands; the points can be redeemed for gifts and prizes. Loyalty programs have become particularly popular among grocery stores.[53] Nearly 7,000 supermarkets now have loyalty programs that offer members discounts, a chance to accumulate points that can be redeemed for rewards, newsletters, and other special services. Loyalty programs are also used by a variety of other retailers, including department stores, home centers, bookstores, and even local bagel shops. Many specialty retailers such as consumer electronics stores also have launched loyalty programs. For example, Best Buy launched its Rewards Zone program in 2003 and the program has grown to include more than 7 million members.

There are a number of reasons why loyalty programs have become so popular. Marketers view these programs as a way of encouraging consumers to use their products or services on a continual basis and as a way of developing strong customer loyalty. Many companies are also realizing the importance of customer retention and understand that the key to retaining and growing market share is building relationships with loyal customers.[54] Frequency programs also provide marketers with the opportunity to develop databases containing valuable information on their customers that can be used to better understand their needs, interests, and characteristics as well as to identify and track a company's most valuable customers. These databases can also be used to target specific programs and offers to customers to increase the amount they purchase and/or to build stronger relationships with them. For example, the WD-40 Fan Club is a loyalty program for the brand which provides members with product information, usage tips, newsletters, downloads of games, and other benefits (Exhibit 16–23). The fan club has more than 100,000 members who educate each other about creative ways to use the solvent and serve as advocates for the brand.[55]

As frequency programs become more common, marketers will be challenged to find ways to use them as a means of differentiating their product, service, business, or retail store. The average American household belongs to 12 loyalty programs but is active in only 40 percent of them.[56] It has been argued that many of the loyalty programs developed by marketers are really short-term promotions that overreward regular users and do little to develop long-term loyalty.[57] A recent study by a loyalty marketing firm found that 66 percent of consumers say that discounts are the main reason they participate in loyalty programs. This study also found that many consumers drop out of loyalty programs because of the length of time it takes to accumulate reward points.[58] Marketers must find ways to make their loyalty programs more than just discount or frequent-buyer programs. This will require the careful management of databases to identify and track valuable customers and their purchase history and the strategic use of targeted loyalty promotions.

**EXHIBIT 16–24**
The Dew Tour provides Mountain Dew with event marketing opportunities

## Event Marketing

Another type of consumer-oriented promotion that has become very popular in recent years is the use of event marketing. It is important to make a distinction between *event marketing* and *event sponsorships,* as the two terms are often used interchangeably yet they refer to different activities. **Event marketing** is a type of promotion where a company or brand is linked to an event or where a themed activity is developed for the purpose of creating experiences for consumers and promoting a product or service. Marketers often do event marketing by associating their product with some popular activity such as a sporting event, concert, fair, or festival. However, marketers also create their own events to use for promotional purposes. For example, PepsiCo has created an irreverent brand image for its popular Mountain Dew brand by associating it with action sports. Extreme sports are about a nonconforming lifestyle from clothes to music, and young people respond to brands that make an authentic connection and become part of the action sports community. In 2005, the brand raised its involvement with action sports to a new level when it became a founding partner of the Dew Tour, a five-event series that features competition in skateboarding, BMX, and freestyle motocross and has expanded into winter sports as well with the Winter Dew Tour (Exhibit 16–24). From an event marketing perspective, an important part of the Dew Tour is the promotional opportunities associated with the various events. At each Dew Tour stop the company's event agency sets up the "Mountain Dew Green Label Experience" which is built around the action sports lifestyle and features custom art, interactive displays, athlete autograph sessions, lounges where fans can hang out and interact with their favorite extreme sport athletes, and the product sampling kitchen where they can try various Mountain Dew flavors, as well as other products.

An **event sponsorship** is an integrated marketing communications activity where a company develops actual sponsorship relations with a particular event and provides financial support in return for the right to display a brand name, logo, or advertising message and be identified as a supporter of the event. Event marketing often takes place as part of a company's sponsorship of activities such as concerts, the arts, social causes, and sporting events. Decisions and objectives for event sponsorships are often part of an organization's public relations activities and are discussed in the next chapter.

Event marketing has become a very popular part of the integrated marketing communications programs of many companies as they view them as excellent promotional opportunities and a way to associate their brands with certain lifestyles, interests, and activities. Events can be an effective way to connect with consumers in an environment where they are comfortable with receiving a promotional message. Moreover, consumers often expect companies to be part of events and welcome their participation as they make the events more entertaining, interesting, and exciting. Marketers can use events to distribute samples as well as information about their products and services or to actually let consumers experience their brands.

## Summary of Consumer-Oriented Promotions and Marketer Objectives

The discussion of the various sales promotion techniques shows that marketers use these tools to accomplish a variety of objectives. As noted at the beginning of the chapter, sales promotion techniques provide consumers with an *extra incentive* or

| Consumer Reward Incentive | Marketing Objective: Induce trial | Customer retention/loading | Support IMC program/ build brand equity |
|---|---|---|---|
| Immediate | • Sampling<br>• Instant coupons<br>• In-store coupons<br>• In-store rebates | • Price-off deals<br>• Bonus packs<br>• In- and on-package free premiums<br>• Loyalty programs | • Events<br>• In- and on-package free premiums |
| Delayed | • Media- and mail-delivered coupons<br>• Mail-in refunds and rebates<br>• Free mail-in premiums<br>• Scanner- and Internet-delivered coupons | • In- and on-package coupons<br>• Mail-in refunds and rebates<br>• Loyalty programs | • Self-liquidating premiums<br>• Free mail-in premiums<br>• Contests and sweepstakes<br>• Loyalty programs |

**FIGURE 16–4**

Consumer-Oriented Sales Promotion Tools for Various Marketing Objectives

*reward* for engaging in a certain form of behavior such as purchasing a brand. For some types of sales promotion tools the incentive the consumer receives is immediate, while for others the reward is delayed and is not realized immediately. Marketers often evaluate sales promotion tools in terms of their ability to accomplish specific objectives and consider whether the impact of the promotion will be immediate or delayed. Figure 16–4 outlines which sales promotion tools can be used to accomplish various objectives of marketers and identifies whether the extra incentive or reward is immediate or delayed.[59]

It should be noted that in Figure 16–4 some of the sales promotion techniques are listed more than once because they can be used to accomplish more than one objective. For example, loyalty programs can be used to retain customers by providing both immediate and delayed rewards. Shoppers who belong to loyalty programs sponsored by supermarkets and receive discounts every time they make a purchase are receiving immediate rewards that are designed to retain them as customers. Some loyalty promotions such as frequency programs used by airlines, car rental companies, and hotels offer delayed rewards by requiring that users accumulate points to reach a certain level or status before the points can be redeemed. Loyalty programs can also be used by marketers to help build brand equity. For example, when an airline or car rental company sends its frequent users upgrade certificates, the practice helps build relationships with these customers and thus contributes to brand equity.

While marketers use consumer-oriented sales promotions to provide current and/or potential customers with an extra incentive, they also use these promotions as part of their marketing program to leverage trade support. Retailers are more likely to stock a brand, purchase extra quantities, or provide additional support such as end-aisle displays when they know a manufacturer is running a promotion during a designated period. The development of promotional programs targeted toward the trade is a very important part of the marketing process and is discussed in the next section.

# TRADE-ORIENTED SALES PROMOTION

## Objectives of Trade-Oriented Sales Promotion

Like consumer-oriented promotions, sales promotion programs targeted to the trade should be based on well-defined objectives and measurable goals and a consideration of what the marketer wants to accomplish. Typical objectives for promotions targeted to marketing intermediaries such as wholesalers and retailers include obtaining distribution and support for new products, maintaining support for established brands, encouraging retailers to display established brands, and building retail inventories.

**Obtain Distribution for New Products** Trade promotions are often used to encourage retailers to give shelf space to new products. Manufacturers recognize that only a limited amount of shelf space is available in supermarkets, drugstores, and other major retail outlets. Thus, they provide retailers with financial incentives to stock and promote new products. While trade discounts or other special price deals are used to encourage retailers and wholesalers to stock a new brand, marketers may use other types of promotions to get them to push the brand. Merchandising allowances can get retailers to display a new product in high-traffic areas of stores, while incentive programs or contests can encourage wholesale or retail store personnel to push a new brand.

**Maintain Trade Support for Established Brands** Trade promotions are often designed to maintain distribution and trade support for established brands. Brands that are in the mature phase of their product life cycle are vulnerable to losing wholesale and/or retail distribution, particularly if they are not differentiated or face competition from new products. Trade deals induce wholesalers and retailers to continue to carry weaker products because the discounts increase their profit margins. Brands with a smaller market share often rely heavily on trade promotions, since they lack the funds required to differentiate themselves from competitors through media advertising.

Even if a brand has a strong market position, trade promotions may be used as part of an overall marketing strategy. For example, Heinz has relied heavily on trade promotions to hold its market share position for many of its brands. Many consumer packaged-goods companies count on trade promotions to maintain retail distribution and support.

**EXHIBIT 16–25**
This brochure shows retailers the various promotions Chicken of the Sea planned to use for its various products

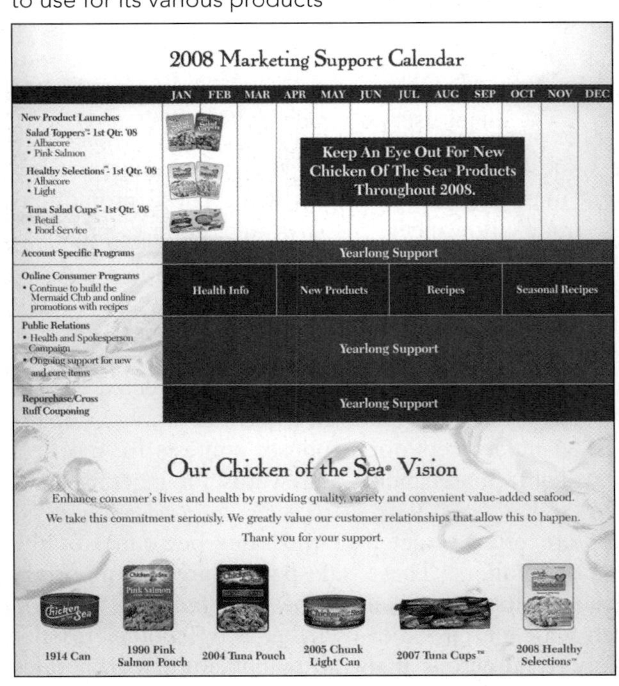


**Encourage Retailers to Display Established Brands** Another objective of trade-oriented promotions is to encourage retailers to display and promote an established brand. Marketers recognize that many purchase decisions are made in the store and promotional displays are an excellent way of generating sales. An important goal is to obtain retail store displays of a product away from its regular shelf location. A typical supermarket has approximately 50 display areas at the ends of aisles, near checkout counters, and elsewhere. Marketers want to have their products displayed in these areas to increase the probability shoppers will come into contact with them. Even a single display can increase a brand's sales significantly during a promotion.

Manufacturers often use multifaceted promotional programs to encourage retailers to promote their products at the retail level. For example, Exhibit 16–25 shows a marketing support calendar that Chicken of the Sea International provides to retailers showing the various promotions the company planned to use during the year for its Chicken of the Sea brands. The company was intending to use a variety of IMC tools including media advertising, public relations, online support of its Mermaid Club loyalty program, and a number of sales promotion tools. These include FSI distribution via direct mail as well as newspapers, account-specific promotions, repurchase/cross-ruff coupons, and event marketing through the Taste of Home Cooking schools, which visit 125 cities nationwide.

**FIGURE 16–5**

Three Forms of Promotion Targeted to Reseller Salespeople

- Product or Program Sales

  Awards are tied to the selling of a product, for example:

  Selling a specified number of cases

  Selling a specified number of units

  Selling a specified number of promotional programs

- New Account Placements

  Awards are tied to:

  The number of new accounts opened

  The number of new accounts ordering a minimum number of cases or units

  Promotional programs placed in new accounts

- Merchandising Efforts

  Awards are tied to:

  Establishing promotional programs (such as theme programs)

  Placing display racks, counter displays, and the like

**Build Retail Inventories** Manufacturers often use trade promotions to build the inventory levels of retailers or other channel members. There are several reasons manufacturers want to load retailers with their products. First, wholesalers and retailers are more likely to push a product when they have high inventory levels rather than storing it in their warehouses or back rooms. Building channel members' inventories also ensures they will not run out of stock and thus miss sales opportunities.

Some manufacturers of seasonal products offer large promotional discounts so that retailers will stock up on their products before the peak selling season begins. This enables the manufacturer to smooth out seasonal fluctuations in its production schedule and passes on some of the inventory carrying costs to retailers or wholesalers. When retailers stock up on a product before the peak selling season, they often run special promotions and offer discounts to consumers to reduce excess inventories.

## Types of Trade-Oriented Promotions

Manufacturers use a variety of trade promotion tools as inducements for wholesalers and retailers. Next we examine some of the most often used types of trade promotions and some factors marketers must consider in using them. These promotions include contests and incentives, trade allowances, displays and point-of-purchase materials, sales training programs, trade shows, and co-op advertising.

**Contests and Incentives** Manufacturers may develop contests or special incentive programs to stimulate greater selling effort and support from reseller management or sales personnel. Contests or incentive programs can be directed toward managers who work for a wholesaler or distributor as well as toward store or department managers at the retail level. Manufacturers often sponsor contests for resellers and use prizes such as trips or valuable merchandise as rewards for meeting sales quotas or other goals.

Contests or special incentives are often targeted at the sales personnel of the wholesalers, distributors/dealers, or retailers. These salespeople are an important link in the distribution chain because they are likely to be very familiar with the market, more frequently in touch with the customer (whether it be another reseller or the ultimate consumer), and more numerous than the manufacturer's own sales organization. Manufacturers often devise incentives or contests for these sales personnel. These programs may involve cash payments made directly to the retailer's or wholesaler's sales staff to encourage them to promote and sell a manufacturer's product. These payments are known as **push money** (pm) or *spiffs*. For example, an appliance manufacturer may pay a $25 spiff to retail sales personnel for selling a certain model or size. In sales contests, salespeople can win trips or valuable merchandise for meeting certain goals established by the manufacturer. As shown in Figure 16–5, these incentives may be tied to product sales, new account placements, or merchandising efforts.

While contests and incentive programs can generate reseller support, they can also be a source of conflict between retail sales personnel and management. Some retailers want to maintain control over the selling activities of their sales staffs. They don't want their salespeople devoting an undue amount of effort to trying to win a contest or receive incentives offered by the manufacturer. Nor do they want their people becoming too aggressive in pushing products that serve their own interests instead of the product or model that is best for the customer.

Many retailers refuse to let their employees participate in manufacturer-sponsored contests or to accept incentive payments. Retailers that do allow them often have strict guidelines and require management approval of the program.

### Trade Allowances

Probably the most common trade promotion is some form of **trade allowance**, a discount or deal offered to retailers or wholesalers to encourage them to stock, promote, or display the manufacturer's products. Types of allowances offered to retailers include buying allowances, promotional or display allowances, and slotting allowances.

**Buying Allowances** A buying allowance is a deal or discount offered to resellers in the form of a price reduction on merchandise ordered during a fixed period. These discounts are often in the form of an **off-invoice allowance**, which means a certain per-case amount or percentage is deducted from the invoice. A buying allowance can also take the form of *free goods;* the reseller gets extra cases with the purchase of specific amounts (for example, 1 free case with every 10 cases purchased).

Buying allowances are used for several reasons. They are easy to implement and are well accepted, and sometimes expected, by the trade. They are also an effective way to encourage resellers to buy the manufacturer's product, since they will want to take advantage of the discounts being offered during the allowance period. Manufacturers offer trade discounts expecting wholesalers and retailers to pass the price reduction through to consumers, resulting in greater sales. However, as discussed shortly, this is often not the case.

**EXHIBIT 16–26**
Chicken of the Sea encourages retailers to use in-store displays of its products

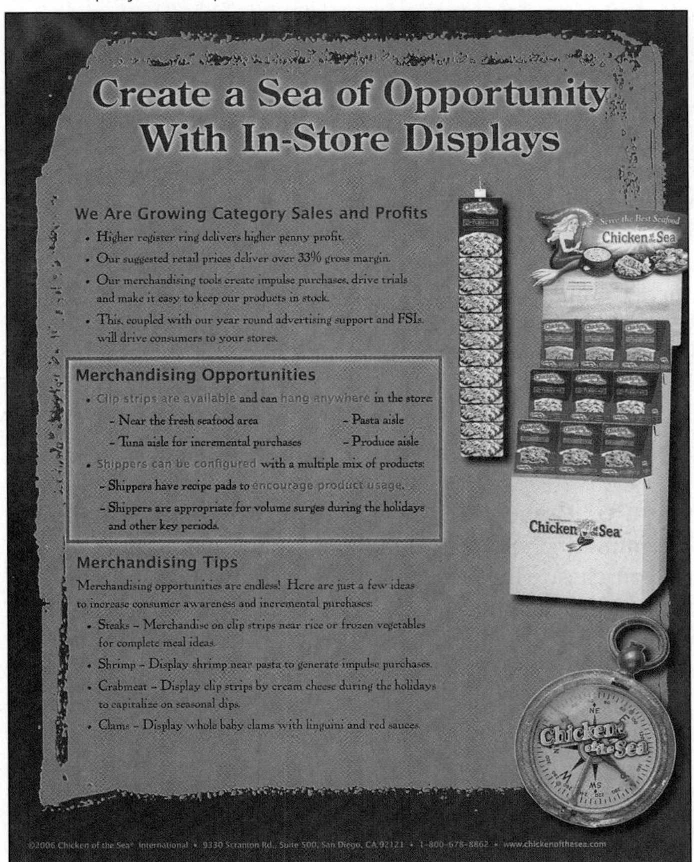


**Promotional Allowances** Manufacturers often give retailers allowances or discounts for performing certain promotional or merchandising activities in support of their brands. These merchandising allowances can be given for providing special displays away from the product's regular shelf position, running in-store promotional programs, or including the product in an ad. The manufacturer generally has guidelines or a contract specifying the activity to be performed to qualify for the promotional allowance. The allowance is usually a fixed amount per case or a percentage deduction from the list price for merchandise ordered during the promotional period.

Exhibit 16–26 shows a trade promotional piece used by Chicken of the Sea International to inform retailers of the merchandising opportunities available for its products and to encourage them to use in-store displays. An important goal of the company's trade marketing efforts is to get retailers to set up more displays of its products in various areas of their stores where related products are sold.

**Slotting Allowances** In recent years, retailers have been demanding a special allowance for agreeing to handle a new product. **Slotting allowances**, also called *stocking allowances, introductory allowances,* or *street money,* are fees retailers charge for providing a slot or position to accommodate the new product. Retailers justify these fees by pointing out the costs associated with taking on so many new products each year, such as redesigning store shelves, entering the product into their computers, finding warehouse space, and briefing store employees on the new product.[60] They also note they are assuming some risk, since so many new product introductions fail.

Slotting fees can range from a few hundred dollars per store to $50,000 or more for an entire retail chain. Manufacturers that want to get their products on the shelves nationally can face several million dollars in slotting fees. Many marketers believe slotting allowances are a form of blackmail or bribery and say some 70 percent of these fees go directly to retailers' bottom lines.

Retailers can continue charging slotting fees because of their power and the limited availability of shelf space in supermarkets relative to the large numbers of products introduced each year. Some retailers have even been demanding **failure fees** if a new product does not hit a minimum sales level within a certain time. The fee is charged to cover the costs associated with stocking, maintaining inventories, and then pulling the product.[61] Large manufacturers with popular brands are less likely to pay slotting fees than smaller companies that lack leverage in negotiating with retailers.

In 1999, the Senate Committee on Small Business began taking action against the practice of using slotting fees in the grocery, drugstore, and computer software industries because of the fees' negative impact on small business.[62] The committee recommended that the Federal Trade Commission and Small Business Administration take steps to limit the use of slotting fees because they are anticompetitive. A study by Paul Bloom, Gregory Gundlach, and Joseph Cannon examined the views of manufacturers, wholesalers, and grocery retailers regarding the use of slotting fees. Their findings suggest that slotting fees shift the risk of new product introductions from retailers to manufacturers and help apportion the supply and demand of new products. They also found that slotting fees lead to higher retail prices, are applied in a discriminatory fashion, and place small marketers at a disadvantage.[63]

**Displays and Point-of-Purchase Materials** The next time you are in a store, take a moment to examine the various promotional materials used to display and sell products. Point-of-purchase (POP) displays are an important promotional tool because they can help a manufacturer obtain more effective in-store merchandising of products. Companies in the United States spend more than $19 billion a year on point-of-purchase materials, including end-of-aisle displays, banners, posters, shelf cards, motion pieces, and stand-up racks, among others. Point-of-purchase displays are very important to marketers since many consumers make their purchase decisions in the store. In fact, some studies estimate that nearly two-thirds of a consumer's buying decisions are made in a retail store. Thus, it is very important for marketers to get the attention of consumers, as well as to communicate a sales or promotional message, through POP displays.

A measurement study from Point-of-Purchase Advertising International (an industry trade association) and the Advertising Research Foundation estimates that the cost-per-thousand-impressions figure for POPs is $6 to $8 for supermarket displays.[64] The CPM figure is based on findings that a grocery store display makes an average of 2,300 to 8,000 impressions per week, depending on store size and volume. Although this study has shown that POP displays are very effective at reaching consumers, difficulties in getting retail stores to comply with requests for displays often make it difficult for marketers to use them.[65] Moreover, many retailers are decreasing the amount of signage and displays they will accept as well as the messages they can communicate. Also, as account-specific promotions become more popular, some retailers are requiring customized POP materials. For example, 7-Eleven has taken over the responsibility for the production of all POP materials from vendors—who must still pay for them. The goal is to give 7-Eleven complete control over its in-store environment.

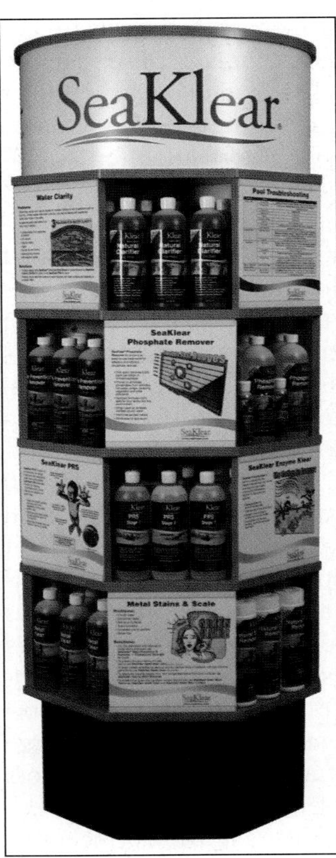


**EXHIBIT 16–27**
This award-winning point-of-purchase display plays an important role in the merchandising of SeaKlear pool and spa products

Despite these challenges, marketers recognize that point-of-purchase displays are an important part of their promotional programs. Many continue to develop innovative methods to display their products efficiently, make them stand out in the retail environment, and communicate a sales message to consumers. It should be noted that the importance of creative POP displays is not limited to grocery or convenience stores. Point-of-purchase displays are also important to companies that distribute their products through other types of retail outlets, such as home improvement, consumer electronic, and specialty retail stores. For example, Exhibit 16–27 shows an award winning POP display created by E-B Display Co. to promote the SeaKlear family of pool and spa treatments. The display holds 16 different pool and spa products and the unique octagonal shape allows for a 360° shoppable display in a relatively small footprint. The display also has large graphic areas to educate consumers regarding specific uses and applications and help them make their purchase decisions.

Many manufacturers help retailers use shelf space more efficiently through **planograms**, which are configurations of products that occupy a shelf section in a store. Some manufacturers are developing computer-based programs that allow retailers to input information from their scanner data and determine the best shelf layouts by experimenting with product movement, space utilization, profit yields, and other factors.[66]

**Sales Training Programs** Another form of manufacturer-sponsored promotional assistance is sales training programs for reseller personnel. Many products sold at the retail level require knowledgeable salespeople who can provide consumers with information about the features, benefits, and advantages of various brands and models. Cosmetics, appliances, computers, consumer electronics, and sporting equipment are examples of products for which consumers often rely on well-informed retail sales personnel for assistance.

Manufacturers provide sales training assistance to retail salespeople in a number of ways. They may conduct classes or training sessions that retail personnel can attend to increase their knowledge of a product or a product line. These training sessions present information and ideas on how to sell the manufacturer's product and may also include motivational components. Sales training classes for retail personnel are often sponsored by companies selling high-ticket items or complex products such as personal computers, cars, or ski equipment.

Another way manufacturers provide sales training assistance to retail employees is through their own sales force. Sales reps educate retail personnel about their product line and provide selling tips and other relevant information. The reps can provide ongoing sales training as they come into contact with retail sales staff members on a regular basis and can update them on changes in the product line, market developments, competitive information, and the like.

Manufacturers also give resellers detailed sales manuals, product brochures, reference manuals, and other material. Many companies provide videocassettes for

**EXHIBIT 16–28**
Trade shows are important for reaching retailers in many industries

retail sales personnel that include product information, product-use demonstrations, and ideas on how to sell their product. These selling aids can often be used to provide information to customers as well.

**Trade Shows** Another important promotional activity targeted to resellers is the **trade show**, a forum where manufacturers can display their products to current as well as prospective buyers. According to the Center for Exhibition Industry Research, more than 100 million people attend the nearly 15,000 trade shows each year in the United States and Canada, and the number of exhibiting companies exceeds 1.3 million. In many industries, trade shows are a major opportunity to display one's product lines and interact with customers. They are often attended by important management personnel from large retail chains as well as by distributors and other reseller representatives.

A number of promotional functions can be performed at trade shows, including demonstrating products, identifying new prospects, gathering customer and competitive information, and even writing orders for a product. Trade shows are particularly valuable for introducing new products, because resellers are often looking for new merchandise to stock. Shows can also be a source of valuable leads to follow up on through sales calls or direct marketing. The social aspect of trade shows is also important. Many companies use them to entertain key customers and to develop and maintain relationships with the trade. An academic study demonstrated that trade shows generate product awareness and interest and can have a measurable economic return.[67] For example, the International-Dairy-Deli-Bakery Association's annual seminar and expo is the leading trade show for manufacturers of dairy, deli, and bakery products. Companies competing in these industries attend the conference to show their new products, make new contacts, and learn about new ideas. Exhibit 16–28 shows the booth used by the California Milk Advisory Board at a recent IDDBA expo.

**Cooperative Advertising** The final form of trade-oriented promotion we examine is **cooperative advertising**, where the cost of advertising is shared by more than one party. There are three types of cooperative advertising. Although the first two are not trade-oriented promotion, we should recognize their objectives and purpose.

**Horizontal cooperative advertising** is advertising sponsored in common by a group of retailers or other organizations providing products or services to the market. For example, automobile dealers who are located near one another in an auto park or along the same street often allocate some of their ad budgets to a cooperative advertising fund. Ads are run promoting the location of the dealerships and encouraging car buyers to take advantage of their close proximity when shopping for a new automobile.

**Ingredient-sponsored cooperative advertising** is supported by raw materials manufacturers; its objective is to help establish end products that include the company's materials and/or ingredients. Companies that often use this type of advertising include Du Pont, which promotes the use of its materials such as Teflon, Thinsulate, and Kevlar in a variety of consumer and industrial products, and NutraSweet, whose artificial sweetener is an ingredient in many food products and beverages. Perhaps the best-known, and most successful, example of this type of cooperative advertising is the "Intel Inside" program, sponsored by Intel Corporation, which the company has been using since 1991.[68] Under this program, computer manufacturers get back 5 percent of what they pay Intel for microprocessors in return for showing the "Intel Inside" logo in their advertising as well as on their PCs. The monies received from Intel must be applied to ads paid for jointly by the PC maker and Intel. Nearly 90 percent of the PC print ads run in the United States carry the "Intel Inside" logo, and the program has helped Intel grow its share of the microprocessor market from 56 percent in 1990 to nearly 80 percent in 2007 (Exhibit 16–29). It is estimated that Intel spends several hundred million dollars each year on its cooperative advertising program. Intel recently made a significant change in the co-op program as companies that participate are now required to spend a minimum of 35 percent of the money that Intel provides on online marketing. The company made the mandated change in the media mix because its research shows that the major influences on consumers' purchasing decisions for personal computers come from some form of online media.[69]

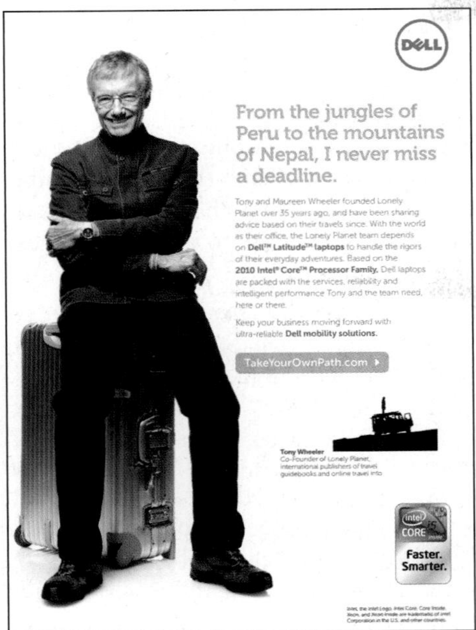


**EXHIBIT 16–29**
The "Intel Inside" cooperative advertising program has been extremely successful

The most common form of cooperative advertising is the trade-oriented form, **vertical cooperative advertising**, in which a manufacturer pays for a portion of the advertising a retailer runs to promote the manufacturer's product and its availability in the retailer's place of business. Manufacturers generally share the cost of advertising run by the retailer on a percentage basis (usually 50/50) up to a certain limit.

**EXHIBIT 16–30**
This Bridgestone Golf ad is an example of vertical cooperative advertising

"DON'T JUST PLAY WHAT THE PROS PLAY."
Retailer name/information goes here
Brandt Snedeker
Lee Trevino
PLAY A BALL THAT FITS YOUR GAME.
BRIDGESTONE GOLF
BRIDGESTONE GOLF
MORE DISTANCE FOR <105 MPH SWINGS.
MORE CONTROL FOR <105 MPH SWINGS.
The first ever Tour performance ball designed for amateur swing speeds is now a series. Introducing the all new RX with longer distance and the new RXS for added control. Now just like Tour players, you have a choice to play the best ball for your game.
FIT IT. BOOM IT. BELIEVE IT.
BRIDGESTONEGOLF.COM
BRIDGESTONE GOLF
PASSION for EXCELLENCE


The amount of cooperative advertising the manufacturer pays for is usually based on a percentage of dollar purchases. If a retailer purchases $100,000 of product from a manufacturer, it may receive 3 percent, or $3,000, in cooperative advertising money. Large retail chains often combine their co-op budgets across all of their stores, which gives them a larger sum to work with and more media options.

Cooperative advertising can take on several forms. Retailers may advertise a manufacturer's product in, say, a newspaper ad featuring a number of different products, and the individual manufacturers reimburse the retailer for their portion of the ad. Or the ad may be prepared by the manufacturer and placed in the local media by the retailer. Exhibit 16–30 shows a cooperative ad format for Bridgestone Golf that retailers in various market areas can use by simply inserting their store name and location.

Once a cooperative ad is run, the retailer requests reimbursement from the manufacturer for its percentage of the media costs. Manufacturers usually have specific requirements the ad must meet to qualify for co-op reimbursement, such as size, use of trademarks, content, and format. Verification that the ad was run is also required, in the form of a tearsheet (print) or an affidavit from the radio or TV station (broadcast) and an invoice.

As with other types of trade promotions, manufacturers have been increasing their cooperative advertising expenditures in recent years. Some companies have been moving money out of national advertising into cooperative advertising because they believe they can have greater impact with ad campaigns in local markets. There is also a trend toward more cooperative advertising programs initiated by retailers, which approach manufacturers with catalogs, promotional events they are planning, or advertising programs they have developed in conjunction with local media and ask them to pay a percentage of the cost. Manufacturers often go along with these requests, particularly when the retailer is large and powerful.[70]

# COORDINATING SALES PROMOTION WITH ADVERTISING AND OTHER IMC TOOLS

Those involved in the promotional process must recognize that sales promotion techniques usually work best in conjunction with advertising and other integrated marketing tools and that the effectiveness of an IMC campaign can be enhanced by consumer-oriented sales promotion efforts. Rather than separate activities competing for a firm's promotional budget, advertising and sales promotion should be viewed as complementary tools. When properly planned and executed to work together, advertising and sales promotion can have a *synergistic effect* much greater than that of either promotional mix element alone.

Proper coordination of sales promotion with other IMC tools is essential for the firm to take advantage of the opportunities offered by each and get the most out of its promotional budget. Successful integration of advertising and sales promotion requires decisions concerning not only the allocation of the budget to each area but also the coordination of the ad and sales promotion themes, proper media support for, and timing of, the various promotional activities, and the target audience reached.

## Budget Allocation

While many companies are spending more money on sales promotion than on media advertising, it is difficult to say just what percentage of a firm's overall promotional budget should be allocated to advertising versus consumer- and trade-oriented promotions. This allocation depends on a number of factors, including the specific promotional objectives of the campaign, the market and competitive situation, and the brand's stage in its life cycle.

Consider, for example, how allocation of the promotional budget may vary according to a brand's stage in the product life cycle. In the introductory stage, a large amount of the budget may be allocated to sales promotion techniques such as sampling and couponing to induce trial. In the growth stage, however, promotional dollars may be used primarily for advertising to stress brand differences and keep the brand name in consumers' minds.

When a brand moves to the maturity stage, advertising is primarily a reminder to keep consumers aware of the brand. Consumer-oriented sales promotions such as coupons, price-offs, premiums, and bonus packs may be needed periodically to maintain consumer loyalty, attract new users, and protect against competition. Trade-oriented promotions are needed to maintain shelf space and accommodate retailers' demands for better margins as well as encourage them to promote the brand. A study on the synergistic effects of advertising and promotion examined a brand in the mature phase of its life cycle and found that 80 percent of its sales at this stage were due to sales promotions. When a brand enters the decline stage of the product life cycle, most of the promotional support will probably be removed and expenditures on sales promotion are unlikely.

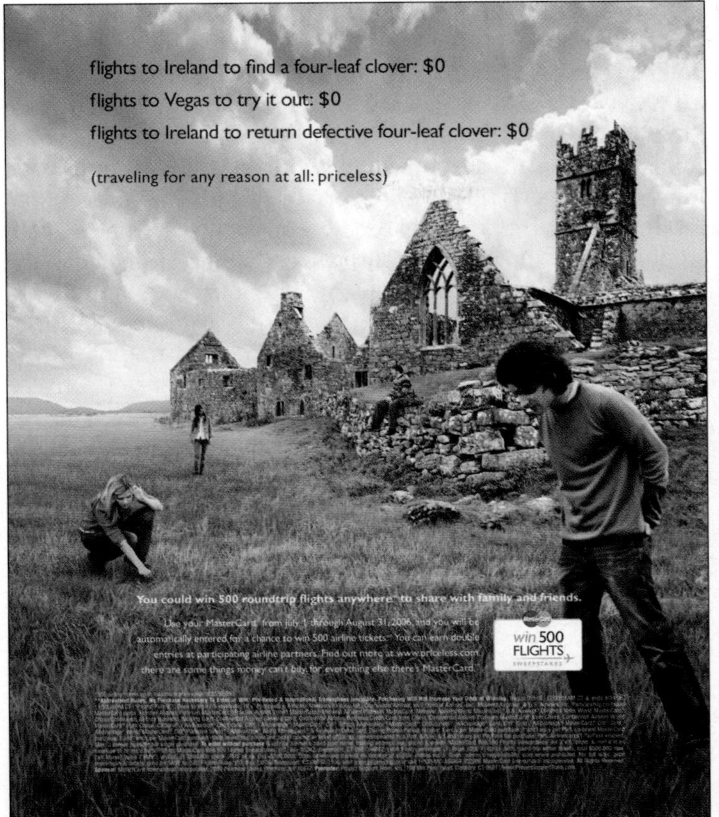

flights to Ireland to find a four-leaf clover: $0
flights to Vegas to try it out: $0
flights to Ireland to return defective four-leaf clover: $0
(traveling for any reason at all: priceless)
You could win 500 roundtrip flights anywhere to share with family and friends.
Use your MasterCard from July 1 through August 31, 2006, and you will be automatically entered for a chance to win 500 airline tickets. You can earn double entries at participating airline partners. Find out more at www.priceless.com.
there are some things money can't buy. for everything else there's MasterCard.
win 500 FLIGHTS
SWEEPSTAKES


**EXHIBIT 16–31**
MasterCard used media advertising to promote the "Win 500 Flights" sweepstakes

## Coordination of Ad and Promotion Themes

To integrate the advertising and sales promotion programs successfully, the theme of consumer promotions should be tied in with the positioning platform for the company and/or their brand wherever possible. Sales promotion tools should attempt to communicate a brand's unique attributes or benefits and to reinforce the sales message or advertising campaign theme. In this way, the sales promotion effort contributes to the consumer franchise-building effort for the brand.

At the same time, media advertising and other IMC tools should be used to draw attention to a sales promotion program such as a contest, sweepstakes, or event or to a special promotion offer such as a price reduction or rebate program. An excellent example of this is the award-winning "Win 500 Flights" sweepstakes that was developed by MasterCard and its promotional agency, Armstrong Partnership. The sweepstakes was developed under the umbrella of MasterCard's "Priceless" campaign theme and thus was designed to deliver on the brand promise that MasterCard understands what matters most to consumers—in this case traveling for any reason at all. The primary objective of the integrated marketing campaign was to drive MasterCard use during the key summer travel season. Consumers using their MasterCard from July 1 to August 31 were automatically entered in the sweepstakes for a chance to win 500 airline tickets to anywhere that could be shared with family and friends. Media advertising including television, print, out-of-home, and online banner ads were used to promote the sweepstakes, along with an extensive public relations campaign. Exhibit 16–31 shows one of the print ads used to promote the "Win 500 Flights" sweepstakes.

## Media Support and Timing

Media support for a sales promotion program is critical and should be coordinated with the media program for the ad campaign. Media advertising is often needed to deliver such sales promotion materials as coupons, sweepstakes, contest entry forms, premium offers, and even samples. It is also needed to inform consumers of a promotional offer as well as to create awareness, interest, and favorable attitudes toward the brand.

By using advertising in conjunction with a sales promotion program, marketers can make consumers aware of the brand and its benefits and increase their responsiveness to the promotion. Consumers are more likely to redeem a coupon or respond to a price-off deal for a brand they are familiar with than one they know nothing about. Moreover, product trial created through sales promotion techniques such as sampling or high-value couponing is more likely to result in long-term use of the brand when accompanied by advertising.[71]

Using a promotion without prior or concurrent advertising can limit its effectiveness and risk damaging the brand's image. If consumers perceive the brand as being promotion dependent or of lesser quality, they are not likely to develop favorable attitudes and long-term loyalty. Conversely, the effectiveness of an ad can be enhanced by a coupon, a premium offer, or an opportunity to enter a sweepstakes or contest.

An example of the effective coordination of advertising and sales promotion is the introductory campaign Unilever developed for its Dove Men+Care line in early 2010. Unilever sent samples of the body and face wash product to more than half the households in the United States along with high value coupons and also used trade promotions targeted to retailers as part of its introductory marketing blitz (Exhibit 16–32). The sales promotion efforts were accompanied by heavy advertising in print and on television including a commercial in the Super Bowl and a follow-up spot featuring New Orleans Saints quarterback Drew Brees, who won the game's MVP award, using the new product while showering.[72] The launch campaign included the use of additional IMC tools including public relations, mobile marketing and digital and social media. A few months after the launch, Unilever used "An Ultimate Baseball Experience" sweepstakes to help drive trials of the new product line.

To coordinate their advertising and sales promotion programs more effectively, many companies are getting their sales promotion agencies more involved in the advertising and promotional planning process. Rather than hiring agencies to develop individual, nonfranchise-building types of promotions with short-term goals and tactics, many firms are having their sales promotion and advertising agencies work together to develop integrated promotional strategies and programs. Figure 16–6 shows how the role of promotional agencies is changing.

## SALES PROMOTION ABUSE

LO 16-5

The increasing use of sales promotion in marketing programs is more than a passing fad. It is a fundamental change in strategic decisions about how companies market their products and services. The value of this increased emphasis on sales promotion has been questioned by several writers, particularly with regard to the lack of adequate planning and management of sales promotion programs.[73]

Are marketers becoming too dependent on this element of the marketing program? As was discussed in IMC Perspective 16–1, consumer and trade promotions can be a very effective tool for generating short-term increases in sales, and many brand managers would rather use a promotion to produce immediate sales than invest in advertising and build the brand's image over an extended time. As the director of sales promotion services at one large ad agency noted: "There's a great temptation for quick sales fixes through promotions. It's a lot easier to offer the consumer an immediate price savings than to differentiate your product from a competitor's."[74]

Overuse of sales promotion can be detrimental to a brand in several ways. A brand that is constantly promoted may lose perceived value. Consumers often end up purchasing a brand because it is on sale, they get a premium, or they have a coupon, rather than basing their decision on a favorable attitude they have developed. When the extra promotional incentive is not available, they switch to another brand. A study by Priya Raghubir and Kim Corfman examined whether price promotions affect pretrial evaluations of a brand.[75] They found that offering a price promotion is more likely to lower a brand's evaluation when the brand has not been promoted previously compared to when it has been frequently promoted; that price promotions are used as a source of information about a brand to a greater extent when the evaluator is not an expert but does have some product or industry knowledge; and that promotions are more likely to result in negative evaluations when they are uncommon in the industry. The findings from this study suggest that marketers must be careful in the use of price promotions as they may inhibit trial of a brand in certain situations.

**EXHIBIT 16–32**
Unilever's launch of its Dove Men+Care line involved the coordination of advertising and sales promotion along with other IMC tools

| Traditional | New and Improved |
|---|---|
| 1. Primarily used to develop short-term tactics or concepts. | 1. Used to develop long- and short-term promotional strategies as well as tactics. |
| 2. Hired/compensated on a project-by-project basis. | 2. Contracted on annual retainer, following formal agency reviews. |
| 3. Many promotion agencies used a mix—each one hired for best task and/or specialty. | 3. One or two exclusive promotion agencies for each division or brand group. |
| 4. One or two contact people from agency. | 4. Full team or core group on the account. |
| 5. Promotion agency never equal to ad agency—doesn't work up front in annual planning process. | 5. Promotion agency works on equal basis with ad agency—sits at planning table up front. |
| 6. No directly accountable for results. | 6. Very much accountable—goes through a rigorous evaluation process. |

**FIGURE 16–6**
The Shifting Role of the Promotion Agency

Alan Sawyer and Peter Dickson have used the concept of *attribution theory* to examine how sales promotion may affect consumer attitude formation.[76] According to this theory, people acquire attitudes by observing their own behavior and considering why they acted in a certain manner. Consumers who consistently purchase a brand because of a coupon or price-off deal may attribute their behavior to the external promotional incentive rather than to a favorable attitude toward the brand. By contrast, when no external incentive is available, consumers are more likely to attribute their purchase behavior to favorable underlying feelings about the brand.

Another potential problem with consumer-oriented promotions is that a **sales promotion trap** or spiral can result when several competitors use promotions extensively.[77] Often a firm begins using sales promotions to differentiate its product or service from the competition. If the promotion is successful and leads to a differential advantage (or even appears to do so), competitors may quickly copy it. When all the competitors are using sales promotions, this not only lowers profit margins for each firm but also makes it difficult for any one firm to hop off the promotional bandwagon.[78] This dilemma is shown in Figure 16–7.

A number of industries have fallen into this promotional trap. In the cosmetics industry, gift-with-purchase and purchase-with-purchase promotional offers were developed as a tactic for getting buyers to sample new products. But they have become a common, and costly, way of doing business.[79] In many areas of the country, supermarkets have gotten into the trap of doubling or even tripling manufacturers' coupons, which cuts into their already small profit margins. Fast-food chains have also fallen into the trap with promotions featuring popular menu items for 99 cents

**FIGURE 16–7**
The Sales Promotion Trap

| | Our Firm | |
|---|---|---|
| All Other Firms | Cut back promotions | Maintain promotions |
| Cut back promotions | Higher profits for all | Market share goes to our firm |
| Maintain promotions | Market share goes to all other firms | Market share stays constant; profits stay low |

CHAPTER 16

**EXHIBIT 16–33**
Wendy's promotes its Value Meals

or one dollar. Fast-food companies such as McDonald's use their dollar menus to offer options to budget-conscious consumers and provide them with consistent everyday values. McDonald's has been ahead of many of its competitors in terms of promoting its value menu and has had popular items such as its double cheeseburger on the menu since its introduction in 2003. However, competitors such as Burger King and Wendy's have recently put popular items on their value meal menus in an effort to keep pace with the industry leader[80] (Exhibit 16–33).

Marketers must consider both the short-term impact of a promotion and its long-term effect on the brand. The ease with which competitors can develop a retaliatory promotion and the likelihood of their doing so should also be considered. Marketers must be careful not to damage the brand franchise with sales promotions or to get the firm involved in a promotional war that erodes the brand's profit margins and threatens its long-term existence. Marketers are often tempted to resort to sales promotions to deal with declining sales and other problems when they should examine such other aspects of the marketing program as channel relations, price, packaging, product quality, or advertising.

After reading this chapter you can see that there are a number of factors that marketers must consider in developing and implementing effective sales promotion programs as they involve much more than just offering consumers an extra economic incentive to purchase a product. Priya Raghub, Jeffrey Inman, and Hans Grande suggest that there are three aspects to consumer promotions including economic, informative, and affective effects.[81] They note that in addition to economic effects, marketers must consider the information and signals a promotional offer conveys to the consumer as well as the affective influences. These include the consumer feelings and emotions aroused by exposure to a promotion or associated with purchasing the brand or company that is offering a deal. By considering all of these effects, managers can design and communicate consumer promotions more efficiently as well as more effectively.

## Summary

For many years, advertising was the major promotional mix element for most consumer-product companies. Over the past two decades, however, marketers have been allocating more of their promotional dollars to sales promotion. There has been a steady increase in the use of sales promotion techniques to influence consumers' purchase behavior. The growing power of retailers, erosion of brand loyalty, increase in consumers' sensitivity to promotions, increase in new product introductions, fragmentation of the consumer market, short-term focus of marketing and brand managers, and increase in advertising clutter are some of the reasons for this increase.

Sales promotions can be characterized as either franchise building or nonfranchise building. The former contribute to the long-term development and reinforcement of brand identity and image; the latter are designed to accelerate the purchase process and generate immediate increases in sales.

Sales promotion techniques can be classified as either trade- or consumer-oriented. A number of consumer-oriented sales promotion techniques were examined in this chapter, including sampling, couponing, premiums, contests and sweepstakes, rebates and refunds, bonus packs, price-off deals, loyalty programs, and event marketing. The characteristics of these promotional tools were examined, along with their advantages and limitations. Various trade-oriented promotions were also examined, including trade contests and incentives, trade allowances, displays and point-of-purchase materials, sales training programs, trade shows, and cooperative advertising.

Advertising and sales promotion should be viewed not as separate activities but rather as complementary tools. When planned and executed properly, advertising and sales promotion can produce a synergistic effect that is greater than the response generated from either promotional mix element alone. To accomplish this, marketers must coordinate budgets, advertising and promotional themes, media scheduling and timing, and target audiences.

Sales promotion abuse can result when marketers become too dependent on the use of sales promotion techniques and sacrifice long-term brand position and image for short-term sales increases. Many industries experience sales promotion traps when a number of competitors use promotions extensively and it becomes difficult for any single firm to cut back on promotion without risking a loss in sales. Overuse of sales promotion tools can lower profit margins and threaten the image and even the viability of a brand.

## Key Terms

**sales promotion** p. 520
**consumer-oriented sales promotion** p. 521
**trade-oriented sales promotion** p. 521
**account-specific marketing** p. 526
**consumer franchise-building (CFB) promotions** p. 528
**nonfranchise-building (non-FB) promotions** p. 530
**sampling** p. 533
**bounce-back coupon** p. 540
**cross-ruff coupon** p. 540
**instant coupon** p. 540
**in-store couponing** p. 540
**premium** p. 542
**self-liquidating premiums** p. 543
**contest** p. 545
**sweepstakes** p. 546
**game** p. 546
**refund** p. 547
**bonus packs** p. 549
**price-off deal** p. 550
**loyalty programs** p. 552
**event marketing** p. 553
**event sponsorship** p. 553
**push money** p. 557
**trade allowance** p. 557
**off-invoice allowance** p. 557
**slotting allowance** p. 558
**failure fees** p. 558
**planograms** p. 559
**trade show** p. 560
**cooperative advertising** p. 560
**horizontal cooperative advertising** p. 560
**ingredient-sponsored cooperative advertising** p. 560
**vertical cooperative advertising** p. 561
**sales promotion trap** p. 565

## Discussion Questions

1. Why do you think Subway's $5 Footlong promotion has been so successful? What factors will determine how long Subway can continue to run the promotion? (LO1)
2. IMC Perspective 16–1 discusses the problems Macy's encountered when it tried to cut back on the use of discount coupons. Analyze the company's decision to abandon its strategy to wean its customers off discount coupons. Do you think they should have given the new strategy more time to take effect before abandoning it? (LO1)
3. What are some of the reasons marketing and brand managers are allocating more of their promotional budget to sales promotion rather than media advertising? Do you agree with critics who argue that the increased use of sales promotion is undermining brand equity for many once-powerful brands? (LO1)
4. What is the difference between a consumer franchise-building promotion and a nonfranchise-building promotion? Find an example of a promotion being used by a company that contributes to the equity of the brand and explain how it does so. (LO2)
5. Evaluate the effectiveness of coupons as a sales promotion tool. How would you respond to critics who argue that they are inefficient since less than 2 percent of coupons are redeemed? (LO3)
6. Discuss the type of company that would be likely to offer discounts to consumers using Groupon.com. What are the pros and cons of a company using this type of promotional offer? (LO3)
7. Discuss the role the Internet is playing with regard to sales promotion. Why are many companies moving promotions such as contests and sweepstakes online? (LO3)
8. Discuss what marketers can do to avoid some of the promotional problems discussed in IMC Perspective 16–2. Do you think the problems that KFC experienced with their coupon promotion in China could have been avoided? (LO3)
9. A recent report by a rebate fulfillment service showed that the average redemption rate for a $50 rebate on a product that costs $200 is only 35 percent. Why do you think redemption rates for rebates are so low? How might these low redemption rates affect a marketer's decision regarding the use of rebates as a promotional tool? (LO3)
10. Describe the various forms of cooperative advertising and the reasons they are used by marketers. (LO3)
11. What is meant by a sales promotion trap or spiral? Evaluate the promotional war that has developed in the fast-food industry as the various competitors promote their 99 cents or dollar menus. What are the options for companies in deciding whether to participate in the promotional war? (LO5)

## AdForum Exercise: "Evaluating Advertising Used for Promotions"

### PART 1

The chapter opener discusses the very successful "Five Dollar Footllong" promotion that Subway has been running for several years. Watch the two Subway commercials provided on the playlist that were created to promote the $5 offer. Discuss the role commercials such as these play in determining the success of the "Five Dollar Footlong" promotion. Do you think the $5 promotion would have been as successful without this type of advertising support? Why or why not?

### PART 2

IMC Perspective 16-1 discusses how Macy's, which is one of the premier retailers in the United States, has become very dependent upon price promotions and "One-day sales" to drive store traffic and revenue. The playlist for Chapter 16 includes three commercials used as part of the national advertising done by Macy's. Watch these three commercials and answer the following questions:

1 Discuss the objectives of each commercial and the role it plays in Macy's overall marketing strategy.

2 How does the "Come Together" commercial differ from the other two spots ("Fourth of July" and "Blues Break")? How might commercials such as the "Come Together" spot help Macy's become less dependent on the use of price-based promotions?

Access to the chapter playlist is available through connect™ MARKETING, www.mcgrawhillconnect.com

A temporary pause. To put you first.

**Why we've temporarily stopped some of our plants:**

As you may have heard, in rare cases, sticking accelerator pedals have occurred in some of our vehicles. We believe we are close to announcing an effective remedy. And we've temporarily halted production at some of our North American plants to focus on the vehicles we've recalled. Why have we taken this unprecedented action? Because it's the right thing to do for our customers.

To find out if your Toyota is affected and to get the very latest information about the recall, please visit:

**toyota.com**

Toyota Customer Experience Center
1-800-331-4331

## LEARNING OBJECTIVES

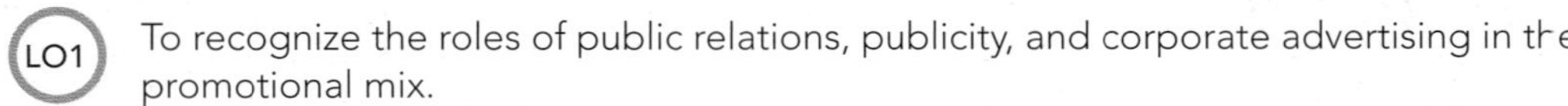

LO1 To recognize the roles of public relations, publicity, and corporate advertising in the promotional mix.

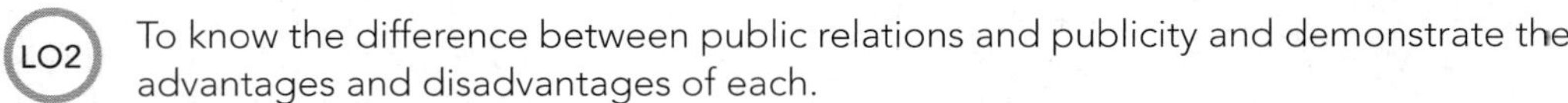

LO2 To know the difference between public relations and publicity and demonstrate the advantages and disadvantages of each.

LO3 To understand the reasons for corporate advertising and its advantages and disadvantages.

LO4 To know the methods for measuring the effects of public relations, publicity, and corporate advertising.

LO5 To understand the different forms of corporate advertising.

# 17 Public Relations, Publicity, and Corporate Advertising

## PUBLIC RELATIONS COMPANIES WORK OVERTIME AND WITH NEW MEDIA TO SOLVE PUBLICITY NIGHTMARES

From a public relations standpoint, the stars must be out of alignment. Perhaps at no other time in the history of the United States has there been two major public relations nightmares in such a short period of time. While PR people have an old saying, "Expect the worst," neither Toyota or BP could have anticipated what was to come. Nor could the traditional public relations agencies have imagined the role both traditional and new media would play.

*Toyota*—Let's start with Toyota, one of the world's most respected automobile brands, which had built its reputation on quality and reliability. An automobile accident in San Diego, California, in which four members of a family were killed in a Lexus while the driver was on a 911 call saying he could not get the car to stop, started the problem. The word quickly spread that there were accelerator sticking problems in other Toyota vehicles as well. Toyota's initial attempt to blame the problem on poor fitting floormats wasn't being bought. Things only got worse, additional problems surfaced, and over a period of months, the auto giant voluntarily recalled millions of vehicles.

Toyota's initial response to the crisis was considered by many to be poorly handled. After first attempting to blame the floormats, Toyota seemed reluctant to admit there was a problem and assume responsibility for handling it. The anticipated traditional deep bow and apology never came. However, as time went on, the PR efforts took root. Toyota apologized and employed a substantial IMC campaign designed to restore consumers' faith in the company. A television commercial was created specifically to address the crisis, acknowledging that Toyota had let down its customers when it came to safety, but also focusing on their half-century of selling quality cars in the United States. A radio spot was also created—media employing both Spanish language and English versions. Newspaper ads were also run talking about how Toyota dealers were working around the clock to make repairs. The website provided continual updates and an answer to commonly held questions. To reach their younger audiences, the company posted the TV commercial on YouTube, and the U.S. sales manager held a live chat at Digg.com. Additional messages were conveyed through social networking sites. The results showed the efforts to be quite successful as Toyota sales rose by 41% the first month after the negative publicity hit.

*BP*—If Toyota was having a bad dream, BP was having a nightmare of major proportions. An oil well explosion and burst pipe at the Deepwater Horizon well spilled an estimated 4.9 million barrels of oil into the Gulf of Mexico off the coast of Louisiana. The problem took 87 days to correct, and the oil slick created by almost three months of leakage spread as far away as Florida—killing wildlife and polluting pristine beaches along the way. CEO Tony Hayward was replaced, and the company reported a $17.2 billion quarterly loss.

BP's response was more immediate than Toyota's but has lasted much longer. The company took a very aggressive approach, holding news conferences, constantly updating the media as to what was happening, and so on. Like Toyota, BP also took to the Internet. Those who went to Google to search for information about the spill would likely notice a banner ad at the top of the page sponsored by BP. Clicking on the banner would link them to a microsite explaining what efforts BP was taking to stop the leak. Ads also appeared on YouTube and Facebook. The information response hub set up in the Gulf of Mexico fed information through Twitter, Facebook, YouTube, and Flickr. Traditional advertising appeared in print and on television (which was criticized by some as an inappropriate expenditure given the cost of the cleanup). BP established facilities in the stricken area in an attempt to compensate those whose businesses and/or jobs have been affected and established a $20 billion compensation fund for those impacted by the spill. To support BP, numerous organizations have devoted time, effort, and money to help out in the cleanup effort. In the meantime, BP has lost more than half of its stock value, and a lot more than that in image, as the spill has become the worst in U.S. history.

At this point, the longterm results of these efforts are still to be determined. For Toyota, things seem to be working out, as sales after experiencing slight negative downturns quickly rebounded, and the company's image is improving. For BP, it's another story; protests continued in the U.S. and Britain for months. Now that the problem itself is solved, the PR efforts will need to be continued for a long time, to clean up that mess.

Sources: Shirley Brady, "BP Confirms CEO Exit, Record Loss," www.brandchannel.com, July 27, 2010; Dale Buss, "Toyota Brand May Be Bouncing Back Already," www.brandchannel.com, April 2, 2010; Noreen O'Leary, "How Toyota Helped Digg Itself Out of Major Trouble," www.brandweek.com, April 4, 2010; Brian Morrissey, "Beleaguered BP Is Getting Aggressive via Social Media," www.adweek.com, June 20, 2010; Chris Woodyard, "Toyota PR Blitz Plays Catch-up after Storm of Problems," www.USA.com, February 10, 2010; Patricia Faulhaber, "Toyota's Messages about Recall Troubles," www.corporate-marketing-branding-suite101.com, February 10, 2010.

The lead-in to this chapter clearly demonstrates the power of publicity—which can be positive or negative. The results often directly impact the companies involved financially as well as in respect to trust, image, and other nonfinancial aspects. As you will see in this chapter, publicity is often out of the control of the marketer, but increasingly the management of publicity is being adopted as a marketing strategy. While attempts to generate positive publicity are nothing new, as these efforts increase, they signify changes in the public relations functions of companies and organizations. Although the importance and role of public relations in the IMC program may be argued, one thing is clear: The role of public relations in the communications program has changed. Like every other aspect of IMC, the public relations function has been changed by the Internet and other new media. While some people may disagree as to the importance and power of this program element, few, if any, would contend that it is business as usual.

LO 17-1

Publicity, public relations, and corporate advertising all have promotional program elements that may be of great benefit to marketers. They are integral parts of the overall promotional effort that must be managed and coordinated with the other elements of the promotional mix. However, these three tools do not always have the specific objectives of product and service promotion, nor do they always involve the same methods you have become accustomed to as you have read this text. Typically, these activities are designed more to change attitudes toward an organization or issue than to promote specific products or affect behaviors directly (though you will see that this role is changing in some organizations). This chapter explores the roles of public relations, publicity, and corporate advertising, the advantages and disadvantages of each, and the process by which they are employed.

# PUBLIC RELATIONS

What is public relations? How does it differ from other elements of marketing discussed thus far? Perhaps a good starting point is to define what the term *public relations* has traditionally meant and then to introduce its new role.

## The Traditional Definition of PR

A variety of books define **public relations (PR)**, but perhaps the most comprehensive definition is that offered by the *Public Relations News* (the weekly newsletter of the industry):

> [T]he management function which evaluates public attitudes, identifies the policies and procedures of an organization with the public interest, and executes a program of action (and communication) to earn public understanding and acceptance.[1]

Public relations is indeed a management function. The term *management* should be used in its broadest sense; it is not limited to business management but extends to other types of organizations, including nonprofit institutions.

In this definition, public relations requires a series of stages, including:

1. The determination and evaluation of public attitudes.
2. The identification of policies and procedures of an organization with a public interest.
3. The development and execution of a communications program designed to bring about public understanding and acceptance.

This process does not occur all at once. An effective public relations program continues over months or even years.

Finally, this definition reveals that public relations involves much more than activities designed to sell a product or service. The PR program may involve some of the promotional program elements previously discussed but use them in a different way. For example, companies may send press releases to announce new products or changes in the organization, companies may organize special events to create goodwill in the community, and companies may use advertising to state the firm's position on a controversial issue.

## The New Role of PR

An increasing number of marketing-oriented companies have established new responsibilities for public relations. PR takes on a much broader (and more marketing-oriented) perspective, designed to promote the organization as well as its products and/or services.

The way that companies and organizations use public relations might best be viewed as a continuum. On one end of the continuum is the use of PR from a traditional perspective. In this perspective, public relations is viewed as a nonmarketing function whose primary responsibility is to maintain mutually beneficial relationships between the organization and its publics. In this case, customers or potential customers are only part of numerous publics—employees, investors, neighbors, special-interest groups, and so on. Marketing and public relations are separate departments; if external agencies are used, they are separate agencies. At the other end of the continuum, public relations is considered primarily a marketing communications function. All noncustomer relationships are perceived as necessary only in a marketing context.[2] In these organizations, public relations reports to marketing. At the same time, for many companies the PR function is moving more and more toward a new role, which is much closer to a marketing function than a traditional one.

In the new role of public relations, managers envision both strong marketing and strong PR departments. Rather than each department operating independently, the two work closely together, blending their talents to provide the best overall image of the firm and its product or service offerings. As noted by Jonah Bloom, there has always been a cultural gulf separating the two departments, but today's information age demands the two camps work together. As noted by Bloom, "You'll struggle to peddle your eco-friendly detergent if your company is being slammed for pouring chemicals into a river."[3] In a poll conducted among members of the Public Relations Society of America (PRSA) and subscribers to *PR News,* 76 percent of respondents stated that they regularly work with the marketing department; 78 percent thought that the marketing department had a positive perception of the PR department, and an equal number indicated the same perception about marketing. While the degree of coordination differed by activity, the study clearly reflects coordination and cooperation.[4]

Writing in *Advertising Age,* William N. Curry notes that organizations must use caution in establishing this relationship because PR and marketing are not the same thing, and when one department becomes dominant, the balance required to operate at maximum efficiency is lost.[5] He says losing sight of the objectives and functions of public relations in an attempt to achieve marketing goals may be detrimental in the long run. Others take an even stronger view that if public relations and marketing distinctions continue to blur, the independence of the PR function will be lost, and it will become much less effective.[6] In fact, as noted by Cutlip, Center, and Broom, marketing and public relations are complementary functions, "with each making unique but complementary contributions to building and maintaining the many relationships essential for organizational survival and growth. To ignore one is to risk failure in the other."[7] This position is consistent with our perception that public relations is an important part of the IMC process, contributing in its own way but also in a way consistent with marketing goals.

## Integrating PR into the Promotional Mix

Given the broader responsibilities of public relations, the issue is how to integrate it into the promotional mix. Companies have a number of ways in which they organize the marketing and public relations functions. Others may outsource the public relations to outside agencies. In this text we regard public relations as an IMC program element. This means that its broad role must include traditional responsibilities, as well as new ones.

Whether public relations takes on a traditional role or a more marketing-oriented one, PR activities are still tied to specific communications objectives. Assessing public attitudes and creating a favorable corporate image are no less important than promoting products or services directly.

## Marketing Public Relations Functions

Thomas L. Harris has referred to public relations activities designed to support marketing objectives as **marketing public relations (MPR)** functions.[8] Marketing objectives that may be aided by public relations activities include raising awareness, informing and educating, gaining understanding, building trust, giving consumers a reason to buy, and motivating consumer acceptance. MPR adds value to the integrated marketing program in a number of ways:

- *Building marketplace excitement before media advertising breaks.* The announcement of a new product, for example, is an opportunity for the marketer to obtain publicity and to dramatize the product, thereby increasing the effectiveness of ads. When Apple introduces any new product from the iPod to the iPad, a great deal of anticipation is created through public relations prior to the availability of the product. The result is that Apple receives a great deal of press coverage and word of mouth. It seems that upon release of any Apple product, consumers wait in lines—sometime for hours—to be the first to own the next innovation.
- *Improving ROI.* By reducing overall marketing costs, while at the same time delivering meaningful marketing outcomes, MPRs help improve ROI.
- *Creating advertising news where there is no product news.* Ads themselves can be the focus of publicity. There seems to be as much hype about the ads on the Super Bowl as there is for the game itself. TV commercials frequently find their ways to social sites on the Internet where they are viewed time and time again and forwarded to others.
- *Introducing a product with little or no advertising.* This strategy has been implemented successfully by a number of companies, including Hewlett-Packard, Segway, Ty, Crayola, and, of course, Apple. Among others, Gillette uses PR as the lead medium in every new product launch.

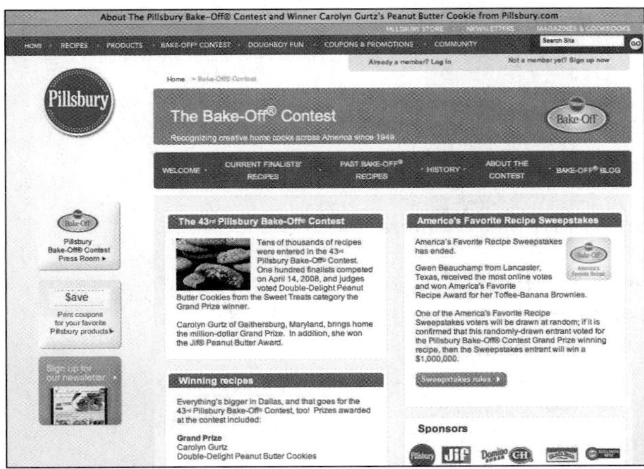

**EXHIBIT 17–1**
The Pillsbury Bake Off has generated positive results since 1949

- *Providing a value-added customer service.* Butterball established a hotline where people can call in to receive personal advice on how to prepare their turkeys. The company handled 25,000 calls during the first holiday season. Many companies provide such services on their Internet sites. Chicken of the Sea provides recipes to visitors of its site (which, of course, suggest using Chicken of the Sea tuna).
- *Building brand-to-customer bonds.* The Pillsbury Bake-Off has led to strong brand loyalty among Pillsbury customers, who compete by submitting baked goods. The contest has taken place annually since 1949, and the winner now receives a $1 million prize! The winning recipes are posted on the Pillsbury website (Exhibit 17–1).
- *Influencing the influentials.* That is, providing information to opinion leaders.

- *Defending products at risk and giving consumers a reason to buy.* By taking constructive actions to defend or promote a company's products, PR can actually give consumers a reason to buy the products. Energizer's national education campaign that urged consumers to change the batteries in their fire alarms when they reset their clocks in the fall resulted in a strong corporate citizen image and increased sales of batteries. Cessna's campaign to convince executives that there are legitimate reasons to buy corporate jets (Exhibit 17–2) is an excellent example of defending a product at risk (Figure 17–1).

**FIGURE 17–1**
Companies Use MPRs

*Cessna*

During the auto industry sales slump, top executives of Detroit's Big Three car companies went to the nation's capital to ask for a bailout. When the execs traveled by private plane rather than drive, the lawmakers and press bashed them for it. Unfortunately, the backlash had a profound negative effect on jet manufacturers, as numerous orders were canceled or deferred. Production was cut by as much as 56%, and as much as one-third of the industry's workers were laid off. One company, Cessna, decided to fight back and give corporate America a reason to buy.

In a hard hitting print campaign starting in *The Wall Street Journal* called "Rise," Cessna challenged business leaders to not be timid, and recognize private planes are not about ego, but about having the right tools to be productive. Cessna said it was time for the other side of the story to be told . In addition to *The Wall Street Journal,* the ads were run in national business newspapers and magazines as well as aviation trade journal, together with an extensive PR campaign.

*Starbucks*

When McDonald's ran a billboard ad attacking Starbucks' four-dollar coffee prices, many marketers thought that the coffee chain would fight back. Instead, Starbucks took the "high road." Rather than directly responding to the McDonald's campaign, Starbucks ran a commercial on the *Saturday Night Live* show just before election day, advertising that they would give out free coffee on November 4, and another ad on CNN and the Weather Channel on the Wednesday before Thanksgiving letting consumers know they would be donating portions of the profits from coffee sales to help African AIDS victims. They also took the philanthropic messages to YouTube, Twitter, and Facebook, believing consumers are now less vain and more conscientious, and would be more likely to respond positively. Interviewed by CBS's Katie Couric, Starbucks' CEO Howard Schultz emphasized that the coffee giant would not respond to competitors' frivolous campaigns.

*KFC*

In an attempt to rebound struggling sales, KFC called in the giant of publicity—Oprah Winfrey—to help out. As most marketers know, sales for anything that Oprah says good things about takes off like a rocket. KFC tied in with the megastar to give away coupons for free samples of their new "Kentucky Grilled Chicken." The response was overwhelming—actually, too much so. The KFC website was overwhelmed by downloads of the coupons, and stores had to turn people away due to the rush. Much of this activity could be attributed to a viral announcement on Twitter. As noted by one marketing expert, the combination of free food and Oprah led to a tsunami—a tsunami of bad publicity for KFC. So the company offered a second promotion, this time a better managed one. More free meals were given away, and KFC hit number 1 on Twitter's trending topics.

**FIGURE 17–2**

Advantages and Disadvantages of MPRs

Sources: Thomas L. Harris, "Marketing PR—The Second Century," Reputation Management, www.prcentral.com, January/February 1999, pp. 1–6.

*Advantages*

- It is a cost-effective way to reach the market.
- It is a highly targeted way to conduct public relations.
- It benefits from the endorsement of independent and objective third parties who have no association with the product.
- It achieves credibility.
- It supports advertising programs by making messages more credible.
- It breaks through the clutter.
- It circumvents consumer resistance to sales efforts.
- There can be improved media involvement among consumers.
- It can create influence among opinion leaders and trendsetters.
- It can improve ROI.

*Disadvantages*

- There is a lack of control over the media.
- It is difficult to tie in slogans and other advertising devices.
- Media time and space are not guaranteed.
- There are no standard effectiveness measures.

As shown in Figure 17–2, Harris notes that there are a number of advantages of using MPRs.

One of the major threats of using an MPR structure, as expressed by Harris, is that public relations functions may become subservient to marketing efforts—a concern expressed by many opponents of MPR. However, if employed properly and used in conjunction with other traditional public relations practices as well as IMC elements, MPR can continue to be used effectively. Weiner also notes that the key to the successful use of MPRs is integration with IMC, though such a task may prove to be difficult to accomplish.

**EXHIBIT 17–2**

Cessna attempts to aid a product at risk

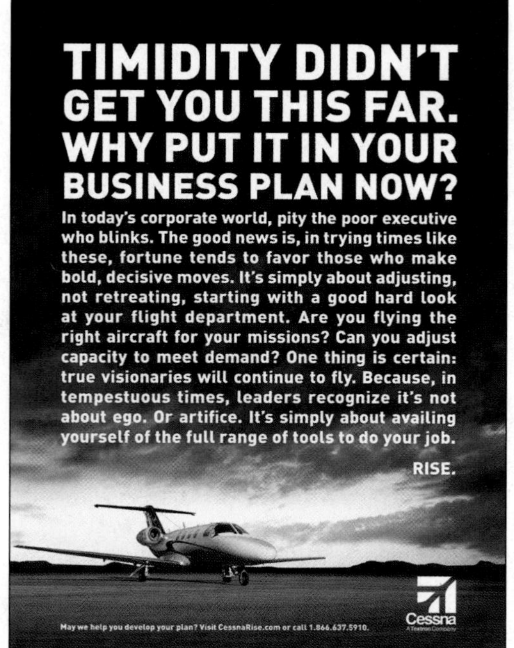


# THE PROCESS OF PUBLIC RELATIONS

The actual process of conducting public relations and integrating it into the promotional mix involves a series of both traditional and marketing-oriented tasks.

## Determining and Evaluating Public Attitudes

You have learned that public relations is concerned with people's attitudes toward the firm or specific issues beyond those directed at a product or service. The first question you may ask is why. Why is the firm so concerned with the public's attitudes?

One reason is that these attitudes may affect sales of the firm's products. A number of companies have experienced sales declines as a result of consumer boycotts. BP, Nestle, Nokia, and Walmart are just a few companies that have had to respond to organized pressures. Likewise, the media must be concerned with the attitudes of the public. When *Fox News*, which is owned by NewsCorp, announced that they would air an interview with O. J. Simpson during sweeps titled "O. J. Simpson: If I Did It, Here's How It Happened" (in regard to accusations that he murdered his wife), a number of Fox affiliates immediately announced they would not carry the program, and media salespersons refused to sell advertising time. In addition, thousands of irate TV watchers e-mailed and phoned local Fox affiliates, as well as NewsCorp, causing them to pull the program, in spite of an estimated loss of $10 million in revenue.[9]

On the other hand, companies can gain favorable impressions and positive attitudes from consumers by doing the right thing. Exhibit 17–3 shows a message sent by Netflix.com as an apology for a late product shipment due to a system failure. The customer was credited 10 percent for the inconvenience. The apology was used as an example of great customer service by bloggers, and created positive attitudes for Netflix.

Second, no one wants to be perceived as a bad citizen. Corporations exist in communities, and their employees generally both work and live there. Negative attitudes carry over to employee morale and may result in a less-than-optimal working environment internally and in the community.

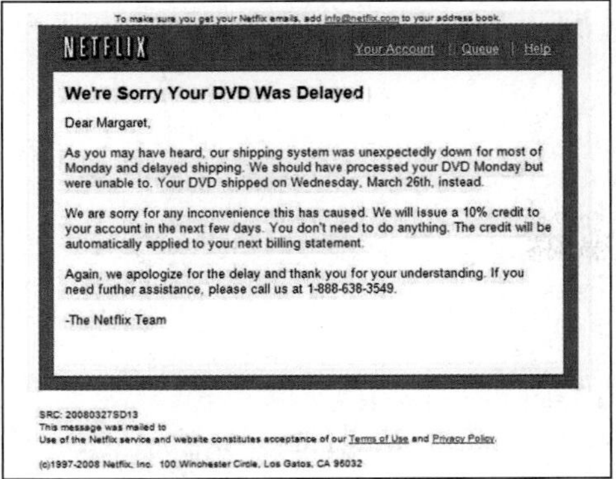
To make sure you get your Netflix emails, add info@netflix.com to your address book.

NETFLIX — Your Account | Queue | Help

**We're Sorry Your DVD Was Delayed**

Dear Margaret,

As you may have heard, our shipping system was unexpectedly down for most of Monday and delayed shipping. We should have processed your DVD Monday but were unable to. Your DVD shipped on Wednesday, March 26th, instead.

We are sorry for any inconvenience this has caused. We will issue a 10% credit to your account in the next few days. You don't need to do anything. The credit will be automatically applied to your next billing statement.

Again, we apologize for the delay and thank you for your understanding. If you need further assistance, please call us at 1-888-638-3549.

-The Netflix Team

SRC: 20080327SD13
This message was mailed to
Use of the Netflix service and website constitutes acceptance of our Terms of Use and Privacy Policy.

(c)1997-2008 Netflix, Inc. 100 Winchester Circle, Los Gatos, CA 95032

**EXHIBIT 17–3**
Netflix gained favor with an e-mail apology

Due to their concerns about public perceptions, many privately held corporations, publicly held companies, utilities, and media survey public attitudes. The reasons for conducting this research are many, but include the following:

1. *It provides input into the planning process.* Once the firm has determined public attitudes, they become the starting point in the development of programs designed to maintain favorable positions or change unfavorable ones.
2. *It serves as an early warning system.* Once a problem exists, it may require substantial time and money to correct. By conducting research, the firm may be able to identify potential problems and handle them effectively before they become serious issues.
3. *It secures support internally.* If research shows a problem or potential problem exists, it will be much easier for the public relations arm to gain the support it needs to address this problem.
4. *It increases the effectiveness of the communication.* The better it understands a problem, the better the firm can design communications to deal with it.

## Establishing a PR Plan

For some companies, their PR programs involve little more than press releases, press kits for trade shows, and new product announcements. Further, these tools are often not designed into a formal public relations effort but rather are used only as needed. In other words, no structured program for conducting PR is evident. As we noted earlier, the public relations process is an ongoing one, requiring formalized policies and procedures for dealing with problems and opportunities. Just as you would not develop an advertising and/or a promotions program without a plan, you should not institute public relations efforts haphazardly. Moreover, the PR plan needs to be integrated into the overall marketing communications program. Figure 17–3 provides some questions marketers should ask to determine whether their PR plan is workable.

Cutlip, Center, and Broom suggest a four-step process for developing a public relations plan: (1) define public relations problems, (2) plan and program, (3) take action and communicate, and (4) evaluate the program.[10] The questions in Figure 17–3 and the four-step planning process tie in with the promotional planning process stressed throughout this text.

## Developing and Executing the PR Program

Because of the broad role that public relations may be asked to play, the PR program may need to extend beyond promotion. A broader definition of the target market, additional communications objectives, and different messages and delivery systems may be employed. Let us examine this process.

**FIGURE 17–3**
Ten Questions for Evaluating Public Relations Plans

1. Does the plan reflect a thorough understanding of the company's business situation?
2. Has the PR program made good use of research and background sources?
3. Does the plan include full analysis of recent editorial coverage?
4. Do the PR people fully understand the product's strengths and weaknesses?
5. Does the PR program describe several cogent, relevant conclusions from the research?
6. Are the program objectives specific and measurable?
7. Does the program clearly describe what the PR activity will be and how it will benefit the company?
8. Does the program describe how its results will be measured?
9. Do the research, objectives, activities, and evaluations tie together?
10. Has the PR department communicated with marketing throughout the development of the program?

**Determining Relevant Target Audiences** The targets of public relations efforts may vary, with different objectives for each. Some may be directly involved in selling the product; others may affect the firm in a different way (e.g., they may be aimed at stockholders or legislators). These audiences may be internal or external to the firm.

**Internal audiences** may include the employees, stockholders, and investors of the firm as well as members of the local community, suppliers, and current customers. As noted in Figure 17–1, Cessna's public relations programs were designed, in part, to reach buyers as well as to improve morale among employees. Why are community members and customers of the firm considered internal rather than external? According to John Marston, it's because these groups are already connected with the organization in some way, and the firm normally communicates with them in the ordinary routine of work.[11] **External audiences** are those people who are not closely connected with the organization (e.g., the public at large).

It may be necessary to communicate with these groups on an ongoing basis for a variety of reasons, ranging from ensuring goodwill to introducing new policies, procedures, or even products. A few examples may help.

**EXHIBIT 17–4**
An example of a newsletter used for internal communication by the College of Business Administration at San Diego University

MAY/JUNE 2010

insideBUSINESS

SDSU COLLEGE OF BUSINESS ADMINISTRATION

**SDSU College of Business Names New Associate Dean**

SDSU'S COLLEGE OF BUSINESS Administration announced the appointment of Dr. Gangaram Singh as the new associate dean for academic affairs. Singh replaces the retiring Dr. Jim Lackritz and will assume his new role on July 1, 2010.

As the associate dean for academic affairs, Singh's responsibilities will include overseeing curriculum and faculty development; supervising academic processes and policies; formulating and managing student policies; and administering the College's accreditation activities.

Singh has been with the SDSU as a professor of management since 1999. During that time, he served as chairman of the College's management department, director of the Center for International Business Education and Research (CIBER), has taught in the Sports Management M.B.A. and the Executive M.B.A. programs, and has been the recipient of numerous awards, honors and grants.

Singh has served on numerous committees and programs at SDSU and was recently named to the city of San Diego's Citizen Revenue Review and Economic Competitiveness Commission. He also sits on the marketing committee of the board of Sharp Hospital and has been deeply involved in founding several local cricket programs. Singh earned his Ph.D.in Industrial Relations from the University of Toronto in 1998.

SAN DIEGO STATE UNIVERSITY
College of Business Administration
*Leadership for the Global Marketplace*

**ALUMNI SPOTLIGHT: ROBERT SCHULTE AND MARC STAHELI**

IT'S A COMMON SCENARIO: A COUPLE OF GUYS that have been friends for years decide to go into business together. They don't know what the business will be, but they know each other very well. So they sit down, determine their business plan, raise the capital and away they go.

This is NOT how Taxcient founders, Robert Schulte ('05, M.B.A.) and Marc Staheli ('01, information services; '05, M.S.B.A.), started their business.

Separately, they each had a plan – they just needed to meet each other for their plans to fall into place.

Staheli had earned an accounting degree in his native Switzerland and had just completed his bachelor's degree in information systems at SDSU. He was working within SDSU's enterprise technology systems group, but realized that he wanted start his own company. "I pursued a master's degree in entrepreneurship because I felt I had the energy and desire to create a company from scratch, either by myself or with a couple of motivated self-starters," he said. He also knew that he wanted "to pursue a technology-related career."

Enter Robert Schulte.

After working as an auditor for the state of California, Schulte already had a game plan. "I purposefully went back to get my graduate degree in entrepreneurship to meet someone who could help me build Taxcient," said Schulte.

The two met in the spring of 2003 during their business plan development course (Management 743) which was taught management professor Dr. Alex DeNoble. "I met Marc in our very first class and we

(. . . CONTINUED ON PAGE 2)

www.sdsu.edu/business tel: (619) 594-5259 fax: (619) 594-1573 email: business@sdsu.edu

**Employees of the Firm** Maintaining morale and showcasing the results of employees' efforts are often prime objectives of the public relations program. Organizational newsletters, notices on bulletin boards, awards ceremonies and events, direct mail, and annual reports are some of the methods used to communicate with these groups. Exhibit 17–4 shows one such internal communication used by the College of Business Administration at San Diego University.

Personal methods of communicating may be as formal as an established grievance committee or as informal as an office Christmas party. Other social events, such as corporate bowling teams or picnics, are also used to create goodwill.

**Stockholders and Investors** You may think an annual report like the one in Exhibit 17–5 provides stockholders and investors only with financial information regarding the firm. While this is one purpose, annual reports are also a communications channel for informing this audience about why the firm is or is not doing well, outlining future plans, and providing other information that goes beyond numbers.

It has become very common for companies to use annual reports for public relations purposes—to generate additional investments, to bring more of their stocks "back home" (i.e., become more locally controlled and managed), and to produce funding to solve specific problems, as well as to promote goodwill.

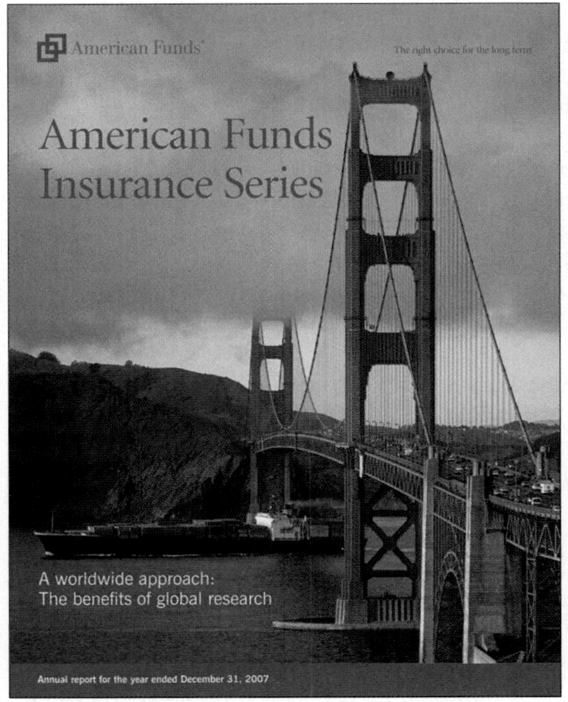


**EXHIBIT 17–5**
Annual reports serve a variety of purposes

**Community Members** People who live and work in the community where a firm is located or doing business are often the target of public relations efforts. Such efforts may involve ads informing the community of activities that the organization is engaged in, for example, reducing air pollution, cleaning up water supplies, or preserving wetlands. (The community can be defined very broadly.) As you can see in Exhibit 17–6, a number of oil companies are involved in this form of public relations, by demonstrating to people that the organization is a good citizen with their welfare in mind.

**Suppliers and Customers** An organization wishes to maintain *goodwill* with its suppliers as well as its consuming public. If consumers think a company is not socially conscious, they may take their loyalties elsewhere. Suppliers may be inclined to do the same.

Sometimes sponsoring a public relations effort results in direct evidence of success. Certainly KFC achieved their goal of getting consumers to try their product. Indirect indications of the success of PR efforts may include more customer loyalty, less antagonism, or greater cooperation between the firm and its suppliers or consumers.

Public relations efforts are often targeted to more than one group, and are a direct result of concerns initiated in the marketplace. As noted earlier, along with potential consumers, trade association members, human resource directors, buyers, and suppliers often constitute the target audience for PR efforts.

Relevant audiences may also include people not directly involved with the firm. The press, educators, civic and business groups, governments, and the financial community can be external audiences.

**EXHIBIT 17–6**
Citgo demonstrates concern for the community

**The Media** Perhaps one of the most critical external publics is the media, which determine what you will read in your newspapers or see on TV, and how this news will be presented. Because of the media's power, they should be informed of the firm's actions. Companies issue press releases and communicate through conferences, interviews, and special events. The media are generally receptive to such information as long as it is handled professionally; reporters are always interested in good stories. In turn, the media are also concerned about how the community perceives them.

**Educators** A number of organizations provide educators with information regarding their activities. The Direct Marketing Association, the Promotional Products Association, and the Outdoor Advertising Association, among others, keep educators informed in an attempt to generate goodwill as well as exposure for their causes. These groups and major

**EXHIBIT 17–7**
The Yellow Pages provide information about the medium

corporations provide information regarding innovations, state-of-the-art research, and other items of interest. The Yellow Pages Association provides materials including case examples and lecture notes specifically designed for educators (Exhibit 17–7).

Educators are a target audience because, like the media, they control the flow of information to certain parties—in this case, people like you. *BusinessWeek,* and *Fortune* magazines attempt to have professors use their magazines in their classes, as does *The Wall Street Journal, The New York Times,* and *Advertising Age,* among others. In addition to selling more magazines, such usage also lends credibility to the media.

**Civic and Business Organizations** The local Jaycees, Kiwanis, and other nonprofit civic organizations also serve as gatekeepers of information. Companies' financial contributions to these groups, speeches at organization functions, and sponsorships are all designed to create goodwill. Corporate executives' service on the boards of nonprofit organizations also generates positive public relations.

**Governments** Public relations often attempts to influence government bodies directly at both local and national levels. Successful lobbying may mean immediate success for a product, while regulations detrimental to the firm may cost it millions. Imagine for a moment what FDA approval of a product can mean for sales, or what could happen to the beer and wine industries if TV advertising were banned. The pharmaceutical industry lobbied hard for permission to advertise prescription drugs directly to the consumer. Within the first five years of approval, an estimated 65 million consumers approached their doctors to inquire about the drugs as a result.[12] In turn, environmentalists, trade unions, and other groups with specific agendas will attempt to influence government legislation in their behalf.

**Financial Groups** In addition to current shareholders, potential shareholders and investors may be relevant target markets for PR efforts. Financial advisors, lending institutions, and others must be kept abreast of new developments as well as of financial information, since they offer the potential for new sources of funding. Press releases and corporate reports play an important role in providing information to these publics.

**EXHIBIT 17–8**
NOAA press release

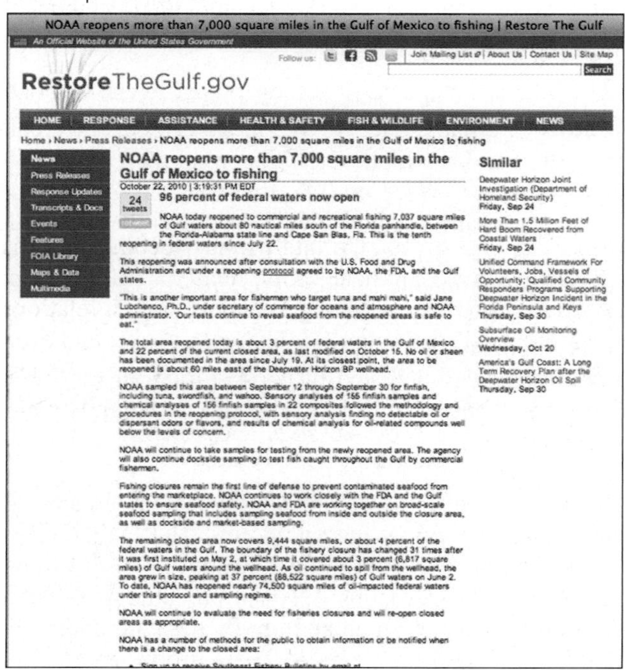
NOAA reopens more than 7,000 square miles in the Gulf of Mexico to fishing | Restore The Gulf

An Official Website of the United States Government

Follow us: | Join Mailing List | About Us | Contact Us | Site Map

Search

RestoreTheGulf.gov

HOME | RESPONSE | ASSISTANCE | HEALTH & SAFETY | FISH & WILDLIFE | ENVIRONMENT | NEWS

Home › News › Press Releases › NOAA reopens more than 7,000 square miles in the Gulf of Mexico to fishing

News
Press Releases
Response Updates
Transcripts & Docs
Events
Features
FOIA Library
Maps & Data
Multimedia

NOAA reopens more than 7,000 square miles in the Gulf of Mexico to fishing

October 22, 2010 | 3:19:31 PM EDT

24 tweets

96 percent of federal waters now open

NOAA today reopened to commercial and recreational fishing 7,037 square miles of Gulf waters about 80 nautical miles south of the Florida panhandle, between the Florida-Alabama state line and Cape San Blas, Fla. This is the tenth reopening in federal waters since July 22.

This reopening was announced after consultation with the U.S. Food and Drug Administration and under a reopening protocol agreed to by NOAA, the FDA, and the Gulf states.

"This is another important area for fishermen who target tuna and mahi mahi," said Jane Lubchenco, Ph.D., under secretary of commerce for oceans and atmosphere and NOAA administrator. "Our tests continue to reveal seafood from the reopened areas is safe to eat."

The total area reopened today is about 3 percent of federal waters in the Gulf of Mexico and 22 percent of the current closed area, as last modified on October 15. No oil or sheen has been documented in the area since July 19. At its closest point, the area to be reopened is about 60 miles east of the Deepwater Horizon BP wellhead.

NOAA sampled this area between September 12 through September 30 for finfish, including tuna, swordfish, and wahoo. Sensory analyses of 155 finfish samples and chemical analyses of 156 finfish samples in 22 composites followed the methodology and procedures in the reopening protocol, with sensory analysis finding no detectable oil or dispersant odors or flavors, and results of chemical analysis for oil-related compounds well below the levels of concern.

NOAA will continue to take samples for testing from the newly reopened area. The agency will also continue dockside sampling to test fish caught throughout the Gulf by commercial fishermen.

Fishing closures remain the first line of defense to prevent contaminated seafood from entering the marketplace. NOAA continues to work closely with the FDA and the Gulf states to ensure seafood safety. NOAA and FDA are working together on broad-scale seafood sampling that includes sampling seafood from inside and outside the closure area, as well as dockside and market-based sampling.

The remaining closed area now covers 9,444 square miles, or about 4 percent of the federal waters in the Gulf. The boundary of the fishery closure has changed 31 times after it was first instituted on May 2, at which time it covered about 3 percent (6,817 square miles) of Gulf waters around the wellhead. As oil continued to spill from the wellhead, the area grew in size, peaking at 37 percent (88,522 square miles) of Gulf waters on June 2. To date, NOAA has reopened nearly 74,500 square miles of oil-impacted federal waters under this protocol and sampling regime.

NOAA will continue to evaluate the need for fisheries closures and will re-open closed areas as appropriate.

NOAA has a number of methods for the public to obtain information or be notified when there is a change to the closed area:

Similar

Deepwater Horizon Joint Investigation (Department of Homeland Security)
Friday, Sep 24

More Than 1.5 Million Feet of Hard Boom Recovered from Coastal Waters
Friday, Sep 24

Unified Command Framework For Volunteers, Jobs, Vessels of Opportunity; Qualified Community Responders Programs Supporting Deepwater Horizon Incident in the Florida Peninsula and Keys
Thursday, Sep 30

Subsurface Oil Monitoring Overview
Wednesday, Oct 20

America's Gulf Coast: A Long Term Recovery Plan after the Deepwater Horizon Oil Spill
Thursday, Sep 30

**Implementing the PR Program** Once the research has been conducted and the target audiences identified, the public relations program must be developed and delivered to the receivers. A number of PR tools are available for this purpose, including press releases, press conferences, exclusives, interviews, and community involvement.

**The Press Release** One of the most important publics is the press. To be used by the press, information must be factual, true, and of interest to the medium as well as to its audience. The source of the **press release** can do certain things to improve the likelihood that the "news" will be disseminated, such as ensuring that it reaches the right target audience, making it interesting, and making it easy to pass along (Exhibit 17–8).

The information in a press release won't be used unless it is of interest to the users of the medium it is sent to. For

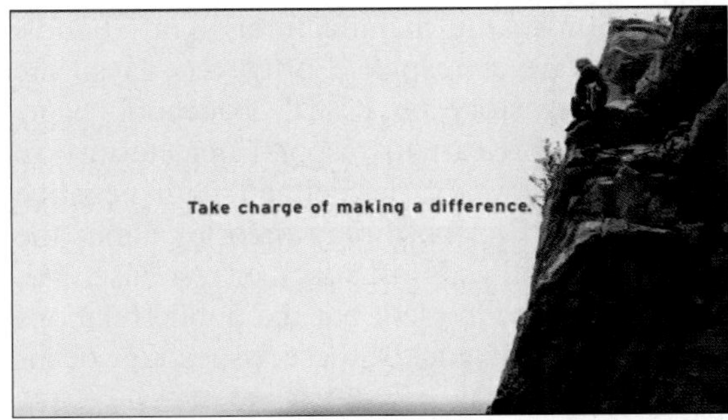

**EXHIBIT 17–9**
American Express gets involved in philanthropic projects

example, financial institutions may issue press releases to business trade media and to the editor of the business section of a general-interest newspaper. Organizations like the PRNewswire and PRLog.org provide services to help disseminate information.

**Press Conferences** We are all familiar with **press conferences** held by political figures. Although used less often by organizations and corporations, this form of delivery can be very effective. The topic must be of major interest to a specific group before it is likely to gain coverage. Usually major accomplishments (such as the awarding of the next Super Bowl or Olympics location), major breakthroughs (such as medical cures), emergencies, or catastrophes warrant a national press conference. On a local level, community events, local developments, and the like may receive coverage. Companies often call press conferences when they have significant news to announce, such as the introduction of a new product or advertising campaign. Sports teams use this tool to attract fan attention and interest when a new star is signed.

**Exclusives** Although most public relations efforts seek a variety of channels for distribution, an alternative strategy is to offer one particular medium exclusive rights to the story if that medium reaches a substantial number of people in the target audience. Offering an **exclusive** may enhance the likelihood of acceptance. As you watch television over the next few weeks, watch for the various networks' and local stations' exclusives. Notice how the media actually use these exclusives to promote themselves.

**Interviews** When you watch TV or read magazines, pay close attention to the personal interviews. Usually someone will raise specific questions, and a spokesperson provided by the firm will answer them. Apple's Steve Jobs appeared in an interview to discuss purported problems with the iPhone 4, while the CEO of BP appeared numerous times to address the Gulf of Mexico oil spill.

**Community Involvement** Many corporations enhance their public image through involvement in the local community. This involvement may take many forms, including membership in local organizations like the Kiwanis or Jaycees and contributions to or participation in community events (Exhibit 17–9).

**The Internet** As mentioned briefly in Chapter 15, the Internet has become a means by which companies and organizations can disseminate public relations information. Just as in the print media, companies have used the Web to establish media relations and government, investor, and community relationships; to deal with crises; and even to conduct cause marketing. Companies have used their websites to address issues, as well as to provide information about products and services, archive press releases, link to other articles and sites, and provide lists of activities and events.

**Social Networks and Blogs** More and more companies and organizations are making use of social networks, blogs, and other 2.0 media (discussed in Chapter 15) for public relations purposes. It is now expected that companies will post information on their websites providing announcements and updates on product releases, recalls, or other issues. In addition, many of these companies are using 2.0 media to disseminate this information as well. Apple made valuable use of blogs and social networks to announce the release of its new iPhone 4, as did Motorola with the Droid X and Sprint. New product information and other news is now a common practice.

At the same time, these new media have required that the public relations functions for their organizations be constantly updated. Within hours after the release of the iPhone 4, information was circulating in regard to technical issues that led to dropped calls. The blogosphere was alive with information, requests, and proposals for solutions and even accusations that Apple knew about the problem before the phone's release.[13] In another instance, a mother reported a problem with Capri Sun to the manufacturer, Kraft Foods. When she did not receive a response after ten days, she posted an account of her story on Kraft's Facebook page. In the seven hours it took Kraft to respond (an eternity in social media time!) Kraft was overwhelmed with negative comments, rumors, and even conspiracy theories about the cause of the problem, as well as Kraft's lack of response. The problem was subsequently addressed, but the public relations problem is reflective of how quickly these issues can occur in today's viral world.[14]

**EXHIBIT 17–10**
Edward Jones promotes its J.D. Power Award

## Advantages and Disadvantages of PR

Like the other program elements, public relations has both advantages and disadvantages.

Advantages include the following:

1. *Credibility.* Because public relations communications are not perceived in the same light as advertising—that is, the public does not realize the organization either directly or indirectly paid for them—they tend to have more credibility. The fact that the media are not being compensated for providing the information may lead receivers to consider the news more truthful and credible. For example, an article in newspapers or magazines discussing the virtues of aspirin may be perceived as much more credible than an ad for a particular brand of aspirin.

   Automotive awards presented in magazines such as *Motor Trend* have long been known to carry clout with potential car buyers. The influential J.D. Power awards are now offered for a variety of reasons (quality, customer satisfaction, service, etc.) in a variety of industries (automobile, financial services, airports, etc.). It has become a common practice for car companies and others to promote their achievements (Exhibit 17–10).

   News about a product may in itself serve as the subject of an ad. Exhibit 17–11 demonstrates how General Mills used favorable publicity from a variety of sources to promote the importance of whole grain in a healthy diet and promote the use of whole grain in its cereals.
2. *Cost.* In both absolute and relative terms, the cost of public relations is very low, especially when the possible effects are considered. While a firm can employ public relations agencies and spend millions of dollars on PR, for smaller companies this form of communication may be the most affordable alternative available. As noted, many services exist to distribute this information at little or no cost. Many public relations programs require little more than the time and expenses associated with putting the program together and getting it distributed, yet they still accomplish their objectives.
3. *Avoidance of clutter.* Because they are typically perceived as news items, public relations messages are not subject to the clutter of ads. A story regarding a new

product introduction or breakthrough is treated as a news item and is likely to receive attention.

4. *Lead generation.* Information about technological innovations, medical breakthroughs, and the like results almost immediately in a multitude of inquiries. These inquiries may give the firm some quality sales leads.
5. *Ability to reach specific groups.* Because some products appeal to only small market segments, it is not feasible to engage in advertising and/or promotions to reach them. If the firm does not have the financial capabilities to engage in promotional expenditures, the best way to communicate to these groups is through public relations. Social networks and blogs have become extremely valuable in this regard.
6. *Image building.* Effective public relations helps to develop a positive image for the organization. A strong image is insurance against later misfortunes. The strength of the Toyota brand name made it possible for Toyota to get through its recent crisis. The ad in Exhibit 17–12 demonstrates how a company can take advantage of a strong brand image.

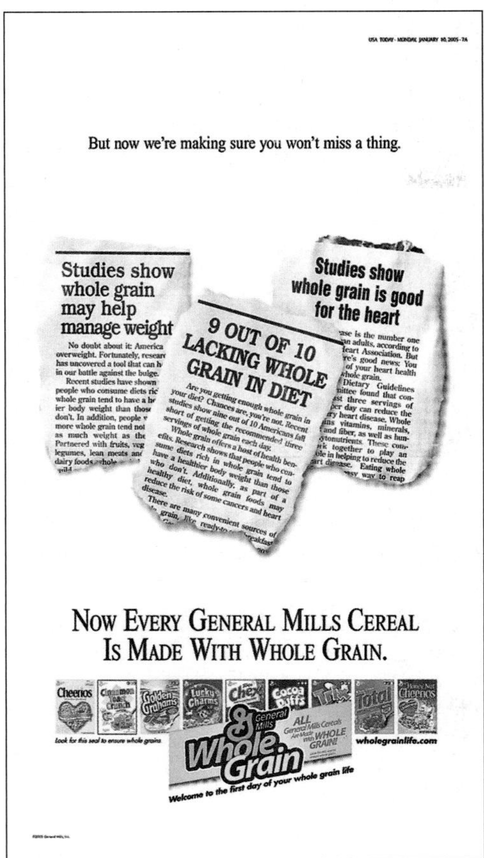


**EXHIBIT 17–11**
General Mills capitalizes on positive publicity

Perhaps the major disadvantage of public relations is the potential for not completing the communications process. While public relations messages can break through the clutter of commercials, the receiver may not make the connection to the source. Many firms' PR efforts are never associated with their sponsors in the public mind.

Public relations may also misfire through mismanagement and a lack of coordination with the marketing department. When marketing and PR departments operate independently, there is a danger of inconsistent communications, redundancies in efforts, and so on.

The key to effective public relations is to establish a good program, worthy of public interest, and to manage it properly. To determine if this program is working, the firm must measure the effectiveness of the PR effort.

**EXHIBIT 17–12**
This Maserati ad demonstrates the value of a strong brand and/or corporate image

**FIGURE 17–4**

Criteria for Measuring the Effectiveness of PR

A system for measuring the effectiveness of the public relations program has been developed by Lotus HAL. The criteria used in the evaluation process follow:

- Total number of impressions over time
- Total number of impressions on the target audience
- Total number of impressions on specific target audiences
- Percentage of positive articles over time
- Percentage of negative articles over time
- Ratio of positive to negative articles
- Percentage of positive/negative articles by subject
- Percentage of positive/negative articles by publication or reporter
- Percentage of positive/negative articles by target audience

## Measuring the Effectiveness of PR

As with the other promotional program elements, it is important to evaluate the effectiveness of the public relations efforts. In addition to determining the contribution of this program element to attaining communications objectives, the evaluation offers other advantages:

1. It tells management what has been achieved through public relations activities.
2. It provides management with a way to measure public relations achievements quantitatively.
3. It gives management a way to judge the quality of public relations achievements and activities.

As outlined in Figure 17–4 a number of criteria may be used to measure the effects of PR programs. Walter Lindenmann recommends that in measuring the effectiveness of a public relations campaign consider whether the target audience (1) *received* the messages, (2) paid *attention* to them, (3) *understood* the messages, and (4) *retained* the messages in any shape or form.[15] Figure 17–5 shows the results of a study conducted in an attempt to determine how public relations professionals currently go about this process. (Note: the study was conducted in the E.U., but as the authors note, the results may be generalized to the United States, the U.K., and other developed countries, as a similar usage pattern exists).[16] Take a minute or two to examine the results of this study in respect to the criteria suggested by Lindenmann.

Mark Weiner, in discussing measures of effectiveness of MPRs, also suggests using the following methods:[17]

- *Media content analysis.* Systematically and objectively identifying the characteristics of messages that appear in the media, analyzing the content to determine trends and perceptions relevant to the product or brand.
- *Survey research.* Quantitatively assessing consumers' attitudes toward the product or brand.
- *Marketing-mix modeling.* Drawing data from multiple sources and integrating them to provide insight into the process.

In summary, the role of public relations in the promotional mix is changing. As PR has become more marketing oriented, the criteria by which the programs are evaluated have also changed. At the same time, nonmarketing activities will continue to be part of the public relations department and part of the basis for evaluation.

# PUBLICITY

**Publicity** refers to the generation of news about a person, product, or service that appears in broadcast or print media. To many marketers, publicity and public

**FIGURE 17–5**

PR Measurement and Evaluation Tools: Frequency of Use and Perceived Effectiveness.

| PR measurement and evaluation tools | How often your organization has used the evaluation technique* | How effective in evaluating the impact of a PR programme is |
|---|---|---|
| Correlation between PR-related changes in coverages and changes in sales and market share | | |
| Regression-based "Marketing Mix Models" | | |
| Impact of PR programme on brand image among stakeholders | 57% | 96% |
| Impact of PR programme on corporate reputation among stakeholders | 54 | 98 |
| Media content analysis-related measures such as share of discussion/voice, key message penetration, tonality, etc. | 63 | 89 |
| Impressions/"Opportunity to see" | | |
| Penetration of key messages in target media | 70 | 91 |
| Clip reports/press cuttings books | 89 | 65 |
| Tracking the effectiveness of internal communications initiatives | 63 | 87 |
| Tracking the effectiveness of PR initiatives conducted via the Internet | | |
| Increasing target awareness of key messages or other key issues | 61 | 91 |
| Word of mouth/buzz creation | | |
| Improving volume of coverages versus competitors | | |
| Advertising value equivalencies (AVEs) | | |
| Reach/penetration of PR-generated coverage within target media | | |
| Correlation between PR-related boosts in coverage and positive changes in target behavior (e.g., website visitation, information requests, product inquiries, purchases.) | | |
| Pre- and post-surveys as a way to measure the impact of events or changes in media coverage | 50 | 93 |
| Focus groups | | |
| Costs per thousand impressions generated by PR programme | | |
| "Gut feel" | | |

*Percentages reported only for variables where significant differences exist.

Source: Baskin, et.al., *Public Relations Review* (36), 2010.

CHAPTER 17

relations are synonymous. In fact, publicity is really a subset of the public relations effort.

But there are several major differences. First, publicity is typically a *short-term* strategy, while public relations is a concerted program extending over a period of time. Second, public relations is designed to provide positive information about the firm and is usually controlled by the firm or its agent. Publicity, on the other hand, is not always positive and is not always under the control of, or paid for by, the organization. Both positive and negative publicity often originates from sources other than the firm.

In most organizations, publicity is controlled and disseminated by the public relations department. In this section, we discuss the role publicity plays in the promotional program and some of the ways marketers use and react to these communications.

## The Power of Publicity

One of the factors that most sets off publicity from the other program elements is the sheer power this form of communication can generate. Unfortunately for marketers, this power is not always realized in the way they would like it to be. Publicity can make or break a product or even a company. At one point, BP's stock dropped to less than one-half of what it was prior to the spill.

Why is publicity so much more powerful than advertising or sales promotion—or even other forms of public relations? First, publicity is highly credible. Unlike advertising and sales promotions, publicity is not usually perceived as being sponsored by the company (in negative instances, it never is). So consumers perceive this information as more objective and place more confidence in it. In fact, media often take great measures to insure their objectivity and promote the fact that they are not influenced by advertisers or other outside sources.

Publicity information may be perceived as endorsed by the medium in which it appears. For example, publicity regarding a breakthrough in the durability of golf balls will go far to promote them if it is reported by *Golf* magazine. *Car & Driver*'s award for car of the year reflects the magazine's perception of the quality of the auto selected.

Still another reason for publicity's power is its news value and the frequency of exposure it generates. When the publicity is positive, companies stand to benefit. When it is not, companies may suffer negative consequences such as lost sales, impacts on image, and even litigation, as shown in the opening vignette of this chapter.

The bottom line is that publicity is news, and people like to pass on information that has news value. Publicity thus results in a significant amount of free, credible, word-of-mouth information regarding the firm and its products.

## The Control and Dissemination of Publicity

In some of the examples cited previously, the control of publicity was not in the hands of the company. In some instances it is the firm's own blunder that allows information to leak out. Companies such as Toyota and BP could do nothing to stop the media from releasing negative information about them. When publicity becomes news, it is reported by the media, sometimes despite efforts by the firm. In these instances, the organization needs to react to the potential threat created by the news. Unfortunately, simply ignoring the problem will not make it go away.

A good example of one company's efforts to respond to adverse publicity is shown in Exhibit 17–13. Tree Top's problems began when all the major news media reported that the chemical Alar, used by some growers to regulate the growth of apples, might cause cancer in children. Despite published statements by reliable scientific and medical authorities (including the surgeon general) that Alar does not cause cancer, a few special-interest groups were able to generate an extraordinary amount of adverse publicity, causing concern among consumers and purchasing agents. A

**EXHIBIT 17–13**
Tree Top responds to the threat of negative publicity

few school districts took apples off their menus, and even applesauce and juice were implicated. Tree Top ran the ad shown in Exhibit 17–13 to state its position and alleviate consumers' fears. It also sent a direct mailing to nutritionists and day care operators. The campaign was successful in assuring consumers of the product's safety and rebuilding their confidence.

In other instances, however, publicity must be managed like any other promotional tool. For example, when Martha Stewart was convicted by the SEC (Securities and Exchange Commission) of insider trading, the negative publicity had severe consequences for her company. Sales dropped, stocks plummeted, and advertisers pulled their ads from her TV program. Many media observers all but buried her brand. However, while still in jail, Stewart cultivated a softer image than her past reputation as a harsh taskmaster, by befriending inmates and dispensing tips for better prison food. Upon her release, stock prices increased, many advertisers returned, and a Martha Stewart *Apprentice* TV show aired. Brand experts said the show of humility was key to Stewart's comeback.[18]

Publicity can also work for marketers. Kids' toys frequently achieve significant sales due to high levels of positive publicity and word-of-mouth advertising. Sales of Cabernet Savignon increased an average of 45 percent in the month after a CBS *60 Minutes* report indicating that daily moderate consumption of red wine can reduce the risk of heart disease, and green tea sales skyrocketed when the word spread that consumption of the product was effective in preventing cancer. Products that contain antioxidents are now very popular due to their health benefits. There are many more examples of the positive impact publicity can have.

Marketers like to have as much control as possible over the time and place where information is released. One way to do this is with the **video news release (VNR)**, a publicity piece produced by publicists so that stations can air it as a news story. The videos almost never mention that they are produced by the subject organization, and most news stations don't mention it either. Many government agencies have used VNRs, as have the American Dental Association, GM, Motorola, and Nokia, among others. The use of VNRs without disclosing the source has led some consumer advocates to protest such actions.

In their efforts to manage publicity and public relations, marketers are continuously learning more about these activities. Courses are offered, websites are devoted to the topic, and books written on how to manage publicity. These books cover how to make a presentation, whom to contact, how to issue a press release, and what to know about each medium addressed, including TV, radio, newspapers, magazines, the Internet, and direct-response advertising. They discuss such alternative media as news conferences, seminars, events, and personal letters, as well as insights on how to deal with government and other legislative bodies. Because this information is too extensive to include as a single chapter in this text, we suggest you peruse one of the many books available on this subject for additional insights.

## Advantages and Disadvantages of Publicity

Publicity offers the advantages of credibility, news value, significant word-of-mouth communications, and a perception of being endorsed by the media. Beyond the

## IMC Perspective 17–1 > > >

### Be Careful, PR Blunders Can Cost a Lot of Money

Two of the biggest negative publicity events of this century (involving Toyota and BP) have cost the companies involved millions of dollars—not just in repairs but in stock prices, media costs, and so forth. While one can make a legitimate argument that these events could have been avoided, sometimes things happen that a company could not foresee, or take steps to avoid, but require a response. All too often, the problem is quickly magnified by today's viral media.

Take Domino's Pizza for example. A couple of Domino's employees decided that it would be funny to make a video of themselves adding their own ingredients to Domino's sandwiches. On the video, one of the employees inserts pieces of pizza into his nose and waves pieces of salami around his rear, then places them on the sandwich, and exalts in the fact that someone would soon be eating them (there was more, but we will spare you!). Within 24 hours of the video's appearance on YouTube, 760,000 views had taken place, and Domino's had a problem. The toll was obvious—negative perceptions of the company increased, its quality rating fell from 5.0 to a negative 2.8 on one brand index measure, and buzz ratings fell on another. The number of blog postings mentioning Domino's increased from 27.4 to 227.5 in one month—most of which were negative. Of course, the employees were fired (what were they thinking?) and arrested, and Domino's began corrective actions. First they made their own video for YouTube in which the company president apologized for the incident, and described how Domino's would take steps to insure it never happened again. The president also held a press conference, and a Twitter campaign was initiated in response. A thank you was sent to the blogger that first reported it and updates were sent to other blogs as well. Of course, Domino's representatives appeared on television and responded through other traditional media as well. You can only imagine what all this cost.

Other companies have experienced similar gaffes. Pepsi ran a promotion in which they gave away free tickets to the New York Yankees opening game at the new Yankee stadium—unfortunately, to a lot less people than expected them. Afterwards a near riot broke out with people pouring Pepsi in the streets gutters and chanting "Pepsi Sucks!" and "Drink Coca-Cola." After police dispersed the mob, Pepsi responded with another giveaway of 500 tickets and free coupons for 12-packs of Pepsi Max. A Burger King ad designed to promote the company's new Texican Whopper offended Mexicans by showing a small *lucha libre* wrestler donning a cape that resembled the Mexican flag. A Mexican diplomat demanded an apology and BK assumed the cost of making a new commercial. And of course, we have already talked about KFC's problem.

But wait, there is a whole new category of blunders caused by and to individuals themselves. First there was Tiger Woods—his bad publicity reportedly cost him about $90 million in lost endorsements. After a domestic violence charge was filed by his girlfriend Rihanna, R&B star, Chris Brown was dropped by Wrigley. A Dunkin' Donuts commercial featuring Rachel Ray was pulled after complaints that the scarf she wore showed support for Muslim extremism and terrorism. Olympic champion Michael Phelps was shown allegedly taking hits from a bong on a cell phone video taken while he was at a friend's party (some friend!). He was dropped by Kellogg, temporarily discontinued by Subway (later to be reinstated), and his celebrity endorsement status took a big hit—particularly on trust and aspiration attributes. (Speedo stood behind and supported him.) Alex Rodriguez is expected to lose numerous endorsement deals after failing a MLB test for steroids. And NFL football player Michael Vick is now an endorser for PETA!

Sometimes we can't avoid trouble. Other times we bring it on ourselves. Either way, it can get very expensive.

Sources: Rupal Parekh and Emily Bryson York, "BK to Revise Ad after Complaints from Mexican Official," www.adage.com, April 14, 2009; Richard Tedesco, "Wrigley's Drops Chris Brown," www.promomagazine.com, February 11, 2009; Emily Bryson York, "Kellogg to Drop Olympian Phelps, February 5, 2009; Emily Bryson York, "Phelps Losing Buzz in Brand Attributes, but Athletic Rating Still High," www.adage.com, February 10, 2009; Mark Feinsand, "Alex Rodriguez Could Take Hit on Any Ad Deals," www.nydailynews.com, February 9, 2009.

potential impact of negative publicity, other major problems arise from the use of publicity: lack of control, timing and accuracy.

**Lack of Control** In the viral world today, there is little control of what information is conveyed. Social networks, blogs, and so on, have expanded the number of recipients of messages, while at the same time opening up the information stream to sources that are not confined by standards that may be imposed on traditional media. The result is that once public, the company or organization has lost control over the information. As can be seen in IMC Perspective 17–1, this can often become a costly experience.

**Timing** Timing of the publicity is not always completely under the control of the marketer. Unless the press thinks the information has very high news value, the timing of the press release is entirely up to the media—if it gets released at all. Thus, the information may be released earlier than desired or too late to make an impact.

**Accuracy** There are numerous ways to generate publicity. Quite often these means are not in the company's control. Unfortunately, the information sometimes gets lost in translation, that is, it is not always reported the way the provider wishes it to be. As a result, inaccurate information, omissions, or other errors may result. Sometimes when you see a publicity piece that was written from a press release, you wonder if the two are even about the same topic.

### Measuring the Effectiveness of Publicity

The methods for measuring the effects of publicity are essentially the same as those discussed earlier under the broader topic of public relations. A well-respected model for measuring the effects of publicity has been developed by Ketchum Public Relations. Using Walter Lindenmann's criteria, the Ketchum Effectiveness Yardstick was perceived as the standard in the industry for decades, and was used by numerous companies. While the Ketchum website makes no mention of the Yardstick communications program, the agency continues to provide effectiveness measures to its clients.

## CORPORATE ADVERTISING



One of the more controversial forms of advertising is **corporate advertising**. Actually an extension of the public relations function, corporate advertising does not promote any one specific product or service. Rather, it is designed to promote the firm overall, by enhancing its image, assuming a position on a social issue or cause, or seeking direct involvement in something. Why is corporate advertising controversial? A number of reasons are offered:

1. *Consumers are not interested in this form of advertising.* Studies have shown that many consumers are not interested in corporate ads. At least part of this may be because consumers do not understand the reasons behind such ads. Of course, much of this confusion results from ads that are not very good from a communications standpoint.

2. *It's a costly form of self-indulgence.* Firms have been accused of engaging in corporate image advertising only to satisfy the egos of top management. This argument stems from the fact that corporate ads are not easy to write. The message to be communicated is not as precise and specific as one designed to position a product, so the top managers often dictate the content of the ad, and the copy reflects their ideas and images of the corporation.
3. *The firm must be in trouble.* Some critics believe the only time firms engage in corporate advertising is when they are in trouble—either in a financial sense or in the public eye—and are advertising to attempt to remedy the problem. There are a number of forms of corporate advertising, each with its own objectives. These critics argue that these objectives have become important only because the firm has not been managed properly.

**EXHIBIT 17–14**
Dow uses corporate image advertising for positioning

4. *Corporate advertising is a waste of money.* Given that the ads do not directly appeal to anyone, are not understood, and do not promote anything specific, critics say the monies could be better spent in other areas. Again, much of this argument has its foundation in the fact that corporate image ads are often intangible. They typically do not ask directly for a purchase; they do not ask for investors. Rather, they present a position or try to create an image. Because they are not specific, many critics believe their purpose is lost on the audience and these ads are not a wise investment of the firm's resources.

Despite these criticisms and others, corporate advertising still enjoys wide usage. A variety of business-to-business and consumer-product companies continue to run corporate image ads, and numerous others have also increased expenditures in this area.

Since the term *corporate advertising* tends to be used as a catchall for any type of advertising run for the direct benefit of the corporation rather than its products or services, much advertising falls into this category. For purposes of this text (and to attempt to bring some perspective to the term), we use it to describe any type of advertising designed to promote the organization itself rather than its products or services.

## Objectives of Corporate Advertising

Corporate advertising may be designed with two goals in mind: (1) creating a positive image for the firm and (2) communicating the organization's views on social, business, and environmental issues. More specific applications include:

- Boosting employee morale and smoothing labor relations.
- Helping newly deregulated industries ease consumer uncertainty and answer investor questions.
- Helping diversified companies establish an identity for the parent firm rather than relying solely on brand names.[19]

**EXHIBIT 17–15**
Whirlpool supports the fight to eliminate poverty housing

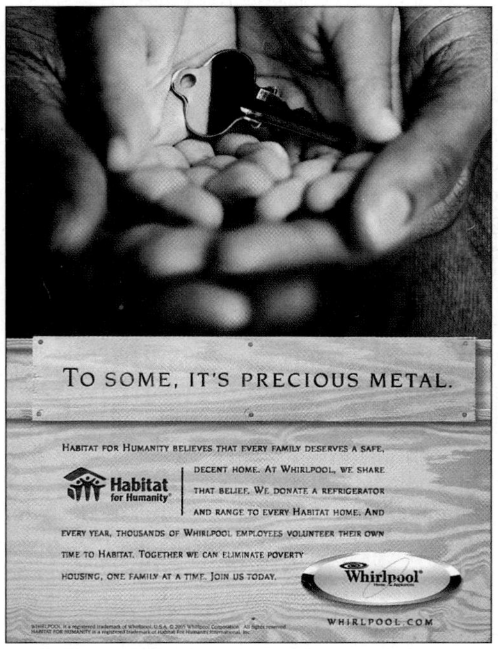


As these objectives indicate, corporate advertising is targeted at both internal and external audiences and involves the promotion of the organization as well as its ideas.

## Types of Corporate Advertising

Marketers seek attainment of corporate advertising's objectives by implementing image, advocacy, or cause-related advertising. Each form is designed to achieve specific goals.

### Image Advertising

One form of corporate advertising is devoted to promoting the organization's overall image. **Image advertising** may accomplish a number of objectives, including creating goodwill both internally and externally, creating a position for the company, and generating resources, both human and financial. A number of methods are used:

1. *General image or positioning ads.* As shown in Exhibit 17–14, ads are often designed to create an image of the firm in the public mind. The exhibit shows how Dow is attempting to create an image of itself as an innovator and leader in putting healthy food

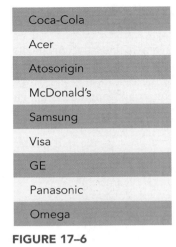

| Coca-Cola |
| --- |
| Acer |
| Atosorigin |
| McDonald's |
| Samsung |
| Visa |
| GE |
| Panasonic |
| Omega |

**FIGURE 17–6**
U.S. Olympic Sponsors and Partners

on the world's table. The ad is designed to demonstrate Dow's concern for science and humanity. A number of companies have created new names—for example, Accenture, Verizon, and Allianz—in an attempt to create a new image.

2. *Sponsorships.* Firms often run corporate image advertising on TV programs or specials. For example, on the National Geographic Channel, a number of companies including Nikon, American Airlines, and others provide sponsorships to associate themselves with the quality programming shown. These and others also sponsor programs on public TV and other educational programs designed to promote the corporation as a good citizen. By associating itself with high-quality or educational programming, companies like Siemens and Starbucks as well as local sponsors hope for a carryover effect that benefits their own images.

   Other examples of sponsorships include those run by American Express (members project), McDonald's (UNICEF), and U.S. Bank (arts, music, and sports programs). Exhibit 17–15 shows Whirlpool's sponsorship of the Habitat for Humanity and its efforts to fight poverty housing. Visa considers sponsorships an important part of its integrated marketing communications. It has sponsored the Olympics, the U.S. decathlon team, U.S. basketball's dream team, the U.S. Gymnastics Federation, the U.S. Open Tennis Championships, and Major League Baseball's All-Star game. The sponsorships are designed to fulfill specific business objectives while providing support for the recipients. Figure 17–6 shows a few of the companies that decided an Olympic sponsorship would be good for them.

3. *Recruiting.* The Grant Thornton ad presented in Exhibit 17–16 is a good example of corporate image advertising designed to attract new employees. If you have a passion for accounting and want to work with others who share that passion, you might be interested in the Grant Thornton accounting firm.

   The Sunday employment section of most major metropolitan newspapers is an excellent place to see this form of corporate image advertising at work. Notice the ads in these papers and consider the images the firms are presenting.

**EXHIBIT 17–16**
Corporate image advertising designed to attract employees

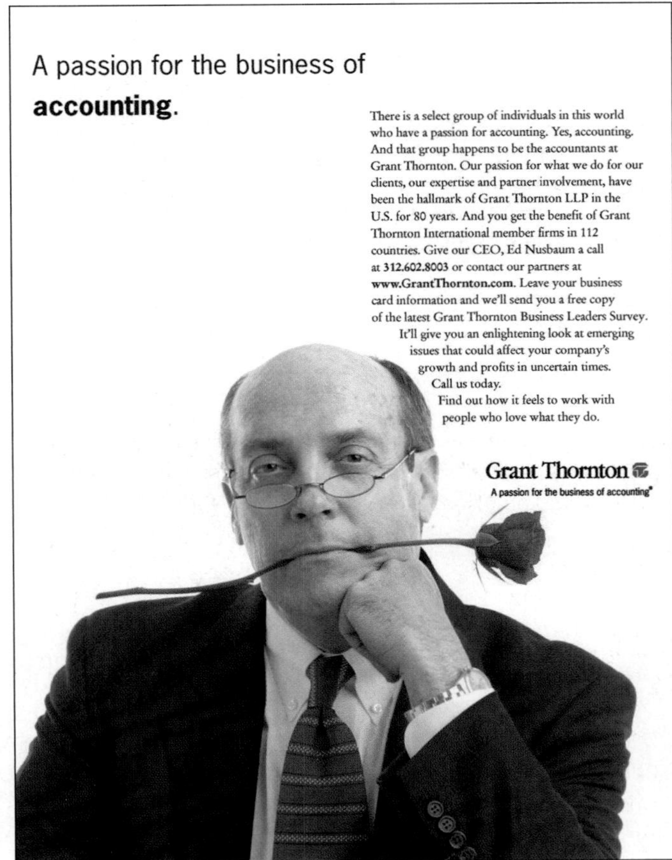

A passion for the business of
**accounting**.
There is a select group of individuals in this world who have a passion for accounting. Yes, accounting. And that group happens to be the accountants at Grant Thornton. Our passion for what we do for our clients, our expertise and partner involvement, have been the hallmark of Grant Thornton LLP in the U.S. for 80 years. And you get the benefit of Grant Thornton International member firms in 112 countries. Give our CEO, Ed Nusbaum a call at 312.602.8003 or contact our partners at www.GrantThornton.com. Leave your business card information and we'll send you a free copy of the latest Grant Thornton Business Leaders Survey. It'll give you an enlightening look at emerging issues that could affect your company's growth and profits in uncertain times.
Call us today.
Find out how it feels to work with people who love what they do.
Grant Thornton
A passion for the business of accounting®

4. *Generating financial support.* Some corporate advertising is designed to generate investments in the corporation. By creating a more favorable image, the firm makes itself attractive to potential stock purchasers and investors. More investments mean more working capital, more monies for research and development, and so on. In this instance, corporate image advertising is almost attempting to make a sale; the product is the firm.

   While there is no concrete evidence that corporate image advertising leads directly to increased investment, many managers believe there is, and that there is a correlation between the price of stock and the amount of corporate advertising done. Firms that spend more on corporate advertising also tend to have higher-priced stocks (though a direct relationship is very difficult to substantiate).

   This thing called *image* is not unidimensional. Many factors affect it. Figure 17–7 shows the results of a survey conducted by *Fortune* magazine on the most admired corporations in the United States. The most admired firms did not

| Rank | Company |
|---|---|
| 1 | Apple |
| 2 | Berkshire Hathaway |
| 3 | Toyota Motor Corp. |
| 4 | Google |
| 5 | Johnson & Johnson |
| 6 | Procter & Gamble |
| 7 | FedEx |
| 8 | Southwest Airlines |
| 9 | General Electric |
| 10 | Microsoft |

**FIGURE 17–7**

*Fortune*'s List of America's Most Admired Companies (2009)

Source: World's Most Admired Companies from *Fortune*, March 16, 2009. Reprinted with permission of PARS International.

gain their positions merely by publicity and word of mouth (nor, we guess, did the least admired).

A positive corporate image cannot be created just from a few advertisements. Quality of products and services, innovation, sound financial practices, good corporate citizenship, and wise marketing are just a few of the factors that contribute to overall image. In addition, the type of product marketed and emotional appeal also contribute. The *Fortune* survey cited above demonstrates that profits and stock performances have little to do with reputation and that once a reputation is acquired, it has lasting power. (Note that this survey was conducted prior to the bad publicity Toyota experienced. It will be interesting to see how the company fares in next year's survey.)

**Event Sponsorships** As we noted in the last section, corporate sponsorships of charities and causes have become a popular form of public relations. While some companies sponsor specific events or causes with primarily traditional public relations objectives in mind, a separate and more marketing-oriented use of sponsorships is also on the increase. Such **event sponsorships** take on a variety of forms, as shown in Figure 17–8. Anything from golf apparel and equipment to concerts, stadiums, and college football bowl games are now candidates for corporate sponsorship. Like any other relationship, however, risks must be assumed by both sides in such agreements. For example, many companies who have had their names placed on stadiums—TWA Dome (St. Louis), PSINet (Baltimore), Fruit of the Loom (Miami)—have gone bankrupt, while others have had their images tarnished—Enron (Enron Field), MCI (MCI Center)—which is not good for the cities. A risk taken by a company in naming a stadium is the cost of hundreds of millions of dollars, which can cause stockholders and consumers concern over the value of such an investment.

After seven straight years of growth, sponsorship spending decreased in 2009, due primarily to the state of the economy. Forecasts for 2010 expect renewed growth in all areas. Companies spent more than $17 billion on event sponsorships in 2010, with sports receiving the majority of event sponsorship monies.[20]

For example, the NASCAR Nextel Cup remains an attractive event to numerous companies, despite the increasing costs of sponsorship (Exhibit 17–17). Many companies are attracted to event sponsorships because effective IMC programs can be built around them, and promotional tieins can be made to local, regional, national, and even international markets. Companies are finding event sponsorships an excellent platform from which to build equity and gain affinity with target audiences as well as a good public relations tool.

**FIGURE 17–8**

Annual Sponsorship Spending in 1996–2010

| | 1996 | 1997 | 1998 | 1999 | 2002 | 2004 | 2008 | 2010 |
|---|---|---|---|---|---|---|---|---|
| Sports | $3,540 | $3,840 | $4,556 | $5,100 | $6,430 | $7,690 | $11,600 | $11,600 |
| Entertainment tours/ attractions | 566 | 650 | 680 | 756 | 865 | 1,060 | 1,610 | 1,740 |
| Festivals, fairs, events | 512 | 558 | 612 | 685 | 834 | 792 | 754 | 781 |
| Causes | 485 | 535 | 544 | 630 | 828 | 991 | 1,500 | 1,610 |
| Arts | 323 | 354 | 408 | 460 | 610 | 612 | 832 | 841 |
| Total | $5,426 | $5,937 | $6,800 | $7,631 | $9,567 | $11,140 | $16,296 | $16,752 |

Source: Adapted from *Cause Marketing Forum*, 2010.

**EXHIBIT 17–17**
NASCAR is an attractive sponsorship for many companies

**Advocacy Advertising** A third major form of corporate advertising addresses social, business, or environmental issues. Such **advocacy advertising** is concerned with propagating ideas and elucidating controversial social issues of public importance in a manner that supports the interests of the sponsor.

While still portraying an image for the company or organization, advocacy advertising does so indirectly, by adopting a position on a particular issue rather than promoting the organization itself. An example of advocacy advertising sponsored by the American Heart Association and the American Stroke Association and advocating support for President Obama's Health Care program is shown in Exhibit 17–18. Advocacy advertising has increased in use over the past few years and has also met with increased criticism. A recent advertising campaign sponsored by the Santa Fe Natural Tobacco company was designed to create a more positive image of tobacco. The two-page ad begins with a statement, "There are some things in our past you should know about," and continues on side two with statements that include the fact that the company has been supporting American farmers since the early 1990s, their tobacco is 100 percent additive-free and it is all grown in the United States. The image of the tobacco industry in the United States has been a negative one for decades despite many attempts to change it. Santa Fe seems to be trying again.

**EXHIBIT 17–18**
An example of an advocacy ad

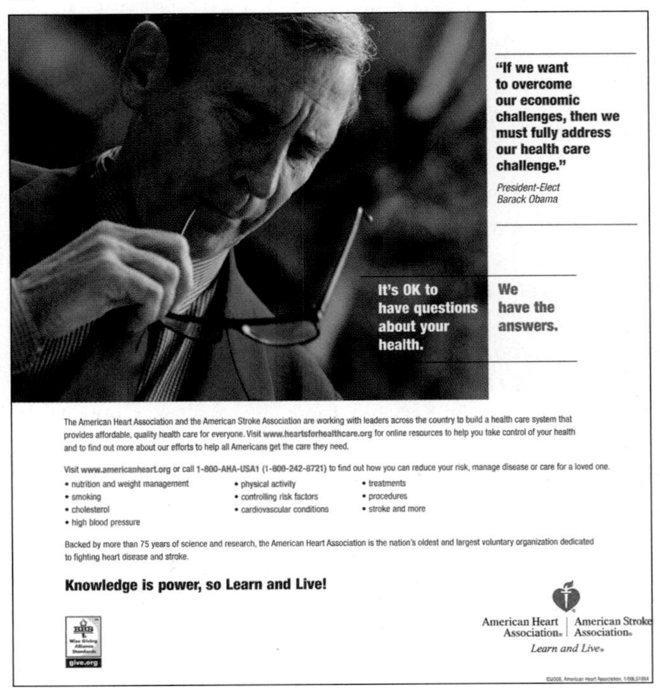


Advocacy ads may be sponsored by a firm or by a trade association and are designed to tell readers how the firm operates or explain management's position on a particular issue. Sometimes the advertising is a response to negative publicity or to the firm's inability to place an important message through its regular public relations channels. At other times, the firm just wants to get certain ideas accepted or to have society understand its concerns.

Another form of advocacy advertising, **issue ads**, are increasingly appearing in the media. While considered a form of advocacy advertising, issue ads may have no affiliation with a corporate or trade sponsor but may be sponsored by an organization to bring attention to what

# IMC Perspective 17–2 > > >

## Häagen-Dazs Generates Buzz on Campus

Häagen-Dazs is the original brand of super premium ice cream and competes against several other brands in this category such as Ben & Jerry's, Dove, and Ciao Bella. The brand has a very loyal, but aging, consumer following, particularly in comparison to its primary competitor—Ben & Jerry's—which has always been rated high in social responsibility based on its dealings with local communities, employees, and environmental policies and programs. Häagen-Dazs was faced with a problem because the brand was losing its share in the ice cream market and finding it more difficult to connect with consumers. One particular market segment where Häagen-Dazs was having problems was college students, who are heavy consumers of ice cream and seen as future brand advocates but were identifying more with Ben & Jerry's which was perceived as more a youthful and approachable brand as well as more environmentally conscious.

Häagen-Dazs had not focused any of its marketing efforts specifically on college students. However, the company and its promotional agency, Alcone Marketing Group, saw a unique opportunity to connect with students by building on a cause-related marketing campaign that had been developed for the brand. Häagen-Dazs's advertising agency, Goodby, Silverstein and Partners had launched a socially conscious campaign to raise awareness of the plight of honey bees, whose population was mysteriously dying off.

The "Häagen-Dazs Loves Honey Bees" campaign noted how the brand had a connection to the cause since honey bees are responsible for pollinating more than a third of all the foods we eat, including many of the ingredients included in various flavors of its all-natural ice creams, sorbets, frozen yogurts, and bars. The campaign provided consumers with a different perspective of Häagen-Dazs, as its previous advertising had focused on the brand and its great ice cream. The cause-related effort included a $250,000 research grant to the agricultural department at Penn State University to study the problem, a new Vanilla Honey Bee brand flavor, and print partnerships with various magazines that included seed-embedded paper insert ads that readers could crumple up and plant in the ground.

Häagen-Dazs saw an opportunity to leverage the highly successful "Help the Honey Bees" campaign with college students as it was a cause with which they could identify, and it provided a way to build a connection between the brand and various colleges and universities across the country. To adapt the campaign to this market, the college-focused campaign was developed based on the theme "Imagine a World Without Bees." The campaign began with a unique print ad that was developed for college newspapers that created a fake newspaper front page and removed every instance of the letter "B." The reverse side of the ad featured a bold four-color ad that explained why the letter B was missing and called attention to the honey bee crisis and how it could impact the world's natural food supply, including all of the natural ingredients in 50 percent of Häagen-Dazs flavors. The ad included a call to action for students to purchase Häagen-Dazs on campus, and for every purchase, a bee-friendly flower would be planted in various places.

**EXHIBIT 17–19**

Issue ads are on the increase

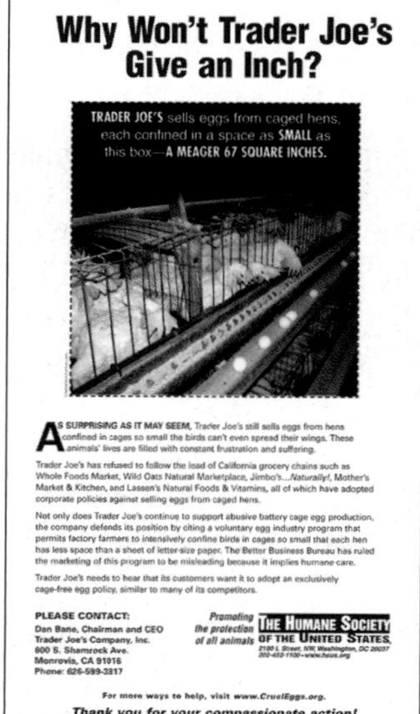


they consider to be an important issue. For example, after failed negotiations between The Humane Society of the United States and grocery store chain Trader Joe's, the animal welfare organization placed an issue ad (Exhibit 17–19). The response from Trader Joe's customers was enormous. And the company publicly announced that it would convert all of its brand eggs to cage free within three months. In 2007, the U.S. Supreme Court ruled that corporate and union sponsorships of issue ads (previously banned) must be permitted to run. Many believed this decision would lead to a significant increase in issue advertising.[21]

Advocacy advertising has been criticized by a number of sources. But as you can see in Exhibit 17–20, this form of communication has been around for a long time. AT&T engaged in issues-oriented advertising way back in 1908 and has continued to employ this form of communication throughout the 21st century. Critics contend that companies with large advertising budgets purchase too much ad space and time and that advocacy ads may be misleading, but the checks and balances of regular product advertising also operate in this area.

For example, a television commercial shown during the 2010 Super Bowl spawned a heated debate (not to mention lots of publicity). The commercial, sponsored by the conservative evangelical organization Focus on Family, included Heisman Trophy winner Tim Tebow and his mother and supported an antiabortion position. The ad was considered inappropriate by many in the media and the public, while others

In addition to the ads in the college papers, the campaign also included sampling events at various campuses where brand ambassadors distributed free samples as well as backpack buttons that contained the phrase "Help Bees Get Busy." Various other forms of nontraditional media were used to drive awareness and participation including dorm room door hangers, table tents, ads on coffee cup sleeves, and wild postings around the campus. Over 23,000 samples of Häagen-Dazs ice cream were distributed across 12 campuses where the campaign was run, and more than 2 million media impressions were generated at these schools. The sampling program was an effective way to introduce college students to the Häagen-Dazs brand and move it into their consideration set against Ben & Jerry's and other super premium brands.

The "Imagine a World Without Bees" campaign was very successful from a number of other perspectives. The program helped generate retail distribution for Häagen-Dazs on a number of college campuses where it had been discontinued, such as the University of California at Davis and UCLA. The groundbreaking creative tactic of taking over the front page of college newspapers with the "missing B" ad also attracted a considerable amount of media attention that resulted in articles in major newspapers such as *The Wall Street Journal* and *The New York Times* and generated a lot of buzz online through various websites and blogs popular among college students. The campaign also won a 2010 Reggie Award from the Promotional Marketing Association as one of the best promotional campaigns of the year.

The success of the "Help the Honey Bees" and the college-focused "Imagine a World Without Bees" marketing campaigns led Häagen-Dazs to extend the campaign for another year. The new effort utilizes social media to target environmentally conscious consumers who are likely to spread the message regarding the plight of the bees and the need to take action. To help expand the effort, the campaign encourages consumers to spread the campaign message on Twitter and is donating $1 per tweet, up to $1,000 a day, to UC Davis to conduct research on the issue and to the Häagen-Dazs Bee Haven, which is a half-acre bee-friendly garden and education center at the school.

Häagen-Dazs feels that the campaign is helping bring attention to the plight of the declining honey bee population among consumers, including a new generation of college students who have been introduced to the issue, as well as the brand, through the unique promotional program that was created to reach them. The company plans to continue to support the cause of the bees and hopes consumers will do the same and enjoy some Häagen-Dazs ice cream while doing so, including the college students who they hope will become future brand advocates.

Sources: Karen Egolf, "Häagen-Dazs Extends Social Media Effort," *Advertising Age*, November 10, 2009, http://adage.com/print?article_id=140412; Michael Bush, "Häagen-Dazs Saves the Honeybees, May 7, 2009, http://adage.com/print?article_id=136486; 2010 Reggie Awards, Promotion Marketing Association, www.pmalink.org/?reggieawards.



saw nothing controversial about it. In hindsight, it appears that the action off the field (that is, in the Super Bowl advertising community) was much greater than that generated by the ad itself.[22]

**Cause-Related Advertising** An increasingly popular method of image building is **cause-related marketing**, in which companies link with charities or nonprofit organizations as contributing sponsors. The company benefits from favorable publicity, while the charity receives much-needed funds. IMC Perspective 17–2 provides an example a cause-related campaign run by Häagen-Dazs. Proponents of cause marketing say that association with a cause may differentiate one brand or store from another, increase consumer acceptance of price increases, generate favorable publicity, and even win over skeptical officials who may have an impact on the company.[23] Cause-marketing relationships can take a variety of forms. Making outright donations to a nonprofit cause, having companies volunteer for the cause, donating materials or supplies, running public service announcements, or even providing event refreshments are some of the ways companies get involved. Exhibit 17–21 shows an innovative campaign sponsored by the Sojourner Center. The campaign was targeted to those attempting to overcome the impact of domestic violence. The award winning campaign was unique given its heavy use of nontraditional

SHE'S A PARTNER IN A
GREAT AMERICAN BUSINESS
SHE is one of 850,000 owners of Bell System securities. They are typical Americans—some young, some middle age, some old. They live in every part of the nation.
One may be a housewife in Pennsylvania. Another a physician in Oregon—a clerk in Illinois—an engineer in Texas—a merchant in Massachusetts—a miner in Nevada—a stenographer in Missouri—a teacher in California—or a telephone employee in Michigan.
For the most part, Bell System stockholders are men and women who have put aside small sums for saving. More than half of them have held their shares for five years or longer. More than 650,000 of these 850,000 security holders own stock in the American Telephone and Telegraph Company—the parent company of the Bell System. More than 225,000 own five shares or less. Over fifty per cent are women. No one owns as much as one per cent of the stock of A. T. & T. In a very real sense, the Bell System is a democracy in business—owned by the people it serves.
More than 270,000 men and women work for the Bell System. One person out of every 150 in this country owns A. T. & T. securities or stock and bonds of associated companies in the Bell System.
BELL TELEPHONE SYSTEM

**EXHIBIT 17–20**
AT&T has used advocacy ads for years

media including cell phone text messaging, e-mail messaging, and the Internet, along with television, radio, posters, and billboards.

At the same time, not all cause marketing is a guarantee of success. Cause marketing requires more than just associating with a social issue, and it takes time and effort. Companies have gotten into trouble by misleading consumers about their relationships, and others have wasted money by supporting a cause that offered little synergism. One survey showed that more than 300 companies associated themselves with breast cancer concerns, but most became lost in sponsorship clutter. Others have simply picked the wrong cause—finding that their customers and potential customers either have little interest in or don't support the cause. In some cases, cause marketing is considered nothing more than shock advertising. Finally, the results of cause-marketing efforts can sometimes be hard to quantify.

## Advantages and Disadvantages of Corporate Advertising

A number of reasons for the increased popularity of corporate advertising become evident when you examine the advantages of this form of communication:

1. *It is an excellent vehicle for positioning the firm.* Firms, like products, need to establish an image or position in the marketplace. Corporate image ads are one way to accomplish this objective. A well-positioned product is much more likely to achieve success than is one with a vague or no image. The same holds true of the firm. Stop and think for a moment about the image that comes to mind when you hear the name Apple, Johnson & Johnson, or Procter & Gamble.

   Now what comes to mind when you hear Unisys, USX, or Navistar? How many consumer brands can you name that fall under ConAgra's corporate umbrella? (Hunts, Chef Boyardee, Pam, Slim-Jims, and many others.) While we are not saying these latter companies are not successful—because they certainly are—we are suggesting their corporate identities (or positions) are not as well entrenched as the identities of those first cited. Companies with strong positive corporate images have an advantage over competitors that may be enhanced when they promote the company overall.

**EXHIBIT 17–21**
This ad was part of a campaign designed to stop domestic violence

2. *It takes advantage of the benefits derived from public relations.* As the PR efforts of firms have increased, the attention paid to these events by the media has lessened (not because they are of any less value, but because there are more events to cover). The net result is that when a company engages in a public relations effort, there is no guarantee it will receive press coverage and publicity. Corporate image advertising gets the message out, and though consumers may not perceive it as positively as information from an objective source, the fact remains that it can communicate what has been done.
3. *It reaches a select target market.* Corporate image advertising should not be targeted to the general public. It is often targeted to investors and managers of other firms rather than to

the general public. It doesn't matter if the general public does not appreciate this form of communication, as long as the target market does. In this respect, this form of advertising may be accomplishing its objectives.

Some of the disadvantages of corporate advertising were alluded to earlier in the chapter. To these criticisms, we can add the following:

1. *Questionable effectiveness.* There is no strong evidence to support the belief that corporate advertising works. Many doubt the data cited earlier that demonstrated a correlation between stock prices and corporate image advertising as some studies show little support for this effect.
2. *Constitutionality and/or ethics.* Some critics contend that since larger firms have more money, they can control public opinion unfairly. This point was resolved in the courts in favor of the advertisers. Nevertheless, many consumers still see such advertising as unfair given the great disparities that sometimes exist in financial resources available to some but not others, and immediately take a negative view of the sponsor.

A number of valid points have been offered for and against corporate advertising. Two things are certain: (1) No one knows who is right, and (2) the use of this communications form continues to increase.

## Measuring the Effectiveness of Corporate Advertising

As you can tell from our discussion of the controversy surrounding corporate advertising, there need to be methods for evaluating whether or not such advertising is effective:

- *Attitude surveys.* One way to determine the effectiveness of corporate advertising is to conduct attitude surveys to gain insights into both the public's and investors' reactions to ads. A study conducted by Janas Sinclair and Tracy Irani on advocacy advertising in the biotechnology industry employed a survey research methodology to demonstrate that public accountability was a good predictor of corporate trustworthiness, and this and the attitude toward the advertiser would predict consumers' attitude toward the ad, biotechnology, and purchase intentions.[24] The Phase II study conducted by market research firm Yankelovich, Skelly & White is one of the best-known applications of this measurement method.[25] The firm measured recall and attitude toward corporate advertisers and found that corporate advertising is more efficient in building recall for a company name than is product advertising alone. Frequent corporate advertisers rated better on virtually all attitude measures than those with low corporate ad budgets.
- *Studies relating corporate advertising and stock prices.* A number of studies have examined the effect of various elements of corporate advertising (position in the magazine, source effects, etc.) on stock prices. These studies have yielded conflicting conclusions, indicating that while the model for such measures seems logical, methodological problems may account for at least some of the discrepancies.
- *Focus group research.* Focus groups have been used to find out what investors want to see in ads and how they react after the ads are developed. As with product-oriented advertising, this method has limitations, although it does allow for some effective measurements.

While the effectiveness of corporate advertising has been measured by some of the methods used to measure product-specific advertising, reported research in this area has not kept pace with that of the consumer market. The most commonly offered reason for this lack of effort is that corporate ads are often the responsibility of those in the highest management positions in the firm, and these parties do not wish to be held accountable. It is interesting that those who should be most concerned with accountability are the most likely to shun this responsibility!

## Summary

This chapter examined the role of the promotional elements of public relations, publicity, and corporate advertising. We noted that these areas are all significant to the marketing and communications effort and are usually considered differently from the other promotional elements. The reasons for this special treatment stem from the facts that (1) they are typically not designed to promote a specific product or service, and (2) in many instances it is harder for the consumer to make the connection between the communication and its intent.

Public relations was shown to be useful in its traditional responsibilities as well as in a more marketing-oriented role. In many firms, PR is a separate department operating independently of marketing; in others, it is considered a support system. Many large firms have an external public relations agency, just as they have an outside ad agency.

In the case of publicity, another factor enters the equation: lack of control over the communication the public will receive. In public relations and corporate advertising, the organization remains the source and retains much more control. Publicity often takes more of a reactive than a proactive approach, yet it may be more instrumental (or detrimental) to the success of a product or organization than all other forms of promotion combined.

While not all publicity can be managed, the marketer must nevertheless recognize its potential impact. Press releases and the management of information are just two of the factors under the company's control. Proper reaction and a strategy to deal with uncontrollable events are also responsibilities.

Corporate advertising was described as controversial, largely because the source of the message is top management, so the rules for other advertising and promoting forms are often not applied. This element of communication definitely has its place in the promotional mix. But to be effective, it must be used with each of the other elements, with specific communications objectives in mind.

Finally, we noted that measures of evaluation and control are required for each of these program elements, just as they are for all others in the promotional mix. We presented some methods for taking such measurements and some evidence showing why it is important to use them. As long as the elements of public relations, publicity, and corporate advertising are considered integral components of the overall communications strategy, they must respect the same rules as the other promotional mix elements to ensure success.

## Key Terms

**public relations (PR)** p. 572
**marketing public relations (MPR)** p. 574
**internal audiences** p. 578
**external audiences** p. 578
**press release** p. 580
**press conference** p. 581
**exclusive** p. 581
**publicity** p. 584
**video news release (VNR)** p. 587
**corporate advertising** p. 589
**image advertising** p. 590
**event sponsorship** p. 592
**advocacy advertising** p. 593
**issue ads** p. 593
**cause-related marketing** p. 595

## Discussion Questions

1. As can be seen in the lead in to this chapter, BP appeared to be less successful than Toyota in the final outcome related to their negative publicity. Give some reasons why this might have happened. What could BP have done differently, if anything? (LO1)
2. Some marketers consider corporate advertising a waste of time and money. What are some of the reasons they feel this way. Take a position pro or con corporate advertising and defend it. (LO3)
3. Explain how social networks can both help and hurt companies in regard to publicity. (LO1)
4. Discuss some of the advantages and disadvantages of public relations. Now do the same for MPRs. (LO3)
5. Why do companies get involved in event sponsorships? Is this an effective strategy? Give examples of event sponsorships that were successful and some that were not. (LO5)
6. The chapter discusses the lack of coordination that often exists between marketing and public relations departments. Discuss some of the reasons this might occur. What can be done to reduce this conflict to achieve greater coordination? (LO1)

7. Examine a number of examples of different types of sponsorships corporations are currently engaging. Analyze the reasons for the sponsorship, and evaluate whether it employs a wise strategy or not. (LO3)

8. The use of MPRs has irked traditional public relations people. Discuss why MPRs may be controversial. Explain the reasons why MPRs should and should not be used. (LO1)

9. The chapter discusses the increasing use of advocacy advertising and issue advertising. Explain what these advertising forms are, and why there has been such an increase in their use by profit and nonprofit organizations. (LO5)

10. There is a saying that "any publicity is good publicity." Discuss what you think about this statement. (LO2)

## AdForum Exercise: "Understanding Corporate Image Advertising"

(see Advertising and Promotion Playlist, Chapter 17)

As more and more companies engage in corporate image advertising, they use this form of advertising to achieve a variety of objectives. Using the playlist for Chapter 17, answer the following questions:

1 What type (from the text) of corporate image advertising is being employed?

2 Why would each of these companies use corporate image advertising (explain individually)?

3 Do you think that the corporate image ads here are likely to achieve the objectives sought? Explain why or why not.

4 Do you think the monies spent on these ads are likely to be effective?

Access to the chapter playlist is available through McGraw Hill connect™ MARKETING, www.mcgrawhillconnect.com

## LEARNING OBJECTIVES

- **LO1** To understand reasons for measuring promotional program effectiveness.
- **LO2** To know the various measures used in assessing promotional program effectiveness.
- **LO3** To understand the requirements of proper effectiveness research.
- **LO4** To evaluate alternative methods for measuring promotional program effectiveness.

# 18 Measuring the Effectiveness of the Promotional Program

## EYE TRACKING—AN OLD TECHNOLOGY FINDS NEW APPLICATIONS IN MEASURING IMC EFFECTIVENESS

The usefulness of eye tracking technology for measuring advertising effectiveness is not new news for the marketer. Back in the late 1970s and early 1980s, advertising researchers were employing this technology to determine where viewers were focusing when they looked at ads and/or TV commercials. One story is that one of the original Tab diet soft drink commercials was changed when viewers focused on the female swimsuit model instead of the product. The commercial was supposedly changed to have her hold the can in front of her body to attract attention. For whatever reason, while proven to be useful, eye tracking never went away, but no one seemed to pay much attention to it. Now all of that is changing.

A number of factors may be contributing to this change. An increased emphasis on accountability and the increased pressure to determine an ad's effectiveness, improved technologies, the advent of new media, and improvements to existing media forms are some of the reasons cited, but it is probably a combination of all of the above. As a result, marketers have found a number of new applications to eye tracking, including:

- *Retail (interior displays/window design):* Eye tracking studies enabling interior designers to choose color, lighting, architecture, and so on, so as to subtly influence the customer's mood. This includes the use of eye catchers to attract passers-by and arouse their curiosity.
- *Package design:* Optimizing the look and feel of the packaging as well as the attention-getting capabilities.
- *Advertisements:* Allowing the advertiser to determine what customers see and to determine the effectiveness of copy and visuals.
- *Online marketing:* From Web design to viewers' attention to display ads, marketers are finding eye tracking a valuable tool to enhance effectiveness.

Researchers use eye movements to tell specifically where viewers are looking, to see if they are reading or scanning, and what catches their first view. They can also tell how much time the viewers spend looking at a specific stimulus and the order in which they view others (if they do!). For example:

- An eye tracking study conducted by Oneupweb asked participants to navigate Facebook, Twitter, and YouTube as they normally would. The study revealed that 65 percent of them engaged with a sponsor within 10 seconds of beginning their search, when asked to search for Pepsi on both Facebook and YouTube (Twitter is not included as they have no search tool). On Facebook, the results showed that their first attention was paid to the sponsored ads, and others were barely, if at all, viewed, while on YouTube, the top six organic results and the first sponsored ad got all the attention. The conclusion? Sponsored ads work better than expected.
- In another Internet study, Jakob Nielsen and Kara Pernice, authors of the book *Eyetracking Web Usability,* tracked how people navigate websites when looking for information. Searches included how to deal with heartburn, shopping for baby presents, and picking cell phone features, among others. Their results indicate that to be effective, an ad should be simple, with those that had only text or text and a separate image being most effective, while those that imposed text on top of images or included animation fared the worse. While the study showed

that people saw 36 percent of the ads on the pages they visited, the time spent viewing them was only one-third of a second. One of the most surprising results was the fact that text only ads scored best. When asked for an explanation, the authors hypothesized that unlike television which is a passive medium, the Web is all about taking action, searching, clicking, and so forth. On the Web, it is the value of content that makes it attractive.

- In a scarier application, a Canadian company now offers an eye-tracking device that can determine when someone looks at a billboard, where they look, and for how long, without one even knowing it—up to 33 feet. It then provides Google-like metrics that greatly improve on existing methods of data collection.
- In Germany, a pre- and posttest research study was designed to measure participants' perceptions and recall of ads through a virtual reality situation in which one drives a van down the street with advertisements on both sides. The eye-tracking and survey results are then combined to determine viewers' unaided/aided recall, recognition and design aspects of the ads. And yes, they can do it at different speeds!

Part of the reason why eye tracking measures have not hit the mainstream, is due to the high cost and obtrusiveness of the measurement equipment (participants have to wear headgear, whether in a lab setting or in the field—for example walking through a department store or supermarket looking weird.) There was also the question about whether the fact that the participants knew they were in a study influenced their behaviors. With advances in technology and decreases in cost—some companies now make the technology available for a rental fee—eye tracking is making a comeback. And the implications seem endless!

Sources: Barbara Kiviat, "Why We Look at Some Web Ads and Not Others, www.time.com, November 8, 2009; Nathania Johnson, "Eye Tracking Study Shows Sponsored Ads Attract Social Media Searchers," July 19, 2009, blog .searchenginewatch.com; Dan Skeen, "Eye-Tracking Device Lets Billboards Know When You Look at Them," www.wired .com, June 12, 2007; G. Theuner, K. Pischke, and T. Bley, "Analysis of Advertising Effectiveness with Eye Tracking," *Proceedings of Measuring Behavior 2008,* Maastricht, The Netherlands, August 26–29, 2008, pp. 229–230.

As noted throughout this text, the increased emphasis on accountability is forcing many companies to evaluate, or reevaluate, their IMC plans. Both clients and agencies are continually striving to determine whether their communications are working and how well they are working relative to other options. As can be seen in the lead-in to this chapter, researchers are continually providing new methods designed to assist in this endeavor. Companies and organizations continue to work together in an attempt to provide answers to these questions, and to develop new ways to measure communications effectiveness.

Measuring the effectiveness of the promotional program is a critical element in the promotional planning process. Research allows the marketing manager to evaluate the performance of specific program elements and provides input into the next period's situation analysis. It is a necessary ingredient to a continuing planning process, yet it is often not carried out.

In this chapter, we discuss some reasons firms should measure the effectiveness of their IMC programs, as well as why many decide not to. We also examine how, when, and where such measurements can be conducted. Most of our attention is devoted to measuring the effects of advertising because much more time and effort have been expended developing evaluation measures in advertising than in the other promotional areas. We will, however, discuss measurement in other areas of the IMC program as well. (In some of these areas, the measures are more directly observable—for example, direct marketing and personal selling.) You'll recall that we addressed the methods used to evaluate many of the other promotional elements in previous chapters.

It is important to understand that in this chapter we are concerned with research that is conducted in an evaluative role—that is, to measure the effectiveness of advertising and promotion and/or to assess various strategies before implementing them. This is not to be confused with research discussed earlier in the text to help develop the promotional program, although the two can (and should) be used together. While evaluative research may occur at various times throughout the promotional process (including the development stage), it is conducted specifically to assess the effects of various strategies. We begin our discussion with the reasons effectiveness should be measured as well as some of the reasons firms do not do so.

# ARGUMENTS FOR AND AGAINST MEASURING EFFECTIVENESS

Almost any time one engages in a project or activity, whether for work or fun, some measure of performance occurs. In sports you may compare your golf score against par or your time on a ski course to other skiers' performance. In business, employees are generally given objectives to accomplish, and their job evaluations are based on their ability to achieve these objectives. Advertising and promotion should not be an exception. It is important to determine how well the communications program is working and to measure this performance against some standards.

## Reasons to Measure Effectiveness

Assessing the effectiveness of ads both before they are implemented and after the final versions have been completed and fielded offers a number of advantages:

LO 18-1

1. *Avoiding costly mistakes.* The top three advertisers in the United States spent over $11 billion in advertising and promotion in 2009. The top 10 spent a total of over $25 billion.[1] This is a lot of money to be throwing around without some understanding of how well it is being spent. If the program is not achieving its objectives, the marketing manager needs to know so he or she can stop spending (wasting) money on it.

   Just as important as the out-of-pocket costs is the opportunity loss due to poor communications. If the advertising and promotions program is not accomplishing its objectives, not only is the money spent lost but so too is the potential gain that could result from an effective program. Thus, measuring the effects of advertising does not just save money. It also helps the firm maximize its investment.
2. *Evaluating alternative strategies.* Typically a firm has a number of strategies under consideration. For example, there may be some question as to the degree to which each medium should be used or whether one message is more effective than another. Or the decision may be between two promotional program elements. We have noted previously that many marketers are shifting dollars from traditional to nontraditional media. For example, Southern Comfort has moved its advertising for its spirits brand from cable TV and magazine ads completely to online properties such as Facebook, Spin, Fader, Hulu, and others.[2] As shown in Figure 18–1 those monies will be allocated to a variety of programs. A key question for the future is to be able to determine how effective each one was. Other companies have also reallocated monies to nontraditional media. In a study conducted by the Anderson Group, 63 percent of advertisers said they planned to spend more monies in social media in the next year.[3] The question is, should research be spent on traditional, on nontraditional, or digital, or on advertising or in what combination? Research may be designed to help the manager determine which strategy is most likely to be effective.

**SOUTHERN COMFORT'S DIGITAL PARTNERSHIPS**

**Facebook:** Fan page featuring custom video, exclusive events, party pics, SMS programs, news, recipes and video clips.

**Spin:** Sponsorship of the top 50 cover songs of all time, with 10 free downloads, "tab covered by" Southern Comfort.

**Playboy:** Presenting sponsorship of the Playboy "Uncovered" series highlighting artists paying tribute to legends who have inspired them.

**The Fader:** "At the Bar" with Southern Comfort series featuring 10 pop-up sessions with local artists performing acoustically and discussing their musical influences.

Fader's 'At the Bar' series

**Pitchfork:** "Faces in the Crowd" series featuring artist interviews by fans, Pitchfork Music Festival, Monolith Festival and Voodoo Experience.

**Thrillist:** E-newsletters touting the brand, story, events and drinks.

**NBC:** Online spots running in and around prime-time NBC shows such as "30 Rock," "The Office," "Jay Leno," "The Tonight Show With Conan O'Brien" and "Saturday Night Live," among others.

**NBC Local:** Friday-through-Sunday takeover of the "What You're Doing Tonight" section, with home-page coverage before each Southern Comfort music-series event.

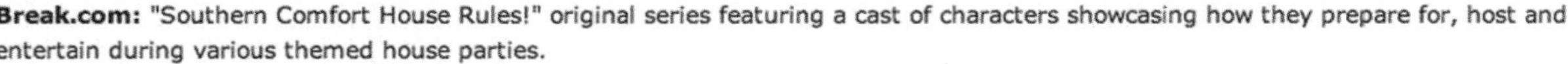

**Break.com:** "Southern Comfort House Rules!" original series featuring a cast of characters showcasing how they prepare for, host and entertain during various themed house parties.

**My Damn Channel:** Sponsorship of "Grace Crashers," an original series starring Grace Helbig as the ultimate party crasher as she and her crew show up unannounced at parties around Halloween, Holiday and Mardi Gras

**Comedy Central:** "Holiday Survival Guide" featuring Comedy Central comedians providing tips for getting out of sticky holiday situations.

**FIGURE 18–1**

Southern Comfort's Digital Partnerships

Source: Reprinted with permission from *Advertising Age*, www.adage.com, July, 2009. Copyright © 2010 Crain Communications..

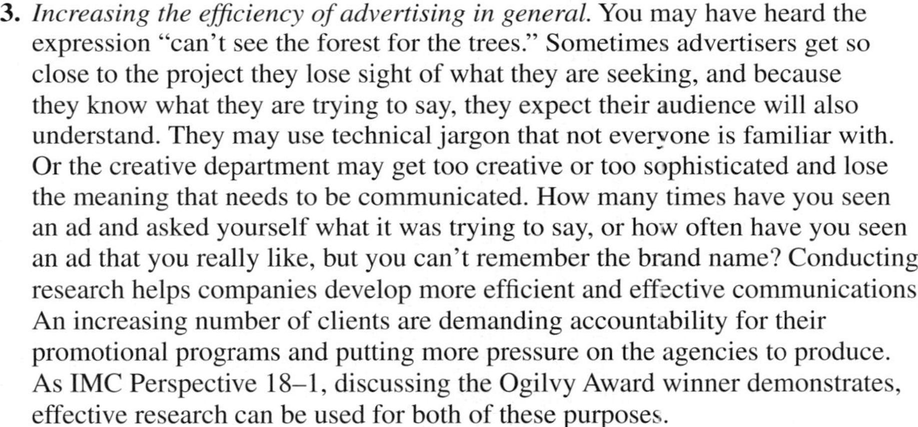

3. *Increasing the efficiency of advertising in general.* You may have heard the expression "can't see the forest for the trees." Sometimes advertisers get so close to the project they lose sight of what they are seeking, and because they know what they are trying to say, they expect their audience will also understand. They may use technical jargon that not everyone is familiar with. Or the creative department may get too creative or too sophisticated and lose the meaning that needs to be communicated. How many times have you seen an ad and asked yourself what it was trying to say, or how often have you seen an ad that you really like, but you can't remember the brand name? Conducting research helps companies develop more efficient and effective communications. An increasing number of clients are demanding accountability for their promotional programs and putting more pressure on the agencies to produce. As IMC Perspective 18–1, discussing the Ogilvy Award winner demonstrates, effective research can be used for both of these purposes.
4. *Determining if objectives are achieved.* In a well-designed IMC plan, specific communication objectives are established. If objectives are attained, new ones need to be established in the next planning period. An assessment of how program elements led to the attainment of the goals should take place, and/or reasons for less-than-desired achievements must be determined. Research should address whether the strategy delivers the stated objectives and how appropriate the measures used to make this assessment are.

## Reasons Not to Measure Effectiveness

While it seems obvious that it makes sense to measure effectiveness, the fact remains that in too many instances this is not done. Whereas advertisers know that it is important

# IMC Perspective 18–1 > > >

## The Grand Ogilvy Award Winner—2010

*Grand Prize Winner: The U.S. Postal Service: A Simpler Way to Ship*—For years, the expedited package shipment industry, which is 95 percent comprised of business to business shipments, has been controlled by two companies—FedEx and UPS. The two giants dominate the industry controlling approximately 86 percent of the market while spending a combined $256 million a year in advertising. To make things harder for a competitor, both offer excellent reliability and customer service, and customer satisfaction is very high. While a third competitor, DHL, ceased U.S. operations in 2009, most of the lost market share has come at the expense of the U.S. Postal Service which had experienced declining sales for 10 straight years, dropping from a high of 20 percent to 13.7 percent share of the market in 2008. (Each share point is 89 million packages or $630 million in sales!) To make things worse, a series of minigroup research and quantitative studies among businesses indicated that the USPS was really not considered a viable option, and that the shippers saw no reason to switch from UPS or FedEx.

Knowing that something had to be done and soon, the USPS established a one-year budget of $30 million for media, search, PR, direct mail, and promotions, and a goal of achieving a 5 percent share increase. A massive Brand Potential Study indicated that a product developed five years earlier—the flat rate box—offered the most potential. The boxes also offered the highest ratings on "provides new information," "is a credible option," "is relevant to me," and "is superior to competitive options." Additional focus group and brand metaphor research provided additional insights into the consumer decision-making process and another study indicated that the two market leaders "owned" the two most important decision making criteria of "on time delivery" and "speed of service." More importantly, the studies revealed the third most important criterion to be "ease of use." No one seemed to be focusing on this criterion. Knowing that the Flat Rate Box option made the process significantly easier, the USPS now had a positioning statement. Further research led to the development of a message strategy to address three truths about shipping packages: (1) weighing packages is a hassle; (2) comprehending shipping rates to other states is confusing; and (3) the shipping process is overly complicated. This led to the campaign theme for Flat Rate Boxes as "A Simpler Way to Ship." Four executions of the ad were created, and all four tested positively in animatic form, and the Millward-Brown awareness and persuasive measures tested extremely well. Because research also showed that people trusted their mail carriers, the campaign featured a carrier as spokesperson.

Once launched, research was employed to determine media weights, cost per lead, and ROI. A number of metrics were employed in the pretests, and tracking was used to determine impact on brand value, inquiries through business response cards, and visits to the microsite. Campaign engagement and sales volume were also monitored on a continuing basis. However, from the start, USPS management made it very clear—the only measure of effectiveness that would count would be an increase in sales volume and revenues. While all of the image and creative stuff was admirable, this campaign *must* generate sales.

And sell it has! Besides generating strong market research scores, the campaign has led to a reversal in the ten year decline in sales and brand share for USPS in the first year. Flat rate shipping volume increased by 59 percent (versus a projected 5–9 percent decline), and sales revenue increased 53 percent. An additional $119 million in sales revenue was generated. In addition, the campaign led to an additional 20,000 leads from high volume shippers, with 3,927 new accounts opened, resulting in an additional $54.1 million in revenue. Over the same period, both FedEx and UPS experienced 21 percent and 19 percent increases respectively. In addition, since the campaign started, prioritymail.com hits have totaled over 2.4 million.

David Ogilvy was right. Strong research leads to winning campaigns!

Source: David Ogilvy Awards, presented by the Advertising Research Foundation, New York, 2010.

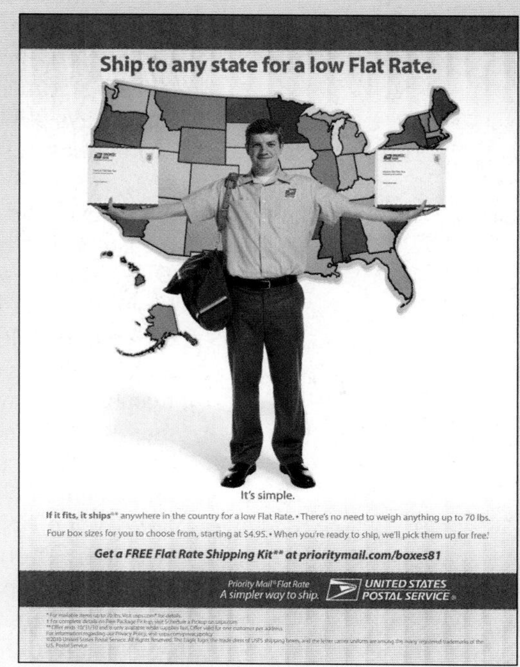


CHAPTER 18

to measure effectiveness, with as many as 90 percent considering it a priority, many do not do so, or if they do, they are not confident of the results. On the positive side, 60 percent of these managers say they plan to increase their expenditures in this area.[4]

Companies give a number of reasons for not measuring the effectiveness of advertising and promotions strategies:

1. *Cost.* Perhaps the most commonly cited reason for not testing (particularly among smaller firms) is the expense. In one of the surveys cited, it was noted that while some companies spend as much as 25 percent of their revenue on marketing and advertising, 70 percent of them spend less than 2 percent on measuring effectiveness.[5] Good research can be expensive, in terms of both time and money. Many managers decide that time is critical and they must implement the program while the opportunity is available. Many believe the monies spent on research could be better spent on improved production of the ad, additional media buys, and the like.

   While the first argument may have some merit, the second does not. Imagine what would happen if a poor campaign were developed or the incentive program did not motivate the target audience. Not only would you be spending money without the desired effects, but the effort could do more harm than good. Spending more money to buy media does not remedy a poor message or substitute for an improper promotional mix. For example, one of the nation's leading brewers watched its test-market sales for a new brand of beer fall short of expectations. The problem, it thought, was an insufficient media buy. The solution, it decided, was to buy all the TV time available that matched its target audience. After two months sales had not improved, and the product was abandoned in the test market. Analysis showed the problem was not in the media but rather in the message, which communicated no reason to buy. Research would have identified the problem, and millions of dollars and a brand might have been saved. The moral: Spending research monies to gain increased exposure to the wrong message is not a sound management decision.
2. *Research problems.* A second reason cited for not measuring effectiveness is that it is difficult to isolate the effects of promotional elements. Each variable in the marketing mix affects the success of a product or service. Because it is often difficult to measure the contribution of each marketing element directly, some managers become frustrated and decide not to test at all. They say, "If I can't determine the specific effects, why spend the money?"

   This argument also suffers from weak logic. While we agree that it is not always possible to determine the dollar amount of sales contributed by promotions, research can provide useful results and, as shown throughout this text, most have metrics to evaluate their performance. As demonstrated by the USPS example in IMC Perspective 18–1, communications effectiveness can be measured and may carry over to sales or other behaviors.
3. *Disagreement on what to test.* The objectives sought in the promotional program may differ by industry, by stage of the product life cycle, or even for different people within the firm. There are numerous ways to measure these and not always a concensus as to what measure should be used. The sales manager may want to see the impact of promotions on sales, top management may wish to know the impact on corporate image, and those involved in the creative process may wish to assess recall and/or recognition of the ad. Lack of agreement on what to test often results in no testing. A study conducted by the AAAA and ANA (Figure 18–2) revealed that many marketers are dissatisfied with their efforts to integrate traditional and digital media, and there is a need to develop appropriate metrics for doing so.

   Again, there is little rationale for this position. With the proper design, many or even all of the above might be measured. Since every promotional element is designed to accomplish specific objectives while contributing to the overall program, research can be used to measure its effectiveness in doing so.

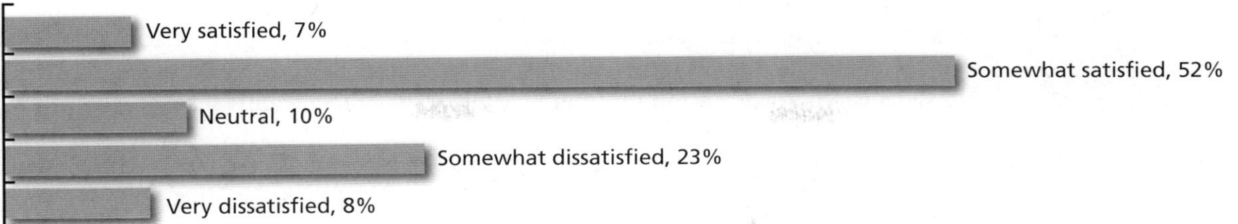


**FIGURE 18–2**

Satisfaction Level of U.S. Marketers with Their Company's Progress in Integrating Traditional and Digital Media, Q1 2009 (% of respondents)

Note: The 122 client-side marketers (members of ANA)

Source: Reprinted with permission of eMarketer.

4. *The objections of creative.* It has been argued by many (and denied by others) that the creative department does not want its work to be tested and many agencies are reluctant to submit their work for testing. This is sometimes true. Ad agencies' creative departments argue that tests are not true measures of the creativity and effectiveness of ads; applying measures stifles their creativity; and the more creative the ad, the more likely it is to be successful. They want permission to be creative without the limiting guidelines marketing may impose. The Chiat/Day ad shown in Exhibit 18–1 reflects how many people in the advertising business feel about this subject.

   At the same time, the marketing manager is ultimately responsible for the success of the product or brand. Given the substantial sums being allocated to advertising and promotion, it is the manager's right, and responsibility, to know how well a specific program—or a specific ad—will perform in the market. Interestingly, in a study examining the 200 most awarded commercials over a 2-year span, it was shown that 86 percent were deemed effective in achieving their goals, versus only 33 percent for other ads—proving that creative ads are effective.[6]

5. *Time.* A final reason given for not testing is a lack of time. Managers believe they already have too much to do and just can't get around to testing, and they don't want to wait to get the message out because they might miss the window of opportunity.

   Planning might be the solution to the first problem. Although many managers are overworked and time poor, research is just too important to skip.

The second argument can also be overcome with proper planning. While timeliness is critical, getting the wrong message out is of little or no value and may even be harmful. There will be occasions where market opportunities require choosing between testing and immediate implementation. But even then some testing may help avoid mistakes or improve effectiveness.

**EXHIBIT 18–1**

Chiat/Day expresses its opinion of recall tests

# CONDUCTING RESEARCH TO MEASURE ADVERTISING EFFECTIVENESS

## What to Test

We now examine how to measure the effects of communications. This section considers what elements to evaluate, as well as where and how such evaluations should occur.

In Chapter 5, we discussed the components of the communications model (source, message, media, receiver) and the importance of each in the promotional program. Marketers need to determine how each is affecting the communications process. Other decisions made in the promotional planning process must also be evaluated.

**Source Factors** An important question is whether the spokesperson being used is effective and how the target market will respond to him or her. Or a product spokesperson may be an excellent source initially but, owing to a variety of reasons, may lose impact over time. As shown in Chapter 17, negative publicity can easily change the value of a source. The fact that so many of the companies using Tiger Woods as a spokesperson terminated their contracts with him was based on the expectation that the target audiences would no longer have positive perceptions of him. The list of celebrities who have fallen out of favor is a long one.

**Message Variables** Both the message and the means by which it is communicated are bases for evaluation. For example, in the beer example discussed earlier, the message never provided a reason for consumers to try the new product. In other instances, the message may not be strong enough to pull readers into the ad by attracting their attention or clear enough to help them evaluate the product. Sometimes the message is memorable but doesn't achieve the other goals set by management. For example, one study examined what effect sexually themed print ads would have on viewers. Among the numerous results was that men favor sex appeals more than women do and that recall of the brands was lower for sexual ads than for nonsexual ones. Whereas men responded that sexual ads have "high stopping power" for them, their lower brand recall seems to indicate that they are paying more attention to other aspects of the ad than the marketers would prefer.[7]

**Media Strategies** Research may be designed in an attempt to determine which media class (for example, broadcast versus print), subclass (newspaper versus magazines), or specific vehicles (which newspapers or magazines) generate the most effective results. Likewise, how does one digital medium compare relative to others, or to traditional media? Perhaps, most importantly, how does each medium contribute to the achievement of overall IMC objectives?

Another factor is the **vehicle option source effect**, "the differential impact that the advertising exposure will have on the same audience member if the exposure occurs in one media option rather than another." People perceive ads differently depending on their context.[8]

Another factor to consider in media decisions involves scheduling. The evaluation of flighting versus pulsing or continuous schedules is important, particularly given the increasing costs of media time. As discussed in Chapter 10, there is evidence to support the fact that continuity may lead to a more effective media schedule than does flighting. Likewise, there may be opportunities associated with increasing advertising weights in periods of downward sales cycles or recessions. The manager experimenting with these alternative schedules and/or budget outlays should attempt to measure their differential impact.

As more and more companies and organizations move toward an integrated media mix, it becomes increasingly important to attempt to determine the individual contributions of various media as well as their synergistic effect. As you will see later in this chapter, progress is being made in this regard, but making such a determination is not a simple task.

**Budgeting Decisions** A number of studies have examined the effects of budget size on advertising effectiveness and the effects of various ad expenditures on sales. Many companies have also attempted to determine whether increasing their ad budget directly increases sales. This relationship is often hard to determine, perhaps because using sales as an indicator of effectiveness ignores the impact of other

**FIGURE 18–3**

Classification of Testing Methods

Source: Reprinted with permission.

| Pretests | | |
|---|---|---|
| *Laboratory Methods* | | |
| Consumer juries | Theater tests | Readability tests |
| Portfolio tests | Rough tests | Comprehension and reaction tests |
| Physiological measures | Concept tests | |
| *Field Methods* | | |
| Dummy advertising vehicles | On-air tests | |
| **Posttests** | | |
| *Field Methods* | | |
| Recall tests | Single-source systems | Recognition tests |
| Association measures | Inquiry tests | Tracking studies |

marketing mix elements. More definitive conclusions may be possible if other dependent variables, such as the communications objectives stated earlier, are used.

## When to Test

Virtually all test measures can be classified according to when they are conducted. **Pretests** are measures taken before the campaign is implemented; **posttests** occur after the ad or commercial has been in the field. A variety of pretests and posttests are available to the marketer, each with its own methodology designed to measure some aspect of the advertising program. Figure 18–3 classifies these testing methods.

**Pretesting** Pretests may occur at a number of points, from as early on as idea generation to rough execution to testing the final version before implementing it. More than one type of pretest may be used. For example, concept testing (which is discussed later in this chapter) may take place at the earliest development of the ad or commercial, when little more than an idea, basic concept, or positioning statement is under consideration. In other instances, layouts of the ad campaign that include headlines, some body copy, and rough illustrations are used. For TV commercials, storyboards and animatics may be tested. In these tests specific shortcomings may be identified, and changes made to enhance certain executional elements. As noted by Cramphorn, the best reason to pretest is to identify winners, to enhance good ads, and to eliminate bad ones. He notes that it is important to know the probable effect the ad will have before committing to its use.[9]

The methodologies employed to conduct pretests vary. In focus groups, participants freely discuss the meanings they get from the ads, consider the relative advantages of alternatives, and even suggest improvements or additional themes. In addition to or instead of the focus groups, consumers are asked to evaluate the ad on a series of rating scales. (Different agencies use different measures.) In-home interviews, mall intercept, Internet surveys, or laboratory methods may be used to gather the data.

The advantage of pretesting at this stage is that feedback is relatively inexpensive. Any problems with the concept or the way it is to be delivered are identified before large amounts of money are spent in development. Sometimes more than one version of the ad is evaluated to determine which is most likely to be effective.

Due to the fact that it costs so much less to find out that an ad may not work prior to making it public, rather than after doing so, it certainly makes sense to pretest.

The disadvantage is that mock-ups, storyboards, or animatics may not communicate nearly as effectively as the final product. The mood-enhancing and/or emotional aspects of the message are very difficult to communicate in this format. Another disadvantage is time delays. Many marketers believe being first in the market offers them a distinct advantage over competitors, so they forgo research to save time and ensure this position.

**Posttesting** Posttesting is also common among both advertisers and ad agencies (with the exception of testing commercials for wearout). Posttesting is designed to (1) determine if the campaign is accomplishing the objectives sought and (2) serve as input into the next period's situation analysis.

## Where to Test

In addition to when to test, decisions must be made as to *where*. These tests may take place in either laboratory or field settings.

**Laboratory** In **laboratory tests**, people are brought to a particular location where they are shown ads and/or commercials. The testers either ask questions about them or measure participants' responses by other methods—for example, pupil dilation, eye tracking, or galvanic skin response.

The major advantage of the lab setting is the *control* it affords the researcher. Changes in copy, illustrations, formats, colors, and the like can be manipulated inexpensively and the differential impact of each assessed. This makes it much easier for the researcher to isolate the contribution of each factor.

The major disadvantage is the lack of *realism*. Perhaps the greatest effect of this lack of realism is a **testing bias**. When people are brought into a lab (even if it has been designed to look like a living room), they may scrutinize the ads much more closely than they would at home. A second problem with this lack of realism is that it cannot duplicate the natural viewing situation, complete with the distractions or comforts of home. Looking at ads in a lab setting may not be the same as viewing at home on the couch, with the spouse, kids, dog, cat, and parakeet chirping in the background. (A bit later you will see that some testing techniques have made progress in correcting this deficiency. No, they did not bring in the dogs and the parakeets.) Overall, however, the control offered by this method probably outweighs the disadvantages, which accounts for the frequent use of lab methods.

**Field Tests** **Field tests** are tests of the ad or commercial under natural viewing situations, complete with the realism of noise, distractions, and the comforts of home. Field tests take into account the effects of repetition, program content, and even the presence of competitive messages.

The major disadvantage of field tests is the lack of control. It may be impossible to isolate causes of viewers' evaluations. If atypical events occur during the test, they may bias the results. Competitors may attempt to sabotage the research. And field tests usually take more time and money to conduct, so the results are not available to be acted on quickly. Thus, realism is gained at the expense of other important factors. It is up to the researcher to determine which trade-offs to make.

## How to Test

Our discussion of what should be tested, when, and where was general and designed to establish a basic understanding of the overall process as well as some key terms. In this section, we discuss more specifically some of the methods commonly used at each stage. First, however, it is important to establish some criteria by which to judge ads and commercials.

**FIGURE 18–4**

Positioning Advertising Copy Testing (PACT)

1. Provide measurements that are relevant to the objectives of the advertising.
2. Require agreement about how the results will be used in advance of each specific test.
3. Provide multiple measurements (because single measurements are not adequate to assess ad performance).
4. Be based on a model of human response to communications—the reception of a stimulus, the comprehension of the stimulus, and the response to the stimulus.
5. Allow for consideration of whether the advertising stimulus should be exposed more than once.
6. Require that the more finished a piece of copy is, the more soundly it can be evaluated and require, as a minimum, that alternative executions be tested in the same degree of finish.
7. Provide controls to avoid the biasing effects of the exposure context.
8. Take into account basic considerations of sample definition.
9. Demonstrate reliability and validity.

Conducting evaluative research is not easy. Twenty-one of the largest U.S. ad agencies have endorsed a set of principles aimed at "improving the research used in preparing and testing ads, providing a better creative product for clients, and controlling the cost of TV commercials."[10] This set of nine principles, called **PACT (Positioning Advertising Copy Testing)**, defines *copy testing* as research "which is undertaken when a decision is to be made about whether advertising should run in the marketplace. Whether this stage utilizes a single test or a combination of tests, its purpose is to aid in the judgment of specific advertising executions."[11] The nine principles of good copy testing are shown in Figure 18–4.

As you can see, advertisers and their clients are concerned about developing *appropriate* testing methods. Adherence to these principles may not make for perfect testing, but it goes a long way toward improving the state of the art and alleviates at least one of the testing problems cited earlier.

## THE TESTING PROCESS



Testing may occur at various points throughout the development of an ad or a campaign: (1) concept generation research; (2) rough, prefinished art, copy, and/or commercial testing; (3) finished art or commercial pretesting; and (4) market testing of ads or commercials (posttesting).

### Concept Generation and Testing

Figure 18–5 describes the process involved in advertising **concept testing**, which is conducted very early in the campaign development process in order to explore the targeted consumer's response to a potential ad or campaign or have the consumer evaluate advertising alternatives. Positioning statements, copy, headlines, and/or illustrations may all be under scrutiny. The material to be evaluated may be just a headline or a rough sketch of the ad. The colors used, typeface, package designs, and even point-of-purchase materials may be evaluated.

One of the more commonly used methods for concept testing is focus groups, which usually consist of 8 to 10 people in the target market for the product. Companies have tested everything from product concepts to advertising concepts using focus groups. For most companies, the focus group is the first step in the research process. The number of focus groups used varies depending on group consensus,

**FIGURE 18–5**
Concept Testing

| *Objective:* |
|---|
| Explores consumers' responses to various ad concepts as expressed in words, pictures, or symbols. |
| *Method:* |
| Alternative concepts are exposed to consumers who match the characteristics of the target audience. Reactions and evaluations of each are sought through a variety of methods, including focus groups, direct questioning, and survey completion. Sample sizes vary depending on the number of concepts to be presented and the consensus of responses. |
| *Output:* |
| Qualitative and/or quantitative data evaluating and comparing alternative concepts. |

strength of response, and/or the degree to which participants like or dislike the concepts. Some companies use 50 or more groups to develop a campaign, although fewer than 10 are usually needed to test a concept sufficiently.

While focus groups continue to be a favorite of marketers, they are often overused. The methodology is attractive in that results are easily obtained, directly observable, and immediate. A variety of issues can be examined, and consumers are free to go into depth in areas they consider important. Also, focus groups don't require quantitative analysis. Unfortunately, many managers are uncertain about research methods that require statistics; and focus groups, being qualitative in nature, don't demand much skill in interpretation. Weaknesses with focus groups are shown in Figure 18–6. Clearly, there are appropriate and inappropriate circumstances for employing this methodology.

Another way to gather consumers' opinions of concepts is mall intercepts, where consumers in shopping malls are approached and asked to evaluate rough ads and/or copy. Rather than participating in a group discussion, individuals assess the ads via questionnaires, rating scales, and/or rankings. New technologies allow for concept testing over the Internet, where advertisers can show concepts simultaneously to consumers throughout the United States, garnering feedback and analyzing the results almost instantaneously. Internet methods are becoming increasingly popular given the cost savings and time efficiencies associated with these research methods, and some research firms now offer hybrid studies that involve a combination of online and traditional measures.

## Rough Art, Copy, and Commercial Testing

Because of the high cost associated with the production of an ad or commercial (many network commercials cost hundreds of thousands of dollars to produce),

**FIGURE 18–6**
Weaknesses Associated with Focus Group Research

- The results are not quantifiable.
- Sample sizes are too small to generalize to larger populations.
- Group influences may bias participants' responses.
- One or two members of the group may steer the conversation or dominate the discussion.
- Consumers become instant "experts."
- Members may not represent the target market. (Are focus group participants a certain type of person?)
- Results may be taken to be more representative and/or definitive than they really are.

A *rough* commercial is an unfinished execution that may fall into three broad categories:

| *Animatic Rough* | *Photomatic Rough* | *Live-Action Rough* |
|---|---|---|
| Succession of drawings/cartoons | Succession of photographs | Live motion |
| Rendered artwork | Real people/scenery | Stand-in/nonunion talent |
| Still frames | Still frames | Nonunion crew |
| Simulated movement: | Simulated movements: | Limited props/minimal opticals |
| Panning/zooming of frame/rapid sequence | Panning/zooming of frame/rapid sequence | Location settings |
| *A Finished Commercial Uses:* | | |
| Live motion/animation | | |
| Highly paid union talent | | |
| Full union crew | | |
| Exotic props/studio sets/special effects | | |

**FIGURE 18–7**

Rough Testing Terminology

advertisers are increasingly spending more monies testing a rendering of the final ad at early stages. Slides of the artwork posted on a screen or animatic and photomatic roughs may be used to test at this stage. (See Figure 18–7 for an explanation of terminology.) Because such tests can be conducted inexpensively, research at this stage is becoming ever more popular.

But cost is only one factor. The test is of little value if it does not provide relevant, accurate information. Rough tests must indicate how the finished commercial would perform. Studies have demonstrated that these testing methods are reliable and the results typically correlate well with the finished ad.

Most of the tests conducted at the rough stage involve lab settings, although some on-air field tests are also available. Popular tests include comprehension and reaction tests and consumer juries. Again, the Internet allows field settings to be employed at this stage.

1. *Comprehension and reaction tests.* One key concern for the advertiser is whether the ad or commercial conveys the meaning intended. The second concern is the reaction the ad generates. Obviously, the advertiser does not want an ad that evokes a negative reaction or offends someone. **Comprehension and reaction tests** are designed to assess these responses (which makes you wonder why some ads are ever brought to the marketplace).

   Tests of comprehension and reaction employ no one standard procedure. Personal interviews, group interviews, and focus groups have all been used for this purpose, and sample sizes vary according to the needs of the client; they typically range from 50 to 200 respondents.
2. *Consumer juries.* This method uses consumers representative of the target market to evaluate the probable success of an ad. **Consumer juries** may be asked to rate a selection of layouts or copy versions presented in pasteups on separate sheets. The objectives sought and methods employed in consumer juries are shown in Figure 18–8.

   While the jury method offers the advantages of control and cost effectiveness, serious flaws in the methodology limit its usefulness:

   - *The consumer may become a self-appointed expert.* One of the benefits sought from the jury method is the objectivity and involvement in the product or service that the targeted consumer can bring to the evaluation process. Sometimes, however, knowing they are being asked to critique ads, participants try

CHAPTER 18

**FIGURE 18–8**

Consumer Juries

| Objective: |
|---|
| Potential viewers (consumers) are asked to evaluate ads and give their reactions to and evaluation of them. When two or more ads are tested, viewers are usually asked to rate or rank order the ads according to their preferences. |
| **Method:** |
| Respondents are asked to view ads and rate them according to either (1) the order of merit method or (2) the paired comparison method. In the former, the respondent is asked to view the ads and then rank them from one to *n* according to their perceived merit. In the latter, ads are compared only two at a time. Each ad is compared to every other ad in the group, and the winner is listed. The best ad is that which wins the most times. Consumer juries typically employ 50 to 100 participants. |
| **Output:** |
| An overall reaction to each ad under construction as well as a rank ordering of the ads based on the viewers' perceptions. |

to become more *expert* in their evaluations, paying more attention and being more critical than usual. The result may be a less than objective evaluation or an evaluation on elements other than those intended.

- *The number of ads that can be evaluated is limited.* Whether *order of merit* or *paired comparison* methods are used, the ranking procedure becomes tedious as the number of alternatives increases. Consider the ranking of 10 ads. While the top two and the bottom two may very well reveal differences, those ranked in the middle may not yield much useful information.

  In the paired comparison method, the number of evaluations required is calculated by the formula

$$\frac{n(n-1)}{2}$$

  If six alternatives are considered, 15 evaluations must be made. As the number of ads increases, the task becomes even more unmanageable.
- *A halo effect is possible.* Sometimes participants rate an ad good on all characteristics because they like a few and overlook specific weaknesses. This tendency, called the **halo effect**, distorts the ratings and defeats the ability to control for specific components. (Of course, the reverse may also occur—rating an ad bad overall due to only a few bad attributes.)
- *Preferences for specific types of advertising may overshadow objectivity.* Ads that involve emotions or pictures may receive higher ratings or rankings than those employing copy, facts, and/or rational criteria. Even though the latter are often more effective in the marketplace, they may be judged less favorably by jurists who prefer emotional appeals.

Some of the problems noted here can be remedied by the use of ratings scales instead of rankings. But ratings are not always valid either. Thus, while consumer juries have been used for years, questions of bias have led researchers to doubt their validity. As a result, a variety of other methods (discussed later in this chapter) are more commonly employed.

## Pretesting of Finished Ads

Pretesting finished ads is one of the more commonly employed studies among marketing researchers and their agencies. At this stage, a finished advertisement or commercial is used; since it has not been presented to the market, changes can still be made.

**FIGURE 18–9**

Gallup & Robinson's Impact System

| *Objective:* |
|---|
| Understanding the performance of individual advertising executions or testing finished products. Evaluation of print advertising in magazines or newspapers. Can also be used to pretest rough advertising executions or posttesting finished products. |
| *Method:* |
| Interviewers contact potential respondents door to door or by telephone and screen for qualification. |
| *Output:* |
| Scores include recall, idea communication, persuasion, brand rating, and ad liking. Diagnostics in regard to ad reactions and brand attributes are also reported. |

Many researchers believe testing the ad in final form provides better information. Several test procedures are available for print and broadcast ads, including both laboratory and field methodologies.

Print methods include portfolio tests, analyses of readability, and dummy advertising vehicles. Broadcast tests include theater tests and on-air tests. Both print and broadcast may use physiological measures.

**Pretesting Finished Print Messages** A number of methods for pretesting finished print ads are available. One is *Gallup & Robinson's Impact System,* described in Figure 18–9. The most common of these methods are portfolio tests, readability tests, and dummy advertising vehicles.

**Portfolio Tests** **Portfolio tests** are a laboratory methodology designed to expose a group of respondents to a portfolio consisting of both control and test ads. Respondents are then asked what information they recall from the ads. The assumption is that the ads that yield the *highest recall* are the most effective.

While portfolio tests offer the opportunity to compare alternative ads directly, a number of weaknesses limit their applicability:

1. Factors other than advertising creativity and/or presentation may affect recall. Interest in the product or product category, the fact that respondents know they are participating in a test, or interviewer instructions (among others) may account for more differences than the ad itself.
2. Recall may not be the best test. Some researchers argue that for certain types of products (those of low involvement) ability to recognize the ad when shown may be a better measure than recall.

One way to determine the validity of the portfolio method is to correlate its results with readership scores once the ad is placed in the field. Whether such validity tests are being conducted or not is not readily known, although the portfolio method remains popular in the industry.

**Readability Tests** The communications efficiency of the copy in a print ad can be tested without reader interviews. This test uses the **Flesch formula**, named after its developer, Rudolph Flesch, to assess readability of the copy by determining the average number of syllables per 100 words. Human interest appeal of the material, length of sentences, and familiarity with certain words are also considered and correlated with the educational background of target audiences. Test results are compared to previously established norms for various target audiences. The test suggests that copy is best comprehended when sentences are short, words are concrete and familiar, and personal references are drawn.

This method eliminates many of the interviewee biases associated with other tests and avoids gross errors in understanding. The norms offer an attractive standard for comparison.

**FIGURE 18–10**
Ipsos-ASI's Next*Print

| *Objective:* |
|---|
| To assist advertisers in copy testing of print advertisements to determine the print ad's impact on the brand (parallels Next*TV pretest methodology). |
| *Method:* |
| Tests are conducted in magazines, in homes. The recall measure consists of 150 responses. Diagnostic measures range from 105 to 150 responses. Highly targeted audiences are available through a version known as the Targeted Print Test. |
| *Output:* |
| Standard scores, related recall, persuasion, and specific diagnostics. |

Disadvantages are also inherent, however. The copy may become too mechanical, and direct input from the receiver is not available. Without this input, contributing elements like creativity cannot be addressed. To be effective, this test should be used only in conjunction with other pretesting methods.

**Dummy Advertising Vehicles** In an improvement on the portfolio test, ads are placed in "dummy" magazines developed by an agency or research firm. The magazines contain regular editorial features of interest to the reader, as well as the test ads, and are distributed to a *random sample* of homes in predetermined geographic areas. Readers are told the magazine publisher is interested in evaluations of editorial content and asked to read the magazines as they normally would. Then they are interviewed on their reactions to both editorial content and ads. Recall, readership, and interest-generating capabilities of the ad are assessed.

The advantage of this method is that it provides a more natural setting than the portfolio test. Readership occurs in the participant's own home, the test more closely approximates a natural reading situation, and the reader may go back to the magazine, as people typically do.

But the dummy magazine shares the other disadvantages associated with portfolio tests. The testing effect is not eliminated, and product interest may still bias the results. Thus, while this test offers some advantages over the portfolio method, it is not a guaranteed measure of the advertising's impact.

While all the previously described measures are available, the most popular form of pretesting of print ads now involves a series of measures. Companies like Millward-Brown and Ipsos-ASI offer copy testing services that have improved upon many of the shortcomings cited above. The tests can be used for rough and/or finished ads and are most commonly conducted in the respondents' homes. For example, Millward-Brown's link copy test includes measures of emotional responses to ads, assessing metrics such as enjoyment, engagement, likes, and dislikes to address overall emotional response. Ipsos-ASI's Next*Print methodology also offers multiple measures, as shown in Figure 18–10.

**Pretesting Finished Broadcast Ads** A variety of methods for pretesting broadcast ads are available. The most popular are theater tests, on-air tests, and physiological measures.

**Theater Tests** In the past, one of the most popular laboratory methods for pretesting finished commercials was **theater testing**. In theater tests participants are invited to view pilots of proposed TV programs. In some instances, the show is actually being tested, but more commonly a standard program is used so audience responses can be compared with normative responses established by previous viewers. Sample sizes range from 250 to 600 participants, with 300 being most typical.

**FIGURE 18–11**
The AD*VANTAGE/ACT Theater Methodology

Advertising Control for Television (ACT), a lab procedure of The MSW Group, uses about 400 respondents representing four cities. It measures initial brand preference by asking participants which brands they most recently purchased. Respondents are then divided into groups of 25 to view a 30-minute program with seven commercials inserted in the middle. Four are test commercials; the other three are control commercials with established viewing norms. After viewing the program, respondents are given a recall test of the commercials. After the recall test, a second 30-minute program is shown, with each test commercial shown again. The second measure of brand preference is taken at this time, with persuasion measured by the percentage of viewers who switched preferences from their most recently purchased brand to one shown in the test commercials.

The methods of theater testing operations vary, though all measure brand preference changes. For example, many of the services now use videotaped programs with the commercials embedded for viewing in one's home or office rather than in a theater. Others establish viewing rooms in malls and/or hotel conference rooms. Some do not take all the measures listed here; others ask the consumers to turn dials or push buttons on a keypad to provide the continual responses. An example of one methodology is shown in Figure 18–11.

Those opposed to theater tests cite a number of disadvantages. First, they say the environment is too artificial. The lab setting is bad enough, but asking respondents to turn dials or, as one service does, wiring people for physiological responses takes them too far from a natural viewing situation. Second, the contrived measure of brand preference change seems too phony to believe. Critics contend that participants will see through it and make changes just because they think they are supposed to. Finally, the group effect of having others present and overtly exhibiting their reactions may influence viewers who did not have any reactions themselves.

Proponents argue that theater tests offer distinct advantages. In addition to control, the established norms (averages of commercials' performances) indicate how one's commercial will fare against others in the same product class that were already tested. Further, advocates say the brand preference measure is supported by actual sales results.

Despite the limitations of theater testing, most major consumer-product companies have used it to evaluate their commercials. This method may have shortcomings, but it allows them to identify strong or weak commercials and to compare them to other ads.



**On-Air Tests** Some of the firms conducting theater tests also insert the commercials into actual TV programs in certain test markets. Typically, the commercials are in finished form, although the testing of ads earlier in the developmental process is becoming more common. This is referred to as an **on-air test** and often includes single-source ad research (discussed later in this chapter). Information Resources, Ipsos-ASI, MSW Group, and Nielsen are well-known providers of on-air tests.

On-air testing techniques offer all the advantages of field methodologies, as well as all the disadvantages. The most commonly employed metric used in an on-air test is **recall**—that is the number of persons able to recall the ad and/or its message. In an examination of real-world advertising tests reported in the *Journal Of Advertising Research,* Hu, et al. conclude that recall and persuasion pretests, while often employed, do not fare well in respect to reliability and/or validity.[12] Nevertheless, most of the testing services have offered evidence of both validity and reliability for on-air pretesting of commercials. Both Ipsos-ASI and MSW Group claim their pretest and posttest results yield the same recall scores 9 out of 10 times—a strong indication of reliability and a good predictor of the effect the ad is likely to have when shown to the population as a whole.

**FIGURE 18–12**

Eye Movement Research

| Objective: |
|---|
| Track viewers' eye movements to determine what viewers read or view in print ads and where their attention is focused in TV commercials, websites, or billboards. |
| **Method:** |
| Fiber optics, digital data processing, and advanced electronics are used to follow eye movements of viewers and/or readers as they process an ad. |
| **Output:** |
| Relationship among what readers see, recall, and comprehend. Scan movement paths on print ads, billboards, commercials, print materials, and websites. (Can also be used to evaluate package designs.) |

In summary, on-air pretesting of finished or rough commercials offers some distinct advantages over lab methods and some indications of the ad's likely success. Whether the measures used are as strong an indication as the providers say still remains in question.

**Physiological Measures** A less common method of pretesting finished commercials involves a laboratory setting in which physiological responses are measured. These measures indicate the receiver's *involuntary* response to the ad, theoretically eliminating biases associated with the voluntary measures reviewed to this point. (Involuntary responses are those over which the individual has no control, such as heartbeat and reflexes.) Physiological measures used to test both print and broadcast ads include pupil dilation, galvanic skin response, eye tracking, and brain waves:

1. *Pupil dilation.* Research in **pupillometrics** is designed to measure dilation and constriction of the pupils of the eyes in response to stimuli. Dilation is associated with action; constriction involves the body's conservation of energy.

   Advertisers have used pupillometrics to evaluate product and package design as well as to test ads. Pupil dilation suggests a stronger interest in (or preference for) an ad or implies arousal or attention-getting capabilities. Other attempts to determine the affective (liking or disliking) responses created by ads have met with less success.

   Because of high costs and some methodological problems, the use of pupillometrics has waned over the past decade. But it can be useful in evaluating certain aspects of advertising.
2. *Galvanic skin response.* Also known as **electrodermal response**, GSR measures the skin's resistance or conductance to a small amount of current passed between two electrodes. Response to a stimulus activates sweat glands, which in turn increases the conductance of the electrical current. Thus, GSR/EDR activity might reflect a reaction to advertising. While there is evidence that GSR/EDR may be useful to determine the effectiveness of ads, difficulties associated with this testing method have resulted in its infrequent use at this time.
3. *Eye tracking.* As seen in the lead-in to this chapter, a methodology that is more commonly employed is **eye tracking** (Figure 18–12), in which viewers are asked to view an ad while a sensor aims a beam of infrared light at the eye. The beam follows the movement of the eye and shows the exact spot on which the viewer is focusing. The continuous reading of responses demonstrates which elements of the ad are attracting attention, how long the viewer is focusing on them, and the sequence in which they are being viewed.

   Eye tracking can identify strengths and weaknesses in an ad. For example, attractive models or background action may distract the viewer's attention away from the brand or product being advertised. The advertiser can remedy this distraction before fielding the ad. In other instances, colors or illustrations may attract attention and create viewer interest in the ad (Exhibit 18–2).

Eye tracking has increasingly been used to measure the effectiveness of websites and online ads, and, as noted earlier, e-mails. Using eye tracking to examine how consumers view homepages, Steve Outing and Laura Roel were able to determine that (1) eyes first fixate on the upper left of the screen, (2) dominant headlines draw attention first, and (3) larger type promotes scanning, while small type encourages reading. The study drew other conclusions as well—too many to mention here.[13]

4. *Brain waves.* **Electroencephalographic (EEG) measures** can be taken from the skull to determine electrical frequencies in the brain. These electrical impulses are used in two areas of research, alpha waves and hemispheric lateralization:
   - **Alpha activity** refers to the degree of brain activation. People are in an alpha state when they are inactive, resting, or sleeping. The theory is that a person in an alpha state is less likely to be processing information (recall correlates negatively with alpha levels) and that attention and processing require moving from this state. By measuring a subject's alpha level while viewing a commercial, researchers can assess the degree to which attention and processing are likely to occur.
   - **Hemispheric lateralization** distinguishes between alpha activity in the left and right sides of the brain. It has been hypothesized that the right side of the brain processes visual stimuli and the left processes verbal stimuli. The right hemisphere is thought to respond more to emotional stimuli, while the left responds to logic. The right determines recognition, while the left is responsible for recall. If these hypotheses are correct, advertisers could design ads to increase learning and memory by creating stimuli to appeal to each hemisphere. However, some researchers believe the brain does not function laterally and an ad cannot be designed to appeal to one side or the other.
   - Using technologies originally designed for the medical field such as positron emission tomography (PET), functional magnetic resonance imaging (fMRI), and electroencephalography (EEG), neuroscientists have teamed up with marketers to examine physiological reactions to ads and brands through brain scan imaging. By monitoring the brain activity directly, scientists are learning how consumers make up their minds by measuring chemical activity and/or changes in the magnetic fields of the brain as well as how they react to commercials.

**EXHIBIT 18–2**
Eye-tracking services like these provided by SensoMotoric Instruments are now available to marketers

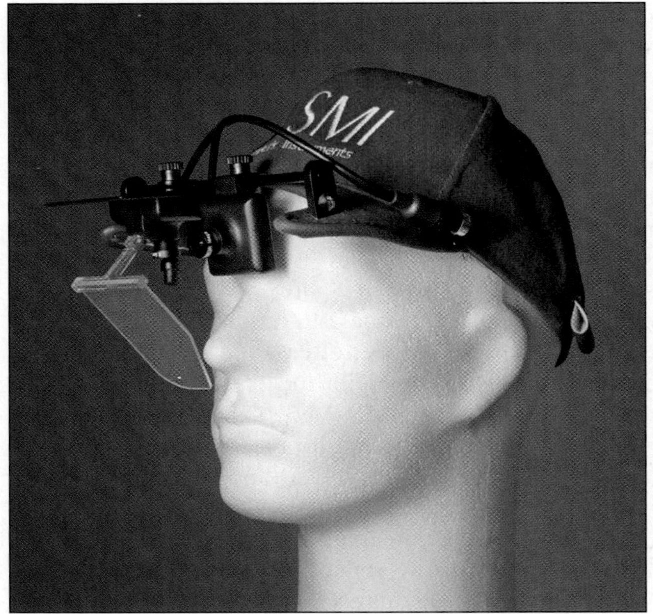


While EEG research has engaged the attention of academic researchers, it has been much less successful in attracting the interest of practitioners, though recently the technology has gained in attractiveness as shown in IMC Technology Perspective 18–1.

## Market Testing of Ads

The fact that the ad and/or campaign has been implemented does not mean there is no longer a need for testing. The pretests were conducted on smaller samples and may in some instances have questionable merit, so the marketer must find out how the ad is doing in the field. In this section, we discuss methods for posttesting

## IMC Technology Perspective 18–1 > > >

### Neuromarketing: Marketing Panacea or Voodoo?

At one time, it seemed, MRI machines were used only in hospitals to diagnose potential health problems. Likewise, heart rates were also the domain of medical offices and hospitals. But times have changed. In the constant search for determining the effectiveness of advertising, marketers have now turned to the use of these measures along with changes in the skin and even facial muscles that are imperceptible to the human eye to examine physiological responses to ads, TV commercials, websites, and video games. The use of neurosciences to test commercials is hailed by some as a major measurement breakthrough, and discounted by others as junk science.

During the 2008 Super Bowl, a company in El Paso, Texas, strapped caps with electrodes that were wirelessly linked to electroencephalography (EEG) machines on the heads of 20 subjects while they watched Super Bowl commercials. The EEG measured and recorded brain activity in millisecond increments to 60 commercials shown on the game. After the physiological measures were taken, the group was orally tested to gauge recall of the commercials' content and brand identification, as well as their preferences for each ad. The top 10 commercials were then ranked (sound familiar?).

Interestingly, but probably not surprisingly, the top 10 list did not match the lists provided by pollsters and focus groups. Nor did it match well with the *USA Today* Ad Meter. The top five commercials in the physiological study were Pepsi's "Bob's House," Coke's "Balloons," Bud Light's "Fly," Audi's "R8/Old Luxury on Notice," and Verizon's "Voyager." Only "Balloons" was on both lists. In fact, only two matched on the top 10 lists—the other being a Budweiser commercial. But, popularity aside, the physiological measures provided some additional insights. Sexy spots fared poorly, 60-second ads scored higher than 30-second ones, and ads with an element of surprise consistently scored high. Sands Research—the company that conducted the research—concluded that, based on this study and others it has conducted, neuromedia analysis is becoming an increasingly sophisticated and cost-efficient method of conducting research into audience engagement and the decision-making process. Many others agree.

The $4.2 billion Nielsen Company, the world's leading audience measurement company recently invested in NeuroFocus, a neuromarketing company, as Fortune 500 companies have shown increased interest in the applications of brainwave research to marketing. For example, some marketers believe that this method of testing consumer responses may be superior to focus groups, given the common knowledge that what consumers say they will do in the groups and what they do are often not the same. They say it's hard to change neurological responses. Other marketing thoughts that have been examined include product desirability, pricing factors, and risk behaviors. Professor Uzma Khan of Stanford University uses neuromarketing to explore larger context issues such as the design and marketing approach of retail stores.

The use of neurosciences for marketing purposes has been employed for some time. Neuromarketing, as it is referred to by some, has been used to test differences in responses to Coke and Pepsi, men's reactions to automobiles, movie trailers, and political ads, to mention a few. As noted by one marketer, there are so many com-

an ad. Some of the tests are similar to the pretests discussed in the previous section and are provided by the same companies.

**Posttests of Print Ads** A variety of print posttests are available, including inquiry tests, recognition tests, and recall tests.

**Inquiry Tests** Used in both consumer and business-to-business market testing, **inquiry tests** are designed to measure advertising effectiveness on the basis of inquiries generated from ads appearing in various print media, often referred to as "bingo cards" such as the one shown in Exhibit 18–3. While still used, the response card is employed less often today as viewers can seek information merely by searching on the URL provided in the ad. The inquiry may take the form of the number of coupons returned, phone calls generated, or direct inquiries through reader cards. If you called in a response to an ad in a local medium recently, perhaps you were asked how you found out about the company or product or where you saw the ad. This is a very simple measure of the ad's or medium's effectiveness.

panies now offering this methodology, they are cluttering up the marketing landscape.

Others are not convinced of the value of neuroscience studies. Andrew Gelman, professor of statistics and political science at Columbia University, contends that the reported correlations between brain activity patterns and thoughts and emotions are "too good to be true." Gelman goes on to say the correlations are so high that they can't be trusted. William Eddy of Carnegie Mellon agrees, noting that, "Correlations of 0.9 are unbelievable in any social science setting." While the supporters of the use of the science are often furious, fighting back with blog posts and online defenses, they have also admitted that some reported correlations are inflated. They also concede that these reports have not been good for the science.

Another nonbeliever is Brian Knutson, a professor of neuroscience and psychology at Stanford University who has compared the use of EEG to "standing outside a baseball stadium and listening to the crowd to figure out what happened" and Neuroscientist Joshua Freedman, chief scientist at FKF Applied Research who considers the results "worse data than you'd get by just talking to people in focus groups." But both Knutson and Freedman are optimistic that neurosciences have potential for marketing studies, Freedman arguing for the superiority of MRI over EEG. Many other neuroscientists and marketers alike are less optimistic, however, contending there have only been promises of success, and that these measures have provided little if any insights. Still others argue that studying the brain in isolation while ignoring the impact of the larger culture just doesn't make sense. Erwin Ephron, a well-respected advertising and media consultant, believes that neuroscience just doesn't go far enough in explaining consumer reactions to ads, while others refer to it straight out as "junk science."

So what is it—a major marketing research breakthrough or just another research methodology that promises more than it delivers? Are we better off just asking people what they think about commercials or wiring them to machines to probe inside their heads? Maybe we should conduct some research?

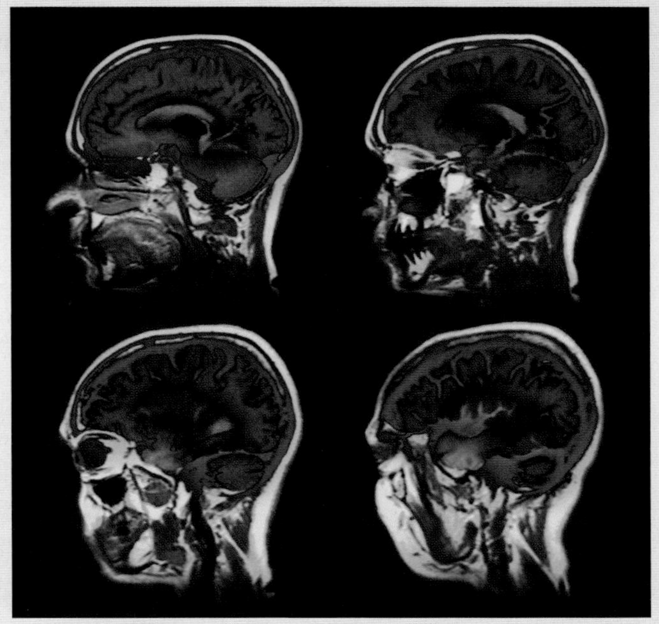

Sources: Sharon Begley, "Of Voodoo and the Brain," www.newsweek.com, February 9, 2009; Rick Ferguson, "Neuromarketing: What the Human Brain Means to Your Campaign," www.chiefmarketer.com, October 27, 2009; Mya Frazier, "Hidden Persuasion or Junk Science?" *Advertising Age,* September 10, 2007, pp. 1, 38–39; Erwin Ephron, "The Open Mind," *Mediaweek,* February 5, 2007, p. 10; Jack Neff, "The Super Bowl Spots That Got Inside Consumers Heads," adage.com, February 7, 2008, pp. 1–3; "Sands Research Conducts Real-Time Brain Imaging of Viewers Exposed to Super Bowl Commercials," www.reuters.com, February 11, 2008, pp. 1–3.



More complex methods of measuring effectiveness through inquiries may involve (1) running the ad in successive issues of the same medium, (2) running **split-run tests**, in which variations of the ad appear in different copies of the same newspaper or magazine, and/or (3) running the same ad in different media. Each of these methods yields information on different aspects of the strategy. The first measures the *cumulative* effects of the campaign; the second examines specific elements of the ad or variations on it. The final method measures the effectiveness of the medium rather than the ad itself.

While inquiry tests may yield useful information, weaknesses in this methodology limit its effectiveness. For example, inquiries may not be a true measure of the attention-getting or information-providing aspects of the ad. The reader may be attracted to an ad, read it, and even store the information but not be motivated to inquire at that particular time. Time constraints, lack of a need for the product or service at the time the ad is run, and other factors may limit the number of inquiries. But receiving a small number of inquiries doesn't mean the ad was not effective; attention, attitude change, awareness, and recall of copy points may all have been

**EXHIBIT 18–3**
Reader response cards are popular in business-to-business markets

**TARGET MARKETING** Receive the information you need to market smarter instantly!
Go to: **www.targetonline.com** and click on free information.

**Or...Fill out this card and either FAX your request today: 215-238-5388 or mail.**

**Free Subscription**

**Do you wish to receive (continue to receive) a FREE subscription to TARGET MARKETING?** ☐ YES ☐ NO

Signature__________ Date__________
Name (please print)__________ Title __________
Company Name __________
Address __________
City/State/Zip __________
Telephone__________ FAX __________
Email Address:__________

1. **TYPE OF BUSINESS AT THIS LOCATION: (Check One)**
   04 ☐ Catalogers, Mail Order Companies
   05 ☐ Retailers, Wholesaler/Distributor
   06 ☐ On-line Merchant
   03 ☐ Financial Services: Banks, Insurance, Credit Cards, Investment
   21 ☐ Fund Raisers: Non-Profit Groups, Charities
   33 ☐ High Technology: Internet Services, Computers, Software, Telecommunications, Office Equipment
   12 ☐ Manufacturers, Package Goods and Other Business-to-Business Marketers
   31 ☐ Non Financial Services Marketers: Associations, Clubs, Educational, Government Agencies, Health Care, Membership Organizations, Personnel Services, Real Estate, Utilities, Communications, Tourism and Travel
   13 ☐ Publishers: Magazines, Books, Newsletters, Newspapers, Book & Record Clubs On-line publications
   01 ☐ Advertising/DM Agencies, Freelance Creative and Consultants
   09 ☐ Mailing List Professionals: Brokers, Compilers, Owners
   20 ☐ Other: (Please Specify) __________
2. **JOB FUNCTION: (Check One)**
   10 ☐ Corporate and General Management (Excluding Sales, Marketing and Advertising Management)
   02 ☐ Marketing, List and Sales Management
   01 ☐ Advertising Promotion and Public Relations Management
   08 ☐ Operational, Technical and Telemarketing Management
   06 ☐ Circulation Management
   11 ☐ Other: (Please Specify) __________
3. **MY FIRM'S MARKETING ACTIVITY: (Check All That Apply)**
   1 ☐ Catalog
   2 ☐ Direct Mail
   09 ☐ Internet
   3 ☐ Telemarketing
   10 ☐ Alternate Media
   5 ☐ Consumer
   6 ☐ Business-to-Business
   7 ☐ International
   8 ☐ None of the Above
4. **IN THE PERFORMANCE OF YOUR JOB, CHECK THE ONE THAT BEST DESCRIBES YOUR PURCHASING AUTHORITY: (Check One)**
   1 ☐ Authorize/Approve Purchase
   2 ☐ Recommend/ Specify Purchase
   3 ☐ No Purchasing Authority

**Free Information**

**Circle the free info number for the products and services that interest you**

| | | | | | | | | | | | |
|---|---|---|---|---|---|---|---|---|---|---|---|
| 001 | 002 | 003 | 004 | 005 | 006 | 007 | 008 | 009 | 010 | 011 | 012 |
| 013 | 014 | 015 | 016 | 017 | 018 | 019 | 020 | 021 | 022 | 023 | 024 |
| 025 | 026 | 027 | 028 | 029 | 030 | 031 | 032 | 033 | 034 | 035 | 036 |
| 037 | 038 | 039 | 040 | 041 | 042 | 043 | 044 | 045 | 046 | 047 | 048 |
| 049 | 050 | 051 | 052 | 053 | 054 | 055 | 056 | 057 | 058 | 059 | 060 |
| 061 | 062 | 063 | 064 | 065 | 066 | 067 | 068 | 069 | 070 | 071 | 072 |
| 073 | 074 | 075 | 076 | 077 | 078 | 079 | 080 | 081 | 082 | 083 | 084 |
| 085 | 086 | 087 | 088 | 089 | 090 | 091 | 092 | 093 | 094 | 095 | 096 |
| 097 | 098 | 099 | 100 | 101 | 102 | 103 | 104 | 105 | 106 | 107 | 108 |
| 109 | 110 | 111 | 112 | 113 | 114 | 115 | 116 | 117 | 118 | 119 | 120 |
| 121 | 122 | 123 | 124 | 125 | 126 | 127 | 128 | 129 | 130 | 131 | 132 |
| 133 | 134 | 135 | 136 | 137 | 138 | 139 | 140 | 141 | 142 | 143 | 144 |
| 145 | 146 | 147 | 148 | 149 | 150 | 151 | 152 | 153 | 154 | 155 | 156 |
| 157 | 158 | 159 | 160 | 161 | 162 | 163 | 164 | 165 | 166 | 167 | 168 |
| 169 | 170 | 171 | 172 | 173 | 174 | 175 | 176 | 177 | 178 | 179 | 180 |

**For Information on Product/Service Categories**
To request information on any of the following areas of interest, check the appropriate free information number:

501 ☐ Agencies/Consultants/Creative Services
502 ☐ Alternate Media/Delivery
503 ☐ Broadcast Media/Services
504 ☐ Call Center Equipment
505 ☐ Credit/Collection Services
506 ☐ Database Management Systems/ Services/Software
507 ☐ Delivery Services
529 ☐ E-mail Marketing
508 ☐ Envelopes/Order Forms/Labels
509 ☐ Fulfillment Services/Operations
510 ☐ Int'l Call Centers
511 ☐ Int'l Delivery Services
512 ☐ Int'l DM Agencies
525 ☐ International DM Services
530 ☐ Internet Services
513 ☐ Lettershop Services
514 ☐ Lists-Business-to-Business
515 ☐ Lists-Consumer
528 ☐ Lists-E-mail
516 ☐ Lists-International
517 ☐ List Services
518 ☐ Mailing Equipment/Services
520 ☐ Paper
521 ☐ Premiums/Promotional Products
522 ☐ Prepress Equipment/Services
523 ☐ Printers
527 ☐ Printing Systems/Equipment
524 ☐ Telemarketing Services

RS0110

achieved. At the other extreme, a person with a particular need for the product may respond to any ad for it, regardless of specific qualities of the ad.

Major advantages of inquiry tests are that they are inexpensive to implement and they provide some feedback with respect to the general effectiveness of the ad or medium used. But they are usually not very effective for comparing different versions or specific creative aspects of an ad.

**Recognition Tests** Perhaps the most common posttest of print ads is the **recognition method**, most closely associated with GfK-Starch. The *Starch Ad Readership Report* lets the advertiser assess the impact of an ad in a single issue of a magazine, over time, and/or across different magazines. Starch measures over 155,000 ads in more than 3,100 issues representing more than 200 consumer magazines per year and provides a number of measures of the ad's effectiveness. The measures used in the Starch test methodology are shown in Figure 18–13. An example of a Starch scored ad is shown in Exhibit 18–4.

Starch claims that (1) the pulling power of various aspects of the ad can be assessed through the control offered, (2) the effectiveness of competitors' ads can be compared through the norms provided, (3) alternative ad executions can be tested, and (4) readership scores are a useful indication of consumers' *involvement* in the ad or campaign. (The theory is that a reader must read and become involved in the ad before the ad can communicate. To the degree that this readership can be shown, it is a direct indication of effectiveness.)

Of these claims, perhaps the most valid is the ability to judge specific aspects of the ad. Some researchers have criticized other aspects of the Starch recognition method (as well as other recognition measures) on the basis of problems of false claiming, interviewer sensitivities, and unreliable scores:

**FIGURE 18–13**
The *GfK Starch Ad Readership Report*

| *Objective:* |
|---|
| Determining recognition of print ads and comparing them to other ads of the same variety or in the same magazine. |
| *Method:* |
| Personal interviewers screen readers for qualifications and determine exposure and readership to specific issues of newspapers, consumer magazines, and business and professional publications. Samples include a minimum of 200 males and females, as well as specific audiences where required. Participants are asked to go through the magazines, looking at the ads, and provide specific responses. |
| *Output:* |
| *Starch Ad Readership Reports* generate three recognition scores: <br>■ Noting score—the percentage of readers who remember seeing the ad. <br>■ Brand-associated score—the percentage of readers who recall seeing or reading any part of the ad identifying the product or brand. <br>■ Read-most score—the percentage of readers who report reading at least half of the copy portion of the ad. Ad norms provide a benchmark to provide a comparison to other ads in the issue. |

1. *False claiming.* Research shows that in recognition tests, respondents may claim to have seen an ad when they did not. False claims may be a result of having seen similar ads elsewhere, expecting that such an ad would appear in the medium, or wanting to please the questioner. Interest in the product category also increases reporting of ad readership. Whether this false claiming is deliberate or not, it leads to an overreporting of effectiveness. On the flip side, factors such as interview fatigue may lead to an underreporting bias—that is, respondents not reporting an ad they did see.
2. *Interviewer sensitivities.* Any time research involves interviewers, there is a potential for bias. Respondents may want to impress the interviewer or fear looking unknowledgeable if they continually claim not to recognize an ad. There may also be variances associated with interviewer instructions, recordings, and so on, regardless of the amount of training and sophistication involved.
3. *Reliability of recognition scores.* Starch admits that the reliability and validity of its readership scores increase with the number of insertions tested, which essentially means that to test just one ad on a single exposure may not produce valid or reliable results.

CHAPTER 18

**EXHIBIT 18–4**
An ad scoring very high on the Starch rating scale.

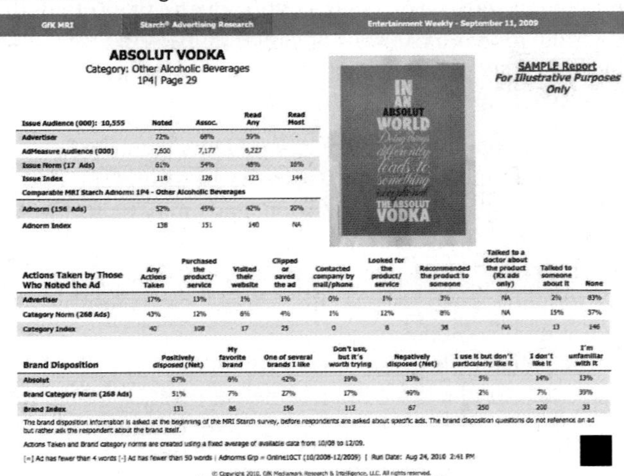
GfK MRI | Starch® Advertising Research | Entertainment Weekly - September 11, 2009

**ABSOLUT VODKA**
Category: Other Alcoholic Beverages
1P4| Page 29



SAMPLE Report
*For Illustrative Purposes Only*

| Issue Audience (000): 10,555 | Noted | Assoc. | Read Any | Read Most |
|---|---|---|---|---|
| Advertiser | 72% | 68% | 59% | - |
| AdMeasure Audience (000) | 7,600 | 7,177 | 6,227 | |
| Issue Norm (17 Ads) | 61% | 54% | 48% | 10% |
| Issue Index | 118 | 126 | 123 | 144 |
| Comparable MRI Starch Adnorm: 1P4 - Other Alcoholic Beverages | | | | |
| Adnorm (156 Ads) | 52% | 45% | 42% | 20% |
| Adnorm Index | 138 | 151 | 140 | NA |

| Actions Taken by Those Who Noted the Ad | Any Actions Taken | Purchased the product/service | Visited their website | Clipped or saved the ad | Contacted company by mail/phone | Looked for the product/service | Recommended the product to someone | Talked to a doctor about the product (Rx ads only) | Talked to someone about it | None |
|---|---|---|---|---|---|---|---|---|---|---|
| Advertiser | 17% | 13% | 1% | 1% | 0% | 1% | 3% | NA | 2% | 83% |
| Category Norm (268 Ads) | 43% | 12% | 6% | 4% | 1% | 12% | 8% | NA | 15% | 57% |
| Category Index | 40 | 108 | 17 | 25 | 0 | 8 | 38 | NA | 13 | 146 |

| Brand Disposition | Positively disposed (Net) | My favorite brand | One of several brands I like | Don't use, but it's worth trying | Negatively disposed (Net) | I use it but don't particularly like it | I don't like it | I'm unfamiliar with it |
|---|---|---|---|---|---|---|---|---|
| Absolut | 67% | 6% | 42% | 19% | 33% | 5% | 14% | 13% |
| Brand Category Norm (268 Ads) | 51% | 7% | 27% | 17% | 49% | 2% | 7% | 39% |
| Brand Index | 131 | 86 | 156 | 112 | 67 | 250 | 200 | 33 |

The brand disposition information is asked at the beginning of the MRI Starch survey, before respondents are asked about specific ads. The brand disposition questions do not reference an ad but rather ask the respondent about the brand itself.

Actions Taken and Brand category norms are created using a fixed average of available data from 10/08 to 12/09.

[=] Ad has fewer than 4 words [-] Ad has fewer than 50 words | Adnorms Grp = Online10CT (10/2008-12/2009) | Run Date: Aug 24, 2010 2:41 PM

© Copyright 2010, GfK Mediamark Research & Intelligence, LLC. All rights reserved.
Advertising Occurrence Data: Copyright 2010 by Kantar Media | Intelligence. All rights reserved.

In sum, despite critics, the Starch readership studies continue to dominate the posttesting of print ads. The value provided by norms and the fact that multiple exposures can improve reliability and validity may underlie the decisions to employ this methodology.

**Recall Tests** There are several tests to measure recall of print ads. Perhaps the best known of these are the Ipsos-ASI Next*Print test and the Gallup & Robinson Magazine Impact Research Service (MIRS) (described in Figure 18–14). These **recall tests** are similar to those discussed in the section on pretesting broadcast ads in that they attempt to measure recall of specific ads.

In addition to having the same interviewer problems as recognition tests, recall tests have other disadvantages. The reader's degree of involvement with the product and/

**FIGURE 18–14**

Gallup & Robinson Magazine Impact Research Service (MIRS)

| *Objective:* |
| --- |
| Tracking recall of advertising (and client's ads) appearing in magazines to assess performance and effectiveness. |
| *Method:* |
| Test magazines are placed in participants' homes and respondents are asked to read the magazine that day. A telephone interview is conducted the second day to assess recall of ads, recall of copy points, and consumers' impressions of the ads. Sample size is 150 people. |
| *Output:* |
| Three measurement scores are provided:<br>■ Proven name registration—the percentage of respondents who can accurately recall the ad.<br>■ Idea communication—the number of sales points the respondents can recall.<br>■ Favorable buying attitude—the extent of favorable purchase reaction to the brand or corporation. |

or the distinctiveness of the appeals and visuals may lead to higher-than-accurate recall scores, although in general the method may lead to lower levels of recall than actually exist (an error the advertiser would be happy with). Critics contend the test is not strong enough to reflect recall accurately, so many ads may score as less effective than they really are, and advertisers may abandon or modify them needlessly.

On the plus side, it is thought that recall tests can assess the ad's impact on memory. Proponents of recall tests say the major concern is not the results themselves but how they are interpreted. Previous studies have shown that the correlation between ad recall and recognition is very high in both newspapers and magazines.

**Posttests of Broadcast Commercials** A variety of methods exist for posttesting broadcast commercials. The most common provide a combination of day-after recall tests, persuasion measures, and diagnostics. Test marketing and tracking studies, including single-source methods, are also employed.

**Day-After Recall Tests** The most popular method of posttesting employed in the broadcasting industry for decades was the *Burke Day-After Recall test.* While a number of companies offered day-after recall methodologies, the "Burke test" for all intents and purposes became the generic name attached to these tests. While popular, day-after recall tests also had problems, including limited samples, high costs, and security issues (ads shown in test markets could be seen by competitors). Because of their common usage, numerous studies have been conducted to determine the efficacy of DAR tests. While these studies have been conducted quite some time ago, the conclusions seem to be relevant today, and merit consideration here. In addition, the following disadvantages with recall tests were also suggested:

1. DAR tests may favor unemotional appeals because respondents are asked to verbalize the message. Thinking messages may be easier to recall than emotional communications, so recall scores for emotional ads may be lower.[14] A number of other studies have also indicated that emotional ads may be processed differently from thinking ones; some ad agencies, for example, Leo Burnett and BBDO Worldwide, have gone so far as to develop their own methods of determining emotional response to ads.[15]
2. Program content may influence recall. The programs in which the ad appears may lead to different recall scores for the same brand. The net result is a potential inaccuracy in the recall score and in the norms used to establish comparisons.

3. A prerecruited sample (Gallup & Robinson) may pay increased attention to the program and the ads contained therein because the respondents know they will be tested the next day. This effect would lead to a higher level of recall than really exists.
4. In addition, studies have shown that recall is a measure that the ad has been received, but not necessarily accepted, and not predictive of sales.[16,17]

The major advantage of day-after recall tests is that they are field tests. The natural setting is supposed to provide a more realistic response profile. These tests are also popular because they provide norms that give advertisers a standard for comparing how well their ads are performing. In addition to recall, a number of different measures of the commercial's effectiveness are now offered, including persuasive measures and diagnostics. (The Burke test itself no longer exists.)

**Persuasive Measures** As noted earlier in our discussion of pretesting broadcast commercials, a measure of a commercial's persuasive effectiveness is gathered by asking consumers to choose a brand that they would want to win in a drawing and then—after exposure to the ad—ask the question again. In theater settings this is accomplished by announcing a series of prize drawings, with viewers indicating which of the brands they would choose if they won. In field settings, it is accomplished by taking a brand preference measure when the video is delivered and then again the next day. Some of the services offer additional persuasion measures, including purchase-intent and frequency-of-purchase criteria. Ipsos-ASI and the ARS Group are two of the more well-known providers of measures of persuasion.

**Diagnostics** In addition to measuring recall and persuasion, copy testing firms also provide diagnostic measures. These measures are designed to garner viewers' evaluations of the ads, as well as how clearly the creative idea is understood and how well the proposition is communicated. Rational and emotional reactions to the ads are also examined. A number of companies offer diagnostic measures, including Gallup & Robinson and Millward Brown, among many others.

**Comprehensive Measures** While each of the measures just described provides specific input into the effectiveness of a commercial, many advertisers are interested in more than just one specific input. Thus, some companies provide comprehensive approaches in which each of the three measures just described can be obtained through one testing program. Figure 18–15 describes one such comprehensive program, Ipsos-ASI's Next*TV test (Exhibit 18–5).



**Test Marketing** Many companies conduct tests designed to measure their advertising effects in specific test markets before releasing them nationally. The markets chosen are representative of the target market. For example, a company may test its ads in Portland, Oregon; San Antonio, Texas; or Buffalo, New York, if the demographic and socioeconomic profiles of these cities match the product's market. A variety of factors may be tested, including reactions to the ads (for example, alternative copy points), the effects of various budget sizes, or special offers. The ads run in finished form in the media where they might normally appear, and effectiveness is measured after the ads run.

The advantage of test marketing of ads is realism. Regular viewing environments are used and the testing effects are minimized. A high degree of control can be attained if the test is designed successfully. For example, an extensive test market study was designed and conducted by Seagram and Time, Inc., over three years to measure the effects of advertising frequency on consumers' buying habits. This study demonstrated just how much could be learned from research conducted in a field setting but with some experimental controls. It also showed that proper research can provide strong insights into the impact of ad campaigns. (Many advertising

**FIGURE 18–15**
Ipsos-ASI's Next*TV

| Objectives: |
|---|
| To assist advertisers in copy testing of their commercials through multiple measures to determine (1) the potential of the commercial for impacting sales, (2) how the ad contributes to brand equity, (3) how well it is in line with existing advertising strategies and objectives, and (4) how to optimize effectiveness. |
| **Method:** |
| Consumers are recruited to evaluate a TV program, with ads embedded into the program as they would be on local prime-time television. Consumers view the program on a videotape in their homes to simulate actual field conditions. (The option to use local cable television programs with commercial inserts is also provided.) |
| **Output:** |
| Related recall (day-after recall) scores; persuasion scores, including brand preference shifts, purchase intent and frequency, brand equity differentiation, and relevance and communication; and reaction diagnostics to determine what viewers take away from the ad and how creative elements contribute to or distract from advertising effectiveness. |

researchers consider this study one of the most conclusive ever conducted in the attempt to demonstrate the effects of advertising on sales.)

The Seagram study also reveals some of the disadvantages associated with test market measures, not the least of which are cost and time. Few firms have the luxury to spend three years and hundreds of thousands of dollars on such a test. In addition, there is always the fear that competitors may discover and intervene in the research process.

A number of companies, including Procter & Gamble and Toyota, have test-marketed interactive commercials. Reckitt—the world's largest manufacturer of household cleaning products—and Whirlpool have joined efforts to test *i*TV ads. Customers were offered three different enticements to interact with the campaign: (1) register to win a Whirlpool dishwasher, (2) register for free samples of Finish Dishwater Freshener, or (3) order money-off coupons for Finish Dishwater Tablets. After eight months of testing, Reckitt reported that the target goal of 35,000 responses was exceeded.[18] Sears and Ford have both tested the impact of ads placed on Gemstar—*TV Guide*'s interactive program guide—while Chrysler has experimented with online gaming to generate leads and stimulate buzz.[19]

Test marketing can provide substantial insight into the effectiveness of advertising if care is taken to minimize the negative aspects of such tests.

**EXHIBIT 18–5**
Ipsos-ASI offers a comprehensive testing measure

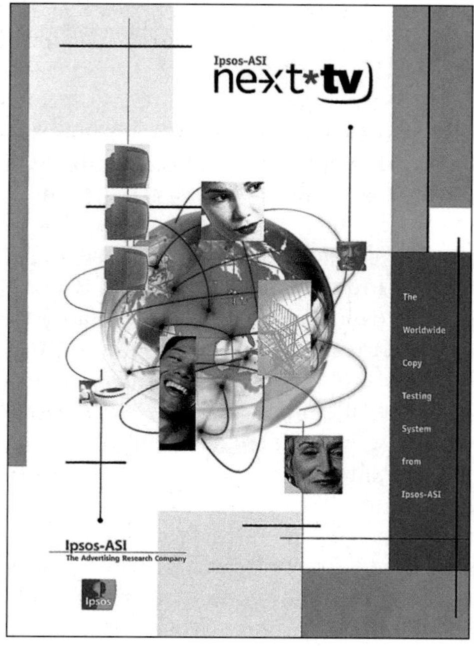


**Single-Source Tracking Studies** Since the 1980s the focus of many research efforts has been on single-source tracking methods. **Single-source tracking methods** track the behaviors of consumers from the television set to the supermarket checkout counter. Participants in a designated area who have cable TV and agree to participate in the studies use optical scanning equipment that identifies their household and gives the research company their demographics. The households are split into matched groups; one group receives an ad while the other does not, or alternate ads are sent to each. Their purchases are recorded from the bar codes of the products bought. Commercial exposures are then correlated with purchase behaviors.

Earlier we mentioned the use of single-source ad research in pretesting commercials. The single-source method can also be used effectively

**EXHIBIT 18–6**
Tracking studies provide useful measures

to posttest ads, allowing for a variety of dependent measures and tracking the effects of increased ad budgets and different versions of ad copy—and even ad effects on sales.

A 10-year study conducted by Information Resources' BehaviorScan service demonstrated long-term effects of advertising on sales. The study examined copy, media schedules, ad budgets, and the impact of trade promotions on sales in 10 markets throughout the United States and concluded that advertising can produce sales growth as long as two years after a campaign ends.[20] (The study also concluded that results of copy recall and persuasion tests were unlikely to predict sales reliably.) A number of single-source methods have been used, among them BehaviorScan (Information Resources) and Integrated Marketing Solutions (IMS). The A. C. Nielsen company's ScanTrack is another commonly employed single-source tracking system.

Many advertisers believe these single-source measures will change the way research is conducted due to the advantages of control and the ability to measure directly the ads' effects on sales. A number of major corporations and ad agencies are now employing this method, including companies and their agencies in the automotive, entertainment, financial services, packaged goods, and pharmaceutical industries among others.

While single-source testing is a valuable tool, it still has some problems. One researcher says, "Scanner data focus on short-term sales effects, and as a result capture only 10 to 30 percent of what advertising does."[21] Others complain that the data are too complicated to deal with, as an overabundance of information is available. Still another disadvantage is the high cost of collecting single-source data. While the complexity of single-source data resulted in a slow adoption rate, this method of tracking advertising effectiveness became widely adopted in the 1990s by the research companies mentioned earlier (Gallup & Robinson, Millward-Brown, and Ipsos-ASI).

**Tracking Print/Broadcast Ads** One of the more useful and adaptable forms of posttesting involves tracking the effects of the ad campaign by taking measurements at regular intervals. **Tracking studies** have been used to measure the effects of advertising on awareness, recall, interest, and attitudes toward the ad and/or brand as well as purchase intentions. (Ad tracking may be applied to both print and broadcast ads but is much more common with the latter.) Personal interviews, phone surveys, mall intercepts, and even mail surveys have been used. Sample sizes typically range from 250 to 500 cases per period (usually quarterly or semiannually). Tracking studies yield perhaps the most valuable information available to the marketing manager for assessing current programs and planning for the future. (See Exhibit 18–6.)

The major advantage of tracking studies is that they can be tailored to each specific campaign and/or situation. A standard set of questions can track effects of the campaign over time or through the consumer purchase funnel. In a study by the research organization Yankelovich and the Television Bureau of Advertising (TVB), it was shown that the effectiveness of advertising depends on the product category and where the consumer is in the purchase funnel. The advertising medium impact varied as the consumer moved through the stages.[22] The effects of various media can also be determined, although with much less effectiveness. Tracking studies have also been used to measure the differential impact of different budget sizes, the effects of flighting, brand or corporate image, and recall of specific copy points. As you will see later in the chapter, however, it is often difficult to quantify some of the measures suggested. Finally, when designed properly, as shown in Figure 18–16, tracking studies offer a high degree of reliability and validity.

**FIGURE 18–16**

Factors That Make or Break Tracking Studies

1. Properly defined objectives
2. Alignment with sales objectives
3. Properly designed measures (e.g., adequate sample size, maximum control over interviewing process, adequate time between tracking periods)
4. Consistency through replication of the sampling plan
5. Random samples
6. Continuous interviewing (that is, not seasonal)
7. Evaluate measures related to behavior (attitudes meet this criterion; recall of ads does not)
8. Critical evaluative questions asked early to eliminate bias
9. Measurement of competitors' performance
10. Skepticism about questions that ask where the advertising was seen or heard (TV always wins)
11. Building of news value into the study
12. "Moving averages" used to spot long-term trends and avoid seasonality
13. Data reported in terms of relationships rather than as isolated facts
14. Integration of key marketplace events with tracking results (e.g., advertising expenditures of self and competitors, promotional activities associated with price changes in ad campaigns, introductions of new brands, government announcements, changes in economic conditions)

Some of the problems of recall and recognition measures are inherent in tracking studies, since many other factors may affect both brand and advertising recall. Despite these limitations, however, tracking studies are a very effective way to assess the effects of advertising campaigns.

In summary, you can see that each of the testing methods considered in this chapter has its strengths and its limitations. You may wonder Can we actually test advertising effectiveness? What can be done to ensure a valid, reliable test? The next section of this chapter suggests some answers.

# ESTABLISHING A PROGRAM FOR MEASURING ADVERTISING EFFECTS

There is no surefire way to test advertising effectiveness. However, in response to pressures to determine the contribution of ads to the overall marketing effort, steps are being taken to improve this measurement task. Let's begin by reviewing the major problems with some existing methods and then examine possible improvements.

## Problems with Current Research Methods

When current testing methods are compared to the criteria established by PACT (see Figure 18–4), it is clear that some of the principles important to good copy testing can be accomplished readily, whereas others require substantially more effort. For example, principle 6 (providing equivalent test ads) should require a minimum of effort. The researcher can easily control the state of completion of the test communications. Also fairly easy are principles 1 and 2 (providing measurements relative to the objectives sought and determining *a priori* how the results will be used).

We have seen throughout this text that each promotional medium, the message, and the budget all consider the marketing and communications objectives sought. The integrated marketing communications planning model establishes the roles of these elements. So by the time one gets to the measurement phase, the criteria by which these programs will be evaluated should simply fall into place.

Slightly more difficult are principles 3, 5, and 8, although again these factors are largely in the control of the researcher. Principle 3 (providing multiple measurements) may require little more than budgeting to make sure more than one test is conducted. At the most, it may require considering two similar measures to ensure reliability. Likewise, principle 5 (exposing the test ad more than once) can be accomplished with a proper research design. Finally, principle 8 (sample definition) requires little more than sound research methodology; any test should use the target audience to assess an ad's effectiveness. You would not use a sample of nondrinkers to evaluate new liquor commercials.

The most difficult factors to control—and the principles that may best differentiate between good and bad testing procedures—are PACT requirements 4, 7, and 9. Fortunately, however, addressing each of these contributes to the attainment of the others.

The best starting point is principle 4, which states the research should be guided by a model of human response to communications that encompasses reception, comprehension, and behavioral response. It is the best starting point, in our opinion, because it is the principle least addressed by practicing researchers. If you recall, Chapter 5 proposed a number of models that could fulfill this principle's requirements. Yet even though these models have existed for quite some time, few if any common research methods attempt to integrate them into their methodologies. Most current methods do little more than provide recall scores, despite the fact many researchers have shown that recall is a poor measure of effectiveness. Models that do claim to measure such factors as attitude change or brand preference change are often fraught with problems that severely limit their reliability. An effective measure must include some relationship to the communications process.

It might seem at first glance that principle 7 (providing a nonbiasing exposure) would be easy to accomplish. But lab measures, while offering control, are artificial and vulnerable to testing effects. And field measures, while more realistic, often lose control. The Seagram and Time study may have the best of both worlds, but it is too large a task for most firms to undertake. Some of the improvements associated with the single-source systems help to solve this problem. In addition, properly designed ad tracking studies provide truer measures of the impact of the communication. As technology develops and more attention is paid to this principle, we expect to see improvements in methodologies soon.

Last but not least is principle 9, the concern for reliability and validity. Most of the measures discussed are lacking in at least one of these criteria, yet these are two of the most critical distinctions between good and bad research. If a study is properly designed, and by that we mean it addresses principles 1 through 8, it should be both reliable and valid.



## Essentials of Effective Testing

Simply put, good tests of advertising effectiveness must address the nine principles established by PACT. One of the easiest ways to accomplish this is by following the decision sequence model in formulating promotional plans.

- *Establish communications objectives.* We have stated that except for a few instances (most specifically direct-response advertising), it is nearly impossible to show the direct impact of advertising on sales. So the marketing objectives established for the promotional program are not usually good measures of communication effectiveness. For example, it is very difficult (or too expensive) to demonstrate the effect of an ad on brand share or on sales. On the other hand, attainment of communications objectives can be measured and leads to the accomplishment of marketing objectives.
- *Use a consumer response model.* Early in this text we reviewed the hierarchy of effects models and cognitive response models, which provide an understanding of the effects of communications and lend themselves to achieving communications goals.
- *Use both pretests and posttests.* From a cost standpoint—both actual cost outlays and opportunity costs—pretesting makes sense. It may mean the difference

between success or failure of the campaign or the product. But it should work in conjunction with posttests, which avoid the limitations of pretests, use much larger samples, and take place in more natural settings. Posttesting may be required to determine the true effectiveness of the ad or campaign.

- *Use multiple measures.* Many attempts to measure the effectiveness of advertising focus on one major dependent variable—perhaps sales, recall, or recognition. As noted earlier in this chapter, advertising may have a variety of effects on the consumer, some of which can be measured through traditional methods, others that require updated thinking (recall the discussion on physiological responses). For a true assessment of advertising effectiveness, a number of measures may be required. The Ogilvy Award winners mentioned earlier all employed multiple measures to track the effects on communications objectives.
- *Understand and implement proper research.* It is critical to understand research methodology. What constitutes a good design? Is it valid and reliable? Does it measure what we need it to? There is no shortcut to this criterion, and there is no way to avoid it if you truly want to measure the effects of advertising.

A major study sponsored by the Advertising Research Foundation (ARF), involving interviews with 12,000 to 15,000 people, addressed some of these issues.[23] While we do not have the space to analyze this study here, note that the research was designed to evaluate measures of copy tests, compare copy testing procedures, and examine some of the PACT principles. Information on this study has been published in a number of academic and trade journals and by the ARF.

# MEASURING THE EFFECTIVENESS OF OTHER PROGRAM ELEMENTS

Throughout this text, we have discussed how and when promotional program elements should be used, the advantages and disadvantages of each, and so on. In many chapters we have discussed measures of effectiveness used to evaluate these programs. In the final section of this chapter, we add a few measures that were not discussed earlier.

## Measuring the Effectiveness of Sales Promotions

Sales promotions are not limited to retailers and resellers of products. Sports marketers have found them a very effective way to attract crowds and have been able to measure their relative effectiveness by the number of fans attending games. Major League Baseball teams have seen their attendance increase for those games in which promotions are offered.

A number of organizations measure sales promotions. One firm, MarketSource, provides marketers with a basis for measuring the effectiveness of their sampling programs. While too involved to discuss in detail here, the program calculates a breakeven rate by dividing the sampling investment by the profit for the user. If the conversions exceed the breakeven rate, the sampling program is successful.[24] Promotion Decisions Inc. examines the impact of freestanding inserts (FSIs) (Figure 18–17).

Other measures of sales promotions are also available. Schnucks (St. Louis), Smitty's Super Valu (Phoenix), and Vons (Los Angeles) have all used pretests with effects measured through scanner data. Others have employed this methodology to examine brand and store switching, alternative promotions, price discounts, and merchandising techniques.[25] Other advertisers use awareness tracking studies and count the number of inquiries, coupon redemptions, and sweepstakes entries. They also track sales during promotional and nonpromotional periods while holding other factors constant.

**FIGURE 18–17**

Measuring the Effects of FSIs

A study by Promotion Decisions Inc. examined the actual purchase data of users and nonusers of 27 coupon promotions in its National Shopper Lab (75,000 households) over a period of 18 months. The findings:

- FSI coupons generated significant trial by new and lapsed users of a product (53%).
- Repeat purchase rates were 11.8% higher among coupon redeemers than nonredeemers.
- 64.2% of repeat volume among coupon redeemers was without a coupon.
- There was no significant difference in share of volume between buyers who used coupons and those who did not.
- Coupons returned between 71% and 79% of their cost within 12 weeks.
- Full-page ads provided higher redemption rates, incremental volume, redemption by new users, and a higher number of repeat buyers than half-page ads.
- Consumers who used coupons were brand loyal.

One recent technological development designed to track the effectiveness of sales promotions at the point of sale is offered by Shopper Trak. Shopper Trak places sensors in the store that track whether a person is coming or going, calculate the shopper's height (to differentiate between adults and children), and gauge traffic patterns. The system helps retailers evaluate the effectiveness of promotions or displays located throughout the store.[26]

## Measuring the Effectiveness of Nontraditional Media

In Chapter 13, we noted that one of the disadvantages of employing nontraditional media is that it is usually difficult to measure the effectiveness of the programs. But some progress has been made, as shown in these examples:

- *The effects of shopping cart signage.* Earlier we discussed sales increases that occurred when shopping cart signage was used. We have also noted throughout this chapter that while increasing sales is a critical goal, many other factors may contribute to or detract from this measure. (It should be noted that these results are provided by the companies that sell these promotional media.) At least one study has examined the effectiveness of shopping cart signage on data besides sales.[27] This study used personal interviews in grocery stores to measure awareness of, attention to, and influence of this medium. Interestingly, it suggests shopping carts are much less effective than the sign companies claim.
- *The effectiveness of ski resort–based media.* In Chapter 13, we discussed advertising on ski chair lifts and other areas to attempt to reach selective demographic groups. Now the Traffic Audit Bureau (TAB) is tracking the effectiveness of this form of advertising to give advertisers more reliable criteria on which to base purchase decisions. The TAB data verify ad placements, while the media vendors have employed Simmons Market Research Bureau and Nielsen Media Research to collect ad impressions and advertising recall information.[28] These measures are combined with sales tracking data to evaluate the medium's effectiveness.
- *The effects of in-store radio and television.* Interactive Market Systems (IMS) introduced software that enables clients to measure the effectiveness of in-store radio. The company planned to introduce similar software designed to measure in-store television advertising effectiveness.[29]
- *The effectiveness of other media.* A number of companies provide effectiveness measures to determine the impact of package designs, POP displays, trade show exhibits, and the like. Nielsen Entertainment and Massive, Inc., now offer a service to measure videogame advertising effectiveness.[30] While it is not possible to list them all here, suffice it to say that if one wants to measure the impact of various IMC elements, the resources are available.

**FIGURE 18–18**

Eight Steps to Measuring Event Sponsorship

1. Narrowly define objectives with specifics.
2. Establish solid strategies against which programming will be benchmarked and measure your programming and effectiveness against the benchmark.
3. Set measurable and realistic goals; make sure everything you do supports them.
4. Enhance, rather than just change, other marketing variables.
5. Don't pull Marketing Plan 101 off the shelf. Programming should be crafted to reflect the particulars of your company's constituencies and target audiences.
6. Define the scope of your involvement. Will it involve multiple areas within the company? Who internally and externally comprises the team?
7. Think "long term." It takes time to build brand equity. Also, think of leveraging your sponsorship through programming for as long as possible, before and after the event.
8. Build evaluation and a related budget into your overall sponsoring program. Include items such as pre- and post-event attitude surveys, media analyses, and sales results.

## Measuring the Effectiveness of Sponsorships

In earlier chapters we discussed the growth in sponsorships and the reasons why organizations have increased their investments in this area. Along with the increased expenditures have come a number of methods for measuring the impact of sponsorships. Essentially, measures of sponsorship effectiveness can be categorized as exposure-based methods or tracking measures:[31]

- *Exposure methods.* Exposure methods can be classified as those that monitor the quantity and nature of the media coverage obtained for the sponsored event and those that estimate direct and indirect audiences. While commonly employed by corporations, scholars have heavily criticized these measures. For example, Michel Pham argues that media coverage is not the objective of sponsorships and should not be considered as a measure of effectiveness. He argues that the measures provide no indication of perceptions, attitude change, or behavioral change and should therefore not be considered as measures of effectiveness.[32]
- *Tracking measures.* These measures are designed to evaluate the awareness, familiarity, and preferences engendered by sponsorship based on surveys. A number of empirical studies have measured recall of sponsors' ads, awareness of and attitudes toward the sponsors and their products, and image effect including brand and corporate images.

A number of companies now measure the effectiveness of sports sponsorships. For example, companies assign a value referred to as media equivalency and assign a monetary value to the amount of exposure the sponsor receives during the event. They review broadcasts and add up the number of seconds a sponsor's product name or logo can be seen clearly (for example, on signs or shirts). A total of 30 seconds is considered the equivalent of a 30-second commercial. (Such measures are of questionable validity.)

Performance Research in Newport, Rhode Island, measures impact on brand awareness and image shifts. PS Productions, a Chicago-based research organization, provides clients with a measure of event sponsorships based on increased sales. PS calculates sales goals based on the cost of the event and the value of extras like donated media, customized displays, ads for key retailers, and tickets given away. An event is a success if it brings in at least that amount in additional sales.

While each of these measures has its advantages and disadvantages most do not go far enough. As noted by John Nardone and Ed See, most marketers limit their sponsorship evaluations to brand awareness and impressions. The key question that needs to be asked, they say, is "how do you do sponsorships that build brand equity and maintain financial responsibility?"[33] We suggest using several in assessing the impact of sponsorships. In addition to those mentioned here, the eight-step process suggested in Figure 18–18 could be used to guide these evaluations.

**FIGURE 18–19**

Measuring Effectiveness Not Only Efficiency

The most important issue for IMC planning is identifying the most appropriate contact mix, i.e., which contacts to prioritize.

| **Questions: Are we . . .** | |
|---|---|
| Being effective: | 1. Doing the right things? |
| Being efficient: | 2. Doing things right? |
| **Current techniques measure only efficiency** | |
| Reach, frequency, GRPs (media surveys) | |
| Weight of market activity (stochastic) | |
| **MCA by integration measures effectiveness and efficiency** | |
| Influence of contacts | |
| Consumer brand experience | |

## Measuring the Effectiveness of Other IMC Program Elements

Many of the organizations mentioned in this chapter offer research services to measure the effectiveness of specific promotional program elements. As we noted at the outset of this chapter, the increased use of integrated marketing communications programs has led to more interest in determining the synergistic effects of all program elements. A review of the Ogilvy Award winners from 1993 to date demonstrates the increased integration of additional media (as opposed to specifically the best advertising campaign) and the value of measuring their contribution to the program's success. Also departing from the specific focus on advertising are the awards given by the London-based *Institute of Practitioners,* which has opened the competition for the first time to nontraditional media as well as public relations, sales promotions, and other entries.[34]

As noted throughout the chapter, a number of studies have been implemented to determine the combined effects of two or more media as well as their synergistic impact. The number of studies being designed to specifically measure synergistic effects continues to increase—most of which demonstrate a higher effectiveness when multiple media are employed. For example, after receiving negative publicity from a number of sources, Walmart increased its public relations activities and its advertising designed to enhance its corporate image. In less than a year, Walmart was able to show significant improvement in its image, which the company directly attributes to the combined use of the two program elements.[35]

Other companies are applying traditional advertising effectiveness measures offered by companies such as Millward Brown and Nielsen Media Research to their online advertising to assess their overall communications effects.[36] One very effective approach to measuring the impact of the IMC program is that provided by the marketing communications research company Integration. Based on the belief that integrated marketing communications improve both the efficiency and the effectiveness of a campaign. Integration contends that most traditional measurement techniques focus only on the former of these (see Figure 18–19). Noting the increased demand for marketing managers to prioritize the media vehicles used to promote their brands, Integration developed Market ContactAudit to measure both the efficiency and the effectiveness of media used to establish contacts with consumers. By measuring consumers' understanding, evaluation, and perceptions of the contacts and their association with the brand, the Market ContactAudit allows marketers to assess the overall effectiveness as well as the relative contribution of individual IMC elements.[37]

All the advertising effectiveness measures discussed here have their inherent strengths and weaknesses. They offer the advertiser some information that may be useful in evaluating the effectiveness of promotional efforts. While not all promotional efforts can be evaluated effectively, progress is being made.

## Summary

This chapter introduced you to issues involved in measuring the effects of advertising and promotions. These issues include reasons for testing, reasons companies do not test, and the review and evaluation of various research methodologies. We arrived at a number of conclusions: (1) Advertising research to measure effectiveness is important to the promotional program, (2) not enough companies test their ads, and (3) problems exist with current research methodologies. In addition, we reviewed the criteria for sound research and suggested some ways to accomplish effective studies.

All marketing managers want to know how well their promotional programs are working. This information is critical to planning for the next period, since program adjustments and/or maintenance are based on evaluation of current strategies. Problems often result when the measures taken to determine such effects are inaccurate or improperly used.

This chapter demonstrated that testing must meet a number of criteria (defined by PACT) to be successful. These evaluations should occur both before and after the campaigns are implemented.

A variety of research methods were discussed, many provided by syndicated research firms such as Ipsos-ASI, MSW, Arbitron, and A. C. Nielsen. Many companies have developed their own testing systems. There has been an increase in testing through the Internet.

Single-source research data were discussed. These single-source systems offer strong potential for improving the effectiveness of ad measures in the future, since commercial exposures and reactions may be correlated to actual purchase behaviors.

It is important to recognize that different measures of effectiveness may lead to different results. Depending on the criteria used, one measure may show that an ad or promotion is effective while another states that it is not. This is why clearly defined objectives and the use of multiple measures are critical to determining the true effects of an IMC program.

## Key Terms

**vehicle option source effect** p. 608
**pretests** p. 609
**posttests** p. 609
**laboratory tests** p. 610
**testing bias** p. 610
**field tests** p. 610
**PACT (Positioning Advertising Copy Testing)** p. 611
**concept testing** p. 611
**comprehension and reaction tests** p. 613
**consumer juries** p. 613
**halo effect** p. 614
**portfolio tests** p. 615
**Flesch formula** p. 615
**theater testing** p. 616
**on-air test** p. 617
**recall** p. 617
**pupillometrics** p. 618
**electrodermal response** p. 618
**eye tracking** p. 618
**electroencephalographic (EEG) measures** p. 619
**alpha activity** p. 619
**hemispheric lateralization** p. 619
**inquiry tests** p. 620
**split-run tests** p. 621
**recognition method** p. 622
**recall tests** p. 623
**single-source tracking methods** p. 626
**tracking studies** p. 627

## Discussion Questions

1. Explain why it is so difficult to measure the effectiveness of an IMC program that uses multiple program elements. (LO3)
2. Discuss the various types of pretests that advertisers employ. Why do marketers pretest ads? What are some reasons why marketers may not pretest? (LO2)
3. What are some of the problems with existing effectiveness measures? Discuss the essentials of effective testing methods. (LO3)
4. The Ogilvy Awards are given to companies and their agencies that have successfully employed research to develop and measure the effectiveness of their campaigns. Google the Ogilvy Awards, pick any of the award winners and discuss why that program was successful. (LO1)
5. Cite examples where advertisers may be able to develop successful ads without the benefit of pretesting. Why would an advertiser decide to make the decision not to pretest? (LO2)
6. What is the difference between a lab testing methodology and a field testing methodology? What are the advantages and disadvantages associated with each? When should each be used? (LO2)
7. The chapter discusses the use of neurosciences to assess viewers' evaluation of commercials. What are the pros and cons associated with these methods? When should advertisers use them? (LO3)
8. Eye tracking methodologies have been used to measure advertising effectiveness in the past. This

methodology had now been used in a variety of other ways. Discuss the use of eye tracking and its applications to advertising and promotion. (LO3)

9. Some companies test their commercials in rough formats described in the chapter. Others only test the commercials in finished form. Discuss some of the advantages and disadvantages of conducting tests at both stages. (LO2)

10. Discuss some of the reasons why some companies decide not to measure the effectiveness of their promotional programs. Explain why this may or may not be a good strategy. (LO1)

## AdForum Exercise: "Examining the Effectiveness of Beer Commercials"

adforum.com

(see Advertising and Promotion Playlist, Chapter 18)

The playlist for Chapter 18 contains a number of beer ads used by some of the top selling domestic brands of beer in the United States. Review each of these commercials and answer the following:

1 What are the specific objectives of each of these ads?

2 How are these ads designed to achieve these objectives?

3 How would you measure the effectiveness of each of these ads?

4 Describe some of the themes that are consistent across the ads? Why do you think the beer companies use these themes?

Access to the chapter playlist is available through McGraw Hill connect™ |MARKETING, www.mcgrawhillconnect.com

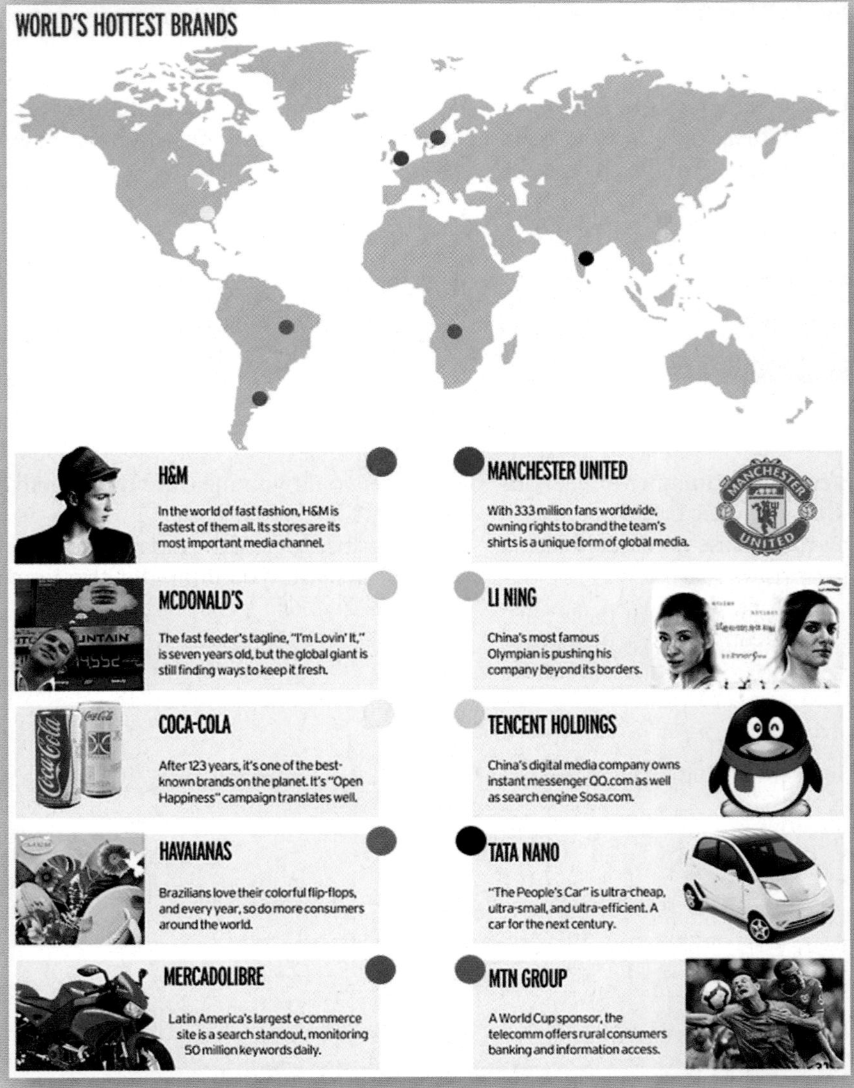

WORLD'S HOTTEST BRANDS
H&M
In the world of fast fashion, H&M is fastest of them all. Its stores are its most important media channel.
MANCHESTER UNITED
With 333 million fans worldwide, owning rights to brand the team's shirts is a unique form of global media.
MANCHESTER UNITED
MCDONALD'S
The fast feeder's tagline, "I'm Lovin' It," is seven years old, but the global giant is still finding ways to keep it fresh.
LI NING
China's most famous Olympian is pushing his company beyond its borders.
COCA-COLA
After 123 years, it's one of the best-known brands on the planet. It's "Open Happiness" campaign translates well.
TENCENT HOLDINGS
China's digital media company owns instant messenger QQ.com as well as search engine Sosa.com.
HAVAIANAS
Brazilians love their colorful flip-flops, and every year, so do more consumers around the world.
TATA NANO
"The People's Car" is ultra-cheap, ultra-small, and ultra-efficient. A car for the next century.
MERCADOLIBRE
Latin America's largest e-commerce site is a search standout, monitoring 50 million keywords daily.
MTN GROUP
A World Cup sponsor, the telecomm offers rural consumers banking and information access.

## LEARNING OBJECTIVES

LO1 To examine the importance of international marketing and the role of international advertising and promotion.

LO2 To review the various factors in the international environment and how they influence advertising and promotion decisions.

LO3 To consider the pros and cons of global versus localized marketing and advertis ng.

LO4 To examine the various decision areas of international advertising.

LO5 To understand the role of other promotional mix elements in the international integrated marketing communications program.

# 19 International Advertising and Promotion

## GLOBAL BRANDS STILL HAVE TO COMPETE LOCALLY

It has been more than a quarter of a century since former Harvard marketing professor Theodore Levitt popularized the idea of globalization in his classic article entitled "The Globalization of Markets" which appeared in the *Harvard Business Review* in 1983. Levitt argued that the world was becoming a global marketplace where people have the same basic needs, wants, desires, and tastes no matter where they live, and called on companies to develop global marketing strategies and true global brands that could be sold under one name around the world. Many multinational companies heeded the call for globalization, and their advertising agencies were given the charge of helping them turn their products into global brands that could be promoted with the same basic advertising theme and approach worldwide.

A number of United States–based companies such as Coca-Cola, IBM, Microsoft, PepsiCo, Google, Intel, and Disney have been successful in turning many of their products and services into global brands. Companies based outside the United States such as Nestlé, Nokia, Toyota, Samsung, Ikea, and Nintendo have done so as well, as the small size of their domestic markets has necessitated that they be adroit at marketing their brands abroad. However, while many companies refer to themselves and/or their various products and services as "global brands," the number that are truly global in scope is actually quite small. Experts note that a true global brand is one that does more than use the same basic product, name, packaging, and advertising around the world. In his book *The Global Brand,* Nigel Hollis, executive vice president and chief global analyst for the Millward Brown Group, defines a global brand as one that has transcended its cultural origins to develop strong relationships with consumers across different countries and cultures. Hollis also notes that the number of truly global brands is quite small as only around 5 percent of the world's brands are marketed in more than six countries.

Surveys conducted by Millward Brown as well as the branding consultancy company Interbrand show that the world's most valuable brands include Google, IBM, Coca-Cola, Marlboro, Microsoft, Vodafone, and McDonald's. Most of these brands have taken a long time to establish themselves across multiple countries and cultures and to develop strong connections with consumers in various regions. However, Hollis notes that even a brand like Coca-Cola will find that it has different strengths of relationships with consumers in various countries. For example, in South Africa 65 percent of consumers have a strong emotional connection or bonding score to the brand while the score is 50 percent in Mexico. However, in a country like India, the bonding score for Coca-Cola is only 10 percent.

Hollis notes that for most of the leading global brands, there is a strong relationship between the length of time in a market with how well accepted the brand is there. The longer the brand has been around and the more people have grown up with it, the more localized the brand is in terms of how it competes in the market and how it is perceived by consumers. While many of the world's leading brands have been able to hold their position, a number of new brands are emerging around the globe. In its 2010 global report, *Advertising Age* identified 30 of the World's Hottest Brands—focusing on the top 10 that are succeeding on a global, regional, and local level. The top brands at the global level included Coca-Cola, BMW, Facebook, Nike, the Nintendo Wii, and H&M. Coca-Cola remains one of the best know brands on the planet and has topped the Interbrand surveys as the world's most valuable brand nearly every year. The company recently initiated a new global advertising campaign using the theme "Open Happiness" which has translated well and resonates with consumers around the world. Swedish based H&M has become one of the fastest growing fashion brands in the world and has been very successful at attracting value-conscious consumers with its affordable, yet stylish, apparel and making the stores themselves its most important media channel.

Among the regional brands on the *Ad Age* hot list are Lenovo, *The Economist* magazine, MTN Group, and MercadoLibre. MTN is South Africa's mobile telephone company, has more than 116 million subscribers, and has become the leading source of agricultural and health care information for remote parts of Africa. The company was one of the leading sponsors of the 2010 World Cup soccer championship, which was held in its home country, and also is a sponsor for the Manchester United soccer team which has more than 330 million fans worldwide. China based Lenovo purchased IBM's personal computer division in 2005 and has become one of the leading brands of personal computers in the world over the past five years. However, the company's primary strength is in its home market as well as in emerging markets such as India. Lenovo is refocusing on its domestic market, particularly China's rural areas and third-, fourth-, and fifth-tier cities which represent a potential market of nearly 700 million first-time computer buyers. Lenovo has developed an innovative integrated marketing program called "PCs for Rural China" which reaches consumers in these areas by presenting free feature films in more than 3,000 villages and small towns. Lenovo commercials are shown before each screening and consumers can visit an interactive Lenovo PC bazaar to learn more about its computers, experiment with them, and pick up brochures with product and service information.

Some of the hottest local brands on the *Ad Age* list are China's Li Ning, India's Tata Nano, and ZipCar from the United States. Li Ning was founded by and named after the Olympic gymnast who was China's first celebrity athlete and also one of its first entrepreneurs. The company operates more than 6,200 retail stores in China and is expanding to other countries. It sells athletic shoes and apparel under its flagship Li Ning brand and competes successfully against major global companies such as Nike, adidas, and Puma. It has adopted many of its competitors' tactics by becoming the official partner of the National Basketball Association in China and by signing sponsorship deals with the national basketball teams of Spain and Argentina and deals with several tennis pros and track athletes. Tata Nano is being marketed as India's "First car for everyone" and has a price that is appropriate for the developing automobile market in India of just $2,000. The "People's Car" is ultra-small as well, as it is only 10 feet long from bumper to bumper and is very fuel efficient.

A number of Internet-based companies are also on the *Advertising Age* hottest brands list such as Facebook and China's Tenscent Holdings, which is the company behind QQ.Com, an instant messaging service with 523 million subscribers. Other technology companies on the list are Soso .com, a search engine whose business is poised to explode since Google has had problems in China, and MercardoLibre which is Latin America's equivalent to eBay. Given the growing role and importance of technology it is not surprising to see them on the list.

Multinational companies will continue their efforts to turn many of their products and services into global brands. However, they are learning that they must now compete against regional and local brands that are improving their product and service quality and have stronger emotional connections to consumers. This means marketers must develop advertising and IMC programs that travel well and transcend markets or adapt them to make them more in tune with local consumers and cultures. While the world seems to be getting smaller every day, cultural perceptions of brands and marketing still vary from country to country and can often be worlds apart.

Sources: Ann Marie Kerwin, "A World of Inspirational Problem-Solving, Savvy Brands and Smart Marketing," *Advertising Age,* June 1, 2010, pp. 4–5; Normand Madden, "Lenovo Sets Its Sights Back to Local," *Advertising Age,* June 22, 2009, http:/adage.com/print?article_id=137481; Normandy Madden, "Two Chinese Brand Break onto World Scene," *Advertising Age,* June 15, 2009, p. 17; Nigel Hollis, The Global Brand (New York: Palgrave MacMillan), 2008.

The primary focus of this book so far has been on integrated marketing communications programs for products and services sold in the U.S. market. Many American companies have traditionally devoted most of their marketing efforts to the domestic market, since they often lack the resources, skills, or incentives to go abroad. This is changing rapidly, however, as U.S. corporations recognize the opportunities that foreign markets offer for new sources of sales and profits as well as the need to market their products internationally. Many companies are striving to develop global brands that can be advertised and promoted the world over.

In this chapter, we look at international advertising and promotion and the various issues marketers must consider in communicating with consumers around the globe. We examine the environment of international marketing and how companies often must adapt their promotional programs to conditions in each country. We review the debate over whether a company should use a global marketing and advertising approach or tailor it specifically for various countries.

We also examine how firms organize for international advertising, select agencies, and consider various decision areas such as research, creative strategy, and media selection. While the focus of this chapter is on international advertising, we also consider other promotional mix elements in international marketing, including sales promotion, personal selling, publicity/public relations, and the Internet. Let's begin by discussing some of the reasons international marketing has become so important to companies.

## THE IMPORTANCE OF INTERNATIONAL MARKETS

LO 19-1

One of the major developments in the business world during the decade of the 90s was the globalization of markets. The emergence of a largely borderless world has created a new reality for all types of companies. Today, world trade is driven by global competition among global companies for global consumers.[1] With the development of faster communication, transportation, and financial transactions, time and distance are no longer barriers to global marketing. Products and services developed in one country quickly find their way to other countries where they are finding enthusiastic acceptance. Consumers around the world wear Nike shoes and Calvin Klein jeans, eat at McDonald's, shave with Gillette razors, use Dell computers, listen to music on Apple iPods, drink Coca-Cola and Pepsi Cola soft drinks and Starbucks coffee, talk on cellular phones made by Nokia, Samsung, and Motorola, and drive cars made by global automakers such as Ford, Honda, and Nissan.[2]

Companies are focusing on international markets for a number of reasons. Many companies in the United States and Western Europe recognize that their domestic markets offer them limited opportunities for expansion because of slow population growth, saturated markets, intense competition, and/or an unfavorable marketing environment. For example, U.S. tobacco companies face declining domestic consumption as a result of restrictions on their marketing and advertising efforts and the growing antismoking sentiment in this country. Cigarette consumption in the United States has declined by 42 percent since its peak in 1981, and advertising spending on cigarettes has fallen by 95 percent since 1985.[3] Companies such as R. J. Reynolds and Philip Morris are turning to markets outside the United States such as Asia and South America, where higher percentages of people smoke, nonsmokers are far more tolerant of the habit, opposition is less organized, and consumers are less litigious.[4]

Another industry that has been impacted by globalization is the beer business, as the major U.S. brewers are now owned by foreign based companies. In 2002 the Miller Brewing Company was purchased by South African Breweries, whose largest markets are in Asia and Africa.[5] Six years later SAB Miller entered into an agreement with Molson Coors Brewing Co. to combine their United States operations and formed MillerCoors with the intention of challenging industry leader Anheuser-Busch, which controls almost 50 percent of the U.S. beer market.[6] However, a few months later Anheuser-Busch was acquired by Belgian brewer InBev and a new entity was created, Anheuser-Busch InBev, which immediately became the world's largest brewer.[7] InBev plans to introduce Anheuser-Busch's flagship Budweiser brand into new markets around the world as well as create new marketing and advertising programs tailored more to the local markets where the brand is already

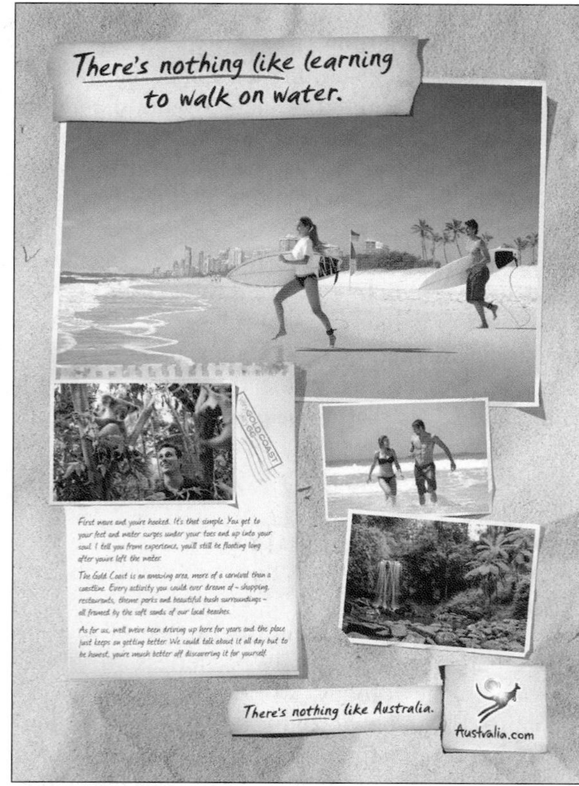


**EXHIBIT 19–1**
Tourism Australia promotes the country as a travel destination with the "There's Nothing Like Australia" campaign

available. While Budweiser has a major presence outside the United States in China, Canada, and the United Kingdom, the brand has limited sales in many other parts of the world such as Africa.[8] Both major brewers recognize that they must move to increase their presence in other countries in order to grow, because beer consumption in the United States has been declining as a result of the recession and changes in consumer lifestyles.[9]

Many companies must focus on foreign markets to survive. Most European nations are relatively small in size and without foreign markets would not have the economies of scale to compete against larger U.S. and Japanese companies. For example, Swiss-based Nestlé and Netherlands-based Unilever are two of the world's largest consumer-product companies because they have learned how to market their brands to consumers in countries around the world. Three of the world's major marketers of cellular telephones are from small countries. Nokia is based in Finland and Samsung and LG are based in Korea. Australia's tourist industry is a major part of its economy and relies heavily on visitors from other countries. Tourism Australia, the federal government agency responsible for the country's international and domestic tourism marketing, recently launched a new global campaign called "There's Nothing Like Australia," which is designed to attract visitors by showcasing the diversity of places to visit and experiences available across the country. The campaign was built with the involvement of the Australian people by having them share their favorite place in the world. The fully integrated campaign uses digital, print, broadcast, and outdoor media as well as direct marketing and point-of-sale ads in travel agencies. During the first phase of the campaign, Australians were invited to share their personal stories of where they live and holiday in Australia as a way to promote the country as a travel destination. Australians uploaded nearly 30,000 stories and images to the website developed for the campaign (www.nothinglikeaustralia.com). For the second phase of the campaign Tourism Australia used the entries to create an interactive digital map of the country which included all of the places and experiences Australians think are special about their country. The various entries were also used to create a series of print ads used in the campaign such as the one shown in Exhibit 19–1.

Companies are also pursuing international markets because of the opportunities they offer for growth and profits. The dramatic economic, social, and political changes around the world in recent years have opened markets in Eastern Europe and China. China's joining of the World Trade Organization in 2001 has provided foreign competitors with access to 1.3 billion potential Chinese consumers, and Western marketers are eager to sell them a variety of products and services.[10] The growing markets of the Far East, Latin America, and other parts of the world present tremendous opportunities to marketers of consumer products and services as well as business-to-business marketers.

Many companies in the United States, as well as in other countries, are also pursuing international markets out of economic necessity as they recognize that globalization is revolutionizing the world far more radically and rapidly that industrial development and technological changes of previous eras. In his influential book, *The World Is Flat: A Brief History of the Twenty-first Century,* Thomas L. Friedman discusses how the economic flattening of the earth is being stimulated by technology that is breaking down barriers that historically inhibited and restricted international trade. He notes that companies in the United States can only prosper if they are able to compete in the global marketplace that encompasses the 95 percent of the world's population that lives beyond our borders.[11]

**EXHIBIT 19–2**
The WD-40 Co. gets much of its sales growth from foreign markets such as Latin America

Most major multinational companies have made the world their market and generate much of their sales and profits from abroad. Gillette sells more than 800 products in over 200 countries while Colgate-Palmolive generates almost 80 percent of its $15 billion in sales from outside North America and Procter & Gamble gets 60 percent of its revenue outside the United States. Starbucks sells lattes around the world as its name and image connect with consumers in Europe and Asia as well as North America. The company has coffee shops in more than 50 countries and operates nearly 6,000 international outlets from Beijing to Sydney to London. Starbucks' projected growth plan includes establishing 30,000 stores worldwide, with at least 15,000 locations outside the United States.[12] Coca-Cola, Pepsi, Nike, KFC, Dell, McDonald's, and many other U.S. companies and brands are known all over the world.

International markets are important to small and mid-size companies as well as the large multinational corporations. Many of these firms can compete more effectively in foreign markets, where they may face less competition or appeal to specific market segments or where products have not yet reached the maturity stage of their life cycle. For example, the WD-40 Co. has saturated the U.S. market with its lubricant product and now gets much of its sales growth from markets in Europe, Asia, Latin America, and Australia (Exhibit 19–2).

Another reason it is increasingly important for U.S. companies to adopt an international marketing orientation is that imports are taking a larger and larger share of the domestic market for many products. The United States has been running a continuing **balance-of-trade deficit**; the monetary value of our imports exceeds that of our exports. American companies are realizing that we are shifting from being an isolated, self-sufficient, national economy to being part of an interdependent *global economy.* This means U.S. corporations must defend against foreign inroads into the domestic market as well as learn how to market their products and services to other countries.

While many U.S. companies are becoming more aggressive in their pursuit of international markets, they face stiff competition from large multinational corporations from other countries. Some of the world's most formidable marketers are European companies such as Unilever, Nestlé, Siemens, Philips, and Renault, as well as the various Japanese car and electronic manufacturers and packaged-goods companies such as Suntory, Shiseido, and Kao.



## THE ROLE OF INTERNATIONAL ADVERTISING AND PROMOTION

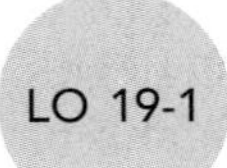
LO 19-1

Advertising and promotion are important parts of the marketing program of firms competing in the global marketplace. An estimated $177 billion was spent on advertising in the United States in 2009, with much of this money being spent by multinational companies headquartered outside this country.[13] Advertising expenditures outside the United States have increased by nearly 60 percent since 1990, reaching an estimated $446 billion in 2009, as global marketers based in the United States, as well as European and Asian countries, increase their worldwide advertising. Figure 19–1 shows the top 10 companies in terms of worldwide advertising spending.

In addition, estimates are that another $500 billion is spent on sales promotion efforts targeted at consumers, retailers, and wholesalers around the world. The United States is still the world's major advertising market, accounting for nearly one-third of the estimated $630 billion in worldwide ad expenditures. Nearly 90 percent of the money spent on advertising products and services around the world is concentrated in the United States and Canada along with the industrialized countries of Western Europe and the Pacific Rim, including Japan, South Korea, and Australia.

| Rank | Advertiser | Headquarters | AD SPENDING (MILLIONS US DOLLARS) | | |
|---|---|---|---|---|---|
| | | | Worldwide | Outside the U.S. | U.S. Spending |
| 1 | Procter & Gamble Co. | Cincinnati, OH | $9,731 | $6,364 | $3,367 |
| 2 | Unilever | London/Rotterdam | 5,717 | 4,965 | 752 |
| 3 | L'Oreal | Paris, France | 4,040 | 3,242 | 798 |
| 4 | General Motors | Detroit, MI | 3,674 | 1,442 | 2,232 |
| 5 | Toyota Motor Corp. | Toyota City, Japan | 3,203 | 2,181 | 1,022 |
| 6 | Coca-Cola Co. | Atlanta, GA | 2,673 | 2,231 | 442 |
| 7 | Johnson & Johnson | New Brunswick, NJ | 2,602 | 1,181 | 1,402 |
| 8 | Ford Motor Co. | Dearborn, MI | 2,448 | 1,436 | 1,012 |
| 9 | Reckitt Benckiser | Slough, Berkshire U.K. | 2,369 | 1,842 | 544 |
| 10 | Nestlé | Vevey, Switzerland | 2,314 | 1,696 | 618 |

**FIGURE 19–1**

Top 10 Companies by Worldwide Advertising Spending

Source: "Global Marketers 2009" *Advertising Age*, http://adage.com/globalmarketers09

However, advertising spending is increasing rapidly in China and in several Latin American countries, such as Mexico and Brazil.

More and more companies recognize that an effective promotional program is important for companies competing in foreign markets. As one international marketing scholar notes:

> Promotion is the most visible as well as the most culture bound of the firm's marketing functions. Marketing includes the whole collection of activities the firm performs in relating to its market, but in other functions the firm relates to the market in a quieter, more passive way. With the promotional function, however, the firm is standing up and speaking out, wanting to be seen and heard.[14]

Many companies have run into difficulties developing and implementing advertising and promotion programs for international markets. Companies that promote their products or services abroad face an unfamiliar marketing environment and customers with different sets of values, customs, consumption patterns, and habits, as well as differing purchase motives and abilities. Languages vary from country to country and even within a country, such as India or Switzerland. Media options are quite limited in many countries, owing to lack of availability or limited effectiveness. These factors demand different creative and media strategies as well as changes in other elements of the advertising and promotional program for foreign markets.

## THE INTERNATIONAL ENVIRONMENT

Just as with domestic marketing, companies engaging in international marketing must care-fully analyze the major environmental factors of each market in which they compete, including economic, demographic, cultural, and political/legal variables. Figure 19–2 shows some of the factors marketers must consider in each category when analyzing the environment of each country or market. These factors are important in evaluating the potential of each country as well as designing and implementing a marketing and promotional program.

**FIGURE 19–2**

Forces in the International Marketing Environment

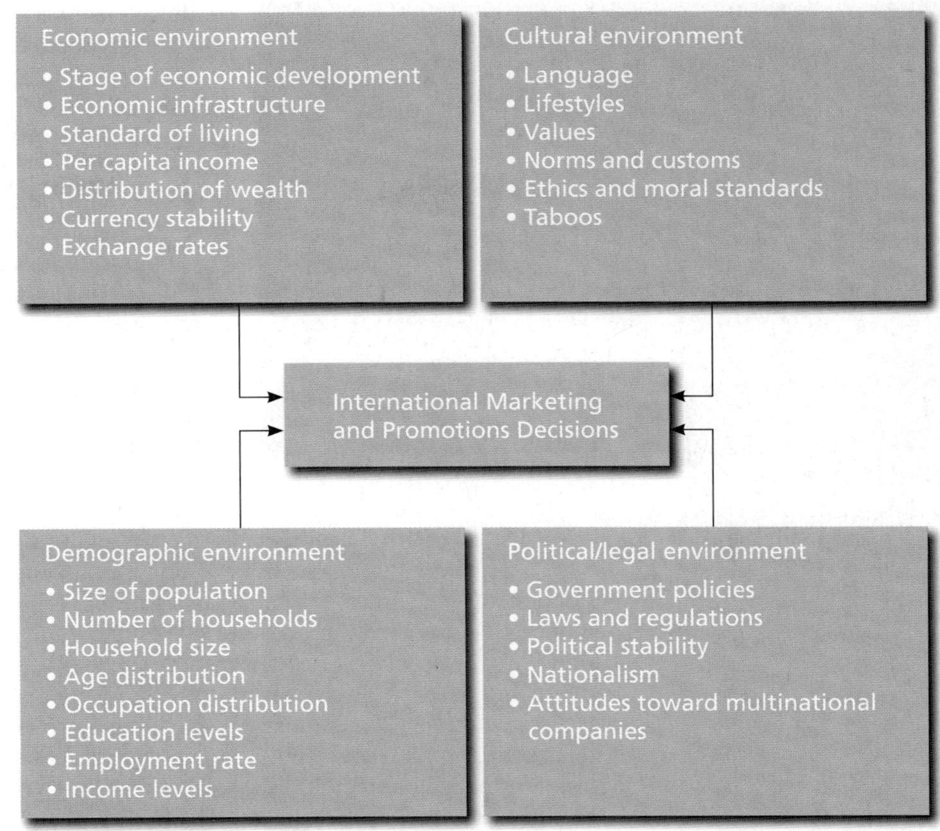


## The Economic Environment

A country's economic conditions indicate its present and future potential for consuming, since products and services can be sold only to countries where there is enough income to buy them. This is generally not a problem in developed countries such as the United States, Canada, Japan, and most of western Europe, where consumers generally have higher incomes and standards of living. Thus, they can and want to purchase a variety of products and services. Developed countries have the **economic infrastructure** in terms of the communications, transportation, financial, and distribution networks needed to conduct business in these markets effectively. By contrast, many developing countries lack purchasing power and have limited communications networks available to firms that want to promote their products or services to these markets.

For most companies, industrialized nations represent the greatest marketing and advertising opportunities. But most of these countries have stable population bases, and their markets for many products and services are already saturated. Many marketers are turning their attention to parts of the world whose economies and consumer markets are growing. Markets in Asia, as well as in Europe and South America, were stagnant for a number of years, which led to reductions in advertising spending in most countries. However, these markets are experiencing strong economic growth, which is resulting in greater consumer spending as well as increases in advertising. Over the past several years, advertising spending in the BRIC nations, which includes Brazil, Russia, India, and China, has grown four times faster than the world average and is expected to reach nearly $50 billion by 2011. Brazil is experiencing stable, solid economic growth after a period of high inflation and economic volatility as is Russia. Much of Brazil's growth is coming from an emerging lower

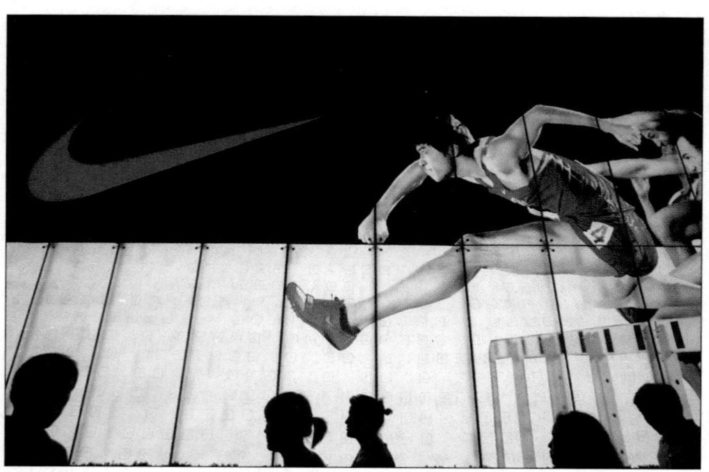

**EXHIBIT 19–3**
Nike uses track star Liu Xiang as an endorser in China

middle class that now represents nearly half of the company's population. Marketers of products such as consumer electronics, mobile phones, and automobiles are targeting this emerging middle class as their disposable income rises in the growing Brazilian economy.[15]

China and India in particular are two countries that are transforming the global economy. The two countries together account for a third of the world's population, and they both have had economic growth rates ranging from 6 to 10 percent over the past several years, which is much greater than other countries in the world. Each country has the fundamentals to sustain the high growth rates including young populations, high savings, and a growing number of consumers who have the ability to purchase, as well as the need for, many products.[16]

Marketers of products such as mobile phones, TVs, personal computers, cars, as well as luxury items such as jewelry and designer clothing are focusing more attention on consumers in India and China.[17] The growing middle class in these countries is also creating growth opportunities for marketers of consumer package-goods products, who are focusing a great deal of attention and spending more on advertising to reach these consumers. For example, China has become Nike's second largest market and the company is spending large amounts of money there on media advertising, promotions, events, and sponsorship of sports teams and athletes such as track star and Olympic gold medalist Liu Xiang (Exhibit 19–3). China has become the fourth-largest advertising market in the world trailing only the United States, Japan, and Germany.

The pent-up demand of China's 1.3 billion emerging consumers makes entering the market a priority for multinational companies and many are developing IMC programs as part of their marketing efforts to capitalize on the strong economic growth taking place there. However, the realities of entering the market are much more difficult because China's diverse customer base encompasses a broad range of economic disparity and cultural complexity. China also lacks the marketing infrastructure that companies take for granted in the West including quality consumer research and distribution systems.

China's cities are classified by a five-tier system based on size, sophistication, purchasing habits, attitudes, and disposable income of the population in each city. Tier one is the most affluent and includes the major cities of Beijing, Shanghai, Guangzhou, and Shenzen. Tier two has about 30 cities, mostly provincial capitals with more than 5 million people. Currently, 70 percent of China's affluent households live in the country's top eight cities. However, it is estimated that by 2012, only 30 percent will live in these cities, as the rural masses move into midsize cities. Most multinational companies have penetrated China's major cities such as Shanghi and Beijing and recognize they must move beyond the prosperous tier one cities and coastal regions if they are to have a future in China.[18] Thus, companies are moving into the middle and lower tiers that include thousands of towns as well as China's smallest villages where 70 percent of the overall market resides. As noted in the chapter opener, companies such as Lenovo are focusing attention on the rural markets of China using road shows that visit fourth- and fifth-tier cities. The efforts have helped the company increase its market share in rural markets in China from 30 percent to 42 percent.[19]

Many multinational companies are also turning their attention to third world countries where consumer markets are slowly emerging. Package-good companies such as Procter & Gamble and Unilever sell products such as soap, toothpaste, shampoo, and laundry detergents to consumers in remote villages. Often they adapt their products for these markets by making them available in single-use sachets that cost the equivalent of pennies rather than dollars and can be easily distributed and sold through the small kiosks found in rural villages. Global Perspective 19–1 discusses the opportunities these markets present as well as the challenges of marketing to them.

## The Demographic Environment

Major demographic differences exist among countries as well as within them. Marketers must consider income levels and distribution, age and occupation distributions of the population, household size, education, and employment rates. In some countries, literacy rates are also a factor; people who cannot read will not respond well to print ads. Demographic data can provide insight into the living standards and lifestyles in a particular country to help companies plan ad campaigns.

Demographic information can reveal the market potential of various foreign markets. India's population was nearly 1.2 billion in 2010. Only China, with 1.3 billion people, has a larger population. Latin America remains one of the world's largest potential markets, although the meager income of most consumers in the region is still a problem. Brazil, the largest consumer market in South America, now has a population of 200 million and is a growing market for many products and services. More than 50 percent of the Latin American market is younger than age 26, and 30 percent is under 15. Moreover, children are the fastest-growing segment of that market. These numbers have caught the attention of international advertisers such as Mattel, Hasbro, Burger King, and others. Indonesia also has a very young population, with more people under the age of 16 than the United States, and they are very receptive to Western ways and products.

**EXHIBIT 19–4**
The tagline used in this TaylorMade ad had to be changed for Asian countries because of translation problems

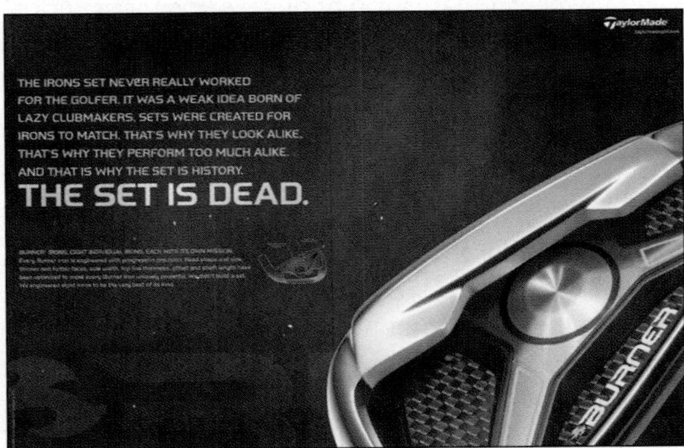

## The Cultural Environment

Another important aspect of the international marketing environment is the culture of each country. Cultural variables marketers must consider include language, customs, tastes, attitudes, lifestyles, values, and ethical/moral standards. Nearly every country exhibits cultural traits that influence not just the needs and wants of consumers but how they go about satisfying them.

Marketers must be sensitive not only in determining what products and services they can sell foreign cultures but also in communicating with them. Advertising is often the most effective way to communicate with potential buyers and create markets in other countries. But it can also be one of the most difficult aspects of the international marketing program because of problems in developing messages that will be understood in various countries.

International advertisers often have problems with language. The advertiser must know not only the native tongue of the country but also its nuances, idioms, and subtleties. International marketers must be aware of the connotations of words and symbols used in their messages and understand how advertising copy and slogans are translated. Marketers often encounter problems in translating their advertising messages and brand names into various languages. The ad for TaylorMade Burner Irons golf clubs shown in Exhibit 19–4 is one example. In the United States and other English speaking countries, the tagline the advertising used is "The Set Is Dead." However, in Asian countries such as Japan and Korea, the word dead in the tagline did not translate well so it was

# Global Perspective 19–1 > > >

## Marketing to the World's Poorest Consumers

Most multinational companies generate the majority of their sales and profits by selling products and services to consumers and businesses in highly developed countries. When they do venture into developing nations such as China, India, Indonesia, or Vietnam, they have traditionally focused on urban areas where incomes are higher and communication, transportation, and distribution systems are available to implement their marketing programs. However, many multinational marketers have begun turning their attention to the 4 billion consumers who live in the remote, rural communities of developing countries. These people are yearning for a better way of life and are eager to become consumers for a variety of products. Marketers also recognize the opportunity this market presents, as over the next 20 years, the number of upper-middle- to upper-income consumers will decline slightly while the developing world will acquire another 2 billion people.

While this emergent trend has been given various labels such as B2-4B (business-to-4-billion), selling to the "bottom of the pyramid" or selling to premarkets, a number of companies are recognizing that they can turn a profit while having a positive effect on people not normally considered potential consumers. However, they also realize that it is a tremendous challenge to market to these consumers. Many of the world's poor live in severe poverty, subsisting on less than $2,000 a year, and are illiterate or nearly so. They often live in tiny villages in remote areas that are completely beyond the reach of mass media and common distribution channels. Their access to and ability to use products is determined by the available infrastructure—water, roads, electricity—or lack thereof. Clearly marketers have to package, price, and distribute their products differently as well as find innovative ways to communicate with these consumers.

So how do global marketers Procter & Gamble, Unilever, Wrigley, Samsung, and many others market products such as toothpaste, shampoo, gum, cell phones, and TVs to consumers in these developing countries? These companies often start by examining the daily lives of these consumers including their needs, aspirations, and habits to better understand what they may want as consumers. In many cases, advertising agencies are following or often leading their clients into these rural areas. For example, Lowe & Partners' office in India, Lowe Lintas, formed Linterland Rural Initiatives, an integrated marketing division designed to provide specialized marketing and communication services to rural India. Linterland works with companies and helps them understand how specialized forms of marketing communications, such as events, road shows, and sampling, are needed to reach the 700 million people who are spread out in nearly a million villages across India that are virtually untouched by mass media. Linterland uses its network of more than 8,500 individual field workers to coordinate and help deliver marketing messages on behalf of a number of consumer product companies.

Leo Burnett, Asia Pacific, recently completed a major project whereby the agency's researchers spent six months living among consumers in rural China and India to observe their routines and better understand them as people. They found that although their incomes are low by Western standards, they compare themselves to the other people in their villages and towns. From their point of view, the most important thing is not that they earn only $2,000 a year but that they can live on this income. They are often brand conscious,

changed to "The Set Is History," which made the meaning of phrase easier to understand.

Advertisers can encounter problems with the connotative meaning of signs and symbols used in their messages. For example, the thumbs-up sign, which signifies affirmation to most Americans, has offensive meaning in some countries such as Russia and Poland if the palm of the hand is visible but is acceptable if the back of the hand is shown. There can also be problems associated with the symbolic meanings of colors. In Japan, as in many Asian countries, white is a color for mourning rather than black, and purple is associated with death in many Latin American countries. An American ad campaign using various shades of green was a disaster in Malaysia, where the color symbolizes death and disease.

Problems arising from language diversity and differences in signs and symbols can usually be best solved with the help of local expertise. Marketers should consult local employees or use an ad agency knowledgeable in the local language that can help verify that the advertiser is saying what it wants to say. Many companies turn to agencies that specialize in translating advertising slogans and copy into foreign languages.[20]

Tastes, traditions, and customs are also an important part of cultural considerations. The customs of a society affect what products and services it will buy and

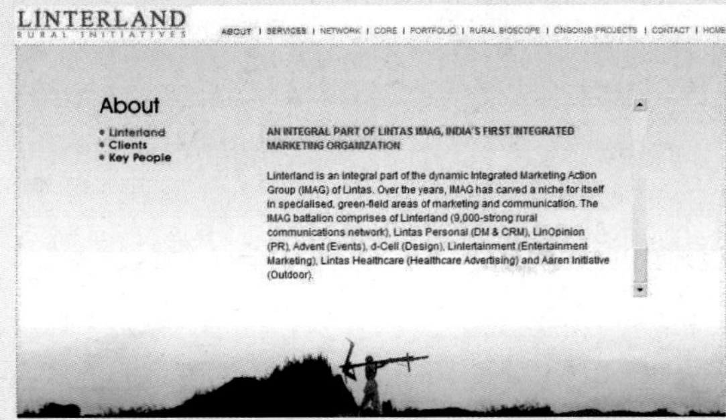


as even for these consumers brands are a way to signal their achievement. However, they buy brands not only for image but as a guarantee of quality. The majority of consumers have products such as mobile phones and televisions and nearly half the Chinese consumers earning only $200 per month have a personal computer. While conventional wisdom has suggested that these consumers are price conscious, in reality they are value conscious and are extremely savvy about what they will buy.

Marketers and their agencies are also focusing attention on marketing their products to consumers on the bottom rungs of the economy in Mexico and Latin America. McCann Worldwide, which is owned by the Interpublic Group, has formed a new division called Barrio and has sent researchers across Latin America to live for a week with families earning as little as $350 a month. The unit has amassed hundreds of hours of video recordings and surveys which are being used to study the taste, purchase patterns, and needs of these consumers and develop a better understanding of consumption in the region's poorer areas. An important finding from the studies is that for the poor in Latin America, food means survival and is related to energy and strength to get through the day. The research is being used to help clients such as Nestlé and Danone position their products and develop advertising messages for low income consumers in Mexico and other Latin American countries.

While packaged-goods retailers have been selling products such as shampoo, soap, and toothpaste to rural villagers for years, many companies are now trying to sell them products such as cell phones, TVs, computers, and even cars. Companies such as Nokia, Motorola, and Samsung are generating strong sales in emerging markets such as China and India with low-cost models aimed at first-time mobile phone users. Word of mouth is the supreme marketing tool for reaching consumers in these rural markets, followed by education and product demonstrations. Integrated marketing agencies such as Linterland and Ogilvy Outreach work with school teachers, village heads, and local health workers to get them to relay their client's marketing messages. For example, in Kaler, a small town of 300 families in India's north-eastern Punjab region, Hyundai was able to reach the marketer's dream—the village headman, an opinion leader whose advice is sought on marriages, crops, and increasingly on which TV set or car to buy.

More developing countries are becoming more stable and open to trade and direct foreign investment, while education levels are also improving. Although investment in these markets still requires a long-term perspective, many companies are recognizing that the billions of people in the third world are eager to become consumers and represent a major growth opportunity. However, the real opportunity for marketers is not in just changing the package sizes and price points of the products they sell in the West. It is in understanding consumers in the developing markets, innovating to meet their needs, and selling them quality products at prices they can afford.

Sources: Michelle Kristula-Green, "How to Market to Asia's Masses," *Advertising Age*, August 6, 2007, pp. 14, 15; Dexter Roberts, "Scrambling to Bring Crest to the Masses," *BusinessWeek*, June 25, 2007, pp. 72–73; Antonio Regalado, "McCann Offers Peek at Lives of Latin America's Poor," *The Wall Street Journal*, December 8, 2008, p. B6.



how they must be marketed. In France, cosmetics are used heavily by men as well as women, and advertising to the male market is common. There are also cultural differences in the grooming and hygiene habits of consumers in various countries. For example, though many U.S. consumers use products like deodorant and shampoo daily, consumers in many other Western countries are not as fanatical about personal hygiene, so consumption of products such as deodorants and mouthwash is much lower than in the United States.

Another aspect of culture that is very important for international marketers to understand is values. **Cultural values** are beliefs and goals shared by members of a society regarding ideal end states of life and modes of conduct. Society shapes consumers' basic values, which affect their behavior and determine how they respond to various situations. For example, cultural values in the United States place a major emphasis on individual activity and initiative, while many Asian societies stress cooperation and conformity to the group. Values and beliefs of a society can also affect its members' attitudes and receptivity toward foreign products and services.[21] Values such as *ethnocentrism,* which refers to the tendency for individuals to view their own group or society as the center of the universe, or nationalism often affect the way consumers in various countries respond to foreign brands or even advertising

**EXHIBIT 19–5**
New Balance shoes have become very popular in France

**EXHIBIT 19–6**
New Balance created a new version of the 576 shoe dedicated to France

messages.[22] For many years, consumers in many European countries were reluctant to buy American brands and there was even a backlash against American imagery. In fact, many U.S. companies doing business in Europe were careful not to flaunt their American roots.

One European country, in particular, where American-made products were not well received for many years is France. The French have always been very protective of their culture; for example, they have quotas for French-language shows on TV and music on the radio. As historian Richard Pells notes: "France, like the U.S., has traditionally seen itself as a country with a mission and a country whose culture and civilization is worthy of being exported around the world."[23] However, in recent years many American brands have become popular in France, particularly among younger consumers. For example, the French subsidiary of New Balance, the Boston-based athletic shoe and apparel company, experienced strong growth in France when its 576 model became *de rigueur* among the fashion elite in the late 1990s (Exhibit 19–5). As sales took off, New Balance kept the nubuck shoes coming in a variety of solid colors and also kept the prices high and distribution limited to perpetuate the luxury goods image of the 576.[24] The shoe has remained popular over the past decade and in 2010 New Balance released a new version of the popular shoe called the 576 "France" which comes in the country's national colors and even has the French flag in the form of embroidery on the heel (Exhibit 19–6). This new 576 marked the first time New Balance had dedicated a shoe to a country.[25]

In recent years, U.S. brands have become popular in many other European countries as well as in Asia. Marketers attribute the rising popularity of many U.S.-made products to the worldwide distribution of American music, films, and TV shows; the growth of the Internet; and the increase in travel to the United States. These factors have made consumers in foreign countries more familiar with American culture, values, and lifestyle.[26]

Japan is one of the more difficult markets for many American advertisers to understand because of its unique values and customs.[27] For example, the Japanese have a very strong commitment to the group; social interdependence and collectivism are as important to them as individualism is to most Americans. Ads stressing individuality and nonconformity have traditionally not done well in Japan, but westernized values have become more prevalent in Japanese advertising in recent years.[28] However, the Japanese dislike ads that confront or disparage the competition and tend to prefer soft rather than hard sells.[29] A study found that Japanese and American magazine ads tend to portray teenage girls in different ways and that the differences correspond to each country's central concepts of self and society. In many American ads teens are associated with images of independence, rebelliousness, determination, and even defiance that are consistent with the American value of individuality. In contrast, Japanese ads tend to portray a happy, playful, childlike, girlish image that is consistent with the Japanese culture's sense of self, which is more dependent on others.[30] Another study examined gender-role portrayals in Japanese magazine advertising and found that some of the previously used hard-line stereotyping of both men and women has softened considerably since the 1980s. Men are not associated as much with stereotypical male traits, while women are shown in more positive ways. The researchers suggest that this may reflect the westernization of the depictions of men and women in Japan.[31]

As advertisers turn their attention to China, more consideration is also being given to understanding the cultural system and values of the world's most populous country. Chinese values are centered around Confucianism, which stresses loyalty and interpersonal relationships. Chinese culture also emphasizes passive acceptance of fate by seeking harmony with nature; inner experiences of meaning and feeling; stability and harmony; close family ties; and tradition.[32] A study of advertising appeals used in China found that advertising reflects these traditional Chinese cultural values. Chinese advertisers tend to base their advertising strategies on creating liking for a product through image and emotional appeals rather than information-laden ads. However, the study also found subtle changes in appeals to cultural values used by advertisers, particularly for ads targeting younger consumers. Youth and modernity appeals were found to be prevalent, reflecting the westernization, as well as the modernization, trend in China.[33] Marketing is just beginning to emerge in China, and advertising is a relatively new social phenomenon, so it will be important for marketers to develop a better understanding of Chinese cultural values and their implication for communications strategy.[34]

Nike recently ran into a problem over a commercial that aired in China showing NBA basketball star LeBron James winning a battle with a Chinese dragon and a kung fu master. The commercial was banned by government regulators who stated that it created indignant feelings among Chinese television viewers because it showed an American sports icon defeating the dragon, a symbol of Chinese culture, and the martial arts master, a symbol of national pride. A statement posted on the website of China's State Administration for Radio, Film, and Television stated that the ad violated the regulation that "all advertisements must uphold national dignity and interest, and respect the motherland's culture." Nike's China marketing director said that it was not the company's intention to show disrespect to the Chinese culture, explaining that the ad was meant to inspire youth to overcome internal fear and obstacles in order to improve themselves. Toyota Motor Co. of Japan also had to retract and issue an apology for an ad that ran in magazines and newspapers in China depicting stone lions, a traditional sign of Chinese power, saluting and bowing to a Prado Land Cruiser sport utility vehicle.[35] A recent study examined perceptions of offensive advertising among Chinese consumers living in Hong Kong and Shanghai. The study found that the central issue related to whether an ad was perceived as offensive by the type of execution and creative tactics used or by the offensiveness of the product or service being advertised. The researchers noted that despite the sophistication and modernization of these two major cities, consumers there remain conservative and, to some extent collectivist, as susceptibility to interpersonal influence affects this evaluation of offensive advertising. They recommended that marketers remain cautious when developing advertising for China and should not take too many risks with offensive advertising.[36]

Religion is another aspect of culture that affects norms, values, and behaviors. For example, in many Arab countries, advertisers must be aware of various taboos resulting from conservative applications of the Islamic religion. Alcohol and pork cannot be advertised. Human nudity is forbidden, as are pictures of anything sacred, such as images of a cross or photographs of Mecca. The faces of women may not

**EXHIBIT 19–7**
PepsiCo and Coca-Cola are targeting the Middle East to grow their soft drink brands

be shown in photos, so cosmetics use drawings of women's faces in ads. In conservative Islamic countries, many religious authorities are opposed to advertising on the grounds that it promotes Western icons and culture and the associated non-Islamic consumerism. Restrictions on advertising still exist in some countries such as Iran, which has particularly averse feelings toward Western-style advertising. However, Western-style ads have become more prevalent in many Middle Eastern countries such as Egypt and Lebanon.

Both Coca-Cola and PepsiCo have taken their cola wars to the Middle East and have been engaged in a battle to win the soft drink allegiance of Arabs, especially the youth, in countries such as Lebanon, Saudi Arabia, Egypt, and even Iran. To reach the youth market, the two companies have used a variety of integrated marketing tools including media advertising, sponsorship of sports teams as well as sporting and musical events, and talent shows as well as branded entertainment (Exhibit 19–7). PepsiCo has been running ads featuring local and international celebrities such as French soccer star Thierry Henry and Christina Aguilera as well as local celebrities such as singer Elissa and pop star Haifa Wehbe. Coca-Cola has used ads featuring the young Arab singer Arjam that have resonated with youth across the Arab region.[37]

## The Political/Legal Environment

The political and legal environment in a country is one of the most important factors influencing the advertising and promotional programs of international marketers. Regulations differ owing to economic and national sovereignty considerations, nationalistic and cultural factors, and the goal of protecting consumers not only from false or misleading advertising but, in some cases, from advertising in general. It is difficult to generalize about advertising regulation at the international level, since some countries are increasing government control of advertising while others are decreasing it. Government regulations and restrictions can affect various aspects of a company's advertising program, including:

- The types of products that may be advertised.
- The content or creative approach that may be used.
- The media that all advertisers (or different classes of advertisers) are permitted to employ.
- The amount of advertising a single advertiser may use in total or in a specific medium.
- The use of foreign languages in ads.
- The use of advertising material prepared outside the country.
- The use of local versus international advertising agencies.
- The specific taxes that may be levied against advertising.

A number of countries ban or restrict the advertising of various products. Cigarette advertising is banned in some or all media in numerous countries besides the United States, including Argentina, Canada, France, Italy, Norway, Sweden, and Switzerland. The Australian government limits tobacco advertising to point of purchase. The ban also excludes tobacco companies from sponsoring sporting events. In Malaysia, a government ban on cigarette-related advertising and sponsorship was initiated in 2003 in an effort to curb the rising number of smokers in the country.[38] In China, tobacco and liquor advertising are banned except in hotels for foreigners. In Europe there has been a longstanding ban on advertising for prescription-drug products, which is designed to keep government-subsidized health care costs under control. The European Union has argued that advertising increases the marketing budgets of drug companies and results in higher prices. The ban prevents prescription-drug companies from mentioning their products even on their websites or in brochures, although some relaxation of these restrictions is being considered by the European Commission for drugs used to treat AIDS, diabetes, and respiratory ailments.[39]

The advertising of tobacco and liquor is banned in India although many companies have tried to get around the ban by using what are known as "surrogate advertisements." Instead of promoting tobacco and liquor products, these TV commercials and print ads market unrelated products that the company also happens to manufacture—such as CDs, playing cards, and bottled water—that carry the same brand name and allow them to build brand awareness. The Indian government has been clamping down on surrogate TV ads in response to complaints by health activists, which is leading marketers to look to other ways to promote their brands such as the branding of sports teams, concerts, and other entertainment events. They are also lobbying the Indian government for more flexibility in enforcing the crackdown such as allowing liquor ads on late night television programs.[40]

Many countries restrict the media advertisers can use. In 1999, the European Commission threw out an appeal against Greece's national ban on toy advertising on daytime television. Thus, advertisers can advertise toys on TV only during the evening hours.[41] Some of the most stringent advertising regulations in the world are found in Scandinavian countries. Commercial TV advertising did not begin in Sweden until 1992, and both Sweden and Denmark limit the amount of time available for commercials. Both Sweden and Norway prohibit domestic advertising that targets children as their governments believe that young people are not able to differentiate between advertising and programming and are not capable of understanding the selling intent of commercials.[42] Saudi Arabia opened its national TV system to commercial advertising in 1986, but advertising is not permitted on the state-run radio system. Advertising in magazines and newspapers in the country is subject to government and religious restrictions.[43]

Many governments have rules and regulations that affect the advertising message. For example, comparative advertising is legal and widely used in the United States and Canada but is illegal in some countries such as Korea and Belgium. In Europe, the European Commission has developed a directive to standardize the basic form and content of comparative advertising and develop a uniform policy.[44] Currently, comparative advertising is legal in many European countries, illegal in some, and legal and rarely used in others such as Great Britain. Many Asian and South American countries have also begun to accept comparative ads. However, Brazil's self-regulatory advertising codes are so strict that few advertisers have been able to create a comparative message that has been approved.[45] Many countries restrict the types of claims advertisers can make, the words they can use, and the way products can be represented in ads. In Greece, specific claims for a product, such as "20 percent fewer calories," are not permitted in an advertising message.[46] Copyright and other legal restrictions make it difficult to maintain the same name from market to market. For example, Diet Coke is known as Coca-Cola Light in Germany, France, and many other countries because of legal restrictions prohibiting the word *diet* (Exhibit 19–8).

**EXHIBIT 19–8**
Diet Coke must use a different name in some countries

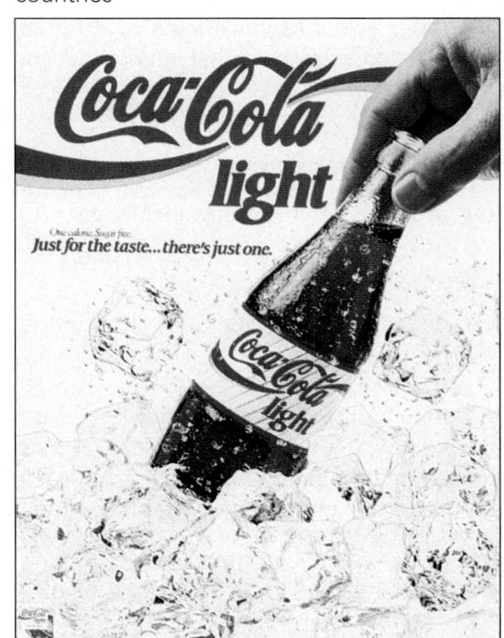


China has also begun cracking down on advertising claims as consumer groups slowly become a more powerful force in the country. For years, government regulation of advertising was less stringent than in developed markets and many companies were very aggressive with their advertising claims. However, government officials have begun enforcing a 1995 law that stipulates that statistical claims and quotations "should be true and accurate with sources clearly indicated." In

2005, the Chinese government launched a crackdown on false and illegal ads with a focus on cosmetic, beauty, health, and pharmaceutical products.[47]

An area that is receiving a great deal of attention in Europe, as well as in the United States, is the marketing and advertising of food products that are considered to contribute to childhood obesity. In 2005, the European Health Commission called upon advertisers of a variety of food products to set their own regulations to curb the advertising of so-called junk food to the 450 million consumers in the European Union. The commission has also recommended that these companies do not advertise directly to children and has even threatened to ban advertising icons such as Ronald McDonald and Tony the Tiger.[48]

# GLOBAL VERSUS LOCALIZED ADVERTISING

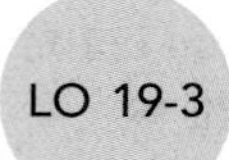


The discussion of differences in the marketing environments of various countries suggests that each market is different and requires a distinct marketing and advertising program. However, in recent years a great deal of attention has focused on the concept of **global marketing**, where a company uses a common marketing plan for all countries in which it operates, thus selling the product in essentially the same way everywhere in the world. **Global advertising** falls under the umbrella of global marketing as a way to implement this strategy by using the same basic advertising approach in all markets.

The debate over standardization versus localization of marketing and advertising programs began years ago.[49] But the idea of global marketing was popularized by Professor Theodore Levitt, who says the worldwide marketplace has become homogenized and consumers' basic needs, wants, and expectations transcend geographic, national, and cultural boundaries.[50] One writer described Levitt's position on global marketing as follows:

> Levitt's vision of total worldwide standardization is global marketing at the extreme. He argues that, thanks to cheap air travel and new telecommunications technology, consumers the world over are thinking—and shopping—increasingly alike. According to Levitt, the New Republic of Technology homogenizes world tastes, wants, and possibilities into global marketing proportions, which allows for world standardized products.[51]

Not everyone agrees with Levitt's global marketing theory, particularly with respect to advertising. Many argue that products and advertising messages must be designed or at least adapted to meet the differing needs of consumers in different countries.[52] We will consider the arguments for and against global marketing and advertising, as well as situations where it is most appropriate.

## Advantages of Global Marketing and Advertising

A global marketing strategy and advertising program offer certain advantages to a company, including the following:

- Economies of scale in production and distribution.
- Lower marketing and advertising costs as a result of reductions in planning and control.
- Lower advertising production costs.
- Abilities to exploit good ideas on a worldwide basis and introduce products quickly into various world markets.
- A consistent international brand and/or company image.
- Simplification of coordination and control of marketing and promotional programs.

Advocates of global marketing and advertising contend that standardized products are possible in all countries if marketers emphasize quality, reliability, and low prices. They say people everywhere want to buy the same products and live the

**EXHIBIT 19–9**
Gillette used global advertising to promote its Fusion razor

same way. Product standardization results in lower design and production costs as well as greater marketing efficiency, which translates into lower prices for consumers. Product standardization and global marketing also enable companies to roll out products faster into world markets, which is becoming increasingly important as product life cycles become shorter and competition increases.

A number of companies, including IBM, DeBeers, Merrill Lynch, British Airways, and American Express, have successfully used the global advertising approach. Gillette has used the "Best a Man Can Get" as its global advertising theme for over a decade and has launched a number of new razor products including the Sensor, Mach3, and Fusion using a global approach.[53] Gillette uses the same advertising theme in each country and maintains websites with similar content and layout, with only language differences. In 2007 Gillette launched a global integrated marketing campaign to promote its revolutionary six-bladed Fusion razor featuring three of most prominent athletes in the world—golfer Tiger Woods, Swiss tennis champion Roger Federer, and French soccer star Thierry Henry (Exhibit 19–9). The integrated campaign was part of the Gillette Champions program, a global sports marketing initiative for the brand, and includes television, print, and online advertising; consumer and trade promotions; and a public relations program.[54] Global Perspective 19–2 discusses how Asics, which is one of the leading brands of running shoes, recently developed a global campaign called "The Cleansing Power of Sport" to help better define the brand and increase its awareness in countries around the world.

## Problems with Global Advertising

Opponents of the standardized global approach argue that very few products lend themselves to global advertising.[55] Differences in culture, market, and economic development; consumer needs and usage patterns; media availabilities; and legal restrictions make it extremely difficult to develop an effective universal approach to marketing and advertising. Advertising may be particularly difficult to standardize because of cultural differences in circumstances, language, traditions, values, beliefs, lifestyle, music, and so on. Moreover, some experts argue that cultures around the world are becoming more diverse, not less so. Thus, advertising's job of informing and persuading consumers and moving them toward using a particular brand can be done only within a given culture.

Consumer usage patterns and perceptions of a product may vary from one country to another, so advertisers must adjust their marketing and advertising approaches to different problems they may face in different markets. For example, when Nestlé introduced its Nescafé instant coffee brand, the company faced at least five different situations in various parts of the world:

1. In the United States, the idea of instant coffee had great penetration but Nescafé had the minor share of the market.
2. In continental Europe, Nescafé had the major share of the market, but the idea of instant coffee was in the early stages.
3. In the tea-drinking countries such as the United Kingdom and Japan, tea drinkers had to be converted not just to coffee but to instant coffee.
4. In Latin America, the preferred coffee was a heavy one that could not be duplicated with an instant version.
5. In Scandinavia, Nestlé had to deal with the ingrained custom of keeping a pot of coffee on the stove from early morning until late at night.

## Global Perspective 19–2 > > >

### Asics Takes "Sound Mind, Sound Body" Message Global

In 1949, Mr. Kihachiro Onitsuka founded his athletic footwear company which was called Onitsuka Co., Ltd., by manufacturing basketball shoes out of his living room in Kobe, Japan. The company operated under the Onitsuka Tiger name until 1977 when the name was changed to Asics, which the founder chose based on the acronym for a famous Latin phrase "Anima sana in corpore sano" that when translated expresses the ancient ideal of "a sound mind, in a sound body." Today Asics is a $2.1 billion global company that offers a full line of performance-driven athletic shoes, sports apparel, and accessories. However, the company competes in a very competitive industry that includes a number of global brands including Nike, adidas, Puma, and Reebok, as well as New Balance, Saucony, and Under Armour.

Like its competitors, Asics recognizes the importance of having a strong global brand presence if it is to accomplish its mission, which is "to become the number one brand of the sports enthusiast." To help attain this objective, in 2010 the company decided to embark on a global advertising campaign to better define the brand and what it represents. The new campaign is called "The Cleansing Power of Sport" and uses exercise, and more specifically running, as a cleansing metaphor. The campaign's pervading theme is executed by showing a runner sprinting through walls of water as words such as fear, stress, insecurity and doubt, rendered in various languages, fall away from his body. Gary Slayton, Asic's vice president of marketing communication, notes that the campaign is "about shedding all those negative things on a daily basis when you get that moment to get out and exercise. It's all about perspective, and readjusting their outlook on their personal lifestyle."

The campaign was developed by the San Diego–based Vitro agency, which has handled Asics's advertising in the United States since 1996 and won the global assignment in 2009. Both client and agency felt that the time was right to embark on a global campaign that would better define the brand and position Asics as one of the leading innovative performance sports brands in the world. Despite the weak economy, Asics has had double-digit sales growth in both footwear and apparel and is now the second leading brand of running shoes, trailing only Nike. A major goal of the global campaign is to help build awareness for the Asics brand and spread its unique "Sound mind, sound body" philosophy. Research conducted by Vitro found that while consumers were not familiar with the acronym behind the Asics name, when explained it resonated well with them and generated positive feelings for the brand.

While some ads for athletic shoes rely on copy-laden ads to promote features and benefits, Vitro decided to use an imagery-based campaign that shows a runner going through walls of water and the "Sound mind, sound body" tagline. By using imagery for the creative execution, the global campaign connects to consumers in any country or region of

Nestlé had to use different advertising strategies for each market; a global campaign would not have been able to address the varying situations adequately. Exhibit 19–10 shows Nescafé ads used in Japan and Norway.[56]

Laundry detergent is another example of a product category where there are differences across various markets make the use of a global campaign difficult.[57] For example, the U.S. market is well behind Western Europe's with regard to washing machine technology and the degree of involvement in washing clothes. In countries such as Germany top-of-the line front loading machines are the norm, and clothes are washed in water at very high temperatures which requires highly specialized

**EXHIBIT 19–10**

(A) Nescafé instant coffee ad used in Japan. (B) Nescafé Gull instant coffee ad used in Norway

(A)

(B)

the world, in any language while being flexible and versatile with respect to its execution and budget. The campaign is anchored by a TV commercial as well as a number of different print executions of the theme. For the campaign to work globally, the message had to be visually iconic and easily translatable. Understandably, the complex graphics and art that make up the negative words posed a challenge. But, through relationships and negotiations, the print was able to be fully customized by language without sacrificing quality. The final campaign was translated into more than a dozen languages.

Adapting the image-based print ads for different countries and languages was not very difficult or expensive. However, doing so for a television commercial, where production costs are much higher, was more of a challenge. Thus, a decision was made to adapt the TV spot in the top five languages and priority regions that would have the budget to contribute to and air it. These languages include English, French, German, Spanish, and Japanese. The win-win here was that the use of different languages allowed the TV spot to be used in most countries and regions, as well as make the brand look bigger and more global in scope.

While television and print ads anchor the global campaign, it is fully integrated and also includes online events and sponsorships, and in-store components. Consistency across all of these touchpoints is a priority so that wherever consumers see the Asics name, it stands out against other global brands such as Nike and adidas, which have larger advertising and promotion budgets. Integration across the various touchpoints allows Asics to look, speak, and act bigger, bolder, and more confident in delivering its singular branding message.

Asics and Vitro feel that "The Cleansing Power of Sport" global campaign will make consumers around the world more aware of this philosophy and better define it for them. Vitro's CEO Tom Sullivan notes that "Sound mind, sound body" is much more than a tagline. "It's the origin of the company name and brand philosophy." Asics does not want runners just to run, but feel better about running and the emotional benefits it delivers and see Asics as the brand that represents the powerful alliance of brand and body.

Sources: Special thanks to Michael Catanzaro, account executive on Asics at Vitro who assisted in the preparation of this global perspective; Eletheria Parpis, "Asics: 'Sound Mind, Sound Body'," *Adweek* February 22, 2010, http://www.adweek.com/aw/content_display/creative/news/e3i45a85038cbfe6e22af34c3024d8.

**EXHIBIT 19–11**
Marketers of laundry products must adapt their products and IMC programs to account for differences in various countries

laundry detergents. Europe accounts for 45 percent of the world's $41 billion in annual spending on laundry products despite having only 11 percent of the population.[58] In other parts of the world such as China and Brazil, the shift to washing machines is a function of economic development and many consumers still cling to traditional laundry habits. Companies that compete in the laundry detergent market such as Unilever, Henkel, and Procter & Gamble have to adapt their products, as well as their integrated marketing programs, to account for differences in technology, water usage, and cultural preferences in various markets (Exhibit 19–11).

Many experts believe that marketing a standardized product the same way all over the world can turn off consumers, alienate employees, and blind a company to diversities in customer needs. Multinational companies can also encounter problems when they use global advertising as local managers in countries or regions often resent the home office standardizing the advertising function and mandating the type of

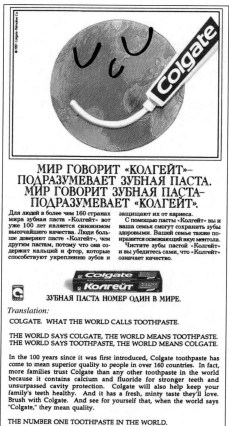

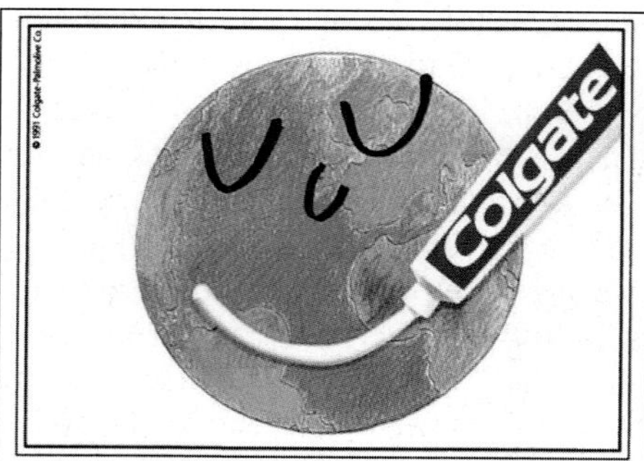
Colgate
МИР ГОВОРИТ «КОЛГЕЙТ»–ПОДРАЗУМЕВАЕТ ЗУБНАЯ ПАСТА.
МИР ГОВОРИТ ЗУБНАЯ ПАСТА–ПОДРАЗУМЕВАЕТ «КОЛГЕЙТ».
Для людей в более чем 160 странах мира зубная паста «Колгейт» вот уже 100 лет является синонимом высочайшего качества. Люди больше доверяют пасте «Колгейт», чем другим пастам, потому что она содержит кальций и фтор, которые способствуют укреплению зубов и защищают их от кариеса.
С помощью пасты «Колгейт» вы и ваша семья смогут сохранить зубы здоровыми. Вашей семье также понравится освежающий вкус ментола.
Чистите зубы пастой «Колгейт» и вы убедитесь сами, что «Колгейт» означает качество.

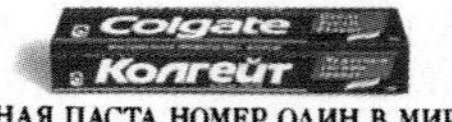
Colgate
Колгейт

ЗУБНАЯ ПАСТА НОМЕР ОДИН В МИРЕ.
*Translation:*
COLGATE. WHAT THE WORLD CALLS TOOTHPASTE.
THE WORLD SAYS COLGATE, THE WORLD MEANS TOOTHPASTE.
THE WORLD SAYS TOOTHPASTE, THE WORLD MEANS COLGATE.
In the 100 years since it was first introduced, Colgate toothpaste has come to mean superior quality to people in over 160 countries. In fact, more families trust Colgate than any other toothpaste in the world because it contains calcium and fluoride for stronger teeth and unsurpassed cavity protection. Colgate will also help keep your family's teeth healthy. And it has a fresh, minty taste they'll love. Brush with Colgate. And see for yourself that, when the world says "Colgate," they mean quality.
THE NUMBER ONE TOOTHPASTE IN THE WORLD.

**EXHIBIT 19–12**
Advertising for Colgate toothpaste uses a consistent visual image, but the copy may vary for different markets

advertising to be used in their markets. Sir Martin Sorrell, Chairman of the United Kingdom–based WPP Group, argues that there are limits to global advertising and that the one-size-fits-all pendulum has gone too far. He urges his executives to focus on consumer needs in the countries they serve and advocates the use of country managers to build contacts and adapt campaigns to local markets.[59]

Some major companies are moving away from a completely standardized approach. For example, the Colgate-Palmolive Co. has used global advertising for many of its brands, including the Colgate, Palmolive, and Ajax product lines, and continues to endorse the use of global appeals. Under its current marketing strategy, however, advertising is often modified for a specific country or region, particularly where local creativity can improve the advertising over the global standard. An example of this approach is the advertising used for Colgate toothpaste in Russia (see Exhibit 19–12). The globe/smile image is used as the visual in nearly every country where Colgate is marketed, but the copy varies.

Some marketing experts claim much of the attention to the advantages of global advertising stems from large ad agencies trying to increase business by encouraging clients to use one agency to handle their marketing communications worldwide.[60] Many large multinational companies are indeed consolidating their business with one or a few agencies who have offices around the world and offer international advertising capabilities. However, the consolidations are often driven by the client's increasing emphasis on global markets.[61]

## When Is Globalization Appropriate?

While globalization of advertising is viewed by many in the advertising industry as a difficult task, some progress has been made in learning what products and services are best suited to worldwide appeals:[62]

1. Brands or messages that can be adapted for a visual appeal, avoiding the problems of trying to translate words into dozens of languages.
2. Brands that are promoted with image campaigns that play to universal needs, values, and emotions.
3. High-tech products and new products coming to the world for the first time, not steeped in the cultural heritage of a country.
4. Products with nationalistic flavor if the country has a reputation in the field.
5. Products that appeal to a market segment with universally similar tastes, interests, needs, and values.

Many companies and brands rely on visual appeals that are easily adapted for use in global advertising campaigns. These companies are often marketing products in the secondary category, such as jewelry, cosmetics, liquor, and cigarettes, which appeal to universal needs, values, and emotions and lend themselves to global campaigns. Marketers recognize that emotions such as joy, sentiment, excitement, and pleasure are universal as are needs/values such as self-esteem, status, and achievement. Thus, it is common for global advertising campaigns to use emotional and image appeals. As one advertising executive notes:

> What it all boils down to is that we are all human. We share the gift of emotional response. We feel things. And we feel them in remarkably similar ways. We speak different languages, we observe different customs, but we are wired to each other and to an ultimate power source that transcends us in a way that makes us subject to a common emotional spectrum.[63]

A number of companies whose products appeal to universal needs, values, and emotions use global advertising. For example, the Lambesis agency created a global advertising campaign for the Italian liqueur brand Campari that celebrated its status

EXHIBIT 19–13
Campari uses global advertising to position the brand as the sophisticated choice of upscale consumers

as the sophisticated choice of upscale drinkers. The campaign celebrates Campari's passionate brand history with iconic high-fashion images used in posterlike print ads and fine art calendars as well as TV commercials featuring actress Jessica Alba. The "Club Campari" global campaign runs in over 30 countries in print, television and outdoor media as well as online. However, in developing this campaign the agency had to account for differences in the way the brand is viewed in different countries, such as Germany where it is enjoyed while watching sunsets; Brazil where it is often consumed pool-side and has a very upbeat image; and Italy where Campari has more of a progressive and cinematic image. The TV commercial developed by Lambesis, which is shown in Exhibit 19–13, effectively combines these various perceptions and images of the brand.

High-tech products such as mobile phones, personal computers, plasma and LCD television sets, video games, and MP3 players are products in the third category. Many of the marketers of high-tech products use global campaigns to promote their brands. For example, Taiwan-based HTC is one of the fastest growing companies in the mobile phone industry and now has 5 percent of the world's smartphone market.[64] The company makes flagship smartphones for many of the world's wireless operators including the Sprint EVO, Verizon Droid, T-Mobile MyTouch, and Vodafone. While HTC works with the wireless carriers to market these brands, the firm has also embarked on a global advertising campaign to help build its own brand image. The YOU global campaign is based on the company's "Quietly Brilliant" positioning and uses the tagline: "You don't need to get a phone. You need a phone that gets you." The goal of the campaign is to drive broad global visibility as well as an understanding of HTC's unique brand promise and corporate philosophy—that it is all about YOU the consumer and not the mobile device.[65] Exhibit 19–14 shows one of the ads from the global campaign.

Products in the fourth category are those that come from countries with national reputations for quality and/or a distinctive image that can be used as the basis for global advertising. These products capitalize on the **country-of-origin effect** which refers to consumers' general perceptions of quality for products made in a given country.[66] Examples include Swiss watches, French wine, and German beer or automobiles. Many U.S. companies are taking advantage of the cachet American products have acquired among consumers in Europe and other international markets. For example, Jeep promotes itself as "the American legend" in Europe and Japan. Brown-Forman has been using an American theme for its Jack Daniel's and Southern Comfort liquor brands since it began selling them in foreign markets more than two decades ago. A number of studies have shown a pronounced effect of country of origin on the quality perceptions of products, with the reputation of specific countries impacting consumers' evaluative judgments of brands.[67] Thus, companies and brands that originate in countries associated with quality may want to take

EXHIBIT 19–14
HTC is using a global campaign to build brand awareness and image

CHAPTER 19

## Global Perspective 19–3 > > >

### Is Country of Origin Important to College Students?

As a college student, it is very likely you are using products made by a company based in a foreign country. You may own a Samsung, LG, or Nokia cell phone, wear Adidas apparel and/or athletic shoes, drink Heineken beer, have Hermes jewelry and accessories, and shop at Ikea for furniture. However, before reading further, stop for a moment and ask yourself if you know the country of origin for each of these brands. If you are like most college students, there is a good chance you may not know the home country of many of these companies. And it is also very likely that you may not really care.

Marketers often proudly promote the country of origin of their products in their advertising messages when they think it can provide them with a competitive advantage. They know that to many consumers "German made" is a sign of quality engineering, "made in Italy" signals style, French products are often synonymous with chic, and Japan is perceived as making the best consumer electronics products. However, a recent study conducted by the marketing consultancy firm Anderson Analytics suggests that while college students may be heavily influenced by brand names, they know very little about where their favorite brands originate. The company surveyed a representative sample of 1,000 U.S. college students from over 375 universities. The students were given a list of 31 brands and asked to match them with their home countries. In addition, they were asked which countries were best at producing certain products, as well as producing quality products overall. The products were from 11 different countries and included well-known global companies/brands such as Motorola, Nokia, Ikea, Volvo, Saab, LG, and Samsung.

The results of the study showed that the vast majority of students are not aware of the country of origin of most brands. Moreover, Japan, the United States and Germany get a lot of undue credit for creating some of the biggest brands because the majority of students identified the brands as coming from these three countries. Brands originating from Finland, Denmark, the Netherlands, Korea, Sweden, and the United Kingdom were the most misidentified. For example, only 4 percent of the college students surveyed knew that cell phone maker Nokia is from Finland, while 53 percent identified the company as being from Japan. Similar results were found for consumer electronics company Samsung. Only 9 percent knew the company was from Korea while 58 percent identified the company as being Japanese. Only 12 percent correctly identified Adidas as being based in Germany, while almost half (48 percent) mistakenly thought that it was a U.S. company.

Brands for which the college students were most able to identify the country of origin were Motorola (38 percent), Lexus (37 percent), Ikea (31 percent), and Hermes (31 percent). A research analyst noted that it was not surprising that Swedish-based Ikea was correctly identified by many of the students since its stylish and inexpensive furniture is popular among the college crowd while French-based Hermes is a popular fashion brand. Motorola and Lexus, which are from the United States and Japan, respectively, were the only two brands that were correctly identified by more than a third of the students.

While college students may not have a clue as to where brands come from, they do have definite opinions about which countries produce the best products. When students were asked whether they believe a country makes quality products, Japan was rated the highest at 82 percent, followed by the United States at 78 percent, Germany at 77 percent, and Italy at 74 percent. Countries rated the lowest

advantage of this in their advertising. However, some marketing experts argue that in today's world of globalization, consumers are only vaguely aware of the country of origin for many of the brands they buy.[68] Thus, marketers need to understand whether product origin is relevant to the consumers in their target market. Global Perspective 19–3 discusses the results of a recent study conducted among college students which indicates that the vast majority of them are unaware of the country from which most brands originate.

In the final category for which globalization is appropriate are products and services that can be sold to common market segments around the world, such as those identified by Salah Hassan and Lea Katsansis.[69] One such segment is the world's elite—people who, by reason of their economically privileged position, can pursue a lifestyle that includes fine jewelry, expensive clothing, quality automobiles, and the like. Marketers of high-quality products such as Bally leather goods, Cartier jewelry, Godiva chocolates, and Louis Vuitton luggage can use global advertising to appeal to the elite market segment around the world. Well-known international brands competing in the luxury goods marketplace often present a singular image of prestige and style to the entire world.

for product quality were Russia, Mexico, and Vietnam. An interesting result of the study was that some brands actually benefited from being misidentified in terms of quality perception while others suffered. For example, Lexus received lower-quality ratings from students who thought it was a U.S. brand than it did from those who knew it was Japanese, while Hermes received lower ratings among students who thought it was a brand from the United Kingdom. The product category with the highest level of misidentification was cell phones. However, country of origin did not affect students' quality perceptions of the various brands, which may be one of the reasons why Korean brands such as LG and Samsung compete with companies such as Nokia and Motorola, despite the overall lower-quality ratings for Korean products.

The results of this study suggest that marketers targeting young people may have little to gain by promoting their products' country of origin in their advertising and other forms of marketing communication. Ted Morris, senior vice president of global alliances at Intel, notes, "They don't care about country of origin because of the way their world has been defined. Being online transcends geography; point of origin is becoming less relevant." Tom Anderson, the managing partner of the company that conducted the study, was surprised how little college students identify brand with their country of origin noting that there is a lot of confusion. However, an analyst at Jupiter Research notes that the results may reflect the lack of consumer experience of younger consumers because geographic associations come into play as consumers age and become more concerned with product quality.

While college students may be somewhat indifferent to country of origin, marketers still need to pay attention to whether students perceive their country's reputation as good, bad, or indifferent. Country of origin does have a positive impact on brand equity when the country is associated with quality and it works the other way as well. However, in this new age of technology-driven globalization and connectedness, the most important factor may be how well products work and what they represent rather than where they originate.

Sources: Beth Snyder Bulik, "Ditch the Flags; Kids Don't Care Where You Come From," *Advertising Age*, June 4, 2007, pp. 1, 59; Adrienne W. Fawcett, "Study Finds College Students Flunk 'Brand Origin 101,'" publications .mediapost.com, June 1, 2007; "Brand & Countries," Anderson Analytics, LLC, 2007.



An example of a marketer of luxury products that uses global advertising is Swiss watchmaker TAG Heuer, who targets upscale consumers, many of whom are world travelers. Thus, the company feels that it is important to have a consistent advertising message and image in each country. Creative elements of TAG Heuer ads such as the layout, logo, pictures of the product, slogan, and tagline remain clear, consistent, and visually recognizable at first glance all over the world. The only element of the ad that changes from country to country is the celebrity ambassador who appears in the ad. For example, Tag Heuer's new "Knights of Time" campaign uses Formula 1 champions Lewis Hamilton and Jenson Button in Europe. In India, the ambassadors include racing champion Karun Chandhok and Bollywood actor Shah Rukh Khan while in the United States the ambassadors include Tiger Woods, Maria Sharapova, and Leonardo DiCaprio (Exhibit 19–15).

Another segment of global consumers who have similar needs and interests and seek similar features and benefits from products and services is teenagers. There are more than 200 million teens in Europe, Latin America, and the Pacific Rim countries of Asia whose lifestyles are converging with those of the 40 million teens in the United States and Canada to create a vast, free-spending global market.[70]

**EXHIBIT 19–15**
TAG Heuer uses a global campaign featuring different celebrity ambassadors for various countries

Teens now have intense exposure to television, magazines, movies, music, travel, and global advertising from companies such as Levi Strauss, Benetton, Nike, Coca-Cola, Pepsi, and many others.

## Global Products, Local Messages

While the pros and cons of global marketing and advertising continue to be debated, many companies are taking an in-between approach by standardizing their products and basic marketing strategy but localizing their advertising messages. This approach recognizes similar desires, goals, needs, and uses for products and services but tailors advertising to the local cultures and conditions in each market. Some agencies call this approach "Think globally, act locally" while others describe it as "global vision with a local touch."

Although some marketers use global ads with little or no modification, most companies adapt their messages to respond to differences in language, market conditions, and other factors. Many global marketers use a strategy called **pattern advertising**; their ads follow a basic approach, but themes, copy, and sometimes even visual elements are adapted to differences in local markets. For example, Unilever's Dove soap uses the same basic advertising and positioning theme globally, but models from Australia, France, Germany, and Italy are used to appeal to women in those countries.

Another company that uses pattern advertising is the TaylorMade golf company, recognized globally as having the leading brand of drivers. However, the brand positioning is different in various countries such as the United States and the United Kingdom. In the United States, TaylorMade is a premium brand founded on innovation while in the United Kingdom it is still somewhat of a value brand, resulting from discounting in the retail environment. Exhibit 19–16 shows ads used by TaylorMade when the British Open Golf Tournament was held at St. Andrews in Scotland, which is considered to be the birthplace of golf. While the ads are similar, the focus in the American ad is on a connection to the game at the highest level, and the ad is used as a simple "Thank you for the game" tribute to St. Andrews. In the United Kingdom, where TaylorMade still needs product validation from association with major golf championships, the focus in the ad was on the historic dominance of events such as the British Open through recent wins and continuing to be the most used driver at major tournaments worldwide.

**EXHIBIT 19–16**
TaylorMade uses pattern advertising with different messages to promote its ads in the United States and United Kingdom

Another way global marketers adapt their campaigns to local markets is by producing a variety of ads with a similar theme and format and allowing managers in various countries or regions to select those messages they believe will work best in their markets. Some companies are also giving local managers more autonomy in adapting global campaign themes to local markets. For example, Coca-Cola developed a new model for its global advertising and brand communication model: Rather than authorizing the heads of individual markets to run their own advertising, various regions of the world are consolidated into a series of hubs or clusters. Although the company provides local marketing support for each cluster, a global team oversees creative work that can be used in various markets, thus allowing for fewer creative executions. Coca-Cola's chief creative officer notes that the new structure "allows us to feel more like global brands with local relevance."[71]

Although many marketers are striving to develop global brands, research suggests most are doing so by using a localized approach. A study of international advertising strategies of successful U.S. multinational corporations found that only 9 percent used totally standardized global advertising for all foreign markets, while 37 percent used all localized advertising. The remaining 54 percent used a combination strategy, standardizing portions of their advertising but adapting it for local markets.[72] Marketers said a major risk of the global approach was a lack of communication owing to cultural differences. Another study found that most U.S. consumer durable goods manufacturers used a localized advertising approach—but most used some standardized messages.[73]

A more recent study of international advertising decision makers found that "think globally, act locally" still appears to be the dominant strategy of international advertisers, but with a slight revision: "Think globally, act regionally."[74] Most of the respondents in this survey said their companies' worldwide headquarters play a dominant role in determining their international advertising messages so they are consistent worldwide. However, there is a trend toward giving regional offices the autonomy to adapt the global theme for their local markets.

Most managers believe it is important to adapt components of their advertising messages—such as the language, models, scenic backgrounds, message content, and symbols—to reflect the culture and frame of reference of consumers in various countries. For example, global branding expert Nigel Hollis notes that research conducted by Millward Brown found that, all things being equal, brands that are identified with local culture will perform better than others.[75] He notes several reasons why it is important for brands to have a strong degree of identity to local culture and advises that the key to global brand success is to connect with consumers at the local level while capitalizing on the advantages offered by operating on a global scale.[76] Many companies are making these tactical adjustments to their advertising messages while still pursuing global strategies that will help them project a consistent global image and turn their products and services into global brands.

# DECISION AREAS IN INTERNATIONAL ADVERTISING

Companies developing advertising and promotional programs for international markets must make certain organizational and functional decisions similar to those for domestic markets. These decisions include organization style, agency selection, advertising research, creative strategy and execution, and media strategy and selection.

## Organizing for International Advertising

One of the first decisions a company must make when it decides to market its products to other countries is how to organize the international advertising and promotion function. This decision is likely to depend on how the company is organized overall for international marketing and business. Three basic options are centralization at the home office or headquarters, decentralization of decision making to local foreign markets, or a combination of the two.

**Centralization** Many companies prefer to *centralize* the international advertising and promotion function so that all decisions about agency selection, research, creative strategy and campaign development, media strategy, and budgeting are made at the firm's home office.

Complete centralization is likely when market and media conditions are similar from one country to another, when the company has only one or a few international agencies handling all of its advertising, when the company can use standardized advertising, or when it desires a consistent image worldwide. Centralization may also be best when a company's international business is small and it operates through foreign distributors or licensees who do not become involved in the marketing and promotional process.

Many companies prefer the centralized organizational structure to protect their foreign investments and keep control of the marketing effort and corporate and/or brand image. Centralization can save money, since it reduces the need for staff and administration at the local subsidiary level. As the trend toward globalized marketing and advertising strategies continues, more companies are likely to move more toward centralization of the advertising function to maintain a unified world brand image rather than presenting a different image in each market. Some foreign managers may actually prefer centralized decision making, as it removes them from the burden of advertising and promotional decisions and saves them from defending local decisions to the home office. However, many marketing and advertising managers in foreign markets oppose centralized control. They say the structure is too rigid and makes it difficult to adapt the advertising and promotional program to local needs and market conditions.

**Decentralization** Under a *decentralized* organizational structure, marketing and advertising managers in each market have the authority to make their own advertising and promotional decisions. Local managers can select ad agencies, develop budgets, conduct research, approve creative themes and executions, and select advertising media. Companies using a decentralized approach put a great deal of faith in the judgment and decision-making ability of personnel in local markets. This approach is often used when companies believe local managers know the marketing situation in their countries the best. They may also be more effective and motivated when given responsibility for the advertising and promotional program in their markets. Decentralization also works well in small or unique markets where headquarters' involvement is not worthwhile or advertising must be tailored to the local market.

International fragrance marketer Chanel, Inc., uses a decentralized strategy. Chanel found that many of its fragrance concepts do not work well globally and decided to localize advertising. For example, the U.S. office has the option of using ads created by the House of Chanel in Paris or developing its own campaigns for the

U.S. market. Chanel executives in the United States think that the French concept of prestige is not the same as Americans' and the artsy ads created in France do not work well in this country.[77]

**Combination** While there is an increasing trend toward centralizing the international advertising function, many companies combine the two approaches. The home office, or headquarters, has the most control over advertising policy, guidelines, and operations in all markets. The international advertising manager works closely with local or regional marketing managers and personnel from the international agency (or agencies) and sets advertising and promotional objectives, has budgetary authority, approves all creative themes and executions, and approves media selection decisions, especially when they are made on a regional basis or overlap with other markets.

Advertising managers in regional or local offices submit advertising plans and budgets for their markets, which are reviewed by the international advertising manager. Local managers play a major role in working with the agency to adapt appeals to their particular markets and select media.

The combination approach allows for consistency in a company's international advertising yet permits local input and adaptation of the promotion program. Most consumer-product companies find that local adaptation of advertising is necessary for foreign markets or regions, but they want to maintain control of the overall worldwide image they project. For example, Levi Strauss recently hired its first global chief marketing officer to oversee the company's marketing operations in over 60 countries and try to make the Levi's brand more competitive against premium denim lines such as True Religion, Seven For All Mankind, and Joe's Jeans.[78] However, the company still provides a great deal of autonomy to regional marketing directors and uses different ad agencies. While Wieden & Kennedy is the company's creative agency for the Americas, Bartle Bogle Hegarty handles Levi's creative work in Europe and Asia.[79]

## Agency Selection

One of the most important decisions for a firm engaged in international marketing is the choice of an advertising agency. The company has three basic alternatives in selecting an agency to handle its international advertising. First, it can choose a major agency with both domestic and overseas offices. Many large agencies have offices all over the world and have become truly international operations. Some Western agencies have opened offices in Eastern Europe and Russia to create ads for the multinational companies participating in the free-market economies that are developing in these countries. Many agencies are moving their offices from Hong Kong to Shanghai to be closer to the world's largest consumer market on the mainland of China.[80]

Many American companies prefer to use a U.S.-based agency with foreign offices; this gives them greater control and convenience and also facilitates coordination of overseas advertising. Companies often use the same agency to handle international and domestic advertising. As discussed in Chapter 3, the flurry of mergers and acquisitions in the ad agency business in recent years, both in the United States and in other countries, has created large global agencies that can meet the international needs of global marketers. A number of multinational companies have consolidated their advertising with one large agency. The consolidation trend began in 1994 when IBM dismissed 40 agencies around the world and awarded its entire account to Ogilvy & Mather Worldwide.[81] A year later, Colgate-Palmolive consolidated all of its global advertising with New York–based Young & Rubicam. The move, which followed the worldwide restructuring of Colgate's manufacturing and distribution system, marked the first time a large multibrand advertiser put all of its billings with one agency.[82]

In 2008 Dell entered into a partnership with the WPP Group, one of the world's largest agency holding companies, to form a new global integrated marketing and

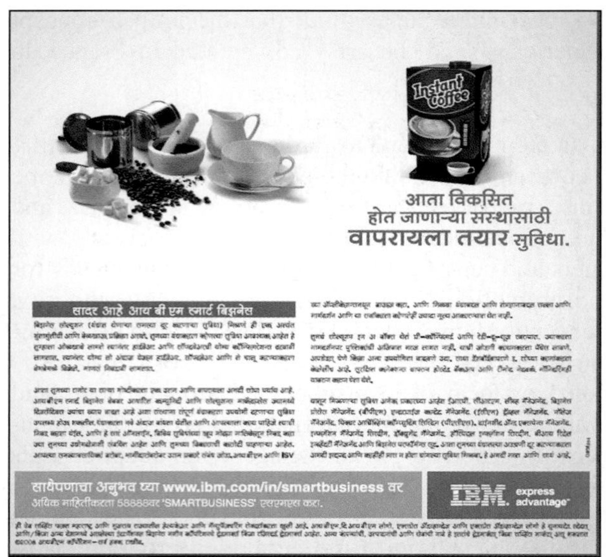


**EXHIBIT 19–17**

IBM uses the Ogilvy & Mather agency to handle all of its global advertising

communications agency that will be staffed by over 1,000 planners, creatives, and other marketing experts to serve the computer makers' global marketing needs.[83] Dell had been working with more than 800 different marketing communication firms around the world and felt that a simpler solution that integrated the various marketing communication disciplines was needed. However, WPP and Dell ran into problems in making the new agency (Enfatico) a viable division within the holding company and in 2009 WPP consolidated the start-up into its Y&R Brands division.[84]

There are a number of reasons why global marketers consolidate their advertising with one agency. Many companies recognize they must develop a consistent global image for the company and/or its brands and speak with one coordinated marketing voice around the world. For example, IBM officials felt the company had been projecting too many images when its advertising was divided among so many agencies. The consolidation enabled IBM to present a single brand identity throughout the world while taking advantage of one of the world's best-known brand names (Exhibit 19–17).

Companies are also consolidating their global advertising in an effort to increase cost efficiencies and gain greater leverage over their agencies. When a major client puts all of its advertising with one agency, that company often becomes the agency's most important account. And, as one IBM executive notes, "You become a magnet for talent and attention."[85] Consolidation can also lead to cost efficiencies. For example, as part of its new agency partnership with the WPP Group, Dell also consolidated all its media planning and buying with the holding company's MediaCom division to take advantage of economies of scale that result from working with a large media specialist organization.[86]

Advertising executives also noted that a major reason for all of the account consolidation is that agencies now have the ability to communicate and manage globally. The Internet, e-mail, and airline connections make it much easier to manage accounts around the globe. Of course, placing an entire global advertising account with one agency can be risky. If the agency fails to deliver an effective campaign, the client has no backup agency to make a fast rebound and the search for a new agency can be very time-consuming. Clients who consolidate also face the problem of selling the idea to regional offices, which often previously enjoyed their own local agency relationships. However, it appears that more and more companies are willing to take these risks and rely on one agency to handle their advertising around the world.

A second alternative for the international marketer is to choose an agency that rather than having its own foreign offices or branches, is affiliated with agencies in other countries or belongs to a network of foreign agencies. A domestic agency may acquire an interest in several foreign agencies or become part of an organization of international agencies. The agency can then sell itself as an international agency offering multinational coverage and contacts. Many of the large agency holding companies such as the WPP Group, Publicis Groupe, Omincom, and the Interpublic Group own agencies throughout the world that can handle their clients' advertising in various countries. For example, the Korean consumer electronics giant Samsung recently awarded its global brand advertising account to Leo Burnett Worldwide, which is part of the Publicis Groupe and has a global network of 96 offices in 84 countries. Samsung also awarded its $600 million global media-buying account to Starcom, the media specialist company that is also part of Publicis.[87]

The advantage of this arrangement is that the client can use a domestic-based agency yet still have access to foreign agencies with detailed knowledge of market conditions, media, and so on in each local market. There may be problems with this approach, however. The local agency may have trouble coordinating and controlling

**FIGURE 19–3**

Criteria for Selecting an Agency to Handle International Advertising

- Ability of agency to cover relevant markets
- Quality of agency work
- Market research, public relations, and other services offered by agency
- Relative roles of company advertising department and agency
- Level of communication and control desired by company
- Ability of agency to coordinate international campaign
- Size of company's international business
- Company's desire for local versus international image
- Company organizational structure for international business and marketing (centralized versus decentralized)
- Company's level of involvement with international operations

independent agencies, and the quality of work may vary among network members. Companies considering this option must ask the local agency about its ability to control the activities of its affiliates and the quality of their work in specific areas such as creative and media.

The third alternative for the international marketer is to select a local agency for each national market in which it sells its products or services. Since local agencies often have the best understanding of the marketing and advertising environment in their country or region, they may be able to develop the most effective advertising.

Some companies like local agencies because they may provide the best talent in each market. In many countries, smaller agencies may, because of their independence, be more willing to take risks and develop the most effective, creative ads. Choosing local agencies also increases the involvement and morale of foreign subsidiary managers by giving them responsibility for managing the promotion function in their markets. Some companies have the subsidiary choose a local agency, since it is often in the best position to evaluate the agency and will work closely with it.

**Criteria for Agency Selection** The selection of an agency to handle a company's international advertising depends on how the firm is organized for international marketing and the type of assistance it needs to meet its goals and objectives in foreign markets. Figure 19–3 lists some criteria a company might use in selecting an agency. In a study conducted among marketing directors of European companies, creative capability was ranked the most important factor in selecting an advertising agency network, followed by understanding the market, understanding marketing goals, and ability to produce integrated communications. Size of the agency and agency reputation were cited as important criteria by less than 2 percent of the respondents.[88] Another recent study found that most clients choose an agency based on its creative reputation and the creative presentation it had made. However, a large number of clients felt their agencies lacked international expertise and account coordination ability.[89]

Some companies choose a combination of the three alternatives just discussed because their involvement in each market differs, as do the advertising environment and situation in each country. Several experts in international marketing and advertising advocate the use of international agencies by international companies, particularly those firms moving toward global marketing and striving for a consistent corporate or brand image around the world. The trend toward mergers and acquisitions and the formation of mega-agencies with global marketing and advertising capabilities suggests the international agency approach will become the preferred arrangement among large companies.

## Advertising Research

Research plays the same important role in the development of international advertising and promotion programs that it does domestically—helping managers make better, more informed decisions. However, many companies do not conduct advertising research in international markets. Probably the main reason for this is the high cost of conducting research in foreign markets, coupled with the limited budgets many firms have for international advertising and promotion. When international markets represent a small percentage of overall sales, investments in research are difficult to justify. Rather than quality marketing information, generalizations based on casual observations of foreign markets have guided the promotional process.

As companies increase their investment in international marketing, they are recognizing the importance of conducting marketing and advertising research to better understand the characteristics and subtleties of consumers in foreign markets. There are a number of areas where research on foreign markets can help firms make better advertising decisions:

- Information on demographic characteristics of markets.
- Information on cultural differences such as norms, lifestyles, and values.
- Information on consumers' product usage, brand attitudes, and media preferences.
- Information on media usage and audience size.
- Copy testing to determine reactions to different types of advertising appeals and executions.
- Research on the effectiveness of advertising and promotional programs in foreign markets.

A great deal of information on international markets is available through secondary sources. One of the most valuable sources of information for companies based in this country is the U.S. Department of Commerce, which works closely with American companies to help them sell their products overseas through its International Trade Administration (ITA) division. The ITA publishes a series of reports that provide valuable information on most major world markets, including economic and marketing data as well as laws and regulations. Information on markets is sometimes available from other countries' government agencies, embassies, or consulates. The ITA also publishes *International Trade Update,* which is a monthly newsletter that provides valuable information on foreign markets and issues related to global business. The Central Intelligence Agency (CIA) publishes the *World Fact Book,* which contains information on more than 270 countries in eight categories, including geography, population, economy, government, communications, transportation, military, and transnational issues (Exhibit 19–18). The information includes data on telephones, radios, television sets, and communication-satellite use for nearly every country in the world and is updated annually. Circulation figures for the world's newspapers are also published every year.

**EXHIBIT 19–18**

The *World FactBook* is a valuable source of information on different countries

The *United Nations Statistical Yearbook,* which is published annually, provides demographic and economic data on more than 200 countries. Yearbooks and other reports are also available for regions such as Latin America, Europe, and Asia. Other international organizations that can provide valuable information on world markets include the International Monetary Fund and regional organizations like the Japanese External Trade Organization and the European Union. The World Bank's annual *World Development Reports* has many national statistics including per capita incomes, literacy rates, imports, exports, and a variety of other information.

Information on product and brand attitudes, usage patterns, and media habits is generally more difficult to find, particularly in developing countries. However, more information is becoming available. Nielsen Global Services provides marketers with key consumer insights for countries around the world. Global Track Consumer is a panel-based product that tracks consumer purchases in nearly 125,000 households using scanning technology or, in some markets, more traditional purchase diaries. Information from the panels is useful for

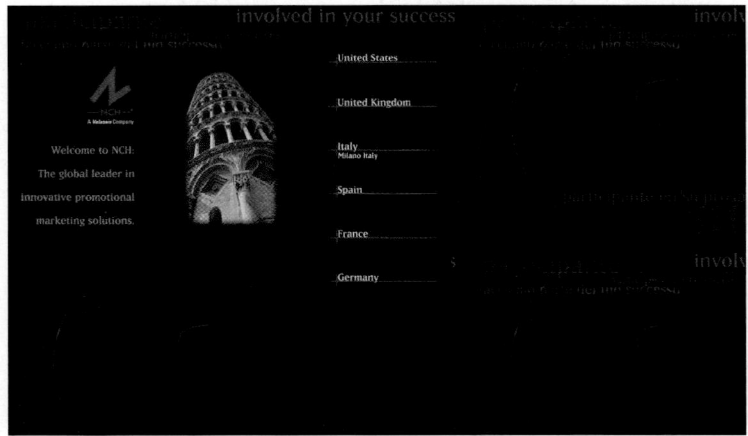


**EXHIBIT 19–19**
NCH Marketing Services is a source of information for coupon usage in various countries

understanding purchase behavior and shopping patterns for different segments of the population across various retail outlets. NCH Marketing Services, Inc. now collects information on coupon distribution and redemption patterns in the United States and a number of European countries (Exhibit 19–19). Data on media usage in various countries have increased over the past decade. However, information on TV audiences is still lacking in many countries.

Much of the information advertisers need must be gathered from research generated by the company and/or ad agency. Consumer needs and wants, purchase motives, and usage patterns often vary from one country to another, and research is needed to understand these differences. Some companies and their agencies conduct psychographic research in foreign markets to determine activities, interests, and opinions as well as product usage patterns. Advertisers should also research consumers' reactions to the advertising appeal and execution style they plan to use in foreign markets. One agency researcher recommends testing the basic premise and/or selling idea to be used in a global campaign first to be sure it is relevant to the target audiences in the markets where it will appear.[90]

## Creative Decisions

Another decision facing the international advertiser is determining the appropriate advertising messages for each market. Creative strategy development for international advertising is basically similar in process and procedure to that for domestic advertising. Advertising and communications objectives should be based on the marketing strategy and market conditions in foreign markets. Major selling ideas must be developed and specific appeals and execution styles chosen.

An important factor in the development of creative strategy is the issue of global versus localized advertising. If the standardized approach is taken, the creative team must develop advertising that will transcend cultural differences and communicate effectively in every country. For example, Tropicana uses a global advertising campaign for its pure premium orange juice. Its ads, though tailored a bit for each market, stress the superior, nearly fresh-squeezed taste of its juice over local brands that are often reconstituted from concentrates.

When companies follow a **localized advertising strategy**, the creative team must determine what type of selling idea, ad appeal, and execution style will work in each market. A product may have to be positioned differently in each market depending on consumers' usage patterns and habits. For example, the Las Vegas Convention and Visitors Authority has taken its popular "What Happens Here Stays Here" campaign to several foreign markets including the United Kingdom and Mexico. Research conducted by the ad agency found that the creative ads were not provocative enough for the United Kingdom, needed to be toned down for Mexico, and could be left alone for western Canada.[91] However, French Canadians in the eastern part of the country are more European-like in their sensibilities and the agency plans to develop alternative taglines and stories for a French-language campaign there. Mexicans were more comfortable with story lines that fit with family customers and were not sexually provocative. For example, one spot featured a young man meeting a group of friends in a Mexican bar and trying to tell them about his first trip to Las Vegas, but being too excited to find the right words (Exhibit 19–20).

**EXHIBIT 19–20**
Television ads for Las Vegas were adapted for the Mexican market

Marketers must also figure out what type of advertising appeal or execution style will be most effective in each market. Emotional appeals such as humor may work well in one country but not in another because of differences in cultural backgrounds and consumer perceptions of what is or is not funny. While humorous appeals are popular in the United States and Britain, they are not used often in Germany, where consumers do not respond favorably to them. German advertising typically uses rational appeals that are text-heavy and contain arguments for a product's superiority.[92] France, Italy, and Brazil are more receptive to sexual appeals and nudity in advertising than are most other societies. The French government recently stepped up its efforts to convince advertisers and their ad agencies to tone down the use of sexual imagery and violence in their advertising.[93] France's Truth in Advertising Commission, which is the main self-regulatory body, has issued new standards regarding the presentation of human beings in advertising.

Countries such as Japan, Brazil, and Thailand appreciate creativity: Humorous and irreverent ads are often needed to catch the attention of consumers. In Thailand, which has become the creative nerve center of Asian advertising, the unusual blend of culture, religion, politics, and language influences the advertising. Thailand's *sabi-sabai* ("take it easy") attitude is partly a product of the country's Buddhist religion, which teaches disciples to forgive and look on the sunny side of life, as well as the country's heritage as a peaceful kingdom. Thailand has a very high literacy rate but few people read as a leisure activity, which results in most ads being visual in nature rather than based upon language.[94] Many marketers have found that ads that are more humorous, irreverent, or adventurous break through the clutter and attract the attention of Thai consumers.

Another country where there is a major emphasis on creativity is India where consumers are not as cynical toward advertising as they are in many other countries, such as the United States.[95] Multinational marketers are recognizing that they must create ads specifically for the Indian market rather than trying to adapt campaigns being used globally or in their domestic markets.

In China, marketers must deal with a very decentralized market with distinct differences in culture, language, food preferences, and lifestyles among the various regions and 2,000 cities. In general, the Chinese place a high emphasis on group and family values. Advertisers must be careful when using humor and sexual appeal, particularly for national campaigns, as language and values vary greatly from province to province. Human interest stories are used as the basis for ads in southern China but less so in cities such as Beijing and Shanghai where residents prefer more information-based ads.[96]

## Media Selection

One of the most challenging areas for international marketers is media strategy and selection. Companies generally find major differences in the media available outside their home markets, and media conditions may vary considerably from one country to another. In less developed countries such as Vietnam, Kenya, and Egypt, most consumers do not have contact with a marketer's advertising and promotion efforts until they enter a store. Packaging and other point-of-purchase elements, rather than media advertising, will have the greatest impact on purchase decisions. On the other hand, advertising bombards consumers in the more affluent countries of Europe, the Pacific Rim, and North America through a variety of print and broadcast as well as interactive media. Media planners face a number of problems in attempting to communicate advertising and promotional messages to consumers in various countries. First, the types of media available are different in different countries. Many homes in developing countries do not have TV sets. For example, in many South and Central African nations (such as Uganda, Tanzania, Kenya, and Zimbabwe), radio is the dominant medium and access to TV sets is very limited. For many years, access to television was limited in countries such as Vietnam, and outdoor advertising was the best way to reach consumers along with point-of-purchase material. However, the number of households with televisions is growing rapidly in less developed countries such as India and Vietnam, as are other media such as the Internet.

The amount of time people spend watching television also varies from one country to the next. In the United States, the average person spends nearly 4.5 hours a day watching television. However, in Europe average daily viewing averages 3.5 hours and ranges from a low of 2.4 hours in Switzerland to a high of 3.9 hours in Greece. Many European countries have hundreds of channels available to cable households or homes with satellite connections.

In some countries, TV advertising is not accepted or the amount of commercial time is severely limited. For example, in Germany advertising is not permitted after 8 p.m. on government-owned channels and is prohibited on Sundays and holidays. However, the restrictions do not apply to Germany's privately owned television stations, which can devote up to 20 percent of their airtime to commercials. In the Netherlands, TV spots are limited to 5 percent of airtime and must be booked up to a year in advance. Programs also do not have fixed time slots for ads, making it impossible to plan commercial buys around desired programs. In some countries, the limited number of channels and demand for commercial time result in extremely high levels of advertising clutter.

The number of TV sets is increasing tremendously in India, but there is still controversy over TV advertising. Commercials are restricted to only 10 percent of programming time and must appear at the beginning or end of a program. Australia lifted a ban on cable TV advertising in 1997. However, some cable channels won't accept any advertising, and Australian consumers will not tolerate as much advertising on cable channels as on free TV networks.[97]

The characteristics of media differ from country to country in terms of coverage, cost, quality of reproduction, restrictions, and the like. In some countries, media rates are negotiable or may fluctuate owing to unstable currencies, economic conditions, or government regulations. For example, in China TV stations charge a local rate for Chinese advertisers, a foreign rate, and a joint venture rate. Although its 1.19 billion TV viewers make China the world's largest television market, the medium is strictly controlled by the Communist Party. State-owned China Central Television (CCTV) controls the national networks. Politics frequently intrude into program selection and scheduling: A show might be delayed for several months to coincide with a key political event, or programs from foreign countries may be pulled off the air.[98] CCTV has developed its own version of an up-front market, as an auction is held each November to sell advertising time on prime-time programming for the coming year. The annual auction is generally considered a barometer for China's media market as local and regional channels will often hold off setting their advertising rates to see the level of demand for advertising time. While CCTV is China's only national broadcaster, it accounts for just 12 percent of the total television advertising revenue in China with the remainder going to local TV channels, provincial satellite channels, and provincial TV stations.[99]

Another problem international advertisers face is obtaining reliable media information such as circulation figures, audience profiles, and costs. Many countries that had only state-owned TV channels are now experiencing a rapid growth in commercial channels, which is providing more market segmentation opportunities. However, reliable audience measurement data are not available, and media buyers often rely on their instincts when purchasing TV time. A number of research companies are developing audience measurement systems for countries in Eastern Europe, Russia, and China. In China, AGB Nielsen Media Research monitors TV-viewing audiences in 11 of China's biggest cities including Beijing, Shanghai, and Guangzhou as well as in the rural parts of several provinces using nearly 10,000 households with people meters.[100] Audience measurement information is also available from CSM Media Research, a company that is a joint venture between CTR Market Research (the leading market research company in China) and TNS Group, a global market information company based in London.

**EXHIBIT 19–21**
*Jelly* is a popular fashion magazine in Japan

The goal of international advertisers is to select media vehicles that reach their target audience most effectively and efficiently. Media selection is often localized even for a centrally planned, globalized campaign. Local agencies or media buyers generally have more knowledge of local media and better opportunities to negotiate rates, and subsidiary operations can maintain control and adapt to media conditions and options in their market. Media planners have two options: using national or local media or using international media.

**Local Media** Many advertisers choose the local media of a country to reach its consumers. Print is the most used medium worldwide, since TV commercial time and the number of homes with TV sets are limited in many countries. Many countries have magazines that are circulated nationwide as well as national or regional newspapers that carry advertising directed to a national audience. Most countries also have magazines that appeal to special interests or activities, allowing for targeting in media selection. For example, Japan has numerous fashion magazines such as *Jelly,* which focuses on runway fashions, as well as street fashion and culture (Exhibit 19–21).

Although restrictions and regulations have limited the development of TV as a dominant advertising medium in many countries, it is a primary medium for obtaining nationwide coverage in most developed countries and offers tremendous creative opportunities. Restrictions on television may be lessening in some countries, and time availability may increase. For example, the number of TV stations and television advertising in Italy have exploded in the past decade since government restrictions against private broadcasting were lifted. Advertising groups are using economic, legal, and political pressure to get more television commercial time from reluctant European governments. The increase in TV channels through direct broadcasting by satellite to many European households (discussed later in this section) is hastening this process.

In addition to print and television, local media available to advertisers include radio, direct mail, billboards, cinema, and transit advertising. These media give international advertisers great flexibility and the opportunity to reach specific market segments and local markets within a country. Most international advertisers rely heavily on national and local media in their media plans for foreign markets.

**International Media** The other way for the international advertiser to reach audiences in various countries is through international media that have multimarket coverage. The primary focus of international media has traditionally been magazines and newspapers. A number of U.S.-based consumer-oriented publications have international editions, including *Time, Newsweek, Reader's Digest,* and *National Geographic* as well as the newspaper *USA Today.* Hearst Magazines International oversees the publication of Hearst's leading consumer magazines around the world. Hearst publishes nearly 200 international editions for distribution in more than 100 countries including *Esquire, Good Housekeeping, Seventeen,* and *Popular Mechanics.* Hearst also publishes *Cosmopolitan,* which with 58 international editions, is the largest selling young women's magazine and has more editions than any other magazine in the world. Other U.S.-based publications with foreign editions include *BusinessWeek, Fortune,* and *The Wall Street Journal.*

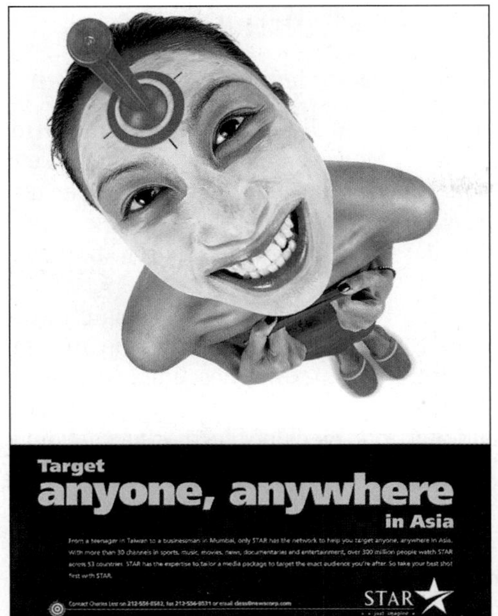

**EXHIBIT 19–22**
STAR TV reaches more than 100 million homes across Asia

A number of U.S.-based publishers are looking for growth by taking their brands to other countries where the number of magazines is still growing and the Internet has less of an impact on advertising revenue. The CEO of Hearst Magazines International has noted that the BRIC countries—Brazil, Russia, India, and China—offer good growth opportunities based on the level of competition, as well as growth in GDP and advertising spending.[101] Over the past several years Hearst has started new editions of magazines such as *Cosmopolitan*, *Harper's Bazaar*, and *Esquire* in India, Vietnam, Spain, and Australia. Another major publisher, Time Inc., has launched new editions of *Sports Illustrated* and *InStyle* in China; *People* and *Sports Illustrated* in India; *Fortune* in Korea; and *InStyle* in Thailand. However, publishing companies must still overcome a number of challenges in foreign countries such as underdeveloped distribution systems, cultural differences, and low cover prices and advertising rates that make it difficult to generate enough revenue to make the magazines profitable.[102]

International publications offer advertisers a way to reach large audiences on a regional or worldwide basis. Readers of these publications are usually upscale, high-income individuals who are desirable target markets for many products and services. There are, however, several problems with these international media that can limit their attractiveness to many advertisers. Their reach in any one foreign country may be low, particularly for specific segments of a market. Also, while they deliver desirable audiences to companies selling business or upscale consumer products and services, they do not cover the mass consumer markets or specialized market segments very well. Other U.S.-based publications in foreign markets do offer advertisers ways to reach specific market segments.

While print remains the dominant medium for international advertising, many companies are turning their attention to international commercial TV. Package-goods companies in particular view TV advertising as the best way to reach mass markets and effectively communicate their advertising messages. Satellite technology has helped spread the growth of TV in other countries and made global television networks a reality. For example, MTV Networks International has a variety of brands that span the globe and are seen in over 500 million households in 160 countries including its flagship MTV network as well as VH1 and Nickelodeon. MTV is still the premier media platform for marketers trying to reach young consumers in countries throughout the world, including Europe, Asia, and Latin America.

A major development affecting broadcasting in Europe, Asia, and Latin America is **direct broadcast by satellite (DBS)** to homes and communities equipped with small, low-cost receiving dishes. A number of satellite networks operate in these regions and beam entertainment programming across several countries. The satellite network market is dominated by the global media conglomerate News Corporation, which was founded by Rupert Murdoch and owns a number of media properties in the United States including the Fox Broadcasting Company. News Corp has a controlling interest in British Sky Broadcasting (BSkyB), which beams more than 300 channels to 7 million subscribers in Britain, and also owns STAR, which is the world's largest satellite network, stretching from the Middle East to India and South Korea and reaching more than 300 million viewers in 53 countries (Exhibit 19–22). News Corp also owns part of Phoenix Satellite Television, which reaches several provinces in China and has greater reach than any other foreign channel, particularly among upscale educated viewers in urban areas such as Beijing, Shanghai, and Guangzhou.[103]

Advances in satellite and communications technology, the expansion of multinational companies with global marketing perspectives, and the development of global ad agencies mean advertisers' use of television as a global medium is likely to increase.

# THE ROLES OF OTHER PROMOTIONAL MIX ELEMENTS IN INTERNATIONAL MARKETING

This chapter has focused on advertising, since it is usually the primary element in the promotional mix of the international marketer. However, as in domestic marketing, promotional programs for foreign markets generally include such other elements as sales promotion, public relations, and digital media. The roles of these other promotional mix elements vary depending on the firm's marketing and promotional strategy in foreign markets.

Sales promotion and public relations can support and enhance advertising efforts; the latter may also be used to create or maintain favorable images for companies in foreign markets. For some firms, personal selling may be the most important promotional element and advertising may play a support role. This final section considers the roles of some of these other promotional mix elements in the international marketing program.

## Sales Promotion

Sales promotion activity in international markets is growing due in part to the transfer of promotion concepts and techniques from country to country and in part to the proliferation of media. The growth also stems from the liberalization of trade, the rise of global brands, the spread of cable and satellite TV, and the deregulation and/or privatization of media. Sales promotion and direct-response agencies have been becoming more common, particularly in Europe and more recently in South American, Asian, and Middle Eastern countries. In many less developed countries, spending on sales promotion often exceeds media spending on TV, radio, and print ads.

As we saw in Chapter 16, sales promotion is one of the fastest-growing areas of marketing in the United States. Companies increasingly rely on consumer- and trade-oriented sales promotion to help sell their products in foreign markets as well. Many of the promotional tools that are effective in the United States, such as free samples, premiums, event sponsorships, contests, coupons, and trade promotions, are also used in foreign markets. For example, Häagen-Dazs estimates it gave out more than 5 million free tastings of its ice cream as part of its successful strategy for entering the European market. Since taste is the major benefit of this premium product, sampling was an appropriate sales promotion tool for entering foreign markets. The WD-40 Company uses samples in the United States as well as foreign markets to educate consumers about the versatility of the product and encourage trial. The sample shown in Exhibit 19–23, which uses the front headline "One Can. One Thousand Uses," was translated into 20 different languages. This makes it possible for the distributors in different countries to use a sampling tool in their local languages. Nestlé introduced its Nescafe brand to China by conducting the world's largest coffee-sampling program. Nescafe samples were passed out across 150 cities in China using 18 teams throughout the country. The sampling program helped increase sales by over 150 percent in the predominantly tea-drinking country.[104]

**EXHIBIT 19–23**
WD-40 uses product samples in various countries to encourage trial

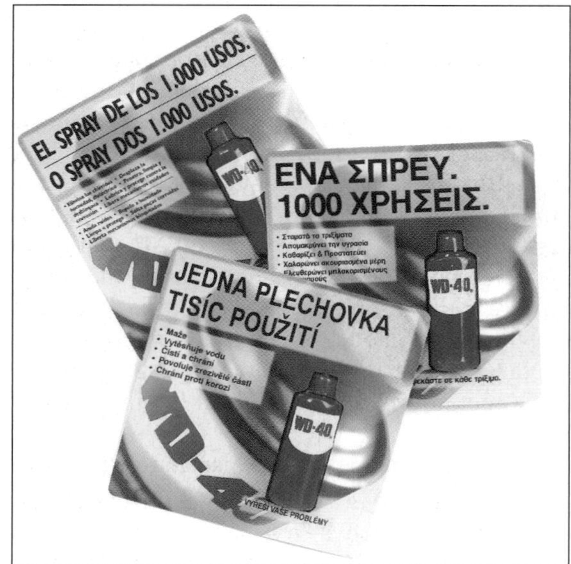


Unlike advertising, which can be done on a global basis, sales promotions must be adapted to local markets. Kamran Kashani and John Quelch noted several important differences among countries that marketers must consider in developing a sales promotion program.[105] They include the stage of economic development, market maturity, consumer perceptions of promotional tools, trade structure, and legal restrictions and regulations:

- *Economic development.* In highly developed countries such as the United States, Canada, Japan, and Western European nations, marketers can choose from a wide range of promotional tools. But in developing countries they must be careful not to use promotional tools such as in- or on-package premiums that would increase the price of the product beyond the reach of most consumers. Free samples and demonstrations are widely used as effective promotional tools in developing countries. But coupons, which are so popular with consumers in the United States, are rarely used because of problems with distribution and resistance from retailers. In the United States and Britain, most coupons are distributed through newspapers (including FSIs) or magazines. Low literacy rates in some countries make print media an ineffective coupon distribution method, so coupons are delivered door to door, handed out in stores, or placed in or on packages. The use of coupons by both marketers as well as consumers is much greater in the United States than other countries as more than 300 billion coupons were distributed and 3.2 billion redeemed in 2009. Coupon distribution and redemption in other countries drops dramatically from the levels seen in the United States, as the United Kingdom is the second largest users of coupons with just over 6 billion distributed in 2009 and 63 million redeemed.
- *Market maturity.* Marketers must also consider the stage of market development for their product or service in various countries when they design sales promotions. To introduce a product to a country, consumer-oriented promotional tools such as sampling, high-value coupons, and cross-promotions with established products and brands are often effective. The competitive dynamics of a foreign market are also often a function of its stage of development. More competition is likely in well-developed mature markets, which will influence the types of sales promotion tools used. For example, there may be competitive pressure to use trade allowances to maintain distribution or consumer promotions that will maintain customer loyalty, such as bonus packs, price-off deals, or coupons.
- *Consumer perceptions.* An important consideration in the design of sales promotion programs is how they are perceived by consumers as well as the trade. Consumer perceptions of various sales promotion tools vary from market to market. For example, Japanese women are less likely to take advantage of contests, coupons, or other promotions than are women in the United States. Premium offers in particular must be adapted to the tastes of consumers in various markets. A study by Huff and Alden examined consumers' opinions toward the use of coupons and sweepstakes in three Asian countries: Taiwan, Malaysia, and Thailand. The study found differences among the three countries with consumers in Taiwan having more negative attitudes and lower levels of use of both sweepstakes and coupons than consumers in Malaysia and Thailand.[106]
- *Trade structure.* In areas with highly concentrated retailing systems, such as northern Europe, the trade situation is becoming much like the United States and Canada as pressure grows for more price-oriented trade and in-store promotions. In southern Europe, the retail industry is highly fragmented and there is less trade pressure for promotions. The willingness and ability of channel members to accommodate sales promotion programs must also be considered. Retailers in many countries do not want to take time to process coupons, post promotional displays, or deal with premiums or packaging that require special handling or storage. In countries like Japan or India, where retailing structures are highly fragmented, stores are too small for point-of-purchase displays or in-store sampling.
- *Regulations.* An important factor affecting the use of sales promotions in foreign countries is the presence of legal restrictions and regulations. Laws affecting sales promotions are generally more restrictive in other countries than in the United States. Some countries ban contests, games, or lotteries, while others

restrict the size or amount of a sample, premium, or prize. For example, fair-trade regulations in Japan limit the maximum value of premiums to 10 percent of the retail price; in France the limit is 5 percent. Canada prohibits games of pure chance unless a skill element is used to determine the winner. In Japan the amount of a prize offer is limited to a certain percentage of the product tied to the promotion.[107] In some countries, a free premium must be related to the nature of the product purchased. Many countries have strict rules when it comes to premium offers for children, and some ban them altogether.

Variations in rules and regulations mean marketers must often develop separate consumer sales promotion programs for each country. Many companies have found it difficult to do any promotions throughout Europe because sales promotion rules differ so much from one country to another. While the treaty on European Union may result in a more standardized legal environment in Europe, laws regarding sales promotion are still likely to vary. This is why many companies use local agencies or international sales promotion companies to develop sales promotion programs for foreign markets.

## Public Relations

Many companies involved in international marketing are recognizing the importance of using public relations to support and enhance their marketing and advertising efforts.[108] Public relations activities are needed to deal with local governments, media, trade associations, and the general public, any of which may feel threatened by the presence of a foreign multinational. The job of PR agencies in foreign markets is not only to help the company sell its products or services but also to present the firm as a good corporate citizen concerned about the future of the country.

Companies generally need a favorable image to be successful in foreign markets. Those perceived negatively may face pressure from the media, local governments, or other relevant publics, or even boycotts by consumers. Often, public relations is needed to deal with specific problems a company faces in international markets. For example, NutraSweet had problems getting its low-calorie sweetener into some markets because of strong sugar lobbies in Australia, Canada, and Europe. These lobbies encouraged the foreign press to pick up some unfavorable news about the product from the U.S. media. The company retained Burson-Marsteller, the second-largest PR company in the world, to help design factual ads about the product and to conduct other PR activities to counter the problems and get the facts out about NutraSweet.

The Coca-Cola Company and PepsiCo have had to deal with public relations problems in India following accusations by a local environmental group that the level of pesticide residues in their products was too high.[109] The Indian government tested the companies' soft drinks and issued an announcement that the companies' products conformed to local quality standards. However, opposition lawmakers pushed the government to institute a public inquiry into the allegations and numerous state governments also began doing their own tests on Coke and Pepsi products. The problems for Coca-Cola in particular became worse when an Indian consumer activist, along with several other nongovernmental organizations, accused the company of a number of other egregious offenses in India and vowed to continue their anti-Coke campaign until the company closed three controversial bottling plants and met a number of other demands. The allegations impacted both Coca-Cola and Pepsi sales in India and have resulted in some states banning the products from educational institutions.[110]

Another company, Häagen-Dazs, recently encountered a public relations problem in India, which resulted from miscommunications in posters used to promote the company's first retail outlet in Delhi. The messages on the posters read: "Exclusive Preview for International Travelers. Access restricted only to holders of international passports," and were intended to create a cosmopolitan image and to suggest that you can experience international places such as the French Riviera by enjoying

Häagen-Dazs. The controversy arose when the Web editor of the *Times of India* posted a blog criticizing the company after a friend was refused entry to the new store and e-mailed him a photo of the ad which the editor posted. The post generated more than 1,000 comments from Indians who were offended by the ad. Häagen-Dazs executives indicated that the people were barred from entering the store only because it was too crowded and apologized for the wording of the ad. The company also terminated its relationship with the advertising agency that created the teaser message. This public relations problem encountered by Häagen-Dazs serves as a reminder to companies doing business in India that the level of national pride is very high in the country and that it has a number of social activists and nongovernment organizations (NGOs) that can utilize social media to quickly create public relations problems for companies.[111]

McDonald's and a number of other companies have had to deal with public relations problems arising from concerns over the nutritional value of their food. The latest controversy erupted in response to a report showing child obesity in France had doubled to 16 percent in 10 years. Concerns over the problem of childhood obesity have spread to other European countries and other food companies such as Kraft, Kellogg, and PepsiCo are also being criticized. As noted earlier, the European Union called on the food industry to regulate so-called junk-food advertising aimed at consumers across the continent.[112]

Marketers in Spain have had to deal with a different type of public relations problem arising from concern over the growing number of eating disorders among young women fixated on their weight and appearance. The Spanish government considered banning the advertising of certain beauty related products and services such as diet products, plastic surgery, and beauty treatments before 10 p.m. The government had also considered but rejected a far more drastic move that would have banned all products advertised as "lite' including a wide range of food and beverage products such as Coke Lite and light beer.[113]

## Digital Media

**Worldwide Growth of the Internet** The Internet is coming of age as a global marketing medium and is becoming an important IMC tool for companies around the world, both large and small. Marketers are using the Internet to promote their companies, build their brands, and engage in e-commerce transactions in their own countries as well as across borders. As more homes and offices become connected to the Internet, its importance as an integrated marketing communications tool and way of transacting business will increase tremendously for companies selling consumer products and services as well as business-to-business marketers.

During its formative years the Internet was largely a North American phenomenon. By the end of the '90s, nearly 54 percent of all online users were in North America and English was the language used on three-fourths of all websites and nearly all e-commerce sites, even though it is the primary language of only 8 percent of the world's population. However, this is changing rapidly. As of 2010, there were more than 1.8 billion Internet users around the world with the largest number of users residing in Asia followed by Europe and North America. China is now the country with the largest number of people online, with an estimated 384 million users, followed by the United States with 220 million, and Japan with 96 million.[114] While the United States has the second highest number of users, its ranks ninth in terms of Internet penetration as a percentage of the population at 76 percent. The country that ranks the highest in Internet users is Norway (91 percent) followed by Sweden (90 percent). Other countries ranking higher than the United States include Netherlands and Australia.

As noted above, China now has the world's largest Internet population as well as broadband penetration at 90 percent. There are key differences in the demographic

**EXHIBIT 19–24**
TaylorMade Golf develops a website specifically for specific countries

and usage behavior of China's "digital elite" as they are younger, better educated, and more likely to be employed full-time versus Internet users in other countries. They also spend more time online and are more involved with Web 2.0 activities such as participating in blogs and chats, posting product ratings and reviews, and using social media. They are also more likely to access the Internet from mobile devices. The look, feel, and features of many Chinese websites are similar to those in the United States and Europe, and China has search (Baidu) and e-commerce (Taobao) sites that function like Google and eBay.[115] Baidu dominates online search in China today as Google closed its China site in March 2010 because of censorship by the Chinese government and intrusion from hackers. Google's retreat from China is only partial as it has retained many of its operations there and continues to offer online mapping and music services. It is expected that Google will work to resolve its disagreements with the Chinese government as the company will not want to turn its back on what has become the world's largest Internet and continues to grow.[116]

Internet usage is also very high in other Asian countries such as Taiwan and South Korea. While English is the dominant language of the Internet, most multinational companies are developing websites in a variety of languages as Internet penetration increases and more consumers around the world go online for information and entertainment.

**Use of Digital Media in International Marketing** Digital media are becoming an integral part of the IMC program of marketers at a global, regional, and local level as Internet penetration increases in countries around the world and marketers become more adept using social media, mobile marketing, and other forms of digital communication. Most multinational marketers now have websites for specific countries and/or regions which allow them to tailor the information they provide to the needs, interests, lifestyles, and subtleties of consumers in these markets. For example, Exhibit 19–24 shows a page from the website used by the TaylorMade Golf Company in Japan. Markets are also using mass media advertising to drive consumers to their websites where they provide them with detailed information about their products and services, encourage them to participate in online promotions, or allow them to make purchases. Business-to-business marketers are also using their websites as well as social media to provide customers with information and conduct business with them.

The use of social media is also becoming prevalent in countries around the world and marketers are making social-networking sites an integral part of their IMC programs. Facebook has become the first truly global social-media brand and has more than 500 million users and expects to reach 1 billion in the next few years.[117] It has become the leading social-networking site in the United States and many European countries, as well as in Australia and Argentina. However, Facebook has very little presence in China and its penetration is also very low in Japan, Korea, and Russia.[118] Local social-networking sites are thriving in many of these countries such as Tencent in China, Nasza-Klasa in Poland, GupShup in India, and Mixi in Japan, which is that country's largest social networking site with nearly 29 million users (Exhibit 19–25). Orkut has more than 20 million users in Brazil compared to only 5 million for Facebook. Google owns the international site and it has become such a popular brand that it is now operated out of Brazil. Some of these social-networking sites do not offer the applications of Facebook or MySpace, but

**EXHIBIT 19–25**
Mixi is the leading social-networking site in Japan

many are improving their capabilities to remain competitive as other sites come into their countries.

As the digital revolution continues, marketers will be making greater use of digital media in their global as well as regional and local IMC programs. The use of social-networking sites will become more prevalent and marketers are also expected to increase their use of mobile marketing techniques as more consumers are now using their mobile devices to access and surf the Internet. Spending on mobile advertising is increasing in the United States, as well as in many other countries where mobile devices are popular including many Asian countries. As consumers become more reliant on the Internet and various forms of digital media for information, entertainment, and socializing, marketers must develop ways to reach them through these contact points.

## Summary

Many U.S. companies are recognizing not only the opportunities but also the necessity of marketing their products and services internationally because of saturated markets and intense competition from both domestic and foreign competitors. Advertising and promotion are important parts of the international marketing program of a multinational corporation. Advertising is generally the most cost-effective way to communicate with buyers and create a market in other countries.

International marketers must carefully analyze the major environmental forces in each market where they compete, including economic, demographic, cultural, and political/ legal factors. These factors are important not only in assessing the potential of each country as a market but also in designing and implementing advertising and promotional programs.

In recent years, much attention has focused on global marketing, where a standard marketing program is used in all markets. Part of global marketing is global advertising, where the same basic advertising approach is used in all markets. Opponents of the global (standardized) approach argue that differences in culture, market and economic conditions, and consumer needs and wants make a universal approach to marketing and advertising impractical. Many companies use an in-between approach, standardizing their basic marketing strategy but localizing advertising messages to fit each market.

There are a number of important decision areas in the development of advertising and promotional programs for international markets. These include organization, agency selection, advertising research, creative strategy and execution, and media strategy and selection.

Sales promotion, personal selling, public relations, and the Internet are also part of the promotional mix of international marketers. Sales promotion programs usually must be adapted to local markets. Factors to consider include stage of market development, market maturity, consumer perceptions of promotional tools, trade structure, and legal restrictions and regulations. PR programs are also important to help international marketers develop and maintain favorable relationships with governments, media, and consumers in foreign countries. The use of digital media such as the Internet, social-networking sites and mobile marketing is becoming an important part of international marketers' IMC programs. Internet penetration is increasing rapidly in most countries and as more consumers go online, marketers are developing websites for various countries and also using other forms of digital media to reach them.

## Key Terms

**balance-of-trade deficit** p. 641
**economic infrastructure** p. 643
**cultural values** p. 647
**global marketing** p. 652
**global advertising** p. 652
**country-of-origin effect** p. 657
**pattern advertising** p. 660
**localized advertising strategy** p. 667
**direct broadcast by satellite (DBS)** p. 671

## Discussion Questions

1. The opening vignette to the chapter discusses how many multinational companies want to turn many of their products and services into global brands. Discuss some of the challenges marketers are facing in competition from regional and local brands and how this might impact their efforts to develop strong global brands. (LO1, LO3)

2. Discuss how the consolidation taking place in the beer industry might impact the marketing strategies of

major brewers such as Anheuser Busch InBev or SAB Miller. What are the implications of the consolidation for their IMC programs? (LO1)

3. Why are so many multinational companies expanding into China? What challenges do markets and advertising agencies face in developing IMC programs for the Chinese market? (LO2)

4. Global Perspective 19–1 discusses how many multinational companies are focusing more attention on the 4 billion consumers who live in the remote, rural communities of developing countries. Discuss the challenges companies face in marketing their products to the world's poorest consumers. How do they have to adapt their IMC programs for these countries? (LO2)

5. Why are international markets so important to companies in the United States as well as other nations? Discuss the role of advertising and other forms of promotion in the international marketing programs of multinational companies. (LO1)

6. What are some of the cultural variables that marketers must consider in developing advertising and promotional programs in a foreign market? Choose one of these cultural variables and discuss how it has created a problem or challenge for a company in developing an advertising and promotional program in a specific country. (LO2)

7. Evaluate the "Cleansing Power of Sport" global advertising campaign being used by Asics which is discussed in Global Perspective 19–2. Do you think it is appropriate to use a global advertising campaign for Asics running shoes? Why or why not? (LO3)

8. What is meant by a country-of-origin effect? Discuss the implications of the results found in the survey by Anderson Analytics (discussed in Global Perspective 19–3), which shows that college students have limited knowledge of the country of origin of most brands. (LO3)

9. What is meant by a global market segment? Provide an example of a company that has identified a global market segment and advertises its product or service the same way around the world to this market. (LO3)

10. Discuss the problems and challenges international marketers face in developing media strategies for foreign markets. (LO4)

11. Discuss the evolving role of the Internet and other digital media in the IMC program of international marketers. How can marketers make effective use of digital media in marketing their products and services in various countries? (LO5)

## AdForum Exercise: "Comparing adidas Soccer Commercials Used in Various Countries"

adforum.com

(See Advertising and Promotion Playlist, Chapter 19)

The playlist for this chapter contains commercials used by the global sports company adidas, which is based in Germany, to promote its soccer shoes, ball, and apparel in various countries including Germany, the United Kingdom, Japan, Netherlands, France, and the United States. Watch the six commercials and answer the following questions:

1 Evaluate the commercials used by adidas in each of the six countries and discuss the similarities and differences among them. What aspects of each spot, if any, do you think are unique to the country where the commercial is used?

2 Discuss whether this commercial can be used outside of the country it is currently being used? What creative aspects of the spot might allow it to be used beyond the specific country and what factors might limit its use?

3 Discuss whether a company like adidas can use a global advertising campaign to promote its soccer products. Which of the six commercials on the playlist do you think would be most appropriate for a global campaign and which spot would be least effective?

Access to the chapter playlist is available through McGraw-Hill connect MARKETING, www.mcgrawhillconnect.com

## LEARNING OBJECTIVES

- LO1 To examine how advertising is regulated, including the role and function of various regulatory agencies.
- LO2 To examine self-regulation of advertising and evaluate its effectiveness.
- LO3 To consider how advertising is regulated by federal and state government agencies, including the Federal Trade Commission.
- LO4 To examine rules and regulations that affect sales promotion, direct marketing, and marketing on the Internet.

# 20 Regulation of Advertising and Promotion

## PRODUCT PLACEMENTS MAY FACE REGULATION

Product placements are nearly as old as television itself as they date back to the early days of TV when the hosts of popular shows such as Milton Berle's *Texaco Star Theater* and Mutual of Omaha's *Wild Kingdom* would promote the sponsor's products. During his tenure as host of *General Electric Theater* from 1954 to 1962, future United States President Ronald Reagan would commonly plug the show's sponsor in introductions, segues, and closing comments by delivering a friendly message about the company that usually ended with the tagline "Progress is our most important product." The mentioning of these companies was never considered a problem because they sponsored the production of the program and were very aboveboard in promoting themselves. However, the number of product placements has increased dramatically over the years and the way brands are integrated into TV shows has also changed, which has led to concern over the practice by various consumer advocacy groups.

Unlike some countries, the United States does not prohibit product placements in the broadcast or motion picture industries. However, the use of undisclosed commercial messages in broadcasting has been regulated for more than 75 years as Section 317 of the Communications Act of 1934, which requires broadcasters to disclose "any money, service, or valuable consideration" that is paid to, or promised to, or charged by the broadcaster in exchange for product placements. However, broadcasters do not have to disclose product placements when they are offered without charge or for a nominal fee. The Federal Communications Commission (FCC) is the governmental agency that has the responsibility to prescribe the appropriate rules and regulations needed to carry out the sponsorship identification requirements. The FCC has basically interpreted the purpose of Section 317 of the Act to be that the viewers in the TV audience must be informed that what they are viewing has been paid for and that the entity paying for the broadcast must be clearly identifiable.

While there are a number of requirements and conditions associated with Section 317, broadcasters usually have been considered in compliance with the regulation by placing an announcement in the credits at the beginning or end of the program stating that "promotion consideration paid for by (name of sponsor)" which remains on the screen long enough to be read or heard by the average viewer. While this single disclosure has been the common practice in the industry, a number of consumer groups have argued that more stringent regulation is needed. They argue that product placements have become more prevalent and also more stealthy in nature as marketers work with producers of TV shows to integrate their brands into their programs. Product placements have definitely become more ubiquitous according to numbers from Nielsen IAG which tracks the number of show segments in which a brand placement appears. In 2009 the number of product placements in prime time increased by 8 percent over 2008. The television programs with the most product placements included *The Jay Leno Show* (1,015), *The Biggest Loser* (704), and *American Idol* (553) while the top brands with TV product placements were AT&T, Coca-Cola, Apple, and Ford.

Although the FCC has enforcement authority against certain forms of product placement, some consumer advocacy groups have argued that for more regulation of the practice is needed. Those expressing concern over product placements range from consumer advocacy groups to pediatricians who are seeking to protect children from the promotion of sugary cereals. One of the leading critics of product placement is Commercial Alert, a nonprofit organization cofounded by consumer activist Ralph Nader, which argues that product placements are inherently deceptive because so many viewers do not realize they are, in fact, advertisements. Another activist group that opposes product placements is Free Press. Corie Wright, an attorney and policy advisor for the group, argues that the practice is deceptive, stating that "Product placements don't allow us to have the usual veil of skepticism we have when we watch a standard commercial." Critics are concerned not just by the prevalence of products appearing in shows but also by the various forms of integration whereby brands are actually written into plotlines such as a *30 Rock* episode in which Alec Baldwin sang the praises of Cisco teleconferencing equipment, or Subway collaborating with producers of *Chuck* and *The Biggest Loser* to work the brand into show plots. The critics argue that the promotion of brands is no longer confined to the commercial breaks, and commercials and content are becoming one and the same, and difficult to distinguish from one another.

Critics are calling upon the FCC to require the TV networks to disclose product placements by using some form of onscreen notification system. Proposals range from requiring programs to run text along the bottom of the screen when a product appears in a scene, to using a flashing red light to alert viewers that a marketer is promoting a product. Some point to a system that is being proposed in the United Kingdom, which plans to begin allowing product placements for the first time in 2011. The European Union approved their use in 2009 but left it up to the individual countries to make their own rules. Regulators in the U.K. are calling for the use of an onscreen symbol, perhaps in the form of a large "P" at the beginning and end of programs to alert audiences to the paid messages embedded in the shows they are about to watch or have just seen.

In 2008 the FCC published a "Notice of Inquiry" and a "Notice of Proposed Rulemaking" to seek public comment on the call for more stringent regulations. The FCC is proposing more frequent and more obvious disclosures during programming with product placements, extension of product integration regulations to cable television, and additional restrictions for children's programming. While little has been done thus far, the television industry is already up in arms as are the marketers who use product placements. Tony Pace, Subway's chief marketing officer opposes disclosures except at the end of a program arguing that "We'd rather seem like a natural part of the show than punch the viewer in the nose with a message like, 'Hey, this is paid for." Producers of television programs as well as the major broadcast and cable networks are also concerned as paid product placements are an important source of revenue that help underwrite the costs of TV shows. Marketers also view product placements as a way to deliver branding messages to consumers who are becoming more difficult to reach during commercial breaks, particularly when they record a show on a DVR and fast-forward through the commercials when watching it.

Proponents of product placements also point to the fact that the Federal Trade Commission, which has broad jurisdiction over advertising practices, has declined to regulate their use. The FTC position has been that they have no basis for doing so since product placements rarely make objective, material claims about a product when used within a show. The FTC has also stated that it would be difficult to develop a "one-size-fits-all" rule or guide that could effectively regulate product placements. Proponents note that the FTC's position supports their argument that further restrictions on these placements are unnecessary since they are not causing any injury to consumers.

Ultimately, it may be consumers who decide the fate of product placements. The time may come when we yearn for a return to the traditional model of television programs whereby ads appear during commercial breaks and we can decide whether we want to watch them. However, until then, it is likely that marketers will continue to look for clever ways to integrate their brands into the TV shows and leave it up to the consumer to figure out why they are there.

Sources: Emma Hall, "U.K. Proposes Product Placement Alert," *Advertising Age*, June 30 2010, http://adage.com/print?article_id=144751; Brian Steinberg, "Don't Like Product Placement? Here's Why It's Your Fault," *Advertising Age*, February 11, 2010, http://adage.com/print?article_id=142069; Daniel Hertzberg, "Blasting Away at Product Placement, *BusinessWeek*, October 26, 2010, p. 60; Richard J. Wegener, "Product Placement & Government Regulation: FCC vs. FTC," paper presented at Promotional Marketing Association's 30th Annual Promotion Marketing Conference, November 20, 2008.

Suppose you are the advertising manager for a consumer-products company and have just reviewed a new commercial your agency created. You are very excited about the ad. It presents new claims about your brand's superiority that should help differentiate it from the competition. However, before you approve the commercial you need answers. Are the claims verifiable? Did researchers use proper procedures to collect and analyze the data and present the findings? Do research results support the claims? Were the right people used in the study? Could any conditions have biased the results?

Before approving the commercial, you have it reviewed by your company's legal department and by your agency's attorneys. If both reviews are acceptable, you send the ad to the major networks, which have their censors examine it. They may ask for more information or send the ad back for modification. (No commercial can run without approval from a network's Standards and Practices Department.)

Even after approval and airing, your commercial is still subject to scrutiny from such state and federal regulatory agencies as the state attorney general's office and the Federal Trade Commission. Individual consumers or competitors who find the ad misleading or have other concerns may file a complaint with the National Advertising Division of the Council of Better Business Bureaus. Finally, disparaged competitors may sue if they believe your ad distorts the facts and misleads consumers. If you lose the litigation, your company may have to retract the claims and pay the competitor damages, sometimes running into millions of dollars.

After considering all these regulatory issues, you must ask yourself if the new ad can meet all these challenges and is worth the risk. Maybe you ought to continue with the old approach that made no specific claims and simply said your brand was great.

Regulatory concerns can play a major role in the advertising decision-making process. Advertisers operate in a complex environment of local, state, and federal rules and regulations. Additionally, a number of advertising and business-sponsored associations, consumer groups and organizations, and the media attempt to promote honest, truthful, and tasteful advertising through their own self-regulatory programs and guidelines. The legal and regulatory aspects of advertising are very complex. Many parties are concerned about the nature and content of advertising and its potential to offend, exploit, mislead, and/or deceive consumers.

Advertising has also become increasingly important in product liability litigation involving products that are associated with consumer injuries. In many of these cases the courts have been willing to consider the impact of advertising on behavior of consumers that leads to injury-causing situations. Thus advertisers must avoid certain practices and proactively engage in others to ensure that their ads are comprehended correctly and do not misrepresent their products or services.[1]

Numerous guidelines, rules, regulations, and laws constrain and restrict advertising. These regulations primarily influence individual advertisers, but they can also affect advertising for an entire industry. For example, cigarette advertising was banned from the broadcast media in 1970, and many groups are pushing for a total ban on the advertising of tobacco products.[2] Legislation now being considered would further restrict the advertising of alcoholic beverages, including beer and wine.[3] Advertising is controlled by internal self-regulation and by external state and federal regulatory agencies such as the Federal Trade Commission (FTC), the Federal Communications Commission (FCC), the Food and Drug Administration (FDA), and the U.S. Postal Service. And recently state attorneys general have become more active in advertising regulation. While only government agencies (federal, state, and local) have the force of law, most advertisers also abide by the guidelines and decisions of internal regulatory bodies. In fact, internal regulation from such groups as the media and the National Advertising Review Board probably has more influence on advertisers' day-to-day operations and decision making than government rules and regulations.

Decision makers on both the client and agency side must be knowledgeable about these regulatory groups, including the intent of their efforts, how they operate, and how they influence and affect advertising and other promotional mix elements. In this chapter, we examine the major sources of advertising regulation, including efforts by the industry at voluntary self-regulation and external regulation by government agencies. We also examine regulations involving sales promotion, direct marketing, and marketing on the Internet.

# SELF-REGULATION

For many years, the advertising industry has practiced and promoted voluntary **self-regulation**. Most advertisers, their agencies, and the media recognize the importance of maintaining consumer trust and confidence. Advertisers also see self-regulation as a way to limit government interference, which, they believe, results in more stringent and troublesome regulations. Self-regulation and control of advertising emanate from all segments of the advertising industry, including individual advertisers and their agencies, business and advertising associations, and the media.

## Self-Regulation by Advertisers and Agencies

Self-regulation begins with the interaction of client and agency when creative ideas are generated and submitted for consideration. Most companies have specific guidelines, standards, and policies to which their ads must adhere. Recognizing that their ads reflect on the company, advertisers carefully scrutinize all messages to ensure they are consistent with the image the firm wishes to project. Companies also review their ads to be sure any claims made are reasonable and verifiable and do not mislead or deceive consumers. Ads are usually examined by corporate attorneys to avoid potential legal problems and their accompanying time, expense, negative publicity, and embarrassment.

Internal control and regulation also come from advertising agencies. Most have standards regarding the type of advertising they either want or are willing to produce, and they try to avoid ads that might be offensive or misleading. Most agencies will ask their clients to provide verification or support for claims the clients might want to make in their advertising and will make sure that adequate documentation or substantiation is available. However, agencies will also take formal steps to protect themselves from legal and ethical perils through agency-client contracts. For example, many liability issues are handled in these contracts. Agencies generally use information provided by clients for advertising claims, and in standard contracts the agency is protected from suits involving the accuracy of those claims. Contracts will also absolve the agency of responsibility if something goes wrong with the advertised product and consumers suffer damages or injury or other product liability claims arise.[4] However, agencies have been held legally responsible for fraudulent or deceptive claims and in some cases have been fined when their clients were found guilty of engaging in deceptive advertising.[5] Many agencies have a creative review board or panel composed of experienced personnel who examine ads for content and execution as well as for their potential to be perceived as offensive, misleading, and/or deceptive. Most agencies also employ or retain lawyers who review the ads for potential legal problems. Exhibit 20–1 shows an ad for a legal firm specializing in advertising and integrated marketing communications law.

**EXHIBIT 20–1**
The Lustigman firm specializes advertising and integrated marketing communications law

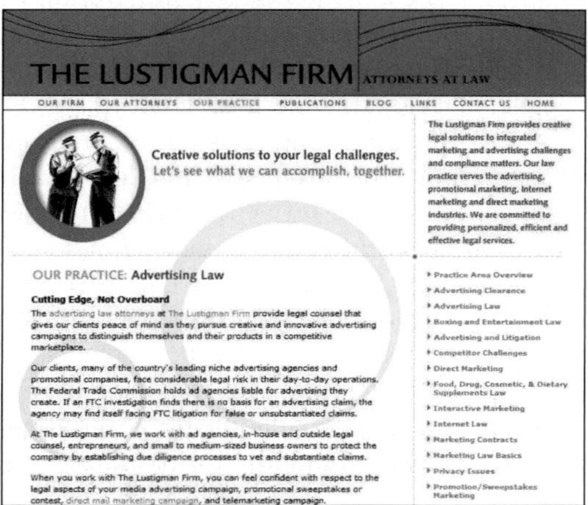


## Self-Regulation by Trade Associations

Like advertisers and their agencies, many industries have also developed self-regulatory programs. This is particularly true in industries whose advertising is prone to controversy, such as liquor and alcoholic beverages, drugs, and various products marketed to children. Many trade and industry associations develop their own advertising guidelines or codes that member companies are expected to abide by.

The Wine Institute, the U.S. Brewers Association, and the Distilled Spirits Council of the United States all have guidelines that member companies are supposed to follow in advertising alcoholic beverages.[6] No specific law prohibits the advertising of hard liquor on radio or television. However, such advertising was effectively

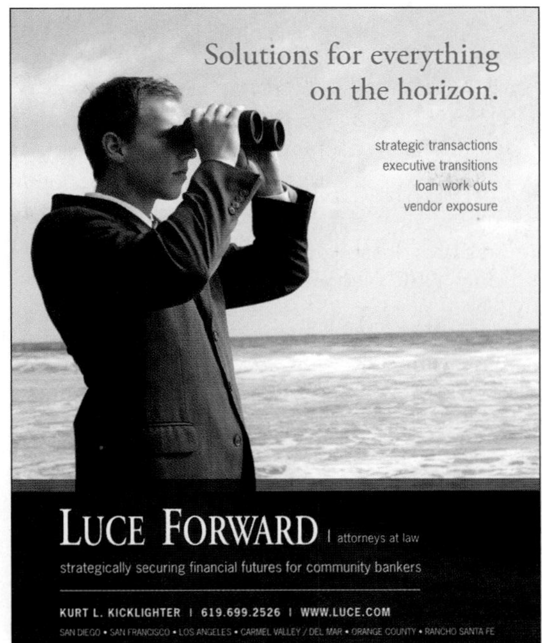


**EXHIBIT 20–2**
Advertising by lawyers has become common

banned for over five decades as a result of a code provision by the National Association of Broadcasters and by agreement of liquor manufacturers and their self-governing body, the Distilled Spirits Council (DISCUS). However, in November 1996, DISCUS amended its code of good practice and overturned its self-imposed ban on broadcast advertising.[7] IMC Perspective 20–1 discusses the reasons why the council decided to overturn the ban, as well as the increase in TV advertising for distilled spirits that has resulted from its decision. Other industry trade associations with advertising codes and guidelines include the Toy Industry Association, the Motion Picture Association of America, and the Pharmaceutical Research and Manufacturers of America whose guidelines for prescription drug advertising are discussed later in the chapter.

Many professions also maintain advertising guidelines through local, state, and national organizations. For years professional associations like the American Medical Association (AMA) and the American Bar Association (ABA) restricted advertising by their members on the basis that such promotional activities lowered members' professional status and led to unethical and fraudulent claims. However, such restrictive codes have been attacked by both government regulatory agencies and consumer groups. They argue that the public has a right to be informed about a professional's services, qualifications, and background and that advertising will improve professional services as consumers become better informed and are better able to shop around.[8]

In 1977, the Supreme Court held that state bar associations' restrictions on advertising are unconstitutional and that attorneys have First Amendment freedom of speech rights to advertise.[9] Many professional associations subsequently removed their restrictions, and advertising by lawyers and other professionals is now common (Exhibit 20–2).[10] In 1982, the Supreme Court upheld an FTC order permitting advertising by dentists and physicians.[11]

Research shows that consumers generally favor increased use of professional advertising. However, professionals continue to have reservations. They worry that advertising has a negative impact on their image, credibility, and dignity and see benefits to consumers as unlikely.[12] Still, advertising by professionals is increasing, particularly among newcomers to medicine, dentistry, and law. Associations such as the AMA and the ABA developed guidelines for members' advertising to help maintain standards and guard against misleading, deceptive, or offensive ads.

The issue of professional advertising, particularly by attorneys, is still debated. Some traditional law firms resist using advertising, particularly on TV, due to concern that it might hurt the profession's image. Many in the legal profession worry that ads soliciting personal injury victims only worsen the public's perception of attorneys. A sizable faction within the American Bar Association (ABA) blames the legal profession's image problem on sleazy ads. The ABA's Commission on Advertising held a series of public hearings on what, if any, restrictive measures to recommend to state ethics panels. Some states restrict the content of attorney ads and the way they can be delivered and require a disclaimer urging consumers not to base their attorney selection on an advertisement. Many attorneys are incensed over efforts to restrict their rights to promote themselves because they use advertising to help build their practices. Several cases are currently being litigated, but ultimately the Supreme Court may have to decide just how far states can go in curtailing advertising.

Although industry associations are concerned with the impact and consequences of members' advertising, they have no legal way to enforce their guidelines. They can only rely on peer pressure from members or other nonbinding sanctions to get advertisers to comply.

## IMC Perspective 20–1 > > >

### Distilled Spirits Use TV Advertising to Boost Sales

For more than five decades, distilled spirits were not advertised on television or radio because of a self-imposed ban by members of the Distilled Spirits Council of the United States (DISCUS). Council members agreed in 1936 to avoid radio advertising and extended the ban to TV in 1948. But Seagram, the second-largest distiller in the world at the time, ended the U.S. spirits industry's long-standing ban on broadcast advertising in June 1996 by airing commercials for its Crown Royal Canadian Whiskey brand on an affiliate in Corpus Christi, Texas.

Seagram issued a statement that it was ending the liquor industry's decades-old practice of not advertising on TV because DISCUS's voluntary code of good practice placed spirits at a competitive disadvantage to beer and wine, which did not have any such restrictions. Seagram also argued that the ban had become outdated as radio and TV have become more targeted and they could pinpoint their advertising message to people of legal drinking age. A number of distillers, eager to turn around the long, slow decline in hard liquor sales, watched Seagram test the water with its TV ads before rolling out their own commercials. Some held discussions with TV stations but waited for a formal amendment to the DISCUS code of good practice before proceeding. The amendments came on November 7, 1996, when DISCUS members voted unanimously to overturn the self-imposed ban on broadcast ads. The DISCUS president noted that spirits makers wanted to break down the public perception that spirits are stronger or more dangerous than beer and wine and thus deserving of harsher social and political treatment.

After the DISCUS ban was lifted, the four major broadcast TV networks, as well as major cable networks such as ESPN and MTV, continued to refuse liquor ads prompting consumer and public interest groups to applaud their actions. In fact, it has been argued that it was really the refusal by TV stations and networks to accept liquor advertising that kept them off the air rather than the DISCUS code. However, the major networks cannot control the practices of affiliate stations they do not own and many of the affiliates began accepting liquor ads, as did local cable channels and independent broadcast stations—although most had restrictions that the ads had to air after 9 P.M.

In December 2001 NBC, which was owned by the General Electric Co. at the time, announced that it would become the first broadcast network to accept hard-liquor advertising. NBC planned to limit the liquor ads to programs where at least 85 percent of viewers are 21 or older, such as during late-night time slots. However, NBC was not joined by the three other major broadcast networks—ABC, CBS, and Fox—in its decision to accept liquor commercials. NBC's decision engendered criticism from members of Congress, federal regulators, the American Medical Association, and many public advocacy groups. Critics of NBC's decision expressed concern that airing liquor ads on TV would glamorize drinking and encourage children and teenagers to drink. Facing a widening backlash over its decision, in March 2002 NBC announced that it was dropping its plans to accept liquor advertising.

The national broadcast networks have continued their self-imposed ban although the amount of liquor advertising on television continues to increase as more than 600 local broadcast and cable stations now accept liquor advertising. Moreover, in 2009 Absolut, the Swedish vodka that has used aggressive advertising and marketing over the past three decades to become one of the world's leading spirit brands, took the bold step of breaking the voluntary ban of spirits advertising on network television by airing a prime-time commercial during the third hour of the *Grammy Awards*. The commercial ran on CBS owned-and-operated stations in 15 of the top markets reaching 31 percent of U.S. TV households and marked the first time a commercial for a distilled spirits product aired on any CBS-owned station. The 30-second spot was an emotion-laden soft sell commercial where the only reference to the brand was at the end when "In an Absolut World" and an understated product shot appeared. According to a CBS representative, local station managers are responsible for determining the suitability of the commercials they air and determined that the Absolut spot was tasteful and appropriate for their late-evening audiences.

Following the initial network airing on the *Grammy's*, Absolut ran the ad on network TV in a number of local markets and media experts, as well as individuals working in the alcohol industry expected other spirits brands to

### Self-Regulation by Businesses

A number of self-regulatory mechanisms have been established by the business community in an effort to control advertising practices.[13] The largest and best known is the **Better Business Bureau (BBB)**, which promotes fair advertising and selling practices across all industries. The BBB was established in 1916 to handle consumer complaints about local business practices and particularly advertising. Local BBBs

follow suit. Industry consultant Arthur Shapiro noted that: "The world has changed since 2001. People are more accepting of spirits advertising. The industry draws the distinction between network, cable, or spot. The consumer doesn't care." The decision by the CBS affiliates to run the spot was also not surprising as the recession has taken its toll on advertising spending and local advertising has been particularly hard hit, making it difficult to turn away a new source of advertising revenue. NBC has also made some small moves back into the category by airing spots on its New York affiliate from Bacardi and Grey Goose.

The alcohol industry has a public responsibility relating to the marketing of its product, since its use is illegal for more than 80 million underage Americans.
Alcohol Marketing and Youth: An Overview
The Center on Alcohol Marketing and Youth

The director of local broadcasting at the Universal McCann media agency has predicted that the spirits category is getting ready to break open, noting that network affiliates would not have considered these ads are now reviewing them as they look for new sources of revenue. However, as might be expected, this is not welcome news for various public advocacy groups. George Hacker, the director of the alcohol policies project at the Center for Science in the Public Interest (CSPI) predicted that brands that advertise on network TV would certainly be held up to scorn and noted that his group was less than delighted by the expansion of spirits advertising into network television. The former executive director of the Center on Alcohol Marketing and Youth at Georgetown University called the move a step backward and refuted the argument that it is acceptable to run the ads after 10 P.M., noting that many young people have TVs in their rooms and this is a heavy viewing time for the groups most at risk.

The liquor industry has also been able to break through several other promotional barriers recently. A major breakthrough occurred when NASCAR lifted its long-standing ban on liquor sponsorships in 2005. For many years, NASCAR officials were skeptical about lifting the ban. However, liquor giants Diageo, Jim Beam Brands, and Brown-Forman started lobbying the racing league in the late 1990s when they saw NASCAR sponsorship as a good fit with their target audience, as well as a symbolic step into mainstream marketing of their brands. Jack Daniels has become a NASCAR sponsor and is also the official sponsor of NASCAR.com's postrace show each week. All of the ads connected to NASCAR must have a strong responsible drinking component. For example, Jack Daniels' sponsorship initiatives include the slogan "Pace Yourself. Drink Responsibly."

In 2009 the distilled spirits industry made inroads into another sport when the National Basketball Association voted to rescind its longtime ban on courtside advertising of hard-liquor brands in an effort to increase revenue during the economic downturn. The NBA is also crafting policies that could allow teams to show ads for hard liquor on their websites, at point-of-sale retail locations, or in arena promotions. The new NBA policy followed moves by Major League Baseball, the National Hockey League, and NASCAR to allow spirits advertising within camera view. However, the National Football League still does not allow any hard liquor signage within camera view in their stadiums. CSPI's George Hacker called the NBA's decision an "act of desperation" and indicated that the advocacy group would not let it pass unnoticed and would be contacting the league.

Restrictions on advertising and other forms of promotion of hard liquor continue to loosen as DISCUS has made major inroads into putting liquor advertising more on par with advertising for beer and wine. DISCUS argues that it gets a high rate of compliance with its marketing code, which has helped the industry gain access to cable television and other channels that were traditionally closed to liquor advertisers. It appears that TV advertising for distilled spirits is here to stay.

Sources: Jeremy Mullman, "The Booze Tube: Spirits Marketers Put Big Bucks into TV," adage.com, July 17, 2006; David Kiley, "A Green Flag for Booze," *BusinessWeek*, March 7, 2005, p. 95; Stuart Elliott, "Facing Outcry, NBC Ends Plan to Run Liquor Ads," *The New York Times*, March 21, 2002, p. C1; Anthony Crupi and Kenneth Hein, "Absolut Takes a Shot at Network Television," *Brandweek*, February 9, 2009, p. 5; Rich Thomaselli, "NBA, MLB Rethink Liquor, Gaming Deals, *Advertising Age*, January 26, 2009, *http://adage.com/print?article_id=134071*.



are located in most large cities throughout the United States and supported entirely by dues of the more than 100,000 member firms.

Local BBBs receive and investigate complaints from consumers and other companies regarding the advertising and selling tactics of businesses in their area. Each local office has its own operating procedures for handling complaints; generally, the office contacts the violator and, if the complaint proves true, requests that the practice be stopped or changed. If the violator does not respond, negative publicity

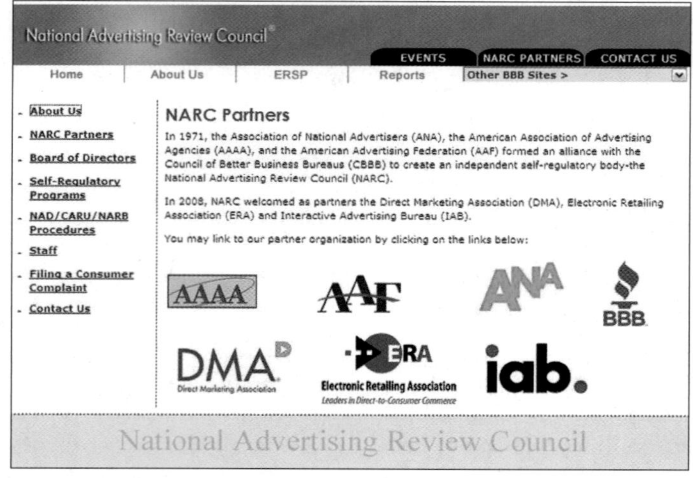


**EXHIBIT 20–3**
The National Advertising Review Council partners with various advertising and marketing organizations to create an effective self-regulatory system

may be used against the firm or the case may be referred to appropriate government agencies for further action.

While BBBs provide effective control over advertising practices at the local level, the parent organization, the **Council of Better Business Bureaus**, plays a major role at the national level, as the third-party administrator of the advertising industry self-regulatory system. Policies and procedures for industry self-regulation are established by the National Advertising Review Council. The system includes three investigative units—the National Advertising Division of the Council of Better Business Bureaus (NAD), the Children's Advertising Review Unit (CARU), and the Electronic Retailing Self-Regulation Program (ERSP)—and an appellate unit, the **National Advertising Review Board (NARB)**. Staffed primarily by attorneys, NAD, CARU, and ERSP review advertising claims that are national in scope. CARU reviews advertising directed to children under the age of 12 and ERSP examines advertising claims in direct-response advertising, including infomercials and home-shopping channels.

## The National Advertising Review Council and the NAD/NARB

In 1971 four associations—the American Advertising Federation (AAF), the American Association of Advertising Agencies (AAAA), the Association of National Advertisers (ANA), and the Council of Better Business Bureaus—joined forces to establish the **National Advertising Review Council (NARC)**. In 2009, the CEOs of three other major marketing organizations—The Direct Marketing Association (DMA), Electronic Retailing Association (ERA), and the Interactive Advertising Bureau—joined the NARC Board of Directors.

NARC's mission is to sustain high standards of truth and accuracy in national advertising. NAD has examined advertising for truth and accuracy since 1971 and has published more than 5,000 decisions, focusing on areas that include product performance claims, superiority claims against competitive products, and all kinds of scientific and technical claims.

Federal law requires that advertisers possess substantiation for their advertising claims before the claims are published. After initiating or receiving a complaint, NAD requests the advertiser's substantiation, reviews the information, and reaches a determination. In cases where the substantiating evidence does not support the claim, NAD recommends that the advertiser modify or discontinue the claim. When an advertiser or a challenger disagrees with the NAD's findings, NAD's decision can be appealed to the NARB for additional review.

The NAD's advertising monitoring program is the source of many of the cases it reviews (Figure 20–1). It also reviews complaints from consumers and consumer groups, trade associations, local BBBs, and competitors. For example, the NAD received a complaint from the Center for Science in the Public Interest, a consumer advocacy group, over an ad run by Campbell Soup for the company's V8 vegetable juice that suggested a link between the tomato-based product and a reduced risk of cancer. Though the NAD decided that Campbell provided competent and reliable evidence to support certain claims, it recommended that the company modify language stating "for prostate cancer, a lower risk is apparent when five or more servings (of tomato products) are consumed per week." Campbell agreed to change the wording of the ad.[14] During the 1970s and '80s, many of the complaints to the NAD came from consumers. However, with the increased use of comparative advertising, the

| Sources | Number | Percent | Decisions | Number | Percent |
|---|---|---|---|---|---|
| Competitor challenges | 134 | 81% | Modified/discontinued | 42 | 30% |
| NAD monitoring | 32 | 19 | Substantiated/modified/discontinued | 42 | 30 |
| Local BBB challenges | 0 | 0 | Administratively closed | 15 | 11 |
| Consumer challenges | 0 | 0 | Compliance | 19 | 14 |
| Total | 166 | 100% | Substantiated | 5 | 4 |
| | | | Referred to government | 15 | 11 |
| | | | Total (28 cases pending) | 138 | 100% |

**FIGURE 20–1**

Sources of NAD Cases and Decisions, 2009

majority of the complaints are now coming from marketers that are challenging competitors' comparisons with their brands.[15] For example, the online dating service eHarmony.com filed a complaint with the NAD over advertising used by competitor Chemistry.com, which claimed that it could use "the latest science of attraction to predict which single men and women one will have a relationship and dating chemistry."[16] Chemistry.com's matchmaking system was developed by an anthropologist who studies mate selection and uses responses to an extensive survey to determine people who might be attracted to one another.

In the Chemistry.com case, the NAD concluded that the dating service could not substantiate many of the advertising claims and ruled that the company should discontinue them. Chemistry's parent company, Match.com, issued a statement saying that it disagreed with some of the NAD's findings but would discontinue the claims at issue.[17]

Advertisers that disagree with NAD's findings have an automatic right to appeal NAD's decision to the National Advertising Review Board. NARB is composed of 70 advertising professionals and prominent public-interest/academia members.

In 2003, for example, Millennium Import Company, importers of Belvedere and Chopin vodka, filed a complaint with the NAD over advertising used by Sidney Frank Importing for its popular Grey Goose vodka brand that claimed it is the world's best-tasting vodka. Millennium argued that the claims were based on the results of a 1998 taste test and communicated a false message to consumers that Grey Goose currently ranked substantially higher than Belvedere in taste testing. After reviewing the case, the NAD ruled in favor of Millennium and Sidney Frank appealed the decision to the National Advertising Review Board, which concurred with the NAD's decision and found the advertising claim for Grey Goose inaccurate and misleading for consumers. Sidney Frank refused to comply with the NAD's and NARB's directive to discontinue or modify their ads and the self-regulatory agency referred the matter to the Federal Trade Commission. Millennium also filed a lawsuit against Sidney Frank in 2004 accusing the company of false advertising and was successful in gaining an injunction preventing Grey Goose from using the claim.[18]

Although the self-regulatory system has no power to order an advertiser to modify or stop running an ad and no sanctions it can impose, advertisers who participate in NAD/CARU/ERSP or NARB proceedings generally comply. When companies refuse to participate in a self-regulatory proceeding or do not comply with the terms of a decision, their disputed advertising may be referred to the most appropriate federal agency for further review.

In 2009, for example, of the 166 cases opened by NAD, 15 were referred to the government, 15 were administratively closed, 42 were modified or discontinued; 42 were substantiated, modified, or discontinued; 5 were substantiated; 15 cases were referred to the government; and 12 cases were appealed (Figure 20–1).[19]

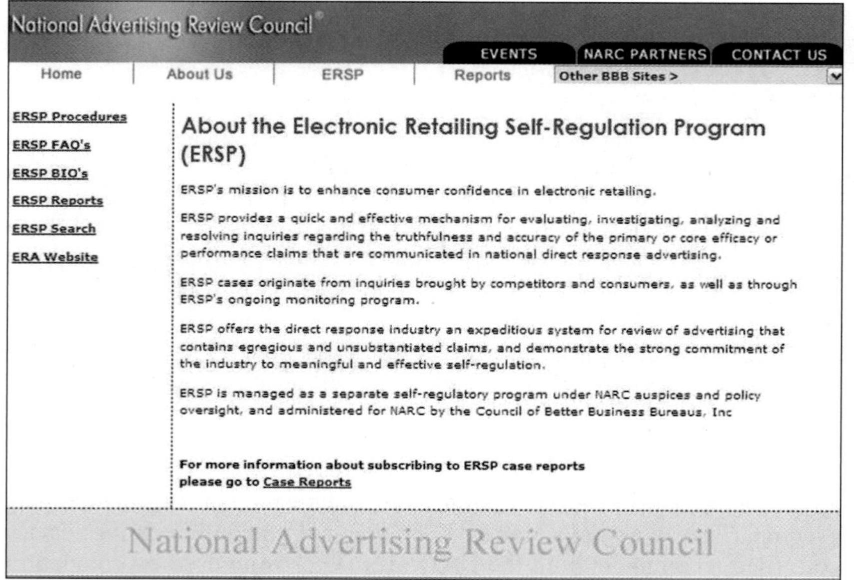

National Advertising Review Council
EVENTS
NARC PARTNERS
CONTACT US
Home
About Us
ERSP
Reports
Other BBB Sites >
ERSP Procedures
ERSP FAQ's
ERSP BIO's
ERSP Reports
ERSP Search
ERA Website
About the Electronic Retailing Self-Regulation Program (ERSP)
ERSP's mission is to enhance consumer confidence in electronic retailing.
ERSP provides a quick and effective mechanism for evaluating, investigating, analyzing and resolving inquiries regarding the truthfulness and accuracy of the primary or core efficacy or performance claims that are communicated in national direct response advertising.
ERSP cases originate from inquiries brought by competitors and consumers, as well as through ERSP's ongoing monitoring program.
ERSP offers the direct response industry an expeditious system for review of advertising that contains egregious and unsubstantiated claims, and demonstrate the strong commitment of the industry to meaningful and effective self-regulation.
ERSP is managed as a separate self-regulatory program under NARC auspices and policy oversight, and administered for NARC by the Council of Better Business Bureaus, Inc
For more information about subscribing to ERSP case reports please go to Case Reports
National Advertising Review Council


**EXHIBIT 20–4**
Electronic Retailing Self-Regulation Program is a new area of self-regulation by the NARC

CARU's activities include the review and evaluation of child-directed advertising in all media, as well as online privacy issues that affect children. The CARU also provides a general advisory service for advertisers and agencies and has developed self-regulatory guidelines for children's advertising. CARU recognizes that the special nature and needs of a youthful audience require particular care and diligence on the part of advertisers. As such, CARU's Self-Regulatory Guidelines for Children's Advertising go beyond truthfulness and accuracy to address children's developing cognitive abilities.

In 2004, the NARC became involved in the self-regulation of electronic retailing when it initiated the Electronic Retailing Self-Regulation Program (ERSP). The program is sponsored by the Electronic Retailing Association (ERA), although it works independently of the ERA to create an unbiased self-regulatory system. The mission of the ERSP is to enhance consumer confidence in electronic retailing, to discourage advertising and marketing in the electronic retailing industry that contains unsubstantiated claims, and to demonstrate a commitment to meaningful and effective self-regulation (Exhibit 20–4). The majority of claims reviewed under the ERSP program are for direct-response TV ads including long- and short-form infomercials. Reviews apply to all aspects of a marketing campaign including radio and Internet marketing. SPAM e-mails along with Internet pop-up ads that lead to further e-commerce are in the ERSP's purview as well as advertising on TV shopping channels.[20]

The NAD also works with various industries to help them develop more effective self-regulatory programs. For example, in 2006 the National Advertising Review Council and the Council for Responsible Nutrition (CRN), a trade association representing dietary supplement manufacturers and ingredient suppliers, developed a dietary supplement advertising review program. The goal of the program was to increase consumer confidence in the truth and accuracy of advertising claims for dietary supplement products and to encourage fair competition within the industry. The year before the monitoring initiative began, the NAD opened less than 10 cases involving dietary supplement advertising. However, during the first three years of the program the NAD opened more than 75 cases, with almost all resulting in voluntary compliance. In 2009 the NAD received a $959,000 grant from the CRN Foundation to extend the program for an additional five years.[21]

The National Advertising Review Council, working through the NAD/CARU/ERSP and NARB is a valuable and effective self-regulatory body. Cases brought to it are handled at a fraction of the cost (and with much less publicity) than those brought to court and are expedited more quickly than those reviewed by a government agency such as the FTC. The system also works because judgments are made by the advertiser's peers, and most companies feel compelled to comply. Firms may prefer self-regulation rather than government intervention in part because they can challenge competitors' unsubstantiated claims and win a more rapid resolution.[22]

**Advertising Associations** Various groups in the advertising industry also favor self-regulation. The two major national organizations, the American Association of Advertising Agencies and the American Advertising Federation, actively monitor and police industrywide advertising practices. The AAAA, which is the major trade association of the ad agency business in the United States, has established

The Board of Directors of the American Association of Advertising Agencies recognizes that when used truthfully and fairly, comparative advertising provides the consumer with needed and useful information.

However, extreme caution should be exercised. The use of comparative advertising, by its very nature, can distort facts and, by implication, convey to the consumer information that misrepresents the truth.

Therefore, the Board believes that comparative advertising should follow certain guidelines:

1. The intent and connotation of the ad should be to inform and never to discredit or unfairly attack competitors, competing products, or services.
2. When a competitive product is named, it should be one that exists in the marketplace as significant competition.
3. The competition should be fairly and properly identified but never in a manner or tone of voice that degrades the competitive product or service.
4. The advertising should compare related or similar properties or ingredients of the product, dimension to dimension, feature to feature.
5. The identification should be for honest comparison purposes and not simply to upgrade by association.
6. If a competitive test is conducted, it should be done by an objective testing source, preferably an independent one, so that there will be no doubt as to the veracity of the test.
7. In all cases the test should be supportive of all claims made in the advertising that are based on the test.
8. The advertising should never use partial results or stress insignificant differences to cause the consumer to draw an improper conclusion.
9. The property being compared should be significant in terms of value or usefulness of the product to the consumer.
10. Comparatives delivered through the use of testimonials should not imply that the testimonial is more than one individual's thought unless that individual represents a sample of the majority viewpoint.

**FIGURE 20–2**

AAAA Policy Statement and Guidelines for Comparative Advertising

Source: Reprinted with permission.

standards of practice and its own creative code. It also issues guidelines for specific types of advertising such as comparative messages (Figure 20–2). The AAF consists of advertisers, agencies, media, and numerous advertising clubs. The association has standards for truthful and responsible advertising, is involved in advertising legislation, and actively influences agencies to abide by its code and principles.

LO 20-2

## Self-Regulation by Media

The media are another important self-regulatory mechanism in the advertising industry. Most media maintain some form of advertising review process and, except for political ads, may reject any they regard as objectionable. Some media exclude advertising for an entire product class; others ban individual ads they think offensive or objectionable. For example, *Reader's Digest* does not accept advertising for tobacco or liquor products. A number of magazines in the United States and other countries refused to run some of Benetton's shock ads on the grounds that their readers would find them offensive or disturbing (Exhibit 20–5).[23]

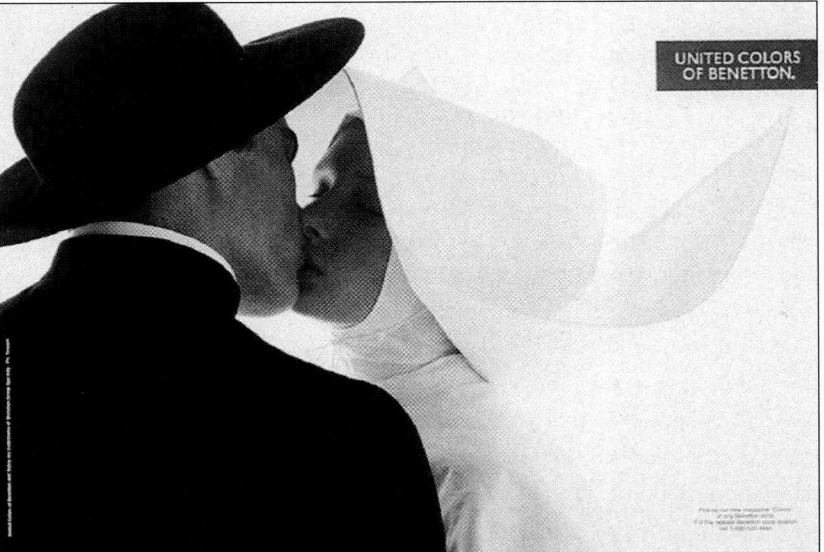


**EXHIBIT 20–5**

A number of magazines refused to run this Benetton ad

Newspapers and magazines have their own advertising requirements and restrictions, which often vary depending on the size and nature of the publication. Large, established publications, such as major newspapers or magazines, often have strict standards regarding the type of advertising they accept. Some magazines, such as *Parents* and *Good Housekeeping,* regularly test the products they advertise and offer a "seal of approval" and refunds if the products are later found to be defective. Such policies are designed to enhance the credibility of the publication and increase the reader's confidence in the products it advertises.

Advertising on television and radio has been regulated for years through codes developed by the industry trade association, the National Association of Broadcasters (NAB). Both the radio code (established in 1937) and the television code (1952) provided standards for broadcast advertising for many years. Both codes prohibited the advertising of certain products, such as hard liquor. They also affected the manner in which products could be advertised. However, in 1982, the NAB suspended all of its code provisions after the courts found that portions (dealing with time standards and required length of commercials in the TV code) were in restraint of trade. While the NAB codes are no longer in force, many individual broadcasters, such as the major TV networks, have incorporated major portions of the code provisions into their own standards.[24]

The four major television networks have the most stringent review process of any media. All four networks maintain standards and practices divisions, which carefully review all commercials submitted to the network or individual affiliate stations. Advertisers must submit for review all commercials intended for airing on the network or an affiliate.

A commercial may be submitted for review in the form of a script, storyboard, animatic, or finished commercial (when the advertiser believes there is little chance of objection). A very frustrating, and often expensive, scenario for both an agency and its client occurs when a commercial is approved at the storyboard stage but then is rejected after it is produced. Commercials are rejected for a variety of reasons, including violence, morbid humor, sex, politics, and religion. Network reviewers also consider whether the proposed commercial meets acceptable standards and is appropriate for certain audiences. For example, different standards are used for ads designated for prime-time versus late-night spots or for children's versus adults' programs (see Figure 20–3). Although most of these guidelines remain in effect, ABC and NBC loosened their rules on celebrity endorsements.[25]

The four major networks receive nearly 50,000 commercials a year for review; nearly two-thirds are accepted, and only 3 percent are rejected. Most problems with

**FIGURE 20–3**

A Sampling of the TV Networks' Guidelines for Children's Advertising

Each of the major TV networks has its own set of guidelines for children's advertising, although the basics are very similar. A few rules, such as the requirement of a static "island" shot at the end, are written in stone; others, however, can sometimes be negotiated. Many of the rules below apply specifically to toys. The networks also have special guidelines for kids' food commercials and for kids' commercials that offer premiums.

- Must not overglamorize product
- No exhortative language, such as "Ask Mom to buy . . ."
- No realistic war settings
- Generally no celebrity endorsements
- Can't use "only" or "just" in regard to price
- Show only two toys per child or maximum of six per commercial
- Five-second "island" showing product against plain background at end of spot
- Animation restricted to one-third of a commercial
- Generally no comparative or superiority claims
- No costumes or props not available with the toy
- No child or toy can appear in animated segments
- Three-second establishing shot of toy in relation to child
- No shots under one second in length
- Must show distance a toy can travel before stopping on its own

**EXHIBIT 20–6**
This humorous "Got milk?" commercial had to be modified slightly to satisfy network censors

the remaining 30 percent are resolved through negotiation, and the ads are revised and resubmitted.[26] Most commercials run after changes are made. For example, censors initially rejected a humorous "Got milk?" spot that showed children watching an elderly neighbor push a wheelbarrow. Suddenly, the man's arms rip off, presumably because he doesn't drink milk. The spot was eventually approved after it was modified so that the man appears unhurt after losing his limbs and there was no expression of pain (Exhibit 20–6).[27]

Network standards regarding acceptable advertising change constantly. The networks first allowed lingerie advertisers to use live models rather than mannequins in 1987. Advertising for contraceptives is now appearing on some stations. The networks also loosened long-standing restrictions on endorsements and competitive advertising claims.[28] Network standards will continue to change as society's values and attitudes toward certain issues and products change. Also, many advertising people believe these changes are a response to competition from independent and cable stations, which tend to be much less stringent in their standards and practices. However, since television is probably the most carefully scrutinized and frequently criticized of all forms of advertising, the networks must be careful not to offend their viewers and detract from advertising's credibility.

For example, a number of advertisers such as Godaddy.com have had ads created for the Super Bowl rejected because the big game has a very large audience that ranges from children to older adults and the networks ruled that the sexually suggestive ads were inappropriate for the tenor of the event.[29] CBS rejected a commercial that ManCrunch .com, a gay dating website, wanted to air on the 2010 Super Bowl showing two young men watching a football game and rooting for their teams and then becoming passionate when their hands meet inside a bowl of chips (Exhibit 20–7). In its rejection letter CBS stated that the ad was not within the network's broadcast standards for Super Bowl Sunday and that it had difficulty verifying ManCrunch's credit status. While CBS indicated that it was open to working with the company on alternative submissions, some gay rights groups complained that the network was discriminating against the company as well as gays by not accepting the ad.[30]

**EXHIBIT 20–7**
CBS rejected a commercial that ManCrunch wanted to run on the Super Bowl

## Appraising Self-Regulation

The three major participants in the advertising process—advertisers, agencies, and the media—work individually and collectively to encourage truthful, ethical, and responsible advertising. The advertising industry views self-regulation as an effective mechanism for controlling advertising abuses and avoiding the use of

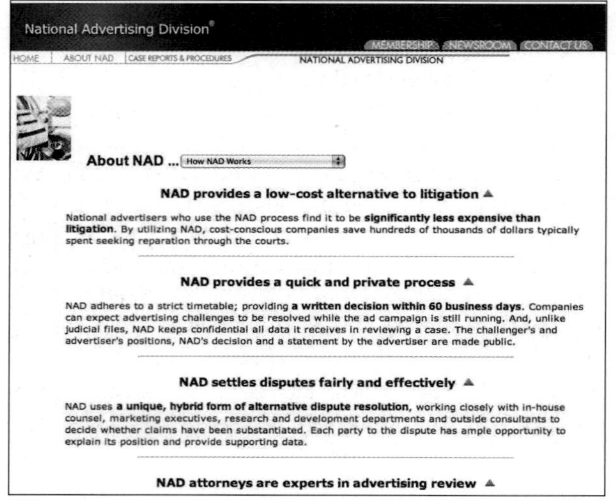


**EXHIBIT 20–8**
The NAD is an effective alternative to government intervention and/or litigation.

offensive, misleading, or deceptive practices, and it prefers this form of regulation to government intervention (Exhibit 20–8). Self-regulation of advertising has been effective and in many instances probably led to the development of more stringent standards and practices than those imposed by or beyond the scope of legislation.

A senior vice president and general counsel at Kraft Foods, while praising the NAD, summarized the feelings of many advertisers toward self-regulation. In his testimonial he stated: "NAD is superior to its competition, which is regulation by the government or regulation by the courts. Accurate, prompt, and inexpensive decisions year in and year out have earned NAD its well-deserved credibility with the industry and with regulators." Former Federal Trade Commission chairman Timothy Murris has described the NAD as a "model of self-regulation." Deborah Platt Majoras, who was the FTC chair from 2004 until 2008, also praised the National Advertising Review Council for running a model program covering national advertising as well as a number of other areas.

There are, however, limitations to self-regulation, and the process has been criticized in a number of areas. For example, the NAD may take six months to a year to resolve a complaint, during which time a company often stops using the commercial anyway. Budgeting and staffing constraints may limit the number of cases the NAD/NARB system investigates and the speed with which it resolves them.[31] And some critics believe that self-regulation is self-serving to the advertisers and advertising industry and lacks the power or authority to be a viable alternative to federal or state regulation.

Many do not believe advertising can or should be controlled solely by self-regulation. They argue that regulation by government agencies is necessary to ensure that consumers get accurate information and are not misled or deceived. Moreover, since advertisers do not have to comply with the decisions and recommendations of self-regulatory groups, it is sometimes necessary to turn to the federal and/or state government.

# FEDERAL REGULATION OF ADVERTISING

Advertising is controlled and regulated through federal, state, and local laws and regulations enforced by various government agencies. The federal government is the most important source of external regulation since many advertising practices come under the jurisdiction of the **Federal Trade Commission**. In addition, depending on the advertiser's industry and product or service, other federal agencies such as the Federal Communications Commission, the Food and Drug Administration, the U.S. Postal Service, and the Bureau of Alcohol, Tobacco, and Firearms may have regulations that affect advertising. We will begin our discussion of federal regulation of advertising by considering the basic rights of marketers to advertise their products and services under the First Amendment.

## Advertising and the First Amendment

Freedom of speech or expression, as defined by the First Amendment to the U.S. Constitution, is the most basic federal law governing advertising in the United States. For many years, freedom of speech protection did not include advertising and other forms of speech that promote a commercial transaction. However, the courts have extended First Amendment protection to **commercial speech**, which is speech that promotes a commercial transaction. There have been a number of landmark cases over the past three decades where the federal courts have issued rulings supporting the coverage of commercial speech by the First Amendment.

In a 1976 case, *Virginia State Board of Pharmacy v. Virginia Citizens Consumer Council,* the U.S. Supreme Court ruled that states cannot prohibit pharmacists from advertising the prices of prescription drugs, because such advertising contains information that helps the consumer choose between products and because the free flow of information is indispensable.[32] As noted earlier, in 1977 the Supreme Court ruled that state bar associations' restrictions on advertising are unconstitutional and attorneys have a First Amendment right to advertise their services and prices.[33] In another landmark case in 1980, *Central Hudson Gas & Electric Corp. v. New York Public Service Commission,* the Supreme Court ruled that commercial speech was entitled to First Amendment protection in some cases. However, the Court ruled that the U.S. Constitution affords less protection to commercial speech than to other constitutionally guaranteed forms of expression. In this case the Court established a four-part test, known as the **Central Hudson Test**, for determining restrictions on commercial speech.[34] In a more recent case, the Supreme Court's 1996 decision in *44 Liquormart, Inc. v. Rhode Island* struck down two state statutes designed to support the state's interest in temperance. The first prohibited the advertising of alcoholic beverage prices in Rhode Island except on signs within a store, while the second prohibited the publication or broadcast of alcohol price ads. The Court ruled that the Rhode Island statutes were unlawful because they restricted the constitutional guarantee of freedom of speech, and the decision signaled strong protection for advertisers under the First Amendment.[35]

In the cases regarding advertising, the U.S. Supreme Court has ruled that freedom of expression must be balanced against competing interests. For example, the courts have upheld bans on the advertising of products that are considered harmful, such as tobacco. The Court has also ruled that only truthful commercial speech is protected, not advertising or other forms of promotion that are false, misleading, or deceptive.

In a recent and important case involving Nike, the California Supreme Court issued a ruling that is likely to impact the way companies engage in public debate regarding issues that affect them. Nike was sued for false advertising under California consumer protection laws for allegedly making misleading statements regarding labor practices and working conditions in its foreign factories. Nike argued that statements the company made to defend itself against the charges should be considered political speech, which is protected by the First Amendment, rather than commercial speech, which is subject to advertising regulations. However, the California high court ruled that statements made by the company to defend itself against the allegations were commercial in nature and thus subject to the state's consumer protection regulations. Nike appealed the case to the U.S. Supreme Court, which sent it back to California for trial to determine if the company's statements were deceptive and misleading. However, Nike settled the case rather than risking a long and costly court battle. While the ruling in this case only applies to California, it is important as the courts ruled that speech in the form of press releases or public statements by company representatives can be considered commercial and subject to consumer protection laws.[36]

The job of regulating advertising at the federal level and determining whether advertising is truthful or deceptive is a major focus of the Federal Trade Commission. We now turn our attention to federal regulation of advertising and the FTC.

## Background on Federal Regulation of Advertising

Federal regulation of advertising originated in 1914 with the passage of the **Federal Trade Commission Act** (FTC Act), which created the FTC, the agency that is today the most active in, and has primary responsibility for, controlling and regulating advertising. The FTC Act was originally intended to help enforce antitrust laws, such as the Sherman and Clayton acts, by helping to restrain unfair methods of competition. The main focus of the first five-member commission was to protect competitors from one another; the issue of false or misleading advertising was not even mentioned. In 1922, the Supreme Court upheld an FTC interpretation that false advertising was an unfair method of competition, but in the 1931 case *FTC v. Raladam Co.,* the Court ruled the commission could not prohibit false advertising unless there was evidence of injury to a competitor.[37] This ruling limited the power of the FTC to protect consumers from false or deceptive advertising and led to a consumer movement that resulted in an important amendment to the FTC Act.

In 1938, Congress passed the **Wheeler-Lea Amendment**. It amended section 5 of the FTC Act to read: "Unfair methods of competition in commerce and unfair or deceptive acts or practices in commerce are hereby declared to be unlawful." The amendment empowered the FTC to act if there was evidence of injury to the public; proof of injury to a competitor was not necessary. The Wheeler-Lea Amendment also gave the FTC the power to issue cease-and-desist orders and levy fines on violators. It extended the FTC's jurisdiction over false advertising of foods, drugs, cosmetics, and therapeutic devices. And it gave the FTC access to the injunctive power of the federal courts, initially only for food and drug products but expanded in 1972 to include all products in the event of a threat to the public's health and safety.

In addition to the FTC, numerous other federal agencies are responsible for, or involved in, advertising regulation. The authority of these agencies is limited, however, to a particular product area or service, and they often rely on the FTC to assist in handling false or deceptive advertising cases.

## The Federal Trade Commission

The FTC is responsible for protecting both consumers and businesses from anticompetitive behavior and unfair and deceptive practices. The major divisions of the FTC include the bureaus of competition, economics, and consumer protection. The Bureau of Competition seeks to prevent business practices that restrain competition and is responsible for enforcing antitrust laws. The Bureau of Economics helps the FTC evaluate the impact of its actions and provides economic analysis and support to antitrust and consumer protection investigations and rule makings. It also analyzes the impact of government regulation on competition and consumers. The Bureau of Consumer Protection's mandate is to protect consumers against unfair, deceptive, or fraudulent practices. This bureau also investigates and litigates cases involving acts or practices alleged to be deceptive or unfair to consumers. The Division of Advertising Practices protects consumers from deceptive and unsubstantiated advertising and enforces the provisions of the FTC Act that forbid misrepresentation, unfairness, and deception in general advertising at the national and regional level (Exhibit 20–9). The Division of Marketing Practices engages in activities that are related to various marketing and warranty practices such as fraudulent telemarketing schemes, 900-number programs, and disclosures relating to franchise and business opportunities.

**EXHIBIT 20–9**
The Division of Advertising Practices protects consumers from deceptive and unsubstantiated advertising claims

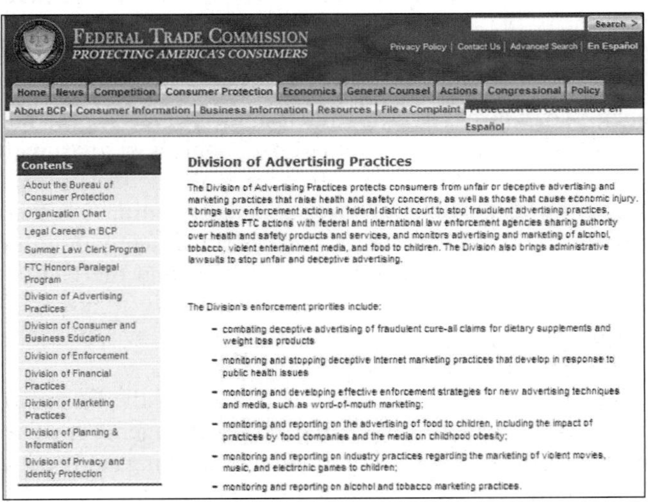

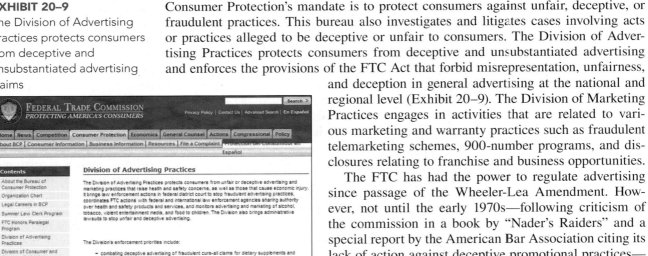

The FTC has had the power to regulate advertising since passage of the Wheeler-Lea Amendment. However, not until the early 1970s—following criticism of the commission in a book by "Nader's Raiders" and a special report by the American Bar Association citing its lack of action against deceptive promotional practices—did the FTC become active in regulating advertising.[38] The authority of the FTC was increased considerably throughout the 1970s. The Magnuson-Moss Act of 1975, an important piece of legislation, dramatically broadened the FTC's powers and substantially increased its budget. The first section of the act dealt with consumers' rights regarding product warranties; it allowed the commission to require restitution for deceptively written warranties where the consumer lost more than $5. The second section, the FTC Improvements Act, empowered the FTC to establish **trade regulation rules (TRRs)**, industrywide rules that define unfair practices before they occur.

During the 1970s, the FTC made enforcement of laws regarding false and misleading advertising a top priority. Several new programs were instituted, budgets were increased, and the commission became a very powerful regulatory agency. However, many of these programs, as well as the expanded powers of the FTC to develop regulations on the basis of "unfairness," became controversial. At the root of this controversy is the fundamental issue of what constitutes unfair advertising.

## The Concept of Unfairness

Under section 5 of the FTC Act, the Federal Trade Commission has a mandate to act against unfair or deceptive advertising practices. However, this statute does not define the terms *unfair* and *deceptive,* and the FTC has been criticized for not doing so itself. While the FTC has taken steps to clarify the meaning of *deception,* people have been concerned for years about the vagueness of the term *unfair.*

Controversy over the FTC's authority to regulate unfair advertising practices began in 1978, when the agency relied on this mandate to formulate its controversial "kid vid" rule restricting advertising to children.[39] This interpretation caused widespread concern in the business community that the term *unfair* could be used to encompass anything FTC commissioners might find objectionable. For example, in a 1980 policy statement the FTC noted that "the precise concept of consumer unfairness is one whose precise meaning is not immediately obvious." Consequently, in 1980 Congress responded by suspending the children's advertising rule and banning the FTC from using unfairness as a legal basis for advertising rulemaking.

The FTC responded to these criticisms in December 1980 by sending Congress a statement containing an interpretation of unfairness. According to FTC policy, the basis for determining **unfairness** is that a trade practice (1) causes substantial physical or economic injury to consumers, (2) could not reasonably be avoided by consumers, and (3) must not be outweighed by countervailing benefits to consumers or competition. The agency also stated that a violation of public policy (such as of other government statutes) could, by itself, constitute an unfair practice or could be used to prove substantial consumer injury. Practices considered unfair are claims made without prior substantiation, claims that might exploit such vulnerable groups as children and the elderly, and instances where consumers cannot make a valid choice because the advertiser omits important information about the product or competing products mentioned in the ad.[40]

The FTC's statement was intended to clarify its interpretation of unfairness and reduce ambiguity over what might constitute unfair practices. However, efforts by the FTC to develop industrywide trade regulation rules that would define unfair practices and have the force and effect of law were limited by Congress in 1980 with the passage of the FTC Improvements Act. Amidst calls to end the stalemate over the FTC's regulation of unfair advertising by having the agency work with Congress to define its advertising authority, in 1994 Congress and the advertising industry agreed on a definition of unfair advertising that is very similar to the FTC's 1980 policy statement discussed earlier. However, the new agreement requires that before the FTC can initiate any industrywide rule, it has to have reason to believe that the unfair or deceptive acts or practices are prevalent.[41]

The FTC does have specific regulatory authority in cases involving deceptive, misleading, or untruthful advertising. The vast majority of advertising cases that the FTC handles concern deception and advertising fraud, which usually involve knowledge of a false claim.

## Deceptive Advertising

In most economies, advertising provides consumers with information they can use to make consumption decisions. However, if this information is untrue or misleads the consumer, advertising is not fulfilling its basic function. Moreover, a study by Peter Drake and Robin Ritchie found that deceptive advertising engenders mistrust, which negatively affects consumers' responses to subsequent advertising from the same source as well as second-party sources. They note that deceptive advertising can seriously undermine the effectiveness and credibility of advertising and marketing in general by making consumers defensive toward future advertising and should be of concern to all marketers.[42] But what constitutes an untruthful or deceptive ad? Deceptive advertising can take a number of forms, ranging from intentionally false or misleading claims to ads that, although true, leave some consumers with a false or misleading impression.

The issue of deception, including its definition and measurement, receives considerable attention from the FTC and other regulatory agencies. One of the problems regulatory agencies deal with in determining deception is distinguishing between false or misleading messages and those that, rather than relying on verifiable or substantiated objective information about a product, make subjective claims or statements, a practice known as puffery. **Puffery** has been legally defined as "advertising or other sales presentations which praise the item to be sold with subjective opinions, superlatives, or exaggerations, vaguely and generally, stating no specific facts."[43] The use of puffery in advertising is common. For example, Bayer aspirin calls itself the "wonder drug that works wonders," Nestlé claims "Nestlé makes the very best chocolate," Snapple advertises that its beverages are "made from the best stuff on Earth," and BMW uses the tagline "The Ultimate Driving Machine." Superlatives such as *greatest, best,* and *finest* are puffs that are often used.

Puffery has generally been viewed as a form of poetic license or allowable exaggeration. The FTC takes the position that because consumers expect exaggeration or inflated claims in advertising, they recognize puffery and don't believe it. But some studies show that consumers may believe puffery and perceive such claims as true.[44] One study found that consumers could not distinguish between a verifiable fact-based claim and puffery and were just as likely to believe both types of claims.[45] Ivan Preston argues that puffery has a detrimental effect on consumers' purchase decisions by burdening them with untrue beliefs and refers to it as "soft-core deception" that should be illegal.[46]

Advertisers' battle to retain the right to use puffery was supported in the latest revision of the Uniform Commercial Code in 1996. The revision switches the burden of proof to consumers from advertisers in cases pertaining to whether certain claims were meant to be taken as promises. The revision states that the buyer must prove that an affirmation of fact (as opposed to puffery) was made, that the buyer was aware of the advertisement, and that the affirmation of fact became part of the agreement with the seller.[47]

The use of puffery as a defense for advertising claims is periodically challenged in court. IMC Perspective 20–2 discusses a legal battle involving Pizza Hut and Papa John's in which the U.S. Supreme Court issued a decision in support of the use of puffery as the basis for a comparative advertising claim, and how Domino's used the ruling as the basis for an ad campaign comparing the taste of their pizza to Papa John's.

A more recent ruling by an appellate court may set new precedents for the use of puffery and comparative advertising. The case was filed in 2006 by Time Warner Cable against its rival DirecTV over commercials the satellite television company was running to promote the superiority of its high definition service over that of cable. One of the spots featured actress Jessica Simpson portraying the Daisy Duke character she played in the movie *The Dukes of Hazzard.* In the spot Simpson says, "Hey 253 days at the gym to get this body and you're not gonna watch me on DirectTV HD? You're not gonna get the best picture out of some fancy big-screen TV without

DirecTV. It's broadcast in 1080 dpi. I don't totally know what that means, but I want it." In the original spot a narrator added, "For picture quality that beats cable, you've got to get DirecTV." However, the spot was revised to say, "For an HD picture that can't be beat, get DirecTV." The campaign also included Internet banner ads featuring a very fuzzy picture identified as "other TV" next to a clear picture labeled "DirecTV."

Although Time Warner was not mentioned by name in the ads, it sued, challenging the campaign's accuracy despite the changes to the original slogan. DirecTV argued that the revised ads never said its picture was better than cable's and claimed the Internet ads were using puffery. A district court judge issued an order stopping DirecTV from running the TV spots and Internet banner ads. However, DirecTV appealed the ruling and in 2007 an appellate panel issued a ruling upholding the ban on the TV spots, but reversing the decision on the Internet ads, noting that no one would believe the fuzzy picture shown represented a real cable picture. The judges ruled that the license to use verbal puffery claims also apply to "grossly exaggerated" images that no consumer would take as fact. The two companies settled the dispute out of court and the case was dropped.[48]

Since unfair and deceptive acts or practices have never been precisely defined, the FTC is continually developing and refining a working definition in its attempts to regulate advertising. The traditional standard used to determine deception was whether a claim had the "tendency or capacity to deceive." However, this standard was criticized for being vague and all-encompassing.

In 1983, the FTC, under Chair James Miller III, put forth a new working definition of **deception**: "The commission will find deception if there is a misrepresentation, omission, or practice that is likely to mislead the consumer acting reasonably in the circumstances to the consumer's detriment."[49] There are three essential elements to this definition of deception.[50] The first element is that the representation, omission, or practice must be *likely to mislead* the consumer. The FTC defines *misrepresentation* as an express or implied statement contrary to fact, whereas a *misleading omission* occurs when qualifying information necessary to prevent a practice, claim, representation, or reasonable belief from being misleading is not disclosed.

The second element is that the act or practice must be considered from the perspective of *the reasonable consumer*. In determining reasonableness, the FTC considers the group to which the advertising is targeted and whether their interpretation of or reaction to the message is reasonable in light of the circumstances. The standard is flexible and allows the FTC to consider factors such as the age, education level, intellectual capacity, and frame of mind of the particular group to which the message or practice is targeted. For example, advertisements targeted to a particular group, such as children or the elderly, are evaluated with respect to their effect on a reasonable member of that group.

The third key element to the FTC's definition of deception is *materiality*. According to the FTC a "material" misrepresentation or practice is one that is likely to affect a consumer's choice or conduct with regard to a product or service. What this means is that the information, claim, or practice in question is important to consumers and, if acted upon, would be likely to influence their purchase decisions. In some cases the information or claims made in an ad may be false or misleading but would not be regarded as material since reasonable consumers would not make a purchase decision on the basis of this information.

Miller's goal was to help the commission determine which cases were worth pursuing and which were trivial. Miller argued that for an ad to be considered worthy of FTC challenge, it should be seen by a substantial number of consumers, it should lead to significant injury, and the problem should be one that market forces are not likely to remedy. However, the revised definition may put a greater burden on the FTC to prove that deception occurred and that the deception influenced the consumers' decision-making process in a detrimental way.

Determining what constitutes deception is still a gray area. Two of the factors the FTC considers in evaluating an ad for deception are (1) whether there are significant

# IMC Perspective 20–2 > > >

## Domino's Joins the Pizza Puffery War

The use of unsubstantiated superlatives such as good, better, and best has long been a staple of American advertising. The Federal Trade Commission views the use of these terms, as well as other forms of marketing bravado, as puffery and takes the position that consumers would not expect these claims to be documented or take them seriously. However, advertisers often see the use of these terms as tantamount to claims of superiority and the advertisers that use them as engaging in comparative advertising. Thus, they expect their competitors can substantiate their claims rather than try to hide behind a thin veil of puffery. In recent years, a number of well-known companies have taken legal action against competitors to stop them from using claims their rivals argue are based on puffery, and thus require no substantiation.

One of the most intense battles regarding the use of puffery was fought by Papa John's and Pizza Hut and went all the way to the United States Supreme Court. The problem began when Papa John's began running ads comparing its product to market leader Pizza Hut using the tagline "Better Ingredients. Better Pizza." Pizza Hut initially filed a complaint with the National Advertising Division of the Council of Better Business Bureaus, but after getting no sympathy from the NAD, the company filed a lawsuit against Papa John's, claiming that the latter's ads were false and misleading. After hearing several weeks of testimony, a jury sided with Pizza Hut, ruling that the slogan was false and misleading because Papa John's had failed to prove its sauce and dough were superior. The judge upheld the jury's decision and ruled that the slogan was acceptable puffery until Papa John's began running ads touting its tomato sauce and pizza dough as superior and issued an injunction against the entire "Better Ingredients. Better Pizza" integrated marketing campaign the company was using.

Papa John's appealed the decision arguing that the judge had misinterpreted the law and claimed the use of the slogan was legally acceptable puffery. The court of appeals handed down a complicated ruling that sided with Papa John's on the puffery issue and lifted the injunction. Pizza Hut petitioned to have the ruling heard by the U.S. Supreme Court on the grounds that the appellate court had required an unusually high standard of evidence from its research studies to prove that consumers had been misled by Papa John's. However, the high court denied the petition and the court of appeals ruling was allowed to stand. The advertising industry was relieved that the Supreme Court ruled in favor of Papa John's because a ruling against the puffery defense could have opened the door for other challenges and a redrawing of the blurry line between so-called puffery and outright false advertising.

Pizza Hut and Papa John's finally ended their battle after spending millions of dollars in legal fees and being criticized for frivolous appeals and wasting the Supreme

omissions of important information and (2) whether advertisers can substantiate the claims made for the product or service. The FTC has developed several programs to address these issues.

**Affirmative Disclosure** An ad can be literally true yet leave the consumer with a false or misleading impression if the claim is true only under certain conditions or circumstances or if there are limitations to what the product can or cannot do. Thus, under its **affirmative disclosure** requirement, the FTC may require advertisers to include certain types of information in their ads so that consumers will be aware of all the consequences, conditions, and limitations associated with the use of a product or service. The goal of affirmative disclosure is to give consumers sufficient information to make an informed decision. An ad may be required to define the testing situation, conditions, or criteria used in making a claim. For example, fuel mileage claims in car ads are based on Environmental Protection Agency (EPA) ratings since they offer a uniform standard for making comparisons. Cigarette ads must contain a warning about the health risks associated with smoking.

An example of an affirmative disclosure ruling is the FTC's case against Campbell Soup for making deceptive and unsubstantiated claims. Campbell's ads, run as part of its "Soup is good food" campaign, linked the low-fat and low-cholesterol

Court's time by having the highest court in the land listen to how they make their pizzas. However, knowing that the legal battle was a disaster for both companies, Domino's (which is the second leading national pizza chain) decided to take advantage of the appellate court ruling that Papa John's "Better Ingredients. Better Pizza" slogan was considered puffery.

In early 2010, Domino's began running a TV commercial showing the company's head chef, Brandon Solano, standing outside of a Federal Court of Appeals building in New Orleans talking about Papa John's and its slogan. In the spot Solano says: "For years Papa John's has been telling us they have better ingredients and better pizza. But when challenged in this court, they stated their slogan is puffery." He then turns to a lawyer standing next to him and asks him: "What's puffery?" Reading from a law book the lawyer says: "Puffery. An exaggerated statement based on opinion. Not fact." Solano then says "Here's what's not puffery" and goes on to explain how Dominos beat Papa John's in a national taste test. The spot ends with Solano stating: "Our pizza tastes better and that's not puffery, that's proven."

The commercial was not the first time Domino's used a comparative taste-test commercial. In late 2008 the pizza chain launched a campaign claiming that consumers preferred its oven-baked sandwiches over Subway's by a two-to-one margin. However, Subway responded to Domino's comparative ads very quickly with a cease-and-desist letter citing concerns about the methodology used in the taste tests and the ability to make fair comparisons between the products. Domino's responded less than a month later with an ad showing its CEO declaring: "Everything's better when it's oven-baked, even a letter from Subway," as he tosses the letter into a pizza oven.

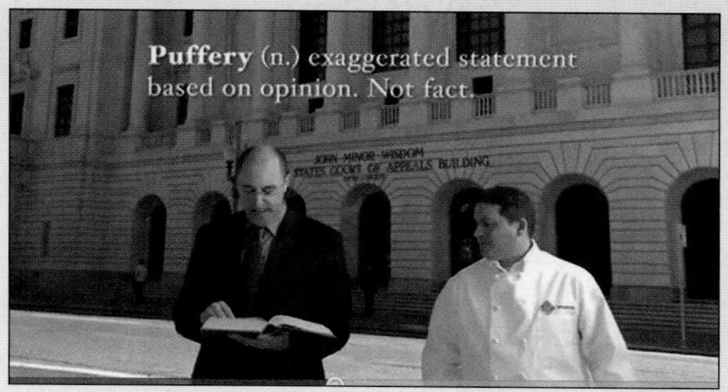


Domino's also added a "Bake the letter" feature on its website where consumers could click a button and watch an image of the letter burn, with a visible Subway logo.

Some experts note that Domino's may be setting itself up for a legal challenge with its comparative ads as both make specific fact claims regarding taste superiority over Papa John's and Subway. However, Domino's chief marketing officer has noted that the company is confident in its consumer research, and its aggressive marketing demonstrates its commitment to gaining a foothold in the sandwich business as well as increasing its share of the pizza market. At this point, the ball is in Papa John's as well as Subway's court and both must decide if they want to call in their lawyers and start the legal battle once again.

Sources: Emily Bryson York, "Domino's Claims Victory with Pizza Makeover Strategy," *Advertising Age*, May 10, 2010, http://adage.com/article_id=143764; Emily Bryson York, "Domino's Doesn't Back Down in Sandwich Skirmish," *Advertising Age*, January 23, 2009, http://adage.com/article_id=134070; Suzanne Vranica, "Pizza Maker's Ads Aims to Top Rival," *The Wall Street Journal*, April 4, 2005, p. B6.

content of its soup with a reduced risk of heart disease. However, the advertising failed to disclose that the soups are high in sodium, which may increase the risk of heart disease. In a consent agreement accepted in 1991, Campbell agreed that, for any soup containing more than 500 milligrams of sodium in an 8-ounce serving, it will disclose the sodium content in any advertising that directly or by implication mentions heart disease in connection with the soup. Campbell also agreed it would not imply a connection between soup and a reduction in heart disease in future advertising.[51]

Another area where the Federal Trade Commission is seeking more specificity from advertisers is in regard to country of origin claims. The FTC has been working with marketers and trade associations to develop a better definition of what the "Made in the USA" label means. The 50-year-old definition used until recently required full manufacturing in the United States, using U.S. labor and parts, with only raw materials from overseas.[52] Many companies argue that in an increasingly global economy, it is becoming very difficult to have 100 percent U.S. content and remain price-competitive. However, the FTC argues that advertising or labeling a product as "Made in the USA" can provide a company with a competitive advantage. For many products some consumers do respond to the claim, as they trust the quality of domestic-made products and/or feel patriotic when they buy American. For example, athletic-shoe maker

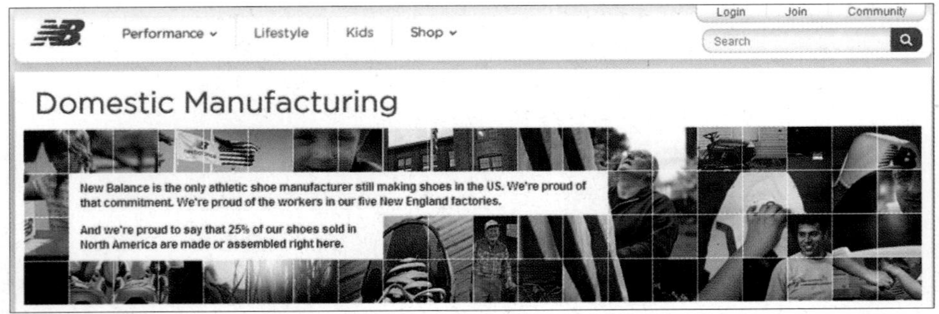


**EXHIBIT 20–10**
New Balance promotes its commitment to U.S. manufacturing

New Balance is a company that promotes its commitment to domestic manufacturing and the fact that 25 percent of its products are made in the United States (Exhibit 20–10).

In December 1998, the FTC issued new guidelines for American-made products. The guidelines spell out what it means by "all or virtually all" in mandating how much U.S. content a product must have to wear a "Made in USA" label or be advertised as such. According to the new FTC guidelines, all significant parts and processing that go into the product must be of U.S. origin and the product should have no or very little foreign content. Companies do not have to receive the approval of the FTC before making a "Made in USA" claim. However, the commission does have the authority to take action against false and unsubstantiated "Made in USA" claims just as it does with other advertising claims.[53]

Another interesting example of a case involving product origin claims is in the wine industry. The U.S. Champagne Bureau recently launched its "Unmask the Truth" ad campaign which has the goals of rallying consumers and demanding lawmakers protect place-of-origin names on wine sold in the United States. The ad, which is shown in Exhibit 20–11, features a mask over a sparkling wine bottle mislabeled "American Champagne" and asks consumers to voice their support for truthful labeling regarding where wine comes from. The campaign is designed to address a loophole in federal law that allows some U.S. sparkling wine producers to mislead consumers by labeling their products "Champagne" even though they do not come from the Champagne region of France. The trade association argues that names of American wine regions such as Napa Valley and Williamette also risk being misused.[54]

**EXHIBIT 20–11**
The U.S. Champagne Bureau is running ads calling for clarification of the region of origin on wine labels

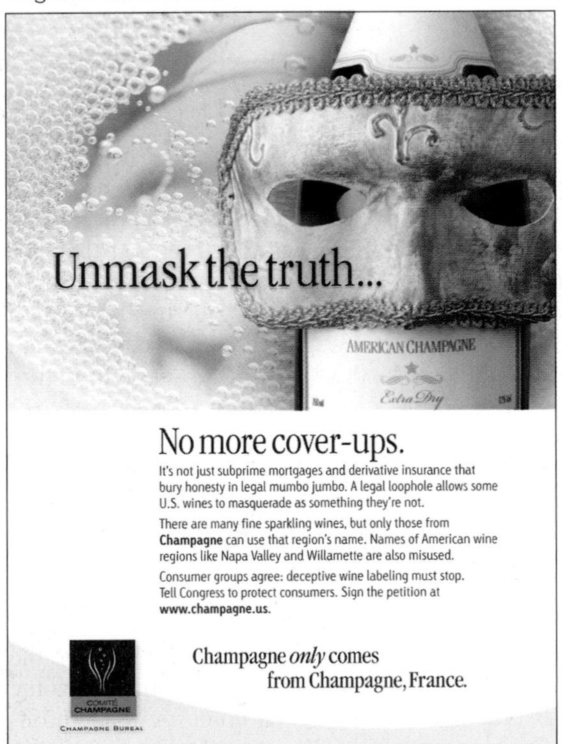


**Advertising Substantiation** A major area of concern to regulatory agencies is whether advertisers can support or substantiate their claims. For many years, there were no formal requirements concerning substantiation of advertising claims. Many companies made claims without any documentation or support such as laboratory tests or clinical studies. In 1971, the FTC's **advertising substantiation** program required advertisers to have supporting documentation for their claims and to prove the claims are truthful.[55] Broadened in 1972, this program now requires advertisers to substantiate their claims before an ad appears. Substantiation is required for all express or implied claims involving safety, performance, efficacy, quality, or comparative price.

The FTC's substantiation program has had a major effect on the advertising industry, because it shifted the burden of proof from the commission to the advertiser. Before the substantiation program, the FTC had to prove that an advertiser's claims were unfair or deceptive.

Ad substantiation seeks to provide a basis for believing advertising claims so consumers can make rational and informed decisions and companies are deterred from making claims they cannot adequately support. The FTC takes the perspective that it is illegal and unfair to consumers for a firm to make a claim for a product without having a "reasonable basis" for the claim.

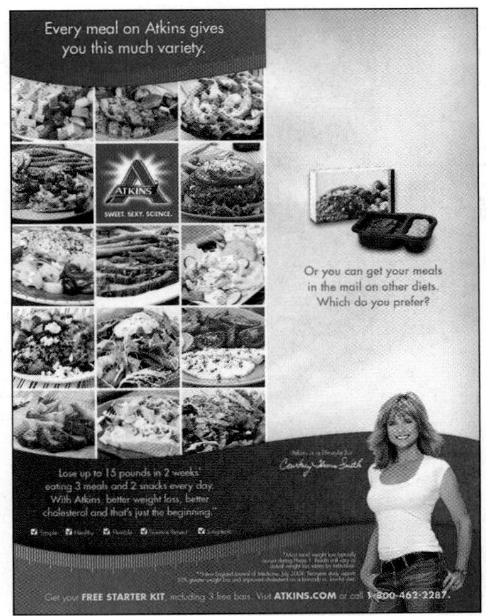


**EXHIBIT 20–12**
Weight-loss program marketers are now required to substantiate their claims as a result of an FTC ruling

In their decision to require advertising substantiation, the commissioners made the following statement:

> Given the imbalance of knowledge and resources between a business enterprise and each of its customers, economically it is more rational and imposes far less cost on society, to require a manufacturer to confirm his affirmative product claims rather than impose a burden on each individual consumer to test, investigate, or experiment for himself. The manufacturer has the ability, the know-how, the equipment, the time and resources to undertake such information, by testing or otherwise, . . . the consumer usually does not.[56]

Many advertisers respond negatively to the FTC's advertising substantiation program. They argue it is too expensive to document all their claims and most consumers either won't understand or aren't interested in the technical data. Some advertisers threaten to avoid the substantiation issue by using puffery claims, which do not require substantiation.

Generally, advertisers making claims covered by the substantiation program must have available prior substantiation of all claims. However, in 1984, the FTC issued a new policy statement that suggested after-the-fact substantiation might be acceptable in some cases and it would solicit documentation of claims only from advertisers that are under investigation for deceptive practices.

In a number of cases, the FTC has ordered advertisers to cease making inadequately substantiated claims. In 1993, the FTC took on the weight-loss industry when it filed a complaint charging that none of five large, well-known diet program marketers had sufficient evidence to back up claims that their customers achieved their weight-loss goals or maintained the loss. Three of the companies agreed to publicize the fact that most weight loss is temporary and to disclose how long their customers kept off the weight they lost. The agreement required the companies to substantiate their weight-loss claims with scientific data and to document claims that their customers keep off the weight by monitoring a group of them for two years[57] (Exhibit 20–12).

Nearly 10 years later, the FTC held a workshop to once again explore the problem of misleading weight-loss promotional pitches. The FTC used the workshop as a forum to suggest that the media should play a more active role in screening ads for diet products and programs. Professor Herbert Rotfeld has evaluated the FTC's efforts to deal with the problem of deceptive advertising in the weight-loss industry and concludes that its efforts to curb the deceptions have largely failed and that new strategies are needed. He argues that there needs to be more media self-regulation of deceptive weight-loss advertising. However, he also notes that if the FTC wants to see greater screening by the media, they need to give executives from the print and broadcast media a stronger incentive to do so by holding the media companies liable for knowingly carrying deceptive claims.[58]

Recently the FTC has stepped up its action against false and unsubstantiated claims in ads and infomercials. A few years ago, the commission fined the Home Shopping Network $1.1 million for making unsubstantiated advertising claims for two weight-loss products, an acne treatment, and a dietary supplement for menopause and premenstrual syndrome. Under the settlement Home Shopping is enjoined from making product claims about curing and treating diseases without "reliable scientific evidence."

## The FTC's Handling of Deceptive Advertising Cases

**Consent and Cease-and-Desist Orders** Allegations of unfair or deceptive advertising come to the FTC's attention from a variety of sources, including competitors, consumers, other government agencies, or the commission's own monitoring and investigations. Once the FTC decides a complaint is justified and warrants further action, it notifies the offender, who then has 30 days to respond. The

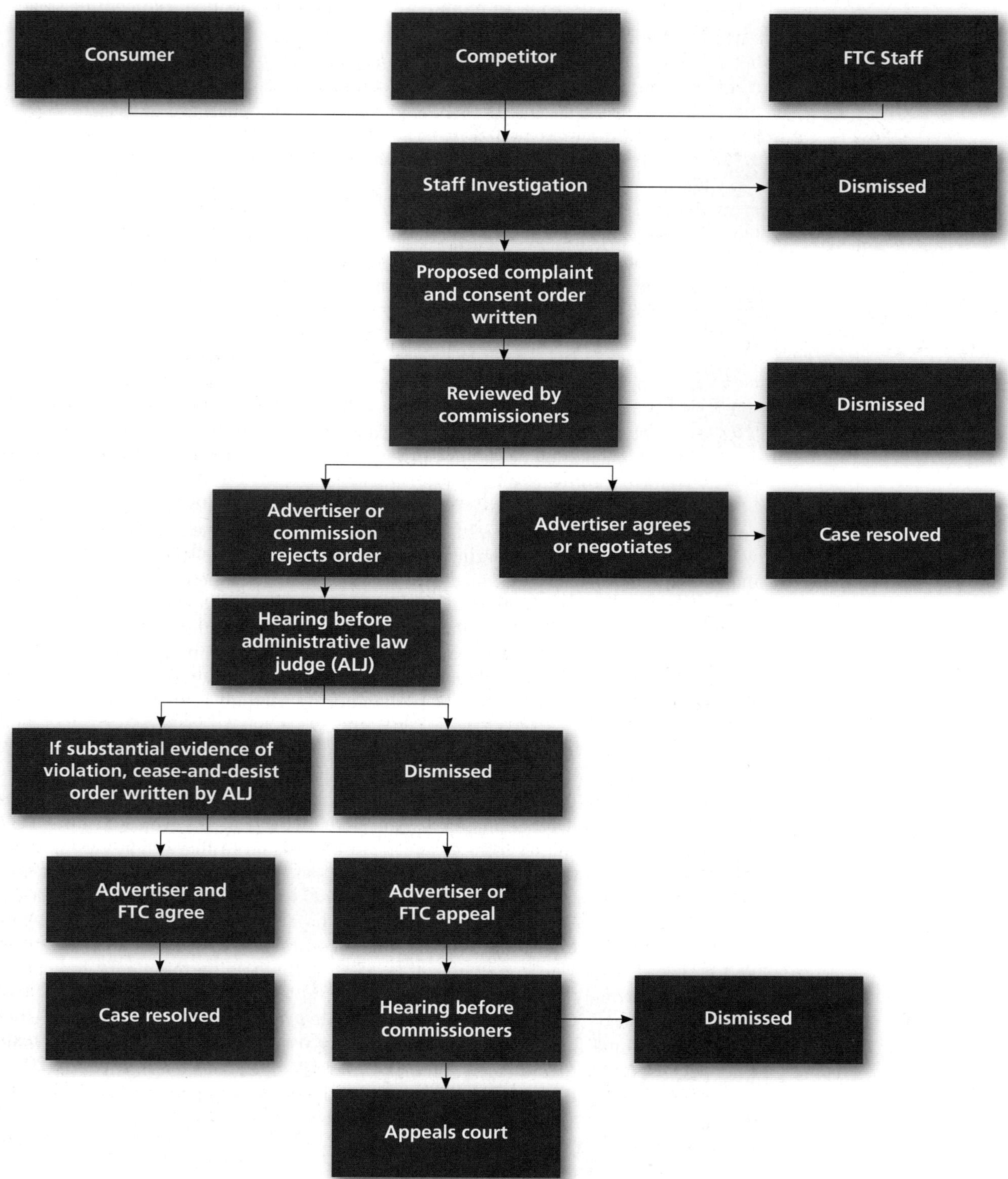


**FIGURE 20–4**

FTC Complaint Procedure

advertiser can agree to negotiate a settlement with the FTC by signing a **consent order**, which is an agreement to stop the practice or advertising in question. This agreement is for settlement purposes only and does not constitute an admission of guilt by the advertiser. Most FTC inquiries are settled by consent orders because they save the advertiser the cost and possible adverse publicity that might result if the case went further.

If the advertiser chooses not to sign the consent decree and contests the complaint, a hearing can be requested before an administrative law judge employed by the FTC but not under its influence. The judge's decision may be appealed to the full five-member commission by either side. The commission either affirms or modifies the order or dismisses the case. If the complaint has been upheld by the administrative law judge and the commission, the advertiser can appeal the case to the federal courts.

The appeal process may take some time, during which the FTC may want to stop the advertiser from engaging in the deceptive practice. The Wheeler-Lea Amendment empowers the FTC to issue a **cease-and-desist order**, which requires that the advertiser stop the specified advertising claim within 30 days and prohibits the advertiser from engaging in the objectionable practice until after the hearing is held. Violation of a cease-and-desist order is punishable by a fine of up to $10,000 a day. Figure 20–4 summarizes the FTC complaint procedure.

**Corrective Advertising** By using consent and cease-and-desist orders, the FTC can usually stop a particular advertising practice it believes is unfair or deceptive. However, even if an advertiser ceases using a deceptive ad, consumers may still remember some or all of the claim. To address the problem of residual effects, in the 1970s, the FTC developed a program known as **corrective advertising**. An advertiser found guilty of deceptive advertising can be required to run additional advertising designed to remedy the deception or misinformation contained in previous ads.

The impetus for corrective advertising was another case involving Campbell Soup, which when making a photo for an ad, placed marbles in the bottom of a bowl of vegetable soup to force the solid ingredients to the surface, creating a false impression that the soup contained more vegetables than it really did. (Campbell Soup argued that if the marbles were not used, all the ingredients would settle to the bottom, leaving an impression of fewer ingredients than actually existed!) While Campbell Soup agreed to stop the practice, a group of law students calling themselves SOUP (Students Opposed to Unfair Practices) argued to the FTC that this would not remedy false impressions created by prior advertising and contended Campbell Soup should be required to run advertising to rectify the problem.[59]

Although the FTC did not order corrective advertising in the Campbell case, it has done so in many cases since then. Profile Bread ran an ad stating each slice contained fewer calories than other brands, but the ad did not mention that slices of Profile bread were thinner than those of other brands. Ocean Spray cranberry juice was found guilty of deceptive advertising because it claimed to have more "food energy" than orange or tomato juice but failed to note it was referring to the technical definition of food energy, which is calories. In each case, the advertisers were ordered to spend 25 percent of their annual media budgets to run corrective ads. The STP Corporation was required to run corrective advertising for claims regarding the ability of its oil additive to reduce oil consumption. Many of the corrective ads run in the STP case appeared in business publications to serve notice to other advertisers that the FTC was enforcing the corrective advertising program. The texts of the corrective messages required in each of these cases are shown in Figure 20–5.

Corrective advertising is probably the most controversial of all the FTC programs.[60] Advertisers argue that corrective advertising infringes on First Amendment rights of freedom of speech. In one of the most publicized corrective advertising cases ever, involving Listerine mouthwash, Warner-Lambert tested the FTC's legal power to order corrective messages.[61] For more than 50 years Warner-Lambert had advertised that gargling with Listerine helped prevent colds and sore throats or lessened their severity because it killed the germs that caused these illnesses. In 1975, the FTC ruled these claims could not be substantiated and ordered Warner-Lambert to stop making them. In addition, the FTC argued that corrective advertising was needed to rectify the erroneous beliefs that had been created by Warner-Lambert as a result of the large amount of advertising it had run for Listerine over the prior 50 years.

**Profile Bread**

"Hi, [celebrity's name] for Profile Bread. Like all mothers, I'm concerned about nutrition and balanced meals. So, I'd like to clear up any misunderstanding you may have about Profile Bread from its advertising or even its name.

"Does Profile have fewer calories than any other breads? No. Profile has about the same per ounce as other breads. To be exact, Profile has seven fewer calories per slice. That's because Profile is sliced thinner. But eating Profile will not cause you to lose weight. A reduction of seven calories is insignificant. It's total calories and balanced nutrition that count. And Profile can help you achieve a balanced meal because it provides protein and B vitamins as well as other nutrients.

"How does my family feel about Profile? Well, my husband likes Profile toast, the children love Profile sandwiches, and I prefer Profile to any other bread. So you see, at our house, delicious taste makes Profile a family affair."

(To be run in 25 percent of brand's advertising, for one year.)

**Ocean Spray**

"If you've wondered what some of our earlier advertising meant when we said Ocean Spray Cranberry Juice Cocktail has more food energy than orange juice or tomato juice, let us make it clear: we didn't mean vitamins and minerals. Food energy means calories. Nothing more.

"Food energy is important at breakfast since many of us may not get enough calories, or food energy, to get off to a good start. Ocean Spray Cranberry Juice Cocktail helps because it contains more food energy than most other breakfast drinks.

"And Ocean Spray Cranberry Juice Cocktail gives you and your family Vitamin C plus a great wake-up taste. It's . . . the other breakfast drink."

(To be run in one of every four ads for one year.)

**STP**

As a result of an investigation by the Federal Trade Commission into certain allegedly inaccurate past advertisements for STP's oil additive, STP Corporation has agreed to a $700,000 settlement. With regard to that settlement, STP is making the following statement:

"It is the policy of STP to support its advertising with objective information and test data. In 1974 and 1975 an independent laboratory ran tests of the company's oil additive which led to claims of reduced oil consumption. However, these tests cannot be relied on to support the oil consumption reduction claim made by STP.

"The FTC has taken the position that, in making the claim, the company violated the terms of a consent order. When STP learned that the test did not support the claim, it stopped advertising containing that claim. New tests have been undertaken to determine the extent to which the oil additive affects oil consumption. Agreement to this settlement does not constitute an admission by STP that the law has been violated. Rather, STP has agreed to resolve the dispute with the FTC to avoid protracted and prohibitively expensive litigation."

**FIGURE 20–5**

Examples of Corrective Advertising Messages

Warner-Lambert argued that the advertising was not misleading and, further, that the FTC did not have the power to order corrective advertising. Warner-Lambert appealed the FTC decision all the way to the Supreme Court, which rejected the argument that corrective advertising violates advertisers' First Amendment rights. The powers of the FTC in the areas of both claim substantiation and corrective advertising were upheld. Warner-Lambert was required to run $10 million worth of corrective ads over a 16-month period stating, "Listerine does not help prevent colds or sore throats or lessen their severity."

Since the Supreme Court ruling in the Listerine case, there have been several other situations where the FTC has ordered corrective advertising on the basis of the "Warner-Lambert test," which considers whether consumers are left with a latent impression that would continue to affect buying decisions and whether corrective ads are needed to remedy the situation.

In a more recent case involving Novartis Consumer Health Corp.'s Doan's Pills, the FTC sent a strong message to advertisers and agencies that it will require marketers to run corrective ads to remedy any misleading impressions that were created through unsubstantiated advertising claims.[62] In this case, Novartis was ordered to spend $8 million, or the equivalent of the average annual ad budget for Doan's Pills over an eight-year period, on corrective ads to remedy any impressions that might exist from previous advertising that the brand is more effective than other analgesics for relieving back pain. Novartis was ordered to include the statement "Although Doan's is an effective pain reliever, there is no evidence that Doan's is more effective than other pain relievers for back pain" on packaging and in ads until $8 million was spent on the campaign. Novartis appealed the FTC decision ordering corrective advertising. However, the U.S. Court of Appeals unanimously upheld the FTC's right to demand corrective advertising in this case. Also at issue in the appeal was the FTC's standard for determining whether a lingering false impression exists from deceptive advertising and whether the commission has to prove that the years of advertising created the false impression or could assume that years of advertising would have done so. The courts described the evidence of lingering effect the FTC had amassed as "thin and somewhat fragmentary," but upheld the commission's decision based on the record as a whole.[63]

The appeals court decision in this case has very important implications for the FTC as well as for advertisers. The ruling reaffirmed the commission's authority to order corrective advertising and gave it greater freedom to use the remedy, whereas a loss could have limited its authority to do so. The ruling also has repercussions for advertisers who expressed concern over the FTC's contention that "corrective advertising is not a drastic remedy" but is an appropriate method for restoring the status quo. Advertisers fear that this is a sign the FTC will be more willing to apply the remedy in future cases. However, FTC officials indicated that the ruling would not substantially change its request for corrective ads. This appears to be the case thus far.

However, in 2009 another federal agency, the Food and Drug Administration (FDA), ordered Bayer to run a six-month, $20 million corrective advertising campaign for Yaz, the company's birth-control product. The FDA ruled that Bayer's marketing and advertising for Yaz, which is the leading nongeneric in the birth-control market, was deceptive and made false claims regarding its efficacy for acne and premenstrual syndrome. Bayer was ordered to spend nearly a third of the $66.7 million it spent in measured media the prior year on corrective ads and was also required to submit all of its advertising for Yaz to the FDA for approval for the next six years.[64]

## Developments in Federal Regulation by the FTC

By the end of the 1970s, the FTC had become a very powerful and active regulator of advertising. However, Congress was concerned about the FTC's broad interpretation of unfairness, which led to the restrictive legislation of the 1980 FTC Improvements Act. During the 1980s, the FTC became less active and cut back its regulatory efforts, due in large part to the Reagan administration's laissez-faire attitude toward the regulation of business in general. Some feared that the FTC had become too narrow in its regulation of national advertising, forcing companies and consumer groups to seek relief from other sources such as state and federal courts or through self-regulatory groups such as the NAD/NARB.[65]

In 1988–89, an 18-member panel chosen by the American Bar Association undertook a study of the FTC as a 20-year follow-up to the 1969 report used by President Richard Nixon to overhaul the commission. The panel's report expressed strong concern over the FTC's lack of sufficient resources and staff to regulate national advertising effectively and called for more funding.

After more than a decade of relative inactivity, the Federal Trade Commission once again became active in the regulation of advertising. The commission showed particular interest in cracking down on misleading advertising in areas such as health, nutrition, weight loss, and environmental claims as well as advertising directed to children and the elderly.[66] The FTC also became more involved with potential fraud and deception through various other promotional methods such as telemarketing, 900 numbers, infomercials, and the Internet. In addition to monitoring deceptive claims made over the Internet, the FTC has become very involved in privacy issues and the collection of personal information on websites.

Robert Pitofsky, who served as FTC chairman during the Clinton administration, focused the commission's attention on developing new policies, particularly as the growth of the Internet created the need for laws and regulations regarding online privacy and ways of protecting children online. However, empirical evidence from a study conducted by Avery Abernethy and George Franke indicates that during this period when the FTC was most active and stringent in requiring advertising substantiation, the objective information contained in advertising actually decreased substantially. Abernethy and Franke suggest that it became more expensive for companies to provide factual information in their ads due to the regulatory burden placed on advertising. Thus, the overall information content of advertising fell, which suggests that increased government regulation can have unintended negative consequences.[67]

Under the Bush administration the FTC focused its attention on the enforcement of existing regulations, particularly in areas such as telemarketing and Internet privacy.[68] The FTC also has focused on eliminating false e-mail advertising and has stepped up its enforcement against senders of deceptive or misleading claims via e-mail. The commission also scrutinized the use of testimonial ads more carefully, particularly with respect to the use of a "results not typical" disclosure in situations where the outcomes are more likely to vary substantially than be typical for most consumers.[69] The FTC has been active in bringing enforcement action against deceptive health claims and companies and principals in the mortgage lending industry for deceptive and unfair practices in servicing mortgage loans. The FTC has also become more involved in the area of environmental marketing and the use of "green" claims for carbon offset, landfill reduction, and sustainable packaging.[70] Deborah Platt Majoras, who was FTC chair during most of the second term of the Bush administration, was a strong proponent of industry self-regulation, but also noted the need for self-regulatory organizations to have sufficient resources to do their job effectively and to be independent of influence from the lobbying efforts of member firms.[71]

**EXHIBIT 20–13**
The FTC issues an *Annual Report* on its activities and initiatives

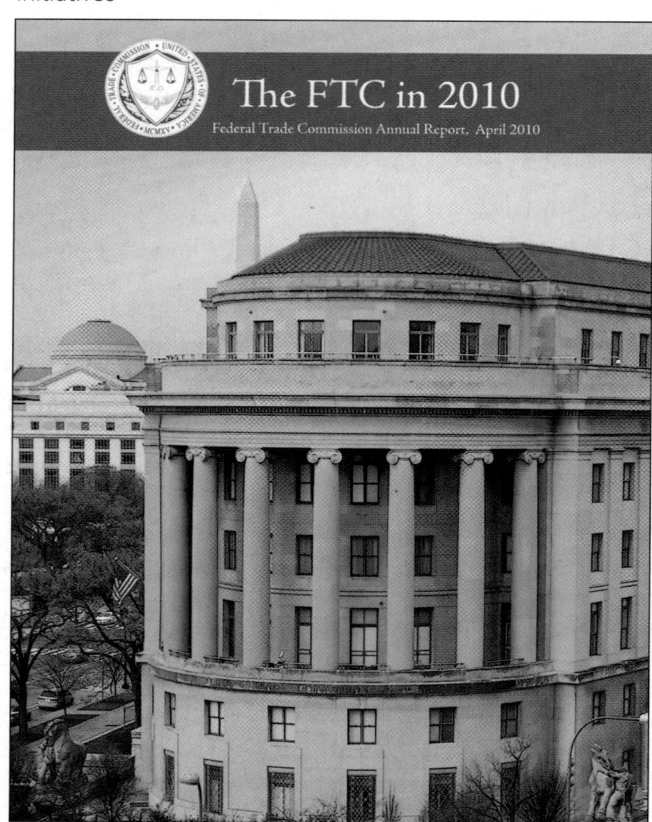

The FTC in 2010
Federal Trade Commission Annual Report, April 2010


Under the Obama administration, the FTC is becoming very active in the regulation of advertising as well as of other marketing practices. The administration, along with the new FTC Chairman Jon Leibowitz, have asked Congress to grant the agency increased powers to protect consumers from deceptive practices by unscrupulous providers of financial services and products. In its 2010 *Annual Report,* the FTC has noted that it intends to step up its efforts to stop fraud that targets financially distressed consumers (Exhibit 20–13). The FTC has joined forces with a number of states and other federal agencies to take action against mortgage modification and foreclosure rescue scams; phony debt reduction and credit repair operations; and payday lenders, get-rich-quick schemes, and bogus government grants.[72] To better protect consumers, Leibowitz is also seeking to streamline the FTC's rulemaking procedures, asking for power to bring charges directly against aiders and abettors of financial fraud and expanding the FTC's remedial powers.

The FTC is expected to take a more regulatory approach under the Obama administration rather than relying on the voluntary self-regulation that was used by the commission during the Bush presidency.[73] The FTC is focusing attention on protecting consumers' online privacy and the collection of sensitive information, particularly for those using social media such as Facebook and Twitter. In 2009 it passed a new set of guidelines for online endorsements that requires bloggers to disclose any "material connection" to an advertiser.[74] The new guidelines also call for self-regulation regarding online behavioral targeting, although it is expected that marketers will face more FTC scrutiny in this area.[75] The Federal Trade Commission will continue to be the primary regulator of advertising and marketing practices in the United States, although the direction of the FTC is likely to be influenced by the political party of the presidential administration.

While the FTC is the major regulator of advertising for products sold in interstate commerce, several other federal agencies and departments also regulate advertising and promotion.

## Additional Federal Regulatory Agencies

**The Federal Communications Commission** The FCC, founded in 1934 to regulate broadcast communication, has jurisdiction over the radio, television, telephone, and telegraph industries. The FCC has the authority to license broadcast stations as well as to remove a license or deny renewal to stations not operating in the public's interest. The FCC's authority over the airways gives it the power to control advertising content and to restrict what products and services can be advertised on radio and TV. The FCC can eliminate obscene and profane programs and/or messages and those it finds in poor taste. While the FCC can purge ads that are deceptive or misleading, it generally works closely with the FTC in the regulation of advertising. For example, the Federal Communications Commission and the FTC held a joint workshop and publicly accused long-distance phone marketers of deceiving consumers in their advertising. Officials of both commissions expressed concern over per-minute ads for long distance and so-called dial-around long-distance services. They also warned long-distance marketers that they would take action if steps were not taken to clean up their advertising.[76]

Many of the FCC's rules and regulations for TV and radio stations have been eliminated or modified. The FCC no longer limits the amount of television time that can be devoted to commercials. (But in 1991, the Children's Television Act went into effect. The act limits advertising during children's programming to 10.5 minutes an hour on weekends and 12 minutes an hour on weekdays.)

Under the Reagan administration, the controversial Fairness Doctrine, which required broadcasters to provide time for opposing viewpoints on important issues, was repealed on the grounds that it was counterproductive. It was argued that the Fairness Doctrine actually reduced discussion of important issues because a broadcaster might be afraid to take on a paid controversial message in case it might be required to provide equal free exposure for opposing viewpoints. It was under this doctrine that the FCC required stations to run commercials about the harmful effects of smoking before passage of the Public Health Cigarette Smoking Act of 1970, which banned broadcast advertising of cigarettes. Many stations still provide time for opposing viewpoints on controversial issues as part of their public service requirement, not necessarily directly related to fairness.

In recent years the FCC has become very active in enforcing laws governing the airing of obscene, indecent, and profane material. For example, in 2004, the commission fined "shock jock" Howard Stern $495,000 for broadcasting indecent content and also levied fines against Clear Channel Communications, the nation's largest owner of radio stations, which carried his syndicated show.[77] Concern over Stern's constant battling with the FCC led to a decision by Clear Channel to drop his daily radio show.[78] Stern subsequently signed a five-year contract with Sirius Satellite radio, the subscription-based radio service, where his show is not subject to FCC regulations. The FCC also stepped up its enforcement of obscenity in the

**EXHIBIT 20–14**
Janet Jackson's "wardrobe malfunction" during the 2004 Super Bowl half-time show led to greater enforcement of obscenity laws by the FCC

wake of the controversy following the baring of Janet Jackson's breast during the halftime show of the 2004 Super Bowl (Exhibit 20–14).[79] These incidents resulted in federal legislation dramatically increasing the amount both radio and television networks and stations can be fined for broadcast obscenity violations. In 2005, the FCC launched a new website explaining its broadcast obscenity, indecency, and profanity rules as well as complaint procedures and enforcement actions.

The FCC has also recently become involved in issues affecting the area of publicity and public relations. In 2005, the commission issued a missive insisting that broadcasters screen video news releases to ensure that they clearly disclose "the nature, source and sponsorship" of the material. The crackdown is designed to address a marketing practice whereby prepackaged promotional videos sent to TV stations by companies, organizations, and government agencies are represented as news stories.[80] And, as discussed in the chapter opener, the FCC is also currently considering the regulation of the use product placements in television shows.

**The Food and Drug Administration** Now under the jurisdiction of the Department of Health and Human Services, the FDA has authority over the labeling, packaging, branding, ingredient listing, and advertising of packaged foods and drug products, as well as cosmetics. The FDA is authorized to require caution and warning labels on potentially hazardous products and also has limited authority over nutritional claims made in food advertising. This agency has the authority to set rules for promoting these products and the power to seize food and drugs on charges of false and misleading advertising.

Like the FTC, the Food and Drug Administration has become a very aggressive regulatory agency in recent years. The FDA has cracked down on a number of commonly used descriptive terms it believes are often abused in the labeling and advertising of food products—for example, *natural, light, no cholesterol, fat free,* and *organic.* The FDA has also become tougher on nutritional claims implied by brand names that might send a misleading message to consumers. For example, Great Foods of America was not permitted to continue using the HeartBeat trademark under which it sold most of its foods. The FDA argued the trademark went too far in implying the foods have special advantages for the heart and overall health.

**EXHIBIT 20–15**
The Nutritional Labeling and Education Act requires that labels be easy for consumers to understand

Many changes in food labeling are a result of the Nutritional Labeling and Education Act, which Congress passed in 1990. Under this law the FDA established legal definitions for a wide range of terms (such as *low fat, light,* and *reduced calories*) and required straightforward labels for all foods beginning in early 1994 (Exhibit 20–15). In its current form the act applies only to food labels, but it may soon affect food advertising as well. The FTC would be asked to ensure that food ads comply with the new FDA standards.

The FDA has also become increasing active in policing health-related claims for food products. In 2009 General Mills received a warning letter from the FDA for violations stemming from claims the company has been making that eating Cheerios cereal can reduce cholesterol by 4 to 6 percent in six weeks. The FDA charged that the claims made for the product based on clinical studies would make it a drug, not a food, because it is intended for use in the prevention, mitigation, and treatment of disease. General Mills has been working with the FDA to resolve the issue as the cholesterol-reduction claims are an important part of the brand's positioning and used as the basis for much of its advertising.[81]

Another regulatory area where the FDA has been heavily involved is the advertising and promotion of tobacco products. In 1996, President Bill Clinton signed an executive order declaring that nicotine is an addictive drug and giving the FDA board jurisdiction to regulate cigarettes and smokeless tobacco. Many of the regulations resulting from this order were designed to keep teenagers from smoking.[82] However, the tobacco industry immediately appealed the order. While continuing to fight its legal battle with the federal government over the FDA regulations, the tobacco makers did agree to settle lawsuits brought by 46 states against the industry in late 1998 by signing the Master Settlement Agreement. This settlement was considered a better deal for the tobacco industry, as many of the onerous cigarette marketing restrictions contained in the original FDA proposal settlement were missing. The agreement allows large outdoor signs at retailers, whereas the original proposal banned all outdoor ads. The original deal banned all use of humans and cartoons in ads, while the current settlement bans only cartoons and even permits their use on cigarette packs. And while the original proposal eliminated sports sponsorships, the current agreement allows each company to continue one national sponsorship.[83]

An important provision of the Master Settlement Agreement was that the tobacco companies agreed not to target youth (those under the age of 18) in the advertising, promotion, and marketing of tobacco products either directly or indirectly. However, over the past several years there has been considerable debate over whether tobacco companies are complying with the agreement. Much of this debate centers on what is called the 15 percent rule, under which the tobacco companies voluntarily pledged not to advertise in magazines that have more than 15 percent of their readers under the age of 18. Some major tobacco companies such as Philip Morris have stopped advertising in magazines that have a substantial number of youth readers, such as *People, Sports Illustrated, Spin,* and *Rolling Stone*. However, other tobacco companies still advertise in these publications, and it appears that there remains a number of battles to fight in the war over the marketing and advertising of cigarettes.[84]

In 2000, the United States Supreme Court ruled that the Food and Drug Administration did not have the authority to regulate tobacco as a drug, and that Congress would have to specifically enact legislation to allow the FDA to regulate tobacco. As a result, all FDA tobacco regulations were dropped. However, in June 2009 Congress passed a tobacco-control bill giving the FDA sweeping new powers over the packaging, manufacturing, and marketing of tobacco products, and it was signed into law by President Obama shortly thereafter. The Family Smoking Prevention and Tobacco Control Act calls for restrictions on marketing and sales to youths including a ban on all outdoor tobacco advertising within 1,000 feet of schools and playgrounds; a ban on all remaining tobacco-brand sponsorships of sports and entertainment events; a ban on free giveaways of non-tobacco products with the purchase of a tobacco product; a limit on advertising in publications with significant teen readership as well as limiting outdoor and point-of-sale advertising, except in adult-only facilities, to black-and-white ads only; and a restriction on ads on vending machines and self-service displays to adult-only facilities.[85]

Immediately following the passage of the landmark legislation, six tobacco companies along with several other entities, including the Association of National Advertisers and the American Civil Liberties Union, filed a lawsuit in federal court challenging the constitutionality of the new law. The suit argues that the marketing and advertising restrictions laid out in the bill fail to comply with free-speech protections provided by the First Amendment.[86] In January 2010, the federal court ruled that the ban on the use of colors and illustrations does indeed violate the First Amendment, but upheld the remaining parts of the new law. While additional appeals by the tobacco companies are expected, the new law will have a significant impact on the marketing and advertising of tobacco products.

A number of consumer advocacy groups as well as health departments in many states run ads warning consumers against the dangers of smoking and tobacco-related diseases. For example, the American Legacy Foundation, which was established as part of the 1998 tobacco settlement and is dedicated to reducing tobacco use, has run a number of hard-hitting ads warning consumers of the risk of smoking. One of the most successful programs developed by the ALF has been truth®,

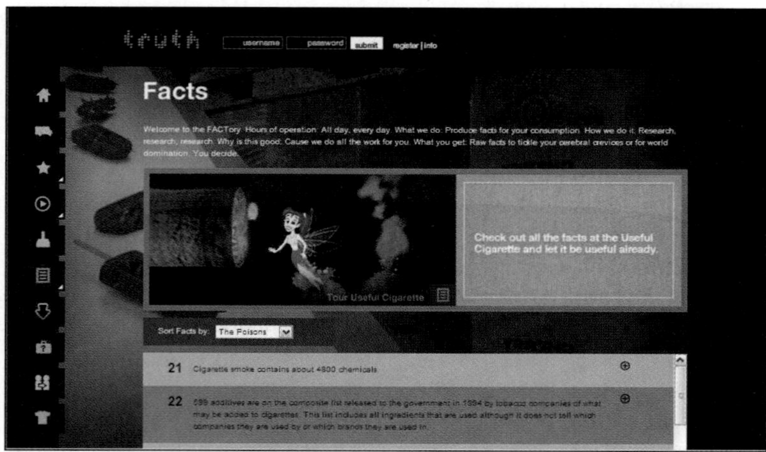


**EXHIBIT 20–16**
truth® has been a very effective youth smoking prevention campaign

which was launched in 2000 and is the largest national youth smoking prevention campaign. Truth® exposes the tactics of the tobacco industry, the truth about addiction, the health effects and consequences of smoking, and is designed to allow teens to make informed choices about tobacco use by giving them the facts about the industry and its products. Truth® is a fully integrated campaign which includes advertising in media that are popular with youth, a summer travel tour that allows teens to engage firsthand with the campaign, and a website (www.thetruth.com) that contains a number of distinctive interactive elements (Exhibit 20–16).

Another area where the Food and Drug Administration has become more involved is the advertising of prescription drugs. Tremendous growth in direct-to-consumer drug advertising has occurred since the FDA issued new guidelines making it easier for pharmaceutical companies to advertise prescription drugs to consumers. A number of studies have been conducted to examine the influence of DTC prescription drug advertising on consumers as well as patient–physician interactions.[87] Ethical Perspective 20–1 discusses the concerns over the increase in direct-to-consumer drug advertising and the guidelines and regulations that have been developed by the FDA to address the issue.

**The U.S. Postal Service** Many marketers use the U.S. mail to deliver advertising and promotional messages. The U.S. Postal Service has control over advertising involving the use of the mail and ads that involve lotteries, obscenity, or fraud. The regulation against fraudulent use of the mail has been used to control deceptive advertising by numerous direct-response advertisers. These firms advertise on TV or radio or in magazines and newspapers and use the U.S. mail to receive orders and payment. Many have been prosecuted by the Post Office Department for use of the mail in conjunction with a fraudulent or deceptive offer.

**Bureau of Alcohol, Tobacco, and Firearms** The Bureau of Alcohol, Tobacco, and Firearms (BATF) is an agency within the Treasury Department that enforces laws, develops regulations, and is responsible for tax collection for the liquor industry. The BATF regulates and controls the advertising of alcoholic beverages. The agency determines what information can be provided in ads as well as what constitutes false and misleading advertising. It is also responsible for including warning labels on alcohol advertising and banning the use of active athletes in beer commercials. The BATF can impose strong sanctions for violators. The advertising of alcoholic beverages has become a very controversial issue, with many consumer and public-interest groups calling for a total ban on the advertising of beer, wine, and liquor.

## The Lanham Act

While most advertisers rely on self-regulatory mechanisms and the FTC to deal with deceptive or misleading advertising by their competitors, many companies are filing lawsuits against competitors they believe are making false claims. One piece of federal legislation that has become increasingly important in this regard is the Lanham Act. This act was originally written in 1947 as the Lanham Trade-Mark Act to protect words, names, symbols, or other devices adopted to identify and distinguish a manufacturer's products. The **Lanham Act** was amended to encompass false advertising by prohibiting "any false description or representation including words or other symbols tending falsely to describe or represent the same." While the

FTC Act did not give individual advertisers the opportunity to sue a competitor for deceptive advertising, civil suits are permitted under the Lanham Act.

More and more companies are using the Lanham Act to sue competitors for their advertising claims, particularly since comparative advertising has become so common. For example, a court ordered Ralston Purina to pay Alpo Petfoods $12 million for damages it caused by making false claims that its Purina Puppy Chow dog food could ameliorate and help prevent joint disease. The court ruled that the claim was based on faulty data and that the company continued the campaign after learning its research was in error. Alpo was awarded the money as compensation for lost revenue and for the costs of advertising it ran in response to the Puppy Chow campaign.[88]

Wilkinson Sword and its advertising agency were found guilty of false advertising and ordered to pay $953,000 in damages to the Gillette Co. Wilkinson had run TV and print ads claiming its Ultra Glide razor and blades produced shaves "six times smoother" than Gillette's Atra Plus blades. This case marked the first time an agency was held liable for damages in connection with false claims made in a client's advertising.[89] Although the agency was later found not liable, the case served as a sobering reminder to agencies that they can be drawn into litigation over advertising they create for their clients. To deal with this problem, many agencies insist on indemnification clauses in contracts with their clients.

Suing competitors for false claims was made even easier with passage of the TradeMark Law Revision Act of 1988. According to this law, anyone is vulnerable to civil action who "misrepresents the nature, characteristics, qualities, or geographical origin of his or her or another person's goods, services, or commercial activities." This wording closed a loophole in the Lanham Act, which prohibited only false claims about one's own goods or services. While many disputes over comparative claims are never contested or are resolved through the NAD, more companies are turning to lawsuits for several reasons: the broad information discovery powers available under federal civil procedure rules, the speed with which a competitor can stop the offending ad through a preliminary injunction, and the possibility of collecting damages.[90] However, companies do not always win their lawsuits. Under the Lanham Act you are required to prove five elements to win a false advertising lawsuit containing a comparative claim.[91] You must prove that:

- False statements have been made about the advertiser's product or your product.
- The ads actually deceived or had the tendency to deceive a substantial segment of the audience.
- The deception was "material" or meaningful and is likely to influence purchasing decisions.
- The falsely advertised products or services are sold in interstate commerce.
- You have been or likely will be injured as a result of the false statements, by either loss of sales or loss of goodwill.

**EXHIBIT 20–17**

Comparative claims involving the Prego and Ragu brands of spaghetti sauce resulted in a lawsuit

Over the years there has been a significant increase in the use of comparative advertising, and it has resulted in more and more companies' suing one another under the Lanham Act. In the mid-90s the Campbell Soup Co. advertised that its Prego brand of spaghetti sauce was thicker than Van Den Bergh Food's Ragu brand. Van Den Bergh sued to have Campbell's comparative ads for Prego halted but lost the case in district court as well as in appeals court. Campbell capitalized on its victory by creating an ad based on it. The ad tweaked Ragu by showing snippets of the comparison ads and then a shot of Prego with a breadstick standing up in the sauce (Exhibit 20–17). The tagline was, "Ragu took us to court. We made our case stand. Just like our breadstick." The two companies finally declared a truce in the spaghetti sauce wars in late 1999.[92]

## Ethical Perspective 20–1 > > >

### Direct-to-Consumer Drug Advertising Continues to Come under Attack

For years, pharmaceutical companies marketed most of their prescription drugs directly to physicians, either through their sales force or by advertising in medical journals. However, in 1997, the Food and Drug Administration (FDA) issued new guidelines to make it easier for pharmaceutical companies to advertise prescription drugs on television as well as in print media. Consumers still must have the explicit permission of a physician to buy a prescription medication so drug companies still have the challenge of motivating consumers to see their doctor while touting their brand as a remedy to the problem. However, with the change in guidelines, direct-to-consumer (DTC) drug advertising has exploded, and pharmaceutical companies are some of the largest consumer advertisers.

Direct-to-consumer drug advertising spending soared from \$859 million in 1997 to over \$5 billion in 2009. Brand-name prescription drugs such as Lipitor, Zoloft, Celebrex, Viagra, and Levitra have become as well-known to consumers as brands of soft drinks. The pharmaceutical companies argue that the increased spending on drug advertising has helped educate consumers about their options and has caused people, who might not do so otherwise, to see doctors about medications. However, a number of physicians, consumers, and health care groups have expressed concern over the increase in drug advertising for several reasons. A major concern is the accuracy of the ads and whether they inform consumers of all the risks associated with taking a drug. Consumer groups asked the Food and Drug Administration to enforce the "fair balance" provision, an FDA regulation governing broadcast commercials that requires drug ads to give both the benefits and the risks of taking a medication.

The FDA is charged with the responsibility of ensuring that drug advertising is fair, balanced, and truthful. However, the number of ads submitted annually for FDA scrutiny, including TV spots, magazine ads, Internet sites, and even pamphlets used by sales representatives has jumped nearly 35 percent over the past 10 years from just over 25,000 to nearly 40,000. However, the number of citation letters issued by the FDA to drug companies for ads that might be false, misleading, or otherwise out of compliance fell from 142 in 1995 to just 43 in 2008. The pharmaceutical companies say that the drop in citations shows that their advertisements are cleaner than before and that they are much more knowledgeable about the FDA guidelines. However, the FDA's director of the Division of Drug Marketing, Advertising, and Communication notes that with its limited resources the division cannot investigate all of the ads, so it focuses on ads deemed most critical: those that appear on television, make unusual claims, or raise a major public health issue.

Consumer advocates have argued for stricter regulations on drug ads noting that while advertisers must include statements about negative side effects or toxicity, the images of people with allergies romping happily outside or of someone who has chronic heartburn downing a pepperoni pizza are what people remember—not the cautionary voiceover. In 2009 the FDA published new advertising guidelines that caution companies not to downplay a drug's risk and/or side effects by using tactics to distract viewers such as loud music or using a typeface smaller than the one used to describe a drug's benefits. Both doctors and critics are also concerned that the ads lead patients to insist on specific drugs when other drugs or lifestyle changes might be better for them.

Concerns over DTC drug advertising escalated in the fall of 2004 when Merck and Co. had to pull its popular antiarthritis medication Vioxx from the market after it was determined that the drug increased patients' risk of heart attack. The industry received more negative publicity in 2009 when Pfizer agreed to pay \$2.3 billion to settle the

In a recent suit brought under the Lanham Act, PepsiCo sued rival Coca-Cola over the advertising for a new version of the latter's Powerade brand sports drink. The issue in the case was an ad campaign promoting Powerade Ion4 as the "complete sports drink" and better than PepsiCo's Gatorade because it contains four electrolytes while Gatorade contains only two. PepsiCo argued that the Powerade superiority claims were false as there was no evidence that the rival brand was better than Gatorade, and that Powerade had the extra electrolytes in only trace amounts anyway. The case ended up in court where a federal judge denied PepsiCo's request that Coca-Cola stop running the comparative ads (because they had already done so). The judge also ruled that the company had not presented sufficient evidence that brand equity or sales of Gatorade had suffered or that Powerade's campaign had caused irreparable injury to PepsiCo. However, the judge did find evidence of possible misconduct by Coca-Cola for referring to Gatorade as incomplete despite largest fraudulent health care marketing case in history. The government accused Pfizer of making false and misleading claims of safety and efficacy to promote Bextra for unapproved uses and for dosages above the approved level from 2002 through April 2005. Pfizer also was forced to stop running TV commercials for its blockbuster drug Lipitor, after the government and other critics charged that the ad misrepresented the credentials of Dr. Robert Jarvik who had endorsed the drug. The ad represented Jarvik as a medical expert when most of his career was spent on the invention of the artificial heart.

In 2007 Congress passed legislation giving the FDA more power to regulate DTC drug advertising. The new bill gives the FDA new power to require drug companies to submit TV ads for review before they run, but it can only recommend changes, not require them. The bill also granted the FDA the power to impose fines on a drug company if its ads are found false and misleading. The fines can amount to $250,000 a day for the first violation in any three-year period and up to $500,000 for any subsequent violation over a three-year period. The FDA will also be able to require that DTC ads disclose specific safety risks as well as clear, conspicuous, and neutral statements about any side effects. With newer drugs, the agency can require that the ads disclose the date the product won FDA approval.

Critics of DTC drug advertising have argued that the legislation did not go far enough as the FDA still does not have the authority to block a company from advertising a medication that carries serious safety concerns. However, the pharmaceutical industry is recognizing that it needs to address the problems with DTC advertising. In 2005, the Pharmaceutical Research and Manufacturers of America (PhRMA), the industry's trade organization, released its Guiding Principles on Direct-to-Consumer Advertisements about Prescription Medications. The voluntary guidelines called for better presentation of risk information and for drug companies to spend an appropriate amount of time to educate health care professionals about a new drug product, including the risks and benefits. However, critics argue that the PhRMA developed its own standards to preempt stricter guidelines that the FDA might impose.

Recently legislators have considered ending the tax deduction for drug ads as a way to raise money to help pay for the federal government's new health care overhaul. Some critics have even called for a total ban on all DTC drug advertising, noting that the United States is one of only two countries that permit the practice. The other is New Zealand where there have been several attempts to ban DTC drug advertising. While it is unlikely that there will be a total ban on this advertising, the message being sent continues to be clear—industry heal thyself.

Sources: Rich Thomaselli, "Medical Groups Mum on DTC Ads," *Advertising Age*, February 28, 2008, pp. 4, 30; Rich Thomaselli, "Pharma Biz Cops to $5 Billion Drug Problem," *Advertising Age*, pp. 3, 39; Rich Thomaselli, "Pfizer to Pay $2.3 Billion in Fraudulent-Marketing Suit," *Advertising Age*, September 2, 2009, http://adage.com/print?article_id=138763; Natasha Singer, "Lawmakers Seek to Curb Drug Commercials," *The New York Times*, July 27, 2009, http://www.nytimes.com/2009/07/27/business/media/27drugads.html.



concerns from one of its research scientists about the claim. Coca-Cola dropped the comparative claims for Powerade and both sides claimed victory in the case.[93]

Marketers using comparative ads have to carefully consider whether their messages have the potential to mislead consumers or may overstate their brand's performance relative to that of competitors. In some cases, a competitor may run an ad challenging a rival's claim if they feel that it misleading or is not based on accurate information. For example, Exhibit 20–18 shows an ad run recently by the TaylorMade Golf Company challenging rival Callaway's claim of its driver being the number one driver used on the Professional Golf Association tour. Note how the ad provides information to substantiate TaylorMade's claim that it is the number one driver on tour. A study by Michael J. Barone and his colleagues provides a framework for developing measures to assess the misleading effects that may arise from various types of comparative advertising.[94]

**EXHIBIT 20–18**
TaylorMade ran this ad to challenge rival Callaway's claim of having the #1 driver on the PGA Tour

# STATE REGULATION

In addition to the various federal rules and regulations, advertisers must also concern themselves with numerous state and local controls. An important early development in state regulation of advertising was the adoption in 44 states of the *Printers Ink* model statutes as a basis for advertising regulation. These statutes were drawn up in 1911 by *Printers Ink,* for many years the major trade publication of the advertising industry. Many states have since modified the original statutes and adopted laws similar to those of the Federal Trade Commission Act for dealing with false and misleading advertising. For example, in California, the Business and Professional Code prohibits "unlawful, unfair, or fraudulent" business practices and "unfair, deceptive, untrue, or misleading advertising."

In addition to recognizing decisions by the federal courts regarding false or deceptive practices, many states have special controls and regulations governing the advertising of specific industries or practices. As the federal government became less involved in the regulation of national advertising during the 1980s, many state attorneys general (AGs) began to enforce state laws regarding false or deceptive advertising. For example, the attorneys general in New York and Texas initiated investigations of Kraft ads claiming the pasteurized cheese used in Cheez Whiz was real cheese.[95] The well-publicized "monster truck" deceptive advertising case involving Volvo and its advertising agency that occurred in the early 90s was initiated by the attorney general's office in the state of Texas.[96]

The **National Association of Attorneys General (NAAG)** moved against a number of national advertisers as a result of inactivity by the FTC during the Reagan administration. In 1987, the NAAG developed enforcement guidelines on airfare advertising that were adopted by more than 40 states. The NAAG has also been involved in other regulatory areas, including car-rental price advertising as well as advertising dealing with nutrition and health claims in food ads. The NAAG's foray into regulating national advertising raises the issue of whether the states working together can create and implement uniform national advertising standards that will, in effect, supersede federal authority. An American Bar Association panel concluded that the Federal Trade Commission is the proper regulator of national advertising and recommended the state AGs focus on practices that harm consumers within a single state.[97] This report also called for cooperation between the FTC and the state attorneys general. In recent years state attorneys general have been working with the FTC and other federal government agencies on false advertising cases. For example, 27 state attorneys general worked with the FDA in the deceptive advertising case for Bayer's Yaz birth control pill that resulted in corrective advertising. A group of state attorneys general also worked with the FTC in a recent case against the makers of Airborne, a multivitamin and herbal supplement whose labels and ads falsely claimed that the product cures and prevents colds. Airborne had been making the false claims since 1999 and agreed to refund the money to consumers who had bought the product, as part of a \$23.3 million class action settlement.[98]

Advertisers are concerned about the trend toward increased regulation of advertising at the state and local levels because it could mean that national advertising campaigns would have to be modified for every state or municipality. Yet the FTC takes the position that businesses that advertise and sell nationwide need a national advertising policy. While the FTC recognizes the need for greater cooperation with the states, the agency believes regulation of national advertising should be its responsibility.[99] Just in case, the advertising industry is still keeping a watchful eye on changes in advertising rules, regulations, and policies at the state and local levels.

## REGULATION OF OTHER PROMOTIONAL AREAS

So far we've focused on the regulation of advertising. However, other elements of the promotional mix also come under the surveillance of federal, state, and local laws and various self-regulatory bodies. This section examines some of the rules, regulations, and guidelines that affect sales promotion, direct marketing, and marketing on the Internet.

### Sales Promotion

Both consumer- and trade-oriented promotions are subject to various regulations. The Federal Trade Commission regulates many areas of sales promotion through the Marketing Practices Division of the Bureau of Consumer Protection. Many promotional practices are also policed by state attorneys general and local regulatory agencies. Various aspects of trade promotion, such as allowances, are regulated by the Robinson-Patman Act, which gives the FTC broad powers to control discriminatory pricing practices.

**Contests and Sweepstakes** As noted in Chapter 16, numerous legal considerations affect the design and administration of contests and sweepstakes, and these promotions are regulated by a number of federal and state agencies. There are two important considerations in developing contests (including games) and sweepstakes. First, marketers must be careful to ensure their contest or sweepstakes is not classified as a *lottery,* which is considered a form of gambling and violates the Federal Trade Commission Act and many state and local laws. A promotion is considered a lottery if a prize is offered, if winning a prize depends on chance and not skill, and if the participant is required to give up something of value in order to participate. The latter requirement is referred to as *consideration* and is the basis on which most contests, games, and sweepstakes avoid being considered lotteries. Generally, as long as consumers are not required to make a purchase to enter a contest or sweepstakes, consideration is not considered to be present and the promotion is not considered a lottery.

The second important requirement in the use of contests and sweepstakes is that the marketer provide full disclosure of the promotion. Regulations of the FTC, as well as many state and local governments, require marketers using contests, games, and sweepstakes to make certain all of the details are given clearly and to follow prescribed rules to ensure the fairness of the game.[100] Disclosure requirements include the exact number of prizes to be awarded and the odds of winning, the duration and termination dates of the promotion, and the availability of lists of winners of various prizes (Exhibit 20–19). The FTC also has specific rules governing the way games and contests are conducted, such as requirements that game pieces be randomly distributed, that a game not be terminated before the distribution of all game pieces, and that additional pieces not be added during the course of a game.

A number of states have responded to concerns over fraud on the part of some contest and sweepstakes operators. In 1995, at least 13 states either passed or tightened prize notification laws, requiring fuller disclosure of rules, odds, and the retail value of prizes. And many of the states are following through with tougher enforcement of these laws. For example, Publishers Clearing House, known for its million-dollar giveaways, agreed to pay $490,000 to 14 states and to

**EXHIBIT 20–19**
Marketers are required to provide consumers with full details of a contest or sweepstakes

2008 SEC MEN'S TOURNAMENT GEORGIA DOME-ATLANTA

WIN A TRIP TO THE CHAMPIONSHIP

**Enter to win an all-expense-paid trip for you and a guest to the 2008 Men's Basketball Championship game in Atlanta, GA in March.**

Offer valid January 1 - January 31, 2008. Only at participating locations. No purchase necessary.

Name: ____________ Please Print

Address: ____________ Apt.#: ____________

City: ____________ State: ____________ Zip: ____________

E-mail (optional): ____________ Telephone (optional): ____________

Outlet Name: ____________

Outlet Address: ____________ City: ____________ State: ____________ Zip: ____________

SEC Basketball Championship Game Sweepstakes Official Rules

NO PURCHASE NECESSARY. A PURCHASE WILL NOT INCREASE YOUR CHANCES OF WINNING. VOID WHERE PROHIBITED. Sweepstakes starts on January 1, 2008 at 12:00:01 a.m. Central Time and ends January 31, 2008 at 11:59:59 p.m. Central Time. ("Sweepstakes Period"). Who may enter: Sweepstakes open only to legal U.S. residents of the United States or the District of Columbia (excluding the residents of Puerto Rico), who are 18 years of age and older as of January 1, 2008. Employees, officers and directors of SOPUS Products ("Sponsor") and its parent companies, affiliates, subsidiaries, distributors, dealers, installers, printers and advertising and promotion agencies, and any and all other companies associated with this Sweepstakes, and members of their immediate families (spouse, parents, siblings and children) or households are not eligible to participate. Subject to all applicable federal, state and local laws and regulations. How to enter: 1) Visit your local participating installer location during the Sweepstakes Period and complete an official entry form (while supplies last), insert into mailing envelope and mail to: Q SEC Basketball Championship Game Sweepstakes #800, P.O. Box 809004, Houston, TX 77280-9921; Or 2) write your name, address, city, state, zip code, home telephone number, installer name (including address) and email address (optional) on a 3" x 5" card and mail to: Q SEC Basketball Championship Game Sweepstakes #800, P.O. Box 809004, Houston, TX 77280-9921. Entry forms must be filled out in full. Enter as often as you like; however, each written entry must be original, separately mailed and handwritten. Written entry forms must be postmarked by January 31, 2008 and received by February 8, 2008. Winning: On or about February 15, 2008, One (1) Grand Prize winner will be selected from among all eligible entries received via a random drawing conducted by independent judges. Sponsor will attempt to notify the potential Grand Prize winner by mail and/or phone on or about February 15, 2008. Judges' decisions are final and binding in all matters related to the Sweepstakes. Odds of winning depend on the total number of eligible entries received. Limit one prize per person or household. Only one (1) Grand Prize will be awarded to one winner. Prizes: One (1) Grand Prize: Prize includes a trip for winner and a guest to the SEC Basketball Championship game in Atlanta, Georgia, March 16, 2008. Trip will include roundtrip coach class airfare from major airport nearest winner's home to Hartsfield-Jackson Atlanta International Airport, (airport, airline, and flight itinerary determined by Sponsor in its sole discretion). Also included is 3 days, 2 night's hotel accommodation in a hotel determined by Sponsor in its sole discretion (single room, double occupancy). 2 tickets to the SEC Basketball Championship game approximate retail value of the prize is $3,000.00. Actual value may vary based on airfare fluctuations and distance between departure and destination. If in the judgment of Sponsor air travel is not required due to winner's proximity to prize location, ground transportation will be substituted for round trip airfare at Sponsor's sole discretion. All expenses and incidental travel costs not expressly stated in the Official Rules of this Sweepstakes, including but not limited to, ground transportation, meals, incidentals, airport fees, parking fees, personal charges at the hotel, etc., are the sole responsibility of the winner. Prize details and availability are subject to change, in which case Sponsor may substitute a prize of equal or greater value. Winner is responsible for all local, state and federal taxes and fees, if any. Prizes are non-transferable, except at Sponsor's sole discretion. No substitutions or cash redemptions, except at Sponsor's sole discretion. Claiming prize: Potential Grand Prize winner will be required to complete and return an affidavit of eligibility, liability, and publicity release within 5 days of notification. (Tennessee residents need not execute publicity release.) In the event of noncompliance with these Official Rules, or if the entrant cannot be contacted at the address on his or her entry form, or if notification is undeliverable, prize will be forfeited and an alternate winner may be selected in a random drawing. Prize will be awarded provided a sufficient number of eligible entries are received. Unless the child of the winner, travel companion must be 18 years of age or older as of the date of departure and must travel on same itinerary as winner. Travel companion will be required to execute a liability/publicity release prior to ticketing airline flight (Tennessee residents need not execute publicity release). Acceptance of prize also constitutes permission to use winner's name, biographical information, voice and/or likeness for Sponsor's promotional and/or advertising purposes without notice or compensation. (Tennessee residents need not so consent.) By participating, entrants agree to be bound by the Official Rules of this Sweepstakes and the decisions of the judges. Conditions: All entries and prize claims become the property of the Sponsor and will not be returned. Neither Sponsor nor Installer location are responsible for (1) lost, late, stolen, misdirected, damaged, illegible, incomplete, or postage-due entries. (2) any incorrect or inaccurate information (3) technical or human error which may occur in the administration of the Sweepstakes or the processing of entries; or (4) any injury or damage to persons or property which may be caused, directly or indirectly, from entrants' participation in the Sweepstakes or receipt or use or misuse of prize. Entries and prize claims void if incomplete, defective, altered, forged or obtained outside authorized channels. Persons found tampering with or abusing any aspect of this Sweepstakes, or whom Sponsor reasonably believes to be causing fraud or disruption will be disqualified. Sponsor reserves the right to cancel, suspend and/or modify the Sweepstakes, or any part of it, if any fraud, technical failure or any other factor beyond Sponsor's control impairs the integrity or proper functioning of the Sweepstakes, as determined by Sponsor in its sole discretion. By participating in this Sweepstakes, entrants hereby agree to release and hold Sponsor, Installer location, Sponsor and Installer location employees, officers, directors, subsidiaries and affiliates and any other entity involved in this Sweepstakes harmless from and against all losses, damages, liabilities, claims, actions, proceedings or judgments, including but not limited to, personal injury, death or damage to or loss of property, arising out of or relating to entrant's entry or participating in this Sweepstakes or use or misuse of any prizes awarded hereunder. The Official Rules shall be governed by the laws of the State of Texas, without giving effect to any choice of law or conflict of law rules, which could cause the application of the laws of any jurisdiction other than the State of Texas. Winners list: To receive a list of winners, send a self-addressed, stamped envelope before December 31, 2008 to: Q SEC Basketball Championship Game Sweepstakes Winner's List #800, P.O. Box 809004, Houston, TX 77280-9921. Sponsor: SOPUS Products, P.O. Box 4427, Houston, TX 77210-4427.

© 2008 SOPUS Products. All rights reserved. 5077853

CHAPTER 20

change some of its language, better defining terms like "finalist" and "tie breaker." It also began to disclose the odds of winning prizes. More recently the controversy resulting from the lawsuits filed against American Family Publishing for misleading consumers regarding their odds of winning large cash prizes in its annual magazine subscription solicitation sweepstakes has led to investigations and stricter regulation of sweepstakes in a number of states. For example, New York passed a law requiring the odds of winning a sweepstakes "must be conspicuously disclosed in the same type face, size and boldness and adjacent to the most prominent listing of the prizes on the front of the first page of the offer." The state law also prohibits statements that someone is a "winner" or that his or her name "has been selected" when no prize has been won. The law carries a fine of $1,000 per incident, which could be $1,000 per letter received by New York residents. Some of the most ambitious legal actions are taking place in individual states, where prosecutors are taking sweepstakes and contest companies to court for misleading and deceptive practices.[101]

**Premiums** Another sales promotion area subject to various regulations is the use of premiums. A common problem associated with premiums is misrepresentation of their value. Marketers that make a premium offer should list its value as the price at which the merchandise is usually sold on its own. Marketers must also be careful in making premium offers to special audiences such as children. While premium offers for children are legal, their use is controversial; many critics argue that they encourage children to request a product for the premium rather than for its value. The Children's Advertising Review Unit has voluntary guidelines concerning the use of premium offers. These guidelines note that children have difficulty distinguishing a product from a premium. If product advertising contains a premium message, care should be taken that the child's attention is focused primarily on the product. The premium message should be clearly secondary. Conditions of a premium offer should be stated simply and clearly. "Mandatory" statements and disclosures should be stated in terms that can be understood by the child audience.[102] However, a recent study of children's advertising commissioned by CARU found the single most prevalent violation involved devoting virtually an entire commercial message to information about a premium. CARU guidelines state that advertising targeted to children must emphasize the product rather than the premium offer.[103]

**Trade Allowances** Marketers using various types of trade allowances must be careful not to violate any stipulations of the Robinson-Patman Act, which prohibits price discrimination. Certain sections of the Robinson-Patman Act prohibit a manufacturer from granting wholesalers and retailers various types of promotional allowances and/or payments unless they are made available to all customers on proportionally equal terms.[104] Another form of trade promotion regulated by the Robinson-Patman Act is vertical cooperative advertising. The FTC monitors cooperative advertising programs to ensure that co-op funds are made available to retailers on a proportionally equal basis and that the payments are not used as a disguised form of price discrimination.

As noted in Chapter 16, another trade promotion area where the FTC is becoming involved is the use of slotting fees or allowances paid to retailers for agreeing to handle a new product. In 1999, the Senate Committee on Small Business charged retailers in the grocery, drugstore, and computer software industries with illegally using slotting fees to lock out competitors and prevent consumers from having their choice of the best products. Packaged-goods marketers and retailers have argued that examining slotting fees alone is unfair since they are just part of a wide variety of inducements marketers use to secure the best shelf space. The FTC is investigating the use of slotting fees as anticompetitive weapons that make it difficult for small-size companies to secure retail shelf space.[105] In 2000, the FTC launched its first direct attack on slotting fees when it accused McCormick & Co., the leading spice maker, of offering discriminatory discounts on its products to several grocery chains.

McCormick agreed to settle a complaint that the discounts were a way of paying some retailers disproportionately more in slotting fees than others. The FTC charged that the slotting fees were a way for McCormick to gain more shelf space at the expense of smaller rivals. The practice that was deemed illegal by the FTC is a standard way of doing business in the grocery trade as well as other industries, and some legal experts have argued that this case could impact the use of slotting fees in the future.[106]

**Direct Marketing** As we saw in Chapter 14, direct marketing is growing rapidly. Many consumers now purchase products directly from companies in response to TV and print advertising or direct selling. The Federal Trade Commission enforces laws related to direct marketing, including mail-order offers, the use of 900 telephone numbers, and direct-response TV advertising. The U.S. Postal Service enforces laws dealing with the use of the mail to deliver advertising and promotional messages or receive payments and orders for items advertised in print or broadcast media.

A number of laws govern the use of mail-order selling. The FTC and the Postal Service police direct-response advertising closely to ensure the ads are not deceptive or misleading and do not misrepresent the product or service being offered. Laws also forbid mailing unordered merchandise to consumers, and rules govern the use of "negative option" plans whereby a company proposes to send merchandise to consumers and expects payment unless the consumer sends a notice of rejection or cancellation.[107] FTC rules also encourage direct marketers to ship ordered merchandise promptly. Companies that cannot ship merchandise within the time period stated in the solicitation (or 30 days if no time is stated) must give buyers the option to cancel the order and receive a full refund.[108]

Another area of direct marketing facing increased regulation is telemarketing. With the passage of the Telephone Consumer Protection Act of 1991, marketers who use telephones to contact consumers must follow a complex set of rules developed by the Federal Communications Commission. These rules require telemarketers to maintain an in-house list of residential telephone subscribers who do not want to be called. Consumers who continue to receive unwanted calls can take the telemarketer to state court for damages of up to $500. The rules also ban telemarketing calls to homes before 8:00 a.m. and after 9:00 p.m., automatic dialer calls, and recorded messages to emergency phones, health care facilities, and numbers for which the call recipient may be charged. They also ban unsolicited junk fax ads and require that fax transmissions clearly indicate the sender's name and fax number.[109]

The Federal Trade Commission has also been actively involved with the regulation of advertising that encourages consumers to call telephone numbers with a 900 prefix, whereupon they are automatically billed for the call. While there are many legitimate uses for 900-number technology, it has also been heavily used for sleazy sex operations, contest scams, and other unscrupulous activities.[110] One area of particular concern to the FTC has been ads targeting children and encouraging them to call 900 numbers. In 1993, the FTC issued its 900-Number Rule for advertising directed at children. The rule restricts advertisers from targeting children under the age of 12 with ads containing 900 numbers unless they provide a bona fide educational service. The rule also requires that 900-number ads directed at those under the age of 18 must contain a "clear and conspicuous" disclosure statement that requires the caller to have parental/guardian permission to complete the call. The rule also obligates advertisers to disclose the cost of the call and give the caller the opportunity to hang up without incurring any costs.[111]

The FTC enacted the 900-Number Rule under the provision that it would be reviewed within four years to consider its costs and benefits.[112] This review was undertaken and the rule was retained and revised, although under a new name. The name was changed to the Pay-Per-Call Rule, and in 1998 the rule was revised to give the FTC the authority to broaden its scope and add new provisions. Among other things, the new provisions combat telephone bill cramming, which is the placing of unauthorized charges on consumers' phone bills.[113]

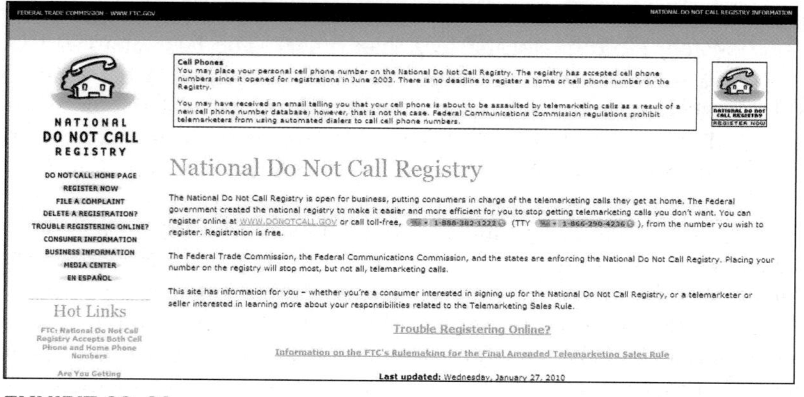

FEDERAL TRADE COMMISSION · WWW.FTC.GOV
NATIONAL DO NOT CALL REGISTRY INFORMATION
Cell Phones
You may place your personal cell phone number on the National Do Not Call Registry. The registry has accepted cell phone numbers since it opened for registrations in June 2003. There is no deadline to register a home or cell phone number on the Registry.
You may have received an email telling you that your cell phone is about to be assaulted by telemarketing calls as a result of a new cell phone number database; however, that is not the case. Federal Communications Commission regulations prohibit telemarketers from using automated dialers to call cell phone numbers.
NATIONAL DO NOT CALL REGISTRY
DO NOT CALL HOME PAGE
REGISTER NOW
FILE A COMPLAINT
DELETE A REGISTRATION?
TROUBLE REGISTERING ONLINE?
CONSUMER INFORMATION
BUSINESS INFORMATION
MEDIA CENTER
EN ESPAÑOL
National Do Not Call Registry
The National Do Not Call Registry is open for business, putting consumers in charge of the telemarketing calls they get at home. The Federal government created the national registry to make it easier and more efficient for you to stop getting telemarketing calls you don't want. You can register online at WWW.DONOTCALL.GOV or call toll-free, 1-888-382-1222 (TTY 1-866-290-4236), from the number you wish to register. Registration is free.
The Federal Trade Commission, the Federal Communications Commission, and the states are enforcing the National Do Not Call Registry. Placing your number on the registry will stop most, but not all, telemarketing calls.
This site has information for you – whether you're a consumer interested in signing up for the National Do Not Call Registry, or a telemarketer or seller interested in learning more about your responsibilities related to the Telemarketing Sales Rule.
Hot Links
FTC: National Do Not Call Registry Accepts Both Cell Phone and Home Phone Numbers
Are You Getting
Trouble Registering Online?
Information on the FTC's Rulemaking for the Final Amended Telemarketing Sales Rule
Last updated: Wednesday, January 27, 2010


**EXHIBIT 20–20**
The National Do Not Call Registry protects consumers from calls by telemarketers

In 2003, Congress approved a Federal Trade Commission proposal for the formation of a National Do Not Call Registry allowing consumers to opt out of most commercial telemarketing.[114] Consumers can place their home phone numbers, as well as personal cell phone numbers, on the National Do Not Call Registry (Exhibit 20–20). Commercial telemarketers must pay a fee to access the registry and generally are prohibited from calling the listed numbers. Telemarketers have three months to comply once a number goes on the list, and a consumer's registration lasts five years. Political and charitable solicitation calls are not affected by the regulation, and telemarketers can call consumers with whom they have an established relationship. Marketers face penalties of $11,000 per incident for calling someone on the list. The Federal Trade Commission, the Federal Communications Commission, and individual states are enforcing the National Do Not Call Registry, which contained nearly 192 million phone numbers as of the end of 2009.

The National Do Not Call Registry affects the direct-marketing industry as it greatly reduces the number of households that telemarketers can call. As might be expected, the direct-marketing industry is strongly opposed to the registry, arguing that it violates their First Amendment rights and, further, that such a program is not needed. The Direct Marketing Association (DMA), which is the primary trade group for the direct-marketing industry, has argued that consumers already have a number of do-not-call options. They can ask to be excluded from an individual company's telemarketing list at the same time they can sign up with state lists or pay $5 to sign up on the voluntary national list maintained by the Direct Marketing Association. The DMA argues that the national registry will impose more bureaucracy on the direct-marketing industry and that the same goal can be achieved by the industry itself with better education and enforcement.

The Direct Marketers Association and the American Teleservices Association, which represent callers, challenged the legality of the registry on the grounds that it took away their rights to First Amendment–protected speech and that it was excessive and poorly drafted, with competitive marketers forced to abide by different rules. However, in February 2004, the U.S. Court of Appeals upheld the registry's validity, ruling that it is a valid commercial speech regulation. The appellate court said that because the registry doesn't affect political or charitable calls and because there is a danger of abusive telemarketing and invasion of consumer privacy from telemarketers, the government has a right to regulate its use. The two major trade associations have been reviewing the ruling and may yet appeal the case to the U.S. Supreme Court.[115]

Direct marketers have been adjusting their telemarketing strategies to deal with the restrictions imposed by the Do Not Call Registry. They are focusing more attention on generating leads through promotional efforts such as sweepstakes and direct-mail programs, prompting consumers to opt in and agree to receive calls from direct marketers.[116] Some industry experts as well as academics argue that the Do Not Call Registry may actually improve telemarketing practice and the general efficiency of the business because direct marketers must focus more attention on consumers who are receptive to receiving their telemarketing calls.[117] However, there is also concern that some companies are finding loopholes in the rules governing the Do Not Call Registry. For example, one technique that has emerged is the use of a marketing tool called a "lead card," which invites a recipient to mail a reply card for free information. However, the cards often fail to warn consumers that by sending a reply, they are giving up their right to avoid telephone solicitations from the sender—even if their phone numbers are listed on the Do Not Call list.[118]

Another tactic being used by some companies to avoid the Do Not Call Registry is to use sweepstakes entry forms as a way to harvest consumers' telephone numbers for telemarketing purposes. When done correctly, this may be a legitimate direct-marketing tool; however the FTC has cracked down on some companies that have violated Do Not Call regulations by calling phone numbers obtained via sweepstakes entry forms. Companies that want to collect telemarketing leads through a sweepstakes entry form must clearly and conspicuously disclose that their entry-form information will be used for telemarketing purposes and include a statement to be signed by consumers expressing agreement under the Do Not Call provision.[119]

The direct-marketing industry is also scrutinized by various self-regulatory groups, such as the Direct Marketing Association and the Direct Selling Association, that have specific guidelines and standards member firms are expected to adhere to and abide by. However, as discussed in IMC Perspective 20–3, some critics argue that these self-regulatory groups are not doing enough to keep consumers from receiving unwanted marketing messages, such as calls from telemarketers and direct-mail offers and solicitations. Thus, it is likely that they will continue to call for more government intervention and regulations.

## Marketing on the Internet

The rapid growth of the Internet as a marketing tool has created a new area of concern for regulators. The same consumer protection laws that apply to commercial activities in other media apply to online as well. The Federal Trade Commission Act, which prohibits "unfair or deceptive acts or practices," encompasses Internet advertising, marketing, and sales. Claims made in Internet ads or on websites must be substantiated, especially when they concern health, safety, or performance, and disclosures are required to prevent ads from being misleading and to ensure that consumers receive material information about the terms of a transaction. There are several areas of particular concern with regard to marketing on the Internet. These include privacy issues, online marketing to children, and the use of spam or unsolicited e-mails for commercial purposes.

The major privacy issue regarding the Internet that has emerged involves undisclosed profiling whereby Web marketers can profile a user on the basis of name, address, demographics, and online/offline purchasing data. Marketers have suggested that profiling offers them an opportunity to target specific niches and reach consumers with custom-tailored messages. However, the FTC has stated that Internet sites that claim they don't collect information but permit advertisers to surreptitiously profile viewer sites are violating consumer protection laws and are open to a charge of deception.[120] In 1999, DoubleClick, the company that is the leader in selling and managing online advertising as well as tracking Web users and now owned by Google, set off a controversy by connecting consumers' names, addresses, and other personal information with information it collects about where consumers go on the Internet. The controversy resulted in the company being investigated by the Federal Trade Commission and lawsuits being filed in some states.[121]

In response to the profiling controversy, companies that collect Internet usage data and information joined together under the banner of the Network Advertising Initiative (NAI) to develop a self-regulatory code.[122] The NAI has developed a set of privacy principles in conjunction with the Federal Trade Commission that provides consumers with explanations of Internet advertising practices and how the practices affect both consumers and the Internet itself. The NAI has also launched a website (www.networkadvertising.org) that provides consumers with information about online advertising practices and gives them the choice to opt out of targeted advertising delivered by NAI member companies (Exhibit 20–21). Another industry-driven initiative is the Platform for Privacy Preferences (P3P), which is a new technology

## IMC Perspective 20–3 > > >

### Direct Mail Comes under Attack

If you are a typical consumer, every time you go to the mailbox it is likely you will find numerous forms of direct mail including advertising circulars, preapproved credit-card applications, postcards, brochures, and catalogs—most of which are unsolicited. It is estimated the typical American household receives about 40 pounds of direct mail each year, despite the fact that much of it goes unopened and only about 2 percent is responded to. Every time you order something over the phone, Internet, or through the mail; subscribe to a magazine; enter a contest or sweepstakes; apply for a credit card or become a member of a group; your name and address is captured and put on a list. While marketers maintain these lists to keep track of their own customers and prospects, they often sell your name and address to another company that wants to reach you—which means you are likely to receive even more unsolicited "junk mail." However, direct mail is the latest traditional marketing tactic being challenged by consumers as they continue to take control over the marketing messages they receive.

Consumer advocacy groups won a major battle against direct marketers at the beginning of the new millennium by lobbying the federal government to create a National Do Not Call Registry to protect consumers from unwanted calls from telemarketers. Since its creation in 2003, Americans have registered 192 million phone numbers on the list, thus shielding themselves from most phone solicitations. Now it appears that consumers are tired of seeing their mailboxes bulging with catalogs as well as other forms of direct mail and want to take action. A number of states are considering legislation to create state-run Do Not Mail list registries that would allow consumers to keep unsolicited direct mail out of their mailboxes.

Thus far, none of the proposed Do Not Mail bills have made it beyond the hearing stage and it may take years before any type of legislation is enacted. However, a number of advocacy groups are not waiting for the government to address the problem and are taking steps to help consumers reduce the amount of unwanted direct mail they are receiving. Sever of these initiatives have been started by groups that are interested in reducing the environmental impact created by the direct-mail industry. Environmental groups claim American households receive 19 billion catalogs of various shapes and sizes each year and estimate that it takes 53 million trees to produce the 3.6 million tons of paper in those catalogs. When the energy required to make the paper and ship the catalog is added in, the groups argue that the process adds 5.2 million tons of carbon dioxide emissions to the atmosphere yearly, equal to the emissions of 2 million cars.

One initiative having a significant impact in terms of reducing the amount of direct mail is Catalog Choice, which was launched in October 2007 by the Ecology Center and is endorsed by the National wildlife Federation and the Natural Resources Defense Council. The mission of Catalog Choice is to reduce the number of repeat and unsolicited catalog mailings, and promote the adoption of sustainable industry best practices. The non-profit group offers an online service that allows people to compile a list of catalogs they do not want to receive. The service then contacts the retailers with a request to take the person's name off their mailing list or makes a downloadable file available that merchants can then feed into their direct-mail database. By 2010, more than 1.2 million people had registered with Catalog Choice and opted out of receiving more than 10 million catalogs. Several hundred merchants have agreed to abide by the site's opt out requests including major companies such as Lands' End, Office Depot, and REI.

The direct-mail industry has noticed the growing popularity of Catalog Choice and other sites that allow

---

that lets consumers screen websites via operating system software. This technology gives consumers greater control over the collection of information by allowing them to specify their privacy preferences electronically and screen out websites that do not meet these preferences. The privacy debate is likely to escalate, and it is expected that legislation will be introduced to force companies to seek consumers' approval before sharing personal information captured from their websites.

While these proposals are aimed at protecting the privacy rights of adults, one of the biggest concerns is over restricting marketers whose activities or websites are targeted at children. These concerns over online marketing to children led to the passage of the **Children's Online Privacy Protection Act** of 1998 **(COPPA)**, which the FTC began enforcing in April 2000.[123] This act places tight restrictions on collecting information from children via the Internet and requires that websites directed at children and young teens have a privacy policy posted on their home page and areas of the site where information is collected. The law also requires websites consumers to have their names removed from mailing lists. The industry's primary trade organization, the Direct Marketing Association, is responding to the attacks on the use of direct mail by its members. A spokesperson for the DMA notes that 1.7 million trees are planted every day in the United States to replace trees cut down for paper and wood products. He also argues that Americans can save 3.3 billion miles of driving if everyone eliminated two trips to a mall per year and shopped by catalog instead. This would prevent a billion tons of carbon emissions from entering the atmosphere and save 290 million gallons of gasoline.

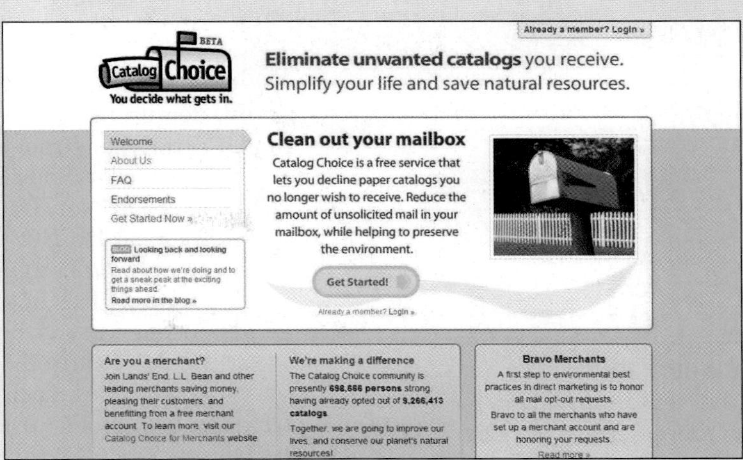


The DMA also notes that it offers a Mail Preference Service (MPS) that, for $1, will put a person's name on a Do Not Mail list for three years. The service is supported by the United States Postal Service and has more than 4.5 million subscribers. The online service prevents companies from adding the person's name to their lists, but it does not stop catalogs and other mail solicitations the person is already receiving. The DMA has also questioned the integrity of the data gathered by third parties such as Catalog Choice and expressed concerns over how marketers can verify the legitimacy of the names and what might be done with them. However, a project manager for Catalog choice notes that this concern is unfounded since the organization uses the same e-mail verification system as the Federal Trade Commission's National Do Not Call Registry.

In 2006 the DMA, along with a number of other mailing community associations and companies, formed a direct-mail advocacy group. Mail Moves America, that is working with state business groups and communicating with legislators about the importance of direct mail for consumers, businesses, and the economy and is lobbying against the creation of a Do Not Mail list. The group notes that direct mail is a large and diverse part of the economy that creates nearly $700 billion of economic activity annually and would be adversely affected if a Do Not Mail bill is passed in any state. MMA also argues that legislation is not needed to provide consumers with options for removing their names from marketing lists, as they already have a variety of options for doing so, ranging from contacting an individual company, to registering their name with the DMA's Mail Preference Service.

Proponents of groups such as Catalog choice acknowledge many people want to get catalogs and other forms of direct mail. However, they argue that American consumers do not want most of the tons of junk mail they receive every year as it comes from companies they have never bought anything from and/or have no interest in buying from. Of course, it will ultimately be consumers who decide if they want to put a no-trespassing sign on their mailboxes and block another point of unwanted media entry into their lives.

Sources: Carol Krol, "Swelling Ranks of 'Do Not Mail' Lists Prompts DMA Response," *BtoB*, February 11, 2008, pp. 26–27; Steven Swanson, "Up to Here in Catalogs? There Is a Solution—Online," *Tribune Business News*, November 4, 2007; Ira Tenowitz and Ken Wheaton, "Do Not Market," *Advertising Age*, March 12, 2007, p. 1, 44; Jenny Rough, "Saving Trees and Your Sanity by Managing Junk Mail," *The Examiner, February* 14, 2010, p. 31.



aimed at children under age 13 to obtain parental permission to collect most types of personal information and to monitor chat rooms and bulletin boards to make sure children do not disclose personal information there. When the law was enacted in 2000, it was left to the FTC to determine how to obtain the required permission, and the FTC temporarily allowed websites to let parents simply return an e-mail to approve certain information. Since then no other solution to the permission issue has surfaced, and the FTC is proposing to make the solution permanent.[124] However, the issue continues to be an area of concern as many marketers close their websites to children under the age of 13, but children under this age will often lie about their ages to gain access to the sites. The prevalence of social media is adding to the problem as many young people want access to fan clubs, blogs, and other websites that allow online interaction.[125]

Concerns over consumer privacy have become a major issue among the government and various regulatory agencies such as the FTC.[126] The federal government

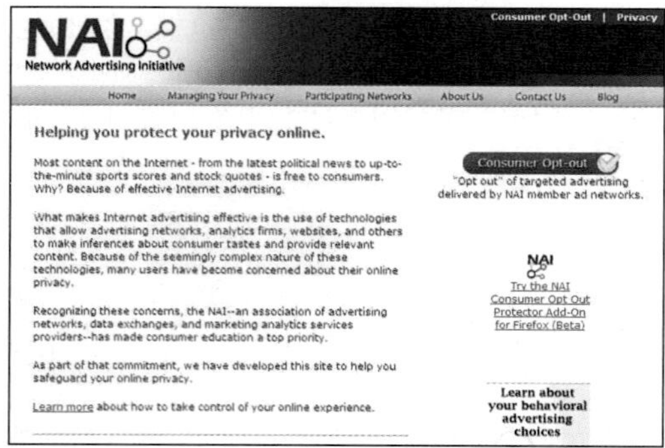


**EXHIBIT 20–21**

The Network Advertising Initiative website provides consumers with information about online advertising practices

is currently considering a number of privacy-related laws, many of which would have an impact on marketing and advertising over the Internet. In late 2007 the FTC requested that marketers voluntarily step up the disclosures they make about data they collect and seek permission from consumers before tracking their Internet surfing behavior.[127] Some privacy advocates have also proposed the creation of a Do Not Track list that would be an Internet version of the National Do Not Call Registry. Under the proposal, advertisers and others who use cookie-based tracking technology would be required to submit lists of their servers to a central regulatory body. Users who do not want to be tracked would download a browser plug-in that would identify those server logs and disallow cookies from them.[128] Some states, such as California, have passed their own online privacy protection acts to protect the privacy of consumers. Consumer groups continue to urge the Federal Trade Commission to step up its actions on privacy protection, including the implementation of a do-not-track registry.[129]

Concerns over privacy have increased with the explosion in the popularity of social media sites such as Facebook, MySpace, Twitter, and others. In June 2010 the FTC settled a complaint against Twitter charging it deceived consumers and put their privacy at risk by failing to safeguard their personal information, marking the agency's first such case against a social networking service. The FTC ordered Twitter to establish a security program subject to government monitoring for the next 10 years. Twitter agreed to the terms in exchange for the FTC not pursuing a civil lawsuit against the company.[130] In May 2010 Facebook announced significant changes to its privacy policies giving users more control over their content, reducing the amount of their information that is available to others, and also making it easier to control whether applications and websites can access their information.[131]

The FTC has also taken action to address the issue of endorsements made through social media sites and blogs and ensure that the same rules apply in this context as they do in traditional advertising and infomercials. In 2009 the agency passed a new set of guidelines for online endorsements that require online endorsers and bloggers to disclose any "material connection" to an advertiser. Under the new guidelines, paid endorsers who post on social media sites such as Facebook or post product reviews on marketer sites such as Amazon can be held liable if they do not identify themselves as such.[132]

Another Internet-related area receiving regulatory attention is **spamming**, which is the sending of unsolicited multiple commercial electronic messages. Spamming has become a major problem; studies show that the typical Internet user spends the equivalent of 10 working days a year dealing with incoming spam.[133] Spam also costs businesses billions of dollars every year in terms of lost worker productivity and network maintenance. Moreover, most of these messages are fraudulent or deceptive in one or more respects.

A number of states have enacted antispamming legislation, and a comprehensive federal antispam bill, the Controlling the Assault of Non-Solicited Pornography and Marketing Act of 2003 (CAN-SPAM Act), went into effect on January 1, 2004. The act's general requirements for commercial e-mails include the following requirements:

- A prohibition against false or misleading transmission information.
- Conspicuous notice of the right to opt-out and a functioning Internet-based mechanism that a recipient may use to request to not receive future commercial e-mail messages from the sender.
- Clear and conspicuous identification that the message is an advertisement.
- A valid physical postal address for the sender.

Violations of the CAN-SPAM law include both civil and criminal penalties including a fine of $250 (calculated on a per e-mail basis) up to a maximum of $2 million.

While the CAN-SPAM Act carries severe penalties for violators, thus far it has done little to stop unsolicited e-mail messages. Spammers have been able to stay one step ahead of law enforcement officials by operating offshore and by constantly moving the Internet hosting source.[134]

## Summary

Regulation and control of advertising stem from internal regulation or self-regulation as well as from external control by federal, state, and local regulatory agencies. For many years the advertising industry has promoted the use of voluntary self-regulation to regulate advertising and limit government interference with and control over advertising. Self-regulation of advertising emanates from all segments of the advertising industry, including advertisers and their agencies, business and advertising associations, and the media.

The NAD/NARB, the primary self-regulatory mechanism for national advertising, has been very effective in achieving its goal of voluntary regulation of advertising. Various media also have their own advertising guidelines. The major television networks maintain the most stringent review process and restrictions.

Traditionally, the federal government has been the most important source of external regulation, with the Federal Trade Commission serving as the major watchdog of advertising in the United States. The FTC protects both consumers and businesses from unfair and deceptive practices and anticompetitive behavior. The FTC became very active in the regulation of advertising during the 1970s when it began several new programs and policies, including affirmative disclosure, advertising substantiation, and corrective advertising. Since 1980 the FTC has not been allowed to implement industrywide rules that would define unfair advertising practices. However, the advertising industry and Congress are nearing agreement on a definition of unfairness, and this power may be restored to the FTC.

In 1983, the FTC developed a new working definition of deceptive advertising. Recently the FTC has become more active in policing false and deceptive advertising. Under the Lanham Act, many companies are taking the initiative by suing competitors that make false claims. Many states, as well as the National Association of Attorneys General, are also active in exercising their jurisdiction over false and misleading advertising.

A number of laws also govern the use of other promotional mix elements, such as sales promotion and direct marketing. The Federal Trade Commission regulates many areas of sales promotion as well as direct marketing. Various consumer-oriented sales promotion tools such as contests, games, sweepstakes, and premiums are subject to regulation. Recently many states have become very active in the regulation of contests and sweepstakes. Trade promotion practices, such as the use of promotional allowances and vertical cooperative advertising, are regulated by the Federal Trade Commission under the Robinson-Patman Act. The FTC also enforces laws in a variety of areas that relate to direct marketing and mail-order selling as well as the Internet, while the FCC has rules governing telemarketing companies.

The rapid growth of the Internet as a marketing tool has created a new area of concern for regulators. The same consumer protection laws that apply to commercial activities in other media apply online as well. Major areas of concern with regard to advertising and marketing on the Internet are privacy, online marketing to children, and spamming or the sending of unsolicited commercial e-mail messages. Concerns over online marketing to children have led to the passage of the Children's Online Privacy Protection Act, which the FTC began enforcing in early 2000. The federal government passed the CAN-SPAM Act, which went into effect on January 1, 2004. This legislation sets stringent requirements for commercial e-mail messages. The Federal Trade Commission has become increasingly concerned over privacy issues related to the increasing popularity of social media and is requiring various sites to protect the privacy of users. The FTC also has issued new guidelines covering online endorsements that require endorsers and bloggers to disclose any material connection to an advertiser.

## Key Terms

**self-regulation** p. 684
**Better Business Bureau (BBB)** p. 686
**Council of Better Business Bureaus** p. 688
**National Advertising Review Board (NARB)** p. 688
**National Advertising Review Council (NARC)** p. 688
**Federal Trade Commission (FTC)** p. 694
**commercial speech** p. 694
**Central Hudson Test** p. 695
**Federal Trade Commission Act** p. 695
**Wheeler-Lea Amendment** p. 696
**trade regulation rules (TRRs)** p. 697
**unfairness** p. 697
**puffery** p. 698
**deception** p. 699
**affirmative disclosure** p. 700
**advertising substantiation** p. 702
**consent order** p. 704
**cease-and-desist order** p. 705
**corrective advertising** p. 705
**Lanham Act** p. 712
**National Association of Attorneys General (NAAG)** p. 716
**Children's Online Privacy Protection Act (COPPA)** p. 722
**spamming** p. 724

## Discussion Questions

1. The chapter opener discusses how the Federal Communications Commission is considering more stringent regulation of product placements in television shows. Evaluate the arguments for and against this policy by the FCC. (LO3)
2. Discuss the need for regulation of advertising and other IMC tools. Do you advocate more or less regulation of advertising and other forms of promotion by governmental agencies such as the Federal Trade Commission and the Food and Drug Administration? (LO1, LO3)
3. Discuss the role the National Advertising Review Council plays in the self-regulation of advertising. Do you view self-regulation as an effective way of protecting consumers from misleading or deceptive advertising? (LO2)
4. IMC Perspective 20–1 discusses the debate over hard liquor companies advertising on television. Do you agree with the DISCUS argument that hard liquor companies are at a competitive disadvantage against beer and wine marketers if they cannot advertise on television? Evaluate the decisions by NASCAR to drop its long-standing bans on sponsorships by hard liquor companies as well as decisions by professional sports leagues such as the NBA to allow spirits advertising within camera view. (LO2)
5. What are the three essential elements required to prove deception under the definition used by the Federal Trade Commission? (LO3)
6. Find several examples of advertising claims or slogans that are based on puffery rather than substantiated claims. Discuss whether you feel these advertising claims can be defended on the basis of puffery. (LO3)
7. Ethical Perspective 20–1 discusses the issue of direct-to-consumer advertising of prescription drugs. Evaluate the new authority the Food and Drug Administration has been given to regulate DTC drug advertising. Do you think the FDA needs more authority to regulate advertising in this area? (LO3)
8. Discuss the Lanham Act and how it affects advertising. What elements are necessary to win a false or deceptive advertising claim under the Lanham Act? (LO3)
9. Discuss how the Do Not Call Registry developed by the Federal Trade Commission is impacting the direct marketing industry. What arguments might direct marketers make in their efforts to have this program rescinded? (LO4)
10. IMC Perspective 20–3 discusses how a number of states are considering legislation that would create Do Not Mail list registries, which would allow consumers to keep unsolicited direct mail out of their mailboxes. Discuss the arguments for and against legislation that would prohibit marketers from sending direct mail to consumers. (LO4)
11. Do you agree with the new guidelines from the Federal Trade Commission requiring bloggers and endorsers to disclose any material connection to an advertiser? How might this impact companies that use social media in their IMC programs? (LO4)

## AdForum Exercise: "Evaluating Advertising Claims from a Legal Perspective"

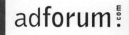

(See Advertising and Promotion Playlist, Chapter 20)

### PART 1

The playlist for this chapter consists of four commercials that use comparative claims including ads for Pizza Hut, Ford, Coors Light, and Miller Lite. Watch the four commercials and answer the following questions:

1 Evaluate the comparative message used by each advertiser with respect to the type of claim being used. What documentation might be required by the company to substantiate the claim, and how it might impact consumer decision making for this brand?

2 Do you think any of the comparative claims made in the commercials for these four brands could result in a lawsuit from a competitor under the Lanham Act? Why or why not?

### PART 2

The playlist includes three commercials for Bayer aspirin. Watch each commercial and answer the following questions:

1 Evaluate the performance claims that are made for Bayer in each commercial and discuss the type of research data that is required to support these claims.

2 Discuss how puffery is used in each commercial and whether it is appropriate or might mislead a consumer who sees these advertisements for Bayer.

Access to the chapter playlist is available through McGraw-Hill connect™ MARKETING, www.mcgrawhillconnect.com

## LEARNING OBJECTIVES

LO1 To consider various perspectives concerning the ethical aspects of advertising and promotion.

LO2 To consider various perspectives concerning the social aspects of advertising and promotion.

LO3 To evaluate the social criticisms of advertising.

LO4 To examine the economic role of advertising and its effects on consumer choice, competition, and product costs and prices.

# 21 Evaluating the Social, Ethical, and Economic Aspects of Advertising and Promotion

## "DERRIERE-ENHANCING" SHOES IGNITE A FOOTWEAR WAR

When critics cite what they think is wrong with advertising, some of the points they make are that it creates materialism, gets people to buy things they don't need, and/or is often untruthful. Sometimes they get examples that provide them with the perfect ammunition to support their case. "Derriere-Enhancing shoes" may just be one of those.

Depending on who you talk to, "toning shoes," the latest craze to hit the market, are either a revolutionary new sneaker, or an overhyped gimmick. The new entry into the $17 billion athletic footwear market is supposed to tone muscles, promote healthy weight loss, and improve the posture of wearers. The shoes can also tighten and shape one's lower body muscles, and—according to at least one advertising claim—make the gym obsolete. While different brands offer their own designs, the oddly shaped shoes generally have some sort of pod and curves in the bottom that create an instability. Adjusting to the shoes leads to an 11 to 41 percent increase in muscle activity to adapt to the imbalance.

Reebok and Skechers have been the leaders in this new shoe market segment, and as a result have achieved significant brand share gains since their introduction. Skechers tripled its share from 5.5 to 16.5 percent, while Reebok went from 3.3 to 8 percent. Herbert Hainer, CEO of Reebok's parent adidas says, "The explosion of growth in this space in such a short period of time eclipses nearly everything I have witnessed in the industry over the last 25 years." Reebok expects to sell over 5 million pairs of the shoes in the United States alone this year. The shoes sell for $100 to $250, and 90 percent of the market to date consists of women who spend a lot of their time on their feet, including nurses, servers, teachers, and hair stylists. Both Skechers and Reebok are already introducing sleeker-looking models for training, running, and hiking, and a company called Fit-Flop is rolling out toning sandals and clogs.

If there is anything that surpasses the growth of toning shoes, it may be the marketing activity behind it. The Skechers website claims their brand will help you "Shape Up While You Walk," by toning your butt, legs, and abdominal muscles; burn calories; fight cellulite; improve your posture and circulation; and reduce joint stress. It is Skechers who claims that their brand will eliminate the need for the gym. Reebok claims that their shoes generate 28 percent more muscle activity in the gluteus maximus and 11 percent more in users hamstrings and calves. According to Reebok, "EasyTone shoes will help tone your butt and legs with every step." In addition to the website and advertising information, Skechers provides an instructional booklet and DVD with each pair of shoes sold. They have also hired Pro Football Hall of Famer and Super Bowl star, Joe Montana as their spokesperson. Competitor MBT has successfully placed their "Anti-Shoe" in the movie *The Joneses,* with sexy mom Demi Moore wearing them while creating envy among her housewife friends. Other brands like Avia and New Balance have also introduced their own lines of toners.

But wait. Something (or someone) is missing. Where is Nike? The leader in the athletic shoe and apparel market doesn't offer a toning shoe, and has no plans to do so in the future. Nike spokesman Derek Kent is even a bit scornful noting, "Unlike today's toning products, we won't ask the consumer to compromise on stability, flexibility, or any other key performance characteristics as they train." Nike says the shoes just don't fit with their performance-obsessed brand image. They are also skeptical of many of the claims being made out there.

And Nike is not alone. Many in the medical profession are not happy about the claims either. Dr. Paul Langer, a podiatrist at Minnesota Orthopaedic Specialists, says "I would never propose that these shoes would replace a conventional fitness routine." Pete McCall, an exercise physiologist with the American Council on Exercise agrees, noting that claims that the shoes make the gym obsolete are "definitely far-fetched." McCall says the shoes do cause the muscles to work harder, but "Whether the shoes or soles create a mechanical advantage, that's the marketing hype." Other experts claim that the shoes don't make good on their marketing claims and could be dangerous and lead to injuries. Perhaps the strongest words come from Barbara de Lateur, distinguished service professor of physical medicine and rehabilitation at Johns Hopkins University's School of Medicine, who says, "Claims that toning shoes can significantly contribute to a person's fitness are utter nonsense." Alison Drury, a buyer who broke her right ankle the first time she wore the shoes would agree, as would a number of other doctors who say the shoe claims are mostly hype.

So as advocates and opponents of the shoes line up on both sides of the battle, at this point we are all left to wonder who is right. The only thing we know for certain is that the critics of advertising have more ammunition to stake the claim that they are.

Sources: Michael McCarthy, "A Revolutionary Sneaker, or Overhyped Gimmick?" *USA Today,* June 30, 2010, pp.1, 2A; Jeremy Mullman, "Nike Women's Biz Gets Pounded as Toning Footwear Kicks Butt," *www.adage.com*, June 2, 2010, Madison Park, "Shoes' Toning Claims Draw Experts' Doubts," *www.cnn.com*, August 14, 2009.

> If I were to name the deadliest subversive force within capitalism, the single greatest source of its waning morality—I would without hesitation name advertising. How else should one identify a force that debases language, drains thought, and undoes dignity?[1]

The primary focus of this text has been on the role of advertising and promotion as marketing activities used to convey information to, and influence the behavior of, consumers. We have been concerned with examining the advertising and promotion function in the context of a business and marketing environment and from a perspective that assumes these activities are appropriate. However, as you can see in this quote from economist Robert Heilbroner, not everyone shares this viewpoint. Advertising and promotion are the most visible of all business activities and are prone to scrutiny by those who are concerned about the methods marketers use to sell their products and services.

Proponents of advertising argue that it is the lifeblood of business—it provides consumers with information about products and services and encourages them to improve their standard of living. They say advertising produces jobs and helps new firms enter the marketplace. Companies employ people who make the products and provide the services that advertising sells. Free market economic systems are based on competition, which revolves around information, and nothing delivers information better and at less cost than advertising.

Not everyone, however, is sold on the value of advertising. Critics argue that most advertising is more propaganda than information; it creates needs and faults consumers never knew they had. Ads suggest that children need cell phones, that our bodies should be leaner, our faces younger, and our houses cleaner. They point to the sultry, scantily clad bodies used in ads to sell everything from perfume to beer to power tools and argue that advertising promotes materialism, insecurity, and greed.

One of the reasons advertising and other forms of integrated marketing communications are becoming increasingly criticized is because they are so prevalent. Not only are there more ads than ever, but there are more places where these ads appear. Advertising professor David Helm notes: "Between the stickered bananas and the ads over the urinals and the ones on the floor of the supermarkets, we're exposed to 3,000 commercial messages a day. That's one every 15 seconds, assuming we sleep for 8 hours, and I'd guess right now there's someone figuring out how to get us while our eyes are closed."[2]

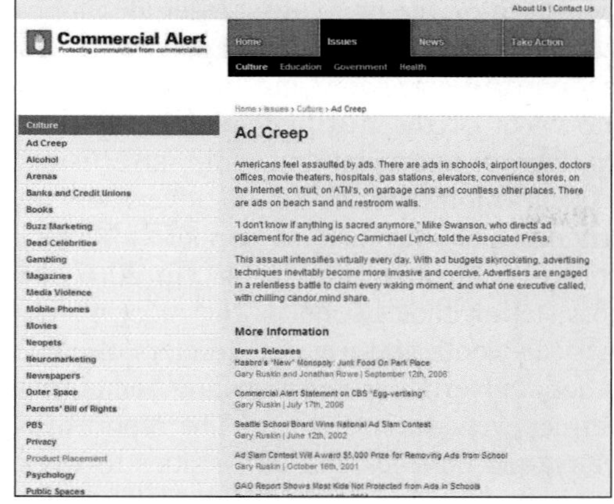


**EXHIBIT 21–1**

Commercial Alert is concerned with the excessive amount of marketing messages consumers receive

As marketers intensify their efforts to get the attention of consumers, resentment against their integrated marketing communications efforts is likely to increase. Concern is growing that there may be a consumer backlash as integrated marketing efforts move to new heights and marketers become increasingly aggressive. Diane Cook, a former advertising executive who founded the AdCenter at Virginia Commonwealth, says: "The growing practice of placing ads and logos everywhere seems a desperate last attempt to make branding work according to the old rules. As telemarketing, advertising, promotions and the rest continue at a frenzied pace, the value of the messages decrease. The system seems headed for a large implosion."[3] Groups such as Commercial Alert are concerned about intrusion of advertising and other types of marketing messages into all aspects of consumers' lives (Exhibit 21–1). Consumer advocacy groups also argue that many companies are obliterating the line between marketing communications and entertainment by creating and delivering ads and other messages that appear to be part of popular culture but have a persuasive intent.[4]

Advertising is a very powerful force, and this text would not be complete without a look at the criticisms regarding its social and economic effects as well as some defenses against these charges. We consider the various criticisms of advertising and promotion from an ethical and social perspective and then appraise the economic effects of advertising.

# ADVERTISING AND PROMOTION ETHICS

In the previous chapter, we examined the regulatory environment in which advertising and promotion operate. While many laws and regulations determine what advertisers can and cannot do, not every issue is covered by a rule. Marketers must often make decisions regarding appropriate and responsible actions on the basis of ethical considerations rather than on what is legal or within industry guidelines. **Ethics** are moral principles and values that govern the actions and decisions of an individual or group.[5]

A particular action may be within the law and still not be ethical. A good example of this involves target marketing. No laws restrict tobacco companies from targeting advertising and promotion for new brands to African-Americans. However, given the high levels of lung cancer and smoking-related illnesses among the black population, many people would consider this an unethical business practice.

Throughout this text we have presented a number of ethical perspectives to show how various aspects of advertising and promotion often involve ethical considerations. Ethical issues must be considered in integrated marketing communications decisions. And advertising and promotion are areas where a lapse in ethical standards or judgment can result in actions that are highly visible and often very damaging to a company.

The role of advertising in society is controversial and has sometimes resulted in attempts to restrict or ban advertising and other forms of promotion to certain groups or for certain products. College students are one such group. The level of alcohol consumption and binge drinking by college students has become a serious problem. Alcohol-related problems have proliferated on college campuses in recent years and have resulted in many negative consequences, including death.[6] Several studies have shown that there has been a significant increase in binge drinking among college students and have advocated a ban on alcohol-related advertising and promotion.[7] Many colleges and universities have imposed restrictions on the marketing of alcoholic beverages to their students. These restrictions include banning sponsorships or support of athletic, musical, cultural, or social events by alcoholic-beverage companies and limiting college newspaper advertising to price and product information ads.

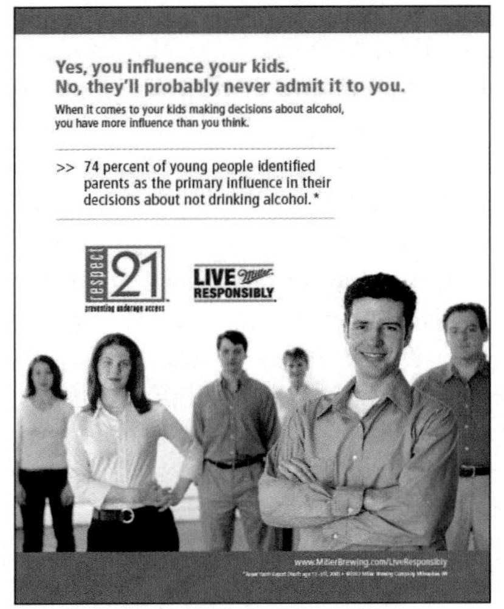


**EXHIBIT 21–2**
This ad is part of a campaign by the Miller Brewing Company to encourage parents to talk to their teenagers about the risks of underage drinking

A great deal of attention is being focused on the issue of whether alcoholic-beverage companies target not only college students but underage drinkers as well. As noted in Chapter 20, the actions of beer, wine, and liquor marketers are being closely scrutinized in the wake of the distilled-spirits industry's decisions to reverse its long-standing ban on television and radio advertising. Many people believe the industry's push to join beer and wine advertisers on television is testing the public's attitudes and may lead to support for more government restrictions and regulations on alcohol advertising.[8] In 2007 the U.S. Surgeon General issued a report stating that alcohol is the most widely used substance of abuse among America's youth and urged marketers of alcoholic beverages to cut back on outdoor advertising and end any remaining college newspaper advertising as well as event sponsorships.[9] The report also called on the media, alcohol marketers, and colleges and universities to work to address the problem by not glamorizing underage alcohol use in movies and TV shows and minimizing youth exposure to alcohol advertising through the media as well as on the Internet.

Companies marketing alcoholic beverages such as beer and liquor recognize the need to reduce alcohol abuse and drunken driving, particularly among young people. Many of these companies have developed programs and ads designed to address this problem. For example, the Miller Brewing Company has been running a campaign that uses ads such as the one shown in Exhibit 21–2 to encourage parents to talk to their kids about the risks of underage drinking. The company has also teamed up with parents, teachers, community organizations, law enforcement officials, and others to ensure progress in the fight against alcohol abuse. The Beer Institute and Distilled Spirits Council of the U.S. marketing codes also ban college newspaper ads, prohibit rite-of-passage ad appeals, and limit some outdoor ads. Both groups also require that ads be placed in media where 70 percent of the audience is 21 or older.

Criticism often focuses on the actions of specific advertisers. Groups like the National Organization for Women and Women Against Pornography have been critical of advertisers for promoting sexual permissiveness and objectifying women in their ads. For example, NOW expressed outrage over a print ad used by fashion brand Dolce & Gabbana that it felt suggested gang rape. The ad features a woman fully clothed in a tight dress and spiked heels, lying on her back, hips raised while a bare-chested man holds her down as four other men look on.[10] The creative director at the agency that handles the advertising for Dolce & Gabbana defended the ad by noting that the company is communicating its Sicilian heritage and "it is coming from a very Latin, passionate, emotional and sexually charged space."[11] NOW protests ads such as this on the Love Your Body: Offensive Ads section of its website as shown in Exhibit 21–3.

**EXHIBIT 21–3**
The National Organization for Women calls attention to ads that are offensive to women on its website

Another company that has received a great deal of criticism for its advertising over the years is Benetton. For nearly two decades the Italian-based clothing company ran numerous "shock" ads containing controversial images such as a black woman nursing a white baby, an AIDS patient and his family moments before his death, and a priest kissing a nun (see Exhibit 20–5). Oliviero Toscani, Benetton's former creative director who developed most of these ads, noted that the controversial images were designed to raise public awareness of social issues and position the company as a cutting-edge, socially conscious marketer.[12] The company's most controversial ads, at least in the United States, were those used in its "Death Row" campaign that ran in 2000. The campaign, aimed at drawing attention to the use of capital punishment in the United States, featured ads showing piercing portraits of death-row inmates (Exhibit 21–4).

The campaign created a storm of controversy; the state of Missouri sued Toscani and Benetton for misrepresenting themselves while interviewing four death-row inmates featured in the campaign. Protests from the families of

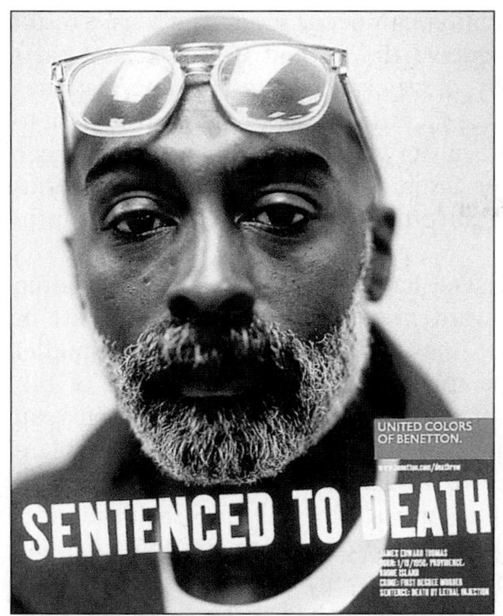


**EXHIBIT 21–4**
Benetton's "Death Row" ads created a major controversy

the inmates' victims and threatened boycotts from enraged consumers resulted in Sears dropping the Benetton line. A year later the lawsuit was settled when Benetton agreed to write letters of apology to the four Missouri families whose relatives were murdered by the inmates featured in the ads and to make a donation to the Missouri Crime Victims Compensation Fund.[13] Since 2000, Benetton has toned down its advertising and now alternates between conventional product campaigns and ads focusing on socially relevant issues such as volunteerism and famine. In 2008 the company launched a new global campaign called "Africa Works" that was designed to put the spotlight on entrepreneurial Africa and the microcredit program spearheaded by Grammy Award winning singer Youssou N'Dour.[14] Exhibit 21–5 shows one of the ads from the campaign.

As you read this chapter, remember that the various perspectives presented reflect judgments of people with different backgrounds, values, and interests. You may see nothing wrong with the ads for cigarettes or beer or sexually suggestive ads. Others, however, may oppose these actions on moral and ethical grounds. While we attempt to present the arguments on both sides of these controversial issues, you will have to draw your own conclusions as to who is right or wrong.

# SOCIAL AND ETHICAL CRITICISMS OF ADVERTISING

Much of the controversy over advertising stems from the ways many companies use it as a selling tool and from its impact on society's tastes, values, and lifestyles. Specific techniques used by advertisers are criticized as deceptive or untruthful, offensive or in bad taste, and exploitative of certain groups, such as children. We discuss each of these criticisms, along with advertisers' responses. We then turn our attention to criticisms concerning the influence of advertising on values and lifestyles, as well as charges that it perpetuates stereotyping and that advertisers exert control over the media.

## Advertising as Untruthful or Deceptive

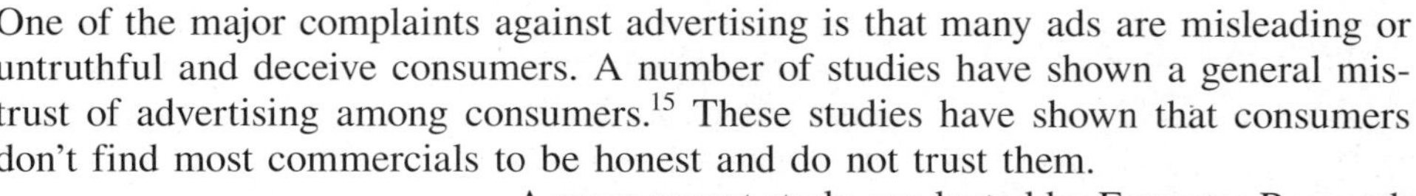

One of the major complaints against advertising is that many ads are misleading or untruthful and deceive consumers. A number of studies have shown a general mistrust of advertising among consumers.[15] These studies have shown that consumers don't find most commercials to be honest and do not trust them.

**EXHIBIT 21–5**
Benetton's advertising continues to focus on socially relevant issues

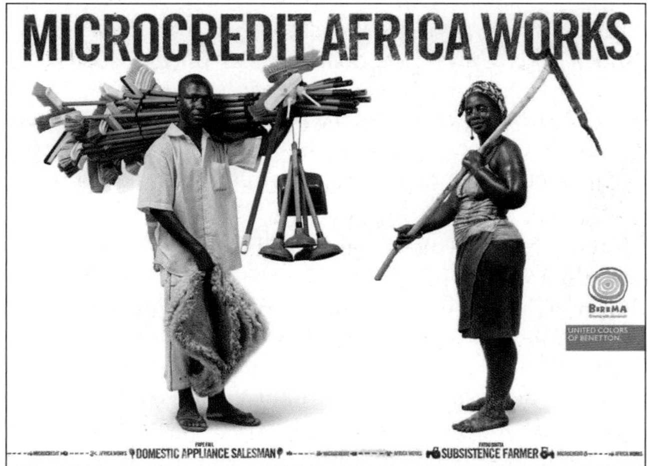


A more recent study conducted by Forrester Research found that consumers mistrust ads for most types of products and rely on word of mouth from friends and family as the most trusted source of information. Brand websites were rated the second most trusted source of information with 8 percent of consumers reporting that they completely trust brand websites versus only 1 to 2 percent for most other media. The study found that consumers ignore most ads because the number and intrusiveness of them is too high and their relevance is too low.[16]

Attempts by industry and government to regulate and control deceptive advertising were discussed in Chapter 20. We noted that advertisers should have a reasonable basis for making a claim about product performance and may be required to provide evidence to support their

CHAPTER 21

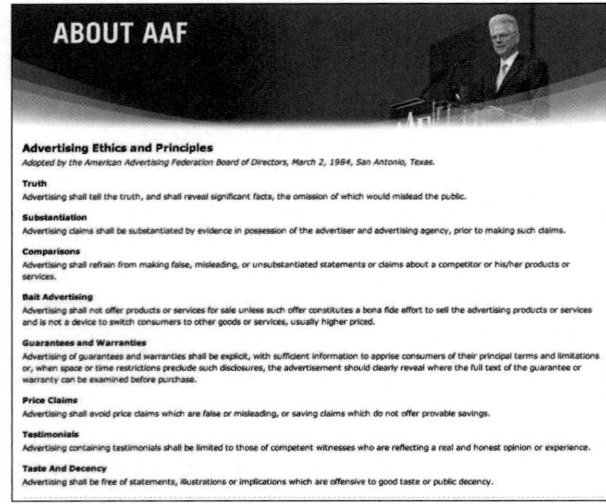

ABOUT AAF

**Advertising Ethics and Principles**

*Adopted by the American Advertising Federation Board of Directors, March 2, 1984, San Antonio, Texas.*

**Truth**

Advertising shall tell the truth, and shall reveal significant facts, the omission of which would mislead the public.

**Substantiation**

Advertising claims shall be substantiated by evidence in possession of the advertiser and advertising agency, prior to making such claims.

**Comparisons**

Advertising shall refrain from making false, misleading, or unsubstantiated statements or claims about a competitor or his/her products or services.

**Bait Advertising**

Advertising shall not offer products or services for sale unless such offer constitutes a bona fide effort to sell the advertising products or services and is not a device to switch consumers to other goods or services, usually higher priced.

**Guarantees and Warranties**

Advertising of guarantees and warranties shall be explicit, with sufficient information to apprise consumers of their principal terms and limitations or, when space or time restrictions preclude such disclosures, the advertisement should clearly reveal where the full text of the guarantee or warranty can be examined before purchase.

**Price Claims**

Advertising shall avoid price claims which are false or misleading, or saving claims which do not offer provable savings.

**Testimonials**

Advertising containing testimonials shall be limited to those of competent witnesses who are reflecting a real and honest opinion or experience.

**Taste And Decency**

Advertising shall be free of statements, illustrations or implications which are offensive to good taste or public decency.

**EXHIBIT 21–6**

Advertising principles of the American Advertising Federation

claims. However, deception can occur more subtly as a result of how consumers perceive the ad and its impact on their beliefs.[17] The difficulty of determining just what constitutes deception, along with the fact that advertisers have the right to use puffery and make subjective claims about their products, tends to complicate the issue. But a concern of many critics is the extent to which advertisers are *deliberately* untruthful or misleading.

Sometimes advertisers have made false or misleading claims or failed to award prizes promoted in a contest or sweepstakes. However, these cases usually involve smaller companies and only a tiny portion of the hundreds of billions of dollars spent on advertising and promotion each year. Most advertisers do not design their messages with the intention to mislead or deceive consumers or run sweepstakes with no intention of awarding prizes. Not only are such practices unethical, but the culprits would damage their reputation and risk prosecution by regulatory groups or government agencies. National advertisers invest large sums of money to develop loyalty to, and enhance the image of, their brands. These companies are not likely to risk hard-won consumer trust and confidence by intentionally deceiving consumers.

The problem of untruthful or fraudulent advertising and promotion exists more at the local level and in specific areas such as mail order, telemarketing, and other forms of direct marketing. Yet there have been many cases where large companies were accused of misleading consumers with their ads or promotions. Some companies test the limits of industry and government rules and regulations to make claims in an attempt to give their brands an advantage in highly competitive markets.

While many critics of advertising would probably agree that most advertisers are not out to deceive consumers deliberately, they are still concerned that consumers may not be receiving enough information to make an informed choice. They say advertisers usually present only information that is favorable to their position and do not always tell consumers the whole truth about a product or service.

Many believe advertising should be primarily informative in nature and should not be permitted to use puffery or embellished messages. Others argue that advertisers have the right to present the most favorable case for their products and services and should not be restricted to just objective, verifiable information.[18] They note that consumers can protect themselves from being persuaded against their will and that the various industry and government regulations suffice to keep advertisers from misleading consumers. Exhibit 21–6 shows the advertising ethics and principles of the American Advertising Federation, which many advertisers use as a guideline in preparing and evaluating their ads.

## Advertising as Offensive or in Bad Taste

Another common criticism of advertising is that ads are offensive, tasteless, irritating, boring, obnoxious, and so on. A number of studies have found that consumers feel most advertising insults their intelligence and that many ads are in poor taste.[19]

**Sources of Distaste** Consumers can be offended or irritated by advertising in a number of ways. Some object when certain products or services such as contraceptives or personal hygiene products are advertised at all. Most media did not accept ads for condoms until the AIDS crisis forced them to reconsider their restrictions. The major TV networks gave their affiliates permission to accept condom advertising in 1987, but the first condom ad did not appear on network TV until 1991.

In 1994, the U.S. Department of Health's Centers for Disease Control and Prevention (CDC) began a new HIV prevention campaign that includes radio and TV commercials urging sexually active people to use latex condoms. The commercials

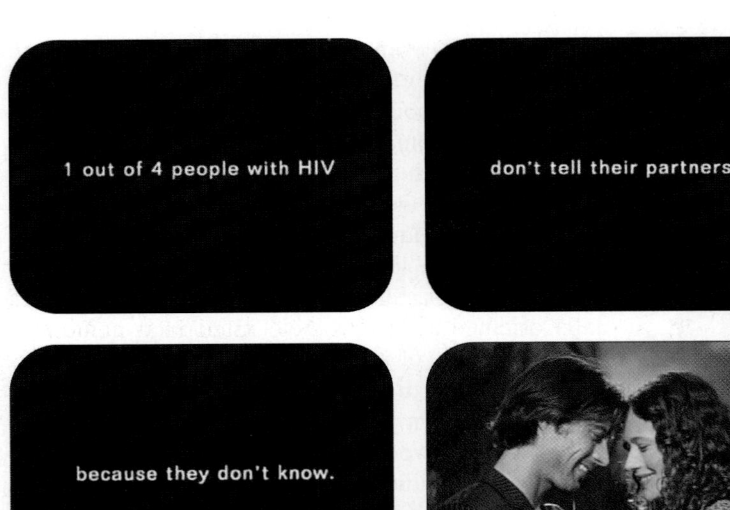

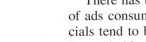

**EXHIBIT 21–7**
Many of the broadcast networks now accept ads for condoms during prime time that promote health-related uses

prompted strong protests from conservative and religious groups, which argued that the government should stress abstinence in preventing the spread of AIDS among young people. NBC and ABC agreed to broadcast all the commercials, while CBS said it would air certain spots.[20]

Advertising for condoms has now been appearing on TV for almost 20 years, but only in late-night time slots or on cable networks. However, in 2005, the broadcast networks agreed to accept commercials for condoms during prime time by agreeing to run heath-oriented ads for the Trojan brand.[21] The tone of the Trojan advertising was informational and provided facts and figures designed to raise viewers' consciousness and awareness about the potential consequences of unprotected sex among those who are sexually active (Exhibit 21–7). In 2007 both CBS and Fox rejected a commercial for Trojan condoms because of concerns about the creative content of the ad. Fox indicated that it rejected the ad because contraceptive advertising must stress health-related uses rather than the prevention of pregnancy.[22]

There has been found to be a strong product class effect with respect to the types of ads consumers perceived as distasteful or irritating. The most irritating commercials tend to be for feminine hygiene products; ads for women's undergarments and hemorrhoid products were close behind. Another study found that consumers are more likely to dislike ads for products they do not use and for brands they would not buy.[23] Ads for personal products have become more common on television and in print, and the public is more accepting of them. However, advertisers must still be careful of how these products are presented and the language and terminology used. There are still many rules, regulations, and taboos advertisers must deal with to have their TV commercials approved by the networks.[24]

Another way advertising can offend consumers is by the type of appeal or the manner of presentation. For example, many people object to appeals that exploit consumer anxieties. Fear appeal ads, especially for products such as deodorants, mouthwash, and dandruff shampoos, are often criticized for attempting to create anxiety and using a fear of social rejection to sell these products. Some ads for home computers were also criticized for attempting to make parents think that if their young children couldn't use a computer, they would fail in school.

**EXHIBIT 21–8**
This Airwalk ad was criticized for being suggestive and symbolizing sexual submission

**Sexual Appeals** The advertising appeals that have received the most criticism for being in poor taste are those using sexual appeals such as suggestiveness and/or nudity. These techniques are often used to gain consumers' attention and may not even be appropriate to the product being advertised. Even if the sexual appeal relates to the product, people may be offended by it.

A common criticism of sexual appeals is that they can demean women (or men) by depicting them as sex objects (such as the Dolce & Gabbana ad discussed earlier). Ads for cosmetics and lingerie are among the most criticized for their portrayal of women as sex objects and for being implicitly suggestive. For example, some women's groups criticized the Airwalk ad shown in Exhibit 21–8, arguing that it showed a submissive and

**EXHIBIT 21–9**
Ads are often criticized for being sexually suggestive

sexually available woman. A critic argued that the ad contained a number of symbolic cues that were sexually suggestive and combined to reinforce an image of the woman's sexual submission to the man.[25]

Critics have been particularly concerned about the use of sexual appeals in the advertising of products such as cigarettes, liquor, and beer. Sexual appeals and risqué images have long been used in advertising for alcoholic beverages. Skyy Spirits has used provocative, sexually oriented ads to promote its popular namesake vodka brand. Some of its ads, which use stylized images placing the brand's distinctive blue bottle in suggestive situations, have been criticized by conservative groups (Exhibit 21–9). However, a company spokesperson has responded to the criticisms by noting, "Style is a maker of interpretation and like with all art we appreciate all points of view."[26]

Attitudes toward the use of sex in advertising is a polarizing issue as opinions regarding its use vary depending upon the individual's values and religious orientation, as well as by age, education, and gender. A recent study found major differences between men and women in their attitudes toward sex in advertising.[27] As you can see in Figure 21–1, while almost half of men said they liked sexual ads, only 8 percent of women felt the same way. Most men (63 percent) indicated that sexual ads have high stopping power and get their attention, but fewer women thought the same (28 percent). Also, most women (58 percent) said there is too much sex in advertising versus only 29 percent of the men. Women were also much more likely than men to say that sexual ads promote a deterioration of moral and social values and that they are demeaning of the models used in them.

**Shock Advertising** With the increasing clutter in the advertising environment, advertisers continue to use sexual appeals and other techniques that offend some people but catch the attention of consumers and may even generate publicity for their companies. In recent years, there has been an increase in what is often referred to as **shock advertising**, in which marketers use nudity, sexual suggestiveness, or other startling images to get consumers' attention. As discussed earlier in the chapter, shock advertising is nothing new; companies such as Benetton and Calvin Klein have been using this tactic in their ads since the 1980s. However, a number of other marketers have been criticized for using shock techniques in their ads as well as in other promotional materials.[28] For example, clothing retailer Abercrombie & Fitch has been criticized numerous times for the content and images used in its quarterly catalogs, which have included sex tips from porn star Jenna Jameson, a spoof interview with a shopping mall Santa portrayed as a pedophile, and nude photos. A few years ago the retailer promoted its Christmas catalog with an advertisement across the plastic covering stating, "Two-hundred and eighty pages of sex and Xmas fun" (Exhibit 21–10).[29] Officials in four states threatened or pursued legal action against the company, which responded by implementing a policy of carding would-be buyers of the catalog to ensure they are at least 18 years old. Abercrombie & Fitch has recently changed its business strategy and moved away from the sultry and sexy advertising, a marketing tool used to create a chic and cool image for the brand but often intimidated the teens who shop in its stores. While the Abercrombie & Fitch brand still has a sexy ethos, the company has eliminated the racy catalogs and ads that offended many parents.[30]

**FIGURE 21–1**

Attitudes toward Sex in Advertising: Men versus Women

Source: From Media Analyzer.

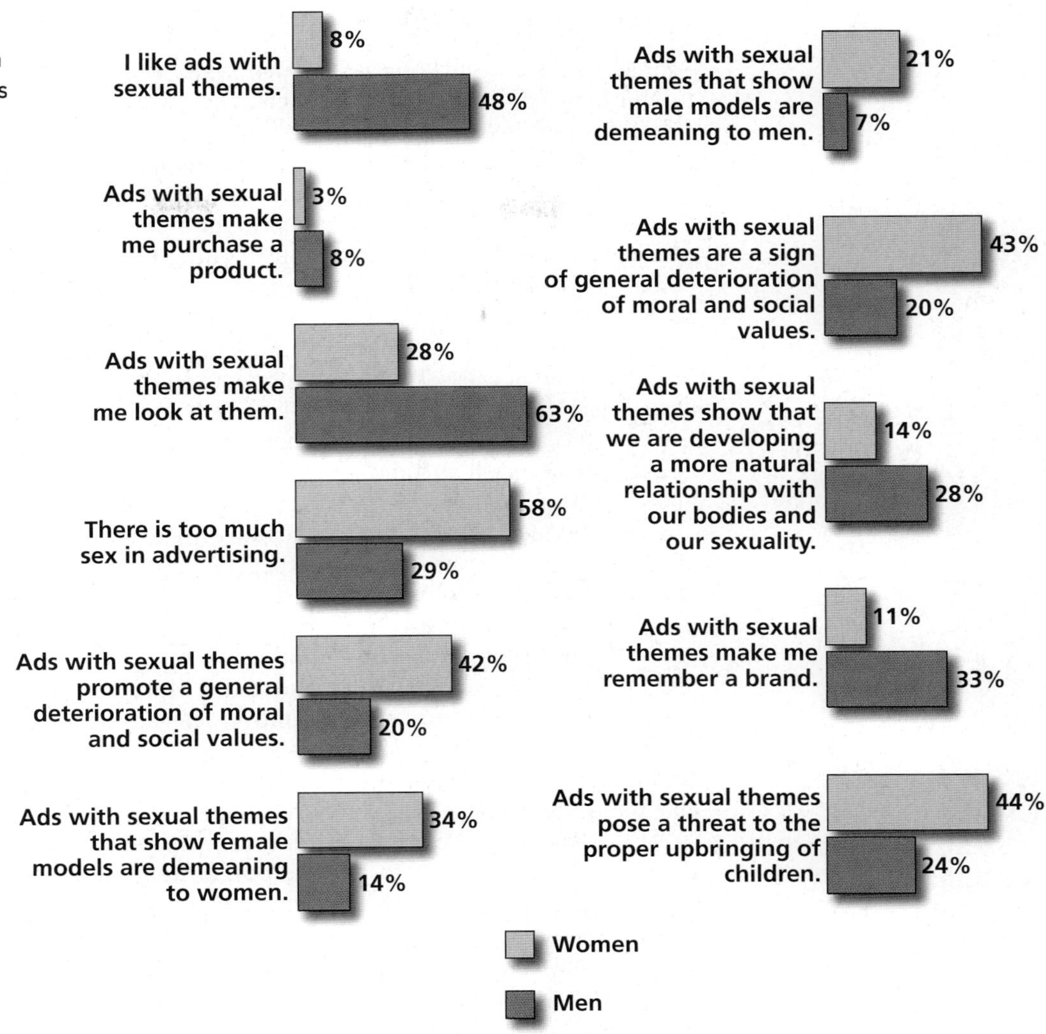
I like ads with sexual themes.
8%
48%
Ads with sexual themes make me purchase a product.
3%
8%
Ads with sexual themes make me look at them.
28%
63%
There is too much sex in advertising.
58%
29%
Ads with sexual themes promote a general deterioration of moral and social values.
42%
20%
Ads with sexual themes that show female models are demeaning to women.
34%
14%
Ads with sexual themes that show male models are demeaning to men.
21%
7%
Ads with sexual themes are a sign of general deterioration of moral and social values.
43%
20%
Ads with sexual themes show that we are developing a more natural relationship with our bodies and our sexuality.
14%
28%
Ads with sexual themes make me remember a brand.
11%
33%
Ads with sexual themes pose a threat to the proper upbringing of children.
44%
24%
Women
Men

**EXHIBIT 21–10**

Abercrombie & Fitch's catalogs were criticized over the use of sex and nudity

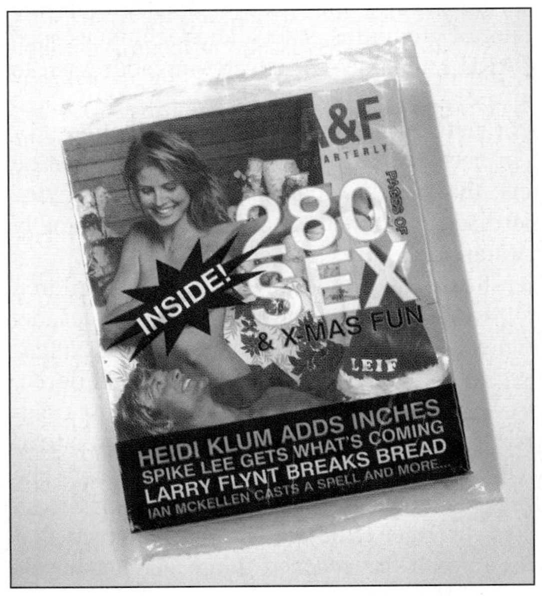
A&F
280
SEX
& X-MAS FUN
INSIDE!
LEIF
HEIDI KLUM ADDS INCHES
SPIKE LEE GETS WHAT'S COMING
LARRY FLYNT BREAKS BREAD
IAN MCKELLEN CASTS A SPELL AND MORE...

Many advertising experts argue that what underlies the increase in the use of shock advertising is the pressure on marketers and their agencies to do whatever it takes to get their ads noticed. However, critics argue that the more advertisers use the tactic, the more shocking the ads have to be to get attention. How far advertisers can go with these appeals will probably depend on the public's reaction. When consumers think the advertisers have gone too far, they are likely to pressure the advertisers to change their ads and the media to stop accepting them.

While marketers and ad agencies often acknowledge that their ads push the limits with regard to taste, they also complain about a double standard that exists for advertising versus editorial television program content. The creative director for Abercrombie & Fitch's agency argues that there is a double standard and hypocrisy in the shock advertising debate: "When advertising uses sex, everybody complains—when editorial does it, nobody cares."[31] Advertisers and agency creative directors argue that even the most suggestive commercials are bland compared with the content of many television programs.

## Advertising and Children

Another controversial topic advertisers must deal with is the issue of advertising to children. TV is a vehicle through which advertisers can reach children easily. Estimates are that children spend an average of 5 hours a day using media including television, video games, and Internet websites and they watch nearly 22 hours of TV a week.[32] A 2007 study conducted by the Kaiser Family Foundation found that children ages 2 to 7 are exposed to an average of 13,904 TV ads a year for all products, while the comparable numbers are 30,155 ads for 8- to 12-year-olds, and 28,655 for teens between the ages of 13 and 17.[33] Approximately 80 percent of all advertising targeted to children falls within four product categories: toys, cereals, candy, and fast-food restaurants.[34] Advertisers spend billions of dollars a year to reach children because TV is an important source of information for them and influences their direct purchases as well as their influence over other family members. Concern has also been expressed about marketers' use of other promotional vehicles and techniques such as radio ads, point-of-purchase displays, premiums in packages, and the use of commercial characters as the basis for TV shows.

Critics argue that children, particularly young ones, are especially vulnerable to advertising because they lack the experience and knowledge to understand and critically evaluate the purpose of persuasive advertising appeals. Research has shown that preschool children cannot differentiate between commercials and programs, do not perceive the selling intent of commercials, and cannot distinguish between reality and fantasy.[35] The study also concluded that children must understand how advertising works in order to use their cognitive defenses against it effectively. Because of children's limited ability to interpret the selling intent of a message or identify a commercial, critics charge that advertising to them is inherently unfair and deceptive and should be banned or severely restricted.

At the other extreme are those who argue that advertising is a part of life and children must learn to deal with it in the **consumer socialization process** of acquiring the skills needed to function in the marketplace. They say existing restrictions are adequate for controlling children's advertising and that marketplace knowledge plays an important role in adolescents' skepticism toward advertising. They contend that greater knowledge of the marketplace appears to give teens a basis by which to evaluate ads and enables them to recognize the persuasion techniques used by advertisers.[36]

Children are also protected from the potential influences of commercials by network censors and industry self-regulatory groups such as the Council of Better Business Bureaus' Children's Advertising Review Unit (CARU). CARU has strict self-regulatory guidelines regarding the type of appeals, product presentation and claims, disclosures and disclaimers, the use of premiums, safety, and techniques such as special effects and animation. The CARU guidelines for advertising addressed to children under 12 are presented in Figure 21–2.

As we saw in Chapter 20, the major networks also have strict guidelines for ads targeted to children. For example, in network TV ads, only 10 seconds can be devoted to animation and special effects; the final 5 seconds are reserved for displaying all the toys shown in the ad and disclosing whether they are sold separately and whether accessories such as batteries are included.[37]

Concerns over advertising and other forms of promotion directed at children diminished somewhat during the late '90s and the early part of the new decade. However, the issue has once again begun receiving a considerable amount of attention as various groups are calling for restrictions on advertising targeted to children. In 2004, the American Psychological Association (APA), the nation's largest organization of psychologists, issued a report criticizing the increasing commercialization of childhood and calling for new curbs on marketing aimed at children.[38] The APA report faulted marketers for taking advantage of an ever-fragmenting media landscape of cable channels and websites to target children. The report noted that marketing activities focused on America's youth has reached unprecedented levels and called for restrictions on advertising in TV programming that appeals primarily

**FIGURE 21–2**

Children's Advertising Review Unit Principles

Source: From Children's Advertising Review Unit.

Six basic principles underlie these guidelines for advertising directed to children:

1. Advertisers should always take into account the level of knowledge, sophistication, and maturity of the audience to which their message is primarily directed. Younger children have a limited capability for evaluating the credibility of information they receive. They also may lack the ability to understand the nature of the personal information they disclose on the Internet. Advertisers, therefore, have a special responsibility to protect children from their own susceptibilities.
2. Realizing that children are imaginative and that make-believe play constitutes an important part of the growing-up process, advertisers should exercise care not to exploit unfairly the imaginative quality of children. Unreasonable expectations of product quality or performance should not be stimulated either directly or indirectly by advertising.
3. Products and content inappropriate for children should not be advertised or promoted directly to children.
4. Recognizing that advertising may play an important part in educating the child, advertisers should communicate information in a truthful and accurate manner and in language understandable to young children with full recognition that the child may learn practices from advertising which can affect his or her health and well-being.
5. Advertisers are urged to capitalize on the potential of advertising to influence behavior by developing advertising that, wherever possible, addresses itself to positive and beneficial social behavior, such as friendship, kindness, honesty, justice, generosity, and respect for others.
6. Care should be taken to incorporate minority and other groups in advertisements in order to present positive and pro-social roles and role models wherever possible. Social stereotyping and appeals to prejudice should be avoided.

These Principles embody the philosophy upon which CARU's mandate is based. The Principles, and not the Guidelines themselves, determine the scope of our review. The Guidelines effectively anticipate and address many of the areas requiring scrutiny in child-directed advertising, but they are illustrative rather than limiting. Where no specific Guideline addresses the issues of concern to CARU, it is these broader Principles that CARU applies in evaluating advertising directed to the uniquely impressionable and vulnerable child audience.

to children under the age of eight and a total ban on advertising in programs aimed at very young children in this group. The report also found that the Internet is a particularly effective, and thus potentially harmful, means of sending advertising messages to children as websites often blur, or even ignore the boundaries between commercial and noncommercial content. Marketing and advertising trade groups have been critical of the report and continue to defend their right to advertise on the basis that parents of younger children, rather than the children themselves, make purchase decisions.[39]

In addition to concerns over the increasing amount of advertising targeted to children, there are a number of other issues that consumer groups and regulatory agencies have raised with respect to young people, These include an increase in the number of ads encouraging children to call 900 numbers, the increase in the number of toy-based programs on TV, and general concerns over the content of children's programming, particularly with regard to violence. The marketing of violent entertainment to minors and the advertising practices and rating systems of the film, music, and electronic game industries are also being monitored very carefully. The issue of what young consumers are watching, listening to, and playing and how much violence that entertainment contains became an area of great concern following a flurry of shootings at schools.

As discussed in the previous chapter, there is also growing concern over how marketers are using the Internet to communicate with and sell to children. Another issue that has received a great deal of attention recently is the role of advertising

# Ethical Perspective 21–1 > > >

## Is It Time to Tax Soft Drinks?—Food Marketers Come under Attack

Obesity is, by far, the leading health problem in the United States. A report in the *Journal of the American Medical Association* found that 31 percent of Americans are obese, up from 23 percent a decade ago, and nearly two-thirds are overweight. America's battle with the bulge begins at a very young age with 13 percent of children age 6 to 11 and 14 percent of kids 14 to 19 overweight, triple the number 20 years ago. Much more than vanity is at stake here as obesity increases the risk of heart disease, cancer, diabetes, and high blood pressure among other ailments. It also accounts for nearly 300,000 deaths a year, ranking second only to cancer.

Health experts point to a number of factors that are responsible for the alarming rise in obesity including an environment that encourages overeating, the eating of unhealthy foods, and a lack of physical activity. Another factor that is increasingly being cited as a major reason for the obesity epidemic is the marketing and advertising practices of the food industry. High-calorie, artery-clogging foods are cheap and plentiful and serving sizes have ballooned in recent years. Fast-food restaurants have been promoting their value menus and offering "supersizes" of menu items such as hamburgers, french fries, and soda. Convenience stores such as 7-Eleven and ampm offer 32-ounce sizes of Big Gulps and Slurpees as well as sodas and other beverages that are high in sugar. Also coming under attack are the high levels of advertising and promotion used to promote food products. The food industry spends an estimated $42 billion a year on advertising and promotion.

While the experts acknowledge that the advertising and promotion done by the food industry are not solely to blame for the fattening of America, they do argue that the marketing tactics used by the industry encourage people to eat more than they should. Consumer and health groups are particularly concerned about the rising obesity problem in children and argue that it is directly related to the amount of advertising they are exposed to every day. According to a report by the Kaiser Family Foundation, children ages 2 to 7 see an average of more than 4,400 food ads per year, those 8 to 12 see more than 7,600,l and teenagers see more than 6,000 food ads over the course of a year. The report notes that children ages 8 to 12 may be the group most affected by the advertising since they watch so much television.

Food companies are recognizing they are under attack and are taking steps to address the concerns by developing more healthy products and changing their advertising and promotion practices. In 2005 Kraft Foods pledged to stop advertising popular snack food items such as Kool-Aid, Chips Ahoy! and Oreo cookies, and Oscar Mayer Lunchables to children under 12. A year earlier Kraft stopped in-school marketing and began its Health & Wellness Advisory Council to revamp its marketing guidelines. Coca-Cola has also recently updated its guidelines to eliminate advertising and sampling to kids under 12 and the company, along with PepsiCo and other beverage marketers, announced a set of voluntary restrictions to limit sales of their drinks in schools.

One of the most significant developments occurred in 2007 when a group of 11 major companies that account for two-thirds of all food advertising and beverage advertising targeted at children—including Coca-Cola, PepsiCo, McDonald's, General Mills, Hershey, and Kellogg—pledged to stop advertising products that do not meet certain nutritional standards to children under the age of 12. Several additional companies including Burger King and ConAgra have also joined the program. The pledges are part of the Children's Food and Beverage Advertising initiative, a voluntary self-regulation program developed by the Council of Better Business Bureaus and the National Advertising Review Council. The initiative originally called for advertisers to devote at least half their advertising directed to children to promote

---

and other marketing practices in contributing to the obesity problem among children as well as adults (see Ethical Perspective 21–1). One area of concern has been the practice of school districts awarding "pouring contracts" to soft-drink companies such as Coca-Cola and PepsiCo to make money for their schools (Exhibit 21–11). These deals have been criticized because of concerns over the nutritional value of soft drinks and snack foods and their contribution to the obesity problem. Many states now require these companies to offer alternative beverages such as fruit juices, juice drinks, and bottled water, as well as healthier snack products, to alleviate this concern.[40]

Advertising to children will remain a controversial topic. Some groups feel that the government is responsible for protecting children from the potentially harmful effects of advertising and other forms of promotion, while others argue that parents are ultimately responsible for doing so. A survey of 12,500 young people up to 18 years of age conducted for *Advertising Age* regarding their attitudes toward advertising and various media found that two-thirds of those surveyed believed the main healthier dietary choices and/or messages that encourage good nutrition or healthy lifestyles. The restrictions on advertising are intended to answer critics' charges that the industry is not doing enough to combat rising childhood obesity.

While a number of food marketers have been taking steps to appease consumers and advocacy groups, many feel that the industry has not gone far enough. In 2009 a proposal to impose a federal tax on soft drinks was defeated in Washington D.C. If imposed, at a penny an ounce on soda and other sugary drinks, the tax supposedly would earn $150 billion over the next decade. The battle has now turned to the states, where the California legislature is vowing to pass a state tax on soft drinks , estimating that obesity costs the state $41 billion/year in medical expenses and reduced productivity. The Center for Science in the Public Interest released a set of far-reaching food marketing guidelines which specify acceptable nutritional content, portion size, packing design, and logo use. The guidelines also seek to control advertising and other forms of marketing communication in TV shows, video games, websites, and books, as well as the use of premiums, in-store displays, and other sale promotion tools. The American Academy of Pediatrics also issued a policy statement demanding that television ads on children's shows be halved and junk food ads on children's shows be banned during shows viewed predominately by those under age 8. Consumer groups continue to monitor the advertising and promotional tactics used by food marketers. For example, in early 2008 McDonald's agreed to terminate its sponsorship of report card covers in Seminole County, Florida, public schools. The jacket covers offered a free Happy Meal to any student with all As and Bs, two or fewer absences, or good behavior. The school system had approached McDonald's for the sponsorship, which had been previously sponsored by Pizza Hut, but parents still protested the promotion.

The food industry, as well as the advertising and marketing community, are concerned about the attacks by the CSPI and other consumer advocacy groups on the food industry. Industry executives do not think they should take the blame for the fattening of America and point to the need for more personal and parental responsibility,

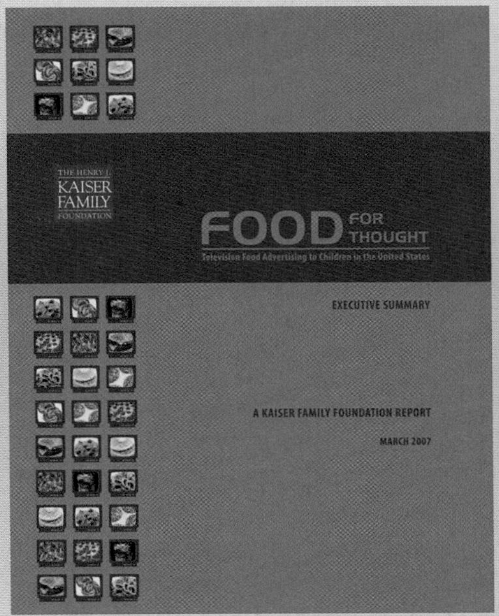


nutritional education, dietary balance and moderation, and physical activity. They are also concerned that the ultimate goal of government regulators and consumer health advocates is putting an end to the marketing and even sale of foods they deem unhealthy. However, many of the food and beverage companies are in the process of developing new products and modifying existing brands to keep them compliant with the new guidelines they have set and make a healthy choice the easy choice for consumers.

Sources: Kim Geiger and Tom Hamburger, "Soft Drink Tax Battle Shifts to States," www.latimes.com, February 21, 2010; Elizabeth Lopatto, "Soft-Drink Tax Could Pare Waistlines Cover Health Care Costs," www.bloomberg.com, September 16, 2009; Emily Bryson York, "McDonald's Discontinues Report-Card Sponsorship," *Advertising Age*, January 21, 2008, p. 37; Ira Teinowitz, "More Major Food Marketers Establish Kids-Advertising Limits," adage.com, July 18, 2007; Brooks Barnes, "Limiting Ads of Junk Food for Children," *The New York Times*, July 18, 2007, p. C1; "Food for Thought: Television Food Advertising to Children in the United States," Kaiser Family Foundation Report, www.kff.org, March 2007; Stephanie Thompson, "Food Fight Breaks Out," *Advertising Age*, January 17, 2005, pp. 1, 25.



goal of advertising is to make them buy things, while only 11 percent felt that its objective is to provide information.[41]

It is important to many companies to communicate directly with children. However, only by being sensitive to the naiveté of children as consumers will they be able to do so freely and avoid potential conflict with those who believe children should be protected from advertising and other forms of promotion.

## Social and Cultural Consequences

Concern is often expressed over the impact of advertising on society, particularly on values and lifestyles. While a number of factors influence the cultural values, lifestyles, and behavior of a society, the overwhelming amount of advertising and its prevalence in the mass media lead many critics to argue that advertising plays a major role in influencing and transmitting social values. In his book *Advertising and Social Change,* Ronald Berman says:

**EXHIBIT 21–11**
Many schools are now restricting the availability of soft drinks and snack products

> The institutions of family, religion, and education have grown noticeably weaker over each of the past three generations. The world itself seems to have grown more complex. In the absence of traditional authority, advertising has become a kind of social guide. It depicts us in all the myriad situations possible to a life of free choice. It provides ideas about style, morality, behavior.[42]

Mike Hughes, president and creative director of the Martin Agency, notes that advertising has a major impact on society: "Ads help establish what is cool in society; their messages contribute to the public dialogue. Gap ads show white, black and Hispanic kids dancing together. Hilfiger ads showed it's cool for people to get along. Ikea showed a gay couple." He argues that advertising agencies have a social and ethical responsibility to consider the impact of the advertising messages they create for their clients.[43]

While there is general agreement that advertising is an important social influence agent, opinions as to the value of its contribution are often negative. Advertising is criticized for encouraging materialism, manipulating consumers to buy things they do not really need, perpetuating stereotypes, and controlling the media.

### Advertising Encourages Materialism

Many critics claim advertising has an adverse effect on consumer values by encouraging **materialism**, a preoccupation with material things rather than intellectual or spiritual concerns. They argue that a major contributor to materialism is advertising that

- Seeks to create needs rather than merely showing how a product or service fulfills them.
- Surrounds consumers with images of the good life and suggests the acquisition of material possessions leads to contentment and happiness and adds to the joy of living.
- Suggests material possessions are symbols of status, success, and accomplishment and/or will lead to greater social acceptance, popularity, sex appeal, and so on.

**EXHIBIT 21–12**
Critics argue that advertising contributes to materialistic values

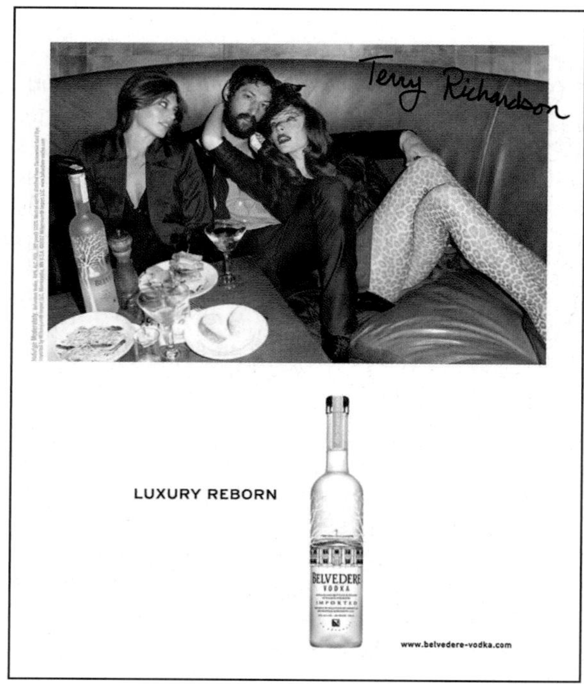


Advertising for products such as expensive automobiles and luxury goods like clothing, jewelry, and alcoholic beverages is often criticized for promoting materialistic values (Exhibit 21–12).

This criticism of advertising assumes that materialism is undesirable and is sought at the expense of other goals. But many believe materialism is an acceptable part of the **Protestant ethic**, which stresses hard work and individual effort and initiative and views the accumulation of material possessions as evidence of success. Others argue that the acquisition of material possessions has positive economic impact by encouraging consumers to keep consuming after their basic needs are met. Many Americans believe economic growth is essential and materialism is both a necessity and an inevitable part of this progress.

It has also been argued that an emphasis on material possessions does not rule out interest in intellectual, spiritual, or cultural values. Defenders of advertising say consumers can be more interested in higher-order goals when basic needs have been met and point out that consumers may purchase material things in the pursuit of nonmaterial goals. For example, a person may buy an expensive stereo system to enjoy music rather than simply to impress someone or acquire a material possession.

Even if we assume materialism is undesirable, there is still the question of whether advertising is responsible for creating and encouraging it. While many critics argue that advertising is a major contributing force to materialistic values, others say advertising merely reflects the values of society rather than shaping them.[44] They argue that consumers' values are defined by the society in which they live and are the results of extensive, long-term socialization or acculturation.

The argument that advertising is responsible for creating a materialistic and hedonistic society is addressed by Stephen Fox in his book *The Mirror Makers: A History of American Advertising and Its Creators.* Fox concludes advertising has become a prime scapegoat for our times and merely reflects society. Regarding the effect of advertising on cultural values, he says:

> To blame advertising now for those most basic tendencies in American history is to miss the point. It is too obvious, too easy, a matter of killing the messenger instead of dealing with the bad news. The people who have created modern advertising are not hidden persuaders pushing our buttons in the service of some malevolent purpose. They are just producing an especially visible manifestation, good and bad, of the American way of life.[45]

The ad shown in Exhibit 21–13 was developed by the American Association of Advertising Agencies and suggests that advertising is a reflection of society's tastes and values, not vice versa. The ad was part of a campaign that addressed criticisms of advertising.

Individuals from a variety of backgrounds are concerned over the values they see driving our society. They believe that materialism, greed, and selfishness increasingly dominate American life and that advertising is a major reason for these undesirable values. The extent to which advertising is responsible for materialism and the desirability of such values are deep philosophical issues that will continue to be part of the debate over the societal value and consequences of advertising.

**EXHIBIT 21–13**
The advertising industry argues that advertising reflects society

### Advertising Makes People Buy Things They Don't Need

A common criticism of advertising is that it manipulates consumers into buying things they do not need. Many critics say advertising should just provide information useful in making purchase decisions and should not attempt to persuade. They view information advertising (which reports price, performance, and other objective criteria) as desirable but persuasive advertising (which plays on consumers' emotions, anxieties, and psychological needs and desires such as status, self-esteem, and attractiveness) as unacceptable. Persuasive advertising is criticized for fostering discontent among consumers and encouraging them to purchase products and services to solve deeper problems.

Defenders of advertising offer a number of rebuttals to these criticisms. First, they point out that a substantial amount of advertising is essentially informational in nature. Also, it is difficult to separate desirable informational advertising from undesirable persuasive advertising. Shelby Hunt, in examining the *information-persuasion dichotomy,* points out that even advertising that most observers would categorize as very informative is often very persuasive. He says, "If advertising critics really believe that persuasive advertising should not be permitted, they are actually proposing that no advertising be allowed, since the purpose of all advertising is to persuade."[46]

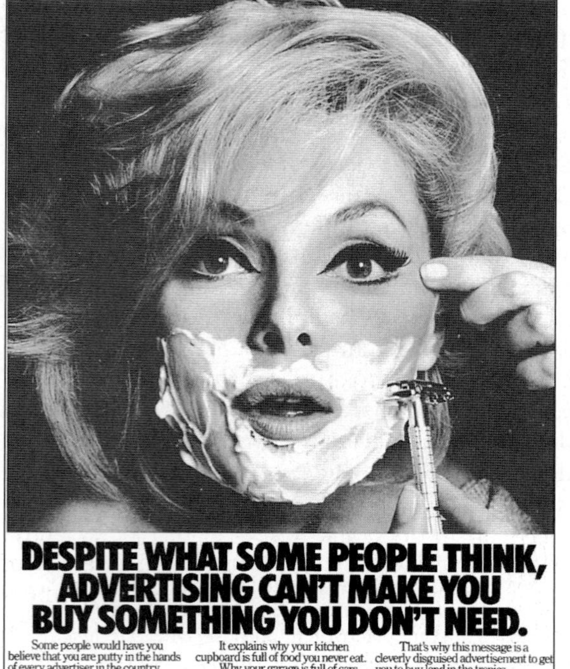

DESPITE WHAT SOME PEOPLE THINK, ADVERTISING CAN'T MAKE YOU BUY SOMETHING YOU DON'T NEED.
Some people would have you believe that you are putty in the hands of every advertiser in the country.
They think that when advertising is put under your nose, your mind turns to oatmeal.
It's mass hypnosis. Subliminal seduction. Brain washing. Mind control. It's advertising.
And you are a pushover for it.
It explains why your kitchen cupboard is full of food you never eat.
Why your garage is full of cars you never drive.
Why your house is full of books you don't read, TV's you don't watch, beds you don't use, and clothes you don't wear.
You don't have a choice. You are forced to buy.
That's why this message is a cleverly disguised advertisement to get you to buy land in the tropics.
Got you again, didn't we? Send in your money.
ADVERTISING
ANOTHER WORD FOR FREEDOM OF CHOICE.
American Association of Advertising Agencies


**EXHIBIT 21–14**

The AAAA responds to the claim that advertising makes consumers buy things they do not need

Defenders of advertising also take issue with the argument that it should be limited to dealing with basic functional needs. In our society, most lower-level needs recognized in Maslow's hierarchy, such as the need for food, clothing, and shelter, are satisfied for most people. It is natural to move from basic needs to higher-order ones such as self-esteem and status or self-actualization. Consumers are free to choose the degree to which they attempt to satisfy their desires, and wise advertisers associate their products and services with the satisfaction of higher-order needs.

Proponents of advertising offer two other defenses against the charge that advertising makes people buy things they do not really need. First, this criticism attributes too much power to advertising and assumes consumers have no ability to defend themselves against it. Second, it ignores the fact that consumers have the freedom to make their own choices when confronted with persuasive advertising. While they readily admit the persuasive intent of their business, advertisers are quick to note it is extremely difficult to make consumers purchase a product they do not want or for which they do not see a personal benefit. If advertising were as powerful as the critics claim, we would not see products with multimillion-dollar advertising budgets failing in the marketplace. The reality is that consumers do have a choice and they are not being forced to buy. Consumers ignore ads for products and services they do not really need or that fail to interest them (see Exhibit 21–14).

**Advertising and Stereotyping** Advertising is often accused of creating and perpetuating stereotypes through its portrayal of women, ethnic minorities, and other groups.

**Women** The portrayal of women in advertising is an issue that has received a great deal of attention through the years. Advertising has received much criticism for stereotyping women and failing to recognize the changing role of women in our society. Critics have argued that advertising often depicts women as preoccupied with beauty, household duties, and motherhood or shows them as decorative objects or sexually provocative figures. The various research studies conducted through the years show a consistent picture of gender stereotyping that has varied little over time. Portrayals of adult women in American television and print advertising have emphasized passivity, deference, lack of intelligence and credibility, and punishment for high levels of efforts. In contrast, men have been portrayed as constructive, powerful, autonomous, and achieving.[47]

Research on gender stereotyping in advertising targeted to children has found a pattern of results similar to that reported for adults. A study found sex-role stereotyping in television advertising targeted at children in the United States as well as in Australia.[48] Boys are generally shown as being more knowledgeable, active, aggressive, and instrumental than girls. Nonverbal behaviors involving dominance and control are associated more with boys than girls. Advertising directed toward children has also been shown to feature more boys than girls, to position boys in more dominant, active roles, and to use male voiceovers more frequently than female ones.[49] A study examining race and gender stereotyping of children's advertising on the Turner Cartoon Network found that the primary target for most of the commercials was active, white boys. Girls were portrayed in traditional roles and shown performing limited passive, indoor activities, while boys were shown in the outdoor world engaging in more exciting and active things.[50]

Feminist groups such as the National Organization for Women (NOW) and the Sexual Assault Prevention and Awareness Center argue that advertising that portrays women as sex objects contributes to violence against women. These groups often protest to advertisers and their agencies about ads they find insulting to women and have even called for boycotts against offending advertisers. NOW has also been critical of advertisers for the way they portray women in advertising for clothing, cosmetics, and other products. The organization feels that many of these ads contribute to the epidemic of eating disorders and smoking among women and girls who hope such means will help them control their weight.[51]

While sexism and stereotyping still exist, advertising's portrayal of women is improving in many areas. Many advertisers have begun to recognize the importance of portraying women realistically. The increase in the number of working women has resulted not only in women having more influence in family decision making but also in more single-female households, which means more independent purchasers.

Researchers Steven Kates and Glenda Shaw-Garlock argue that the transformed social positioning of women in North American society is perhaps the most important social development of this century.[52] They note that as women have crossed the boundary from the domestic sphere to the professional arena, expectations and representations of women have changed as well. For example, a number of magazines, such as *MS.* and *Working Mother,* now incorporate and appeal to the sociocultural shifts in women's lives. Many advertisers are now depicting women in a diversity of roles that reflect their changing place in society. In many ads, the stereotypic character traits attributed to women have shifted from weak and dependent to strong and autonomous. The ad for Network Solutions shown in Exhibit 21–15 is an example of how advertisers are changing the way they portray women in their ads. One reason for the changes in the way women are portrayed in advertising is the emergence of females in key agency roles. Women advertising executives are likely to be more sensitive to the portrayal of their own gender and to strengthen the role of women beyond stereotypical housewives or a position of subservience to men.[53]

**EXHIBIT 21–15**
Many advertisers now portray women in powerful roles

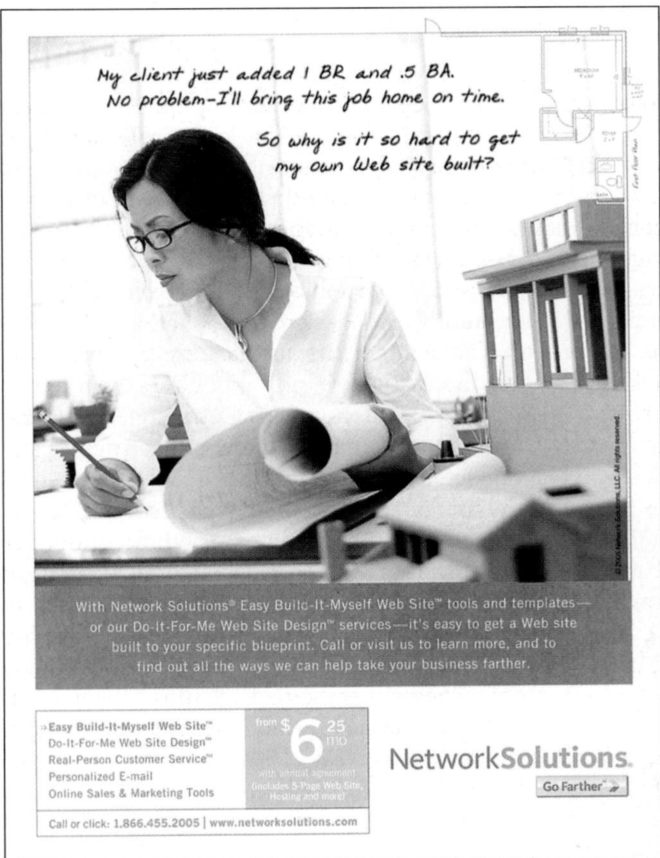


**African-Americans and Hispanics** African-Americans and Hispanics have also been the target of stereotyping in advertising. For many years, advertisers virtually ignored all nonwhite ethnic groups as identifiable subcultures and viable markets. Ads were rarely targeted to these ethnic groups, and the use of blacks and Hispanics as spokespeople, communicators, models, or actors in ads was very limited.

Several studies in the late 1980s and early 90s examined the incidence of minorities in advertising. A study conducted in 1987 found that 11 percent of the people appearing in commercials were African-Americans while another study conducted two years later found that African-Americans appeared in 26 percent of all ads on network TV that used live models but Hispanics appeared in only 6 percent.[54,55] Almost ten years later studies showed that 17 percent of prime-time network TV ads featured African-Americans as dominant characters and the majority of commercials featured them in minor roles.[56]

A content analysis study by Linzee Locke compared the presence of African-Americans in prime-time TV commercials on the BET and MTV cable networks in 2003. The study found that 26 percent of the commercials with live models on BET included African-Americans while 33 percent of the commercials aired on MTV included African-American models. The study also found that commercials on MTV

**EXHIBIT 21–16**
Banana Republic broke ground with this ad showing an interracial couple.

were more racially integrated than those on BET. On MTV, 87 percent of the commercials containing African-Americans were racially integrated compared to 45 percent of BET commercials. BET showed more black-only commercials (54 percent), while only 13 percent of the ads on MTV used all African-American actors. Locke noted that commercials airing on MTV include far more African-Americans than the average network and suggested that this may reflect the acceptance and crossover appeal of African-American culture to the network's younger target audience.[57]

Ads are increasingly likely to be racially integrated. Some advertisers have begun breaking the taboo against suggesting interracial attraction. For example, Banana Republic, and many other retailers, commonly run interracial ads (Exhibit 21–16). Advertisers are also finding that advertising developed specifically for the African-American market, such as the Levi's ad shown in Exhibit 21–17, is an effective way of reaching this ethnic market. A study by Corliss L. Green found that ads targeting African-Americans through racially targeted media, especially with race-based products, benefit from featuring African-American models with a dominant presence in the ad.

Another minority group that has received attention recently from those researching advertising and stereotyping is Asian-Americans, whose affluence, high education, work ethic, and growth rate have made this group a popular target market. A study of prime-time TV commercials found that Asian male and female models are overrepresented in terms of their proportion of the U.S. population (3.6 percent), appearing in 8.4 percent of the commercials. However, Asian models were more likely than members of other minority groups to appear in background roles, and Asian women were rarely depicted in major roles. The study also found that portrayals of Asian-Americans put more emphasis on the work ethic and less on other aspects of their lives.[58]

There is little question that advertising has been guilty of stereotyping women and ethnic groups in the past and, in some cases, still does so. But as the role of women changes, advertisers are changing their portrayals to remain accurate and appeal to their target audience. Advertisers are also trying to increase the incidence of minority groups in ads while avoiding stereotypes and negative role portrayals. They are being careful to avoid ethnic stereotyping and striving to develop advertising that has specific appeals to various ethnic groups. Increases in the size and purchasing power of ethnic minorities are leading companies to give more attention to multicultural marketing. However, as discussed in Diversity Perspective 21–1, many companies are still struggling to connect with multicultural consumers, which may be due, at least in part, to the lack of African-Americans and other ethnic minorities working in the advertising industry.

**EXHIBIT 21–17**
Many marketers are creating ads specifically for the African-American market

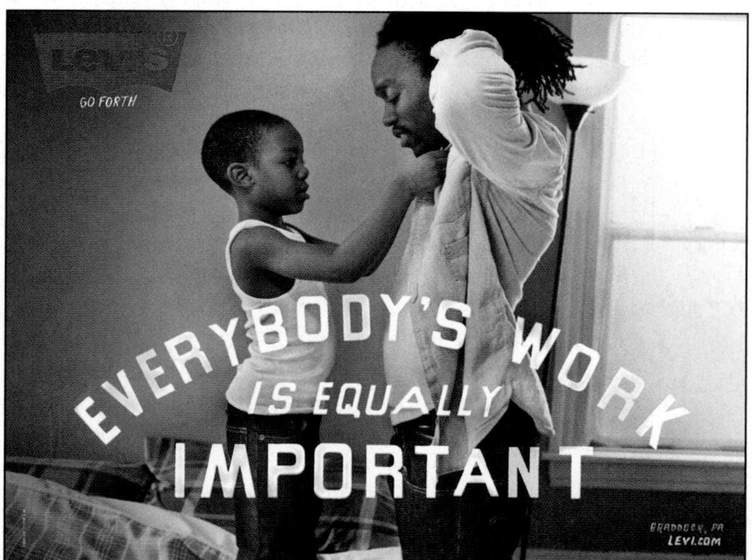


**Other Groups** While the focus here has been on women and ethnic minorities, some other groups feel they are victims of stereotyping by advertisers. Many groups in our society are battling against stereotyping and discrimination, and companies must consider whether their ads might offend them. Creative personnel in agencies sometimes feel restricted as their ideas are squelched out of concern that they might offend someone or be misinterpreted. However, advertisers must be sensitive to the portrayal of specific types of people in their ads, for both ethical and commercial reasons. For example, both Volkswagen and General Motors received protests from mental health groups over commercials considered insensitive to the problem of suicide. The Volkswagen spot showed a young man about to commit suicide by jumping off a roof after he is seen expressing his unhappiness with the state of the world, but ultimately opts not to do so after he learns that there are three VW models available for under $17,000. Volkswagen ended up pulling the spot after receiving protests from a number of suicide prevention groups.[59] The General Motors ad, which premiered on the Super Bowl, created a controversy by showing a robot that gets fired for dropping a bolt on the assembly line, takes a succession of lesser jobs, and eventually jumps off a bridge in despair. GM agreed to change the ad, which was designed to show the company's obsession with product quality, after discussing concerns about it with the American Foundation for Suicide Prevention.[60]

One area where significant changes have taken place recently is in advertising targeted to gay consumers. In 1995 Ikea broke new ground with a TV commercial featuring a gay couple shopping for furniture. For years beer companies targeted this market by placing ads in local gay media to support or sponsor AIDS awareness, Gay Pride festivals, and the Gay Games. A number of beer companies, including Anheuser-Busch and Miller Brewing Co., now run gay-specific, brand-specific ads in national gay publications.

A number of other companies, including Virgin Mobile and SKYY Blue, also now run ads with gay themes, although they generally confine them to magazines and newspapers targeting the gay market. While a TV commercial or print ad with a gay reference occasionally runs in the mainstream media, it usually is so subtle or ambiguous that many heterosexuals do not perceive it as a gay message.

More advertisers are turning to gay themes in their mainstream commercials, though often subtly. However, few run these ads on network television; they limit them to spot TV and local stations in more gay-friendly cities such as New York, Los Angeles, and San Francisco. The Miller Brewing Co. took a bold step by airing one of the first gay-themed commercials on network television. One ad was for Miller Lite beer and showed a gay couple holding hands in a straight bar to the dismay of two women who are interested in them. Levi Strauss recently created a spot with alternative endings, one of which was designed to appeal to the gay market. The spot featured a young, attractive male in his second-floor apartment slipping on his Levi's. The motion of yanking up his jeans inexplicably causes the street below his apartment to get pulled up as well, crashing through his floor and bringing with it an attractive female in a telephone booth who he walks away with. In a version of the ad that aired on Logo, MTV's gay cable network seen in more than 27 million homes, an attractive man is in the phone booth and the two men run off together in the same manner as their heterosexual counterparts.[61]

**EXHIBIT 21–18**
Snickers offended the gay community with its Super Bowl commercial

A recent commercial that was not well received by the gay community was a spot for Snickers candy bars that also aired during the 2007 Super Bowl. The "mechanics" spot depicted two auto mechanics who end up sharing a Snickers bar and an inadvertent kiss and then ripping out chest hair to do something "manly" (Exhibit 21–18). Snickers also created a micro website featuring alternate endings to the commercial, such as the mechanics beating each other with wrenches as well as other players from the Super Bowl teams reactions to them. Gay-rights groups complained to the parent company of Snickers, Masterfood USA—a subsidiary of Mars—that

## Diversity Perspective 21–1 > > >

### Advertisers Increase Efforts in Multicultural Marketing

Most marketers recognize the changing racial and ethnic diversity of the marketplace. The expansion of ethnic populations has become one of the most powerful social and economic dynamics in America over the past generation. Approximately one in three United States' residents is African-American, Asian-American, Hispanic, or American Indian, constituting a market exceeding 103 million. By 2042 they will be the majority of the U.S. population. A number of companies are developing multicultural programs that reflect to appeal to these groups. However, while marketers are spending more money than ever to connect with multicultural consumers, many are struggling in their efforts to do so.

A survey conducted by Brandiosity, a consulting firm specializing in multisegment marketing, found that 84 percent of marketers believe multicultural marketing is critical to their business, although there is still a good deal of confusion among top marketing executives regarding their understanding of multicultural markets. The survey was conducted for the executive search firm of Heidrick & Struggles, which commissioned the study to better understand what type of talent companies are looking for to target multicultural segments. The survey found that companies use a variety of approaches to communicate with the multicultural market by employing general and multicultural agencies and research service providers.

One of the reasons many companies may be struggling with their multicultural marketing efforts is the lack of diversity among their employees, as well as in the staffs of the advertising agencies that handle their marketing communication programs. The American Association of Advertising Agencies (4As) found that total minority employment at the large agencies they surveyed was 20 percent in 2007 versus 18 percent in 2002. Minorities accounted for only 14 percent of total creative employment versus 11 percent five years earlier. The advertising industry was recently reprimanded by New York City's Commission on Human Rights after an investigation into minority hiring practices among the largest advertising agencies in the city. The chair of the commission noted, "The findings revealed a disappointingly low number of minorities, especially African-Americans, held managerial, professional and creative positions and that little had changed over 40 years when the commission last held hearings on the issue." As a result of the investigation, 15 of the largest ad agencies in the city signed an agreement pledging to increase minority hiring and retention.

Several reasons have been offered as to why minority employment is low. First, ad agencies have to compete against other employers for talented employees and advertising's lower pay scale versus other industries is widely cited as a barrier to hiring and retaining minorities. Also, the advertising industry is centered in cities such as New York, Chicago, and Los Angeles, which have very high costs of living and the parents of many minorities cannot afford to support them in the early years of their new careers. Some of the agencies are addressing the problem by developing programs to attract and retain minority talent. For example, the Interpublic Group offers its 10 top minority candidates jobs in Inter-Act, a two-year talent and diversity program. Industry groups such as the 4As and American Advertising Federation (AAF) offer multicultural advertising internship programs to college students. For example, the AAF has run its Most Promising Minority Student program to help connect candidates with ad agencies, media agencies, and marketers for more than a decade.

the spots were homophobic and encouraged violence and prejudice against gays. Masterfoods noted that the commercial was only trying to be humorous and attract the attention of the core Snickers consumer. However, the company agreed to stop running the ad and removed the website.[62]

**Advertising and the Media** The fact that advertising plays such an important role in financing the media has led to concern that advertisers may influence or even control the media. It is well documented that *economic censorship* occurs, whereby the media avoid certain topics or even present biased news coverage, in acquiescence to advertiser demands.[63] In fact, Professors Lawrence Soley and Robert Craig say, "The assertion that advertisers attempt to influence what the public sees, hears, and reads in the mass media is perhaps the most damning of all criticisms of advertising, but this criticism isn't acknowledged in most advertising textbooks."[64] We will address this important issue in this book by considering arguments on both sides.

**Arguments Supporting Advertiser Control** Advertising is the primary source of revenue for nearly all the news and entertainment media in the United States.

Many in the advertising industry feel Madison Avenue will not bridge the diversity divide until there is more pressure from clients for agencies to develop advertising that reflects the dynamics of a changing consumer market. In 2010, The Interactive Advertising Bureau (IAB) formed the IAB Multicultural Council to focus on key issues that impact marketing and advertising within the multicultural marketplace including audience measurement in online media. In addition, the council will work to educate marketers and agencies on how to create successful digital marketing strategies to reach multicultural markets, equip multicultural publishers with the tools necessary to address the needs of marketers who want to reach diverse populations, and assist marketers who use interactive media to reach these market segments. Some companies are leading the way in the area of multicultural marketing. For example, Procter & Gamble, the largest advertiser in the world, recently launched an initiative called "My Black Is Beautiful." P&G recognized the need for the campaign after its research found that 77 percent of black women were concerned about the way they are portrayed in the media and 71 percent felt they were portrayed worse than other women, despite the fact that they spend on average three times more than the general market on beauty products.

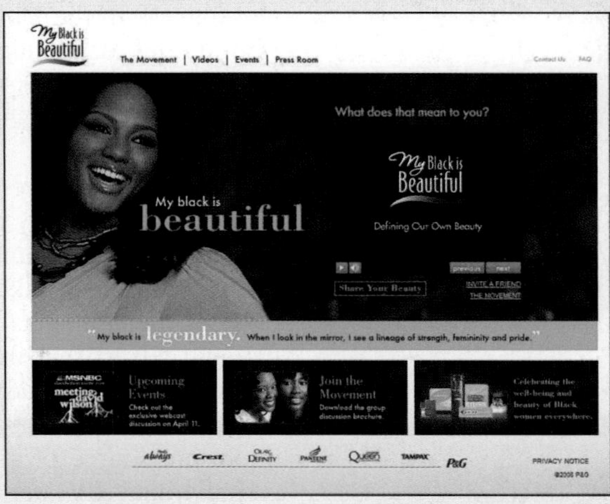


Other companies are changing their strategies as well. Ford rolled out a "Ready Pa'Tu Mundo" (Ready for Your World) program for the 2011 Ford Fiesta that includes a social media, digital, and Web platform focusing on young, bilingual Hispanics between the ages of 18 to 34. Ford has recognized that the multicultural audience is one of the largest consumer groups in the small car segment, and that they are heavy users of Twitter, Facebook, and YouTube as well as Univision and CNN. General Mills also gets it. The cereal company relaunched its Spanish-language effort "Que Rica Vida" (What a Rich Life) to include a more robust Web presence with more Spanish content. The company has already seen double-digit sales growth as a result. State Farm Insurance has employed branded entertainment strategies through its Hispanic agencies by creating a real band of Mexican musicians to show how the company helps immigrants realize their American dreams.

While marketers realize they still have a lot to learn about multicultural markets, many have a strong motivation to do so. As noted by Chief Marketing Officer Neil Golden of McDonald's, "Ethnic segments are leading lifestyle trends." They are also accounting for 40 percent of McDonald's sales in the United States alone.

Sources: Laura Martinez, "New Messaging Needed to Reach 'New Majority,'" *Advertising Age*, June 21, 2010, pp. 4–5; ____, "The Interactive Advertising Bureau; IAB Forms Multicultural Council," *Marketing Weekly News*, June 12, 2010, p. 101; Beth Snyder Bulik, "Marketers: We Don't Get How to Do Diversity," *Advertising Age*, February 25, 2008, pp. 1, 25; Jack Neff, "'My Black Is Beautiful,'" *Advertising Age*, August 27, 2007, pp. 1, 21; Lisa Sanders, "NYC Ad Agencies Scramble to Hit Diversity Targets," *Advertising Age*, January 15, 2007, pp. 1, 33; Patricia L. Gatling, "New York Ad Agencies and Equal Opportunity," *The Wall Street Journal*, October 18, 2006, p. A21; Lisa Sanders, "NYC Slams Madison Ave. for Woeful Lack of Diversity," *Advertising Age*, March 6, 2006, pp. 1, 41.

Some critics charge that the media's dependence on advertisers' support makes them susceptible to various forms of influence, including exerting control over the editorial content of magazines and newspapers; biasing editorial opinions to favor the position of an advertiser; limiting coverage of a controversial story that might reflect negatively on a company; and influencing the program content of television.

Newspapers and magazines receive nearly 70 percent of their revenue from advertising; commercial TV and radio derive virtually all their income from advertisers. Small, financially insecure newspapers, magazines, or broadcast stations are the most susceptible to pressure from advertisers, particularly companies that account for a large amount of the media outlet's advertising revenue. A local newspaper may be reluctant to print an unfavorable story about a car dealer or supermarket chain on whose advertising it depends. For example, a few years ago more than 40 car dealers canceled their ads in the *San Jose Mercury News* when the paper printed an article titled "A Car Buyer's Guide to Sanity." The dealers objected to the tone of the article, which they felt implied consumers should consider car dealers unethical adversaries in the negotiation process.[65] A recent study by Soontae An and Lori Bergen surveyed advertising directors at 219 daily newspapers in the United States and found frequent conflicts between the business side and editorial side of the newspaper operations. Advertising directors at small newspapers or chain-owned newspapers were more likely to endorse scenarios where editorial integrity was compromised to please, or refrain from offending, their advertisers.[66]

While larger, more financially stable media should be less susceptible to an advertiser's influence, they may still be reluctant to carry stories detrimental to companies that purchase large amounts of advertising time or space. For example, since cigarette commercials were taken off radio and TV in 1970, tobacco companies have allocated most of their budgets to the print media. The tobacco industry outspends all other national advertisers in newspapers, and cigarettes constitute the second-largest category of magazine advertising (behind transportation). This has led to charges that magazines and newspapers avoid articles on the hazards of smoking to protect this important source of ad revenue.[67]

Individual TV stations and even the major networks also can be influenced by advertisers. Programming decisions are made largely on the basis of what shows will attract the most viewers and thus be most desirable to advertisers. Critics say this often results in lower-quality television as educational, cultural, and informative programming is usually sacrificed for shows that get high ratings and appeal to the mass markets. It is well recognized that advertisers often avoid TV shows that deal with controversial issues. Most advertisers also have contract stipulations allowing them to cancel a media buy if, after prescreening a show, they are uncomfortable with its content or feel sponsorship of it may reflect poorly on their company.

Advertisers have also been accused of pressuring the networks to change their programming. Many advertisers have withdrawn commercials from programs that contain too much sex or violence, often in response to threatened boycotts of their products by consumers if they advertise on these shows. For example, groups such as the American Family Association have been fighting sex and violence in TV programs by calling for boycotts. A number of companies, including Procter & Gamble, Mars Inc., and Kraft Foods, pulled their advertising from certain shows while others have not responded to their actions.

**Arguments against Advertiser Control** The commercial media's dependence on advertising means advertisers can exert influence on their character, content, and coverage of certain issues. However, media executives offer several reasons why advertisers do not exert undue influence over the media.

First, they point out it is in the best interest of the media not to be influenced too much by advertisers. To retain public confidence, they must report the news fairly and accurately without showing bias or attempting to avoid controversial issues. Media executives point to the vast array of topics they cover and the investigative reporting they often do as evidence of their objectivity. They want to build a large audience for their publications or stations so that they can charge more for advertising space and time.

Media executives also note that an advertiser needs the media more than they need any individual advertiser, particularly when the medium has a large audience or does a good job of reaching a specific market segment. Many publications and stations have a broad base of advertising support and can afford to lose an advertiser that attempts to exert too much influence. This is particularly true for the larger, more established, financially secure media. For example, a consumer-product company would find it difficult to reach its target audience without network TV and could not afford to boycott a network if it disagreed with a station's editorial policy or program content. Even the local advertiser in a small community may be dependent on the local newspaper, since it may be the most cost-effective media option available.

Most magazine and newspaper publishers insist they do not allow advertiser pressure to influence their editorial content. They argue that they have long regarded the formal separation of their news and business departments as essential to their independence and credibility. This separation is often referred to as "The Wall" and is often spoken of with a mixture of reverence and trepidation.[68] Many magazines and newspapers have traditionally discouraged employees on the publishing side—including advertising, circulation, and other business departments—from interacting with those on the editorial side, who write and edit the articles. This is done by separating editorial and advertising offices, barring the sales force from reading articles before they are printed, and prohibiting editorial employees from participating in advertising sales calls.

Most print media are very concerned over maintaining the concept of The Wall and ensuring that decisions on the writing, editing, and publishing of stories are made on journalistic merit rather than on whether they will attract or repel advertisers. However, the new economics of the publishing industry is making it difficult to maintain the separation: Competition from cable TV, direct mail, and the Internet is increasing, and newspaper and magazine readership and revenues continue to decline. There have been several well-publicized situations in recent years where major magazines and newspapers were found to have given favorable editorial consideration to an advertiser.[69] However, the media usually hold their ground when challenged by companies that threaten to pull their advertising, or even do so, when they find editorial coverage objectionable. For example, in April 2005 General Motors canceled all of its advertising in the *Los Angeles Times* after a series of articles in the newspaper were unflattering to the automaker. GM, which was spending an estimated $21 million in the *Times* each year, claimed that "factual errors and misrepresentations" in various articles led it to withdraw its advertising in the paper. The paper had run several articles that were critical of certain General Motors' vehicles, such as the Hummer and Pontiac G6, and also suggested that some senior GM executives should be dismissed because of the company's sales and profit woes. GM's advertising boycott of the *Los Angeles Times* lasted four months and was finally ended after executives from the two sides met to resolve their differences.[70]

The media in the United States are basically supported by advertising; this means we can enjoy them for free or for a fraction of what they would cost without advertising. The alternative to an advertiser-supported media system is support by users through higher subscription costs for the print media and a fee or pay-per-view system with TV. The ad in Exhibit 21–19, part of a campaign by the International Advertising Association, explains how advertising lowers the cost of print media for consumers. Another alternative is government-supported media like those in many other countries, but this runs counter to most people's desire for freedom of the press. Although not perfect, our system of advertising-supported media provides the best option for receiving information and entertainment.

**EXHIBIT 21–19**
This ad points out how advertising lowers the cost of newspapers for consumers

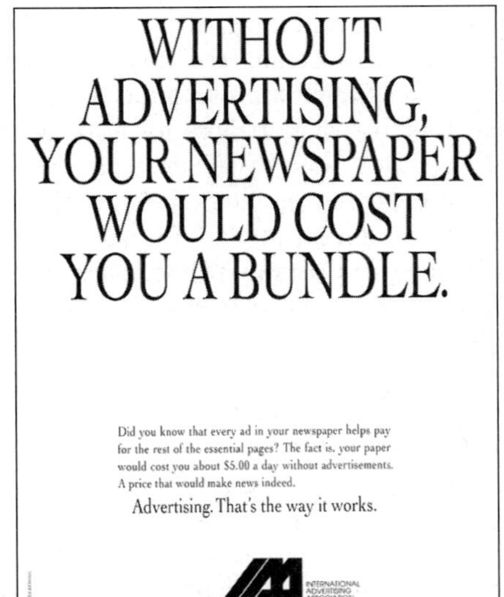

WITHOUT ADVERTISING, YOUR NEWSPAPER WOULD COST YOU A BUNDLE.
Did you know that every ad in your newspaper helps pay for the rest of the essential pages? The fact is, your paper would cost you about $5.00 a day without advertisements. A price that would make news indeed.
Advertising. That's the way it works.
INTERNATIONAL ADVERTISING ASSOCIATION
The global partnership of advertisers, agencies and media.


## Summarizing Social Effects

We have examined a number of issues and have attempted to analyze the arguments for and against them. Many people have reservations about the impact of advertising and promotion on society. The numerous rules, regulations, policies, and guidelines marketers comply with do not cover every advertising and promotional situation. Moreover, what one individual views as distasteful or unethical may be acceptable to another.

Negative opinions regarding advertising and other forms of promotion have been around almost as long as the field itself, and it is unlikely they will ever disappear. However, the industry must address the various concerns about the effects of advertising and other forms of promotion on society. Advertising is a very powerful institution, but it will remain so only as long as consumers have faith in the ads they see and hear every day. Many of the problems discussed here can be avoided if individual decision makers make ethics an important element of the IMC planning process.

**EXHIBIT 21–20**
The Partnership for a Drug Free America and ONDCP use advertising to deal with the problem of prescription-drug abuse

**EXHIBIT 21–21**
This ad campaign for the Boys & Girls Club is an example of the pro bono work often done by advertising agencies for nonprofit organizations

The primary focus of this discussion of social effects has been on the way advertising is used (or abused) in the marketing of products and services. It is important to note that advertising and other IMC tools, such as direct marketing and public relations, are also used to promote worthy causes and to deal with problems facing society (drunk driving, drug abuse, and the AIDS crisis, among others). For example, the Partnership for a Drug Free America and the U.S. government's Office of National Drug Control Policy (ONDCP) work together on advertising campaigns designed to help fight the war on drugs in the United States. The advertising effort has been effective in helping reduce the use of illicit street drugs. However, the abuse of prescription drugs is increasing and the Partnership and ONDCP are using ads such as the one shown in Exhibit 21–20 to address this problem.[71] Campaigns for nonprofit organizations and worthy causes are often developed pro bono by advertising agencies, and free advertising time and space are donated by the media. Exhibit 21–21 shows an ad from a very successful public service campaign for the Boys & Girls Clubs of America featuring actor Denzel Washington. The campaign is designed to establish an image to distinguish the Boys & Girls Clubs from other public service groups and to encourage adults to organize clubs.

## ECONOMIC EFFECTS OF ADVERTISING

Advertising plays an important role in a free-market system like ours by making consumers aware of products and services and providing them with information for decision making. Advertising's economic role goes beyond this basic function,

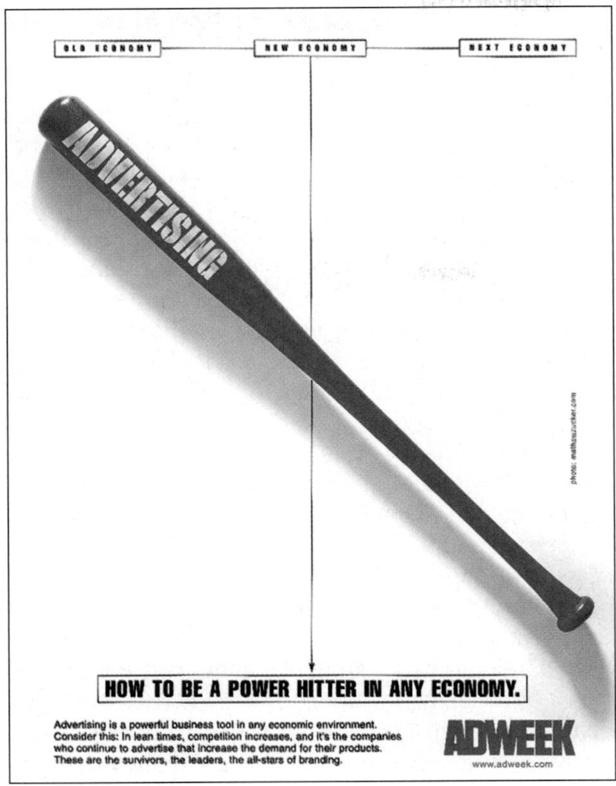


**EXHIBIT 21–22**
This ad promotes the economic value of advertising

however. It is a powerful force that can affect the functioning of our entire economic system (Exhibit 21–22).

Advertising can encourage consumption and foster economic growth. It not only informs customers of available goods and services but also facilitates entry into markets for a firm or a new product or brand; leads to economies of scale in production, marketing, and distribution, which in turn lead to lower prices; and hastens the acceptance of new products and the rejection of inferior products.

Critics of advertising view it as a detrimental force that not only fails to perform its basic function of information provision adequately but also adds to the cost of products and services and discourages competition and market entry, leading to industrial concentration and higher prices for consumers.

In their analysis of advertising, economists generally take a macroeconomic perspective: They consider the economic impact of advertising on an entire industry or on the economy as a whole rather than its effect on an individual company or brand. Our examination of the economic impact of advertising focuses on these broader macro-level issues. We consider its effects on consumer choice, competition, and product costs and prices.

## Effects on Consumer Choice

Some critics say advertising hampers consumer choice, as large advertisers use their power to limit our options to a few well-advertised brands. Economists argue that advertising is used to achieve (1) **differentiation**, whereby the products or services of large advertisers are perceived as unique or better than competitors', and (2) brand loyalty, which enables large national advertisers to gain control of the market, usually at the expense of smaller brands.

Larger companies often end up charging higher prices and achieve a more dominant position in the market than smaller firms that cannot compete against them and their large advertising budgets. When this occurs, advertising not only restricts the choice alternatives to a few well-known, heavily advertised brands but also becomes a substitute for competition based on price or product improvements.

**EXHIBIT 21–23**
Virgin Atlantic Airways chair Richard Branson acknowledges the importance of advertising

Heavily advertised brands dominate the market in certain product categories, such as soft drinks, beer, and cereals. But advertising generally does not create brand monopolies and reduce the opportunities for new products to be introduced to consumers. In most product categories, a number of different brands are on the store shelves and thousands of new products are introduced every year. In 2010, there were over 100 brands of bottled water on the market. The opportunity to advertise gives companies the incentive to develop new brands and improve their existing ones. When a successful new product such as a personal computer is introduced, competitors quickly follow and use advertising to inform consumers about their brand and attempt to convince them it is superior to the original. Companies like Virgin Atlantic Airways recognize that advertising has been an important part of their success (Exhibit 21–23).

## Effects on Competition

One of the most common criticisms economists have about advertising concerns its effects on competition. They argue that power in the hands of large firms with huge advertising budgets creates a **barrier to entry**, which makes it difficult for other firms to enter the market. This results in less competition and higher prices. Economists note that smaller firms already in the market find it difficult to compete against the large advertising budgets of the industry leaders and are often driven out of business. For example, in the U.S. beer industry, the number of national brewers has declined dramatically. In their battle for market share, industry giants Anheuser-Busch and Miller increased their ad budgets substantially and reaped market shares that total over 60 percent. Anheuser-Busch alone spends over $800 million on advertising a year. However, these companies are spending much less per barrel than smaller firms, making it very difficult for the latter to compete.

Large advertisers clearly enjoy certain competitive advantages. First, there are **economies of scale** in advertising, particularly with respect to factors such as media costs. Firms such as Procter & Gamble and PepsiCo, which spend several billion dollars a year on advertising and promotion, are able to make large media buys at a reduced rate and allocate them to their various products.

Large advertisers usually sell more of a product or service, which means they may have lower production costs and can allocate more monies to advertising, so they can afford the costly but more efficient media like network television. Their large advertising outlays also give them more opportunity to differentiate their products and develop brand loyalty. To the extent that these factors occur, smaller competitors are at a disadvantage and new competitors are deterred from entering the market.

While advertising may have an anticompetitive effect on a market, there is no clear evidence that advertising alone reduces competition, creates barriers to entry, and thus increases market concentration. High levels of advertising are not always found in industries where firms have a large market share. These findings run contrary to many economists' belief that industries controlled by a few firms have high advertising expenditures, resulting in stable brand shares for market leaders.

**EXHIBIT 21–24**
Virgin America relied on advertising to help the airline enter the U.S. market

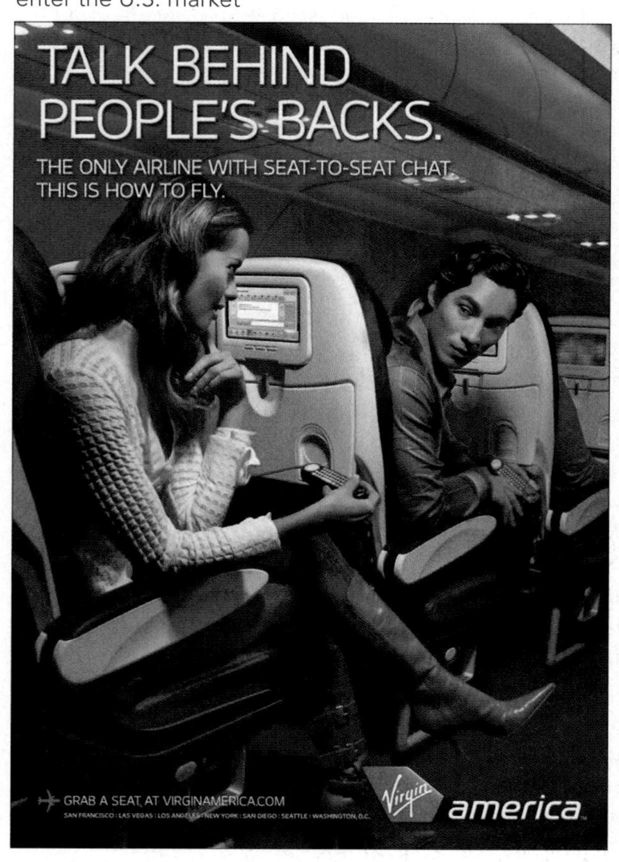


Defenders of advertising say it is unrealistic to attribute a firm's market dominance and barriers to entry solely to advertising. There are a number of other factors, such as price, product quality, distribution effectiveness, production efficiencies, and competitive strategies. For many years, products such as Coors beer and Hershey chocolate bars were dominant brands even though these companies spent little on advertising. Hershey did not advertise at all until 1970. For 66 years, the company relied on the quality of its products, its favorable reputation and image among consumers, and its extensive channels of distribution to market its brands. Industry leaders often tend to dominate markets because they have superior product quality and the best management and competitive strategies, not simply the biggest advertising budgets.[72]

While market entry against large, established competitors is difficult, companies with a quality product at a reasonable price often find a way to break in. Moreover, they usually find that advertising actually facilitates their market entry by making it possible to communicate the benefits and features of their new product or brand to consumers. For example, the airline Virgin America was launched in the United States in 2007. The company relied on media advertising to inform consumers of its low fares and innovative features and services which help differentiate it from other airlines.[73] Among the innovations offered by Virgin America are an in-flight entertainment system with video touch screens, a food ordering system, and a seat-to-seat chat service, which is promoted in the ad shown in Exhibit 21–24.

## Effects on Product Costs and Prices

A major area of debate among economists, advertisers, consumer advocates, and policymakers concerns the effects of advertising on product costs and prices. Critics argue that advertising increases the prices consumers pay for products and services. First, they say the large sums of money spent advertising a brand constitute an expense that must be covered and the consumer ends up paying for it through higher prices. As discussed in the previous chapter, concern has been expressed that the tremendous increase in direct-to-consumer drug advertising by pharmaceutical companies in recent years is driving up the cost of prescription drugs. Critics argue that the millions of dollars spent on advertising and other forms of promotion are an expense that must be covered by charging higher prices.[74]

A second way advertising can result in higher prices is by increasing product differentiation and adding to the perceived value of the product in consumers' minds. The fundamental premise is that advertising increases the perceived differences between physically homogeneous products and enables advertised brands to command a premium price without an increase in quality.

Critics of advertising generally point to the differences in prices between national brands and private-label brands that are physically similar, such as aspirin or tea bags, as evidence of the added value created by advertising. They see consumers' willingness to pay more for heavily advertised national brands rather than purchasing the lower-priced, nonadvertised brand as wasteful and irrational. The prescription drug industry is again a very good example of this, as critics argue that the increase in advertising is encouraging consumers to request brand-name drugs and steering them away from lower-priced generics.[75] However, consumers do not always buy for rational, functional reasons. The emotional, psychological, and social benefits derived from purchasing a national brand are important to many people. Moreover, say researchers Albion and Farris,

> Unfortunately there seems to be no single way to measure product differentiation, let alone determine how much is excessive or attributable to the effects of advertising . . . Both price insensitivity and brand loyalty could be created by a number of factors such as higher product quality, better packaging, favorable use experience and market position. They are probably related to each other but need not be the result of advertising.[76]

Proponents of advertising offer several other counterarguments to the claim that advertising increases prices. They acknowledge that advertising costs are at least partly paid for by consumers. But advertising may help lower the overall cost of a product more than enough to offset them. For example, advertising may help firms achieve economies of scale in production and distribution by providing information to and stimulating demand among mass markets. These economies of scale help cut the cost of producing and marketing the product, which can lead to lower prices—if the advertiser chooses to pass the cost savings on to the consumer. The ad in Exhibit 21–25, from a campaign sponsored by the American Association of Advertising Agencies, emphasizes this point.

**EXHIBIT 21–25**
This ad refutes the argument that reducing advertising expenditures will lead to lower prices

ADVERTISING MAKES THINGS COST MORE, RIGHT?
DRiNKS 5¢ 4¢
Drinks 5¢ 4¢ 3¢
We admit it. Advertising has a tremendous impact on prices. But you may be surprised by what *kind* of impact.
In addition to being informative, educational and sometimes entertaining, advertising can actually lower prices.
It works like this: Advertising spurs competition which holds down prices. And since advertising also creates a mass market for products, it can bring down the cost of producing each product, a savings that can be passed on to consumers.
Moreover, competition created by advertising provides an incentive for manufacturers to produce new and better products.
Which means advertising can not only reduce prices, but it can also help you avoid lemons.
ADVERTISING
ANOTHER WORD FOR FREEDOM OF CHOICE.
American Association of Advertising Agencies


Advertising can also lower prices by making a market more competitive, which usually leads to greater price competition. It has been shown that for some products, advertising has helped to keep the costs down. Finally, advertising is a means to market entry rather than a deterrent and helps stimulate product innovation, which makes markets more competitive and helps keep prices down.

Overall, it is difficult to reach any firm conclusions regarding the relationship between advertising and prices. After an extensive review of this area, Farris and Albion concluded, "The evidence connecting manufacturer advertising to prices is neither complete nor definitive . . . consequently, we cannot say whether advertising is a tool of market efficiency or market power without further research."[77]

| Advertising = Market Power | | Advertising = Information |
|---|---|---|
| Advertising affects consumer preferences and tastes, changes product attributes, and differentiates the product from competitive offerings. | Advertising | Advertising informs consumers about product attributes but does not change the way they value those attributes. |
| Consumers become brand loyal and less price sensitive and perceive fewer substitutes for advertised brands. | Consumer buying behavior | Consumers become more price sensitive and buy best "value." Only the relationship between price and quality affects elasticity for a given product. |
| Potential entrants must overcome established brand loyalty and spend relatively more on advertising. | Barriers to entry | Advertising makes entry possible for new brands because it can communicate product attributes to consumers. |
| Firms are insulated from market competition and potential rivals; concentration increases, leaving firms with more discretionary power. | Industry structure and market power | Consumers can compare competitive offerings easily and competitive rivalry increases. Efficient firms remain, and as the inefficient leave, new entrants appear; the effect on concentration is ambiguous. |
| Firms can change higher prices and are not as likely to compare on quality or price dimensions. Innovation may be reduced. | Market conduct | More informed consumers pressure firms to lower prices and improve quality; new entrants facilitate innovation. |
| High prices and excessive profits accrue to advertisers and give them even more incentive to advertise their products. Output is restricted compared with conditions of perfect competition. | Market performance | Industry prices decrease. The effect on profits due to increased competition and increased efficiency is ambiguous. |

**FIGURE 21–3**

Two Schools of Thought on Advertising's Role in the Economy

## Summarizing Economic Effects

Economists' perspectives can be divided into two principal schools of thought that make different assumptions regarding the influence of advertising on the economy.[78] Figure 21–3 summarizes the main points of the "advertising equals market power" and "advertising equals information" perspectives.

**Advertising Equals Market Power** The belief that advertising equals market power reflects traditional economic thinking and views advertising as a way to change consumers' tastes, lower their sensitivity to price, and build brand loyalty among buyers of advertised brands. This results in higher profits and market power for large advertisers, reduces competition in the market, and leads to higher prices and fewer choices for consumers. Proponents of this viewpoint generally have negative attitudes regarding the economic impact of advertising.

**Advertising Equals Information** The belief that advertising equals information takes a more positive view of advertising's economic effects. This model sees advertising as providing consumers with useful information, increasing their price sensitivity (which moves them toward lower-priced products), and increasing competition in the market. Advertising is viewed as a way to communicate with consumers and tell them about a product and its major features and attributes. More informed and knowledgeable consumers pressure companies to provide high-quality products

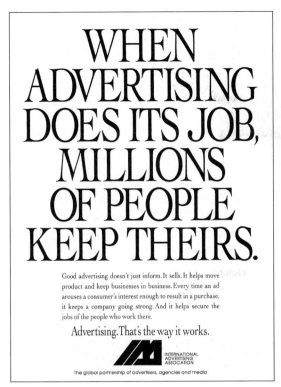

WHEN ADVERTISING DOES ITS JOB, MILLIONS OF PEOPLE KEEP THEIRS.

Good advertising doesn't just inform. It sells. It helps move product and keep businesses in business. Every time an ad arouses a consumer's interest enough to result in a purchase, it keeps a company going strong. And it helps secure the jobs of the people who work there.

Advertising. That's the way it works.

The global partnership of advertisers, agencies and media

**EXHIBIT 21–26**
This ad is part of a global campaign by the International Advertising Association to educate consumers about the economic value of advertising

at lower prices. Efficient firms remain in the market, whereas inefficient firms leave as new entrants appear. Proponents of this model believe the economic effects of advertising are favorable and think it contributes to more efficient and competitive markets.

There is considerable evidence that advertising does provide the information consumers need to make purchase decisions. Avery Abernethy and George Franke performed a meta-analysis of studies examining the information content of advertising and found that more than 84 percent of 91,000 ads analyzed in these studies contain at least one information cue. The most commonly provided types of information included performance, availability, components, price, and quality, all of which are important to consumers in making an informed choice.[79]

It is unlikely the debate over the economic effects and value of advertising will be resolved soon. Many economists will continue to take a negative view of advertising and its effects on the functioning of the economy, while advertisers will continue to view it as an efficient way for companies to communicate with their customers and an essential component of our economic system. The International Advertising Association has been running a campaign for several years to convince consumers around the world of the economic value of advertising. Ads like the one shown in Exhibit 21–26 are used in countries where consumers may be less familiar with the concept of advertising. The goal of the campaign is to get consumers in these countries to recognize the role advertising plays in contributing to their economic well-being.

The advertising industry in the United States continually promotes the value of advertising. Major advertising associations, such as the American Association of Advertising Agencies (AAAA), the American Advertising Federation (AAF), along with trade associations for various media often run campaigns reminding the general public of advertising's contributions to the economy as well as to consumers' social well-being. However, sometimes the industry must also remind advertisers themselves of the value of advertising. Recently the American Advertising Federation, which is the advertising industry's primary trade organization, decided to take action to change the way advertising is viewed by companies. The AAF decided that the best way to get marketers to recognize the value of advertising was to practice what it preaches, and thus an integrated marketing communications campaign was developed to redefine advertising in the eyes of corporate executives.

The campaign was targeted at corporate executives who were responsible for establishing and maintaining budget levels for advertising. The theme of the campaign is "Advertising. The way great brands get to be great brands," cautions corporate executives not to neglect their brand development. The Great Brands campaign promoted the economic power of advertising by featuring companies synonymous with quality advertising and for whom advertising has played a critical role in building brand equity. Exhibit 21–27 shows one of the ads from the campaign featuring Intel, the market leader for computer chips and microprocessors.

Figure 21–4, excerpts from a speech given by famous adman Leo Burnett, summarizes the perspective of most advertising people on the economic effects of advertising. Advertising and marketing experts agree that advertising and promotion play an important role in helping to expand consumer demand for new products and services and in helping marketers differentiate their existing brands.

**EXHIBIT 21–27**
The AAF promotes the value of advertising in building strong brands

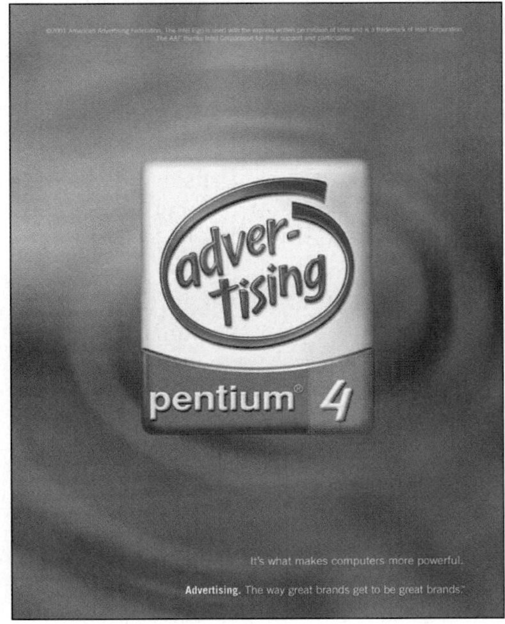


CHAPTER 21

**FIGURE 21–4**

This Message Describes the Positive Economic Effects of Advertising

Source: Excerpts from a speech given by Leo Burnett on the American Association of Advertising Agencies' 50th anniversary, April 20, 1967.

To me it means that if we believe to any degree whatsoever in the economic system under which we live, in a high standard of living and in high employment, advertising is the most efficient known way of moving goods in practically every product class.

My proof is that millions of businessmen have chosen advertising over and over again in the operations of their business. Some of their decisions may have been wrong, but they must have thought they were right or they wouldn't go back to be stung twice by the same kind of bee.

It's a pretty safe bet that in the next 10 years many Americans will be using products and devices that no one in this room has even heard of. Judging purely by past performance, American advertising can be relied on to make them known and accepted overnight at the lowest possible prices.

Advertising, of course, makes possible our unparalleled variety of magazines, newspapers, business publications, and radio and television stations.

It must be said that without advertising we would have a far different nation, and one that would be much the poorer—not merely in material commodities, but in the life of the spirit.

Leo Burnett

## Summary

Advertising is a very powerful institution and has been the target of considerable criticism regarding its social and economic impact. The criticism of advertising concerns the specific techniques and methods used as well as its effect on societal values, tastes, lifestyles, and behavior. Critics argue that advertising is deceptive and untruthful; that it is often offensive, irritating, or in poor taste; and that it exploits certain groups, such as children. Many people believe advertising should be informative only and advertisers should not use subjective claims, puffery, embellishment, or persuasive techniques.

Advertising often offends consumers by the type of appeal or manner of presentation used; sexually suggestive ads and nudity receive the most criticism. Advertisers say their ads are consistent with contemporary values and lifestyles and are appropriate for the target audiences they are attempting to reach. Advertising to children is an area of particular concern, since critics argue that children lack the experience, knowledge, and ability to process and evaluate persuasive advertising messages rationally. Although an FTC proposal to severely restrict advertising to children was defeated, it remains an issue.

The pervasiveness of advertising and its prevalence in the mass media have led critics to argue that it plays a major role in influencing and transmitting social values. Advertising has been charged with encouraging materialism; manipulating consumers to buy things they do not really want or need; perpetuating stereotypes through its portrayal of certain groups such as women, minorities, and the elderly; and controlling the media.

Advertising has also been scrutinized with regard to its economic effects. The basic economic role of advertising is to give consumers information that helps them make consumption decisions. Some people view advertising as a detrimental force that has a negative effect on competition, product costs, and consumer prices. Economists' perspectives regarding the effects of advertising follow two basic schools of thought: the advertising equals market power model and the advertising equals information model. Arguments consistent with each perspective were considered in analyzing the economic effects of advertising.

## Key Terms

**ethics** p. 731
**shock advertising** p. 736
**consumer socialization process** p. 738
**materialism** p. 742
**Protestant ethic** p. 742
**differentiation** p. 753
**barrier to entry** p. 754
**economies of scale** p. 754

## Discussion Questions

1. The lead in to the chapter discusses the new "toner" shoes that are marketed as having the ability to improve ones' figure, among other claims. The shoes and the claims have been controversial, as many doctors do not believe they are true. Discuss the social and ethical issues surrounding these shoes. Should these claims be allowed to be made? (LO1)
2. What are shock ads? Do you think they are designed to create sales, or to bring attention to specific issues? Do they work? (LO2)
3. Over the years, and again very recently, there have been calls to eliminate or severely restrict advertising to children. Discuss the social and ethical issues as to whether advertising to children should be permitted. Support your position. (LO1)
4. The lead in to the chapter notes that some doctors and competitors claim that the new "toner" shoes do not work. Others suggest that the mere fact that consumers think they work and—as a result—exercise more, is enough to warrant their claims. Discuss these arguments. (LO2)
5. Ethical Perspective 21–1 discusses how the food and beverage industry is coming under attack over the advertising of fast food, snack products, and soft drinks. Do you think marketers of these products are responsible for the increase in obesity, particularly among young people? How should the industry respond to this criticism and efforts to limit their advertising and promotion programs? (LO3)
6. Groups such as Commercial Alert are concerned about the intrusion of advertising and other types of marketing messages into all aspects of consumers' lives. Discuss some of the reasons consumer watchdog groups are critical of advertising and other types of marketing practices. (LO2)
7. Evaluate the Dolce & Gabbana ad shown in Exhibit 21–3. Do you agree with the National Organization for Women's position that this ad is offensive to women? (LO3)
8. A common criticism of advertising is that it stereotypes women. Discuss the ways this might occur. Do you think the Airwalk ad shown in Exhibit 21–8 is suggestive and symbolizes sexual submission? (LO3)
9. Discuss how attitudes toward the use of sex in advertising differ between men and women. Discuss the implications of these attitudinal differences for marketers who are developing ads for each sex. (LO1)
10. The chapter discusses how many marketers are struggling with their multicultural marketing efforts and suggests that one reason may be the lack of diversity in advertising agencies. What are some of the reasons for the low number of minorities, such as African-Americans, working in advertising? How can the industry address this problem? (LO2)

## AdForum Exercise: "Examining the Social and Ethical Aspects of Advertising"

adforum.com

(see Advertising and Promotion Playlist, Chapter 21)

The playlist for Chapter 21 contains a number of ads, half of which are from the United States and half from other countries. Each reflects a social and/or ethical issue discussed in the chapter. Review each of these commercials and answer the following:

1 What objective is each ad trying to accomplish? Do you think they will achieve this objective?

2 Given the various media used, are some ads appropriate for one medium but not another? Explain.

3 Do you notice any differences between the U.S. and foreign ads?

Access to the chapter playlist is available through McGraw-Hill connect™ MARKETING, www.mcgrawhillconnect.com

Your enterprise information is exploding, along with the demands to make it all mobile.

NOW IT'S UP TO YOU TO MAKE IT WORK.

When businesses get serious about **INFORMATION MANAGEMENT AND MOBILITY** they get Sybase.

Ready to get serious about taking your data infrastructure to the next level? Choose the company that 81 of Fortune 100 organizations rely on to securely deliver decision-ready information to the point of action while providing the IT control you need: Sybase. Our modular software helps your IT staff to break down the complex barriers in your data flow, ensuring information moves seamlessly and securely between data sources and points of action. So if you're ready to make the Unwired Enterprise a reality, let Sybase help you deliver some serious results. To learn more, visit www.sybase.com/getserious

SYBASE

# 22 Personal Selling

## LEARNING OBJECTIVES

LO1 To understand the role of personal selling in the integrated marketing communications program.

LO2 To know the advantages and disadvantages of personal selling as a promotional program element.

LO3 To understand how personal selling is combined with other elements in an IMC program.

LO4 To know methods used to determine the effectiveness of the personal selling effort.

**GO TO WWW.MHHE.COM/BELCH9E TO ACCESS CHAPTER 22.**

# GLOSSARY OF ADVERTISING AND PROMOTION TERMS

*Note: Numbers in parentheses after term indicate chapter(s) where term is discussed.*

**absolute costs (10)** The actual total cost of placing an ad in a particular media vehicle.

**account executive (3)** The individual who serves as the liaison between the advertising agency and the client. The account executive is responsible for managing all of the services the agency provides to the client and representing the agency's point of view to the client.

**account planner (3)** Advertising agency personnel who gather information that is relevant to a client's product or service and can be used in the development of the creative strategy, as well as other aspects of an IMC campaign.

**account planning (8)** The process of conducting research and gathering all relevant information about a client's product, service, brand, and consumers in the target audience for use in the development of creative strategy as well as other aspects of an IMC campaign.

**account specific marketing (16)** Development of customized promotional programs for individual retail accounts by marketers.

**ad execution–related thoughts (5)** A type of thought or cognitive response a message recipient has concerning factors related to the execution of the ad such as creativity, visual effects, color, and style.

**adjacencies (11)** Commercial spots purchased from local television stations that generally appear during the time periods adjacent to network programs.

**advertising (1)** Any paid form of nonpersonal communication about an organization, product, service, or idea by an identified sponsor.

**advertising agency (3)** A firm that specializes in the creation, production, and placement of advertising messages and may provide other services that facilitate the marketing communications process.

**advertising appeal (9)** The basis or approach used in an advertising message to attract the attention or interest of consumers and/or influence their feelings toward the product, service, or cause.

**advertising campaign (8)** A comprehensive advertising plan that consists of a series of messages in a variety of media that center on a single theme or idea.

**advertising creativity (8)** The ability to generate fresh, unique, and appropriate ideas that can be used as solutions to communication problems.

**advertising manager (3)** The individual in an organization who is responsible for the planning, coordinating, budgeting, and implementing of the advertising program.

**advertising substantiation (21)** A Federal Trade Commission regulatory program that requires advertisers to have documentation to support the claims made in their advertisements.

**advocacy advertising (17)** Advertising that is concerned with the propagation of ideas and elucidation of social issues of public importance in a manner that supports the position and interest of the sponsor.

**aerial advertising (13)** A form of outdoor advertising where messages appear in the sky in the form of banners pulled by airplanes, skywriting, and on blimps.

**affect referral decision rule (4)** A type of decision rule where selections are made on the basis of an overall impression or affective summary evaluation of the various alternatives under consideration.

**affiliates (11)** Local television stations that are associated with a major network. Affiliates agree to preempt time during specified hours for programming provided by the network and carry the advertising contained in the program.

**affirmative disclosure (20)** A Federal Trade Commission program whereby advertisers may be required to include certain types of information in their advertisements so consumers will be aware of all the consequences, conditions, and limitations associated with the use of the product or service.

**affordable method (7)** A method of determining the budget for advertising and promotion where all other budget areas are covered and remaining monies are available for allocation.

**AIDA model (5)** A model that depicts the successive stages a buyer passes through in the personal selling process including attention, interest, desire, and action.

**alpha activity (18)** A measure of the degree of brain activity that can be used to assess an individual's reactions to an advertisement.

**alternative media (13)** A term commonly used in advertising to describe support media.

**animatic (8, 18)** A preliminary version of a commercial whereby a videotape of the frames of a storyboard is produced along with an audio soundtrack.

**arbitrary allocation (7)** A method for determining the budget for advertising and promotion based on arbitrary decisions of executives.

**attitude toward the ad (5)** A message recipient's affective feelings of favorability or unfavorability toward an advertisement.

**attractiveness (6)** A source characteristic that makes him or her appealing to a message recipient. Source attractiveness can be based on similarity, familiarity, or likability.

**audimeter (11)** An electric measurement device that is hooked to a television set to record when the set is turned on and the channel to which it is tuned.

**average frequency (10)** The number of times the average household reached by a media schedule is exposed to a media vehicle over a specified period.

**average quarter-hour (AQH) figure (11)** The average number of persons listening to a particular station for at least five minutes during a 15-minute period. Used by Arbitron in measuring the size of radio audiences.

**average quarter-hour rating (11)** The average quarter-hour figure estimate expressed as a percentage of the population being measured. Used by Arbitron in measuring the size of radio audiences.

**average quarter-hour share (11)** The percentage of the total listening audience tuned to each station as a percentage of the total listening audience in the survey area. Used by Arbitron in measuring the size of radio audiences.

**balance-of-trade deficit (19)** A situation where the monetary value of a country's imports exceeds its exports.

**banner ad (15)** An ad on a webpage that may be "hot-linked" to the advertiser's site.

**barrier to entry (21)** Conditions that make it difficult for a firm to enter the market in a particular industry, such as high advertising budgets.

**behavioral targeting (15)** A basis for target marketing based on consumers' website surfing behaviors.

**behavioristic segmentation (2)** A method of segmenting a market by dividing customers into groups based on their usage, loyalties, or buying responses to a product or service.

**benchmark measures (7)** Measures of a target audience's status concerning response hierarchy variables such as awareness, knowledge, image, attitudes, preferences, intentions, or behavior. These measures are taken at the beginning of an advertising or promotional campaign to determine the degree to which a target audience must be changed or moved by a promotional campaign.

**benefit segmentation (2)** A method of segmenting markets on the basis of the major benefits consumers seek in a product or service.

**Better Business Bureau (BBB) (20)** An organization established and funded by businesses that operate primarily at the local level to monitor activities of companies and promote fair advertising and selling practices.

**billings (3)** The amount of client money agencies spend on media purchases and other equivalent activities. Billings are often used as a way of measuring the size of advertising agencies.

**bleed pages (12)** Magazine advertisements where the printed area extends to the edge of the page, eliminating any white margin or border around the ad.

**blog (15)** Also known as a weblog, a blog is a Web-based publication consisting primarily of periodic articles written and provided in reverse chronological order. Blogs may reflect the writings of an individual, community political organization, or corporation.

**body copy (9)** The main text portion of a print ad. Also often referred to as copy.

**bonus packs (16)** Special packaging that provides consumers with extra quantity of merchandise at no extra charge over the regular price.

**bounce-back coupon (16)** A coupon offer made to consumers as an inducement to repurchase the brand.

**brand development index (BDI) (10)** An index that is calculated by taking the percentage of a brand's total sales that occur in a given market as compared to the percentage of the total population in the market.

**brand equity (2)** The intangible asset of added value or goodwill that results from the favorable image, impressions of differentiation, and/or the strength of consumer attachment of a company name, brand name, or trademark.

**brand loyalty (4)** Preference by a consumer for a particular brand that results in continual purchase of it.

**brand manager (3)** The person responsible for the planning, implementation, and control of the marketing program for an individual brand.

**branded entertainment (13)** The combined use of an audiovisual program (such as TV, radio, podcast, or videocast) and a brand to market a product or service. The purpose of a branded entertainment program is to entertain, while at the same time provide the opportunity for brands or products to be promoted.

**buildup approach (7)** A method of determining the budget for advertising and promotion by determining the specific tasks that have to be performed and estimating the costs of performing them. See objective and task method.

**cable television (11)** A form of television where signals are carried to households by wire rather than through the airways.

**campaign theme (8)** The central message or idea that is communicated in all advertising and other promotional activities.

**carryover effect (7)** A delayed or lagged effect whereby the impact of advertising on sales can occur during a subsequent time period.

**category development index (CDI) (10)** An index that is calculated by taking the percentage of a product category's total sales that occur in a given market area as compared to the percentage of the total population in the market.

**category management system (3)** An organizational system whereby managers have responsibility for the marketing programs for a particular category or line of products.

**cause-related marketing (17)** Image-related advertising in which companies link with charities or nonprofit organizations as contributing sponsors.

**cease-and-desist order (20)** An action by the Federal Trade Commission that orders a company to stop engaging in a practice that is considered deceptive or misleading until a hearing is held.

**Central Hudson Test (20)** A four-part test used by the courts for determining restrictions on commercial speech.

**central route to persuasion (5)** One of two routes to persuasion recognized by the elaboration likelihood model. The central route to persuasion views a message recipient as very active and involved in the communications process and as having the ability and motivation to attend to and process a message.

**centralized system (3)** An organizational system whereby advertising along with other marketing activities such as sales, marketing research, and planning are divided along functional lines and are run from one central marketing department.

**channel (5)** The method or medium by which communication travels from a source or sender to a receiver.

**Children's Online Privacy Protection Act of 1998 (20)** Federal legislation which places restrictions on information collected from children via the Internet and requires that websites directed at children have a privacy policy posted on their home page and areas of the site where information is collected.

**city zone (12)** A category used for newspaper circulation figures that refers to a market area composed of the city where the paper is published and contiguous areas similar in character to the city.

**classical conditioning (4)** A learning process whereby a conditioned stimulus that elicits a response is paired with a neutral stimulus that does not elicit any particular response. Through repeated exposure, the neutral stimulus comes to elicit the same response as the conditioned stimulus.

**classified advertising (12)** Advertising that runs in newspapers and magazines that generally contains text only and is arranged under subheadings according to the product, service, or offering. Employment, real estate, and automotive ads are the major forms of classified advertising.

**clients (3)** The organizations with the products, services, or causes to be marketed and for which advertising agencies and other marketing promotional firms provide services.

**clipping service (7)** A service which clips competitors' advertising from local print media allowing the company to monitor the types of advertising that are running or to estimate their advertising expenditures.

**clutter (6, 11)** The nonprogram material that appears in a broadcast environment, including commercials, promotional messages for shows, public service announcements, and the like.

**cognitive dissonance (4)** A state of psychological tension or postpurchase doubt that a consumer may experience after making a purchase decision. This tension often leads the consumer to try to reduce it by seeking supportive information.

**cognitive responses (5)** Thoughts that occur to a message recipient while reading, viewing, and/or hearing a communication.

**collateral services (3)** Companies that provide companies with specialized services such as package design, advertising production, and marketing research.

**combination rates (12)** A special space rate or discount offered for advertising in two or more periodicals. Combination rates are often offered by publishers who own both morning and evening editions of a newspaper in the same market.

**commercial rating (11)** Measures of the average viewership of a television commercial both live and up to three days after the ads are played back on a digital video recorder (DVR).

**commercial speech (20)** Speech that promotes a commercial transaction.

**commission system (3)** A method of compensating advertising agencies whereby the agency receives a specified commission (traditionally 15 percent) from the media on any advertising time or space it purchases.

**communication (5)** The passing of information, exchange of ideas, or process of establishing shared meaning between a sender and a receiver.

**communication objectives (1, 7)** Goals that an organization seeks to achieve through its promotional program in terms of communication effects such as creating awareness, knowledge, image, attitudes, preferences, or purchase intentions.

**communications task (7)** Under the DAGMAR approach to setting advertising goals and objectives, something that can be performed by and attributed to advertising such as awareness, comprehension, conviction, and action.

**comparative advertising (6, 9)** The practice of either directly or indirectly naming one or more competitors in an advertising message and usually making a comparison on one or more specific attributes or characteristics.

**competitive advantage (2)** Something unique or special that a firm does or possesses that provides an advantage over its competitors.

**competitive parity method (7)** A method of setting the advertising and promotion budget based on matching the absolute level of percentage of sales expenditures of the competition.

**compliance (6)** A type of influence process where a receiver accepts the position advocated by a source to obtain favorable outcomes or to avoid punishment.

**comprehension and reaction tests (18)** Advertising testing to ensure receivers comprehend the message and to gauge their reaction to the same.

**computer simulation models (7)** Quantitative-based models that are used to determine the relative contribution of advertising expenditures on sales response.

**concave-downward function model (7)** An advertising/sales response function that views the incremental effects of advertising on sales as decreasing.

**concentrated marketing (2)** A type of marketing strategy whereby a firm chooses to focus its marketing efforts on one particular market segment.

**concept testing (18)** A method of pretesting alternative ideas for an advertisement or campaign by having consumers provide their responses and/or reactions to the creative concept.

**conditioned response (4)** In classical conditioning, a response that occurs as a result of exposure to a conditioned stimulus.

**conditioned stimulus (4)** In classical conditioning, a stimulus that becomes associated with an unconditioned stimulus and capable of evoking the same response or reaction as the unconditioned stimulus.

**consent order (20)** A settlement between a company and the Federal Trade Commission whereby an advertiser agrees to stop the advertising or practice in question. A consent order is for settlement purposes only and does not constitute an admission of guilt.

**consumer behavior (4)** The process and activities that people engage in when searching for, selecting, purchasing, using, evaluating, and disposing of products and services so as to satisfy their needs and desires.

**consumer franchise-building promotions (16)** Sales promotion activities that communicate distinctive brand attributes and contribute to the development and reinforcement of brand identity.

**consumer juries (18)** A method of pretesting advertisements by using a panel of consumers who are representative of the target audience and provide ratings, rankings, and/or evaluations of advertisements.

**consumer-oriented sales promotion (16)** Sales promotion techniques that are targeted to the ultimate consumer such as coupons, samples, contests, rebates, sweepstakes, and premium offers.

**consumer socialization process (21)** The process by which an individual acquires the skills needed to function in the marketplace as a consumer.

**contact point (1)** Each and every opportunity a consumer has to see or hear about a company and/or its brands or have an encounter or experience with it.

**content sponsorship (15)** The sponsor not only provides dollars in return for name association on the Internet but participates in the provision of content itself.

**contest (16)** A promotion whereby consumers compete for prizes or money on the basis of skills or ability, and winners are determined by judging the entries or ascertaining which entry comes closest to some predetermined criteria.

**contextual ads (15)** Internet advertising placed on the basis of the content of the webpage.

**continuity (10)** A media scheduling strategy where a continuous pattern of advertising is used over the time span of the advertising campaign.

**contribution margin (7)** The difference between the total revenue generated by a product or brand and its total variable costs.

**controlled circulation basis (12)** Distribution of a publication free to individuals a publisher believes are of importance and responsible for making purchase decisions or are prescreened for qualification on some other basis.

**cooperative advertising (2, 16)** Advertising program in which a manufacturer pays a certain percentage of the expenses a retailer or distributor incurs for advertising the manufacturer's product in a local market area.

**copywriter (3, 8)** Individual who helps conceive the ideas for ads and commercials and writes the words or copy for them.

**corporate advertising (17)** Advertising designed to promote overall awareness of a company or enhance its image among a target audience.

**corrective advertising (20)** An action by the Federal Trade Commission whereby an advertiser can be required to run advertising messages designed to remedy the deception or misleading impression created by its previous advertising.

**cost per order (CPO) (14)** A measure used in direct marketing to determine the number of orders generated relative to the cost of running the advertisement.

**cost per ratings point (10)** A computation used by media buyers to compare the cost efficiency of broadcast programs that divides the cost of commercial time on a program by the audience rating.

**cost per thousand (10)** A computation used in evaluating the relative cost of various media vehicles that represents the cost of exposing 1,000 members of a target audience to an advertising message.

**cost-plus system (3)** A method of compensating advertising agencies whereby the agency receives a fee based on the cost of the work it performs plus an agreed-on amount for profit.

**Council of Better Business Bureaus (20)** The parent office of local offices of the Better Business Bureau. The council assists in the development of codes and standards for ethical and responsible business and advertising practices.

**counterargument (5)** A type of thought or cognitive response a receiver has that is counter or opposed to the position advocated in a message.

**country-of-origin effect (19)** The impact on consumers' perceptions of products and/or brands that results from where the products are manufactured.

**coverage (10)** A measure of the potential audience that might receive an advertising message through a media vehicle.

**creative boutique (3)** An advertising agency that specializes in and provides only services related to the creative aspects of advertising.

**creative brief (8)** A document that specifies the basic elements of the creative strategy such as the basic problem or issue the advertising must address, the advertising and communications objectives, target audience, major selling idea or key benefits to communicate, campaign theme or appeal, and supportive information or requirements.

**creative execution style (9)** The manner or way in which a particular advertising appeal is transformed into a message.

**creative strategy (8)** A determination of what an advertising message will say or communicate to a target audience.

**creative tactics (8)** A determination of how an advertising message will be implemented so as to execute the creative strategy.

**credibility (6)** The extent to which a source is perceived as having knowledge, skill, or experience relevant to a communication topic and can be trusted to give an unbiased opinion or present objective information on the issue.

**cross-media advertising (12)** An arrangement where opportunities to advertise in several different types of media are offered by a single company or a partnership of various media providers.

**cross/multimagazine deals (12)** An arrangement where two or more publishers offer their magazines to an advertiser as one media package.

**cross-ruff coupon (16)** A coupon offer delivered on one product that is redeemable for the purchase of another product. The other product is usually one made by the same company but may involve a tie-in with another manufacturer.

**cultural values (19)** Refers to beliefs and goals shared by members of a society regarding ideal end-states of life and modes of conduct.

**culture (4)** The complexity of learned meanings, values, norms, and customs shared by members of a society.

**cume (11)** A term used for cumulative audience, which is the estimated total number of different people who listened to a radio station for a minimum of five minutes during a particular daypart.

**DAGMAR (7)** An acronym that stands for defining advertising goals for measured advertising results. An approach to setting advertising goals and objectives developed by Russell Colley.

**daily inch rate (10)** A cost figure used in periodicals based on an advertisement placed one inch deep and one column wide (whatever the column inch).

**database (14)** A listing of current and/or potential customers for a company's product or service that can be used for direct-marketing purposes.

**database marketing (14)** The use of specific information about individual customers and/or prospects to implement more effective and efficient marketing communications.

**day-after recall scores (18)** A measure used in on-air testing of television commercials by various marketing research companies. The day-after recall score represents the percentage of viewers surveyed who can remember seeing a particular commercial.

**dayparts (11)** The time segments into which a day is divided by radio and television networks and stations for selling advertising time.

**decentralized system (3)** An organizational system whereby planning and decision-making responsibility for marketing, advertising, and promotion lies with a product/brand manager or management team rather than a centralized department.

**deception (20)** According to the Federal Trade Commission, a misrepresentation, omission, or practice that is likely to mislead the consumer acting reasonably in the circumstances to the consumer's detriment.

**decoding (5)** The process by which a message recipient transforms and interprets a message.

**demographic segmentation (2)** A method of segmenting a market based on the demographic characteristics of consumers.

**departmental system (3)** The organization of an advertising agency into departments based on functions such as account services, creative, media, marketing services, and administration.

**designated market area (DMA) (11)** The geographic areas used by the Nielsen Station Index in measuring audience size. DMAs are nonoverlapping areas consisting of groups of counties from which stations attract their viewers.

**differentiated marketing (2)** A type of marketing strategy whereby a firm offers products or services to a number of market segments and develops separate marketing strategies for each.

**differentiation (21)** A situation where a particular company or brand is perceived as unique or better than its competitors.

**digital billboards (13)** Billboards using digital imagery that changes every 6 to 8 seconds.

**direct broadcast satellite (DBS) (19)** A television signal delivery system whereby programming is beamed from satellites to special receiving dishes mounted in the home or yard.

**direct channel (2)** A marketing channel where a producer and ultimate consumer interact directly with one another.

**direct headline (9)** A headline that is very straightforward and informative in terms of the message it is presenting and the target audience it is directed toward. Direct headlines often include a specific benefit, promise, or reason for a consumer to be interested in a product or service.

**direct marketing (1, 14)** A system of marketing by which an organization communicates directly with customers to generate a response and/or transaction.

**direct-marketing agency (3)** A company that provides a variety of direct-marketing services to their clients including database management, direct mail, research, media service, creative, and production.

**direct-marketing media (14)** Media that are used for direct-marketing purposes including direct mail, telemarketing, print, and broadcast.

**direct-response advertising (1, 14)** A form of advertising for a product or service that elicits a sales response directly from the advertiser.

**direct-response media (14)** Media used to seek a direct response from the consumer, including direct mail, telemarketing, etc.

**direct selling (14)** The direct personal presentation, demonstration, and sale of products and services to consumers usually in their homes or at their jobs.

**directional medium (13)** Advertising media that are not used to create awareness or demand for products or services but rather to inform customers as to where purchases can be made once they have decided to buy. The Yellow Pages are an example of a directional medium.

**display advertising (12)** Advertising in newspapers and magazines that uses illustrations, photos, headlines, and other visual elements in addition to copy text.

**dissonance/attribution model (5)** A type of response hierarchy where consumers first behave, then develop attitudes or feelings as a result of that behavior, and then learn or process information that supports the attitude and behavior.

**e-commerce (15)** Direct selling of goods and services through the Internet.

**e-mail (15)** Messages sent electronically over the Internet.

**economic infrastructure (19)** A country's communications, transportation, financial, and distribution networks.

**economies of scale (7, 21)** A decline in costs with accumulated sales or production. In advertising, economies of scale often occur in media purchases as the relative costs of advertising time and/or space may decline as the size of the media budget increases.

**effective reach (10)** A measure of the percentage of a media vehicle's audience reached at each effective frequency increment.

**80/20 rule (2)** The principle that 80 percent of sales volume for a product or service is generated by 20 percent of the customers.

**elaboration likelihood model (ELM) (5)** A model that identifies two processes by which communications can lead to persuasion—central and peripheral routes.

**electrodermal response (18)** A measure of the resistance the skin offers to a small amount of current passed between two electrodes. Used as a measure of consumers' reaction level to an advertisement.

**electroencephalographic (EEG) measures (18)** Measures of the electrical impulses in the brain that are sometimes used as a measure of reactions to advertising.

**emotional appeals (6, 9)** Advertising messages that appeal to consumers' feelings and emotions.

**encoding (5)** The process of putting thoughts, ideas, or information into a symbolic form.

**ethics (21)** Moral principles and values that govern the actions and decisions of an individual or group.

**ethnographic research (8)** A research technique that involves observing or studying consumers in their natural environment.

**evaluative criteria (4)** The dimensions or attributes of a product or service that are used to compare different alternatives.

**event marketing (16)** A type of promotion where a company or brand is linked to an event, or where a themed activity is developed for the purpose of creating experiences for consumers and promoting a product or service.

**event sponsorship (16, 17)** A type of promotion whereby a company develops sponsorship relations with a particular event such as a concert, sporting event, or other activity.

**exchange (1)** Trade of something of value between two parties such as a product or service for money. The core phenomenon or domain for study in marketing.

**exclusive (17)** A public relations tactic whereby one particular medium is offered exclusive rights to a story.

**external analysis (1)** The phase of the promotional planning process that focuses on factors such as the characteristics of an organization's customers, market segments, positioning strategies, competitors, and marketing environment.

**external audiences (17)** In public relations, a term used in reference to individuals who are outside of or not closely connected to the organization such as the general public.

**external search (4)** The search process whereby consumers seek and acquire information from external sources such as advertising, other people, or public sources.

**eye tracking (18)** A method for following the movement of a person's eyes as he or she views an ad or commercial. Eye tracking is used for determining which portions or sections of an ad attract a viewer's attention and/or interest.

**failure fee (16)** A trade promotion arrangement whereby a marketer agrees to pay a penalty fee if a product stocked by a retailer does not meet agreed-upon sales levels.

**fear appeals (6)** An advertising message that creates anxiety in a receiver by showing negative consequences that can result from engaging in (or not engaging in) a particular behavior.

**Federal Trade Commission (FTC) (20)** The federal agency that has the primary responsibility for protecting consumers and businesses from anticompetitive behavior and unfair and deceptive practices. The FTC regulates advertising and promotion at the federal level.

**Federal Trade Commission Act (20)** Federal legislation passed in 1914 that created the Federal Trade Commission and gave it the responsibility to monitor deceptive or misleading advertising and unfair business practices.

**fee-commission combination (3)** A type of compensation system whereby an advertising agency establishes a fixed monthly fee for its services to a client and media commissions received by the agency are credited against the fee.

**feedback (5)** Part of the message recipient's response that is communicated back to the sender. Feedback can take a variety of forms and provides a sender with a way of monitoring how an intended message is decoded and received.

**field of experience (5)** The experiences, perceptions, attitudes, and values that senders and receivers of a message bring to a communication situation.

**field tests (18)** Tests of consumer reactions to an advertisement that are taken under natural viewing situations rather than in a laboratory.

**financial audit (3)** An aspect of the advertising agency evaluation process that focuses on how the agency conducts financial affairs related to serving a client.

**fixed-fee arrangement (3)** A method of agency compensation whereby the agency and client agree on the work to be done and the amount of money the agency will be paid for its services.

**flat rates (12)** A standard newspaper advertising rate where no discounts are offered for large-quantity or repeated space buys.

**Flesch formula (18)** A test used to assess the difficulty level of writing based on the number of syllables and sentences per 100 words.

**flighting (10)** A media scheduling pattern in which periods of advertising are alternated with periods of no advertising.

**focus groups (4, 8)** A qualitative marketing research method whereby a group of 10 to 12 consumers from the target market is led through a discussion regarding a particular topic such as a product, service, or advertising campaign.

**frequency (10)** The number of times a target audience is exposed to a media vehicle(s) in a specified period.

**frequency programs (16)** A type of promotional program that rewards customers for continuing to purchase the same brand of a product or service over time (also referred to as continuity or loyalty programs).

**full-service agency (3)** An advertising agency that offers clients a full range of marketing and communications services including the planning, creating, producing, and placing of advertising messages and other forms of promotion.

**functional consequences (4)** Outcomes of product or service usage that are tangible and can be directly experienced by a consumer.

**game (16)** A promotion that is a form of sweepstakes because it has a chance element or odds of winning associated with it. Games usually involve game card devices that can be rubbed or opened to unveil a winning number or prize description.

**gatefolds (12)** An oversize magazine page or cover that is extended and folded over to fit into the publication. Gatefolds are used to extend the size of a magazine advertisement and are always sold at a premium.

**general advertising rates (12)** Rates charged by newspapers to display advertisers outside the paper's designated market areas and to any classification deemed by the publisher to be general in nature.

**general preplanning input (8)** Information gathering and/or market research studies on trends, developments, and happenings in the marketplace that can be used to assist in the initial stages of the creative process of advertising.

**geographic segmentation (2)** A method of segmenting a market on the basis of different geographic units or areas.

**global advertising (19)** The use of the same basic advertising message in all international markets.

**global marketing (19)** A strategy of using a common marketing plan and program for all countries in which a company operates, thus selling the product or services the same way everywhere in the world.

**gross ratings points (GRPs) (10)** A measure that represents the total delivery or weight of a media schedule during a specified time period. GRPs are calculated by multiplying the reach of the media schedule by the average frequency.

**group system (3)** The organization of an advertising agency by dividing it into groups consisting of specialists from various departments such as creative, media, marketing services, and other areas. These groups work together to service particular accounts.

**guerrilla marketing (13)** The use of nontraditional media to market one's product often employing atypical efforts, and often attempting to capitalize on competitor's promotional efforts.

**halo effect (18)** The tendency for evaluations of one attribute or aspect of a stimulus to distort reactions to its other attributes or properties.

**headline (9)** Words in the leading position of the advertisement; the words that will be read first or are positioned to draw the most attention.

**hemisphere lateralization (18)** The notion that the human brain has two relatively distinct halves or hemispheres with each being responsible for a specific type of function. The right side is responsible for visual processing while the left side conducts verbal processing.

**heuristics (4)** Simplified or basic decision rules that can be used by a consumer to make a purchase choice, such as buy the cheapest brand.

**hierarchy of effects model (5)** A model of the process by which advertising works that assumes a consumer must pass through a sequence of steps from initial awareness to eventual action. The stages include awareness, interest, evaluation, trial, and adoption.

**hierarchy of needs (4)** Abraham Maslow's theory that human needs are arranged in an order or hierarchy based on their importance. The need hierarchy includes physiological, safety, social/love and belonging, esteem, and self-actualization needs.

**hit (15)** The number of times that a specific component of a website is accessed.

**horizontal cooperative advertising (16)** A cooperative advertising arrangement where advertising is sponsored in common by a group of retailers or other organizations providing products or services to a market.

**households using television (HUT) (11)** The percentage of homes in a given area that are watching television during a specific time period.

**identification (6)** The process by which an attractive source influences a message recipient. Identification occurs when the receiver is motivated to seek some type of relationship with the source and adopt a similar position in terms of beliefs, attitudes, preferences, or behavior.

**image advertising (8, 17)** Advertising that creates an identity for a product or service by emphasizing psychological meaning or symbolic association with certain values, lifestyles, and the like.

**image transfer (11)** A radio advertising technique whereby the images of a television commercial are implanted into a radio spot.

**incentive-based system (3)** A form of compensation whereby an advertising agency's compensation level depends on how well it meets predetermined performance goals such as sales or market share.

**index numbers (10)** A ratio used to describe the potential of a market. The index number is derived by dividing the percentage of users in a market segment by the percentage of population in the same segment and multiplying by 100.

**indirect channel (2)** A marketing channel where intermediaries such as wholesalers and retailers are utilized to make a product available to the customer.

**indirect headlines (9)** Headlines that are not straightforward with respect to identifying a product or service or providing information regarding the point of an advertising message.

**infomercials (14)** Television commercials that are very long, ranging from several minutes to an hour. Infomercials are designed to provide consumers with detailed information about a product or service.

**information processing model (5)** A model of advertising effects developed by William McGuire that views the receiver of a message as an information processor and problem solver. The model views the receiver as passing through a response hierarchy that includes a series of stages including message presentation, attention, comprehension, acceptance or yielding, retention, and behavior.

**informational/rational appeals (9)** Advertising appeals that focus on the practical, functional, or utilitarian need for a product or service and emphasize features, benefits, or reasons for owning or using the brand.

**ingredient-sponsored cooperative advertising (16)** Advertising supported by raw material manufacturers with the objective being to help establish end products that include materials and/or ingredients supplied by the company.

**inherent drama (8)** An approach to advertising that focuses on the benefits or characteristics that lead a consumer to purchase a product or service and uses dramatic elements to emphasize them.

**in-house agency (3)** An advertising agency set up, owned, and operated by an advertiser that is responsible for planning and executing the company's advertising program.

**ink-jet imaging (12)** A printing process where a message is reproduced by projecting ink onto paper rather than mechanical plates. Ink-jet imaging is being offered by many magazines to allow advertisers to personalize their messages.

**innovation adoption model (5)** A model that represents the stages a consumer passes through in the adoption process for an innovation such as a new product. The series of steps includes awareness, interest, evaluation, trial, and adoption.

**inquiry tests (18)** Tests designed to measure advertising effectiveness on the basis of inquiries or responses generated from the ad such as requests for information, number of phone calls, or number of coupons redeemed.

**inside cards (13)** A form of transit advertising where messages appear on cards or boards inside of vehicles such as buses, subways, or trolleys.

**instant coupons (16)** Coupons attached to a package that can be removed and redeemed at the time of purchase.

**in-store couponing (16)** The distribution of coupons in retail stores through various methods such as tear-off pads, handouts, and on-shelf or electronic dispensers.

**in-store media (13)** Advertising and promotional media that are used inside of a retail store such as point-of-purchase displays, ads on shopping carts, coupon dispensers, and display boards.

**integrated marketing communications (1)** A strategic business process used to develop, execute, and evaluate coordinated, measurable, persuasive brand communications programs over time with consumers, customers, prospects, employees, associates, and other targeted relevant external and internal audiences. The goal is to generate both short-term financial returns and build long-term brand and shareholder value.

**integrated marketing communications management (1)** The process of planning, executing, evaluating, and controlling the use of various promotional mix elements to effectively communicate with a target audience.

**integrated marketing communications objectives (7)** Statements of what various aspects of the integrated marketing communications program will accomplish with respect to factors such as communication tasks, sales, market share, and the like.

**integrated marketing communications plan (1)** A document that provides the framework for developing, implementing, and controlling an organization's integrated marketing communications program.

**integration processes (4)** The way information such as product knowledge, meanings, and beliefs is combined to evaluate two or more alternatives.

**interactive agency (3)** An organization that specializes in the creation of interactive media such as CD-ROMs, kiosks, and websites.

**interactive media (1, 10)** A variety of media that allows the consumer to interact with the source of the message, actively receiving information and altering images, responding to questions, and so on.

**interactive TV (15)** Television programs that allow the viewer to interact with the program or ads.

**interconnects (11)** Groups of cable systems joined together for advertising purposes.

**internal analysis (1)** The phase of the promotional planning process that focuses on the product/service offering and the firm itself including the capabilities of the firm and its ability to develop and implement a successful integrated marketing communications program.

**internal audiences (17)** In public relations, a term used to refer to individuals or groups inside of the organization or with a close connection to it.

**internal search (4)** The process by which a consumer acquires information by accessing past experiences or knowledge stored in memory.

**internalization (6)** The process by which a credible source influences a message recipient. Internalization occurs when the receiver is motivated to have an objectively correct position on an issue and the receiver will adopt the opinion or attitude of the credible communicator if he or she believes the information from this source represents an accurate position on the issue.

**Internet (15)** A worldwide means of exchanging information and communicating through a series of interconnected computers.

**interstitial (15)** An advertisement that appears in a window on your computer screen while you are waiting for a webpage to load.

**issue advertising (issue ads) (17)** A form of advocacy advertising in which the advertiser wishes to bring attention to what they consider to be an important issue.

**jingles (9)** Songs about a brand or company that usually carry the advertising theme and a simple message.

**laboratory tests (18)** Tests of consumer reactions to advertising under controlled conditions.

**Lanham Act (20)** A federal law that permits a company to register a trademark for its exclusive use. The Lanham Act was amended to encompass false advertising and prohibits any false description or representation including words or other symbols tending falsely to describe or represent the same.

**layout (9)** The physical arrangement of the various parts of an advertisement including the headline, subheads, illustrations, body copy, and any identifying marks.
**link (15)** An electronic connection between two websites.
**local advertising (11)** Advertising done by companies within the limited geographic area where they do business.
**localized advertising strategy (19)** Developing an advertising campaign specifically for a particular country or market rather than using a global approach.
**low-involvement hierarchy (5)** A response hierarchy whereby a message recipient is viewed as passing from cognition to behavior to attitude change.
**loyalty programs (16)** Programs designed to encourage repeat purchase or patronage of a specific brand of a product or service.

**magazine networks (12)** A group of magazines owned by one publisher or assembled by an independent network that offers advertisers the opportunity to buy space in a variety of publications through a package deal.
**mailing list (14)** A type of database containing names and addresses of present and/or potential customers who can be reached through a direct-mail campaign.
**major selling idea (8)** The basis for the central theme or message idea in an advertising campaign.
**marginal analysis (7)** A principle of resource allocation that balances incremental revenues against incremental costs.
**market opportunities (2)** Areas where a company believes there are favorable demand trends, needs, and/or wants that are not being satisfied, and where it can compete effectively.
**market segmentation (2)** The process of dividing a market into distinct groups that have common needs and will respond similarly to a marketing action.
**market segments (2)** Identifiable groups of customers sharing similar needs, wants, or other characteristics that make them likely to respond in a similar fashion to a marketing program.
**marketing (1)** The activity, set of institutions, and processes for creating, communicating, delivering, and exchanging offerings that have value for customers, clients, partners, and society at large.
**marketing channels (2)** The set of interdependent organizations involved in the process of making a product or service available to customers.
**marketing mix (2)** The controllable elements of a marketing program including product, price, promotion, and place.
**marketing objectives (1, 7)** Goals to be accomplished by an organization's overall marketing program such as sales, market share, or profitability.
**marketing plan (1)** A written document that describes the overall marketing strategy and programs developed for an organization, a particular product line, or a brand.
**marketing public relations (MPR) (17)** Public relations activities designed to support marketing objectives and programs.
**mass media (5)** Nonpersonal channels of communication that allow a message to be sent to many individuals at one time.
**materialism (21)** A preoccupation with material things rather than intellectual or spiritual concerns.
**media buying services (3)** Independent companies that specialize in the buying of media, particularly radio and television time.
**media objectives (10)** The specific goals an advertiser has for the media portion of the advertising program.
**media organizations (3)** One of the four major participants in the integrated marketing communications process whose function is to provide information or entertainment to subscribers, viewers, or readers while offering marketers an environment for reaching audiences with print and broadcast messages.
**media planning (10)** The series of decisions involved in the delivery of an advertising message to prospective purchasers and/or users of a product or service.
**media specialist companies (3)** Companies that specialize in the buying of advertising media time and space, particularly for radio and television.
**media strategies (10)** Plans of action for achieving stated media objectives such as which media will be used for reaching a target audience, how the media budget will be allocated, and how advertisements will be scheduled.
**media vehicle (10)** The specific program, publication, or promotional piece used to carry an advertising message.
**medium (10)** The general category of communication vehicles that are available for communicating with a target audience such as broadcast, print, direct mail, and outdoor.
**message (5)** A communication containing information or meaning that a source wants to convey to a receiver.
**mnemonics (4)** Basic cues such as symbols, rhymes, and associations that facilitate the learning and memory process.
**mobile (15)** Type of services accessed through a portable communications device.
**mobile billboards (13)** An out-of-home medium in which advertisements are able to be transported to different locations (signs painted on automobiles, trailers pulling billboards, and the like).
**motivation research (4)** Qualitative research designed to probe the consumer's subconscious and discover deeply rooted motives for purchasing a product.
**motive (4)** Something that compels or drives a consumer to take a particular action.
**multiattribute attitude model (4)** A model of attitudes that views an individual's evaluation of an object as being a function of the beliefs that he or she has toward the object on various attributes and the importance of these attributes.
**multiplexing (11)** An arrangement where multiple channels are transmitted by one cable network.

**narrowcasting (11)** The reaching of a very specialized market through programming aimed at particular target audiences. Cable television networks offer excellent opportunities for narrowcasting.
**National Advertising Review Board (NARB) (20)** A part of the National Advertising Division of the Council of Better Business Bureaus. The NARB is the advertising industry's primary self-regulatory body.
**National Advertising Review Council (NARC) (20)** An organization founded by the Council of Better Business Bureaus and various advertising industry groups to promote high standards of truth, accuracy, morality, and social responsibility in national advertising.
**National Association of Attorneys General (20)** An organization consisting of state attorneys general that is involved in the regulation of advertising and other business practices.
**national spot advertising (11)** All nonnetwork advertising done by a national advertiser in local markets.
**needledrop (9)** A term used in the advertising industry to refer to music that is prefabricated, multipurpose, and conventional and can be used in a commercial when a particular normative effect is desired.
**negotiated commission (3)** A method of compensating advertising agencies whereby the client and agency negotiate the commission structure rather than relying on the traditional 15 percent media commission.

**Nielsen Television Index (11)** A service that provides daily and weekly estimates of the size and composition of national television viewing audiences for the network shows.

**noise (5)** Extraneous factors that create unplanned distortion or interference in the communications process.

**nonfranchise-building promotions (16)** Sales promotion activities that are designed to accelerate the purchase decision process and generate an immediate increase in sales but do little or nothing to communicate information about a brand and contribute to its identity and image.

**nonmeasured media (13)** A term commonly used in the advertising industry to describe support media.

**nontraditional media (13)** Newer media including various forms of support media such as entertainment marketing, guerrilla marketing, product placements, and the like, as well as Internet and interactive media, such as blogs, podcasts, and more.

**objective and task method (7)** A build-up approach to budget setting involving a three-step process: (1) determining objectives, (2) determining the strategies and tasks required to attain these objectives, and (3) estimating the costs associated with these strategies and tasks.

**off-invoice allowance (16)** A promotional discount offered to retailers or wholesalers whereby a certain per-case amount or percentage is deducted from the invoice.

**on-air tests (18)** Testing the effectiveness of television commercials by inserting test ads into actual TV programs in certain test markets.

**one-sided message (6)** Communications in which only positive attributes or benefits of a product or service are presented.

**one-step approach (14)** A direct-marketing strategy in which the medium is used directly to obtain an order (for example, television direct-response ads).

**open rate structure (12)** A rate charged by newspapers in which discounts are available based on frequency or bulk purchases of space.

**operant conditioning (instrumental conditioning) (4)** A learning theory that views the probability of a behavior as being dependent on the outcomes or consequences associated with it.

**out-of-home advertising (13)** The variety of advertising forms including outdoor, transit, skywriting, and other media viewed outside the home.

**outside posters (13)** Outdoor transit posters appearing on buses, taxis, trains, subways, and trolley cars.

**PACT (Positioning Advertising Copy Testing) (18)** A set of principles endorsed by 21 of the largest U.S. ad agencies aimed at improving the research used in preparing and testing ads, providing a better creative product for clients, and controlling the cost of TV commercials.

**paid search (15)** Also referred to as search engine advertising in which advertisers pay only when a consumer clicks on their ad or link from a search engine page.

**participations (11)** The situation where several advertisers buy commercial time or spots on network television.

**pass-along rate (10)** An estimate of the number of readers of a magazine in addition to the original subscriber or purchaser.

**pass-along readership (12)** The audience that results when the primary subscriber or purchaser of a magazine gives the publication to another person to read, or when the magazine is read in places such as waiting rooms in doctors' offices.

**pattern advertising (19)** Advertisements that follow a basic global approach although themes, copy, and sometimes even visual elements may be adjusted.

**payout plan (7)** A budgeting plan that determines the investment value of the advertising and promotion appropriation.

**people meter (11)** An electronic device that automatically records a household's television viewing, including channels watched, number of minutes of viewing, and members of the household who are watching.

**percentage charges (3)** The markups charged by advertising agencies for services provided to clients.

**percentage of sales method (7)** A budget method in which the advertising and/or promotions budget is set based on a percentage of sales of the product.

**perception (4)** The process by which an individual receives, selects, organizes, and interprets information to create a meaningful picture of the world.

**peripheral route to persuasion (5)** In the elaboration likelihood model, one of two routes to persuasion in which the receiver is viewed as lacking the ability or motivation to process information and is not likely to be engaging in detailed cognitive processing.

**personal selling (1, 10)** Person-to-person communication in which the seller attempts to assist and/or persuade prospective buyers to purchase the company's product or service or to act on an idea.

**persuasion matrix (6)** A communications planning model in which the stages of the response process (dependent variables) and the communications components (independent variables) are combined to demonstrate the likely effect that the independent variables will have on the dependent variables.

**planograms (16)** A planning configuration of products that occupy a shelf section in a store that is used to provide more efficient shelf space utilization.

**podcasting (15)** A medium using the Internet to distribute files for downloading into iPods and other MP3 players.

**pop-under (15)** Ads that pop-up as the user is leaving the website.

**pop-ups (15)** Advertisement windows on the Internet usually larger than a banner ad and smaller than a full screen.

**portable people meter (11)** A wearable pager-sized device that electronically traces what consumers listen to on the radio by detecting inaudible identification codes that are embedded in the programming.

**portfolio tests (18)** A laboratory methodology designed to expose a group of respondents to a portfolio consisting of both control and test print ads.

**positioning (2)** The art and science of fitting the product or service to one or more segments of the market in such a way as to set it meaningfully apart from competition.

**posttests (18)** Ad effectiveness measures that are taken after the ad has appeared in the marketplace.

**preferred position rate (12)** A rate charged by newspapers that ensures the advertiser the ad will appear in the position required and/or in a specific section of the newspaper.

**premium (16)** An offer of an item of merchandise or service either free or at a low price that is used as an extra incentive for purchasers.

**preprinted inserts (12)** Advertising distributed through newspapers that is not part of the newspaper itself, but is printed by the advertiser and then taken to the newspaper to be inserted.

**press conference (17)** The calling together of the press to announce significant news and/or events.

**press release (17)** Factual and interesting information released to the press.

**pretests (18)** Advertising effectiveness measures that are taken before the implementation of the advertising campaign.

**price-off deal (16)** A promotional strategy in which the consumer receives a reduction in the regular price of the brand.

**primacy effect (6)** A theory that the first information presented in the message will be the most likely to be remembered.

**primary circulation (12)** The number of copies of a magazine distributed to original subscribers.

**problem detection (8)** A creative research approach in which consumers familiar with a product (or service) are asked to generate an exhaustive list of problems encountered in its use.

**problem recognition (4)** The first stage in the consumer's decision-making process in which the consumer perceives a need and becomes motivated to satisfy it.

**product integrations (13)** The act of integrating the product into television program content.

**product placement (13)** A form of advertising and promotion in which products are placed in television shows and/or movies to gain exposure.

**product/service-specific preplanning input (8)** Specific studies provided to the creative department on the product or service, the target audience, or a combination of the two.

**product symbolism (2)** The meaning that a product or brand has to consumers.

**program rating (10, 11)** The percentage of TV households in an area that are tuned to a program during a specific time period.

**promotion (1)** The coordination of all seller-initiated efforts to set up channels of information and persuasion to sell goods and services or to promote an idea.

**promotional mix (1)** The tools used to accomplish an organization's communications objective. The promotional mix includes advertising, direct marketing, sales promotion, publicity/public relations, and personal selling.

**promotional products marketing (13)** The advertising or promotional medium or method that uses promotional products such as ad specialties, premiums, business gifts, awards, prizes, or commemoratives.

**promotional pull strategy (2)** A strategy in which advertising and promotion efforts are targeted at the ultimate consumers to encourage them to purchase the manufacturer's brand.

**promotional push strategy (2)** A strategy in which advertising and promotional efforts are targeted to the trade to attempt to get them to promote and sell the product to the ultimate consumer.

**Protestant ethic (21)** A perspective of life that stresses hard work and individual effort and initiative and views the accumulation of material possessions as evidence of success.

**psychoanalytic theory (4)** An approach to the study of human motivations and behaviors pioneered by Sigmund Freud.

**psychographic segmentation (2)** Dividing the product on the basis of personality and/or lifestyles.

**psychosocial consequences (4)** Purchase decision consequences that are intangible, subjective, and personal.

**public relations (1, 17)** The management function that evaluates public attitudes, identifies the policies and procedures of an individual or organization with the public interest, and executes a program to earn public understanding and acceptance.

**public relations firm (3)** An organization that develops and implements programs to manage a company's publicity, image, and affairs with consumers and other relevant publics.

**publicity (1, 17)** Communications regarding an organization, product, service, or idea that are not directly paid for or run under identified sponsorship.

**puffery (20)** Advertising or other sales presentations that praise the item to be sold using subjective opinions, superlatives, or exaggerations, vaguely and generally, stating no specific facts.

**pulsing (10)** A media scheduling method that combines flighting and continuous scheduling.

**pupillometrics (18)** An advertising effectiveness methodology designed to measure dilation and constriction of the pupils of the eye in response to stimuli.

**purchase intention (4)** The predisposition to buy a certain brand or product.

**push money (16)** Cash payments made directly to the retailers' or wholesalers' sales force to encourage them to promote and sell a manufacturer's product.

**qualitative audit (3)** An audit of the advertising agency's efforts in planning, developing, and implementing the client's communications programs.

**qualitative media effect (6)** The positive or negative influence the medium may contribute to the message.

**ratings point (11)** A measurement used to determine television viewing audiences in which one ratings point is the equivalent of 1 percent of all of the television households in a particular area tuned to a specific program.

**reach (10)** The number of different audience members exposed at least once to a media vehicle (or vehicles) in a given period.

**readers per copy (10)** A cost comparison figure used for magazines that estimates audience size based on pass-along readership.

**really simple syndication (RSS) (15)** (*see* RSS)

**recall tests (18)** Advertising effectiveness tests designed to measure advertising recall.

**receiver (5)** The person or persons with whom the sender of a message shares thoughts or information.

**recency (10)** The idea that advertising will have the most effect on someone who is in the market for the product, and that planners should attempt to reach that consumer as close as possible to their purchase decision.

**recency effect (6)** The theory that arguments presented at the end of the message are considered to be stronger and therefore are more likely to be remembered.

**recency planning (10)** Media planning that attempts to reach the consumer in the period of time just before their purchase decision.

**recognition method (18)** An advertising effectiveness measure of print ads that allows the advertiser to assess the impact of an ad in a single issue of a magazine over time and/or across alternative magazines.

**reference group (4)** A group whose perspectives, values, or behavior is used by an individual as the basis for his or her judgments, opinions, and actions.

**refund (16)** An offer by a manufacturer to return a portion of a product's purchase price, usually after the consumer supplies a proof of purchase.

**refutational appeal (6)** A type of message in which both sides of the issue are presented in the communication, with arguments offered to refute the opposing viewpoint

**reinforcement (4)** The rewards or favorable consequences associated with a particular response.

**relative cost (10)** The relationship between the price paid for advertising time or space and the size of the audience delivered; it is used to compare the prices of various media vehicles.

**relevance (8)** The degree to which the various elements of an advertisement are meaningful, useful, or valuable to the consumer.

**reminder advertising (9)** Advertising designed to keep the name of the product or brand in the mind of the receiver.

**repositioning (2)** The changing of a product or brand's positioning.

**resellers (2)** Intermediaries in the marketing channel such as wholesalers, distributors, and retailers.

**response (5)** The set of reactions the receiver has after seeing, hearing, or reading a message.

**retail advertising rates (12)** Rates newspapers charge to advertisers that conduct business or sell goods and services within the paper's designated market area.

**retail trading zone (12)** The market outside the city zone whose residents regularly trade with merchants within the city zone.

**RFM scoring method (14)** The Postal Service's recommendation for scoring the value of database entries, based on recency, frequency, and monetary transactions.

**rich media (15)** A term for advanced technology used in Internet ads, such as a streaming video, which allows interaction and special effects.

**ROI (7)** Return on investment is a measure used to determine the returns received on advertising and other IMC element investments.

**ROI budgeting method (return on investment) (7)** A budgeting method in which advertising and promotions are considered investments, and thus measurements are made in an attempt to determine the returns achieved by these investments.

**RSS (15)** Really simple syndication is a specification that uses XML to organize and format Web-based content in a standard way to provide RSS feeds, which consist of titles and brief descriptions of other online articles.

**run of paper (ROP) (12)** A rate quoted by newspapers that allows the ad to appear on any page or in any position desired by the medium.

**S-shaped response curve (7)** A sales response model that attempts to show sales responses to various levels of advertising and promotional expenditures.

**sales promotion (1, 16)** Marketing activities that provide extra value or incentives to the sales force, distributors, or the ultimate consumer and can stimulate immediate sales.

**sales promotion agency (3)** An organization that specializes in the planning and implementation of promotional programs such as contests, sweepstakes, sampling, premiums, and incentive offers for its clients.

**sales promotion trap (16)** A spiral that results when a number of competitors extensively use promotions. One firm uses sales promotions to differentiate its product or service and other competitors copy the strategy, resulting in no differential advantage and a loss of profit margins to all.

**salient attributes (2)** Attributes considered important to consumers in the purchase decision process.

**salient beliefs (4)** Beliefs concerning specific attributes or consequences that are activated and form the basis of an attitude.

**sampling (16)** A variety of procedures whereby consumers are given some quantity of a product for no charge to induce trial.

**scatter market (11)** A period for purchasing television advertising time that runs throughout the TV season.

**schedules of reinforcement (4)** The schedule by which a behavioral response is rewarded.

**script (9)** A written version of the commercial that provides a detailed description of its video and audio content.

**search engine optimization (SEO) (15)** The process of improving ranking in search engine results.

**selective attention (4)** A perceptual process in which consumers choose to attend to some stimuli and not others.

**selective binding (12)** A computerized production process that allows the creation of hundreds of copies of a magazine in one continuous sequence.

**selective comprehension (4)** The perceptual process whereby consumers interpret information based on their own attitudes, beliefs, motives, and experiences.

**selective exposure (4)** A process whereby consumers choose whether or not to make themselves available to media and message information.

**selective learning (5)** The process whereby consumers seek information that supports the choice made and avoid information that fails to bolster the wisdom of a purchase decision.

**selective perception (4)** The perceptual process involving the filtering or screening of exposure, attention, comprehension, and retention.

**selective retention (4)** The perceptual process whereby consumers remember some information but not all.

**selectivity (12)** The ability of a medium to reach a specific target audience.

**self-liquidating premiums (16)** Premiums that require the consumer to pay some or all of the cost of the premium plus handling and mailing costs.

**self-regulation (20)** The practice by the advertising industry of regulating and controlling advertising to avoid interference by outside agencies such as the government.

**sensation (4)** The immediate and direct response of the senses (taste, smell, sight, touch, and hearing) to a stimulus such as an advertisement, package, brand name, or point-of-purchase display.

**shaping (4)** The reinforcement of successive acts that lead to a desired behavior pattern or response.

**share of audience (11)** The percentage of households watching television in a special time period that are tuned to a specific program.

**shock advertising (21)** Advertising in which marketers use nudity, sexual suggestiveness, or other startling images to get consumers' attention.

**single-source tracking (18)** A research method designed to track the behaviors of consumers from the television set to the supermarket checkout counter.

**situational determinants (4)** Influences originating from the specific situation in which consumers are to use the product or brand.

**sleeper effect (6)** A phenomenon in which the persuasiveness of a message increases over time.

**slogan (or tagline) (8)** A statement or phrase consisting of a few words that succinctly expresses the company image, identity, and/or positioning a company or brand wants to communicate.

**slotting allowance (16)** Fees that must be paid to retailers to provide a "slot" or position to accommodate a new product on the store shelves.

**social class (4)** Relatively homogeneous divisions of society into which people are grouped based on similar lifestyles, values, norms, interests, and behaviors.
**social media (15)** Media created to be shared freely.
**social network (15)** A network of business or social contacts.
**source (5, 6)** The sender—person, group, or organization—of the message.
**source bolsters (5)** Favorable cognitive thoughts generated toward the source of a message.
**source derogations (5)** Negative thoughts generated about the source of a communication.
**source power (6)** The power of a source as a result of his or her ability to administer rewards and/or punishments to the receiver.
**spam (15, 20)** Unsolicited commercial e-mail.
**spamming (20)** The sending of unsolicited multiple commercial electronic messages.
**specialized marketing communication services (3)** Organizations that provide marketing communication services in their areas of expertise including direct marketing, public relations, and sales promotion firms.
**specialty advertising (13)** An advertising, sales promotion, and motivational communications medium that employs useful articles of merchandise imprinted with an advertiser's name, message, or logo.
**split run test (18)** An advertising effectiveness measure in which different versions of an ad are run in alternate copies of the same newspaper and/or magazine.
**split runs (12)** Two or more versions of a print ad are printed in alternative copies of a particular issue of a magazine.
**sponsorship (11)** When the advertiser assumes responsibility for the production and usually the content of a television program as well as the advertising that appears within it.
**sponsorships (15)** When advertisers sponsor content on a website, it is considered a sponsorship.
**spot advertising (11)** Commercials shown on local television stations, with the negotiation and purchase of time being made directly from the individual stations.
**standard advertising unit (SAU) (12)** A standard developed in the newspaper industry to make newspaper purchasing rates more comparable to other media that sell space and time in standard units.
**standard learning model (5)** Progression by the consumers through a learn-feel-do hierarchical response.
**station reps (11)** Individuals who act as sales representatives for a number of local stations and represent them in dealings with national advertisers.
**storyboard (8)** A series of drawings used to present the visual plan or layout of a proposed commercial.
**strategic marketing plan (2)** The planning framework for specific marketing activities.
**subcultures (4)** Smaller groups within a culture that possess similar beliefs, values, norms, and patterns of behavior that differentiate them from the larger cultural mainstream.
**subheads (9)** Secondary headlines in a print ad.
**subliminal perception (4)** The ability of an individual to perceive a stimulus below the level of conscious awareness.
**superagencies (3)** Large external agencies that offer integrated marketing communications on a worldwide basis.
**superstations (11)** Independent local stations that send their signals via satellite to cable operators that, in turn, make them available to subscribers (WWOR, WPIX, WGN, WSBK, WTBS).
**support advertising (14)** A form of direct marketing in which the ad is designed to support other forms of advertising appearing in other media.
**support argument (5)** Consumers' thoughts that support or affirm the claims being made by a message.
**support media (13)** Those media used to support or reinforce messages sent to target markets through other more "dominant" and/or more traditional media.
**survey of buying power (10)** An index that provides information regarding population, effective buying income, and total retail sales in an area.
**sweeps periods (10, 11)** The times of year in which television audience measures are taken (February, May, July, and November).
**sweepstakes (16)** A promotion whereby consumers submit their names for consideration in the drawing or selection of prizes and winners are determined purely by chance. Sweepstakes cannot require a proof of purchase as a condition for entry.
**syndicated programs (11)** Shows sold or distributed to local stations.

**target CPM (TCPM) (10)** A relative cost comparison that calculates CPMs based on the target audience as opposed to the overall audience.
**target marketing (2)** The process of identifying the specific needs of segments, selecting one or more of these segments as a target, and developing marketing programs directed to each.
**target ratings points (TRPs) (10)** The number of persons in the primary target audience that the media buy will reach—and the number of times.
**teaser advertising (9)** An ad designed to create curiosity and build excitement and interest in a product or brand without showing it.
**telemarketing (14)** Selling products and services by using the telephone to contact prospective customers.
**telemedia (14)** The use of telephone and voice information services (800, 900, 976 numbers) to market, advertise, promote, entertain, and inform.
**television households (11)** The number of households in a market that own a television set.
**television network (11)** The provider of news and programming to a series of affiliated local television stations.
**terminal posters (13)** Floor displays, island showcases, electronic signs, and other forms of advertisements that appear in train or subway stations, airline terminals, and the like.
**testing bias (18)** A bias that occurs in advertising effectiveness measures because respondents know they are being tested and thus alter their responses.
**theater testing (18)** An advertising effectiveness pretest in which consumers view ads in a theater setting and evaluate these ads on a variety of dimensions.
**top-down approaches (7)** Budgeting approaches in which the budgetary amount is established at the executive level and monies are passed down to the various departments.
**total audience (television) (11)** The total number of homes viewing any five-minute part of a television program.
**total audience/readership (12)** A combination of the total number of primary and pass-along readers multiplied by the circulation of an average issue of a magazine.
**tracking studies (18)** Advertising effectiveness measures designed to assess the effects of advertising on awareness, recall, interest, and attitudes toward the ad as well as purchase intentions.

**trade advertising (2)** Advertising targeted to wholesalers and retailers.

**trade allowance (16)** A discount or deal offered to retailers or wholesalers to encourage them to stock, promote, or display a manufacturer's product.

**trade-oriented sales promotion (16)** A sales promotion designed to motivate distributors and retailers to carry a product and make an extra effort to promote or "push" it to their customers.

**trade regulation rules (TRRs) (20)** Industrywide rules that define unfair practices before they occur. Used by the Federal Trade Commission to regulate advertising and promotion.

**trade show (16)** A type of exhibition or forum where manufacturers can display their products to current as well as prospective buyers.

**traditional media (13)** Commonly thought of media that have been employed for years. These include advertising, sales promotions, public relations, and direct marketing.

**transformational ad (9)** An ad that associates the experience of using the advertised brand with a unique set of psychological characteristics that would not typically be associated with the brand experience to the same degree without exposure to the advertisement.

**transit advertising (13)** Advertising targeted to target audiences exposed to commercial transportation facilities, including buses, taxis, trains, elevators, trolleys, airplanes, and subways.

**two-sided message (6)** A message in which both good and bad points about a product or claim are presented.

**two-step approach (14)** A direct-marketing strategy in which the first effort is designed to screen or qualify potential buyers, while the second effort has the responsibility of generating the response.

**undifferentiated marketing (2)** A strategy in which market segment differences are ignored and one product or service is offered to the entire market.

**unduplicated reach (10)** The number of persons reached once with a media exposure.

**unfairness (20)** A concept used by the Federal Trade Commission to determine unfair or deceptive advertising practices. Unfairness occurs when a trade practice causes substantial physical or economic injury to consumers, could not be avoided by consumers, and must not be outweighed by countervailing benefits to consumers or competition.

**unique selling proposition (USP) (8)** An advertising strategy that focuses on a product or service attribute that is distinctive to a particular brand and offers an important benefit to the customer.

**up-front market (11)** A buying period that takes place prior to the upcoming television season when the networks sell a large part of their commercial time.

**user-provided content (9, 15)** Advertising and/or other forms of content provided by consumers or other nonprofessional sources.

**value (1)** The customer's perception of all of the benefits of a product or service weighed against the costs of acquiring and consuming it.

**vehicle option source effect (18)** The differential impact the advertising exposure will have on the same audience member if the exposure occurs in one media option rather than another.

**vertical cooperative advertising (16)** A cooperative arrangement under which a manufacturer pays for a portion of the advertising a retailer runs to promote the manufacturer's product and its availability in the retailer's place of business.

**video news release (VNR) (17)** News stories produced by publicists so that television stations may air them as news.

**voiceover (9)** A message or action on the screen in a commercial that is narrated or described by a narrator who is not visible.

**want (4)** A felt need shaped by a person's knowledge, culture, and personality.

**waste coverage (10)** A situation where the coverage of the media exceeds the target audience.

**wearout (6)** The tendency for a television or radio commercial to lose its effectiveness when it is seen and/or heard repeatedly.

**Web 2.0 (15)** Web applications that facilitate interactive information sharing, interoperability, user-centered design, and interactivity.

**webcasting (15)** A system for pushing out site information to Web users rather than waiting for them to find the site on their own. (Often referred to as push technologies.)

**website (15)** The information made available to users of the Internet by the provider.

**Wheeler-Lea Amendment (20)** An act of Congress passed in 1938 that amended section 5 of the FTC Act to read that unfair methods of competition in commerce and unfair or deceptive acts or practices in commerce are declared unlawful.

**wireless (15)** A communications network that allows access, as well as transmissions to and from the Internet to travel over the air waves, rather than fixed land lines.

**word-of-mouth communications (5)** Social channels of communication such as friends, neighbors, associates, co-workers, or family members.

**World Wide Web (WWW) (15)** Commonly referred to as the Web. The commercial component of the Internet.

**Yellow Pages (13)** A telephone directory providing names of companies that provide specific products and/or services.

**Yellow Pages advertising (13)** Advertisements that appear in the various Yellow Pages–type phone directories.

**zapping (11)** The use of a remote control device to change channels and switch away from commercials.

**zero-based communications planning (7)** An approach to planning the integrated marketing communications program that involves determining what tasks need to be done and what marketing communication functions should be used to accomplish them and to what extent.

**zipping (11)** Fast-forwarding through commercials during the playback of a program previously recorded on a VCR.

# ENDNOTES

## Chapter One

1. Bob Garfield. *The Chaos Scenario,* (Nashville, TN: Stielstra Publishing, 2009).
2. "Media Advertising & Non-Advertising Marketing Communications Investment Report 2009–2010," *Jack Myers Media Business Report* (Rhinebeck, NY; M.E.D.I.Advisory Group LLC, December 7, 2009).
3. Ibid.
4. Nat Ives and Michael Bush, "Growth Returns to Global Ad Spending in 2010—Modestly and Unevenly," *Advertising Age,* http://adage.com/printe?article_id=140929.
5. Suzanne Vranica, "For Ad Industry, 2010 Promises Scant Relief," *The Wall Street Journal,* December 24, 2009, p. B5.
6. "AMA Approves New Marketing-Definition," *Marketing News,* March 1, 1985, p. 1.
7. Richard P. Bagozzi, "Marketing as Exchange," *Journal of Marketing* 39 (October 1975), pp. 32–39.
8. Lisa M. Keefe, "Marketing Defined," *Marketing News,* January 15, 2008, pp. 28–29.
9. Frederick E. Webster, Jr., "Defining the New Marketing Concept," *Marketing Management* 3, no. 4 (1993), pp. 22–31.
10. Adrienne Ward Fawcett, "Integrated Marketing—Marketers Convinced: Its Time Has Arrived," *Advertising Age,* November 6, 1993, pp. S1–2.
11. "Do Your Ads Need a SuperAgency?" *Fortune,* April 27, 1991, pp. 81–85; Faye Rice, "A Cure for What Ails Advertising?" *Fortune,* December 16, 1991, pp. 119–22.
12. Scott Hume, "Campus Adopts 'New' Advertising," *Advertising Age,* September 23, 1991, p. 17.
13. Don E. Schultz, "Integrated Marketing Communications: Maybe Definition Is in the Point of View," *Marketing News,* January 18, 1993, p. 17.
14. Ibid.
15. Joep P. Cornelissen and Andrew R. Lock, "Theoretical Concept or Management Fashion? Examining the Significance of IMC," *Journal of Advertising Research* (September–October 2000), pp. 7–15.
16. Philip J. Kitchen, Joanne Brignell, Tao Li, and Graham Spickett Jones, "The Emergence of IMC: A Theoretical Perspective," *Journal of Advertising Research* (March 2004), pp. 19–30.
17. Don E. Schultz, "IMC Receives More Appropriate Definition," *Marketing News,* September 15, 2004, pp. 8–9.
18. Joep P. Cornelissen and Andrew R. Lock, "Theoretical Concept or Managemet Fashion? Examining the Significance of IMC."
19. Harlan E. Spotts, David R. Lambert, and Mary L. Joyce, "Marketing Déjà Vu: The Discovery of Integrated Marketing Communications," *Journal of Marketing Education,* 20(3) (December 1998), pp. 210–18.
20. Tom Duncan and Sandra E. Moriarty, "A Communication-Based Model for Managing Relationships," *Journal of Marketing* 62(2) (April 1998), pp. 1–13.
21. Anthony J. Tortorici, "Maximizing Marketing Communications Through Horizontal and Vertical Orchestration," *Public Relations Quarterly* 36(1) (1991), pp. 20–22.
22. Emily Steel, "Advertising's Brave New World: Different Lineup of Players Emerges with Online's Rise, *The Wall Street Journal,* May 25, 2007, p. B1.
23. W. Glynn Mangold and David J. Faulds, "Social Media: The New Hybrid Element of the Promotion Mix," *Business Horizons* 52(4), July/August 2009, pp. 52, 357–365.
24. Nat Ives, "Consumers Bugged by Many Ads," *Advertising Age,* December 1, 2008, http://adage.com/printe?article_id=132867.
25. Eric Tegler, "Ford is Counting on Army of 100 Bloggers to Launch Fiesta," *Advertising Age,* April 29, 2009, http://adage.com/printe?article_id=136045.
26. Bob Garfield. "The Chaos Scenario 2.0 the Post Advertising Age," *Advertising Age,* March 26, 2007: pp. 1, 12–14; Sergio Zyman, *The End of Marketing As We Know It* (New York: HarperBusiness, 1999); Joe Cappo, "Agencies: Change or Die," *Advertising Age,* December 7, 1992, p. 26.
27. Andrew Hampp, "Five Best Branded-Entertainment Deals of 2009, *Advertising Age,* http://adage.com/print?article_id=141218.
28. "World Internet Usage and Population Statistics," http://www.internetworldstats.com/stats.htm., 2009.
29. *Social Media and Young Adults*, February 2010, http://www.pewinternet.org/Reports/2010/Social-Media-and-Young-Adults.aspx.
30. Werner Reinhartz, Manfred Krafft, and Wayne D. Hoyer, "The Customer Relationship Management Process: Its Measurement and Impact on Performance," *Journal of Marketing Research* 41 (August 2005), pp. 293–305.
31. Kevin Lane Keller, "The Brand Report Card," *Harvard Business Review* 78(1) (January/February 2000), pp. 3–10.
32. Kevin Lane Keller, "Conceptualizing, Measuring, and Managing Customer-Based Brand Equity," *Journal of Marketing,* 57 (January 1993), pp. 1–22.
33. Michael L. Ray, *Advertising and Communication Management* (Englewood Cliffs, NJ: Prentice Hall, 1982).
34. Ralph S. Alexander, ed., *Marketing Definitions* (Chicago: American Marketing Association, 1965), p. 9.
35. "Network Television Cost and CPM Trends," Trends in Media, Television Bureau of Advertising, New York. http://www.tvb.org/rcentral.
36. Kenneth Hein, "Study: TV Ads More Effective Than Ever, *Adweek,* February 25, 2009, Adweek.com.
37. Rita Chang, "Marketers Say Hello to Long-Awaited Mobile Technology," *Advertising Age,* http://adage.com/print?article_id=135248; Alice Z. Cuneo, "Mobile Marketing Based on Place is Finally Making Strides," *Advertising Age,* March 31, 2008, p. 24; Alice Z. Cuneo, "Wireless

Giants Leap into Third-Screen Marketing," *adage.com,* September 11, 2006.

**38.** Stephanie Startz, "Starbucks Offers iPhone App and 'Local' Branding to Regain Its Footing," *Brand Channel,* September 24, 2009, http://www.brandchannel.com/home/post/2009/09/24/Starbucks-Offer.

**39.** Andrew Adam Newman, "For Those Who Want Their Cereal Extra Manly," *The New York Times,* July 23, 2009, p. B3.

**40.** "2009 PROMO Industry Trends Report," *Promo,* http://promomagazine.com/09-industry-trends-report/.

**41.** Stephanie Thompson, "Food Fight Breaks Out," *Advertising Age,* January 17, 2005, pp. 1, 25.

**42.** Kate Linebaugh and Norihiko Shirouzu, "Toyota Halts Sales over Safety Issue," *The Wall Street Journal*, January 26, 2010, p. B2.

**43.** Kathy Jackson, "Toyota Sales Strategy Threatens Pricing Power," *Advertising Age,* March 22, 2010, http://adage.com/print?article_id=142997.

**44.** H. Frazier Moore and Bertrand R. Canfield, *Public Relations: Principles, Cases, and Problems,* 7th ed. (Burr Ridge, IL: Richard D. Irwin, 1977), p. 5.

**45.** Jooyoung Kim, Hye Jin Yoon, and Sun Young Lee, "Integrating Advertising and Publicity, *Journal of Advertising* 39(1), Spring 2010, pp. 97–114; Paul Holmes, "Marketers See a Greater Role for Public Relations in the Marketing Mix," *Advertising Age,* January 24, 2005, pp. C4–10; Jack Neff, "Ries' Thesis: Ads Don't Build Brands, PR Does," *Advertising Age,* July 15, 2002, pp. 14–15.

**46.** Tom Duncan, *Principles of Advertising & IMC,* 2nd edition (New York: McGraw-Hill/Irwin, 2005).

**47.** Ibid.

**48.** Steve Rubel, "Facebook Will Rule the Web during the Next Decade," *Advertising Age,* March 15, 2010, http://adage.com/print?article_id=142765.

**49.** Karlene Lukovitz, "Naked Juice Launches Viral Eco Campaign," *MediaPost News: Marketing Daily,* http://mediapost.com/publications/?fa=articles=113460.

## Chapter Two

**1.** Stuart Elliott, "It's a Find Broth of a Campaign," NYTimes.com, November 2, 2009.

**2.** Vincent Boland, Scheherazade Daneshkhu, "Top-end Brands Lose Their Sparkle in Recession," *Financial Times,* October 29, 2009, p. 17.

**3.** Geoff Mulvihill, "Retro "Bop" Boosting V8 Sales," *North Jersey Media Group Inc.*, October 1, 2007.

**4.** Ted Goldammer, *The Beer Brewer's Handbook,* 2nd ed., 2008.

**5.** Dale Buss, "Can Harley Ride the New Wave?" *Brandweek,* October 25, 2004, pp. 20–22.

**6.** www.SegundaJuventud.com.

**7.** www.aarpmagazine.com.

**8.** Edward M. Tauber, "Research on Food Consumption Values Finds Four Market Segments: Good Taste Still Tops," *Marketing News,* May 15, 1981, p. 17; Rebecca C. Quarles, "Shopping Centers Use Fashion Lifestyle Research to Make Marketing Decisions," *Marketing News,* January 22, 1982, p. 18; and "Our Auto, Ourselves," *Consumer Reports,* June 1985, p. 375.

**9.** Judith Graham, "New VALS2 Takes Psychological Route," *Advertising Age,* February 13, 1989, p. 24.

**10.** *Ayer's Dictionary of Advertising Terms* (Philadelphia: Ayer Press, 1976).

**11.** Andrew M. Carlo, "The Comfort Zone," *Home Channel News,* May 24, 2004, pp. 3, 29; Davis A. Aaker and John G. Myers, *Advertising Management,* 3rd ed. (Englewood Cliffs, NJ: Prentice Hall, 1987), p. 125.

**12.** Jack Trout and Al Ries, "Positioning Cuts through Chaos in the Marketplace," *Advertising Age,* May 1, 1972, pp. 51–53.

**13.** Jack Trout, "Branding Can't Exist without Positioning," *Advertising Age,* March 14, 2005, p. 28.

**14.** David A. Aaker and J. Gary Shansby, "Positioning Your Product," *Business Horizons,* May–June 1982, pp. 56–62.

**15.** Aaker and Myers, *Advertising Management.*

**16.** Natalie Zmuda, "Gatorade Not Just for Elite Athletes Anymore," January 30, 2009, www.adage.com.

**17.** J. Paul Peter and Jerry C. Olson, *Consumer Behavior* (Burr Ridge, IL: Richard D. Irwin, 1987), p. 505.

**18.** Michael R. Solomon, "The Role of Products as Social Stimuli: A Symbolic Interactionism Perspective," *Journal of Consumer Research* 10 (December 1983), pp. 319–29.

**19.** Don. E. Schultz, Stanley I. Tannenbaum, and Robert F. Lauterborn, *Integrated Marketing Communications* (Lincolnwood, IL: NTC Publishing Group, 1993), p. 72.

**20.** J. Paul Peter and Jerry C. Olson, *Consumer Behavior,* p. 571.

**21.** Jack Neff, "Study: TV Spots Reduce Consumers' Sensitivity to Price Change," *Advertising Age,* October 10, 2007.

**22.** Roger A. Kerin, Steven W. Hartley, Eric N. Berkowitz, and William Rudelius, *Marketing,* 8th ed. (Burr Ridge, IL: Irwin/McGraw Hill, 2006).

**23.** David W. Stewart, Gary L. Frazier, and Ingrid Martin, "Integrated Channel Management: Merging the Communication and Distribution Functions of the Firm," in *Integrated Communication: Synergy of Persuasive Voices,* pp. 185–215, Esther Thorson and Jeri Moore (eds.) (Mahwah, NJ.: Lawrence Earlbaum Associates, 1996).

## Chapter Three

**1.** Jack Neff, "P&G Redefines the Brand Manager," *Advertising Age,* October 13, 1997, pp. 1, 18, 20.

**2.** Thomas J. Cosse and John E. Swan, "Strategic Marketing Planning by Product Managers—Room for Improvement?" *Journal of Marketing* 47 (Summer 1983), pp. 92–102.

**3.** "Behind the Tumult at P&G," *Fortune,* March 7, 1994, pp. 74–82; "Category Management: New Tools Changing Life for Manufacturers, Retailers," *Marketing News,* September 25, 1989, pp. 2, 19.

**4.** Timothy Dewhirst and Brad Davis, "Brand Strategy and Integrated Marketing Communications, *Journal of Advertising* 34, no. 4 (Winter 2005), pp. 81–92.

**5.** Cosse and Swan, "Strategic Marketing Planning by Product Managers—Room for Improvement?"

**6.** Victor P. Buell, *Organizing for Marketing/Advertising Success* (New York: Association of National Advertisers, 1982).

**7.** Jean Halliday, "GM Puts Final Nail in Coffin of Brand-Management Effort," *Advertising Age,* April 5, 2004, p. 8.

**8.** Jack Neff, "Why It's Time to Do Away with the Brand Manager," *Advertising Age,* October 12, 2009, http://adage.com/print?article_id=139593; Tom Hinkes, "Our Biggest Brands Can No Longer Be Managed by Nerds, *Advertising Age,* March 17, 2010, http://adage.com/print?article_id=142841.

9. M. Louise Ripley, "What Kind of Companies Take Their Advertising In-House?" *Journal of Advertising Research* 31(4) (October/November 1991), pp. 73–80.
10. Rupal Parekh, "Thinking of Pulling a CareerBuilder? Pros and Cons of Bringing an Account In-house," *Advertising Age,* May 18, 2009, http://adage.com/print?article_id=136701.
11. Ibid.
12. Rupal Parekh and Michael Bush, "WPP Folds Ill-Fated Dell Agency Enfatico into Y&R Brands" *Advertising Age,* April 9, 2009, http://adage.com/print?article_id=135910.
13. Bruce Horovitz, "Some Companies Say the Best Ad Agency Is No Ad Agency at All," *Los Angeles Times,* July 19, 1989, Sec IV, p. 5.
14. Suzanne Vranica, "Google, Expanding Its Reach, Taps Into Madison Avenue," *The Wall Street Journal,* September 19, 2007, p. B3.
15. Joan Voight, "The Outsiders," *Adweek,* October 4, 2004, pp. 32–35.
16. "Best Buy Awards Accounts to BBDO and Crispin Porter," *The New York Times,* June 18, 2007, p. C6.
17. Jeremy Mullman and Rupal Parekh, "Best Buy to Rely on Crispin at BBDO's Expense," *Advertising Age,* December 18, 2008, http://adage.com/print?article_id=133401.
18. Aaron Baar and Noreen O'Leary, "Second City, Second Thoughts," *Adweek,* May 14, 2007, pp. 8–9.
19. Alice Z. Cuneo, "Not So Golden Anymore," *Advertising Age,* January 24, 2005, pp. 1, 53; Kate MacArthur, "Chicago Blues," *Advertising Age,* September 10, 2001, pp. 1, 12; Anthony Vagnoni, "Gotham Regains Some Lost Luster as Center of U.S. Agency Creativity," *Advertising Age,* April 12, 1999, pp. 1, 10.
20. Sally Goll Beatty, "Global Needs Challenge Midsize Agencies," *The Wall Street Journal,* December 14, 1995, p. B9.
21. "Agency Report 2010," *Advertising Age,* April 26, 2010, pp. 22, 23.
22. Bob Lammons, "A Good Account Exec Makes a Big Difference," *Marketing News,* June 3, 1996, p. 12.
23. Jon Steel, *Truth, Lies & Advertising: The Art of Account Planning* (New York: Wiley, 1998).
24. Quote in Alice Z. Cuneo, "Account Planners at a Crossroads," adage.com, July 30, 2007.
25. Anthony Vagnoni, "Small Fries," *Advertising Age,* March 4, 2002, pp. 20, 22.
26. Michael Bush, "Why the $7B Media-Consolidation Windfall Isn't Good News for Small Shops, *Advertising Age,* March 15, 2010, pp. 1, 26.
27. David Beals, *Trends in Agency Compensation,* 14th Edition, Association of National Advertisers, 2007.
28. Ibid.
29. Chris Kuenne, "Why Ad Agencies Need to Embrace Value-Based Compensation," *Advertising Age,* March 22, 2010, http://adage.com/print?article_id=142915.
30. David Beals, *Trends in Agency Compensation.*
31. Jack Neff and Bradley Johnson, "P&G Pushes More Performance Pay," *Advertising Age,* May 10, 2004, pp. 1, 2; Kathryn Kranhold, "P&G Expands Its Program to Tie Agency Pay to Brand Performance," *The Wall Street Journal,* September 16, 1999, p. B12.
32. Jeremy Mullman and Natalie Zmuda, "Coke Pushes Pay-for-Performance Model," *Advertising Age,* April 27, 2009, http://adage.com/print?article_id=136266.
33. Jeremy Mullman, "Anheuser-Busch Whacks Retainers for Its Agencies, *Advertising Age,* February 16, 2009, http://adage.com/print?article_id=136266; Kate MacArthur, "McD's Squeezes Agency Fees," November 11, 2002, *Advertising Age,* pp. 1, 45; Jack Neff, "Feeling the Squeeze," *Advertising Age,* June 4, 2001, pp. 1, 14; Jean Halliday, "GM to Scrap Agency Commissions," *Advertising Age,* November 16, 1998, pp. 1, 57.
34. Marissa Miley, "Most Marketers Cutting Budgets, Renegotiating with Agencies, *Advertising Age,* February 10, 2009, http://adage.com/print?article_id=134526.
35. Jack Neff, "ANA Survey: Agency-Performance Reviews Are Now Business as Usual, *Advertising Age,* September 14, 2009, http://adage.com/print?article_id=138983.
36. Report on the Agency-Advertiser Value Survey, American Association of Advertising Agencies/Association of National Advertisers, August 2007.
37. Tim Williams and Ronald Baker, "New Value-Based Comp Model Needed, *adage.com,* June 11, 2007.
38. Teressa Iezzi, "What's to Become of Long-Term Marketer, Agency Relationships?," *Advertising Age,* March 26, 2007, p. 17; Joanne Lipman, "Study Shows Clients Jump Ship Quickly," *The Wall Street Journal,* May 21, 1992, p. B6.
39. Jeremy Mullman, "State Farm Sounding Like Its Rivals to Stay on Top of Them, *Advertising Age,* March 29, 2010, http://adage.com/print?article_id=143020; Brian Steinberg and Chad Terhune, "PepsiCo Switches Its Ad Account for Diet Pepsi to DDB Worldwide," *The Wall Street Journal,* December 7, 2004, p. B4.
40. Kevin Goldman, "Global Companies Hone Agency Rosters," *The Wall Street Journal,* July 25, 1995, p. B8; Sally Goll Beatty, "Young & Rubicam Is Only One for Colgate," *The Wall Street Journal,* December 1, 1995, p. B6.
41. Kathleen Sampley, "Love's Labors Lost: Behind the Breakups," *Adweek,* August 1, 2005, p. 8; Fred Beard, "Marketing Client Role Ambiguity as a Source of Dissatisfaction in Client–Ad Agency Relationships," *Journal of Advertising Research,* (September/October 1996), pp. 9–20; Paul Michell, Harold Cataquet, and Stephen Hague, "Establishing the Causes of Disaffection in Agency-Client Relations," *Journal of Advertising Research* 32, no. 2, 1992, pp. 41–48; Peter Doyle, Marcel Corstiens, and Paul Michell, "Signals of Vulnerability in Agency-Client Relations," *Journal of Marketing* 44 (Fall 1980), pp. 18–23; and Daniel B. Wackman, Charles Salmon, Caryn C. Salmon, "Developing an Advertising Agency–Client Relationship," *Journal of Advertising Research* 26, no. 6 (December 1986/January 1987), pp. 21–29.
42. Jeremy Mullman. "Man Flaws: Why Miller and Crispin Couldn't Stop Lite from Stumbling," *Advertising Age,* March 26, 2007, pp. 1, 28.
43. Joan Voight and Wendy Melillo, "Study: Clients Want Multiple Partners," *Adweek,* May 14, 2007, pp. 20–21.
44. Suzanne Vranica, "Pinched Firms Woo Rivals' Happy Clients," *The Wall Street Journal,* March 4, 2002, p. B8.
45. Jennifer Comiteau, "What Agencies Think of Search Consultants," *Adweek,* August 4, 2003, pp. 14–16.
46. Fred K. Beard, "Exploring the Use of Advertising Agency Review Consultants," *Journal of Advertising*

*Research* 42(1) (January/February) 2002, pp. 39–50.

**47.** "Agency A-List," *Advertising Age,* January 25, 2010, pp. 10–19.

**48.** Rupal Parekh, "Agency A-List: Crispin Porter + Bogusky, *Advertising Age*, January 19, 2009, pp. 22–23; Eleftheria Parpis, "U.S. Agency of the Year," *Adweek*, January 8, 2007, pp. 18–19.

**49.** Kate McArthur, "Burger King Sets High Score with Its Adver-games," *Advertising Age*, January 8, 2007, http://adage.com/print?article_id=114158.

**50.** Jack Neff, "Ries' Thesis: Ads Don't Build Brands, PR Does," *Advertising Age*, July 15, 2002, pp. 14–15; Prema Nakra, "The Changing Role of Public Relations in Marketing Communications," *Public Relations Quarterly*, 1 (1991), pp. 42–45.

**51.** Betsy Spathmann, "Sudden Impact," *Promo*, April 1999, pp. 42–48.

**52.** Quote in: Laura Q. Hughes and Kate MacArthur, "Soft Boiled," *Advertising Age*, May 28, 2001, pp. 3, 54.

**53.** Study cited in: Michael Bush, "Memo to Marketers: It's Your Fault if Your Shops Flounder," *Advertising Age*, March 29, 2010, http://adage.com/print?article_id=142010.

**54.** William N. Swain, "Perceptions of IMC after a Decade of Development: Who's at the Wheel and How Can We Measure Success," *Journal of Advertising Research* (March 2004), pp. 46–67; Philip J. Kitchen and Don E. Schultz, "A Multi-Country Comparison of the Drive for IMC" Journal of Advertising Research, January/February 1999, pp. 21–38.

**55.** David N. McArthur and Tom Griffin, "A Marketing Management View of Integrated Marketing Communications," *Journal of Advertising Research* 37, no. 5 (September/October) 1997, pp. 19–26; and Adrienne Ward Fawcett, "Integrated Marketing—Marketers Convinced: Its Time Has Arrived," *Advertising Age*, November 6, 1993, pp. S1–2.

**56.** Claire Atkinson, "Tracking the Challenges of Integrated Marketing," *Television Weekly*, March 17, 2003, Vol. 22, p. 11.

**57.** Joan Voight and Wendy Melillo, "Study: Clients Want Multiple Partners."

**58.** Quoted in Michael Bush, "Memo to Marketers: It's Your Fault if Your Shops Flounder."

## Chapter Four

**1.** Dirk Zeims, "The Morphological Approach for Unconscious Consumer Motivation Research," *Journal of Advertising Research* 44(2) June 2004, pp. 210–15.

**2.** Jeffrey Ball, "But How Does It Make You Feel?," *The Wall Street Journal,* May 3, 1999, p. B1.

**3.** Jagdish N. Sheth, "The Role of Motivation Research in Consumer Psychology" (Faculty Working Paper, University of Illinois, Champaign: 1974); Bill Abrams, "Charles of the Ritz Discovers What Women Want," *The Wall Street Journal,* August 20, 1981, p. 29; Ernest Dichter, *Getting Motivated* (New York: Pergamon Press, 1979).

**4.** Ball, "But How Does It Make You Feel?"

**5.** Gary Strauss, "TV Sex: Uncut, Unavoidable," *USA Today,* January 20, 2010, p. 1.

**6.** Joanne Lipman, "Leaders Turning Up Their Noses at 'Scent Strips' Ads in Magazines," *Wall Street Journal,* December 6, 1989, p. 1.

**7.** Gord Hotchkiss, "400 Ads a Day and Counting," MediaPost.com, November 14, 2007, p. 1.

**8.** Gordon W. Allport, "Attitudes," in *Handbook of Social Psychology,* ed. C. M. Murchison (Winchester, MA: Clark University Press, 1935), p. 810.

**9.** Robert B. Zajonc and Hazel Markus, "Affective and Cognitive Factors in Preferences," *Journal of Consumer Research* 9(2) (June 1982), pp. 123–31.

**10.** Joel B. Cohen, Paul W. Minniard, and Peter R. Dickson, "Information Integration: An Information Processing Perspective," in *Advances in Consumer Research* 7, ed. Jerry C. Olson (Ann Arbor, MI: Association for Consumer Research, 1980), pp. 161–70.

**11.** James F. Engel, "The Psychological Consequences of a Major Purchase Decision," in *Marketing in Transition,* (ed.) William S. Decker (Chicago: American Marketing Association, 1963), pp. 462–75.

**12.** Leon G. Schiffman and Leslie Lazar Kannuk, *Consumer Behavior,* 4th ed. (Englewood Cliffs, NJ: Prentice Hall, 1991), p. 192.

**13.** Gerald J. Gorn, "The Effects of Music in Advertising on Choice: A Classical Conditioning Approach," *Journal of Marketing* 46 (Winter 1982), pp. 94–101.

**14.** James J. Kellaris, Anthony D. Cox, and Dena Cox, "The Effect of Background Music on Ad Processing: A Contingency Explanation," *Journal of Marketing* 57(4) (Fall 1993), p. 114.

**15.** Brian C. Deslauries and Peter B. Everett, "The Effects of Intermittent and Continuous Token Reinforcement on Bus Ridership," *Journal of Applied Psychology* 62 (August 1977), pp. 369–75.

**16.** Lyman E. Ostlund, "Role Theory and Group Dynamics," in *Consumer Behavior: Theoretical Sources,* eds. Scott Ward and Thomas S. Robertson (Englewood Cliffs, NJ: Prentice Hall, 1973), pp. 230–75.

## Chapter Five

**1.** Wilbur Schram, *The Process and Effects of Mass Communications* (Urbana: University of Illinois Press, 1955).

**2.** Ibid.

**3.** Kate Niederhoffer, Rob Mooth, David Wiesenfeld and Jonathon Gordon, "The Origin and Impact of CPG New-Product Buzz: Emerging Trends and Implications," *Journal of Advertising Research,* December 2007, pp. 420–426; Catharine P. Taylor, "Pssst! How Do You Measure Buzz," *Adweek,* October 24, 2005, pp. 26–28. Robert E. Smith and Christine A. Vogt, "The Effects of Integrating Advertising and Negative Word-of-Mouth Communications on Message Processing and Response," *Journal of Consumer Psychology* 4, no. 2 (1995), pp. 133–51; Barry L. Bayus, "Word of Mouth: The Indirect Effect of Marketing Efforts," *Journal of Advertising Research* 25 (3) (June/July 1985), pp. 31–39.

**4.** Robert Brenner, "I Sold It Through the Grapevine," *BusinessWeek,* May 26, 2006, pp. 32–34; Garry Khermouch and Jeff Green, Buzz Marketing, *BusinessWeek,* July 30, 2001, pp. 50–56.

**5.** Michael Learmoth, "Doritos, Google, Super Bowl Ads Storm Chart," *Advertising Age,* February 18, 2010, http://adage.com/print?article-id=142151; Emily Bryson York, "Doritos Wants 'Crash the Super Bowl' Spot to Hit No. 1," *Advertising Age,* January 23,

2009, http://adage.com/print?article-id=134063.

6. Kamu High, Brian Morrissey and Eleftheria Parpis, "The 'Evolution' of Advertising," *Adweek,* June 25, 2007, pp. 6–7.
7. Ed Keller and Brad Fay, "The Role of Advertising in Word of Mouth," *Journal of Advertising Research* 49(2), June 2009, pp. 154–163; Ed Keller and Jon Berry, "Word-of-Mouth: The Real Action is Offline," *Advertising Age,* December 4, 2006, p. 20.
8. Larry Yu, "How Companies Turn Buzz into Sales," *MIT Sloan Management Review*" (Winter 2005), pp. 5–6.
9. Suzanne Vranica, "Getting Buzz Marketers to Fess Up," *The Wall Street Journal,* February 9, 2005, p. B9.
10. Ibid.
11. Quote by Gordon S. Bower in *Fortune,* October 14, 1985, p. 11.
12. Meg James, "Over 50 and Out of Favor," *The Los Angeles Times,* May 10, 2005, pp. A1, 10.
13. Thomas V. Bonoma and Leonard C. Felder, "Nonverbal Communication in Marketing: Toward Communicational Analysis," *Journal of Marketing Research* (May 1977), pp. 169–80.
14. Jacob Jacoby and Wayne D. Hoyer, "Viewer Miscomprehension of Televised Communication: Selected Findings," *Journal of Marketing* 46(4) (Fall 1982), pp. 12–26; Jacoby and Hoyer, "The Comprehension and Miscomprehension of Print Communications: An Investigation of Mass Media Magazines," *Advertising Education Foundation Study,* New York, 1987.
15. E. K. Strong, *The Psychology of Selling* (New York: McGraw-Hill, 1925), p. 9.
16. Robert J. Lavidge and Gary A. Steiner, "A Model for Predictive Measurements of Advertising Effectiveness," *Journal of Marketing* 24 (October 1961), pp. 59–62.
17. Everett M. Rogers, *Diffusion of Innovations* (New York: Free Press, 1962), pp. 79–86.
18. "Shiny New Things: What Digital Adopters Want, How to Reach Them, and Why Every Marketer Should Pay Attention," *Advertising Age Insights White Paper,* March 15, 2010.
19. William J. McGuire, "An Information Processing Model of Advertising Effectiveness," in *Behavioral and Management Science in Marketing,* eds. Harry J. Davis and Alvin J. Silk (New York: Ronald Press, 1978), pp. 156–80.
20. Michael L. Ray, "Communication and the Hierarchy of Effects," in *New Models for Mass Communication Research,* ed. P. Clarke (Beverly Hills, CA: Sage, 1973), pp. 147–75.
21. Herbert E. Krugman, "The Impact of Television Advertising: Learning without Involvement," *Public Opinion Quarterly* 29 (Fall 1965), pp. 349–56.
22. Scott A. Hawkins and Stephen J. Hoch, "Low-Involvement Learning: Memory without Evaluation," *Journal of Consumer Research* 19, no. 2 (September 1992), pp. 212–25.
23. Harry W. McMahan, "Do Your Ads Have VIP?" *Advertising Age,* July 14, 1980, pp. 50–51.
24. Robert E. Smith, "Integrating Information from Advertising and Trial: Processes and Effects on Consumer Response to Product Information," *Journal of Marketing Research* 30 (May 1993), pp. 204–19.
25. DeAnna S. Kempf and Russell N. Laczniak, "Advertising's Influence on Subsequent Product Trial Processing," *Journal of Advertising* 30, no. 3, Fall 2001, pp. 27–38.
26. Judith L. Zaichkowsky, "Conceptualizing Involvement," *Journal of Advertising* 15, no. 2 (1986), pp. 4–14; Anthony G. Greenwald and Clark Leavitt, "Audience Involvement in Advertising: Four Levels," *Journal of Consumer Research* 11, no. 1 (June 1984), pp. 581–92.
27. Richard Vaughn, "How Advertising Works: A Planning Model," *Journal of Advertising Research* 20, no. 5 (October 1980), pp. 27–33.
28. Richard Vaughn, "How Advertising Works: A Planning Model Revisited," *Journal of Advertising Research* 26, no. 1 (February/March 1986), pp. 57–66.
29. Beth Snyder Bulik, "Is There an Expensive Washing Machine in Your Future?," *Advertising Age,* November 5, 2007, p. 10.
30. Jerry C. Olson, Daniel R. Toy, and Phillip A. Dover, "Mediating Effects of Cognitive Responses to Advertising on Cognitive Structure," in *Advances in Consumer Research* 5, ed. H. Keith Hunt (Ann Arbor, MI: Association for Consumer Research, 1978), pp. 72–78.
31. Anthony A. Greenwald, "Cognitive Learning, Cognitive Response to Persuasion and Attitude Change," in *Psychological Foundations of Attitudes,* eds. A. G. Greenwald, T. C. Brock, and T. W. Ostrom (New York: Academic Press, 1968); Peter L. Wright, "The Cognitive Processes Mediating Acceptance of Advertising," *Journal of Marketing Research* 10 (February 1973), pp. 53–62; Brian Wansink, Michael L. Ray, and Rajeev Batra, "Increasing Cognitive Response Sensitivity," *Journal of Advertising* 23, no. 2 (June 1994), pp. 65–76.
32. Peter Wright, "Message Evoked Thoughts, Persuasion Research Using Thought Verbalizations," *Journal of Consumer Research* 7, no. 2 (September 1980), pp. 151–75.
33. Scott B. Mackenzie, Richard J. Lutz, and George E. Belch, "The Role of Attitude toward the Ad as a Mediator of Advertising Effectiveness: A Test of Competing Explanations," *Journal of Marketing Research* 23 (May 1986), pp. 130–43; Rajeev Batra and Michael L. Ray, "Affective Responses Mediating Acceptance of Advertising," *Journal of Consumer Research* 13 (September 1986), pp. 234–49; Tim Ambler and Tom Burne, "The Impact of Affect on Memory of Advertising," *Journal of Advertising Research* 29, no. 3 (March/April 1999), pp. 25–34.
34. Ronald Alsop, "TV Ads That Are Likeable Get Plus Rating for Persuasiveness," *The Wall Street Journal,* February 20, 1986, p. 23.
35. David J. Moore and William D. Harris, "Affect Intensity and the Consumer's Attitude toward High Impact Emotional Advertising Appeals," *Journal of Advertising* 25, no. 2 (Summer 1996), pp. 37–50; Andrew A. Mitchell and Jerry C. Olson, "Are Product Attribute Beliefs the Only Mediator of Advertising Effects on Brand Attitude?" *Journal of Marketing Research* 18 (August 1981), pp. 318–32.
36. David J. Moore, William D. Harris, and Hong C. Chen, "Affect Intensity: An Individual Difference Response to Advertising Appeals," *Journal of Consumer Research* 22 (September 1995), pp. 154–64; Julie Edell and Marian C. Burke, "The Power of Feelings in Understanding Advertising Effects," *Journal of Consumer Research* 14 (December 1987), pp. 421–33.
37. Richard E. Petty and John T. Cacioppo, "Central and Peripheral Routes to Persuasion: Application to Advertising,"

in *Advertising and Consumer Psychology,* eds. Larry Percy and Arch Woodside (Lexington, MA: Lexington Books, 1983), pp. 3–23.

**38.** Ibid.

**39.** Richard E. Petty, John T. Cacioppo, and David Schumann, "Central and Peripheral Routes to Advertising Effectiveness: The Moderating Role of Involvement," *Journal of Consumer Research* 10 (September 1983), pp. 135–46.

**40.** Demetrios Vakratsas and Tim Ambler, "How Advertising Works: What Do We Really Know?" *Journal of Marketing* 63 (January 1999), pp. 26–43.

**41.** Bruce F. Hall, "A New Model for Measuring Advertising Effects," *Journal of Advertising Research* 42, no. 2, (March/April 2002), pp. 23–31.

**42.** Thomas E. Barry, "In Defense of the Hierarchy of Effects: A Rejoinder to Weilbacher," *Journal of Advertising Research,"* (May/June 2002), pp. 44–47.

**43.** William M. Weilbacher, "Point of View: Does Advertising Cause a 'Hierarchy of Effects'?," *Journal of Advertising Research* 41, no. 6 (November/December 2001), pp. 19–26.

## Chapter Six

**1.** William J. McGuire, "An Information Processing Model of Advertising Effectiveness," in *Behavioral and Management Science in Marketing,* Harry J. Davis and Alvin J. Silk (eds.) (New York: Ronald Press, 1978), pp. 156–80.

**2.** V. Kumar, J. Andrew Petersen, and Robert P. Leone, "How Valuable is Word of Mouth?," Harvard Business Review, October 2007, pp. 139–46; Garry Khermouch and Jeff Green, "Buzz Marketing," *BusinessWeek,* July 30, 2001, pp. 50–56.

**3.** Herbert C. Kelman, "Processes of Opinion Change," *Public Opinion Quarterly* 25 (Spring 1961), pp. 57–78.

**4.** William J. McGuire, "The Nature of Attitudes and Attitude Change," in *Handbook of Social Psychology,* 2nd ed., eds. G. Lindzey and E. Aronson (Cambridge, MA: Addison-Wesley, 1969), pp. 135–214; Daniel J. O'Keefe, "The Persuasive Effects of Delaying Identification of High- and Low-Credibility Communicators: A Meta-Analytic Review," *Central States Speech Journal* 38 (1987), pp. 63–72.

**5.** Rebecca Ohanian, "The Impact of Celebrity Spokespersons' Image on Consumers' Intention to Purchase," *Journal of Advertising Research,* 21 (February/March 1991), pp. 46–54.

**6.** Lacey Rose, "The 10 Most Trusted Celebrities, *Forbes.com,* January 25, 2010, http://www.forbes.com/2010/01/25/most-trusted-celebrities-business-entertainment-trust.html.

**7.** David P. Hamilton, "Celebrities Help 'Educate' Public on New Drugs," *The Wall Street Journal,* April 22, 2002, p. B1.

**8.** James Bandler, "How Companies Pay TV Experts for On-Air Product Mentions," *The Wall Street Journal,* April 19, 2005, pp. A1, 12.

**9.** Karen Benezra and Jennifer Gilbert, "The CEO as Brand," *Chief Executive,* www.chiefexecutive.net, Vol. 174, January 2002.

**10.** "Business Celebrities," *BusinessWeek,* June 23, 1986, pp. 100–107.

**11.** Bruce Horovitz and Theresa Howard, "Wendy's Loses Its Legend," *USA TODAY,* January 9, 2002, pp. 1, 2B.

**12.** Frank Green, "Masters of the Pitch," *The San Diego Union-Tribune,"* January 30, 2000, pp. 1, 6.

**13.** Barbara Lippert, "A Winner Out of the Gates," *Adweek,* September 22, 2008, p. 28.

**14.** Emily Bryson York and Brooke Capps, "Dave Disciples Flip Wigs over Trendy Wendy," *Advertising Age,* September 3, 2007, pp. 1, 22; Kate MacArthur, "Wendy's Set to Unveil New Brand Spokesperson," *adage.com,* February 18, 2004.

**15.** Rupal Parekh and Kunur Patel, "Ten Things to Think Hard About before Featuring the Chairman in Advertising," *Advertising Age,* September 14, 2009, http://adage.com/print?article_id=138984.

**16.** Erick Reidenback and Robert Pitts, "Not All CEOs Are Created Equal as Advertising Spokespersons: Evaluating the Effective CEO Spokesperson," *Journal of Advertising* 20, no. 3 (1986), pp. 35–50; Roger Kerin and Thomas E. Barry, "The CEO Spokesperson in Consumer Advertising: An Experimental Investigation," in *Current Issues in Research in Advertising,* eds. J. H. Leigh and C. R. Martin (Ann Arbor: University of Michigan, 1981), pp. 135–48; and J. Poindexter, "Voices of Authority," *Psychology Today,* August 1983.

**17.** Frank Green, "Masters of the Pitch."

**18.** A. Eagly and S. Chaiken, "An Attribution Analysis of the Effect of Communicator Characteristics on Opinion Change," *Journal of Personality and Social Psychology* 32 (1975), pp. 136–44.

**19.** For a review of these studies, see Brian Sternthal, Lynn Philips, and Ruby Dholakia, "The Persuasive Effect of Souce Credibility: A Situational Analysis," *Public Opinion Quarterly* 42 (Fall 1978), pp. 285–314.

**20.** Brian Sternthal, Ruby Dholakia, and Clark Leavitt, "The Persuasive Effects of Source Credibility: Tests of Cognitive Response," *Journal of Consumer Research* 4, no. 4 (March 1978), pp. 252–60; Robert R. Harmon and Kenneth A. Coney, "The Persuasive Effects of Source Credibility in Buy and Lease Situations," *Journal of Marketing Research* 19 (May 1982), pp. 255–60.

**21.** For a review, see Noel Capon and James Hulbert, "The Sleeper Effect: An Awakening," *Public Opinion Quarterly* 37 (1973), pp. 333–58.

**22.** Darlene B. Hannah and Brian Sternthal, "Detecting and Explaining the Sleeper Effect," *Journal of Consumer Research* 11(2) (September 1984), pp. 632–42.

**23.** H. C. Triandis, *Attitudes and Attitude Change* (New York: Wiley, 1971).

**24.** J. Mills and J. Jellison, "Effect on Opinion Change Similarity between the Communicator and the Audience He Addresses," *Journal of Personality and Social Psychology* 9, no. 2 (1969), pp. 153–56.

**25.** Arch G. Woodside and J. William Davenport, Jr., "The Effect of Salesman Similarity and Expertise on Consumer Purchasing Behavior," *Journal of Marketing Research* 11 (May 1974), pp. 198–202; Paul Busch and David T. Wilson, "An Experimental Analysis of a Salesman's Expert and Referent Bases of Social Power in the Buyer-Seller Dyad," *Journal of Marketing Research* 13 (February 1976), pp. 3–11.

**26.** Louise Story, "Seeing Stars," *The New York Times,* October 12, 2006, p. C1; Rich Thomaselli, "Searching for Michael Jordan," *Advertising Age,* September 5, 2005, p. 12.

27. George E. Belch and Michael A. Belch, "A Content Analysis Study of the Use of Celebrities in Magazine Advertising," unpublished working paper, Center for Integrated Marketing Communications, San Diego State University, 2009.
28. Kurt Badenhausen, The World's Highest-Paid Athletes," *Forbes.com,* August 10, 2009, http://www.forbes.com/2009/08/10/tiger-woods-schumacher-business-sports-top-earning-athletes.html.
29. Jason Stein "Inside Chrysler's Celine Dion Advertising Disaster," *adage.com,* November 24, 2003.
30. Valerie Folkes, "Recent Attribution Research in Consumer Behavior: A Review and New Directions," *Journal of Consumer Research* 14 (March 1988), pp. 548–65; John C. Mowen and Stephen W. Brown, "On Explaining and Predicting the Effectiveness of Celebrity Endorsers," in *Advances in Consumer Research* 8 (Ann Arbor, MI: Association for Consumer Research, 1981), pp. 437–41.
31. Bruce Horovitz, "Armstrong Rolls to Market Gold," *USA TODAY,* May 4, 2000, pp. 1, 2B.
32. Stephen Rae, "How Celebrities Make Killings on Commercials," *Cosmopolitan,* January 1997, pp. 164–67.
33. Lee Hawkins and Suzanne Vranica, "McDonald's Bets LeBron James Won't Be a Tiger," *The Wall Street Journal,* February 1, 2010, ABI/INFORM Global (Document ID: 1951480801).
34. Charles Atkin and M. Block, "Effectiveness of Celebrity Endorsers," *Journal of Advertising Research* 23(1) (February/March 1983), pp. 57–61.
35. Joe Pereira, "New Balance Sneaker Ads Jab at Pro Athletes' Pretensions," *The Wall Street Journal,* March 10, 2005, p. B1.
36. Brian D. Till and Terence A. Shimp, "Endorsers in Advertising: The Case of Negative Celebrity Information," *Journal of Advertising* 27, no. 1, Spring 1998, pp. 67–82.
37. Rich Thomaselli, "Kobe Kept on the Marketing Bench, *Advertising Age,* September 13, 2004, p. 16.
38. "Vitamin Water Planning Full Marketing Campaign around Kobe Bryant," *Sports Business Daily,* May 13, 2008, http://www.sportsbusinessdaily.com/article/120800.
39. Emily Bryson York, "Phelps Brand Takes a Hit," *Advertising Age,* February 9, 2009, pp, 1, 2.
40. Jeremy Mullman, "Is Nike Next? AirTran Drops Scandal-Prone Vick," *Advertising Age,* June 4, 2007, p 6; Jeremy Mullman, "Nike Suspends Vick from Endorser Roster," *adage.com,* July 27, 2007.
41. Stephanie Thompson, "Heroin Chic Ok, Cocaine Use Not," *Advertising Age,* September 26, 2005, pp. 3, 80.
42. James Tenser, "Endorser Qualities Count More Than Ever," *Advertising Age,* November 8, 2004, pp. S2, 4.
43. Rich Thomaselli, "GM Ending Tiger Woods Endorsement Deal," *Advertising Age,* November 24, 2008, http://adagecom/print?article_id=132810.
44. _______., "Tiger Woods' Agent: No More Car Sponsors for Tiger," Advertising Age, December 1, 2008, http://adagecom/print?article_id=132877.
45. Anital Elberse and Jeroen Verleun, "Brand Alliance and the Value of Reflected Glory," unpublished working paper, Harvard Business School, January 2010.
46. Dave McCaughan, "The Fine Art of Matching a Celebrity with a Brand," *Advertising Age,* April 16, 2007, p. 34; Betsy Cummings, "Star Power," *Sales and Marketing Management,* April 2001, pp. 52–59; Michael A. Kamins, "An Investigation into the 'Match-Up' Hypothesis in Celebrity Advertising," *Journal of Advertising* 19, no. 1 (1990), pp. 4–13.
47. Grant McCracken, "Who Is the Celebrity Endorser? Cultural Foundations of the Endorsement Process," *Journal of Consumer Research* 16, no. 3 (December 1989), pp. 310–21.
48. Ibid., p. 315.
49. "Electrolux Taps Kelly Ripa to Launch New Premium Kitchen Appliance Line in North America, *PR Newswire,* April 14, 2008.
50. Peter Wonacott, "Yao-Mania: Hoop Star's Visit Evokes Beatles 1964," *The Wall Street Journal,* October 15, 2004, pp. B1, 7; Josh Tyrangiel, "The Center of Attention," *Time,* February 10, 2003, pp. 68–70.
51. B. Zafer Erdogan, Michael J. Baker, and Stephen Tagg, "Selecting Celebrity Endorsers: The Practitioner's Perspective," *Journal of Advertising Research* 41, no. 43 (May/June 2001), pp. 39–48.
52. For an excellent review of these studies, see Marilyn Y. Jones, Andrea J. S. Stanaland, and Betsy D. Gelb, "Beefcake and Cheesecake: Insights for Advertisers," *Journal of Advertising* 27, no. 2 (Summer 1998), pp. 32–51; W. B. Joseph, "The Credibility of Physically Attractive Communicators," *Journal of Advertising* 11, no. 3 (1982), pp. 13–23.
53. Michael Solomon, Richard Ashmore, and Laura Longo, "The Beauty Match-Up Hypothesis: Congruence between Types of Beauty and Product Images in Advertising," *Journal of Advertising* 21, no. 4, pp. 23–34; M. J. Baker and Gilbert A. Churchill, Jr., "The Impact of Physically Attractive Models on Advertising Evaluations," *Journal of Marketing Research* 14 (November 1977), pp. 538–55.
54. Robert W. Chestnut, C. C. La Chance, and A. Lubitz, "The Decorative Female Model: Sexual Stimuli and the Recognition of the Advertisements," *Journal of Advertising* 6 (Fall 1977), pp. 11–14; Leonard N. Reid and Lawrence C. Soley, "Decorative Models and Readership of Magazine Ads," *Journal of Advertising Research* 23, no. 2 (April/May 1983), pp. 27–32.
55. Amanda B. Bower, "Highly Attractive Models in Advertising and the Women Who Loathe Them: The Implications of Negative Affect for Spokesperson Effectiveness," *Journal of Advertising* 30, no. 3, (Fall 2001), pp. 51–63; Amanda B. Bower and Stacy Landreth, "Is Beauty Best? Highly Versus Normally Attractive Models in Advertising," *Journal of Advertising* 30, no. 1, pp. 1–12.
56. Jack Neff, "In Dove Ads, Normal Is the New Beautiful," *Advertising Age,* September 27, 2004, pp. 1, 80.
57. Michelle Jeffers, "Behind Dove's 'Real Beauty'," *Adweek,* September 12, 2005, pp. 34–35.
58. Herbert E. Krugman, "On Application of Learning Theory to TV Copy Testing," *Public Opinion Quarterly* 26 (1962), pp. 626–39.
59. C. I. Hovland and W. Mandell, "An Experimental Comparison of Conclusion Drawing by the Communicator and by the Audience," *Journal of Abnormal and Social Psychology* 47 (July 1952), pp. 581–88.
60. Alan G. Sawyer and Daniel J. Howard, "Effect of Omitting Conclusions in Advertisements to Involved and Uninvolved Audiences," *Journal of Mar-*

*keting Research* 28 (November 1991), pp. 467–74.

61. Paul Chance, "Ads without Answers Make Brain Itch," *Psychology Today* 9 (1975), p. 78.

62. Connie Pechmann, "Predicting When Two-Sided Ads Will Be More Effective Than One-Sided Ads," *Journal of Marketing Research,* 24 (November 1992), pp. 441–53; George E. Belch, "The Effects of Message Modality on One- and Two-Sided Advertising Messages," in *Advances in Consumer Research* 10, eds. Richard P. Bagozzi and Alice M. Tybout (Ann Arbor, MI: Association for Consumer Research, 1983), pp. 21–26.

63. Robert E. Settle and Linda L. Golden, "Attribution Theory and Advertiser Credibility," *Journal of Marketing Research* 11 (May 1974), pp. 181–85; Edmund J. Faison, "Effectiveness of One-Sided and Two-Sided Mass Communications in Advertising," *Public Opinion Quarterly* 25 (Fall 1961), pp. 468–69.

64. Martin Eisend, "Two-sided Advertising: A Meta-Analysis," *International Journal of Research in Marketing* 23, June 2006, pp. 187–98.

65. Joel A. Baglole, "Cough Syrup Touts 'Awful Taste' in U.S.," *The Wall Street Journal,* December 15, 1999, p. B10.

66. Alan G. Sawyer, "The Effects of Repetition of Refutational and Supportive Advertising Appeals," *Journal of Marketing Research* 10 (February 1973), pp. 23–37; George J. Szybillo and Richard Heslin, "Resistance to Persuasion: Inoculation Theory in a Marketing Context," *Journal of Marketing Research* 10 (November 1973), pp. 396–403.

67. Andrew A. Mitchell, "The Effect of Verbal and Visual Components of Advertisements on Brand Attitudes and Attitude toward the Advertisement," *Journal of Consumer Research* 13 (June 1986), pp. 12–24; Julie A. Edell and Richard Staelin, "The Information Processing of Pictures in Advertisements," *Journal of Consumer Research* 10, no. 1 (June 1983), pp. 45–60; Elizabeth C. Hirschmann, "The Effects of Verbal and Pictorial Advertising Stimuli on Aesthetic, Utilitarian and Familiarity Perceptions," *Journal of Advertising* 15, no. 2 (1986), pp. 27–34.

68. Jolita Kisielius and Brian Sternthal, "Detecting and Explaining Vividness Effects in Attitudinal Judgments," *Journal of Marketing Research* 21 (1) (1984), pp. 54–64.

69. H. Rao Unnava and Robert E. Burnkrant, "An Imagery-Processing View of the Role of Pictures in Print Advertisements," *Journal of Marketing Research* 28 (May 1991), pp. 226–31.

70. Susan E. Heckler and Terry L. Childers, "The Role of Expectancy and Relevancy in Memory for Verbal and Visual Information: What Is Incongruency?" *Journal of Consumer Research* 18, no. 4 (March 1992), pp. 475–92.

71. Michael J. Houston, Terry L. Childers, and Susan E. Heckler, "Picture-Word Consistency and the Elaborative Processing of Advertisements," *Journal of Marketing Research* 24 (November 1987), pp. 359–69.

72. William L. Wilkie and Paul W. Farris, "Comparative Advertising: Problems and Potential," *Journal of Marketing* 39 (1975), pp. 7–15.

73. For a review of comparative advertising studies, see Cornelia Pechmann and David W. Stewart, "The Psychology of Comparative Advertising," in *Attention, Attitude and Affect in Response to Advertising,* eds. E. M. Clark, T. C. Brock, and D. W. Stewart (Hillsdale, NJ: Lawrence Erlbaum, 1994), pp. 79–96; Thomas S. Barry, "Comparative Advertising: What Have We Learned in Two Decades?" *Journal of Advertising Research* 33, no. 2 (1993), pp. 19–29.

74. Jeremy Mullman, "Is Miller a Sucker to Throw a Punch at A-B?," *Advertising Age,* pp. 1, 60.

75. Emily Bryson York, "Brand vs Brand: Attack Ads on the Rise," *Advertising Age,* October 27, 2008, http://adage.com/print?article_id=132028.

76. Michael Learmonth, "Apple Takes Hits from Windows 7 Droid but Prevails," *Advertising Age,* October 29, 2009, http://adagecom/print?article_id=140007.

77. Rupal Parekh, "Microsoft Changes 'Laptop Hunters' Ad After Apple Complains," *Advertising Age,* July 23, 2009, http://adagecom/print?article_id=138117.

78. Patrick Meirick, "Cognitive Responses to Negative and Comparative Political Advertising," *Journal of Advertising* 31, no. 1, (Spring 2002), pp. 49–59.

79. Bruce E. Pinkleton, Nam-Hyun Um, and Erica Weintraub Austin, "An Exploration of the Effects of Negative Political Advertising on Political Decision Making," *Journal of Advertising* 31 (1) (Spring 2002), pp. 13–25.

80. Bruce E. Pinkleton, "The Effects of Negative Comparative Political Advertising on Candidate Evaluations and Advertising Evaluations: An Exploration," *Journal of Advertising* 26, no. 1 (1997), pp. 19–29.

81. Michael L. Ray and William L. Wilkie, "Fear: The Potential of an Appeal Neglected by Marketing," *Journal of Marketing* 34 (January 1970), pp. 54–62.

82. Brian Sternthal and C. Samuel Craig, "Fear Appeals Revisited and Revised," *Journal of Consumer Research* 1 (December 1974), pp. 22–34.

83. Punam Anand Keller and Lauren Goldberg Block, "Increasing the Persuasiveness of Fear Appeals: The Effect of Arousal and Elaboration," *Journal of Consumer Research* 22, no. 4 (March 1996), pp. 448–60.

84. John F. Tanner, Jr., James B. Hunt, and David R. Eppright, "The Protection Motivation Model: A Normative Mode of Fear Appeals," *Journal of Marketing* 55 (July 1991), pp. 36–45.

85. Ibid.

86. Sternthal and Craig, "Fear Appeals Revisited and Revised."

87. Herbert Jack Rotfeld, "The Textbook Effect: Conventional Wisdom, Myth and Error in Marketing," *Journal of Marketing* 64 (April 2000), pp. 122–27.

88. For a discussion of the use of humor in advertising, see C. Samuel Craig and Brian Sternthal, "Humor in Advertising," *Journal of Marketing* 37 (October 1973), pp. 12–18.

89. Bobby J. Calder and Brian Sternthal, "Television Commercial Wearout: An Information Processing View," *Journal of Marketing Research* 17 (May 1980) pp. 173–87.

90. Dottie Enroco, "Humorous Touch Resonates with Consumers," *USA TODAY,* May 13, 1996, p. 3B.

91. Yong Zhang, "Response to Humorous Advertising: The Moderating Effect of Need for Cognition," *Journal of Advertising* 25, no. 1 (Spring 1996), pp. 15–32; Marc G. Weinberger and Charles S. Gulas, "The Impact of Humor in Advertising: A Review," *Journal of Advertising* 21 (December 1992), pp. 35–59.

92. Marc G. Weinberger and Leland Campbell, "The Use of Humor in Radio Advertising," *Journal of Advertising Research* 31 (December/January 1990–91), pp. 44–52.
93. Yong Zhang and George M. Zinkhan, "Responses to Humorous Ads," *Journal of Advertising,* Winter 2006, pp. 113–27.
94. Thomas J. Madden and Marc G. Weinberger, "Humor in Advertising: A Practitioner View," *Journal of Advertising Research* 24, no. 4 (August/September 1984), pp. 23–26.
95. Harold C. Cash and W. J. E. Crissy, "Comparison of Advertising and Selling: The Salesman's Role in Marketing," *Psychology of Selling* 12 (1965), pp. 56–75.
96. Marshall McLuhan, *Understanding Media: The Extensions of Man* (New York: McGraw-Hill, 1966).
97. Marvin E. Goldberg and Gerald J. Gorn, "Happy and Sad TV Programs: How They Affect Reactions to Commercials," *Journal of Consumer Research* 14, no. 3 (December 1987), pp. 387–403.
98. Andrew B. Aylesworth and Scott B. MacKenzie, "Context Is Key: The Effect of Program-Induced Mood on Thoughts about the Ad," *Journal of Advertising* 27, no. 2 (Summer 1998), pp. 17–32.
99. Michael T. Elliott and Paul Surgi Speck, "Consumer Perceptions of Advertising Clutter and Its Impact across Various Media," *Journal of Advertising Research* 38 (1) (January/February 1998), pp. 29–41; Peter H. Webb, "Consumer Initial Processing in a Difficult Media Environment," *Journal of Consumer Research* 6(3) (December 1979), pp. 225–36.
100. John Consoli, "TV Ad Clutter Showing Minimal Increase," *Mediaweek .com,* April 23, 2007; Andrew Hampp, "ABC, the Most Cluttered of Them All," *adage.com,* April 24, 2007.
101. Katy Bachman, Clutter Makes TV Ads Less Effective, *Mediaweek,* February 9, 2010, http://www.adweek.com/aw/content_display/news/media/e3i4fe3d67e44c8b3ad4c3fcbfe797fc862.
102. Steve McClellan, "Buyers, Now Try to Skirt Clutter With Sponsor Deals," *Adweek,* October 31, 2005, p. 9.

## Chapter Seven

1. Mya Frazier, "GEICO's Big Spending Pays Off, Study Says," www.adage .com, June 26,2007.
2. Nina M. Lentini, "Heinz Credits Marketing Strategy for 19% Profit Hike," www.mediapostpublications.com, November 30, 2007.
3. Donald S. Tull, "The Carry-Over Effect of Advertising," *Journal of Marketing,* (April 1965), pp. 46–53.
4. Darral G. Clarke, "Econometric Measurement of the Duration of Advertising Effect on Sales," *Journal of Marketing Research* 23 (November 1976), pp. 345–57.
5. Philip Kotler, *Marketing Decision Making: A Model Building Approach* (New York: Holt, Rinehart & Winston, 1971), Ch. 5.
6. Becky Ebenkamp, "You Can Teach an Old Hot Dog Brand Some New Design Tricks," *Brandweek,* Sept. 28, 2009.
7. Stephanie Thompson, "Kelloggs Roars Back with Out-of-Box Sds," *Advertising Age,* May 3, 2004, pp. 4–5.
8. Noreen O'Leary, "Why the New Caribou Coffee Logo Features Less Caribou," *Brandweek,* March 1, 2010, p.7.
9. Russell H. Colley, *Defining Advertising Goals for Measured Advertising Results* (New York: Association of National Advertisers, 1961).
10. Don E. Schultz, Dennis Martin, and William Brown, *Strategic Advertising Campaigns,* 2nd ed. (Lincolnwood, IL: Crain Books, 1984).
11. Michael L. Ray, "Consumer Initial Processing: Definitions, Issues, Applications," in *Buyer/Consumer Information Processing,* (ed.) G. David Hughes (Chapel Hill: University of North Carolina Press, 1974); David A. Aaker and John G. Myers, *Advertising Management,* 2nd ed. (Englewood Cliffs, NJ: Prentice Hall, 1982), pp. 122–23.
12. Aaker and Myers, *Advertising Management.*
13. Steven W. Hartley and Charles H. Patti, "Evaluating Business-to-Business Advertising: A Comparison of Objectives and Results," *Journal of Advertising Research* 28 (April/May 1988), pp. 21–27.
14. Study cited in Robert F. Lauterborn, "How to Know If Your Advertising Is Working," *Journal of Advertising Research* 25 (February/March 1985), pp. RC 9–11.
15. Don E. Schultz, "Integration Helps You Plan Communications from Outside-In," *Marketing News,* March 15, 1993, p. 12.
16. Thomas R. Duncan, "To Fathom Integrated Marketing, Dive!" *Advertising Age,* October 11, 1993, p. 18.
17. G. Tellis and K. Tellis. Research on Advertising in a Recession. *Journal of Advertising Research* 49 (3) (2009), pp. 304–27. Retrieved from Communication & Mass Media Complete database.
18. Robert L. Steiner, "The Paradox of Increasing Returns to Advertising," *Journal of Advertising Research,* (February/March 1987), pp. 45–53.
19. David A. Aaker and James M. Carman, "Are You Overadvertising?" *Journal of Advertising Research* 22 (4) (August/September 1982), pp. 57–70.
20. Julian A. Simon and Johan Arndt, "The Shape of the Advertising Response Function," *Journal of Advertising Research* 20 (4) (1980), pp. 11–28.
21. Melvin E. Salveson, "Management's Criteria for Advertising Effectiveness," in *Proceedings, 5th Annual Conference, Advertising Research Foundation,* (New York, 1959), p. 25.
22. Boonghee Yoo and Rujirutana Mandhachitara, "Estimating Advertising Effects on Sales in a Competitive Setting," *Journal of Advertising Research* 43 (3) (2003), pp. 310–20.
23. Dan Lippe, "Media scorecard: How ROI Adds Up," *Advertising Age,* June 20, 2005, pp. S-6, 42.
24. Mike Beirne and Kenneth Hein, "Marketers' Mantra: It's ROI, or I'm Fired!" *Brandweek,* October 18, 2004, pp. 14–15.
25. Joe Mandese, "Half of Media Buys Driven by ROI, TV, Online Dominate," *www.mediapost.com,* April 20, 2005, pp. 1–3.
26. Wayne Friedman, "ROI Measurement Still Falls Short," *TelevisionWeek,* January 31, 2005, p. 19.
27. Hillary Chura, "Advertising ROI Still Elusive Metric," *Advertising Age,* July 26, 2004, p. 8.
28. James O. Peckham, "Can We Relate Advertising Dollars to Market Share Objectives?" in *How Much to Spend for Advertising,* ed. M. A. McNiven (New York: Association of National Advertisers, 1969), p. 30.
29. George S. Low and Jakki Mohr, "Setting Advertising and Promotion Budgets in Multi-Brand Companies," *Journal of Advertising Research* 39 (1) (January/February 1999), pp. 667–78.

30. John P. Jones, "Ad Spending: Maintaining Market Share," *Harvard Business Review* 68 (1) (January/February 1990), pp. 38–42; James C. Schroer, "Ad Spending: Growing Market Share," *Harvard Business Review* 68 (1) (January/February 1990), pp. 44–48.
31. Randall S. Brown, "Estimating Advantages to Large-Scale Advertising," *Review of Economics and Statistics* 60 (August 1978), pp. 428–37.
32. Kent M. Lancaster, "Are There Scale Economies in Advertising?" *Journal of Business* 59 (3) (1986), pp. 509–26.
33. Johan Arndt and Julian Simon, "Advertising and Economics of Scale: Critical Comments on the Evidence," *Journal of Industrial Economics* 32 (2) (December 1983), pp. 229–41; Aaker and Carman, "Are You Overadvertising?"
34. George S. Low and Jakki J. Mohr, "The Budget Allocation between Advertising and Sales Promotion: Understanding the Decision Process," *AMA Educators' Proceedings, Summer 1991* (Chicago: American Marketing Association 1991), pp. 448–57.

## Chapter Eight

1. Joshua Levine, "Fizz, Fizz-Plop, Plop," *Fortune,* June 21, 1993, p. 139.
2. Jeremy Mullman and Stephanie Thompson, "Burnett's Stumble Continues as Altoids Slips Away," *Advertising Age,* January 5, 2007, http://www.adage.com/print?article_id=114094.
3. Bob Garfield, "Award Winners' Edge: That's Entertainment," *Advertising Age,* August 3, 2004, pp. 16–17; Brent Bouchez, "Trophies Are Meaningless," *Advertising Age,* July 30, 2001, p. 16; Vanessa O'Connell, "Ad Slump Deflates Awards Show," *The Wall Street Journal,* May 21, 2002, p. B2; Jennifer Pendleton, "Awards-Creatives Defend Pursuit of Prizes," *Advertising Age,* April 25, 1988, pp. 1, 7.
4. Elizabeth C. Hirschman, "Role-Based Models of Advertising Creation and Production," *Journal of Advertising* 18, no. 4 (1989), pp. 42–53.
5. Ibid., p. 51.
6. Cyndee Miller, "Study Says 'Likability' Surfaces as Measure of TV Ad Success," *Marketing News,* January 7, 1991, pp. 6, 14; Ronald Alsop, "TV Ads That Are Likeable Get Plus Rating for Persuasiveness," *The Wall Street Journal,* February 20, 1986, p. 23.
7. Brian D. Till and Daniel W. Baack, "Recall and Persuasion: Does Creativity Matter?," *Journal of Advertising* 34 (3) (2005), pp. 47–57.
8. Robert E. Smith, Scott B. MacKenzie, Xiaojing Yang, Laura Buchholz, William K. Darley, and Xiaojing Yang, "Modeling the Determinants and Effects of Creativity in Advertising," *Marketing Science* 26 (6), pp. 819–33; Robert E. Smith and Xiaojing Yang, "Toward a General Theory of Creativity in Advertising: Examining the Role of Divergence," *Marketing Theory* 4 (1/2), pp. 29–55.
9. Deborah J. MacInnis and Bernard J. Jaworski, "Information Processing from Advertisements: Toward an Integrative Framework," *Journal of Marketing* 53 (4) (October 1989), pp. 1–23.
10. Jeff Cioletti, "In a Changing World, There's Only One Absolut," *Beverage World,* July 2007, pp. 20–25; Stuart Elliott, "In an 'Absolut World,' a Vodka Could Use the Same Ads for More Than 25 Years," *The New York Times,* April 27, 2007, p. C3.
11. Robert E. Smith, Jiemiao Chen, and Xiaojing Yang, "The Impact of Advertising Creativity on the Hierarchy of Effects," *Journal of Advertising* 37 (4) (Winter 2008), pp. 47–61.
12. Robert E. Smith, Scott B. MacKenzie, Xiaojing Yang, Laura Buchholz, William K. Darley, and Xiaojing Yang, "Modeling the Determinants and Effects of Creativity in Advertising."
13. Swee Hoon Ang, Yih Hwai Lee, and Siew Meng Leong, "The Ad Creativity Cube: Conceptualization and Initial Validation," *Journal of the Academy of Marketing Science* 35 (23), pp. 220–32; Arthur J. Kover, Stephen M. Goldenberg, and William L. James, "Creativity vs. Effectiveness? An Integrative Classification for Advertising," *Journal of Advertising Research* 35 (November/December 1995), pp. 29–38.
14. Robert E. Smith, Scott B. MacKenzie, Xiaojing Yang, Laura Buchholz, William K. Darley, and Xiaojing Yang, "Modeling the Determinants and Effects of Creativity in Advertising."
15. For an interesting discussion on the embellishment of advertising messages, see William M. Weilbacher, *Advertising,* 2nd ed. (New York: Macmillan, 1984), pp. 180–82.
16. David Ogilvy, *Confessions of an Advertising Man* (New York: Atheneum, 1963); Hanley Norins, *The Compleat Copywriter* (New York: McGraw-Hill, 1966).
17. Hank Sneiden, *Advertising Pure and Simple* (New York: ANACOM, 1977).
18. Quoted in Valerie H. Free, "Absolut Original," *Marketing Insights,* Summer 1991, p. 65.
19. Jeff Jensen, "Marketer of the Year," *Advertising Age,* December 16, 1996, pp. 1, 16.
20. Cathy Taylor, "Risk Takers: Wieden & Kennedy," *Adweek's Marketing Week,* March 23, 1992, pp. 26, 27.
21. "Residence Inn by Marriott Breaks Out of the Box with New Ad Campaign Featuring Exotic Acrobatic Performers," *PR Newswire,* July 19, 2007.
22. Anthony Vagnoni, "Creative Differences," *Advertising Age,* November 17, 1997, pp. 1, 28, 30.
23. Jonathon Cranin, "Has Advertising Gone the Way of the Cosa Nostra?" *Advertising Age,* June 6, 2005.
24. Anthony Vagnoni, "Creative Differences."
25. Jonathon Cranin, "Has Advertising Gone the Way of the Cosa Nostra?"
26. Arthur J. Kover, "Copywriters' Implicit Theories of Communication: An Exploration," *Journal of Consumer Research* 21 (4) (March 1995), pp. 596–611.
27. Sheila L. Sasser and Scott Koslow, "Desperately Seeking Advertising Creativity," *Journal of Advertising* 37 (4) (Winter 2008), pp. 5–19.
28. James Webb Young, *A Technique for Producing Ideas,* 3rd ed. (Chicago: Crain Books, 1975), p. 42.
29. Graham Wallas, *The Art of Thought* (New York: Harcourt Brace), 1926.
30. Debra Goldman, "Origin of the Species: Has the Planner Finally Evolved into the Agency's Most Potent Creature?" *Adweek,* April 10, 1995, pp. 28–38.
31. Jon Steel, *Truth, Lies & Advertising: The Art of Account Planning* (New York: Wiley, 1998).
32. Sandra E. Moriarty, *Creative Advertising: Theory and Practice* (Englewood Cliffs, NJ: Prentice Hall, 1986).
33. E. E. Norris, "Seek Out the Consumer's Problem," *Advertising Age,* March 17, 1975, pp. 43–44.
34. Thomas L. Greenbaum, "Focus Groups Can Play a Part in Evaluating Ad Copy," *Marketing News,* September 13, 1993, pp. 24–25.

35. Emily Steel, "The New Focus Groups: Online Networks, Proprietary Panels Help Consumer Companies Shape Product Ads," *The Wall Street Journal,* January 14, 2008, p. B6.

36. Jennifer Comiteau, "Why the Traditional Focus Group Is Dying," *Adweek,* October 31, 2005, pp. 24–25, 32; Stephanie Thompson, "'Tipping Point' Guru Takes on Focus Groups," *Advertising Age,* January 24, 2005, pp. 4, 54; Malcolm Gladwell, "*Blink: The Power of Thinking Without Thinking*" (New York: Little, Brown and Company, 2004).

37. David Kiley, "Shoot the Focus Group," *BusinessWeek,* November 14, 2005, pp. 120–21.

38. Stephanie Thompson, "'Tipping Point' Guru Takes on Focus Groups."

39. Eric J. Arnould and Melanie Wallendorf, "Market-Oriented Ethnography: Interpretation Building and Marketing Strategy Formulation," *Journal of Marketing Research* 31 (November 1994), pp. 388–96.

40. "White Gold," 2009 Bronze Effie Winner, Effie Awards, http://www.effie.org/winners/showcase/2009/3686.

41. Stephen Winzenburg, "Your Advertising Slogans Are Crummy. Can't You Do Better, *Advertising Age,* January 14, 2008, p. 15; John Mathes, "Taglines That Stick; Here's How to Create an Effective Brand Summation Line. How Long Should It Be? Is It the Same as Your Brand Positioning? How Often Do You Need to Refresh It?," *ABA Bank Marketing,* December 1, 2008, pp. 22–25.

42. John Sutherland, Lisa Duke, and Avery Abernethy, "A Model of Marketing Information Flow," *Journal of Advertising* 22, no. 4 (Winter 2004), pp. 39–52.

43. A. Jerome Jeweler, *Creative Strategy in Advertising* (Belmont, CA: Wadsworth, 1981).

44. John O'Toole, *The Trouble with Advertising,* 2nd ed. (New York: Random House, 1985), p. 131.

45. David Ogilvy, *Ogilvy on Advertising* (New York: Crown, 1983), p. 16.

46. Arthur J. Kover, "Copywriters' Implicit Theories of Communication: An Exploration."

47. John R. Rossiter, "Defining the Necessary Components of Creative, Effective Ads," *Journal of Advertising Research* 37 (4) (Winter 2008), pp. 139–44.

48. Rosser Reeves, *Reality in Advertising* (New York: Knopf, 1961), pp. 47, 48.

49. Shelly Branch and Frances A. McMorris, "Irate Firms Take Comparisons to Court," *The Wall Street Journal,* December 22, 1999, p. B8.

50. Jeremy Mullman, "Hey, Those A-B Brands Look Like Miller Beers," *Advertising Age,* June 11, 2009, http://adagecom/print?article_id=137260; _______., "Miller Lightens Its Load: Will Go National with MGD 64 by Fall," *Advertising Age,* http://adage.com/print?article_id=127945.

51. Ogilvy, *Confessions of an Advertising Man.*

52. Martin Mayer, *Madison Avenue, U.S.A.* (New York: Pocket Books, 1958).

53. Jeremy Mullman, "Hallmark Reminds Consumers That Little Things Mean a Lot," *Advertising Age,* http://adage.com/print?article_id=135625.

54. Al Ries and Jack Trout, *Positioning: The Battle for Your Mind,* New York: McGraw-Hill, 1985; Jack Trout and Al Ries, "The Positioning Era Cometh," *Advertising Age,* April 24, 1972, pp. 35–38; May 1, 1972, pp. 51–54; May 8, 1972, pp. 114–16.

55. Jack Trout, "Brands Can't Exist without Positioning," *Advertising Age,* March 14, 2005, p. 28.

56. Jean Halliday, "Sometimes Oil and Oil Don't Mix," *Advertising Age,* March 4, 2002, pp. 4, 62.

57. Rajeev Batra, John G. Myers, and David A. Aaker, *Advertising Management,* 5th ed. (Upper Saddle River, NJ: Prentice Hall, 1996).

58. Anthony Vagnoni, "They Might Be Giants," *Advertising Age,* April 27, 1998, pp. 1, 20, 24.

59. _______., "Goodby, Silverstein Do 'Intelligent Work' with a Sales Pitch," *Advertising Age,* April 27, 1998, pp. 20, 24.

60. _______., "Having Ad Bosses Focus on the Work Key to Cult of Clow," *Advertising Age,* April 27, 1998, pp. 22, 24.

61. Ira Teinowitz, "Agencies Using Creativity to Save Themselves," adage.com, April 9, 2008.

62. Eleftheria Parpis, "U.S. Agency of the Year–2007: Goodby, Silverstein," *Adweek,* January 7, 2008, p. 20.

## Chapter Nine

1. Sandra E. Moriarty, *Creative Advertising: Theory and Practice,* 2nd ed. (Englewood Cliffs, NJ: Prentice Hall, 1991), p. 76.

2. William M. Weilbacher, *Advertising,* 2nd ed. (New York: Macmillan, 1984), p. 197.

3. William Wells, John Burnett, and Sandra Moriarty, *Advertising* (Englewood Cliffs, NJ: Prentice Hall, 1989), p. 330.

4. Hamish Pringle and Peter Field, "Why Emotional Messages Beat Rational Ones," *Advertising Age,* March 2, 2009, http://adage.com/print?article_id=134920; Stuart J. Agres, "Emotion in Advertising: An Agency Point of View," in *Emotion in Advertising: Theoretical and Practical Explanations,* eds. Stuart J. Agres, Julie A. Edell, and Tony M. Dubitsky (Westport, CT: Quorom Books, 1991).

5. Edward Kamp and Deborah J. Macinnis, "Characteristics of Portrayed Emotions in Commercials: When Does What Is Shown in Ads Affect Viewers?" *Journal of Advertising Research* (November/December 1995), pp. 19–28.

6. For a review of research on the effect of mood states on consumer behavior, see Meryl Paula Gardner, "Mood States and Consumer Behavior: A Critical Review," *Journal of Consumer Research* 12, no. 3 (December 1985), pp. 281–300.

7. Cathy Madison, "Researchers Work Advertising into an Emotional State," *Adweek,* November 5, 1990, p. 30.

8. Hamish Pringle and Peter Field, *Brand Immortality, How Brands Can Live Long and Prosper* (London: Kogan Page Limited), 2009.

9. Hamish Pringle and Peter Field, "Why Emotional Messages Beat Rational Ones."

10. Kate Macarthur, "Big Mac's Back," *Advertising Age,* March 13, 2004, pp. S1–8.

11. Emily Bryson York, "McDonald's Unveils 'I'm Lovin' It '2.0," *Advertising Age,* April 22, 2010, http://adage.com/print?article_id=143453.

12. Christopher P. Puto and William D. Wells, "Informational and Transformational Advertising: The Different Effects of Time," in *Advances in Consumer Research* 11, ed. Thomas C. Kinnear (Ann Arbor, MI: Association for Consumer Research, 1984), p. 638.

13. Ibid.

14. Kenneth Hein, "Strategy: Skyy Set the Stage in Sultry Cinematic Scenes," *Adweek,* June 17, 2002.
15. David Ogilvy and Joel Raphaelson, "Research on Advertising Techniques That Work and Don't Work," *Harvard Business Review,* July/August 1982, p. 18.
16. "New American Airlines TV Commercials Created by TIM Advertising Capture 'Smart Travelers' Perspective, *PR Newswire,* March 22, 2010.
17. *Topline,* No. 4 (September 1989), McCann-Erickson, New York.
18. Xiang Fang, Surendra Singh, and Rohini Ahluwalia, " An Examination of Different Explanations for the Mere Exposure Effect, *Journal of Consumer Research,* June 2007, pp. 97–103.
19. Robert Zajonc, "Attitudinal Effects of Mere Exposure," *Journal of Personality and Social Psychology Monographs*" (No. 2, Part 2), pp. 1–27.
20. John Young, "Making Online Ad Suck Less in 8 Easy Steps," *Advertising Age,* April 10, 2010, http://adage.com/print?article_id=143368.
21. Quote by Irwin Warren, cited in Enrico, in "Teaser Ads Grab Spotlight," *USA Today,* July 6, 1995, pp. 1, 2B.
22. Jonathan Lemonnier, "Doritos Got a Winning Spot, Creators Won Recognition," *Advertising Age,* http://adage.com/print?article_id=122990.
23. Emily Bryson York and Jeremy Mullman, "DDB, Crispin Goodby Can't Compete With Doritos Crotch Joke," *Advertising Age,* February 2, 2009, http://adage.com/print?article_id=134270.
24. Michael Learmonth, "Brands Team Up for User-Generated-Ad Contest," *Advertising Age,* March 23, 2009, http://adage.com/print?article_id=125422.
25. Martin Mayer, *Madison Avenue, U.S.A.* (New York: Pocket Books, 1958), p. 64.
26. Sally Beatty, "P&G to Ad Agencies: Please Rewrite Our Old Formulas," *The Wall Street Journal,* November 5, 1998, pp. B1, 10; Alecia Swasy, "P&G Tries Bolder Ads—With Caution," *The Wall Street Journal,* May 7, 1990, pp. B1, 7.
27. Lynn Coleman, "Advertisers Put Fear into the Hearts of Their Prospects," *Marketing News,* August 15, 1988, p. 1.
28. Ibid.
29. Bob Garfield, "Listerine Eschews 'Creativity' for an Ad That Actually Works," *Advertising Age,* September 20, 2004, p. 57.
30. Theresa Howard, "Schwab Ads' Message Goes for a Tone of 'Candid and Real'," *USA Today,* January 16, 2006, p. 5B.
31. ________., "Aflac Duck Give Wings to Insurer's Name Recognition," *USA Today,* May 17, 2001, p. B9.
32. Barbara B. Stern, "Classical and Vignette Television Advertising: Structural Models, Formal Analysis, and Consumer Effects," *Journal of Consumer Research* 20, no. 4 (March 1994), pp. 601–15; John Deighton, Daniel Romer, and Josh McQueen, "Using Drama to Persuade," *Journal of Consumer Research* 15, no. 3 (December 1989), pp. 335–43.
33. Moriarty, *Creative Advertising,* p. 77.
34. Mario Pricken, *Creative Advertising,* (New York: Thames & Hudson, 2009).
35. W. Keith Hafer and Gordon E. White, *Advertising Writing,* 3rd ed. (St. Paul, MN: West Publishing, 1989), p. 98.
36. Carol Marie Cooper, "Who Says Talk Is Cheap," *The New York Times,* October 22, 1998, pp. C1, 5; and Wendy Brandes, "Star Power Leaves Some Voice-Over Artists Speechless," *The Wall Street Journal,* June 2, 1995, p. B6.
37. David Allan, "A Content Analysis of Music Placement in Prime-Time Advertising," *Journal of Advertising Research* (September 2008), pp. 404–14.
38. Linda M. Scott, "Understanding Jingles and Needledrop: A Rhetorical Approach to Music in Advertising," *Journal of Consumer Research* 17, no. 2 (September 1990), pp. 223–36.
39. Kineta Hung, "Framing Meaning Perceptions with Music: The Case of Teaser Ads," *Journal of Advertising* 30, no. 3 (Fall 2001), pp. 39–49; Russell I. Haley, Jack Richardson, and Beth Baldwin, "The Effects of Nonverbal Communications in Television Advertising," *Journal of Advertising Research,* (July/August 1984) 24, no. 4, pp. 11–18.
40. Natalie Zmuda, "Pass or Fail, Pepsi's Refresh Will Be Case for Marketing Textbooks," *Advertising Age,* February 8, 2010, http://adage.com/print?article_id=141973.
41. Steve Oakes, "Evaluating Empirical Research into Music in Advertising: A Congruity Perspective," *Journal of Advertising Research,* March 2007, pp. 38–50.
42. Gerald J. Gorn, "The Effects of Music in Advertising on Choice Behavior: A Classical Conditioning Approach," *Journal of Marketing* 46 (Winter 1982), pp. 94–100.
43. Donna DeMarco, "TV Ads Go Pop: Advertisers Marry Modern Music with Their Products," *Washington Times,* May 12, 2002, p. A1.
44. Matthew Boyle, "The Accidental Hero," *BusinessWeek,* November 5, 2009, http://www.businessweek.com/print/magazine/content/09_46/b4155058815908.htm.
45. Stephanie Thompson, "Promotions: Nostalgia Bolognese," *Brandweek,* April 14, 1997.
46. Quote from: Suzanne Vranica, "P&G Dusts Off a Familiar Tune," *The Wall Street Journal,* March 3, 2005, p. B2.
47. Ibid.
48. "Results of 4A's 2008 Television Production Costs Survey," American Association of Advertising Agencies, Bulletin # 7115, December 15, 2009.
49. Jack Neff, "Industry Explores New Compensation Model for Talent," *Advertising Age,* May 3, 2010, http://adage.com/print?article_id=143638.
50. Jack Neff, "Why P&G Won't Win Many Cannes Lions," *Advertising Age,* June 13, 2005, pp. 3, 45; Beatty, "P&G to Ad Agencies."
51. Meg James, "Over 50 and Out of Flavor," *Los Angeles Times,* May 10, 2005, pp. A1, 10.
52. Rupel Parekh, "Brand Awareness Was Only Half the Battle for Aflac," *Advertising Age*, June 22, 2009, http://adage.com/print?article_id=137392; Suzanne Vranica, "Aflac Partly Muzzles Iconic Duck," *The Wall Street Journal,* December 2, 2004, p. B8.
53. Jack Neff, "Method Pulls 'Shiny Suds' Ad After Sexism Complaints," *Advertising Age,* December 2, 2009, http://adage.com/print?article_id=140830. Bob Garfield, "Why Method Did Right in Pulling the Plug on 'Shiny Suds'," *Advertising Age,* December 7, 2009, http://adage.com/print?article_id=140894.

## Chapter Ten

1. Jamie Turner, "Top 52 Social Media Platforms Every Marketer Should Know," www.60secondmarketer.com, April 9, 2010.

2. Jim Surmanek, *Advertising Media A to Z,* McGraw-Hill, 2003.
3. Matthew Creamer, "Ad Groups Back Switch from 'Frequency' to 'Engagement,'" *adage.com*, July 21, 2005.
4. Jeff Cusack, "Chuck Shows the Value of Audience Engagement," www.filmindustry.suite101.com, May 1, 2009.
5. Chuck Ross, "Study Finds for Continuity vs. Flights," *Advertising Age,* April 19, 1999, p. 2.
6. Joseph W. Ostrow, "Setting Frequency Levels: An Art or a Science?" *Journal of Advertising Research* 24 (August/September 1984), pp. i9–11.
7. David Crane, "Arnold vs. Calbuzz, Meg's Ad Buy; Memo to Media," www.calbluzz.com, March 10, 2010.
8. Scott Walker, "Ratings and TV Advertising Sales," www.tvadvertising.suite101.com, April 2, 2008.
9. David Berger, "How Much to Spend," *Foote, Cone & Belding Internal Report,* in Michael L. Rothschild, *Advertising* (Lexington, MA: Heath, 1987), p. 468.
10. David W. Olson, "Real World Measures of Advertising Effectiveness for New Products," *Speech to the 26th Annual Conference of the Advertising Research Foundation,* New York, March 18, 1980.
11. Joseph W. Ostrow, "What Level Frequency?" *Advertising Age,* November 1981, pp. 13–18.
12. Jack Myers, "More Is Indeed Better," *Media Week,* September 6, 1993, pp. 14–18.
13. Jim Surmanek, "One-Hit or Miss: Is a Frequency of One Frequently Wrong?" *Advertising Age,* November 27, 1995, p. 46.
14. Erwin Ephron, "Back to the Future," www.ephrononmedia.com, April 14, 2010.
15. Joseph W. Ostrow, "What Level Frequency?"
16. Erwin Ephron, "Recency Planning," www.ephrononmedia.com, March 18, 1998.
17. Erwin Ephron, "Sitting on the Shelf," www.ephrononmedia.com, October 1, 2009.

## Chapter Eleven

1. *The Radio Marketing Guide,* (New York: Radio Advertising Bureau, 2010), www.rab.com.
2. "114 Million U.S. Television Homes Estimated for 2009–2010 Season," *Nielsen Wire,* August 28, 2009, www.blog.nielsen.com.
3. "Network Television Cost and CPM Trends," *Trends in Media* (Television Bureau of Advertising, New York), www.tvb.org/rcentral.
4. Rebecca Dana and Stephanie King, "Answer to Vexing Question: Who's Not Watching Ads," *The Wall Street Journal,* October 17, 2009, p. B2; Lex van Meurs, "Zapp! A Study on Switching Behavior during Commercial Breaks," *Journal of Advertising Research* (January/February 1998), pp. 43–53; John J. Cronin, "In-Home Observations of Commercial Zapping Behavior," *Journal of Current Issues and Research in Advertising,* Vol. 17, No. 2 (Fall 1995), pp. 69–75.
5. "Results of 4A's 2008 Television Production Costs Survey," American Association of Advertising Agencies, Bulletin #7115, December 15, 2009.
6. Brian Grow, "Hispanic Nation," *BusinessWeek,* March 15, 2004, pp. 58–70.
7. "Network Television Commercial Activity by Length of Commercial," *Trends in Television* (New York: Television Bureau of Advertising), www.tvb.org/rcentral.
8. Steve McClellan "Buyers, Nets Try to Skirt Clutter with Sponsor Deals," *Adweek,* October 31, 2005, p. 9.
9. John J. Cronin and Nancy Menelly, "Discrimination vs. Avoidance: 'Zipping' of Television Commercials," *Journal of Advertising* 21, no. 2 (June 1992), pp. 1–7.
10. Suzanne Vranica, "TiVo Serves Up Portrait of the Ad-Zappers," *The Wall Street Journal,* November 8, 2007, p. B5.
11. John J. Cronin, "In-Home Observations of Commercial Zapping Behavior."
12. Carrie Heeter and Bradley S. Greenberg, "Profiling the Zappers," *Journal of Advertising Research,* April/May 1985, pp. 9–12; Fred S. Zufryden, James H. Pedrick, and Avu Sandaralingham, "Zapping and Its Impact on Brand Purchase Behavior," *Journal of Advertising Research* 33 (January/February 1993), pp. 58–66; Patricia Orsini, "Zapping: A Man's World," Spring Television Report, *Adweek's Marketing Week,* April 8, 1991, p. 3.
13. Lex van Meurs, "Zapp! A Study on Switching Behavior during Commercial Breaks," *Journal of Advertising Research* 38(1) (January/February 1998), pp. 43–53.
14. Alan Ching Biu Tse and Rub P. W. Lee, "Zapping Behavior During Commercial Breaks," *Journal of Advertising Research* 41(3) (May/June 2001), pp. 25–29.
15. Suzanne Vranica, "CW Newsmagazine Is Pitch within Pitch," *The Wall Street Journal,* September 21, 2007, p. B3.
16. ________., "NBC Hopes Live Spot Puts Life into Ads," *The Wall Street Journal,* June 8, 2007, p. B3.
17. Kim Masters, "In the Age of TiVo, Advertisers Scramble to Keep Up," www.npr.org, May 16, 2007.
18. Brooks Barnes, "ABC, Cox Bar Ad Skipping in Video on Demand," *The Wall Street Journal,* May 8, 2007, p. B8.
19. John Consoli, "DVR Viewing Delays Clear Ratings Picture," *Adweek,* October 1, 2007, p. 6; Brooks Barnes and Emily Steel, "Lagging Online, TV Stations Get Moving," *The Wall Street Journal,* April 11, 2007, pp. B1, 3.
20. Linda F. Alwitt and Paul R. Prabhaker, "Identifying Who Dislikes Television Advertising: Not by Demographics Alone," *Journal of Advertising Research* 32, no. 5 (1992), pp. 30–42.
21. Banwari Mittal, "Public Assessment of TV Advertising: Faint Praise and Harsh Criticism," *Journal of Advertising Research* 34, no. 1 (1994), pp. 35–53.
22. Lucy L. Henke, "Young Children's Perceptions of Cigarette Brand Advertising Symbols: Awareness, Affect, and Target Market Identification," *Journal of Advertising* 24, no. 4 (Winter 1995), pp. 13–28.
23. Bill Mann, "What's with CW? Result of Merger between WB and UPN Targets 18-and-Ups," *The Press Democrat,* December 16, 2007, p. D8.
24. Brooks Barnes and Miriam Jordan, "Big Four TV Networks Get a Wake-Up Call—in Spanish," *The Wall Street Journal,* May 2, 2005, pp. B1, 6.
25. Brian Steinberg, "*Sunday Night Football* Remains Costliest TV Show," *Advertising Age,* October 26, 2009, p. 8.
26. 'Idol' Showing Age but Still Delivering Golden Eggs for Fox," *Advertising Age,* June 7, 2010, http://adage.com/print?article_id=144263; Brian Steinberg, "Fox Makes Out Like Ban-

dit with 'Idol' and Bowl," *Advertising Age,* December 17, 2007, pp. 1, 34.

27. Brian Steinberg, "TV Nets Notice Uptick in 'Just in Time' Ad Buying," *Advertising Age,* September 7, 2009, http://adage.com/print?article_id=138856.
28. Brian Steinberg, "More Networks Are Pulling the Plugs," *The Wall Street Journal,* October 15, 2004, p. B2.
29. Sally Goll Beatty, "MSNBC Already Waging Marketing War," *The Wall Street Journal,* July 9, 1996, p. B8.
30. Joe Flint and Stefan Fatsis, "Comcast Mulls Sports Network to Rival ESPN," *The Wall Street Journal,* July 27, 2005, pp. B1, 3.
31. Brian Steinberg, "Broadcast TV or Cable, It's All the Same to Consumers," *Advertising Age,* March 23, 2009, http://adage.com/print?article_id=135246.
32. Joe Flint and Stefan Fatsis, "ESPN Snatches NFL on Monday; NBC Scores, Too," *The Wall Street Journal,* April 19, 2005, pp. B1, 9.
33. Gary Levin, "Arbitron Exits from Ratings Race," *Advertising Age,* October 25, 1993, p. 4.
34. A.J. Frutkin, "Do Sweeps Still Matter," *Mediaweek.com,* April 30, 2007.
35. "Measuring TV Audience," *Broadcast Engineering,* October 1, 2007, p. 26.
36. Brian Steinberg and Andrew Hampp, "Commercial Ratings? Nets Talk TiVo Instead," *Advertising Age,* June 4, 2007, pp. 1, 60.
37. Steve McClellan, "Taking the 'Break' Out of Commercial Pods," *Adweek,* March 16, 2007, p. 9.
38. "Nielsen Appoints Client Advisory Committees for Its Anytime Anywhere Media Measurement (A2/M2) Initiative," *PR Newswire,* October 16, 2006.
39. Kate Fitzgerald, "Campus Viewing Stirs a Romp, *Advertising Age,* April 9, 2007, http://adage.com/print?article_id=115950.
40. Andrew Hampp, "Nielsen Adds Ratings for Away-From-Home TV Networks," *Advertising Age,* April 14, 2010, http://adage.com/print?article_id=143308.
41. Andrew Hampp, "Upfront Metric of Choice: Engagement?," adage.com, April 9, 2007.
42. Cristel Russell, Andrew T. Norman, and Susan E. Heckler, "People and Their Television Shows: An Exploration into The Construct of Audience Connectedness," *Marketing Letters* 10 (4), pp. 387–401.
43. Brian Steinberg, "Viewer-Engagement Rankings Signal Change for TV Industry," *Advertising Age,* May 10, 2010, http://adage.com/print?article_id=143754.
44. *The Radio Marketing Guide,* (New York: Radio Advertising Bureau, 2010), www.rab.com.
45. Ibid.
46. Verne Gay, "Image Transfer: Radio Ads Make Aural History," *Advertising Age,* January 24, 1985, p. 1.
47. "The Benefits of Synergy: Moving Money into Radio" (New York: Radio Ad Effectiveness Lab, Inc.) December 2004, www.radioadlal.com.
48. Avery Abernethy, "Differences between Advertising and Program Exposure for Car Radio Listening," *Journal of Advertising Research* 31, no. 2 (April/May 1991), pp. 33–42.
49. *The Radio Marketing Guide* (New York: Radio Advertising Bureau, 2010), www.rab.com.
50. Martin Peers, "Radio Produces Both Gains and Skeptics," *The Wall Street Journal,* January 1, 1999, p. B6.
51. Andrew Hampp, "Liberty Media Rides in to Rescue Sirius XM," *Advertising Age,* February 17, 2009, http://adage.com/print?article_id=134661.
52. Heather Green, Tom Lowry, Catherine Young, and David Kiley, "The New Radio Revolution, *BusinessWeek,* March 14, 2005, pp. 32–35.
53. Martin Peers, "Radio Produces Both Gains and Skeptics."
54. Heather Green et al., "The New Radio Revolution."
55. Andrew Hampp, "Contextual Radio Ads: Clear Channel's New Pitch to National Marketers, "*Advertising Age,* January 15, 2010, http://adage.com/print?article_id=141533.
56. Jon Fine. "A Better Measure of Old Media," *BusinessWeek,* July 9, 2007, p. 20.

## Chapter Twelve

1. An excellent resource on the role of magazines as advertising media vehicles is the Association of Magazine Media website at www.magazine.org.
2. Herbert E. Krugman, "The Measurement of Advertising Involvement," *Public Opinion Quarterly* 30 (Winter 1966–67), pp. 583–96.
3. *Magazines the Medium of Action: A Comprehensive Guide and Handbook 2009/2010* (New York: Magazine Publishers of America, www.magazine.org/handbook).
4. *Samir Husni's Guide to New Magazines,* 24th Edition (Taylor, MS: Nautilus Publishing 2009).
5. Brian Steinberg, "Gimmicky Magazine Inserts Aim to Grab Page Flippers," *The Wall Street Journal,* August 8, 2005, pp. B1, 2.
6. Scott Donaton and Pat Sloan, "Ad 'Printaculars' under Scrutiny," *Advertising Age,* February 12, 1990, p. 3.
7. *Magazines the Medium of Action: A Comprehensive Guide and Handbook 2009/2010.*
8. Ibid.
9. Sarah Ellison, "Good Housekeeping Touts Its Test Lab to Seek New Readers' Seal of Approval," *The Wall Street Journal,* October 11, 2006, pp. B1, 4.
10. Steve Fajen, "Numbers Aren't Everything," *Media Decisions* 10 (June 1975), pp. 65–69.
11. *Magazines the Medium of Action: A Comprehensive Guide and Handbook 2009/2010.*
12. Ibid.
13. Sally Goll Beatty, "Philip Morris Starts Lifestyle Magazine," *The Wall Street Journal,* September 16, 1996, pp. B1, 8.
14. Jack Neff, "P&G to Launch Customer Beauty Magazine *Rouge* in U.S.," *Advertising Age,* October 7, 2009, http://adage.com/print?article_id=139515.
15. Jack Neff, "P&G Extends Online Custom Publishing," *Advertising Age,* March 22, 2004, pp. 24–25.
16. Jon Fine, "Audit Bureau to Change How It Counts Circulation," adage.com, July 17, 2001.
17. _______., "ABC Feels Heat of Circ Scandals," *Advertising Age,* January 17, 2005, pp. 1, 26.
18. _______., "ABC Intensifies Effort to Root Out Circ Fraud," *Advertising Age,* November 15, 2004, pp. 4, 49.
19. Study cited in Jim Surmanek, *Media Planning: A Practical Guide* (Lincolnwood, IL: Crain Books, 1985).
20. "How Advertising Readership Is Influenced by Ad Size," Report no. 110.1, *Cahners Advertising Research,* Newton, MA; "Larger Advertisements Get Higher Readership," *LAP Report no. 3102,* McGraw-Hill Research, New York; "Effect of Size, Color and

Position on Number of Responses to Recruitment Advertising," *LAP Report no. 3116,* McGraw-Hill Research, New York.

21. "Almost Everything You Want to Know about Positioning in Magazines," study by Roper Starch Worldwide, Inc., 1999.
22. "Readership by Advertising Unit Type," *Magazine Dimensions,* 2001, Media Dynamics, Inc., http://www.magazine.org/resources/fact_sheets/adv.
23. Nat Ives, "Why Ad Pages Won't Ever Fully Return to Mags," *Advertising Age,* July 27, 2009, http://adage.com/print?article_id=138131; Nat Ives, "Mags March Calmly into Face of Chaos," adage.com, April 23, 2007.
24. ______., "The Last Page," *Advertising Age,* December 15, 2009, http://adage.com/print?article_id=132779.
25. ______., "What Life Is Like for Titles after They Leave Print," *Advertising Age,* November 16, 2009, http://adage.com/print?article_id=140541.
26. Lucia Moses. "The Heat Is On," *Mediaweek,* August 6, 2007, pp. 20–21.
27. Nat Ives, "Business Magazines Face Harsh Reality," *Advertising Age,* November 2, 2009, http://adage.com/print?article_id=140117.
28. ______., "Glamour Is Magazine of the Year but New York Takes the Most Prizes," *Advertising Age,* April 23, 2010, http://adage.com/print?article_id=143471.
29. ______., "Many Magazines That Cut Subscription Prices Lose Subscribers Anyway," *Advertising Age,* February 5, 2010, http://adage.com/print?article_id=141945.
30. _______., "Mags March Calmly into Face of Chaos."
31. _______., "Magazines to Sell Subscriptions within Facebook's News Feed," *Advertising Age,* May 12, 2010, http://adage.com/print?article_id=143813.
32. _______., "Magazines' Pitch to Marketers: Our Ads Will Work—We Promise," *Advertising Age,* May 10, 2010, http://adage.com/print?article_id=143773.
33. *Magazines the Medium of Action: A Comprehensive Guide and Handbook 2009/2010.*
34. "NAA Daily and Sunday Newspaper Section Readership Reports" (Vienna, VA: Newspaper Association of America, 2008), www.naa.org/trendsandnumbers/readership.
35. Andrew Vanacore, "U.S. Newspaper Circulation down 8.7% in Latest Survey," *USA Today,* April 26, 2010, http://www.usatoday.com/cleanprint/?1276093954708.
36. Ann Marie Kerwin, "After a Long Lobbying Effort, *New York Times* Wins New Ad Status," *Advertising Age,* February 22, 1999, p. 24.
37. Ann Marie Kerwin, "Big-City Dailies Eye National Stage," *Advertising Age,* February 22, 1999, p. 24.
38. "Christian Science Monitor to Drop Daily Print Publication, Go Online Only," *Advertising Age,* October 28, 2008, http://adage.com/print?article_id=132086.
39. Hanna Liebman, "NAA Network Ready to Roll," *Mediaweek,* December 13, 1993, p. 18.
40. David Washburn, "*Union-Tribune* to Offer Free Classified Ads to Individuals," *The San Diego Union Tribune,* August 8, 2005, pp. H1, 4.
41. Nat Ives, "Newspapers' Paid Circulation Losses Shrink," *Advertising Age,* April 26, 2010, http://adage.com/print?article_id=143509; Paul E. Steiger, "Read All About It," *The Wall Street Journal,*" December 29, 2007, pp. A1, 8; Brian Steinberg, "Newspaper Woes Are Black and White," *The Wall Street Journal,* December 15, 2004, p. B3.
42. ______., "Newspaper Subscribers Stick around Longer, Pay More," *Advertising Age,* September 30, 2009, http://adage.com/print?article_id=139346.
43. NAA Daily and Sunday Newspaper Section Readership Reports.
44. "Brandy, Bon Jovi, Barbara Bush, Elway, Hill, and Streep Return for Fourth Flight of NAA National Ad Campaign," news release, Newspaper Association of America, 1999 (http://www.naa.org).
45. Ann Marie Kerwin, "Print's Power Play," *Advertising Age: The Next Century,* special issue, 1999.
46. Newspaper websites, Newspaper Association of America, 2010, http://www.naa.org/TrendsandNumbers/Newspaper-websites.aspx.
47. Julia Angwin, "Newspapers Set To Jointly Sell Ads on Web Sites," *The Wall Street Journal,* January 10, 2007, pp. A1, 8.
48. Ibid.

## Chapter Thirteen

1. *Outdoor Advertising Association,* 2010.
2. *Product Acceptance and Research,* 2007.
3. David Kaplan, "Agency Offers In-Store Insight: End-Aisles, Print Surpass TV," www.mediapost.com, June 23, 2005.
4. *American Public Transportation Association,* 2010.
5. *Outdoor Advertising Association,* 2010.
6. Ibid.
7. Mukesh Bhargava and Naveen Donthu, "Sales Response to Outdoor Advertising," *Journal of Advertising Research,* 39 (3), July/August 1999.
8. *American Public Transportation Association,* 2010.
9. Andrew Hampp, "Outdoor Ad Industry Finally Gets Its Improved Metrics," www.adage.com, March 30, 2010.
10. *Promotional Products Association International,* 2010.
11 Ibid.
12. Ibid.
13. Ibid.
14. Yellow Pages Association, 2010.
15. Ibid.
16. Ibid.
17. Ibid.
18. Ibid.
19. Ibid.
20. Ibid.
21. _______., "Catch a Commercial at the Movies," October 29, 2007.
22. Sarah McBride, "In Theaters: Commercials Aplenty," *The Wall Street Journal,* February 8, 2007.
23. Hank, Kim, "Regal Pre-movie Package Boosts Recall," *Advertising Age,* June 7, 2004, p. 21.
24. Sarah McBride, "Cinema Surpassed DVD Sales in 2009," www.wsj.com, January 4, 2010.
25. Erik Sass, "Movie Metrics: Cinema Ads Click with Viewers," www.mediapost.com, April 13, 2010.
26. Jon Lafayette, "Study Says Theater Spots Deliver Ad Message," www.tvweek.com, February 4, 2009.
27. Katy Bachman, "Taco Bell Goes Cinematic with Ad Campaign," www.mediaweek.com, June 28, 2009.
28. T.L. Stanley, " A Place For Everything," *Next,* March 1, 2010, pp.12–13.
29. Shahnaz Mahmud, "Branded Content, Mobile to Grow," *Adweek,* August 8, 2007.

30. Michael Belch and Cristel A. Russell," A Managerial Investigation into the Product Placement Industry," *Journal of Advertising Research,* March, 2005, pp. 73–92.
31. David G. Kennedy, "Coming of Age in Consumerdom," *American Demographics,* April 2004, p. 14.
32. Marc Graser, "Movie Placement Creates Demand for Nonexistent Shoe," www.adage.com. January 31, 2005, pp. 1–2.
33. Jim Edwards, "Will Product Placement Get Its Own Dot-Comeuppance?" *Brandweek,* July 25, 2005, p. 13.
34. Brian Steinberg, "'Modern Family' Featured an iPad, but ABC Didn't Collect," www.adage.com, April 1, 2010.
35. Louis Story, "Creating the Content to Go with the Ad Spot," *The New York Times,* November 3, 2006.
36. Brian Steinberg, "Desperate Spokeswives: A New Marriage with Ads," www.adage.com, September 28, 2009.
37. David G. Kennedy, "Coming of Age in Consumerdom."
38. David Kaplan, "Product Placement: Well-Placed among Consumers."
39. Gail Schiller, "Tie-ins Often Sobering for Liquor Firms," *Hollywood Reporter,* August 1, 2005, pp. 1–3; MarinInstitute.org, 2006.
40. John Consoli, "80% TV Viewers Approve Product Placement," www.insidebrandedentertainment.com, March 28, 2005, p. 1.
41. David G. Kennedy, "Coming of Age in Consumerdom."
42. Harris Interactive, "Attitudes of US Children and Teens toward Advertising Tactics, by Age, May 2006," *eMarketer,* 2006.
43. Steve McClellan, "Branded Entertainment Finding Its Place(ment)," www.insidebrandedentertainment.com, March 28, 2005, pp. 1–3.
44. Michael Belch and Cristel A. Russell, "A Managerial Investigation into the Product Placement Industry," *Journal of Advertising Research,* March 2005, pp. 73–92.
45. Lorin Cipolla, "Guerilla Marketing Goes Mainstream: AMA Conference," www.promomagazine.com, February 17, 2004, p. 1.
46. Betsy Spethmann, Patricia Odell, Tim Parry, Amy Johannes, "Guerilla Marketing Grows Up," www.PROMOXtra.com, January 12, 2005, pp. 1–4.
47. Todd Wasserman, "Planning A Branding Ambush? Better Bring That Digital Gadget First," *Next,* January 11, 2010, p. 8.
48. Robert Klara, "Herd on the Street," www.brandweek.com, December 5, 2008.
49. _______., "ESA Facts," www.theesa.com, May 22, 2010.
50. _______., "Outcast Sees High Recall for At-the-Pump Network: Nielsen," www.mediabuyerplanner.com, May 6, 2009.
51. PRN.com.

## Chapter Fourteen

1. Direct Marketing Association, 2010.
2. *Direct Marketing Association Statistical Fact Book 2010,* New York: Direct Marketing Association, 2010.
3. Ibid.
4. *Bureau of Labor Statistics,* 2010.
5. Erik Sass, "Survey Results Make a Case for Direct Mail," *Media Post,* June 12, 2007.
6. Herbert Kanzenstein and William S. Sachs, *Direct Marketing,* 2nd ed. (New York: Macmillan, 1992).
7. *Statistical Fact Book 2010,* New York: Direct Marketing Association.
8. Ibid.
9. Ibid.
10. Louise Lee, "Catalogs Everywhere: Net Shopping Isn't Rendering Them Obsolete. It's Just Changing Their Role," *BusinessWeek,* December 4, 2006.
11. Elaine Underwood, "Is There a Future for the TV Mall?," *Brandweek,* March 25, 1996, pp. 24–26.
12. www.responsemagazine.com, April 2010.
13. *Statistical Fact Book 2010.*
14. Marianna Morello, "Print Media + DRTV = Retail Success," *Response,* September 2002, p. 6.
15. David Kaplan, "OnStar Positions New TV Ad Format: The 'Documercial,'" www.mediapost.com, April 14, 2005, pp. 1–2.
16. expoTV.com, 2010.
17. Iris Dorbian, "Home Shopping Sales Up in Q1," *DM News,* May 17, 2010, p. 2.
18. *Statistical Fact Book 2010.*
19. *Direct Selling Association* 2010.
20. U.S. Postal Service, "Industry Facts and Figures, 2004," *Postal News, 2008. www.retailing.org*, September 9, 2005, pp. 1–2; *Statistical Fact Book 2007,* New York: Direct Marketing Association, 2010.
21. _______., "Jupiter Predicts Consumers to Receive over 3,900 Spam E-mails Annually by 2007," *www.directmag.com*, September 18, 2002.
22. U.S. Postal Service, *Postal News, 2008.*

## Chapter Fifteen

1. TVB/Yankelovich, "How Media Works," April 2009.
2. "Retail E-Commerce Growth Resumes Double-Digit Growth," *eMarketer,* March 2010.
3. Andrea Chang, "Retail Chains are Embracing Their Online Stores," www.latimes.com, June 18, 2010.
4. Wikipedia.org, 2010.
5. Andrew Stem, "8 Ways to Improve Your Click-Through Rate," Direct Marketing, February 1, 2010, pp. 1–3.
6. Anita Davis, "Banner Ads Drive Search Behavior: Study," www.brandrepublic.asia, May 13, 2009.
7. Tessa Wegert, "Banner Ads: Beyond the Click," *eMarketer,* May 18, 2009.
8. Xiang Fang, Surendra Singh, and Rohini Ahluwalia, "An Examination of Different Explanations for the Mere Exposure Effect," *Journal of Consumer Research,* June 2007.
9. "Consumers Unhappy with Web Site Simply Go Away," www.CenterforMediaResearch.com, August 23, 2005, pp. 1–2.
10. Cong Li and Robert Meeds, "Different Forced-Exposure Levels of Internet Advertising: An Experimental Study of Pop-Up Ads and Interstitials," *American Academy of Advertising Conference Proceedings,* 2005, pp. 200–208.
11. Abbey Klaassen, "The State of Search Marketing: 2009," www.adage.com, November 2, 2009.
12. Wikipedia.org, 2010.
13. Wikipedia.org, 2010.
14. Ian Schafer, "What Is Rich Media, Really?" www.clickz.com, September 23, 2005, p. 1.
15. "Online's Slice of Ad Spending Grows Worldwide," *eMarketer,* September 30, 2009.
16. Wikipedia.org, 2010.
17. Wikipedia.org, 2010.
18. Wikipedia.org, 2010.
19. "Podcasting Goes Mainstream," *eMarketer,* March 4, 2009.
20. Chris Sherman, "What Is RSS, and Why Should You Care?" www.searchenginewatch.com, August 30, 2005, pp. 1–4.

21. Pingdom, "Internet 2009 in Numbers," royal.pingdom.com., January 22, 2010.
22. *Statistical Fact Book 2010,* New York: Direct Marketing Association.
23. www.Wikipedia.com
24. "Measurement Guidelines and Measurement Certification," www.iab.net, 2006.
25. Jack Neff, " Study: ROI May Be Measurable in Facebook, MySpace after All," www.adage.com, April 13, 2009.
26. Measurement Guidelines and Measurement Certification, www.iab.net, 2006.
27. Steve Latham, "Why Marketers Are Not Investing Online," *Media Post,* February 13, 2008.
28. Jeremy Mullman and Alice Cuneo, "Nike Setting the Place in Interactive-TV Race," *Advertising Age,* August 13, 2007.
29. Paul Sakuma, "Google Joins Up with Sony, Intel, & Logitech for Interactive TV Plan, www.csmonitor.com, May 20, 2010.
30. _______., "Mobile Marketing Emerges with Couponing," www.news@mediapost.com, April 22, 2010.
31. Mark Walsh, "Ace Hardware Snags 30% More in Mobile Effort," www.mediapost.com, July 8, 2009.


## Chapter Sixteen


1. Louis J. Haugh, "Defining and Redefining," *Advertising Age,* February 14, 1983, p. M44.
2. "Best Loyalty Program: Kellogg's Movie Lover's Collection DVD Continuity," *PROMO,* October 2007, p. 48.
3. Scott A. Nielsen, John Quelch, and Caroline Henderson, "Consumer Promotions and the Acceleration of Product Purchases," in *Research on Sales Promotion: Collected Papers,* ed. Katherine E. Jocz (Cambridge, MA: Marketing Science Institute, 1984).
4. J. Jeffrey Inman and Leigh McAlister, "Do Coupon Expiration Dates Affect Consumer Behavior?" *Journal of Marketing Research,* Vol. 3, August 1994, pp. 23–28.
5. "2009 PROMO Industry Trends Report," *PROMO,* December 1, 2009, http://promagazine.com/09-industry-trends-report/index.html.
6. Ibid.
7. Betsy Spethman, "Is Promotion a Dirty Word?," *PROMO,* March 2001, pp. 64–72.
8. "Clutter: Extras, Extras!" www.promomagazine.com, August 1, 2001.
9. Ibid.
10. Ellen Byron and Suzanne Vranica, "Scanners Check Out Who's Browsing," *The Wall Street Journal,* September 27, 2006, p. B2.
11. Matthew Boyle, "Brand Killers," *Fortune,* August 11, 2003, pp. 89–100.
12. Jack Neff, "Stuck-in-Middle Walmart Starts to Lose Share," *Advertising Age,* March 8, 2010, http://adage.com/article?article_id=142650.
13. Andy Serwer, "Bruised in Bentonville," *Fortune,* April 18, 2005, pp. 84–89.
14. "The Effects of Promotion Stimuli on Consumer Purchase Behavior," Promotion Decisions, Inc. (Glenview, IL, 1999).
15. Betsy Spethman, "Tuning In at the Shelf," *PROMO 13th Annual Source Book,* 2006, pp. 22–24.
16. Leigh McAlister, "A Model of Consumer Behavior," *Marketing Communications,* April 1987.
17. "Too Many Choices," *The Wall Street Journal,* April 20, 2001, p. B1.
18. Al Urbanski, "Techno Promo," *PROMO,* August 1998, pp. 48–52, 146, 147.
19. Leonard M. Lodish and Carl F. Mela, "If Brands Are Built over Years, Why Are They Managed over Quarters?" *Harvard Business Review,* July–August 2007, pp. 104–12.
20. Annette Bourdea, "Rocket Launcher—Unilever's Jillian McLaughlin Prepped for the Massive Sunsilk Launch by Immersing Her Team in the Demo's World—and the Method Paid Off," *Strategy,* August 2006, p. 16.
21. *NCH Reporter, No. 1* (Nielsen Clearing House, 1983).
22. *The Magazine Handbook,* no. 9 (New York: Magazine Publishers of America, 1991).
23. Leonard M. Lodish and Carl F. Mela, "If Brands Are Built over Years, Why Are They Managed over Quarters?"; Judann Dagnoli, "Jordan Hits Ad Execs for Damaging Brands," *Advertising Age,* November 4, 1991, p. 47.
24. R.M. Prentice, "How to Split Your Marketing Funds between Advertising and Promotion Dollars," *Advertising Age,* January 10, 1977, pp. 41–42, 44.
25. Betsy Spethman, "Money and Power," *Brandweek,* March 15, 1993, p. 21.
26. Tim Parry, "Happy Customers," *PROMO,* April 2005, pp. AR 21–23.
27. Miller Taste Challenge, 2005 Reggie Awards—Promotion Marketing Association, www.pmalink.org/awards/reggie2005/index.
28. "2010 Reggie Awards Multi-Cultural/Ethnic," http://www.pmalink.org/?reggieawards.
29. "Trial and Conversion VI: Consumers' Reactions to Samples and Demonstrations," *Promotional Marketing Association, Inc.,* 2002.
30. Natalie Zmuda, "Facebook Turns Focus Group with Splenda Product-Sampling App," *Advertising Age,* July 13, 2009, http://adage.com/article?article_id=137851.
31. "2010 Coupon Facts Report," (Deerfield, IL: NCH Marketing Services).
32. J. Jeffrey Inman and Leigh McAlister, "Do Coupon Expiration Dates Affect Consumer Behavior?"
33. Jack Neff, "Coupons Get Clipped," *Advertising Age,* November 5, 2001, pp. 1, 47.
34. Karen Holt, "Coupon Crimes," *PROMO,* April 2004, pp. 23–26, 70.
35. "2010 Coupon Facts Report."
36. Ibid.
37. Jack Neff, "Coupons Get Clipped."
38. _______., "P&G Extends Co-branded Coupons," *Advertising Age,* June 3, 1996, p. 9; Richard Sale, "Not Your Mother's Coupon," *PROMO,* April 1999, pp. 56–61.
39. _______., "Package-good Players Just Can't Quit Coupons," *Advertising Age,* May 14, 2007, p. 8.
40. Stephanie Kang, "Coupons Gain New Market on Cellphones," *The Wall Street Journal,* September 11, 2007, p. B8.
41. Emily Bryson York, "BK 'Sacrifices'" Whopper Facebook Application," *Advertising Age,* January 15, 2009, http://adage.com/print?article_id=133800.
42. Survey by Oxtoby-Smith, Inc., cited in "Many Consumers View Rebates as a Bother," *The Wall Street Journal,* April 13, 1989, p. B1.
43. William R. Dean, "Irresistible But Not Free of Problems," *Advertising Age,* October 6, 1980, pp. S1–12.
44. William A. Robinson, "What Are Promos' Weak and Strong Points?" *Advertising Age,* April 7, 1980, p. 54.

45. Richard Sale, "Serving Up Sweeps," *PROMO,* August 1999, pp. 70–78; "Sweepstakes Fever," *Forbes,* October 3, 1988, pp. 164–66.
46. "Next-Tech," *PROMO,* July 2005, pp. 24–27.
47. Jonathon Lemennier, "Doritos Got a Winning Spot. Creators Won Recognition," *Advertising Age,* January 9, 2008, http://adage.com/print?article_id=122990.
48. Bob Woods, "Picking a Winner," *PROMO,* August 1998, pp. 57–62; Richard Sale, "Sweeping the Courts," *PROMO,* May 1998, pp. 148–52; 422–45; Maxine S. Lans, "Legal Hurdles Big Part of Promotions Game," *Marketing News,* October 24, 1994, pp. 15–16.
49. Kimberly Palmer, "Why Shoppers Love to Hate Rebates," www.usnews.com, January 18, 2008.
50. Peter Tat, William A. Cunningham III, and Emin Babakus, "Consumer Perceptions of Rebates," *Journal of Advertising Research,* 28(4), August/September 1988, pp. 45–50.
51. Brian Grow, "The Great Rebate Runaround," *BusinessWeek,* December 5, 2005, pp. 34–37.
52. Edward A. Blair and E. Lair Landon, "The Effects of Reference Prices in Retail Advertisements," *Journal of Marketing* 45, no. 2, Spring 1981, pp. 61–69.
53. Betsy Spethman, "Switching Loyalty," *PROMO,* July 2002, pp. 40–45.
54. "Retailers Should Overhaul Loyalty Programs: Survey," promomagazine.com, August 22, 2007.
55. R. J. Igneizi, "WD-40@50," *The San Diego Union Tribune*, November 10, 2003, pp. D1, 4.
56. "Top of Wallett," promomagazine.com, July 1, 2007.
57. Betsy Spethman, "Switching Loyalty."
58. Kathleen M. Joyce, "Keeping the Faith," *PROMO's 12th Annual Source Book 2005,* p. 24.
59. Adapted from: Terrence A. Shimp, *Advertising Promotion and Supplemental Aspects of Integrated Marketing Communication,* 6th ed. (Mason, Ohio: South-Western, 2003), p. 524.
60. William L. Wilkie, Debra M. Desrochers, and Gregory T. Gundlach, "Marketing Research and Public Policy: The Case of Slotting Fees," *Journal of Marketing & Public Policy* 21 (2), Fall 2002, pp. 275–88; Frank Green, "Battling for Shelf Control," *San Diego Union-Tribune,* November 19, 1996, pp. C1, 6, 7.
61. "Want Shelf Space at the Supermarket? Ante Up," *BusinessWeek,* August 7, 1989, pp. 60–61.
62. Ira Teinowitz, "Senators Berate Industry Abuse of Slotting Fees," *Advertising Age,* September 20, 1999, pp. 3, 66.
63. Paul N. Bloom, Gregory T. Gundlach, and Joseph P. Cannon, "Slotting Allowances and Fees: Schools of Thought and Views of Practicing Managers," *Journal of Marketing* 64, April 2000, pp. 92–108.
64. "Crunching the Numbers," *PROMO,* May 1, 2001, pp. 49–50.
65. Matthew Kinsman, "No Pain, No Gain," *PROMO,* January 2002, pp. 26–28.
66. Tom Steinhagen, "Space Management Shapes Up with Planograms," *Marketing News,* November 12, 1990, p. 7.
67. Srinath Gopalakrishna, Gary L. Lilien, Jerome D. Williams, and Ian K. Sequeria, "Do Trade Shows Pay Off?" *Journal of Marketing* 59, July 1995, pp. 7–83.
68. Tobi Elkin, "Co-op Crossroads," *Advertising Age,* November 15, 1999, pp. 1, 24, 26.
69. Stuart Elliott, "'Intel Inside' Ad Campaign Shifts Focus to the Web," *International Herald Tribune,* www.iht.com, October 11, 2007.
70. Cynthia Rigg, "Hard Times Means Growth for Co-op Ads," *Advertising Age,* November 12, 1990, p. 24.
71. Edwin L. Artzt, "The Lifeblood of Brands," *Advertising Age,* November 4, 1991, p. 32.
72. Jack Neff and Rupal Parekh, "Dove Takes Its New Men's Line to the Super Bowl," *Advertising Age,* January 5, 2010, http://adage.com/print?article_id=141312.
73. Leonard M. Lodish and Carl F. Mela, "If Brands Are Built Over Years, Why Are They Managed over Quarters?"; Jack Neff, "The New Brand Management," *Advertising Age,* November 8, 1999, pp. S2, 18; Benson P. Shapiro, "Improved Distribution with Your Promotional Mix," *Harvard Business Review,* March/April 1977, p. 116; and Roger A. Strang, "Sales Promotion—Fast Growth, Faulty Management," *Harvard Business Review,* July/August 1976, p. 119.
74. Quote by Thomas E. Hamilton, Director of Sales Promotion Service, William Esty Advertising, cited in Felix Kessler, "The Costly Couponing Craze," *Fortune,* June 9, 1986, p. 84.
75. Priya Raghubir and Kim Corfman, "When Do Price Promotions Affect Pretrial Brand Evaluations?" *Journal of Marketing Research* 36 (May 1999), pp. 211–22.
76. Alan G. Sawyer and Peter H. Dickson, "Psychological Perspectives on Consumer Response to Sales Promotion," in *Research on Sales Promotion: Collected Papers,* ed. Katherine E. Jacz (Cambridge, MA: Marketing Science Institute, 1984).
77. William E. Myers, "Trying to Get Out of the Discounting Box," *Adweek,* November 11, 1985, p. 2.
78. Leigh McAlister, "Managing the Dynamics of Promotional Change," in *Looking at the Retail Kaleidoscope, Forum IX* (Stamford, CT: Donnelley Marketing, April 1988).
79. "Promotions Blemish Cosmetic Industry," *Advertising Age,* May 10, 1984, pp. 22–23, 26; Cliff Edwards, "Everyone Loves a Freebie—Except Dell's Rivals," *BusinessWeek,* July 22, 2002, p. 41.
80. Lauren Shepherd, "Customers Getting More Burger for the Buck," *San Diego Union-Tribune,* February 13, 2008, pp. C1, 3.
81. Priya Raghubir, J. Jeffrey Inman, and Hans Grande, "The Three Faces of Price Promotions," *California Management Review* (Summer 2004), p. 23–42.

## Chapter Seventeen

1. www.publicrelationsnewspr.com
2. Scott M. Cutlip, Allen H. Center, and Glen M. Broom, *Effective Public Relations,* 10th ed. (Upper Saddle River, NJ: Prentice Hall, 2009).
3. Jonah Bloom, "The Cultural Gulf That Separates Marketing and PR," *Advertising Age,* March 11, 2007.
4. "PR News/PRSA Survey," *PR News,* May 25, 2005, p. 1.
5. N. Curry, "PR Isn't Marketing," *Advertising Age,* December 18, 1991, p. 18.
6. Martha M. Lauzen, "Imperialism and Encroachment in Public Relations," *Public Relations Review* 17 (3) (Fall 1991), pp. 245–55.
7. Cutlip, Center, and Broom, *Effective Public Relations.*
8. Thomas L. Harris, "How MPR Adds Value to Integrated Marketing

Communications," *Public Relations Quarterly,* Summer 1993, pp. 13–18.

9. Wayne Friedman, "Fox's O.J Dilemma: An $8M Question," *Media Post,* November 20, 2006.
10. Cutlip, Center, and Broom, *Effective Public Relations.*
11. John E. Marston, *Modern Public Relations* (New York: McGraw-Hill, 1979).
12. "Pfizer Announces Improvements to Consumer Advertising for Prescription Medicines," *Pfizer News Release,* www.pfizer.com, 2005.
13. Chang, "Did Apple Fail to Detect iPhone 4g Antenna Problem Beforehand," www.lanewsmonitor.com, June 26, 2010.
14. Laura Crovo, "The Art of Kraft-ing a Social Media Response," www.mghus.com, June, 24, 2010.
15. Walter K. Lindenmann, "Public Relations Research for Planning and Evaluation,"www.instituteforpr.org, 2006.
16. Otis Baskin, Joe Hahn, Samuel Seaman, and Dan Reines, "Perceived Effectiveness and Implementation of Public Relations Measurement and Evaluation Tools among European Providers and Consumers of PR Services," *Public Relations Review* 36, 2010, pp. 105–111.
17. Mark Weiner, "Marketing PR Revolution," *Communication World,* January/February 2005, pp. 1–5.
18. Michele Gershberg, "Maratha Stewart Sticks to Kinder, Gentler TV Image," www.reuters.com, September 28, 2005, pp. 1–3.
19. Jaye S. Niefeld, "Corporate Advertising," *Industrial Marketing,* July 1980, pp. 64–74.
20. _______., "The Growth of Cause Marketing," *Cause Marketing Forum,* 2010.
21. Wayne Friedman, "Supreme Court OKs Corporate-Sponsored Issue Ads," *Media Post,* June 27, 2007.
22. Stuart Elliott, "An Advocacy Ad Stirs a National Debate," www.nytimes.com, February 1, 2010.
23. Harvey Meyer, "When the Cause Is Just," *Journal of Business Strategy* (November/December 1999), pp. 27–31.
24. Janas Sinclair and Tracy Irani, "Advocacy Advertising for Biotechnology," *Journal of Advertising* (Fall 2005), pp. 59–74.
25. Bob Donath, "Corporate Communications," *Industrial Marketing,* July 1980, pp. 53–57.

## Chapter Eighteen

1. *Advertising Age,* June 21, 2010, p. 10.
2. "Southern Comfort's Digital Partnerships," www.adage.com, July 21, 2009, p. 1.
3. "Marketers Moving to Social Media," www.emarketer.com, March 23, 2009, p. 1.
4. Spike Cramphorn, "What Advertising Testing Might Have Been, If We Had Only Known," *Journal of Advertising Research,* 44(2), June 2004, pp. 170–180.
5. Robyn Greenspan, "Marketers Missing Measurements," www.clickz.com, June 4, 2004, pp. 1–2.
6. Noreen O'Leary, "Does Creativity Count?" *Adweek,* December 11, 2000, pp. 30–34.
7. Tim Nudd, "Does Sex Really Sell?," *Adweek,* October 17, 2005, pp. 14–17.
8. David A. Aaker and John G. Myers, *Advertising Management,* 3rd ed., (Englewood Cliffs, NJ: Prentice-Hall, 1987), p. 474.
9. Cramphorn, "What Advertising Testing Might Have Been."
10. "21 Ad Agencies Endorse Copy-Testing Principles," *Marketing News* 15 (February 19, 1982), p. 1.
11. Ibid.
12. Ye, Hu, Leonard Lodish, Abba Krieger and Babak Hayati, "An Update of Real-World TV Advertising Tests," *Journal of Advertising Research* June, 2009, pp. 201–206.
13. Steve Outing and Laura Ruel, "The Best of Eyetrack III: What We Saw When We Looked Through Their Eyes," www.poynterextra.org, 2004, pp. 1–9.
14. Hubert A. Zielske, "Does Day-after Recall Penalize 'Feeling Ads'?," *Journal of Advertising Research* 22(1) (1982), pp. 19–22.
15. Arthur J. Kover, "Why Copywriters Don't Like Advertising Research—and What Kind of Research Might They Accept," *Journal of Advertising Research* 36 (March/April 1996), pp. RC8–RC10; Gary Levin, "Emotion Guides BBDO's Ad Tests," *Advertising Age,* January 29, 1990, p. 12.
16. Terry Haller, "Day-after Recall to Persist Despite JWT Study; Other Criteria Looming," *Marketing News,* May 18, 1979, p. 4.
17. Mark Mellman, "Ad Recall Doesn't Equal Effectiveness," www.TheHill.com, July 7, 2005, p. 1.
18. Ravi Chandiramani, "Reckitt Launches Debut iTV Campaign for Finish," *Marketing,* January 10, 2002, p. 9.
19. Kipp Cheng, "IPG Platform Gains Major Advertisers," *Adweek,* July 23, 2001, p. 5.
20. Gary Levin, "Tracing Ads' Impact," *Advertising Age,* November 12, 1990, p. 49.
21. Jeffrey L. Seglin, "The New Era of Ad Measurement," *Adweek's Marketing Week,* January 23, 1988, p. 24.
22. "Yankelovich Study Shows Advertising's Effects Vary, Depending on Category and Purchase Funnel Stage," www.tvb.org, April 16, 2009, p. 1.
23. Russell I. Haley and Allan L. Baldinger, "The ARF Copy Research Validity Project," *Journal of Advertising Research* (April/May 1991), pp. 11–32.
24. Glenn Heitsmith, "Something for Nothing," *Promo,* September 1993, pp. 30, 31, 93.
25. Ibid.
26. "Journeying Deeper into the Minds of Shoppers," *BusinessWeek,* February 4, 1991, p. 85.
27. David W. Schumann, Jennifer Grayson, Johanna Ault, Kerri Hargrove, Lois Hollingsworth, Russell Ruelle, and Sharon Seguin, "The Effectiveness of Shopping Cart Signage: Perceptual Measures Tell a Different Story," *Journal of Advertising Research* 31 (February/ March 1991), pp. 17–22.
28. June Bryan Kim, "Research Makes Ski Run Easier," *Advertising Age,* August 18, 1991, p. 30.
29. Steve McClellan, "New Software to Track In-Store Radio," *Adweek,* October 10, 2005, p. 10.
30. Mike Shields, "Massive, Nielsen: In-Game Ads Boost Brands," www.adweek.com, Aug 8, 2007, pp. 1–3.
31. Michel Tuan Pham, "The Evaluation of Sponsorship Effectiveness: A Model and Some Methodological Considerations," Gestion 2000, pp. 47–65.
32. Ibid.
33. John Nardone and Ed See, "Measure Sponsorship to Drive Sales-Shift Gears: Move Beyond Perceiving Them as Mere Brand Builders and Instead Assess ROI," *Advertising Age,* March 5, 2007.
34. "2008 David Ogilvy Awards Finalists," *The ARF,* 2008.
35. Teresa F. Lindeman, "Good Wal-Mart, Bad Wal-Mart; Retail Giant Hopes to Combat Negative Public-

ity," *Knight Ridder Tribune Business News,* April 10, 2005, pp. 1–6.

**36.** "Advertisers Demand More Accountability for Digital Media," *Center for Media Research,* February 22, 2007, pp. 1–2.

**37.** Marek Winearz, "The Market Contact Audit," www.integration-imc.com.

## Chapter Nineteen

**1.** Richard S. Post and Penelope N. Post, *Global Brand Integrity Management* (New York: McGraw-Hill, 2008); David A. Aaker and Erich Joachimsthaler, "The Lure of Global Branding," *Harvard Business Review,* (November/December 1999), pp. 137–44.

**2.** David Kiley and Burt Helm, "The Great Trust Offensive," *BusinessWeek,* September 28, 2009, pp. 38–42.

**3.** Bradley Johnson, "Up in Smoke: Documents from the Annals of Tobacco Marketing," *Advertising Age,* March 20, 2010, http://adage.com/print?article_id=142928.

**4.** Deborah Game, "Match Game," *Marketing News,* November 11, 2002, pp. 1, 11–12; John A. Byrne, "Philip Morris: Inside America's Most Reviled Company," *BusinessWeek,* November 29, 1999, pp. 176–92.

**5.** Hillary Chura, "Beer Giant SAB Wins Approval for Miller Acquisition," *Advertising Age,* July 1, 2002, http://adage.com/print?article_id=35024.

**6.** Jeremy Mullman and Ira Teinowitz, "Justice Department Approves MillerCoors Merger," *Advertising Age,* June 5, 2008, http://adage.com/print?article_id=127562.

**7.** Jeremy Mullman, "Anheuser-Busch, InBev Deal Officially Sealed," *Advertising Age,* November 18, 2008, http://adage.com/print?article_id=132651.

**8.** Jeremy Mullman, "A-B InBev Wants Bud to Go Global with Coke as a Model," *Advertising Age,* http://adage.com/print?article_id=138648.

**9.** Jeremy Mullman, "Americans Downing Less Beer, Sparking Brawl among Brewers," *Advertising Age,* May 31, 2010, http://adage.com/print?article_id=144156.

**10.** Paula Lyon Andruss, "Slow Boat to China," *Marketing News,* September 10, 2001, pp. 1, 11–12; Normandy Madden, "China Ad Opportunities to Grow with WTO Deal," *Advertising Age International,* January 2000, p. 6.

**11.** Thomas H. Friedman, *The World Is Flat* (New York: Farrar, Straus and Giroux, 2005).

**12.** Barbara Kiviat, "Wake Up and Sell the Coffee," *Time,* April 7, 2008, pp. 44–50.

**13.** Laurel Wentz and Bradley Johnson, "Top 100 Global Advertisers Heap Their Spending Abroad," *Advertising Age,* November 30, 2009, http://adage.com/print?article_id=140723.

**14.** Vern Terpstra, *International Marketing,* 4th ed. (New York: Holt, Rinehart & Winston/Dryden Press, 1987), p. 427.

**15.** Claudia Penteado, "Emerging Lower Middle Class Fires Up Marketers in Brazil," *Advertising Age,* June 14, 2010, p. 12.

**16.** Noreen O'Leary, "The Rise of BRIC," *Adweek,* February 4–11, 2008, pp. 32–37, 65. _______.," Bright Lights, Big Challenges," *Adweek,* January 15, 2007, pp. 22–33.

**17.** _______., "The Lay of the Land," *Adweek,* February 5, 2007, pp. 14–21; Marc Gunther, "MTV's Passage to India," *Fortune,* August 9, 2004, pp. 117–25.

**18.** Normandy Madden, "China's Lower-Tier Cities Offer Most Growth," *Advertising Age,* June 11, 2010, http://adage.com/print?article_id=144416.

**19.** Normandy Madden, "Lenovo Sets Its Sights Back to Local Consumers," *Advertising Age,* June 22, 2009, http://adage.com/print?article_id=137481; Jane Spencer, "In China, Lenovo Sets Sights on Rural Market," *The Wall Street Journal,* August 6, 2007, p. B2.

**20.** Mark Lasswell, "Lost in Translation," *Business 2.0,* August 2004, pp. 68–70.

**21.** George E. Belch and Michael A. Belch, "Toward Development of a Model and Scale for Assessing Consumer Receptivity to Foreign Products and Global Advertising," in *European Advances in Consumer Research* 1, ed. Gary J. Bamossy and W. Fred van Raaij (Provo, UT: Association for Consumer Research, 1993), pp. 52–57.

**22.** Subhash Sharma, Terrence Shimp, and Jeongshin Shin, "Consumer Ethnocentrism: A Test of Antecedents and Moderators," *Journal of the Academy of Marketing Science* (Winter 1995), pp. 26–37.

**23.** Shelly Pannill, "The Road to Richesse," *Sales & Marketing Management,*" November 1999, pp. 89–96.

**24.** Ibid.

**25.** L. Ruano, "New Balance 576 'France' Release Recap," May 9, 2010, http://hypebeast.com/2010/05/balance-576-france-release-recap.

**26.** Steve Hamm, "Borders Are So 20th Century," *BusinessWeek,* September 22, 2003, pp. 68–73.

**27.** For an excellent discussion of various elements of Japanese culture such as language and its implications for promotion, see John F. Sherry, Jr., and Eduardo G. Camargo, "May Your Life Be Marvelous: English Language Labeling and the Semiotics of Japanese Promotion," *Journal of Consumer Research* 14 (September 1987), pp. 174–88.

**28.** Barbara Mueller, "Reflections on Culture: An Analysis of Japanese and American Advertising Appeals," *Journal of Advertising Research,* June/July 1987, pp. 51–59.

**29.** Barbara Mueller, "Standardization vs. Specialization: An Examination of Westernization in Japanese Advertising," *Journal of Advertising Research* 31 (1) (January/February 1992), pp. 15–24; and Johny K. Johanson, "The Sense of Nonsense: Japanese TV Advertising," *Journal of Advertising* 23, no. 1 (March 1994), pp. 17–26.

**30.** Michael L. Maynard and Charles R. Taylor, "Girlish Images across Cultures: Analyzing Japanese versus U.S. *Seventeen* Magazine Ads," *Journal of Advertising* 28, no. 1 (Spring 1999), pp. 39–49.

**31.** John B. Ford, Patricia Kramer Voli, Earl D. Honeycutt, Jr., and Susan L. Casey, "Gender Role Portrayals in Japanese Advertising: A Magazine Content Analysis," *Journal of Advertising* 27, no. 1 (Spring 1998).

**32.** Francis Hsu, *Americans and Chinese: Passage to Differences* (Honolulu, HI: University Press of Hawaii 1981).

**33.** Carolyn A. Lin, "Cultural Values Reflected in Chinese and American Television Advertising," *Journal of Advertising* 30 (4), pp. 83–94.

**34.** Don E. Schultz, "New Systems Make China Next Hot Spot," *Marketing News,* January 7, 2002, p. 5.

**35.** Geoffrey A. Fowler, "China Bans Nike's LeBron Ad As Offensive to Nation's Dignity," *The Wall Street Journal,* December 7, 2004, p. B4.

**36.** Gerard Prendergast, Wah-Leung Cheung, and Douglas West, "How Far Is Too Far? The Antecedents of Offensive Advertising in Modern China,"

*Journal of Advertising Research,* December 2008, pp. 484–95.

**37.** Raed Rafei, Cola Marketers Target Mideast," *Los Angeles Times,* February 4, 2008, pp. C1, 4.

**38.** "Malaysia Bans 'Sly' Tobacco Ads," *Marketing News,* September 1, 2002, p. 7.

**39.** Vanessa Fuhrmans, "In Europe, Prescription-Drug Ads Are Banned—and Health Costs Lower," *The Wall Street Journal,* March 15, 2002, pp. B1, 4.

**40.** Niraj Sheth, "India Liquor, Tobacco Firms Shift Tack," *The Wall Street Journal,* May 6, 2008, p. B8.

**41.** Jeremy Slate, "EC Lets Stand Toy Ad Ban," *Advertising Age International,* August 1999, pp. 1, 11.

**42.** Sam Loewenberg, "Effort in EU to Ban TV Ads Aimed at Kids Gains Steam," *Los Angeles Times,* July 9, 2001, p. C3.

**43.** Safran S. Al-Makaty, G. Norman van Tubergen, S. Scott Whitlow, and Douglas S. Boyd, "Attitudes toward Advertising in Islam," *Journal of Advertising Research* 36 (3) (May/June 1996), pp. 16–26; Marian Katz, "No Women, No Alcohol; Learn Saudi Taboos before Placing Ads," *International Advertiser,* February 1986, pp. 11–12.

**44.** Naveen Donthu, "A Cross-Country Investigation of Recall of and Attitude toward Comparative Advertising," *Journal of Advertising* 27, no. 2 (Summer 1998), pp. 111–22.

**45.** Derek Turner, "Coke Pops Brazilian Comparative Ad," *Advertising Age,* September 9, 1991, p. 24.

**46.** J. Craig Andrews, Steven Lysonski, and Srinivas Durvasula, "Understanding Cross-Cultural Student Perceptions of Advertising in General: Implications for Advertising Educators and Practitioners," *Journal of Advertising* 20, no. 2 (June 1991), pp. 15–28.

**47.** Jonathan Cheng, "China Demands Concrete Proof of Ad Claims," *The Wall Street Journal,* July 8, 2005, pp. B1, 4.

**48.** Stephanie Thompson, "Europe Slams Icons as Food Fights Back," *Advertising Age,* January 31, 2005, pp. 1, 38.

**49.** Robert D. Buzzell, "Can You Standardize Multinational Marketing?" *Harvard Business Review,* (November/December 1968), pp. 102–13; Ralph Z. Sorenson and Ulrich E. Wiechmann, "How Multinationals View Marketing," *Harvard Business Review* (May/June 1975), p. 38.

**50.** Theodore Levitt, "The Globalization of Markets," *Harvard Business Review* (May/June 1983), pp. 92–102; Theodore Levitt, *The Marketing Imagination* (New York: Free Press, 1986).

**51.** Anne B. Fisher, "The Ad Biz Gloms onto Global," *Fortune,* November 12, 1984, p. 78.

**52.** Maduh Agrawal, "Review of a 40-Year Debate in International Advertising," *International Marketing Review* 12(1), pp. 26–48; William L. James and John S. Hill, "International Advertising Messages, To Adapt or Not to Adapt (That Is the Question)," *Journal of Advertising Research* 31 (June/July 1991), pp. 65–71; Keith Reinhad and W. E. Phillips, "Global Marketing: Experts Look at Both Sides," *Advertising Age,* April 15, 1988, p. 47; Anthony Rutigliano, "The Debate Goes On: Global vs. Local Advertising," *Management Review,* June 1986, pp. 27–31.

**53.** Bernhard Warner, "IQ News: Gillette's Mach 3 Media Hits Web: European Site Next?," *AdweekOnline,* August 24, 1998.

**54.** Jack Neff, "Gillette Signs Three Sports Giants for Global Effort," *adage.com,* February 5, 2007.

**55.** Kevin Goldman, "Professor Who Started Debate on Global Ads Still Backs Theory," *The Wall Street Journal,* October 13, 1992, p. B8.

**56.** Examples from speech by Eugene H. Kummel, chairman emeritus, McCann-Erickson Worldwide, and Koji Oshita, president and CEO, McCann-Erickson, Hakuhodo, Japan, in San Diego, California, October 19, 1988; Margo Sugarman, "Nescafé Israel Entry Redefines Coffee Market," *Advertising Age International,* April 1997, p. i12.

**57.** Jack Neff, "The Dirt on Laundry Trends around The World," *Advertising Age,* June 14, 2010, p. 8.

**58.** Ibid.

**59.** Eric White and Jeffrey A. Trachtenberg, "One Size Doesn't Fit All," *The Wall Street Journal,* October 1, 2003, pp. B1, 2.

**60.** Joanne Lipman, "Marketers Turn Sour on Global Sales Pitch," *The Wall Street Journal,* May 12, 1988, p. 1.

**61.** Sally Goll Beatty, "Global Needs Challenge Midsize Agencies," *The Wall Street Journal,* December 14, 1995, p. B9.

**62.** Criteria cited by Edward Meyer, CEO, Grey Advertising, in Rebecca Fannin, "What Agencies Really Think of Global Theory," *Marketing & Media Decisions,* December 1984, p. 74.

**63.** Quote cited in Reinhard and Phillips, "Global Marketing," p. 47.

**64.** Niraj Sheth and Roger Cheng, "HTC Draws Growing Attention in Smartphones," *The Wall Street Journal,* June 7, 2010, p. B1.

**65.** Rita Chang, "Can HTC Make Its Smartphone as Familiar as Apple or Blackberry?" *Advertising Age,* September 7, 2009, http://adage.com/print?article_id=138837.

**66.** Durairaj Maheswaran, "Country of Origin as a Stereotype: Effects on Product Evaluations," *Journal of Consumer Research,* September 1994, pp. 354–65.

**67.** Paul Chao, "The Moderating Effects of Country of Assembly, Country of Parts, and Country of Design on Hybrid Product Evaluations," *Journal of Advertising* 20, no. 4, Winter 2001, pp. 67–82.

**68.** Beth Snyder Bulik, "Ditch the Flags, Kids Don't Care Where You Come From," *Advertising Age,* June 4, 2007, pp. 1, 59.

**69.** Salah S. Hassan and Lea P. Katsansis, "Identification of Global Consumer Segments: A Behavioral Framework," *Journal of International Consumer Marketing* 3 (2), (1991), pp. 11–28.

**70.** Arundhati Parmar, "Global Youth United," *Marketing News,* October 28, 2002, pp. 1, 49; "Ready to Shop until They Drop," *BusinessWeek,* June 22, 1998, pp. 104–10; "Teens Seen as the First Truly Global Consumers," *Marketing News,* March 27, 1995, p. 9; Shawn Tully, "Teens: The Most Global Market of All," *Fortune,* May 16, 1994, pp. 90–97.

**71.** Teressa Iezzi, "Emotional Juice," *Creativity,* March 2004, pp. 10, 30–32.

**72.** Robert E. Hite and Cynthia L. Fraser, "International Advertising Strategies of Multinational Corporations," *Journal of Advertising Research* 28 (4) (August/September 1988), pp. 9–17.

**73.** Ali Kanso, "International Advertising Strategies: Global Commitment to Local Vision," *Journal of Advertising Research,* January/February 1992, pp. 10–14.

74. Jan Jaben, "Ad Decision-Makers Favor Regional Angle, *Advertising Age* International, May 1995, pp. i3, 16.
75. Nigel Hollis, *The Global Brand* (New York: Palgrave MacMillan, 2008).
76. Nigel Hollis, "Global Brands, Local Cultures," *Research World,* July/August 2009, pp. 20–24; Piet Levy, "10 Minutes with Nigel Hollis," *Marketing News* August 30, 2009, pp. 18–19.
77. Penelope Rowlands, "Global Approach Doesn't Always Make Scents," *Advertising Age International,* January 17, 1994, pp. i–1, 38.
78. Natalie Zmuda, "Levi's Names Jaime Szulc Its First Global CMO," *Advertising Age,* August 26, 2009, http://adage.com/print?article_id=138569.
79. Rupal Parekh, "Wieden Wins Levi's Creative Review," *Advertising Age,* December 12, 2008, http://adage.com/print?article_id=133244.
80. Normandy Madden, "Shanghai Rises as Asia's Newest Marketing Capital," *Advertising Age,* October 14, 2002, pp. 1, 13.
81. Kevin Goldman, "Global Companies Hone Agency Rosters," *The Wall Street Journal,* July 25, 1995, p. B8.
82. Sally Goll Beatty, "Young & Rubicam Is Only One for Colgate," *The Wall Street Journal,* December 1, 1995, p. B6.
83. Rupal Parekh, "Dell Picks WPP for $4.5B Marketing Account," *adage.com,* December 2, 2007.
84. Rupal Parekh and Michael Bush, "WPP Folds Ill-Fated Dell Agency Enfatico Into Y&R Brands," *Advertising Age,* April 9, 2009, http://adage.com/print?article_id=135910.
85. Kevin Goldman, "Global Companies Hone Agency Rosters."
86. Megan Mcilroy and Rupal Parekh, "MediaCom to Lead Media Strategy for Dell," *adage.com,* December 14, 2007.
87. Megan Mcilroy, "Samsung Hands $600 Million Media-Buying Biz to Starcom," *adage.com,* November 7, 2007.
88. "Advertising Is Indeed Going Global," Market Europe, October 1997, pp. 8–10.
89. Anne-Marie Crawford, "Clients and Agencies Split over Ad Superstars," *www.adageglobal.com,* May 2001, p. 16.
90. Joseph T. Plummer, "The Role of Copy Research in Multinational Advertising," *Journal of Advertising Research,* October/November 1986, p. 15; Piet Levy, "Live Like Locals," *Marketing News,* August 30, 2009, p. 14.
91. Joan Voight, "Exporting Las Vegas," *Adweek,* September 3, 2007, pp. 14–15.
92. Erin White, "German Ads Get More Daring, But Some Firms Aren't Pleased," *The Wall Street Journal,* November 22, 2002, p. B6.
93. Larry Speer, "French Government Attacks 'Sexist' Ads," *Ad Age Global,* May 2001, p. 7.
94. Normandy Madden, "Looking for the Next Brazil? Try Thailand," *Advertising Age,* April 11, 2005, p. 22.
95. Stephanie King, "Indian Ads Come into Their Own," *The Wall Street Journal,* December 12, 2007, p. B4.
96. Normandy Madden, "Two Chinas," *Advertising Age,* August 16, 2004, pp. 1, 22.
97. Rochell Burbury, "Australia Ends Ban on Cable TV Spots," *Advertising Age International,* March 1997, p. i22.
98. Leslie Chang, "Cracking China's Huge TV Market," *The Wall Street Journal,* August 1, 2000, pp. B1, 4.
99. Normandy Madden, "Vibrant Bidding at the CCTV Auction Indicates Healthy Economy and Media Inflation," *Advertising Age,* November 18, 2009, http://adage.com/print?article_id=140600.
100. Jane Lanhee Lee, "TV Marketers Aim to Reap Rural China's Fertile Land," July 30, 2007, *The Wall Street Journal,* p. B2.
101. Nat Ives, "For Pubs, Going Global Comes with Challenges," *Advertising Age,* June 14, 2010, p. 17.
102. Ibid.
103. Ronal Grover and Tom Lowry, "Rupert's World," *BusinessWeek,* January 19, 2004, pp. 51–60.
104. Noreen O'Leary, "The Lay of the Land."
105. Kamran Kashani and John A. Quelch, "Can Sales Promotion Go Global?" *Business Horizons,* May/June 1990, pp. 37–43.
106. Lenard C. Huff and Dana L. Alden, "An Investigation of Consumer Response to Sales Promotion in Developing Markets: A Three Country Analysis," *Journal of Advertising Research,* May/June 1998, pp. 47–56.
107. Douglas J. Wood and Linda A. Goldstein, "A Lawyer's Guide to Going Global," *Promo Magazine,* Special Report, August 1998, p. S11.
108. "Foreign Ads Go Further with PR," *International Advertiser,* December 1986, p. 30.
109. Joanna Slater, "Coca-Cola, Pepsi Pass India's Test on Pesticides," *The Wall Street Journal,* August 22, 2003, p. B5.
110. Brian Bremner and Nandini Lakshman, "India: Behind the Scare over Pesticides in Pepsi and Coke," *BusinessWeek,* September 4, 2006, p. 43; Steve Stecklow, 'How a Global Web of Activists Gives Coke Problems in India," *The Wall Street Journal,* June 27, 2005, pp. A1, 6.
111. Laurel Wentz, "Haagen-Dazs Teaser Ad Offends Indians," *Advertising Age,* December 29, 2009, http://adage.com/print?article_id=141246.
112. Sam Loewenberg, "Effort in EU to Ban TV Ads Aimed at Kids Gains Steam."
113. Emma Hall, "Spain to Ban Some Diet, Beauty TV Ads before 10 P.M.," *Advertising Age,* January 20, 2010, http://adage.com/print?article_id=141610.
114. "Internet World Stats: Usage and Population Statistics," 2010, http://www.internetworldstats.com/stats.htm.
115. Cate Riegner, "Wired China: The Power of the World's Largest Internet Population, *Journal of Advertising Research,* December 2008, pp. 496–505.
116. David Wolf, "With Google Out, Will Baidu Reign in China?" *Advertising Age,* March 16, 2010, http://adage.com/print?article_id=142285.
117. Rupal Parekh, "How Facebook Plans to Get 1 Billion Global Users," *Advertising Age,* June 23, 2010, http://adage.com/print?article_id=14268.
118. Kunur Patel, Valentia Vescovi, and Aixa Rocca, "Profiling the Facebooks of the World," *Advertising Age,* June 14, 2010, p. 6.


## Chapter Twenty


1. Fred W. Morgan and Jeffrey J. Stoltman, "Advertising and Product Liability Litigation," *Journal of Advertising* 26, no. 2 (Summer 1997), pp. 63–75.
2. Ira Teinowitz, "Curb Proposal Raises Tobacco Marketers' Ire," *Advertising Age,* March 18, 2002, p. 70; Myron Levin, "U.S. to Pursue Lawsuit to

Curb Cigarette Marketing," *Los Angeles Times,* March 12, 2002, pp. C1, 15.

3. Christopher Lawton, "Beer Industry Tests FTC's Patience," *The Wall Street Journal,* February 2, 2005, p. B2.
4. Alice Z. Cuneo, "Of Contracts and Claims; Agencies Face Liability Issues," *Advertising Age,* January 31, 2000, p. 25.
5. Steven W. Colford and Raymond Serafin, "Scali Pays for Volvo Ad: FTC," *Advertising Age,* August 26, 1991, p. 4; Alice Z. Cuneo, "Can an Agency Be Guilty of Malpractice?" *Advertising Age,* January 31, 2000, pp. 24–25.
6. Priscilla A. LaBarbera, "Analyzing and Advancing the State of the Art of Advertising Self-Regulation," *Journal of Advertising* 9, no. 4 (1980), p. 30.
7. Ian P. Murphy, "Competitive Spirits: Liquor Industry Turns to TV Ads," *Marketing News,* December 2, 1996, pp. 1, 17.
8. John F. Archer, "Advertising of Professional Fees: Does the Consumer Have a Right to Know?" *South Dakota Law Review* 21 (Spring 1976), p. 330.
9. Bates v. State of Arizona, 97 S.Ct. 2691. 45, *U.S. Law Week* 4895 (1977).
10. Charles Laughlin, "Ads on Trial," *Link,* May 1994, pp. 18–22; "Lawyers Learn the Hard Sell—And Companies Shudder," *BusinessWeek,* June 10, 1985, p. 70.
11. Bruce H. Allen, Richard A. Wright, and Louis E. Raho, "Physicians and Advertising," *Journal of Health Care Marketing* 5 (Fall 1985), pp. 39–49.
12. Robert E. Hite and Cynthia Fraser, "Meta-Analyses of Attitudes toward Advertising by Professionals," *Journal of Marketing* 52, no. 3 (July 1988), pp. 95–105.
13. Priscilla A. LaBarbera, "Analyzing and Advancing the State of the Art of Advertising Self-Regulation."
14. Shelly Branch, "Campbell Is in the Soup on V8 Ad," *The Wall Street Journal,* April 26, 2002, p. B4.
15. Jack Neff, "Household Brands Counterpunch," *Advertising Age,* November 1, 1999, p. 26.
16. Jessica E. Vascellaro, "Regulators Say Love Ain't 'Chemistry' after All," *The Wall Street Journal,* September 17, 2007, p. B5.
17. Ibid.
18. "Millennium Import Company, Importers of Belvedere and Chopin Vodkas, File Motion for Preliminary and Permanent Injunction against Grey Goose," *Business Wire,* January 26, 2004, p. 1.
19. "NAD Case Reports, 2009 Summary" (National Advertising Division, Council of Better Business Bureaus) 35, no. 1 (January 2010), p. 2.
20. "The Electronic Retailing Self-Regulation Program: Policy and Procedures," The National Advertising Review Council, www.narcpartners.org/ersp.
21. Linda Bean, "CRN Foundation Announces Five-Year Grant to NAD," November 9, 2009, http://www.bbb.org/us/post/crn-foundation-announces-five-year-grant-to-nad-859.
22. Dorothy Cohen, "The FTC's Advertising Substantiation Program," *Journal of Marketing* 44, no. 1 (Winter 1980), pp. 26–35.
23. Eric J. Lyman, "The True Colors of Toscani," *www.adageglobal.com,* September 2001, pp. 22–23.
24. Lynda M. Maddox and Eric J. Zanot, "The Suspension of the National Association of Broadcasters' Code and Its Effects on the Regulation of Advertising," *Journalism Quarterly* 61 (Summer 1984), pp. 125–30, 156.
25. Joe Mandese, "ABC Loosens Rules," *Advertising Age,* September 9, 1991, pp. 2, 8.
26. Avery M. Abernethy and Jan LeBlanc Wicks, "Self-regulation and Television Advertising: A Replication and Extension," *Journal of Advertising Research* 41(3) (May/June 2001), pp. 31–37; Eric Zanot, "Unseen but Effective Advertising Regulation: The Clearance Process," *Journal of Advertising* 14(4) (1985), p. 48.
27. Joanne Voight and Wendy Melillo, "To See or Not to See?" *Adweek,* March 11, 2002, p. 30.
28. Mandese, "ABC Loosens Rules."
29. Hoag Levins, "Fox Killed Second Airing of Super Bowl Godaddy Ad," *Advertising Age,* February 8, 2005, http://adage.com/print?article_id=45076.
30. Jermey Mullman and Ken Wheaton, "Mancrunch Swears This Isn't a Super Bowl Stunt (Updated)," *Advertising Age,* January 20, 2010, http://adage.com/print?article_id=141816.
31. Steven W. Colford, "Speed Up the NAD, Industry Unit Told," *Advertising Age,* May 1, 1989, p. 3.
32. Virginia State Board of Pharmacy v. Virginia Citizens Consumer Council, 425 U.S. 748, 96 S.Ct. 1817, 48 L. Ed. 2d 346 (1976).
33. Bates v. State of Arizona.
34. Central Hudson Gas & Electric v. Public Service Commission, 447 U.S. 557,100 S. Ct. 2343, 65 L. Ed. 2d 341 (1980).
35. 44 Liquormart, Inc. v. Rhode Island, 517 U.S. 484 (1996).
36. Erik L. Collins, Lynn Zoch, and Christopher S. McDonald, "When Professional Worlds Collide: Implications of Kasky v. Nike for Corporate Reputation," *Management, Public Relations Review* 30, no. 4, November 2004, pp. 411–18; Anne Gearan, "High Court Passes Up Decision on Nike Case," *The San Diego Union-Tribune,* June 27, 2003, p. C1.
37. *FTC v. Raladam Co.,* 258 U.S. 643 (1931).
38. Edward Cox, R. Fellmeth, and J. Schultz, *The Consumer and the Federal Trade Commission* (Washington, DC: American Bar Association, 1969); and American Bar Association, *Report of the American Bar Association to Study the Federal Trade Commission* (Washington, DC: The Association, 1969).
39. *FTC Staff Report on Advertising to Children* (Washington, DC: Government Printing Office, 1978).
40. *Federal Trade Commission Improvement Act of 1980,* P. L., No. 96-252.
41. Bruce Silverglade, "Does FTC Have an 'Unfair' Future?," *Advertising Age,* March 26, 1994, p. 20.
42. Peter R. Darke and Robin J. Ritchie, "The Defensive Consumer: Advertising Deception, Defensive Processing, and Distrust," *Journal of Marketing Research* 44 (February 2007), 114–27.
43. Ivan L. Preston, *The Great American Blow-Up: Puffery in Advertising and Selling* (Madison: University of Wisconsin Press, 1975), p. 3.
44. Isabella C. M. Cunningham and William H. Cunningham, "Standards for Advertising Regulation," *Journal of Marketing* 41 (October 1977), pp. 91–97; Herbert J. Rotfeld and Kim B. Rotzell, "Is Advertising Puffery Believed?" *Journal of Advertising* 9 (3) (1980), pp. 16–20.
45. Herbert J. Rotfeld and Kim B. Rotzell, "Puffery vs. Fact Claims—Really Different?" in *Current Issues and Research in Advertising,* ed. James H. Leigh and Claude R. Martin, Jr. (Ann

Arbor: University of Michigan, 1981), pp. 85–104.

46. Preston, *The Great American Blow-Up.*
47. Chuck Ross, "Marketers Fend Off Shift in Rules for Ad Puffery," *Advertising Age,* February 19, 1996, p. 41.
48. Ira Teinowitz, "A Victory for Puffery," *Advertising Age,* August 10, 2007, http://adage.com/print?article_id=119812.
49. Federal Trade Commission, "Policy Statement on Deception," 45 ATRR 689 (October 27, 1983), p. 690.
50. For an excellent discussion and analysis of these three elements of deception, see Gary T. Ford and John E. Calfee, "Recent Developments in FTC Policy on Deception," *Journal of Marketing* 50, no. 3 (July 1986), pp. 86–87.
51. Ray O. Werner, ed., "Legal Developments in Marketing," *Journal of Marketing* 56 (January 1992), p. 102.
52. Ira Teinowitz, "FTC Strives to Clarify 'Made in USA' Rules," *Advertising Age,* April 29, 1996, p. 12.
53. Kalpana Srinivasan, "FTC Spells Out Tough Standards for 'Made in USA,'" *Marketing News,* January 18, 1999, p. 18.
54. "Champagne Bureau; Ad Campaign Urges Consumers to 'Unmask the Truth' about Champagne & Wine Place Names," *Marketing Weekly News,* December 26, 2009, p. 41.
55. Cohen, "The FTC's Advertising Substantiation Program."
56. *Trade Regulation Reporter,* Par. 20,056 at 22,033, 1970–1973 Transfer Binder, Federal Trade Commission, July 1972.
57. John E. Califee, "FTC's Hidden Weight-Loss Ad Agenda," *Advertising Age,* October 25, 1993, p. 29.
58. Chester S. Galloway, Herbert Jack Rotfeld, and Jeff I. Richards, "Holding Media Responsible for Deceptive Weight-Loss Advertising," *West Virginia Law Review* 107, no. 2 (Winter 2005), pp. 353–84; Herbert Jack Rotfeld, "Desires versus the Reality of Self-Regulation," *The Journal of Consumer Affairs* 27, no. 2 (Winter 2003), pp. 424–27.
59. For an excellent description of the Campbell Soup corrective advertising case, see Dick Mercer, "Tempest in a Soup Can," *Advertising Age,* October 17, 1994, pp. 25, 28–29.
60. William L. Wilkie, Dennis L. McNeill, and Michael B. Mazis, "Marketing's 'Scarlet Letter': The Theory and Practice of Corrective Advertising," *Journal of Marketing* 48 (Spring 1984), pp. 11–31.
61. *Warner-Lambert Co. v. Federal Trade Commission,* CCH P61, 563A-D.C., August 1977 and CCH P61, 646 CA-D.C., September 1977.
62. Bruce Ingersoll, "FTC Orders Novartis to Correct Claims," *The Wall Street Journal,* May 28, 1999, p. B2; Ira Teinowitz, "Doan's Decision Worries Marketers," *Advertising Age,* May 31, 1999, p. 74.
63. Ira Teinowitz, "Doan's Decision Sets Precedent for Corrective Ads," *adage.com,* September 4, 2000.
64. Rich Thomaselli, "What Bayer Campaign Means for Pharma Ads," *Advertising Age,* February 16, 2009, http://adage.com/print?article_id=134624.
65. "Deceptive Ads: The FTC's Laissez-Faire Approach Is Backfiring," *BusinessWeek,* December 2, 1985, p. 136.
66. Bruce Ingersoll, "FTC Action Snares Home Shopping, iMall," *The Wall Street Journal,* April 16, 1999, p. B2.
67. Avery M. Abernethy and George R. Franke, "The Information Content of Advertising: A Meta-Analysis," *Journal of Advertising* 25, no. 2 (Summer 1996), pp. 1–17.
68. Ira Teinowitz, "Chairman Muris Promises Evolution at FTC," *Advertising Age,* June 25, 2001, pp. 3, 42.
69. _______., "Beales Makes Regulation Academic as FTC Director," Advertising Age, December 10, 2001, p. 66.
70. Laurie Sullivan, "FTC Pushes Up Hearings on Environmental Marketing Guides," *Mediapost.com,* November 29, 2007.
71. Doug Wood and Anthony Diresta, "When Concerns Arise, We Will Not Be Silent," *The Advertiser,* December 2007, pp. 46–54.
72. *The FTC in 2010: Federal Trade Commission Annual Report,* April 2010, http://ftc.gov/os/2010/04/2010ChairmansReport.pdf.
73. Ira Teinowitz, "FTC to Marketers: Self-Regulate Behavioral Targeting," *Advertising Age,* February 12, 2009, http://adage.com/print?article_id=134587.
74. Michael Bush, "Blogger Be Warned: FTC May Monitor What You Say," *Advertising Age,* April 13, 2009, http://adage.com/print?article_id=135938.
75. Ira Teinowitz, "FTC to Marketers: Self Regulate Behavioral Targeting."
76. _______., "FCC, FTC Vow 'Action' against Phone Ads," *Advertising Age,* November 8, 1999, p. 129.
77. _______., "Howard Stern to Abandon FM Radio," *Advertising Age,* October 6, 2004, http://adage.com/print?article_id=41266.
78. _______., "Clear Channel Drops Howard Stern," *Advertising Age,* February 26, 2004, http://adage.com/print?article_id=39530.
79. _______., "FCC To Probe Super Bowl Halftime Breast Incident," *Advertising Age,* February 2, 2004, http://adage.com/print?article_id=39341.
80. _______ and Matthew Creamer, "Fake News Videos Unmasked in FCC crackdown," *Advertising Age,* April 18, 2005, http://adage.com/print?article_id=102295.
81. Rich Thomaselli, "Cheerios First in FDA Firing Line. Who's Next?," *Advertising Age,* May 18, 2009, http://adage.com/print?article_id=136704.
82. Sheryl Stolberg, "Clinton Imposes Wide Crackdown on Tobacco Firms," *Los Angeles Times,* August 24, 1996, pp. A1, 10.
83. Joy Johnson Wilson, "Summary of the Attorneys General Master Tobacco Settlement Agreement," National Conference of State Legislators, www.academic.udayton.edu/health/syllabi/tobacco/summary.
84. Charles King III, and Michael Siegel, "The Master Settlement Agreement with the Tobacco Industry and Cigarette Advertising in Magazines," *The New England Journal of Medicine* 345, August 16, 2001, pp. 504–11.
85. Rich Thomaselli, "FDA Set to Take Control of Tobacco Regulation," *Advertising Age,* June 11, 2009, http://adage.com/print?article_id=137253.
86. _______., "ANA Mounts Suit to Block Tobacco Legislation," *Advertising Age,* June 16, 2009, http://adage.com/print?article_id=137355.
87. Jisu Huh and Rita Langteau, "Presumed Influence of Direct-To-Consumer (DTC) Prescription Drug Advertising on Patients: The Physician's Perspective," *Journal of Advertising* 36, no. 3 (Fall 2007), pp. 151–72; Sejung Marina Choi and Wei-Na Lee, "Understanding the Impact of Direct-To-Consumer (DTC) Pharmaceutical Advertising on Patient-Physician Interaction," *Journal of Advertising* 36, no. 3 (Fall 2007), pp. 137–49.

88. Steven W. Colford, "$12 Million Bite," *Advertising Age,* December 2, 1991, p. 4.
89. Jan Joben, "A Setback for Competitive Ads?" *Business Marketing,* October 1992, p. 34.
90. Bruce Buchanan and Doron Goldman, "Us vs. Them: The Minefield of Comparative Ads," *Harvard Business Review,* May/June 1989, pp. 38–50.
91. Maxine Lans Retsky, "Lanham Have It: Law and Comparative Ads," *Marketing News,* November 8, 1999, p. 16.
92. Judann Pollack, "Prego Prevails in Battle over Comparative Ad," *Advertising Age,* September 1, 1996, p. 12; Michael Fumento, "Free-a the Papa!," *Forbes,* February 21, 2000, p. 53.
93. Natali Zmuda and Rupal Parekh," "Judge Rules in Powerade-Gatorade Court Battle, but Dispute Lives On," *Advertising Age,* August 6, 2009, http://adage.com/print?article_id=138327.
94. Michael J. Barone, Randall L. Rose, Paul W. Minniard, and Kenneth C. Manning, "Enhancing the Detection of Misleading Comparative Advertising," *Journal of Advertising Research* 39 (5) (September/October 1999), pp. 43–50.
95. "Deceptive Ads: The FTC's Laissez-Faire Approach."
96. Jennifer Lawrence, "State Ad Rules Face Showdown," *Advertising Age,* November 28, 1988, p. 4.
97. Steven Colford, "ABA Panel Backs FTC over States," *Advertising Age,* April 10, 1994, p. 1.
98. "Airborne to Pay $23.3 Million for False Advertising," *Natural Standard Blog,* March 21, 2008, http://blog.naturalstandard.com/natural-standard-blog/2008/03/airborne.
99. S. J. Diamond, "New Director Putting Vigor Back into FTC," *Los Angeles Times,* March 29, 1991, pp. D1, 4.
100. Federal Trade Commission, "Trade Regulation Rule: Games of Chance in the Food Retailing and Gasoline Industries," 16 CFR, Part 419 (1982).
101. Richard Sale, "Sweeping the Courts," *Promo,* May 1998, pp. 42–45, 148–52; Ira Teinowitz and Carol Krol, "Multiple States Scrutinize Sweepstakes Mailings," *Advertising Age,* February 9, 1998, p. 41; Mark Pawlosky, "States Rein in Sweepstakes, Game Operators," *The Wall Street Journal,* July 3, 1995, pp. B1, 3.
102. "Children Advertising Review Unit Self Regulatory Guidelines for Children's Advertising," Council of Better Business Bureaus, 2003, www.caru.org/guidelines/index.
103. Steven W. Colford, "Top Kid TV Offender: Premiums," *Advertising Age,* April 29, 1991, p. 52.
104. Federal Trade Commission, "Guides for Advertising Allowances and Other Merchandising Payments and Services," 16 CFR, Part 240 (1983).
105. William L. Wilkie, Debra M. Desrochers, and Gregory T. Gundlach, "Marketing Research and Public Policy: The Case of Slotting Fees," *Journal of Marketing & Public Policy* 21(2) (Fall 2002), pp. 275–88.
106. Ira Teinowitz, "FTC, McCormick Reach Accord on Slotting Fees," *Advertising Age,* March 13, 2000, p. 75.
107. Federal Trade Commission, "Trade Regulation Rule: Use of Negative Option Plans by Sellers in Commerce, 16 CFR, Part 42 (1982).
108. For a more thorough discussion of legal aspects of sales promotion and mail-order practices, see Dean K. Fueroghne, *Law & Advertising* (Chicago: Copy Workshop, 1995).
109. Mary Lu Carnevale, "FTC Adopts Rules to Curb Telemarketing," *The Wall Street Journal,* September 18, 1992, pp. B1, 10.
110. Scott Hume, "900 Numbers: The Struggle for Respect," *Advertising Age,* February 18, 1991, p. S1.
111. Federal Register, "Rules and Regulations," August 9, 1993, 42364–42406.
112. "Commission to Seek Public Comment on 900-Number Rule Revisions," *Federal Trade Commission Press Release,* October 23, 1998; Russell N. Laczniak, Les Carlson, and Ann Walsh, "Antecedents of Mothers' Attitudes toward the FTC's Rule for 900-Number Advertising Directed at Children," *Journal of Current Issues and Research in Advertising* 21, no. 2 (Fall 1999), pp. 49–58.
113. "US FTC: FTC Workshop to Address Proposed Changes to Its Pay-per-Call-Rule," *M2 Presswire,* May 20, 1999.
114. Ira Teinowitz, "Congress Approves National 'Do Not Call'," *Advertising Age,* February 13, 2003, http://adage.com/print?article_id=36837.
115. Ira Teinowitz, "'Do Not Call' Law Upheld As Constitutional," *Advertising Age,* February 17, 2004, http://adage.com/print?article_id=39453.
116. ______., "'Do Not Call' Does Not Hurt Direct Marketers," *Advertising Age,* April 11, 2005, pp. 3, 95.
117. Herbert Jack Rotfeld, "Do-not-call as the US Government's Improvement to Telemarketing Efficiency," *Journal of Consumer Marketing* 21, no. 4, 2004, pp. 242–44.
118. Jennifer Levitz and Kelly Greene, "Marketers Use Trickery to Evade No-Call Lists," *The Wall Street Journal,* October 26, 2007, pp. A1, 8.
119. Natasha Shabani, "Are You Using Sweepstakes to Skirt the Do-Not-Call List?," *Advertising Age,* April 12, 2010, http //adage.com/print?article_id=143190.
120. Ira Teinowitz and Jennifer Gilbert, "FTC Chairman: Stop Undisclosed Profiling on Net," *Advertising Age,* November 8, 1999, p. 2.
121. Andrea Petersen, "DoubleClick Reverses Course after Privacy Outcry," *The Wall Street Journal,* March 3, 2000, pp. B1, 6; Jennifer Gilbert and Ira Teinowitz, "Privacy Debate Continues to Rage," *Advertising Age,* February 7, 2000, pp. 44, 46.
122. "NAI Launches Privacy-awareness Web Site," *Advertising Age,* May 28, 2001, http://adage.com/print?article_id=11226; ' Online Advertisers Launch Two Consumer Privacy Tools," Network Advertising Initiative, May 23, 2001, www.networkadvertising.org/aboutnai.
123. James Heckman, "COPPA to Bring No Surprises, Hefty Violation Fines in April," *Marketing News,* January 31, 2000, p. 6.
124. Ira Teinowitz, "FTC Proposal on Kids' Privacy Raises Ire of Watchdog Groups," *Advertising Age,* March 14, 2005, http://adage.com/print?article_id=102494.
125. Larry Dobrow, "Privacy Issues Loom for Marketers," *Advertising Age,* March 13, 2006, http://adage.com/print?article_id=107066.
126. Betsy Spethmann, "Private Eyes," *Promo,* January 2002, pp. 37–43; "Protecting Consumers' Privacy: 2002 and Beyond," Remarks of FTC Chairman Timothy J. Muris at The Privacy 2001 Conference, Cleveland, Ohio, October 4, 2001, www.ftc.gov/speeches/muris/privisp1002.
127. Ira Teinowitz, Why Ignoring New Voluntary FTC Privacy Guidelines Could Be Perilous," *adage.com,* December 28, 2007.

128. Abbey Klaassen and Ira Teinowitz," A Push for Web Version of the Do-Not-Call List," *adage.com,* November 5, 2007.
129. Ira Teinowitz, "Consumer Groups Push Obama for 'Do Not Track' List," *Advertising Age,* December 16, 2008, http://adage.com/print?article_id=133329.
130. Bryon Acohido, "FTC tells Twitter to Protect the Private Data of Its Users," *USA Today,* June 25, 2010, p. 3B.
131. Mark Zuckerberg, "Making Control Simple," *The Facebook Blog,* May 26, 2010, http://blog.facebook.com/blog.php?post=391922327130.
132. Abbey Klaassen and Michael Learmonth, "What You Need to Know about the New FTC Endorsement Rules—and Why," *Advertising Age,* October 12, 2009, http://adage.com/print?article_id=139595.
133. Ira Teinowitz, "U.S. House Passes Anti-Spam Measure in Dawn Session," *Advertising Age,* November 23, 2003, http://adage.com/print?article_id=38896; Spethmann, "Private Eyes;" Lisa Takeuchi Cullen, "Some More Spam, Please," *Time,* November 11, 2002, pp. 58–62.
134. Tom Zeller Jr. "Federal Law Hasn't Curbed Junk e-mail," *The San Diego Union-Tribune,* February, 1, 2005, pp. C1, 5.

## Chapter Twenty-One

1. Robert L. Heilbroner, "Demand for the Supply Side," *New York Review of Books* 38 (June 11, 1981), p. 40.
2. David Helm, "Advertising's Overdue Revolution," speech given to the Adweek Creative Conference, October 1, 1999.
3. Joan Voight, "The Consumer Rebellion," *Adweek,* January 10, 2000, pp. 46–50.
4. Claire Atkinson, "FTC and FCC Nearing Product-Placement Decisions," *adage.com,* October 29, 2004; Daniel Eisenberg, "Its an Ad, Ad, Ad, World," *Time,* September 2, 2002, pp. 38–41.
5. Eric N. Berkowitz, Roger A. Kerin, Steven W. Hartley, William Rudelius, *Marketing,* 7th ed. (Burr Ridge, IL: Irwin/McGraw-Hill, 2003), p. 21.
6. Je Eun Lee, Meichum Kuo, and Hang Lee, "College Binge Drinking in the 1990s: A Continuing Problem. Results of the Harvard School of Public Health 1999 College Alcohol Study," *Journal of American Collegiate Health* 48(5), 2000, pp. 199–210; Jim O Hara, "New Study Shows Underage Youth a Target of Alcohol Marketing: Youth Are More Likely To See Alcohol Advertising Than Adults," *U.S. Newswire,* September 24, 2002.
7. Jennifer Christie, Dan Fisher, John C. Kozup, Scott Smith, Scott Burton and Elizabeth H. Creyer, "The Effects of Bar-Sponsored Beverage Promotions Across Binge and Nonbinge Drinkers," *Journal of Public Policy & Marketing* 20(2), (Fall 2001), pp. 240–53.
8. Mike Beirne, "In The Name of Responsibility," *BrandWeek,* May 12, 2003, pp. 32–36; Ira Teinowitz, "Booze-Hounded," *Advertising Age,* March 25, 2002, pp. 1, 27.
9. Ira Teinowitz, "Underage-drinking Report Calls for Voluntary Alcohol Cutbacks," *adage.com,* March 6, 2007.
10. Sandra O'Loughlin and Steve Miller, "Marketers Struggle with the 'Dark' Side," *Brandweek,* February 19, 2007, pp. 4–5.
11. Quote in Ibid.
12. Stephanie Bentley, "Benetton Risks Fresh Outrage," *Marketing Week,* September 13, 1996, p. 9; Gary Levin, "Benetton Ad Lays Bare the Bloody Toll of War," *Advertising Age,* February 21, 1994, p. 38.
13. Jerry Della Famina, "Benetton Ad Models Are Dressed to Kill Sales," *The Wall Street Journal,* March 20, 2000, p. A34.
14. "Benetton Supports and Promotes Africa for Africans. In Partnership With Youssou N'Dour," www.benetton.com/africaworks-press, February 13, 2008.
15. Stephanie O'Donohoe, "Attitudes to Advertising: A Review of British and American Research," *International Journal of Advertising* 14 (1995), pp. 245–61.
16. Patricia Odell, "Consumers Feel Assaulted by Ads: Forrester," *Promo Xtra,* www.promomaazine.com/news, September 21, 2004.
17. Gita Venkataramini Johar, "Consumer Involvement and Deception from Implied Advertising Claims," *Journal of Marketing Research* 32 (August 1995), pp. 267–79; J. Edward Russo, Barbara L. Metcalf, and Debra Stephens, "Identifying Misleading Advertising," *Journal of Consumer Research* 8 (September 1981), pp. 119–31.
18. Shelby D. Hunt, "Informational vs. Persuasive Advertising: An Appraisal," *Journal of Advertising,* Summer 1976, pp. 5–8.
19. "The Take on You," *Adweek,* September 24, 2007, pp. 14–15; Banwari Mittal, "Public Assessment of TV Advertising: Faint Praise and Harsh Criticism," *Journal of Advertising Research* 34 (January/February 1994), pp. 35–53; J. C. Andrews, "The Dimensionality of Beliefs toward Advertising in General," *Journal of Advertising* 18, no. 1 (1989), pp. 26–35.
20. Helen Cooper, "CDC Advocates Use of Condoms in Blunt AIDS-Prevention Spots," *The Wall Street Journal,* January 5, 1994, p. B1.
21. Jack Neff, "Trojan Ads Ready for Prime Time: NBC," *Advertising Age,* May 16, 2005, p. 3.
22. Claude Brodesser-Akner, "Sex on TV Is Ok as Long as It's Not Safe," *adage.com,* September 17, 2007.
23. Stephen A. Greyser, "Irritation in Advertising," *Journal of Advertising Research* 13 (February 1973), pp. 3–10.
24. Joan Voight and Wendy Melillo, "Rough Cut," *Adweek,* March 11, 2002, pp. 27–29; Joanne Lipman, "Censored Scenes: Why You Rarely See Some Things in Television Ads," *The Wall Street Journal,* August 17, 1987, p. 17.
25. For an interesting analysis of an interpretation of this ad from a literary theory perspective see Aaron C. Ahuvia, "Social Criticism of Advertising: On the Role of Literary Theory and the Use of Data," *Journal of Advertising* 27, no. 1 (Spring 1998), pp. 143–62.
26. James B. Arndorfer, "Skyy Hit The Limit with Racy Ad: Critics," *Advertising Age,* February 7, 2005, p. 6.
27. Tim Nudd, "Does Sex Really Sell?," *Adweek,* October 17, 2005, pp. 14–17.
28. Michael McCarthy, "Shockvertising Jolts Ad Viewers," *USA Today,* February 23, 2000, p. 6B.
29. Leanne Potts, "Retailers, Ads Bare Flesh for Bottom Line," *Albuquerque Journal,* December 20, 2002, p. D1.
30. Stephanie Kang, "Abercrombie & Fitch Tries to Be Less Haughty, More Nice," *The Wall Street Journal,* June 17, 2005, pp. B1, 2.
31. Rebecca Quick, "Is Ever-So-Hip Abercrombie & Fitch Losing Its Edge with Teens?" *The Wall Street Journal,* February 22, 2000, pp. B1, 4.

**32.** "Report of the APA Task Force on Advertising and Children," February 20, 2004, www.apa.org/releases/childrenads.

**33.** "Food for Thought: Television Food Advertising to Children in the United States," Kaiser Family Foundation Report, www.kff.org, March 2007.

**34.** Dale Kunkel, "Children and Television Advertising, in D.G. Singer and J. L. Singer (eds.), *The Handbook of Children and Media* (Thousand Oaks, CA.: Sage Publications, 2001), pp. 375–94.

**35.** Merrie Brucks, Gary M. Armstrong, and Marvin E. Goldberg, "Children's Use of Cognitive Defenses against Television Advertising: A Cognitive Response Approach," *Journal of Consumer Research* 14, no. 4 (March 1988), pp. 471–82.

**36.** Tamara F. Mangleburg and Terry Bristol, "Socialization and Adolescents' Skepticism toward Advertising," *Journal of Advertising* 27, no. 3 (Fall 1998), pp. 11–21.

**37.** Ronald Alsop, "Watchdogs Zealously Censor Advertising Targeted to Kids," *The Wall Street Journal,* September 5, 1985, p. 35.

**38.** "Report of the APA Task Force on Advertising and Children," February 20, 2004.

**39.** Tiffany Meyers, "Marketing to Kids Comes under Fresh Attack," *Advertising Age,* February 21, 2005, pp. S2, 8.

**40.** Betsy McKay, "Soda Marketers Will Cut Back Sales to Schools," *The Wall Street Journal,* August 17, 2005, pp. B1, 3.

**41.** Dan Lippe, "What Children Say about Media and Advertising," *adage.com,* February 4, 2002.

**42.** Ronald Berman, *Advertising and Social Change* (Beverly Hills, CA: Sage, 1981), p. 13.

**43.** Quote in Joan Voight, "The Consumer Rebellion."

**44.** Morris B. Holbrook, "Mirror Mirror on the Wall, What's Unfair in the Reflections on Advertising," *Journal of Marketing* 5 (July 1987), pp. 95–103; Theodore Levitt, "The Morality of Advertising," *Harvard Business Review* (July/August 1970), pp. 84–92.

**45.** Stephen Fox, *The Mirror Makers: A History of American Advertising and Its Creators* (New York: Morrow, 1984), p. 330.

**46** Hunt, "Informational vs. Persuasive Advertising."

**47.** Daniel J. Brett and Joanne Cantor, "The Portrayal of Men and Women in U.S. Television Commercials: A Recent Content Analysis and Trends of 15 Years," *Sex Roles* 18, no. 9/10 (1998), pp. 595–608; John B. Ford and Michael La Tour, "Contemporary Perspectives of Female Role Portrayals in Advertising," *Journal of Current Issues and Research in Advertising* 28, no. 1 (1996), pp. 81–93.

**48.** Beverly A. Browne, "Gender Stereotypes in Advertising on Children's Television in the 1990s: A Cross-National Analysis," *Journal of Advertising* 27, no. 1 (Spring 1998), pp. 83–96.

**49.** Richard H. Kolbe, "Gender Roles in Children's Advertising: A Longitudinal Content Analysis," in *Current Issues and Research in Advertising,* ed. James H. Leigh and Claude R. Martin, Jr. (Ann Arbor: University of Michigan, 1990), pp. 197–206.

**50.** Debra Merskin, "Boys Will Be Boys: A Content Analysis of Gender and Race in Children's Advertisements on the Turner Cartoon Network," *Journal of Current Issues and Research in Advertising* 24 (1) (Spring 2002), pp. 51–60.

**51.** Cate Terwilliger, "'Love Your Body Day' Auraria Event Takes Aim at 'Offensive' Images, Ads," *Denver Post,* September 23, 1999, p. E3.

**52.** Steven M. Kates and Glenda Shaw-Garlock, "The Ever Entangling Web: A Study of Ideologies and Discourses in Advertising to Women," *Journal of Advertising* 28, no. 2 (Summer 1999), pp. 33–49.

**53.** Suzanne Vranica, "Stereotypes of Women Persist in Ads," *The Wall Street Journal,* October 17, 2003, p. B4.

**54.** Thomas H. Stevenson, "How Are Blacks Portrayed in Business Ads?" Industrial Marketing Management 20 (1991), pp. 193–99; Helen Czepic and J. Steven Kelly, "Analyzing Hispanic Roles in Advertising," in *Current Issues and Research in Advertising,* ed. James H. Leigh and Claude Martin (Ann Arbor: University of Michigan, 1983), pp. 219–40; R. F. Busch, Allan S. Resnik, and Bruce L. Stern, "A Content Analysis of the Portrayal of Black Models in Magazine Advertising," in *American Marketing Association Proceedings: Marketing in the 1980s,* ed. Richard P. Bagozzi (Chicago: American Marketing Association, 1980); F. Busch, Allan S. Resnik, and Bruce L. Stern, "There Are More Blacks in TV Commercials," *Journal of Advertising Research* 17 (1977), pp. 21–25.

**55.** James Stearns, Lynette S. Unger, and Steven G. Luebkeman, "The Portrayal of Blacks in Magazine and Television Advertising," in *AMA Educator's Proceedings,* ed. Susan P. Douglas and Michael R. Solomon (Chicago: American Marketing Association, 1987).

**56.** Julia Bristor, Renee Gravois Lee, and Michelle Hunt, "Race and Ideology: African American Images in Television Advertising," *Journal of Public Policy and Marketing* 14 (Spring 1995), pp. 48–59.

**57.** Linzee D. Locke, "A Content Analysis: African Americans Presence in Prime Time Advertisements, on BET and MTV Networks," The University of Iowa, Online Communications Studies Resources.

**58.** Charles R. Taylor and Barbara B. Stern, "Asian-Americans: Television Advertising and the 'Model Minority' Stereotype," *Journal of Advertising* 26 no. 2 (Summer 1997), pp. 47–61.

**59.** Bruce Horovitz, "Mental Health Groups Slam Volkswagen Ad," *USA Today,* February 15, 2007, p. B1.

**60.** Brooke Capps, "Suicide Prevention Group Tells GM to Yank Robot Spot," *adage.com,* February 7, 2007.

**61.** Andrew Happ,, "An Ad in Which Boy Gets Girl. . .or Boy," *adage.com,* August 6, 2007.

**62.** Stephanie Thompson, "Mars Pulls Snickers Super Bowl Spot," *adage .com,* February 6, 2007.

**63.** Jef I. Richards and John H. Murphy, II, "Economic Censorship and Free Speech: The Circle of Communication between Advertisers, Media and Consumers," *Journal of Current Issues and Research in Advertising* 18, no. 1 (Spring 1996), pp. 21–33.

**64.** Lawrence C. Soley and Robert L. Craig, "Advertising Pressure on Newspapers: A Survey," *Journal of Advertising,* December 1992, pp. 1–10.

**65.** Mark Simon, "Mercury News Ad Dispute Cooling Off: Advertisers Return While Reporters Stew," *San Francisco Business Chronicle,* July 15, 1994, p. B1.

**66.** Soontae An and Lori Bergen, "Advertiser Pressure on Daily Newspapers," *Journal of Advertising* 36, no. 2 (Summer 2007), pp. 111–21.

**67.** Janet Guyon, "Do Publications Avoid Anti-Cigarette Stories to Protect Ad Dollars?" *The Wall Street Journal,* November 22, 1982, pp. 1, 20; Elizabeth M. Whelan, "When Newsweek and Time Filtered Cigarette Copy," *The Wall Street Journal,* November 1, 1984, p. 3; "RJR Swears Off Saatchi and Nabisco Is in a Sweat," *BusinessWeek,* April 18, 1988, p. 36.

**68.** David Shaw, "An Uneasy Alliance of News and Ads," *Los Angeles Times,* March 29, 1998, pp. A1, 28.

**69.** Steven T. Goldberg, "Do the Ads Tempt the Editors?" *Kiplingers Personal Finance,* (May 1996), pp. 45–49.

**70.** Nat Ives, "GM Ends 'L.A.Times' Boycott, Resumes Advertising," *adage .com,* August 2, 2005.

**71.** "Major New Initiative Launched Targeting Prescription Drug Abuse," The Partnership for a Drug Free America, www.drugfree.org, January 14, 2008.

**72.** Robert D. Buzzell, Bradley T. Gale, and Ralph G. M. Sultan, "Market Share—A Key to Profitability," *Harvard Business Review,* (January/February 1975), pp. 97–106.

**73.** "Virgin America Launches New National Ad Campaign; Fashion-Feel Campaign Targets Non-Traditional Media and Spotlights In-Flight Team Members," *PR Newswire,* February 5, 2008.

**74.** Paul W. Farris and Mark S. Albion, "The Impact of Advertising on the Price of Consumer Products," *Journal of Marketing,* 44 no. 3 (Summer 1980), pp. 17–35.

**75.** Buron, "Reining in Drug Advertising."

**76.** Farris and Albion, "The Impact of Advertising on the Price of Consumer Products"

**77.** _______., "The Impact of Advertising," p. 30.

**78.** _______., "The Impact of Advertising."

**79.** Avery M. Abernethy and George R. Franke, "The Information Content of Advertising,: A Meta-Analysis," *Journal of Advertising* 25, no. 2, (Summer 1996), pp. 1–17.

# PHOTO CREDITS

## Chapter 1

p.2: Used with permission of Volkswagen Group of America, Inc. ®; p.5: Used with permission of Volkswagen Group of America, Inc. ®; p.7: American Red Cross; p.9: Courtesy of the Movado Group; p.11: Courtesy of Google; p.12: Courtesy of Ford Motor Co. and Team Detroit; p.13: MediaFlo USA Inc.; p.17: © PRNewsFoto/McDonald's/AP Photos; p.19 (top): Courtesy of American Advertising Federation; p.19 (bottom): Courtesy of GE and AMV BBDO; p.21: Courtesy of Under Armour Inc.; p.22: Bazaarvoice Interaction Suite; p.23: WHEATIES FUEL is a registered trademark of General Mills and is used with permission; p.24: Courtesy of Chicken of the Sea International; p.25: American Honda Motor Company; p.32: Starbucks Coffee Company; p.33: Courtesy of Naked Juice

## Chapter 2

p.40: Courtesy of GEICO; p.43: Courtesy of Manischewitz; p.44 (top): PRNewsFoto/Mercedes-Benz USA/AP Photos; p.44 (bottom): The Coca-Cola Company; p.45 (top): Courtesy of Campbell Soup Company; p. 45 (bottom): Reproduced with the permission of Malt-O-Meal Company, Minneapolis, Minnesota; p.47: Miller Brewing Company; p.48: Courtesy Big Red, Incorporated; p.50 (top): Courtesy of iVillage and NBC Universal; p. 50 (bottom): Courtesy of AARP; p.51: © PRNewsFoto/Verizon Wireless/AP Photos; p.52: Courtesy of AT&T Intellectual Property. Used with permission.; p.54 (top): Courtesy of Unilever; p.54 (bottom): © PRNewsFoto/Burt's Bees/AP Photos; p.55 (top): Courtesy of Pepsi-Cola Company; p.55 (bottom): PRNewsFoto/Iconix Brand Group, Inc./AP Photos; p.56 (top): Courtesy of Intuit ®; p.56 (bottom): Use of the ARM & HAMMER, ARM & HAMMER logo, distinctive trade dress and other content of the Arm & Hammer web site is with the express permission of Church & Dwight Co., Inc., Princeton, New Jersey © Church & Dwight Co.; p.57 (top left): PRNewsFoto/Campbell Soup Company/AP Photos; p.57 (top right): Courtesy of DC Shoes; p. 57 (bottom left): PR Newswire/AP Photos; p. 57 (bottom right): PRNewsFoto/Gatorade/AP Photos; p.58: © Jason LaVeris/Getty Images; p.59: Courtesy of Rolex; p.60 (top): Courtesy of WD-40 Company; p.60 (bottom): PR Newswire/AP Photos

## Chapter 3

p.66: Courtesy of Under Armour Inc., p.70: Courtesy of National Geographic Society; p.73 (both): Courtesy of P&G; p.74: Courtesy of P&G; p.77: PRNewsFoto/Kraft Foods/AP Photos; p.80: © TongRo Image Stock/Alamy; p.81 (left): Courtesy of Advertising Age; p.81 (right): © Copyright Mentus; p.85: © John Kuczala; p.87: Courtesy of Droga5; p.88: © Initiative; p.97: Courtesy of Hyundai Motors of America; p.98: Tumbleweeds reprinted with special permission of NAS, Inc., p.99: The BURGER KING® trademarks and advertising materials are used with permission from Burger King Brands, Inc.; p.100: Courtesy of Protocol Integrated Direct Marketing; p.101: Courtesy of Don Jagoda Associates, Inc., Melville, NY; p.102 (top): Courtesy of Agency.com; p.102 (bottom): Courtesy of AvenueSocial

## Chapter 4

p.108: Brian Harkin/The New York Times/Redux Pictures; p.111: Courtesy of Tommy Bahama; p.112 (top): NICODERM®, CQ®, COMMITTED QUITTERS® and design, SmartControl™, Shield Trade Dress/Designs are trademarks owned by and/or licensed to GlaxoSmithKline; p.112 (bottom): Courtesy of Vertical Marketing; p.113: © 2008 Kimberly-Clark Worldwide, Inc.; p.114 (left): Courtesy of Consumer Healthcare Products Association; p.114 (right):The PORSCHE CREST, PORSCHE, 911 and the distinctive shape of the PORSCHE 911 automobile are registered trademarks in the United States of Dr. Ing. h.c.F. Porsche AG. Used with permission of Porsche Cars North America, Inc. Copyrighted by Porsche Cars North America, Inc. Photographer: Erik Chmil; p.116: Courtesy of Joe's Jeans; p.118 (top): Courtesy of Tropicana; p.118 (bottom): American Association of Advertising Agencies; p.119: Courtesy of Alberto-Culver Company; p.122: Photo by Walter Daran/Time Life Pictures/Getty Images; p.123: Copyright © 2007 Michigan Economic Development Corporation; p.125 (top): Courtesy of Michelin North America, Inc.; p.125 (bottom): © PRNewsFoto/Levi Strauss & Co/AP Photos; p.127: Courtesy of CDW Corporation; p.128: Courtesy of Ameriprise Financial Inc.; p.130: PRNewsFoto/Elizabeth Arden, Inc./AP Photos; p.131: Courtesy of Kyocera; p.135 (top left): Courtesy of the Procter & Gamble Company; p.135 (top right): © Markwins Beauty Products 2008, National Ad Campaign for Tropez Cosmetics, Designed by Jane Hjellum; p.135 (bottom): PRNewsFoto/Jaguar/AP Photos; p.136 (top left): Courtesy of United States Navy; p.136 (top right): Courtesy Quality Social

## Chapter 5

p.142: Courtesy of Ford Motor Co. and Team Detroit; p.147: Courtesy California Milk Processor Board; p.148: Courtesy AP Photo/PR Newswire; p.149 (top): Courtesy of Coach, Inc.; p.149 (bottom): © 2010 Frito-Lay North America, Inc. All rights reserved; p.150: Courtesy of the Procter & Gamble Company and Getty Images; p.152: Courtesy of AARP; p.156 (top): VISTAKON®, Division of Johnson & Johnson Vision Care, Inc.; p.156 (bottom): Courtesy Sony Corporation of America; p.158: Courtesy of Advertising Age; p.160: Courtesy of Acura; p.161: Used with permission of VISA, USA. Photography © Karen Moscowitz/Getty Images; p.162: Courtesy H.J. Heinz Company LLP. Used with permission; p.163: © Eveready Battery Company, Inc. Printed with permission; p.165: Courtesy of LG Electronics; p.166: Used with permission of the Procter & Gamble Company; p.169: Courtesy of Advertising Age; p.170: Courtesy Old World Industries

## Chapter 6

p.176: © AP Photos; p.180: © PRNewsFoto/Milk Processors Education Board/AP Photos; p.181: Courtesy of Unilever; p.182: Splash News and Pictures/Newscom; p.184: Courtesy of Jerome's Furniture; p.187 (top): PRNewsFoto/Cole Haan/AP Photos; p.187 (bottom): Courtesy of PowerBar; p.188: PRNewsFoto/YES! Golf/AP Photos; p.191: Courtesy of Electrolux; p.192 (left to right): Courtesy of Gatorade and ad provided by Fleishman; Courtesy of Coty, Inc.; © 2010 VF Jeanswear Limited Partnership; p.196: Courtesy of Unilever; p.197: Courtesy of Take Pride in America; p.198: Courtesy of White Wave, Inc.; p.199 (top): Courtesy of Novartis Consumer Health Canada Inc.; p.199 (bottom): Sterling-Rice Group; p.200: Courtesy of Domino's Pizza Inc.; p.202: Nestle Waters North America; p.203 (top): Courtesy of Miller Brewing Company; p.203 (bottom): © Apple Computer, Inc. Used with permission. All rights reserved. Apple ® and the Apple logo are registered trademarks of Apple Computer, Inc.; p.205: Courtesy of Australasian New Car Assessment Program (ANCAP); p.208: Courtesy of Facebook, Inc.; p.210: Cover image courtesy of Travel + Leisure. Photograph by Susan Seubert

## Chapter 7

p.214: Courtesy Television Bureau of Advertising, Inc. All Rights Reserved; p.217 (left): Courtesy Standard Bank Group; p.217 (right): All Rights Reserved and Owned by the Qatar Foundation; p.221: Courtesy Kayem Foods, Inc.; p.222 (top): © 2010 Mercury Insurance Group. All Rights Reserved.; p.222 (bottom): Courtesy of J.C. Penney Company, Inc.; p.223:

Courtesy Consolidated Edison, Inc.; p.224: © 2010 Caribou Coffee, Inc. All Rights Reserved; p.227: © 2011 Hyundai Sonata; p.228: Performics, a division of VNC Communications, Inc.; p.231: Courtesy San Diego Zoo; p.233: © American Association of Advertising Agencies; p.234: Photo by Apic/Getty Images

## Chapter 8

p.256: Courtesy Cannes Lions International Advertising Festival. Cannes Lions 2010 Grand Prix Winner; p.259: Courtesy of BMW of North America, LLC; p.260: Courtesy of the Wm. Wrigley Jr. Company; p.263: © www .barackobama.com; p.264: Courtesy V&S Vin and Spirit AB. Imported by the Absolut Spirits Co., New York, NY; p.266: PR Newswire/Nike/ AP Photos; p.267: PR Newswire/AP Photos; p.268: Mediaweek material used with permission of e5 Global Media, LLC; p.271: © Sharon Hoogstratem; p.272: Courtesy of Young & Rubicam, Inc.; p.273: Courtesy of Aflac; p.274: Courtesy California Milk Processor Board; p.275: Courtesy of Skyy Spirits, LLC; p.277: The Las Vegas Convention and Visitors Authority; p.279: © 2009 Tacori; p.281: Courtesy of United Technologies Corporation; p.283: Courtesy of Hitachi, Ltd.; p.284: Courtesy Colgate-Palmolive Company; p.285 (top): Bebe Stores, Inc. All Rights reserved; p.285 (bottom): Courtesy Hallmark; p.286: Courtesy General Electric; p.287: © SOPUS Products. All Rights reserved.

## Chapter 9

p.290: Courtesy of Mountain Dew; p.293: Courtesy of Acura; p.294 (top): RED BULL and the Double Bull Device are the registered trademarks of Red Bull GmbH; p.294 (bottom): Courtesy of HP; p.295: Courtesy of TaylorMade Golf Company, Inc.; p.296: Milk Processor Education Program/PR News Foto/AP Photos; p.297: Courtesy of Skyy Spirits, LLC; p.298: Courtesy of American Airlines; p.299 (top): Courtesy of MasterCard; p.299 (bottom): Nature Valley® is a registered trademark of General Mills and is used with permission; p.302: Courtesy Hyundai Motor America; p.303 (top): Courtesy of Ford Motor Co. and Team Detroit; p.303 (bottom): Courtesy of Kinerase. Kinerase is a registered trademark of Valeant Pharmaceuticals International; p.304 (top): Photo and Ad by Arnell; p.304 (bottom): Courtesy of Jenny Craig; p.305: Makers of Listerine; p.306 (top): Courtesy of Charles Schwab & Co., Inc. Member SIPC, animation by Bob Sabiston and Susan Sabiston-FlatBlack Films, with thanks to Larry Poindexter; p.306 (bottom): Courtesy of Aflac; p.307 (left): Courtesy of Singapore Airlines; p.307 (right): Bebe Stores, Inc.; p.309: AP Photos; p.310: Courtesy BASF Corporation; p.311: © 2010 Visa Corporation; p.312 (left): Used with permission of Volkswagen Group of America, Inc.; p.312 (right): Courtesy of GEICO; p.313 (top): PR Newswire/AP Photos; p.313 (bottom): © The Coca-Cola Company; p.320: © Apple Inc. Used with permission. All rights reserved. Apple ® and the Apple logo are registered trademarks of Apple Inc.; p.321: Courtesy of Skyy Spirits, LLC; p.322: Courtesy of Golf Pride

## Chapter 10

p.326: Photo courtesy of James Cope; p.329: Photograph courtesy of NBC Universal, Inc.; p.337: Mindset Media, LLC

## Chapter 11

p.362: Courtesy of Alex Ostroy; p.365: Courtesy of Hitachi America, Limited and Lambesis; p.367: Courtesy of NBC Universal; p.369: Courtesy of You Tube; p.370: Courtesy of TiVo Inc., p.371: © Game Show Network: p.373: Courtesy of the CW Television Network; p.374: Courtesy of Univision; p.377: Courtesy of SNTA, Inc.; p.381: Courtesy of Versus, 2008; p.382 (top): New York Interconnect copyright 2010; p.382 (bottom): Courtesy of CNBC; p.383: ABC/Photofest; p.385: Courtesy ESPN; p.387: Courtesy of Nielsen Media Research; p.388: Courtesy of WJZ TV; p.389: © Comedy Central/Photofest; p.391: Courtesy of TiVo Inc.; p.392: Courtesy of Radio Advertising Bureau; p.395 (all): Courtesy of Radio Advertising Bureau; p.396: Courtesy of Arbitron; p.397: AP Photos; p.398: Courtesy of Sound Mind Inc. and Premiere Radio Networks and Rush Limbaugh; p.400: Courtesy of Arbitron

## Chapter 12

p.404: Courtesy Sony Corporation of America; p.407: Courtesy of Virgo Publishing; p.409 (top): *Transworld Snowboarding*® magazine is a publication of Bonnier Corporation. © 2010 Bonnier Corporation. All rights reserved.; p.409 (bottom): BEEF Magazine; p.410: Courtesy of Samir Husni, Ph.D.-Mr. Magazine ™; p.411: Courtesy of Jones Agency; p.413: Courtesy of Jen Blankenship; p.414 (top): Courtesy of BMW of North America LLC; p.414 (bottom): Supernatural materials courtesy of The WB Television Network; p.415 (top): Courtesy of WD-40 Company; p.415 (bottom): Courtesy of Hearst/ Good Housekeeping; p.419: Courtesy of P&G; p.421: Audit Bureau Circulations; p.422: Courtesy of SRDS; p.423: Courtesy of Ivy League Magazine Network; p.424: Courtesy of ESPN; p.425: Courtesy of Parent & Child Magazine and Kleenex® brand tissue ; p.427: Courtesy of Magazines Publishers Association; p.428: Courtesy of The Wall Street Journal; p.429: Courtesy of Parade Publications; p.431: Courtesy of The Daily Aztec; p.432 (top): Courtesy of The San Diego Union Tribune; p.432 (bottom): Courtesy of Bridgestone Golf, Inc.; p.433: Courtesy of Chicago Tribune; p.434: Courtesy of The San Diego Union Tribune; p.435: Courtesy of The Los Angeles Times; p.437: Newspaper National Network, LP; p.440: "Bee Movie" ™ & © 2007 Dream Works Animation LLC, used courtesy of Dream Works Animation LLC; Ad Courtesy of Newspaper Association of America; p.441: Courtesy of The San Diego Union Tribune

## Chapter 13

p.444: Dave M. Benett/Getty Images; p.449 (left): Courtesy of Outdoor Advertising Association of America; p.449 (right): Photograph courtesy of Toshiba; p.450: Courtesy of Outdoor Advertising Association of America; p.451: The Goodyear Tire and Rubber Company; p.452: Courtesy of Outdoor Advertising Association of America; p.453: Courtesy of Outdoor Advertising Association of America; p.459: Courtesy of Yellow Pages Association; p.462: © The Jersey Journal/Landov Images; p.467 (top): Used with permission of KFC Corporation; p.467 (bottom): AP Photos; p.468: © Charlie Neuman/Zuma Press

## Chapter 14

p.472: Courtesy of New York Jets LLC; p.476: Courtesy of Bose® Corporation; p.477: Courtesy of Costco Wholesale; p.478 (top): Courtesy of Pinehurst and Acura; p.480: Courtesy of American Airlines; p.482 (top): Courtesy of Maserati North America, Inc.; p.482 (bottom): Courtesy of Deliver Magazine and Jude Buffum; p.483 (top): Courtesy of Nielsen Business Media; p.483 (bottom): Road Runner Sports-World's Largest Running Store; p.484 (top): Executive Visions Inc/PRNewsFoto/AP Photos; p.484 (bottom): Used by permission of Lenox, Inc.; p.485: Courtesy of CMedia; p.486: Courtesy of CUTCO Company

## Chapter 15

p.492: Courtesy Purple Door Communications; p.497: © 2008 Kimberly-Clark Worldwide, Inc.; p.498 (top): Courtesy of SweetBling.com; p.498 (bottom): RED BULL and the Double Bull Device are the registered trademarks of Red Bull GmbH; p.499 (top): Courtesy of OluKai Premium Footwear; p.499 (bottom): These materials have been reproduced with the permission of eBay Inc. © 2008 EBAY INC. All Rights Reserved; p.501 (top): Courtesy of Grantastic Designs, Inc.; p.501 (bottom): Courtesy of Google; p.503: Courtesy of Google; p.506: © Rob Kim/Landov Images; p.507: PRNewsFoto/Ghirardelli Chocolate Company/AP Photos; p.508: © IAB; p.509: Courtesy of Chrysler Group LLC; p.514: Courtesy of Google; p.515: © AP Photos

## Chapter 16

p.518: Courtesy of Subway; p.521: © 2006 Kellogg North America Company. The copyright in and to the images is and shall remain the sole property of Kellogg North American Company; p.523 (top): Channellock, Inc., Meadville, PA 16335; p.523 (bottom): Courtesy of Aspen Marketing Services; p.525: BumbleBee Foods LLC; p.527: Courtesy of Wal-Mart, Inc.; p.529:

© McGraw-Hill Companies/Jill Braaten, photographer; p.530: Courtesy of Ryan Partnership; p.531: Use of the ARM & HAMMER, ARM & HAMMER logo, distinctive trade dress and other content of the Arm & Hammer website is with the express permission of Church & Dwight Co., Inc., Princeton, New Jersey © Church & Dwight Co., p.532: Courtesy of Miller Brewing Company; p.533: Courtesy of Kleenex®, a registered trademark of Kimberly-Clark Worldwide; p.534: Courtesy of © Jack In The Box Inc. 2010; p.535 (top): ArmorAll Products Corporation; p.535 (bottom): Courtesy of StartSampling, Inc.; p.539: Courtesy of ValPak Direct Marketing Systems, Inc.; p.540 (top): © McGraw-Hill Companies/Jill Braaten, photographer; p.540 (bottom): California Milk Advisory Board; p.542: Courtesy of Cellfire; p.543 (top): PRNewsFoto/DreamWorks Animation SKG, Inc./AP Photos; p.543 (bottom): Courtesy of American Airlines; p.545: Courtesy of Groupon; p.546: Courtesy of Levi's; p.547: Used with permission from Penzoil/Quaker State Company; p.550: ArmorAll Products Corporation; p.551 (top): www.CartoonStock.com; p.551 (bottom): KAO Brands Company; p.552: Courtesy of WD-40 Company; p.553: Courtesy of Mountain Dew; p.555: Courtesy of Chicken of The Sea International; p.557: Courtesy of Chicken of The Sea International; p.559: Courtesy of SeaKlear; p.560: Courtesy of the California Milk Advisory Board; p.561 (top): Courtesy of Intel; p.561 (bottom): Courtesy of Bridgestone Golf, Inc.; p.563: Courtesy of MasterCard; p.564: Courtesy of Unilever; p.566: Courtesy of Wendy's International

## Chapter 17

p.570: © 2010 Toyota Motor Sales USA, Inc.; p.575: Courtesy of General Mills; p.576: Image Courtesy of Cessna Aircraft Company; p.578: Courtesy of San Diego State University; p.579 (top): Courtesy of Capital Group; p.579 (bottom): Ad courtesy of CITGO Petroleum Corporation; p.580 (top): Courtesy Yellow Pages Association; p.580 (bottom): Courtesy PR Newswire; p.581: Courtesy American Express; p.582: Courtesy of Edward Jones Investments; p.583 (top): Courtesy of the General Mills Archives; p.583 (bottom): Courtesy Maserati North America and Ross Design; p.587: Used by permission of Tree Top, Inc.; p.590 (top): Courtesy Draftcb, Albert Watson photographer; p.590 (bottom): WHIRLPOOL is a registered trademark of Whirlpool, U.S.A. © 2005 Whirlpool Corporation. All rights reserved. HABITAT FOR HUMANITY is a registered trademark of Habitat for Humanity International, Inc.; p.591: Grant Thornton brand-building advertising; p.593 (top): Darrell Ingham/Getty Images; p.593 (bottom): ©2008, American Heart Association; p.594: Courtesy of The Humane Society of the United States; p.595: © Harold Feinstein www.haroldfeinstein.com; p.596 (top): Courtesy of AT&T Archives and History Center; p.596 (bottom): Courtesy of Arizona Department of Health Services

## Chapter 18

p.600: Courtesy of SensoMotoric Instruments (SMI); p.604: Courtesy of Advertising Age; p.605: Courtesy of United States Postal Service; p.607: Courtesy of Chiat/Day/Mogo Inc. Advertising; p.619: Courtesy of SensoMotoric Instruments (SMI); p.621: Jim Wehtje/Getty Images; p.622: With permission from Target Marketing/NAPCO; p.623: Courtesy of GfK MRI Starch Advertising Research; p.626: Courtesy of Ipsos-ASI, Inc.; p.627: Courtesy of Decision Analyst, Inc.

## Chapter 19

p.636: Courtesy Advertising Age; p.640: Courtesy Australian Tourist Commission™ © The Brand Australia Trademark is the subject of copyright and is a trademark of the Australia Tourist Commission, 2010; p.641: Used by permission of WD-40 Company; p.644: © Newscom Photos; p.645: © 2010 Taylor Made Golf Company, Inc. All rights reserved. TaylorMade is a part of the Adidas Group; p.647: © Linterland 2006; p.648: Courtesy of New Balance Athletic Shoe, Inc.; p.650: © Gordon Sinclair/Alamy; p.651: Coca-Cola and Coca-Cola Light are registered trademarks of The Coca-Cola Company. Permission granted by the Coca-Cola Company; p.653: Courtesy of Procter & Gamble; p.654: Courtesy Nestle; p.655 (top): © Asics Corporation; p.655 (bottom): Courtesy of Advertising Age; p.656: Courtesy The Colgate-Palmolive Company; P.657 (top): © Davide Campari-Milano S.P.A. All rights reserved; p.657 (bottom): Copyright © 2009 HTC Corporation. All rights reserved; p.659: © RF/Corbis; p.660: Courtesy of TAG Heuer; p.661: Courtesy TaylorMade Golf Company, Inc.; p.664: Courtesy IBM; p.666: Source: Central Intelligence Agency; p.667 (top): Courtesy NCH Marketing Services, Inc.; p.667 (bottom): Courtesy of Las Vegas Convention and Visitors Authority; p.670: Copyright © 1999-2010 LiveJournal, Inc. All rights reserved; p.671: STAR Creative Team; p.672: Courtesy WD-40 Company. Photography by Sharon Hoogstraten; p.676 (top): Courtesy of Taylor Made Golf Company, Inc.; p.676 (bottom): Courtesy mixi, Inc.

## Chapter 20

p.680: © Fox Broadcasting Co./Photofest; p.684: Courtesy of the Lustigman Firm, Attorneys at Law; p.685: Courtesy Luce, Forward, Hamilton & Scripps LLP; p.687: © The Center on Alcohol Marketing and Youth; p.688: Courtesy National Advertising Review Council; p.690: Courtesy National Advertising Review Council; p.691: Courtesy Benetton Cosmetics Corporation. Photo by O. Toscani; p.693 (top): Courtesy California Milk Advisory Board; p.693 (bottom): www.ManCrunch.com; p.694: Courtesy National Advertising Review Council; p.696: Courtesy Federal Trade Commission; p.701: Courtesy of Domino's Pizza Inc.; p.702 (top): : Courtesy of New Balance Athletic Shoe, Inc. p.702 (bottom): Courtesy of The Champagne Bureau; p.703: © PRNewsFoto/Atkins Nutritional Inc./AP Photos; p.708: Courtesy of Federal Trade Commission; p.710 (top): © Frank Micelotta/Getty Images; p.710 (bottom): © Dennis MacDonald/Alamy; p.712: Courtesy of American Legacy Foundation; p.713: Courtesy Campbell Soup Company; p.715: © Susan VanEtten/PhotoEdit; p.716: Courtesy of TaylorMade Golf Company, Inc. p.717: Used with permission from Penzoil/Quaker State Company; p.720: Source: National Do Not Call Registry; p.723: Copyright © 2007 CatalogChoice.org. All Rights Reserved; p.724: Courtesy of National Advertising Initiative

## Chapter 21

p.728: © Chris Jackson/Getty Images; p.731: Courtesy of Commercial Alert; p.732 (top): Courtesy Miller Brewing Company; p.732 (bottom): Courtesy of the National Organization for Women; p.733 (top): Courtesy Cannes Lions International Advertising Festival; p.733 (bottom): Courtesy of United Colors of Benetton; p.734: Courtesy American Advertising Federation; p.735 (top): Reprinted with permission of Church & Dwight Virginia Co., Inc.; p.735 (bottom): Courtesy Airwalk; p.736: Courtesy of Skyy Spirits, LLC; p.737: © Sharon Hoogstratem; p.741: Courtesy of Kaiser Foundation; p.742 (top): © Tim Boyle/Getty Images; p.742 (bottom): Courtesy AP Photos /PR Newswire; p.743: © American Association of Advertising Agencies; p.744: © American Association of Advertising Agencies; p.745: Courtesy of Network Solutions. © Copyright 2005 Network Solutions. All rights reserved; p.746 (top): © Flickr; p.746 (bottom): © PRNewsFoto/The Levi's brand/AP Photos; p.747: Courtesy AP Photos , PR Newswire; p.749: Courtesy the Procter & Gamble Company; p.751: Courtesy International Advertising Association; p.752 (left): Source: Office of National Drug Control Policy; p.752 (right): Courtesy of Boys & Girls Clubs of America; p.753 (top): Courtesy of *ADWEEK;* p.753 (bottom): © American Association of Advertising Agencies; p.754: Courtesy AP Photos , PR Newswire; p.755: © American Association of Advertising Agencies; p.757 (top): Courtesy International Advertising Association; p.757 (bottom): Courtesy of American Advertising Federation

## Chapter 22

p.2: Courtesy of Sybase; p.8: Copyright © 2007 SAS Institute Inc. All Rights Reserved. Reproduced with permission of SAS Institute Inc., Cary, NC. USA; p.9: Courtesy of CDW; p.10: Courtesy of *info*USA®; p.15: © 2010 Dell Inc. All Rights Reserved; p.16: © Newscom; p.17: Courtesy of Phone Works, LLC; p.18 (top): Courtesy of Oracle Corporation; p.18 (bottom): Courtesy of GoToMeeting®: p.19: PRNewsFoto/NetSuite Inc./Newscom

# NAME AND COMPANY INDEX

## A



## B

## C

## D



## E



## F

## J



## K



## L



## M

## N

## O



## P



## Q



## R

## S

## T



## U



## V



## W

# SUBJECT INDEX

## A

## B



## C

# D

## E



## F

## J



## K



## L

## Q



## R



## S

# T

## U

## W

## Y



## Z